Bill James presents. . .

STATS™
Major League Handbook
1998

STATS, Inc. • Bill James

STATS
PUBLISHING

Published by STATS Publishing
A Division of Sports Team Analysis & Tracking Systems, Inc.

Cover by Ron Freer

Photo by Tony Inzerillo of The Sporting Views

First Edition: November, 1997

Printed in the United States of America

ISBN 1-884064-42-6

Acknowledgments

When we began the *STATS Major League Handbook* eight years ago, STATS had all of six full-time employees. Now we have more than 10 times that number. That's an amazing success story, and we'd like to use this space to thank the people who continue to help our company grow and prosper.

John Dewan, STATS President and CEO, is the man who made it all happen. John's leadership has made us the number-one source for sports statistics in America, and he's not about to rest on his laurels. Helping John with all the details is his able assistant, Heather Schwarze.

The Systems department crunches all the numbers in the *Handbook*, along with all the other data our company produces; we're continually awed by how they do it. Systems is led by Sue Dewan, Mike Canter and Art Ashley, with the assistance of Andrew Bernstein, Dave Carlson, Drew Faust, Kevin Goldstein, Mike Hammer, Stefan Kretschmann, Steve Moyer, Brent Osland, Dean Peterson, David Pinto, Pat Quinn, Allan Spear, Kevin Thomas and Jeff Schinski. A special tip of the cap goes to Stefan, the chief programmer for this book.

The Operations Department gathers our data and ensures its accuracy right down to the last intentional walk. Doug Abel manages Ops in smooth fashion; his staff consists of Jeff Chernow, Brian Cousins, Jason Kinsey, Jim Osborne, John Sasman, Matt Senter, Joseph Weindel and Peter Woelflein.

Publications, headed by yours truly, takes those numbers and fashions them into books, magazines and other useful products for the home. My All-Star staff consists of Jim Callis, Ethan Cooperson, Kevin Fullam, Jim Henzler, Chuck Miller, Tony Nistler and Mat Olkin. The Fantasy Department, which produces some of the most innovative sports games in existence, consists of Mike Wenz, Jim Musso, Dan Ford and Oscar Palacios.

The Marketing and Sales Departments spread the word about our products to clients around the world (and they probably won't stop there!). Steve Byrd heads up Marketing with help from Marc Elman, Ron Freer, Corey Roberts and Walter Lis. Jim Capuano leads the Sales team with the assistance of Kristen Beauregard, Leena Sheth and Lori Smith. The Departments responsible for Finances and Administration, headed by Bob Meyerhoff, manage the important day-to-day details of our office, from paper clips all the way up to six-figure contracts. Bob's staff consists of Steve Drago, Angela Gabe, Mark Hong, Betty Moy, Carol Savier and Taasha Schroeder. Stephanie Seburn leads our Human Resources Department with help from Tracy Lickton, and Susan Zamechek manages the Administrative staff, which consists of Grant Blair, Ken Gilbert, Sherlinda Johnson, Antoinette Kelly and Kacey Schueler Poulos.

Finally, our deep thanks to Bill James. Without Bill, some of us would still be delivering mail.

— Don Zminda

This book is dedicated to the memory of
my father, Paul Abel. He held positions of trust
throughout a career of distinguished service to others.
His spirit and example live on.
— Doug Abel

Table of Contents

Introduction

Some numbers have all the fun. How many headlines do home runs grab in a given day? Just ask Mark McGwire or Ken Griffey Jr. How many articles make some sort of reference to strikeouts? Curt Shilling and Pedro Martinez can give you a pretty good idea. How often do the subjects of batting averages or wins or saves come up around the water cooler? Tony Gwynn, Roger Clemens and Randy Myers would all give the same answer: plenty.

And why not? They're the stars of the show. . . the numbers that keep the turnstiles turning and the registers ringing, and you'll find them all in the ninth edition of the STATS *Major League Handbook*. But that's not even close to *all* you'll find in these pages. Hey, we love the glitz and glamour just as much as the next fan, but what about the hundreds, heck, thousands, of *other* figures that play such a key role in the outcome of each and every game. Don't worry, they're in here, too.

Holds, CERA, Range Factor, Park Index, OBP, GDP, Slow Hooks, Cheap Wins, Batters Faced, Total Chances, Pitchouts—just to name a few. They may not be the sexiest stats around, but they'll tell you as much about why a team won or lost as any one of the headline-grabbers. They'll tell you that the Yankees got a big shot in the arm from their middle relievers, that Turner Field was a tough place to hit homers and that no big leaguer was better at getting on base than Frank Thomas. Throw in our exclusive Pitchers Hitting, Lefty/Righty and Player Projections sections, and you have the headlines, the stories and the stories-within-the-stories of the 1997 season.

From homers to holds. . . it's in here, and all by the beginning of November. Now *that's* worth a few headlines!

—Tony Nistler

What's Official and What's Not

The statistics in this book are technically unofficial. The official Major League Baseball averages are not released until December, but we can't wait that long. If you compare these stats with the official ones, you'll find no major differences. That said, we do *not* agree with the unofficial stats released by Major League Baseball at the end of the season in the following three instances—all involving intentional walks:

- Rickey Henderson vs. Mike Mohler, SD@Oak (7/1/97), 7th inning

- Mike Lansing vs. Robb Nen, Mon@Fla (7/14/97), 12th inning

- Wally Joyner vs. Kevin Brown, SD@Fla (7/21/97), 5th inning

In all three cases, we have counted these walks as intentional and confirmed this with the individual teams involved. As always, we take extraordinary efforts to ensure accuracy.

Career Stats

The career data section of this book includes the records of all players who saw major league action in 1997.

You probably know what most of the abbreviations stand for, but just in case:

Age is seasonal age based on July 1, 1998.

For Batters, **B** = Bats; **T** = Throws; **DH** = Designated Hitter; **PH** = Pinch Hitter; **G** = Games; **AB** = At Bats; **H** = Hits; **2B** = Doubles; **3B** = Triples; **HR** = Home Runs; **Hm** = Home Runs at Home; **Rd** = Home Runs on the Road; **TB** = Total Bases; **R** = Runs; **RBI** = Runs Batted In; **TBB** = Total Bases on Balls; **IBB** = Intentional Bases on Balls; **SO** = Strikeouts; **HBP** = Times Hit by Pitches; **SH** = Sacrifice Hits; **SF** = Sacrifice Flies; **SB** = Stolen Bases; **CS** = Times Caught Stealing; **SB%** = Stolen Base Percentage; **GDP** = Times Grounded into Double Plays; **Avg** = Batting Average; **OBP** = On-Base Percentage; **SLG** = Slugging Percentage.

For Pitchers, **SP** = Starting Pitcher; **RP** = Relief Pitcher; **G** = Games Pitched; **GS** = Games Started; **CG** = Complete Games; **GF** = Games Finished; **IP** = Innings Pitched; **BFP** = Batters Facing Pitcher; **H** = Hits Allowed; **R** = Runs Allowed; **ER** = Earned Runs Allowed; **HR** = Home Runs Allowed; **SH** = Sacrifice Hits Allowed; **SF** = Sacrifice Flies Allowed; **HB** = Hit Batsmen; **TBB** = Total Bases on Balls; **IBB** = Intentional Bases on Balls; **SO** = Strikeouts; **WP** = Wild Pitches; **Bk** = Balks; **W** = Wins; **L** = Losses; **Pct.** = Winning Percentage; **ShO** = Shutouts; **Sv** = Saves; **Op** = Save Opportunities; **Hld** = Holds; **ERA** = Earned Run Average.

An asterisk (*) by a player's minor league stats indicates that these are his 1997 minor league numbers only; previous minor league experience is not included. Figures in **boldface** indicate the player led the league in that category.

For players who played for more than one major league team in a season, stats for each team are shown just above the bottom-line career totals.

Some Class-A and Rookie Leagues are denoted with a "+" or "-" (like A+) to indicate the caliber of competition within the classification.

Jeff Abbott

Bats: R **Throws:** L **Pos:** PH-8; LF-5; RF-4; DH-3; CF-1   **Ht:** 6'1" **Wt:** 235 **Born:** 8/17/72 **Age:** 25

								BATTING											BASERUNNING				PERCENTAGES		
Year Team	Lg	G	AB	H	2B	3B	HR	(Hm	Rd)	TB	R	RBI	TBB	IBB	SO	HBP	SH	SF	SB	CS	SB%	GDP	Avg	OBP	SLG
1994 White Sox	R	4	15	7	1	0	1	—	—	11	4	3	4	0	0	0	0	0	2	1	.67	1	.467	.579	.733
Hickory	A	63	224	88	16	6	6	—	—	134	47	48	38	1	33	1	1	1	2	1	.67	4	.393	.481	.598
1995 Pr William	A+	70	264	92	16	0	4	—	—	120	41	47	26	0	25	2	1	5	7	1	.88	8	.348	.404	.455
Birmingham	AA	55	197	63	11	1	3	—	—	85	25	28	19	2	20	2	3	2	1	3	.25	3	.320	.382	.431
1996 Nashville	AAA	113	440	143	27	1	14	—	—	214	64	60	32	1	50	2	1	0	12	4	.75	12	.325	.373	.486
1997 Nashville	AAA	118	465	152	35	3	11	—	—	226	88	63	41	0	52	5	2	3	12	7	.63	12	.327	.385	.486
1997 Chicago	AL	19	38	10	1	0	1	(0	1)	14	8	2	0	0	6	0	0	0	0	0	.00	3	.263	.263	.368

Kurt Abbott

Bats: R **Throws:** R **Pos:** 2B-54; PH-29; LF-10; SS-7; 3B-4; DH-2   **Ht:** 6'0" **Wt:** 185 **Born:** 6/2/69 **Age:** 29

								BATTING											BASERUNNING				PERCENTAGES		
Year Team	Lg	G	AB	H	2B	3B	HR	(Hm	Rd)	TB	R	RBI	TBB	IBB	SO	HBP	SH	SF	SB	CS	SB%	GDP	Avg	OBP	SLG
1993 Oakland	AL	20	61	15	1	0	3	(0	3)	25	11	9	3	0	20	0	3	0	2	0	1.00	3	.246	.281	.410
1994 Florida	NL	101	345	86	17	3	9	(4	5)	136	41	33	16	1	98	5	3	2	3	0	1.00	5	.249	.291	.394
1995 Florida	NL	120	420	107	18	7	17	(12	5)	190	60	60	36	4	110	5	2	5	4	3	.57	6	.255	.318	.452
1996 Florida	NL	109	320	81	18	7	8	(6	2)	137	37	33	22	1	99	3	4	0	3	3	.50	7	.253	.307	.428
1997 Florida	NL	94	252	69	18	2	6	(1	5)	109	35	30	14	3	68	1	6	0	3	1	.75	5	.274	.315	.433
5 ML YEARS		444	1398	358	72	19	43	(23	20)	597	184	165	91	9	395	14	18	7	15	7	.68	26	.256	.307	.427

Bob Abreu

Bats: L **Throws:** R **Pos:** RF-43; PH-11; LF-10; CF-1   **Ht:** 6'0" **Wt:** 160 **Born:** 3/11/74 **Age:** 24

								BATTING											BASERUNNING				PERCENTAGES		
Year Team	Lg	G	AB	H	2B	3B	HR	(Hm	Rd)	TB	R	RBI	TBB	IBB	SO	HBP	SH	SF	SB	CS	SB%	GDP	Avg	OBP	SLG
1991 Astros	R	56	183	55	7	3	0	—	—	68	21	20	17	0	27	1	2	3	10	6	.63	3	.301	.358	.372
1992 Asheville	A	135	480	140	21	4	8	—	—	193	81	48	63	1	79	3	0	3	15	11	.58	5	.292	.375	.402
1993 Osceola	A+	129	474	134	21	17	5	—	—	204	62	55	51	1	90	1	1	3	10	14	.42	8	.283	.352	.430
1994 Jackson	AA	118	400	121	25	9	16	—	—	212	61	73	42	3	81	3	0	6	12	10	.55	2	.303	.368	.530
1995 Tucson	AAA	114	415	126	24	17	10	—	—	214	72	75	67	9	120	1	0	8	16	14	.53	6	.304	.395	.516
1996 Tucson	AAA	132	484	138	14	16	13	—	—	223	86	68	83	3	111	2	2	2	24	18	.57	5	.285	.391	.461
1997 Jackson	AA	3	12	2	1	0	0	—	—	3	2	0	1	0	5	0	0	0	0	0	.00	0	.167	.231	.250
New Orleans	AAA	47	194	52	9	4	2	—	—	75	25	22	21	2	49	0	1	3	7	4	.64	4	.268	.335	.387
1996 Houston	NL	15	22	5	1	0	0	(0	0)	6	1	1	2	0	3	0	0	0	0	0	.00	1	.227	.292	.273
1997 Houston	NL	59	188	47	10	2	3	(3	0)	70	22	26	21	0	48	1	0	3	7	2	.78	0	.250	.329	.372
2 ML YEARS		74	210	52	11	2	3	(3	0)	76	23	27	23	0	51	1	0	3	7	2	.78	1	.248	.325	.362

Juan Acevedo

Pitches: Right **Bats:** Right **Pos:** RP-23; SP-2   **Ht:** 6'2" **Wt:** 218 **Born:** 5/5/70 **Age:** 28

		HOW MUCH HE PITCHED						WHAT HE GAVE UP											THE RESULTS					
Year Team	Lg	G	GS	CG	GF	IP	BFP	H	R	ER	HR	SH	SF	HB	TBB	IBB	SO	WP	Bk	W	L	Pct.	ShO	Sv-Op	Hld	ERA
1992 Bend	A-	1	0	0	0	2	13	4	3	3	0	1	0	1	1	0	3	0	0	0	0	.000	0	0- --	—	13.50
Visalia	A+	12	12	1	0	64.2	289	75	46	39	2	2	2	3	33	0	37	1	2	3	4	.429	0	0- --	—	5.43
1993 Central Val	A+	27	20	1	3	118.2	529	119	68	58	8	5	4	9	58	0	107	12	4	9	8	.529	0	0- --	—	4.40
1994 New Haven	AA	26	26	5	0	174.2	697	142	56	46	16	4	3	5	38	0	161	4	5	17	6	.739	2	0- --	—	2.37
1995 Colo Sprngs	AAA	3	3	0	0	14.2	68	18	11	10	0	1	1	2	7	0	7	2	1	1	1	.500	0	0- --	—	6.14
Norfolk	AAA	2	2	0	0	3	9	0	0	0	0	0	1	0	1	0	2	0	0	0	0	.000	0	0- --	—	0.00
1996 Norfolk	AAA	19	19	2	0	102.2	472	116	70	68	15	3	7	8	53	0	83	11	1	4	8	.333	1	0- --	—	5.96
1997 Norfolk	AAA	18	18	1	0	116.2	487	111	55	50	7	4	3	4	34	1	99	2	4	6	6	.500	0	0- --	—	3.86
1995 Colorado	NL	17	11	0	0	65.2	291	82	53	47	15	4	2	6	20	2	40	2	1	4	6	.400	0	0-0	—	6.44
1997 New York	NL	25	2	0	4	47.2	215	52	24	19	6	2	5	4	22	2	33	0	1	3	1	.750	0	0-4	4	3.59
2 ML YEARS		42	13	0	4	113.1	506	134	77	66	21	6	7	10	42	4	73	2	2	7	7	.500	0	0-4	4	5.24

Mark Acre

Pitches: Right **Bats:** Right **Pos:** RP-15   **Ht:** 6'8" **Wt:** 240 **Born:** 9/16/68 **Age:** 29

		HOW MUCH HE PITCHED						WHAT HE GAVE UP											THE RESULTS					
Year Team	Lg	G	GS	CG	GF	IP	BFP	H	R	ER	HR	SH	SF	HB	TBB	IBB	SO	WP	Bk	W	L	Pct.	ShO	Sv-Op	Hld	ERA
1997 Edmonton *	AAA	43	0	0	26	47.2	209	48	27	22	5	3	1	1	20	5	46	2	0	3	4	.429	0	11- --	—	4.15
1994 Oakland	AL	34	0	0	6	34.1	147	24	13	13	4	3	1	1	23	3	21	1	0	5	1	.833	0	0-1	3	3.41
1995 Oakland	AL	43	0	0	10	52	236	52	35	33	7	1	2	2	28	2	47	2	1	1	2	.333	0	0-4	2	5.71
1996 Oakland	AL	22	0	0	11	25	124	38	17	17	4	1	0	2	9	4	18	0	0	1	3	.250	0	2-3	2	6.12
1997 Oakland	AL	15	0	0	5	15.2	75	21	10	10	1	0	1	0	8	0	12	0	0	2	0	1.000	0	0-2	0	5.74
4 ML YEARS		114	0	0	32	127	582	135	75	73	16	5	4	5	68	9	98	3	1	9	6	.600	0	2-10	7	5.17

Terry Adams

Pitches: Right **Bats:** Right **Pos:** RP-74   **Ht:** 6'3" **Wt:** 205 **Born:** 3/6/73 **Age:** 25

		HOW MUCH HE PITCHED						WHAT HE GAVE UP											THE RESULTS					
Year Team	Lg	G	GS	CG	GF	IP	BFP	H	R	ER	HR	SH	SF	HB	TBB	IBB	SO	WP	Bk	W	L	Pct.	ShO	Sv-Op	Hld	ERA
1995 Chicago	NL	18	0	0	9	18	86	22	15	13	0	0	0	0	10	1	15	1	0	1	1	.500	0	1-1	0	6.50
1996 Chicago	NL	69	0	0	22	101	423	84	36	33	6	7	3	1	49	6	78	5	1	3	6	.333	0	4-8	11	2.94
1997 Chicago	NL	74	0	0	39	74	341	91	43	38	3	1	2	1	40	6	64	6	0	2	9	.182	0	18-22	11	4.62

3

Year Team		HOW MUCH HE PITCHED			WHAT HE GAVE UP												THE RESULTS					
	Lg	G GS CG GF	IP	BFP	H	R	ER	HR SH SF HB	TBB IBB	SO	WP	Bk	W	L	Pct.	ShO	Sv-Op	Hld	ERA
3 ML YEARS		161 0 0 68	193	850	197	94	84	9 8 5 2	99 13	157	12	1	6	16	.273	0	23-31	22	3.92

Willie Adams

Pitches: Right **Bats:** Right **Pos:** SP-12; RP-1   **Ht:** 6'7" **Wt:** 215 **Born:** 10/8/72 **Age:** 25

Year Team	Lg	G GS CG GF	IP	BFP	H	R	ER	HR SH SF HB	TBB IBB	SO	WP	Bk	W	L	Pct.	ShO	Sv-Op	Hld	ERA
1993 Madison	A	5 5 0 0	18.2	84	21	10	7	2 1 1 0	8 0	22	1	1	0	2	.000	0	0- -	—	3.38
1994 Modesto	A+	11 5 0 6	45.1	181	41	17	17	7 2 0 0	10 0	42	2	3	7	1	.875	0	2- -	—	3.38
Huntsville	AA	10 10 0 0	60.2	256	58	32	29	3 2 3 5	23 2	33	1	1	4	3	.571	0	0- -	—	4.30
1995 Huntsville	AA	13 13 0 0	80.2	330	75	33	27	8 2 1 2	17 0	72	1	0	6	5	.545	0	0- -	—	3.01
Edmonton	AAA	11 10 1 1	68	288	73	35	33	2 2 2 6	15 5	40	3	0	2	5	.286	0	0- -	—	4.37
1996 Edmonton	AAA	19 19 3 0	112	466	95	49	47	12 1 1 6	39 2	80	4	0	10	4	.714	1	0- -	—	3.78
1997 Edmonton	AAA	13 12 0 0	75.1	345	105	57	54	13 2 4 2	19 3	58	3	1	5	4	.556	0	0- -	—	6.45
1996 Oakland	AL	12 12 1 0	76.1	329	76	39	34	11 3 2 5	23 3	68	2	0	3	4	.429	1	0-0	0	4.01
1997 Oakland	AL	13 12 0 0	58.1	282	73	53	53	9 3 5 4	32 2	37	2	0	3	5	.375	0	0-0	0	8.18
2 ML YEARS		25 24 1 0	134.2	611	149	92	87	20 6 7 9	55 5	105	4	0	6	9	.400	1	0-0	0	5.81

Joel Adamson

Pitches: Left **Bats:** Left **Pos:** RP-24; SP-6   **Ht:** 6'4" **Wt:** 185 **Born:** 7/2/71 **Age:** 26

Year Team	Lg	G GS CG GF	IP	BFP	H	R	ER	HR SH SF HB	TBB IBB	SO	WP	Bk	W	L	Pct.	ShO	Sv-Op	Hld	ERA
1990 Princeton	R+	12 8 1 3	48	204	55	27	21	2 1 0 3	12 1	39	6	7	2	5	.286	0	1- -	—	3.94
1991 Spartanburg	A	14 14 1 0	81	333	72	29	23	5 2 4 3	22 0	84	3	2	4	4	.500	1	0- -	—	2.56
Clearwater	A+	5 5 0 0	29.2	125	28	12	10	1 2 1 1	7 0	20	2	1	2	1	.667	0	0- -	—	3.03
1992 Clearwater	A+	15 15 1 0	89.2	378	90	35	34	4 2 3 7	19 0	52	0	1	5	6	.455	1	0- -	—	3.41
Reading	AA	10 10 2 0	59	255	68	36	28	10 3 1 0	13 1	35	3	0	3	6	.333	0	0- -	—	4.27
1993 Edmonton	AAA	5 5 0 0	26	125	39	21	20	5 1 1 0	13 0	7	0	1	1	2	.333	0	0- -	—	6.92
High Desert	A+	22 20 6 1	129.2	571	160	83	66	13 3 4 4	30 0	72	5	7	5	5	.500	3	0- -	—	4.58
1994 Portland	AA	33 11 2 16	91.1	402	95	51	44	9 5 2 5	32 5	59	0	0	5	6	.455	2	7- -	—	4.34
1995 Charlotte	AAA	19 18 2 0	115	471	113	51	42	12 0 3 6	20 0	80	4	2	8	4	.667	0	0- -	—	3.29
1996 Charlotte	AAA	44 8 0 14	97.2	424	108	48	41	15 3 3 3	28 2	84	1	0	6	6	.500	0	3- -	—	3.78
1997 Tucson	AAA	6 6 0 0	33	138	38	16	16	4 1 1 2	8 0	24	3	1	2	1	.667	0	0- -	—	4.36
1996 Florida	NL	9 0 0 1	11	56	18	9	9	1 2 1 1	7 0	7	0	0	0	0	.000	0	0-0	0	7.36
1997 Milwaukee	AL	30 6 0 3	76.1	324	78	36	30	13 4 2 5	19 0	56	0	1	5	3	.625	0	0-0	1	3.54
2 ML YEARS		39 6 0 4	87.1	380	96	45	39	14 6 3 6	26 0	63	0	1	5	3	.625	0	0-0	1	4.02

Rick Aguilera

Pitches: Right **Bats:** Right **Pos:** RP-61   **Ht:** 6'5" **Wt:** 203 **Born:** 12/31/61 **Age:** 36

Year Team	Lg	G GS CG GF	IP	BFP	H	R	ER	HR SH SF HB	TBB IBB	SO	WP	Bk	W	L	Pct.	ShO	Sv-Op	Hld	ERA
1985 New York	NL	21 19 2 1	122.1	507	118	49	44	8 7 4 2	37 2	74	5	2	10	7	.588	0	0- -	—	3.24
1986 New York	NL	28 20 2 2	141.2	605	145	70	61	15 6 5 7	36 1	104	5	3	10	7	.588	0	0- -	—	3.88
1987 New York	NL	18 17 1 0	115	494	124	53	46	12 7 2 3	33 2	77	9	0	11	3	.786	0	0-0	1	3.60
1988 New York	NL	11 3 0 2	24.2	111	29	20	19	2 2 0 1	10 2	16	1	1	0	4	.000	0	0-0	1	6.93
1989 NYN-Min		47 11 3 19	145	594	130	51	45	8 7 1 3	38 4	137	4	3	9	11	.450	0	7-11	1	2.79
1990 Minnesota	AL	56 0 0 54	65.1	268	55	27	20	5 0 0 4	19 6	61	3	0	5	3	.625	0	32-39	0	2.76
1991 Minnesota	AL	63 0 0 60	69	275	44	20	18	3 1 3 1	30 6	61	0	0	4	5	.444	0	42-51	0	2.35
1992 Minnesota	AL	64 0 0 61	66.2	273	60	28	21	7 1 2 1	17 4	52	5	0	2	6	.250	0	41-48	0	2.84
1993 Minnesota	AL	65 0 0 61	72.1	287	60	25	25	9 2 1 1	14 3	59	1	0	4	3	.571	0	34-40	0	3.11
1994 Minnesota	AL	44 0 0 40	44.2	201	57	23	18	7 4 1 0	10 3	46	2	0	1	4	.200	0	23-29	0	3.63
1995 Min-Bos	AL	52 0 0 51	55.1	223	46	16	16	6 1 4 1	13 1	52	0	0	3	3	.500	0	32-36	0	2.60
1996 Minnesota	AL	19 19 2 0	111.1	484	124	69	67	20 1 3 3	27 1	83	6	0	8	6	.571	0	0-0	0	5.42
1997 Minnesota	AL	61 0 0 57	68.1	285	65	29	29	9 5 3 2	22 3	68	3	0	5	4	.556	0	26-33	0	3.82
1989 New York	NL	36 0 0 19	69.1	284	59	19	18	3 5 1 2	21 3	80	3	3	6	6	.500	0	7-11	1	2.34
Minnesota	AL	11 11 3 0	75.2	310	71	32	27	5 2 0 1	17 1	57	1	0	3	5	.375	0	0-0	0	3.21
1995 Minnesota	AL	22 0 0 21	25	99	20	7	7	2 0 2 1	6 1	29	0	0	1	1	.500	0	12-15	0	2.52
Boston	AL	30 0 0 30	30.1	124	26	9	9	4 1 2 0	7 0	23	0	0	2	2	.500	0	20-21	0	2.67
13 ML YEARS		549 89 10 408	1101.2	4607	1057	480	429	111 44 29 29	306 38	890	47	9	72	66	.522	0	237- -	—	3.50

Jose Alberro

Pitches: Right **Bats:** Right **Pos:** RP-6; SP-4   **Ht:** 6'2" **Wt:** 190 **Born:** 6/29/69 **Age:** 29

Year Team	Lg	G GS CG GF	IP	BFP	H	R	ER	HR SH SF HB	TBB IBB	SO	WP	Bk	W	L	Pct.	ShO	Sv-Op	Hld	ERA
1997 Okla City *	AAA	16 16 1 0	91.2	387	90	44	43	6 2 1 5	29 1	59	3	1	5	6	.455	1	0- -	—	4.22
Columbus *	AAA	1 1 1 0	8	32	5	4	3	1 0 1 1	1 0	6	0	0	1	0	1.000	0	0- -	—	3.38
1995 Texas	AL	12 0 0 7	20.2	101	26	18	17	2 0 1 1	12 1	10	2	0	0	0	.000	0	0-0	0	7.40
1996 Texas	AL	5 1 0 1	9.1	46	14	6	6	1 0 1 0	7 1	2	0	0	0	1	.000	0	0-0	0	5.79
1997 Texas	AL	10 4 0 2	28.1	143	37	33	25	4 2 1 1	17 1	11	3	0	0	3	.000	0	0-0	0	7.94
3 ML YEARS		27 5 0 10	58.1	290	77	57	48	7 2 3 2	36 3	23	5	0	0	4	.000	0	0-0	1	7.41

4

Scott Aldred

Pitches: Left Bats: Left Pos: SP-15; RP-2 Ht: 6'4" Wt: 215 Born: 6/12/68 Age: 30

Year Team	Lg	G	GS	CG	GF	IP	BFP	H	R	ER	HR	SH	SF	HB	TBB	IBB	SO	WP	Bk	W	L	Pct.	ShO	Sv-Op	Hld	ERA
1997 Salt Lake *	AAA	7	7	0	0	39.2	187	56	39	31	4	1	2	1	16	1	23	7	0	3	3	.500	0	0- -	-	7.03
1990 Detroit	AL	4	3	0	0	14.1	63	13	6	6	0	2	1	1	10	1	7	0	0	1	2	.333	0	0-0	0	3.77
1991 Detroit	AL	11	11	1	0	57.1	253	58	37	33	9	3	2	0	30	2	35	3	1	2	4	.333	0	0-0	0	5.18
1992 Detroit	AL	16	13	0	0	65	304	80	51	49	12	4	3	3	33	4	34	1	0	3	8	.273	0	0-0	0	6.78
1993 Col-Mon	NL	8	0	0	2	12	65	19	14	12	2	2	0	1	10	1	9	2	0	1	0	1.000	0	0-1	0	9.00
1996 Det-Min	AL	36	25	0	0	165.1	748	194	125	114	29	7	7	6	68	4	111	10	1	6	9	.400	0	0-0	1	6.21
1997 Minnesota	AL	17	15	0	0	77.1	350	102	66	66	20	2	1	3	28	2	33	7	0	2	10	.167	0	0-0	0	7.68
1993 Colorado	NL	5	0	0	1	6.2	40	10	10	8	1	2	0	1	9	1	5	1	0	0	0	.000	0	0-0	0	10.80
Montreal	NL	3	0	0	1	5.1	25	9	4	4	1	0	0	0	1	0	4	1	0	1	0	1.000	0	0-1	0	6.75
1996 Detroit	AL	11	8	0	0	43.1	217	60	52	45	9	3	2	3	26	3	36	6	1	0	4	.000	0	0-0	1	9.35
Minnesota	AL	25	17	0	0	122	531	134	73	69	20	4	5	3	42	1	75	4	0	6	5	.545	0	0-0	1	5.09
6 ML YEARS		92	67	1	2	391.1	1783	466	299	280	72	20	14	14	179	14	229	23	2	15	33	.313	0	0-1	1	6.44

Manny Alexander

Bats: R Throws: R Pos: SS-54; 2B-35; PH-8; 3B-1 Ht: 5'10" Wt: 160 Born: 3/20/71 Age: 27

Year Team	Lg	G	AB	H	2B	3B	HR	(Hm	Rd)	TB	R	RBI	TBB	IBB	SO	HBP	SH	SF	SB	CS	SB%	GDP	Avg	OBP	SLG
1997 St. Lucie *	A+	1	4	1	0	0	0	—	—	1	0	0	0	0	1	0	0	0	0	0	.00	0	.250	.250	.250
1992 Baltimore	AL	4	5	1	0	0	0	(0	0)	1	1	0	0	0	3	0	0	0	0	0	.00	0	.200	.200	.200
1993 Baltimore	AL	3	0	0	0	0	0	(0	0)	0	1	0	0	0	0	0	0	0	0	0	.00	0	.000	.000	.000
1995 Baltimore	AL	94	242	57	9	1	3	(2	1)	77	35	23	20	0	30	2	4	0	11	4	.73	2	.236	.299	.318
1996 Baltimore	AL	54	68	7	0	0	0	(0	0)	7	6	4	3	0	27	0	2	0	3	3	.50	2	.103	.141	.103
1997 NYN-ChN	NL	87	248	66	12	4	3	(0	3)	95	37	22	17	3	54	3	3	1	13	1	.93	6	.266	.320	.383
1997 New York	NL	54	149	37	9	3	2	(0	2)	58	26	15	9	1	38	1	1	1	11	0	1.00	3	.248	.294	.389
Chicago	NL	33	99	29	3	1	1	(0	1)	37	11	7	8	2	16	2	2	0	2	1	.67	3	.293	.358	.374
5 ML YEARS		242	563	131	21	5	6	(2	4)	180	80	49	40	3	114	5	9	1	27	8	.77	10	.233	.289	.320

Antonio Alfonseca

Pitches: Right Bats: Right Pos: RP-17 Ht: 6'5" Wt: 235 Born: 4/16/72 Age: 26

Year Team	Lg	G	GS	CG	GF	IP	BFP	H	R	ER	HR	SH	SF	HB	TBB	IBB	SO	WP	Bk	W	L	Pct.	ShO	Sv-Op	Hld	ERA
1991 Expos	R	11	10	0	0	51	225	46	33	22	2	1	4	3	25	0	38	1	0	3	3	.500	0	0- -	-	3.88
1992 Expos	R	12	10	1	0	66	282	55	31	27	0	2	6	3	35	0	62	8	2	3	4	.429	1	0- -	-	3.68
1993 Jamestown	A-	15	4	0	3	33.2	151	31	26	23	3	0	2	3	22	1	29	4	1	2	2	.500	0	1- -	-	6.15
1994 Kane County	A	32	9	0	7	86.1	361	78	41	39	5	2	3	2	21	1	74	14	0	6	5	.545	0	0- -	-	4.07
1995 Portland	AA	19	17	1	0	96.1	405	81	43	39	6	3	3	4	42	1	75	5	4	9	3	.750	0	0- -	-	3.64
1996 Charlotte	AAA	14	13	0	1	71.2	321	86	47	44	6	1	4	3	22	0	51	2	0	4	4	.500	0	1- -	-	5.53
1997 Charlotte	AAA	46	0	0	20	58.1	246	58	34	28	8	2	2	2	20	3	45	3	2	7	2	.778	0	7- -	-	4.32
1997 Florida	NL	17	0	0	2	25.2	123	36	16	14	3	1	0	1	10	3	19	1	0	1	3	.250	0	0-2	0	4.91

Edgardo Alfonzo

Bats: R Throws: R Pos: 3B-143; SS-12; PH-7; 2B-3 Ht: 5'11" Wt: 187 Born: 11/8/73 Age: 24

Year Team	Lg	G	AB	H	2B	3B	HR	(Hm	Rd)	TB	R	RBI	TBB	IBB	SO	HBP	SH	SF	SB	CS	SB%	GDP	Avg	OBP	SLG
1995 New York	NL	101	335	93	13	5	4	(0	4)	128	26	41	12	1	37	1	4	4	1	1	.50	7	.278	.301	.382
1996 New York	NL	123	368	96	15	2	4	(2	2)	127	36	40	25	2	56	0	9	5	2	0	1.00	8	.261	.304	.345
1997 New York	NL	151	518	163	27	2	10	(4	6)	224	84	72	63	0	56	5	8	5	11	6	.65	4	.315	.391	.432
3 ML YEARS		375	1221	352	55	9	18	(6	12)	479	146	153	100	3	149	6	21	14	14	7	.67	19	.288	.342	.392

Luis Alicea

Bats: B Throws: R Pos: 2B-105; 3B-12; PH-12; DH-6 Ht: 5'9" Wt: 177 Born: 7/29/65 Age: 32

Year Team	Lg	G	AB	H	2B	3B	HR	(Hm	Rd)	TB	R	RBI	TBB	IBB	SO	HBP	SH	SF	SB	CS	SB%	GDP	Avg	OBP	SLG
1988 St. Louis	NL	93	297	63	10	4	1	(1	0)	84	20	24	25	4	32	2	4	2	1	1	.50	12	.212	.276	.283
1991 St. Louis	NL	56	68	13	3	0	0	(0	0)	16	5	0	8	0	19	0	0	0	1	0	1.00	0	.191	.276	.235
1992 St. Louis	NL	85	265	65	9	11	2	(2	0)	102	26	32	27	1	40	4	2	4	2	5	.29	5	.245	.320	.385
1993 St. Louis	NL	115	362	101	19	3	3	(2	1)	135	50	46	47	2	54	4	1	7	11	1	.92	9	.279	.362	.373
1994 St. Louis	NL	88	205	57	12	5	5	(3	2)	94	32	29	30	4	38	3	1	5	4	5	.44	1	.278	.373	.459
1995 Boston	AL	132	419	113	20	3	6	(4	1)	157	64	44	63	0	61	7	13	9	13	10	.57	10	.270	.367	.375
1996 St. Louis	NL	129	380	98	26	3	5	(4	1)	145	54	42	52	10	78	5	4	6	11	3	.79	4	.258	.350	.382
1997 Anaheim	AL	128	388	98	16	7	5	(2	3)	143	59	37	69	3	65	8	4	2	22	8	.73	6	.253	.375	.369
8 ML YEARS		826	2384	608	115	36	27	(14	13)	876	310	254	321	24	387	33	29	33	64	34	.65	45	.255	.347	.367

Jermaine Allensworth

Bats: Right Throws: Right Pos: CF-104; PH-5 Ht: 6'0" Wt: 190 Born: 1/11/72 Age: 26

Year Team	Lg	G	AB	H	2B	3B	HR	(Hm	Rd)	TB	R	RBI	TBB	IBB	SO	HBP	SH	SF	SB	CS	SB%	GDP	Avg	OBP	SLG
1993 Welland	A-	67	263	81	16	4	1	—	—	108	44	32	24	0	38	12	2	1	18	3	.86	2	.308	.390	.411
1994 Carolina	AA	118	452	109	26	8	1	—	—	154	63	34	39	0	79	11	5	3	16	14	.53	2	.241	.315	.341

Year Team	Lg	G	AB	H	2B	3B	HR	(Hm	Rd)	TB	R	RBI	TBB	IBB	SO	HBP	SH	SF	SB	CS	SB%	GDP	Avg	OBP	SLG
1995 Carolina	AA	56	219	59	14	2	1	—	—	80	37	14	25	0	34	5	2	0	13	8	.62	4	.269	.357	.365
Calgary	AAA	51	190	60	13	4	3	—	—	90	46	11	13	0	30	5	1	0	13	4	.76	3	.316	.375	.474
1996 Calgary	AAA	95	352	116	23	6	8	—	—	175	77	43	39	6	61	7	1	1	25	5	.83	4	.330	.406	.497
1997 Calgary	AAA	5	20	8	3	1	0	—	—	13	5	1	2	0	4	0	0	0	1	1	.50	0	.400	.455	.650
1996 Pittsburgh	NL	61	229	60	9	3	4	(4	0)	87	32	31	23	0	50	4	2	2	11	6	.65	2	.262	.337	.380
1997 Pittsburgh	NL	108	369	94	18	2	3	(1	2)	125	55	43	44	1	79	7	9	6	14	7	.67	5	.255	.340	.339
2 ML YEARS		169	598	154	27	5	7	(5	2)	212	87	74	67	1	129	11	11	8	25	13	.66	7	.258	.339	.355

Carlos Almanzar

Pitches: Right **Bats:** Right **Pos:** RP-4   **Ht:** 6'2" **Wt:** 166 **Born:** 11/6/73 **Age:** 24

Year Team	Lg	G	GS	CG	GF	IP	BFP	H	R	ER	HR	SH	SF	HB	TBB	IBB	SO	WP	Bk	W	L	Pct.	ShO	Sv-Op	Hld	ERA
1994 Medicne Hat	R+	14	14	0	0	84.2	351	82	38	27	2	7	1	1	19	0	77	3	2	7	4	.636	0	0-	—	2.87
1995 Knoxville	AA	35	19	0	7	126.1	546	144	77	56	10	3	6	3	32	1	93	4	1	3	12	.200	0	2-	—	3.99
1996 Knoxville	AA	54	0	0	29	94.2	418	106	58	51	13	1	2	3	33	6	105	3	0	7	8	.467	0	9-	—	4.85
1997 Knoxville	AA	21	0	0	19	25.2	109	30	14	14	2	2	2	0	5	1	25	0	0	1	1	.500	0	8-	—	4.91
Syracuse	AAA	32	0	0	17	51	189	30	9	8	2	2	1	2	8	0	47	2	0	5	1	.833	0	3-	—	1.41
1997 Toronto	AL	4	0	0	2	3.1	12	1	1	1	1	0	0	0	1	0	4	0	0	0	1	.000	0	0-0	0	2.70

Roberto Alomar

Bats: Both **Throws:** Right **Pos:** 2B-109; PH-7; DH-2   **Ht:** 6'0" **Wt:** 185 **Born:** 2/5/68 **Age:** 30

Year Team	Lg	G	AB	H	2B	3B	HR	(Hm	Rd)	TB	R	RBI	TBB	IBB	SO	HBP	SH	SF	SB	CS	SB%	GDP	Avg	OBP	SLG
1988 San Diego	NL	143	545	145	24	6	9	(5	4)	208	84	41	47	5	83	3	16	0	24	6	.80	15	.266	.328	.382
1989 San Diego	NL	158	623	184	27	1	7	(3	4)	234	82	56	53	4	76	1	17	8	42	17	.71	10	.295	.347	.376
1990 San Diego	NL	147	586	168	27	5	6	(4	2)	223	80	60	48	1	72	2	5	5	24	7	.77	16	.287	.340	.381
1991 Toronto	AL	161	637	188	41	11	9	(6	3)	278	88	69	57	3	86	4	16	5	53	11	.83	5	.295	.354	.436
1992 Toronto	AL	152	571	177	27	8	8	(5	3)	244	105	76	87	5	52	5	6	2	49	9	.84	8	.310	.405	.427
1993 Toronto	AL	153	589	192	35	6	17	(8	9)	290	109	93	80	5	67	5	4	5	55	15	.79	13	.326	.408	.492
1994 Toronto	AL	107	392	120	25	4	8	(4	4)	177	78	38	51	2	41	2	7	3	19	8	.70	14	.306	.386	.452
1995 Toronto	AL	130	517	155	24	7	13	(7	6)	232	71	66	47	3	45	0	6	7	30	3	.91	16	.300	.354	.449
1996 Baltimore	AL	153	588	193	43	4	22	(10	4)	310	132	94	90	10	65	1	8	12	17	6	.74	14	.328	.411	.527
1997 Baltimore	AL	112	412	137	23	2	14	(10	4)	206	64	60	40	2	43	3	7	7	9	3	.75	10	.333	.390	.500
10 ML YEARS		1416	5460	1659	296	54	113	(66	47)	2402	893	653	600	40	630	26	92	54	322	85	.79	121	.304	.372	.440

Sandy Alomar Jr

Bats: Right **Throws:** Right **Pos:** C-119; PH-7; DH-1   **Ht:** 6'5" **Wt:** 215 **Born:** 6/18/66 **Age:** 32

Year Team	Lg	G	AB	H	2B	3B	HR	(Hm	Rd)	TB	R	RBI	TBB	IBB	SO	HBP	SH	SF	SB	CS	SB%	GDP	Avg	OBP	SLG
1988 San Diego	NL	1	1	0	0	0	0	(0	0)	0	0	0	0	0	0	0	0	0	0	0	.00	0	.000	.000	.000
1989 San Diego	NL	7	19	4	1	0	1	(1	0)	8	1	6	3	1	3	0	0	0	0	0	.00	1	.211	.318	.421
1990 Cleveland	AL	132	445	129	26	2	9	(5	4)	186	60	66	25	2	46	2	5	6	4	1	.80	10	.290	.326	.418
1991 Cleveland	AL	51	184	40	9	0	0	(0	0)	49	10	7	8	1	24	4	2	1	0	4	.00	4	.217	.264	.266
1992 Cleveland	AL	89	299	75	16	0	2	(1	1)	97	22	26	13	3	32	5	3	0	3	3	.50	7	.251	.293	.324
1993 Cleveland	AL	64	215	58	7	1	6	(3	3)	85	24	32	11	0	28	6	1	4	3	1	.75	3	.270	.318	.395
1994 Cleveland	AL	80	292	84	15	1	14	(4	10)	143	44	43	25	2	31	2	0	1	8	4	.67	7	.288	.347	.490
1995 Cleveland	AL	66	203	61	6	0	10	(4	6)	97	32	35	7	0	26	3	4	1	3	1	.75	8	.300	.332	.478
1996 Cleveland	AL	127	418	110	23	0	11	(3	8)	166	53	50	19	0	42	3	2	2	1	0	1.00	20	.263	.299	.397
1997 Cleveland	AL	125	451	146	37	0	21	(9	12)	246	63	83	19	2	48	3	6	1	0	2	.00	16	.324	.354	.545
10 ML YEARS		742	2527	707	140	4	74	(30	44)	1077	309	348	130	11	281	28	23	16	22	16	.58	76	.280	.320	.426

Moises Alou

Bats: R **Throws:** R **Pos:** LF-91; CF-54; RF-22; PH-3   **Ht:** 6'3" **Wt:** 195 **Born:** 7/3/66 **Age:** 31

Year Team	Lg	G	AB	H	2B	3B	HR	(Hm	Rd)	TB	R	RBI	TBB	IBB	SO	HBP	SH	SF	SB	CS	SB%	GDP	Avg	OBP	SLG
1990 Pit-Mon	NL	16	20	5	0	1	0	(0	0)	6	4	0	0	0	3	0	0	0	0	0	.00	1	.200	.200	.300
1992 Montreal	NL	115	341	96	28	2	9	(6	3)	155	53	56	25	0	46	1	5	5	16	2	.89	5	.282	.328	.455
1993 Montreal	NL	136	482	138	29	6	18	(10	8)	233	70	85	38	9	53	5	3	7	17	6	.74	9	.286	.340	.483
1994 Montreal	NL	107	422	143	31	5	22	(9	13)	250	81	78	42	10	63	2	0	5	7	6	.54	7	.339	.397	.592
1995 Montreal	NL	93	344	94	22	0	14	(4	10)	158	48	58	29	6	56	9	0	4	4	3	.57	9	.273	.342	.459
1996 Montreal	NL	143	540	152	28	2	21	(14	7)	247	87	96	49	7	83	2	0	7	9	4	.69	15	.281	.339	.457
1997 Florida	NL	150	538	157	29	5	23	(12	11)	265	88	115	70	9	85	4	0	7	9	5	.64	13	.292	.373	.493
1990 Pittsburgh	NL	2	5	1	0	0	0	(0	0)	1	0	0	0	0	0	0	0	0	0	0	.00	1	.200	.200	.200
Montreal	NL	14	15	3	0	1	0	(0	0)	5	4	0	0	0	3	0	1	0	0	0	.00	0	.200	.200	.333
7 ML YEARS		760	2687	784	167	21	107	(55	52)	1314	431	488	253	41	389	23	9	35	62	26	.70	59	.292	.354	.489

Wilson Alvarez

Pitches: Left **Bats:** Left **Pos:** SP-33   **Ht:** 6'1" **Wt:** 235 **Born:** 3/24/70 **Age:** 28

Year Team	Lg	G	GS	CG	GF	IP	BFP	H	R	ER	HR	SH	SF	HB	TBB	IBB	SO	WP	Bk	W	L	Pct.	ShO	Sv-Op	Hld	ERA
1989 Texas	AL	1	1	0	0	0	5	3	3	3	2	0	0	0	2	0	0	0	0	0	1	.000	0	0-0	0	0.00
1991 Chicago	AL	10	9	2	0	56.1	237	47	26	22	9	3	1	0	29	0	32	2	0	3	2	.600	1	0-0	0	3.51

6

Year Team	Lg	G	GS	CG	GF	IP	BFP	H	R	ER	HR	SH	SF	HB	TBB	IBB	SO	WP	Bk	W	L	Pct.	ShO	Sv-Op	Hld	ERA
1992 Chicago	AL	34	9	0	4	100.1	455	103	64	58	12	3	4	4	65	2	66	2	0	5	3	.625	0	1-1	3	5.20
1993 Chicago	AL	31	31	1	0	207.2	877	168	78	68	14	13	6	7	122	8	155	2	1	15	8	.652	1	0-0	0	2.95
1994 Chicago	AL	24	24	2	0	161.2	682	147	72	62	16	6	3	0	62	1	108	3	0	12	8	.600	1	0-0	0	3.45
1995 Chicago	AL	29	29	3	0	175	769	171	96	84	21	6	5	2	93	4	118	1	2	8	11	.421	0	0-0	0	4.32
1996 Chicago	AL	35	35	0	0	217.1	946	216	106	102	21	5	2	4	97	3	181	2	0	15	10	.600	1	0-0	0	4.22
1997 ChA-SF		33	33	2	0	212	896	180	97	82	18	10	6	4	91	4	179	5	1	13	11	.542	1	0-0	0	3.48
1997 Chicago	AL	22	22	2	0	145.2	613	126	61	49	9	6	5	3	55	1	110	4	0	9	8	.529	1	0-0	0	3.03
San Francisco	NL	11	11	0	0	66.1	283	54	36	33	9	4	1	1	36	3	69	1	1	4	3	.571	0	0-0	0	4.48
8 ML YEARS		197	171	10	4	1130.1	4867	1035	542	481	113	46	27	21	561	22	839	17	4	71	54	.568	4	1-1	3	3.83

Rich Amaral

Bats: R **Throws:** R **Pos:** LF-39; PH-38; 1B-14; 2B-11; CF-9; RF-6; DH-3; 3B-1; **Ht:** 6'0" **Wt:** 175 **Born:** 4/1/62 **Age:** 36

Year Team	Lg	G	AB	H	2B	3B	HR	(Hm	Rd)	TB	R	RBI	TBB	IBB	SO	HBP	SH	SF	SB	CS	SB%	GDP	Avg	OBP	SLG
1991 Seattle	AL	14	16	1	0	0	0	(0	0)	1	2	0	1	0	5	1	0	0	0	0	.00	1	.063	.167	.063
1992 Seattle	AL	35	100	24	3	0	1	(0	1)	30	9	7	5	0	16	0	4	0	4	2	.67	4	.240	.276	.300
1993 Seattle	AL	110	373	108	1	1	1	(0	1)	137	53	44	33	0	54	3	7	5	19	11	.63	5	.290	.348	.367
1994 Seattle	AL	77	228	60	10	2	4	(2	2)	86	37	18	24	1	28	1	7	2	5	1	.83	3	.263	.333	.377
1995 Seattle	AL	90	238	67	14	2	2	(1	1)	91	45	19	21	0	33	1	1	0	21	2	.91	3	.282	.342	.382
1996 Seattle	AL	118	312	91	11	3	1	(1	0)	111	69	29	47	0	55	5	4	1	25	6	.81	6	.292	.392	.356
1997 Seattle	AL	89	190	54	5	0	1	(0	1)	62	34	21	10	0	34	3	5	2	12	8	.60	7	.284	.327	.326
7 ML YEARS		533	1457	405	67	8	10	(4	6)	518	249	138	141	1	225	14	28	10	86	30	.74	29	.278	.345	.356

Ruben Amaro

Bats: B **Throws:** R **Pos:** PH-65; CF-37; LF-26; RF-15; 1B-1 **Ht:** 5'10" **Wt:** 175 **Born:** 2/12/65 **Age:** 33

Year Team	Lg	G	AB	H	2B	3B	HR	(Hm	Rd)	TB	R	RBI	TBB	IBB	SO	HBP	SH	SF	SB	CS	SB%	GDP	Avg	OBP	SLG
1991 California	AL	10	23	5	1	0	0	(0	0)	6	0	2	3	1	3	0	0	0	0	0	.00	1	.217	.308	.261
1992 Philadelphia	NL	126	374	82	15	6	7	(5	2)	130	43	34	37	1	54	9	4	2	11	5	.69	11	.219	.303	.348
1993 Philadelphia	NL	25	48	16	2	2	1	(0	1)	25	7	6	6	0	5	0	3	1	0	0	.00	1	.333	.400	.521
1994 Cleveland	AL	26	23	5	1	0	2	(0	2)	12	5	5	2	0	3	0	0	0	2	1	.67	0	.217	.280	.522
1995 Cleveland	AL	28	60	12	3	0	1	(1	0)	18	5	7	4	0	6	2	2	0	1	3	.25	1	.200	.273	.300
1996 Philadelphia	NL	61	117	37	10	0	2	(1	1)	53	14	15	9	0	18	3	1	0	0	0	.00	3	.316	.380	.453
1997 Philadelphia	NL	117	175	41	6	1	2	(1	1)	55	18	21	21	0	24	2	0	2	1	1	.50	4	.234	.320	.314
7 ML YEARS		393	820	198	38	9	15	(8	7)	299	92	90	82	2	113	16	10	5	15	10	.60	21	.241	.321	.365

Brady Anderson

Bats: Left **Throws:** Left **Pos:** CF-124; DH-25; PH-3 **Ht:** 6'1" **Wt:** 195 **Born:** 1/18/64 **Age:** 34

Year Team	Lg	G	AB	H	2B	3B	HR	(Hm	Rd)	TB	R	RBI	TBB	IBB	SO	HBP	SH	SF	SB	CS	SB%	GDP	Avg	OBP	SLG
1988 Bos-Bal	AL	94	325	69	13	4	1	(1	0)	93	31	21	23	0	75	4	11	1	10	6	.63	3	.212	.272	.286
1989 Baltimore	AL	94	266	55	12	2	4	(2	2)	83	44	16	43	6	45	3	5	0	16	4	.80	4	.207	.324	.312
1990 Baltimore	AL	89	234	54	5	2	3	(1	2)	72	24	24	31	2	46	5	4	5	15	2	.88	4	.231	.327	.308
1991 Baltimore	AL	113	256	59	12	3	2	(1	1)	83	40	27	38	0	44	5	11	3	12	5	.71	1	.230	.338	.324
1992 Baltimore	AL	159	623	169	28	10	21	(15	6)	280	100	80	98	14	98	9	10	9	53	16	.77	2	.271	.373	.449
1993 Baltimore	AL	142	560	147	36	8	13	(2	11)	238	87	66	82	4	99	10	4	0	24	12	.67	4	.263	.363	.425
1994 Baltimore	AL	111	453	119	25	5	12	(7	5)	190	78	48	57	3	75	10	3	2	31	1	.97	4	.263	.356	.419
1995 Baltimore	AL	143	554	145	33	10	16	(10	6)	246	108	64	87	4	111	10	4	2	26	7	.79	3	.262	.371	.444
1996 Baltimore	AL	149	579	172	37	5	50	(19	31)	369	117	110	76	1	106	22	6	4	21	8	.72	11	.297	.396	.637
1997 Baltimore	AL	151	590	170	39	7	18	(8	10)	277	97	73	84	6	105	19	2	1	18	12	.60	1	.288	.393	.469
1988 Boston	AL	41	148	34	5	3	0	(1	0)	45	14	12	15	0	35	4	4	1	4	2	.67	2	.230	.315	.304
Baltimore	AL	53	177	35	8	1	1	(1	0)	48	17	9	8	0	40	0	7	0	6	4	.60	1	.198	.232	.271
10 ML YEARS		1245	4440	1159	240	56	140	(66	74)	1931	726	529	619	40	804	97	62	33	226	73	.76	40	.261	.361	.435

Brian Anderson

Pitches: Left **Bats:** Both **Pos:** SP-8 **Ht:** 6'1" **Wt:** 190 **Born:** 4/26/72 **Age:** 26

Year Team	Lg	G	GS	CG	GF	IP	BFP	H	R	ER	HR	SH	SF	HB	TBB	IBB	SO	WP	Bk	W	L	Pct.	ShO	Sv-Op	Hld	ERA
1997 Buffalo *	AAA	15	15	1	0	85.2	348	78	33	29	13	2	1		15	0	60	1	1	7	1	.875	1	0--	—	3.05
1993 California	AL	4	1	0	3	11.1	45	11	5	5	1	0	0	0	2	0	4	0	0	0	0	.000	0	0-0	0	3.97
1994 California	AL	18	18	0	0	101.2	441	120	63	59	13	3	3	0	27	0	47	5	5	7	5	.583	0	0-0	0	5.22
1995 California	AL	18	17	1	0	99.2	433	110	66	65	24	5	5	3	30	2	45	1	3	6	8	.429	0	0-0	0	5.87
1996 Cleveland	AL	10	9	0	0	51.1	215	58	29	28	9	2	3	0	14	1	21	2	0	3	1	.750	0	0-0	1	4.91
1997 Cleveland	AL	8	8	0	0	48	199	55	28	25	7	0	5	0	11	0	22	1	0	4	2	.667	0	0-0	0	4.69
5 ML YEARS		58	53	1	3	312	1333	354	191	182	54	10	19	8	84	3	139	9	8	20	16	.556	0	0-0	0	5.25

Garret Anderson

Bats: L **Throws:** L **Pos:** LF-130; CF-27; DH-4; RF-4; PH-2 **Ht:** 6'3" **Wt:** 190 **Born:** 6/30/72 **Age:** 26

Year Team	Lg	G	AB	H	2B	3B	HR	(Hm	Rd)	TB	R	RBI	TBB	IBB	SO	HBP	SH	SF	SB	CS	SB%	GDP	Avg	OBP	SLG
1994 California	AL	5	13	5	0	0	0	(0	0)	5	0	1	0	0	2	0	0	0	0	0	.00	0	.385	.385	.385
1995 California	AL	106	374	120	19	1	16	(7	9)	189	50	69	19	4	65	1	2	4	6	2	.75	8	.321	.352	.505

Year Team	Lg	G	AB	H	2B	3B	HR	(Hm	Rd)	TB	R	RBI	TBB	IBB	SO	HBP	SH	SF	SB	CS	SB%	GDP	Avg	OBP	SLG
1996 California	AL	150	607	173	33	2	12	(7	5)	246	79	72	27	5	84	0	5	3	7	9	.44	22	.285	.314	.405
1997 Anaheim	AL	154	624	189	36	3	8	(5	3)	255	76	92	30	6	70	2	1	5	10	4	.71	20	.303	.334	.409
4 ML YEARS		415	1618	487	88	6	36	(19	17)	695	205	234	76	15	221	3	8	12	23	15	.61	50	.301	.331	.430

Shane Andrews

Bats: Right **Throws:** Right **Pos:** 3B-18   **Ht:** 6'1" **Wt:** 215 **Born:** 8/28/71 **Age:** 26

Year Team	Lg	G	AB	H	2B	3B	HR	(Hm	Rd)	TB	R	RBI	TBB	IBB	SO	HBP	SH	SF	SB	CS	SB%	GDP	Avg	OBP	SLG
1997 Ottawa *	AAA	3	12	3	0	0	1	—	—	6	3	1	1	0	0	0	0	0	0	0	.00	1	.250	.308	.500
Wst Plm Bch *	A+	5	17	3	2	0	1	—	—	8	2	5	2	0	7	0	0	1	0	0	.00	0	.176	.250	.471
1995 Montreal	NL	84	220	47	10	1	8	(2	6)	83	27	31	17	2	68	1	1	2	1	1	.50	4	.214	.271	.377
1996 Montreal	NL	127	375	85	15	2	19	(8	11)	161	43	64	35	8	119	2	0	2	3	1	.75	2	.227	.295	.429
1997 Montreal	NL	18	64	13	3	0	4	(2	2)	28	10	9	3	0	20	0	0	2	0	0	.00	0	.203	.232	.438
3 ML YEARS		229	659	145	28	3	31	(12	19)	272	80	104	55	10	207	3	1	6	4	2	.67	6	.220	.281	.413

Luis Andujar

Pitches: Right **Bats:** Right **Pos:** RP-9; SP-8   **Ht:** 6'2" **Wt:** 175 **Born:** 11/22/72 **Age:** 25

	HOW MUCH HE PITCHED						WHAT HE GAVE UP										THE RESULTS						
Year Team	Lg	G	GS	CG	GF	IP	BFP	H	R	ER	HR	SH	SF	HB	TBB	IBB	SO	WP	Bk	W	L	Pct.	ShO	Sv-Op	Hld	ERA
1997 Syracuse *	AAA	13	5	1	7	39	169	37	25	24	6	2	2	3	14	1	29	1	1	1	6	.143	0	1--	--	5.54
1995 Chicago	AL	5	5	0	0	30.1	128	26	12	11	4	0	0	1	14	2	9	0	0	2	1	.667	0	0-0	0	3.26
1996 ChA-Tor	AL	8	7	0	0	37.1	170	46	30	29	8	1	4	1	16	0	11	1	0	1	3	.250	0	0-0	0	6.99
1997 Toronto	AL	17	8	0	5	50	244	76	45	36	9	3	4	0	21	1	28	2	0	0	6	.000	0	0-0	0	6.48
1996 Chicago	AL	5	5	0	0	23	113	32	22	21	4	1	2	0	15	0	6	0	0	0	2	.000	0	0-0	0	8.22
Toronto	AL	3	2	0	0	14.1	57	14	8	8	4	0	2	1	1	0	5	1	0	1	1	.500	0	0-0	0	5.02
3 ML YEARS		30	20	0	5	117.2	542	148	87	76	21	4	8	2	51	3	48	3	0	3	10	.231	0	0-0	1	5.81

Eric Anthony

Bats: Left **Throws:** Left **Pos:** PH-29; LF-17; RF-4   **Ht:** 6'2" **Wt:** 195 **Born:** 11/8/67 **Age:** 30

Year Team	Lg	G	AB	H	2B	3B	HR	(Hm	Rd)	TB	R	RBI	TBB	IBB	SO	HBP	SH	SF	SB	CS	SB%	GDP	Avg	OBP	SLG
1997 Okla City *	AAA	9	36	16	2	0	2	—	—	24	3	9	2	0	7	0	0	1	0	0	.00	0	.444	.462	.667
Albuquerque *	AAA	27	105	36	6	1	7	—	—	65	18	27	11	1	28	0	0	1	2	3	.40	0	.343	.402	.619
1989 Houston	NL	25	61	11	2	0	4	(2	2)	25	7	7	9	2	16	0	0	0	0	0	.00	1	.180	.286	.410
1990 Houston	NL	84	239	46	8	0	10	(5	5)	84	26	29	29	3	78	2	1	6	5	0	1.00	4	.192	.279	.351
1991 Houston	NL	39	118	18	6	0	1	(0	1)	27	11	7	12	1	41	0	0	2	1	0	1.00	0	.153	.227	.229
1992 Houston	NL	137	440	105	15	1	19	(9	10)	179	45	80	38	5	98	1	0	4	5	4	.56	7	.239	.298	.407
1993 Houston	NL	145	486	121	19	4	15	(5	10)	193	70	66	49	2	88	2	0	7	3	5	.38	9	.249	.319	.397
1994 Seattle	AL	79	262	62	14	1	10	(3	7)	108	31	30	23	4	66	0	0	2	6	2	.75	7	.237	.297	.412
1995 Cincinnati	NL	47	134	36	6	0	5	(3	2)	57	19	23	13	2	30	0	0	3	2	1	.67	1	.269	.327	.425
1996 Cin-Col	NL	79	185	45	8	0	12	(4	8)	89	32	22	32	2	56	0	0	3	1	0	1.00	3	.243	.353	.481
1997 Los Angeles	NL	47	74	18	3	2	2	(1	1)	31	8	5	12	1	18	0	0	0	2	0	1.00	2	.243	.349	.419
1996 Cincinnati	NL	47	123	30	6	0	8	(3	5)	60	22	13	22	2	36	0	0	0	0	0	.00	2	.244	.359	.488
Colorado	NL	32	62	15	2	0	4	(1	3)	29	10	9	10	0	20	0	0	3	1	0	1.00	1	.242	.342	.468
9 ML YEARS		682	1999	462	81	8	78	(32	46)	793	249	269	217	22	491	5	3	19	24	14	.63	34	.231	.305	.397

Kevin Appier

Pitches: Right **Bats:** Right **Pos:** SP-34   **Ht:** 6'2" **Wt:** 195 **Born:** 12/6/67 **Age:** 30

	HOW MUCH HE PITCHED						WHAT HE GAVE UP										THE RESULTS						
Year Team	Lg	G	GS	CG	GF	IP	BFP	H	R	ER	HR	SH	SF	HB	TBB	IBB	SO	WP	Bk	W	L	Pct.	ShO	Sv-Op	Hld	ERA
1989 Kansas City	AL	6	5	0	0	21.2	106	34	22	22	3	0	3	0	12	1	10	0	0	1	4	.200	0	0-0	0	9.14
1990 Kansas City	AL	32	24	3	1	185.2	784	179	67	67	13	5	9	6	54	2	127	6	1	12	8	.600	3	0-0	0	2.76
1991 Kansas City	AL	34	31	6	1	207.2	881	205	97	79	13	8	6	2	61	3	158	7	1	13	10	.565	3	0-0	1	3.42
1992 Kansas City	AL	30	30	3	0	208.1	852	167	59	57	10	8	3	2	68	5	150	4	0	15	8	.652	0	0-0	0	2.46
1993 Kansas City	AL	34	34	5	0	238.2	953	183	74	68	8	3	5	1	81	3	186	5	0	18	8	.692	1	0-0	0	2.56
1994 Kansas City	AL	23	23	1	0	155	653	137	68	66	11	9	7	4	63	7	145	11	1	7	6	.538	0	0-0	0	3.83
1995 Kansas City	AL	31	31	4	0	201.1	832	163	90	87	14	3	3	8	80	1	185	5	0	15	10	.600	1	0-0	0	3.89
1996 Kansas City	AL	32	32	5	0	211.1	874	192	87	85	17	7	4	5	75	2	207	10	1	14	11	.560	1	0-0	0	3.62
1997 Kansas City	AL	34	34	4	0	235.2	972	215	96	89	24	4	4	4	74	2	196	14	1	9	13	.409	4	0-0	0	3.40
9 ML YEARS		256	244	31	2	1665.1	6907	1475	660	610	113	47	44	32	568	26	1364	62	5	104	78	.571	10	0-0	1	3.30

Alex Arias

Bats: Right **Throws:** Right **Pos:** 3B-37; PH-31; SS-11   **Ht:** 6'3" **Wt:** 185 **Born:** 11/20/67 **Age:** 30

Year Team	Lg	G	AB	H	2B	3B	HR	(Hm	Rd)	TB	R	RBI	TBB	IBB	SO	HBP	SH	SF	SB	CS	SB%	GDP	Avg	OBP	SLG
1992 Chicago	NL	32	99	29	6	0	0	(0	0)	35	14	7	11	0	13	2	1	0	0	0	.00	4	.293	.375	.354
1993 Florida	NL	96	249	67	5	1	2	(1	1)	80	27	20	27	0	18	3	1	1	1	1	.50	5	.269	.344	.321
1994 Florida	NL	59	113	27	5	0	0	(0	0)	32	4	15	9	0	19	1	1	1	0	1	.00	1	.239	.298	.283
1995 Florida	NL	94	216	58	9	2	3	(2	1)	80	22	26	22	1	20	2	3	3	1	0	1.00	8	.269	.337	.370
1996 Florida	NL	100	224	62	11	2	3	(1	2)	86	27	26	17	1	28	3	1	1	2	0	1.00	2	.277	.335	.384
1997 Florida	NL	74	93	23	2	0	1	(0	1)	28	13	11	12	0	12	3	4	0	0	1	.00	6	.247	.352	.301
6 ML YEARS		455	994	266	38	5	9	(4	5)	341	107	105	98	2	110	14	11	8	4	3	.57	30	.268	.339	.343

George Arias

Bats: Right **Throws:** Right **Pos:** 3B-9; PH-6; DH-1   **Ht:** 5'11" **Wt:** 190 **Born:** 3/12/72 **Age:** 26

						BATTING												BASERUNNING				PERCENTAGES		
Year Team	Lg	G	AB	H	2B	3B	HR	(Hm | Rd)	TB	R	RBI	TBB	IBB	SO	HBP	SH	SF	SB	CS	SB%	GDP	Avg	OBP	SLG
1993 Cedar Rapds	A	74	253	55	13	3	9	—	—	101	31	41	31	1	65	3	1	2	6	1	.86	6	.217	.308	.399
1994 Lk Elsinore	A+	134	514	144	28	3	23	—	—	247	89	80	58	1	111	5	3	4	6	3	.67	9	.280	.356	.481
1995 Midland	AA	134	520	145	19	10	30	—	—	274	91	104	63	1	119	5	1	5	3	1	.75	11	.279	.359	.527
1996 Vancouver	AAA	59	243	82	24	0	9	—	—	133	49	55	20	2	38	3	0	2	2	1	.67	5	.337	.392	.547
1997 Vancouver	AAA	105	401	112	28	3	11	—	—	179	71	60	39	4	51	4	1	5	3	4	.43	17	.279	.345	.446
Las Vegas	AAA	10	30	10	4	1	1			19	4	5	3	0	8	0	0	0	0	0	.00	1	.333	.394	.633
1996 California	AL	84	252	60	8	1	6	(5 | 1)	88	19	28	16	2	50	0	6	0	2	0	1.00	6	.238	.284	.349
1997 Ana-SD		14	28	7	1	0	0	(0 | 0)	8	3	3	0	0	1	0	0	0	0	0	.00	2	.250	.250	.286
1997 Anaheim	AL	3	6	2	0	0	0	(0 | 0)	2	1	1	0	0	0	0	0	0	0	0	.00	0	.333	.333	.333
San Diego	NL	11	22	5	1	0	0	(0 | 0)	6	2	2	0	0	1	0	0	0	0	0	.00	2	.227	.227	.273
2 ML YEARS		98	280	67	9	1	6	(5 | 1)	96	22	31	16	2	51	0	6	0	2	0	1.00	8	.239	.280	.343

Rene Arocha

Pitches: Right **Bats:** Right **Pos:** RP-6   **Ht:** 6'0" **Wt:** 205 **Born:** 2/24/66 **Age:** 32

		HOW MUCH HE PITCHED						WHAT HE GAVE UP										THE RESULTS						
Year Team	Lg	G	GS	CG	GF	IP	BFP	H	R	ER	HR	SH	SF	HB	TBB	IBB	SO	WP	Bk	W	L	Pct.	ShO	Sv-Op Hld	ERA
1997 Phoenix *	AAA	18	18	1	0	111.2	470	121	59	59	17	3	2	4	27	0	68	3	0	7	3	.700	0	0-- —	4.76
Columbus *	AAA	4	1	0	1	9.2	37	7	2	2	0	0	1	0	2	0	10	0	0	1	0	1.000	0	0-- —	1.86
1993 St. Louis	NL	32	29	1	0	188	774	197	89	79	20	8	5	3	31	2	96	3	1	11	8	.579	0	0-- —	3.78
1994 St. Louis	NL	45	7	1	25	83	360	94	42	37	9	5	1	4	21	4	62	2	0	4	4	.500	1	11-12 6	4.01
1995 St. Louis	NL	41	0	0	13	49.2	216	55	24	22	6	8	2	3	18	4	25	2	0	3	5	.375	0	0-7 14	3.99
1997 San Francisco	NL	6	0	0	2	10.1	54	17	14	13	2	1	1	1	5	2	7	0	0	0	0	.000	0	0-1 0	11.32
4 ML YEARS		124	36	2	40	331	1404	363	169	151	37	22	9	11	75	12	190	7	1	18	17	.514	1	11-20 20	4.11

Andy Ashby

Pitches: Right **Bats:** Right **Pos:** SP-30   **Ht:** 6'5" **Wt:** 190 **Born:** 7/11/67 **Age:** 30

		HOW MUCH HE PITCHED						WHAT HE GAVE UP										THE RESULTS						
Year Team	Lg	G	GS	CG	GF	IP	BFP	H	R	ER	HR	SH	SF	HB	TBB	IBB	SO	WP	Bk	W	L	Pct.	ShO	Sv-Op Hld	ERA
1991 Philadelphia	NL	8	8	0	0	42	186	41	28	28	5	1	3	3	19	0	26	6	0	1	5	.167	0	0-0	6.00
1992 Philadelphia	NL	10	8	0	0	37	171	42	31	31	6	2	1	1	21	0	24	2	0	1	3	.250	0	0-0	7.54
1993 Col-SD	NL	32	21	0	3	123	577	168	100	93	19	6	7	4	56	5	77	6	3	3	10	.231	0	1-1	6.80
1994 San Diego	NL	24	24	4	0	164.1	682	145	75	62	16	11	3	3	43	12	121	5	0	6	11	.353	0	0-0	3.40
1995 San Diego	NL	31	31	2	0	192.2	800	180	79	63	17	10	4	11	62	3	150	7	0	12	10	.545	2	0-0	2.94
1996 San Diego	NL	24	24	1	0	150.2	612	147	60	54	17	6	2	3	34	1	85	3	0	9	5	.643	0	0-0	3.23
1997 San Diego	NL	30	30	2	0	200.2	851	207	108	92	17	13	6	5	49	2	144	3	0	9	11	.450	0	0-0	4.13
1993 Colorado	NL	20	9	0	3	54	277	89	54	51	5	3	3	3	32	4	33	2	3	0	4	.000	0	1-1	8.50
San Diego	NL	12	12	0	0	69	300	79	46	42	14	3	4	1	24	1	44	4	0	3	6	.333	0	0-0	5.48
7 ML YEARS		159	146	9	3	910.1	3879	930	481	423	97	49	27	30	284	23	627	32	3	41	55	.427	2	1-1	4.18

Billy Ashley

Bats: Right **Throws:** Right **Pos:** PH-37; LF-35   **Ht:** 6'7" **Wt:** 235 **Born:** 7/11/70 **Age:** 27

						BATTING												BASERUNNING				PERCENTAGES		
Year Team	Lg	G	AB	H	2B	3B	HR	(Hm	Rd)	TB	R	RBI	TBB	IBB	SO	HBP	SH	SF	SB	CS	SB%	GDP	Avg	OBP	SLG
1992 Los Angeles	NL	29	95	21	5	0	2	(2	0)	32	6	6	5	0	34	0	0	0	0	0	.00	2	.221	.260	.337
1993 Los Angeles	NL	14	37	9	0	0	0	(0	0)	9	0	0	2	0	11	0	0	0	0	0	.00	0	.243	.282	.243
1994 Los Angeles	NL	2	6	2	1	0	0	(0	0)	3	0	0	0	0	2	0	0	0	0	0	.00	0	.333	.333	.500
1995 Los Angeles	NL	81	215	51	5	0	8	(6	2)	80	17	27	25	4	88	2	0	2	0	0	.00	8	.237	.320	.372
1996 Los Angeles	NL	71	110	22	2	1	9	(5	4)	53	18	25	21	1	44	1	0	1	0	0	.00	3	.200	.331	.482
1997 Los Angeles	NL	71	131	32	7	0	6	(4	2)	57	12	19	8	0	46	1	0	0	0	0	.00	2	.244	.293	.435
6 ML YEARS		268	594	137	20	1	25	(17	8)	234	53	77	61	5	225	4	0	3	0	0	.00	15	.231	.305	.394

Paul Assenmacher

Pitches: Left **Bats:** Left **Pos:** RP-75   **Ht:** 6'3" **Wt:** 210 **Born:** 12/10/60 **Age:** 37

		HOW MUCH HE PITCHED						WHAT HE GAVE UP										THE RESULTS						
Year Team	Lg	G	GS	CG	GF	IP	BFP	H	R	ER	HR	SH	SF	HB	TBB	IBB	SO	WP	Bk	W	L	Pct.	ShO	Sv-Op Hld	ERA
1986 Atlanta	NL	61	0	0	27	68.1	287	61	23	19	5	7	1	0	26	4	56	2	3	7	3	.700	0	7-- —	2.50
1987 Atlanta	NL	52	0	0	10	54.2	251	58	41	31	8	2	1	1	24	4	39	0	0	1	1	.500	0	2-6 10	5.10
1988 Atlanta	NL	64	0	0	32	79.1	329	72	28	27	4	8	1	1	32	11	71	7	0	8	7	.533	0	5-11 8	3.06
1989 Atl-ChN	NL	63	0	0	17	76.2	331	74	37	34	3	9	3	1	28	8	79	3	1	3	4	.429	0	0-3 13	3.99
1990 Chicago	NL	74	1	0	21	103	426	90	33	32	10	10	3	1	36	8	95	2	0	7	2	.778	0	10-20 10	2.80
1991 Chicago	NL	75	0	0	31	102.2	427	85	41	37	10	8	4	3	31	6	117	4	0	7	8	.467	0	15-24 14	3.24
1992 Chicago	NL	70	0	0	23	68	298	72	32	31	6	1	2	3	26	5	67	4	0	4	4	.500	0	8-13 20	4.10
1993 ChN-NYA		72	0	0	21	56	237	54	21	21	5	4	0	1	22	6	45	0	0	4	3	.571	0	0-5 17	3.38
1994 Chicago	AL	44	0	0	11	33	134	26	13	13	2	1	3	1	13	2	29	1	0	1	2	.333	0	1-3 14	3.55
1995 Cleveland	AL	47	0	0	12	38.1	160	32	13	12	3	1	2	3	12	3	40	1	0	6	2	.750	0	0-1 9	2.82
1996 Cleveland	AL	63	0	0	25	46.2	201	46	18	16	1	4	2	4	14	5	44	2	0	4	2	.667	0	1-3 13	3.09
1997 Cleveland	AL	75	0	0	20	49	205	43	17	16	5	1	2	1	15	5	53	4	0	5	0	1.000	0	4-5 20	2.94
1989 Atlanta	NL	49	0	0	14	57.2	247	55	26	23	2	7	2	1	16	7	64	3	1	1	3	.250	0	0-2 7	3.59
Chicago		14	0	0	3	19	84	19	11	11	1	2	1	0	12	1	15	0	0	2	1	.667	0	0-1 6	5.21
1993 Chicago	NL	46	0	0	15	38.2	166	44	15	15	5	0	0	0	13	3	34	0	0	2	1	.667	0	0-4 12	3.49
New York	AL	26	0	0	6	17.1	71	10	6	6	0	4	0	1	9	3	11	0	0	2	2	.500	0	0-1 5	3.12

		HOW MUCH HE PITCHED						WHAT HE GAVE UP											THE RESULTS					
Year Team	Lg	G	GS	CG	GF	IP	BFP	H	R	ER	HR	SH	SF	HB	TBB	IBB	SO	WP	Bk	W	L	Pct.	ShO	Sv-Op	Hld	ERA
12 ML YEARS		760	1	0	250	775.2	3286	713	317	289	62	56	24	20	279	67	735	30	4	57	38	.600	0	53- -	—	3.35

Pedro Astacio

Pitches: Right **Bats:** Right **Pos:** SP-31; RP-2   **Ht:** 6'2" **Wt:** 195 **Born:** 11/28/69 **Age:** 28

		HOW MUCH HE PITCHED						WHAT HE GAVE UP											THE RESULTS					
Year Team	Lg	G	GS	CG	GF	IP	BFP	H	R	ER	HR	SH	SF	HB	TBB	IBB	SO	WP	Bk	W	L	Pct.	ShO	Sv-Op	Hld	ERA
1992 Los Angeles	NL	11	11	4	0	82	341	80	23	18	1	3	2	2	20	4	43	1	0	5	5	.500	4	0-0	0	1.98
1993 Los Angeles	NL	31	31	3	0	186.1	777	165	80	74	14	7	8	5	68	5	122	8	9	14	9	.609	2	0-0	0	3.57
1994 Los Angeles	NL	23	23	3	0	149	625	142	77	71	18	6	5	4	47	4	108	4	0	6	8	.429	1	0-0	0	4.29
1995 Los Angeles	NL	48	11	1	7	104	436	103	53	49	12	5	3	4	29	5	80	5	0	7	8	.467	1	0-1	2	4.24
1996 Los Angeles	NL	35	32	0	0	211.2	885	207	86	81	18	11	5	9	67	9	130	6	2	9	8	.529	0	0-0	0	3.44
1997 LA-Col	NL	33	31	2	2	202.1	862	200	98	93	24	9	7	9	61	0	166	6	3	12	10	.545	1	0-0	0	4.14
1997 Los Angeles	NL	26	24	2	2	153.2	654	151	75	70	15	9	5	4	47	0	115	4	3	7	9	.438	1	0-0	0	4.10
Colorado	NL	7	7	0	0	48.2	208	49	23	23	9	0	2	5	14	0	51	2	0	5	1	.833	0	0-0	0	4.25
6 ML YEARS		181	139	13	9	935.1	3926	897	417	386	87	41	30	33	292	27	649	30	14	53	48	.525	9	0-1	2	3.71

Rich Aurilia

Bats: Right **Throws:** Right **Pos:** SS-36; PH-13   **Ht:** 6'1" **Wt:** 170 **Born:** 9/2/71 **Age:** 26

		BATTING															BASERUNNING				PERCENTAGES		
Year Team	Lg	G	AB	H	2B	3B	HR	(Hm | Rd)	TB	R	RBI	TBB	IBB	SO	HBP	SH	SF	SB	CS	SB%	GDP	Avg	OBP	SLG
1997 Phoenix *	AAA	8	34	10	2	0	1	—	—	15	9	5	5	0	4	0	0	0	2	1	.67	1	.294	.385	.441
1995 San Francisco	NL	9	19	9	3	0	2	(0 | 2)	18	4	4	1	0	2	0	1	1	1	0	1.00	1	.474	.476	.947
1996 San Francisco	NL	105	318	76	7	1	3	(1 | 2)	94	27	26	25	2	52	1	6	2	4	1	.80	1	.239	.295	.296
1997 San Francisco	NL	46	102	28	8	0	5	(1 | 4)	51	16	19	8	0	15	0	1	2	1	1	.50	3	.275	.321	.500
3 ML YEARS		160	439	113	18	1	10	(2 | 8)	163	47	49	34	2	69	1	8	5	6	2	.75	5	.257	.309	.371

Brad Ausmus

Bats: Right **Throws:** Right **Pos:** C-129; PH-12   **Ht:** 5'11" **Wt:** 190 **Born:** 4/14/69 **Age:** 29

		BATTING															BASERUNNING				PERCENTAGES		
Year Team	Lg	G	AB	H	2B	3B	HR	(Hm | Rd)	TB	R	RBI	TBB	IBB	SO	HBP	SH	SF	SB	CS	SB%	GDP	Avg	OBP	SLG
1993 San Diego	NL	49	160	41	8	1	5	(4 | 1)	66	18	12	6	0	28	0	0	0	2	0	1.00	2	.256	.283	.413
1994 San Diego	NL	101	327	82	12	1	7	(6 | 1)	117	45	24	30	12	63	1	6	2	5	1	.83	8	.251	.314	.358
1995 San Diego	NL	103	328	96	16	4	5	(2 | 3)	135	44	34	31	3	56	2	4	4	16	5	.76	6	.293	.363	.412
1996 SD-Det		125	375	83	16	0	5	(2 | 3)	114	46	35	39	1	72	5	6	2	4	8	.33	8	.221	.302	.304
1997 Houston	NL	130	425	113	25	1	4	(1 | 3)	152	45	44	38	4	78	3	6	6	14	6	.70	8	.266	.326	.358
1996 San Diego	NL	50	149	27	4	0	1	(0 | 1)	34	16	13	13	0	27	3	1	0	1	4	.20	4	.181	.261	.228
Detroit	AL	75	226	56	12	0	4	(2 | 2)	80	30	22	26	1	45	2	5	2	3	4	.43	4	.248	.328	.354
5 ML YEARS		508	1615	415	77	7	26	(15 | 11)	584	198	149	144	20	297	11	22	14	41	20	.67	32	.257	.320	.362

Bruce Aven

Bats: R **Throws:** R **Pos:** LF-10; RF-2; PH-2; CF-1   **Ht:** 5'9" **Wt:** 180 **Born:** 3/4/72 **Age:** 26

		BATTING															BASERUNNING				PERCENTAGES		
Year Team	Lg	G	AB	H	2B	3B	HR	(Hm | Rd)	TB	R	RBI	TBB	IBB	SO	HBP	SH	SF	SB	CS	SB%	GDP	Avg	OBP	SLG
1994 Watertown	A-	61	220	73	14	5	5	—	—	112	49	33	20	0	45	12	2	5	12	3	.80	1	.332	.409	.509
1995 Kinston	A+	130	479	125	23	5	23	—	—	227	70	69	41	3	109	13	0	1	15	9	.63	7	.261	.335	.474
1996 Canton-Akrn	AA	131	481	143	31	4	23	—	—	251	91	79	43	0	101	17	0	3	22	6	.79	9	.297	.373	.522
Buffalo	AAA	3	9	6	0	0	1	—	—	9	5	2	1	0	1	0	0	0	0	1	.00	0	.667	.727	1.000
1997 Buffalo	AAA	121	432	124	27	3	17	—	—	208	69	77	50	0	99	11	2	5	10	3	.77	10	.287	.371	.481
1997 Cleveland	AL	13	19	4	1	0	0	(0 | 0)	5	4	2	1	0	5	0	0	0	0	1	.00	0	.211	.250	.263

Steve Avery

Pitches: Left **Bats:** Left **Pos:** SP-18; RP-4   **Ht:** 6'4" **Wt:** 205 **Born:** 4/14/70 **Age:** 28

		HOW MUCH HE PITCHED						WHAT HE GAVE UP											THE RESULTS					
Year Team	Lg	G	GS	CG	GF	IP	BFP	H	R	ER	HR	SH	SF	HB	TBB	IBB	SO	WP	Bk	W	L	Pct.	ShO	Sv-Op	Hld	ERA
1997 Sarasota *	A+	1	1	0	0	3	11	2	0	0	0	0	0	0	1	0	3	0	0	0	0	.000	0	0- -	—	0.00
Red Sox *	R	1	1	0	0	6	25	5	3	1	0	0	0	0	0	0	8	0	0	0	0	.000	0	0- -	—	1.50
Pawtucket *	AAA	1	1	0	0	5	19	1	0	0	0	0	0	0	3	0	1	0	0	1	0	1.000	0	0- -	—	0.00
1990 Atlanta	NL	21	20	1	1	99	466	121	79	62	7	14	4	2	45	2	75	5	1	3	11	.214	0	0-0	0	5.64
1991 Atlanta	NL	35	35	3	0	210.1	868	189	89	79	21	8	4	3	65	0	137	4	1	18	8	.692	1	0-0	0	3.38
1992 Atlanta	NL	35	35	2	0	233.2	969	216	95	83	14	12	8	0	71	3	129	7	3	11	11	.500	2	0-0	0	3.20
1993 Atlanta	NL	35	35	3	0	223.1	891	216	81	73	14	12	8	0	43	5	125	3	1	18	6	.750	1	0-0	0	2.94
1994 Atlanta	NL	24	24	1	0	151.2	628	127	71	68	15	4	6	4	55	4	122	5	2	8	3	.727	0	0-0	0	4.04
1995 Atlanta	NL	29	29	3	0	173.1	724	165	92	90	22	6	4	6	52	4	141	3	0	7	13	.350	1	0-0	0	4.67
1996 Atlanta	NL	24	23	1	0	131	567	146	70	65	10	7	3	4	40	8	86	5	0	7	10	.412	0	0-0	0	4.47
1997 Boston	AL	22	18	0	1	96.2	453	127	76	69	15	1	4	2	49	0	51	4	0	6	7	.462	0	0-0	1	6.42
8 ML YEARS		225	219	14	2	1319	5566	1307	653	589	118	64	41	21	420	26	866	36	8	78	69	.531	6	0-0	1	4.02

Bobby Ayala

Pitches: Right Bats: Right Pos: RP-71   Ht: 6'3" Wt: 210 Born: 7/8/69 Age: 28

		HOW MUCH HE PITCHED						WHAT HE GAVE UP											THE RESULTS						
Year Team	Lg	G	GS	CG	GF	IP	BFP	H	R	ER	HR	SH	SF	HB	TBB	IBB	SO	WP	Bk	W	L	Pct.	ShO	Sv-Op	Hld	ERA
1992 Cincinnati	NL	5	5	0	0	29	127	33	15	14	1	2	0	1	13	2	23	0	0	2	1	.667	0	0-0	0	4.34
1993 Cincinnati	NL	43	9	0	8	98	450	106	72	61	16	9	2	7	45	4	65	5	0	7	10	.412	0	3-5	6	5.60
1994 Seattle	AL	46	0	0	40	56.2	236	42	25	18	2	1	2	0	26	0	76	2	0	4	3	.571	0	18-24	6	2.86
1995 Seattle	AL	63	0	0	50	71	320	73	42	35	9	2	3	6	30	4	77	3	0	6	5	.545	0	19-27	2	4.44
1996 Seattle	AL	50	0	0	26	67.1	285	65	45	44	10	2	2	2	25	3	61	2	0	6	3	.667	0	3-6	7	5.88
1997 Seattle	AL	71	0	0	33	96.2	403	91	45	41	14	3	6	3	41	3	92	6	0	10	5	.667	0	8-12	15	3.82
6 ML YEARS		278	14	0	157	418.2	1821	410	244	213	52	19	15	19	180	16	394	18	0	35	27	.565	0	51-74	30	4.58

Manny Aybar

Pitches: Right Bats: Right Pos: SP-12   Ht: 6'1" Wt: 165 Born: 10/5/74 Age: 23

		HOW MUCH HE PITCHED						WHAT HE GAVE UP											THE RESULTS						
Year Team	Lg	G	GS	CG	GF	IP	BFP	H	R	ER	HR	SH	SF	HB	TBB	IBB	SO	WP	Bk	W	L	Pct.	ShO	Sv-Op	Hld	ERA
1994 Cardinals	R	13	13	1	0	72.1	295	69	25	17	2	4	4	9	0	0	79	4	3	6	1	.857	0	0--	—	2.12
1995 Savannah	A	18	18	2	0	112.2	461	82	46	38	8	7	4	2	36	0	99	8	1	3	8	.273	1	0--	—	3.04
St. Pete	A+	9	9	0	0	48.1	202	42	27	18	4	0	1	1	16	0	43	7	1	2	5	.286	0	0--	—	3.35
1996 Arkansas	AA	20	20	0	0	121	507	120	53	41	10	6	3	0	34	0	83	3	3	6	6	.571	0	0--	—	3.05
Louisville	AAA	5	5	0	0	30.2	123	26	12	11	1	0	1	0	7	0	25	3	2	2	2	.500	0	0--	—	3.23
1997 Louisville	AAA	22	22	3	0	137	579	131	60	53	10	2	4	4	45	2	114	7	3	5	8	.385	2	0--	—	3.48
1997 St. Louis	NL	12	12	0	0	68	295	66	33	32	8	4	4	2	29	0	41	1	1	2	4	.333	0	0-0	0	4.24

Carlos Baerga

Bats: Both Throws: Right Pos: 2B-131; PH-8   Ht: 5'11" Wt: 200 Born: 11/4/68 Age: 29

		BATTING																	BASERUNNING				PERCENTAGES		
Year Team	Lg	G	AB	H	2B	3B	HR	Hm	Rd	TB	R	RBI	TBB	IBB	SO	HBP	SH	SF	SB	CS	SB%	GDP	Avg	OBP	SLG
1990 Cleveland	AL	108	312	81	17	2	7	(3	4)	123	46	47	16	2	57	4	1	5	0	2	.00	4	.260	.300	.394
1991 Cleveland	AL	158	593	171	28	2	11	(2	9)	236	80	69	48	5	74	6	4	3	3	2	.60	12	.288	.346	.398
1992 Cleveland	AL	161	657	205	32	1	20	(9	11)	299	92	105	35	10	76	13	2	9	10	2	.83	15	.312	.354	.455
1993 Cleveland	AL	154	624	200	28	6	21	(8	13)	303	105	114	34	7	68	6	3	13	15	4	.79	17	.321	.355	.486
1994 Cleveland	AL	103	442	139	32	2	19	(8	11)	232	81	80	10	1	45	6	3	8	8	2	.80	10	.314	.333	.525
1995 Cleveland	AL	135	557	175	28	2	15	(7	8)	252	87	90	35	6	31	3	0	5	1	1	.50	23	.314	.355	.452
1996 Cle-NYN		126	507	129	28	0	12	(5	7)	193	59	66	21	0	27	9	2	5	1	1	.50	23	.254	.293	.381
1997 New York	NL	133	467	131	25	1	9	(4	5)	185	53	52	20	1	54	3	3	5	2	6	.25	13	.281	.311	.396
1996 Cleveland	AL	100	424	113	25	0	10	(5	5)	168	54	55	16	0	25	7	2	4	1	1	.50	15	.267	.302	.396
New York	NL	26	83	16	3	0	2	(0	2)	25	5	11	5	0	2	2	0	1	0	0	.00	8	.193	.253	.301
8 ML YEARS		1078	4159	1231	218	16	114	(46	68)	1823	603	623	219	32	432	50	18	53	50	21	.70	109	.296	.335	.438

Jeff Bagwell

Bats: Right Throws: Right Pos: 1B-159; PH-3; DH-1   Ht: 6'0" Wt: 195 Born: 5/27/68 Age: 30

		BATTING																	BASERUNNING				PERCENTAGES		
Year Team	Lg	G	AB	H	2B	3B	HR	Hm	Rd	TB	R	RBI	TBB	IBB	SO	HBP	SH	SF	SB	CS	SB%	GDP	Avg	OBP	SLG
1991 Houston	NL	156	554	163	26	4	15	(6	9)	242	79	82	75	5	116	13	1	7	7	4	.64	12	.294	.387	.437
1992 Houston	NL	162	586	160	34	6	18	(8	10)	260	87	96	84	13	97	12	2	13	10	6	.63	17	.273	.368	.444
1993 Houston	NL	142	535	171	37	4	20	(9	11)	276	76	88	62	6	73	3	0	9	13	4	.76	20	.320	.388	.516
1994 Houston	NL	110	400	147	32	2	39	(23	16)	300	104	116	65	14	65	4	0	10	15	4	.79	12	.368	.451	.750
1995 Houston	NL	114	448	130	29	0	21	(10	11)	222	88	87	79	12	102	6	0	6	12	5	.71	9	.290	.399	.496
1996 Houston	NL	162	568	179	48	2	31	(16	15)	324	111	120	135	20	114	10	0	6	21	7	.75	15	.315	.451	.570
1997 Houston	NL	162	566	162	40	2	43	(22	21)	335	109	135	127	27	122	16	0	8	31	10	.76	10	.286	.425	.592
7 ML YEARS		1008	3657	1112	246	20	187	(94	93)	1959	654	724	627	97	689	64	3	59	109	40	.73	95	.304	.409	.536

Scott Bailes

Pitches: Left Bats: Left Pos: RP-24   Ht: 6'2" Wt: 171 Born: 12/18/62 Age: 35

		HOW MUCH HE PITCHED						WHAT HE GAVE UP											THE RESULTS						
Year Team	Lg	G	GS	CG	GF	IP	BFP	H	R	ER	HR	SH	SF	HB	TBB	IBB	SO	WP	Bk	W	L	Pct.	ShO	Sv-Op	Hld	ERA
1997 Okla City *	AAA	44	0	0	20	43	189	46	22	19	5	4	1	1	13	2	37	2	2	2	3	.400	0	4--	—	3.98
1986 Cleveland	AL	62	10	0	22	112.2	500	123	70	62	12	7	4	1	43	5	60	4	2	10	10	.500	0	7--	—	4.95
1987 Cleveland	AL	39	17	0	15	120.1	551	145	75	62	21	4	6	4	47	1	65	3	0	7	8	.467	0	6-8	1	4.64
1988 Cleveland	AL	37	21	5	7	145	617	149	89	79	22	5	4	2	46	0	53	2	3	9	14	.391	0	0-2	4	4.90
1989 Cleveland	AL	34	11	0	9	113.2	473	116	57	54	7	5	5	3	29	4	47	3	0	5	9	.357	0	0-1	4	4.28
1990 California	AL	27	0	0	6	35.1	173	46	30	25	8	1	5	1	20	0	16	0	0	2	0	1.000	0	0-0	4	6.37
1991 California	AL	42	0	0	14	51.2	219	46	24	24	5	3	2	4	22	5	41	2	0	1	2	.333	0	0-1	8	4.18
1992 California	AL	32	0	0	10	38.2	200	59	34	32	7	1	2	1	28	4	25	2	1	3	1	.750	0	0-0	4	7.45
1997 Texas	AL	24	0	0	7	22	91	18	9	7	2	2	1	0	10	2	14	0	0	1	0	1.000	0	0-0	0	2.86
8 ML YEARS		297	59	5	90	639.1	2824	697	390	345	84	28	29	16	245	21	321	16	6	38	44	.463	2	13--	—	4.86

Cory Bailey

Pitches: Right Bats: Right Pos: RP-7   Ht: 6'1" Wt: 202 Born: 1/24/71 Age: 27

		HOW MUCH HE PITCHED						WHAT HE GAVE UP											THE RESULTS						
Year Team	Lg	G	GS	CG	GF	IP	BFP	H	R	ER	HR	SH	SF	HB	TBB	IBB	SO	WP	Bk	W	L	Pct.	ShO	Sv-Op	Hld	ERA
1997 Okla City *	AAA	42	0	0	33	50.1	219	49	20	19	1	3	1	0	23	7	38	4	0	3	4	.429	0	15--	—	3.40

Year Team	Lg	HOW MUCH HE PITCHED						WHAT HE GAVE UP												THE RESULTS						
		G	GS	CG	GF	IP	BFP	H	R	ER	HR	SH	SF	HB	TBB	IBB	SO	WP	Bk	W	L	Pct.	ShO	Sv-Op	Hld	ERA
Phoenix *	AAA	13	0	0	11	17.1	70	16	4	3	0	1	1	0	6	1	14	1	0	4	0	1.000	0	3--	—	1.56
1993 Boston	AL	11	0	0	5	15.2	66	12	7	6	0	1	1	0	12	3	11	2	1	0	1	.000	0	0-0	0	3.45
1994 Boston	AL	5	0	0	2	4.1	24	10	6	6	2	0	0	0	3	1	4	0	0	0	1	.000	0	0-1	0	12.46
1995 St. Louis	NL	3	0	0	0	3.2	15	2	3	3	0	0	0	0	2	1	5	1	0	0	0	.000	0	0-0	0	7.36
1996 St. Louis	NL	51	0	0	12	57	251	57	21	19	1	2	1	1	30	3	38	3	0	5	2	.714	0	0-1	10	3.00
1997 San Francisco	NL	7	0	0	4	9.2	45	15	9	9	1	0	1	0	4	0	5	0	0	0	1	.000	0	0-0	0	8.38
5 ML YEARS		77	0	0	23	90.1	401	96	46	43	4	3	3	1	51	8	63	6	1	5	5	.500	0	0-2	10	4.28

Roger Bailey

Pitches: Right **Bats:** Right **Pos:** SP-29

Ht: 6'1" **Wt:** 180 **Born:** 10/3/70 **Age:** 27

Year Team	Lg	HOW MUCH HE PITCHED						WHAT HE GAVE UP												THE RESULTS						
		G	GS	CG	GF	IP	BFP	H	R	ER	HR	SH	SF	HB	TBB	IBB	SO	WP	Bk	W	L	Pct.	ShO	Sv-Op	Hld	ERA
1995 Colorado	NL	39	6	0	9	81.1	360	88	49	45	9	7	2	1	39	3	33	7	1	7	6	.538	0	0-0	5	4.98
1996 Colorado	NL	24	11	0	4	83.2	385	94	64	58	7	2	4	1	52	0	45	3	0	2	3	.400	0	1-1	0	6.24
1997 Colorado	NL	29	29	5	0	191	835	210	103	91	27	7	4	13	70	2	84	4	0	9	10	.474	2	0-0	0	4.29
3 ML YEARS		92	46	5	13	356	1580	392	216	194	43	16	10	15	161	5	162	14	1	18	19	.486	2	1-1	5	4.90

Harold Baines

Bats: Left **Throws:** Left **Pos:** DH-121; PH-16; RF-1

Ht: 6'2" **Wt:** 195 **Born:** 3/15/59 **Age:** 39

Year Team	Lg	BATTING															BASERUNNING				PERCENTAGES		
		G	AB	H	2B	3B	HR	(Hm | Rd)	TB	R	RBI	TBB	IBB	SO	HBP	SH	SF	SB	CS	SB%	GDP	Avg	OBP	SLG
1980 Chicago	AL	141	491	125	23	6	13	(3 | 10)	199	55	49	19	7	65	1	2	5	2	4	.33	15	.255	.281	.405
1981 Chicago	AL	82	280	80	11	7	10	(3 | 7)	135	42	41	12	4	41	2	0	2	6	2	.75	6	.286	.318	.482
1982 Chicago	AL	161	608	165	29	8	25	(11 | 14)	285	89	105	49	10	95	0	2	9	10	3	.77	12	.271	.321	.469
1983 Chicago	AL	156	596	167	33	2	20	(12 | 8)	264	76	99	49	13	85	1	3	6	7	5	.58	15	.280	.333	.443
1984 Chicago	AL	147	569	173	28	10	29	(16 | 13)	308	72	94	54	9	75	0	1	5	1	2	.33	12	.304	.361	.541
1985 Chicago	AL	160	640	198	29	3	22	(13 | 9)	299	86	113	42	8	89	1	0	10	1	1	.50	23	.309	.348	.467
1986 Chicago	AL	145	570	169	29	2	21	(8 | 13)	265	72	88	38	9	89	2	0	8	2	1	.67	14	.296	.338	.465
1987 Chicago	AL	132	505	148	26	4	20	(12 | 8)	242	59	93	46	2	82	1	0	2	0	0	.00	12	.293	.352	.479
1988 Chicago	AL	158	599	166	39	1	13	(5 | 8)	246	55	81	67	14	109	1	0	7	0	0	.00	21	.277	.347	.411
1989 ChA-Tex	AL	146	505	156	29	1	16	(5 | 11)	235	73	72	73	13	79	1	0	4	0	3	.00	15	.309	.395	.465
1990 Tex-Oak	AL	135	415	118	15	1	16	(9 | 7)	183	52	65	67	10	80	0	2	6	0	2	.00	17	.284	.378	.441
1991 Oakland	AL	141	488	144	25	1	20	(11 | 9)	231	76	90	72	22	67	1	0	5	1	1	.00	12	.295	.383	.473
1992 Oakland	AL	140	478	121	18	0	16	(10 | 6)	187	58	76	59	6	61	0	0	6	1	3	.25	11	.253	.331	.391
1993 Baltimore	AL	118	416	130	22	0	20	(12 | 8)	212	64	78	57	9	52	0	1	6	0	0	.00	14	.313	.390	.510
1994 Baltimore	AL	94	326	96	12	1	16	(11 | 5)	158	44	54	30	6	49	1	0	4	0	1	.00	14	.294	.356	.485
1995 Baltimore	AL	127	385	115	19	1	24	(7 | 17)	208	60	63	70	13	45	0	0	4	0	0	.00	17	.299	.403	.540
1996 Chicago	AL	143	495	154	29	0	22	(9 | 13)	249	80	95	73	7	62	1	0	3	3	1	.75	20	.311	.399	.503
1997 ChA-Bal	AL	137	452	136	23	0	16	(6 | 10)	207	55	67	55	11	62	1	0	3	1	1	.50	12	.301	.375	.458
1989 Chicago	AL	96	333	107	20	1	13	(4 | 9)	168	55	56	60	13	52	1	0	3	0	1	.00	11	.321	.423	.505
Texas	AL	50	172	49	9	0	3	(1 | 2)	67	18	16	13	0	27	0	0	1	0	2	.00	4	.285	.333	.390
1990 Texas	AL	103	321	93	10	1	13	(6 | 7)	144	41	44	47	9	63	0	0	3	0	0	.00	13	.290	.377	.449
Oakland	AL	32	94	25	5	0	3	(3 | 0)	39	11	21	20	1	17	0	2	2	0	2	.00	4	.266	.381	.415
1997 Chicago	AL	93	318	97	18	0	12	(5 | 7)	151	40	52	41	10	47	0	0	2	1	0	.00	9	.305	.382	.475
Baltimore	AL	44	134	39	5	0	4	(1 | 3)	56	15	15	14	1	15	0	0	1	0	1	.00	3	.291	.356	.418
18 ML YEARS		2463	8818	2561	439	48	339	(163 | 176)	4113	1168	1423	932	173	1287	13	9	92	33	32	.51	257	.290	.356	.466

James Baldwin

Pitches: Right **Bats:** Right **Pos:** SP-32

Ht: 6'3" **Wt:** 210 **Born:** 7/15/71 **Age:** 26

Year Team	Lg	HOW MUCH HE PITCHED						WHAT HE GAVE UP												THE RESULTS						
		G	GS	CG	GF	IP	BFP	H	R	ER	HR	SH	SF	HB	TBB	IBB	SO	WP	Bk	W	L	Pct.	ShO	Sv-Op	Hld	ERA
1995 Chicago	AL	6	4	0	0	14.2	81	32	22	21	6	0	0	0	9	1	10	1	0	0	1	.000	0	0-0	0	12.89
1996 Chicago	AL	28	28	0	0	169	719	168	88	83	24	2	2	4	57	3	127	12	1	11	6	.647	0	0-0	0	4.42
1997 Chicago	AL	32	32	1	0	200	879	205	128	117	19	3	6	5	83	3	140	14	3	12	15	.444	0	0-0	0	5.27
3 ML YEARS		66	64	1	0	383.2	1679	405	238	221	49	5	8	9	149	7	277	27	4	23	22	.511	0	0-0	0	5.18

Brian Banks

Bats: B **Throws:** R **Pos:** LF-15; PH-11; 1B-5; DH-1; 3B-1; RF-1

Ht: 6'3" **Wt:** 200 **Born:** 9/28/70 **Age:** 27

Year Team	Lg	BATTING															BASERUNNING				PERCENTAGES		
		G	AB	H	2B	3B	HR	(Hm | Rd)	TB	R	RBI	TBB	IBB	SO	HBP	SH	SF	SB	CS	SB%	GDP	Avg	OBP	SLG
1993 Helena	R+	12	48	19	1	1	2	—	—	28	8	8	11	0	8	0	0	1	1	2	.33	2	.396	.500	.583
Beloit	A	38	147	36	5	1	4	—	—	55	21	19	7	0	34	1	0	1	2	1	.33	1	.245	.284	.374
1994 Stockton	A+	67	246	58	9	1	4	—	—	81	29	28	38	2	46	2	3	2	3	8	.27	8	.236	.340	.329
Beloit	A	65	237	71	13	1	9	—	—	113	41	47	29	5	40	2	1	4	11	1	.92	3	.300	.375	.477
1995 El Paso	AA	128	441	136	39	10	12	—	—	231	81	78	81	6	113	3	3	3	9	9	.50	10	.308	.413	.524
1996 New Orleans	AAA	137	487	132	29	7	16	—	—	223	71	64	66	3	105	2	2	7	17	8	.68	6	.271	.356	.458
1997 Tucson	AAA	98	378	112	26	3	10	—	—	174	53	63	35	2	83	1	2	5	7	3	.70	6	.296	.353	.460
1996 Milwaukee	AL	4	7	4	2	0	1	(0 | 1)	9	2	2	1	0	2	0	0	0	0	0	.00	0	.571	.625	1.286
1997 Milwaukee	AL	28	68	14	1	0	1	(0 | 1)	18	9	8	6	0	17	0	0	1	0	1	.00	1	.206	.267	.265
2 ML YEARS		32	75	18	3	0	2	(0 | 2)	27	11	10	7	0	19	0	0	1	0	1	.00	1	.240	.301	.360

Willie Banks

Pitches: Right **Bats:** Right **Pos:** RP-4; SP-1   **Ht:** 6'1" **Wt:** 200 **Born:** 2/27/69 **Age:** 29

		HOW MUCH HE PITCHED						WHAT HE GAVE UP										THE RESULTS					
Year Team	Lg	G	GS	CG	GF	IP	BFP	H	R	ER	HR	SH	SF	HB	TBB	IBB	SO	WP	Bk	W	L	Pct.	ShO	Sv-Op	Hld	ERA
1997 Columbus *	AAA	33	24	1	5	154	662	164	87	73	18	3	3	4	45	0	130	7	0	14	5	.737	0	3--	--	4.27
1991 Minnesota	AL	5	3	0	2	17.1	85	21	15	11	1	0	0	0	12	0	16	3	0	1	1	.500	0	0-0	0	5.71
1992 Minnesota	AL	16	12	0	2	71	324	80	46	45	6	2	5	2	37	0	37	5	1	4	4	.500	0	0-0	0	5.70
1993 Minnesota	AL	31	30	0	1	171.1	754	186	91	77	17	4	4	3	78	2	138	9	5	11	12	.478	0	0-0	0	4.04
1994 Chicago	NL	23	23	1	0	138.1	598	139	88	83	16	5	2	2	56	3	91	8	1	8	12	.400	1	0-0	0	5.40
1995 ChN-LA-Fla	NL	25	15	0	2	90.2	430	106	71	57	14	6	3	2	58	7	62	9	1	2	6	.250	0	0-1	1	5.66
1997 New York	AL	5	1	0	1	14	57	9	3	3	0	2	0	1	6	0	8	0	0	3	0	1.000	0	0-1	0	1.93
1995 Chicago	NL	10	0	0	2	11.2	73	27	23	20	5	1	1	0	12	4	9	3	0	0	1	.000	0	0-1	1	15.43
Los Angeles	NL	6	6	0	0	29	138	36	21	13	2	1	1	0	16	2	23	4	1	0	2	.000	0	0-0	0	4.03
Florida	NL	9	9	0	0	50	219	43	27	24	7	4	1	0	30	1	30	2	0	2	3	.400	0	0-0	0	4.32
6 ML YEARS		105	84	1	8	502.2	2248	541	314	276	54	18	14	10	247	12	352	34	8	29	35	.453	1	0-2	1	4.94

Manuel Barrios

Pitches: Right **Bats:** Right **Pos:** RP-2   **Ht:** 6'0" **Wt:** 185 **Born:** 9/21/74 **Age:** 23

		HOW MUCH HE PITCHED						WHAT HE GAVE UP										THE RESULTS					
Year Team	Lg	G	GS	CG	GF	IP	BFP	H	R	ER	HR	SH	SF	HB	TBB	IBB	SO	WP	Bk	W	L	Pct.	ShO	Sv-Op	Hld	ERA
1994 Quad City	A	43	0	0	11	65	295	73	44	43	4	5	2	7	23	4	63	8	2	0	6	.000	0	4--	--	5.95
1995 Quad City	A	50	0	0	48	52	219	44	16	13	1	2	1	4	17	1	55	1	0	1	5	.167	0	23--	--	2.25
1996 Jackson	AA	60	0	0	53	68.1	298	60	29	18	4	4	2	3	29	5	69	3	0	6	4	.600	0	23--	--	2.37
1997 New Orleans	AAA	57	0	0	17	82.2	350	70	32	30	5	10	4	1	34	9	77	2	0	4	8	.333	0	0--	--	3.27
1997 Houston	NL	2	0	0	0	3	18	6	4	4	0	0	0	0	3	0	3	0	0	0	0	.000	0	0-0	1	12.00

Tony Barron

Bats: Right **Throws:** Right **Pos:** RF-53; PH-5   **Ht:** 6'0" **Wt:** 185 **Born:** 8/17/66 **Age:** 31

		BATTING																	BASERUNNING				PERCENTAGES		
Year Team	Lg	G	AB	H	2B	3B	HR	(Hm	Rd)	TB	R	RBI	TBB	IBB	SO	HBP	SH	SF	SB	CS	SB%	GDP	Avg	OBP	SLG
1987 Great Falls	R+	53	171	51	13	2	3	—	—	77	33	30	13	2	49	5	1	3	5	3	.63	1	.298	.359	.450
1988 Bakersfield	A+	12	20	5	2	0	0	—	—	7	1	4	1	1	5	0	0	0	0	0	.00	1	.250	.286	.350
Salem	A-	73	261	79	6	3	9	—	—	118	54	38	25	1	75	10	6	0	36	7	.84	2	.303	.385	.452
1989 Vero Beach	A+	105	324	79	7	5	4	—	—	108	45	40	17	1	90	4	2	3	26	12	.68	9	.244	.287	.333
1990 Vero Beach	A+	111	344	102	21	3	6	—	—	147	58	60	30	1	82	7	2	5	42	7	.86	9	.297	.360	.427
1991 San Antonio	AA	73	200	47	2	2	9	—	—	80	35	31	28	2	44	3	0	1	8	3	.73	11	.235	.336	.400
1992 San Antonio	AA	28	97	39	4	1	7	—	—	66	18	22	6	1	22	2	0	1	7	3	.70	3	.402	.443	.680
Albuquerque	AAA	78	286	86	18	2	6	—	—	126	40	33	17	1	65	2	2	0	6	4	.60	15	.301	.344	.441
1993 Albuquerque	AAA	107	259	75	22	1	8	—	—	123	42	36	27	1	59	2	2	2	6	5	.55	7	.290	.359	.475
1994 Jacksnville	AA	108	402	119	19	3	18	—	—	198	60	55	26	1	85	4	1	3	18	5	.78	19	.296	.343	.493
Calgary	AAA	2	8	2	0	0	2	—	—	8	2	2	0	0	0	0	0	0	0	0	.00	0	.250	.250	1.000
1995 Tacoma	AAA	9	25	5	0	0	0	—	—	5	4	2	2	0	3	1	0	0	0	0	.00	0	.200	.286	.200
Harrisburg	AA	29	103	30	5	0	10	—	—	65	20	23	10	0	21	2	0	0	0	0	.00	8	.291	.365	.631
Ottawa	AAA	50	147	36	10	0	10	—	—	76	20	22	14	1	22	2	0	1	0	2	.00	3	.245	.317	.517
1996 Harrisburg	AA	18	67	19	3	1	5	—	—	39	12	12	6	1	19	0	0	0	1	0	1.00	1	.284	.342	.582
Ottawa	AAA	105	394	126	29	2	14	—	—	201	58	59	20	1	74	9	3	1	9	4	.69	12	.320	.366	.510
1997 Scranton-WB	AAA	92	329	108	21	4	18	—	—	191	51	78	27	4	64	12	0	3	3	4	.43	11	.328	.396	.581
1996 Montreal	NL	1	1	0	0	0	0	(0	0)	0	0	0	0	0	1	0	0	0	0	0	.00	0	.000	.000	.000
1997 Philadelphia	NL	57	189	54	12	1	4	(3	1)	80	22	24	12	0	38	2	2	3	0	1	.00	0	.286	.330	.423
2 ML YEARS		58	190	54	12	1	4	(3	1)	80	22	24	12	0	39	2	2	3	0	1	.00	0	.284	.329	.421

Kimera Bartee

Bats: Both **Throws:** Right **Pos:** PH-8; DH-3; LF-3; CF-3   **Ht:** 6'0" **Wt:** 175 **Born:** 7/21/72 **Age:** 25

		BATTING																	BASERUNNING				PERCENTAGES		
Year Team	Lg	G	AB	H	2B	3B	HR	(Hm	Rd)	TB	R	RBI	TBB	IBB	SO	HBP	SH	SF	SB	CS	SB%	GDP	Avg	OBP	SLG
1993 Bluefield	R+	66	264	65	15	2	4	—	—	96	59	37	44	0	66	3	3	2	27	6	.82	0	.246	.358	.364
1994 Frederick	A+	130	514	150	22	4	10	—	—	210	97	57	56	1	117	7	14	4	44	9	.83	7	.292	.367	.409
1995 Orioles	R	5	21	5	0	0	1	—	—	8	5	3	3	0	2	0	0	0	1	1	.50	0	.238	.333	.381
Bowie	AA	53	218	62	9	1	3	—	—	82	45	19	23	1	45	1	3	2	22	7	.76	1	.284	.352	.376
Rochester	AAA	15	52	8	2	1	0	—	—	12	5	3	0	0	16	0	2	1	0	0	.00	0	.154	.151	.231
1997 Toledo	AAA	136	501	109	13	7	3	—	—	145	67	33	52	1	154	4	12	4	33	9	.79	3	.218	.294	.289
1996 Detroit	AL	110	217	55	6	1	1	(0	1)	66	32	14	17	0	77	0	13	0	20	10	.67	1	.253	.308	.304
1997 Detroit	AL	12	5	1	0	0	0	(0	0)	1	4	0	2	0	2	1	0	0	3	1	.75	0	.200	.500	.200
2 ML YEARS		122	222	56	6	1	1	(0	1)	67	36	14	19	0	79	1	13	0	23	11	.68	1	.252	.314	.302

Richard Batchelor

Pitches: Right **Bats:** Right **Pos:** RP-23   **Ht:** 6'1" **Wt:** 195 **Born:** 4/8/67 **Age:** 31

		HOW MUCH HE PITCHED						WHAT HE GAVE UP										THE RESULTS					
Year Team	Lg	G	GS	CG	GF	IP	BFP	H	R	ER	HR	SH	SF	HB	TBB	IBB	SO	WP	Bk	W	L	Pct.	ShO	Sv-Op	Hld	ERA
1990 Greensboro	A	27	0	0	18	51.1	200	39	15	9	1	0	2	0	14	1	38	2	0	2	2	.500	0	8--	--	1.58
1991 Ft. Laud	A+	50	0	0	41	62	269	55	28	19	1	6	1	1	22	5	58	4	0	4	7	.364	0	25--	--	2.76
Albany-Colo	AA	1	0	0	1	1	9	5	5	5	0	1	0	0	1	0	0	0	0	0	0	.000	0	0--	--	45.00
1992 Albany-Colo	AA	58	0	0	34	70.2	320	79	40	33	5	1	2	6	34	3	45	4	0	4	5	.444	0	7--	--	4.20
1993 Albany-Colo	AA	36	0	0	32	40.1	162	27	9	4	1	1	0	1	12	0	40	3	0	1	3	.250	0	19--	--	0.89
Columbus	AAA	15	0	0	14	16.1	74	14	5	5	0	0	1	0	8	1	17	3	0	1	1	.500	0	6--	--	2.76

13

Year Team	Lg	G	GS	CG	GF	IP	BFP	H	R	ER	HR	SH	SF	HB	TBB	IBB	SO	WP	Bk	W	L	Pct.	ShO	Sv-Op	Hld	ERA
		HOW MUCH HE PITCHED						**WHAT HE GAVE UP**												**THE RESULTS**						
1994 Louisville	AAA	53	0	0	13	81.1	347	85	40	32	7	5	3	3	32	6	50	7	0	1	2	.333	0	0- -	—	3.54
1995 Louisville	AAA	50	6	0	7	85	352	85	39	31	5	4	3	7	16	2	61	0	0	5	4	.556	0	0- -	—	3.28
1996 Louisville	AAA	51	0	0	44	54.2	246	59	29	25	5	4	2	2	19	5	57	5	0	5	2	.714	0	28- -	—	4.12
1997 Louisville	AAA	12	0	0	10	14	66	18	9	7	1	0	2	1	6	2	10	2	0	2	2	.000	0	5- -	—	4.50
Las Vegas	AAA	15	0	0	4	21	93	23	15	15	2	1	1	1	8	2	19	5	0	3	0	1.000	0	0- -	—	6.43
1993 St. Louis	NL	9	0	0	2	10	45	14	12	9	1	1	2	0	3	1	4	0	0	0	0	.000	0	0- -	—	8.10
1996 St. Louis	NL	11	0	0	7	15	54	9	2	2	0	1	0	0	1	0	11	0	0	2	0	1.000	0	0-0	1	1.20
1997 StL-SD	NL	23	0	0	8	28.2	138	40	23	19	2	3	0	3	14	2	18	1	1	3	1	.750	0	0-0	0	5.97
1997 St. Louis	NL	10	0	0	3	16	76	21	12	8	0	2	0	2	7	1	8	0	1	1	1	.500	0	0-1	0	4.50
San Diego	NL	13	0	0	5	12.2	62	19	11	11	2	1	0	1	7	1	10	1	0	2	0	1.000	0	0-1	0	7.82
3 ML YEARS		43	0	0	17	53.2	237	63	37	30	3	5	2	3	18	3	33	1	1	5	1	.833	0	0-2	1	5.03

Jason Bates

Bats: B **Throws:** R **Pos:** PH-26; 2B-22; SS-16; 3B-6   **Ht:** 5'11" **Wt:** 185 **Born:** 1/5/71 **Age:** 27

Year Team	Lg	G	AB	H	2B	3B	HR	(Hm	Rd)	TB	R	RBI	TBB	IBB	SO	HBP	SH	SF	SB	CS	SB%	GDP	Avg	OBP	SLG
		BATTING																	**BASERUNNING**				**PERCENTAGES**		
1997 Colo Spmgs *	AAA	35	135	32	6	1	3			49	21	18	13	0	36	2	1	1	3	.25	1	.237	.311	.363
1995 Colorado	NL	116	322	86	17	4	8	(4	4)	135	42	46	42	3	70	2	2	0	3	6	.33	4	.267	.355	.419
1996 Colorado	NL	88	160	33	8	1	1	(1	0)	46	19	9	23	1	34	2	1	1	2	1	.67	7	.206	.312	.288
1997 Colorado	NL	62	121	29	10	0	3	(1	2)	48	17	11	15	1	27	3	0	0	0	1	.00	3	.240	.338	.397
3 ML YEARS		266	603	148	35	5	12	(6	6)	229	78	66	80	5	131	7	3	1	5	8	.38	14	.245	.340	.380

Miguel Batista

Pitches: Right **Bats:** Right **Pos:** SP-6; RP-5   **Ht:** 6'0" **Wt:** 160 **Born:** 2/19/71 **Age:** 27

Year Team	Lg	G	GS	CG	GF	IP	BFP	H	R	ER	HR	SH	SF	HB	TBB	IBB	SO	WP	Bk	W	L	Pct.	ShO	Sv-Op	Hld	ERA
		HOW MUCH HE PITCHED						**WHAT HE GAVE UP**												**THE RESULTS**						
1990 Expos	R	9	6	0	1	40.1	167	31	16	9	0	1	2	1	19	0	22	1	1	4	3	.571	0	0- -	—	2.01
Rockford	A	3	2	0	0	12.1	63	16	13	12	2	0	1	4	5	0	7	3	0	0	1	.000	0	0- -	—	8.76
1991 Rockford	A	23	23	2	0	133.2	592	126	74	60	1	6	8	6	57	0	90	12	2	11	5	.688	1	0- -	—	4.04
1992 Wst Plm Bch	A+	24	24	1	0	135.1	585	130	69	57	3	4	4	6	54	1	92	9	4	7	7	.500	0	0- -	—	3.79
1993 Harrisburg	AA	26	26	0	0	141	627	139	79	68	11	4	5	4	86	0	91	8	5	13	5	.722	0	0- -	—	4.34
1994 Harrisburg	AA	3	3	0	0	11.1	49	8	3	3	0	0	0	0	9	0	5	2	0	0	1	.000	0	0- -	—	2.38
1995 Charlotte	AAA	34	18	0	4	116.1	516	118	79	62	11	1	1	1	60	2	58	12	1	6	12	.333	0	0- -	—	4.80
1996 Charlotte	AAA	47	2	0	14	77	360	93	57	46	4	4	4	6	39	0	56	16	1	4	3	.571	0	4- -	—	5.38
1997 Iowa	AAA	31	14	2	4	122	509	117	60	57	19	3	3	0	38	1	95	8	1	9	4	.692	2	0- -	—	4.20
1992 Pittsburgh	NL	1	0	0	1	2	13	4	2	2	1	0	0	0	3	0	1	0	0	0	0	.000	0	0-0	0	9.00
1996 Florida	NL	9	0	4	11.1		49	9	8	7	0	3	0	0	7	2	6	1	0	0	0	.000	0	0-0	0	5.56
1997 Chicago	NL	11	6	0	2	36.1	168	36	24	23	4	4	4	1	24	2	27	2	0	0	5	.000	0	0-0	0	5.70
3 ML YEARS		21	6	0	7	49.2	230	49	34	32	5	7	4	1	34	4	34	3	0	0	5	.000	0	0-0	0	5.80

Tony Batista

Bats: R **Throws:** R **Pos:** SS-61; PH-7; 3B-4; DH-1; 2B-1   **Ht:** 6'0" **Wt:** 165 **Born:** 12/9/73 **Age:** 24

Year Team	Lg	G	AB	H	2B	3B	HR	(Hm	Rd)	TB	R	RBI	TBB	IBB	SO	HBP	SH	SF	SB	CS	SB%	GDP	Avg	OBP	SLG
		BATTING																	**BASERUNNING**				**PERCENTAGES**		
1992 Athletics	R	45	167	41	6	2	0	—	—	51	32	22	15	0	29	2	5	0	1	0	1.00	4	.246	.315	.305
1993 Athletics	R	24	104	34	6	2	2	—	—	50	21	17	6	1	14	0	0	2	6	2	.75	1	.327	.357	.481
Tacoma	AAA	4	12	2	1	0	0	—	—	3	1	1	1	0	4	1	0	0	0	0	.00	0	.167	.286	.250
1994 Modesto	A+	119	466	131	26	3	17	—	—	214	91	68	54	1	108	4	1	3	7	7	.50	10	.281	.357	.459
1995 Huntsville	AA	120	419	107	23	1	16	—	—	180	55	61	29	0	98	2	6	3	7	8	.47	8	.255	.305	.430
1996 Edmonton	AAA	57	205	66	17	4	8	—	—	115	33	40	15	0	30	2	1	1	2	1	.67	8	.322	.372	.561
1997 Edmonton	AAA	33	124	39	10	1	3	—	—	60	25	21	17	0	18	1	1	2	2	2	.50	4	.315	.396	.484
1996 Oakland	AL	74	238	71	10	2	6	(1	5)	103	38	25	19	0	49	1	0	2	7	3	.70	2	.298	.350	.433
1997 Oakland	AL	68	188	38	10	1	4	(0	4)	62	22	18	14	0	31	2	3	0	2	2	.50	8	.202	.265	.330
2 ML YEARS		142	426	109	20	3	10	(1	9)	165	60	43	33	0	80	3	3	2	9	5	.64	10	.256	.313	.387

Danny Bautista

Bats: R **Throws:** R **Pos:** LF-48; PH-22; RF-10; CF-1   **Ht:** 5'11" **Wt:** 170 **Born:** 5/24/72 **Age:** 26

Year Team	Lg	G	AB	H	2B	3B	HR	(Hm	Rd)	TB	R	RBI	TBB	IBB	SO	HBP	SH	SF	SB	CS	SB%	GDP	Avg	OBP	SLG
		BATTING																	**BASERUNNING**				**PERCENTAGES**		
1997 Richmond *	AAA	46	170	48	10	3	2	—	—	70	28	28	19	0	30	1	2	1	1	0	1.00	9	.282	.356	.412
1993 Detroit	AL	17	61	19	3	0	1	(0	1)	25	6	9	1	0	10	0	0	1	3	1	.75	1	.311	.317	.410
1994 Detroit	AL	31	99	23	4	1	4	(1	3)	41	12	15	3	0	18	0	0	1	1	2	.33	1	.232	.255	.414
1995 Detroit	AL	89	271	55	9	0	7	(3	4)	85	28	27	12	0	68	0	6	0	4	1	.80	6	.203	.237	.314
1997 Atlanta	NL	64	103	25	3	2	3	(1	2)	41	14	9	5	1	24	1	2	3	2	0	1.00	3	.226	.323	.321
1996 Detroit	AL	25	64	16	2	0	2	(1	1)	24	12	8	9	0	15	0	0	0	1	2	.33	1	.250	.342	.375
Atlanta	NL	17	20	3	0	0	0	(0	0)	3	1	1	2	0	5	1	0	0	0	0	.00	1	.150	.261	.150
5 ML YEARS		243	618	141	21	3	17	(6	11)	219	73	69	32	1	140	2	8	2	11	6	.65	17	.228	.268	.354

Jose Bautista

Pitches: Right **Bats:** Right **Pos:** RP-32 **Ht:** 6'2" **Wt:** 205 **Born:** 7/26/64 **Age:** 33

Year Team	Lg	G	GS	CG	GF	IP	BFP	H	R	ER	HR	SH	SF	HB	TBB	IBB	SO	WP	Bk	W	L	Pct.	ShO	Sv-Op	Hld	ERA
1997 Louisville *	AAA	11	0	0	2	17.1	56	3	0	0	0	0	3	0	2	1	11	0	0	2	0	1.000	0	0- -	0	0.00
1988 Baltimore	AL	33	25	3	5	171.2	721	171	86	82	21	2	3	7	45	3	76	4	5	6	15	.286	0	0-0	0	4.30
1989 Baltimore	AL	15	10	0	4	78	325	84	46	46	17	1	1	1	15	0	30	0	0	3	4	.429	0	0-0	0	5.31
1990 Baltimore	AL	22	0	0	9	26.2	112	28	15	12	4	1	1	0	7	3	15	2	0	1	0	1.000	0	0-0	5	4.05
1991 Baltimore	AL	5	0	0	3	5.1	34	13	10	10	1	0	0	1	5	0	3	1	0	0	1	.000	0	0-0	0	16.88
1993 Chicago	NL	58	7	1	14	111.2	459	105	38	35	11	4	3	5	27	3	63	4	1	10	3	.769	0	2-2	7	2.82
1994 Chicago	NL	58	0	0	24	69.1	293	75	30	30	10	5	4	3	17	7	45	2	1	4	5	.444	0	1-4	14	3.89
1995 San Francisco	NL	52	6	0	19	100.2	451	120	77	72	24	8	5	5	26	3	45	1	2	3	8	.273	0	0-0	5	6.44
1996 San Francisco	NL	37	1	0	12	69.2	289	66	32	26	10	4	3	2	15	5	28	0	0	3	4	.429	0	0-1	2	3.36
1997 Det-StL		32	0	0	7	52.2	241	70	42	39	7	4	0	3	14	4	23	2	1	2	2	.500	0	0-0	2	6.66
1997 Detroit	AL	21	0	0	4	40.1	185	55	32	30	6	1	0	2	12	3	19	1	1	2	2	.500	0	0-0	1	6.69
St. Louis	NL	11	0	0	3	12.1	56	15	10	9	1	3	0	1	2	1	4	1	0	0	0	.000	0	0-0	1	6.57
9 ML YEARS		312	49	4	97	685.2	2925	732	376	352	106	29	20	27	171	28	328	16	10	32	42	.432	0	3-7	35	4.62

Trey Beamon

Bats: Left **Throws:** Right **Pos:** PH-28; LF-15; RF-5 **Ht:** 6'3" **Wt:** 195 **Born:** 2/11/74 **Age:** 24

							BATTING										BASERUNNING				PERCENTAGES		
Year Team	Lg	G	AB	H	2B	3B	HR	(Hm | Rd)	TB	R	RBI	TBB	IBB	SO	HBP	SH	SF	SB	CS	SB%	GDP	Avg	OBP	SLG
1992 Pirates	R	13	39	12	1	0	1	—	—	16	9	6	4	1	0	0	0	0	0	1	.00	0	.308	.372	.410
Welland	A-	19	69	20	5	0	3	—	—	34	15	9	8	0	9	0	0	0	4	3	.57	6	.290	.364	.493
1993 Augusta	A	104	373	101	18	6	0	—	—	131	64	45	48	2	60	6	0	4	19	6	.76	12	.271	.360	.351
1994 Carolina	AA	112	434	140	18	9	5	—	—	191	69	47	33	4	53	5	4	3	24	9	.73	8	.323	.375	.440
1995 Calgary	AAA	118	452	151	29	5	5	—	—	205	74	62	39	4	55	2	2	3	18	8	.69	7	.334	.387	.454
1996 Calgary	AAA	111	378	109	15	3	5	—	—	145	62	52	55	6	63	6	3	5	16	3	.84	12	.288	.383	.384
1997 Las Vegas	AAA	90	329	108	19	4	5	—	—	150	64	49	48	1	58	9	2	2	14	6	.70	11	.328	.425	.456
1996 Pittsburgh	NL	24	51	11	2	0	0	(0 | 0)	13	7	6	4	0	6	0	1	0	1	1	.50	0	.216	.273	.255
1997 San Diego	NL	43	65	18	3	0	0	(0 | 0)	21	5	7	2	0	17	1	0	1	1	2	.33	1	.277	.309	.323
2 ML YEARS		67	116	29	5	0	0	(0 | 0)	34	12	13	6	0	23	1	1	1	2	3	.40	1	.250	.293	.293

Rod Beck

Pitches: Right **Bats:** Right **Pos:** RP-73 **Ht:** 6'1" **Wt:** 236 **Born:** 8/3/68 **Age:** 29

Year Team	Lg	G	GS	CG	GF	IP	BFP	H	R	ER	HR	SH	SF	HB	TBB	IBB	SO	WP	Bk	W	L	Pct.	ShO	Sv-Op	Hld	ERA
1991 San Francisco	NL	31	0	0	10	52.1	214	53	22	22	4	4	2	1	13	2	38	0	1	1	1	.500	0	1-1	1	3.78
1992 San Francisco	NL	65	0	0	42	92	352	62	20	18	4	6	2	2	15	2	87	5	2	3	3	.500	0	17-23	4	1.76
1993 San Francisco	NL	76	0	0	71	79.1	309	57	20	19	11	6	3	3	13	4	86	4	0	3	1	.750	0	48-52	0	2.16
1994 San Francisco	NL	48	0	0	47	48.2	207	49	17	15	10	3	3	0	13	2	39	0	0	2	4	.333	0	28-28	0	2.77
1995 San Francisco	NL	60	0	0	52	58.2	255	60	31	29	7	4	3	2	21	3	42	2	0	5	6	.455	0	33-43	0	4.45
1996 San Francisco	NL	63	0	0	58	62	248	56	23	23	9	0	2	1	10	2	48	1	0	0	9	.000	0	35-42	0	3.34
1997 San Francisco	NL	73	0	0	66	70	281	67	31	27	7	1	0	2	8	2	53	1	0	7	4	.636	0	37-45	1	3.47
7 ML YEARS		416	0	0	346	463	1866	404	164	153	52	24	15	11	93	17	393	13	2	21	28	.429	0	199-234	6	2.97

Rich Becker

Bats: L **Throws:** L **Pos:** CF-115; RF-13; PH-12; LF-9 **Ht:** 5'10" **Wt:** 199 **Born:** 2/1/72 **Age:** 26

							BATTING										BASERUNNING				PERCENTAGES		
Year Team	Lg	G	AB	H	2B	3B	HR	(Hm | Rd)	TB	R	RBI	TBB	IBB	SO	HBP	SH	SF	SB	CS	SB%	GDP	Avg	OBP	SLG
1993 Minnesota	AL	3	7	2	2	0	0	(0 | 0)	4	3	0	5	0	4	0	0	0	1	1	.50	0	.286	.583	.571
1994 Minnesota	AL	28	98	26	3	0	1	(1 | 0)	32	12	8	13	0	25	0	1	0	6	1	.86	2	.265	.351	.327
1995 Minnesota	AL	106	392	93	15	1	2	(1 | 1)	116	45	33	34	0	95	4	6	2	8	9	.47	9	.237	.303	.296
1996 Minnesota	AL	148	525	153	31	4	12	(8 | 4)	228	92	71	68	1	118	2	5	4	19	5	.79	14	.291	.372	.434
1997 Minnesota	AL	132	443	117	22	3	10	(4 | 6)	175	61	45	62	1	130	1	2	2	17	5	.77	4	.264	.354	.395
5 ML YEARS		417	1465	391	73	8	25	(14 | 11)	555	213	157	182	2	372	7	14	8	51	21	.71	29	.267	.349	.379

Robbie Beckett

Pitches: Left **Bats:** Right **Pos:** RP-2 **Ht:** 6'5" **Wt:** 225 **Born:** 7/16/72 **Age:** 25

Year Team	Lg	G	GS	CG	GF	IP	BFP	H	R	ER	HR	SH	SF	HB	TBB	IBB	SO	WP	Bk	W	L	Pct.	ShO	Sv-Op	Hld	ERA
1990 Padres	R	10	10	0	0	49.1	236	40	28	24	1	3	1	2	45	0	54	8	3	2	5	.286	0	0- -	—	4.38
Riverside	A+	3	3	0	0	16.2	76	18	13	13	0	1	0	0	11	0	11	1	1	2	1	.667	0	0- -	—	7.02
1991 Chston-SC	A	28	26	1	0	109.1	545	115	111	100	5	1	8	3	117	0	96	20	2	2	14	.125	0	0- -	—	8.23
1992 Waterloo	A	24	24	1	0	120.2	578	77	88	64	4	1	1	8	140	1	147	20	4	4	10	.286	1	0- -	—	4.77
1993 Rancho Cuca	A+	37	10	0	14	83.2	413	75	62	56	7	1	7	2	93	1	88	25	3	2	4	.333	0	4- -	—	6.02
1994 Wichita	AA	33	0	0	14	40	188	40	28	26	2	4	2	1	40	0	59	10	0	1	3	.250	0	2- -	—	5.85
Las Vegas	AAA	23	0	0	11	23.2	134	27	36	31	4	0	3	0	39	0	30	7	0	0	1	.000	0	0- -	—	11.79
1995 Memphis	AA	36	8	2	11	86.1	400	65	57	46	3	2	3	10	73	4	98	19	0	3	4	.429	1	0- -	—	4.80
1996 Portland	AA	3	3	0	0	13	66	17	9	9	1	1	2	0	13	0	7	1	0	1	0	1.000	0	0- -	—	6.23
New Haven	AA	30	4	0	11	48.2	219	38	30	26	7	4	3	1	46	5	55	3	0	6	3	.667	0	0- -	—	4.81
Colo Spngs	AAA	12	0	0	4	12.1	55	6	6	3	0	1	0	1	11	0	15	2	0	0	2	.000	0	1- -	—	2.19
1997 Colo Spngs	AAA	45	1	0	17	54.1	267	61	49	41	12	1	3	2	47	2	67	13	0	1	3	.250	0	1- -	—	6.79
1996 Colorado	NL	5	0	0	2	5.1	31	6	8	8	3	0	1	0	9	0	6	1	0	0	0	.000	0	0-1	0	13.50
1997 Colorado	NL	2	0	0	2	1.2	9	1	1	1	0	0	0	0	1	1	2	0	0	0	0	.000	0	0- -	0	5.40

Year Team	Lg	G	GS	CG	GF	IP	BFP	H	R	ER	HR	SH	SF	HB	TBB	IBB	SO	WP	Bk	W	L	Pct.	ShO	Sv-Op	Hld	ERA
2 ML YEARS		7	0	0	4	7	38	7	9	9	3	0	1	0	10	1	8	1	0	0	0	.000	0	0-1	0	11.57

Matt Beech

Pitches: Left **Bats:** Left **Pos:** SP-24   **Ht:** 6'2" **Wt:** 190 **Born:** 1/20/72 **Age:** 26

Year Team	Lg	G	GS	CG	GF	IP	BFP	H	R	ER	HR	SH	SF	HB	TBB	IBB	SO	WP	Bk	W	L	Pct.	ShO	Sv-Op	Hld	ERA
1994 Batavia	A-	4	3	0	1	18.2	80	9	4	4	0	1	0	4	12	0	27	0	0	2	1	.667	0	0- —		1.93
Spartanburg	A	10	10	4	0	69.2	274	51	23	20	7	0	1	3	23	0	83	5	3	4	4	.500	1	0- —		2.58
1995 Clearwater	A+	15	15	0	0	86	363	87	45	40	5	3	2	3	30	0	85	6	0	9	4	.692	0	0- —		4.19
Reading	AA	14	13	0	0	79	345	67	33	26	7	6	2	6	33	1	70	4	1	2	4	.333	0	0- —		2.96
1996 Reading	AA	21	21	0	0	133.1	547	108	57	47	16	2	5	4	32	0	132	9	0	11	6	.647	0	0- —		3.17
Scranton-WB	AAA	2	2	0	0	15	57	9	6	4	3	0	0	0	1	0	14	0	0	2	0	1.000	0	0- —		2.40
1997 Clearwater	A+	1	1	0	0	5.2	22	1	1	0	0	0	0	0	4	0	9	0	0	0	0	.000	0	0- —		0.00
Scranton-WB	AAA	5	5	1	0	30	127	24	20	19	5	1	0	0	10	0	38	2	0	3	1	.750	0	0- —		5.70
1996 Philadelphia	NL	8	8	0	0	41.1	182	49	32	32	8	2	6	3	11	0	33	0	0	1	4	.200	0	0-0	0	6.97
1997 Philadelphia	NL	24	24	0	0	136.2	602	147	81	77	25	7	6	5	57	9	120	6	2	4	9	.308	0	0-0	0	5.07
2 ML YEARS		32	32	0	0	178	784	196	113	109	33	9	12	8	68	9	153	6	2	5	13	.278	0	0-0	0	5.51

Tim Belcher

Pitches: Right **Bats:** Right **Pos:** SP-32   **Ht:** 6'3" **Wt:** 220 **Born:** 10/19/61 **Age:** 36

Year Team	Lg	G	GS	CG	GF	IP	BFP	H	R	ER	HR	SH	SF	HB	TBB	IBB	SO	WP	Bk	W	L	Pct.	ShO	Sv-Op	Hld	ERA
1987 Los Angeles	NL	6	5	0	1	34	135	30	11	9	2	2	1	0	7	0	23	0	1	4	2	.667	0	0-0	0	2.38
1988 Los Angeles	NL	36	27	4	5	179.2	719	143	65	58	8	6	1	2	51	7	152	4	1	12	6	.667	1	4-5	0	2.91
1989 Los Angeles	NL	39	30	10	6	230	937	182	81	72	20	6	6	7	80	5	200	7	2	15	12	.556	8	1-1	1	2.82
1990 Los Angeles	NL	24	24	5	0	153	627	136	76	68	17	5	6	2	48	0	102	6	1	9	9	.500	2	0-0	0	4.00
1991 Los Angeles	NL	33	33	2	0	209.1	880	189	76	61	10	11	3	2	75	3	156	7	0	10	9	.526	1	0-0	0	2.62
1992 Cincinnati	NL	35	34	2	1	227.2	949	201	104	99	17	12	11	3	80	2	149	3	1	15	14	.517	1	0-0	0	3.91
1993 Cin-ChA		34	33	5	0	208.2	886	198	108	103	19	8	4	8	74	4	135	6	0	12	11	.522	3	0-0	0	4.44
1994 Detroit	AL	25	25	3	0	162	750	192	124	106	21	3	3	4	78	10	76	6	1	7	15	.318	0	0-0	0	5.89
1995 Seattle	AL	28	28	1	0	179.1	802	188	101	90	19	4	5	5	88	5	96	6	0	10	12	.455	0	0-0	0	4.52
1996 Kansas City	AL	35	35	4	0	238.2	1021	262	117	104	28	6	10	6	68	4	113	7	0	15	11	.577	1	0-0	0	3.92
1997 Kansas City	AL	32	32	3	0	213.1	927	242	128	119	31	7	4	5	70	2	113	1	0	13	12	.520	1	0-0	0	5.02
1993 Cincinnati	NL	22	22	4	0	137	590	134	72	68	11	6	3	7	47	4	101	6	0	9	6	.600	2	0-0	0	4.47
Chicago	AL	12	11	1	0	71.2	296	64	36	35	8	2	1	1	27	0	34	0	0	3	5	.375	1	0-0	0	4.40
11 ML YEARS		327	306	39	13	2035.2	8633	1963	991	889	192	70	54	44	719	42	1315	59	7	122	113	.519	18	5-6	1	3.93

Stan Belinda

Pitches: Right **Bats:** Right **Pos:** RP-84   **Ht:** 6'3" **Wt:** 215 **Born:** 8/6/66 **Age:** 31

Year Team	Lg	G	GS	CG	GF	IP	BFP	H	R	ER	HR	SH	SF	HB	TBB	IBB	SO	WP	Bk	W	L	Pct.	ShO	Sv-Op	Hld	ERA
1989 Pittsburgh	NL	8	0	0	2	10.1	46	13	8	7	0	0	0	0	2	0	10	1	0	0	1	.000	0	0-0	2	6.10
1990 Pittsburgh	NL	55	0	0	17	58.1	245	48	23	23	4	2	2	1	29	3	55	1	0	3	4	.429	0	8-13	9	3.55
1991 Pittsburgh	NL	60	0	0	37	78.1	318	50	30	30	10	4	3	4	35	4	71	0	0	7	5	.583	0	16-20	6	3.45
1992 Pittsburgh	NL	59	0	0	42	71.1	299	58	26	25	8	4	6	0	29	5	57	1	0	6	4	.600	0	18-24	0	3.15
1993 Pit-KC		63	0	0	44	69.2	287	65	31	30	6	3	2	2	17	4	55	2	0	4	2	.667	0	19-23	8	3.88
1994 Kansas City	AL	37	0	0	10	49	220	47	36	28	6	0	3	5	24	3	37	1	0	2	2	.500	0	1-2	5	5.14
1995 Boston	AL	63	0	0	30	69.2	285	51	25	24	5	0	4	4	28	3	57	2	0	8	1	.889	0	10-14	17	3.10
1996 Boston	AL	31	0	0	10	28.2	139	31	22	21	3	1	0	4	20	1	18	2	0	2	1	.667	0	2-4	7	6.59
1997 Cincinnati	NL	84	0	0	18	99.1	420	84	42	41	11	6	5	9	33	6	114	5	0	1	5	.167	0	1-5	28	3.71
1993 Pittsburgh	NL	40	0	0	37	42.1	171	35	18	17	4	1	2	1	11	4	30	0	0	3	1	.750	0	19-22	0	3.61
Kansas City	AL	23	0	0	7	27.1	116	30	13	13	2	2	0	1	6	0	25	2	0	1	1	.500	0	0-1	8	4.28
9 ML YEARS		460	0	0	210	534.2	2259	447	243	229	53	20	25	29	217	29	474	17	0	33	25	.569	0	75-105	82	3.85

David Bell

Bats: R **Throws:** R **Pos:** 3B-35; 2B-23; SS-13; PH-5   **Ht:** 5'10" **Wt:** 170 **Born:** 9/14/72 **Age:** 25

Year Team	Lg	G	AB	H	2B	3B	HR	(Hm	Rd)	TB	R	RBI	TBB	IBB	SO	HBP	SH	SF	SB	CS	SB%	GDP	Avg	OBP	SLG
1997 Arkansas *	AA	9	32	7	2	0	1	—	—	12	3	3	2	0	2	0	0	1	1	0	1.00	1	.219	.265	.375
Louisville *	AAA	6	22	5	0	0	1	—	—	8	3	4	0	0	6	1	0	1	0	0	.00	0	.227	.250	.364
1995 Cle-StL		41	146	36	7	2	2	(1	1)	53	13	19	4	0	25	2	0	1	1	2	.33	0	.247	.275	.363
1996 St. Louis	NL	62	145	31	6	0	1	(1	0)	40	12	9	10	2	22	1	0	1	1	1	.50	3	.214	.268	.276
1997 St. Louis	NL	66	142	30	7	2	1	(1	0)	44	9	12	10	2	28	0	2	1	1	0	1.00	2	.211	.261	.310
1995 Cleveland	AL	2	2	0	0	0	0	(0	0)	0	0	0	0	0	0	0	0	0	0	0	.00	0	.000	.000	.000
St. Louis	NL	39	144	36	7	2	2	(1	1)	53	13	19	4	0	25	2	0	1	1	2	.33	0	.250	.278	.368
3 ML YEARS		169	433	97	20	4	4	(3	1)	137	34	40	24	4	75	3	2	3	3	3	.50	5	.224	.268	.316

Derek Bell

Bats: R **Throws:** R **Pos:** RF-89; CF-36; PH-6; DH-1   **Ht:** 6'2" **Wt:** 215 **Born:** 12/11/68 **Age:** 29

Year Team	Lg	G	AB	H	2B	3B	HR	(Hm	Rd)	TB	R	RBI	TBB	IBB	SO	HBP	SH	SF	SB	CS	SB%	GDP	Avg	OBP	SLG
1997 New Orleans *	AAA	5	13	2	0	0	0	—	—	2	0	1	1	0	1	0	0	0	1	0	1.00	3	.154	.214	.154

Year Team	Lg	G	AB	H	2B	3B	HR	(Hm Rd)	TB	R	RBI	TBB	IBB	SO	HBP	SH	SF	SB	CS	SB%	GDP	Avg	OBP	SLG
1991 Toronto	AL	18	28	4	2	0	0	(0 1)	4	5	1	6	0	5	1	0	0	3	2	.60	0	.143	.314	.143
1992 Toronto	AL	61	161	39	6	3	2	(2 0)	57	23	15	15	1	34	5	2	1	7	2	.78	6	.242	.324	.354
1993 San Diego	NL	150	542	142	19	1	21	(12 9)	226	73	72	23	5	122	12	0	8	26	5	.84	7	.262	.303	.417
1994 San Diego	NL	108	434	135	20	0	14	(8 6)	197	54	54	29	5	88	1	0	2	24	8	.75	14	.311	.354	.454
1995 Houston	NL	112	452	151	21	2	8	(3 5)	200	63	86	33	2	71	8	0	6	27	9	.75	10	.334	.385	.442
1996 Houston	NL	158	608	165	40	3	17	(8 9)	262	84	113	40	8	123	8	0	9	29	3	.91	18	.263	.311	.418
1997 Houston	NL	129	493	136	29	3	15	(7 8)	216	67	71	40	3	94	12	0	2	15	7	.68	16	.276	.344	.438
7 ML YEARS		736	2737	772	135	12	77	(40 37)	1162	369	412	186	24	537	47	2	28	131	36	.78	71	.282	.335	.425

Jay Bell

Bats: Right **Throws:** Right **Pos:** SS-149; PH-6; 3B-4   **Ht:** 6'0" **Wt:** 182 **Born:** 12/11/65 **Age:** 32

Year Team	Lg	G	AB	H	2B	3B	HR	(Hm Rd)	TB	R	RBI	TBB	IBB	SO	HBP	SH	SF	SB	CS	SB%	GDP	Avg	OBP	SLG
1986 Cleveland	AL	5	14	5	2	0	1	(0 1)	10	3	4	2	0	3	0	0	0	0	0	.00	0	.357	.438	.714
1987 Cleveland	AL	38	125	27	9	1	2	(1 1)	44	14	13	8	0	31	1	3	0	2	0	1.00	0	.216	.269	.352
1988 Cleveland	AL	73	211	46	5	1	2	(2 0)	59	23	21	21	0	53	1	1	2	4	2	.67	3	.218	.289	.280
1989 Pittsburgh	NL	78	271	70	13	3	2	(1 1)	95	33	27	19	0	47	1	10	2	5	3	.63	9	.258	.307	.351
1990 Pittsburgh	NL	159	583	148	28	7	7	(1 6)	211	93	52	65	0	109	3	39	6	10	6	.63	14	.254	.329	.362
1991 Pittsburgh	NL	157	608	164	32	8	16	(7 9)	260	96	67	52	1	99	4	30	3	10	6	.63	15	.270	.330	.428
1992 Pittsburgh	NL	159	632	167	36	9	9	(5 4)	242	87	55	55	0	103	4	19	2	7	5	.58	12	.264	.326	.383
1993 Pittsburgh	NL	154	604	187	32	9	9	(3 6)	264	102	51	77	6	122	6	13	1	16	10	.62	16	.310	.392	.437
1994 Pittsburgh	NL	110	424	117	35	4	9	(3 6)	187	68	45	49	1	82	3	8	3	2	0	1.00	15	.276	.353	.441
1995 Pittsburgh	NL	138	530	139	28	4	13	(8 5)	214	79	55	55	1	110	4	3	1	5	5	.29	13	.262	.336	.404
1996 Pittsburgh	NL	151	527	132	29	3	13	(7 6)	206	65	71	54	5	108	5	6	6	6	4	.60	10	.250	.323	.391
1997 Kansas City	AL	153	573	167	28	3	21	(10 11)	264	89	92	71	2	101	4	3	9	10	6	.63	13	.291	.368	.461
12 ML YEARS		1375	5102	1369	277	49	104	(48 56)	2056	752	553	528	16	968	36	135	35	74	47	.61	120	.268	.339	.403

Albert Belle

Bats: Right **Throws:** Right **Pos:** LF-154; DH-7   **Ht:** 6'2" **Wt:** 210 **Born:** 8/25/66 **Age:** 31

Year Team	Lg	G	AB	H	2B	3B	HR	(Hm Rd)	TB	R	RBI	TBB	IBB	SO	HBP	SH	SF	SB	CS	SB%	GDP	Avg	OBP	SLG
1989 Cleveland	AL	62	218	49	8	4	7	(3 4)	86	22	37	12	0	55	2	0	2	2	2	.50	4	.225	.269	.394
1990 Cleveland	AL	9	23	4	0	0	1	(1 0)	7	1	3	1	0	6	0	1	0	0	0	.00	1	.174	.208	.304
1991 Cleveland	AL	123	461	130	31	2	28	(8 20)	249	60	95	25	2	99	5	0	5	3	1	.75	24	.282	.323	.540
1992 Cleveland	AL	153	585	152	23	1	34	(15 19)	279	81	112	52	5	128	4	1	8	8	2	.80	18	.260	.320	.477
1993 Cleveland	AL	159	594	172	36	3	38	(20 18)	328	93	129	76	13	96	8	1	14	23	12	.66	18	.290	.370	.552
1994 Cleveland	AL	106	412	147	35	2	36	(21 15)	294	90	101	58	9	71	5	1	4	9	6	.60	5	.357	.438	.714
1995 Cleveland	AL	143	546	173	52	1	50	(25 25)	377	121	126	73	6	80	6	0	4	5	2	.71	24	.317	.401	.690
1996 Cleveland	AL	158	602	187	38	3	48	(22 26)	375	124	148	99	15	87	7	0	7	11	0	1.00	20	.311	.410	.623
1997 Chicago	AL	161	634	174	45	1	30	(14 16)	311	90	116	53	6	105	6	0	7	4	4	.50	26	.274	.332	.491
9 ML YEARS		1074	4075	1188	268	17	272	(129 143)	2306	682	867	449	55	727	43	4	52	65	29	.69	140	.292	.364	.566

Mark Bellhorn

Bats: B **Throws:** R **Pos:** 3B-40; 2B-17; PH-11; DH-3; SS-1   **Ht:** 6'0" **Wt:** 190 **Born:** 8/23/74 **Age:** 23

Year Team	Lg	G	AB	H	2B	3B	HR	(Hm Rd)	TB	R	RBI	TBB	IBB	SO	HBP	SH	SF	SB	CS	SB%	GDP	Avg	OBP	SLG
1995 Modesto	A+	56	229	59	12	0	6	— —	89	35	31	27	0	52	4	2	0	5	2	.71	9	.258	.346	.389
1996 Huntsville	AA	131	468	117	24	5	10	— —	181	84	71	73	7	124	4	7	4	19	2	.90	7	.250	.353	.387
1997 Edmonton	AAA	70	241	79	18	3	11	— —	136	54	46	64	2	59	2	3	0	6	6	.50	4	.328	.472	.564
1997 Oakland	AL	68	224	51	9	1	6	(3 3)	80	33	19	32	0	70	0	5	0	7	1	.88	1	.228	.324	.357

Rafael Belliard

Bats: Right **Throws:** Right **Pos:** SS-53; PH-20; 2B-7   **Ht:** 5'6" **Wt:** 160 **Born:** 10/24/61 **Age:** 36

Year Team	Lg	G	AB	H	2B	3B	HR	(Hm Rd)	TB	R	RBI	TBB	IBB	SO	HBP	SH	SF	SB	CS	SB%	GDP	Avg	OBP	SLG
1982 Pittsburgh	NL	9	2	1	0	0	0	(0 0)	1	3	0	0	0	0	0	0	0	1	0	1.00	0	.500	.500	.500
1983 Pittsburgh	NL	4	1	0	0	0	0	(0 0)	0	1	0	0	0	0	0	0	0	0	0	.00	0	.000	.000	.000
1984 Pittsburgh	NL	20	22	5	0	0	0	(0 0)	5	3	0	0	0	1	0	0	0	4	1	.80	0	.227	.227	.227
1985 Pittsburgh	NL	17	20	4	0	0	0	(0 0)	4	1	1	0	0	5	0	0	0	0	0	.00	0	.200	.200	.200
1986 Pittsburgh	NL	117	309	72	5	2	0	(0 0)	81	33	31	26	6	54	3	11	1	12	2	.86	8	.233	.298	.262
1987 Pittsburgh	NL	81	203	42	4	3	1	(0 1)	55	26	15	20	6	25	3	2	1	5	1	.83	4	.207	.286	.271
1988 Pittsburgh	NL	122	286	61	0	4	0	(0 0)	69	28	11	26	3	47	4	5	0	7	1	.88	10	.213	.288	.241
1989 Pittsburgh	NL	67	154	33	4	0	0	(0 0)	37	10	8	8	2	22	0	3	0	5	2	.71	1	.214	.253	.240
1990 Pittsburgh	NL	47	54	11	3	0	0	(0 0)	14	10	6	5	0	13	1	1	0	1	2	.33	2	.204	.283	.259
1991 Atlanta	NL	149	353	88	9	2	0	(0 0)	101	36	27	22	2	63	2	7	1	3	1	.75	4	.249	.296	.286
1992 Atlanta	NL	144	285	60	6	1	0	(0 0)	68	20	14	14	4	43	3	13	0	0	1	.00	15	.211	.255	.239
1993 Atlanta	NL	91	79	18	0	0	0	(0 0)	23	6	6	4	0	13	3	3	0	0	0	.00	1	.228	.291	.291
1994 Atlanta	NL	46	120	29	7	1	0	(0 0)	38	9	9	2	1	29	2	2	1	0	2	.00	4	.242	.264	.317
1995 Atlanta	NL	75	180	40	2	1	0	(0 0)	44	12	7	6	2	28	2	4	0	2	2	.50	2	.222	.255	.244
1996 Atlanta	NL	87	142	24	7	0	0	(0 0)	31	9	3	2	0	22	0	3	0	3	1	.75	2	.169	.179	.218
1997 Atlanta	NL	72	71	15	3	0	1	(0 1)	21	9	3	1	0	17	0	4	0	0	1	.00	1	.211	.219	.296
16 ML YEARS		1148	2281	503	55	14	2	(0 2)	592	216	141	136	26	383	23	58	6	43	17	.72	51	.221	.271	.260

Rigo Beltran

Pitches: Left **Bats:** Left **Pos:** RP-31; SP-4   **Ht:** 5'11" **Wt:** 185 **Born:** 11/13/69 **Age:** 28

Year Team	Lg	G	GS	CG	GF	IP	BFP	H	R	ER	HR	SH	SF	HB	TBB	IBB	SO	WP	Bk	W	L	Pct.	ShO	Sv-Op	Hld	ERA
1991 Hamilton	A-	21	4	0	4	48	206	41	17	14	4	4	2	2	19	0	69	3	12	5	2	.714	0	0--	--	2.63
1992 Savannah	A	13	13	2	0	83	316	38	20	20	4	1	0	4	40	0	106	8	6	6	1	.857	1	0--	--	2.17
St. Pete	A+	2	2	0	0	8	30	6	0	0	0	1	0	0	2	0	3	0	6	0	0	.000	0	0--	--	0.00
1993 Arkansas	AA	18	16	0	1	88.2	376	74	39	32	8	5	0	6	38	1	82	11	4	5	5	.500	0	0--	--	3.25
1994 Arkansas	AA	4	4	1	0	28	95	12	3	2	2	1	0	0	3	0	21	0	0	4	0	1.000	1	0--	--	0.64
Louisville	AAA	23	23	1	0	138.1	624	147	82	78	15	7	7	5	68	2	87	18	5	11	11	.500	0	0--	--	5.07
1995 Louisville	AAA	24	24	0	0	129.2	575	156	81	75	12	2	8	5	34	0	92	4	2	8	9	.471	0	0--	--	5.21
1996 Louisville	AAA	38	16	3	5	130.1	548	132	67	63	17	2	4	5	24	1	132	8	1	8	6	.571	1	0--	--	4.35
1997 Louisville	AAA	9	8	1	1	54.1	227	45	17	14	7	0	1	1	21	0	46	0	0	5	2	.714	0	0--	--	2.32
1997 St. Louis	NL	35	4	0	16	54.1	224	47	25	21	3	6	3	0	17	0	50	1	0	1	2	.333	0	1-1	2	3.48

Marvin Benard

Bats: L **Throws:** L **Pos:** PH-51; RF-18; LF-14; CF-6; DH-1   **Ht:** 5'9" **Wt:** 180 **Born:** 1/20/70 **Age:** 28

Year Team	Lg	G	AB	H	2B	3B	HR	(Hm	Rd)	TB	R	RBI	TBB	IBB	SO	HBP	SH	SF	SB	CS	SB%	GDP	Avg	OBP	SLG
1997 Phoenix *	AAA	17	60	20	5	0	0	--	--	25	14	5	11	0	9	1	0	0	4	3	.57	3	.333	.444	.417
1995 San Francisco	NL	13	34	13	2	0	1	(0	1)	18	5	4	1	0	7	0	0	0	1	0	1.00	1	.382	.400	.529
1996 San Francisco	NL	135	488	121	17	4	5	(2	3)	161	89	27	59	2	84	4	6	1	25	11	.69	8	.248	.333	.330
1997 San Francisco	NL	84	114	26	4	0	1	(0	1)	33	13	13	13	0	29	2	0	1	3	1	.75	2	.228	.315	.289
3 ML YEARS		232	636	160	23	4	7	(2	5)	212	107	44	73	2	120	6	6	2	29	12	.71	11	.252	.333	.333

Alan Benes

Pitches: Right **Bats:** Right **Pos:** SP-23   **Ht:** 6'5" **Wt:** 215 **Born:** 1/21/72 **Age:** 26

Year Team	Lg	G	GS	CG	GF	IP	BFP	H	R	ER	HR	SH	SF	HB	TBB	IBB	SO	WP	Bk	W	L	Pct.	ShO	Sv-Op	Hld	ERA
1995 St. Louis	NL	3	3	0	0	16	76	24	15	15	2	1	0	1	4	0	20	3	0	1	2	.333	0	0-0	0	8.44
1996 St. Louis	NL	34	32	3	1	191	840	192	120	104	27	15	9	7	87	3	131	5	1	13	10	.565	1	0-0	0	4.90
1997 St. Louis	NL	23	23	0	0	161.2	666	128	60	52	13	5	4	4	68	3	160	9	2	9	9	.500	0	0-0	0	2.89
3 ML YEARS		60	58	5	1	368.2	1582	344	195	171	42	21	13	12	159	6	311	17	3	23	21	.523	1	0-0	0	4.17

Andy Benes

Pitches: Right **Bats:** Right **Pos:** SP-26   **Ht:** 6'6" **Wt:** 245 **Born:** 8/20/67 **Age:** 30

Year Team	Lg	G	GS	CG	GF	IP	BFP	H	R	ER	HR	SH	SF	HB	TBB	IBB	SO	WP	Bk	W	L	Pct.	ShO	Sv-Op	Hld	ERA
1997 Louisville *	AAA	1	1	0	0	5	18	3	1	1	1	0	0	0	1	0	5	0	0	0	0	.000	0	0--	--	1.80
Arkansas *	AA	1	1	0	0	7	26	2	1	1	0	0	0	0	1	0	6	0	0	1	0	1.000	0	0--	--	1.29
Pr William *	A+	1	1	0	0	5	19	3	1	0	0	0	0	0	1	0	9	0	0	0	0	.000	0	0--	--	0.00
1989 San Diego	NL	10	10	0	0	66.2	280	51	28	26	7	6	2	1	31	0	66	0	3	6	3	.667	0	0-0	0	3.51
1990 San Diego	NL	32	31	2	1	192.1	811	177	87	77	18	5	6	1	69	5	140	2	5	10	11	.476	0	0-0	0	3.60
1991 San Diego	NL	33	33	4	0	223	908	194	76	75	23	5	4	4	59	7	167	3	4	15	11	.577	1	0-0	0	3.03
1992 San Diego	NL	34	34	2	0	231.1	961	230	90	86	14	19	6	5	61	6	169	1	1	13	14	.481	2	0-0	0	3.35
1993 San Diego	NL	34	34	4	0	230.2	968	200	111	97	23	10	6	4	86	7	179	14	2	15	15	.500	2	0-0	0	3.78
1994 San Diego	NL	25	25	2	0	172.1	717	155	82	74	20	11	1	1	51	2	189	4	6	6	14	.300	2	0-0	0	3.86
1995 SD-Sea		31	31	1	0	181.2	809	193	107	96	18	4	8	6	78	5	171	15	0	11	9	.550	1	0-0	0	4.76
1996 St. Louis	NL	36	34	3	1	230.1	963	215	107	98	28	2	6	6	77	7	160	6	0	18	10	.643	1	1-1	0	3.83
1997 St. Louis	NL	26	26	0	0	177	727	149	64	61	9	6	7	5	61	4	175	7	0	10	7	.588	0	0-0	0	3.10
1995 San Diego	NL	19	19	1	0	118.2	518	121	65	55	10	3	4	4	45	3	126	3	0	4	7	.364	1	0-0	0	4.17
Seattle	AL	12	12	0	0	63	291	72	42	41	8	1	4	2	33	2	45	2	0	7	2	.778	0	0-0	0	5.86
9 ML YEARS		261	258	18	2	1705.1	7144	1564	752	690	160	68	46	33	573	43	1416	42	15	104	94	.525	9	1-1	0	3.64

Armando Benitez

Pitches: Right **Bats:** Right **Pos:** RP-71   **Ht:** 6'4" **Wt:** 220 **Born:** 11/3/72 **Age:** 25

Year Team	Lg	G	GS	CG	GF	IP	BFP	H	R	ER	HR	SH	SF	HB	TBB	IBB	SO	WP	Bk	W	L	Pct.	ShO	Sv-Op	Hld	ERA
1994 Baltimore	AL	3	0	0	1	10	42	8	1	1	0	0	0	1	4	0	14	0	0	0	0	.000	0	0-0	0	0.90
1995 Baltimore	AL	44	0	0	18	47.2	221	37	33	30	8	2	3	5	37	2	56	3	1	1	5	.167	0	2-5	6	5.66
1996 Baltimore	AL	18	0	0	18	14.1	56	7	6	6	2	0	1	0	6	0	20	1	0	1	0	1.000	0	4-5	1	3.77
1997 Baltimore	AL	71	0	0	26	73.1	307	49	22	20	7	2	4	1	43	5	106	1	0	4	5	.444	0	9-10	20	2.45
4 ML YEARS		136	0	0	53	145.1	626	101	62	57	17	4	8	7	90	7	196	5	1	6	10	.375	0	15-20	27	3.53

Yamil Benitez

Bats: Right **Throws:** Right **Pos:** LF-31; RF-22; PH-1   **Ht:** 6'2" **Wt:** 195 **Born:** 5/10/72 **Age:** 26

Year Team	Lg	G	AB	H	2B	3B	HR	(Hm	Rd)	TB	R	RBI	TBB	IBB	SO	HBP	SH	SF	SB	CS	SB%	GDP	Avg	OBP	SLG
1990 Expos	R	22	83	19	1	0	1	--	--	23	6	5	8	0	18	0	0	0	0	0	.00	1	.229	.297	.277
1991 Expos	R	54	197	47	9	5	5	--	--	81	20	38	12	1	55	1	1	5	10	5	.67	3	.239	.279	.411
1992 Albany	A	33	79	13	3	2	1	--	--	23	6	6	5	1	49	0	0	0	2	0	.00	1	.165	.214	.291
Jamestown	A-	44	162	44	6	6	3	--	--	71	24	23	14	0	52	2	1	0	19	1	.95	5	.272	.337	.438
1993 Burlington	A	111	411	112	21	5	15	--	--	188	70	61	29	3	99	3	6	3	18	7	.72	8	.273	.323	.457

Year Team	Lg	G	AB	H	2B	3B	HR	(Hm	Rd)	TB	R	RBI	TBB	IBB	SO	HBP	SH	SF	SB	CS	SB%	GDP	Avg	OBP	SLG
1994 Harrisburg	AA	126	475	123	18	4	17	—	—	200	58	91	36	2	134	2	1	4	18	15	.55	12	.259	.311	.421
1995 Ottawa	AAA	127	474	123	24	6	18	—	—	213	66	69	44	3	128	2	2	2	14	6	.70	10	.259	.324	.449
1996 Ottawa	AAA	114	439	122	20	2	23	—	—	215	56	81	28	5	120	1	0	6	11	4	.73	5	.278	.319	.490
1997 Omaha	AAA	92	329	97	14	1	21	—	—	176	61	71	24	1	82	1	0	4	12	3	.80	8	.295	.341	.535
1995 Montreal	NL	14	39	15	2	1	2	(1	1)	25	8	7	1	0	7	0	0	0	0	2	.00	1	.385	.400	.641
1996 Montreal	NL	11	12	2	0	0	0	(0	0)	2	0	2	0	0	4	0	0	0	0	0	.00	0	.167	.167	.167
1997 Kansas City	AL	53	191	51	7	1	8	(5	3)	84	22	21	10	0	49	1	2	2	2	2	.50	2	.267	.307	.440
3 ML YEARS		78	242	68	9	2	10	(6	4)	111	30	30	11	0	60	1	2	0	2	4	.33	3	.281	.315	.459

Mike Benjamin

Bats: R **Throws:** R **Pos:** 3B-19; SS-16; PH-11; 2B-5; 1B-4; DH-1; P-1   **Ht:** 6'0" **Wt:** 169 **Born:** 11/22/65 **Age:** 32

Year Team	Lg	G	AB	H	2B	3B	HR	(Hm	Rd)	TB	R	RBI	TBB	IBB	SO	HBP	SH	SF	SB	CS	SB%	GDP	Avg	OBP	SLG
1997 Pawtucket *	AAA	33	105	26	4	1	4	—	—	44	12	12	8	0	20	2	2	0	4	1	.80	2	.248	.313	.419
1989 San Francisco	NL	14	6	1	0	0	0	(0	0)	1	6	0	0	0	1	0	0	0	0	0	.00	0	.167	.167	.167
1990 San Francisco	NL	22	56	12	3	1	2	(2	0)	23	7	3	3	1	10	0	0	0	1	0	1.00	0	.214	.254	.411
1991 San Francisco	NL	54	106	13	3	0	2	(0	2)	22	12	8	7	2	26	2	3	2	1	0	1.00	1	.123	.188	.208
1992 San Francisco	NL	40	75	13	2	1	1	(0	1)	20	4	3	4	1	15	0	3	0	1	0	1.00	3	.173	.215	.267
1993 San Francisco	NL	63	146	29	7	0	4	(3	1)	48	22	16	9	2	23	4	6	0	0	0	.00	3	.199	.264	.329
1994 San Francisco	NL	38	62	16	5	1	1	(1	0)	26	9	9	5	1	16	3	5	0	5	0	1.00	1	.258	.343	.419
1995 San Francisco	NL	68	186	41	6	0	3	(1	2)	56	19	12	8	3	51	1	7	0	11	1	.92	3	.220	.256	.301
1996 Philadelphia	NL	35	103	23	5	1	4	(0	4)	42	13	13	12	5	21	2	1	0	3	1	.75	2	.223	.316	.408
1997 Boston	AL	49	116	27	9	1	0	(0	0)	38	12	7	4	0	27	1	1	1	2	3	.40	2	.233	.262	.328
9 ML YEARS		383	856	175	40	5	17	(7	10)	276	104	71	52	15	190	13	26	3	26	5	.84	15	.204	.260	.322

Shayne Bennett

Pitches: Right **Bats:** Right **Pos:** RP-16   **Ht:** 6'5" **Wt:** 200 **Born:** 4/10/72 **Age:** 26

Year Team	Lg	G	GS	CG	GF	IP	BFP	H	R	ER	HR	SH	SF	HB	TBB	IBB	SO	WP	Bk	W	L	Pct.	ShO	Sv-Op	Hld	ERA
1993 Red Sox	R	2	1	0	1	7	25	2	1	1	0	1	0	1	0	1	4	1	0	0	0	.000	0	1--	—	1.29
Ft. Laud	A+	23	0	0	18	31.1	128	26	8	6	1	4	1	0	11	1	23	2	2	1	2	.333	0	6--	—	1.72
1994 Sarasota	A+	15	8	0	4	48.1	216	46	31	24	1	2	1	3	27	0	28	1	1	1	6	.143	0	3--	—	4.47
1995 Sarasota	A+	52	0	0	43	59.2	255	50	23	17	3	4	2	4	21	4	69	5	1	2	5	.286	0	24--	—	2.56
Trenton	AA	10	0	0	6	10.2	48	16	6	6	0	3	1	0	3	0	6	1	0	0	1	.000	0	3--	—	5.06
1996 Harrisburg	AA	53	0	0	27	92.2	393	83	32	26	6	3	3	5	35	2	89	2	2	8	8	.500	0	12--	—	2.53
1997 Harrisburg	AA	23	1	0	7	47	210	47	28	23	6	3	1	4	20	0	38	1	0	4	2	.667	0	2--	—	4.40
Ottawa	AAA	25	0	0	21	34.1	142	23	8	6	0	2	1	2	21	1	29	2	0	1	1	.333	0	14--	—	1.57
1997 Montreal	NL	16	0	0	3	22.2	98	21	9	8	2	1	3	0	9	3	8	0	0	0	1	.000	0	0-0	0	3.18

Jeff Berblinger

Bats: Right **Throws:** Right **Pos:** 2B-4; PH-3   **Ht:** 6'0" **Wt:** 190 **Born:** 11/19/70 **Age:** 27

Year Team	Lg	G	AB	H	2B	3B	HR	(Hm	Rd)	TB	R	RBI	TBB	IBB	SO	HBP	SH	SF	SB	CS	SB%	GDP	Avg	OBP	SLG
1993 Glens Falls	A-	38	138	43	9	0	2	—	—	58	26	21	11	0	14	3	1	3	9	4	.69	2	.312	.368	.420
St. Pete	A+	19	70	13	1	0	0	—	—	14	7	5	5	0	10	1	2	0	3	1	.75	1	.186	.250	.200
1994 Savannah	A	132	479	142	27	7	8	—	—	207	86	67	52	0	85	25	6	5	24	5	.83	8	.296	.390	.432
1995 Arkansas	AA	87	332	106	15	4	5	—	—	144	66	29	48	1	40	9	1	2	16	16	.50	2	.319	.417	.434
1996 Arkansas	AA	134	500	144	32	7	11	—	—	223	78	53	52	0	66	8	3	7	23	10	.70	9	.288	.360	.446
1997 Louisville	AAA	133	513	135	19	7	11	—	—	201	63	58	55	3	98	1	1	5	24	12	.67	15	.263	.339	.392
1997 St. Louis	NL	7	5	0	0	0	0	(0	0)	0	1	0	0	0	1	0	1	0	0	0	.00	0	.000	.000	.000

Jason Bere

Pitches: Right **Bats:** Right **Pos:** SP-6   **Ht:** 6'3" **Wt:** 215 **Born:** 5/26/71 **Age:** 27

Year Team	Lg	G	GS	CG	GF	IP	BFP	H	R	ER	HR	SH	SF	HB	TBB	IBB	SO	WP	Bk	W	L	Pct.	ShO	Sv-Op	Hld	ERA
1997 White Sox *	R	2	2	0	0	5	16	2	0	0	0	0	0	0	0	0	5	0	0	0	0	.000	0	0--	—	0.00
Hickory *	A	1	1	0	0	3	13	4	2	2	0	0	0	0	0	0	3	0	0	0	0	.000	0	0--	—	6.00
Birmingham *	AA	2	2	0	0	7	33	8	7	6	2	0	0	1	2	0	7	0	0	1	0	1.000	0	0--	—	7.71
Nashville *	AAA	4	4	0	0	19.1	85	23	13	12	2	0	0	1	7	0	13	1	0	1	1	.500	0	0--	—	5.59
1993 Chicago	AL	24	24	1	0	142.2	610	109	60	55	12	4	2	5	81	0	129	8	0	12	5	.706	0	0-0	0	3.47
1994 Chicago	AL	24	24	0	0	141.2	608	119	65	60	17	4	4	1	80	0	127	6	0	12	2	.857	0	0-0	0	3.81
1995 Chicago	AL	27	27	1	0	137.2	668	151	120	110	21	4	7	6	106	6	110	8	0	8	15	.348	0	0-0	0	7.19
1996 Chicago	AL	5	5	0	0	16.2	93	26	19	19	3	1	1	0	18	1	19	2	0	0	1	.000	0	0-0	0	10.26
1997 Chicago	AL	6	6	0	0	28.2	123	20	15	15	4	1	1	3	17	0	21	1	0	4	2	.667	0	0-0	0	4.71
5 ML YEARS		86	86	2	0	467.1	2102	425	279	259	57	14	15	15	302	7	406	21	0	36	25	.590	0	0-0	0	4.99

Sean Bergman

Pitches: Right **Bats:** Right **Pos:** RP-35; SP-9   **Ht:** 6'4" **Wt:** 230 **Born:** 4/11/70 **Age:** 28

Year Team	Lg	G	GS	CG	GF	IP	BFP	H	R	ER	HR	SH	SF	HB	TBB	IBB	SO	WP	Bk	W	L	Pct.	ShO	Sv-Op	Hld	ERA
1993 Detroit	AL	9	6	1	1	39.2	189	47	29	25	6	3	2	1	23	3	19	3	1	1	4	.200	0	0-0	0	5.67
1994 Detroit	AL	3	3	0	0	17.2	82	22	11	11	2	0	1	0	7	0	12	1	0	2	1	.667	0	0-0	0	5.60

		HOW MUCH HE PITCHED						WHAT HE GAVE UP											THE RESULTS					
Year Team	Lg	G	GS	CG	GF	IP	BFP	H	R	ER	HR	SH	SF	HB	TBB	IBB	SO	WP	Bk	W	L	Pct.	ShO	Sv-Op	Hld	ERA
1995 Detroit	AL	28	28	1	0	135.1	630	169	95	77	19	5	3	4	67	8	86	13	0	7	10	.412	1	0-0	—	5.12
1996 San Diego	NL	41	14	0	11	113.1	482	119	63	55	14	8	4	2	33	3	85	7	2	6	8	.429	0	0-0	1	4.37
1997 San Diego	NL	44	9	0	13	99	451	126	72	67	11	7	4	3	38	4	74	6	0	2	4	.333	0	0-2	1	6.09
5 ML YEARS		125	60	2	25	405	1834	483	270	235	52	23	14	11	168	18	276	30	3	18	27	.400	1	0-2	2	5.22

Geronimo Berroa

Bats: Right **Throws:** Right **Pos:** RF-83; DH-69; PH-8   **Ht:** 6'0" **Wt:** 195 **Born:** 3/18/65 **Age:** 33

		BATTING																		BASERUNNING				PERCENTAGES		
Year Team	Lg	G	AB	H	2B	3B	HR	(Hm	Rd)	TB	R	RBI	TBB	IBB	SO	HBP	SH	SF		SB	CS	SB%	GDP	Avg	OBP	SLG
1989 Atlanta	NL	81	136	36	4	0	2	(1	1)	46	7	9	7	1	32	0	0	0		0	1	.00	2	.265	.301	.338
1990 Atlanta	NL	7	4	0	0	0	0	(0	0)	0	0	0	1	1	1	0	0	0		0	0	.00	0	.000	.200	.000
1992 Cincinnati	NL	13	15	4	1	0	0	(0	0)	5	2	0	2	0	1	1	0	0		0	1	.00	1	.267	.389	.333
1993 Florida	NL	14	34	4	1	0	0	(0	0)	5	3	0	2	0	7	0	0	0		0	0	.00	2	.118	.167	.147
1994 Oakland	AL	96	340	104	18	2	13	(4	9)	165	55	65	41	0	62	3	0	7		7	2	.78	5	.306	.379	.485
1995 Oakland	AL	141	546	152	22	3	22	(10	12)	246	87	88	63	2	98	1	0	6		7	4	.64	12	.278	.351	.451
1996 Oakland	AL	153	586	170	32	1	36	(21	15)	312	101	106	47	0	122	4	0	6		0	3	.00	16	.290	.344	.532
1997 Oak-Bal	AL	156	561	159	25	0	26	(11	15)	262	88	90	76	4	120	4	0	7		4	4	.50	18	.283	.369	.467
1997 Oakland	AL	73	261	81	12	0	16	(6	10)	141	40	42	36	2	58	1	0	1		3	2	.60	12	.310	.395	.540
Baltimore	AL	83	300	78	13	0	10	(5	5)	121	48	48	40	2	62	3	0	6		1	2	.33	6	.260	.347	.403
8 ML YEARS		661	2222	629	103	6	99	(47	52)	1041	343	358	239	8	443	13	0	26		18	15	.55	56	.283	.352	.468

Sean Berry

Bats: Right **Throws:** Right **Pos:** 3B-85; PH-12; DH-3   **Ht:** 5'11" **Wt:** 200 **Born:** 3/22/66 **Age:** 32

		BATTING																		BASERUNNING				PERCENTAGES		
Year Team	Lg	G	AB	H	2B	3B	HR	(Hm	Rd)	TB	R	RBI	TBB	IBB	SO	HBP	SH	SF		SB	CS	SB%	GDP	Avg	OBP	SLG
1997 New Orleans *	AAA	3	9	3	0	0	0	—	—	3	1	0	3	0	3	0	0	0		0	0	.00	0	.333	.500	.333
1990 Kansas City	AL	8	23	5	1	1	0	(0	0)	8	2	4	2	0	5	0	0	0		0	0	.00	0	.217	.280	.348
1991 Kansas City	AL	31	60	8	3	0	0	(0	0)	11	5	1	5	0	23	1	0	0		0	0	.00	1	.133	.212	.183
1992 Montreal	NL	24	57	19	1	0	1	(0	1)	23	5	4	1	0	11	0	0	0		2	1	.67	1	.333	.345	.404
1993 Montreal	NL	122	299	78	15	2	14	(5	9)	139	50	49	41	6	70	2	3	6		12	2	.86	4	.261	.348	.465
1994 Montreal	NL	103	320	89	19	2	11	(4	7)	145	43	41	32	7	50	3	2	2		14	0	1.00	7	.278	.347	.453
1995 Montreal	NL	103	314	100	22	1	14	(5	9)	166	38	55	25	1	53	2	2	5		3	8	.27	5	.318	.367	.529
1996 Houston	NL	132	431	121	38	1	17	(4	13)	212	55	95	23	1	58	9	2	4		12	6	.67	11	.281	.328	.492
1997 Houston	NL	96	301	77	24	1	8	(4	4)	127	37	43	25	1	53	5	1	6		1	5	.17	8	.256	.318	.422
8 ML YEARS		619	1805	497	123	8	65	(22	43)	831	235	292	154	16	323	22	10	23		44	22	.67	37	.275	.336	.460

Damon Berryhill

Bats: Both **Throws:** Right **Pos:** C-51; PH-23; 1B-1   **Ht:** 6'0" **Wt:** 205 **Born:** 12/3/63 **Age:** 34

		BATTING																		BASERUNNING				PERCENTAGES		
Year Team	Lg	G	AB	H	2B	3B	HR	(Hm	Rd)	TB	R	RBI	TBB	IBB	SO	HBP	SH	SF		SB	CS	SB%	GDP	Avg	OBP	SLG
1997 Phoenix *	AAA	4	13	5	0	0	0	—	—	5	0	1	2	2	1	0	0	0		0	0	.00	0	.385	.467	.385
1987 Chicago	NL	12	28	5	1	0	0	(0	0)	6	2	1	3	0	5	0	0	0		0	1	.00	1	.179	.258	.214
1988 Chicago	NL	95	309	80	19	1	7	(5	2)	122	19	38	17	5	56	0	3	3		1	0	1.00	11	.259	.295	.395
1989 Chicago	NL	91	334	86	13	0	5	(2	3)	114	37	41	16	4	54	2	4	5		1	0	1.00	13	.257	.291	.341
1990 Chicago	NL	17	53	10	4	0	1	(1	0)	17	6	9	5	1	14	0	0	1		0	0	.00	3	.189	.254	.321
1991 ChN-Atl	NL	63	160	30	7	0	5	(3	2)	52	13	14	11	1	42	1	0	1		1	2	.33	7	.188	.243	.325
1992 Atlanta	NL	101	307	70	16	1	10	(6	4)	118	21	43	17	4	67	1	0	3		0	2	.00	4	.228	.268	.384
1993 Atlanta	NL	115	335	82	18	2	8	(6	2)	128	24	43	21	2	64	2	2	3		0	0	.00	7	.245	.291	.382
1994 Boston	AL	82	255	67	17	2	6	(3	3)	106	30	34	19	0	59	0	0	2		0	1	.00	6	.263	.312	.416
1995 Cincinnati	NL	34	82	15	3	0	2	(2	0)	24	6	11	10	2	19	0	1	4		0	0	.00	3	.183	.260	.293
1997 San Francisco	NL	73	167	43	8	0	3	(2	1)	60	17	23	20	5	29	0	0	0		0	0	.00	5	.257	.335	.359
1991 Chicago	NL	62	159	30	7	0	5	(3	2)	52	13	14	11	1	41	1	0	1		1	2	.33	2	.189	.244	.327
Atlanta	NL	1	1	0	0	0	0	(0	0)	0	0	0	0	0	1	0	0	0		0	0	.00	0	.000	.000	.000
10 ML YEARS		683	2030	488	106	6	47	(30	17)	747	175	257	139	23	409	6	10	23		3	6	.33	53	.240	.288	.368

Mike Bertotti

Pitches: Left **Bats:** Left **Pos:** RP-9   **Ht:** 6'1" **Wt:** 185 **Born:** 1/18/70 **Age:** 28

		HOW MUCH HE PITCHED						WHAT HE GAVE UP												THE RESULTS					
Year Team	Lg	G	GS	CG	GF	IP	BFP	H	R	ER	HR	SH	SF	HB	TBB	IBB	SO	WP	Bk	W	L	Pct.	ShO	Sv-Op	Hld	ERA
1997 Nashville *	AAA	21	20	1	0	107.2	505	91	70	64	17	1	7	2	105	0	87	15	0	5	9	.357	0	0--	—	5.35
1995 Chicago	AL	4	4	0	0	14.1	80	23	20	20	6	0	3	3	11	0	15	2	1	1	1	.500	0	0-0	0	12.56
1996 Chicago	AL	15	2	0	4	28	130	28	18	16	5	0	1	0	20	3	19	4	0	2	0	1.000	0	0-1	2	5.14
1997 Chicago	AL	9	0	0	2	3.2	23	9	3	3	0	0	1	0	2	0	4	0	1	0	0	.000	0	0-0	0	7.36
3 ML YEARS		28	6	0	6	46	233	60	41	39	11	0	5	3	33	3	38	6	2	3	1	.750	0	0-1	2	7.63

Brian Bevil

Pitches: Right **Bats:** Right **Pos:** RP-18   **Ht:** 6'3" **Wt:** 190 **Born:** 9/5/71 **Age:** 26

		HOW MUCH HE PITCHED						WHAT HE GAVE UP												THE RESULTS					
Year Team	Lg	G	GS	CG	GF	IP	BFP	H	R	ER	HR	SH	SF	HB	TBB	IBB	SO	WP	Bk	W	L	Pct.	ShO	Sv-Op	Hld	ERA
1991 Royals	R	13	12	2	1	65.1	262	56	20	14	0	1	0	2	19	0	70	3	3	5	3	.625	0	0--	—	1.93
1992 Appleton	A	26	26	4	0	156	646	129	67	59	17	5	4	5	63	0	168	9	0	9	7	.563	2	0--	—	3.40
1993 Wilmington	A+	12	12	2	0	74.1	286	46	21	19	2	2	2	4	23	0	61	4	0	7	1	.875	0	0--	—	2.30

Year Team	Lg	HOW MUCH HE PITCHED						WHAT HE GAVE UP													THE RESULTS						
		G	GS	CG	GF	IP	BFP	H	R	ER	HR	SH	SF	HB	TBB	IBB	SO	WP	Bk	W	L	Pct.	ShO	Sv-Op	Hld	ERA
Memphis	AA	6	6	0	0	33	146	36	17	16	4	2	2	0	14	0	26	3	0	3	3	.500	0	0- -	—	4.36
1994 Memphis	AA	17	17	0	0	100	408	75	42	39	6	3	5	3	40	0	78	12	0	5	4	.556	0	0- -	—	3.51
1995 Omaha	AAA	6	6	0	0	22	119	40	31	23	7	1	0	3	14	1	10	2	0	1	3	.250	0	0- -	—	9.41
Wichita	AA	15	15	0	0	74	334	85	51	48	7	0	3	3	35	0	57	7	0	5	7	.417	0	0- -	—	5.84
1996 Wichita	AA	13	13	2	0	75.2	301	56	22	17	4	1	3	2	26	0	74	6	0	9	2	.818	0	0- -	—	2.02
Omaha	AAA	12	12	0	0	67.2	289	62	36	31	10	0	0	5	19	0	73	6	0	7	5	.583	0	0- -	—	4.12
1997 Wichita	AA	4	2	0	2	8	38	11	8	5	0	0	1	1	4	0	10	1	0	0	0	.000	0	0- -	—	5.63
Omaha	AAA	26	3	0	12	39	171	34	22	19	8	1	2	2	22	0	47	0	0	2	1	.667	0	1- -	—	4.38
1996 Kansas City	AL	3	1	0	1	11	44	9	7	7	2	0	1	0	5	0	7	0	0	1	0	1.000	0	0-0	1	5.73
1997 Kansas City	AL	18	0	0	11	16.1	72	16	13	12	1	0	2	1	9	2	13	2	0	1	2	.333	0	1-5	1	6.61
2 ML YEARS		21	1	0	12	27.1	116	25	20	19	3	0	3	1	14	2	20	2	0	2	2	.500	0	1-5	2	6.26

Dante Bichette

Bats: R **Throws:** R **Pos:** LF-128; RF-16; PH-7; DH-5   **Ht:** 6'3" **Wt:** 235 **Born:** 11/18/63 **Age:** 34

Year Team	Lg	BATTING																	BASERUNNING				PERCENTAGES		
		G	AB	H	2B	3B	HR	(Hm	Rd)	TB	R	RBI	TBB	IBB	SO	HBP	SH	SF	SB	CS	SB%	GDP	Avg	OBP	SLG
1988 California	AL	21	46	12	2	0	0	(0	0)	14	1	8	0	0	7	0	0	4	0	0	.00	0	.261	.240	.304
1989 California	AL	48	138	29	7	0	3	(2	1)	45	13	15	6	0	24	0	0	2	3	0	1.00	3	.210	.240	.326
1990 California	AL	109	349	89	15	1	15	(8	7)	151	40	53	16	1	79	3	1	2	5	2	.71	9	.255	.292	.433
1991 Milwaukee	AL	134	445	106	18	3	15	(6	9)	175	53	59	22	4	107	1	1	6	14	8	.64	9	.238	.272	.393
1992 Milwaukee	AL	112	387	111	27	2	5	(3	2)	157	37	41	16	3	74	3	2	3	18	7	.72	13	.287	.318	.406
1993 Colorado	NL	141	538	167	43	5	21	(11	10)	283	93	89	28	2	99	7	0	8	14	8	.64	7	.310	.348	.526
1994 Colorado	NL	116	484	147	33	2	27	(15	12)	265	74	95	19	3	70	4	0	2	21	8	.72	17	.304	.334	.548
1995 Colorado	NL	139	579	197	38	2	40	(31	9)	359	102	128	22	5	96	4	0	7	13	9	.59	16	.340	.364	.620
1996 Colorado	NL	159	633	198	39	3	31	(22	9)	336	114	141	45	4	105	6	0	10	31	12	.72	18	.313	.359	.531
1997 Colorado	NL	151	561	173	31	2	26	(20	6)	286	81	118	30	1	90	3	0	7	6	5	.55	13	.308	.343	.510
10 ML YEARS		1130	4160	1229	253	20	183	(118	65)	2071	608	747	204	23	751	31	4	51	125	59	.68	105	.295	.329	.498

Mike Bielecki

Pitches: Right **Bats:** Right **Pos:** RP-50   **Ht:** 6'3" **Wt:** 200 **Born:** 7/31/59 **Age:** 38

Year Team	Lg	HOW MUCH HE PITCHED						WHAT HE GAVE UP													THE RESULTS						
		G	GS	CG	GF	IP	BFP	H	R	ER	HR	SH	SF	HB	TBB	IBB	SO	WP	Bk	W	L	Pct.	ShO	Sv-Op	Hld	ERA
1984 Pittsburgh	NL	4	0	0	1	4.1	17	4	0	0	0	1	0	0	0	0	1	0	1	0	0	.000	0	0- -	—	0.00
1985 Pittsburgh	NL	12	7	0	1	45.2	211	45	26	23	5	4	0	1	31	1	22	1	1	2	3	.400	0	0- -	—	4.53
1986 Pittsburgh	NL	31	27	0	0	148.2	667	149	87	77	10	7	6	2	83	3	83	7	5	6	11	.353	0	0- -	—	4.66
1987 Pittsburgh	NL	8	8	2	0	45.2	192	43	25	24	6	5	2	1	12	0	25	3	0	2	3	.400	0	0-0	0	4.73
1988 Chicago	NL	19	5	0	7	48.1	215	55	22	18	4	1	4	0	16	1	33	3	3	2	2	.500	0	0-1	1	3.35
1989 Chicago	NL	33	33	4	0	212.1	882	187	82	74	16	9	3	0	81	8	147	9	4	18	7	.720	3	0-0	1	3.14
1990 Chicago	NL	36	29	0	6	168	749	188	101	92	13	16	4	5	70	11	103	11	0	8	11	.421	0	1-1	0	4.93
1991 ChN-Atl	NL	41	25	0	9	173.2	727	171	91	86	18	10	6	2	56	6	75	6	0	13	11	.542	0	0-1	0	4.46
1992 Atlanta	NL	19	14	1	0	80.2	336	77	27	23	2	3	2	1	27	1	62	4	0	2	4	.333	1	0-1	0	2.57
1993 Cleveland	AL	13	13	0	0	68.2	317	90	47	45	8	0	2	2	23	3	38	1	0	4	5	.444	0	0-0	0	5.90
1994 Atlanta	NL	19	1	0	7	27	115	28	12	12	2	1	0	1	12	1	18	0	1	2	0	1.000	0	0-0	0	4.00
1995 California	AL	22	11	0	2	75.1	334	80	56	50	15	2	5	3	31	1	45	3	0	4	6	.400	0	0-0	0	5.97
1996 Atlanta	NL	40	5	0	8	75.1	317	63	24	22	8	0	3	0	33	6	71	2	0	4	3	.571	0	2-2	3	2.63
1997 Atlanta	NL	50	0	0	7	57.1	250	56	33	26	9	3	1	1	21	3	60	1	0	3	7	.300	0	0-0	0	4.08
1991 Chicago	NL	39	25	0	8	172	718	169	91	86	18	10	6	2	54	6	72	6	0	13	11	.542	0	0-1	0	4.50
Atlanta	NL	2	0	0	1	1.2	9	2	0	0	0	0	0	0	2	0	3	0	0	0	0	.000	0	0-0	0	0.00
14 ML YEARS		347	178	7	48	1231	5329	1236	633	572	116	62	38	19	496	45	783	51	15	70	73	.490	4	5- -	—	4.18

Steve Bieser

Bats: L **Throws:** R **Pos:** PH-31; CF-13; LF-9; C-2; RF-1   **Ht:** 5'10" **Wt:** 170 **Born:** 8/4/67 **Age:** 30

Year Team	Lg	BATTING																	BASERUNNING				PERCENTAGES		
		G	AB	H	2B	3B	HR	(Hm	Rd)	TB	R	RBI	TBB	IBB	SO	HBP	SH	SF	SB	CS	SB%	GDP	Avg	OBP	SLG
1989 Batavia	A-	25	75	18	3	1	1	—	—	26	13	13	12	0	20	2	2	2	2	1	.67	1	.240	.352	.347
1990 Batavia	A-	54	160	37	11	1	0	—	—	50	36	12	26	1	20	1	2	2	13	2	.87	3	.231	.339	.313
1991 Spartanburg	A	60	168	41	6	0	0	—	—	47	25	13	31	0	35	3	4	3	17	4	.81	4	.244	.366	.280
1992 Clearwater	A+	73	203	58	6	5	0	—	—	74	33	10	39	3	28	9	8	0	8	8	.50	2	.286	.422	.365
Reading	AA	33	139	38	5	4	0	—	—	51	20	8	6	0	25	4	4	0	8	3	.73	3	.273	.322	.367
1993 Reading	AA	53	170	53	6	3	1	—	—	68	21	19	15	1	24	2	1	0	9	5	.64	2	.312	.374	.400
Scranton-WB	AAA	26	83	21	4	0	0	—	—	25	3	4	2	0	14	1	1	0	3	0	1.00	0	.253	.279	.301
1994 Scranton-WB	AAA	93	228	61	13	1	0	—	—	76	42	15	17	1	40	5	4	2	12	8	.60	2	.268	.329	.333
1995 Scranton-WB	AAA	95	245	66	12	6	1	—	—	93	37	33	22	1	56	10	6	2	14	5	.74	5	.269	.351	.380
1996 Ottawa	AAA	123	382	123	24	4	1	—	—	158	63	32	35	4	55	6	23	2	27	7	.79	6	.322	.386	.414
1997 Norfolk	AAA	41	122	20	5	0	0	—	—	25	6	4	9	0	20	5	2	0	4	3	.57	1	.164	.250	.205
1997 New York	NL	47	69	17	3	0	0	(0	0)	20	16	4	7	1	20	4	0	1	2	3	.40	0	.246	.346	.290

Craig Biggio

Bats: Right **Throws:** Right **Pos:** 2B-160; PH-4; DH-1   **Ht:** 5'11" **Wt:** 180 **Born:** 12/14/65 **Age:** 32

Year Team	Lg	BATTING																	BASERUNNING				PERCENTAGES		
		G	AB	H	2B	3B	HR	(Hm	Rd)	TB	R	RBI	TBB	IBB	SO	HBP	SH	SF	SB	CS	SB%	GDP	Avg	OBP	SLG
1988 Houston	NL	50	123	26	6	1	3	(1	2)	43	14	5	7	2	29	0	1	0	6	1	.86	1	.211	.254	.350
1989 Houston	NL	134	443	114	21	2	13	(6	7)	178	64	60	49	8	64	6	6	5	21	3	.88	7	.257	.336	.402
1990 Houston	NL	150	555	153	24	2	4	(2	2)	193	53	42	53	1	79	3	5	4	25	11	.69	11	.276	.342	.348

Year Team	Lg	G	AB	H	2B	3B	HR	(Hm	Rd)	TB	R	RBI	TBB	IBB	SO	HBP	SH	SF	SB	CS	SB%	GDP	Avg	OBP	SLG
1991 Houston	NL	149	546	161	23	4	4	(0	4)	204	79	46	53	3	71	2	5	3	19	6	.76	2	.295	.358	.374
1992 Houston	NL	162	613	170	32	3	6	(3	3)	226	96	39	94	9	95	7	5	2	38	15	.72	5	.277	.378	.369
1993 Houston	NL	155	610	175	41	5	21	(8	13)	289	98	64	77	7	93	10	4	5	15	17	.47	10	.287	.373	.474
1994 Houston	NL	114	437	139	44	5	6	(4	2)	211	88	56	62	1	58	8	2	2	39	4	.91	5	.318	.411	.483
1995 Houston	NL	141	553	167	30	2	22	(6	16)	267	123	77	80	1	85	22	11	7	33	8	.80	6	.302	.406	.483
1996 Houston	NL	162	605	174	24	4	15	(7	8)	251	113	75	75	0	72	27	8	8	25	7	.78	10	.288	.386	.415
1997 Houston	NL	162	619	191	37	8	22	(7	15)	310	146	81	84	6	107	34	0	7	47	10	.82	5	.309	.415	.501
10 ML YEARS		1379	5104	1470	282	36	116	(44	72)	2172	874	545	634	38	753	119	51	40	268	82	.77	57	.288	.377	.426

Willie Blair

Pitches: Right **Bats:** Right **Pos:** SP-27; RP-2   **Ht:** 6'1" **Wt:** 185 **Born:** 12/18/65 **Age:** 32

Year Team	Lg	G	GS	CG	GF	IP	BFP	H	R	ER	HR	SH	SF	HB	TBB	IBB	SO	WP	Bk	W	L	Pct.	ShO	Sv-Op	Hld	ERA
1997 W Michigan *	A	1	1	0	0	5	16	1	0	0	0	0	0	0	0	0	7	0	0	0	0	.000	0	0- -	—	0.00
Toledo *	AAA	1	1	0	0	7	25	1	1	0	0	0	0	0	2	0	4	0	0	0	0	.000	0	0- -	—	0.00
1990 Toronto	AL	27	6	0	8	68.2	297	66	33	31	4	0	4	1	28	4	43	3	0	3	5	.375	0	0-0	1	4.06
1991 Cleveland	AL	11	5	0	1	36	168	58	27	27	7	1	2	1	10	0	13	1	0	2	3	.400	0	0-1	0	6.75
1992 Houston	NL	29	8	0	1	78.2	331	74	47	35	5	4	3	2	25	2	48	2	0	5	7	.417	0	0-0	1	4.00
1993 Colorado	NL	46	18	1	5	146	664	184	90	77	20	10	8	3	42	4	84	6	1	6	10	.375	0	0-0	3	4.75
1994 Colorado	NL	47	1	0	13	77.2	365	98	57	50	9	3	1	4	39	3	68	4	0	0	5	.000	0	3-6	2	5.79
1995 San Diego	NL	40	12	0	11	114	485	112	60	55	11	8	2	2	45	3	83	4	0	7	5	.583	0	0-0	3	4.34
1996 San Diego	NL	60	0	0	17	88	377	80	52	45	13	4	3	7	29	5	67	2	0	2	6	.250	0	1-5	4	4.60
1997 Detroit	AL	29	27	2	0	175	739	186	85	81	18	3	6	3	46	2	90	6	1	16	8	.667	0	0-0	0	4.17
8 ML YEARS		289	77	3	56	784	3426	858	451	401	87	33	29	23	264	23	496	28	2	41	49	.456	0	4-12	13	4.60

Henry Blanco

Bats: Right **Throws:** Right **Pos:** PH-2; 1B-1; 3B-1   **Ht:** 5'11" **Wt:** 168 **Born:** 8/29/71 **Age:** 26

Year Team	Lg	G	AB	H	2B	3B	HR	(Hm	Rd)	TB	R	RBI	TBB	IBB	SO	HBP	SH	SF	SB	CS	SB%	GDP	Avg	OBP	SLG
1990 Dodgers	R	60	178	39	8	0	1	—	—	50	23	19	26	0	43	1	0	4	7	2	.78	6	.219	.316	.281
1991 Vero Beach	A+	5	7	1	0	0	0	—	—	1	0	0	2	0	0	0	0	0	0	0	.00	0	.143	.333	.143
Great Falls	R+	62	216	55	7	1	5	—	—	79	35	28	27	0	39	1	2	3	6	3	.33	5	.255	.336	.366
1992 Bakersfield	A+	124	401	94	21	2	5	—	—	134	42	52	51	3	91	9	10	9	10	6	.63	10	.234	.328	.334
1993 San Antonio	AA	117	374	73	19	1	10	—	—	124	33	42	29	0	80	4	2	1	3	3	.50	7	.195	.260	.332
1994 San Antonio	AA	132	405	93	23	2	6	—	—	138	36	38	53	2	67	2	5	3	6	6	.50	12	.230	.320	.341
1995 San Antonio	AA	88	302	77	18	4	12	—	—	139	37	48	29	2	52	4	0	1	1	1	.50	4	.255	.328	.460
Albuquerque	AAA	29	97	22	4	1	2	—	—	34	11	13	10	1	23	0	1	2	0	0	.00	3	.227	.294	.351
1996 San Antonio	AA	92	307	82	14	1	5	—	—	113	39	40	28	2	38	0	3	5	2	3	.40	8	.267	.324	.368
Albuquerque	AAA	2	6	1	0	0	0	—	—	1	1	0	0	0	3	0	0	0	0	0	.00	0	.167	.167	.167
1997 Albuquerque	AAA	91	294	92	20	1	6	—	—	132	38	47	37	2	63	1	1	3	7	4	.64	7	.313	.388	.449
1997 Los Angeles	NL	3	5	2	0	0	1	(0	1)	5	1	1	0	0	1	0	0	0	0	0	.00	0	.400	.400	1.000

Jeff Blauser

Bats: Right **Throws:** Right **Pos:** SS-149; PH-3; DH-1   **Ht:** 6'1" **Wt:** 180 **Born:** 11/8/65 **Age:** 32

Year Team	Lg	G	AB	H	2B	3B	HR	(Hm	Rd)	TB	R	RBI	TBB	IBB	SO	HBP	SH	SF	SB	CS	SB%	GDP	Avg	OBP	SLG
1987 Atlanta	NL	51	165	40	6	3	2	(1	1)	58	11	15	18	1	34	3	1	0	7	3	.70	4	.242	.328	.352
1988 Atlanta	NL	18	67	16	3	1	2	(2	0)	27	7	7	2	0	11	1	3	1	0	1	.00	1	.239	.268	.403
1989 Atlanta	NL	142	456	123	24	2	12	(5	7)	187	63	46	38	2	101	1	8	4	5	2	.71	7	.270	.325	.410
1990 Atlanta	NL	115	386	104	24	3	8	(5	3)	158	46	39	35	1	70	5	3	0	3	5	.38	4	.269	.338	.409
1991 Atlanta	NL	129	352	91	14	3	11	(7	4)	144	49	54	54	4	59	2	4	3	5	6	.45	4	.259	.358	.409
1992 Atlanta	NL	123	343	90	19	3	14	(5	9)	157	61	46	46	2	82	4	7	3	5	5	.50	2	.262	.354	.458
1993 Atlanta	NL	161	597	182	29	2	15	(4	11)	260	110	73	85	0	109	16	5	7	16	6	.73	13	.305	.401	.436
1994 Atlanta	NL	96	380	98	21	4	6	(3	3)	145	56	45	38	0	64	5	5	4	1	3	.25	11	.258	.329	.382
1995 Atlanta	NL	115	431	91	16	2	12	(7	5)	147	60	31	57	2	107	12	2	2	8	6	.57	7	.211	.319	.341
1996 Atlanta	NL	83	265	65	14	1	10	(4	6)	111	48	35	40	3	54	6	0	1	6	0	1.00	7	.245	.356	.419
1997 Atlanta	NL	151	519	160	31	4	17	(9	8)	250	90	70	70	6	101	20	5	9	5	1	.83	13	.308	.405	.482
11 ML YEARS		1184	3961	1060	201	28	109	(50	59)	1644	601	461	483	21	792	75	43	36	61	37	.62	72	.268	.355	.415

Ron Blazier

Pitches: Right **Bats:** Right **Pos:** RP-36   **Ht:** 6'5" **Wt:** 205 **Born:** 7/30/71 **Age:** 26

Year Team	Lg	G	GS	CG	GF	IP	BFP	H	R	ER	HR	SH	SF	HB	TBB	IBB	SO	WP	Bk	W	L	Pct.	ShO	Sv-Op	Hld	ERA
1990 Princeton	R+	14	13	1	1	78.2	331	79	46	39	10	1	3	4	29	1	45	3	1	3	5	.375	0	0- -	—	4.46
1991 Batavia	A-	24	8	0	8	72.1	312	81	40	37	11	2	1	3	17	3	77	2	1	7	5	.583	0	2- -	—	4.60
1992 Spartanburg	A	30	21	2	6	159.2	640	141	55	47	10	2	5	5	32	0	149	4	0	14	7	.667	0	0- -	—	2.65
1993 Clearwater	A+	27	23	1	1	155.1	663	171	80	68	8	4	4	6	40	5	86	1	1	9	8	.529	0	0- -	—	3.94
1994 Clearwater	A+	29	29	0	0	173.1	715	197	73	65	15	4	6	9	36	1	120	2	2	13	5	.722	0	0- -	—	3.38
1995 Reading	AA	56	3	0	17	106.2	431	93	44	39	11	5	2	0	31	7	102	2	1	4	5	.444	0	1- -	—	3.29
1996 Scranton-WB	AAA	33	0	0	23	42	168	33	15	12	1	1	2	2	9	2	38	1	0	4	0	1.000	0	12- -	—	2.57
1997 Clearwater	A+	15	0	0	9	30.2	123	24	11	10	0	1	1	0	8	1	45	7	1	2	3	.400	0	3- -	—	2.93
Scranton-WB	AAA	11	0	0	8	14.2	68	17	9	6	4	1	1	0	3	0	10	0	0	0	3	.000	0	1- -	—	3.68
1996 Philadelphia	NL	27	0	0	9	38.1	173	49	30	25	6	3	2	0	10	3	25	3	0	3	1	.750	0	0-0	0	5.87
1997 Philadelphia	NL	36	0	0	7	53.2	240	62	31	30	4	0	1	0	21	3	42	2	0	1	1	.500	0	0-0	0	5.03

Year Team	Lg	HOW MUCH HE PITCHED						WHAT HE GAVE UP											THE RESULTS					
		G	GS	CG	GF	IP	BFP	H	R	ER	HR	SH	SF	HB	TBB	IBB	SO	WP	Bk	W	L	Pct.	ShO	Sv-Op	Hld	ERA
2 ML YEARS		63	0	0	16	92	413	111	61	55	14	4	6	0	31	6	67	5	0	4	2	.667	0	0-0	0	5.38

Mike Blowers

Bats: R **Throws:** R **Pos:** 1B-49; PH-18; 3B-10; LF-5; DH-1; RF-1   **Ht:** 6'2" **Wt:** 210 **Born:** 4/24/65 **Age:** 33

Year Team	Lg	BATTING																BASERUNNING				PERCENTAGES		
		G	AB	H	2B	3B	HR	(Hm | Rd)	TB	R	RBI	TBB	IBB	SO	HBP	SH	SF	SB	CS	SB%	GDP	Avg	OBP	SLG
1989 New York	AL	13	38	10	0	0	0	(0 | 0)	10	2	3	3	0	13	0	0	0	0	0	.00	1	.263	.317	.263
1990 New York	AL	48	144	27	4	0	5	(1 | 4)	46	16	21	12	1	50	1	0	0	1	0	1.00	3	.188	.255	.319
1991 New York	AL	15	35	7	0	0	1	(0 | 1)	10	3	1	4	0	3	0	1	0	0	0	.00	1	.200	.282	.286
1992 Seattle	AL	31	73	14	3	0	1	(0 | 1)	20	7	2	6	0	20	0	1	0	0	0	.00	3	.192	.253	.274
1993 Seattle	AL	127	379	106	23	3	15	(8 | 7)	180	55	57	44	3	98	2	3	1	1	5	.17	12	.280	.357	.475
1994 Seattle	AL	85	270	78	13	0	9	(3 | 6)	118	37	49	25	2	60	1	1	3	2	2	.50	12	.289	.348	.437
1995 Seattle	AL	134	439	113	24	1	23	(17 | 6)	208	59	96	53	0	128	0	3	3	2	1	.67	18	.257	.335	.474
1996 Los Angeles	NL	92	317	84	19	2	6	(4 | 2)	125	31	38	37	2	77	1	0	3	0	0	.00	11	.265	.341	.394
1997 Seattle	AL	68	150	44	5	0	5	(5 | 0)	64	22	20	21	1	33	0	4	2	0	0	.00	4	.293	.376	.427
9 ML YEARS		613	1845	483	91	6	65	(38 | 27)	781	232	287	205	9	482	5	13	12	6	8	.43	65	.262	.335	.423

Doug Bochtler

Pitches: Right **Bats:** Right **Pos:** RP-54   **Ht:** 6'3" **Wt:** 200 **Born:** 7/5/70 **Age:** 27

Year Team	Lg	HOW MUCH HE PITCHED						WHAT HE GAVE UP											THE RESULTS					
		G	GS	CG	GF	IP	BFP	H	R	ER	HR	SH	SF	HB	TBB	IBB	SO	WP	Bk	W	L	Pct.	ShO	Sv-Op	Hld	ERA
1995 San Diego	NL	34	0	0	11	45.1	181	38	18	18	5	2	1	0	19	0	45	1	0	4	4	.500	0	1-4	8	3.57
1996 San Diego	NL	63	0	0	17	65.2	278	45	25	22	6	5	2	1	39	8	68	8	2	2	4	.333	0	3-7	20	3.02
1997 San Diego	NL	54	0	0	13	60.1	281	51	35	32	3	4	3	1	50	4	46	5	0	3	6	.333	0	2-3	9	4.77
3 ML YEARS		151	0	0	41	171.1	740	134	78	72	14	11	6	2	108	12	159	14	2	9	14	.391	0	6-14	37	3.78

Brian Boehringer

Pitches: Right **Bats:** Both **Pos:** RP-34   **Ht:** 6'2" **Wt:** 190 **Born:** 1/8/70 **Age:** 28

Year Team	Lg	HOW MUCH HE PITCHED						WHAT HE GAVE UP											THE RESULTS					
		G	GS	CG	GF	IP	BFP	H	R	ER	HR	SH	SF	HB	TBB	IBB	SO	WP	Bk	W	L	Pct.	ShO	Sv-Op	Hld	ERA
1997 Yankees *	R	1	1	0	0	2	7	1	0	0	0	0	0	0	0	0	2	0	0	0	0	.000	0	0--	—	0.00
Tampa *	A+	3	3	0	0	9	40	9	5	5	1	1	0	0	5	0	8	0	0	0	1	.000	0	0--	—	5.00
1995 New York	AL	7	3	0	0	17.2	99	24	27	27	5	0	1	1	22	1	10	3	0	0	3	.000	0	0-1	0	13.75
1996 New York	AL	15	3	0	1	46.1	205	46	28	28	6	3	3	1	21	2	37	1	0	2	4	.333	0	0-1	4	5.44
1997 New York	AL	34	0	0	11	48	210	39	16	14	4	3	2	0	32	6	53	2	0	3	2	.600	0	0-3	5	2.63
3 ML YEARS		56	6	0	12	112	514	109	71	69	15	6	6	2	75	9	100	6	0	5	9	.357	0	0-5	9	5.54

Tim Bogar

Bats: R **Throws:** R **Pos:** SS-80; 3B-14; PH-5; 1B-1   **Ht:** 6'2" **Wt:** 198 **Born:** 10/28/66 **Age:** 31

Year Team	Lg	BATTING																BASERUNNING				PERCENTAGES		
		G	AB	H	2B	3B	HR	(Hm | Rd)	TB	R	RBI	TBB	IBB	SO	HBP	SH	SF	SB	CS	SB%	GDP	Avg	OBP	SLG
1993 New York	NL	78	205	50	13	0	3	(1 | 2)	72	19	25	14	2	29	3	1	1	0	1	.00	2	.244	.300	.351
1994 New York	NL	50	52	8	0	0	2	(0 | 2)	14	5	5	4	1	11	0	2	1	1	0	1.00	1	.154	.211	.269
1995 New York	NL	78	145	42	7	0	1	(0 | 1)	52	17	21	9	0	25	0	2	1	1	0	1.00	2	.290	.329	.359
1996 New York	NL	91	89	19	4	0	0	(0 | 0)	23	17	6	8	0	20	2	3	2	1	3	.25	0	.213	.287	.258
1997 Houston	NL	97	241	60	14	4	4	(3 | 1)	94	30	30	24	1	42	3	3	4	4	1	.80	4	.249	.320	.390
5 ML YEARS		394	732	179	38	4	10	(4 | 6)	255	88	87	59	4	127	8	11	9	7	5	.58	9	.245	.304	.348

Wade Boggs

Bats: L **Throws:** R **Pos:** 3B-76; DH-19; PH-14; P-1   **Ht:** 6'2" **Wt:** 197 **Born:** 6/15/58 **Age:** 40

Year Team	Lg	BATTING																BASERUNNING				PERCENTAGES		
		G	AB	H	2B	3B	HR	(Hm | Rd)	TB	R	RBI	TBB	IBB	SO	HBP	SH	SF	SB	CS	SB%	GDP	Avg	OBP	SLG
1982 Boston	AL	104	338	118	14	1	5	(4 | 1)	149	51	44	35	4	21	0	4	4	1	0	1.00	9	.349	.406	.441
1983 Boston	AL	153	582	210	44	7	5	(2 | 3)	283	100	74	92	2	36	1	3	7	3	3	.50	15	.361	.444	.486
1984 Boston	AL	158	625	203	31	4	6	(5 | 1)	260	109	55	89	6	44	0	8	4	3	2	.60	11	.325	.407	.416
1985 Boston	AL	161	653	240	42	3	8	(6 | 2)	312	107	78	96	5	61	4	3	2	2	1	.67	20	.368	.450	.478
1986 Boston	AL	149	580	207	47	2	8	(3 | 5)	282	107	71	105	14	44	0	4	4	0	4	.00	11	.357	.453	.486
1987 Boston	AL	147	551	200	40	6	24	(10 | 14)	324	108	89	105	19	48	2	1	8	1	3	.25	19	.363	.461	.588
1988 Boston	AL	155	584	214	45	6	5	(4 | 1)	286	128	58	125	18	34	3	0	7	2	3	.40	23	.366	.476	.490
1989 Boston	AL	156	621	205	51	7	3	(2 | 1)	279	113	54	107	19	51	7	0	7	2	6	.25	19	.330	.430	.449
1990 Boston	AL	155	619	187	44	5	6	(3 | 3)	259	89	63	87	19	68	1	0	6	0	0	.00	14	.302	.386	.418
1991 Boston	AL	144	546	181	42	2	8	(6 | 2)	251	93	51	89	25	32	1	0	6	1	2	.33	16	.332	.421	.460
1992 Boston	AL	143	514	133	22	4	7	(4 | 3)	184	62	50	74	19	31	4	0	6	1	3	.25	10	.259	.353	.358
1993 New York	AL	143	560	169	26	1	2	(1 | 1)	203	83	59	74	4	49	0	1	9	0	1	.00	10	.302	.378	.363
1994 New York	AL	97	366	125	19	1	11	(6 | 5)	179	61	55	61	3	29	1	2	4	2	1	.67	10	.342	.433	.489
1995 New York	AL	126	460	149	22	4	5	(4 | 1)	194	76	63	74	5	50	0	0	7	1	1	.50	13	.324	.412	.422
1996 New York	AL	132	501	156	29	2	2	(2 | 0)	195	80	41	67	7	32	0	1	5	1	2	.33	10	.311	.389	.389
1997 New York	AL	104	353	103	23	1	4	(0 | 4)	140	55	28	48	3	38	0	2	4	0	1	.00	3	.292	.373	.397
16 ML YEARS		2227	8453	2800	541	56	109	(62 | 47)	3780	1422	933	1328	172	668	23	29	90	20	33	.38	209	.331	.420	.447

Brian Bohanon

Pitches: Left **Bats:** Left **Pos:** SP-14; RP-5 | **Ht:** 6'3" **Wt:** 220 **Born:** 8/1/68 **Age:** 29

		HOW MUCH HE PITCHED						WHAT HE GAVE UP										THE RESULTS						
Year Team	Lg	G	GS	CG	GF	IP	BFP	H	R	ER	HR	SH	SF	HB	TBB	IBB	SO	WP	Bk	W	L	Pct.	ShO	Sv-Op	Hld	ERA
1997 Norfolk *	AAA	15	14	4	0	96	404	88	37	28	9	2	1	3	32	0	84	2	0	9	3	.750	0	0- -	—	2.63
1990 Texas	AL	11	6	0	1	34	158	40	30	25	6	0	3	2	18	0	15	1	0	0	3	.000	0	0-0	0	6.62
1991 Texas	AL	11	11	1	0	61.1	273	66	35	33	4	2	5	2	23	0	34	3	1	4	3	.571	0	0-0	0	4.84
1992 Texas	AL	18	7	0	3	45.2	220	57	38	32	7	0	2	1	25	0	29	2	0	1	1	.500	0	0-0	0	6.31
1993 Texas	AL	36	8	0	4	92.2	418	107	54	49	8	2	5	4	46	3	45	10	0	4	4	.500	0	0-1	1	4.76
1994 Texas	AL	11	5	0	1	37.1	169	51	31	30	7	1	0	1	8	1	26	5	0	2	2	.500	0	0-0	0	7.23
1995 Detroit	AL	52	10	0	7	105.2	474	121	68	65	10	0	5	4	41	5	63	3	0	1	1	.500	0	1-1	10	5.54
1996 Toronto	AL	20	0	0	6	22	112	27	19	19	4	0	2	2	19	4	17	2	0	1	0	1.000	0	1-1	2	7.77
1997 New York	NL	19	14	0	0	94.1	412	95	49	40	9	6	0	4	34	2	66	3	1	6	4	.600	0	0-0	0	3.82
8 ML YEARS		178	61	1	22	493	2236	564	324	293	55	11	22	20	214	15	295	29	2	18	19	.486	0	2-3	13	5.35

Barry Bonds

Bats: Left **Throws:** Left **Pos:** LF-159 | **Ht:** 6'1" **Wt:** 190 **Born:** 7/24/64 **Age:** 33

		BATTING																	BASERUNNING				PERCENTAGES		
Year Team	Lg	G	AB	H	2B	3B	HR	(Hm	Rd)	TB	R	RBI	TBB	IBB	SO	HBP	SH	SF	SB	CS	SB%	GDP	Avg	OBP	SLG
1986 Pittsburgh	NL	113	413	92	26	3	16	(9	7)	172	72	48	65	2	102	2	2	2	36	7	.84	4	.223	.330	.416
1987 Pittsburgh	NL	150	551	144	34	9	25	(12	13)	271	99	59	54	3	88	3	0	3	32	10	.76	4	.261	.329	.492
1988 Pittsburgh	NL	144	538	152	30	5	24	(14	10)	264	97	58	72	14	82	2	0	2	17	11	.61	3	.283	.368	.491
1989 Pittsburgh	NL	159	580	144	34	6	19	(7	12)	247	96	58	93	22	93	1	1	4	32	10	.76	9	.248	.351	.426
1990 Pittsburgh	NL	151	519	156	32	3	33	(14	19)	293	104	114	93	15	83	3	0	6	52	13	.80	8	.301	.406	.565
1991 Pittsburgh	NL	153	510	149	28	5	25	(12	13)	262	95	116	107	25	73	4	0	13	43	13	.77	8	.292	.410	.514
1992 Pittsburgh	NL	140	473	147	36	5	34	(15	19)	295	109	103	127	32	69	5	0	7	39	8	.83	9	.311	.456	.624
1993 San Francisco	NL	159	539	181	38	4	46	(21	25)	365	129	123	126	43	79	2	0	7	29	12	.71	11	.336	.458	.677
1994 San Francisco	NL	112	391	122	18	1	37	(15	22)	253	89	81	74	18	43	6	0	3	29	9	.76	3	.312	.426	.647
1995 San Francisco	NL	144	506	149	30	7	33	(16	17)	292	109	104	120	22	83	5	0	4	31	10	.76	12	.294	.431	.577
1996 San Francisco	NL	158	517	159	27	3	42	(23	19)	318	122	129	151	30	76	1	0	6	40	7	.85	11	.308	.461	.615
1997 San Francisco	NL	159	532	155	26	5	40	(24	16)	311	123	101	145	34	87	8	0	5	37	8	.82	13	.291	.446	.585
12 ML YEARS		1742	6069	1750	359	56	374	(182	192)	3343	1244	1094	1227	260	958	42	3	62	417	118	.78	95	.288	.408	.551

Ricky Bones

Pitches: Right **Bats:** Right **Pos:** RP-17; SP-13 | **Ht:** 6'0" **Wt:** 193 **Born:** 4/7/69 **Age:** 29

		HOW MUCH HE PITCHED						WHAT HE GAVE UP										THE RESULTS						
Year Team	Lg	G	GS	CG	GF	IP	BFP	H	R	ER	HR	SH	SF	HB	TBB	IBB	SO	WP	Bk	W	L	Pct.	ShO	Sv-Op	Hld	ERA
1997 Tucson *	AAA	8	7	0	1	42	173	40	18	13	2	0	0	3	8	0	22	0	1	5	0	1.000	0	0- -	—	2.79
1991 San Diego	NL	11	11	0	0	54	234	57	33	29	3	0	4	0	18	0	31	4	0	4	6	.400	0	0-0	0	4.83
1992 Milwaukee	AL	31	28	0	0	163.1	705	169	90	83	27	2	5	9	48	0	65	3	2	9	10	.474	0	0-0	0	4.57
1993 Milwaukee	AL	32	31	3	1	203.2	883	222	122	110	28	5	7	8	63	3	63	6	1	11	11	.500	0	0-0	0	4.86
1994 Milwaukee	AL	24	24	4	0	170.2	708	166	76	65	17	4	5	3	45	1	57	8	0	10	9	.526	1	0-0	0	3.43
1995 Milwaukee	AL	32	31	3	0	200.1	877	218	108	103	26	3	11	4	83	2	77	5	2	10	12	.455	0	0-0	0	4.63
1996 Mil-NYA	AL	36	24	0	2	152	699	184	115	105	30	5	5	10	68	2	63	2	0	7	14	.333	0	0-0	3	6.22
1997 Cin-KC		30	13	1	4	96	450	133	81	72	12	3	8	7	36	4	44	1	0	4	8	.333	0	0-1	2	6.75
1996 Milwaukee	AL	32	23	0	2	145	658	170	104	94	28	4	4	9	62	2	59	2	0	7	14	.333	0	0-0	3	5.83
New York	AL	4	1	0	0	7	41	14	11	11	2	1	1	1	6	0	4	0	0	0	0	.000	0	0-0	0	14.14
1997 Cincinnati	NL	9	2	0	2	17.2	98	31	22	20	2	1	2	2	11	2	8	0	0	0	1	.000	0	0-0	0	10.19
Kansas City	AL	21	11	1	2	78.1	352	102	59	52	10	2	6	5	25	2	36	1	0	4	7	.364	0	0-1	2	5.97
7 ML YEARS		196	162	11	7	1040	4556	1149	625	567	143	22	45	41	361	12	400	29	5	55	70	.440	1	0-1	5	4.91

Bobby Bonilla

Bats: B **Throws:** R **Pos:** 3B-149; DH-3; 1B-2; PH-1 | **Ht:** 6'4" **Wt:** 240 **Born:** 2/23/63 **Age:** 35

		BATTING																	BASERUNNING				PERCENTAGES		
Year Team	Lg	G	AB	H	2B	3B	HR	(Hm	Rd)	TB	R	RBI	TBB	IBB	SO	HBP	SH	SF	SB	CS	SB%	GDP	Avg	OBP	SLG
1986 ChA-Pit		138	426	109	16	4	3	(2	1)	142	55	43	62	3	88	2	5	1	8	5	.62	9	.256	.352	.333
1987 Pittsburgh	NL	141	466	140	33	3	15	(7	8)	224	58	77	39	4	64	2	0	8	3	5	.38	8	.300	.351	.481
1988 Pittsburgh	NL	159	584	160	32	7	24	(9	15)	278	87	100	85	19	82	4	0	8	3	5	.38	4	.274	.366	.476
1989 Pittsburgh	NL	163	616	173	37	10	24	(13	11)	302	96	86	76	20	93	1	0	8	8	8	.50	10	.281	.358	.490
1990 Pittsburgh	NL	160	625	175	39	7	32	(13	19)	324	112	120	45	9	103	1	0	15	4	3	.57	11	.280	.322	.518
1991 Pittsburgh	NL	157	577	174	44	6	18	(9	9)	284	102	100	90	8	67	2	0	11	2	4	.33	14	.302	.391	.492
1992 New York	NL	128	438	109	23	0	19	(5	14)	189	62	70	66	10	73	1	0	1	4	3	.57	11	.249	.348	.432
1993 New York	NL	139	502	133	21	3	34	(18	16)	262	81	87	72	11	96	0	0	8	3	3	.50	12	.265	.352	.522
1994 New York	NL	108	403	117	24	1	20	(8	12)	203	60	67	55	9	101	0	0	2	1	3	.25	10	.290	.374	.504
1995 NYN-Bal		141	554	182	37	8	28	(14	14)	319	96	99	54	10	79	2	0	4	0	5	.00	22	.329	.388	.576
1996 Baltimore	AL	159	595	171	27	5	28	(9	19)	292	107	116	75	7	85	5	0	17	1	3	.25	13	.287	.363	.491
1997 Florida	NL	153	562	167	39	3	17	(8	9)	263	77	96	73	8	94	5	0	8	6	6	.50	18	.297	.378	.468
1986 Chicago	AL	75	234	63	10	2	2	(2	0)	83	27	26	33	2	49	1	2	1	4	1	.80	4	.269	.361	.355
Pittsburgh	NL	63	192	46	6	2	1	(0	1)	59	28	17	29	1	39	1	3	0	4	4	.50	5	.240	.342	.307
1995 New York	NL	80	317	103	25	4	18	(7	11)	190	49	53	31	10	48	1	0	2	0	3	.00	11	.325	.385	.599
Baltimore	AL	61	237	79	12	4	10	(7	3)	129	47	46	23	0	31	1	0	2	0	2	.00	11	.333	.392	.544
12 ML YEARS		1746	6348	1810	372	57	262	(115	147)	3082	993	1061	792	118	1025	25	5	88	43	53	.45	142	.285	.362	.486

Aaron Boone

Bats: Right **Throws:** Right **Pos:** 3B-13; PH-4; 2B-1   **Ht:** 6'2" **Wt:** 190 **Born:** 3/9/73 **Age:** 25

Year Team	Lg	G	AB	H	2B	3B	HR	(Hm	Rd)	TB	R	RBI	TBB	IBB	SO	HBP	SH	SF	SB	CS	SB%	GDP	Avg	OBP	SLG
1994 Billings	R+	67	256	70	15	5	7	—	—	116	48	55	36	3	35	3	0	6	6	3	.67	7	.273	.362	.453
1995 Chattanooga	AA	23	66	15	3	0	0	—	—	18	6	3	5	0	12	0	1	2	2	0	1.00	5	.227	.274	.273
Winston-Sal	A+	108	395	103	19	1	14	—	—	166	61	50	43	7	77	9	4	2	11	7	.61	4	.261	.345	.420
1996 Chattanooga	AA	136	548	158	44	7	17	—	—	267	86	95	38	4	77	5	1	4	21	10	.68	5	.288	.338	.487
1997 Indianapols	AAA	131	476	138	30	4	22	—	—	242	79	75	40	3	81	1	3	3	12	4	.75	11	.290	.344	.508
1997 Cincinnati	NL	16	49	12	1	0	0	(0	0)	13	5	5	2	0	5	0	1	0	1	0	1.00	1	.245	.275	.265

Bret Boone

Bats: Right **Throws:** Right **Pos:** 2B-136; PH-5   **Ht:** 5'10" **Wt:** 180 **Born:** 4/6/69 **Age:** 29

Year Team	Lg	G	AB	H	2B	3B	HR	(Hm	Rd)	TB	R	RBI	TBB	IBB	SO	HBP	SH	SF	SB	CS	SB%	GDP	Avg	OBP	SLG
1997 Indianapols *	AAA	3	7	2	1	0	0	—	—	3	1	1	2	0	2	0	0	0	1	0	1.00	0	.286	.444	.429
1992 Seattle	AL	33	129	25	4	0	4	(2	2)	41	15	15	4	0	34	1	1	0	1	1	.50	4	.194	.224	.318
1993 Seattle	AL	76	271	68	12	2	12	(7	5)	120	31	38	17	1	52	4	6	4	2	3	.40	6	.251	.301	.443
1994 Cincinnati	NL	108	381	122	25	2	12	(5	7)	187	59	68	24	1	74	8	5	6	3	4	.43	10	.320	.368	.491
1995 Cincinnati	NL	138	513	137	34	2	15	(6	9)	220	63	68	41	0	84	6	5	5	5	1	.83	14	.267	.326	.429
1996 Cincinnati	NL	142	520	121	21	3	12	(7	5)	184	56	69	31	0	100	3	5	9	3	2	.60	9	.233	.275	.354
1997 Cincinnati	NL	139	443	99	25	1	7	(4	3)	147	40	46	45	4	101	4	4	5	5	5	.50	11	.223	.298	.332
6 ML YEARS		636	2257	572	121	10	62	(31	31)	899	264	304	162	6	445	26	26	29	19	16	.54	54	.253	.307	.398

Josh Booty

Bats: Right **Throws:** Right **Pos:** 3B-4   **Ht:** 6'3" **Wt:** 210 **Born:** 4/29/75 **Age:** 23

Year Team	Lg	G	AB	H	2B	3B	HR	(Hm	Rd)	TB	R	RBI	TBB	IBB	SO	HBP	SH	SF	SB	CS	SB%	GDP	Avg	OBP	SLG
1994 Marlins	R	10	36	8	0	0	1	—	—	11	5	2	5	0	8	0	1	0	1	0	1.00	2	.222	.317	.306
Elmira	A-	4	16	4	1	0	0	—	—	5	1	1	0	0	4	0	0	0	1	0	1.00	1	.250	.250	.313
1995 Kane County	A	31	109	11	2	0	1	—	—	16	6	6	11	0	45	0	0	1	1	0	1.00	1	.101	.182	.147
Elmira	A-	74	287	63	18	1	6	—	—	101	33	37	19	0	85	5	0	2	4	4	.50	12	.220	.278	.352
1996 Kane County	A	128	475	98	25	1	21	—	—	188	62	87	46	0	195	1	1	6	2	3	.40	11	.206	.275	.396
1997 Portland	AA	122	448	94	19	2	20	—	—	177	42	69	27	1	166	1	0	4	2	2	.50	12	.210	.254	.395
1996 Florida	NL	2	2	1	0	0	0	(0	0)	1	1	0	0	0	0	0	0	0	0	0	.00	1	.500	.500	.500
1997 Florida	NL	4	5	3	0	0	0	(0	0)	3	2	1	1	0	1	0	0	0	0	0	.00	0	.600	.667	.600
2 ML YEARS		6	7	4	0	0	0	(0	0)	4	3	1	1	0	1	0	0	0	0	0	.00	1	.571	.625	.571

Pedro Borbon

Pitches: Left **Bats:** Left **Pos:** RP   **Ht:** 6'1" **Wt:** 205 **Born:** 11/15/67 **Age:** 30

		HOW MUCH HE PITCHED						WHAT HE GAVE UP											THE RESULTS					
Year Team	Lg	G	GS	CG	GF	IP	BFP	H	R	ER	HR	SH	SF	HB	TBB	IBB	SO	WP	Bk	W	L	Pct.	ShO	Sv-Op	Hld	ERA
1992 Atlanta	NL	2	0	0	2	1.1	7	2	1	1	0	0	0	0	1	1	1	0	0	1	0	1.000	0	0-0	0	6.75
1993 Atlanta	NL	3	0	0	2	1.2	11	3	4	4	0	1	0	0	3	0	2	0	0	0	0	.000	0	0-0	0	21.60
1995 Atlanta	NL	41	0	0	19	32	143	29	12	11	2	3	1	1	17	4	33	0	1	2	2	.500	0	2-4	6	3.09
1996 Atlanta	NL	43	0	0	19	36	140	26	12	11	1	4	0	1	7	0	31	0	0	3	0	1.000	0	1-1	4	2.75
4 ML YEARS		89	0	0	40	71	301	60	29	27	3	8	1	2	28	5	67	0	1	5	3	.625	0	3-5	10	3.42

Pat Borders

Bats: Right **Throws:** Right **Pos:** C-53; PH-2   **Ht:** 6'2" **Wt:** 195 **Born:** 5/14/63 **Age:** 35

Year Team	Lg	G	AB	H	2B	3B	HR	(Hm	Rd)	TB	R	RBI	TBB	IBB	SO	HBP	SH	SF	SB	CS	SB%	GDP	Avg	OBP	SLG
1988 Toronto	AL	56	154	42	6	3	5	(2	3)	69	15	21	3	0	24	0	2	1	0	0	.00	5	.273	.285	.448
1989 Toronto	AL	94	241	62	11	1	3	(1	2)	84	22	29	11	2	45	1	1	2	2	1	.67	7	.257	.290	.349
1990 Toronto	AL	125	346	99	24	2	15	(10	5)	172	36	49	18	2	57	0	1	3	0	1	.00	17	.286	.319	.497
1991 Toronto	AL	105	291	71	17	0	5	(2	3)	103	22	36	11	1	45	1	6	3	0	0	.00	8	.244	.271	.354
1992 Toronto	AL	138	480	116	26	2	13	(7	6)	185	47	53	33	3	75	2	1	5	1	1	.50	11	.242	.290	.385
1993 Toronto	AL	138	488	124	30	0	9	(6	3)	181	38	55	20	2	66	2	7	3	2	2	.50	18	.254	.285	.371
1994 Toronto	AL	85	295	73	13	1	3	(3	0)	97	24	26	15	0	50	1	1	5	1	1	.50	7	.247	.284	.329
1995 KC-Hou		63	178	37	8	1	4	(1	3)	59	15	13	9	2	29	0	1	0	0	0	.00	3	.208	.246	.331
1996 StL-Cal-ChA		76	220	61	7	0	5	(3	2)	83	15	18	9	0	43	0	5	0	0	2	.00	4	.277	.306	.377
1997 Cleveland	AL	55	159	47	7	1	4	(0	4)	68	17	15	9	0	27	2	0	0	0	2	.00	5	.296	.341	.428
1995 Kansas City	AL	52	143	33	8	1	4	(1	3)	55	14	13	7	1	22	0	0	0	0	0	.00	1	.231	.267	.385
Houston	NL	11	35	4	0	0	0	(0	0)	4	1	0	2	1	7	0	1	0	0	0	.00	2	.114	.162	.114
1996 St. Louis	NL	26	69	22	3	0	0	(0	0)	25	3	4	1	0	14	0	1	0	0	1	.00	1	.319	.329	.362
California	AL	19	57	13	3	0	2	(2	0)	22	6	8	3	0	11	0	1	0	0	1	.00	1	.228	.267	.386
Chicago	AL	31	94	26	1	0	3	(1	2)	36	6	6	5	0	18	0	3	0	0	0	.00	2	.277	.313	.383
10 ML YEARS		935	2852	732	149	11	66	(35	31)	1101	251	315	138	12	461	8	24	17	6	10	.38	85	.257	.291	.386

Mike Bordick

Bats: Right **Throws:** Right **Pos:** SS-153   **Ht:** 5'11" **Wt:** 175 **Born:** 7/21/65 **Age:** 32

Year Team	Lg	G	AB	H	2B	3B	HR	(Hm	Rd)	TB	R	RBI	TBB	IBB	SO	HBP	SH	SF	SB	CS	SB%	GDP	Avg	OBP	SLG
1990 Oakland	AL	25	14	1	0	0	0	(0	0)	1	0	0	1	0	4	0	0	0	0	0	.00	0	.071	.133	.071
1991 Oakland	AL	90	235	56	5	1	0	(0	0)	63	21	21	14	0	37	3	12	1	3	4	.43	3	.238	.289	.268
1992 Oakland	AL	154	504	151	19	4	3	(3	0)	187	62	48	40	2	59	9	14	5	12	6	.67	10	.300	.358	.371
1993 Oakland	AL	159	546	136	21	2	3	(2	1)	170	60	48	60	2	58	11	10	6	10	10	.50	9	.249	.332	.311
1994 Oakland	AL	114	391	99	18	4	2	(1	1)	131	38	37	38	1	44	3	3	5	7	2	.78	9	.253	.320	.335
1995 Oakland	AL	126	428	113	13	0	8	(2	6)	150	46	44	35	2	48	5	7	3	11	3	.79	5	.264	.325	.350
1996 Oakland	AL	155	525	126	18	4	5	(2	3)	167	46	54	52	0	59	1	4	5	5	6	.45	8	.240	.307	.318
1997 Baltimore	AL	153	509	120	19	1	7	(5	2)	162	55	46	33	1	66	2	12	4	0	2	.00	23	.236	.283	.318
8 ML YEARS		976	3152	802	113	16	28	(15	13)	1031	328	298	273	8	375	34	62	29	48	33	.59	70	.254	.318	.327

Toby Borland

Pitches: Right **Bats:** Right **Pos:** RP-16   **Ht:** 6'6" **Wt:** 193 **Born:** 5/29/69 **Age:** 29

Year Team	Lg	G	GS	CG	GF	IP	BFP	H	R	ER	HR	SH	SF	HB	TBB	IBB	SO	WP	Bk	W	L	Pct.	ShO	Sv-Op	Hld	ERA
1997 Pawtucket *	AAA	28	2	0	13	47.1	213	50	22	21	5	0	0	2	25	3	46	5	0	2	0	1.000	0	2--	—	3.99
1994 Philadelphia	NL	24	0	0	7	34.1	144	31	10	9	1	1	0	4	14	3	26	4	0	1	0	1.000	0	1-1	0	2.36
1995 Philadelphia	NL	50	0	0	18	74	339	81	37	31	3	3	2	5	37	1	59	12	0	1	3	.250	0	6-9	11	3.77
1996 Philadelphia	NL	69	0	0	11	90.2	399	83	51	41	9	4	1	3	43	3	76	10	0	7	3	.700	0	0-2	10	4.07
1997 NYN-Bos		16	0	0	5	16.2	89	17	14	14	2	0	0	3	21	0	8	3	0	1	0	.000	0	1-2	1	7.56
1997 New York	NL	13	0	0	5	13.1	65	11	9	9	1	0	0	1	14	0	7	3	0	0	1	.000	0	1-2	1	6.08
Boston	AL	3	0	0	0	3.1	24	6	5	5	1	0	0	2	7	0	1	0	0	0	0	.000	0	0-0	0	13.50
4 ML YEARS		159	0	0	41	215.2	971	212	112	95	15	8	3	15	115	13	169	29	0	9	7	.563	0	8-14	22	3.96

Joe Borowski

Pitches: Right **Bats:** Right **Pos:** RP-21   **Ht:** 6'2" **Wt:** 225 **Born:** 5/4/71 **Age:** 27

Year Team	Lg	G	GS	CG	GF	IP	BFP	H	R	ER	HR	SH	SF	HB	TBB	IBB	SO	WP	Bk	W	L	Pct.	ShO	Sv-Op	Hld	ERA
1997 Richmond *	AAA	21	0	0	4	37.2	159	32	16	15	3	2	0	1	19	2	34	4	0	1	2	.333	0	2--	—	3.58
1995 Baltimore	AL	6	0	0	3	7.1	30	5	1	1	0	0	0	0	4	0	3	0	0	0	0	.000	0	0-0	0	1.23
1996 Atlanta	NL	22	0	0	8	26	121	33	15	14	4	5	0	1	13	4	15	1	0	2	4	.333	0	0-0	1	4.85
1997 Atl-NYA		21	0	0	9	26	123	29	13	12	2	1	0	0	20	5	8	0	0	2	3	.400	0	0-0	2	4.15
1997 Atlanta	NL	20	0	0	8	24	111	27	11	10	2	1	0	0	16	4	6	0	0	2	2	.500	0	0-0	2	3.75
New York	AL	1	0	0	1	2	12	2	2	2	0	0	0	0	4	1	2	0	0	0	1	.000	0	0-0	0	9.00
3 ML YEARS		49	0	0	20	59.1	274	67	29	27	6	6	0	1	37	9	26	1	0	4	7	.364	0	0-0	3	4.10

Shawn Boskie

Pitches: Right **Bats:** Right **Pos:** RP-19; SP-9   **Ht:** 6'3" **Wt:** 200 **Born:** 3/28/67 **Age:** 31

Year Team	Lg	G	GS	CG	GF	IP	BFP	H	R	ER	HR	SH	SF	HB	TBB	IBB	SO	WP	Bk	W	L	Pct.	ShO	Sv-Op	Hld	ERA
1990 Chicago	NL	15	15	1	0	97.2	415	99	42	40	8	8	2	1	31	3	49	3	2	5	6	.455	0	0-0	0	3.69
1991 Chicago	NL	28	20	0	2	129	582	150	78	75	14	8	6	5	52	4	62	1	1	4	9	.308	0	0-0	0	5.23
1992 Chicago	NL	23	18	0	2	91.2	393	96	55	51	14	9	6	4	36	3	39	5	1	5	11	.313	0	0-0	0	5.01
1993 Chicago	NL	39	2	0	10	65.2	277	63	30	25	7	4	1	7	21	2	39	5	0	5	3	.625	0	0-3	6	3.43
1994 ChN-Phi-Sea		22	15	1	1	90.2	394	92	58	51	15	2	3	3	30	3	61	7	0	4	7	.364	0	0-1	0	5.06
1995 California	AL	20	20	1	0	111.2	494	127	73	70	16	4	6	7	25	0	51	4	0	7	7	.500	0	0-0	0	5.64
1996 California	AL	37	28	1	1	189.1	860	226	126	112	40	6	4	13	67	7	133	10	0	12	11	.522	0	0-0	1	5.32
1997 Baltimore	AL	28	9	0	8	77	349	95	57	55	14	2	7	2	26	1	50	1	0	6	6	.500	0	1-1	1	6.43
1994 Chicago	NL	2	0	0	0	3.2	14	3	0	0	0	0	0	0	0	0	2	1	0	0	0	.000	0	0-0	0	0.00
Philadelphia	NL	18	14	1	1	84.1	367	85	56	49	14	2	3	3	29	2	59	6	0	4	6	.400	0	0-1	0	5.23
Seattle	AL	2	1	0	0	2.2	13	4	2	2	1	0	0	0	1	1	0	0	0	0	1	.000	0	0-0	0	6.75
8 ML YEARS		212	127	4	24	852.2	3764	948	519	479	128	43	35	42	288	23	484	36	4	48	60	.444	0	1-5	8	5.06

Ricky Bottalico

Pitches: Right **Bats:** Left **Pos:** RP-69   **Ht:** 6'1" **Wt:** 208 **Born:** 8/26/69 **Age:** 28

Year Team	Lg	G	GS	CG	GF	IP	BFP	H	R	ER	HR	SH	SF	HB	TBB	IBB	SO	WP	Bk	W	L	Pct.	ShO	Sv-Op	Hld	ERA
1994 Philadelphia	NL	3	0	0	3	3	13	3	0	0	0	0	0	0	1	0	3	0	0	0	0	.000	0	0-0	0	0.00
1995 Philadelphia	NL	62	0	0	20	87.2	350	50	25	24	7	3	1	4	42	3	87	1	0	5	3	.625	0	1-5	20	2.46
1996 Philadelphia	NL	61	0	0	56	67.2	269	47	24	24	6	4	2	2	23	2	74	3	0	4	5	.444	0	34-38	0	3.19
1997 Philadelphia	NL	69	0	0	61	74	324	68	31	30	7	1	2	2	42	4	89	3	0	2	5	.286	0	34-41	0	3.65
4 ML YEARS		195	0	0	140	232.1	956	168	80	78	20	8	5	8	108	9	253	7	0	11	13	.458	0	69-84	20	3.02

Kent Bottenfield

Pitches: Right **Bats:** Right **Pos:** RP-64   **Ht:** 6'3" **Wt:** 237 **Born:** 11/14/68 **Age:** 29

Year Team	Lg	G	GS	CG	GF	IP	BFP	H	R	ER	HR	SH	SF	HB	TBB	IBB	SO	WP	Bk	W	L	Pct.	ShO	Sv-Op	Hld	ERA
1992 Montreal	NL	10	4	0	2	32.1	135	26	9	8	1	1	2	1	11	1	14	0	0	1	2	.333	0	1-1	1	2.23
1993 Mon-Col	NL	37	25	1	2	159.2	710	179	102	90	24	21	4	6	71	3	63	4	1	5	10	.333	0	0-0	0	5.07
1994 Col-SF	NL	16	1	0	3	26.1	121	33	18	18	2	1	0	2	10	0	15	2	0	3	1	.750	0	1-1	0	6.15

			HOW MUCH HE PITCHED			WHAT HE GAVE UP										THE RESULTS						
Year Team	Lg	G GS CG GF	IP	BFP	H	R	ER	HR SH SF HB	TBB	IBB	SO	WP	Bk	W	L	Pct.	ShO	Sv-Op	Hld	ERA
1996 Chicago	NL	48 0 0 10	61.2	258	59	25	18	3 5 0 3	19	4	33	2	0	3	5	.375	0	1-3	4	2.63
1997 Chicago	NL	64 0 0 20	84	361	82	39	36	13 4 4 2	35	7	74	2	0	2	3	.400	0	2-4	8	3.86
1993 Montreal	NL	23 11 0 2	83	373	93	49	38	11 11 1 5	33	2	33	4	1	2	5	.286	0	0-0	0	4.12
Colorado	NL	14 14 1 0	76.2	337	86	53	52	13 10 3 1	38	1	30	0	0	3	5	.375	0	0-0	0	6.10
1994 Colorado	NL	15 1 0 3	24.2	112	28	16	16	1 1 0 2	10	0	15	2	0	3	1	.750	0	1-1	0	5.84
San Francisco	NL	1 0 0 0	1.2	9	5	2	2	1 0 0 0	0	0	0	0	0	0	0	.000	0	0-0	0	10.80
5 ML YEARS		175 30 1 37	364	1585	379	193	170	43 32 10 14	146	15	199	10	1	14	21	.400	0	5-9	13	4.20

Rafael Bournigal

Bats: Right **Throws:** Right **Pos:** SS-74; PH-9; 2B-7 **Ht:** 5'11" **Wt:** 165 **Born:** 5/12/66 **Age:** 32

					BATTING												BASERUNNING			PERCENTAGES		
Year Team	Lg	G	AB	H	2B 3B HR	(Hm Rd)	TB	R	RBI	TBB	IBB	SO	HBP	SH	SF	SB	CS	SB%	GDP	Avg	OBP	SLG
1997 Modesto *	A+	7	21	5	1 0 0	— —	6	0	2	3	0	2	0	0	0	0	0	.00	1	.238	.333	.286
1992 Los Angeles	NL	10	20	3	1 0 0	(0 0)	4	1	0	1	0	2	1	0	0	0	0	.00	0	.150	.227	.200
1993 Los Angeles	NL	8	18	9	1 0 0	(0 0)	10	0	3	0	0	2	0	0	0	0	0	.00	0	.500	.500	.556
1994 Los Angeles	NL	40	116	26	3 1 0	(0 0)	31	2	11	9	1	5	2	5	0	0	0	.00	4	.224	.291	.267
1996 Oakland	AL	88	252	61	14 2 0	(0 0)	79	33	18	16	0	19	1	8	0	4	3	.57	6	.242	.290	.313
1997 Oakland	AL	79	222	62	9 0 1	(0 1)	74	29	20	16	1	19	4	7	0	2	1	.67	11	.279	.339	.333
5 ML YEARS		225	628	161	28 3 1	(0 1)	198	65	52	42	2	47	8	20	0	6	4	.60	21	.256	.311	.315

Mike Bovee

Pitches: Right **Bats:** Right **Pos:** RP-3 **Ht:** 5'10" **Wt:** 200 **Born:** 8/21/73 **Age:** 24

			HOW MUCH HE PITCHED			WHAT HE GAVE UP						THE RESULTS							
Year Team	Lg	G GS CG GF	IP	BFP	H	R	ER	HR SH SF HB	TBB IBB	SO	WP	Bk	W	L	Pct.	ShO	Sv-Op	Hld	ERA
1991 Royals	R	11 11 0 0	61.2	251	52	19	14	1 0 1 1	12 0	76	4	0	3	1	.750	0	0--	—	2.04
1992 Appleton	A	28 24 1 0	149.1	618	143	85	59	8 4 9 3	41 1	120	13	3	9	10	.474	0	0--	—	3.56
1993 Rockford	A	20 20 2 0	109	469	118	58	51	1 4 4 6	30 0	111	15	0	5	9	.357	0	0--	—	4.21
1994 Wilmington	A+	28 26 0 1	169.2	675	149	58	50	10 4 3 4	32 0	154	8	1	13	4	.765	0	0--	—	2.65
1995 Wichita	AA	20 20 1 0	114	486	118	60	53	12 2 4 2	43 0	72	4	0	8	6	.571	0	0--	—	4.18
1996 Wichita	AA	27 27 3 0	176.2	783	223	113	95	21 9 8 6	40 1	102	10	0	10	11	.476	2	0--	—	4.84
1997 Midland	AA	20 13 3 1	102	424	117	53	48	7 3 5 4	23 0	61	7	0	8	2	.800	0	0--	—	4.24
Vancouver	AAA	12 12 1 0	89	377	92	38	34	7 4 2 7	25 0	71	4	0	4	3	.571	0	0--	—	3.44
1997 Anaheim	AL	3 0 0 3	3.1	14	3	2	2	1 0 0 0	1 0	5	0	0	0	0	.000	0	0-0	0	5.40

Shane Bowers

Pitches: Right **Bats:** Right **Pos:** SP-5 **Ht:** 6'4" **Wt:** 213 **Born:** 7/27/71 **Age:** 26

			HOW MUCH HE PITCHED			WHAT HE GAVE UP						THE RESULTS							
Year Team	Lg	G GS CG GF	IP	BFP	H	R	ER	HR SH SF HB	TBB IBB	SO	WP	Bk	W	L	Pct.	ShO	Sv-Op	Hld	ERA
1993 Elizabethtn	R+	3 1 0 4	11.1	48	13	7	6	0 1 1 0	1 0	13	3	0	2	0	1.000	0	0--	—	4.76
1994 Ft. Wayne	A	27 11 1 9	81.2	333	76	32	30	3 5 1 6	18 1	72	8	0	6	4	.600	0	5--	—	3.31
Ft. Myers	A+	13 0 0 5	17.2	85	28	7	7	1 0 0 0	4 0	19	2	0	0	0	.000	0	0--	—	3.57
1995 Ft. Myers	A+	23 23 1 0	145.2	580	119	43	35	6 2 4 12	32 1	103	6	1	13	5	.722	0	0--	—	2.16
1996 Hardware City	AA	27 22 1 1	131	569	134	71	61	15 2 3 6	42 1	96	11	0	6	8	.429	0	0--	—	4.19
1997 New Britain	AA	14 13 1 0	71.1	299	65	29	27	6 2 3 4	22 0	59	2	0	7	2	.778	1	0--	—	3.41
Salt Lake	AAA	9 9 1 0	56.1	247	64	35	30	12 1 4 3	14 0	46	2	0	6	2	.750	0	0--	—	4.79
1997 Minnesota	AL	5 5 0 0	19	92	27	20	17	2 0 1 1	8 0	7	1	0	0	3	.000	0	0-0	0	8.05

Darren Bragg

Bats: L **Throws:** R **Pos:** CF-118; RF-41; PH-12; 3B-1; LF-1 **Ht:** 5'9" **Wt:** 180 **Born:** 9/7/69 **Age:** 28

					BATTING												BASERUNNING			PERCENTAGES		
Year Team	Lg	G	AB	H	2B 3B HR	(Hm Rd)	TB	R	RBI	TBB	IBB	SO	HBP	SH	SF	SB	CS	SB%	GDP	Avg	OBP	SLG
1994 Seattle	AL	8	19	3	1 0 0	(0 0)	4	4	2	1	5	0	0	0	0	0	0	.00	0	.158	.238	.211
1995 Seattle	AL	52	145	34	5 1 3	(1 2)	50	20	12	18	1	37	4	1	2	9	0	1.00	0	.234	.331	.345
1996 Sea-Bos	AL	127	417	109	26 2 10	(7 3)	169	74	47	69	6	74	4	2	7	14	9	.61	5	.261	.366	.405
1997 Boston	AL	153	513	132	35 2 9	(3 6)	198	65	57	61	5	102	3	5	4	10	6	.63	16	.257	.337	.386
1996 Seattle	AL	69	195	53	12 1 7	(4 3)	88	36	25	33	4	35	2	1	4	8	5	.62	2	.272	.376	.451
Boston	AL	58	222	56	14 1 3	(3 0)	81	38	22	36	2	39	2	1	3	6	4	.60	3	.252	.357	.365
4 ML YEARS		340	1094	278	67 5 22	(11 11)	421	163	118	150	13	218	11	8	13	33	15	.69	23	.254	.346	.385

Mark Brandenburg

Pitches: Right **Bats:** Right **Pos:** RP-31 **Ht:** 6'0" **Wt:** 180 **Born:** 7/14/70 **Age:** 27

			HOW MUCH HE PITCHED			WHAT HE GAVE UP						THE RESULTS							
Year Team	Lg	G GS CG GF	IP	BFP	H	R	ER	HR SH SF HB	TBB IBB	SO	WP	Bk	W	L	Pct.	ShO	Sv-Op	Hld	ERA
1997 Sarasota *	A+	1 0 0 1	3	12	3	0	0	0 0 0 0	1 0	1	0	0	0	0	.000	0	0--	—	0.00
Pawtucket *	AAA	9 0 0 4	18.2	73	13	6	5	2 0 1 1	3 1	23	0	0	2	1	.667	0	0--	—	2.41
1995 Texas	AL	11 0 0 5	27.1	123	36	18	18	5 0 1 1	7 1	21	0	1	0	1	.000	0	0-0	1	5.93
1996 Tex-Bos	AL	55 0 0 13	76	338	76	35	29	8 3 4 3	33 2	66	0	1	5	5	.500	0	0-2	12	3.43
1997 Boston	AL	31 0 0 5	41	186	49	25	25	3 2 2 2	16 3	34	0	0	0	0	.000	0	0-0	3	5.49
1996 Texas	AL	26 0 0 8	47.2	215	48	22	17	3 3 2 2	25 1	37	0	1	1	3	.250	0	0-1	2	3.21
Boston	AL	29 0 0 5	28.1	123	28	13	12	5 0 2 1	8 1	29	0	0	4	2	.667	0	0-1	10	3.81
3 ML YEARS		97 0 0 23	144.1	647	161	78	72	16 5 7 6	56 6	121	0	2	5	8	.385	0	0-2	16	4.49

Jeff Branson

Bats: L **Throws:** R **Pos:** 2B-33; 3B-33; PH-30; SS-13; DH-1   **Ht:** 6'0" **Wt:** 180 **Born:** 1/26/67 **Age:** 31

							BATTING												BASERUNNING				PERCENTAGES		
Year Team	Lg	G	AB	H	2B	3B	HR	(Hm	Rd)	TB	R	RBI	TBB	IBB	SO	HBP	SH	SF	SB	CS	SB%	GDP	Avg	OBP	SLG
1997 Indianapolis *	AAA	15	57	12	3	0	1	—	—	18	7	4	6	0	10	0	1	0	0	0	.00	1	.211	.286	.316
1992 Cincinnati	NL	72	115	34	7	1	0	(0	0)	43	12	15	5	2	16	0	2	1	0	1	.00	4	.296	.322	.374
1993 Cincinnati	NL	125	381	92	15	1	3	(2	1)	118	40	22	19	2	73	0	8	4	4	1	.80	4	.241	.275	.310
1994 Cincinnati	NL	58	109	31	4	1	6	(1	5)	55	18	16	5	2	16	0	2	0	0	0	.00	4	.284	.316	.505
1995 Cincinnati	NL	122	331	86	18	2	12	(9	3)	144	43	45	44	14	69	2	1	6	2	1	.67	9	.260	.345	.435
1996 Cincinnati	NL	129	311	76	16	4	9	(5	4)	127	34	37	31	4	67	1	7	3	2	0	1.00	9	.244	.312	.408
1997 Cin-Cle		94	170	34	7	1	3	(3	0)	52	14	12	14	1	40	1	1	2	1	2	.33	4	.200	.262	.306
1997 Cincinnati	NL	65	98	15	3	1	1	(1	0)	23	9	5	7	1	23	0	1	0	1	0	1.00	3	.153	.210	.235
Cleveland	AL	29	72	19	4	0	2	(2	0)	29	5	7	7	0	17	1	0	2	0	2	.00	1	.264	.329	.403
6 ML YEARS		600	1417	353	67	10	33	(20	13)	539	161	147	118	25	281	4	21	16	9	5	.64	34	.249	.305	.380

Jeff Brantley

Pitches: Right **Bats:** Right **Pos:** RP-13   **Ht:** 5'10" **Wt:** 190 **Born:** 9/5/63 **Age:** 34

		HOW MUCH HE PITCHED						WHAT HE GAVE UP										THE RESULTS					
Year Team	Lg	G	GS	CG	GF	IP	BFP	H	R	ER	HR	SH	SF	HB	TBB	IBB	SO	WP	Bk	W	L	Pct.	ShO	Sv-Op	Hld	ERA
1988 San Francisco	NL	9	1	0	2	20.2	88	22	13	13	2	1	0	1	6	1	11	0	1	0	1	.000	0	1-1	0	5.66
1989 San Francisco	NL	59	1	0	15	97.1	422	101	50	44	10	7	3	2	37	8	69	3	2	7	1	.875	0	0-1	11	4.07
1990 San Francisco	NL	55	0	0	32	86.2	361	77	18	15	3	2	2	3	33	6	61	0	3	5	3	.625	0	19-24	8	1.56
1991 San Francisco	NL	67	0	0	39	95.1	411	78	27	26	8	4	4	5	52	10	81	6	0	5	2	.714	0	15-19	12	2.45
1992 San Francisco	NL	56	4	0	32	91.2	381	67	32	30	8	7	3	3	45	5	86	3	1	7	7	.500	0	7-9	3	2.95
1993 San Francisco	NL	53	12	0	9	113.2	496	112	60	54	19	5	5	7	46	2	76	3	4	5	6	.455	0	0-3	10	4.28
1994 Cincinnati	NL	50	0	0	35	65.1	262	46	20	18	6	5	1	0	28	5	63	1	0	6	6	.500	0	15-21	1	2.48
1995 Cincinnati	NL	56	0	0	49	70.1	283	53	22	22	11	2	3	1	20	3	62	2	2	3	2	.600	0	28-32	0	2.82
1996 Cincinnati	NL	66	0	0	61	71	288	54	21	19	7	4	5	0	28	6	76	2	0	1	2	.333	0	44-49	0	2.41
1997 Cincinnati	NL	13	0	0	9	11.2	53	9	5	5	2	0	0	2	7	1	16	2	0	1	1	.500	0	1-3	0	3.86
10 ML YEARS		484	18	0	283	723.2	3045	619	268	246	76	37	26	24	302	47	601	22	13	40	31	.563	0	130-16	245	3.06

Brent Brede

Bats: L **Throws:** L **Pos:** RF-40; 1B-15; PH-10; LF-3; DH-1   **Ht:** 6'4" **Wt:** 190 **Born:** 9/13/71 **Age:** 26

							BATTING												BASERUNNING				PERCENTAGES		
Year Team	Lg	G	AB	H	2B	3B	HR	(Hm	Rd)	TB	R	RBI	TBB	IBB	SO	HBP	SH	SF	SB	CS	SB%	GDP	Avg	OBP	SLG
1990 Elizabethtn	R+	46	143	35	5	0	0	—	—	40	39	14	30	0	29	0	0	1	14	0	1.00	2	.245	.374	.280
1991 Kenosha	A	53	156	30	3	2	0	—	—	37	12	10	16	0	31	0	5	3	4	5	.44	8	.192	.263	.237
Elizabethtn	R+	68	253	61	13	0	3	—	—	83	24	36	30	2	48	1	2	4	13	4	.76	7	.241	.319	.328
1992 Kenosha	A	110	363	88	15	0	0	—	—	103	44	29	53	1	77	4	4	3	10	12	.45	8	.242	.343	.284
1993 Ft. Myers	A+	53	182	60	10	1	0	—	—	72	27	27	32	3	19	1	2	0	8	4	.67	6	.330	.433	.396
1994 Ft. Myers	A+	116	419	110	21	4	2	—	—	145	49	45	63	3	60	0	3	1	18	4	.82	7	.263	.358	.346
1995 Hardware City	AA	134	449	123	28	2	3	—	—	164	71	39	69	2	82	3	5	6	14	6	.70	13	.274	.371	.365
1996 Salt Lake	AAA	132	483	168	38	8	11	—	—	255	102	86	87	9	87	3	4	5	14	6	.70	4	.348	.446	.528
1997 Salt Lake	AAA	84	328	116	27	4	9	—	—	178	82	76	47	0	62	2	0	5	4	2	.67	8	.354	.432	.543
1996 Minnesota	AL	10	20	6	0	1	0	(0	0)	8	2	2	1	0	5	0	0	0	0	0	.00	1	.300	.333	.400
1997 Minnesota	AL	61	190	52	11	1	3	(2	1)	74	25	21	21	0	38	1	1	1	7	2	.78	1	.274	.347	.389
2 ML YEARS		71	210	58	11	2	3	(2	1)	82	27	23	22	0	43	1	1	1	7	2	.78	2	.276	.346	.390

Billy Brewer

Pitches: Left **Bats:** Left **Pos:** RP-28   **Ht:** 6'1" **Wt:** 175 **Born:** 4/15/68 **Age:** 30

		HOW MUCH HE PITCHED						WHAT HE GAVE UP										THE RESULTS					
Year Team	Lg	G	GS	CG	GF	IP	BFP	H	R	ER	HR	SH	SF	HB	TBB	IBB	SO	WP	Bk	W	L	Pct.	ShO	Sv-Op	Hld	ERA
1997 Visalia *	A+	2	2	0	0	3	15	1	1	0	0	0	1	0	4	0	5	0	0	0	0	.000	0	0--	—	0.00
Edmonton *	AAA	7	1	0	2	8	36	8	5	5	2	0	1	0	6	0	11	1	0	0	0	.000	0	1--	—	5.63
Scrnton-WB *	AAA	11	0	0	6	9	41	10	7	3	2	2	0	0	5	1	9	0	0	2	1	.667	0	1--	—	3.00
1993 Kansas City	AL	46	0	0	14	39	157	31	16	15	6	1	1	0	20	4	28	2	1	2	2	.500	0	0-2	5	3.46
1994 Kansas City	AL	50	0	0	17	38.2	157	28	11	11	4	2	2	2	16	1	25	3	0	4	1	.800	0	3-7	12	2.56
1995 Kansas City	AL	48	0	0	13	45.1	209	54	28	28	9	1	0	2	20	1	31	5	1	2	4	.333	0	0-4	7	5.56
1996 New York	AL	4	0	0	1	5.2	32	7	6	6	0	0	0	0	8	0	8	0	0	1	0	1.000	0	0-0	0	9.53
1997 Oak-Phi		28	0	0	5	24	105	19	11	11	3	0	3	0	13	0	17	1	0	1	2	.333	0	0-2	5	4.13
1997 Oakland	AL	3	0	0	1	2	12	4	3	3	1	0	1	0	2	0	1	0	0	0	0	.000	0	0-0	0	13.50
Philadelphia	NL	25	0	0	4	22	93	15	8	8	2	0	2	0	11	0	16	1	0	1	2	.333	0	0-2	5	3.27
5 ML YEARS		176	0	0	50	152.2	660	139	72	71	22	4	6	4	77	6	109	11	2	10	9	.526	0	3-15	29	4.19

Tilson Brito

Bats: R **Throws:** R **Pos:** 2B-27; 3B-27; SS-14; PH-4   **Ht:** 6'0" **Wt:** 175 **Born:** 5/28/72 **Age:** 26

							BATTING												BASERUNNING				PERCENTAGES		
Year Team	Lg	G	AB	H	2B	3B	HR	(Hm	Rd)	TB	R	RBI	TBB	IBB	SO	HBP	SH	SF	SB	CS	SB%	GDP	Avg	OBP	SLG
1992 Blue Jays	R	54	189	58	10	4	3	—	—	85	36	36	22	1	22	6	0	5	16	8	.67	5	.307	.387	.450
Knoxville	AA	7	24	5	1	2	0	—	—	10	2	2	0	0	9	0	0	0	0	0	.00	0	.208	.208	.417
1993 Dunedin	A+	126	465	125	21	3	6	—	—	170	80	44	59	0	60	10	10	3	27	16	.63	8	.269	.361	.366
1994 Knoxville	AA	139	476	127	17	7	5	—	—	173	61	57	35	2	68	8	9	7	33	12	.73	7	.267	.323	.363
1995 Syracuse	AAA	90	327	79	16	3	7	—	—	122	49	32	29	0	69	4	2	1	17	8	.68	6	.242	.310	.373
1996 Syracuse	AAA	108	400	111	22	8	10	—	—	179	63	54	38	1	65	5	3	4	11	10	.52	8	.278	.345	.448
1997 Modesto	A+	4	9	3	1	0	1	—	—	7	3	3	2	0	1	2	0	0	0	0	.00	0	.333	.538	.778

Year Team	Lg	G	AB	H	2B	3B	HR	(Hm	Rd)	TB	R	RBI	TBB	IBB	SO	HBP	SH	SF	SB	CS	SB%	GDP	Avg	OBP	SLG
1996 Toronto	AL	26	80	19	7	0	1	(1	0)	29	10	7	10	0	18	3	2	0	1	1	.50	0	.238	.344	.363
1997 Tor-Oak	AL	66	172	41	5	1	2	(2	0)	54	17	14	10	0	38	2	2	2	1	0	1.00	2	.238	.285	.314
1997 Toronto	AL	49	126	28	3	0	0	(0	0)	31	9	8	9	0	28	2	0	2	1	0	1.00	2	.222	.281	.246
Oakland	AL	17	46	13	2	1	2	(2	0)	23	8	6	1	0	10	0	2	0	0	0	.00	0	.283	.298	.500
2 ML YEARS		92	252	60	12	1	3	(3	0)	83	27	21	20	0	56	5	4	2	2	1	.67	2	.238	.305	.329

Doug Brocail

Pitches: Right **Bats:** Left **Pos:** RP-57; SP-4   **Ht:** 6'5" **Wt:** 235 **Born:** 5/16/67 **Age:** 31

Year Team	Lg	G	GS	CG	GF	IP	BFP	H	R	ER	HR	SH	SF	HB	TBB	IBB	SO	WP	Bk	W	L	Pct.	ShO	Sv-Op	Hld	ERA
1992 San Diego	NL	3	3	0	0	14	64	17	10	10	2	2	0	0	5	0	15	0	0	0	0	.000	0	0-0	0	6.43
1993 San Diego	NL	24	24	0	0	128.1	571	143	75	65	16	10	8	4	42	4	70	4	1	4	13	.235	0	0-0	0	4.56
1994 San Diego	NL	12	0	0	4	17	78	21	13	11	1	1	1	2	5	3	11	1	0	0	0	.000	0	0-1	0	5.82
1995 Houston	NL	36	7	0	12	77.1	339	87	40	36	10	1	1	4	22	2	39	1	1	6	4	.600	0	1-1	0	4.19
1996 Houston	NL	23	4	0	4	53	231	58	31	27	7	3	2	2	23	1	34	0	0	1	5	.167	0	0-0	1	4.58
1997 Detroit	AL	61	4	0	20	78	332	74	31	28	10	1	3	3	36	4	60	6	0	3	4	.429	0	2-9	16	3.23
6 ML YEARS		159	42	0	40	367.2	1615	400	200	177	46	18	15	15	133	14	229	12	3	14	26	.350	0	3-11	17	4.33

Chris Brock

Pitches: Right **Bats:** Right **Pos:** SP-6; RP-1   **Ht:** 6'0" **Wt:** 180 **Born:** 2/5/70 **Age:** 28

Year Team	Lg	G	GS	CG	GF	IP	BFP	H	R	ER	HR	SH	SF	HB	TBB	IBB	SO	WP	Bk	W	L	Pct.	ShO	Sv-Op	Hld	ERA
1992 Idaho Falls	R+	15	15	1	0	78	333	61	27	20	3	3	2	3	48	0	72	12	8	6	4	.600	0	0--	--	2.31
1993 Macon	A	14	14	1	0	80	333	61	37	24	3	1	0	2	33	0	92	8	1	7	5	.583	0	0--	--	2.70
Durham	A+	12	12	1	0	79	335	63	28	22	7	1	2	5	35	0	67	6	0	5	2	.714	0	0--	--	2.51
1994 Greenville	AA	25	23	2	0	137.1	576	128	68	57	9	4	4	5	47	0	94	8	3	7	6	.538	2	0--	--	3.74
1995 Richmond	AAA	22	9	0	5	60	270	68	37	36	2	3	3	1	27	2	43	1	2	2	8	.200	0	0--	--	5.40
1996 Richmond	AAA	26	25	3	0	150.1	652	137	95	78	20	3	8	6	61	0	112	9	0	10	11	.476	0	0--	--	4.67
1997 Richmond	AAA	20	19	0	0	118.2	497	97	50	44	9	8	4	1	51	0	83	8	1	10	6	.625	0	0--	--	3.34
1997 Atlanta	NL	7	6	0	1	30.2	144	34	23	19	2	3	4	0	19	2	16	2	1	0	0	.000	0	0-0	0	5.58

Rico Brogna

Bats: Left **Throws:** Left **Pos:** 1B-145; PH-7   **Ht:** 6'2" **Wt:** 205 **Born:** 4/18/70 **Age:** 28

Year Team	Lg	G	AB	H	2B	3B	HR	(Hm	Rd)	TB	R	RBI	TBB	IBB	SO	HBP	SH	SF	SB	CS	SB%	GDP	Avg	OBP	SLG
1992 Detroit	AL	9	26	5	1	0	1	(1	0)	9	3	3	3	0	5	0	0	0	0	0	.00	0	.192	.276	.346
1994 New York	NL	39	131	46	11	2	7	(2	5)	82	16	20	6	0	29	0	1	0	1	0	1.00	0	.351	.380	.626
1995 New York	NL	134	495	143	27	2	22	(13	9)	240	72	76	39	7	111	2	2	2	0	0	.00	10	.289	.342	.485
1996 New York	NL	55	188	48	10	1	7	(5	2)	81	18	30	19	1	50	0	0	4	0	0	.00	4	.255	.318	.431
1997 Philadelphia	NL	148	543	137	36	1	20	(9	11)	235	68	81	33	4	116	0	0	4	12	3	.80	12	.252	.293	.433
5 ML YEARS		385	1383	379	85	6	57	(30	27)	647	177	210	100	12	311	2	3	10	13	3	.81	28	.274	.322	.468

Scott Brosius

Bats: R **Throws:** R **Pos:** 3B-107; SS-30; RF-11; LF-6; CF-6; PH-3   **Ht:** 6'1" **Wt:** 185 **Born:** 8/15/66 **Age:** 31

Year Team	Lg	G	AB	H	2B	3B	HR	(Hm	Rd)	TB	R	RBI	TBB	IBB	SO	HBP	SH	SF	SB	CS	SB%	GDP	Avg	OBP	SLG
1997 Modesto *	A+	2	3	1	0	0	0	—	—	1	1	1	1	0	1	0	0	0	0	0	.00	0	.333	.500	.333
1991 Oakland	AL	36	68	16	5	0	2	(1	1)	27	9	4	3	0	11	0	1	0	3	1	.75	2	.235	.268	.397
1992 Oakland	AL	38	87	19	2	0	4	(1	3)	33	13	13	3	1	13	2	0	1	3	0	1.00	0	.218	.258	.379
1993 Oakland	AL	70	213	53	10	1	6	(3	3)	83	26	25	14	0	37	1	3	2	6	0	1.00	6	.249	.296	.390
1994 Oakland	AL	96	324	77	14	1	14	(9	5)	135	31	49	24	0	57	2	4	6	2	6	.25	7	.238	.289	.417
1995 Oakland	AL	123	349	102	19	2	17	(12	5)	176	69	46	41	0	67	8	1	4	4	2	.67	5	.262	.342	.452
1996 Oakland	AL	114	428	130	25	0	22	(15	7)	221	73	71	59	4	85	7	1	5	7	2	.78	11	.304	.393	.516
1997 Oakland	AL	129	479	97	20	1	11	(7	4)	152	59	41	34	1	102	4	5	4	9	4	.69	9	.203	.259	.317
7 ML YEARS		606	1988	494	95	5	76	(48	28)	827	280	249	178	6	372	24	15	22	34	15	.69	40	.248	.315	.416

Adrian Brown

Bats: Both **Throws:** Right **Pos:** CF-35; PH-10; RF-3   **Ht:** 6'0" **Wt:** 175 **Born:** 2/7/74 **Age:** 24

Year Team	Lg	G	AB	H	2B	3B	HR	(Hm	Rd)	TB	R	RBI	TBB	IBB	SO	HBP	SH	SF	SB	CS	SB%	GDP	Avg	OBP	SLG
1992 Pirates	R	39	121	31	2	2	0	—	—	37	11	12	0	0	12	2	0	0	8	4	.67	3	.256	.268	.306
1993 Lethbridge	R+	69	282	75	12	9	3	—	—	114	47	27	17	1	34	5	3	0	22	7	.76	8	.266	.319	.404
1994 Augusta	A	79	308	80	17	1	1	—	—	102	41	18	14	0	38	0	6	0	19	12	.61	2	.260	.292	.331
1995 Augusta	A	76	287	86	15	4	4	—	—	121	64	31	33	0	23	1	3	2	25	14	.64	2	.300	.372	.422
Lynchburg	A+	54	215	52	5	2	1	—	—	64	30	14	12	0	20	1	4	1	11	6	.65	3	.242	.284	.298
1996 Lynchburg	A+	52	215	69	9	3	4	—	—	96	39	25	14	1	24	2	1	0	18	9	.67	1	.321	.368	.447
Carolina	AA	84	341	101	11	3	3	—	—	127	48	25	25	3	40	1	5	1	27	11	.71	4	.296	.345	.372
1997 Carolina	AA	37	145	44	4	4	2	—	—	62	29	15	18	1	12	2	3	0	9	5	.64	1	.303	.388	.428
Calgary	AAA	62	248	79	10	1	1	—	—	94	53	19	27	1	38	0	2	2	20	4	.83	9	.319	.383	.379
1997 Pittsburgh	NL	48	147	28	6	0	1	(0	1)	37	17	10	13	0	18	4	2	1	8	4	.67	3	.190	.273	.252

Brant Brown

Bats: Left **Throws:** Left **Pos:** LF-27; 1B-12; PH-9 **Ht:** 6'3" **Wt:** 205 **Born:** 6/22/71 **Age:** 27

							BATTING										BASERUNNING				PERCENTAGES		
Year Team	Lg	G	AB	H	2B	3B	HR	(Hm | Rd)	TB	R	RBI	TBB	IBB	SO	HBP	SH	SF	SB	CS	SB%	GDP	Avg	OBP	SLG
1992 Peoria	A	70	248	68	14	0	3	—	—	91	28	27	24	2	49	1	3	5	3	4	.43	4	.274	.335	.367
1993 Daytona	A+	75	266	91	8	7	3	—	—	122	26	33	11	0	38	1	4	0	8	7	.53	5	.342	.371	.459
Orlando	AA	28	110	35	11	3	4	—	—	64	17	23	6	1	18	4	0	1	2	1	.67	2	.318	.372	.582
1994 Orlando	AA	127	470	127	30	6	5	—	—	184	54	37	37	3	86	5	2	0	11	15	.42	10	.270	.330	.391
1995 Orlando	AA	121	446	121	27	4	6	—	—	174	67	53	39	2	77	3	11	3	8	5	.62	6	.271	.332	.390
1996 Iowa	AAA	94	342	104	25	3	10	—	—	165	48	43	19	1	65	3	0	0	6	6	.50	10	.304	.346	.482
1997 Iowa	AAA	71	256	77	19	3	16	—	—	150	51	51	31	2	44	1	1	1	6	6	.50	5	.301	.379	.586
1996 Chicago	NL	29	69	21	1	0	5	(3 | 2)	37	11	9	2	1	17	1	0	1	3	3	.50	1	.304	.329	.536
1997 Chicago	NL	46	137	32	7	1	5	(3 | 2)	56	15	15	7	0	28	3	1	0	2	1	.67	2	.234	.286	.409
2 ML YEARS		75	206	53	8	1	10	(6 | 4)	93	26	24	9	1	45	4	1	1	5	4	.56	3	.257	.300	.451

Emil Brown

Bats: R **Throws:** R **Pos:** PH-37; LF-30; CF-8; RF-4 **Ht:** 6'2" **Wt:** 195 **Born:** 12/29/74 **Age:** 23

							BATTING										BASERUNNING				PERCENTAGES		
Year Team	Lg	G	AB	H	2B	3B	HR	(Hm	Rd)	TB	R	RBI	TBB	IBB	SO	HBP	SH	SF	SB	CS	SB%	GDP	Avg	OBP	SLG
1994 Athletics	R	32	86	19	1	1	3	—	—	31	13	12	13	0	12	4	0	0	5	1	.83	2	.221	.350	.360
1995 W Michigan	A	124	459	115	17	3	3	—	—	147	63	67	52	0	77	11	0	6	35	19	.65	17	.251	.337	.320
1996 Athletics	R	4	15	4	3	0	0	—	—	7	5	2	3	0	2	1	0	0	1	1	.50	0	.267	.421	.467
Modesto	A+	57	211	64	10	1	10	—	—	106	50	47	32	1	51	6	0	2	13	5	.72	5	.303	.406	.502
1997 Pittsburgh	NL	66	95	17	2	1	2	(1	1)	27	16	6	10	1	32	7	0	0	5	1	.83	1	.179	.304	.284

Kevin Brown

Pitches: Right **Bats:** Right **Pos:** SP-33 **Ht:** 6'4" **Wt:** 195 **Born:** 3/14/65 **Age:** 33

		HOW MUCH HE PITCHED						WHAT HE GAVE UP											THE RESULTS						
Year Team	Lg	G	GS	CG	GF	IP	BFP	H	R	ER	HR	SH	SF	HB	TBB	IBB	SO	WP	Bk	W	L	Pct.	ShO	Sv-Op	Hld	ERA
1986 Texas	AL	1	1	0	0	5	19	6	2	2	0	0	0	0	0	0	4	0	0	1	0	1.000	0	0-0	0	3.60
1988 Texas	AL	4	4	1	0	23.1	110	33	15	11	2	1	0	1	8	0	12	1	0	1	1	.500	0	0-0	0	4.24
1989 Texas	AL	28	28	7	0	191	798	167	81	71	10	3	6	4	70	2	104	7	2	12	9	.571	0	0-0	0	3.35
1990 Texas	AL	26	26	6	0	180	757	175	84	72	13	2	7	3	60	3	88	9	2	12	10	.545	2	0-0	0	3.60
1991 Texas	AL	33	33	0	0	210.2	934	233	116	103	17	6	4	13	90	5	96	12	3	9	12	.429	0	0-0	0	4.40
1992 Texas	AL	35	35	11	0	265.2	1108	262	117	98	11	7	8	10	76	2	173	8	2	21	11	.656	1	0-0	0	3.32
1993 Texas	AL	34	34	12	0	233	1001	228	105	93	14	5	3	15	74	5	142	8	1	15	12	.556	3	0-0	0	3.59
1994 Texas	AL	26	25	3	1	170	760	218	109	91	18	2	7	6	50	3	123	7	0	7	9	.438	0	0-0	0	4.82
1995 Baltimore	AL	26	26	3	0	172.1	706	155	73	69	10	5	2	9	48	1	117	3	1	10	9	.526	1	0-0	0	3.60
1996 Florida	NL	32	32	5	0	233	906	187	60	49	8	4	4	16	33	2	159	6	1	17	11	.607	3	0-0	0	1.89
1997 Florida	NL	33	33	6	0	237.1	976	214	77	71	10	5	1	14	66	7	205	7	1	16	8	.667	2	0-0	0	2.69
11 ML YEARS		278	277	54	1	1921.1	8075	1878	839	730	113	40	42	91	575	30	1223	68	12	121	92	.568	12	0-0	0	3.42

Kevin L. Brown

Bats: Right **Throws:** Right **Pos:** C-4; PH-1 **Ht:** 6'2" **Wt:** 200 **Born:** 4/21/73 **Age:** 25

							BATTING										BASERUNNING				PERCENTAGES		
Year Team	Lg	G	AB	H	2B	3B	HR	(Hm	Rd)	TB	R	RBI	TBB	IBB	SO	HBP	SH	SF	SB	CS	SB%	GDP	Avg	OBP	SLG
1994 Hudson Vall	A-	68	232	57	19	1	6	—	—	96	33	32	23	0	86	4	0	6	0	1	.00	4	.246	.317	.414
1995 Charlotte	A+	107	355	94	25	1	11	—	—	154	48	57	50	0	96	9	1	4	2	3	.40	9	.265	.366	.434
Okla City	AAA	3	10	4	1	0	0	—	—	5	1	0	2	0	4	0	0	0	2	0	.00	0	.400	.500	.500
1996 Tulsa	AA	128	460	121	27	1	26	—	—	228	77	86	73	0	150	11	0	6	0	3	.00	5	.263	.373	.496
1997 Okla City	AAA	116	403	97	18	2	19	—	—	176	56	50	38	1	111	5	1	2	2	2	.50	11	.241	.313	.437
1996 Texas	AL	3	4	0	0	0	0	(0	0)	0	1	1	2	0	2	1	0	0	0	0	.00	0	.000	.375	.000
1997 Texas	AL	4	5	2	0	0	1	(0	1)	5	1	1	0	0	0	0	0	0	0	0	.00	0	.400	.400	1.000
2 ML YEARS		7	9	2	0	0	1	(0	1)	5	2	2	2	0	2	1	0	0	0	0	.00	0	.222	.385	.556

Jacob Brumfield

Bats: R **Throws:** R **Pos:** CF-24; LF-14; PH-12; RF-10; DH-4 **Ht:** 6'0" **Wt:** 185 **Born:** 5/27/65 **Age:** 33

							BATTING										BASERUNNING				PERCENTAGES		
Year Team	Lg	G	AB	H	2B	3B	HR	(Hm	Rd)	TB	R	RBI	TBB	IBB	SO	HBP	SH	SF	SB	CS	SB%	GDP	Avg	OBP	SLG
1997 Dunedin *	A+	6	25	4	0	0	0	—	—	4	2	2	0	0	6	0	0	0	1	1	.50	0	.160	.160	.160
1992 Cincinnati	NL	24	30	4	0	0	0	(0	0)	4	6	2	2	1	4	1	0	0	6	0	1.00	0	.133	.212	.133
1993 Cincinnati	NL	103	272	73	17	3	6	(1	5)	114	40	23	21	4	47	1	3	2	20	8	.71	1	.268	.321	.419
1994 Cincinnati	NL	68	122	38	10	2	4	(3	1)	64	36	11	15	0	18	0	2	2	6	3	.67	3	.311	.381	.525
1995 Pittsburgh	NL	116	402	109	23	2	4	(4	0)	148	64	26	37	0	71	5	0	1	22	12	.65	3	.271	.339	.368
1996 Pit-Tor		119	388	99	28	2	14	(8	6)	173	63	60	29	2	75	4	1	4	15	4	.79	14	.255	.311	.446
1997 Toronto		58	174	36	5	1	2	(1	1)	49	22	10	14	0	31	1	1	1	4	4	.50	4	.207	.268	.282
1996 Pittsburgh	NL	29	80	20	9	0	2	(0	2)	35	11	8	5	1	17	0	0	1	3	1	.75	4	.250	.291	.438
Toronto	AL	90	308	79	19	2	12	(8	4)	138	52	52	24	1	58	4	1	3	12	3	.80	10	.256	.316	.448
6 ML YEARS		488	1388	359	83	10	30	(17	13)	552	231	142	118	7	246	12	7	10	73	31	.70	25	.259	.320	.398

30

Jim Bruske

Pitches: Right **Bats:** Right **Pos:** RP-28 **Ht:** 6'1" **Wt:** 185 **Born:** 10/7/64 **Age:** 33

Year Team	Lg	G	GS	CG	GF	IP	BFP	H	R	ER	HR	SH	SF	HB	TBB	IBB	SO	WP	Bk	W	L	Pct.	ShO	Sv-Op	Hld	ERA
1986 Batavia	A-	1	0	0	1	1	7	1	2	2	0	0	0	0	3	0	3	2	0	0	0	.000	0	0- -	—	18.00
1989 Canton-Akrn	AA	2	0	0	2	2	11	3	3	3	0	0	0	0	2	0	1	1	0	0	0	.000	0	0- -	—	13.50
1990 Canton-Akrn	AA	32	13	3	6	118	511	118	53	43	6	2	3	4	42	2	62	5	0	9	3	.750	2	0- -	—	3.28
1991 Canton-Akrn	AA	17	11	0	3	80.1	337	73	36	31	3	0	1	2	27	3	35	2	0	5	2	.714	0	1- -	—	3.47
Colo Sprngs	AAA	7	1	0	3	25.2	100	19	9	7	3	0	1	0	8	0	13	1	1	4	0	1.000	0	2- -	—	2.45
1992 Colo Sprngs	AAA	7	0	0	1	17.2	83	24	11	9	2	0	0	2	6	1	8	2	0	2	0	1.000	0	0- -	—	4.58
Jackson	AA	13	9	1	1	61.2	258	54	23	18	2	2	2	4	14	1	48	1	1	4	3	.571	0	0- -	—	2.63
1993 Jackson	AA	15	15	1	0	97.1	391	86	34	25	6	1	1	2	22	1	83	2	0	9	5	.643	0	0- -	—	2.31
Tucson	AAA	12	9	0	1	66.2	290	77	36	28	4	2	1	0	18	2	42	3	0	4	2	.667	0	1- -	—	3.78
1994 Tucson	AAA	7	7	0	0	39	170	47	22	18	2	1	0	1	8	0	25	2	0	3	1	.750	0	0- -	—	4.15
1995 Albuquerque	AAA	43	6	0	13	114	492	128	54	52	6	4	4	3	41	2	99	3	0	7	5	.583	0	4- -	—	4.11
1996 Albuquerque	AAA	36	0	0	21	62	270	63	34	28	4	3	4	3	21	6	51	1	0	5	2	.714	0	4- -	—	4.06
1997 Las Vegas	AAA	16	9	0	0	68	294	73	41	37	8	2	1	3	22	1	67	2	0	5	4	.556	0	0- -	—	4.90
1995 Los Angeles	NL	9	0	0	3	10	45	12	7	5	0	0	0	1	4	0	5	1	0	0	0	.000	0	1-1	0	4.50
1996 Los Angeles	NL	11	0	0	5	12.2	58	17	8	8	2	0	0	1	3	1	12	1	0	0	0	.000	0	0-0	0	5.68
1997 San Diego	NL	28	0	0	6	44.2	193	37	22	18	4	2	3	1	25	1	32	4	0	4	1	.800	0	0-1	5	3.63
3 ML YEARS		48	0	0	14	67.1	296	66	37	31	6	2	3	3	32	2	49	6	0	4	1	.800	0	1-2	5	4.14

Damon Buford

Bats: Right **Throws:** Right **Pos:** CF-117; PH-13; DH-3 **Ht:** 5'10" **Wt:** 170 **Born:** 6/12/70 **Age:** 28

Year Team	Lg	G	AB	H	2B	3B	HR	(Hm	Rd)	TB	R	RBI	TBB	IBB	SO	HBP	SH	SF	SB	CS	SB%	GDP	Avg	OBP	SLG
1993 Baltimore	AL	53	79	18	5	0	2	(0	2)	29	18	9	9	0	19	1	1	0	2	2	.50	1	.228	.315	.367
1994 Baltimore	AL	4	2	1	0	0	0	(0	0)	1	2	0	0	0	1	0	0	0	0	0	.00	0	.500	.500	.500
1995 Bal-NYN		68	168	34	5	0	4	(2	2)	51	30	14	25	0	35	5	3	3	10	8	.56	3	.202	.318	.304
1996 Texas	AL	90	145	41	9	0	6	(3	3)	68	30	20	15	0	34	0	1	1	8	5	.62	3	.283	.348	.469
1997 Texas	AL	122	366	82	18	0	8	(4	4)	124	49	39	30	0	83	3	3	2	18	7	.72	8	.224	.287	.339
1995 Baltimore	AL	24	32	2	0	0	0	(0	0)	2	6	2	6	0	7	0	3	1	3	1	.75	0	.063	.205	.063
New York	NL	44	136	32	5	0	4	(2	2)	49	24	12	19	0	28	5	0	2	7	7	.50	3	.235	.346	.360
5 ML YEARS		337	760	176	37	0	20	(9	11)	273	129	82	79	0	172	9	8	6	38	22	.63	15	.232	.309	.359

Jay Buhner

Bats: Right **Throws:** Right **Pos:** RF-154; PH-3; DH-2 **Ht:** 6'3" **Wt:** 210 **Born:** 8/13/64 **Age:** 33

Year Team	Lg	G	AB	H	2B	3B	HR	(Hm	Rd)	TB	R	RBI	TBB	IBB	SO	HBP	SH	SF	SB	CS	SB%	GDP	Avg	OBP	SLG
1987 New York	AL	7	22	5	2	0	0	(0	0)	7	0	1	1	0	6	0	0	0	0	0	.00	1	.227	.261	.318
1988 NYA-Sea	AL	85	261	56	13	1	13	(8	5)	110	36	38	28	1	93	6	1	3	1	1	.50	5	.215	.302	.421
1989 Seattle	AL	58	204	56	15	1	9	(7	2)	100	27	33	19	0	55	2	0	1	2	2	.50	6	.275	.341	.490
1990 Seattle	AL	51	163	45	12	0	7	(2	5)	78	16	33	17	1	50	4	0	1	2	2	.50	6	.276	.357	.479
1991 Seattle	AL	137	406	99	14	4	27	(14	13)	202	64	77	53	5	117	6	2	4	0	1	.00	10	.244	.337	.498
1992 Seattle	AL	152	543	132	16	3	25	(9	16)	229	69	79	71	2	146	6	1	8	0	6	.00	12	.243	.333	.422
1993 Seattle	AL	158	563	153	28	3	27	(13	14)	268	91	98	100	11	144	2	2	4	2	5	.29	12	.272	.379	.476
1994 Seattle	AL	101	358	100	23	4	21	(8	13)	194	74	68	66	3	63	5	2	5	0	1	.00	7	.279	.394	.542
1995 Seattle	AL	126	470	123	23	0	40	(21	19)	266	86	121	60	7	120	1	2	6	0	1	.00	15	.262	.343	.566
1996 Seattle	AL	150	564	153	29	0	44	(21	23)	314	107	138	84	5	159	9	0	10	0	1	.00	11	.271	.369	.557
1997 Seattle	AL	157	540	131	18	2	40	(13	27)	273	104	109	119	3	175	5	0	1	0	0	.00	23	.243	.383	.506
1988 New York	AL	25	69	13	0	0	3	(1	2)	22	8	13	3	0	25	3	0	1	0	0	.00	1	.188	.250	.319
Seattle	AL	60	192	43	13	1	10	(7	3)	88	28	25	25	1	68	3	1	2	1	1	.50	4	.224	.320	.458
11 ML YEARS		1182	4094	1053	193	18	253	(116	137)	2041	674	795	618	38	1128	46	10	47	6	22	.21	102	.257	.357	.499

Jim Bullinger

Pitches: Right **Bats:** Right **Pos:** SP-25; RP-11 **Ht:** 6'2" **Wt:** 190 **Born:** 8/21/65 **Age:** 32

Year Team	Lg	G	GS	CG	GF	IP	BFP	H	R	ER	HR	SH	SF	HB	TBB	IBB	SO	WP	Bk	W	L	Pct.	ShO	Sv-Op	Hld	ERA
1992 Chicago	NL	39	9	1	15	85	380	72	44	44	9	9	4	4	54	6	36	4	0	2	8	.200	0	7-7	4	4.66
1993 Chicago	NL	15	0	0	6	16.2	75	18	9	8	1	0	1	0	9	0	10	0	0	1	0	1.000	0	1-1	3	4.32
1994 Chicago	NL	33	10	1	10	100	412	87	43	40	6	3	3	1	34	2	72	4	1	6	2	.750	0	2-2	1	3.60
1995 Chicago	NL	24	24	1	0	150	665	152	80	69	14	12	5	3	65	7	93	5	1	12	8	.600	1	0-0	0	4.14
1996 Chicago	NL	37	20	1	6	129.1	598	144	101	94	15	8	5	8	68	5	90	7	0	6	10	.375	1	1-1	0	6.54
1997 Montreal	NL	36	25	2	4	155.1	697	165	106	96	17	8	6	12	74	5	87	7	0	7	12	.368	2	0-1	0	5.56
6 ML YEARS		184	88	6	41	636.1	2827	638	388	351	62	40	24	34	304	25	388	27	2	34	40	.459	4	11-12	8	4.96

Dave Burba

Pitches: Right **Bats:** Right **Pos:** SP-27; RP-3 **Ht:** 6'4" **Wt:** 240 **Born:** 7/7/66 **Age:** 31

Year Team	Lg	G	GS	CG	GF	IP	BFP	H	R	ER	HR	SH	SF	HB	TBB	IBB	SO	WP	Bk	W	L	Pct.	ShO	Sv-Op	Hld	ERA
1990 Seattle	AL	6	0	0	2	8	35	8	6	4	0	2	0	1	2	0	4	0	0	0	0	.000	0	0-0	0	4.50
1991 Seattle	AL	22	2	0	11	36.2	153	34	16	15	6	0	0	0	14	3	16	1	0	2	2	.500	0	1-1	0	3.68
1992 San Francisco	NL	23	11	0	4	70.2	318	80	43	39	4	2	4	2	31	2	47	1	1	2	7	.222	0	0-0	0	4.97
1993 San Francisco	NL	54	5	0	9	95.1	408	95	49	45	14	6	3	3	37	5	88	4	0	10	3	.769	0	0-0	10	4.25
1994 San Francisco	NL	57	0	0	13	74	322	59	39	36	5	3	1	6	45	3	84	3	0	3	6	.333	0	0-3	11	4.38

31

Year Team	Lg	G	GS	CG	GF	IP	BFP	H	R	ER	HR	SH	SF	HB	TBB	IBB	SO	WP	Bk	W	L	Pct.	ShO	Sv-Op	Hld	ERA
		HOW MUCH HE PITCHED						WHAT HE GAVE UP												THE RESULTS						
1995 SF-Cin	NL	52	9	1	7	106.2	451	90	50	47	9	4	1	0	51	3	96	5	0	10	4	.714	1	0-1	5	3.97
1996 Cincinnati	NL	34	33	0	0	195	849	179	96	83	18	5	12	2	97	9	148	9	1	11	13	.458	0	0-0	0	3.83
1997 Cincinnati	NL	30	27	2	1	160	706	157	88	84	22	6	3	9	73	10	131	6	0	11	10	.524	0	0-0	0	4.73
1995 San Francisco	NL	37	0	0	7	43.1	191	38	26	24	5	3	1	0	25	2	46	2	0	4	2	.667	0	0-1	5	4.98
Cincinnati	NL	15	9	1	0	63.1	260	52	24	23	4	1	0	0	26	1	50	3	0	6	2	.750	1	0-0	0	3.27
8 ML YEARS		278	87	3	47	746.1	3242	702	387	353	78	28	24	23	350	35	614	29	2	49	45	.521	1	1-5	26	4.26

John Burke

Pitches: Right **Bats:** Both **Pos:** SP-9; RP-8 **Ht:** 6'4" **Wt:** 215 **Born:** 2/9/70 **Age:** 28

Year Team	Lg	G	GS	CG	GF	IP	BFP	H	R	ER	HR	SH	SF	HB	TBB	IBB	SO	WP	Bk	W	L	Pct.	ShO	Sv-Op	Hld	ERA
		HOW MUCH HE PITCHED						WHAT HE GAVE UP												THE RESULTS						
1992 Bend	A-	10	10	0	0	41	173	38	13	11	3	1	0	0	18	0	32	0	3	2	0	1.000	0	0--	--	2.41
1993 Central Val	A+	20	20	2	0	119	521	104	62	42	5	7	2	3	64	0	114	8	1	8	7	.467	0	0--	--	3.18
Colo Sprngs	AAA	8	8	0	0	48.2	206	44	22	17	0	3	2	2	23	0	38	1	0	3	2	.600	0	0--	--	3.14
1994 Colo Sprngs	AAA	8	0	0	3	11	72	16	25	24	0	0	1	2	22	0	6	5	0	0	0	.000	0	0--	--	19.64
Asheville	A	4	4	0	0	17	61	5	3	2	1	0	0	0	5	0	16	1	0	1	0	1.000	0	0--	--	1.06
1995 Colo Sprngs	AAA	19	17	0	1	87	376	79	46	44	7	2	3	1	48	0	65	5	1	7	1	.875	0	1--	--	4.55
1996 Salem	A+	3	3	0	0	12	54	10	12	8	1	1	0	0	9	0	12	4	0	0	1	.000	0	0--	--	6.00
Colo Sprngs	AAA	24	9	0	10	63.2	293	75	46	42	3	1	5	2	28	0	54	5	0	2	4	.333	0	1--	--	5.94
1997 Colo Sprngs	AAA	3	3	0	0	17	85	23	14	11	1	0	0	0	14	0	15	2	0	1	2	.333	0	--	--	5.82
1996 Colorado	NL	11	0	0	3	15.2	75	21	13	13	3	0	1	1	7	0	19	1	0	2	1	.667	0	0-0	1	7.47
1997 Colorado	NL	17	9	0	1	59	288	83	46	43	13	1	3	6	26	0	39	4	0	2	5	.286	0	0-0	1	6.56
2 ML YEARS		28	9	0	4	74.2	363	104	59	56	16	1	4	7	33	0	58	5	0	4	6	.400	0	0-0	2	6.75

John Burkett

Pitches: Right **Bats:** Right **Pos:** SP-30 **Ht:** 6'3" **Wt:** 215 **Born:** 11/28/64 **Age:** 33

Year Team	Lg	G	GS	CG	GF	IP	BFP	H	R	ER	HR	SH	SF	HB	TBB	IBB	SO	WP	Bk	W	L	Pct.	ShO	Sv-Op	Hld	ERA
		HOW MUCH HE PITCHED						WHAT HE GAVE UP												THE RESULTS						
1997 Okla City *	AAA	1	1	0	0	5	23	6	2	2	1	0	0	0	2	0	3	0	0	1	0	1.000	0	0--	--	3.60
1987 San Francisco	NL	3	0	0	1	6	28	7	4	3	2	1	0	1	3	0	5	0	0	0	0	.000	0	0-0	0	4.50
1990 San Francisco	NL	33	32	2	1	204	857	201	92	86	18	6	5	4	61	7	118	3	5	14	7	.667	0	1-1	0	3.79
1991 San Francisco	NL	36	34	3	0	206.2	890	223	103	96	19	8	8	10	60	2	131	5	2	12	11	.522	1	0-0	0	4.18
1992 San Francisco	NL	32	32	3	0	189.2	799	194	96	81	13	11	4	4	45	6	107	0	0	13	9	.591	1	0-0	0	3.84
1993 San Francisco	NL	34	34	2	0	231.2	942	224	100	94	18	8	4	11	40	4	145	1	2	22	7	.759	1	0-0	0	3.65
1994 San Francisco	NL	25	25	0	0	159.1	676	176	72	64	14	12	5	7	36	7	85	2	0	6	8	.429	0	0-0	0	3.62
1995 Florida	NL	30	30	4	0	188.1	810	208	95	90	22	10	0	6	57	5	126	2	1	14	14	.500	0	0-0	0	4.30
1996 Fla-Tex		34	34	2	0	222.2	934	229	117	105	19	12	6	5	58	4	153	0	0	11	12	.478	1	0-0	0	4.24
1997 Texas	AL	30	30	2	0	189.1	828	240	106	96	20	4	7	4	30	1	139	1	0	9	12	.429	1	0-0	0	4.56
1996 Florida	NL	24	24	1	0	154	645	154	84	74	15	11	4	3	42	2	108	0	0	6	10	.375	0	0-0	0	4.32
Texas	AL	10	10	1	0	68.2	289	75	33	31	4	1	2	2	16	2	47	0	0	5	2	.714	1	0-0	0	4.06
9 ML YEARS		257	251	18	2	1597.2	6764	1702	785	715	145	72	39	52	390	36	1011	14	6	101	80	.558	4	1-1	1	4.03

Ellis Burks

Bats: Right **Throws:** Right **Pos:** CF-89; LF-67; PH-10 **Ht:** 6'2" **Wt:** 198 **Born:** 9/11/64 **Age:** 33

Year Team	Lg	G	AB	H	2B	3B	HR	(Hm	Rd)	TB	R	RBI	TBB	IBB	SO	HBP	SH	SF	SB	CS	SB%	GDP	Avg	OBP	SLG
		BATTING																	BASERUNNING				PERCENTAGES		
1987 Boston	AL	133	558	152	30	2	20	(11	9)	246	94	59	41	0	98	2	4	1	27	6	.82	1	.272	.324	.441
1988 Boston	AL	144	540	159	37	5	18	(8	10)	260	93	92	62	1	89	3	4	6	25	9	.74	8	.294	.367	.481
1989 Boston	AL	97	399	121	19	6	12	(6	6)	188	73	61	36	2	52	5	2	4	21	5	.81	8	.303	.365	.471
1990 Boston	AL	152	588	174	33	8	21	(10	11)	286	89	89	48	4	82	1	2	2	9	11	.45	18	.296	.349	.486
1991 Boston	AL	130	474	119	33	3	14	(8	6)	200	56	56	39	2	81	6	2	3	6	11	.35	7	.251	.314	.422
1992 Boston	AL	66	235	60	8	3	8	(4	4)	98	35	30	25	2	48	1	0	2	5	2	.71	5	.255	.327	.417
1993 Chicago	AL	146	499	137	24	4	17	(7	10)	220	75	74	60	2	97	4	3	8	6	9	.40	11	.275	.352	.441
1994 Colorado	NL	42	149	48	8	3	13	(7	6)	101	33	24	16	3	39	0	0	0	3	1	.75	3	.322	.388	.678
1995 Colorado	NL	103	278	74	10	6	14	(8	6)	138	41	49	39	0	72	2	1	1	7	3	.70	7	.266	.359	.496
1996 Colorado	NL	156	613	211	45	8	40	(23	17)	392	142	128	61	2	114	6	3	2	32	6	.84	19	.344	.408	**.639**
1997 Colorado	NL	119	424	123	19	2	32	(17	15)	242	91	82	47	0	75	3	1	2	7	2	.78	17	.290	.363	.571
11 ML YEARS		1288	4757	1378	266	50	209	(109	100)	2371	822	744	474	18	847	33	22	31	148	65	.69	104	.290	.356	.498

Jeromy Burnitz

Bats: L **Throws:** R **Pos:** RF-124; CF-26; PH-14; LF-5 **Ht:** 6'0" **Wt:** 190 **Born:** 4/15/69 **Age:** 29

Year Team	Lg	G	AB	H	2B	3B	HR	(Hm	Rd)	TB	R	RBI	TBB	IBB	SO	HBP	SH	SF	SB	CS	SB%	GDP	Avg	OBP	SLG
		BATTING																	BASERUNNING				PERCENTAGES		
1993 New York	NL	86	263	64	10	6	13	(6	7)	125	49	38	38	4	66	1	2	2	3	6	.33	2	.243	.339	.475
1994 New York	NL	45	143	34	4	0	3	(2	1)	47	26	15	23	0	45	1	1	0	1	1	.50	2	.238	.347	.329
1995 Cleveland	AL	9	7	4	1	0	0	(0	0)	5	4	0	0	0	0	0	0	0	0	0	.00	0	.571	.571	.714
1996 Cle-Mil	AL	94	200	53	14	0	9	(5	4)	94	38	40	33	2	47	4	0	2	4	1	.80	4	.265	.377	.470
1997 Milwaukee	AL	153	494	139	37	8	27	(18	9)	273	85	85	75	8	111	5	3	0	20	13	.61	8	.281	.382	.553
1996 Cleveland	AL	71	128	36	10	0	7	(4	3)	67	30	26	25	1	31	2	0	0	2	1	.67	3	.281	.406	.523
Milwaukee	AL	23	72	17	4	0	2	(1	1)	27	8	14	8	1	16	2	0	2	2	0	1.00	1	.236	.321	.375
5 ML YEARS		387	1107	294	66	14	52	(31	21)	544	202	178	169	14	269	11	6	4	28	21	.57	16	.266	.367	.491

Terry Burrows

Pitches: Left **Bats:** Left **Pos:** RP-13 **Ht:** 6'1" **Wt:** 185 **Born:** 11/28/68 **Age:** 29

		HOW MUCH HE PITCHED					WHAT HE GAVE UP											THE RESULTS					
Year Team	Lg	G	GS	CG	GF	IP	BFP	H	R	ER	HR	SH	SF	HB	TBB	IBB	SO	WP	Bk	W	L	Pct.	ShO	Sv-Op	Hld	ERA
1997 Las Vegas *	AAA	31	1	0	10	33.2	160	44	24	24	3	1	0	1	19	3	26	1	1	1	5	.167	0	2- -	—	6.42
Edmonton *	AAA	13	0	0	3	27	127	35	18	17	2	1	2	0	15	2	24	2	0	2	2	.500	0	0- -	—	5.67
1994 Texas	AL	1	0	0	0	1	5	1	1	1	1	0	0	0	1	0	0	0	0	0	0	.000	0	0-0	0	9.00
1995 Texas	AL	28	3	0	6	44.2	207	60	37	32	11	0	0	2	19	0	22	4	0	2	2	.500	0	1-3	6	6.45
1996 Milwaukee	AL	8	0	0	4	12.2	58	12	4	4	2	1	0	1	10	0	5	0	0	2	0	1.000	0	0-0	0	2.84
1997 San Diego	NL	13	0	0	4	10.1	52	12	13	12	1	1	0	1	8	1	8	0	0	0	2	.000	0	0-0	1	10.45
4 ML YEARS		50	3	0	14	68.2	322	85	55	49	15	2	0	4	38	1	35	4	0	4	4	.500	0	1-3	7	6.42

Mike Busby

Pitches: Right **Bats:** Right **Pos:** SP-3 **Ht:** 6'4" **Wt:** 210 **Born:** 12/27/72 **Age:** 25

		HOW MUCH HE PITCHED					WHAT HE GAVE UP										THE RESULTS					
Year Team	Lg	G	GS	CG	GF	IP	BFP	H	R	ER	HR	SH	SF	HB	TBB	IBB	SO	WP	Bk	W	L	Pct.	ShO	Sv-Op	Hld	ERA
1991 Cardinals	R	11	11	0	0	59	267	67	35	23	1	0	2	2	29	0	71	3	1	4	3	.571	0	0- -	—	3.51
1992 Savannah	A	28	28	1	0	149.2	665	145	96	61	11	1	7	17	67	0	84	16	1	4	13	.235	0	0- -	—	3.67
1993 Savannah	A	23	21	1	0	143.2	579	116	49	39	8	6	4	10	31	0	125	5	2	12	2	.857	1	0- -	—	2.44
1994 St. Pete	A+	26	26	1	0	151.2	663	166	82	75	11	8	5	14	49	1	89	5	2	6	13	.316	0	0- -	—	4.45
1995 Arkansas	AA	20	20	1	0	134	565	125	63	49	8	3	3	6	35	1	95	5	0	7	6	.538	0	0- -	—	3.29
Louisville	AAA	6	6	1	0	38.1	154	28	18	14	2	2	2	3	11	0	26	2	0	2	2	.500	0	0- -	—	3.29
1996 Louisville	AAA	14	14	0	0	72	343	89	57	51	11	3	1	6	44	1	53	7	2	2	5	.286	0	0- -	—	6.38
1997 Louisville	AAA	15	14	1	0	93.2	395	95	49	48	12	0	1	7	30	1	65	8	0	4	8	.333	1	0- -	—	4.61
1996 St. Louis	NL	1	1	0	0	4	28	9	13	8	4	1	0	1	4	0	4	0	0	0	1	.000	0	0-0	0	18.00
1997 St. Louis	NL	3	3	0	0	14.1	67	24	14	14	2	1	1	0	4	0	6	0	0	0	2	.000	0	0-0	0	8.79
2 ML YEARS		4	4	0	0	18.1	95	33	27	22	6	2	1	1	8	0	10	0	0	0	3	.000	0	0-0	0	10.80

Homer Bush

Bats: Right **Throws:** Right **Pos:** 2B-8; PH-7 **Ht:** 5'10" **Wt:** 175 **Born:** 11/12/72 **Age:** 25

		BATTING															BASERUNNING				PERCENTAGES		
Year Team	Lg	G	AB	H	2B	3B	HR	(Hm | Rd)	TB	R	RBI	TBB	IBB	SO	HBP	SH	SF	SB	CS	SB%	GDP	Avg	OBP	SLG
1991 Padres	R	32	127	41	3	2	0	—	—	48	16	16	4	1	33	1	0	0	11	7	.61	2	.323	.348	.378
1992 Chston-SC	A	108	367	86	10	5	0	—	—	106	37	18	13	0	85	3	0	2	14	11	.56	3	.234	.265	.289
1993 Waterloo	A	130	472	152	19	3	5	—	—	192	63	51	19	0	87	1	1	1	39	14	.74	10	.322	.349	.407
1994 Rancho Cuca	A+	39	161	54	10	3	0	—	—	70	37	16	9	0	29	4	1	1	9	2	.82	2	.335	.383	.435
Wichita	AA	59	245	73	11	4	3	—	—	101	35	14	10	0	39	3	1	0	20	7	.74	6	.298	.333	.412
1995 Memphis	AA	108	432	121	12	5	5	—	—	158	53	37	15	0	83	2	4	0	34	12	.74	6	.280	.307	.366
1996 Las Vegas	AAA	32	116	42	11	1	2	—	—	61	24	3	3	1	33	2	5	0	3	5	.38	2	.362	.388	.526
1997 Las Vegas	AAA	38	155	43	10	1	3	—	—	64	25	14	7	0	40	2	1	4	5	1	.83	1	.277	.310	.413
Columbus	AAA	74	275	68	10	3	2	—	—	90	36	26	25	0	56	1	7	4	12	7	.63	6	.247	.308	.327
1997 New York	AL	10	11	4	0	0	0	(0 | 0)	4	2	3	0	0	0	0	0	0	0	0	.00	0	.364	.364	.364

Brett Butler

Bats: L **Throws:** L **Pos:** CF-49; LF-47; PH-15; DH-1 **Ht:** 5'10" **Wt:** 161 **Born:** 6/15/57 **Age:** 41

		BATTING															BASERUNNING				PERCENTAGES		
Year Team	Lg	G	AB	H	2B	3B	HR	(Hm | Rd)	TB	R	RBI	TBB	IBB	SO	HBP	SH	SF	SB	CS	SB%	GDP	Avg	OBP	SLG
1981 Atlanta	NL	40	126	32	2	3	0	(0 | 0)	40	17	4	19	0	17	0	0	0	9	1	.90	0	.254	.352	.317
1982 Atlanta	NL	89	240	52	2	0	0	(0 | 0)	54	35	7	25	0	35	0	3	0	21	8	.72	1	.217	.291	.225
1983 Atlanta	NL	151	549	154	21	13	5	(4 | 1)	216	84	37	54	3	56	2	3	5	39	23	.63	5	.281	.344	.393
1984 Cleveland	AL	159	602	162	25	9	3	(1 | 2)	214	108	49	86	1	62	4	11	6	52	22	.70	6	.269	.361	.355
1985 Cleveland	AL	152	591	184	28	14	5	(1 | 4)	255	106	50	63	2	42	1	6	8	47	20	.70	8	.311	.377	.431
1986 Cleveland	AL	161	587	163	17	14	4	(0 | 4)	220	92	51	70	1	65	4	17	5	32	15	.68	8	.278	.356	.375
1987 Cleveland	AL	137	522	154	25	8	9	(4 | 5)	222	91	41	91	0	55	1	2	2	33	16	.67	3	.295	.399	.425
1988 San Francisco	NL	157	568	163	27	9	6	(1 | 5)	226	109	43	97	4	64	4	8	2	43	20	.68	2	.287	.393	.398
1989 San Francisco	NL	154	594	168	22	4	4	(2 | 2)	210	100	36	59	2	69	3	13	3	31	16	.66	4	.283	.349	.354
1990 San Francisco	NL	160	622	192	20	9	3	(3 | 0)	239	108	44	90	1	62	6	7	7	51	19	.73	3	.309	.397	.384
1991 Los Angeles	NL	161	615	182	13	5	2	(2 | 0)	211	112	38	108	4	79	1	4	2	38	28	.58	3	.296	.401	.343
1992 Los Angeles	NL	157	553	171	14	11	3	(1 | 2)	216	86	39	95	2	67	3	24	1	41	21	.66	4	.309	.413	.391
1993 Los Angeles	NL	156	607	181	21	10	1	(0 | 1)	225	80	42	86	1	69	5	14	4	39	19	.67	6	.298	.387	.371
1994 Los Angeles	NL	111	417	131	13	9	8	(2 | 6)	186	79	33	68	0	52	2	7	2	27	8	.77	2	.314	.411	.446
1995 NYN-LA	NL	129	513	154	18	9	1	(0 | 1)	193	78	38	67	2	51	0	10	6	32	8	.80	5	.300	.377	.376
1996 Los Angeles	NL	34	131	35	1	1	0	(0 | 0)	38	22	8	9	0	22	1	1	3	8	3	.73	1	.267	.313	.290
1997 Los Angeles	NL	105	343	97	8	3	0	(0 | 0)	111	52	18	42	0	40	1	15	0	15	10	.60	1	.283	.363	.324
1995 New York	NL	90	367	114	13	7	1	(0 | 1)	144	54	25	43	2	42	0	6	2	21	7	.75	4	.311	.381	.392
Los Angeles	NL	39	146	40	5	2	0	(0 | 0)	49	24	13	24	0	9	0	4	4	11	1	.92	1	.274	.368	.336
17 ML YEARS		2213	8180	2375	277	131	54	(21 | 33)	3076	1359	578	1129	23	907	38	147	51	558	257	.68	62	.290	.377	.376

Rich Butler

Bats: Left **Throws:** Right **Pos:** LF-3; PH-3; DH-1 **Ht:** 6'1" **Wt:** 180 **Born:** 5/1/73 **Age:** 25

		BATTING															BASERUNNING				PERCENTAGES		
Year Team	Lg	G	AB	H	2B	3B	HR	(Hm | Rd)	TB	R	RBI	TBB	IBB	SO	HBP	SH	SF	SB	CS	SB%	GDP	Avg	OBP	SLG
1991 Blue Jays	R	59	213	56	6	7	0	—	—	76	30	13	17	1	45	0	4	0	10	6	.63	0	.263	.317	.357
1992 Myrtle Bch	A	130	441	100	14	1	2	—	—	122	43	43	37	1	90	7	6	0	11	15	.42	6	.227	.297	.277
1993 Dunedin	A+	110	444	136	19	8	11	—	—	204	68	65	48	10	64	3	1	4	11	13	.46	4	.306	.375	.459

33

Year Team	Lg	G	AB	H	2B	3B	HR	(Hm	Rd)	TB	R	RBI	TBB	IBB	SO	HBP	SH	SF	SB	CS	SB%	GDP	Avg	OBP	SLG
Knoxville	AA	6	21	2	0	1	0	—	—	4	3	0	3	0	5	0	0	0	0	0	.00	0	.095	.208	.190
1994 Knoxville	AA	53	192	56	7	4	3	—	—	80	29	22	19	1	31	2	1	1	7	4	.64	1	.292	.360	.417
Syracuse	AAA	94	302	73	6	2	3	—	—	92	34	27	22	0	66	0	2	1	8	8	.50	6	.242	.292	.305
1995 Syracuse	AAA	69	199	32	4	2	2	—	—	46	20	14	9	0	45	0	1	1	2	3	.40	5	.161	.196	.231
Knoxville	AA	58	217	58	12	3	4	—	—	88	27	33	25	1	41	2	1	0	11	3	.79	5	.267	.348	.406
1996 Dunedin	A+	10	28	2	0	0	0	—	—	2	1	0	5	0	9	0	0	0	4	1	.80	1	.071	.212	.071
1997 Syracuse	AAA	137	537	161	30	9	24	—	—	281	93	87	60	2	107	4	3	3	20	7	.74	11	.300	.373	.523
1997 Toronto	AL	7	14	4	1	0	0	(0	0)	5	3	2	0	0	3	0	0	0	0	1	.00	0	.286	.375	.357

Rob Butler

Bats: L **Throws:** L **Pos:** PH-22; CF-14; RF-8; LF-4   **Ht:** 5'11" **Wt:** 185 **Born:** 4/10/70 **Age:** 28

Year Team	Lg	G	AB	H	2B	3B	HR	(Hm	Rd)	TB	R	RBI	TBB	IBB	SO	HBP	SH	SF	SB	CS	SB%	GDP	Avg	OBP	SLG
1997 Scrnton-WB *	AAA	21	71	20	4	0	0	—	—	24	8	9	1	0	9	0	0	0	0	0	.00	4	.282	.292	.338
1993 Toronto	AL	17	48	13	4	0	0	(0	0)	17	8	2	7	0	12	1	0	0	2	2	.50	0	.271	.375	.354
1994 Toronto	AL	41	74	13	0	1	0	(0	0)	15	13	5	7	0	8	1	4	2	0	1	.00	3	.176	.250	.203
1997 Philadelphia	NL	43	89	26	9	1	0	—	—	37	10	13	5	0	8	0	0	1	1	0	1.00	2	.292	.326	.416
3 ML YEARS		101	211	52	13	2	0	(0	0)	69	31	20	19	0	28	2	4	3	3	3	.50	5	.246	.311	.327

Paul Byrd

Pitches: Right **Bats:** Right **Pos:** RP-27; SP-4   **Ht:** 6'1" **Wt:** 185 **Born:** 12/3/70 **Age:** 27

Year Team	Lg	G	GS	CG	GF	IP	BFP	H	R	ER	HR	SH	SF	HB	TBB	IBB	SO	WP	Bk	W	L	Pct.	ShO	Sv-Op	Hld	ERA
1997 Richmond *	AAA	3	3	0	0	17	64	14	6	6	2	1	0	1	1	0	14	1	0	2	1	.667	0	0– –	—	3.18
1995 New York	NL	17	0	0	6	22	91	18	6	5	1	0	1	1	7	1	26	1	2	2	0	1.000	0	0– –	3	2.05
1996 New York	NL	38	0	0	14	46.2	204	48	22	22	7	1	1	0	21	4	31	3	0	1	2	.333	0	0-2	3	4.24
1997 Atlanta	NL	31	4	0	9	53	236	47	34	31	6	2	2	4	28	4	37	3	1	4	4	.500	0	0-0	1	5.26
3 ML YEARS		86	4	0	29	121.2	531	113	62	58	14	3	5	5	56	9	94	7	3	7	6	.538	0	0-2	7	4.29

Jose Cabrera

Pitches: Right **Bats:** Right **Pos:** RP-12   **Ht:** 6'0" **Wt:** 160 **Born:** 3/24/72 **Age:** 26

Year Team	Lg	G	GS	CG	GF	IP	BFP	H	R	ER	HR	SH	SF	HB	TBB	IBB	SO	WP	Bk	W	L	Pct.	ShO	Sv-Op	Hld	ERA
1992 Burlington	R+	13	13	1	0	92.1	367	74	27	18	6	2	0	2	18	0	79	3	1	8	3	.727	0	0– –	—	1.75
1993 Columbus	A	26	26	1	0	155.1	624	122	54	46	8	2	4	1	53	2	105	8	4	11	6	.647	0	0– –	—	2.67
1994 Kinston	A+	24	24	0	0	133.2	575	134	64	66	15	6	3	5	43	0	110	5	5	4	13	.235	0	0– –	—	4.44
1995 Canton-Akrn	AA	24	11	1	4	85	350	83	32	31	7	1	6	1	21	1	61	0	2	5	3	.625	1	0– –	—	3.28
1996 Bakersfield	A+	7	7	0	0	41.1	183	40	25	18	7	2	2	1	21	0	52	5	0	2	2	.500	0	0– –	—	3.92
Kinston	A+	4	3	0	0	17.2	68	7	2	2	0	1	1	1	8	0	19	3	0	1	1	.500	0	0– –	—	1.02
Canton-Akrn	AA	15	9	1	4	62.1	278	78	45	39	10	2	3	1	17	2	40	4	0	4	3	.571	0	0– –	—	5.63
1997 Buffalo	AAA	5	0	0	2	15	57	8	2	2	2	0	0	1	7	1	11	1	0	3	0	1.000	0	0– –	—	1.20
New Orleans	AAA	31	0	0	5	46	181	31	13	13	2	1	0	2	13	3	48	0	0	2	2	.500	0	0– –	—	2.54
1997 Houston	NL	12	0	0	6	15.1	57	6	2	2	1	0	3	0	6	0	18	0	0	0	0	.000	0	0-1	2	1.17

Orlando Cabrera

Bats: Right **Throws:** Right **Pos:** PH-9; SS-6; 2B-4   **Ht:** 5'9" **Wt:** 150 **Born:** 11/2/74 **Age:** 23

Year Team	Lg	G	AB	H	2B	3B	HR	(Hm	Rd)	TB	R	RBI	TBB	IBB	SO	HBP	SH	SF	SB	CS	SB%	GDP	Avg	OBP	SLG
1993 Expos	R	11	0	0	0	0	0	—	—	0	0	0	0	0	0	0	0	0	0	0	.00	0	.000	.000	.000
1994 Expos	R	22	73	23	4	1	0	—	—	29	13	11	5	0	8	0	1	0	5	0	1.00	2	.315	.359	.397
1995 Wst Plm Bch	A+	3	5	1	0	0	0	—	—	1	0	0	0	0	1	0	0	0	0	0	.00	0	.200	.200	.200
Vermont	A-	65	248	70	12	5	3	—	—	101	37	33	16	0	28	1	2	4	15	8	.65	3	.282	.323	.407
1996 Delmarva	A	134	512	129	28	4	14	—	—	207	86	65	54	4	63	5	5	4	51	18	.74	4	.252	.327	.404
1997 Wst Plm Bch	A+	69	279	77	19	2	5	—	—	115	56	26	27	0	33	0	1	4	32	12	.73	1	.276	.340	.412
Harrisburg	AA	35	133	41	13	2	5	—	—	73	34	20	15	0	18	0	1	0	7	2	.78	0	.308	.378	.549
Ottawa	AAA	31	122	32	5	2	2	—	—	47	17	14	7	0	16	2	1	3	8	1	.89	0	.262	.306	.385
1997 Montreal	NL	16	18	4	0	0	0	(0	0)	4	4	2	1	0	3	0	1	0	1	2	.33	1	.222	.263	.222

Greg Cadaret

Pitches: Left **Bats:** Left **Pos:** RP-15   **Ht:** 6'3" **Wt:** 215 **Born:** 2/27/62 **Age:** 36

Year Team	Lg	G	GS	CG	GF	IP	BFP	H	R	ER	HR	SH	SF	HB	TBB	IBB	SO	WP	Bk	W	L	Pct.	ShO	Sv-Op	Hld	ERA
1997 Buffalo *	AAA	29	1	0	13	50	231	46	31	27	3	1	2	1	35	2	49	8	0	2	2	.500	0	4– –	—	4.86
Vancouver *	AAA	9	0	0	3	14.1	56	11	5	5	1	0	0	0	4	0	16	1	0	0	1	.000	0	3– –	—	3.14
1987 Oakland	AL	29	0	0	7	39.2	176	37	22	20	6	2	2	1	24	1	30	1	0	6	2	.750	0	0-1	3	4.54
1988 Oakland	AL	58	0	0	16	71.2	311	60	26	23	2	5	3	1	36	1	64	5	3	5	2	.714	0	3-4	17	2.89
1989 Oak-NYA	AL	46	13	3	7	120	531	130	62	54	7	3	5	2	57	4	80	6	2	5	5	.500	0	0-2	6	4.05
1990 New York	AL	54	6	0	9	121.1	525	120	62	56	8	9	4	1	64	5	80	14	0	5	4	.556	0	3-4	8	4.15
1991 New York	AL	68	5	0	17	121.2	517	110	52	49	8	6	3	2	59	6	105	3	1	8	6	.571	0	3-7	11	3.62
1992 New York	AL	46	11	1	9	103.2	471	104	53	49	12	3	3	2	74	7	73	5	1	4	8	.333	1	1-3	4	4.25
1993 Cin-KC		47	0	0	18	48	220	54	24	23	4	4	0	2	30	5	25	2	0	3	2	.600	0	1-1	5	4.31
1994 Tor-Det	AL	38	0	0	17	40	191	41	24	21	4	0	0	0	33	5	29	9	0	1	1	.500	0	2-2	4	4.73

		HOW MUCH HE PITCHED						WHAT HE GAVE UP												THE RESULTS							
Year Team	Lg	G	GS	CG	GF	IP	BFP	H	R	ER	HR	SH	SF	HB	TBB	IBB	SO	WP	Bk	W	L	Pct.	ShO	Sv-Op	Hld	ERA
1997 Anaheim	AL	15	0	0	6	13.2	61	11	5	5	1	1	0	2	8	2	11	3	0	0	0	.000	0	0-0	1	3.29
1989 Oakland	AL	26	0	0	6	27.2	119	21	9	7	0	0	2	0	19	3	14	0	0	0	0	.000	0	0-1	5	2.28
New York	AL	20	13	3	1	92.1	412	109	53	47	7	3	3	2	38	1	66	6	2	5	5	.500	1	0-1	1	4.58
1993 Cincinnati	NL	34	0	0	15	32.2	158	40	19	18	3	3	0	1	23	5	23	2	0	2	1	.667	0	1-1	4	4.96
Kansas City	AL	13	0	0	3	15.1	62	14	5	5	0	1	0	1	7	0	2	0	0	1	1	.500	0	0-0	1	2.93
1994 Toronto	AL	21	0	0	8	20	100	24	15	13	4	0	0	0	17	2	15	6	0	0	1	.000	0	0-0	1	5.85
Detroit	AL	17	0	0	9	20	91	17	9	8	0	0	0	0	16	3	14	3	0	1	0	1.000	0	2-2	0	3.60
9 ML YEARS		401	35	4	106	679.2	3003	667	330	300	51	33	20	13	385	36	497	48	7	37	30	.552	2	13-24	62	3.97

Miguel Cairo

Bats: Right **Throws:** Right **Pos:** 2B-9; PH-7; SS-2   **Ht:** 6'0" **Wt:** 160 **Born:** 5/4/74 **Age:** 24

		BATTING																BASERUNNING				PERCENTAGES		
Year Team	Lg	G	AB	H	2B	3B	HR	(Hm	Rd)	TB	R	RBI	TBB	IBB	SO	HBP	SH	SF	SB	CS	SB%	GDP	Avg	OBP	SLG
1992 Dodgers	R	21	76	23	5	2	0	—	—	32	10	9	2	0	6	2	2	1	1	0	1.00	1	.303	.333	.421
Vero Beach	A+	36	125	28	0	0	0	—	—	28	7	7	11	0	12	0	3	1	5	3	.63	3	.224	.285	.224
1993 Vero Beach	A+	89	343	108	10	1	1	—	—	123	49	23	26	0	22	7	10	0	23	16	.59	2	.315	.375	.359
1994 Bakersfield	A+	133	533	155	23	4	2	—	—	192	76	48	34	3	37	6	15	4	44	23	.66	9	.291	.338	.360
1995 San Antonio	AA	107	435	121	20	1	1	—	—	146	53	41	26	0	32	5	4	4	33	16	.67	6	.278	.323	.336
1996 Syracuse	AAA	120	465	129	14	4	3	—	—	160	71	48	26	1	44	8	5	5	27	9	.75	5	.277	.323	.344
1997 Iowa	AAA	135	569	159	35	4	5	—	—	217	82	46	24	0	54	6	6	3	40	15	.73	9	.279	.314	.381
1996 Toronto	AL	9	27	6	2	0	0	(0	0)	8	5	1	2	0	9	1	0	0	0	0	.00	1	.222	.300	.296
1997 Chicago	NL	16	29	7	1	0	0	(0	0)	8	7	1	2	0	3	1	0	0	0	0	.00	0	.241	.313	.276
2 ML YEARS		25	56	13	3	0	0	(0	0)	16	12	2	4	0	12	2	0	0	0	0	.00	1	.232	.306	.286

Mike Cameron

Bats: R **Throws:** R **Pos:** CF-102; RF-37; PH-5; DH-3   **Ht:** 6'2" **Wt:** 190 **Born:** 1/8/73 **Age:** 25

		BATTING																BASERUNNING				PERCENTAGES		
Year Team	Lg	G	AB	H	2B	3B	HR	(Hm	Rd)	TB	R	RBI	TBB	IBB	SO	HBP	SH	SF	SB	CS	SB%	GDP	Avg	OBP	SLG
1991 White Sox	R	44	136	30	3	0	0	—	—	33	21	11	11	0	29	4	1	0	13	2	.87	3	.221	.283	.243
1992 Utica	A-	28	87	24	1	4	2	—	—	39	15	12	11	0	26	0	1	1	3	7	.30	0	.276	.354	.448
South Bend	A	35	114	26	8	1	1	—	—	39	19	9	10	0	37	4	3	1	2	3	.40	0	.228	.310	.342
1993 South Bend	A	122	411	98	14	5	0	—	—	122	52	30	27	0	101	6	2	5	19	10	.66	8	.238	.292	.297
1994 Pr William	A+	131	468	116	15	17	6	—	—	183	86	48	60	2	101	8	2	0	22	10	.69	6	.248	.343	.391
1995 Birmingham	AA	107	350	87	20	5	11	—	—	150	64	60	54	0	104	6	5	4	21	12	.64	9	.249	.355	.429
1996 Birmingham	AA	123	473	142	34	12	28	—	—	284	120	77	71	6	117	12	3	4	39	15	.72	5	.300	.402	.600
1997 Nashville	AAA	30	120	33	7	3	6	—	—	64	21	17	18	0	31	3	0	2	4	2	.67	0	.275	.378	.533
1995 Chicago	AL	28	38	7	2	0	1	(0	1)	12	4	2	3	0	15	0	0	3	0	0	.00	0	.184	.244	.316
1996 Chicago	AL	11	11	1	0	0	0	(0	0)	1	1	0	1	0	3	0	0	0	0	1	.00	0	.091	.167	.091
1997 Chicago	AL	116	379	98	18	3	14	(10	4)	164	63	55	55	1	105	5	2	5	23	2	.92	8	.259	.356	.433
3 ML YEARS		155	428	106	20	3	15	(10	5)	177	68	57	59	1	123	5	5	5	23	3	.88	8	.248	.342	.414

Ken Caminiti

Bats: Both **Throws:** Right **Pos:** 3B-133; PH-4   **Ht:** 6'0" **Wt:** 200 **Born:** 4/21/63 **Age:** 35

		BATTING																BASERUNNING				PERCENTAGES		
Year Team	Lg	G	AB	H	2B	3B	HR	(Hm	Rd)	TB	R	RBI	TBB	IBB	SO	HBP	SH	SF	SB	CS	SB%	GDP	Avg	OBP	SLG
1987 Houston	NL	63	203	50	7	1	3	(2	1)	68	10	23	12	1	44	0	2	1	0	0	.00	6	.246	.287	.335
1988 Houston	NL	30	83	15	2	0	1	(0	1)	20	5	7	5	0	18	0	0	1	0	0	.00	3	.181	.225	.241
1989 Houston	NL	161	585	149	31	3	10	(3	7)	216	71	72	51	9	93	3	3	4	4	1	.80	8	.255	.316	.369
1990 Houston	NL	153	541	131	20	2	4	(2	2)	167	52	51	48	7	97	0	4	3	9	4	.69	15	.242	.302	.309
1991 Houston	NL	152	574	145	30	3	13	(9	4)	220	65	80	46	7	85	5	3	4	4	5	.44	18	.253	.312	.383
1992 Houston	NL	135	506	149	31	2	13	(7	6)	223	68	62	44	13	68	1	2	4	10	4	.71	14	.294	.350	.441
1993 Houston	NL	143	543	142	31	0	13	(5	8)	212	75	75	49	10	88	0	1	3	8	5	.62	15	.262	.321	.390
1994 Houston	NL	111	406	115	28	2	18	(6	12)	201	63	75	43	13	71	2	0	3	4	3	.57	8	.283	.352	.495
1995 San Diego	NL	143	526	159	33	0	26	(16	10)	270	74	94	69	8	94	1	0	6	12	5	.71	11	.302	.380	.513
1996 San Diego	NL	146	546	178	37	2	40	(20	20)	339	109	130	78	16	99	4	0	10	11	5	.69	15	.326	.408	.621
1997 San Diego	NL	137	486	141	28	0	26	(15	11)	247	92	90	80	9	118	3	0	7	11	2	.85	12	.290	.389	.508
11 ML YEARS		1374	4999	1374	278	15	167	(85	82)	2183	684	759	525	93	875	19	14	47	73	34	.68	125	.275	.343	.437

Casey Candaele

Bats: Both **Throws:** Right **Pos:** 2B-9; PH-6; DH-1; 3B-1   **Ht:** 5'9" **Wt:** 165 **Born:** 1/12/61 **Age:** 37

		BATTING																BASERUNNING				PERCENTAGES		
Year Team	Lg	G	AB	H	2B	3B	HR	(Hm	Rd)	TB	R	RBI	TBB	IBB	SO	HBP	SH	SF	SB	CS	SB%	GDP	Avg	OBP	SLG
1997 Buffalo *	AAA	79	311	71	21	0	7	—	—	113	39	38	31	2	43	1	4	4	1	6	.14	12	.228	.297	.363
1986 Montreal	NL	30	104	24	4	1	0	(0	0)	30	9	6	5	0	15	0	0	1	3	5	.38	3	.231	.264	.288
1987 Montreal	NL	138	449	122	23	4	1	(1	0)	156	62	23	38	3	28	2	4	2	7	10	.41	5	.272	.330	.347
1988 Mon-Hou	NL	57	147	25	8	1	0	(0	0)	35	11	5	11	1	17	0	3	0	1	1	.50	7	.170	.228	.238
1990 Houston	NL	130	262	75	8	6	3	(1	2)	104	30	22	31	5	42	1	4	0	7	5	.58	4	.286	.364	.397
1991 Houston	NL	151	461	121	20	7	4	(1	3)	167	44	50	40	7	49	0	1	3	9	3	.75	5	.262	.319	.362
1992 Houston	NL	135	320	69	12	1	1	(0	1)	85	19	18	24	3	36	3	7	6	1	1	.88	5	.213	.269	.266
1993 Houston	NL	75	121	29	8	0	1	(0	1)	40	18	7	10	0	14	0	0	0	2	3	.40	0	.240	.298	.331
1996 Cleveland	AL	24	44	11	2	0	0	(0	1)	16	8	4	1	0	9	0	0	0	0	0	.00	0	.250	.267	.364
1997 Cleveland	AL	14	26	8	1	0	0	(0	0)	9	5	4	1	0	1	0	0	0	0	1	1.00	0	.308	.333	.346
1988 Montreal	NL	36	116	20	5	1	0	(0	0)	27	9	4	10	1	11	0	2	0	1	0	1.00	7	.172	.238	.233
Houston	NL	21	31	5	3	0	0	(0	0)	8	2	1	1	0	6	0	1	0	0	0	.00	0	.161	.188	.258

				BATTING																	BASERUNNING				PERCENTAGES		
Year Team	Lg	G	AB	H	2B	3B	HR	(Hm	Rd)	TB	R	RBI	TBB	IBB	SO	HBP	SH	SF		SB	CS	SB%	GDP	Avg	OBP	SLG
9 ML YEARS		754	1934	483	86	20	11	(4	7)	642	206	139	161	19	211	6	19	12		37	28	.57	29	.250	.308	.332

Tom Candiotti

Pitches: Right **Bats:** Right **Pos:** RP-23; SP-18   **Ht:** 6'2" **Wt:** 221 **Born:** 8/31/57 **Age:** 40

		HOW MUCH HE PITCHED						WHAT HE GAVE UP											THE RESULTS					
Year Team	Lg	G	GS	CG	GF	IP	BFP	H	R	ER	HR	SH	SF	HB	TBB	IBB	SO	WP	Bk	W	L	Pct.	ShO	Sv-Op	Hld	ERA
1983 Milwaukee	AL	10	8	2	1	55.2	233	62	21	20	4	0	2	2	16	0	21	0	0	4	4	.500	1	0--	—	3.23
1984 Milwaukee	AL	8	6	0	0	32.1	147	38	21	19	5	0	0	0	10	0	23	1	0	2	2	.500	0	0--	—	5.29
1986 Cleveland	AL	36	34	17	1	252.1	1078	234	112	100	18	3	9	8	106	0	167	12	4	16	12	.571	3	0--	—	3.57
1987 Cleveland	AL	32	32	7	0	201.2	888	193	132	107	28	8	10	4	93	2	111	13	2	7	18	.280	2	0-0	0	4.78
1988 Cleveland	AL	31	31	11	0	216.2	903	225	86	79	15	12	5	6	53	3	137	5	7	14	8	.636	1	0-0	0	3.28
1989 Cleveland	AL	31	31	4	0	206	847	188	80	71	10	6	4	4	55	5	124	4	8	13	10	.565	0	0-0	0	3.10
1990 Cleveland	AL	31	29	3	1	202	856	207	92	82	23	4	3	6	55	1	128	9	3	15	11	.577	1	0-0	0	3.65
1991 Cle-Tor	AL	34	34	6	0	238	981	202	82	70	12	4	11	6	73	1	167	11	0	13	13	.500	0	0-0	0	2.65
1992 Los Angeles	NL	32	30	6	1	203.2	839	177	78	68	13	20	6	3	63	5	152	9	2	11	15	.423	2	0-0	0	3.00
1993 Los Angeles	NL	33	32	2	0	213.2	898	192	86	74	12	15	9	6	71	1	155	6	0	8	10	.444	1	0-0	0	3.12
1994 Los Angeles	NL	23	22	5	0	153	652	149	77	70	9	9	8	5	54	2	102	9	0	7	7	.500	0	0-0	0	4.12
1995 Los Angeles	NL	30	30	1	0	190.1	812	187	93	74	18	7	5	9	58	2	141	7	0	7	14	.333	1	0-0	0	3.50
1996 Los Angeles	NL	28	27	1	0	152.1	657	172	91	76	18	8	5	3	43	3	79	3	1	9	11	.450	0	0-0	0	4.49
1997 Los Angeles	NL	41	18	0	6	135	573	128	60	54	21	3	2	11	40	4	89	4	0	10	7	.588	0	0-0	2	3.60
1991 Cleveland	AL	15	15	3	0	108.1	442	88	35	27	6	1	7	2	28	0	86	6	0	7	6	.538	0	0-0	0	2.24
Toronto	AL	19	19	3	0	129.2	539	114	47	43	6	3	4	4	45	1	81	5	0	6	7	.462	0	0-0	0	2.98
14 ML YEARS		400	364	65	10	2452.2	10364	2354	1111	964	206	99	79	73	790	29	1596	93	27	136	142	.489	11	0--	—	3.54

John Cangelosi

Bats: B **Throws:** L **Pos:** PH-54; LF-34; CF-23; RF-6; P-1   **Ht:** 5'8" **Wt:** 160 **Born:** 3/10/63 **Age:** 35

				BATTING																BASERUNNING				PERCENTAGES		
Year Team	Lg	G	AB	H	2B	3B	HR	(Hm	Rd)	TB	R	RBI	TBB	IBB	SO	HBP	SH	SF		SB	CS	SB%	GDP	Avg	OBP	SLG
1985 Chicago	AL	5	2	0	0	0	0	(0	0)	0	2	0	0	0	1	1	1	0		0	0	.00	0	.000	.333	.000
1986 Chicago	AL	137	438	103	16	3	2	(1	1)	131	65	32	71	0	61	7	6	3		50	17	.75	5	.235	.349	.299
1987 Pittsburgh	NL	104	182	50	8	3	4	(2	2)	76	44	18	46	1	33	3	1	1		21	6	.78	3	.275	.427	.418
1988 Pittsburgh	NL	75	118	30	4	1	0	(0	0)	36	18	8	17	0	16	1	3	0		9	4	.69	0	.254	.353	.305
1989 Pittsburgh	NL	112	160	35	4	2	0	(0	0)	43	18	9	35	2	20	3	1	2		11	8	.58	1	.219	.365	.269
1990 Pittsburgh	NL	58	76	15	2	0	0	(0	0)	17	13	1	11	0	12	1	2	0		7	2	.78	2	.197	.307	.224
1992 Texas	AL	73	85	16	2	0	1	(0	1)	21	12	6	18	0	16	0	3	0		6	5	.55	0	.188	.330	.247
1994 New York	NL	62	111	28	4	0	0	(0	0)	32	14	4	19	1	20	2	3	0		5	1	.83	1	.252	.371	.288
1995 Houston	NL	90	201	64	5	2	2	(0	2)	79	46	18	48	2	42	4	2	1		21	5	.81	3	.318	.457	.393
1996 Houston	NL	108	262	69	11	4	1	(1	0)	91	49	16	44	0	41	5	1	1		17	9	.65	4	.263	.378	.347
1997 Florida	NL	103	192	47	8	0	1	(1	0)	58	28	12	19	1	33	3	1	1		5	1	.83	3	.245	.321	.302
11 ML YEARS		927	1827	457	64	15	11	(7	4)	584	309	124	328	7	295	30	24	9		152	58	.72	22	.250	.371	.320

Jose Canseco

Bats: R **Throws:** R **Pos:** DH-60; RF-27; LF-19; PH-4   **Ht:** 6'4" **Wt:** 240 **Born:** 7/2/64 **Age:** 33

				BATTING																BASERUNNING				PERCENTAGES		
Year Team	Lg	G	AB	H	2B	3B	HR	(Hm	Rd)	TB	R	RBI	TBB	IBB	SO	HBP	SH	SF		SB	CS	SB%	GDP	Avg	OBP	SLG
1985 Oakland	AL	29	96	29	3	0	5	(4	1)	47	16	13	4	0	31	0	0	1		1	1	.50	1	.302	.330	.490
1986 Oakland	AL	157	600	144	29	1	33	(14	19)	274	85	117	65	1	175	8	0	9		15	7	.68	12	.240	.318	.457
1987 Oakland	AL	159	630	162	35	3	31	(16	15)	296	81	113	50	2	157	2	0	9		15	3	.83	16	.257	.310	.470
1988 Oakland	AL	158	610	187	34	0	42	(16	26)	347	120	124	78	10	128	10	1	6		40	16	.71	15	.307	.391	.569
1989 Oakland	AL	65	227	61	9	1	17	(8	9)	123	40	57	23	4	69	2	0	6		6	3	.67	4	.269	.333	.542
1990 Oakland	AL	131	481	132	14	2	37	(18	19)	261	83	101	72	8	158	5	0	5		19	10	.66	9	.274	.371	.543
1991 Oakland	AL	154	572	152	32	1	44	(16	28)	318	115	122	78	8	152	9	0	5		26	6	.81	16	.266	.359	.556
1992 Oak-Tex	AL	119	439	107	15	0	26	(15	11)	200	74	87	63	2	128	6	0	4		6	7	.46	16	.244	.344	.456
1993 Texas	AL	60	231	59	14	1	10	(6	4)	105	30	46	16	2	62	3	0	3		6	6	.50	6	.255	.308	.455
1994 Texas	AL	111	429	121	19	2	31	(17	14)	237	88	90	69	8	114	5	0	2		15	8	.65	20	.282	.386	.552
1995 Boston	AL	102	396	121	25	1	24	(10	14)	220	64	81	42	4	93	7	0	5		4	0	1.00	9	.306	.378	.556
1996 Boston	AL	96	360	104	22	1	28	(17	11)	212	68	82	63	3	82	6	0	3		3	1	.75	7	.289	.400	.589
1997 Oakland	AL	108	388	91	19	0	23	(10	13)	179	56	74	51	1	122	3	0	4		8	2	.80	15	.235	.325	.461
1992 Oakland	AL	97	366	90	11	0	22	(12	10)	167	66	72	48	2	104	3	0	4		5	7	.42	15	.246	.335	.456
Texas	AL	22	73	17	4	0	4	(3	1)	33	8	15	15	1	24	3	0	0		1	0	1.00	1	.233	.385	.452
13 ML YEARS		1449	5459	1470	270	13	351	(167	184)	2819	920	1107	674	53	1471	66	1	62		164	70	.70	146	.269	.353	.516

Dan Carlson

Pitches: Right **Bats:** Right **Pos:** RP-6   **Ht:** 6'1" **Wt:** 185 **Born:** 1/26/70 **Age:** 28

		HOW MUCH HE PITCHED						WHAT HE GAVE UP											THE RESULTS					
Year Team	Lg	G	GS	CG	GF	IP	BFP	H	R	ER	HR	SH	SF	HB	TBB	IBB	SO	WP	Bk	W	L	Pct.	ShO	Sv-Op	Hld	ERA
1990 Everett	A-	17	11	0	3	62.1	279	60	42	37	5	1	4	1	33	1	77	9	5	2	6	.250	0	0--	—	5.34
1991 Clinton	A	27	27	5	0	181.1	740	149	69	62	11	3	3	2	76	0	164	18	5	16	7	.696	3	0--	—	3.08
1992 Shreveport	AA	27	27	4	0	186	765	166	85	66	15	5	3	4	61	0	139	3	3	15	9	.625	1	0--	—	3.19
1993 Phoenix	AAA	13	12	0	0	70	320	79	54	51	12	2	1	5	32	1	48	4	0	5	6	.455	0	0--	—	6.56
Shreveport	AA	15	15	2	0	100.1	397	86	30	25	9	4	4	0	26	3	81	5	0	7	4	.636	1	0--	—	2.24
1994 Phoenix	AAA	31	22	0	2	151.1	665	173	80	78	21	3	9	1	55	1	117	10	0	13	6	.684	0	1--	—	4.64
1995 Phoenix	AAA	23	22	2	1	132.2	582	138	67	63	11	7	7	3	66	0	93	6	1	9	5	.643	0	0--	—	4.27
1996 Phoenix	AAA	33	15	2	3	146.2	604	135	61	56	18	5	5	2	46	0	123	3	0	13	6	.684	0	1--	—	3.44

Year Team	Lg	G	GS	CG	GF	IP	BFP	H	R	ER	HR	SH	SF	HB	TBB	IBB	SO	WP	Bk	W	L	Pct.	ShO	Sv-Op	Hld	ERA
1997 Bakersfield	A+	2	2	0	0	6	22	3	0	0	0	0	0	0	1	0	7	0	0	0	0	.000	0	0--	—	0.00
Phoenix	AAA	29	14	0	7	109	451	102	53	47	12	3	3	2	36	1	108	6	1	13	3	.813	0	3--	—	3.88
1996 San Francisco	NL	5	0	0	3	10	46	13	6	3	2	0	2	0	2	0	4	0	0	1	0	1.000	0	0-0	0	2.70
1997 San Francisco	NL	6	0	0	2	15.1	72	20	14	13	5	0	1	0	8	1	14	0	0	0	0	.000	0	0-0	0	7.63
2 ML YEARS		11	0	0	5	25.1	118	33	20	16	7	0	3	0	10	1	18	0	0	1	0	1.000	0	0-0	0	5.68

Rafael Carmona

Pitches: Right **Bats:** Left **Pos:** RP-4 **Ht:** 6'2" **Wt:** 185 **Born:** 10/2/72 **Age:** 25

Year Team	Lg	G	GS	CG	GF	IP	BFP	H	R	ER	HR	SH	SF	HB	TBB	IBB	SO	WP	Bk	W	L	Pct.	ShO	Sv-Op	Hld	ERA
1997 Tacoma *	AAA	32	5	0	19	59.1	263	52	31	25	7	2	1	2	35	2	56	3	2	2	5	.286	0	4--	—	3.79
1995 Seattle	AL	15	3	0	6	47.2	230	55	31	30	9	1	5	2	34	1	28	3	1	2	4	.333	0	1-2	0	5.66
1996 Seattle	AL	53	1	0	15	90.1	415	95	47	43	11	7	2	3	55	9	62	4	0	8	3	.727	0	1-5	8	4.28
1997 Seattle	AL	4	0	0	1	5.2	22	3	3	2	1	0	0	0	2	0	6	1	0	0	0	.000	0	0-0	0	3.18
3 ML YEARS		72	4	0	22	143.2	667	153	81	75	21	8	7	5	91	10	96	8	1	10	7	.588	0	2-7	8	4.70

Chris Carpenter

Pitches: Right **Bats:** Right **Pos:** SP-13; RP-1 **Ht:** 6'6" **Wt:** 215 **Born:** 4/27/75 **Age:** 23

Year Team	Lg	G	GS	CG	GF	IP	BFP	H	R	ER	HR	SH	SF	HB	TBB	IBB	SO	WP	Bk	W	L	Pct.	ShO	Sv-Op	Hld	ERA
1994 Medicne Hat	R+	15	15	0	0	84.2	366	76	40	26	3	2	3	8	39	0	80	9	2	6	3	.667	0	0--	—	2.76
1995 Dunedin	A+	15	15	0	0	99.1	420	83	29	24	3	2	4	5	50	0	56	9	3	3	5	.375	0	0--	—	2.17
Knoxville	AA	12	12	0	0	64.1	287	71	47	37	3	1	4	1	31	1	53	9	0	3	7	.300	0	0--	—	5.18
1996 Knoxville	AA	28	28	1	0	171.1	755	161	94	75	13	9	3	8	91	4	150	8	2	7	9	.438	0	0--	—	3.94
1997 Syracuse	AAA	19	19	3	0	120	499	113	64	60	16	2	1	3	53	0	97	6	0	4	9	.308	2	0--	—	4.50
1997 Toronto	AL	14	13	1	1	81.1	374	108	55	46	7	1	2	2	37	0	55	7	1	3	7	.300	1	0-0	0	5.09

Chuck Carr

Bats: Both **Throws:** Right **Pos:** CF-82; PH-16; LF-1 **Ht:** 5'10" **Wt:** 165 **Born:** 8/10/68 **Age:** 29

Year Team	Lg	G	AB	H	2B	3B	HR	(Hm	Rd)	TB	R	RBI	TBB	IBB	SO	HBP	SH	SF	SB	CS	SB%	GDP	Avg	OBP	SLG
1997 New Orleans *	AAA	19	65	16	1	0	0	—	—	17	8	3	8	0	14	0	0	0	5	3	.63	1	.246	.329	.262
1990 New York	NL	4	2	0	0	0	0	(0	0)	0	0	0	0	0	2	0	0	0	1	0	1.00	0	.000	.000	.000
1991 New York	NL	12	11	2	0	0	0	(0	0)	2	1	1	0	0	2	0	0	0	1	0	1.00	0	.182	.182	.182
1992 St. Louis	NL	22	64	14	3	0	0	(0	0)	17	8	3	9	0	6	0	3	0	10	2	.83	0	.219	.315	.266
1993 Florida	NL	142	551	147	19	2	4	(3	1)	182	75	41	49	0	74	2	7	4	58	22	.73	6	.267	.327	.330
1994 Florida	NL	106	433	114	19	2	2	(1	1)	143	61	30	22	1	71	5	6	2	32	8	.80	5	.263	.305	.330
1995 Florida	NL	105	308	70	20	0	2	(1	1)	96	54	20	46	1	49	2	7	2	25	11	.69	2	.227	.330	.312
1996 Milwaukee	AL	27	106	29	6	1	1	(0	1)	40	18	11	6	0	21	0	0	1	5	4	.56	1	.274	.310	.377
1997 Mil-Hou		89	238	59	14	2	4	(3	1)	89	37	17	17	2	48	1	3	1	12	5	.71	0	.248	.305	.374
1997 Milwaukee	AL	26	46	6	3	0	0	(0	0)	9	3	0	2	0	11	1	1	0	1	0	1.00	0	.130	.184	.196
Houston	NL	63	192	53	11	2	4	(3	1)	80	34	17	15	2	37	2	6	1	11	5	.69	0	.276	.333	.417
8 ML YEARS		507	1713	435	81	7	13	(8	5)	569	254	123	149	4	273	12	30	10	144	52	.73	14	.254	.316	.332

Giovanni Carrara

Pitches: Right **Bats:** Right **Pos:** SP-2 **Ht:** 6'2" **Wt:** 230 **Born:** 3/4/68 **Age:** 30

Year Team	Lg	G	GS	CG	GF	IP	BFP	H	R	ER	HR	SH	SF	HB	TBB	IBB	SO	WP	Bk	W	L	Pct.	ShO	Sv-Op	Hld	ERA
1997 Rochester *	AAA	8	8	1	0	46.2	196	45	23	23	4	1	3	2	16	0	48	1	0	4	2	.667	0	0--	—	4.44
Indianapols *	AAA	19	18	2	0	120.2	509	111	50	47	12	5	0	3	51	3	105	1	1	12	5	.706	0	0--	—	3.51
1995 Toronto	AL	12	7	1	2	48.2	229	64	46	39	10	1	2	1	25	1	27	1	0	2	4	.333	0	0-0	0	7.21
1996 Tor-Cin		19	5	0	4	38	188	54	36	34	11	1	0	2	25	3	23	1	0	1	1	.500	0	0-1	0	8.05
1997 Cincinnati	NL	2	2	0	0	10.1	49	14	9	9	4	1	0	0	6	1	5	0	0	0	1	.000	0	0-0	0	7.84
1996 Toronto	AL	11	0	0	3	15	76	23	19	19	5	0	0	0	12	2	10	1	0	0	0	.000	0	0-1	0	11.40
Cincinnati	NL	8	5	0	1	23	112	31	17	15	6	1	0	2	13	1	13	0	0	1	0	1.000	0	0-0	0	5.87
3 ML YEARS		33	14	1	6	97	466	132	91	82	25	3	2	3	56	5	55	2	0	3	6	.333	0	0-1	0	7.61

Hector Carrasco

Pitches: Right **Bats:** Right **Pos:** RP-66 **Ht:** 6'2" **Wt:** 180 **Born:** 10/22/69 **Age:** 28

Year Team	Lg	G	GS	CG	GF	IP	BFP	H	R	ER	HR	SH	SF	HB	TBB	IBB	SO	WP	Bk	W	L	Pct.	ShO	Sv-Op	Hld	ERA
1997 Indianapols *	AAA	3	0	0	2	4.1	20	5	3	3	1	0	0	0	3	0	4	0	0	0	0	.000	0	1--	—	6.23
1994 Cincinnati	NL	45	0	0	29	56.1	237	42	17	14	3	5	0	2	30	1	41	3	1	5	6	.455	0	6-8	3	2.24
1995 Cincinnati	NL	64	0	0	28	87.1	391	86	45	40	1	2	6	2	46	5	64	15	0	2	7	.222	0	5-9	11	4.12
1996 Cincinnati	NL	56	0	0	10	74.1	325	58	37	31	6	4	4	1	45	5	59	8	1	4	3	.571	0	0-2	15	3.75
1997 Cin-KC		66	0	0	22	86	388	80	46	42	7	4	3	8	41	5	76	11	2	2	8	.200	0	0-2	8	4.40
1997 Cincinnati	NL	38	0	0	11	51.1	223	51	25	21	3	3	1	4	25	2	46	3	2	1	2	.333	0	0-0	5	3.68
Kansas City	AL	28	0	0	11	34.2	151	29	21	21	4	1	2	4	16	3	30	8	0	1	6	.143	0	0-2	3	5.45
4 ML YEARS		231	0	0	89	304	1341	266	145	127	17	15	13	13	162	16	240	37	4	13	24	.351	0	11-21	37	3.76

Joe Carter

Bats: R **Throws:** R **Pos:** DH-64; 1B-42; LF-41; RF-10   **Ht:** 6'3" **Wt:** 215 **Born:** 3/7/60 **Age:** 38

Year Team	Lg	G	AB	H	2B	3B	HR	(Hm	Rd)	TB	R	RBI	TBB	IBB	SO	HBP	SH	SF	SB	CS	SB%	GDP	Avg	OBP	SLG
1983 Chicago	NL	23	51	9	1	1	0	(0	0)	12	6	1	0	0	21	0	1	0	1	0	1.00	1	.176	.176	.235
1984 Cleveland	AL	66	244	67	6	1	13	(9	4)	114	32	41	11	0	48	1	0	1	2	4	.33	2	.275	.307	.467
1985 Cleveland	AL	143	489	128	27	0	15	(5	10)	200	64	59	25	2	74	2	3	4	24	6	.80	9	.262	.298	.409
1986 Cleveland	AL	162	663	200	36	9	29	(14	15)	341	108	121	32	3	95	5	1	8	29	7	.81	8	.302	.335	.514
1987 Cleveland	AL	149	588	155	27	2	32	(9	23)	282	83	106	27	6	105	9	1	4	31	6	.84	8	.264	.304	.480
1988 Cleveland	AL	157	621	168	36	6	27	(16	11)	297	85	98	35	6	82	7	1	6	27	5	.84	6	.271	.314	.478
1989 Cleveland	AL	162	651	158	32	4	35	(16	19)	303	84	105	39	8	112	8	2	5	13	5	.72	6	.243	.292	.465
1990 San Diego	NL	162	634	147	27	1	24	(12	12)	248	79	115	48	18	93	7	0	8	22	6	.79	12	.232	.290	.391
1991 Toronto	AL	162	638	174	42	3	33	(23	10)	321	89	108	49	12	112	10	0	9	20	9	.69	6	.273	.330	.503
1992 Toronto	AL	158	622	164	30	7	34	(21	13)	310	97	119	36	4	109	11	1	13	12	5	.71	14	.264	.309	.498
1993 Toronto	AL	155	603	153	33	5	33	(21	12)	295	92	121	47	5	113	9	0	10	8	3	.73	10	.254	.312	.489
1994 Toronto	AL	111	435	118	25	2	27	(18	9)	228	70	103	33	6	64	2	0	13	11	0	1.00	6	.271	.317	.524
1995 Toronto	AL	139	558	141	23	0	25	(13	12)	239	70	76	37	5	87	3	0	5	12	1	.92	11	.253	.300	.428
1996 Toronto	AL	157	625	158	35	7	30	(14	16)	297	84	107	44	2	106	7	0	6	7	6	.54	12	.253	.306	.475
1997 Toronto	AL	157	612	143	30	4	21	(11	10)	244	76	102	40	5	105	7	0	9	8	2	.80	12	.234	.284	.399
15 ML YEARS		2063	8034	2083	410	52	378	(202	176)	3731	1119	1382	503	82	1326	88	10	101	227	65	.78	123	.259	.306	.464

Raul Casanova

Bats: Both **Throws:** Right **Pos:** C-92; PH-13; DH-1   **Ht:** 5'11" **Wt:** 200 **Born:** 8/23/72 **Age:** 25

Year Team	Lg	G	AB	H	2B	3B	HR	(Hm	Rd)	TB	R	RBI	TBB	IBB	SO	HBP	SH	SF	SB	CS	SB%	GDP	Avg	OBP	SLG
1990 Mets	R	23	65	5	0	0	0	—	—	5	4	1	4	0	16	0	0	0	0	1	.00	2	.077	.130	.077
1991 Mets	R	32	111	27	4	2	0	—	—	35	19	9	12	0	22	2	1	1	3	0	1.00	4	.243	.325	.315
Kingsport	R+	5	18	1	0	0	0	—	—	1	0	0	1	0	10	0	0	0	0	0	.00	1	.056	.105	.056
1992 Columbia	A	5	18	3	0	0	0	—	—	3	2	1	1	0	4	0	0	0	0	0	.00	2	.167	.211	.167
Kingsport	R+	42	137	37	9	1	4	—	—	60	25	27	26	2	25	4	0	0	3	1	.75	7	.270	.401	.438
1993 Waterloo	A	76	227	58	12	0	6	—	—	88	32	30	21	2	46	1	5	0	0	1	.00	5	.256	.321	.388
1994 Rancho Cuca	A+	123	471	160	27	2	23	—	—	260	83	120	43	2	97	9	0	3	1	4	.20	16	.340	.403	.552
1995 Memphis	AA	89	306	83	18	0	12	—	—	137	42	44	25	2	51	4	0	4	4	1	.80	7	.271	.330	.448
1996 Jacksnville	AA	8	30	10	2	0	4	—	—	24	5	9	2	0	7	0	0	0	0	0	.00	0	.333	.375	.800
Toledo	AAA	49	161	44	11	0	8	—	—	79	23	28	20	0	24	2	1	4	0	0	.00	11	.273	.353	.491
1997 Toledo	AAA	12	41	8	0	0	1	—	—	11	1	3	3	0	8	0	0	1	0	0	.00	1	.195	.244	.268
1996 Detroit	AL	25	85	16	1	0	4	(1	3)	29	6	9	6	0	18	0	0	0	0	0	.00	6	.188	.242	.341
1997 Detroit	AL	101	304	74	10	1	5	(5	0)	101	27	24	26	1	48	3	0	1	1	1	.50	10	.243	.308	.332
2 ML YEARS		126	389	90	11	1	9	(6	3)	130	33	33	32	1	66	3	0	1	1	1	.50	16	.231	.294	.334

Sean Casey

Bats: Left **Throws:** Right **Pos:** DH-3; PH-3; 1B-1   **Ht:** 6'4" **Wt:** 215 **Born:** 7/2/74 **Age:** 23

Year Team	Lg	G	AB	H	2B	3B	HR	(Hm	Rd)	TB	R	RBI	TBB	IBB	SO	HBP	SH	SF	SB	CS	SB%	GDP	Avg	OBP	SLG
1995 Watertown	A-	55	207	68	18	0	2	—	—	92	26	37	18	4	21	1	0	3	3	0	1.00	6	.329	.380	.444
1996 Kinston	A+	92	344	114	31	0	12	—	—	187	62	57	36	3	47	6	0	2	1	1	.50	5	.331	.402	.544
1997 Akron	AA	62	241	93	19	1	10	—	—	144	38	66	23	2	34	5	0	1	0	1	.00	5	.386	.448	.598
Buffalo	AAA	20	72	26	7	0	5	—	—	48	12	18	9	0	11	1	0	0	0	0	.00	0	.361	.439	.667
1997 Cleveland	AL	6	10	2	0	0	0	(0	0)	2	1	1	1	0	2	1	0	0	0	0	.00	0	.200	.333	.200

Larry Casian

Pitches: Left **Bats:** Right **Pos:** RP-44   **Ht:** 6'0" **Wt:** 175 **Born:** 10/28/65 **Age:** 32

Year Team	Lg	G	GS	CG	GF	IP	BFP	H	R	ER	HR	SH	SF	HB	TBB	IBB	SO	WP	Bk	W	L	Pct.	ShO	Sv-Op	Hld	ERA
1990 Minnesota	AL	5	3	0	1	22.1	90	26	9	8	2	0	1	0	4	0	11	0	0	2	1	.667	0	0-0	0	3.22
1991 Minnesota	AL	15	0	0	4	18.1	87	28	16	15	4	0	0	1	7	2	6	2	0	0	0	.000	0	0-0	1	7.36
1992 Minnesota	AL	6	0	0	1	6.2	28	7	2	2	0	0	0	1	0	0	2	0	0	1	0	1.000	0	0-0	1	2.70
1993 Minnesota	AL	54	0	0	8	56.2	241	59	23	19	1	3	3	1	14	2	31	2	0	5	3	.625	0	1-3	15	3.02
1994 Min-Cle	AL	40	0	0	10	49	231	73	43	40	12	7	2	2	16	3	20	1	0	1	5	.167	0	1-1	6	7.35
1995 Chicago	NL	42	0	0	5	23.1	107	23	6	5	1	1	2	0	15	6	11	2	0	1	0	1.000	0	0-3	4	1.93
1996 Chicago	NL	35	0	0	4	24	90	14	5	5	2	2	1	1	11	3	15	1	0	1	1	.500	0	0-1	5	1.88
1997 ChN-KC		44	0	0	7	36.1	164	48	24	23	8	1	3	1	8	2	23	1	0	0	3	.000	0	0-2	5	5.70
1994 Minnesota	AL	33	0	0	8	40.2	188	57	34	32	11	6	2	2	12	2	18	0	0	1	3	.250	0	1-1	5	7.08
Cleveland	AL	7	0	0	2	8.1	43	16	9	8	1	1	0	0	4	1	2	1	0	0	2	.000	0	0-0	1	8.64
1997 Chicago	NL	12	0	0	1	9.2	49	16	9	8	3	0	2	1	2	1	7	0	0	0	1	.000	0	0-0	0	7.45
Kansas City	AL	32	0	0	6	26.2	115	32	15	15	5	1	1	0	6	1	16	1	0	0	2	.000	0	0-2	5	5.06
8 ML YEARS		241	3	0	40	236.2	1038	278	128	117	30	14	12	6	76	18	119	9	0	11	13	.458	0	2-10	38	4.45

Vinny Castilla

Bats: Right **Throws:** Right **Pos:** 3B-157; PH-2   **Ht:** 6'1" **Wt:** 200 **Born:** 7/4/67 **Age:** 30

Year Team	Lg	G	AB	H	2B	3B	HR	(Hm	Rd)	TB	R	RBI	TBB	IBB	SO	HBP	SH	SF	SB	CS	SB%	GDP	Avg	OBP	SLG
1991 Atlanta	NL	12	5	1	0	0	0	(0	0)	1	1	0	0	0	2	0	1	0	0	0	.00	0	.200	.200	.200
1992 Atlanta	NL	9	16	4	1	0	0	(0	0)	5	1	1	1	1	4	1	0	0	0	0	.00	0	.250	.333	.313
1993 Colorado	NL	105	337	86	9	7	9	(5	4)	136	36	30	13	4	45	2	0	5	2	5	.29	10	.255	.283	.404

38

Year Team	Lg	G	AB	H	2B	3B	HR	(Hm	Rd)	TB	R	RBI	TBB	IBB	SO	HBP	SH	SF	SB	CS	SB%	GDP	Avg	OBP	SLG
1994 Colorado	NL	52	130	43	11	1	3	(1	2)	65	16	18	7	1	23	0	1	3	2	1	.67	3	.331	.357	.500
1995 Colorado	NL	139	527	163	34	2	32	(23	9)	297	82	90	30	2	87	4	4	6	2	8	.20	15	.309	.347	.564
1996 Colorado	NL	160	629	191	34	2	40	(27	13)	345	97	113	35	7	88	5	0	4	7	2	.78	20	.304	.343	.548
1997 Colorado	NL	159	612	186	25	2	40	(21	19)	335	94	113	44	9	108	8	0	4	2	4	.33	17	.304	.356	.547
7 ML YEARS		636	2256	674	114	12	124	(77	47)	1184	327	365	130	24	357	20	6	22	15	20	.43	65	.299	.339	.525

Alberto Castillo

Bats: Right Throws: Right Pos: C-34; PH-3   Ht: 6'0" Wt: 184 Born: 2/10/70 Age: 28

Year Team	Lg	G	AB	H	2B	3B	HR	(Hm	Rd)	TB	R	RBI	TBB	IBB	SO	HBP	SH	SF	SB	CS	SB%	GDP	Avg	OBP	SLG
1997 Norfolk *	AAA	34	83	18	1	0	1	—	—	22	4	8	17	1	16	0	3	1	1	0	1.00	3	.217	.347	.265
1995 New York	NL	13	29	3	0	0	0	(0	0)	3	2	0	3	0	9	1	0	0	0	0	.00	0	.103	.212	.103
1996 New York	NL	6	11	4	0	0	0	(0	0)	4	1	0	0	0	4	0	0	0	0	0	.00	0	.364	.364	.364
1997 New York	NL	35	59	12	1	0	0	(0	0)	13	3	7	9	0	16	1	2	1	0	1	.00	3	.203	.304	.220
3 ML YEARS		54	99	19	1	0	0	(0	0)	20	6	7	12	0	29	2	2	1	1	1	.50	3	.192	.283	.202

Carlos Castillo

Pitches: Right Bats: Right Pos: RP-35; SP-2   Ht: 6'2" Wt: 240 Born: 4/21/75 Age: 23

Year Team	Lg	G	GS	CG	GF	IP	BFP	H	R	ER	HR	SH	SF	HB	TBB	IBB	SO	WP	Bk	W	L	Pct.	ShO	Sv-Op	Hld	ERA
1994 White Sox	R	12	12	0	0	59	239	53	20	17	4	2	2	2	10	0	57	3	4	4	3	.571	0	0--	—	2.59
Hickory	A	3	1	0	2	12	42	3	0	0	0	0	0	1	2	0	17	0	0	2	0	1.000	0	0--	—	0.00
1995 Hickory	A	14	12	2	2	79.2	343	85	42	33	11	1	3	3	18	0	67	3	6	5	6	.455	0	1--	—	3.73
1996 South Bend	A	20	19	5	1	133.1	557	131	74	60	12	3	9	5	29	0	128	9	6	9	9	.500	0	0--	—	4.05
Pr William	A+	6	6	4	0	43.1	180	45	22	19	0	3	5	2	4	1	30	1	1	2	4	.333	0	0--	—	3.95
1997 Nashville	AAA	4	0	0	4	6	24	4	1	1	0	0	0	0	0	0	4	0	0	0	0	.000	0	3--	—	1.50
1997 Chicago	AL	37	2	0	14	66.1	295	68	35	33	9	0	4	1	33	3	43	3	0	2	1	.667	0	1-1	3	4.48

Frank Castillo

Pitches: Right Bats: Right Pos: SP-33; RP-1   Ht: 6'1" Wt: 200 Born: 4/1/69 Age: 29

Year Team	Lg	G	GS	CG	GF	IP	BFP	H	R	ER	HR	SH	SF	HB	TBB	IBB	SO	WP	Bk	W	L	Pct.	ShO	Sv-Op	Hld	ERA
1991 Chicago	NL	18	18	4	0	111.2	467	107	56	54	5	6	3	0	33	2	73	5	1	6	7	.462	0	0-0	0	4.35
1992 Chicago	NL	33	33	0	0	205.1	856	179	91	79	19	11	5	6	63	6	135	11	0	10	11	.476	0	0-0	0	3.46
1993 Chicago	NL	29	25	2	0	141.1	614	162	83	76	20	10	3	9	39	4	84	5	3	5	8	.385	0	0-0	0	4.84
1994 Chicago	NL	4	4	1	0	23	96	25	13	11	3	1	0	0	5	0	19	0	0	2	1	.667	0	0-0	0	4.30
1995 Chicago	NL	29	29	2	0	188	795	179	76	67	22	11	3	6	52	4	135	3	1	11	10	.524	2	0-0	0	3.21
1996 Chicago	NL	33	33	1	0	182.1	789	209	112	107	28	4	5	8	46	4	139	2	1	7	16	.304	1	0-0	0	5.28
1997 ChN-Col	NL	34	33	0	0	184.1	830	220	121	111	25	17	2	8	69	4	126	3	0	12	12	.500	0	0-0	0	5.42
1997 Chicago	NL	20	19	0	0	98	446	113	64	59	9	11	0	4	44	1	67	1	0	6	9	.400	0	0-0	0	5.42
Colorado	NL	14	14	0	0	86.1	384	107	57	52	16	6	2	4	25	3	59	2	0	6	3	.667	0	0-0	0	5.42
7 ML YEARS		180	175	10	0	1036	4447	1081	551	505	122	60	21	37	307	24	711	29	6	53	65	.449	3	0-0	0	4.39

Luis Castillo

Bats: Both Throws: Right Pos: 2B-70; PH-6   Ht: 5'11" Wt: 155 Born: 9/12/75 Age: 22

Year Team	Lg	G	AB	H	2B	3B	HR	(Hm	Rd)	TB	R	RBI	TBB	IBB	SO	HBP	SH	SF	SB	CS	SB%	GDP	Avg	OBP	SLG
1994 Marlins	R	57	216	57	8	0	0	—	—	65	49	16	37	0	36	1	2	1	31	12	.72	1	.264	.371	.301
1995 Kane County	A	89	340	111	4	4	0	—	—	123	71	23	55	1	50	0	4	1	41	18	.69	1	.326	.419	.362
1996 Portland	AA	109	420	133	15	7	1	—	—	165	83	35	66	4	68	2	6	1	51	28	.65	2	.317	.411	.393
1997 Charlotte	AAA	37	130	46	5	0	0	—	—	51	25	5	16	0	22	0	3	0	8	6	.57	1	.354	.425	.392
1996 Florida	NL	41	164	43	2	1	1	(0	1)	50	26	8	14	0	46	0	2	0	17	4	.81	0	.262	.320	.305
1997 Florida	NL	75	263	63	8	0	0	(0	0)	71	27	8	27	0	53	0	1	0	16	10	.62	6	.240	.310	.270
2 ML YEARS		116	427	106	10	1	1	(0	1)	121	53	16	41	0	99	0	3	0	33	14	.70	6	.248	.314	.283

Tony Castillo

Pitches: Left Bats: Left Pos: RP-64   Ht: 5'10" Wt: 190 Born: 3/1/63 Age: 35

Year Team	Lg	G	GS	CG	GF	IP	BFP	H	R	ER	HR	SH	SF	HB	TBB	IBB	SO	WP	Bk	W	L	Pct.	ShO	Sv-Op	Hld	ERA
1988 Toronto	AL	14	0	0	6	15	54	10	5	5	2	0	2	0	2	0	14	0	0	1	0	1.000	0	0-0	1	3.00
1989 Tor-Atl		29	0	0	9	27	127	31	19	17	3	4	1	4	14	6	15	3	0	1	2	.333	0	1-1	6	5.67
1990 Atlanta	NL	52	3	0	7	76.2	337	93	41	36	5	4	4	1	20	3	64	2	2	5	1	.833	0	1-2	3	4.23
1991 Atl-NYN	NL	17	3	0	6	32.1	148	40	16	12	4	2	1	0	11	1	18	0	0	2	1	.667	0	0-0	1	3.34
1993 Toronto	AL	51	0	0	10	50.2	211	44	19	19	4	5	2	0	22	5	28	1	0	3	2	.600	0	0-1	13	3.38
1994 Toronto	AL	41	0	0	8	68	291	66	22	19	7	3	3	3	28	1	43	0	0	5	2	.714	0	1-4	13	2.51
1995 Toronto	AL	55	0	0	31	72.2	298	64	27	26	7	3	5	3	24	1	58	0	0	1	5	.167	0	13-21	5	3.22
1996 Tor-ChA	AL	55	0	0	13	95	398	95	45	38	10	3	5	3	24	2	57	3	0	5	4	.556	0	2-6	9	3.60
1997 Chicago	AL	64	0	0	20	62.1	283	74	48	34	6	9	0	1	23	7	42	0	0	4	4	.500	0	4-9	15	4.91
1989 Toronto	AL	17	0	0	8	17.2	65	23	14	12	2	0	4	0	10	5	10	3	0	1	1	.500	0	1-1	2	6.11
Atlanta	NL	12	0	0	1	9.1	41	8	5	5	0	1	0	0	4	1	5	0	0	0	1	.000	0	0-0	4	4.82
1991 Atlanta	NL	7	0	0	5	8.2	44	13	9	7	3	1	0	0	5	0	8	0	0	1	1	.500	0	0-0	1	7.27
New York	NL	10	3	0	1	23.2	104	27	7	5	1	1	1	0	6	1	10	0	0	2	0	1.000	0	0-0	1	1.90

Year Team	Lg	G	GS	CG	GF	IP	BFP	H	R	ER	HR	SH	SF	HB	TBB	IBB	SO	WP	Bk	W	L	Pct.	ShO	Sv-Op	Hld	ERA
1996 Toronto	AL	40	0	0	7	72.1	304	72	38	34	9	3	2	2	20	1	48	2	0	2	3	.400	0	1-2	6	4.23
Chicago	AL	15	0	0	6	22.2	94	23	7	4	1	0	3	1	4	1	9	1	0	3	1	.750	0	1-4	3	1.59
9 ML YEARS		378	6	0	110	499.2	2147	517	242	206	45	32	26	12	168	26	319	9	2	27	21	.563	0	22-44	66	3.71

Juan Castro

Bats: R **Throws:** R **Pos:** SS-22; 2B-14; PH-6; 3B-3   **Ht:** 5'10" **Wt:** 163 **Born:** 6/20/72 **Age:** 26

							BATTING									BASERUNNING				PERCENTAGES		
Year Team	Lg	G	AB	H	2B	3B	HR	(Hm	Rd)	TB	R	RBI	TBB	IBB	SO	HBP	SH	SF	SB	CS	SB%	GDP	Avg	OBP	SLG
1997 Albuquerque *	AAA	27	101	31	5	2	2	—	—	46	11	11	4	0	20	0	1	2	1	0	1.00	5	.307	.327	.455
1995 Los Angeles	NL	11	4	1	0	0	0	(0	0)	1	0	0	1	0	1	0	0	0	0	0	.00	0	.250	.400	.250
1996 Los Angeles	NL	70	132	26	5	3	0	(0	0)	37	16	5	10	0	27	0	4	0	1	0	1.00	3	.197	.254	.280
1997 Los Angeles	NL	40	75	11	3	1	0	(0	0)	16	3	4	7	1	20	0	2	0	0	0	.00	2	.147	.220	.213
3 ML YEARS		121	211	38	8	4	0			54	19	9	18	1	48	0	6	0	1	0	1.00	5	.180	.245	.256

Frank Catalanotto

Bats: Left **Throws:** Right **Pos:** 2B-6; PH-6; DH-3   **Ht:** 6'0" **Wt:** 170 **Born:** 4/27/74 **Age:** 24

							BATTING									BASERUNNING				PERCENTAGES		
Year Team	Lg	G	AB	H	2B	3B	HR	(Hm	Rd)	TB	R	RBI	TBB	IBB	SO	HBP	SH	SF	SB	CS	SB%	GDP	Avg	OBP	SLG
1992 Bristol	R+	50	10	2	0	0	—	—		12	6	4	8	0	8	0	0	0	0	1	.00	0	.200	.310	.240
1993 Bristol	R+	55	199	61	9	5	3	—	—	89	37	22	15	1	19	3	3	0	3	6	.33	3	.307	.364	.447
1994 Fayetteville	A	119	458	149	24	8	3	—	—	198	72	56	37	1	54	3	5	1	4	5	.44	4	.325	.379	.432
1995 Jacksnville	AA	134	491	111	19	5	8	—	—	164	66	48	49	4	56	9	6	4	13	8	.62	9	.226	.306	.334
1996 Jacksnville	AA	132	497	148	34	6	17	—	—	245	105	67	74	8	69	11	3	3	15	14	.52	8	.298	.398	.493
1997 Toledo	AAA	134	500	150	32	3	16	—	—	236	75	68	47	6	80	10	1	6	12	11	.52	9	.300	.368	.472
1997 Detroit	AL	13	26	8	2	0	0	(0	0)	10	2	3	3	0	7	0	0	0	0	0	.00	0	.308	.379	.385

Mike Cather

Pitches: Right **Bats:** Right **Pos:** RP-35   **Ht:** 6'2" **Wt:** 195 **Born:** 12/17/70 **Age:** 27

								WHAT HE GAVE UP											THE RESULTS					
Year Team	Lg	G	GS	CG	GF	IP	BFP	H	R	ER	HR	SH	SF	HB	TBB	IBB	SO	WP	Bk	W	L	Pct.	ShO	Sv-Op	Hld	ERA
1993 Rangers	R	25	0	0	17	30.2	124	20	7	6	0	0	3	9	0	30	0	1	1	1	.500	0	4- -	—	1.76
1994 Charlotte	A+	44	0	0	37	60.1	270	56	33	26	2	3	2	3	40	3	53	1	0	8	6	.571	0	6- -	—	3.88
1995 Tulsa	AA	18	0	0	12	21.2	90	20	11	8	0	4	1	1	7	5	15	0	0	2	2	.000	0	0- -	—	3.32
Winnipeg	IND	27	0	0	24	31	123	18	6	5	1	2	0	0	12	3	35	2	0	4	2	.667	0	8- -	—	1.45
1996 Greenville	AA	53	0	0	18	87.2	384	89	42	36	2	6	2	8	29	5	61	2	1	3	4	.429	0	5- -	—	3.70
1997 Greenville	AA	22	0	0	2	37.1	153	37	18	18	2	1	2	6	7	1	29	0	0	5	2	.714	0	1- -	—	4.34
Richmond	AAA	13	0	0	10	26	102	17	6	5	1	2	0	1	9	1	22	0	0	0	0	.000	0	3- -	—	1.73
1997 Atlanta	NL	35	0	0	10	37.2	155	23	12	10	1	2	0	2	19	4	29	0	0	2	4	.333	0	0-3	4	2.39

Domingo Cedeno

Bats: B **Throws:** R **Pos:** 2B-65; SS-43; PH-21; 3B-3; DH-2   **Ht:** 6'0" **Wt:** 170 **Born:** 11/4/68 **Age:** 29

							BATTING									BASERUNNING				PERCENTAGES		
Year Team	Lg	G	AB	H	2B	3B	HR	(Hm | Rd)	TB	R	RBI	TBB	IBB	SO	HBP	SH	SF	SB	CS	SB%	GDP	Avg	OBP	SLG
1997 Tulsa *	AA	2	9	4	0	1	0	—	—	6	0	0	0	0	3	0	0	0	0	0	.00	0	.444	.444	.667
Okla City *	AAA	6	28	10	2	0	0	—	—	12	0	2	0	0	6	0	0	0	0	1	.00	1	.357	.357	.429
1993 Toronto	AL	15	46	8	0	0	0	(0 | 0)	8	5	7	1	0	10	0	2	1	1	0	1.00	2	.174	.188	.174
1994 Toronto	AL	47	97	19	2	3	0	(0 | 0)	27	14	10	10	0	31	0	3	4	1	2	.33	1	.196	.261	.278
1995 Toronto	AL	51	161	38	6	1	4	(1 | 3)	58	18	14	10	0	35	2	1	0	0	1	.00	3	.236	.289	.360
1996 Tor-ChA	AL	89	301	82	12	2	2	(0 | 2)	104	46	20	15	0	64	2	8	3	6	3	.67	7	.272	.308	.346
1997 Texas	AL	113	365	103	19	6	4	(2 | 2)	146	49	36	27	0	77	2	2	1	3	3	.50	5	.282	.334	.400
1996 Toronto	AL	77	282	79	10	2	2	(0 | 2)	99	44	17	15	0	60	2	7	1	5	3	.63	6	.280	.320	.351
Chicago	AL	12	19	3	2	0	0	(0 | 0)	5	2	3	0	0	4	0	1	2	1	0	1.00	1	.158	.143	.263
5 ML YEARS		315	970	250	39	12	10	(3 | 7)	343	132	87	63	0	217	6	16	9	11	9	.55	18	.258	.304	.354

Roger Cedeno

Bats: B **Throws:** R **Pos:** CF-55; LF-13; PH-13; RF-4   **Ht:** 6'1" **Wt:** 165 **Born:** 8/16/74 **Age:** 23

							BATTING									BASERUNNING				PERCENTAGES		
Year Team	Lg	G	AB	H	2B	3B	HR	(Hm | Rd)	TB	R	RBI	TBB	IBB	SO	HBP	SH	SF	SB	CS	SB%	GDP	Avg	OBP	SLG
1997 Albuquerque *	AAA	29	113	40	4	4	2	—	—	58	21	9	22	0	16	1	0	0	5	5	.50	1	.354	.463	.513
1995 Los Angeles	NL	40	42	10	2	0	0	(0 | 0)	12	4	3	3	0	10	0	0	1	1	0	1.00	1	.238	.283	.286
1996 Los Angeles	NL	86	211	52	11	1	2	(0 | 2)	71	26	18	24	0	47	1	2	0	5	1	.83	0	.246	.326	.336
1997 Los Angeles	NL	80	194	53	10	2	3	(3 | 0)	76	31	17	25	2	44	3	3	2	9	1	.90	1	.273	.362	.392
3 ML YEARS		206	447	115	23	3	5	(3 | 2)	159	61	38	52	2	101	4	5	3	15	2	.88	2	.257	.338	.356

Norm Charlton

Pitches: Left **Bats:** Both **Pos:** RP-71   **Ht:** 6'3" **Wt:** 205 **Born:** 1/6/63 **Age:** 35

								WHAT HE GAVE UP											THE RESULTS					
Year Team	Lg	G	GS	CG	GF	IP	BFP	H	R	ER	HR	SH	SF	HB	TBB	IBB	SO	WP	Bk	W	L	Pct.	ShO	Sv-Op	Hld	ERA
1988 Cincinnati	NL	10	10	0	0	61.1	259	60	27	27	6	1	2	2	20	2	39	3	2	4	5	.444	0	0-0	0	3.96
1989 Cincinnati	NL	69	0	0	27	95.1	393	67	38	31	5	9	2	2	40	7	98	2	4	8	3	.727	0	0-1	8	2.93

HOW MUCH HE PITCHED								WHAT HE GAVE UP												THE RESULTS						
Year Team	Lg	G	GS	CG	GF	IP	BFP	H	R	ER	HR	SH	SF	HB	TBB	IBB	SO	WP	Bk	W	L	Pct.	ShO	Sv-Op	Hld	ERA
1990 Cincinnati	NL	56	16	1	13	154.1	650	131	53	47	10	7	2	4	70	4	117	9	1	12	9	.571	1	2-3	9	2.74
1991 Cincinnati	NL	39	11	0	10	108.1	438	92	37	35	6	7	1	6	34	4	77	11	0	3	5	.375	0	1-4	3	2.91
1992 Cincinnati	NL	64	0	0	46	81.1	341	79	39	27	7	7	3	3	26	4	90	8	0	4	2	.667	0	26-34	7	2.99
1993 Seattle	AL	34	0	0	29	34.2	141	22	12	9	4	0	1	0	17	0	48	6	0	1	3	.250	0	18-21	1	2.34
1995 Phi-Sea		55	0	0	27	69.2	284	46	31	26	4	4	2	4	31	3	70	6	1	4	6	.400	0	14-16	12	3.36
1996 Seattle	AL	70	0	0	50	75.2	323	68	37	34	7	3	2	1	38	1	73	9	0	4	7	.364	0	20-27	8	4.04
1997 Seattle	AL	71	0	0	38	69.1	343	89	59	56	7	7	0	4	47	2	55	7	1	3	8	.273	0	14-25	9	7.27
1995 Philadelphia	NL	25	0	0	5	22	102	23	19	18	2	1	1	3	15	3	12	1	0	2	5	.286	0	0-1	9	7.36
Seattle	AL	30	0	0	22	47.2	182	23	12	8	2	3	1	1	16	0	58	5	1	2	1	.667	0	14-15	3	1.51
9 ML YEARS		468	37	1	240	750	3172	654	333	292	56	45	15	26	323	27	667	61	9	43	48	.473	1	95-131	57	3.50

Anthony Chavez

Pitches: Right **Bats:** Right **Pos:** RP-7   **Ht:** 5'10" **Wt:** 180 **Born:** 10/22/70 **Age:** 27

HOW MUCH HE PITCHED								WHAT HE GAVE UP												THE RESULTS						
Year Team	Lg	G	GS	CG	GF	IP	BFP	H	R	ER	HR	SH	SF	HB	TBB	IBB	SO	WP	Bk	W	L	Pct.	ShO	Sv-Op	Hld	ERA
1992 Boise	A-	14	0	0	2	16	75	22	13	7	0	0	0	0	4	2	21	3	0	1	1	.500	0	0- -	—	3.94
1993 Cedar Rapds	A	41	0	0	35	59.1	252	44	17	10	1	6	2	2	24	2	87	3	1	4	5	.444	0	16- -	—	1.52
Midland	AA	5	0	0	3	8.2	41	11	5	4	1	0	1	0	4	1	9	3	0	0	0	.000	0	1- -	—	4.15
1994 Lk Elsinore	A+	12	0	0	7	13.1	75	21	19	15	0	2	1	2	11	2	12	2	0	5	0	.000	0	1- -	—	10.13
Cedar Rapds	A	39	1	0	34	50	227	48	33	24	0	3	2	2	28	4	52	7	0	4	3	.571	0	16- -	—	4.32
1995 Vancouver	AAA	8	0	0	5	12	46	7	4	2	0	1	0	0	4	0	8	0	0	2	0	1.000	0	1- -	—	1.50
Midland	AA	7	0	0	6	9	42	13	9	8	1	0	0	1	1	0	4	1	0	0	1	.000	0	2- -	—	8.00
Lk Elsinore	A+	33	0	0	14	44.2	206	51	28	21	2	2	3	4	19	2	49	5	0	3	0	1.000	0	0- -	—	4.23
1996 Lk Elsinore	A+	10	0	0	8	13.2	53	8	4	3	0	0	0	3	3	0	16	0	0	3	0	1.000	0	4- -	—	1.98
Midland	AA	31	0	0	16	72.2	322	81	40	34	4	6	7	2	24	2	55	3	1	4	4	.333	0	1- -	—	4.21
1997 Midland	AA	33	1	0	15	47	200	53	23	22	1	3	2	3	15	1	35	4	0	1	2	.333	0	6- -	—	4.21
Vancouver	AAA	28	0	0	26	28.1	111	21	8	8	2	0	1	1	6	0	22	3	0	4	1	.800	0	15- -	—	2.54
1997 Anaheim	AL	7	0	0	2	9.2	41	7	1	1	1	1	0	1	5	1	10	0	0	0	0	.000	0	0-0	0	0.93

Raul Chavez

Bats: Right **Throws:** Right **Pos:** C-13; PH-4   **Ht:** 5'11" **Wt:** 175 **Born:** 3/18/73 **Age:** 25

BATTING																		BASERUNNING				PERCENTAGES		
Year Team	Lg	G	AB	H	2B	3B	HR	(Hm	Rd)	TB	R	RBI	TBB	IBB	SO	HBP	SH	SF	SB	CS	SB%	GDP	Avg	OBP	SLG
1990 Astros	R	48	155	50	8	1	0	—	—	60	23	23	7	0	12	2	2	1	5	3	.63	7	.323	.358	.387
1991 Burlington	A	114	420	108	17	0	3	—	—	134	54	41	25	1	64	10	3	4	1	4	.20	13	.257	.312	.319
1992 Asheville	A	95	348	99	22	1	2	—	—	129	37	40	16	1	39	4	1	4	1	1	.50	12	.284	.261	.264
1993 Osceola	A+	58	197	45	5	1	0	—	—	52	13	16	8	0	19	1	1	1	1	1	.50	12	.228	.261	.264
1994 Jackson	AA	89	251	55	7	0	1	—	—	65	17	22	17	3	41	2	2	1	1	0	1.00	5	.219	.273	.259
1995 Jackson	AA	58	188	54	8	0	4	—	—	74	16	25	8	1	17	3	4	2	0	4	.00	7	.287	.323	.394
Tucson	AAA	32	103	27	5	0	0	—	—	32	14	10	8	0	13	2	1	1	0	1	.00	7	.262	.325	.311
1996 Ottawa	AAA	60	198	49	10	0	2	—	—	65	15	24	11	0	31	1	4	0	0	2	.00	7	.247	.290	.328
1997 Ottawa	AAA	92	310	76	17	0	4	—	—	105	31	46	18	1	42	4	3	3	1	3	.25	9	.245	.293	.339
1996 Montreal	NL	4	5	1	0	0	0	(0	0)	1	0	1	0	1	0	0	0	0	1	0	1.00	1	.200	.333	.200
1997 Montreal	NL	13	26	7	0	0	0	(0	0)	7	0	2	0	0	5	0	0	0	1	0	1.00	0	.269	.259	.269
2 ML YEARS		17	31	8	0	0	0	(0 | 0)	8	0	3	1	2	1	0	6	0	0	0	2	1.00	1	.258	.273	.258

Robinson Checo

Pitches: Right **Bats:** Right **Pos:** RP-3; SP-2   **Ht:** 6'1" **Wt:** 185 **Born:** 9/9/71 **Age:** 26

HOW MUCH HE PITCHED								WHAT HE GAVE UP												THE RESULTS						
Year Team	Lg	G	GS	CG	GF	IP	BFP	H	R	ER	HR	SH	SF	HB	TBB	IBB	SO	WP	Bk	W	L	Pct.	ShO	Sv-Op	Hld	ERA
1997 Sarasota	A+	11	11	0	0	56	250	54	37	33	9	3	5	1	27	0	63	4	5	1	4	.200	0	0- -	—	5.30
Trenton	AA	1	1	0	0	7.2	29	6	3	2	1	0	1	0	1	0	9	0	0	1	0	1.000	0	0- -	—	2.35
Pawtucket	AAA	9	9	2	0	55.1	220	41	22	21	8	1	0	0	16	0	56	3	0	4	2	.667	1	0- -	—	3.42
1997 Boston	AL	5	2	0	1	13.1	54	12	5	5	0	0	0	0	3	0	14	0	0	1	1	.500	0	0-0	1	3.38

Jason Christiansen

Pitches: Left **Bats:** Right **Pos:** RP-39   **Ht:** 6'5" **Wt:** 230 **Born:** 9/21/69 **Age:** 28

HOW MUCH HE PITCHED								WHAT HE GAVE UP												THE RESULTS						
Year Team	Lg	G	GS	CG	GF	IP	BFP	H	R	ER	HR	SH	SF	HB	TBB	IBB	SO	WP	Bk	W	L	Pct.	ShO	Sv-Op	Hld	ERA
1997 Carolina *	AA	8	1	0	3	15	63	17	7	7	1	0	0	0	5	0	25	0	0	0	1	.000	0	1- -	—	4.20
1995 Pittsburgh	NL	63	0	0	13	56.1	255	49	28	26	5	8	3	3	34	9	53	4	1	1	3	.250	0	0-4	12	4.15
1996 Pittsburgh	NL	33	0	0	9	44.1	205	56	34	33	7	2	3	1	19	2	38	4	1	3	3	.500	0	0-2	5	6.70
1997 Pittsburgh	NL	39	0	0	9	33.2	154	37	11	11	2	0	0	2	17	3	37	4	0	3	0	1.000	0	0-2	8	2.94
3 ML YEARS		135	0	0	31	134.1	614	142	73	70	14	8	6	6	70	14	128	12	2	7	6	.538	0	0-8	22	4.69

Archi Cianfrocco

Bats: R **Throws:** R **Pos:** 1B-39; 3B-38; 2B-12; PH-9; SS-5; RF-2   **Ht:** 6'5" **Wt:** 215 **Born:** 10/6/66 **Age:** 31

BATTING																		BASERUNNING				PERCENTAGES		
Year Team	Lg	G	AB	H	2B	3B	HR	(Hm	Rd)	TB	R	RBI	TBB	IBB	SO	HBP	SH	SF	SB	CS	SB%	GDP	Avg	OBP	SLG
1992 Montreal	NL	86	232	56	5	2	6	(3	3)	83	25	30	11	0	66	1	1	3	3	0	1.00	2	.241	.276	.358
1993 Mon-SD	NL	96	296	72	11	2	12	(6	6)	123	30	48	17	1	69	3	2	5	2	0	1.00	9	.243	.287	.416
1994 San Diego	NL	59	146	32	8	0	4	(3	1)	52	9	13	3	0	39	4	1	2	2	0	1.00	2	.219	.252	.356

Year Team	Lg	G	AB	H	2B	3B	HR	(Hm	Rd)	TB	R	RBI	TBB	IBB	SO	HBP	SH	SF	SB	CS	SB%	GDP	Avg	OBP	SLG
		BATTING																	BASERUNNING				PERCENTAGES		
1995 San Diego	NL	51	118	31	7	0	5	(1	4)	53	22	31	11	1	28	2	0	1	0	2	.00	3	.263	.333	.449
1996 San Diego	NL	79	192	54	13	3	2	(0	2)	79	21	32	8	0	56	2	0	1	1	0	1.00	4	.281	.315	.411
1997 San Diego	NL	89	220	54	12	0	4	(3	1)	78	25	26	25	1	80	3	1	2	7	1	.88	11	.245	.328	.355
1993 Montreal	NL	12	17	4	1	0	1	(0	1)	8	3	1	0	0	5	0	0	0	0	0	.00	0	.235	.235	.471
San Diego	NL	84	279	68	10	2	11	(6	5)	115	27	47	17	1	64	3	2	5	2	0	1.00	9	.244	.289	.412
6 ML YEARS		460	1204	299	56	7	33	(16	17)	468	132	180	75	3	338	15	5	13	15	3	.83	31	.248	.298	.389

Jeff Cirillo

Bats: Right **Throws:** Right **Pos:** 3B-150; PH-4; DH-2 **Ht:** 6'2" **Wt:** 188 **Born:** 9/23/69 **Age:** 28

Year Team	Lg	G	AB	H	2B	3B	HR	(Hm	Rd)	TB	R	RBI	TBB	IBB	SO	HBP	SH	SF	SB	CS	SB%	GDP	Avg	OBP	SLG
		BATTING																	BASERUNNING				PERCENTAGES		
1994 Milwaukee	AL	39	126	30	9	0	3	(1	2)	48	17	12	11	0	16	2	0	0	0	1	.00	4	.238	.309	.381
1995 Milwaukee	AL	125	328	91	19	4	9	(6	3)	145	57	39	47	0	42	4	1	4	7	2	.78	8	.277	.371	.442
1996 Milwaukee	AL	158	566	184	46	5	15	(6	9)	285	101	83	58	0	69	7	6	6	4	9	.31	14	.325	.391	.504
1997 Milwaukee	AL	154	580	167	46	2	10	(6	4)	247	74	82	60	0	74	14	4	3	4	3	.57	13	.288	.367	.426
4 ML YEARS		476	1600	472	120	11	37	(19	18)	725	249	216	176	0	201	27	11	13	15	15	.50	39	.295	.372	.453

Dave Clark

Bats: L **Throws:** R **Pos:** PH-76; LF-24; DH-4; RF-1 **Ht:** 6'2" **Wt:** 209 **Born:** 9/3/62 **Age:** 35

Year Team	Lg	G	AB	H	2B	3B	HR	(Hm	Rd)	TB	R	RBI	TBB	IBB	SO	HBP	SH	SF	SB	CS	SB%	GDP	Avg	OBP	SLG
		BATTING																	BASERUNNING				PERCENTAGES		
1986 Cleveland	AL	18	58	16	1	0	3	(1	2)	26	10	9	7	0	11	0	2	1	1	0	1.00	1	.276	.348	.448
1987 Cleveland	AL	29	87	18	5	0	3	(1	2)	32	11	12	2	0	24	0	0	0	1	0	1.00	4	.207	.225	.368
1988 Cleveland	AL	63	156	41	4	1	3	(2	1)	56	11	18	17	2	28	0	0	1	0	2	.00	8	.263	.333	.359
1989 Cleveland	AL	102	253	60	12	0	8	(4	4)	96	21	29	30	5	63	0	1	1	0	2	.00	7	.237	.317	.379
1990 Chicago	NL	84	171	47	4	2	5	(3	2)	70	22	20	8	1	40	0	0	2	7	1	.88	4	.275	.304	.409
1991 Kansas City	AL	11	10	2	0	0	0	(0	0)	2	1	1	1	0	1	0	0	0	0	0	.00	0	.200	.273	.200
1992 Pittsburgh	NL	23	33	7	0	0	2	(2	0)	13	3	7	6	0	8	0	0	1	0	0	.00	0	.212	.325	.394
1993 Pittsburgh	NL	110	277	75	11	2	11	(8	3)	123	43	46	38	5	58	1	0	2	1	0	1.00	10	.271	.358	.444
1994 Pittsburgh	NL	86	223	66	11	1	10	(7	3)	109	37	46	22	0	48	0	1	3	2	2	.50	5	.296	.355	.489
1995 Pittsburgh	NL	77	196	55	6	0	4	(2	2)	73	30	24	24	1	38	1	0	2	3	3	.50	9	.281	.359	.372
1996 Pit-LA	NL	107	226	61	12	2	8	(6	2)	101	28	36	34	3	53	0	0	1	2	1	.67	6	.270	.364	.447
1997 Chicago	NL	102	143	43	8	0	5	(1	4)	66	19	32	19	3	34	2	0	2	1	0	1.00	2	.301	.386	.462
1996 Pittsburgh	NL	92	211	58	12	2	8	(6	2)	98	28	35	31	3	51	0	0	1	2	1	.67	6	.275	.366	.464
Los Angeles	NL	15	15	3	0	0	0	(0	0)	3	0	1	3	0	2	0	0	0	0	0	.00	0	.200	.333	.200
12 ML YEARS		812	1833	491	74	8	62	(37	25)	767	236	280	208	20	406	4	4	16	18	11	.62	56	.268	.341	.418

Mark Clark

Pitches: Right **Bats:** Right **Pos:** SP-31; RP-1 **Ht:** 6'5" **Wt:** 225 **Born:** 5/12/68 **Age:** 30

Year Team	Lg	G	GS	CG	GF	IP	BFP	H	R	ER	HR	SH	SF	HB	TBB	IBB	SO	WP	Bk	W	L	Pct.	ShO	Sv-Op	Hld	ERA
		HOW MUCH HE PITCHED						WHAT HE GAVE UP												THE RESULTS						
1991 St. Louis	NL	7	2	0	1	22.1	93	17	10	10	3	0	3	0	11	0	13	2	0	1	1	.500	0	0-0	1	4.03
1992 St. Louis	NL	20	20	1	0	113.1	488	117	59	56	12	7	4	0	36	2	44	4	0	3	10	.231	1	0-0	0	4.45
1993 Cleveland	AL	26	15	1	1	109.1	454	119	55	52	18	1	1	1	25	1	57	1	0	7	5	.583	0	0-0	2	4.28
1994 Cleveland	AL	20	20	4	0	127.1	540	133	61	54	14	2	7	4	40	0	60	9	1	11	3	.786	1	0-0	0	3.82
1995 Cleveland	AL	22	21	2	0	124.2	552	143	77	73	13	3	6	4	42	0	68	8	0	9	7	.563	0	0-0	0	5.27
1996 New York	NL	32	32	2	0	212.1	883	217	98	81	20	8	4	3	48	8	142	6	2	14	11	.560	0	0-0	0	3.43
1997 NYN-ChN	NL	32	31	3	0	205	866	213	96	87	24	9	4	4	59	3	123	4	1	14	8	.636	0	0-0	0	3.82
1997 New York	NL	23	22	1	0	142	608	158	74	67	18	9	2	3	47	2	72	4	0	8	7	.533	0	0-0	0	4.25
Chicago	NL	9	9	2	0	63	258	55	22	20	6	0	2	1	12	1	51	0	1	6	1	.857	0	0-0	0	2.86
7 ML YEARS		159	141	13	2	914.1	3876	959	456	413	104	30	29	16	261	14	507	34	4	59	45	.567	2	0-0	3	4.07

Terry Clark

Pitches: Right **Bats:** Right **Pos:** SP-9; RP-4 **Ht:** 6'2" **Wt:** 195 **Born:** 10/10/60 **Age:** 37

Year Team	Lg	G	GS	CG	GF	IP	BFP	H	R	ER	HR	SH	SF	HB	TBB	IBB	SO	WP	Bk	W	L	Pct.	ShO	Sv-Op	Hld	ERA
		HOW MUCH HE PITCHED						WHAT HE GAVE UP												THE RESULTS						
1997 Buffalo *	AAA	25	10	4	7	94.2	390	86	34	30	8	3	2	2	30	0	63	4	0	7	3	.700	1	3--	—	2.85
1988 California	AL	15	15	2	0	94	410	120	54	53	8	2	5	0	31	6	39	5	2	6	6	.500	1	0-0	0	5.07
1989 California	AL	4	2	0	2	11	48	13	8	6	0	2	1	0	3	0	7	2	1	0	2	.000	0	0-0	0	4.91
1990 Houston	NL	1	1	0	0	4	25	9	7	6	0	1	0	0	3	0	2	0	0	0	0	.000	0	0-0	0	13.50
1995 Atl-Bal		41	0	0	13	42.2	184	43	17	17	3	4	1	1	20	5	20	2	0	2	5	.286	0	1-1	7	3.59
1996 KC-Hou		17	0	0	8	23.2	124	44	25	23	4	0	0	1	9	2	17	4	0	1	3	.250	0	0-0	1	8.75
1997 Cle-Tex	AL	13	9	0	2	57	256	70	41	38	6	1	2	2	23	1	24	1	0	1	7	.125	0	0-0	0	6.00
1995 Atlanta	NL	3	0	0	1	3.2	18	3	2	2	0	0	0	0	5	0	2	1	0	0	0	.000	0	0-0	0	4.91
Baltimore	AL	38	0	0	12	39	166	40	15	15	3	4	1	1	15	5	18	1	0	2	5	.286	0	1-1	7	3.46
1996 Kansas City	AL	12	0	0	5	17.1	87	28	15	15	3	0	0	0	7	1	12	3	0	1	1	.500	0	0-0	1	7.79
Houston	NL	5	0	0	3	6.1	37	16	10	8	1	0	0	1	2	1	5	1	0	0	2	.000	0	0-0	0	11.37
1997 Cleveland	AL	4	4	0	0	26.1	118	29	21	18	3	1	2	0	13	1	13	0	0	0	3	.000	0	0-0	0	6.15
Texas	AL	9	5	0	2	30.2	138	41	20	20	3	0	0	2	10	0	11	1	0	1	4	.200	0	0-0	0	5.87
6 ML YEARS		91	27	2	25	232.1	1047	299	152	143	21	10	9	4	89	14	109	14	3	10	23	.303	1	1-1	8	5.54

Tony Clark

Bats: Both **Throws:** Right **Pos:** 1B-158; DH-1 **Ht:** 6'7" **Wt:** 245 **Born:** 6/15/72 **Age:** 26

		BATTING																	BASERUNNING				PERCENTAGES		
Year Team	Lg	G	AB	H	2B	3B	HR	(Hm	Rd)	TB	R	RBI	TBB	IBB	SO	HBP	SH	SF	SB	CS	SB%	GDP	Avg	OBP	SLG
1995 Detroit	AL	27	101	24	5	1	3	(0	3)	40	10	11	8	0	30	0	0	0	0	0	.00	2	.238	.294	.396
1996 Detroit	AL	100	376	94	14	0	27	(17	10)	189	56	72	29	1	127	0	0	6	0	1	.00	7	.250	.299	.503
1997 Detroit	AL	159	580	160	28	3	32	(18	14)	290	105	117	93	13	144	3	0	11	1	3	.25	11	.276	.376	.500
3 ML YEARS		286	1057	278	47	4	62	(35	27)	519	171	200	130	14	301	3	0	11	1	4	.20	20	.263	.342	.491

Will Clark

Bats: Left **Throws:** Left **Pos:** 1B-100; DH-7; PH-6 **Ht:** 6'1" **Wt:** 200 **Born:** 3/13/64 **Age:** 34

		BATTING																	BASERUNNING				PERCENTAGES		
Year Team	Lg	G	AB	H	2B	3B	HR	(Hm	Rd)	TB	R	RBI	TBB	IBB	SO	HBP	SH	SF	SB	CS	SB%	GDP	Avg	OBP	SLG
1986 San Francisco	NL	111	408	117	27	2	11	(7	4)	181	66	41	34	10	76	3	9	4	4	7	.36	3	.287	.343	.444
1987 San Francisco	NL	150	529	163	29	5	35	(22	13)	307	89	91	49	11	98	5	3	2	5	17	.23	2	.308	.371	.580
1988 San Francisco	NL	162	575	162	31	6	29	(14	15)	292	102	109	100	27	129	4	0	10	9	1	.90	9	.282	.386	.508
1989 San Francisco	NL	159	588	196	38	9	23	(9	14)	321	104	111	74	14	103	5	0	8	8	3	.73	6	.333	.407	.546
1990 San Francisco	NL	154	600	177	25	5	19	(8	11)	269	91	95	62	9	97	3	0	13	8	2	.80	7	.295	.357	.448
1991 San Francisco	NL	148	565	170	32	7	29	(17	12)	303	84	116	51	12	91	2	0	4	4	2	.67	5	.301	.359	.536
1992 San Francisco	NL	144	513	154	40	1	16	(11	5)	244	69	73	73	23	82	4	0	11	12	7	.63	5	.300	.384	.476
1993 San Francisco	NL	132	491	139	27	2	14	(5	9)	212	82	73	63	6	68	6	1	6	5	1	.83	5	.283	.367	.432
1994 Texas	AL	110	389	128	24	2	13	(9	4)	195	73	80	71	11	59	3	0	6	5	5	.50	10	.329	.431	.501
1995 Texas	AL	123	454	137	27	3	16	(10	6)	218	85	92	68	6	50	4	0	11	0	1	.00	11	.302	.389	.480
1996 Texas	AL	117	436	124	25	1	13	(9	4)	190	69	72	64	5	67	5	0	7	2	1	.67	10	.284	.377	.436
1997 Texas	AL	110	393	128	29	1	12	(6	6)	195	56	51	49	11	62	3	0	5	0	3	.00	4	.326	.400	.496
12 ML YEARS		1620	5941	1795	354	44	230	(127	103)	2927	970	1004	758	145	982	47	13	87	59	44	.57	73	.302	.381	.493

Royce Clayton

Bats: Right **Throws:** Right **Pos:** SS-153; PH-2 **Ht:** 6'0" **Wt:** 183 **Born:** 1/2/70 **Age:** 28

		BATTING																	BASERUNNING				PERCENTAGES		
Year Team	Lg	G	AB	H	2B	3B	HR	(Hm	Rd)	TB	R	RBI	TBB	IBB	SO	HBP	SH	SF	SB	CS	SB%	GDP	Avg	OBP	SLG
1991 San Francisco	NL	9	26	3	1	0	0	(0	0)	4	0	2	1	0	6	0	0	0	0	0	.00	1	.115	.148	.154
1992 San Francisco	NL	98	321	72	7	4	4	(3	1)	99	31	24	26	3	63	0	3	2	8	4	.67	11	.224	.281	.308
1993 San Francisco	NL	153	549	155	21	5	6	(5	1)	204	54	70	38	2	91	5	8	7	11	10	.52	16	.282	.331	.372
1994 San Francisco	NL	108	385	91	14	6	3	(1	2)	126	38	30	30	2	74	3	3	2	23	3	.88	7	.236	.295	.327
1995 San Francisco	NL	138	509	124	29	3	5	(2	3)	174	56	58	38	1	109	3	4	3	24	9	.73	7	.244	.298	.342
1996 St. Louis	NL	129	491	136	20	4	6	(6	0)	182	64	35	33	4	89	1	2	4	33	15	.69	13	.277	.321	.371
1997 St. Louis	NL	154	576	153	39	5	9	(5	4)	229	75	61	33	4	109	3	2	5	30	10	.75	19	.266	.306	.398
7 ML YEARS		789	2857	734	131	27	33	(22	11)	1018	318	280	199	16	541	15	22	23	129	51	.72	74	.257	.306	.356

Roger Clemens

Pitches: Right **Bats:** Right **Pos:** SP-34 **Ht:** 6'4" **Wt:** 230 **Born:** 8/4/62 **Age:** 35

		HOW MUCH HE PITCHED						WHAT HE GAVE UP											THE RESULTS					
Year Team	Lg	G	GS	CG	GF	IP	BFP	H	R	ER	HR	SH	SF	HB	TBB	IBB	SO	WP	Bk	W	L	Pct.	ShO	Sv-Op	Hld	ERA
1984 Boston	AL	21	20	5	0	133.1	575	146	67	64	13	2	3	2	29	3	126	4	0	9	4	.692	1	0-0	0	4.32
1985 Boston	AL	15	15	3	0	98.1	407	83	38	36	5	1	2	1	37	0	74	1	3	7	5	.583	1	0-0	0	3.29
1986 Boston	AL	33	33	10	0	254	997	179	77	70	21	4	6	4	67	0	238	11	3	24	4	.857	1	0-0	0	2.48
1987 Boston	AL	36	36	18	0	281.2	1157	248	100	93	19	6	4	9	83	4	256	4	3	20	9	.690	7	0-0	0	2.97
1988 Boston	AL	35	35	14	0	264	1063	217	93	86	17	6	3	6	62	4	291	4	2	18	12	.600	8	0-0	0	2.93
1989 Boston	AL	35	35	8	0	253.1	1044	215	101	88	20	9	5	8	93	5	230	7	0	17	11	.607	3	0-0	0	3.13
1990 Boston	AL	31	31	7	0	228.1	919	193	59	49	7	7	5	7	54	3	209	8	0	21	6	.778	4	0-0	0	1.93
1991 Boston	AL	35	35	13	0	271.1	1077	219	93	79	15	6	8	5	65	12	241	6	0	18	10	.643	4	0-0	0	2.62
1992 Boston	AL	32	32	11	0	246.2	989	203	80	66	11	5	5	9	62	5	208	3	0	18	11	.621	5	0-0	0	2.41
1993 Boston	AL	29	29	2	0	191.2	808	175	99	95	17	5	7	11	67	4	160	3	1	11	14	.440	1	0-0	0	4.46
1994 Boston	AL	24	24	3	0	170.2	692	124	62	54	15	2	5	4	71	1	168	4	0	9	7	.563	1	0-0	0	2.85
1995 Boston	AL	23	23	0	0	140	623	141	70	65	15	2	3	14	60	0	132	9	0	10	5	.667	0	0-0	0	4.18
1996 Boston	AL	34	34	6	0	242.2	1032	216	106	98	19	4	7	4	106	2	257	8	1	10	13	.435	2	0-0	0	3.63
1997 Toronto	AL	34	34	9	0	264	1044	204	65	60	9	5	2	12	68	1	292	4	0	21	7	.750	3	0-0	0	2.05
14 ML YEARS		417	416	109	0	3040	12428	2563	1110	1003	203	64	65	98	924	44	2882	76	18	213	118	.644	41	0-0	0	2.97

Chris Clemons

Pitches: Right **Bats:** Right **Pos:** RP-3; SP-2 **Ht:** 6'4" **Wt:** 225 **Born:** 10/31/72 **Age:** 25

		HOW MUCH HE PITCHED						WHAT HE GAVE UP											THE RESULTS					
Year Team	Lg	G	GS	CG	GF	IP	BFP	H	R	ER	HR	SH	SF	HB	TBB	IBB	SO	WP	Bk	W	L	Pct.	ShO	Sv-Op	Hld	ERA
1994 White Sox	R	2	2	0	0	7	27	5	3	3	0	0	0	0	1	0	5	0	0	0	1	.000	0	0- -	—	3.86
Hickory	A	12	12	0	0	69.1	290	74	37	34	5	4	2	5	18	0	42	6	0	4	2	.667	0	0- -	—	4.41
1995 Pr William	A+	27	27	1	0	137	606	136	78	72	18	4	4	11	64	2	92	2	0	7	12	.368	0	0- -	—	4.73
1996 Pr William	A+	6	6	0	0	36	150	36	16	9	6	0	2	4	8	0	26	1	0	1	4	.200	0	0- -	—	2.25
Birmingham	AA	19	16	1	2	94.1	400	91	39	33	7	0	1	6	40	2	69	1	1	5	2	.714	0	0- -	—	3.15
1997 Nashville	AAA	22	21	1	1	124.2	543	115	73	63	15	2	3	4	65	0	70	6	1	5	5	.500	1	0- -	—	4.55
1997 Chicago	AL	5	2	0	3	12.2	67	19	13	12	4	0	0	1	11	0	8	1	0	0	2	.000	0	0-0	0	8.53

Brad Clontz

Pitches: Right **Bats:** Right **Pos:** RP-51 **Ht:** 6'1" **Wt:** 180 **Born:** 4/25/71 **Age:** 27

Year Team	Lg	G	GS	CG	GF	IP	BFP	H	R	ER	HR	SH	SF	HB	TBB	IBB	SO	WP	Bk	W	L	Pct.	ShO	Sv-Op	Hld	ERA
1997 Richmond *	AAA	16	0	0	11	22	77	10	1	0	0	2	0	1	2	1	24	0	0	0	0	.000	0	6--	--	0.00
1995 Atlanta	NL	59	0	0	14	69	295	71	29	28	5	3	2	4	22	4	55	0	0	8	1	.889	0	4-6	6	3.65
1996 Atlanta	NL	81	0	0	11	80.2	350	78	53	51	11	5	4	2	33	8	49	0	1	6	3	.667	0	1-6	17	5.69
1997 Atlanta	NL	51	0	0	16	48	203	52	24	20	3	0	2	1	18	3	42	1	0	5	1	.833	0	1-2	0	3.75
3 ML YEARS		191	0	0	41	197.2	848	201	106	99	19	8	8	7	73	15	146	1	1	19	5	.792	0	6-14	23	4.51

Ken Cloude

Pitches: Right **Bats:** Right **Pos:** SP-9; RP-1 **Ht:** 6'1" **Wt:** 180 **Born:** 1/9/75 **Age:** 23

Year Team	Lg	G	GS	CG	GF	IP	BFP	H	R	ER	HR	SH	SF	HB	TBB	IBB	SO	WP	Bk	W	L	Pct.	ShO	Sv-Op	Hld	ERA
1994 Mariners	R	12	7	0	2	52.1	209	36	22	12	1	2	2	6	19	0	61	9	0	3	4	.429	0	0--	--	2.06
1995 Wisconsin	A	25	25	4	0	161	677	137	64	58	8	1	7	8	63	4	140	10	1	9	8	.529	0	0--	--	3.24
1996 Lancaster	A+	28	28	1	0	168.1	727	167	94	79	15	4	6	8	60	0	161	6	1	15	4	.789	0	0--	--	4.22
1997 Memphis	AA	22	22	3	0	132.2	567	131	62	57	15	4	2	11	48	2	124	7	0	11	7	.611	2	0--	--	3.87
1997 Seattle	AL	10	9	0	0	51	219	41	32	29	8	1	1	3	26	0	46	2	0	4	2	.667	0	0-0	0	5.12

Danny Clyburn

Bats: Right **Throws:** Right **Pos:** LF-1; PH-1 **Ht:** 6'4" **Wt:** 220 **Born:** 4/6/74 **Age:** 24

Year Team	Lg	G	AB	H	2B	3B	HR	(Hm	Rd)	TB	R	RBI	TBB	IBB	SO	HBP	SH	SF	SB	CS	SB%	GDP	Avg	OBP	SLG
1992 Pirates	R	39	149	51	9	0	4	—	—	72	26	25	5	0	20	1	0	2	7	3	.70	4	.342	.363	.483
1993 Augusta	A	127	457	121	21	4	9	—	—	177	55	66	37	1	97	5	0	0	5	5	.50	7	.265	.327	.387
1994 Salem	A+	118	461	126	19	0	22	—	—	211	57	90	20	2	96	0	0	5	4	5	.44	7	.273	.300	.458
1995 Winston-Sal	A+	59	227	59	10	2	11	—	—	106	27	41	13	1	59	4	0	2	2	4	.33	5	.260	.309	.467
Frederick	A+	15	45	9	4	0	0	—	—	13	4	4	4	0	18	2	0	0	1	1	.50	0	.200	.294	.289
High Desert	A+	45	160	45	3	1	12	—	—	86	20	37	17	1	41	4	0	3	2	1	.67	3	.281	.359	.538
1996 Bowie	AA	95	365	92	14	5	18	—	—	170	51	55	17	1	88	4	0	4	4	3	.57	5	.252	.290	.466
1997 Rochester	AAA	137	520	156	33	5	20	—	—	259	91	76	53	3	107	8	0	1	14	4	.78	7	.300	.372	.498
1997 Baltimore	AL	2	3	0	0	0	0	(0	0)	0	0	0	0	0	2	0	0	0	0	0	.00	0	.000	.000	.000

Greg Colbrunn

Bats: Right **Throws:** Right **Pos:** 1B-78; PH-34; DH-5 **Ht:** 6'0" **Wt:** 200 **Born:** 7/26/69 **Age:** 28

Year Team	Lg	G	AB	H	2B	3B	HR	(Hm	Rd)	TB	R	RBI	TBB	IBB	SO	HBP	SH	SF	SB	CS	SB%	GDP	Avg	OBP	SLG
1992 Montreal	NL	52	168	45	8	0	2	(1	1)	59	12	18	6	1	34	2	0	4	3	2	.60	1	.268	.294	.351
1993 Montreal	NL	70	153	39	9	0	4	(2	2)	60	15	23	6	1	33	1	1	3	4	2	.67	1	.255	.282	.392
1994 Florida	NL	47	155	47	10	0	6	(3	3)	75	17	31	9	0	27	2	0	3	1	1	.50	3	.303	.345	.484
1995 Florida	NL	138	528	146	22	1	23	(12	11)	239	70	89	22	4	69	6	0	4	11	3	.79	15	.277	.311	.453
1996 Florida	NL	141	511	146	26	2	16	(7	9)	224	60	69	25	1	76	14	0	5	4	5	.44	22	.286	.333	.438
1997 Min-Atl		98	271	76	17	0	7	(3	4)	114	27	35	10	1	49	2	1	2	1	2	.33	8	.280	.309	.421
1997 Minnesota	AL	70	217	61	14	0	5	(2	3)	90	24	26	8	1	38	1	0	2	1	2	.33	7	.281	.307	.415
Atlanta	NL	28	54	15	3	0	2	(1	1)	24	3	9	2	0	11	1	1	0	0	0	.00	1	.278	.316	.444
6 ML YEARS		546	1786	499	92	3	58	(28	30)	771	201	265	78	8	288	27	2	20	24	15	.62	50	.279	.316	.432

Michael Coleman

Bats: Right **Throws:** Right **Pos:** CF-7; PH-1 **Ht:** 5'11" **Wt:** 180 **Born:** 8/16/75 **Age:** 22

Year Team	Lg	G	AB	H	2B	3B	HR	(Hm	Rd)	TB	R	RBI	TBB	IBB	SO	HBP	SH	SF	SB	CS	SB%	GDP	Avg	OBP	SLG
1994 Red Sox	R	25	95	26	6	1	3	—	—	43	15	15	10	0	20	3	0	1	5	3	.63	3	.274	.358	.453
Utica	A-	23	65	11	2	0	1	—	—	16	16	3	14	0	21	0	3	0	11	1	.92	0	.169	.316	.246
1995 Michigan	A	112	422	113	16	2	11	—	—	166	70	61	40	1	93	6	6	3	29	5	.85	7	.268	.338	.393
1996 Sarasota	A+	110	407	100	20	5	1	—	—	133	54	36	38	1	86	8	7	3	24	5	.83	10	.246	.320	.327
1997 Trenton	AA	102	385	116	17	8	14	—	—	191	56	58	41	1	89	5	9	4	20	7	.74	5	.301	.372	.496
Pawtucket	AAA	28	113	36	9	2	7	—	—	70	27	19	12	0	27	2	0	1	4	2	.67	2	.319	.391	.619
1997 Boston	AL	8	24	4	1	0	0	(0	0)	5	2	2	0	0	11	0	1	0	1	0	1.00	0	.167	.167	.208

Vince Coleman

Bats: Both **Throws:** Right **Pos:** PH-4; LF-2; DH-1; CF-1 **Ht:** 6'1" **Wt:** 185 **Born:** 9/22/61 **Age:** 36

Year Team	Lg	G	AB	H	2B	3B	HR	(Hm	Rd)	TB	R	RBI	TBB	IBB	SO	HBP	SH	SF	SB	CS	SB%	GDP	Avg	OBP	SLG
1985 St. Louis	NL	151	636	170	20	10	1	(1	0)	213	107	40	50	1	115	0	5	5	110	25	.81	3	.267	.320	.335
1986 St. Louis	NL	154	600	139	13	8	0	(0	0)	168	94	29	60	0	98	2	3	5	107	14	.88	4	.232	.301	.280
1987 St. Louis	NL	151	623	180	14	10	3	(3	0)	223	121	43	70	0	126	3	5	1	109	22	.83	4	.289	.363	.358
1988 St. Louis	NL	153	616	160	20	10	3	(2	1)	209	77	38	49	4	111	1	8	5	81	27	.75	4	.260	.313	.339
1989 St. Louis	NL	145	563	143	21	9	2	(1	1)	188	94	28	50	0	90	2	7	2	65	10	.87	6	.254	.316	.334
1990 St. Louis	NL	124	497	145	18	9	6	(1	5)	199	73	39	35	1	88	2	4	1	77	17	.82	6	.292	.340	.400
1991 New York	NL	72	278	71	7	5	1	(0	1)	91	45	17	39	0	47	0	1	0	37	14	.73	3	.255	.347	.327
1992 New York	NL	71	229	63	11	1	2	(2	0)	82	37	21	27	3	41	2	2	1	24	9	.73	1	.275	.355	.358
1993 New York	NL	92	373	104	14	8	2	(2	0)	140	64	25	21	1	58	0	3	2	38	13	.75	2	.279	.316	.375

Year Team	Lg	G	AB	H	2B	3B	HR	(Hm	Rd)	TB	R	RBI	TBB	IBB	SO	HBP	SH	SF	SB	CS	SB%	GDP	Avg	OBP	SLG
1994 Kansas City	AL	104	438	105	14	12	2	(1	1)	149	61	33	29	0	72	1	4	5	50	8	.86	2	.240	.285	.340
1995 KC-Sea	AL	115	455	131	23	6	5	(3	2)	181	66	29	37	2	80	2	5	1	42	16	.72	8	.288	.343	.398
1996 Cincinnati	NL	33	84	13	1	1	1	(1	0)	19	10	4	9	0	31	0	1	0	12	2	.86	0	.155	.237	.226
1997 Detroit	AL	6	14	1	0	0	0	(0	0)	1	0	0	1	0	3	0	0	0	0	0	.00	1	.071	.133	.071
1995 Kansas City	AL	75	293	84	13	4	4	(2	2)	117	39	20	27	1	48	1	2	1	26	9	.74	7	.287	.348	.399
Seattle	AL	40	162	47	10	2	1	(1	0)	64	27	9	10	1	32	1	3	0	16	7	.70	1	.290	.335	.395
13 ML YEARS		1371	5406	1425	176	89	28	(21	7)	1863	849	346	477	12	960	15	48	24	752	177	.81	45	.264	.324	.345

Darnell Coles

Bats: Right   **Throws:** Right   **Pos:** PH-16; 3B-3; LF-2   **Ht:** 6'1"   **Wt:** 180   **Born:** 6/2/62   **Age:** 36

Year Team	Lg	G	AB	H	2B	3B	HR	(Hm	Rd)	TB	R	RBI	TBB	IBB	SO	HBP	SH	SF	SB	CS	SB%	GDP	Avg	OBP	SLG
1983 Seattle	AL	27	92	26	7	0	1	(0	1)	36	9	6	7	0	12	0	1	0	0	3	.00	8	.283	.333	.391
1984 Seattle	AL	48	143	23	3	1	0	(0	0)	28	15	6	17	0	26	2	3	0	1	1	.67	5	.161	.259	.196
1985 Seattle	AL	27	59	14	4	0	1	(0	1)	21	8	5	9	0	17	1	0	2	0	1	.00	0	.237	.338	.356
1986 Detroit	AL	142	521	142	30	2	20	(12	8)	236	67	86	45	3	84	6	1	3	6	2	.75	8	.273	.333	.453
1987 Det-Pit		93	268	54	13	1	10	(8	2)	99	34	39	34	3	43	3	5	3	1	4	.20	4	.201	.295	.369
1988 Pit-Sea		123	406	106	23	2	15	(10	5)	178	52	70	37	1	67	7	2	10	4	3	.57	8	.261	.326	.438
1989 Seattle	AL	146	535	135	21	3	10	(4	6)	192	54	59	27	1	61	6	2	3	5	4	.56	13	.252	.294	.359
1990 Sea-Det		89	215	45	7	1	3	(3	0)	63	22	20	16	2	38	1	1	2	0	4	.00	4	.209	.265	.293
1991 San Francisco	NL	11	14	3	0	0	0	(0	0)	3	1	0	0	0	2	0	0	0	0	0	.00	1	.214	.214	.214
1992 Cincinnati	NL	55	141	44	11	2	3	(1	2)	68	16	18	3	0	15	0	3	2	1	0	1.00	1	.312	.322	.482
1993 Toronto	AL	64	194	49	9	1	4	(3	1)	72	26	26	16	1	29	4	1	2	1	1	.50	3	.253	.319	.371
1994 Toronto	AL	48	143	30	6	1	4	(1	3)	50	15	15	10	0	25	1	0	2	0	0	.00	2	.210	.263	.350
1995 St. Louis	NL	63	138	31	7	0	3	(3	0)	47	13	16	16	1	20	3	0	1	0	0	.00	5	.225	.316	.341
1997 Colorado	NL	21	22	7	1	0	1	(0	1)	11	1	2	0	0	6	1	0	0	0	0	.00	1	.318	.348	.500
1987 Detroit	AL	53	149	27	5	1	4	(3	1)	46	14	15	15	1	23	2	2	1	0	1	.00	1	.181	.263	.309
Pittsburgh	NL	40	119	27	8	0	6	(5	1)	53	20	24	19	2	20	1	3	2	1	3	.25	3	.227	.333	.445
1988 Pittsburgh	NL	68	211	49	13	1	5	(1	4)	79	20	36	20	1	41	3	0	7	1	1	.50	3	.232	.299	.374
Seattle	AL	55	195	57	10	1	10	(9	1)	99	32	34	17	0	26	4	2	3	3	2	.60	5	.292	.356	.508
1990 Seattle	AL	37	107	23	5	1	2	(2	0)	36	9	16	4	1	17	1	0	1	0	4	.00	3	.215	.248	.336
Detroit	AL	52	108	22	2	0	1	(1	0)	27	13	4	12	1	21	0	1	1	0	0	.00	1	.204	.281	.250
14 ML YEARS		957	2891	709	142	14	75	(45	30)	1104	333	368	237	12	445	35	25	35	20	23	.47	58	.245	.307	.382

Lou Collier

Bats: Right   **Throws:** Right   **Pos:** SS-18; PH-3   **Ht:** 5'10"   **Wt:** 180   **Born:** 8/21/73   **Age:** 24

Year Team	Lg	G	AB	H	2B	3B	HR	(Hm	Rd)	TB	R	RBI	TBB	IBB	SO	HBP	SH	SF	SB	CS	SB%	GDP	Avg	OBP	SLG
1993 Welland	A-	50	201	61	6	2	1	—	—	74	35	19	12	0	31	5	1	2	8	7	.53	2	.303	.356	.368
1994 Augusta	A	85	318	89	14	4	7	—	—	135	48	40	25	0	53	8	0	3	32	10	.76	4	.280	.345	.425
Salem	A+	43	158	42	4	1	6	—	—	66	25	16	15	0	29	6	2	2	5	8	.38	4	.266	.348	.418
1995 Lynchburg	A+	114	399	110	19	3	4	—	—	147	68	38	51	4	60	7	3	3	31	11	.74	3	.276	.365	.368
1996 Carolina	AA	119	443	124	20	3	3	—	—	159	76	49	48	4	73	7	2	6	29	9	.76	11	.280	.355	.359
1997 Calgary	AAA	112	397	131	31	5	1	—	—	175	65	48	37	2	47	6	8	3	12	7	.63	13	.330	.393	.441
1997 Pittsburgh	NL	18	37	5	0	0	0	(0	0)	5	3	3	1	0	11	0	0	0	1	0	1.00	1	.135	.158	.135

Bartolo Colon

Pitches: Right   **Bats:** Right   **Pos:** SP-17; RP-2   **Ht:** 6'0"   **Wt:** 185   **Born:** 5/24/75   **Age:** 23

		HOW MUCH HE PITCHED						WHAT HE GAVE UP										THE RESULTS						
Year Team	Lg	G	GS	CG	GF	IP	BFP	H	R	ER	HR	SH	SF	HB	TBB	IBB	SO	WP	Bk	W	L	Pct.	ShO	Sv-Op	Hld	ERA
1994 Burlington	R+	12	12	0	0	66	291	46	32	23	3	2	1	4	44	0	84	6	2	7	4	.636	0	0--	—	3.14
1995 Kinston	A+	21	21	0	0	128.2	493	91	31	28	8	1	2	0	39	0	152	4	3	13	3	.813	0	0--	—	1.96
1996 Canton-Akrn	AA	13	12	0	0	62	253	44	17	12	2	0	1	2	25	0	56	3	1	2	2	.500	0	0--	—	1.74
Buffalo	AAA	8	0	0	1	15	69	16	10	10	2	1	0	2	8	0	19	2	0	0	0	.000	0	0--	—	6.00
1997 Buffalo	AAA	10	10	1	0	56.2	230	45	15	14	4	2	1	0	23	0	54	1	1	7	1	.875	1	0--	—	2.22
1997 Cleveland	AL	19	17	1	0	94	427	107	66	59	12	4	1	3	45	1	66	5	1	4	7	.364	0	0-0	0	5.65

David Cone

Pitches: Right   **Bats:** Left   **Pos:** SP-29   **Ht:** 6'1"   **Wt:** 190   **Born:** 1/2/63   **Age:** 35

		HOW MUCH HE PITCHED						WHAT HE GAVE UP										THE RESULTS						
Year Team	Lg	G	GS	CG	GF	IP	BFP	H	R	ER	HR	SH	SF	HB	TBB	IBB	SO	WP	Bk	W	L	Pct.	ShO	Sv-Op	Hld	ERA
1986 Kansas City	AL	11	0	0	5	22.2	108	29	14	14	2	0	0	1	13	1	21	3	0	0	0	.000	0	0--	—	5.56
1987 New York	NL	21	13	1	3	99.1	420	87	46	41	11	4	3	5	44	1	68	2	4	5	6	.455	0	1-1	2	3.71
1988 New York	NL	35	28	8	0	231.1	936	178	67	57	10	11	5	4	80	7	213	10	10	20	3	.870	4	0-0	1	2.22
1989 New York	NL	34	33	7	0	219.2	910	183	92	86	20	6	4	4	74	6	190	14	4	14	8	.636	2	0-0	0	3.52
1990 New York	NL	31	30	6	1	211.2	860	177	84	76	21	4	6	1	65	1	233	10	4	14	10	.583	2	0-0	0	3.23
1991 New York	NL	34	34	5	0	232.2	966	204	95	85	13	13	7	5	73	2	241	17	1	14	14	.500	2	0-0	0	3.29
1992 NYN-Tor		35	34	7	0	249.2	1055	201	91	78	15	6	9	12	111	7	261	12	1	17	10	.630	5	0-0	0	2.81
1993 Kansas City	AL	34	34	6	0	254	1060	205	102	94	20	7	9	10	114	2	191	14	2	11	14	.440	1	0-0	0	3.33
1994 Kansas City	AL	23	23	4	0	171.2	690	130	60	56	15	1	5	7	54	0	132	5	1	16	5	.762	3	0-0	0	2.94
1995 Tor-NYA	AL	30	30	6	0	229.1	954	195	91	91	24	2	9	8	88	2	191	11	1	18	8	.692	2	0-0	0	3.57
1996 New York	AL	11	11	1	0	72	295	50	25	23	3	1	5	2	34	0	71	4	1	7	2	.778	1	0-0	0	2.88
1997 New York	AL	29	29	1	0	195	805	155	67	61	17	3	2	4	86	2	222	14	2	12	6	.667	0	0-0	0	2.82
1992 New York	NL	27	27	7	0	196.2	831	162	75	63	12	6	9	9	82	5	214	9	1	13	7	.650	5	0-0	0	2.88

45

Year Team	Lg	G	GS	CG	GF	IP	BFP	H	R	ER	HR	SH	SF	HB	TBB	IBB	SO	WP	Bk	W	L	Pct.	ShO	Sv-Op	Hld	ERA
Toronto	AL	8	7	0	0	53	224	39	16	15	3	0	3	3	29	2	47	3	0	4	3	.571	0	0-0	0	2.55
1995 Toronto	AL	17	17	5	0	130.1	537	113	53	49	12	2	1	5	41	2	102	6	1	9	6	.600	2	0-0	0	3.38
New York	AL	13	13	1	0	99	417	82	42	42	12	0	1	1	47	0	89	5	0	9	2	.818	0	0-0	0	3.82
12 ML YEARS		328	299	52	9	2189	9059	1794	838	762	171	58	58	61	836	31	2034	116	31	148	86	.632	21	1- —		3.13

Jeff Conine

Bats: Right **Throws:** Right **Pos:** 1B-145; PH-19; LF-1   **Ht:** 6'1" **Wt:** 220 **Born:** 6/27/66 **Age:** 32

								BATTING												BASERUNNING				PERCENTAGES		
Year Team	Lg	G	AB	H	2B	3B	HR	(Hm	Rd)	TB	R	RBI	TBB	IBB	SO	HBP	SH	SF	SB	CS	SB%	GDP	Avg	OBP	SLG
1990 Kansas City	AL	9	20	5	2	0	0	(0	0)	7	3	2	2	0	5	0	0	0	0	0	.00	1	.250	.318	.350
1992 Kansas City	AL	28	91	23	5	2	0	(0	0)	32	10	9	8	1	23	0	0	0	0	0	.00	1	.253	.313	.352
1993 Florida	NL	162	595	174	24	3	12	(5	7)	240	75	79	52	2	135	5	0	6	2	2	.50	14	.292	.351	.403
1994 Florida	NL	115	451	144	27	6	18	(8	10)	237	60	82	40	4	92	1	0	4	1	2	.33	8	.319	.373	.525
1995 Florida	NL	133	483	146	26	2	25	(13	12)	251	72	105	66	5	94	1	0	12	2	0	1.00	13	.302	.379	.520
1996 Florida	NL	157	597	175	32	2	26	(15	11)	289	84	95	62	1	121	4	0	7	1	4	.20	17	.293	.360	.484
1997 Florida	NL	151	405	98	13	1	17	(7	10)	164	46	61	57	3	89	2	0	2	2	0	1.00	11	.242	.337	.405
7 ML YEARS		755	2642	765	129	16	98	(48	50)	1220	350	433	287	16	559	13	0	31	8	8	.50	65	.290	.358	.462

Jim Converse

Pitches: Right **Bats:** Left **Pos:** RP-3   **Ht:** 5'9" **Wt:** 180 **Born:** 8/17/71 **Age:** 26

Year Team	Lg	G	GS	CG	GF	IP	BFP	H	R	ER	HR	SH	SF	HB	TBB	IBB	SO	WP	Bk	W	L	Pct.	ShO	Sv-Op	Hld	ERA
1997 Omaha *	AAA	6	3	0	1	17.1	75	18	13	13	3	0	2	1	9	0	13	0	0	2	1	.667	0	0- —		6.75
Yankees *	R	3	3	0	0	4.2	21	5	1	1	0	0	0	0	1	0	8	0	0	0	0	.000	0	0- —		1.93
Columbus *	AAA	10	1	0	5	19	86	22	8	7	1	0	0	0	11	1	13	1	0	0	2	.000	0	1- —		3.32
1993 Seattle	AL	4	4	0	0	20.1	93	23	12	12	0	0	1	0	14	2	10	0	0	1	3	.250	0	0-0	0	5.31
1994 Seattle	AL	13	8	0	1	48.2	253	73	49	47	5	2	3	1	40	4	39	3	0	0	5	.000	0	0-0	0	8.69
1995 Sea-KC	AL	15	1	0	4	23.1	109	28	17	17	2	2	0	0	16	2	14	2	0	1	3	.250	0	1-1	1	6.56
1997 Kansas City	AL	3	0	0	1	5	23	4	2	2	0	2	0	0	5	0	3	0	0	0	0	.000	0	0-0	0	3.60
1995 Seattle	AL	6	1	0	3	11	55	16	9	9	2	1	0	0	8	0	9	0	0	0	3	.000	0	1-1	1	7.36
Kansas City	AL	9	0	0	1	12.1	54	12	8	8	0	1	0	0	8	2	5	2	0	1	0	1.000	0	0-0	0	5.84
4 ML YEARS		35	13	0	6	97.1	478	128	80	78	9	4	4	1	75	8	66	5	0	2	11	.154	0	1-1	1	7.21

Dennis Cook

Pitches: Left **Bats:** Left **Pos:** RP-59   **Ht:** 6'3" **Wt:** 190 **Born:** 10/4/62 **Age:** 35

Year Team	Lg	G	GS	CG	GF	IP	BFP	H	R	ER	HR	SH	SF	HB	TBB	IBB	SO	WP	Bk	W	L	Pct.	ShO	Sv-Op	Hld	ERA
1988 San Francisco	NL	4	4	1	0	22	86	9	8	7	1	0	3	0	11	1	13	1	0	2	1	.667	1	0-0	0	2.86
1989 SF-Phi	NL	23	18	2	1	121	499	110	59	50	18	5	2	2	38	6	67	4	2	7	8	.467	1	0-0	1	3.72
1990 Phi-LA	NL	47	16	2	4	156	663	155	74	68	20	7	7	2	56	9	64	6	3	9	4	.692	1	1-2	4	3.92
1991 Los Angeles	NL	20	1	0	5	17.2	69	12	3	1	0	1	2	0	7	1	8	0	0	1	0	1.000	0	0-1	1	0.51
1992 Cleveland	AL	32	25	1	1	158	669	156	79	67	29	3	3	2	50	2	96	4	5	5	7	.417	0	0-0	0	3.82
1993 Cleveland	AL	25	6	0	2	54	233	62	36	34	9	3	2	2	16	1	34	0	1	5	5	.500	0	0-2	2	5.67
1994 Chicago	AL	38	1	0	8	33	143	29	17	13	4	3	0	0	14	3	26	0	1	3	1	.750	0	0-1	3	3.55
1995 Cle-Tex	AL	46	1	0	10	57.2	255	63	32	29	9	4	5	2	26	3	53	1	0	0	2	.000	0	2-2	6	4.53
1996 Texas	AL	60	0	0	9	70.1	298	53	34	32	2	3	5	7	35	7	64	0	0	5	2	.714	0	0-2	11	4.09
1997 Florida	NL	59	0	0	12	62.1	272	64	28	27	4	1	1	2	28	4	63	0	0	1	2	.333	0	0-2	13	3.90
1989 San Francisco	NL	2	2	1	0	15	58	13	3	3	1	0	0	0	5	0	9	1	0	1	0	1.000	1	0-0	0	1.80
Philadelphia	NL	21	16	1	1	106	441	97	56	47	17	5	2	2	33	6	58	3	2	6	8	.429	1	0-0	1	3.99
1990 Philadelphia	NL	42	13	2	4	141.2	594	132	61	56	13	5	5	2	54	9	58	6	3	8	3	.727	1	1-2	3	3.56
Los Angeles	NL	5	3	0	0	14.1	69	23	13	12	7	2	2	0	2	0	6	0	0	1	1	.500	0	0-0	1	7.53
1995 Cleveland	AL	11	0	0	1	12.2	62	16	9	9	3	1	0	1	10	2	13	0	0	0	0	.000	0	0-0	1	6.39
Texas	AL	35	1	0	9	45	193	47	23	20	6	3	5	1	16	1	40	1	0	0	2	.000	0	2-2	5	4.00
10 ML YEARS		354	71	6	52	752	3187	713	370	328	96	30	30	19	281	37	488	16	12	38	32	.543	3	3-12	41	3.93

Steve Cooke

Pitches: Left **Bats:** Right **Pos:** SP-32   **Ht:** 6'6" **Wt:** 236 **Born:** 1/14/70 **Age:** 28

Year Team	Lg	G	GS	CG	GF	IP	BFP	H	R	ER	HR	SH	SF	HB	TBB	IBB	SO	WP	Bk	W	L	Pct.	ShO	Sv-Op	Hld	ERA
1992 Pittsburgh	NL	11	0	0	8	23	91	22	9	9	2	0	0	0	4	1	10	0	0	2	0	1.000	0	1-1	1	3.52
1993 Pittsburgh	NL	32	32	3	0	210.2	882	207	101	91	20	13	6	3	59	4	132	3	3	10	10	.500	1	0-0	0	3.89
1994 Pittsburgh	NL	25	23	2	1	134.1	590	157	79	75	21	9	3	5	46	7	74	3	0	4	11	.267	0	0-0	0	5.02
1996 Pittsburgh	NL	3	0	0	1	8.1	41	11	7	7	1	0	1	0	5	0	7	1	0	0	0	.000	0	0-0	0	7.56
1997 Pittsburgh	NL	32	32	0	0	167.1	756	184	95	80	15	18	5	9	77	11	109	8	1	9	15	.375	0	0-0	0	4.30
5 ML YEARS		103	87	5	10	543.2	2360	581	291	262	61	40	15	17	191	23	332	15	4	25	36	.410	1	1-1	1	4.34

Ron Coomer

Bats: R **Throws:** R **Pos:** 3B-119; PH-10; 1B-9; DH-7; RF-7   **Ht:** 5'11" **Wt:** 195 **Born:** 11/18/66 **Age:** 31

								BATTING												BASERUNNING				PERCENTAGES		
Year Team	Lg	G	AB	H	2B	3B	HR	(Hm	Rd)	TB	R	RBI	TBB	IBB	SO	HBP	SH	SF	SB	CS	SB%	GDP	Avg	OBP	SLG
1995 Minnesota	AL	37	101	26	3	1	5	(2	3)	46	15	19	9	0	11	1	0	0	0	1	.00	9	.257	.324	.455
1996 Minnesota	AL	95	233	69	12	1	12	(5	7)	119	34	41	17	1	24	0	0	3	3	0	1.00	10	.296	.340	.511

					BATTING														BASERUNNING				PERCENTAGES		
Year Team	Lg	G	AB	H	2B	3B	HR	(Hm Rd)	TB	R	RBI	TBB	IBB	SO	HBP	SH	SF	SB	CS	SB%	GDP	Avg	OBP	SLG
1997 Minnesota	AL	140	523	156	30	2	13	(4 9)	229	63	85	22	5	91	0	0	5	4	3	.57	11	.298	.324	.438
3 ML YEARS		272	857	251	45	4	30	(11 19)	394	112	145	48	6	126	1	0	8	7	4	.64	30	.293	.328	.460

Scott Cooper

Bats: L **Throws:** R **Pos:** 3B-39; PH-35; 1B-8; DH-5   **Ht:** 6'3" **Wt:** 215 **Born:** 10/13/67 **Age:** 30

					BATTING														BASERUNNING				PERCENTAGES		
Year Team	Lg	G	AB	H	2B	3B	HR	(Hm Rd)	TB	R	RBI	TBB	IBB	SO	HBP	SH	SF	SB	CS	SB%	GDP	Avg	OBP	SLG
1990 Boston	AL	2	1	0	0	0	0	(0 0)	0	0	0	0	0	1	0	0	0	0	0	.00	0	.000	.000	.000
1991 Boston	AL	14	35	16	4	2	0	(0 0)	24	6	7	2	0	2	0	0	0	0	0	.00	0	.457	.486	.686
1992 Boston	AL	123	337	93	21	0	5	(2 3)	129	34	33	37	0	33	0	2	2	1	1	.50	5	.276	.346	.383
1993 Boston	AL	156	526	147	29	3	9	(3 6)	209	67	63	58	15	81	5	4	3	5	2	.71	8	.279	.355	.397
1994 Boston	AL	104	369	104	16	4	13	(9 4)	167	49	53	30	2	65	1	1	5	0	3	.00	6	.282	.333	.453
1995 St. Louis	NL	118	374	86	18	2	3	(1 2)	117	29	40	49	3	85	3	0	4	0	3	.00	9	.230	.321	.313
1997 Kansas City	AL	75	159	32	6	1	3	(3 0)	49	12	15	17	0	32	2	2	2	1	1	.50	4	.201	.283	.308
7 ML YEARS		592	1801	478	94	12	33	(18 15)	695	197	211	193	20	299	11	9	16	7	10	.41	32	.265	.337	.386

Rocky Coppinger

Pitches: Right **Bats:** Right **Pos:** SP-4; RP-1   **Ht:** 6'5" **Wt:** 250 **Born:** 3/19/74 **Age:** 24

		HOW MUCH HE PITCHED						WHAT HE GAVE UP												THE RESULTS					
Year Team	Lg	G	GS	CG	GF	IP	BFP	H	R	ER	HR	SH	SF	HB	TBB	IBB	SO	WP	Bk	W	L	Pct.	ShO	Sv-Op	Hld	ERA
1994 Bluefield	R+	14	13	0	1	73.1	302	51	24	20	5	0	3	2	40	0	88	5	0	4	3	.571	0	0--	—	2.45
1995 Frederick	A+	11	11	2	0	68.2	272	46	16	12	3	3	1	0	24	0	91	1	0	7	1	.875	1	0--	—	1.57
Bowie	AA	13	13	2	0	83.2	352	58	33	25	7	0	4	3	43	0	62	4	1	6	2	.750	2	0--	—	2.69
Rochester	AAA	5	5	0	0	34.2	140	23	5	4	2	0	2	1	17	0	19	0	0	3	0	1.000	0	0--	—	1.04
1996 Rochester	AAA	12	12	0	0	73	315	65	36	34	6	1	2	0	39	1	81	4	1	4	6	.400	0	0--	—	4.19
1997 Orioles	R	3	3	0	0	10	36	7	3	2	0	0	0	1	0	0	13	0	0	0	0	.000	0	0--	—	1.80
Bowie	AA	3	3	0	0	15	65	15	9	8	4	1	0	1	3	0	15	0	0	1	1	.500	0	0--	—	4.80
Rochester	AAA	3	3	0	0	14.2	69	16	10	9	2	0	0	0	11	0	9	0	0	1	2	.333	0	0--	—	5.52
1996 Baltimore	AL	23	22	0	1	125	548	126	76	72	25	2	5	2	60	1	104	4	0	10	6	.625	0	0-0	0	5.18
1997 Baltimore	AL	5	4	0	1	20	95	21	14	14	2	0	1	1	16	1	22	1	0	1	1	.500	0	0-0	0	6.30
2 ML YEARS		28	26	0	2	145	643	147	90	86	27	2	6	3	76	2	126	5	0	11	7	.611	0	0-0	0	5.34

Joey Cora

Bats: Both **Throws:** Right **Pos:** 2B-142; PH-11   **Ht:** 5'8" **Wt:** 162 **Born:** 5/14/65 **Age:** 33

					BATTING														BASERUNNING				PERCENTAGES		
Year Team	Lg	G	AB	H	2B	3B	HR	(Hm Rd)	TB	R	RBI	TBB	IBB	SO	HBP	SH	SF	SB	CS	SB%	GDP	Avg	OBP	SLG
1987 San Diego	NL	77	241	57	7	2	0	(0 0)	68	23	13	28	1	26	1	5	1	15	11	.58	4	.237	.317	.282
1989 San Diego	NL	12	19	6	1	0	0	(0 0)	7	5	1	1	0	0	0	0	0	1	0	1.00	0	.316	.350	.368
1990 San Diego	NL	51	100	27	3	0	0	(0 0)	30	12	2	6	1	9	0	0	0	8	3	.73	1	.270	.311	.300
1991 Chicago	AL	100	228	55	2	3	0	(0 0)	63	37	18	20	0	21	5	4	3	11	6	.65	1	.241	.313	.276
1992 Chicago	AL	68	122	30	7	1	0	(0 0)	39	27	9	22	1	13	4	2	3	10	3	.77	2	.246	.371	.320
1993 Chicago	AL	153	579	155	15	13	2	(0 2)	202	95	51	67	0	63	9	19	4	20	8	.71	14	.268	.351	.349
1994 Chicago	AL	90	312	86	13	4	2	(2 0)	113	55	30	38	0	32	2	11	5	8	4	.67	6	.276	.353	.362
1995 Seattle	AL	120	427	127	19	2	3	(1 2)	159	64	39	37	0	31	6	13	4	18	7	.72	5	.297	.359	.372
1996 Seattle	AL	144	530	154	37	6	6	(2 4)	221	90	45	35	1	32	7	6	5	5	5	.50	9	.291	.340	.417
1997 Seattle	AL	149	574	172	40	4	11	(4 7)	253	105	54	53	2	49	5	8	9	6	7	.46	6	.300	.359	.441
10 ML YEARS		964	3132	869	144	35	24	(9 15)	1155	513	262	307	6	276	39	72	34	102	54	.65	53	.277	.346	.369

Wil Cordero

Bats: R **Throws:** R **Pos:** LF-137; DH-2; PH-2; 2B-1   **Ht:** 6'2" **Wt:** 195 **Born:** 10/3/71 **Age:** 26

					BATTING														BASERUNNING				PERCENTAGES		
Year Team	Lg	G	AB	H	2B	3B	HR	(Hm Rd)	TB	R	RBI	TBB	IBB	SO	HBP	SH	SF	SB	CS	SB%	GDP	Avg	OBP	SLG
1992 Montreal	NL	45	126	38	4	1	2	(1 1)	50	17	8	9	0	31	1	1	0	0	0	.00	3	.302	.353	.397
1993 Montreal	NL	138	475	118	32	2	10	(8 2)	184	56	58	34	8	60	7	4	1	12	3	.80	12	.248	.308	.387
1994 Montreal	NL	110	415	122	30	3	15	(5 10)	203	65	63	41	3	62	6	2	3	16	3	.84	8	.294	.363	.489
1995 Montreal	NL	131	514	147	35	2	10	(2 8)	216	64	49	36	4	88	9	1	4	9	5	.64	11	.286	.341	.420
1996 Boston	AL	59	198	57	14	0	3	(2 1)	80	29	37	11	4	31	2	1	1	2	1	.67	8	.288	.330	.404
1997 Boston	AL	140	570	160	26	3	18	(11 7)	246	82	72	31	7	122	4	0	4	1	3	.25	11	.281	.320	.432
6 ML YEARS		623	2298	642	141	11	58	(29 29)	979	313	287	162	26	394	29	9	13	40	15	.73	53	.279	.333	.426

Francisco Cordova

Pitches: Right **Bats:** Right **Pos:** SP-29   **Ht:** 5'11" **Wt:** 163 **Born:** 4/26/72 **Age:** 26

		HOW MUCH HE PITCHED						WHAT HE GAVE UP												THE RESULTS					
Year Team	Lg	G	GS	CG	GF	IP	BFP	H	R	ER	HR	SH	SF	HB	TBB	IBB	SO	WP	Bk	W	L	Pct.	ShO	Sv-Op	Hld	ERA
1996 Pittsburgh	NL	59	6	0	41	99	414	103	49	45	11	1	0	2	20	6	95	2	1	4	7	.364	0	12-18	3	4.09
1997 Pittsburgh	NL	29	29	2	0	178.2	744	175	80	72	14	3	7	9	49	4	121	4	0	11	8	.579	2	0-0	0	3.63
2 ML YEARS		88	35	2	41	277.2	1158	278	129	117	25	4	7	11	69	10	216	6	1	15	15	.500	2	12-18	3	3.79

Marty Cordova

Bats: Right **Throws:** Right **Pos:** LF-101; DH-2; PH-2   **Ht:** 6'0" **Wt:** 193 **Born:** 7/10/69 **Age:** 28

						BATTING										BASERUNNING				PERCENTAGES		
Year Team	Lg	G	AB	H	2B	3B	HR	(Hm	Rd)	TB	R	RBI	TBB	IBB	SO	HBP	SH	SF	SB	CS	SB%	GDP	Avg	OBP	SLG
1997 Salt Lake *	AAA	6	24	9	4	0	1	—	—	16	5	4	2	0	3	0	0	0	1	0	1.00	0	.375	.423	.667
1995 Minnesota	AL	137	512	142	27	4	24	(16	8)	249	81	84	52	1	111	10	0	5	20	7	.74	10	.277	.352	.486
1996 Minnesota	AL	145	569	176	46	1	16	(10	6)	272	97	111	53	4	96	8	0	9	11	5	.69	18	.309	.371	.478
1997 Minnesota	AL	103	378	93	18	4	15	(4	11)	164	44	51	30	2	92	3	0	2	5	3	.63	13	.246	.305	.434
3 ML YEARS		385	1459	411	91	9	55	(30	25)	685	222	246	135	7	299	21	0	16	36	15	.71	41	.282	.348	.469

Rheal Cormier

Pitches: Left **Bats:** Left **Pos:** SP-1   **Ht:** 5'10" **Wt:** 187 **Born:** 4/23/67 **Age:** 31

		HOW MUCH HE PITCHED						WHAT HE GAVE UP										THE RESULTS					
Year Team	Lg	G	GS	CG	GF	IP	BFP	H	R	ER	HR	SH	SF	HB	TBB	IBB	SO	WP	Bk	W	L	Pct.	ShO	Sv-Op	Hld	ERA
1991 St. Louis	NL	11	10	2	1	67.2	281	74	35	31	5	1	3	2	8	1	38	2	1	4	5	.444	0	0-0	0	4.12
1992 St. Louis	NL	31	30	3	1	186	772	194	83	76	15	11	3	5	33	2	117	4	2	10	10	.500	1	0-0	0	3.68
1993 St. Louis	NL	38	21	1	4	145.1	619	163	80	70	18	10	4	4	27	3	75	6	0	7	6	.538	0	0-0	0	4.33
1994 St. Louis	NL	7	7	0	0	39.2	169	40	24	24	6	1	2	3	7	0	26	2	0	3	2	.600	0	0-0	0	5.45
1995 Boston	AL	48	12	0	3	115	488	131	60	52	12	6	2	3	31	2	69	4	0	7	5	.583	0	0-2	9	4.07
1996 Montreal	NL	33	27	1	1	159.2	674	165	80	74	16	4	8	9	41	3	100	8	0	7	10	.412	1	0-0	0	4.17
1997 Montreal	NL	1	1	0	0	1.1	9	4	5	5	1	0	0	0	1	0	0	0	0	0	1	.000	0	0-0	0	33.75
7 ML YEARS		169	108	7	10	714.2	3012	771	367	332	73	33	22	26	148	11	425	26	3	38	39	.494	1	0-2	9	4.18

Jim Corsi

Pitches: Right **Bats:** Right **Pos:** RP-52   **Ht:** 6'1" **Wt:** 220 **Born:** 9/9/61 **Age:** 36

		HOW MUCH HE PITCHED						WHAT HE GAVE UP										THE RESULTS					
Year Team	Lg	G	GS	CG	GF	IP	BFP	H	R	ER	HR	SH	SF	HB	TBB	IBB	SO	WP	Bk	W	L	Pct.	ShO	Sv-Op	Hld	ERA
1997 Pawtucket *	AAA	2	0	0	1	2.1	10	2	0	0	0	0	0	0	1	0	3	0	0	0	0	.000	0	1-—	—	0.00
Red Sox *	R	3	2	0	0	4	14	2	1	0	0	0	0	0	0	0	6	0	0	0	1	1.000	0	0-—	—	0.00
1988 Oakland	AL	11	1	0	7	21.1	89	20	10	9	1	3	3	0	6	1	10	1	1	0	1	.000	0	0-0	0	3.80
1989 Oakland	AL	22	0	0	14	38.1	149	26	8	8	2	2	2	1	10	0	21	0	0	1	2	.333	0	0-0	2	1.88
1991 Houston	NL	47	0	0	15	77.2	322	76	37	32	6	3	2	0	23	5	53	1	1	0	5	.000	0	0-3	4	3.71
1992 Oakland	AL	32	0	0	16	44	185	44	12	7	2	4	2	0	18	2	19	0	0	4	2	.667	0	0-0	4	1.43
1993 Florida	NL	15	0	0	6	20.1	97	28	15	15	1	3	1	0	10	3	7	0	0	0	0	.000	0	0-0	1	6.64
1995 Oakland	AL	38	0	0	7	45	187	31	14	11	2	5	1	2	26	1	26	0	0	2	4	.333	0	2-4	13	2.20
1996 Oakland	AL	56	0	0	19	73.2	312	71	33	33	6	9	2	3	34	4	43	1	0	6	0	1.000	0	3-6	10	4.03
1997 Boston	AL	52	0	0	14	57.2	251	56	26	22	1	3	3	4	21	7	40	2	0	5	3	.625	0	2-9	11	3.43
8 ML YEARS		273	1	0	98	378	1592	352	155	137	21	32	16	10	148	23	219	5	2	18	19	.486	0	7-22	45	3.26

Craig Counsell

Bats: Left **Throws:** Right **Pos:** 2B-51; PH-4   **Ht:** 6'0" **Wt:** 170 **Born:** 8/21/70 **Age:** 27

						BATTING										BASERUNNING				PERCENTAGES		
Year Team	Lg	G	AB	H	2B	3B	HR	(Hm	Rd)	TB	R	RBI	TBB	IBB	SO	HBP	SH	SF	SB	CS	SB%	GDP	Avg	OBP	SLG
1992 Bend	A-	18	61	15	6	1	0	—	—	23	11	8	9	1	10	1	1	0	1	2	.33	2	.246	.352	.377
1993 Central Val	A+	131	471	132	26	3	5	—	—	179	79	59	95	1	68	3	5	4	14	8	.64	8	.280	.401	.380
1994 New Haven	AA	83	300	84	20	1	5	—	—	121	47	37	37	4	32	5	1	2	4	1	.80	6	.280	.366	.403
1995 Colo Spmgs	AAA	118	399	112	22	6	5	—	—	161	60	53	34	7	47	2	3	6	10	2	.83	12	.281	.336	.404
1996 Colo Spmgs	AAA	25	75	18	3	0	2	—	—	27	17	10	24	1	7	0	0	0	4	3	.57	2	.240	.424	.360
1997 Colo Spmgs	AAA	96	376	126	31	6	5	—	—	184	77	63	45	3	38	6	7	6	12	2	.86	6	.335	.409	.489
1995 Colorado	NL	3	1	0	0	0	0	(0	0)	0	0	0	1	0	0	0	0	0	0	0	.00	0	.000	.500	.000
1997 Col-Fla	NL	52	164	49	9	2	1	(1	0)	65	20	16	18	2	17	3	3	1	1	1	.50	5	.299	.376	.396
1997 Colorado	NL	1	0	0	0	0	0	(0	0)	0	0	0	0	0	0	0	0	0	0	0	.00	0	.000	.000	.000
Florida	NL	51	164	49	9	2	1	(1	0)	65	20	16	18	2	17	3	3	1	1	1	.50	5	.299	.376	.396
2 ML YEARS		55	165	49	9	2	1	(1	0)	65	20	16	19	2	17	3	3	1	1	1	.50	5	.297	.378	.394

Tim Crabtree

Pitches: Right **Bats:** Right **Pos:** RP-37   **Ht:** 6'4" **Wt:** 195 **Born:** 10/13/69 **Age:** 28

		HOW MUCH HE PITCHED						WHAT HE GAVE UP										THE RESULTS					
Year Team	Lg	G	GS	CG	GF	IP	BFP	H	R	ER	HR	SH	SF	HB	TBB	IBB	SO	WP	Bk	W	L	Pct.	ShO	Sv-Op	Hld	ERA
1997 St. Cathrns *	A-	2	1	0	0	3	12	3	2	1	0	0	0	0	0	0	3	0	0	0	0	.000	0	0-—	—	3.00
Syracuse *	AAA	3	0	0	2	3.2	19	7	4	4	1	1	0	0	1	0	3	0	0	0	0	.000	0	1-—	—	9.82
1995 Toronto	AL	31	0	0	19	32	140	30	16	11	1	0	1	2	13	0	21	2	0	0	2	.000	0	0-2	1	3.09
1996 Toronto	AL	53	0	0	21	67.1	284	59	26	19	4	2	2	3	22	4	57	3	0	5	3	.625	0	1-5	17	2.54
1997 Toronto	AL	37	0	0	16	40.2	199	65	32	32	7	4	2	2	17	3	26	4	0	3	3	.500	0	2-5	8	7.08
3 ML YEARS		121	0	0	56	140	624	154	74	62	12	6	5	7	52	7	104	9	0	8	8	.500	0	3-12	26	3.99

Joe Crawford

Pitches: Left **Bats:** Left **Pos:** RP-17; SP-2   **Ht:** 6'3" **Wt:** 225 **Born:** 5/2/70 **Age:** 28

		HOW MUCH HE PITCHED						WHAT HE GAVE UP										THE RESULTS					
Year Team	Lg	G	GS	CG	GF	IP	BFP	H	R	ER	HR	SH	SF	HB	TBB	IBB	SO	WP	Bk	W	L	Pct.	ShO	Sv-Op	Hld	ERA
1991 Kingsport	R+	19	0	0	16	32.1	118	16	5	4	0	0	0	1	8	0	43	3	1	0	0	.000	0	11-—	—	1.11
Columbia	A	3	0	0	2	3	9	0	0	0	0	0	0	0	0	0	6	0	0	0	0	.000	0	0-—	—	0.00
1992 St. Lucie	A+	25	1	0	16	43.2	174	29	18	10	1	1	3	0	15	3	32	1	3	3	3	.500	0	3-—	—	2.06

48

Year Team	Lg	G	GS	CG	GF	IP	BFP	H	R	ER	HR	SH	SF	HB	TBB	IBB	SO	WP	Bk	W	L	Pct.	ShO	Sv-Op	Hld	ERA
1993 St. Lucie	A+	34	0	0	19	37	156	38	15	15	0	2	0	2	14	5	24	0	0	3	3	.500	0	5--	—	3.65
1994 St. Lucie	A+	33	0	0	15	42.2	155	22	8	7	1	1	2	2	9	2	31	1	0	1	1	.500	0	5--	—	1.48
Binghamton	AA	13	0	0	6	14.2	70	20	10	9	2	0	2	0	8	0	9	0	0	1	0	1.000	0	0--	—	5.52
1995 Binghamton	AA	42	1	0	15	60.2	239	48	17	15	4	3	7	5	17	4	43	3	1	7	2	.778	0	0--	—	2.23
Norfolk	AAA	8	0	0	1	18.2	70	9	5	4	0	1	0	0	4	0	13	0	0	1	1	.500	0	0--	—	1.93
1996 Binghamton	AA	7	7	1	0	49.2	190	34	10	8	4	2	0	0	9	1	34	1	2	5	1	.833	1	0--	—	1.45
Norfolk	AAA	20	16	2	2	96.2	403	98	45	37	10	3	1	4	20	1	68	0	1	6	5	.545	1	0--	—	3.44
1997 Norfolk	AAA	16	16	0	0	99.2	431	109	45	39	6	5	5	1	31	0	72	4	2	8	2	.800	0	0--	—	3.52
1997 New York	NL	19	2	0	9	46.1	182	36	18	17	7	2	0	0	13	1	25	0	1	4	3	.571	0	0-0	0	3.30

Doug Creek

Pitches: Left   Bats: Left   Pos: SP-3   Ht: 5'10"   Wt: 205   Born: 3/1/69   Age: 29

Year Team	Lg	G	GS	CG	GF	IP	BFP	H	R	ER	HR	SH	SF	HB	TBB	IBB	SO	WP	Bk	W	L	Pct.	ShO	Sv-Op	Hld	ERA
1997 Phoenix *	AAA	25	23	2	0	129.2	583	140	76	71	15	6	0	4	66	0	137	7	2	8	6	.571	0	0--	—	4.93
1995 St. Louis	NL	6	0	0	1	6.2	24	2	0	0	0	0	0	0	3	0	10	0	0	0	0	.000	0	0-0	0	0.00
1996 San Francisco	NL	63	0	0	15	48.1	220	45	41	35	11	1	0	2	32	2	38	2	0	0	2	.000	0	0-1	7	6.52
1997 San Francisco	NL	3	3	0	0	13.1	64	12	12	10	1	0	0	0	14	0	14	0	0	1	2	.333	0	0-0	0	6.75
3 ML YEARS		72	3	0	16	68.1	308	59	53	45	12	1	0	2	49	2	62	2	0	1	4	.200	0	0-1	7	5.93

Felipe Crespo

Bats: Both   Throws: Right   Pos: 3B-7; PH-4; DH-2; 2B-1   Ht: 5'11"   Wt: 195   Born: 3/5/73   Age: 25

Year Team	Lg	G	AB	H	2B	3B	HR	(Hm	Rd)	TB	R	RBI	TBB	IBB	SO	HBP	SH	SF	SB	CS	SB%	GDP	Avg	OBP	SLG
1991 Medicne Hat	R+	49	184	57	11	4	4	—	—	88	40	31	25	0	31	3	2	2	6	4	.60	2	.310	.397	.478
1992 Myrtle Bch	A	81	263	74	14	3	1	—	—	97	43	29	58	2	38	4	4	5	7	7	.50	1	.281	.412	.369
1993 Dunedin	A+	96	345	103	16	8	6	—	—	153	51	39	47	3	40	4	5	2	18	5	.78	9	.299	.387	.443
1994 Knoxville	AA	129	502	135	30	4	8	—	—	197	74	49	57	3	95	2	4	1	20	8	.71	5	.269	.345	.392
1995 Syracuse	AAA	88	347	102	20	5	13	—	—	171	56	41	41	4	56	2	1	1	12	7	.63	5	.294	.371	.493
1996 Dunedin	A+	9	34	11	1	0	2	—	—	18	3	6	2	1	3	0	0	0	1	1	.50	5	.324	.361	.529
Syracuse	AAA	98	355	100	25	0	8	—	—	149	53	58	56	2	39	9	2	4	10	11	.48	7	.282	.389	.420
1997 Syracuse	AAA	80	290	75	12	0	12	—	—	123	53	26	46	0	38	4	2	2	7	7	.50	1	.259	.365	.424
1996 Toronto	AL	22	49	9	4	0	0	(0	0)	13	6	4	12	0	13	3	0	1	1	0	1.00	1	.184	.375	.265
1997 Toronto	AL	12	28	8	0	1	1	(0	1)	13	3	5	2	0	4	0	1	0	0	0	.00	0	.286	.333	.464
2 ML YEARS		34	77	17	4	1	1	(0	1)	26	9	9	14	0	17	3	1	1	1	0	1.00	1	.221	.362	.338

Tripp Cromer

Bats: R   Throws: R   Pos: 2B-17; SS-10; PH-2; 3B-1   Ht: 6'2"   Wt: 170   Born: 11/21/67   Age: 30

Year Team	Lg	G	AB	H	2B	3B	HR	(Hm	Rd)	TB	R	RBI	TBB	IBB	SO	HBP	SH	SF	SB	CS	SB%	GDP	Avg	OBP	SLG
1997 Albuquerque *	AAA	43	140	45	8	6	5	—	—	80	25	24	14	1	34	1	1	3	4	1	.80	0	.321	.380	.571
1993 St. Louis	NL	10	23	2	0	0	0	(0	0)	2	1	0	1	0	6	0	0	0	0	0	.00	0	.087	.125	.087
1994 St. Louis	NL	2	0	0	0	0	0	(0	0)	0	1	0	0	0	0	0	0	0	0	0	.00	0	.000	.000	.000
1995 St. Louis	NL	105	345	78	19	0	5	(2	3)	112	36	18	14	2	66	4	1	5	0	0	.00	14	.226	.261	.325
1997 Los Angeles	NL	28	86	25	3	0	4	(2	2)	40	8	20	6	3	16	0	2	1	0	1	.00	2	.291	.333	.465
4 ML YEARS		145	454	105	22	0	9	(4	5)	154	46	38	21	5	88	4	3	6	0	1	.00	16	.231	.268	.339

Jim Crowell

Pitches: Left   Bats: Right   Pos: SP-1; RP-1   Ht: 6'4"   Wt: 225   Born: 5/14/74   Age: 24

Year Team	Lg	G	GS	CG	GF	IP	BFP	H	R	ER	HR	SH	SF	HB	TBB	IBB	SO	WP	Bk	W	L	Pct.	ShO	Sv-Op	Hld	ERA
1995 Watertown	A-	12	9	0	0	56.2	241	50	22	18	1	0	2	1	27	1	48	2	1	5	2	.714	0	0--	—	2.86
1996 Columbus	A	28	28	3	0	165.1	710	163	89	76	16	9	5	9	69	0	104	12	0	7	10	.412	0	0--	—	4.14
1997 Kinston	A+	17	17	0	0	114	461	96	41	30	4	3	2	8	26	0	94	3	0	9	4	.692	0	0--	—	2.37
Akron	AA	3	3	0	0	18	80	13	12	9	2	1	1	1	11	0	7	1	0	1	0	1.000	0	0--	—	4.50
Chattanooga	AA	3	3	0	0	19	75	19	6	6	2	1	1	0	5	0	14	0	0	2	1	.667	0	0--	—	2.84
Indianapols	AAA	3	3	1	0	19.2	85	19	7	6	1	0	2	0	8	0	6	1	0	1	1	.500	1	0--	—	2.75
1997 Cincinnati	NL	2	1	0	1	6.1	36	12	7	7	2	2	0	0	5	0	3	0	0	0	1	.000	0	0-0	0	9.95

Deivi Cruz

Bats: Right   Throws: Right   Pos: SS-147   Ht: 5'11"   Wt: 160   Born: 6/11/75   Age: 23

Year Team	Lg	G	AB	H	2B	3B	HR	(Hm	Rd)	TB	R	RBI	TBB	IBB	SO	HBP	SH	SF	SB	CS	SB%	GDP	Avg	OBP	SLG
1993 Giants	R	28	82	28	3	0	0	—	—	31	8	15	4	0	5	0	3	1	3	0	1.00	3	.341	.368	.378
1994 Giants	R	18	53	16	8	0	0	—	—	24	10	5	5	0	3	1	1	1	0	1	.00	1	.302	.367	.453
1995 Burlington	A	16	58	8	1	0	1	—	—	12	2	9	4	0	7	0	1	0	1	1	.50	1	.138	.194	.207
Bellingham	A-	62	223	66	17	0	3	—	—	92	32	26	19	3	21	0	1	2	6	3	.67	5	.296	.348	.413
1996 Burlington	A	127	517	152	27	2	9	—	—	210	72	64	35	3	49	4	4	3	12	5	.71	20	.294	.342	.406
1997 Detroit	AL	147	436	105	26	0	2	(0	2)	137	35	40	14	0	55	0	14	3	3	6	.33	9	.241	.263	.314

Ivan Cruz

Bats: Left **Throws:** Left **Pos:** PH-6; DH-4; 1B-3; LF-1   **Ht:** 6'3" **Wt:** 210 **Born:** 5/3/68 **Age:** 30

							BATTING											BASERUNNING				PERCENTAGES		
Year Team	Lg	G	AB	H	2B	3B	HR	(Hm | Rd)	TB	R	RBI	TBB	IBB	SO	HBP	SH	SF	SB	CS	SB%	GDP	Avg	OBP	SLG
1989 Niagara Fal	A-	64	226	62	11	2	7	—	—	98	43	40	27	4	29	3	0	1	2	0	1.00	2	.274	.358	.434
1990 Lakeland	A+	118	414	118	23	2	11	—	—	178	61	73	49	3	71	5	2	4	8	1	.89	8	.285	.364	.430
1991 Toledo	AAA	8	29	4	0	0	1	—	—	7	2	4	2	0	12	1	0	0	0	0	.00	0	.138	.219	.241
London	AA	121	443	110	21	0	9	—	—	158	45	47	36	5	74	4	1	2	3	3	.50	12	.248	.309	.357
1992 London	AA	134	524	143	25	1	14	—	—	212	71	104	37	1	102	4	0	6	1	1	.50	16	.273	.322	.405
1993 Toledo	AAA	115	402	91	18	4	13	—	—	156	44	50	30	2	85	3	0	2	1	1	.50	5	.226	.284	.388
1994 Toledo	AAA	97	303	75	11	2	15	—	—	135	36	43	28	0	83	2	0	3	1	0	1.00	7	.248	.313	.446
1995 Toledo	AAA	11	36	7	2	0	0	—	—	9	5	3	6	0	9	0	0	1	0	0	.00	1	.194	.302	.250
Jacksnville	AA	108	397	112	17	1	31	—	—	224	65	93	60	15	94	0	0	3	0	0	.00	7	.282	.374	.564
1996 Columbus	AAA	130	446	115	26	0	28	—	—	225	84	96	48	3	99	8	2	9	2	4	.33	9	.258	.335	.504
1997 Columbus	AAA	116	417	125	35	1	24	—	—	234	69	95	65	10	78	11	0	4	4	5	.44	8	.300	.404	.561
1997 New York	AL	11	20	5	1	0	0	(0 | 0)	6	0	3	2	0	4	0	0	0	0	0	.00	0	.250	.318	.300

Jacob Cruz

Bats: Left **Throws:** Left **Pos:** RF-10; PH-7; LF-2   **Ht:** 6'1" **Wt:** 175 **Born:** 1/28/73 **Age:** 25

							BATTING											BASERUNNING				PERCENTAGES		
Year Team	Lg	G	AB	H	2B	3B	HR	(Hm	Rd)	TB	R	RBI	TBB	IBB	SO	HBP	SH	SF	SB	CS	SB%	GDP	Avg	OBP	SLG
1994 San Jose	A+	31	118	29	7	0	0	—	—	36	14	12	9	0	22	2	2	2	0	2	.00	6	.246	.305	.305
1995 Shreveport	AA	127	458	136	33	1	13	—	—	210	88	77	57	6	72	8	4	2	9	8	.53	15	.297	.383	.459
1996 Phoenix	AAA	121	435	124	26	4	7	—	—	179	60	75	62	5	77	10	2	11	5	9	.36	16	.285	.378	.411
1997 Phoenix	AAA	127	493	178	45	3	12	—	—	265	97	95	64	9	64	3	0	5	18	3	.86	11	.361	.434	.538
1996 San Francisco	NL	33	77	18	3	0	3	(3	0)	30	10	10	12	0	24	2	1	0	0	1	.00	2	.234	.352	.390
1997 San Francisco	NL	16	25	4	1	0	0	(0	0)	5	3	3	3	0	4	0	0	1	0	0	.00	3	.160	.241	.200
2 ML YEARS		49	102	22	4	0	3	(3	0)	35	13	13	15	0	28	2	1	1	0	1	.00	5	.216	.325	.343

Nelson Cruz

Pitches: Right **Bats:** Right **Pos:** RP-19   **Ht:** 6'1" **Wt:** 185 **Born:** 9/13/72 **Age:** 25

		HOW MUCH HE PITCHED						WHAT HE GAVE UP										THE RESULTS						
Year Team	Lg	G	GS	CG	GF	IP	BFP	H	R	ER	HR	SH	SF	HB	TBB	IBB	SO	WP	Bk	W	L	Pct.	ShO	Sv-Op	Hld	ERA
1991 Expos	R	12	8	1	0	48.1	207	40	18	13	1	3	1	2	19	0	34	2	3	2	4	.333	1	0- --	---	2.42
1995 Bristol	R+	1	0	0	1	1	6	2	1	1	0	0	1	1	0	0	0	0	0	0	0	.000	0	0- --	---	9.00
Hickory	A	44	0	0	29	66.2	285	65	31	20	6	3	1	4	15	2	68	5	0	2	7	.222	0	9- --	---	2.70
Pr William	A+	9	0	0	7	19.1	75	12	1	1	1	0	0	2	6	0	18	0	0	1	1	.667	0	1- --	---	0.47
1996 Birmingham	AA	37	18	2	8	149	627	150	65	53	10	7	6	8	41	2	142	3	1	6	6	.500	1	1- --	---	3.20
1997 Nashville	AAA	21	20	1	0	123.1	533	139	75	70	20	1	4	9	31	0	93	1	2	11	7	.611	0	0- --	---	5.11
1997 Chicago	AL	19	0	0	5	26.1	116	29	19	19	6	1	0	0	9	1	23	3	0	0	2	.000	0	0-0	6	6.49

Jose Cruz Jr

Bats: Both **Throws:** Right **Pos:** LF-100; CF-4; PH-2   **Ht:** 6'0" **Wt:** 190 **Born:** 4/19/74 **Age:** 24

							BATTING											BASERUNNING				PERCENTAGES		
Year Team	Lg	G	AB	H	2B	3B	HR	(Hm	Rd)	TB	R	RBI	TBB	IBB	SO	HBP	SH	SF	SB	CS	SB%	GDP	Avg	OBP	SLG
1995 Everett	A-	3	11	5	0	0	0	—	—	5	6	2	3	0	3	0	0	0	1	0	1.00	0	.455	.571	.455
Riverside	A+	35	144	37	7	1	7	—	—	67	34	29	24	1	50	0	0	2	3	1	.75	1	.257	.359	.465
1996 Lancaster	A+	53	203	66	17	1	6	—	—	103	38	43	39	1	33	0	0	6	7	1	.88	4	.325	.423	.507
Port City	AA	47	181	51	10	2	3	—	—	74	39	31	27	4	38	0	0	1	5	0	1.00	8	.282	.373	.409
Tacoma	AAA	22	76	18	1	2	6	—	—	41	15	15	18	1	12	0	1	0	1	1	.50	2	.237	.383	.539
1997 Tacoma	AAA	50	190	51	16	2	6	—	—	89	33	30	34	1	44	1	1	0	3	0	1.00	4	.268	.382	.468
1997 Sea-Tor	AL	104	395	98	19	1	26	(11	15)	197	59	68	41	2	117	0	1	5	7	2	.78	5	.248	.315	.499
1997 Seattle	AL	49	183	49	12	1	12	(7	5)	99	28	34	13	0	45	0	1	1	1	0	1.00	3	.268	.315	.541
Toronto	AL	55	212	49	7	0	14	(4	10)	98	31	34	28	2	72	0	0	4	6	2	.75	2	.231	.316	.462

John Cummings

Pitches: Left **Bats:** Left **Pos:** RP-19   **Ht:** 6'3" **Wt:** 200 **Born:** 5/10/69 **Age:** 29

		HOW MUCH HE PITCHED						WHAT HE GAVE UP										THE RESULTS						
Year Team	Lg	G	GS	CG	GF	IP	BFP	H	R	ER	HR	SH	SF	HB	TBB	IBB	SO	WP	Bk	W	L	Pct.	ShO	Sv-Op	Hld	ERA
1997 Toledo *	AAA	19	0	0	5	16.1	70	13	6	5	2	2	2	1	6	1	7	0	0	2	1	.667	0	0- --	---	2.76
1993 Seattle	AL	10	8	1	0	46.1	207	59	34	31	6	0	2	2	16	2	19	1	1	0	6	.000	0	0-0	0	6.02
1994 Seattle	AL	17	8	0	2	64	285	66	43	40	7	1	3	0	37	2	33	3	1	2	4	.333	0	0-0	0	5.63
1995 Sea-LA		39	0	0	11	44.1	195	46	24	20	3	3	3	0	17	6	25	5	1	3	1	.750	0	0-0	6	4.06
1996 LA-Det		25	0	0	8	37	182	48	27	22	4	3	2	2	22	4	29	1	0	3	4	.429	0	0-1	1	5.35
1997 Detroit	AL	19	0	0	2	24.2	119	32	22	15	3	2	0	0	14	1	8	3	0	2	0	1.000	0	0-0	4	5.47
1995 Seattle	AL	4	0	0	0	5.1	30	8	8	7	0	1	2	0	7	2	4	4	1	0	0	.000	0	0-0	0	11.81
Los Angeles	NL	35	0	0	11	39	165	38	16	13	3	2	1	0	10	4	21	1	0	3	1	.750	0	0-0	6	3.00
1996 Los Angeles	NL	4	0	0	1	5.1	30	12	7	4	1	1	1	2	2	1	5	0	0	0	1	.000	0	0-0	0	6.75
Detroit	AL	21	0	0	7	31.2	152	36	20	18	3	2	1	2	20	3	24	1	0	3	3	.500	0	0-1	1	5.12
5 ML YEARS		110	16	1	23	216.1	988	251	150	128	23	9	10	4	106	15	114	13	3	10	15	.400	0	0-1	11	5.33

Midre Cummings

Bats: L **Throws:** R **Pos:** CF-53; PH-40; LF-14; RF-13   **Ht:** 6'0" **Wt:** 203 **Born:** 10/14/71 **Age:** 26

							BATTING										BASERUNNING				PERCENTAGES		
Year Team	Lg	G	AB	H	2B	3B	HR	(Hm | Rd)	TB	R	RBI	TBB	IBB	SO	HBP	SH	SF	SB	CS	SB%	GDP	Avg	OBP	SLG
1993 Pittsburgh	NL	13	36	4	1	0	0	(0 | 0)	5	5	3	4	0	9	0	0	1	0	0	.00	1	.111	.195	.139
1994 Pittsburgh	NL	24	86	21	4	0	1	(1 | 0)	28	11	12	4	0	18	1	0	1	0	0	.00	0	.244	.283	.326
1995 Pittsburgh	NL	59	152	37	7	1	2	(1 | 1)	52	13	15	13	3	30	0	1	0	1	0	1.00	1	.243	.303	.342
1996 Pittsburgh	NL	24	85	19	3	1	3	(2 | 1)	33	11	7	0	0	16	0	1	1	0	0	.00	0	.224	.221	.388
1997 Pit-Phi	NL	115	314	83	22	6	4	(3 | 1)	129	35	31	31	0	56	1	2	2	2	3	.40	3	.264	.330	.411
1997 Pittsburgh	NL	52	106	20	6	2	3	(2 | 1)	39	11	8	8	0	26	1	1	0	0	0	.00	1	.189	.252	.368
Philadelphia	NL	63	208	63	16	4	1	(1 | 0)	90	24	23	23	0	30	0	1	2	2	3	.40	2	.303	.369	.433
5 ML YEARS		235	673	164	37	8	10	(7 | 3)	247	75	68	52	3	129	2	3	5	3	3	.50	5	.244	.298	.367

Will Cunnane

Pitches: Right **Bats:** Right **Pos:** RP-46; SP-8   **Ht:** 6'2" **Wt:** 175 **Born:** 4/24/74 **Age:** 24

			HOW MUCH HE PITCHED					WHAT HE GAVE UP									THE RESULTS						
Year Team	Lg	G	GS	CG	GF	IP	BFP	H	R	ER	HR	SH	SF	HB	TBB	IBB	SO	WP	Bk	W	L	Pct.	ShO	Sv-Op	Hld	ERA
1993 Marlins	R	16	9	0	4	66.2	290	75	32	20	1	3	0	0	8	0	64	2	1	3	3	.500	0	2- —	—	2.70
1994 Kane County	A	32	16	5	6	138.2	540	110	27	22	2	4	1	6	23	4	106	5	1	11	3	.786	4	1- —	—	1.43
1995 Portland	AA	21	21	1	0	117.2	497	120	48	48	10	3	0	5	34	1	83	2	0	9	2	.818	1	0- —	—	3.67
1996 Portland	AA	25	25	4	0	151.2	631	156	73	63	15	5	2	1	30	6	101	4	0	10	12	.455	1	0- —	—	3.74
1997 San Diego	NL	54	8	0	16	91.1	430	114	69	59	11	1	1	5	49	3	79	3	0	6	3	.667	0	0-2	4	5.81

Chad Curtis

Bats: R **Throws:** R **Pos:** LF-56; CF-55; PH-11; RF-9   **Ht:** 5'10" **Wt:** 175 **Born:** 11/6/68 **Age:** 29

							BATTING										BASERUNNING				PERCENTAGES		
Year Team	Lg	G	AB	H	2B	3B	HR	(Hm	Rd)	TB	R	RBI	TBB	IBB	SO	HBP	SH	SF	SB	CS	SB%	GDP	Avg	OBP	SLG
1997 Akron *	AA	4	18	7	1	0	3	—	—	17	5	6	0	0	3	1	0	0	1	1	.00	1	.389	.421	.944
1992 California	AL	139	441	114	16	2	10	(5	5)	164	59	46	51	2	71	6	5	4	43	18	.70	10	.259	.341	.372
1993 California	AL	152	583	166	25	3	6	(3	3)	215	94	59	70	2	89	4	7	7	48	24	.67	16	.285	.361	.369
1994 California	AL	114	453	116	23	4	11	(8	3)	180	67	50	37	0	69	5	1	2	25	11	.69	10	.256	.317	.397
1995 Detroit	AL	144	586	157	29	3	21	(11	10)	255	96	67	70	4	93	7	0	7	27	15	.64	12	.268	.349	.435
1996 Det-LA	AL	147	504	127	25	1	12	(3	9)	190	85	46	70	0	88	1	6	6	18	11	.62	15	.252	.341	.377
1997 Cle-NYA	AL	115	349	99	22	1	15	(4	11)	168	59	55	43	1	59	5	2	9	12	6	.67	7	.284	.362	.481
1996 Detroit	AL	104	400	105	20	1	10	(2	8)	157	65	37	53	0	73	1	6	6	16	10	.62	14	.263	.346	.393
Los Angeles	NL	43	104	22	5	0	2	(1	1)	33	20	9	17	0	15	0	0	0	2	1	.67	1	.212	.322	.317
1997 Cleveland	AL	22	29	6	1	0	3	(1	2)	16	8	5	7	0	10	0	0	0	0	0	.00	1	.207	.361	.552
New York	AL	93	320	93	21	1	12	(3	9)	152	51	50	36	1	49	5	2	9	12	6	.67	6	.291	.362	.475
6 ML YEARS		811	2916	779	140	14	75	(34	41)	1172	460	323	341	8	469	28	27	37	173	85	.67	70	.267	.346	.402

Omar Daal

Pitches: Left **Bats:** Left **Pos:** RP-39; SP-3   **Ht:** 6'3" **Wt:** 185 **Born:** 3/1/72 **Age:** 26

			HOW MUCH HE PITCHED					WHAT HE GAVE UP									THE RESULTS						
Year Team	Lg	G	GS	CG	GF	IP	BFP	H	R	ER	HR	SH	SF	HB	TBB	IBB	SO	WP	Bk	W	L	Pct.	ShO	Sv-Op	Hld	ERA
1997 Ottawa *	AAA	2	2	0	0	8	36	10	6	5	1	0	0	0	1	0	9	1	0	0	1	.000	0	0- —	—	5.63
Syracuse *	AAA	5	5	1	0	33.2	128	18	2	2	0	1	0	0	10	0	29	2	1	3	0	1.000	1	0- —	—	0.53
1993 Los Angeles	NL	47	0	0	12	35.1	155	36	20	20	5	2	2	0	21	3	19	1	2	2	3	.400	0	0-1	7	5.09
1994 Los Angeles	NL	24	0	0	5	13.2	55	12	5	5	1	1	0	0	5	0	9	1	0	0	0	.000	0	0-0	3	3.29
1995 Los Angeles	NL	28	0	0	0	20	100	29	16	16	1	1	1	1	15	4	11	0	1	4	0	1.000	0	0-1	4	7.20
1996 Montreal	NL	64	6	0	9	87.1	366	74	40	39	10	2	2	1	37	3	82	1	1	4	5	.444	0	0-4	9	4.02
1997 Mon-Tor		42	3	0	6	57.1	270	82	48	45	7	7	1	2	21	3	44	2	0	2	3	.400	0	1-3	3	7.06
1997 Montreal	NL	33	0	0	6	30.1	150	48	35	33	4	5	1	2	15	3	16	1	0	1	2	.333	0	1-3	3	9.79
Toronto	AL	9	3	0	0	27	120	34	13	12	3	2	0	0	6	0	28	1	0	1	1	.500	0	0-0	0	4.00
5 ML YEARS		205	9	0	32	213.2	946	233	129	125	24	13	6	4	99	13	165	5	5	12	11	.522	0	1-9	26	5.27

Jeff D'Amico

Pitches: Right **Bats:** Right **Pos:** SP-23   **Ht:** 6'7" **Wt:** 250 **Born:** 12/27/75 **Age:** 22

			HOW MUCH HE PITCHED					WHAT HE GAVE UP									THE RESULTS						
Year Team	Lg	G	GS	CG	GF	IP	BFP	H	R	ER	HR	SH	SF	HB	TBB	IBB	SO	WP	Bk	W	L	Pct.	ShO	Sv-Op	Hld	ERA
1995 Beloit	A	21	20	3	0	132	523	102	40	35	7	3	2	4	31	2	119	6	1	13	3	.813	1	0- —	—	2.39
1996 El Paso	AA	13	13	3	0	96	387	89	42	34	10	0	2	2	13	0	76	0	1	5	4	.556	0	0- —	—	3.19
1997 Beloit	A	1	1	0	0	3	10	0	0	0	0	0	0	0	1	0	7	0	0	0	0	.000	0	0- —	—	0.00
1996 Milwaukee	AL	17	17	0	0	86	367	88	53	52	21	3	3	0	31	0	53	1	1	6	6	.500	0	0-0	0	5.44
1997 Milwaukee	AL	23	23	1	0	135.2	585	139	81	71	25	4	4	8	43	2	94	3	1	9	7	.563	1	0-0	0	4.71
2 ML YEARS		40	40	1	0	221.2	952	227	134	123	46	7	7	8	74	2	147	4	2	15	13	.536	1	0-0	0	4.99

Johnny Damon

Bats: L **Throws:** L **Pos:** CF-65; LF-48; RF-47; PH-19; DH-5   **Ht:** 6'2" **Wt:** 190 **Born:** 11/5/73 **Age:** 24

							BATTING										BASERUNNING				PERCENTAGES		
Year Team	Lg	G	AB	H	2B	3B	HR	(Hm	Rd)	TB	R	RBI	TBB	IBB	SO	HBP	SH	SF	SB	CS	SB%	GDP	Avg	OBP	SLG
1995 Kansas City	AL	47	188	53	11	5	3	(1	2)	83	32	23	12	0	22	1	2	3	7	0	1.00	2	.282	.324	.441
1996 Kansas City	AL	145	517	140	22	5	6	(3	3)	190	61	50	31	3	64	3	10	5	25	5	.83	4	.271	.313	.368
1997 Kansas City	AL	146	472	130	12	8	8	(3	5)	182	70	48	42	2	70	3	6	1	16	10	.62	3	.275	.338	.386

				BATTING													BASERUNNING				PERCENTAGES		
Year Team	Lg	G	AB	H	2B	3B	HR	(Hm | Rd)	TB	R	RBI	TBB	IBB	SO	HBP	SH	SF	SB	CS	SB%	GDP	Avg	OBP	SLG
3 ML YEARS		338	1177	323	45	18	17	(7 | 10)	455	163	121	85	5	156	7	18	9	48	15	.76	9	.274	.325	.387

Danny Darwin

Pitches: Right **Bats:** Right **Pos:** SP-24; RP-7   **Ht:** 6'3" **Wt:** 202 **Born:** 10/25/55 **Age:** 42

		HOW MUCH HE PITCHED						WHAT HE GAVE UP										THE RESULTS					
Year Team	Lg	G	GS	CG	GF	IP	BFP	H	R	ER	HR	SH	SF	HB	TBB	IBB	SO	WP	Bk	W	L	Pct.	ShO	Sv-Op	Hld	ERA
1978 Texas	AL	3	1	0	2	8.2	36	11	4	4	0	0	1	0	1	0	8	0	0	1	0	1.000	0	0- –	—	4.15
1979 Texas	AL	20	6	1	4	78	313	50	36	35	5	3	6	5	30	2	58	0	1	4	4	.500	0	0- –	—	4.04
1980 Texas	AL	53	2	0	35	109.2	468	98	37	32	4	5	7	2	50	7	104	3	0	13	4	.765	0	8- –	—	2.63
1981 Texas	AL	22	22	6	0	146	601	115	67	59	12	8	3	6	57	5	98	1	0	9	9	.500	2	0-0	0	3.64
1982 Texas	AL	56	1	0	41	89	394	95	38	34	6	10	5	2	37	8	61	2	1	10	8	.556	0	7- –	—	3.44
1983 Texas	AL	28	26	9	0	183	780	175	86	71	9	7	7	3	62	3	92	2	0	8	13	.381	2	0- –	—	3.49
1984 Texas	AL	35	32	5	2	223.2	955	249	110	98	19	3	3	4	54	2	123	3	0	8	12	.400	1	0- –	—	3.94
1985 Milwaukee	AL	39	29	11	8	217.2	919	212	112	92	34	7	9	4	65	4	125	6	0	8	18	.308	1	2- –	—	3.80
1986 Mil-Hou		39	22	6	6	184.2	759	170	81	65	16	6	9	3	44	1	120	7	1	11	10	.524	1	0- –	—	3.17
1987 Houston	NL	33	30	3	0	195.2	833	184	87	78	17	8	3	5	69	12	134	3	1	9	10	.474	1	0-0	1	3.59
1988 Houston	NL	44	20	3	9	192	804	189	86	82	20	10	9	7	48	9	129	1	2	8	13	.381	0	3-3	3	3.84
1989 Houston	NL	68	0	0	26	122	482	92	34	32	8	8	5	2	33	9	104	2	3	11	4	.733	0	7-11	8	2.36
1990 Houston	NL	48	17	3	14	162.2	646	136	42	40	11	4	2	4	31	4	109	0	2	11	4	.733	0	2-4	0	2.21
1991 Boston	AL	12	12	0	0	68	292	71	39	39	15	1	2	4	15	1	42	2	0	3	6	.333	0	0-0	0	5.16
1992 Boston	AL	51	15	2	21	161.1	688	159	76	71	11	7	5	5	53	9	124	5	0	9	9	.500	0	3-6	1	3.96
1993 Boston	AL	34	34	2	0	229.1	919	196	93	83	31	6	9	3	49	8	130	5	1	15	11	.577	1	0-0	0	3.26
1994 Boston	AL	13	13	0	0	75.2	350	101	54	53	13	1	5	1	24	6	54	0	0	7	5	.583	0	0-0	0	6.30
1995 Tor-Tex	AL	20	15	1	0	99	448	131	87	82	25	3	5	4	31	3	58	2	0	3	10	.231	0	0-0	0	7.45
1996 Pit-Hou	NL	34	25	0	1	164.2	677	160	79	69	16	8	7	12	27	3	96	3	3	10	11	.476	0	0-2	1	3.77
1997 ChA-SF		31	24	1	0	157.1	692	181	86	76	26	7	6	2	45	1	92	1	2	5	11	.313	0	0-0	0	4.35
1986 Milwaukee	AL	27	14	5	4	130.1	537	120	62	51	13	5	6	3	35	1	80	5	0	6	8	.429	1	0- –	—	3.52
Houston	NL	12	8	1	2	54.1	222	50	19	14	3	1	3	0	9	0	40	2	1	5	2	.714	0	0- –	—	2.32
1995 Toronto	AL	13	11	1	0	65	303	91	60	55	13	3	5	3	24	2	36	1	0	1	8	.111	0	0-0	0	7.62
Texas	AL	7	4	0	0	34	145	40	27	27	12	0	0	1	7	1	22	1	0	2	2	.500	0	0-0	0	7.15
1996 Pittsburgh	NL	19	19	0	0	122.1	493	117	48	41	9	5	4	6	16	0	69	3	3	7	9	.438	0	0-0	0	3.02
Houston	NL	15	6	0	1	42.1	184	43	31	28	7	3	3	6	11	3	27	0	0	3	2	.600	0	0-0	0	5.95
1997 Chicago	NL	21	17	1	0	113.1	496	130	60	52	21	4	5	1	31	1	62	1	2	4	8	.333	0	0-0	0	4.13
San Francisco	NL	10	7	0	0	44	196	51	26	24	5	3	1	1	14	0	30	0	0	1	3	.250	0	0-0	0	4.91
20 ML YEARS		683	346	53	169	2868	12056	2775	1334	1195	298	112	108	78	825	97	1861	48	17	163	172	.487	9	32- –	—	3.75

Jeff Darwin

Pitches: Right **Bats:** Right **Pos:** RP-14   **Ht:** 6'3" **Wt:** 180 **Born:** 7/6/69 **Age:** 28

		HOW MUCH HE PITCHED						WHAT HE GAVE UP										THE RESULTS					
Year Team	Lg	G	GS	CG	GF	IP	BFP	H	R	ER	HR	SH	SF	HB	TBB	IBB	SO	WP	Bk	W	L	Pct.	ShO	Sv-Op	Hld	ERA
1997 Nashville *	AAA	47	0	0	36	53.2	244	60	32	27	8	3	1	2	24	4	44	6	0	4	3	.571	0	22- –	—	4.53
1994 Seattle	AL	2	0	0	1	4	22	7	6	6	1	0	0	1	3	1	1	0	0	0	0	.000	0	0-0	0	13.50
1996 Chicago	AL	22	0	0	9	30.2	124	26	10	10	5	1	0	2	9	1	15	0	0	0	1	.000	0	0-1	2	2.93
1997 Chicago	AL	14	0	0	6	13.2	65	17	8	8	1	0	1	0	7	0	9	3	0	0	1	.000	0	0-1	2	5.27
3 ML YEARS		38	0	0	16	48.1	211	50	24	24	7	1	1	3	19	2	25	3	0	0	2	.000	0	0-1	4	4.47

Darren Daulton

Bats: L **Throws:** R **Pos:** RF-73; 1B-42; PH-16; DH-7; LF-1   **Ht:** 6'2" **Wt:** 207 **Born:** 1/3/62 **Age:** 36

					BATTING													BASERUNNING				PERCENTAGES		
Year Team	Lg	G	AB	H	2B	3B	HR	(Hm	Rd)	TB	R	RBI	TBB	IBB	SO	HBP	SH	SF	SB	CS	SB%	GDP	Avg	OBP	SLG
1983 Philadelphia	NL	2	3	1	0	0	0	(0	0)	1	1	0	1	0	1	0	0	0	0	0	.00	0	.333	.500	.333
1985 Philadelphia	NL	36	103	21	3	1	4	(0	4)	38	14	11	16	0	37	0	0	0	3	0	1.00	1	.204	.311	.369
1986 Philadelphia	NL	49	138	31	4	0	8	(4	4)	59	18	21	38	3	41	1	2	2	2	3	.40	1	.225	.391	.428
1987 Philadelphia	NL	53	129	25	6	0	3	(1	2)	40	10	13	16	1	37	0	4	1	0	0	.00	0	.194	.281	.310
1988 Philadelphia	NL	58	144	30	6	0	1	(0	1)	39	13	12	17	1	26	0	0	2	2	1	.67	2	.208	.288	.271
1989 Philadelphia	NL	131	368	74	12	2	8	(2	6)	114	29	44	52	8	58	2	1	1	2	1	.67	4	.201	.303	.310
1990 Philadelphia	NL	143	459	123	30	1	12	(5	7)	191	62	57	72	9	72	2	3	4	7	1	.88	6	.268	.367	.416
1991 Philadelphia	NL	89	285	56	12	0	12	(8	4)	104	36	42	41	4	66	2	2	5	5	0	1.00	4	.196	.297	.365
1992 Philadelphia	NL	145	485	131	32	5	27	(17	10)	254	80	109	88	11	103	6	0	6	11	2	.85	3	.270	.385	.524
1993 Philadelphia	NL	147	510	131	35	4	24	(10	14)	246	90	105	117	12	111	2	0	8	5	0	1.00	2	.257	.392	.482
1994 Philadelphia	NL	69	257	77	17	1	15	(7	8)	141	43	56	33	2	43	1	0	1	4	1	.80	2	.300	.380	.549
1995 Philadelphia	NL	98	342	85	19	3	9	(7	2)	137	44	55	55	2	52	5	0	2	3	0	1.00	4	.249	.359	.401
1996 Philadelphia	NL	5	12	2	0	0	0	(0	0)	2	3	0	7	0	5	1	0	0	0	0	.00	0	.167	.500	.167
1997 Phi-Fla	NL	136	395	104	21	8	14	(6	8)	183	68	63	76	5	74	2	0	9	6	1	.86	4	.263	.378	.463
1997 Philadelphia	NL	84	269	71	13	6	11	(6	5)	129	46	42	54	4	57	1	0	7	4	0	1.00	3	.264	.381	.480
Florida	NL	52	126	33	8	2	3	(0	3)	54	22	21	22	1	17	1	0	2	2	1	.67	1	.262	.371	.429
14 ML YEARS		1161	3630	891	197	25	137	(67	70)	1549	511	588	629	58	726	24	12	41	50	10	.83	35	.245	.357	.427

Chili Davis

Bats: Both **Throws:** Right **Pos:** DH-133; PH-9   **Ht:** 6'3" **Wt:** 217 **Born:** 1/17/60 **Age:** 38

					BATTING													BASERUNNING				PERCENTAGES		
Year Team	Lg	G	AB	H	2B	3B	HR	(Hm	Rd)	TB	R	RBI	TBB	IBB	SO	HBP	SH	SF	SB	CS	SB%	GDP	Avg	OBP	SLG
1981 San Francisco	NL	8	15	2	0	0	0	(0	0)	2	1	0	1	0	2	0	0	0	2	0	1.00	1	.133	.188	.133
1982 San Francisco	NL	154	641	167	27	6	19	(6	13)	263	86	76	45	2	115	2	7	6	24	13	.65	13	.261	.308	.410

							BATTING												BASERUNNING				PERCENTAGES		
Year Team	Lg	G	AB	H	2B	3B	HR	(Hm Rd)	TB	R	RBI	TBB	IBB	SO	HBP	SH	SF	SB	CS	SB%	GDP	Avg	OBP	SLG
1983 San Francisco	NL	137	486	113	21	2	11	(7 4)	171	54	59	55	6	108	0	3	9	10	12	.45	9	.233	.305	.352
1984 San Francisco	NL	137	499	157	21	6	21	(7 14)	253	87	81	42	6	74	1	2	2	12	8	.60	13	.315	.368	.507
1985 San Francisco	NL	136	481	130	25	2	13	(7 6)	198	53	56	62	12	74	0	1	7	15	7	.68	16	.270	.349	.412
1986 San Francisco	NL	153	526	146	28	3	13	(7 6)	219	71	70	84	23	96	1	2	5	16	13	.55	11	.278	.375	.416
1987 San Francisco	NL	149	500	125	22	1	24	(9 15)	221	80	76	72	15	109	2	0	4	16	9	.64	8	.250	.344	.442
1988 California	AL	158	600	161	29	3	21	(11 10)	259	81	93	56	14	118	0	1	10	9	10	.47	13	.268	.326	.432
1989 California	AL	154	560	152	24	1	22	(6 16)	244	81	90	61	12	109	0	3	6	3	0	1.00	21	.271	.340	.436
1990 California	AL	113	412	109	17	1	12	(10 2)	164	58	58	61	4	89	0	0	3	1	2	.33	14	.265	.357	.398
1991 Minnesota	AL	153	534	148	34	1	29	(14 15)	271	84	93	95	13	117	1	0	4	5	6	.45	9	.277	.385	.507
1992 Minnesota	AL	138	444	128	27	2	12	(6 6)	195	63	66	73	11	76	3	0	9	4	5	.44	11	.288	.386	.439
1993 California	AL	153	573	139	32	0	27	(13 14)	252	74	112	71	12	135	1	0	5	4	1	.80	18	.243	.327	.440
1994 California	AL	108	392	122	18	1	26	(14 12)	220	72	84	69	11	84	1	0	6	3	2	.60	12	.311	.410	.561
1995 California	AL	119	424	135	23	0	20	(11 9)	218	81	86	89	12	79	0	0	3	3	3	.50	12	.318	.429	.514
1996 California	AL	145	530	155	24	0	28	(15 13)	263	73	95	86	11	99	0	1	6	5	2	.71	18	.292	.387	.496
1997 Kansas City	AL	140	477	133	20	0	30	(21 9)	243	85	16	96	11	96	1	0	4	6	3	.67	15	.279	.386	.509
17 ML YEARS		2255	8094	2222	392	29	328	(164 164)	3655	1170	1285	1107	180	1580	13	20	90	138	96	.59	214	.275	.359	.452

Eric Davis

Bats: Right **Throws:** Right **Pos:** RF-30; DH-12; PH-1   **Ht:** 6'3" **Wt:** 190 **Born:** 5/29/62 **Age:** 36

							BATTING												BASERUNNING				PERCENTAGES		
Year Team	Lg	G	AB	H	2B	3B	HR	(Hm Rd)	TB	R	RBI	TBB	IBB	SO	HBP	SH	SF	SB	CS	SB%	GDP	Avg	OBP	SLG
1984 Cincinnati	NL	57	174	39	10	1	10	(3 7)	81	33	30	24	0	48	1	0	1	10	2	.83	1	.224	.320	.466
1985 Cincinnati	NL	56	122	30	3	3	8	(1 7)	63	26	18	7	0	39	0	2	0	16	3	.84	1	.246	.287	.516
1986 Cincinnati	NL	132	415	115	15	3	27	(12 15)	217	97	71	68	5	100	1	0	3	80	11	.88	6	.277	.378	.523
1987 Cincinnati	NL	129	474	139	23	4	37	(17 20)	281	120	100	84	8	134	1	0	3	50	6	.89	6	.293	.399	.593
1988 Cincinnati	NL	135	472	129	18	3	26	(14 12)	231	81	93	65	10	124	3	0	3	35	3	.92	11	.273	.363	.489
1989 Cincinnati	NL	131	462	130	14	2	34	(15 19)	250	74	101	68	12	116	1	0	11	21	7	.75	16	.281	.367	.541
1990 Cincinnati	NL	127	453	118	26	2	24	(13 11)	220	84	86	60	6	100	2	0	3	21	3	.88	7	.260	.347	.486
1991 Cincinnati	NL	89	285	67	10	0	11	(5 6)	110	39	33	48	5	92	5	0	2	14	2	.88	4	.235	.353	.386
1992 Los Angeles	NL	76	267	61	8	1	5	(1 4)	86	21	32	36	2	71	3	0	2	19	1	.95	9	.228	.325	.322
1993 LA-Det		131	451	107	18	1	20	(10 10)	187	71	68	55	7	106	1	0	4	35	7	.83	12	.237	.319	.415
1994 Detroit	AL	37	120	22	4	0	3	(3 0)	35	19	13	18	0	45	0	0	0	5	0	1.00	4	.183	.290	.292
1996 Cincinnati	NL	129	415	119	20	0	26	(8 18)	217	81	83	70	3	121	6	1	4	23	9	.72	8	.287	.394	.523
1997 Baltimore	AL	42	158	48	11	0	8	(7 1)	83	29	25	14	0	47	1	0	3	6	0	1.00	4	.304	.358	.525
1993 Los Angeles	NL	108	376	88	17	0	14	(7 7)	147	57	53	41	6	88	1	0	4	33	5	.87	8	.234	.308	.391
Detroit	AL	23	75	19	1	1	6	(3 4)	40	14	15	14	1	18	0	0	0	2	2	.50	4	.253	.371	.533
13 ML YEARS		1271	4268	1124	180	20	239	(109 130)	2061	775	753	617	58	1143	25	3	39	335	54	.86	87	.263	.357	.483

Mark Davis

Pitches: Left **Bats:** Left **Pos:** RP-19   **Ht:** 6'4" **Wt:** 215 **Born:** 10/19/60 **Age:** 37

			HOW MUCH HE PITCHED						WHAT HE GAVE UP												THE RESULTS					
Year Team	Lg	G	GS	CG	GF	IP	BFP	H	R	ER	HR	SH	SF	HB	TBB	IBB	SO	WP	Bk	W	L	Pct.	ShO	Sv-Op	Hld	ERA
1997 High Desert *	A+	16	0	0	5	20.1	82	17	6	6	1	0	0	0	4	0	28	3	0	3	1	.750	0	0- -	—	2.66
Tucson *	AAA	17	0	0	10	22.2	96	19	9	9	1	1	3	1	12	1	19	1	1	0	2	.000	0	2- -	—	3.57
1980 Philadelphia	NL	2	1	0	0	7	30	4	2	2	0	0	0	0	5	0	5	0	0	0	0	.000	0	0- -	—	2.57
1981 Philadelphia	NL	9	9	0	0	43	194	49	37	37	7	2	4	0	24	0	29	1	1	1	4	.200	0	0-0	0	7.74
1983 San Francisco	NL	20	20	2	0	111	469	93	51	43	14	2	4	3	50	4	83	8	1	6	4	.600	2	0-0	0	3.49
1984 San Francisco	NL	46	27	1	6	174.2	766	201	113	104	25	10	10	5	54	12	124	8	4	5	17	.227	0	0- -	—	5.36
1985 San Francisco	NL	77	1	0	38	114.1	465	89	49	45	13	13	1	3	41	7	131	6	1	5	12	.294	0	7- -	—	3.54
1986 San Francisco	NL	67	2	0	20	84.1	342	63	33	28	6	5	5	1	34	7	90	3	0	5	7	.417	0	4- -	—	2.99
1987 SF-SD	NL	63	11	1	18	133	566	123	64	59	14	7	2	6	59	8	98	6	2	9	8	.529	0	2-4	2	3.99
1988 San Diego	NL	62	0	0	52	98.1	402	70	24	22	2	7	1	0	42	11	102	9	1	5	10	.333	0	28-34	3	2.01
1989 San Diego	NL	70	0	0	65	92.2	370	66	21	19	6	3	4	2	31	1	92	8	0	4	3	.571	0	44-48	1	1.85
1990 Kansas City	AL	53	3	0	28	68.2	334	71	43	39	9	2	2	0	52	3	73	6	0	2	7	.222	0	6-10	1	5.11
1991 Kansas City	AL	29	5	0	8	62.2	276	55	36	31	6	2	5	1	39	0	47	1	0	6	3	.667	0	1-2	2	4.45
1992 KC-Atl		27	6	0	11	53	261	64	44	42	9	1	5	1	41	2	34	5	1	2	3	.400	0	0-0	0	7.13
1993 Phi-SD	NL	60	0	0	13	69.2	327	79	37	33	10	4	1	0	44	7	70	2	1	1	5	.167	0	4-7	5	4.26
1994 San Diego	NL	20	0	0	3	16.1	81	20	18	16	4	1	0	0	13	1	15	0	0	0	0	.000	0	0-0	4	8.82
1997 Milwaukee	AL	3	0	0	3	16.1	72	21	10	10	4	1	0	0	5	0	14	0	0	0	3	.000	0	0-1	3	5.51
1987 San Francisco	NL	20	11	1	1	70.2	301	72	38	37	9	3	2	4	28	1	51	4	2	4	5	.444	0	0-1	1	4.71
San Diego	NL	43	0	0	17	62.1	265	51	26	22	5	4	0	2	31	7	47	2	0	5	3	.625	0	2-3	2	3.18
1992 Kansas City	AL	13	6	0	4	36.1	176	42	31	29	6	1	4	0	28	0	19	1	0	1	3	.250	0	0-0	0	7.18
Atlanta	NL	14	0	0	7	16.2	85	22	13	13	3	0	1	1	13	2	15	4	1	1	0	1.000	0	0-0	0	7.02
1993 Philadelphia	NL	25	0	0	4	31.1	154	35	22	18	4	1	0	1	24	1	28	1	0	1	2	.333	0	0-1	3	5.17
San Diego	NL	35	0	0	9	38.1	173	44	15	15	6	3	1	0	20	6	42	1	1	0	3	.000	0	4-6	2	3.52
15 ML YEARS		624	85	4	265	1145	4955	1068	582	530	129	60	44	28	534	63	1007	63	12	51	84	.378	2	96- -	—	4.17

Russ Davis

Bats: Right **Throws:** Right **Pos:** 3B-117; PH-4; DH-1   **Ht:** 6'0" **Wt:** 195 **Born:** 9/13/69 **Age:** 28

							BATTING												BASERUNNING				PERCENTAGES		
Year Team	Lg	G	AB	H	2B	3B	HR	(Hm Rd)	TB	R	RBI	TBB	IBB	SO	HBP	SH	SF	SB	CS	SB%	GDP	Avg	OBP	SLG
1994 New York	AL	4	14	2	0	0	0	(0 0)	2	0	1	0	0	4	0	0	0	0	0	.00	1	.143	.143	.143
1995 New York	AL	40	98	27	5	2	2	(2 0)	42	14	12	10	0	26	1	0	0	0	0	.00	0	.276	.349	.429
1996 Seattle	AL	51	167	39	9	0	5	(3 2)	63	24	18	17	1	50	2	4	0	2	0	1.00	1	.234	.312	.377
1997 Seattle	AL	119	420	114	29	1	20	(11 9)	205	57	63	27	2	100	2	3	2	6	2	.75	11	.271	.317	.488
4 ML YEARS		214	699	182	43	3	27	(16 11)	312	95	94	54	3	180	5	7	2	8	2	.80	13	.260	.317	.446

Tim Davis

Pitches: Left   **Bats:** Left   **Pos:** RP-2   **Ht:** 5'11"   **Wt:** 165   **Born:** 7/14/70   **Age:** 27

		HOW MUCH HE PITCHED				WHAT HE GAVE UP												THE RESULTS					
Year Team	Lg	G	GS	CG	GF	IP	BFP	H	R	ER	HR	SH	SF	HB	TBB	IBB	SO	WP	Bk	W	L	Pct.	ShO	Sv-Op	Hld	ERA
1997 Tacoma *	AAA	1	1	0	0	5	22	4	2	2	0	0	0	0	3	0	5	0	0	1	0	1.000	0	0- -	-	3.60
1994 Seattle	AL	42	1	0	12	49.1	225	57	25	22	4	3	3	1	25	5	28	6	0	2	2	.500	0	2-4	5	4.01
1995 Seattle	AL	5	5	0	0	24	117	30	21	17	2	0	1	0	18	2	19	0	0	2	1	.667	0	0-0	0	6.38
1996 Seattle	AL	40	0	0	4	42.2	187	43	21	19	4	1	1	2	17	1	34	0	0	2	2	.500	0	0-0	5	4.01
1997 Seattle	AL	2	0	0	1	6.2	31	6	5	5	1	0	0	1	4	0	10	0	0	0	0	.000	0	0-0	0	6.75
4 ML YEARS		89	6	0	17	122.2	560	136	72	63	11	4	5	4	64	8	91	6	0	6	5	.545	0	2-4	10	4.62

Roland de la Maza

Pitches: Right   **Bats:** Right   **Pos:** RP-1   **Ht:** 6'0"   **Wt:** 175   **Born:** 11/11/71   **Age:** 26

		HOW MUCH HE PITCHED				WHAT HE GAVE UP												THE RESULTS					
Year Team	Lg	G	GS	CG	GF	IP	BFP	H	R	ER	HR	SH	SF	HB	TBB	IBB	SO	WP	Bk	W	L	Pct.	ShO	Sv-Op	Hld	ERA
1997 Kansas City	AL	1	0	0	0	2	9	1	1	1	0	0	0	0	1	0	1	1	0	0	0	.000	0	0-0	0	4.50

Rick DeHart

Pitches: Left   **Bats:** Left   **Pos:** RP-23   **Ht:** 6'1"   **Wt:** 180   **Born:** 3/21/70   **Age:** 28

		HOW MUCH HE PITCHED				WHAT HE GAVE UP												THE RESULTS					
Year Team	Lg	G	GS	CG	GF	IP	BFP	H	R	ER	HR	SH	SF	HB	TBB	IBB	SO	WP	Bk	W	L	Pct.	ShO	Sv-Op	Hld	ERA
1992 Albany	A	38	10	1	15	117	476	91	42	32	11	5	5	4	40	1	133	5	6	9	6	.600	1	3- -	—	2.46
1993 San Berndno	A+	9	9	0	0	53.1	237	56	28	18	4	3	1	0	25	0	44	0	0	4	3	.571	0	0- -	—	3.04
Harrisburg	AA	12	7	0	1	34	163	45	31	29	5	1	2	2	19	0	18	2	0	2	4	.333	0	0- -	—	7.68
Wst Plm Bch	A+	7	7	1	0	42	175	42	14	14	0	1	1	1	17	0	33	2	0	1	3	.250	1	0- -	—	3.00
1994 Wst Plm Bch	A+	30	20	3	5	136.1	566	132	61	51	12	7	2	3	34	0	88	7	1	9	7	.563	2	0- -	—	3.37
1995 Harrisburg	AA	35	12	0	4	93	417	94	62	50	13	4	6	5	39	3	64	4	4	6	7	.462	0	0- -	—	4.84
1996 Harrisburg	AA	30	2	0	14	43.2	196	46	19	13	4	1	2	3	19	0	30	1	0	1	2	.333	0	1- -	—	2.68
1997 Ottawa	AAA	43	0	0	14	63	264	60	33	28	6	2	1	4	22	2	57	1	0	4	0	.000	0	2- -	—	4.00
1997 Montreal	NL	23	0	0	7	29.1	130	33	21	18	7	1	2	0	14	4	29	2	0	2	1	.667	0	0-1	1	5.52

Mike DeJean

Pitches: Right   **Bats:** Right   **Pos:** RP-55   **Ht:** 6'2"   **Wt:** 205   **Born:** 9/28/70   **Age:** 27

		HOW MUCH HE PITCHED				WHAT HE GAVE UP												THE RESULTS					
Year Team	Lg	G	GS	CG	GF	IP	BFP	H	R	ER	HR	SH	SF	HB	TBB	IBB	SO	WP	Bk	W	L	Pct.	ShO	Sv-Op	Hld	ERA
1992 Oneonta	A-	20	0	0	19	20.2	78	3	2	1	1	0	0	0	3	0	20	0	0	0	0	.000	0	16- -	—	0.44
1993 Greensboro	A	20	0	0	18	18	87	22	12	10	1	1	1	0	8	2	16	1	0	2	3	.400	0	9- -	—	5.00
1994 Tampa	A	34	0	0	33	34	156	39	15	9	1	1	2	2	13	0	22	2	0	0	2	.000	0	16- -	—	2.38
Albany-Colo	AA	16	0	0	10	24.2	110	22	14	12	1	4	1	2	15	3	13	6	0	0	2	.000	0	4- -	—	4.38
1995 Norwich	AA	59	0	0	40	78.1	323	58	29	26	5	2	3	5	34	2	57	4	1	5	5	.500	0	20- -	—	2.99
1996 New Haven	AA	16	0	0	15	22.1	90	29	9	8	2	0	1	0	8	0	12	2	0	0	0	.000	0	11- -	—	3.22
Colo Sprngs	AAA	30	0	0	17	40.1	186	52	24	23	3	0	0	2	21	3	31	2	0	0	2	.000	0	1- -	—	5.13
1997 Colo Sprngs	AAA	10	0	0	10	10	50	17	6	6	0	0	1	0	7	1	9	0	0	0	1	.000	0	4- -	—	5.40
New Haven	AA	2	0	0	0	3	14	3	2	2	0	0	0	1	2	0	2	0	0	0	0	.000	0	0- -	—	6.00
1997 Colorado	NL	55	0	0	15	67.2	295	74	34	30	4	3	1	3	24	2	38	2	0	5	0	1.000	0	2-4	13	3.99

Carlos Delgado

Bats: Left   **Throws:** Right   **Pos:** 1B-119; DH-33; PH-16   **Ht:** 6'3"   **Wt:** 206   **Born:** 6/25/72   **Age:** 26

		BATTING																		BASERUNNING				PERCENTAGES		
Year Team	Lg	G	AB	H	2B	3B	HR	(Hm	Rd)	TB	R	RBI	TBB	IBB	SO	HBP	SH	SF	SB	CS	SB%	GDP	Avg	OBP	SLG
1993 Toronto	AL	2	1	0	0	0	0	(0	0)	0	0	0	1	0	0	0	0	0	0	0	.00	0	.000	.500	.000
1994 Toronto	AL	43	130	28	2	0	9	(5	4)	57	17	24	25	4	46	3	0	1	1	1	.50	5	.215	.352	.438
1995 Toronto	AL	37	91	15	3	0	3	(2	1)	27	7	11	6	0	26	0	0	2	0	0	.00	1	.165	.212	.297
1996 Toronto	AL	138	488	132	28	2	25	(12	13)	239	68	92	58	2	139	9	0	8	0	0	.00	13	.270	.353	.490
1997 Toronto	AL	153	519	136	42	3	30	(17	13)	274	79	91	64	9	133	8	0	4	0	3	.00	6	.262	.350	.528
5 ML YEARS		373	1229	311	75	5	67	(36	31)	597	171	218	154	15	344	20	0	15	1	4	.20	25	.253	.342	.486

Wilson Delgado

Bats: Both   **Throws:** Right   **Pos:** PH-5; 2B-3; SS-1   **Ht:** 5'11"   **Wt:** 165   **Born:** 7/15/75   **Age:** 22

		BATTING																		BASERUNNING				PERCENTAGES		
Year Team	Lg	G	AB	H	2B	3B	HR	(Hm	Rd)	TB	R	RBI	TBB	IBB	SO	HBP	SH	SF	SB	CS	SB%	GDP	Avg	OBP	SLG
1994 Mariners	R	39	149	56	5	4	0	—	—	69	30	10	15	0	24	1	0	0	13	5	.72	0	.376	.436	.463
Appleton	A	9	31	6	0	0	0	—	—	6	2	0	0	0	8	0	0	0	0	0	.00	2	.194	.194	.194
1995 Port City	AA	13	41	8	4	0	0	—	—	12	3	1	6	0	8	0	0	0	0	0	.00	1	.195	.298	.293
Wisconsin	A	19	70	17	3	0	0	—	—	20	13	7	3	0	15	0	2	0	3	0	1.00	1	.243	.274	.286
Burlington	A	93	365	113	20	3	5	—	—	154	52	37	32	1	57	2	2	1	9	9	.50	7	.310	.368	.422
San Jose	A+	1	2	0	0	0	0	—	—	0	1	0	0	0	0	0	0	0	0	0	.00	0	.000	.000	.000
1996 San Jose	A+	121	462	124	19	6	2	—	—	161	59	54	48	0	89	2	4	4	8	2	.80	8	.268	.337	.348
Phoenix	AAA	12	43	6	0	1	0	—	—	8	1	1	3	1	7	0	0	0	0	1	.00	1	.140	.196	.186
1997 Phoenix	AAA	119	416	120	22	4	9	—	—	177	47	59	24	4	70	1	6	4	9	3	.75	9	.288	.326	.425
1996 San Francisco	NL	6	22	8	0	0	0	(0	0)	8	3	2	1	0	5	2	0	0	1	0	1.00	1	.364	.440	.364
1997 San Francisco	NL	8	7	1	1	0	0	(0	0)	2	1	0	0	0	2	0	1	0	0	0	.00	0	.143	.143	.286
2 ML YEARS		14	29	9	1	0	0	(0	0)	10	4	2	1	0	7	2	1	0	1	0	1.00	1	.310	.375	.345

David Dellucci

Bats: Left Throws: Left Pos: PH-9; RF-6; DH-5; LF-3 Ht: 5'10" Wt: 180 Born: 10/31/73 Age: 24

Year Team	Lg	G	AB	H	2B	3B	HR	(Hm	Rd)	TB	R	RBI	TBB	IBB	SO	HBP	SH	SF	SB	CS	SB%	GDP	Avg	OBP	SLG
1995 Bluefield	R+	20	69	23	5	1	2	—	—	36	11	12	6	1	7	1	0	1	3	1	.75	1	.333	.390	.522
Frederick	A+	28	96	27	3	0	1	—	—	33	16	10	12	1	10	3	0	0	1	2	.33	3	.281	.378	.344
1996 Frederick	A+	59	185	60	11	1	4	—	—	85	33	28	38	3	34	0	0	1	5	6	.45	2	.324	.438	.459
Bowie	AA	66	251	73	14	1	2	—	—	95	27	33	28	1	56	1	2	1	2	7	.22	4	.291	.363	.378
1997 Bowie	AA	107	385	126	29	3	20	—	—	221	71	55	58	1	69	5	0	1	11	4	.73	6	.327	.421	.574
1997 Baltimore	AL	17	27	6	1	0	1	(0	1)	10	3	3	4	1	7	1	0	0	0	0	.00	2	.222	.344	.370

Rich DeLucia

Pitches: Right Bats: Right Pos: RP-36 Ht: 6'0" Wt: 185 Born: 10/7/64 Age: 33

Year Team	Lg	G	GS	CG	GF	IP	BFP	H	R	ER	HR	SH	SF	HB	TBB	IBB	SO	WP	Bk	W	L	Pct.	ShO	Sv-Op	Hld	ERA
1990 Seattle	AL	5	5	1	0	36	144	30	9	8	2	2	0	0	9	0	20	0	0	1	2	.333	0	0-0	0	2.00
1991 Seattle	AL	32	31	0	0	182	779	176	107	103	31	5	14	4	78	4	98	10	0	12	13	.480	0	0-0	0	5.09
1992 Seattle	AL	30	11	0	6	83.2	382	100	55	51	13	2	2	2	35	1	66	1	0	3	6	.333	0	1-3	3	5.49
1993 Seattle	AL	30	1	0	11	42.2	195	46	24	22	5	1	1	1	23	3	48	4	0	3	6	.333	0	0-4	6	4.64
1994 Cincinnati	NL	8	0	0	2	10.2	47	9	6	5	4	0	0	0	5	0	15	1	0	0	0	.000	0	0-0	0	4.22
1995 St. Louis	NL	56	1	0	8	82.1	342	63	38	31	9	5	2	3	36	2	76	5	0	8	7	.533	0	0-1	9	3.39
1996 San Francisco	NL	56	0	0	20	61.2	279	62	44	40	8	4	2	3	31	6	55	7	0	3	6	.333	0	3-7	8	5.84
1997 SF-Ana		36	0	0	13	44	186	35	21	19	5	2	2	1	27	2	44	2	0	6	4	.600	0	3-7	8	3.89
1997 San Francisco	NL	3	0	0	0	1.2	12	6	3	2	0	0	0	0	0	0	2	1	0	0	0	.000	0	0-0	1	10.80
Anaheim	AL	33	0	0	13	42.1	174	29	18	17	5	2	2	1	27	2	42	1	0	6	4	.600	0	3-7	7	3.61
8 ML YEARS		253	49	1	60	543	2354	521	304	279	77	21	23	14	244	18	422	30	0	36	44	.450	0	4-17	37	4.62

Delino DeShields

Bats: Left Throws: Right Pos: 2B-147; PH-8 Ht: 6'1" Wt: 175 Born: 1/15/69 Age: 29

Year Team	Lg	G	AB	H	2B	3B	HR	(Hm	Rd)	TB	R	RBI	TBB	IBB	SO	HBP	SH	SF	SB	CS	SB%	GDP	Avg	OBP	SLG
1990 Montreal	NL	129	499	144	28	6	4	(3	1)	196	69	45	66	3	96	4	1	2	42	22	.66	10	.289	.375	.393
1991 Montreal	NL	151	563	134	15	4	10	(3	7)	187	83	51	95	2	151	2	8	5	56	23	.71	6	.238	.347	.332
1992 Montreal	NL	135	530	155	19	8	7	(1	6)	211	82	56	54	4	108	3	9	3	46	15	.75	10	.292	.359	.398
1993 Montreal	NL	123	481	142	17	7	2	(2	0)	179	75	29	72	3	64	3	4	2	43	10	.81	6	.295	.389	.372
1994 Los Angeles	NL	89	320	80	11	3	2	(1	1)	103	51	33	54	0	53	0	1	1	27	7	.79	9	.250	.357	.322
1995 Los Angeles	NL	127	425	109	18	3	8	(2	6)	157	66	37	63	4	83	1	3	0	39	14	.74	6	.256	.353	.369
1996 Los Angeles	NL	154	581	130	12	8	5	(3	2)	173	75	41	53	7	124	1	2	5	48	11	.81	12	.224	.288	.298
1997 St. Louis	NL	150	572	169	26	14	11	(6	5)	256	92	58	55	1	72	3	7	6	55	14	.80	5	.295	.357	.448
8 ML YEARS		1058	3971	1063	146	53	49	(21	28)	1462	593	350	512	24	751	17	35	25	356	116	.75	64	.268	.352	.368

Elmer Dessens

Pitches: Right Bats: Right Pos: RP-3 Ht: 6'0" Wt: 190 Born: 1/13/72 Age: 26

Year Team	Lg	G	GS	CG	GF	IP	BFP	H	R	ER	HR	SH	SF	HB	TBB	IBB	SO	WP	Bk	W	L	Pct.	ShO	Sv-Op	Hld	ERA
1995 Carolina	AA	27	27	1	0	152	638	170	62	42	10	11	4	3	21	3	68	7	2	15	8	.652	0	0- —	—	2.49
1996 Calgary	AAA	6	6	0	0	34.1	150	40	14	12	5	2	1	1	15	1	15	2	1	2	2	.500	0	0- —	—	3.15
Carolina	AA	5	1	0	2	11.2	55	15	8	7	1	0	0	1	4	0	7	0	0	0	1	.000	0	0- —	—	5.40
1996 Pittsburgh	NL	15	3	0	1	25	112	40	23	23	2	3	1	0	4	0	13	0	0	0	2	.000	0	0-0	3	8.28
1997 Pittsburgh	NL	3	0	0	1	3.1	13	2	0	0	0	0	0	1	0	0	2	0	0	0	0	.000	0	0-0	0	0.00
2 ML YEARS		18	3	0	2	28.1	125	42	23	23	2	3	1	1	4	0	15	0	0	0	2	.000	0	0-0	3	7.31

Mike Devereaux

Bats: R Throws: R Pos: RF-24; PH-6; LF-5; CF-3 Ht: 6'0" Wt: 195 Born: 4/10/63 Age: 35

Year Team	Lg	G	AB	H	2B	3B	HR	(Hm	Rd)	TB	R	RBI	TBB	IBB	SO	HBP	SH	SF	SB	CS	SB%	GDP	Avg	OBP	SLG
1987 Los Angeles	NL	19	54	12	3	0	0	(0	0)	15	7	4	3	0	10	0	1	0	3	1	.75	0	.222	.263	.278
1988 Los Angeles	NL	30	43	5	1	0	0	(0	0)	6	4	2	2	0	10	0	0	0	0	1	.00	0	.116	.156	.140
1989 Baltimore	AL	122	391	104	14	3	8	(4	4)	148	55	46	36	0	60	2	2	3	22	11	.67	7	.266	.329	.379
1990 Baltimore	AL	108	367	88	18	1	12	(6	6)	144	48	49	28	0	48	0	4	4	13	12	.52	10	.240	.291	.392
1991 Baltimore	AL	149	608	158	27	10	19	(10	9)	262	82	59	47	2	115	2	7	4	16	9	.64	13	.260	.313	.431
1992 Baltimore	AL	156	653	180	29	11	24	(14	10)	303	76	107	44	4	94	4	0	9	10	8	.56	14	.276	.321	.464
1993 Baltimore	AL	131	527	132	31	3	14	(8	6)	211	72	75	43	0	99	1	2	4	3	3	.50	13	.250	.306	.400
1994 Baltimore	AL	85	301	61	8	2	9	(5	4)	100	35	33	22	0	72	1	2	4	1	2	.33	6	.203	.256	.332
1995 ChA-Atl		121	388	116	24	1	11	(5	6)	175	55	63	27	3	62	0	0	3	8	6	.57	11	.299	.342	.451
1996 Baltimore	AL	127	323	74	11	2	8	(5	3)	113	49	34	34	0	53	2	2	2	8	2	.80	8	.229	.305	.350
1997 Texas	AL	29	72	15	3	0	0	(0	0)	18	8	7	7	0	10	0	0	1	1	0	1.00	6	.208	.275	.250
1995 Chicago	AL	92	333	102	21	1	10	(4	6)	155	48	55	25	3	51	0	0	3	6	6	.50	10	.306	.352	.465
Atlanta	NL	29	55	14	3	0	1	(1	0)	20	7	8	2	0	11	0	0	0	2	0	1.00	1	.255	.281	.364
11 ML YEARS		1077	3727	945	169	33	105	(57	48)	1495	491	479	293	6	633	12	20	34	85	55	.61	82	.254	.307	.401

Alex Diaz

Bats: B Throws: R Pos: RF-20; PH-7; LF-3; 1B-1; 2B-1   Ht: 5'11" Wt: 180 Born: 10/5/68 Age: 29

Year Team	Lg	G	AB	H	2B	3B	HR	(Hm	Rd)	TB	R	RBI	TBB	IBB	SO	HBP	SH	SF	SB	CS	SB%	GDP	Avg	OBP	SLG
1997 Norfolk *	AAA	7	26	2	1	0	0	—	—	3	0	1	2	0	3	0	0	0	0	0	.00	2	.077	.143	.115
Okla City *	AAA	105	426	122	25	2	12	—	—	187	65	49	33	3	53	3	0	3	26	7	.79	19	.286	.340	.439
1992 Milwaukee	AL	22	9	1	0	0	0	(0	0)	1	5	1	0	0	0	0	0	0	3	2	.60	0	.111	.111	.111
1993 Milwaukee	AL	32	69	22	2	0	0	(0	0)	24	9	1	0	0	12	0	3	0	5	3	.63	3	.319	.319	.348
1994 Milwaukee	AL	79	187	47	5	7	1	(0	1)	69	17	17	10	1	19	0	3	3	5	5	.50	5	.251	.285	.369
1995 Seattle	AL	103	270	67	14	0	3	(3	0)	90	44	27	13	2	27	2	5	2	18	8	.69	5	.248	.286	.333
1996 Seattle	AL	38	79	19	2	0	1	(1	0)	24	11	5	2	0	8	2	0	1	6	3	.67	2	.241	.274	.304
1997 Texas	AL	28	90	20	4	0	2	(0	2)	30	8	12	5	0	13	1	0	1	1	1	.50	3	.222	.268	.333
6 ML YEARS		302	704	176	27	7	7	(4	3)	238	94	63	30	3	79	5	11	7	38	22	.63	16	.250	.283	.338

Eddy Diaz

Bats: R Throws: R Pos: 2B-14; PH-3; 3B-1; SS-1   Ht: 5'10" Wt: 160 Born: 9/29/71 Age: 26

Year Team	Lg	G	AB	H	2B	3B	HR	(Hm	Rd)	TB	R	RBI	TBB	IBB	SO	HBP	SH	SF	SB	CS	SB%	GDP	Avg	OBP	SLG
1991 Bellingham	A-	61	246	68	14	1	3	—	—	93	48	23	24	1	33	1	3	2	9	2	.82	4	.276	.341	.378
1992 San Berndno	A+	114	436	119	15	2	9	—	—	165	80	39	38	0	46	6	12	2	33	16	.67	11	.273	.338	.378
1993 Appleton	A	46	189	63	14	2	3	—	—	90	28	33	15	2	13	0	0	0	13	9	.59	7	.333	.382	.476
Jacksnville	AA	77	259	65	16	0	6	—	—	99	36	26	17	1	31	2	7	4	6	3	.67	5	.251	.298	.382
1994 Jacksnville	AA	104	340	84	20	0	8	—	—	128	43	42	21	1	23	2	9	3	13	5	.72	8	.247	.292	.376
1995 Tacoma	AAA	11	36	12	2	0	0	—	—	14	5	5	4	0	2	0	0	0	0	0	.00	0	.333	.400	.389
Port City	AA	110	421	110	22	0	16	—	—	180	66	47	40	3	39	8	1	4	9	7	.56	9	.261	.334	.428
1996 Tacoma	AAA	107	422	118	28	4	13	—	—	193	63	58	15	1	38	10	5	2	3	4	.43	9	.280	.318	.457
1997 Tucson	AAA	94	356	117	24	3	9	—	—	174	65	70	26	0	25	9	3	8	0	1	.00	7	.329	.381	.489
1997 Milwaukee	AL	16	50	11	2	1	0	(0	0)	15	4	7	1	0	5	0	0	0	0	0	.00	3	.220	.235	.300

Einar Diaz

Bats: Right Throws: Right Pos: C-5   Ht: 5'10" Wt: 165 Born: 12/28/72 Age: 25

Year Team	Lg	G	AB	H	2B	3B	HR	(Hm	Rd)	TB	R	RBI	TBB	IBB	SO	HBP	SH	SF	SB	CS	SB%	GDP	Avg	OBP	SLG
1992 Burlington	R+	52	178	37	3	0	1	—	—	43	19	14	20	0	9	3	2	2	2	3	.40	4	.208	.296	.242
1993 Burlington	R+	60	231	69	15	3	5	—	—	105	40	33	8	0	7	4	2	4	7	3	.70	5	.299	.328	.455
Columbus	A	1	5	0	0	0	0	—	—	0	0	0	0	0	1	0	0	0	0	0	.00	1	.000	.000	.000
1994 Columbus	A	120	491	137	23	2	16	—	—	212	67	71	17	0	34	21	1	1	4	4	.50	18	.279	.330	.432
1995 Kinston	A+	104	373	98	21	0	6	—	—	137	46	43	12	2	29	8	1	4	3	6	.33	6	.263	.297	.367
1996 Canton-Akrn	AA	104	395	111	26	2	3	—	—	150	47	35	12	0	22	9	1	1	3	2	.60	11	.281	.317	.380
1997 Buffalo	AAA	109	336	86	18	2	3	—	—	117	40	31	18	1	34	5	4	2	2	6	.25	12	.256	.302	.348
1996 Cleveland	AL	4	1	0	0	0	0	(0	0)	0	0	0	0	0	0	0	0	0	0	0	.00	0	.000	.000	.000
1997 Cleveland	AL	5	7	1	1	0	0	(0	0)	2	1	1	0	0	2	0	0	0	0	0	.00	0	.143	.143	.286
2 ML YEARS		9	8	1	1	0	0	(0	0)	2	1	1	0	0	2	0	0	0	0	0	.00	0	.125	.125	.250

Jason Dickson

Pitches: Right Bats: Left Pos: SP-32; RP-1   Ht: 6'0" Wt: 190 Born: 3/30/73 Age: 25

Year Team	Lg	G	GS	CG	GF	IP	BFP	H	R	ER	HR	SH	SF	HB	TBB	IBB	SO	WP	Bk	W	L	Pct.	ShO	Sv-Op	Hld	ERA
1994 Boise	A-	9	7	0	0	44.1	190	40	22	19	3	1	2		18	1	37	3	2	3	1	.750	0	1--	—	3.86
1995 Cedar Rapds	A	25	25	9	0	173	708	151	71	55	12	4	3	8	45	0	134	7	2	14	6	.700	1	0--	—	2.86
1996 Midland	AA	8	8	3	0	55.1	228	55	27	22	3	2	0	0	10	0	40	3	0	5	2	.714	1	0--	—	3.58
Vancouver	AAA	18	18	7	0	130.1	553	134	73	55	9	2	4	5	40	1	70	4	4	7	11	.389	0	0--	—	3.80
1996 California	AL	7	7	0	0	43.1	192	52	22	22	6	2	1	1	18	1	20	1	1	1	4	.200	0	0-0	0	4.57
1997 Anaheim	AL	33	32	2	1	203.2	888	236	111	97	32	4	5	7	56	3	115	4	1	13	9	.591	1	0-0	0	4.29
2 ML YEARS		40	39	2	1	247	1080	288	133	119	38	6	6	8	74	4	135	5	2	14	13	.519	1	0-0	0	4.34

Mike Difelice

Bats: Right Throws: Right Pos: C-91; PH-2; 1B-1   Ht: 6'2" Wt: 205 Born: 5/28/69 Age: 29

Year Team	Lg	G	AB	H	2B	3B	HR	(Hm	Rd)	TB	R	RBI	TBB	IBB	SO	HBP	SH	SF	SB	CS	SB%	GDP	Avg	OBP	SLG
1991 Hamilton	A-	43	157	33	5	0	4	—	—	50	10	15	9	0	40	1	0	0	1	5	.17	3	.210	.257	.318
1992 Hamilton	A-	18	58	20	3	0	2	—	—	29	11	9	4	1	7	1	1	0	2	0	1.00	0	.345	.397	.500
St. Pete	A+	17	53	12	3	0	0	—	—	15	0	4	3	0	11	0	0	2	0	0	.00	3	.226	.259	.283
1993 Springfield	A	8	20	7	1	0	0	—	—	8	5	3	2	0	3	1	0	0	0	1	.00	0	.350	.435	.400
St. Pete	A+	30	97	22	2	0	0	—	—	24	5	8	11	1	13	1	2	2	0	1	.00	4	.227	.306	.247
1994 Arkansas	AA	71	200	50	11	2	2	—	—	71	19	15	12	0	48	2	1	2	0	1	.00	9	.250	.296	.355
1995 Arkansas	AA	62	176	47	10	1	1	—	—	62	14	24	23	0	29	3	2	1	0	2	.00	13	.267	.360	.352
Louisville	AAA	21	63	17	4	0	0	—	—	21	8	3	5	0	11	0	0	0	1	0	1.00	4	.270	.324	.333
1996 Louisville	AAA	79	246	70	13	0	9	—	—	110	25	33	20	1	43	1	0	2	0	3	.00	15	.285	.338	.447
1997 Arkansas	AA	1	3	1	1	0	0	—	—	2	0	0	1	0	0	0	0	0	0	0	.00	0	.333	.500	.667
Louisville	AAA	4	4	1	0	0	0	—	—	1	0	0	0	0	2	0	0	0	0	0	.00	0	.250	.250	1.000
1996 St. Louis	NL	4	7	2	1	0	0	(0	0)	3	0	2	0	0	3	0	0	0	0	0	.00	0	.286	.286	.429
1997 St. Louis	NL	93	260	62	10	1	4	(1	3)	86	16	30	19	0	61	3	6	1	1	1	.50	11	.238	.297	.331
2 ML YEARS		97	267	64	11	1	4	(1	3)	89	16	32	19	0	62	3	6	1	1	1	.50	11	.240	.297	.333

Jerry Dipoto

Pitches: Right **Bats:** Right **Pos:** RP-74 **Ht:** 6'2" **Wt:** 200 **Born:** 5/24/68 **Age:** 30

Year Team	Lg	G	GS	CG	GF	IP	BFP	H	R	ER	HR	SH	SF	HB	TBB	IBB	SO	WP	Bk	W	L	Pct.	ShO	Sv-Op	Hld	ERA
1993 Cleveland	AL	46	0	0	26	56.1	247	57	21	15	0	3	2	1	30	7	41	0	0	4	4	.500	0	11-17	6	2.40
1994 Cleveland	AL	7	0	0	1	15.2	79	26	14	14	1	0	4	1	10	0	9	0	0	0	0	.000	0	0-0	1	8.04
1995 New York	NL	58	0	0	26	78.2	330	77	41	33	2	6	3	4	29	8	49	3	1	4	6	.400	0	2-6	8	3.78
1996 New York	NL	57	0	0	21	77.1	364	91	44	36	5	7	4	3	45	8	52	3	3	7	2	.778	0	0-5	3	4.19
1997 Colorado	NL	74	0	0	33	95.2	422	108	56	50	6	3	7	4	33	5	74	4	1	5	3	.625	0	16-21	10	4.70
5 ML YEARS		242	0	0	107	323.2	1442	359	176	148	14	19	20	13	147	28	225	10	5	20	15	.571	0	29-49	28	4.12

Gary DiSarcina

Bats: Right **Throws:** Right **Pos:** SS-153; PH-2 **Ht:** 6'2" **Wt:** 190 **Born:** 11/19/67 **Age:** 30

Year Team	Lg	G	AB	H	2B	3B	HR	(Hm	Rd)	TB	R	RBI	TBB	IBB	SO	HBP	SH	SF	SB	CS	SB%	GDP	Avg	OBP	SLG
1989 California	AL	2	0	0	0	0	0	(0	0)	0	0	0	0	0	0	0	0	0	0	0	.00	0	.000	.000	.000
1990 California	AL	18	57	8	1	1	0	(0	0)	11	8	0	3	0	10	0	1	0	1	0	1.00	3	.140	.183	.193
1991 California	AL	18	57	12	2	0	0	(0	0)	14	5	3	3	0	4	2	2	0	0	0	.00	0	.211	.274	.246
1992 California	AL	157	518	128	19	0	3	(2	1)	156	48	42	20	0	50	7	5	3	9	7	.56	15	.247	.283	.301
1993 California	AL	126	416	99	20	1	3	(2	1)	130	44	45	15	0	38	6	5	3	5	7	.42	13	.238	.273	.313
1994 California	AL	112	389	101	14	2	3	(2	1)	128	53	33	18	0	28	2	10	2	3	7	.30	10	.260	.294	.329
1995 California	AL	99	362	111	28	6	5	(1	4)	166	61	41	20	0	25	2	7	3	7	4	.64	10	.307	.344	.459
1996 California	AL	150	536	137	26	4	5	(2	3)	186	62	48	21	0	36	2	16	1	2	1	.67	16	.256	.286	.347
1997 Anaheim	AL	154	549	135	28	2	4	(2	2)	179	52	47	17	0	29	4	8	5	7	8	.47	18	.246	.271	.326
9 ML YEARS		836	2884	731	138	16	23	(11	12)	970	333	259	117	0	220	25	54	17	34	34	.50	85	.253	.287	.336

Glenn Dishman

Pitches: Left **Bats:** Right **Pos:** SP-4; RP-3 **Ht:** 6'1" **Wt:** 195 **Born:** 11/5/70 **Age:** 27

Year Team	Lg	G	GS	CG	GF	IP	BFP	H	R	ER	HR	SH	SF	HB	TBB	IBB	SO	WP	Bk	W	L	Pct.	ShO	Sv-Op	Hld	ERA
1997 Toledo *	AAA	21	18	1	2	114	467	112	53	49	12	3	3	2	32	0	77	4	1	7	6	.538	0	1- -	—	3.87
1995 San Diego	NL	19	16	0	1	97	421	104	60	54	11	6	3	4	34	1	43	3	1	4	8	.333	0	0-0	0	5.01
1996 SD-Phi	NL	7	1	0	4	9.1	42	12	8	8	2	0	1	0	3	0	3	1	0	0	0	.000	0	0-0	0	7.71
1997 Detroit	AL	7	4	0	1	29	125	30	18	17	4	1	2	2	8	0	20	0	0	1	2	.333	0	0-0	0	5.28
1996 San Diego	NL	3	0	0	2	2.1	11	3	2	2	0	0	0	0	1	0	1	0	1	0	0	.000	0	0-0	0	7.71
Philadelphia	NL	4	1	0	2	7	31	9	6	6	2	0	1	0	2	0	3	0	0	0	0	.000	0	0-0	0	7.71
3 ML YEARS		33	21	0	6	135.1	588	146	86	79	17	7	6	6	45	1	66	4	1	5	10	.333	0	0-0	0	5.25

Doug Drabek

Pitches: Right **Bats:** Right **Pos:** SP-31 **Ht:** 6'1" **Wt:** 185 **Born:** 7/25/62 **Age:** 35

Year Team	Lg	G	GS	CG	GF	IP	BFP	H	R	ER	HR	SH	SF	HB	TBB	IBB	SO	WP	Bk	W	L	Pct.	ShO	Sv-Op	Hld	ERA
1986 New York	AL	27	21	0	0	131.2	561	126	64	60	13	5	2	3	50	1	76	2	0	7	8	.467	0	0- -	0	4.10
1987 Pittsburgh	NL	29	28	1	0	176.1	721	165	86	76	22	3	4	0	46	2	120	5	1	11	12	.478	1	0-0	0	3.88
1988 Pittsburgh	NL	33	32	3	0	219.1	880	194	83	75	21	7	5	6	50	4	127	4	1	15	7	.682	1	0-0	0	3.08
1989 Pittsburgh	NL	35	34	8	1	244.1	994	215	83	76	21	13	7	3	69	3	123	3	0	14	12	.538	5	0-0	0	2.80
1990 Pittsburgh	NL	33	33	9	0	231.1	918	190	78	71	15	10	3	3	56	2	131	6	0	22	6	.786	3	0-0	0	2.76
1991 Pittsburgh	NL	35	35	5	0	234.2	977	245	92	80	16	12	6	3	62	6	142	5	0	15	14	.517	2	0-0	0	3.07
1992 Pittsburgh	NL	34	34	10	0	256.2	1021	218	84	79	17	8	6	6	54	8	177	11	1	15	11	.577	4	0-0	0	2.77
1993 Houston	NL	34	34	7	0	237.2	991	242	108	100	18	14	8	3	60	12	157	12	0	9	18	.333	2	0-0	0	3.79
1994 Houston	NL	23	23	6	0	164.2	657	132	58	52	14	5	6	2	45	2	121	2	0	12	6	.667	2	0-0	0	2.84
1995 Houston	NL	31	31	2	0	185	797	205	94	98	18	4	3	8	54	4	143	8	1	10	9	.526	1	0-0	0	4.77
1996 Houston	NL	30	30	1	0	175.1	786	208	102	89	21	12	8	7	60	5	137	9	0	7	9	.438	0	0-0	0	4.57
1997 Chicago	AL	31	31	0	0	169.1	731	170	109	108	30	4	2	4	69	5	85	12	2	12	11	.522	0	0-0	0	5.74
12 ML YEARS		375	366	52	3	2426.1	10034	2310	1051	964	226	97	62	48	675	54	1539	79	6	149	123	.548	21	0- -	—	3.58

Darren Dreifort

Pitches: Right **Bats:** Right **Pos:** RP-48 **Ht:** 6'2" **Wt:** 205 **Born:** 5/18/72 **Age:** 26

Year Team	Lg	G	GS	CG	GF	IP	BFP	H	R	ER	HR	SH	SF	HB	TBB	IBB	SO	WP	Bk	W	L	Pct.	ShO	Sv-Op	Hld	ERA
1997 Albuquerque *	AAA	2	2	0	0	5.2	19	2	1	1	1	0	0	0	1	0	3	0	0	0	0	- -	0	- -	—	1.59
1994 Los Angeles	NL	27	0	0	15	29	148	45	21	20	0	3	0	4	15	3	22	1	0	0	5	.000	0	6-9	3	6.21
1996 Los Angeles	NL	19	0	0	5	23.2	106	23	13	13	2	3	1	0	12	4	24	2	1	1	4	.200	0	0-2	1	4.94
1997 Los Angeles	NL	48	0	0	15	63	265	45	21	20	3	5	2	1	34	2	63	3	1	5	2	.714	0	4-7	9	2.86
3 ML YEARS		94	0	0	35	115.2	519	113	55	53	5	11	3	5	61	9	109	6	2	6	11	.353	0	10-18	13	4.12

Rob Ducey

Bats: L **Throws:** R **Pos:** LF-43; RF-19; PH-16; CF-12 **Ht:** 6'2" **Wt:** 180 **Born:** 5/24/65 **Age:** 33

Year Team	Lg	G	AB	H	2B	3B	HR	(Hm	Rd)	TB	R	RBI	TBB	IBB	SO	HBP	SH	SF	SB	CS	SB%	GDP	Avg	OBP	SLG
1997 Tacoma *	AAA	23	74	24	8	0	0	—	—)	32	8	11	8	2	15	3	0	0	0	0	.00	0	.324	.412	.432
1987 Toronto	AL	34	48	9	1	0	1	(1	0)	13	12	6	8	0	10	0	0	1	2	0	1.00	0	.188	.298	.271
1988 Toronto	AL	27	54	17	4	1	0	(0	0)	23	15	6	5	0	7	0	2	2	1	0	1.00	1	.315	.361	.426

Year Team	Lg	G	AB	H	2B	3B	HR	(Hm	Rd)	TB	R	RBI	TBB	IBB	SO	HBP	SH	SF	SB	CS	SB%	GDP	Avg	OBP	SLG
1989 Toronto	AL	41	76	16	4	0	0	(0	0)	20	5	7	9	1	25	0	1	0	2	1	.67	2	.211	.294	.263
1990 Toronto	AL	19	53	16	5	0	0	(0	0)	21	7	7	7	0	15	1	0	1	1	1	.50	1	.302	.387	.396
1991 Toronto	AL	39	68	16	2	2	1	(0	1)	25	8	4	6	0	26	0	1	0	2	0	1.00	1	.235	.297	.368
1992 Tor-Cal	AL	54	80	15	4	0	0	(0	0)	19	7	2	5	0	22	0	0	1	2	4	.33	1	.188	.233	.238
1993 Texas	AL	27	85	24	6	3	2	(2	0)	42	15	9	10	2	17	0	2	2	2	3	.40	1	.282	.351	.494
1994 Texas	AL	11	29	5	1	0	0	(0	0)	6	1	1	2	0	1	0	0	0	0	0	.00	1	.172	.226	.207
1997 Seattle	AL	76	143	41	15	2	5	(0	5)	75	25	10	6	0	31	0	0	2	3	3	.50	3	.287	.311	.524
1992	AL	23	21	1	1	0	0	(0	0)	2	3	0	0	0	10	0	0	0	0	1	.00	0	.048	.048	.095
California	AL	31	59	14	3	0	0	(0	0)	17	4	2	5	0	12	0	0	1	2	3	.40	1	.237	.292	.288
9 ML YEARS		328	636	159	42	8	9	(3	6)	244	95	52	58	3	154	1	6	9	15	12	.56	10	.250	.310	.384

Mariano Duncan

Bats: Right **Throws:** Right **Pos:** 2B-80; LF-6; DH-2 **Ht:** 6'0" **Wt:** 185 **Born:** 3/13/63 **Age:** 35

Year Team	Lg	G	AB	H	2B	3B	HR	(Hm	Rd)	TB	R	RBI	TBB	IBB	SO	HBP	SH	SF	SB	CS	SB%	GDP	Avg	OBP	SLG
1985 Los Angeles	NL	142	562	137	24	6	6	(1	5)	191	74	39	38	4	113	3	13	4	38	8	.83	9	.244	.293	.340
1986 Los Angeles	NL	109	407	93	7	0	8	(2	6)	124	47	30	30	1	78	2	5	1	48	13	.79	6	.229	.284	.305
1987 Los Angeles	NL	76	261	56	8	1	6	(3	3)	84	31	18	17	1	62	2	6	1	11	1	.92	4	.215	.267	.322
1989 LA-Cin	NL	94	258	64	15	2	3	(2	1)	92	32	21	8	0	51	5	2	0	9	5	.64	3	.248	.284	.357
1990 Cincinnati	NL	125	435	133	22	11	10	(5	5)	207	67	55	24	4	67	4	4	4	13	7	.65	10	.306	.345	.476
1991 Cincinnati	NL	100	333	86	7	4	12	(10	2)	137	46	40	12	0	57	3	5	3	5	4	.56	0	.258	.288	.411
1992 Philadelphia	NL	142	574	153	40	3	8	(3	5)	223	71	50	17	0	108	5	5	4	23	3	.88	15	.267	.292	.389
1993 Philadelphia	NL	124	496	140	26	4	11	(5	6)	207	68	73	12	0	88	4	4	2	6	5	.55	13	.282	.304	.417
1994 Philadelphia	NL	88	347	93	22	1	8	(6	2)	141	49	48	17	1	72	4	2	4	10	2	.83	10	.268	.306	.406
1995 Phi-Cin	NL	81	265	76	14	2	6	(3	3)	112	36	36	5	0	62	1	1	5	1	3	.25	7	.287	.297	.423
1996 New York	AL	109	400	136	34	3	8	(5	3)	200	62	56	9	1	77	1	2	5	4	3	.57	10	.340	.352	.500
1997 NYA-Tor	AL	89	339	80	14	0	1	(1	0)	97	36	25	12	0	78	3	1	0	6	3	.67	6	.236	.268	.286
1989 Los Angeles	NL	49	84	21	5	1	0	(0	0)	28	9	8	0	0	15	2	1	0	3	3	.50	1	.250	.267	.333
Cincinnati	NL	45	174	43	10	1	3	(2	1)	64	23	13	8	0	36	3	1	0	6	2	.75	2	.247	.292	.368
1995 Philadelphia	NL	52	196	56	12	1	3	(1	2)	79	20	23	0	0	43	1	1	3	1	2	.33	6	.286	.285	.403
Cincinnati	NL	29	69	20	2	1	3	(2	1)	33	16	13	5	0	19	0	0	2	0	1	.00	1	.290	.329	.478
1997 New York	NL	50	172	42	8	0	1	(1	0)	53	16	13	6	0	39	0	1	0	2	1	.67	2	.244	.270	.308
Toronto	AL	39	167	38	6	0	0	(0	0)	44	20	12	6	0	39	3	0	0	4	2	.67	4	.228	.267	.263
12 ML YEARS		1279	4677	1247	233	37	87	(46	41)	1815	619	491	201	12	913	37	50	33	174	57	.75	93	.267	.300	.388

Todd Dunn

Bats: R **Throws:** R **Pos:** LF-19; DH-14; PH-10; RF-7; CF-2 **Ht:** 6'5" **Wt:** 220 **Born:** 7/29/70 **Age:** 27

Year Team	Lg	G	AB	H	2B	3B	HR	(Hm	Rd)	TB	R	RBI	TBB	IBB	SO	HBP	SH	SF	SB	CS	SB%	GDP	Avg	OBP	SLG
1993 Helena	R+	43	150	46	11	2	10	—	—	91	33	42	22	1	52	6	1	2	5	2	.71	2	.307	.411	.607
1994 Beloit	A	129	429	94	13	2	23	—	—	180	72	63	50	3	131	6	4	4	18	8	.69	6	.219	.307	.420
1995 Stockton	A+	67	249	73	20	2	7	—	—	118	44	40	19	2	67	2	1	1	14	3	.82	5	.293	.347	.474
1996 El Paso	AA	98	359	122	24	5	19	—	—	213	72	78	45	1	84	2	2	4	13	4	.76	11	.340	.412	.593
1997 Tucson	AAA	93	332	101	31	4	18	—	—	194	66	66	39	1	83	8	0	1	5	5	.50	11	.304	.389	.584
1996 Milwaukee	AL	6	10	3	1	0	0	(0	0)	4	2	1	0	0	3	0	0	0	0	0	.00	1	.300	.300	.400
1997 Milwaukee	AL	44	118	27	5	0	3	(2	1)	41	17	9	2	0	39	0	0	0	3	0	1.00	2	.229	.242	.347
2 ML YEARS		50	128	30	6	0	3	(2	1)	45	19	10	2	0	42	0	0	0	3	0	1.00	3	.234	.246	.352

Shawon Dunston

Bats: Right **Throws:** Right **Pos:** SS-126; LF-7; PH-3 **Ht:** 6'1" **Wt:** 180 **Born:** 3/21/63 **Age:** 35

Year Team	Lg	G	AB	H	2B	3B	HR	(Hm	Rd)	TB	R	RBI	TBB	IBB	SO	HBP	SH	SF	SB	CS	SB%	GDP	Avg	OBP	SLG
1985 Chicago	NL	74	250	65	12	4	4	(3	1)	97	40	18	19	3	42	0	1	3	11	3	.79	3	.260	.310	.388
1986 Chicago	NL	150	581	145	37	3	17	(10	7)	239	66	68	21	5	114	3	4	2	13	11	.54	5	.250	.278	.411
1987 Chicago	NL	95	346	85	18	3	5	(3	2)	124	40	22	10	1	68	1	0	2	12	3	.80	6	.246	.267	.358
1988 Chicago	NL	155	575	143	23	6	9	(5	4)	205	69	56	16	8	108	2	4	2	30	9	.77	6	.249	.271	.357
1989 Chicago	NL	138	471	131	20	6	9	(3	6)	190	52	60	30	15	86	1	6	4	19	11	.63	7	.278	.320	.403
1990 Chicago	NL	146	545	143	22	8	17	(7	10)	232	73	66	15	1	87	3	4	6	25	5	.83	9	.262	.283	.426
1991 Chicago	NL	142	492	128	22	7	12	(7	5)	200	59	50	23	5	64	4	4	11	21	6	.78	9	.260	.292	.407
1992 Chicago	NL	18	73	23	3	1	0	(0	0)	28	8	2	3	0	13	0	0	0	2	3	.40	0	.315	.342	.384
1993 Chicago	NL	7	10	4	2	0	0	(0	0)	6	3	2	0	0	1	0	0	0	0	0	.00	0	.400	.400	.600
1994 Chicago	NL	88	331	92	19	0	11	(2	9)	144	38	35	16	3	48	2	5	2	3	8	.27	4	.278	.313	.435
1995 Chicago	NL	127	477	141	30	6	14	(8	6)	225	58	69	10	3	75	6	7	3	10	5	.67	8	.296	.317	.472
1996 San Francisco	NL	82	287	86	12	2	5	(3	2)	117	27	25	13	0	40	1	5	1	8	0	1.00	8	.300	.331	.408
1997 ChN-Pit	NL	132	490	147	22	5	14	(10	4)	221	71	57	8	0	75	3	5	5	32	8	.80	9	.300	.312	.451
1997 Chicago	NL	114	419	119	18	4	9	(7	2)	172	57	41	8	0	64	3	3	4	29	7	.81	7	.284	.300	.411
Pittsburgh	NL	18	71	28	4	1	5	(3	2)	49	14	16	0	0	11	0	2	1	3	1	.75	2	.394	.389	.690
13 ML YEARS		1354	4928	1333	242	51	117	(61	56)	2028	604	530	184	44	821	26	45	40	186	72	.72	74	.270	.298	.412

Todd Dunwoody

Bats: Left **Throws:** Left **Pos:** CF-8; LF-6; PH-6 **Ht:** 6'1" **Wt:** 195 **Born:** 4/11/75 **Age:** 23

Year Team	Lg	G	AB	H	2B	3B	HR	(Hm	Rd)	TB	R	RBI	TBB	IBB	SO	HBP	SH	SF	SB	CS	SB%	GDP	Avg	OBP	SLG
1993 Marlins	R	31	109	21	2	2	0	—	—	27	13	7	7	0	28	2	1	1	5	0	1.00	2	.193	.252	.248

Year Team	Lg	G	AB	H	2B	3B	HR	(Hm	Rd)	TB	R	RBI	TBB	IBB	SO	HBP	SH	SF	SB	CS	SB%	GDP	Avg	OBP	SLG
1994 Kane County	A	15	45	5	0	0	1	—	—	8	7	1	5	0	17	0	1	0	1	0	1.00	1	.111	.200	.178
Marlins	R	46	169	44	6	6	1	—	—	65	32	25	21	1	28	4	1	1	11	3	.79	1	.260	.354	.385
1995 Kane County	A	132	494	140	20	8	14	—	—	218	89	89	52	7	105	8	2	9	39	11	.78	7	.283	.355	.441
1996 Portland	AA	138	552	153	30	6	24	—	—	267	88	93	45	6	149	7	0	5	24	19	.56	10	.277	.337	.484
1997 Charlotte	AAA	107	401	105	16	7	23	—	—	204	74	62	39	2	129	3	0	1	25	3	.89	8	.262	.331	.509
1997 Florida	NL	19	50	13	2	2	2	(0	2)	25	7	7	7	0	21	1	0	0	2	0	1.00	1	.260	.362	.500

Roberto Duran

Pitches: Left **Bats:** Left **Pos:** RP-13   **Ht:** 6'0" **Wt:** 167 **Born:** 3/6/73 **Age:** 25

Year Team	Lg	G	GS	CG	GF	IP	BFP	H	R	ER	HR	SH	SF	HB	TBB	IBB	SO	WP	Bk	W	L	Pct.	ShO	Sv-Op	Hld	ERA
1992 Dodgers	R	9	8	0	0	38.2	166	22	17	12	1	1	1	2	31	0	57	8	0	4	3	.571	0	0- —	—	2.79
Vero Beach	A+	2	1	0	0	5	24	6	5	5	1	0	0	1	4	0	5	1	0	0	0	.000	0	0- —	—	9.00
1993 Vero Beach	A+	8	0	0	2	9.2	43	10	4	4	0	0	0	0	8	1	9	0	0	1	1	.500	0	0- —	—	3.72
Yakima	A-	20	3	0	6	40	201	37	34	31	3	1	2	6	42	0	50	10	0	2	2	.500	0	0- —	—	6.98
1994 Bakersfield	A+	42	4	0	29	65.1	300	61	43	35	5	3	4	5	48	0	86	6	0	6	5	.545	0	10- —	—	4.82
1995 Vero Beach	A+	23	22	0	0	101.1	446	82	42	38	8	3	1	1	70	0	114	12	0	7	4	.636	0	0- —	—	3.38
1996 Dunedin	A+	8	8	1	0	48.1	188	31	9	6	1	1	1	2	19	0	54	5	0	3	1	.750	1	0- —	—	1.12
Knoxville	AA	19	16	0	1	80.2	366	72	52	46	8	1	1	3	61	1	74	13	2	4	6	.400	0	0- —	—	5.13
1997 Jacksnville	AA	50	0	0	34	60.2	265	41	19	16	2	2	5	2	39	0	95	11	0	4	2	.667	0	16- —	—	2.37
1997 Detroit	AL	13	0	0	1	10.2	56	7	9	9	0	0	1	3	15	0	11	1	1	0	0	.000	0	0-0	0	7.59

Ray Durham

Bats: Both **Throws:** Right **Pos:** 2B-153; DH-1; PH-1   **Ht:** 5'8" **Wt:** 170 **Born:** 11/30/71 **Age:** 26

Year Team	Lg	G	AB	H	2B	3B	HR	(Hm	Rd)	TB	R	RBI	TBB	IBB	SO	HBP	SH	SF	SB	CS	SB%	GDP	Avg	OBP	SLG
1995 Chicago	AL	125	471	121	27	6	7	(1	6)	181	68	51	31	2	83	6	5	4	18	5	.78	8	.257	.309	.384
1996 Chicago	AL	156	557	153	33	5	10	(3	7)	226	79	65	58	4	95	10	7	7	30	4	.88	6	.275	.350	.406
1997 Chicago	AL	155	634	172	27	5	11	(3	8)	242	106	53	61	0	96	6	2	8	33	16	.67	14	.271	.337	.382
3 ML YEARS		436	1662	446	87	16	28	(7	21)	649	253	169	150	6	274	22	14	19	81	25	.76	28	.268	.334	.390

Jermaine Dye

Bats: Right **Throws:** Right **Pos:** RF-75; PH-4; LF-1   **Ht:** 6'4" **Wt:** 210 **Born:** 1/28/74 **Age:** 24

Year Team	Lg	G	AB	H	2B	3B	HR	(Hm	Rd)	TB	R	RBI	TBB	IBB	SO	HBP	SH	SF	SB	CS	SB%	GDP	Avg	OBP	SLG
1993 Braves	R	31	124	43	14	0	0	—	—	57	17	27	5	0	13	5	0	1	5	0	1.00	5	.347	.393	.460
Danville	R+	25	94	26	6	1	2	—	—	40	6	12	8	1	10	0	0	2	4	1	.80	2	.277	.327	.426
1994 Macon	A	135	506	151	41	1	15	—	—	239	73	98	33	1	82	8	0	8	19	10	.66	10	.298	.346	.472
1995 Greenville	AA	104	403	115	26	4	15	—	—	194	50	71	27	2	74	1	2	4	4	8	.33	9	.285	.329	.481
1996 Richmond	AAA	36	142	33	7	1	6	—	—	60	25	19	5	0	25	1	0	0	3	0	1.00	3	.232	.264	.423
1997 Omaha	AAA	39	144	44	6	0	10	—	—	80	21	25	9	1	25	1	0	1	0	2	.00	3	.306	.348	.556
1996 Atlanta	NL	98	292	82	16	0	12	(4	8)	134	32	37	8	0	67	3	0	3	1	4	.20	11	.281	.304	.459
1997 Kansas City	AL	75	263	62	14	0	7	(3	4)	97	26	22	17	0	51	1	1	1	2	1	.67	6	.236	.284	.369
2 ML YEARS		173	555	144	30	0	19	(7	12)	231	58	59	25	0	118	4	1	4	3	5	.38	17	.259	.294	.416

Damion Easley

Bats: R **Throws:** R **Pos:** 2B-137; SS-21; PH-8; DH-4   **Ht:** 5'11" **Wt:** 185 **Born:** 11/11/69 **Age:** 28

Year Team	Lg	G	AB	H	2B	3B	HR	(Hm	Rd)	TB	R	RBI	TBB	IBB	SO	HBP	SH	SF	SB	CS	SB%	GDP	Avg	OBP	SLG
1992 California	AL	47	151	39	5	0	1	(1	0)	47	14	12	8	0	26	3	2	1	9	5	.64	2	.258	.307	.311
1993 California	AL	73	230	72	13	2	2	(0	2)	95	33	22	28	2	35	3	1	2	6	6	.50	5	.313	.392	.413
1994 California	AL	88	316	68	16	1	6	(4	2)	104	41	30	29	0	48	4	4	2	4	5	.44	8	.215	.288	.329
1995 California	AL	114	357	77	14	2	4	(1	3)	107	35	35	32	1	47	6	6	4	5	2	.71	11	.216	.288	.300
1996 Cal-Det	AL	49	112	30	2	0	4	(1	3)	44	14	17	10	0	25	1	5	1	3	1	.75	0	.268	.331	.393
1997 Detroit	AL	151	527	139	37	3	22	(12	10)	248	97	72	68	3	102	16	4	5	28	13	.68	18	.264	.362	.471
1996 California	AL	28	45	7	1	0	2	(1	1)	14	4	7	6	0	12	0	3	0	0	0	.00	0	.156	.255	.311
Detroit	AL	21	67	23	1	0	2	(0	2)	30	10	10	4	0	13	1	2	1	3	1	.75	0	.343	.384	.448
6 ML YEARS		522	1693	425	87	8	39	(19	20)	645	234	188	175	6	283	33	22	15	55	32	.63	44	.251	.330	.381

Angel Echevarria

Bats: Right **Throws:** Right **Pos:** PH-8; RF-3; LF-2; CF-2   **Ht:** 6'3" **Wt:** 219 **Born:** 5/25/71 **Age:** 27

Year Team	Lg	G	AB	H	2B	3B	HR	(Hm	Rd)	TB	R	RBI	TBB	IBB	SO	HBP	SH	SF	SB	CS	SB%	GDP	Avg	OBP	SLG
1992 Bend	A-	57	205	46	4	1	5	—	—	67	24	30	19	1	54	2	0	0	1	0	.89	5	.224	.296	.327
1993 Central Val	A+	104	358	97	16	2	6	—	—	135	45	52	44	0	74	5	5	3	6	5	.55	7	.271	.356	.377
1994 Central Val	A+	50	192	58	8	1	6	—	—	86	28	35	9	0	25	4	0	3	2	2	.50	6	.302	.341	.448
New Haven	AA	58	205	52	6	0	8	—	—	82	25	32	15	1	46	2	0	2	4	3	.33	8	.254	.308	.400
1995 New Haven	AA	124	453	136	30	1	21	—	—	231	78	100	56	3	93	8	0	7	8	3	.73	8	.300	.382	.510
1996 Colo Spngs	AAA	110	415	140	19	2	16	—	—	211	67	74	38	3	81	3	0	4	3	5	.37	4	.337	.393	.508
1997 Colo Spngs	AAA	77	295	95	24	0	13	—	—	158	59	80	28	0	47	6	1	4	6	2	.75	8	.322	.387	.536
1996 Colorado	NL	26	21	6	0	0	0	(0	0)	6	2	6	2	0	5	1	0	2	0	0	.00	0	.286	.346	.286
1997 Colorado	NL	15	20	5	0	0	0	(0	0)	5	4	0	2	0	5	0	0	0	0	0	.00	0	.250	.318	.350

			BATTING																BASERUNNING				PERCENTAGES		
Year Team	Lg	G	AB	H	2B	3B	HR	(Hm	Rd)	TB	R	RBI	TBB	IBB	SO	HBP	SH	SF	SB	CS	SB%	GDP	Avg	OBP	SLG
2 ML YEARS		41	41	11	2	0	0	(0	0)	13	6	6	4	0	10	1	0	2	0	0	.00	0	.268	.333	.317

Dennis Eckersley

Pitches: Right **Bats:** Right **Pos:** RP-57   **Ht:** 6'2" **Wt:** 195 **Born:** 10/3/54 **Age:** 43

		HOW MUCH HE PITCHED						WHAT HE GAVE UP										THE RESULTS						
Year Team	Lg	G	GS	CG	GF	IP	BFP	H	R	ER	HR	SH	SF	HB	TBB	IBB	SO	WP	Bk	W	L	Pct.	ShO	Sv-Op	Hld	ERA
1975 Cleveland	AL	34	24	6	5	186.2	794	147	61	54	16	6	7	7	90	8	152	4	2	13	7	.650	2	2- -	—	2.60
1976 Cleveland	AL	36	30	9	3	199.1	821	155	82	76	13	10	4	5	78	2	200	6	1	13	12	.520	3	1- -	—	3.43
1977 Cleveland	AL	33	33	12	0	247.1	1006	214	100	97	31	11	6	7	54	11	191	3	0	14	13	.519	3	0-0	0	3.53
1978 Boston	AL	35	35	16	0	268.1	1121	258	99	89	30	7	8	7	71	8	162	3	0	20	8	.714	3	0-0	0	2.99
1979 Boston	AL	33	33	17	0	246.2	1018	234	89	82	29	10	6	6	59	4	150	1	1	17	10	.630	2	0-0	0	2.99
1980 Boston	AL	30	30	8	0	197.2	818	188	101	94	25	7	8	2	44	7	121	0	0	12	14	.462	0	0-0	0	4.28
1981 Boston	AL	23	23	8	0	154	649	160	82	73	9	6	5	3	35	2	79	0	0	9	8	.529	2	0-0	0	4.27
1982 Boston	AL	33	33	11	0	224.1	926	228	101	93	31	4	4	2	43	3	127	1	0	13	13	.500	3	0-0	0	3.73
1983 Boston	AL	28	28	2	0	176.1	787	223	119	110	27	1	5	6	39	4	77	1	0	9	13	.409	0	0-0	0	5.61
1984 Bos-ChN		33	33	4	0	225	932	223	97	90	21	11	9	5	49	9	114	3	2	14	12	.538	0	0-0	0	3.60
1985 Chicago	NL	25	25	6	0	169.1	664	145	61	58	15	6	2	3	19	4	117	0	3	11	7	.611	2	0-0	0	3.08
1986 Chicago	NL	33	32	1	0	201	862	226	109	102	21	13	10	3	43	3	137	2	5	6	11	.353	0	0-0	0	4.57
1987 Oakland	AL	54	2	0	33	115.2	460	99	41	39	11	3	3	3	17	3	113	1	0	6	8	.429	0	16-20	2	3.03
1988 Oakland	AL	60	0	0	53	72.2	279	52	20	19	5	1	3	1	11	2	70	0	2	4	2	.667	0	45-53	1	2.35
1989 Oakland	AL	51	0	0	46	57.2	206	32	10	10	5	0	4	1	3	0	55	0	0	4	0	1.000	0	33-39	1	1.56
1990 Oakland	AL	63	0	0	61	73.1	262	41	9	5	2	0	1	0	4	1	73	0	0	4	2	.667	0	48-50	0	0.61
1991 Oakland	AL	67	0	0	59	76	299	60	26	25	11	1	0	1	9	3	87	1	0	5	4	.556	0	43-51	0	2.96
1992 Oakland	AL	69	0	0	65	80	309	62	17	17	5	3	0	1	11	6	93	0	0	7	1	.875	0	51-54	0	1.91
1993 Oakland	AL	64	0	0	52	67	276	67	32	31	7	2	2	2	13	4	80	0	0	2	4	.333	0	36-46	0	4.16
1994 Oakland	AL	45	0	0	39	44.1	193	49	26	21	5	1	0	1	13	2	47	0	0	5	4	.556	0	19-25	0	4.26
1995 Oakland	AL	52	0	0	48	50.1	212	53	29	27	5	1	2	1	11	0	40	0	0	4	6	.400	0	29-38	0	4.83
1996 St. Louis	NL	63	0	0	53	60	251	65	26	22	8	1	3	4	6	2	49	0	0	0	6	.000	0	30-34	4	3.30
1997 St. Louis	NL	57	0	0	47	53	218	49	24	23	9	2	0	2	8	0	45	2	0	1	5	.167	0	36-43	0	3.91
1984 Boston	AL	9	9	2	0	64.2	270	71	38	36	10	3	3	1	13	2	33	2	0	4	4	.500	0	0-0	0	5.01
Chicago	NL	24	24	2	0	160.1	662	152	59	54	11	8	6	4	36	7	81	1	2	10	8	.556	0	0-0	0	3.03
23 ML YEARS		1021	361	100	564	3246	13363	3030	1361	1257	341	107	92	73	730	88	2379	28	16	193	170	.532	20	389- -	—	3.49

Jim Edmonds

Bats: L **Throws:** L **Pos:** CF-115; 1B-11; DH-8; PH-3   **Ht:** 6'1" **Wt:** 190 **Born:** 6/27/70 **Age:** 28

			BATTING																BASERUNNING				PERCENTAGES		
Year Team	Lg	G	AB	H	2B	3B	HR	(Hm	Rd)	TB	R	RBI	TBB	IBB	SO	HBP	SH	SF	SB	CS	SB%	GDP	Avg	OBP	SLG
1993 California	AL	18	61	15	4	1	0	(0	0)	21	5	4	2	1	16	0	0	0	0	2	.00	1	.246	.270	.344
1994 California	AL	94	289	79	13	1	5	(3	2)	109	35	37	30	3	72	1	1	1	4	2	.67	3	.273	.343	.377
1995 California	AL	141	558	162	30	4	33	(16	17)	299	120	107	51	4	130	5	1	5	1	4	.20	10	.290	.352	.536
1996 California	AL	114	431	131	28	3	27	(17	10)	246	73	66	46	2	101	4	0	2	4	0	1.00	8	.304	.375	.571
1997 Anaheim	AL	133	502	146	27	0	26	(14	12)	251	82	80	60	5	80	4	0	5	5	7	.42	8	.291	.368	.500
5 ML YEARS		500	1841	533	102	9	91	(50	41)	926	315	294	189	15	399	14	2	13	14	15	.48	30	.290	.358	.503

Robert Eenhoorn

Bats: Right **Throws:** Right **Pos:** 3B-5; 2B-3; SS-2; PH-1   **Ht:** 6'3" **Wt:** 185 **Born:** 2/9/68 **Age:** 30

			BATTING																BASERUNNING				PERCENTAGES		
Year Team	Lg	G	AB	H	2B	3B	HR	(Hm	Rd)	TB	R	RBI	TBB	IBB	SO	HBP	SH	SF	SB	CS	SB%	GDP	Avg	OBP	SLG
1997 Vancouver *	AAA	120	455	140	29	5	12	—	—	215	77	58	25	2	59	7	12	5	1	4	.20	10	.308	.350	.473
1994 New York	AL	3	4	2	1	0	0	(0	0)	3	1	0	0	0	0	0	0	0	0	0	.00	0	.500	.500	.750
1995 New York	AL	5	14	2	1	0	0	(0	0)	3	1	2	1	0	3	0	0	0	0	0	.00	1	.143	.200	.214
1996 NYA-Cal	AL	18	29	5	0	0	0	(0	0)	5	3	2	2	0	5	0	1	2	0	0	.00	0	.172	.212	.172
1997 Anaheim	AL	11	20	7	1	0	1	(1	0)	11	2	6	0	0	2	0	0	1	0	0	.00	0	.350	.333	.550
1996 New York	AL	12	14	1	0	0	0	(0	0)	1	2	2	2	0	3	0	1	2	0	0	.00	0	.071	.167	.071
California	AL	6	15	4	0	0	0	(0	0)	4	1	0	0	0	2	0	0	0	0	0	.00	0	.267	.267	.267
4 ML YEARS		37	67	16	3	0	1	(1	0)	22	7	10	3	0	10	0	1	3	0	0	.00	1	.239	.260	.328

Joey Eischen

Pitches: Left **Bats:** Left **Pos:** RP-1   **Ht:** 6'1" **Wt:** 190 **Born:** 5/25/70 **Age:** 28

		HOW MUCH HE PITCHED						WHAT HE GAVE UP										THE RESULTS						
Year Team	Lg	G	GS	CG	GF	IP	BFP	H	R	ER	HR	SH	SF	HB	TBB	IBB	SO	WP	Bk	W	L	Pct.	ShO	Sv-Op	Hld	ERA
1997 Indianapolis *	AAA	26	5	0	7	42.2	173	41	7	6	1	2	0	1	13	1	26	2	0	1	0	1.000	0	2- -	—	1.27
1994 Montreal	NL	1	0	0	0	0.2	7	4	4	4	0	0	0	1	0	0	1	0	0	0	0	.000	0	0-0	0	54.00
1995 Los Angeles	NL	17	0	0	8	20.1	95	19	9	7	1	0	0	2	11	1	15	1	0	0	0	.000	0	0-0	1	3.10
1996 LA-Det		52	0	0	14	68.1	308	75	36	32	7	3	2	4	34	7	51	4	0	1	2	.333	0	0-2	2	4.21
1997 Cincinnati	NL	1	0	0	0	1.1	7	2	2	1	0	0	0	0	2	1	0	0	0	0	0	.000	0	0-0	0	6.75
1996 Los Angeles	NL	28	0	0	11	43.1	198	48	25	23	4	3	1	4	20	4	36	1	0	0	1	.000	0	0-0	1	4.78
Detroit	AL	24	0	0	3	25	110	27	11	9	3	0	1	0	14	3	15	3	0	1	1	.500	0	0-2	1	3.24
4 ML YEARS		71	0	0	22	90.2	417	100	51	44	8	3	2	7	46	8	69	6	0	1	2	.333	0	0-2	3	4.37

60

Jim Eisenreich

Bats: L **Throws:** L **Pos:** PH-44; LF-42; 1B-29; RF-13; DH-4; CF-1   **Ht:** 5'11" **Wt:** 195 **Born:** 4/18/59 **Age:** 39

Year Team	Lg	G	AB	H	2B	3B	HR	(Hm	Rd)	TB	R	RBI	TBB	IBB	SO	HBP	SH	SF	SB	CS	SB%	GDP	Avg	OBP	SLG
1982 Minnesota	AL	34	99	30	6	0	2	(1	1)	42	10	9	11	0	13	1	0	0	0	0	.00	1	.303	.378	.424
1983 Minnesota	AL	2	7	2	1	0	0	(0	0)	3	1	0	1	0	1	0	0	0	0	0	.00	0	.286	.375	.429
1984 Minnesota	AL	12	32	7	1	0	0	(0	0)	8	1	3	2	1	4	0	0	2	2	0	1.00	1	.219	.250	.250
1987 Kansas City	AL	44	105	25	8	2	4	(3	1)	49	10	21	7	2	13	0	0	3	1	1	.50	2	.238	.278	.467
1988 Kansas City	AL	82	202	44	8	1	1	(0	1)	57	26	19	6	1	31	0	2	4	9	3	.75	2	.218	.236	.282
1989 Kansas City	AL	134	475	139	33	7	9	(4	5)	213	64	59	37	9	44	0	3	4	27	8	.77	8	.293	.341	.448
1990 Kansas City	AL	142	496	139	29	7	5	(2	3)	197	61	51	42	2	51	1	2	4	12	14	.46	7	.280	.335	.397
1991 Kansas City	AL	135	375	113	22	3	2	(2	0)	147	47	47	20	1	35	1	3	6	5	3	.63	10	.301	.333	.392
1992 Kansas City	AL	113	353	95	13	3	2	(1	1)	120	31	28	24	4	36	0	0	3	11	6	.65	6	.269	.313	.340
1993 Philadelphia	NL	153	362	115	17	4	7	(3	4)	161	51	54	26	5	36	1	3	2	5	0	1.00	6	.318	.363	.445
1994 Philadelphia	NL	104	290	87	15	4	4	(3	1)	122	42	43	33	3	31	1	3	2	6	2	.75	8	.300	.371	.421
1995 Philadelphia	NL	129	377	119	22	2	10	(5	5)	175	46	55	38	4	44	1	2	5	10	0	1.00	6	.316	.375	.464
1996 Philadelphia	NL	113	338	122	24	3	3	(1	2)	161	45	41	31	9	32	1	0	3	11	1	.92	7	.361	.413	.476
1997 Florida	NL	120	293	82	19	1	2	(2	0)	109	36	34	30	4	28	1	3	4	0	0	.00	7	.280	.345	.372
14 ML YEARS		1317	3804	1119	218	37	51	(27	24)	1564	471	464	308	45	399	8	21	42	99	38	.72	72	.294	.345	.411

Cal Eldred

Pitches: Right **Bats:** Right **Pos:** SP-34   **Ht:** 6'4" **Wt:** 236 **Born:** 11/24/67 **Age:** 30

Year Team	Lg	G	GS	CG	GF	IP	BFP	H	R	ER	HR	SH	SF	HB	TBB	IBB	SO	WP	Bk	W	L	Pct.	ShO	Sv-Op	Hld	ERA
1991 Milwaukee	AL	3	3	0	0	16	73	20	9	8	2	0	0	0	6	0	10	0	0	2	0	1.000	0	0-0	0	4.50
1992 Milwaukee	AL	14	14	2	0	100.1	394	76	21	20	4	1	0	2	23	0	62	3	0	11	2	.846	1	0-0	0	1.79
1993 Milwaukee	AL	36	36	8	0	258	1087	232	120	115	32	5	12	10	91	5	180	2	0	16	16	.500	1	0-0	0	4.01
1994 Milwaukee	AL	25	25	6	0	179	769	158	96	93	23	5	7	4	84	0	98	2	0	11	11	.500	0	0-0	0	4.68
1995 Milwaukee	AL	4	4	0	0	23.2	104	24	10	9	4	1	0	1	10	0	18	1	1	1	1	.500	0	0-0	0	3.42
1996 Milwaukee	AL	15	15	0	0	84.2	363	82	43	42	8	0	4	4	38	0	50	1	0	4	4	.500	0	0-0	0	4.46
1997 Milwaukee	AL	34	34	1	0	202	885	207	118	112	31	4	6	9	89	0	122	5	0	13	15	.464	1	0-0	0	4.99
7 ML YEARS		131	131	17	0	863.2	3675	799	417	399	104	16	29	30	341	5	540	14	1	58	49	.542	3	0-0	0	4.16

Kevin Elster

Bats: Right **Throws:** Right **Pos:** SS-39   **Ht:** 6'2" **Wt:** 200 **Born:** 8/3/64 **Age:** 33

Year Team	Lg	G	AB	H	2B	3B	HR	(Hm	Rd)	TB	R	RBI	TBB	IBB	SO	HBP	SH	SF	SB	CS	SB%	GDP	Avg	OBP	SLG
1986 New York	NL	19	30	5	1	0	0	(0	0)	6	3	0	3	1	8	0	0	0	0	0	.00	0	.167	.242	.200
1987 New York	NL	5	10	4	2	0	0	(0	0)	6	1	1	0	0	1	0	0	0	0	0	.00	1	.400	.400	.600
1988 New York	NL	149	406	87	11	1	9	(6	3)	127	41	37	35	12	47	3	6	0	2	0	1.00	5	.214	.282	.313
1989 New York	NL	151	458	106	25	2	10	(5	5)	165	52	55	34	11	77	2	6	8	4	3	.57	13	.231	.283	.360
1990 New York	NL	92	314	65	20	1	9	(2	7)	114	36	45	30	2	54	1	1	6	2	0	1.00	4	.207	.274	.363
1991 New York	NL	115	348	84	16	2	6	(3	3)	122	33	36	40	6	53	1	1	4	2	3	.40	4	.241	.318	.351
1992 New York	NL	6	18	4	0	0	0	(0	0)	4	0	0	0	0	2	0	0	0	0	0	.00	0	.222	.222	.222
1994 New York	AL	7	20	0	0	0	0	(0	0)	0	0	0	1	0	6	0	1	0	0	0	.00	0	.000	.048	.000
1995 NYA-Phi		36	70	13	5	1	1	(1	0)	23	11	9	8	1	19	1	2	2	0	0	.00	1	.186	.272	.329
1996 Texas	AL	157	515	130	32	2	24	(9	15)	238	79	99	52	1	138	2	16	11	4	1	.80	8	.252	.317	.462
1997 Pittsburgh	NL	39	138	31	6	2	7	(3	4)	62	14	25	21	0	39	1	2	2	0	2	.00	1	.225	.327	.449
1995 New York	NL	10	17	2	1	0	0	(0	0)	3	1	0	1	0	5	0	0	0	0	0	.00	0	.118	.167	.176
Philadelphia	NL	26	53	11	4	1	1	(1	0)	20	10	9	7	1	14	1	2	2	0	0	.00	1	.208	.302	.377
11 ML YEARS		776	2327	529	118	11	66	(29	37)	867	270	307	224	34	444	11	35	33	14	9	.61	38	.227	.294	.373

Alan Embree

Pitches: Left **Bats:** Left **Pos:** RP-66   **Ht:** 6'2" **Wt:** 190 **Born:** 1/23/70 **Age:** 28

Year Team	Lg	G	GS	CG	GF	IP	BFP	H	R	ER	HR	SH	SF	HB	TBB	IBB	SO	WP	Bk	W	L	Pct.	ShO	Sv-Op	Hld	ERA
1992 Cleveland	AL	4	4	0	0	18	81	19	14	14	3	0	2	1	8	0	12	1	0	0	2	.000	0	0-0	0	7.00
1995 Cleveland	AL	23	0	0	8	24.2	111	23	16	14	2	2	2	0	16	0	23	1	0	3	2	.600	0	1-1	6	5.11
1996 Cleveland	AL	24	0	0	2	31	141	30	26	22	10	1	3	0	21	3	33	3	0	1	1	.500	0	0-0	1	6.39
1997 Atlanta	NL	66	0	0	15	46	190	36	13	13	1	4	1	2	20	2	45	3	1	3	1	.750	0	0-0	16	2.54
4 ML YEARS		117	4	0	25	119.2	523	108	69	63	16	7	8	3	65	5	113	8	2	7	6	.538	0	1-1	23	4.74

Angelo Encarnacion

Bats: Right **Throws:** Right **Pos:** C-11   **Ht:** 5'8" **Wt:** 177 **Born:** 4/18/73 **Age:** 25

Year Team	Lg	G	AB	H	2B	3B	HR	(Hm	Rd)	TB	R	RBI	TBB	IBB	SO	HBP	SH	SF	SB	CS	SB%	GDP	Avg	OBP	SLG
1997 Las Vegas *	AAA	79	253	62	12	1	3	—	—	85	27	23	15	1	32	1	1	0	1	5	.17	9	.245	.290	.336
1995 Pittsburgh	NL	58	159	36	7	2	2	(2	0)	53	18	10	13	5	28	0	3	0	1	1	.50	2	.226	.285	.333
1996 Pittsburgh	NL	7	22	7	2	0	0	(0	0)	9	3	1	0	0	5	0	0	0	0	0	.00	0	.318	.318	.409
1997 Anaheim	AL	11	17	7	1	0	1	(0	1)	11	2	4	0	0	1	0	0	0	2	0	1.00	1	.412	.412	.647
3 ML YEARS		76	198	50	10	2	3	(2	1)	73	23	15	13	5	34	0	3	0	3	1	.75	4	.253	.299	.369

Juan Encarnacion

Bats: Right **Throws:** Right **Pos:** RF-10; CF-2; PH-1 **Ht:** 6'2" **Wt:** 160 **Born:** 3/8/76 **Age:** 22

								BATTING												BASERUNNING				PERCENTAGES		
Year Team	Lg	G	AB	H	2B	3B	HR	(Hm	Rd)	TB	R	RBI	TBB	IBB	SO	HBP	SH	SF		SB	CS	SB%	GDP	Avg	OBP	SLG
1994 Fayetteville	A	24	83	16	1	1	1	—	—	22	6	4	8	1	36	1	0	0		1	1	.50	2	.193	.272	.265
Bristol	R+	54	197	49	7	1	4	—	—	70	16	31	13	1	54	5	1	1		9	2	.82	2	.249	.310	.355
Lakeland	A+	3	6	2	0	0	0	—	—	2	1	0	0	0	3	1	0	0		0	0	.00	0	.333	.429	.333
1995 Fayetteville	A	124	457	129	31	7	16	—	—	222	62	72	30	0	113	8	1	2		5	6	.45	10	.282	.336	.486
1996 Lakeland	A+	131	499	120	31	2	15	—	—	200	54	58	24	2	104	12	0	3		11	5	.69	10	.240	.290	.401
1997 Jacksnville	AA	131	493	159	31	4	26	—	—	276	91	90	43	6	86	19	0	6		17	3	.85	8	.323	.394	.560
1997 Detroit	AL	11	33	7	1	1	1	(1	0)	13	3	5	3	0	12	2	0	0		3	1	.75	1	.212	.316	.394

Todd Erdos

Pitches: Right **Bats:** Right **Pos:** RP-11 **Ht:** 6'1" **Wt:** 190 **Born:** 11/21/73 **Age:** 24

		HOW MUCH HE PITCHED						WHAT HE GAVE UP											THE RESULTS					
Year Team	Lg	G	GS	CG	GF	IP	BFP	H	R	ER	HR	SH	SF	HB	TBB	IBB	SO	WP	Bk	W	L	Pct.	ShO	Sv-Op Hld	ERA
1992 Padres	R	12	9	1	2	57.2	233	36	28	17	1	3	1	3	18	0	61	8	3	3	4	.429	0	0- —	2.65
Spokane	A-	2	2	0	0	13	53	9	2	1	0	1	0	1	5	0	11	0	0	1	0	1.000	0	0- —	0.69
1993 Waterloo	A	11	11	0	0	47.2	235	64	51	44	9	2	3	4	31	2	27	8	1	1	9	.100	0	0- —	8.31
Spokane	A-	16	15	0	0	90.1	384	73	39	32	13	4	2	3	53	2	64	1	1	5	6	.455	0	0- —	3.19
1995 Rancho Cuca	A+	1	0	0	0	2.2	13	5	4	4	0	0	1	0	0	0	4	0	0	0	0	.000	0	0- —	13.50
Clinton	A	5	1	0	1	5	27	4	4	3	0	0	0	0	8	1	1	2	0	0	0	.000	0	0- —	5.40
Idaho Falls	R+	32	0	0	20	41.1	185	34	19	16	1	3	2	5	30	2	48	8	0	5	3	.625	0	1- —	3.48
1996 Rancho Cuca	A+	55	0	0	41	67.1	305	63	33	28	2	7	2	6	37	3	82	6	0	3	3	.500	0	17- —	3.74
1997 Mobile	AA	55	0	0	50	59	244	45	22	22	4	2	1	0	22	4	49	2	1	1	4	.200	0	27- —	3.36
1997 San Diego	NL	11	0	0	2	13.2	64	17	9	8	1	0	0	0	4	0	13	3	0	2	0	1.000	0	0-0	5.27

John Ericks

Pitches: Right **Bats:** Right **Pos:** RP-10 **Ht:** 6'7" **Wt:** 251 **Born:** 9/16/67 **Age:** 30

		HOW MUCH HE PITCHED						WHAT HE GAVE UP											THE RESULTS					
Year Team	Lg	G	GS	CG	GF	IP	BFP	H	R	ER	HR	SH	SF	HB	TBB	IBB	SO	WP	Bk	W	L	Pct.	ShO	Sv-Op Hld	ERA
1997 Pirates *	R	9	8	0	0	13	50	5	5	5	0	0	0	0	5	0	18	1	1	0	0	.000	0	0- —	3.46
Calgary *	AAA	6	0	0	1	7	39	14	11	10	0	0	1	2	1	0	10	1	0	0	0	.000	0	0- —	12.86
1995 Pittsburgh	NL	19	18	1	0	106	472	108	59	54	7	5	5	2	50	4	80	11	1	3	9	.250	0	0-0	4.58
1996 Pittsburgh	NL	28	4	0	13	46.2	213	56	35	30	11	1	0	1	19	2	46	2	0	4	5	.444	0	8-10	5.79
1997 Pittsburgh	NL	10	0	0	10	9.1	39	7	3	2	1	0	0	0	4	0	6	0	0	1	0	1.000	0	6-7	1.93
3 ML YEARS		57	22	1	23	162	724	171	97	86	19	6	6	2	73	6	132	13	1	8	14	.364	0	14-17	4.78

Scott Erickson

Pitches: Right **Bats:** Right **Pos:** SP-33; RP-1 **Ht:** 6'4" **Wt:** 230 **Born:** 2/2/68 **Age:** 30

		HOW MUCH HE PITCHED						WHAT HE GAVE UP											THE RESULTS					
Year Team	Lg	G	GS	CG	GF	IP	BFP	H	R	ER	HR	SH	SF	HB	TBB	IBB	SO	WP	Bk	W	L	Pct.	ShO	Sv-Op Hld	ERA
1990 Minnesota	AL	19	17	1	1	113	485	108	49	36	9	5	2	5	51	4	53	3	0	8	4	.667	0	0-0	2.87
1991 Minnesota	AL	32	32	5	0	204	851	189	80	72	13	5	7	6	71	3	108	4	0	20	8	.714	3	0-0	3.18
1992 Minnesota	AL	32	32	5	0	212	888	197	86	80	18	9	7	8	83	3	101	6	1	13	12	.520	3	0-0	3.40
1993 Minnesota	AL	34	34	1	0	218.2	976	266	138	126	17	10	13	10	71	1	116	5	0	8	19	.296	0	0-0	5.19
1994 Minnesota	AL	23	23	2	0	144	654	173	95	87	15	3	4	9	59	0	104	10	0	8	11	.421	1	0-0	5.44
1995 Min-Bal	AL	32	31	7	1	196.1	836	213	108	105	18	3	3	5	67	0	106	3	0	13	10	.565	2	0-0	4.81
1996 Baltimore	AL	34	34	6	0	222.1	968	262	137	124	21	5	5	11	66	4	100	1	0	13	12	.520	0	0-0	5.02
1997 Baltimore	AL	34	33	3	0	221.2	922	218	100	91	16	3	4	5	61	5	131	11	0	16	7	.696	2	0-0	3.69
1995 Minnesota	AL	15	15	0	0	87.2	390	102	61	58	11	2	1	4	32	0	45	1	0	4	6	.400	0	0-0	5.95
Baltimore	AL	17	16	7	1	108.2	446	111	47	47	7	1	2	1	35	0	61	2	2	9	4	.692	2	0-0	3.89
8 ML YEARS		240	236	30	2	1532	6580	1626	793	721	127	43	45	59	529	20	819	43	3	99	83	.544	11	0-0	4.24

Darin Erstad

Bats: L **Throws:** L **Pos:** 1B-126; DH-9; PH-8; CF-1 **Ht:** 6'2" **Wt:** 210 **Born:** 6/4/74 **Age:** 24

								BATTING												BASERUNNING				PERCENTAGES		
Year Team	Lg	G	AB	H	2B	3B	HR	(Hm	Rd)	TB	R	RBI	TBB	IBB	SO	HBP	SH	SF		SB	CS	SB%	GDP	Avg	OBP	SLG
1995 Angels	R	4	18	10	1	0	0	—	—	11	2	1	1	0	1	0	0	0		1	0	1.00	0	.556	.579	.611
Lk Elsinore	A+	25	113	41	7	3	5	—	—	69	24	24	6	0	22	0	0	1		3	0	1.00	0	.363	.392	.611
1996 Vancouver	AAA	85	351	107	22	5	6	—	—	157	63	41	44	4	53	3	1	2		11	6	.65	5	.305	.385	.447
1996 California	AL	57	208	59	5	1	4	(1	3)	78	34	20	17	1	29	0	1	3		3	3	.50	3	.284	.333	.375
1997 Anaheim	AL	139	539	161	34	4	16	(8	8)	251	99	77	51	4	86	4	5	6		23	8	.74	5	.299	.360	.466
2 ML YEARS		196	747	220	39	5	20	(9	11)	329	133	97	68	5	115	4	6	9		26	11	.70	8	.295	.353	.440

Kelvim Escobar

Pitches: Right **Bats:** Right **Pos:** RP-27 **Ht:** 6'1" **Wt:** 205 **Born:** 4/11/76 **Age:** 22

		HOW MUCH HE PITCHED						WHAT HE GAVE UP											THE RESULTS					
Year Team	Lg	G	GS	CG	GF	IP	BFP	H	R	ER	HR	SH	SF	HB	TBB	IBB	SO	WP	Bk	W	L	Pct.	ShO	Sv-Op Hld	ERA
1994 Blue Jays	R	11	10	1	0	65	257	56	23	17	0	1	2	18	0	64	5	3	4	4	.500	0	0- —	2.35
1995 Medicne Hat	R+	14	14	1	0	69.1	307	66	47	44	6	2	5	6	33	0	75	4	3	3	.500	1	0- —	5.71
1996 Dunedin	A+	18	18	1	0	110.1	460	101	44	33	5	2	1	3	33	0	113	7	2	9	5	.643	0	0- —	2.69
Knoxville	AA	10	10	0	0	54	238	61	36	32	7	0	1	0	24	0	44	6	1	3	4	.429	0	0- —	5.33

Year Team	Lg	G	GS	CG	GF	IP	BFP	H	R	ER	HR	SH	SF	HB	TBB	IBB	SO	WP	Bk	W	L	Pct.	ShO	Sv-Op	Hld	ERA
1997 Dunedin	A+	3	2	0	0	12	55	16	9	5	0	1	1	1	3	0	16	1	0	0	1	.000	0	0--	—	3.75
Knoxville	AA	5	5	1	0	24.1	108	20	13	10	1	0	0	2	16	0	31	1	2	2	1	.667	0	0--	—	3.70
1997 Toronto	AL	27	0	0	23	31	139	28	12	10	1	2	0	0	19	2	36	0	0	3	2	.600	0	14-17	1	2.90

Vaughn Eshelman

Pitches: Left **Bats:** Left **Pos:** RP-15; SP-6   **Ht:** 6'3" **Wt:** 210 **Born:** 5/22/69 **Age:** 29

		HOW MUCH HE PITCHED						WHAT HE GAVE UP												THE RESULTS						
Year Team	Lg	G	GS	CG	GF	IP	BFP	H	R	ER	HR	SH	SF	HB	TBB	IBB	SO	WP	Bk	W	L	Pct.	ShO	Sv-Op	Hld	ERA
1997 Pawtucket *	AAA	14	13	0	1	66.2	281	63	38	36	4	7	4	5	22	0	57	3	0	3	4	.429	0	1--	—	4.86
1995 Boston	AL	23	14	0	4	81.2	356	86	47	44	3	0	3	1	36	0	41	4	0	6	3	.667	0	0-0	1	4.85
1996 Boston	AL	39	10	0	1	87.2	428	112	79	69	13	3	5	2	58	4	59	4	0	6	3	.667	0	0-0	8	7.08
1997 Boston	AL	21	6	0	6	42.2	198	58	32	30	3	1	2	2	17	5	18	2	0	3	3	.500	0	0-1	0	6.33
3 ML YEARS		83	30	0	11	212	982	256	158	143	19	4	10	5	111	9	118	10	0	15	9	.625	0	0-1	9	6.07

Alvaro Espinoza

Bats: R **Throws:** R **Pos:** SS-17; 2B-14; PH-5; 3B-1   **Ht:** 6'0" **Wt:** 190 **Born:** 2/19/62 **Age:** 36

		BATTING																	BASERUNNING				PERCENTAGES		
Year Team	Lg	G	AB	H	2B	3B	HR	(Hm	Rd)	TB	R	RBI	TBB	IBB	SO	HBP	SH	SF	SB	CS	SB%	GDP	Avg	OBP	SLG
1997 Tacoma *	AAA	4	12	4	0	0	0	—	—	4	1	1	2	0	1	0	0	0	0	0	.00	0	.333	.429	.333
1984 Minnesota	AL	1	0	0	0	0	0	(0	0)	0	0	0	0	0	0	0	0	0	0	0	.00	0	.000	.000	.000
1985 Minnesota	AL	32	57	15	2	0	0	(0	0)	17	5	9	1	0	9	1	3	0	0	1	.00	2	.263	.288	.298
1986 Minnesota	AL	37	42	9	1	0	0	(0	0)	10	4	1	1	0	10	0	2	0	0	1	.00	0	.214	.233	.238
1988 New York	AL	3	3	0	0	0	0	(0	0)	0	0	0	0	0	0	0	0	0	0	0	.00	0	.000	.000	.000
1989 New York	AL	146	503	142	23	1	0	(0	0)	167	51	41	14	1	60	1	23	3	3	3	.50	14	.282	.301	.332
1990 New York	AL	150	438	98	12	2	2	(0	2)	120	31	20	16	0	54	5	11	2	1	2	.33	13	.224	.258	.274
1991 New York	AL	148	480	123	23	2	5	(2	3)	165	51	33	16	0	57	2	9	2	4	1	.80	10	.256	.282	.344
1993 Cleveland	AL	129	263	73	15	0	4	(3	1)	100	34	27	8	0	36	1	8	3	2	2	.50	7	.278	.298	.380
1994 Cleveland	AL	90	231	55	13	0	1	(1	0)	71	27	19	6	0	33	1	4	2	1	3	.25	7	.238	.258	.307
1995 Cleveland	AL	66	143	36	4	0	2	(0	2)	46	15	17	2	0	16	1	2	2	0	2	.00	3	.252	.264	.322
1996 Cle-NYN	AL	107	246	66	11	4	8	(3	5)	110	31	27	10	0	37	3	8	2	1	3	.25	8	.268	.303	.443
1997 Seattle	AL	33	72	13	1	0	0	(0	0)	14	3	7	2	0	12	1	3	0	1	1	.50	2	.181	.213	.194
1996 Cleveland	AL	59	112	25	4	2	4	(1	3)	45	12	11	6	0	18	3	3	1	1	1	.50	4	.223	.279	.402
New York	NL	48	134	41	7	2	4	(2	2)	64	19	16	4	0	19	0	5	1	0	2	.00	4	.306	.324	.478
12 ML YEARS		942	2478	630	105	9	22	(9	13)	819	252	201	76	1	324	16	73	16	13	19	.41	66	.254	.279	.331

Bobby Estalella

Bats: Right **Throws:** Right **Pos:** C-11; PH-3   **Ht:** 6'1" **Wt:** 195 **Born:** 8/23/74 **Age:** 23

		BATTING																	BASERUNNING				PERCENTAGES		
Year Team	Lg	G	AB	H	2B	3B	HR	(Hm	Rd)	TB	R	RBI	TBB	IBB	SO	HBP	SH	SF	SB	CS	SB%	GDP	Avg	OBP	SLG
1993 Martinsville	R+	35	122	36	11	0	3	—	—	56	14	19	14	2	24	2	0	0	0	1	.00	6	.295	.377	.459
Clearwater	A+	11	35	8	0	0	0	—	—	8	4	4	2	0	3	0	0	0	0	0	.00	1	.229	.270	.229
1994 Spartanburg	A	86	299	65	19	1	9	—	—	113	34	41	31	0	85	1	1	4	0	0	.00	5	.217	.290	.378
Clearwater	A+	13	46	12	1	0	2	—	—	19	3	9	3	0	17	0	2	1	0	0	.00	1	.261	.300	.413
1995 Clearwater	A+	117	404	105	24	1	15	—	—	176	61	58	56	2	76	2	3	4	0	3	.00	12	.260	.350	.436
Reading	AA	10	34	8	1	0	2	—	—	15	5	9	4	1	7	1	0	0	0	0	.00	1	.235	.333	.441
1996 Reading	AA	111	365	89	14	2	23	—	—	176	48	72	67	5	104	5	1	4	2	4	.33	7	.244	.365	.482
Scranton-WB	AAA	11	36	9	3	0	3	—	—	21	7	8	5	0	10	0	0	0	0	0	.00	1	.250	.341	.583
1997 Scranton-WB	AAA	123	433	101	32	0	16	—	—	181	63	65	56	0	109	9	0	2	3	0	1.00	14	.233	.332	.418
1996 Philadelphia	NL	7	17	6	0	0	2	(0	2)	12	5	4	1	0	6	0	0	0	0	0	1.00	0	.353	.389	.706
1997 Philadelphia	NL	13	29	10	1	0	4	(1	3)	23	9	9	7	0	7	0	0	0	1	0	1.00	2	.345	.472	.793
2 ML YEARS		20	46	16	1	0	6	(1	5)	35	14	13	8	0	13	0	0	0	1	0	1.00	2	.348	.444	.761

Shawn Estes

Pitches: Left **Bats:** Right **Pos:** SP-32   **Ht:** 6'2" **Wt:** 185 **Born:** 2/18/73 **Age:** 25

		HOW MUCH HE PITCHED						WHAT HE GAVE UP												THE RESULTS						
Year Team	Lg	G	GS	CG	GF	IP	BFP	H	R	ER	HR	SH	SF	HB	TBB	IBB	SO	WP	Bk	W	L	Pct.	ShO	Sv-Op	Hld	ERA
1995 San Francisco	NL	3	3	0	0	17.1	76	16	14	13	2	0	0	1	5	0	14	4	0	0	3	.000	0	0-0	0	6.75
1996 San Francisco	NL	11	11	0	0	70	305	63	30	28	3	5	0	2	39	3	60	4	0	3	5	.375	0	0-0	0	3.60
1997 San Francisco	NL	32	32	3	0	201	849	162	80	71	12	13	2	8	100	2	181	10	2	19	5	.792	2	0-0	0	3.18
3 ML YEARS		46	46	3	0	288.1	1230	241	124	112	17	18	2	11	144	5	255	18	2	22	13	.629	2	0-0	0	3.50

Tony Eusebio

Bats: Right **Throws:** Right **Pos:** C-43; PH-17   **Ht:** 6'2" **Wt:** 210 **Born:** 4/27/67 **Age:** 31

		BATTING																	BASERUNNING				PERCENTAGES		
Year Team	Lg	G	AB	H	2B	3B	HR	(Hm	Rd)	TB	R	RBI	TBB	IBB	SO	HBP	SH	SF	SB	CS	SB%	GDP	Avg	OBP	SLG
1991 Houston	NL	10	19	2	1	0	0	(0	0)	3	4	0	6	0	8	0	0	0	0	0	.00	1	.105	.320	.158
1994 Houston	NL	55	159	47	9	1	5	(1	4)	73	18	30	8	0	33	0	2	5	0	1	.00	4	.296	.320	.459
1995 Houston	NL	113	368	110	21	1	6	(5	1)	151	46	58	31	1	59	3	1	5	0	2	.00	12	.299	.354	.410
1996 Houston	NL	58	152	41	7	2	1	(1	0)	55	15	19	18	2	20	0	0	2	0	1	.00	5	.270	.343	.362
1997 Houston	NL	60	164	45	2	0	1	(0	1)	50	12	18	19	1	27	4	0	0	0	1	.00	4	.274	.364	.305
5 ML YEARS		296	862	245	40	4	13	(7	6)	332	95	125	82	4	147	7	3	12	0	5	.00	26	.284	.347	.385

Tom Evans

Bats: Right **Throws:** Right **Pos:** 3B-12   **Ht:** 6'1" **Wt:** 195 **Born:** 7/9/74 **Age:** 23

								BATTING											BASERUNNING				PERCENTAGES		
Year Team	Lg	G	AB	H	2B	3B	HR	(Hm	Rd)	TB	R	RBI	TBB	IBB	SO	HBP	SH	SF	SB	CS	SB%	GDP	Avg	OBP	SLG
1992 Medicne Hat	R+	52	166	36	3	0	1	—	—	42	17	21	33	0	29	1	1	1	4	3	.57	4	.217	.348	.253
1993 Hagerstown	A	119	389	100	25	1	7	—	—	148	47	54	53	2	61	3	0	4	9	2	.82	7	.257	.347	.380
1994 Hagerstown	A	95	322	88	16	2	13	—	—	147	52	48	51	1	80	1	1	1	2	1	.67	3	.273	.373	.457
1995 Dunedin	A+	130	444	124	29	3	9	—	—	186	63	66	51	0	80	8	3	7	7	2	.78	10	.279	.359	.419
1996 Knoxville	AA	120	394	111	27	1	17	—	—	191	87	65	115	0	113	9	0	2	4	0	1.00	7	.282	.452	.485
1997 Dunedin	A+	15	42	11	2	0	2	—	—	19	8	4	11	0	10	4	0	1	0	0	.00	0	.262	.448	.452
Syracuse	AAA	107	376	99	17	1	15	—	—	163	60	65	53	1	104	9	1	3	1	2	.33	4	.263	.365	.434
1997 Toronto	AL	12	38	11	2	0	1	(1	0)	16	7	2	2	0	10	1	0	0	0	1	.00	0	.289	.341	.421

Carl Everett

Bats: B **Throws:** R **Pos:** CF-71; RF-65; PH-29; LF-9   **Ht:** 6'0" **Wt:** 190 **Born:** 6/3/71 **Age:** 27

								BATTING											BASERUNNING				PERCENTAGES		
Year Team	Lg	G	AB	H	2B	3B	HR	(Hm	Rd)	TB	R	RBI	TBB	IBB	SO	HBP	SH	SF	SB	CS	SB%	GDP	Avg	OBP	SLG
1993 Florida	NL	11	19	2	0	0	0	(0	0)	2	0	0	1	0	9	0	0	0	1	0	1.00	0	.105	.150	.105
1994 Florida	NL	16	51	11	1	0	2	(2	0)	18	7	6	3	0	15	0	0	0	4	0	1.00	0	.216	.259	.353
1995 New York	NL	79	289	75	13	1	12	(9	3)	126	48	54	39	2	67	2	1	0	2	5	.29	11	.260	.352	.436
1996 New York	NL	101	192	46	8	1	1	(1	0)	59	29	16	21	2	53	4	1	1	6	0	1.00	4	.240	.326	.307
1997 New York	NL	142	443	110	28	3	14	(11	3)	186	58	57	32	3	102	7	3	2	17	9	.65	3	.248	.308	.420
5 ML YEARS		349	994	244	50	5	29	(23	6)	391	142	133	96	7	246	13	5	3	30	14	.68	18	.245	.319	.393

Bryan Eversgerd

Pitches: Left **Bats:** Right **Pos:** RP-3   **Ht:** 6'1" **Wt:** 190 **Born:** 2/11/69 **Age:** 29

		HOW MUCH HE PITCHED						WHAT HE GAVE UP											THE RESULTS					
Year Team	Lg	G	GS	CG	GF	IP	BFP	H	R	ER	HR	SH	SF	HB	TBB	IBB	SO	WP	Bk	W	L	Pct.	ShO	Sv-Op	Hld	ERA
1997 Okla City *	AAA	26	7	0	5	76.1	339	91	48	36	12	4	2	2	24	2	43	5	1	1	3	.250	0	0-1	0	4.24
1994 St. Louis	NL	40	1	0	8	67.2	283	75	36	34	8	5	2	2	20	1	47	3	1	2	3	.400	0	0-0	1	4.52
1995 Montreal	NL	25	0	0	5	21	95	22	13	12	2	1	2	1	9	2	8	1	0	0	0	.000	0	0-0	3	5.14
1997 Texas	AL	3	0	0	1	1.1	12	5	3	3	0	0	0	0	3	0	2	0	0	0	2	.000	0	0-0	0	20.25
3 ML YEARS		68	1	0	14	90	390	102	52	49	10	6	4	3	32	3	57	4	1	2	5	.286	0	0-1	3	4.90

Scott Eyre

Pitches: Left **Bats:** Left **Pos:** SP-11   **Ht:** 6'1" **Wt:** 190 **Born:** 5/30/72 **Age:** 26

		HOW MUCH HE PITCHED						WHAT HE GAVE UP											THE RESULTS					
Year Team	Lg	G	GS	CG	GF	IP	BFP	H	R	ER	HR	SH	SF	HB	TBB	IBB	SO	WP	Bk	W	L	Pct.	ShO	Sv-Op	Hld	ERA
1992 Butte	R+	15	14	2	0	80.2	339	71	30	26	6	1	0	4	39	0	94	6	1	7	3	.700	1	0-—	—	2.90
1993 Chston-SC	A	26	26	0	0	143.2	597	115	74	55	6	3	6	6	59	1	154	2	1	11	7	.611	0	0-—	—	3.45
1994 South Bend	A	19	18	2	1	111.2	481	108	56	43	7	2	4	3	37	0	111	8	3	8	4	.667	0	0-—	—	3.47
1995 White Sox	R	9	9	0	0	27.1	106	16	7	7	0	0	1	1	12	0	40	2	0	2	0	.000	0	0-—	—	2.30
1996 Birmingham	AA	27	27	0	0	158.1	709	170	90	77	12	3	6	8	79	3	137	12	0	12	7	.632	0	0-—	—	4.38
1997 Birmingham	AA	22	22	0	0	126.2	538	110	61	54	14	1	1	5	55	2	127	9	1	13	5	.722	0	0-—	—	3.84
1997 Chicago	AL	11	11	0	0	60.2	267	62	36	34	11	1	2	1	31	1	36	2	0	4	4	.500	0	0-0	0	5.04

Jorge Fabregas

Bats: Left **Throws:** Right **Pos:** C-113; PH-12; 1B-1   **Ht:** 6'3" **Wt:** 214 **Born:** 3/13/70 **Age:** 28

								BATTING											BASERUNNING				PERCENTAGES		
Year Team	Lg	G	AB	H	2B	3B	HR	(Hm	Rd)	TB	R	RBI	TBB	IBB	SO	HBP	SH	SF	SB	CS	SB%	GDP	Avg	OBP	SLG
1994 California	AL	43	127	36	3	0	0	(0	0)	39	12	16	7	1	18	0	1	0	2	1	.67	5	.283	.321	.307
1995 California	AL	73	227	56	10	0	1	(1	0)	69	24	22	17	0	28	0	3	1	0	2	.00	9	.247	.298	.304
1996 California	AL	90	254	73	6	0	2	(1	1)	85	18	26	17	3	27	0	3	5	0	1	.00	7	.287	.326	.335
1997 Ana-ChA	AL	121	360	93	11	1	7	(1	6)	127	33	51	14	0	46	1	6	4	1	1	.50	16	.258	.285	.353
1997 Anaheim	AL	21	38	3	1	0	0	(0	0)	4	2	3	3	0	3	0	2	0	0	0	.00	2	.079	.146	.105
Chicago	AL	100	322	90	10	1	7	(1	6)	123	31	48	11	0	43	1	4	4	1	1	.50	14	.280	.302	.382
4 ML YEARS		327	968	258	30	1	10	(3	7)	320	87	115	55	4	119	1	13	10	3	5	.38	37	.267	.304	.331

Steve Falteisek

Pitches: Right **Bats:** Right **Pos:** RP-5   **Ht:** 6'2" **Wt:** 200 **Born:** 1/28/72 **Age:** 26

		HOW MUCH HE PITCHED						WHAT HE GAVE UP											THE RESULTS					
Year Team	Lg	G	GS	CG	GF	IP	BFP	H	R	ER	HR	SH	SF	HB	TBB	IBB	SO	WP	Bk	W	L	Pct.	ShO	Sv-Op	Hld	ERA
1992 Jamestown	A-	15	15	2	0	96	407	84	47	38	3	4	1	5	31	2	82	9	10	4	3	.273	0	0-—	—	3.56
1993 Burlington	A	14	14	0	0	76.1	345	86	59	50	4	4	1	2	35	0	63	4	1	3	5	.375	0	0-—	—	5.90
1994 Wst Plm Bch	A+	27	24	1	0	159.2	658	144	72	45	3	0	6	3	49	0	91	11	4	9	4	.692	0	0-—	—	2.54
1995 Harrisburg	AA	25	25	5	0	168	707	152	74	55	3	7	5	11	64	4	112	6	1	9	6	.600	0	0-—	—	2.95
Ottawa	AAA	3	3	1	0	23	86	17	4	3	0	0	0	1	5	0	18	0	1	2	0	1.000	1	0-—	—	1.17
1996 Ottawa	AAA	12	12	0	0	58	272	75	45	41	10	1	0	5	25	0	26	3	0	2	5	.286	0	0-—	—	6.36
Harrisburg	AA	17	17	1	0	115.2	492	111	60	49	9	7	0	5	48	1	62	5	3	6	5	.545	0	0-—	—	3.81
1997 Ottawa	AAA	22	22	1	0	125	555	135	67	55	10	7	7	5	54	1	56	12	1	6	9	.400	0	0-—	—	3.96
1997 Montreal	NL	5	0	0	2	8	34	8	4	3	0	2	2	1	3	0	2	0	0	0	0	.000	0	0-0	0	3.38

Sal Fasano

Bats: Right **Throws:** Right **Pos:** C-12; PH-2; DH-1   **Ht:** 6'2" **Wt:** 220 **Born:** 8/10/71 **Age:** 26

Year Team	Lg	G	AB	H	2B	3B	HR	(Hm	Rd)	TB	R	RBI	TBB	IBB	SO	HBP	SH	SF	SB	CS	SB%	GDP	Avg	OBP	SLG
1993 Eugene	A-	49	176	47	11	1	10	—	—	90	25	36	19	2	49	6	0	2	4	3	.57	1	.267	.355	.511
1994 Rockford	A	97	345	97	16	1	25	—	—	190	61	81	33	4	66	16	0	5	8	3	.73	10	.281	.366	.551
Wilmington	A+	23	90	29	7	0	7	—	—	57	15	32	13	0	24	0	0	0	0	0	.00	3	.322	.408	.633
1995 Wilmington	A+	23	88	20	2	1	2	—	—	30	12	7	5	0	16	1	0	0	0	0	.00	4	.227	.277	.341
Wichita	AA	87	317	92	19	2	20	—	—	175	60	66	27	1	61	16	0	2	3	6	.33	8	.290	.373	.552
1996 Omaha	AAA	29	104	24	4	0	4	—	—	40	12	15	6	0	21	1	0	1	0	1	.00	3	.231	.277	.385
1997 Wichita	AA	40	131	31	5	0	13	—	—	75	27	27	20	0	35	7	0	3	0	2	.00	2	.237	.360	.573
Omaha	AAA	49	152	25	7	0	4	—	—	44	17	14	12	1	53	5	0	1	0	0	.00	1	.164	.247	.289
1996 Kansas City	AL	51	143	29	2	0	6	(1	5)	49	20	19	14	0	25	2	1	0	1	1	.50	3	.203	.283	.343
1997 Kansas City	AL	13	38	8	2	0	1	(0	1)	13	4	1	1	0	12	0	0	0	0	0	.00	1	.211	.231	.342
2 ML YEARS		64	181	37	4	0	7	(1	6)	62	24	20	15	0	37	2	1	0	1	1	.50	4	.204	.273	.343

Jeff Fassero

Pitches: Left **Bats:** Left **Pos:** SP-35   **Ht:** 6'1" **Wt:** 195 **Born:** 1/5/63 **Age:** 35

		HOW MUCH HE PITCHED						WHAT HE GAVE UP										THE RESULTS						
Year Team	Lg	G	GS	CG	GF	IP	BFP	H	R	ER	HR	SH	SF	HB	TBB	IBB	SO	WP	Bk	W	L	Pct.	ShO	Sv-Op	Hld	ERA
1991 Montreal	NL	51	0	0	30	55.1	223	39	17	15	1	6	0	1	17	1	42	4	0	2	5	.286	0	8-11	7	2.44
1992 Montreal	NL	70	0	0	22	85.2	368	81	35	27	1	5	2	2	34	6	63	7	1	8	7	.533	0	1-7	12	2.84
1993 Montreal	NL	56	15	1	10	149.2	616	119	50	38	7	7	4	0	54	0	140	5	0	12	5	.706	0	1-3	6	2.29
1994 Montreal	NL	21	21	1	0	138.2	569	119	54	46	13	7	2	1	40	4	119	6	0	8	6	.571	0	0-0	0	2.99
1995 Montreal	NL	30	30	1	0	189	833	207	102	91	15	19	7	3	74	3	164	7	1	13	14	.481	0	0-0	0	4.33
1996 Montreal	NL	34	34	5	0	231.2	967	217	95	85	20	16	5	3	55	3	222	5	2	15	11	.577	1	0-0	0	3.30
1997 Seattle	AL	35	35	2	0	234.1	1010	226	108	94	21	7	10	3	84	6	189	13	2	16	9	.640	1	0-0	0	3.61
7 ML YEARS		297	135	10	62	1084.1	4586	1008	461	396	78	67	30	12	358	23	939	47	6	74	57	.565	2	10-21	25	3.29

Alex Fernandez

Pitches: Right **Bats:** Right **Pos:** SP-32   **Ht:** 6'1" **Wt:** 215 **Born:** 8/13/69 **Age:** 28

		HOW MUCH HE PITCHED						WHAT HE GAVE UP										THE RESULTS						
Year Team	Lg	G	GS	CG	GF	IP	BFP	H	R	ER	HR	SH	SF	HB	TBB	IBB	SO	WP	Bk	W	L	Pct.	ShO	Sv-Op	Hld	ERA
1990 Chicago	AL	13	13	3	0	87.2	378	89	40	37	6	5	0	3	34	0	61	1	0	5	5	.500	0	0-0	0	3.80
1991 Chicago	AL	34	32	2	1	191.2	827	186	100	96	16	7	11	2	88	2	145	4	1	9	13	.409	0	0-0	1	4.51
1992 Chicago	AL	29	29	4	0	187.2	804	199	100	89	21	6	4	8	50	3	95	3	0	8	11	.421	2	0-0	0	4.27
1993 Chicago	AL	34	34	3	0	247.1	1004	221	95	86	27	9	3	6	67	5	169	8	0	18	9	.667	1	0-0	0	3.13
1994 Chicago	AL	24	24	4	0	170.1	712	163	83	73	25	4	6	1	50	4	122	3	1	11	7	.611	3	0-0	0	3.86
1995 Chicago	AL	30	30	5	0	203.2	858	200	98	86	19	4	6	0	65	7	159	3	0	12	8	.600	2	0-0	0	3.80
1996 Chicago	AL	35	35	6	0	258	1071	248	100	99	34	5	7	7	72	4	200	5	0	16	10	.615	1	0-0	0	3.45
1997 Florida	NL	32	32	5	0	220.2	904	193	93	88	25	14	5	4	69	2	183	9	0	17	12	.586	1	0-0	0	3.59
8 ML YEARS		231	229	32	1	1567	6558	1499	719	654	173	54	42	31	495	27	1134	36	2	96	75	.561	10	0-0	1	3.76

Osvaldo Fernandez

Pitches: Right **Bats:** Right **Pos:** SP-11   **Ht:** 6'2" **Wt:** 190 **Born:** 11/4/68 **Age:** 29

		HOW MUCH HE PITCHED						WHAT HE GAVE UP										THE RESULTS						
Year Team	Lg	G	GS	CG	GF	IP	BFP	H	R	ER	HR	SH	SF	HB	TBB	IBB	SO	WP	Bk	W	L	Pct.	ShO	Sv-Op	Hld	ERA
1997 Phoenix	AAA	2	2	0	0	12	47	10	5	4	1	1	2	0	3	1	4	1	0	0	0	.000	0	0- -	—	3.00
1996 San Francisco	NL	30	28	2	1	171.2	760	193	95	88	20	12	5	10	57	4	106	6	2	7	13	.350	0	0-0	0	4.61
1997 San Francisco	NL	11	11	0	0	56.1	256	74	39	31	9	4	1	0	15	2	31	2	1	3	4	.429	0	0-0	0	4.95
2 ML YEARS		41	39	2	1	228	1016	267	134	119	29	16	6	10	72	6	137	8	3	10	17	.370	0	0-0	0	4.70

Sid Fernandez

Pitches: Left **Bats:** Left **Pos:** SP-1   **Ht:** 6'1" **Wt:** 230 **Born:** 10/12/62 **Age:** 35

		HOW MUCH HE PITCHED						WHAT HE GAVE UP										THE RESULTS						
Year Team	Lg	G	GS	CG	GF	IP	BFP	H	R	ER	HR	SH	SF	HB	TBB	IBB	SO	WP	Bk	W	L	Pct.	ShO	Sv-Op	Hld	ERA
1997 New Orleans *	AAA	2	2	0	0	8.1	34	7	4	4	0	0	0	0	3	0	7	2	0	0	1	.000	0	0- -	—	4.32
1983 Los Angeles	NL	2	1	0	0	6	33	7	4	4	0	0	0	1	7	0	9	0	0	0	1	.000	0	0- -	—	6.00
1984 New York	NL	15	15	0	0	90	371	74	40	35	8	5	5	0	34	3	62	1	4	6	6	.500	0	0-0	0	3.50
1985 New York	NL	26	26	3	0	170.1	685	108	56	53	14	4	3	2	80	3	180	3	2	9	9	.500	0	0-0	0	2.80
1986 New York	NL	32	31	2	1	204.1	855	161	82	80	13	9	7	2	91	1	200	6	0	16	6	.727	1	1-1	0	3.52
1987 New York	NL	28	27	3	0	156	665	130	75	66	16	3	6	8	67	8	134	2	0	12	8	.600	1	0-0	0	3.81
1988 New York	NL	31	31	1	0	187	751	127	69	63	15	2	7	6	70	1	189	4	9	12	10	.545	1	0-0	0	3.03
1989 New York	NL	35	32	6	0	219.1	883	157	73	69	21	4	4	6	75	3	198	1	3	14	5	.737	1	0-0	1	2.83
1990 New York	NL	30	30	2	0	179.1	735	130	79	69	18	7	6	5	67	4	181	1	0	9	14	.391	1	0-0	0	3.46
1991 New York	NL	8	8	0	0	44	177	36	18	14	4	5	1	0	9	0	31	0	0	1	3	.250	0	0-0	0	2.86
1992 New York	NL	32	32	5	0	214.2	865	162	67	65	12	12	11	4	67	4	193	4	0	14	11	.560	2	0-0	0	2.73
1993 New York	NL	18	18	1	0	119.2	469	82	42	39	17	3	1	3	36	0	81	2	0	5	6	.455	1	0-0	0	2.93
1994 Baltimore	AL	19	19	2	0	115.1	494	109	66	66	27	4	3	2	46	2	95	1	0	6	6	.500	0	0-0	0	5.15
1995 Bal-Phi	AL	19	18	0	1	92.2	400	84	51	47	20	2	1	1	38	2	110	0	1	6	5	.545	0	0-0	0	4.56
1996 Philadelphia	NL	11	11	0	0	63	264	50	25	24	5	2	2	1	26	2	77	1	0	3	6	.333	0	0-0	0	3.43
1997 Houston	NL	1	1	0	0	5	21	4	2	2	1	0	0	0	2	0	3	0	0	1	0	1.000	0	0-0	—	3.60
1995 Baltimore	AL	8	7	0	1	28	137	36	26	23	9	1	0	1	17	2	31	0	0	0	4	.000	0	0-0	0	7.39
Philadelphia	NL	11	11	0	0	64.2	263	48	25	24	11	1	0	1	21	0	79	0	1	6	1	.857	0	0-0	0	3.34
15 ML YEARS		307	300	25	2	1866.2	7668	1421	749	696	191	62	57	41	715	33	1743	22	19	114	96	.543	9	1- -	—	3.36

Tony Fernandez

Bats: B **Throws:** R **Pos:** 2B-109; SS-10; PH-6; DH-1   **Ht:** 6'2" **Wt:** 175 **Born:** 6/30/62 **Age:** 36

Year Team	Lg	G	AB	H	2B	3B	HR	(Hm	Rd)	TB	R	RBI	TBB	IBB	SO	HBP	SH	SF	SB	CS	SB%	GDP	Avg	OBP	SLG
1983 Toronto	AL	15	34	9	1	1	0	(0	0)	12	5	2	2	0	2	1	1	0	0	1	.00	1	.265	.324	.353
1984 Toronto	AL	88	233	63	5	3	3	(1	2)	83	29	19	17	0	15	0	2	2	5	7	.42	3	.270	.317	.356
1985 Toronto	AL	161	564	163	31	10	2	(1	1)	220	71	51	43	2	41	2	7	2	13	6	.68	12	.289	.340	.390
1986 Toronto	AL	**163**	**687**	213	33	9	10	(4	6)	294	91	65	27	0	52	4	5	4	25	12	.68	8	.310	.338	.428
1987 Toronto	AL	146	578	186	29	8	5	(1	4)	246	90	67	51	3	48	5	4	4	32	12	.73	14	.322	.379	.426
1988 Toronto	AL	154	648	186	41	4	5	(3	2)	250	76	70	45	3	65	4	3	4	15	5	.75	9	.287	.335	.386
1989 Toronto	AL	140	573	147	25	9	11	(2	9)	223	64	64	29	1	51	3	2	10	22	6	.79	9	.257	.291	.389
1990 Toronto	AL	161	635	175	27	17	4	(2	2)	248	84	66	71	4	70	7	2	6	26	13	.67	17	.276	.352	.391
1991 San Diego	NL	145	558	152	27	5	4	(1	3)	201	81	38	55	0	74	0	7	1	23	9	.72	12	.272	.337	.360
1992 San Diego	NL	155	622	171	32	4	4	(3	1)	223	84	37	56	4	62	4	9	3	20	20	.50	6	.275	.337	.359
1993 NYN-Tor	AL	142	526	147	23	11	5	(1	4)	207	65	64	56	3	45	1	8	3	21	10	.68	16	.279	.348	.394
1994 Cincinnati	NL	104	366	102	18	6	8	(3	5)	156	50	50	44	8	40	5	4	3	12	7	.63	5	.279	.361	.426
1995 New York	AL	108	384	94	20	2	5	(3	2)	133	57	45	42	4	40	4	3	5	6	6	.50	14	.245	.322	.346
1997 Cleveland	AL	120	409	117	21	1	11	(7	4)	173	55	44	22	0	47	2	6	3	6	6	.50	11	.286	.323	.423
1993 New York	NL	48	173	39	5	2	1	(0	1)	51	20	14	25	0	19	1	3	2	6	2	.75	3	.225	.323	.295
Toronto	AL	94	353	108	18	9	4	(1	3)	156	45	50	31	3	26	0	5	1	15	8	.65	13	.306	.361	.442
14 ML YEARS		1802	6817	1925	333	90	77	(32	45)	2669	902	682	560	32	652	42	63	50	226	120	.65	137	.282	.338	.392

Mike Fetters

Pitches: Right **Bats:** Right **Pos:** RP-51   **Ht:** 6'4" **Wt:** 224 **Born:** 12/19/64 **Age:** 33

		HOW MUCH HE PITCHED						WHAT HE GAVE UP											THE RESULTS						
Year Team	Lg	G	GS	CG	GF	IP	BFP	H	R	ER	HR	SH	SF	HB	TBB	IBB	SO	WP	Bk	W	L	Pct.	ShO	Sv-Op	Hld	ERA
1997 Tucson *	AAA	2	0	0	0	1.2	8	1	2	2	0	0	1	0	1	0	0	2	0	0	0	.000	0	0- -	-	10.80
1989 California	AL	1	0	0	0	3.1	16	5	4	3	1	0	0	0	1	0	4	2	0	0	0	.000	0	0-0	0	8.10
1990 California	AL	26	2	0	10	67.2	291	77	33	31	9	1	0	2	20	0	35	3	0	1	1	.500	0	1-1	1	4.12
1991 California	AL	19	4	0	8	44.2	206	53	29	24	4	1	0	3	28	2	24	4	0	2	5	.286	0	0-1	0	4.84
1992 Milwaukee	AL	50	0	0	11	62.2	243	38	15	13	3	5	2	7	24	2	43	4	1	5	1	.833	0	2-5	8	1.87
1993 Milwaukee	AL	45	0	0	14	59.1	246	59	29	22	4	5	5	2	22	4	23	0	0	3	3	.500	0	0-0	0	3.34
1994 Milwaukee	AL	42	0	0	31	46	202	41	16	13	0	2	3	1	27	5	31	3	1	1	4	.200	0	17-20	3	2.54
1995 Milwaukee	AL	40	0	0	34	34.2	163	40	16	13	3	2	1	0	20	4	33	5	0	0	3	.000	0	22-27	1	3.38
1996 Milwaukee	AL	61	0	0	55	61.1	268	65	28	23	4	0	4	1	26	4	53	5	0	3	3	.500	0	32-38	1	3.38
1997 Milwaukee	AL	51	0	0	20	70.1	298	62	30	27	4	6	4	1	33	3	62	2	1	1	5	.167	0	6-11	11	3.45
9 ML YEARS		335	6	0	183	450	1933	440	200	169	32	22	19	17	201	24	308	28	3	16	25	.390	0	80-103	34	3.38

Cecil Fielder

Bats: Right **Throws:** Right **Pos:** DH-89; 1B-8; PH-2   **Ht:** 6'3" **Wt:** 250 **Born:** 9/21/63 **Age:** 34

Year Team	Lg	G	AB	H	2B	3B	HR	(Hm	Rd)	TB	R	RBI	TBB	IBB	SO	HBP	SH	SF	SB	CS	SB%	GDP	Avg	OBP	SLG
1985 Toronto	AL	30	74	23	4	0	4	(2	2)	39	6	16	6	0	16	0	0	1	0	0	.00	2	.311	.358	.527
1986 Toronto	AL	34	83	13	2	0	4	(0	4)	27	7	13	6	0	27	1	0	0	0	0	.00	3	.157	.222	.325
1987 Toronto	AL	82	175	47	7	1	14	(10	4)	98	30	32	20	2	48	1	0	1	0	1	.00	6	.269	.345	.560
1988 Toronto	AL	74	174	40	6	1	9	(6	3)	75	24	23	14	0	53	1	0	1	0	1	.00	6	.230	.289	.431
1990 Detroit	AL	159	573	159	25	1	**51**	(25	26)	339	104	**132**	90	11	**182**	5	0	5	0	1	.00	15	.277	.377	**.592**
1991 Detroit	AL	**162**	624	163	25	0	44	(27	17)	320	102	**133**	78	12	151	6	0	4	0	0	.00	17	.261	.347	.513
1992 Detroit	AL	155	594	145	22	0	35	(18	17)	272	80	**124**	73	8	151	2	0	7	0	0	.00	14	.244	.325	.458
1993 Detroit	AL	154	573	153	23	0	30	(20	10)	266	80	117	90	15	125	4	0	5	0	1	.00	22	.267	.368	.464
1994 Detroit	AL	109	425	110	16	2	28	(12	16)	214	67	90	50	4	110	2	0	4	0	0	.00	17	.259	.337	.504
1995 Detroit	AL	136	494	120	18	1	31	(16	15)	233	70	82	75	8	116	5	0	4	0	1	.00	17	.243	.346	.472
1996 Det-NYA	AL	160	591	149	20	0	39	(18	21)	286	85	117	87	12	139	5	0	5	2	0	1.00	18	.252	.350	.484
1997 New York	AL	98	361	94	15	0	13	(6	7)	148	40	61	51	3	87	7	0	6	0	0	.00	14	.260	.358	.410
1996 Detroit	AL	107	391	97	12	0	26	(9	17)	187	55	80	63	8	91	3	0	3	2	0	1.00	11	.248	.354	.478
New York		53	200	52	8	0	13	(9	4)	99	30	37	24	4	48	2	0	2	0	0	.00	7	.260	.342	.495
12 ML YEARS		1353	4741	1216	183	6	302	(160	142)	2317	695	940	640	75	1205	39	0	43	2	5	.29	151	.256	.347	.489

Mike Figga

Bats: Right **Throws:** Right **Pos:** DH-1; C-1; PH-1   **Ht:** 6'0" **Wt:** 200 **Born:** 7/31/70 **Age:** 27

Year Team	Lg	G	AB	H	2B	3B	HR	(Hm	Rd)	TB	R	RBI	TBB	IBB	SO	HBP	SH	SF	SB	CS	SB%	GDP	Avg	OBP	SLG
1990 Yankees	R	40	123	35	1	1	2	—	—	44	19	18	17	2	33	1	0	1	4	2	.67	2	.285	.373	.358
1991 Pr William	A+	55	174	34	6	0	3	—	—	49	15	17	19	0	51	0	2	1	2	1	.67	9	.195	.273	.282
1992 Pr William	A+	3	10	2	1	0	0	—	—	3	0	0	2	0	3	0	0	0	1	0	1.00	0	.200	.333	.300
Ft. Laud	A+	80	249	44	13	0	1	—	—	60	12	15	13	1	78	2	3	0	3	1	.75	7	.177	.223	.241
1993 San Berndno	A+	83	308	82	17	1	25	—	—	176	48	71	17	0	84	2	2	3	2	3	.40	7	.266	.306	.571
Albany-Colo	AA	6	22	5	0	0	0	—	—	5	3	2	2	0	9	0	0	0	1	0	1.00	1	.227	.292	.227
1994 Albany-Colo	AA	1	2	1	1	0	0	—	—	2	1	0	0	0	1	0	0	0	0	0	.00	0	.500	.500	1.000
Tampa	A+	111	420	116	17	5	15	—	—	188	48	75	22	1	94	2	1	5	3	0	1.00	12	.276	.312	.448
1995 Norwich	AA	109	399	108	22	4	13	—	—	177	59	61	43	3	90	1	2	6	1	0	1.00	10	.271	.339	.444
Columbus	AAA	8	25	7	1	0	1	—	—	11	2	3	0	0	5	0	1	0	0	0	.00	2	.280	.357	.440
1996 Columbus	AAA	4	11	3	1	0	0	—	—	4	3	0	1	0	3	0	0	0	0	0	.00	0	.273	.333	.364
1997 Columbus	AAA	110	390	95	14	4	12	—	—	153	48	54	18	0	104	2	1	3	3	3	.50	9	.244	.278	.392
1997 New York	AL	2	4	0	0	0	0	(0	0)	0	0	0	0	0	0	0	0	0	0	0	.00	0	.000	.000	.000

Chuck Finley

Pitches: Left **Bats:** Left **Pos:** SP-25 **Ht:** 6'6" **Wt:** 214 **Born:** 11/26/62 **Age:** 35

		HOW MUCH HE PITCHED					WHAT HE GAVE UP											THE RESULTS						
Year Team	Lg	G	GS	CG	GF	IP	BFP	H	R	ER	HR	SH	SF	HB	TBB	IBB	SO	WP	Bk	W	L	Pct.	ShO	Sv-Op	Hld	ERA
1997 Lk Elsinore *	A+	2	2	0	0	9	36	5	3	2	0	0	0	0	4	0	12	0	0	0	0	.000	0	0- --	--	2.00
1986 California	AL	25	0	0	7	46.1	198	40	17	17	2	4	0	1	23	1	37	2	0	3	1	.750	0	0- --	0	3.30
1987 California	AL	35	3	0	17	90.2	405	102	54	47	7	2	2	3	43	3	63	4	3	2	7	.222	0	0-2	0	4.67
1988 California	AL	31	31	2	0	194.1	831	191	95	90	15	7	10	6	82	7	111	5	8	9	15	.375	0	0-0	0	4.17
1989 California	AL	29	29	9	0	199.2	827	171	64	57	13	7	3	2	82	0	156	4	2	16	9	.640	1	0-0	0	2.57
1990 California	AL	32	32	7	0	236	962	210	77	63	17	12	3	2	81	3	177	9	0	18	9	.667	2	0-0	0	2.40
1991 California	AL	34	34	4	0	227.1	955	205	102	96	23	4	3	8	101	1	171	6	3	18	9	.667	2	0-0	0	3.80
1992 California	AL	31	31	4	0	204.1	885	212	99	90	24	10	10	3	98	2	124	6	0	7	12	.368	1	0-0	0	3.96
1993 California	AL	35	35	13	0	251.1	1065	243	108	88	22	11	7	6	82	1	187	8	1	16	14	.533	2	0-0	0	3.15
1994 California	AL	25	25	7	0	183.1	774	178	95	88	21	9	6	3	71	0	148	10	0	10	10	.500	2	0-0	0	4.32
1995 California	AL	32	32	2	0	203	880	192	106	95	20	4	5	7	93	1	195	13	1	15	12	.556	1	0-0	0	4.21
1996 California	AL	35	35	4	0	238	1037	241	124	110	27	7	9	11	94	5	215	17	2	15	16	.484	1	0-0	0	4.16
1997 Anaheim	AL	25	25	3	0	164	690	152	79	77	20	3	4	5	65	0	155	10	2	13	6	.684	1	0-0	0	4.23
12 ML YEARS		369	312	55	24	2238.1	9509	2137	1020	918	211	80	62	57	915	24	1739	94	22	142	120	.542	13	0- --	--	3.69

Steve Finley

Bats: Left **Throws:** Left **Pos:** CF-140; PH-10 **Ht:** 6'2" **Wt:** 180 **Born:** 3/12/65 **Age:** 33

		BATTING																BASERUNNING				PERCENTAGES		
Year Team	Lg	G	AB	H	2B	3B	HR	(Hm	Rd)	TB	R	RBI	TBB	IBB	SO	HBP	SH	SF	SB	CS	SB%	GDP	Avg	OBP	SLG
1997 Mobile *	AA	1	4	2	0	0	1	—	—	5	1	2	1	0	2	0	0	0	0	0	.00	0	.500	.600	1.250
Rncho Cuca *	A+	4	14	4	0	0	2	—	—	10	3	3	3	0	2	1	0	0	1	0	1.00	0	.286	.444	.714
1989 Baltimore	AL	81	217	54	5	2	2	(0	2)	69	35	25	15	1	30	1	6	2	17	3	.85	3	.249	.298	.318
1990 Baltimore	AL	142	464	119	16	4	3	(1	2)	152	46	37	32	3	53	2	10	5	22	9	.71	8	.256	.304	.328
1991 Houston	NL	159	596	170	28	10	8	(0	8)	242	84	54	42	5	65	2	10	6	34	18	.65	8	.285	.331	.406
1992 Houston	NL	162	607	177	29	13	5	(5	0)	247	84	55	58	6	63	3	16	2	44	9	.83	10	.292	.355	.407
1993 Houston	NL	142	545	145	15	13	8	(1	7)	210	69	44	28	1	65	3	6	3	19	6	.76	8	.266	.304	.385
1994 Houston	NL	94	373	103	16	5	11	(4	7)	162	64	33	28	0	52	2	13	1	13	7	.65	3	.276	.329	.434
1995 San Diego	NL	139	562	167	23	8	10	(4	6)	236	104	44	59	5	62	3	4	2	36	12	.75	8	.297	.366	.420
1996 San Diego	NL	161	655	195	45	9	30	(15	15)	348	126	95	56	5	87	4	1	5	22	8	.73	20	.298	.354	.531
1997 San Diego	NL	143	560	146	26	5	28	(5	23)	266	101	92	43	2	92	3	2	7	15	3	.83	10	.261	.313	.475
9 ML YEARS		1223	4579	1276	203	69	105	(35	70)	1932	713	479	361	28	569	23	68	33	222	75	.75	78	.279	.332	.422

John Flaherty

Bats: Right **Throws:** Right **Pos:** C-124; PH-6 **Ht:** 6'1" **Wt:** 200 **Born:** 10/21/67 **Age:** 30

		BATTING																BASERUNNING				PERCENTAGES		
Year Team	Lg	G	AB	H	2B	3B	HR	(Hm	Rd)	TB	R	RBI	TBB	IBB	SO	HBP	SH	SF	SB	CS	SB%	GDP	Avg	OBP	SLG
1992 Boston	AL	35	66	13	2	0	0	(0	0)	15	3	2	3	0	7	0	1	1	0	0	.00	0	.197	.229	.227
1993 Boston	AL	13	25	3	2	0	0	(0	0)	5	3	2	2	0	6	1	1	0	0	0	.00	0	.120	.214	.200
1994 Detroit	AL	34	40	6	1	0	0	(0	0)	7	2	4	1	0	11	0	2	1	0	1	.00	1	.150	.167	.175
1995 Detroit	AL	112	354	86	22	1	11	(6	5)	143	39	40	18	0	47	3	8	2	0	0	.00	8	.243	.284	.404
1996 Det-SD	AL	119	416	118	24	0	13	(8	5)	181	40	64	17	2	61	3	4	4	3	3	.50	13	.284	.314	.435
1997 San Diego	NL	129	439	120	21	1	9	(4	5)	170	38	46	33	7	62	0	2	5	4	4	.50	11	.273	.323	.387
1996 Detroit	AL	47	152	38	12	0	4	(2	2)	62	18	23	8	1	25	1	3	1	1	0	1.00	5	.250	.290	.408
San Diego	NL	72	264	80	12	0	9	(6	3)	119	22	41	9	1	36	2	1	3	2	3	.40	8	.303	.327	.451
6 ML YEARS		442	1340	346	72	2	33	(18	15)	521	125	158	74	9	194	7	18	10	7	8	.47	33	.258	.298	.389

Huck Flener

Pitches: Left **Bats:** Both **Pos:** RP-7; SP-1 **Ht:** 5'11" **Wt:** 175 **Born:** 2/25/69 **Age:** 29

		HOW MUCH HE PITCHED					WHAT HE GAVE UP											THE RESULTS						
Year Team	Lg	G	GS	CG	GF	IP	BFP	H	R	ER	HR	SH	SF	HB	TBB	IBB	SO	WP	Bk	W	L	Pct.	ShO	Sv-Op	Hld	ERA
1997 Syracuse *	AAA	20	20	1	0	124	524	126	71	57	14	3	3	2	43	1	58	6	2	6	6	.500	1	0- --	--	4.14
1993 Toronto	AL	6	0	0	0	6.2	30	7	3	3	0	0	0	0	4	1	2	1	0	0	0	.000	0	0-0	2	4.05
1996 Toronto	AL	15	11	0	0	70.2	309	68	40	36	9	0	4	1	33	1	44	1	0	3	2	.600	0	0-0	0	4.58
1997 Toronto	AL	8	1	0	3	17.1	97	40	19	19	3	0	1	0	6	0	9	2	0	0	1	.000	0	0-0	0	9.87
3 ML YEARS		29	12	0	4	94.2	436	115	62	58	12	0	5	1	43	2	55	4	0	3	3	.500	0	0-0	2	5.51

Darrin Fletcher

Bats: Left **Throws:** Right **Pos:** C-83; PH-15 **Ht:** 6'1" **Wt:** 200 **Born:** 10/3/66 **Age:** 31

		BATTING																BASERUNNING				PERCENTAGES		
Year Team	Lg	G	AB	H	2B	3B	HR	(Hm	Rd)	TB	R	RBI	TBB	IBB	SO	HBP	SH	SF	SB	CS	SB%	GDP	Avg	OBP	SLG
1989 Los Angeles	NL	5	8	4	0	0	1	(1	0)	7	1	2	1	0	0	0	0	0	0	0	.00	0	.500	.556	.875
1990 LA-Phi	NL	11	23	3	1	0	0	(0	0)	4	3	1	0	0	6	0	0	0	0	0	.00	0	.130	.167	.174
1991 Philadelphia	NL	46	136	31	8	0	1	(1	0)	42	5	12	5	0	15	0	1	0	0	1	.00	2	.228	.255	.309
1992 Montreal	NL	83	222	54	10	2	2	(0	2)	74	13	26	14	3	28	2	2	4	0	2	.00	8	.243	.289	.333
1993 Montreal	NL	133	396	101	20	1	9	(5	4)	150	33	60	34	2	40	6	5	4	0	0	.00	7	.255	.320	.379
1994 Montreal	NL	94	285	74	18	1	10	(4 | 6)	124	28	57	25	4	23	4	0	0	0	0	12	.00	6	.260	.314	.435
1995 Montreal	NL	110	350	100	21	1	11	(3	8)	156	42	45	32	1	23	4	1	2	0	1	.00	15	.286	.351	.446
1996 Montreal	NL	127	394	105	22	0	12	(6	6)	163	41	57	27	4	42	6	1	3	0	0	.00	13	.266	.321	.414
1997 Montreal	NL	96	310	86	20	1	17	(10	7)	159	39	55	17	3	35	5	0	0	1	1	.50	6	.277	.323	.513
1990 Los Angeles	NL	2	1	0	0	0	0	(0	0)	0	0	0	0	0	1	0	0	0	0	0	.00	0	.000	.000	.000
Philadelphia	NL	9	22	3	1	0	0	(0	0)	4	3	1	0	0	5	0	0	0	0	0	.00	0	.136	.174	.182

			BATTING																	BASERUNNING				PERCENTAGES		
Year Team	Lg	G	AB	H	2B	3B	HR	(Hm	Rd)	TB	R	RBI	TBB	IBB	SO	HBP	SH	SF		SB	CS	SB%	GDP	Avg	OBP	SLG
9 ML YEARS		705	2124	558	120	6	63	(31	32)	879	205	315	156	17	212	26	10	27		1	5	.17	57	.263	.317	.414

Bryce Florie

Pitches: Right **Bats:** Right **Pos:** RP-24; SP-8 **Ht:** 5'11" **Wt:** 190 **Born:** 5/21/70 **Age:** 28

		HOW MUCH HE PITCHED						WHAT HE GAVE UP											THE RESULTS						
Year Team	Lg	G	GS	CG	GF	IP	BFP	H	R	ER	HR	SH	SF	HB	TBB	IBB	SO	WP	Bk	W	L	Pct.	ShO	Sv-Op	Hld	ERA
1994 San Diego	NL	9	0	0	4	9.1	37	8	1	1	0	0	1	0	3	0	8	1	0	0	0	.000	0	0-0	0	0.96
1995 San Diego	NL	47	0	0	10	68.2	290	49	30	23	8	5	1	4	38	3	68	7	2	2	2	.500	0	1-4	9	3.01
1996 SD-Mil		54	0	0	16	68.1	312	65	40	36	4	1	3	6	40	5	63	6	1	2	3	.400	0	0-3	8	4.74
1997 Milwaukee	AL	32	8	0	6	75	332	74	43	36	4	1	4	3	42	2	53	4	1	4	4	.500	0	0-1	0	4.32
1996 San Diego	NL	39	0	0	11	49.1	222	45	24	22	1	0	1	6	27	3	51	3	1	2	2	.500	0	0-1	4	4.01
Milwaukee	AL	15	0	0	5	19	90	20	16	14	3	1	2	0	13	2	12	3	0	0	1	.000	0	0-2	4	6.63
4 ML YEARS		142	8	0	36	221.1	971	196	114	96	16	7	9	13	123	10	192	18	4	8	9	.471	0	1-8	17	3.90

Cliff Floyd

Bats: L **Throws:** R **Pos:** PH-25; LF-24; 1B-9; CF-9; RF-6 **Ht:** 6'4" **Wt:** 235 **Born:** 12/5/72 **Age:** 25

			BATTING																	BASERUNNING				PERCENTAGES		
Year Team	Lg	G	AB	H	2B	3B	HR	(Hm	Rd)	TB	R	RBI	TBB	IBB	SO	HBP	SH	SF		SB	CS	SB%	GDP	Avg	OBP	SLG
1997 Charlotte *	AAA	39	131	48	10	0	9	—	—	85	27	33	10	1	29	1	0	0		7	2	.78	3	.366	.415	.649
1993 Montreal	NL	10	31	7	0	0	1	(0	1)	10	3	2	0	0	9	0	0	0		0	0	.00	0	.226	.226	.323
1994 Montreal	NL	100	334	94	19	4	4	(2	2)	133	43	41	24	0	63	3	2	3		10	3	.77	3	.281	.332	.398
1995 Montreal	NL	29	69	9	1	0	1	(0	1)	13	6	8	7	0	22	1	0	0		3	0	1.00	1	.130	.221	.188
1996 Montreal	NL	117	227	55	15	4	6	(3	3)	96	29	26	30	1	52	5	1	3		7	1	.88	3	.242	.340	.423
1997 Florida	NL	61	137	32	9	1	6	(2	4)	61	23	19	24	0	33	2	1	1		6	2	.75	3	.234	.354	.445
5 ML YEARS		317	798	197	44	9	18	(8	10)	313	104	96	85	1	179	11	4	7		26	6	.81	10	.247	.325	.392

Chad Fonville

Bats: B **Throws:** R **Pos:** PH-9; 2B-5; SS-2; CF-2; DH-1; LF-1 **Ht:** 5'6" **Wt:** 155 **Born:** 3/5/71 **Age:** 27

			BATTING																	BASERUNNING				PERCENTAGES		
Year Team	Lg	G	AB	H	2B	3B	HR	(Hm	Rd)	TB	R	RBI	TBB	IBB	SO	HBP	SH	SF		SB	CS	SB%	GDP	Avg	OBP	SLG
1997 Albuquerque *	AAA	102	371	81	5	2	0	—	—	90	49	22	30	0	39	3	3	2		23	10	.70	3	.218	.281	.243
1995 Mon-LA	NL	102	320	89	6	1	0	(0	0)	97	43	16	23	1	42	1	6	0		20	7	.74	3	.278	.328	.303
1996 Los Angeles	NL	103	201	41	4	1	0	(0	0)	47	34	13	17	1	31	0	3	0		7	2	.78	1	.204	.266	.234
1997 LA-ChA		18	23	3	0	0	0	(0	0)	3	2	2	3	0	4	0	1	0		2	1	.67	0	.130	.231	.130
1995 Montreal	NL	14	12	4	0	0	0	(0	0)	4	2	0	0	0	3	0	0	0		0	2	.00	0	.333	.333	.333
Los Angeles	NL	88	308	85	6	1	0	(0	0)	93	41	16	23	1	39	1	6	0		20	5	.80	3	.276	.328	.302
1997 Los Angeles	NL	9	14	2	0	0	0	(0	0)	2	1	1	2	0	3	0	0	0		0	1	.00	0	.143	.250	.143
Chicago	AL	9	9	1	0	0	0	(0	0)	1	1	1	1	0	1	0	1	0		2	0	1.00	0	.111	.200	.111
3 ML YEARS		223	544	133	10	2	0	(0	0)	147	79	31	43	2	77	1	10	0		29	8	.78	4	.244	.301	.270

Tom Fordham

Pitches: Left **Bats:** Left **Pos:** RP-6; SP-1 **Ht:** 6'2" **Wt:** 205 **Born:** 2/20/74 **Age:** 24

		HOW MUCH HE PITCHED						WHAT HE GAVE UP											THE RESULTS						
Year Team	Lg	G	GS	CG	GF	IP	BFP	H	R	ER	HR	SH	SF	HB	TBB	IBB	SO	WP	Bk	W	L	Pct.	ShO	Sv-Op	Hld	ERA
1993 White Sox	R	3	0	0	1	10	41	9	2	2	0	0	0	0	3	0	12	1	0	1	1	.500	0	0- --	--	1.80
Sarasota	A+	2	0	0	1	5	21	3	1	0	0	0	0	0	3	2	5	1	1	0	0	.000	0	0- --	--	0.00
Hickory	A	8	8	1	0	48.2	194	36	21	21	3	1	6	0	21	0	27	3	2	4	3	.571	0	0- --	--	3.88
1994 Hickory	A	17	17	1	0	109	452	101	47	38	10	1	1	3	30	1	121	5	4	10	5	.667	1	0- --	--	3.14
South Bend	A	11	11	1	0	74.2	315	82	46	36	4	4	3	0	14	0	48	4	4	4	5	.500	1	0- --	--	4.34
1995 Pr William	A+	13	13	1	0	84	340	66	20	19	7	2	1	2	35	2	78	1	0	9	0	1.000	1	0- --	--	2.04
Birmingham	AA	14	14	2	0	82.2	348	79	35	31	9	2	2	4	28	2	61	3	0	6	3	.667	1	0- --	--	3.38
1996 Birmingham	AA	6	6	0	0	37.1	147	26	13	11	4	0	2	0	14	1	37	2	0	2	1	.667	0	0- --	--	2.65
Nashville	AAA	22	22	3	0	140.2	589	117	60	54	15	4	2	4	69	1	118	7	1	10	8	.556	2	0- --	--	3.45
1997 Nashville	AAA	21	20	2	0	114	493	113	64	60	14	1	5	1	53	1	90	6	1	4	7	.462	0	0- --	--	4.74
1997 Chicago	AL	7	1	0	1	17.1	78	17	13	12	2	1	2	1	10	2	10	0	0	0	1	.000	0	0-1	1	6.23

Brook Fordyce

Bats: Right **Throws:** Right **Pos:** C-30; PH-17; DH-1 **Ht:** 6'1" **Wt:** 185 **Born:** 5/7/70 **Age:** 28

			BATTING																	BASERUNNING				PERCENTAGES		
Year Team	Lg	G	AB	H	2B	3B	HR	(Hm	Rd)	TB	R	RBI	TBB	IBB	SO	HBP	SH	SF		SB	CS	SB%	GDP	Avg	OBP	SLG
1989 Kingsport	R+	69	226	74	15	0	9	—	—	116	45	38	30	1	26	1	3	2		10	6	.63	3	.327	.405	.513
1990 Columbia	A	104	372	117	29	1	10	—	—	178	45	54	39	0	42	0	1	2		4	1	.80	18	.315	.378	.478
1991 St. Lucie	A+	115	406	97	19	3	7	—	—	143	42	55	37	2	51	4	0	6		4	5	.44	7	.239	.305	.352
1992 Binghamton	AA	118	425	118	30	0	11	—	—	181	59	61	37	1	78	4	3	6		1	2	.33	13	.278	.337	.426
1993 Norfolk	AAA	116	409	106	21	2	2	—	—	137	33	40	26	3	62	5	3	6		2	2	.50	10	.259	.307	.335
1994 Norfolk	AAA	66	229	60	13	3	3	—	—	88	26	32	19	1	26	1	2	1		1	0	1.00	9	.262	.320	.384
1995 Buffalo	AAA	58	176	44	13	0	0	—	—	57	18	9	14	0	20	2	3	0		1	0	1.00	1	.250	.313	.324
1996 Indianapolis	AAA	107	374	103	20	3	16	—	—	177	48	64	25	3	56	1	1	4		2	1	.67	5	.275	.319	.473
1997 Indianapolis	AAA		47	11	2	0	2	—	—	19	7	6	5	0	6	1	0	0		1	1	.50	3	.234	.321	.404
1995 New York	NL	4	2	1	1	0	0	(0	0)	2	1	0	1	0	0	0	0	0		0	0	.00	0	.500	.667	1.000
1996 Cincinnati	NL	4	7	2	1	0	0	(0	0)	3	0	1	3	0	1	0	0	0		0	0	.00	0	.286	.500	.429
1997 Cincinnati	NL	47	96	20	5	0	1	(1	0)	28	7	8	4	1	15	0	0	0		0	1	.00	2	.208	.267	.292

		BATTING																				BASERUNNING				PERCENTAGES		
Year Team	Lg	G	AB	H	2B	3B	HR	(Hm	Rd)	TB	R	RBI	TBB	IBB	SO	HBP	SH	SF		SB	CS	SB%	GDP		Avg	OBP	SLG
3 ML YEARS		55	105	23	7	0	1	(1	0)	33	8	9	12	1	16	0	0	1		2	0	1.00	0		.219	.297	.314

Tony Fossas

Pitches: Left **Bats:** Left **Pos:** RP-71   **Ht:** 6'0" **Wt:** 198 **Born:** 9/23/57 **Age:** 40

		HOW MUCH HE PITCHED						WHAT HE GAVE UP											THE RESULTS						
Year Team	Lg	G	GS	CG	GF	IP	BFP	H	R	ER	HR	SH	SF	HB	TBB	IBB	SO	WP	Bk	W	L	Pct.	ShO	Sv-Op	Hld	ERA
1988 Texas	AL	5	0	0	1	5.2	28	11	3	3	0	0	0	0	2	0	0	1	0	0	0	.000	0	0-0	0	4.76
1989 Milwaukee	AL	51	0	0	16	61	256	57	27	24	3	7	3	1	22	7	42	1	3	2	2	.500	0	1-3	13	3.54
1990 Milwaukee	AL	32	0	0	9	29.1	146	44	23	21	5	2	1	0	10	2	24	0	0	2	3	.400	0	0-2	8	6.44
1991 Boston	AL	64	0	0	18	57	244	49	27	22	3	5	0	3	28	9	29	2	0	3	2	.600	0	1-2	18	3.47
1992 Boston	AL	60	0	0	17	29.2	129	31	9	8	1	3	0	1	15	3	19	0	0	1	1	.333	0	2-3	14	2.43
1993 Boston	AL	71	0	0	19	40	175	38	28	23	4	0	1	2	15	4	39	1	1	1	1	.500	0	0-2	13	5.18
1994 Boston	AL	44	0	0	14	34	151	35	18	18	6	2	0	1	15	1	31	1	0	2	0	1.000	0	1-1	9	4.76
1995 St. Louis	NL	58	0	0	20	36.2	145	28	6	6	1	2	1	1	10	3	40	1	0	3	0	1.000	0	0-0	19	1.47
1996 St. Louis	NL	65	0	0	11	47	209	43	19	14	7	1	1	0	21	3	36	3	0	0	4	.000	0	2-7	15	2.68
1997 St. Louis	NL	71	0	0	14	51.2	239	62	32	22	7	3	1	1	26	3	41	0	0	2	7	.222	0	0-1	16	3.83
10 ML YEARS		521	0	0	139	392	1722	398	192	161	37	25	8	10	163	35	301	10	4	16	21	.432	0	7-21	125	3.70

Kevin Foster

Pitches: Right **Bats:** Right **Pos:** SP-25; RP-1   **Ht:** 6'1" **Wt:** 170 **Born:** 1/13/69 **Age:** 29

		HOW MUCH HE PITCHED						WHAT HE GAVE UP											THE RESULTS						
Year Team	Lg	G	GS	CG	GF	IP	BFP	H	R	ER	HR	SH	SF	HB	TBB	IBB	SO	WP	Bk	W	L	Pct.	ShO	Sv-Op	Hld	ERA
1993 Philadelphia	NL	2	1	0	0	6.2	40	13	11	11	3	0	0	0	7	0	6	2	0	1	0	.000	0	0-0	0	14.85
1994 Chicago	NL	13	13	0	0	81	337	70	31	26	7	1	1	1	35	1	75	1	1	3	4	.429	0	0-0	0	2.89
1995 Chicago	NL	30	28	0	1	167.2	703	149	90	84	32	4	6	6	65	4	146	2	2	12	11	.522	0	0-0	0	4.51
1996 Chicago	NL	17	16	1	0	87	386	98	63	60	16	5	4	2	35	3	53	2	0	7	6	.538	0	0-0	0	6.21
1997 Chicago	NL	26	25	1	0	146.1	637	141	79	75	27	9	7	2	66	4	118	3	0	10	7	.588	0	0-0	0	4.61
5 ML YEARS		88	83	2	1	488.2	2103	471	274	256	85	19	18	11	208	12	398	10	3	32	29	.525	0	0-0	0	4.71

Keith Foulke

Pitches: Right **Bats:** Right **Pos:** RP-19; SP-8   **Ht:** 6'0" **Wt:** 195 **Born:** 10/19/72 **Age:** 25

		HOW MUCH HE PITCHED						WHAT HE GAVE UP											THE RESULTS						
Year Team	Lg	G	GS	CG	GF	IP	BFP	H	R	ER	HR	SH	SF	HB	TBB	IBB	SO	WP	Bk	W	L	Pct.	ShO	Sv-Op	Hld	ERA
1994 Everett	A-	4	4	0	0	19.1	79	17	4	2	0	1	0	2	3	0	22	0	0	2	0	1.000	0	0--	—	0.93
1995 San Jose	A+	28	26	3	0	177.1	723	166	85	69	16	10	3	7	32	0	168	6	2	13	6	.684	1	0--	—	3.50
1996 Shreveport	AA	27	27	4	0	182.2	712	149	61	56	16	6	7	3	35	0	129	6	1	12	7	.632	2	0--	—	2.76
1997 Phoenix	AAA	12	12	0	0	76	321	79	38	38	11	2	5	6	15	0	54	1	0	5	4	.556	0	0--	—	4.50
Nashville	AAA	1	1	0	0	4.2	20	8	3	3	1	0	0	0	0	0	4	1	0	0	0	.000	0	0--	—	5.79
1997 SF-ChA		27	8	0	5	73.1	326	88	52	52	13	3	1	4	23	2	54	1	0	4	5	.444	0	3-6	5	6.38
San Francisco	NL	11	8	0	0	44.2	209	60	41	41	9	2	0	4	18	1	33	1	0	1	5	.167	0	0-1	0	8.26
Chicago	AL	16	0	0	5	28.2	117	28	11	11	4	1	1	0	5	1	21	0	0	3	0	1.000	0	3-5	5	3.45

Andy Fox

Bats: L **Throws:** R **Pos:** 3B-11; PH-9; 2B-5; DH-2; SS-2; RF-2   **Ht:** 6'4" **Wt:** 205 **Born:** 1/12/71 **Age:** 27

		BATTING																	BASERUNNING				PERCENTAGES		
Year Team	Lg	G	AB	H	2B	3B	HR	(Hm	Rd)	TB	R	RBI	TBB	IBB	SO	HBP	SH	SF	SB	CS	SB%	GDP	Avg	OBP	SLG
1989 Yankees	R	40	141	35	9	2	3	—	—	57	26	25	31	1	29	2	0	2	6	1	.86	1	.248	.386	.404
1990 Greensboro	A	134	455	99	19	4	9	—	—	153	68	55	92	5	132	4	1	2	26	5	.84	14	.218	.353	.336
1991 Pr William	A+	126	417	96	22	4	2	—	—	152	60	46	81	3	104	6	1	9	15	13	.54	7	.230	.357	.365
1992 Pr William	A+	125	473	113	18	3	7	—	—	158	75	42	54	1	81	6	4	0	28	14	.67	7	.239	.325	.334
1993 Albany-Colo	AA	65	236	65	16	1	3	—	—	92	44	24	32	1	54	0	2	0	12	6	.67	1	.275	.362	.390
1994 Albany-Colo	AA	121	472	105	20	3	11	—	—	164	75	43	62	3	102	2	4	1	22	13	.63	4	.222	.315	.347
1995 Norwich	AA	44	175	36	3	5	5	—	—	64	23	17	19	0	36	0	1	1	8	1	.89	3	.206	.282	.366
Columbus	AAA	82	302	105	16	6	9	—	—	160	61	37	43	1	41	4	2	3	22	4	.85	5	.348	.432	.530
1997 Columbus	AAA	95	318	87	11	4	6	—	—	124	66	33	54	5	64	1	2	5	28	11	.72	5	.274	.380	.390
1996 New York	AL	113	189	37	4	0	3	(1	2)	50	26	13	20	0	28	1	9	0	11	3	.79	2	.196	.276	.265
1997 New York	AL	22	31	7	1	0	0	(0	0)	8	13	1	7	0	9	0	2	0	2	1	.67	1	.226	.368	.258
2 ML YEARS		135	220	44	5	0	3	(1	2)	58	39	14	27	0	37	1	11	0	13	4	.76	3	.200	.290	.264

Chad Fox

Pitches: Right **Bats:** Right **Pos:** RP-30   **Ht:** 6'3" **Wt:** 175 **Born:** 9/3/70 **Age:** 27

		HOW MUCH HE PITCHED						WHAT HE GAVE UP											THE RESULTS						
Year Team	Lg	G	GS	CG	GF	IP	BFP	H	R	ER	HR	SH	SF	HB	TBB	IBB	SO	WP	Bk	W	L	Pct.	ShO	Sv-Op	Hld	ERA
1992 Princeton	R+	15	8	0	4	49.1	238	55	43	26	2	1	1	2	34	1	37	6	2	4	2	.667	0	0--	—	4.74
1993 Chston-WV	A	27	26	0	0	135.2	638	138	100	81	7	6	8	13	97	0	81	15	1	9	12	.429	0	0--	—	5.37
1994 Winston-Sal	A+	25	25	1	0	156.1	674	121	74	67	18	5	5	9	94	0	137	20	1	12	5	.706	0	0--	—	3.86
1995 Chattanooga	AA	20	17	0	1	80	363	76	49	45	2	2	2	3	52	1	56	14	0	4	5	.444	0	0--	—	5.06
1996 Richmond	AAA	18	18	1	0	93.1	415	91	57	49	9	8	6	3	49	1	87	8	1	3	10	.231	0	0--	—	4.73
1997 Richmond	AAA	31	0	0	7	24.1	105	24	10	10	1	2	1	0	14	0	25	4	0	0	1	1.000	0	0--	—	3.70
1997 Atlanta	NL	30	0	0	8	27.1	120	24	12	10	4	0	0	0	16	0	28	4	0	0	1	.000	0	0-1	7	3.29

John Franco

Pitches: Left **Bats:** Left **Pos:** RP-59 **Ht:** 5'10" **Wt:** 185 **Born:** 9/17/60 **Age:** 37

		HOW MUCH HE PITCHED						WHAT HE GAVE UP											THE RESULTS						
Year Team	Lg	G	GS	CG	GF	IP	BFP	H	R	ER	HR	SH	SF	HB	TBB	IBB	SO	WP	Bk	W	L	Pct.	ShO	Sv-Op	Hld	ERA
1984 Cincinnati	NL	54	0	0	30	79.1	335	74	28	23	3	4	4	2	36	4	55	2	0	6	2	.750	0	4--	—	2.61
1985 Cincinnati	NL	67	0	0	33	99	407	83	27	24	5	11	1	1	40	8	61	4	0	12	3	.800	0	12--	—	2.18
1986 Cincinnati	NL	74	0	0	52	101	429	90	40	33	7	8	3	2	44	12	84	4	2	6	6	.500	0	29--	—	2.94
1987 Cincinnati	NL	68	0	0	60	82	344	76	26	23	6	5	2	0	27	6	61	1	0	8	5	.615	0	32-41	0	2.52
1988 Cincinnati	NL	70	0	0	61	86	336	60	18	15	3	5	1	0	27	3	46	1	2	6	6	.500	0	39-42	1	1.57
1989 Cincinnati	NL	60	0	0	50	80.2	345	77	35	28	3	7	3	0	36	8	60	3	2	4	8	.333	0	32-39	1	3.12
1990 New York	NL	55	0	0	48	67.2	287	66	22	19	4	3	1	0	21	2	56	7	2	5	3	.625	0	33-39	0	2.53
1991 New York	NL	52	0	0	48	55.1	247	61	27	18	2	3	0	1	18	4	45	6	0	5	9	.357	0	30-35	0	2.93
1992 New York	NL	31	0	0	30	33	128	24	6	6	1	0	2	0	11	2	20	0	0	6	2	.750	0	15-17	1	1.64
1993 New York	NL	35	0	0	30	36.1	172	46	24	21	6	4	1	1	19	3	29	5	0	4	3	.571	0	10-17	0	5.20
1994 New York	NL	47	0	0	43	50	216	47	20	15	2	2	1	1	19	0	42	1	0	1	4	.200	0	30-36	0	2.70
1995 New York	NL	48	0	0	41	51.2	213	48	17	14	4	4	1	0	17	2	41	0	0	5	3	.625	0	29-36	0	2.44
1996 New York	NL	51	0	0	44	54	235	54	15	11	2	6	0	0	21	0	48	2	0	4	3	.571	0	28-36	0	1.83
1997 New York	NL	59	0	0	53	60	244	49	18	17	3	5	1	1	20	2	53	6	0	5	3	.625	0	36-42	0	2.55
14 ML YEARS		771	0	0	623	936	3938	855	323	267	51	67	21	9	356	56	701	42	8	77	60	.562	0	359--	—	2.57

Julio Franco

Bats: R **Throws:** R **Pos:** DH-70; 2B-35; 1B-14; PH-2 **Ht:** 6'1" **Wt:** 190 **Born:** 8/23/61 **Age:** 36

		BATTING															BASERUNNING				PERCENTAGES		
Year Team	Lg	G	AB	H	2B	3B	HR	(Hm | Rd)	TB	R	RBI	TBB	IBB	SO	HBP	SH	SF	SB	CS	SB%	GDP	Avg	OBP	SLG
1982 Philadelphia	NL	16	29	8	1	0	0	(0 | 0)	9	3	3	2	1	4	0	1	0	2	2	.00	1	.276	.323	.310
1983 Cleveland	AL	149	560	153	24	8	8	(6 | 2)	217	68	80	27	1	50	0	2	3	6	32	12	.73	21	.273	.306	.388
1984 Cleveland	AL	160	658	188	22	5	3	(1 | 2)	229	82	79	43	1	68	6	1	10	19	10	.66	23	.286	.331	.348
1985 Cleveland	AL	160	636	183	33	4	6	(3 | 3)	242	97	90	54	2	74	4	0	9	13	9	.59	26	.288	.343	.381
1986 Cleveland	AL	149	599	183	30	5	10	(4 | 6)	253	80	74	32	1	66	0	4	0	5	10	7	.59	28	.306	.338	.422
1987 Cleveland	AL	128	495	158	24	3	8	(3 | 5)	212	86	52	57	2	56	3	0	5	32	9	.78	23	.319	.389	.428
1988 Cleveland	AL	152	613	186	23	6	10	(3 | 7)	251	88	54	56	4	72	2	1	4	25	11	.69	17	.303	.361	.409
1989 Texas	AL	150	548	173	31	5	13	(9 | 4)	253	80	92	66	11	69	1	0	6	21	3	.88	27	.316	.386	.462
1990 Texas	AL	157	582	172	27	1	11	(7 | 4)	234	96	69	82	3	83	2	2	2	31	10	.76	12	.296	.383	.402
1991 Texas	AL	146	589	201	27	3	15	(7 | 8)	279	108	78	65	8	78	3	0	2	36	9	.80	13	.341	.408	.474
1992 Texas	AL	35	107	25	7	0	2	(2 | 0)	38	19	8	15	2	17	0	1	0	1	1	.50	3	.234	.328	.355
1993 Texas	AL	144	532	154	31	3	14	(6 | 8)	233	85	84	62	4	95	1	5	7	9	3	.75	16	.289	.360	.438
1994 Chicago	AL	112	433	138	19	2	20	(10 | 10)	221	72	98	62	4	75	5	0	5	8	1	.89	14	.319	.406	.510
1996 Cleveland	AL	112	432	139	20	1	14	(7 | 7)	203	72	76	61	2	82	3	0	3	8	8	.50	14	.322	.407	.470
1997 Cle-Mil	AL	120	430	116	16	1	7	(5 | 2)	155	68	44	69	4	116	1	1	4	15	6	.71	17	.270	.369	.360
1997 Cleveland	AL	78	289	82	13	1	3	(2 | 1)	106	46	25	38	2	75	0	1	0	8	5	.62	13	.284	.367	.367
Milwaukee	AL	42	141	34	3	0	4	(3 | 1)	49	22	19	31	2	41	1	0	4	7	1	.88	4	.241	.373	.348
15 ML YEARS		1890	7243	2177	335	47	141	(72 | 69)	3029	1104	981	753	50	1005	33	15	68	260	101	.72	255	.301	.366	.418

Matt Franco

Bats: L **Throws:** R **Pos:** PH-71; 3B-39; 1B-13; DH-1; LF-1 **Ht:** 6'2" **Wt:** 200 **Born:** 8/19/69 **Age:** 28

		BATTING															BASERUNNING				PERCENTAGES		
Year Team	Lg	G	AB	H	2B	3B	HR	(Hm | Rd)	TB	R	RBI	TBB	IBB	SO	HBP	SH	SF	SB	CS	SB%	GDP	Avg	OBP	SLG
1987 Wytheville	R+	62	202	50	10	1	1	—	—	65	25	21	26	1	41	0	0	0	4	1	.80	3	.248	.333	.322
1988 Wytheville	R+	20	79	31	9	1	0	—	—	42	14	16	7	0	5	0	0	0	0	1	.00	2	.392	.442	.532
Geneva	A-	44	164	42	2	0	3	—	—	53	19	21	19	3	13	0	0	1	2	0	1.00	7	.256	.332	.323
1989 Chston-WV	A	109	377	102	16	1	5	—	—	135	42	48	57	0	40	0	5	4	2	2	.50	10	.271	.363	.358
Peoria	A	16	58	13	4	0	0	—	—	17	4	9	5	0	5	1	0	1	0	1	.00	1	.224	.292	.293
1990 Peoria	A	123	444	125	33	2	6	—	—	180	52	65	43	2	39	1	1	2	4	4	.50	19	.282	.346	.406
1991 Winston-Sal	A+	104	307	66	12	1	4	—	—	92	47	40	46	2	41	2	2	6	4	1	.80	6	.215	.316	.300
1992 Charlotte	AA	108	343	97	18	3	2	—	—	127	35	31	26	1	46	1	0	3	3	3	.50	4	.283	.332	.370
1993 Orlando	AA	68	237	75	20	1	7	—	—	118	31	37	29	2	30	2	1	2	3	6	.33	2	.316	.393	.498
Iowa	AAA	62	199	58	17	4	5	—	—	98	24	29	16	3	30	1	0	1	4	1	.80	6	.291	.342	.492
1994 Iowa	AAA	128	437	121	32	4	11	—	—	194	63	71	52	5	66	2	2	5	3	3	.50	7	.277	.353	.444
1995 Iowa	AAA	121	455	128	28	5	6	—	—	184	51	58	37	5	44	0	1	6	1	1	.50	11	.281	.331	.404
1996 Norfolk	AAA	133	508	164	40	2	7	—	—	229	74	81	36	3	55	3	1	9	5	2	.71	10	.323	.365	.451
1997 Norfolk	AAA	7	26	7	2	0	0	—	—	9	5	0	2	1	2	1	0	0	0	0	.00	0	.269	.345	.346
1995 Chicago	NL	16	17	5	1	0	0	(0 | 0)	6	3	1	0	0	4	0	0	0	0	0	.00	0	.294	.294	.353
1996 New York	NL	14	31	6	1	0	1	(0 | 1)	10	3	2	1	0	5	1	0	1	0	0	.00	1	.194	.235	.323
1997 New York	NL	112	163	45	5	0	5	(3 | 2)	65	21	21	13	4	23	0	0	0	1	0	1.00	4	.276	.330	.399
3 ML YEARS		142	211	56	7	0	6	(3 | 3)	81	27	24	14	4	32	1	0	1	1	0	1.00	5	.265	.313	.384

Micah Franklin

Bats: Both **Throws:** Right **Pos:** RF-9; PH-6; LF-4 **Ht:** 6'0" **Wt:** 205 **Born:** 4/25/72 **Age:** 26

		BATTING															BASERUNNING				PERCENTAGES		
Year Team	Lg	G	AB	H	2B	3B	HR	(Hm | Rd)	TB	R	RBI	TBB	IBB	SO	HBP	SH	SF	SB	CS	SB%	GDP	Avg	OBP	SLG
1990 Kingsport	R+	39	158	41	9	2	7	—	—	75	29	25	8	0	44	1	0	2	4	1	.80	2	.259	.296	.475
1991 Pittsfield	A-	26	94	27	4	2	0	—	—	35	17	14	21	0	20	1	2	1	12	3	.80	3	.287	.419	.372
Erie	A-	39	153	37	4	0	2	—	—	47	28	8	25	0	35	2	0	1	4	5	.44	3	.242	.354	.307
1992 Billings	R+	75	251	84	13	2	11	—	—	134	58	60	53	3	65	10	0	3	18	17	.51	3	.335	.472	.534
1993 Winston-Sal	A+	20	69	16	1	1	3	—	—	28	10	6	10	1	19	2	1	0	0	1	.00	1	.232	.346	.406
Chston-WV	A	102	343	90	14	4	17	—	—	163	56	68	47	4	109	18	3	6	6	1	.86	4	.262	.374	.475
1994 Winston-Sal	A+	42	150	45	7	0	21	—	—	115	44	44	27	5	48	6	0	1	7	0	1.00	1	.300	.424	.767

Year Team	Lg	G	AB	H	2B	3B	HR	(Hm	Rd)	TB	R	RBI	TBB	IBB	SO	HBP	SH	SF	SB	CS	SB%	GDP	Avg	OBP	SLG
Chattanooga AA		79	279	77	17	0	10	—	—	124	46	40	33	3	79	13	0	3	2	2	.50	3	.276	.375	.444
1995 Calgary AAA		110	358	105	28	0	21	—	—	196	64	71	47	8	95	1	0	5	3	3	.50	7	.293	.372	.547
1996 Toledo AAA		53	179	44	10	1	7	—	—	77	32	21	27	0	60	3	0	0	3	2	.60	1	.246	.354	.430
Louisville AAA		86	289	67	18	3	15	—	—	136	43	53	40	2	71	8	1	3	2	3	.40	4	.232	.338	.471
1997 Louisville AAA		99	326	72	14	1	12	—	—	124	49	48	51	4	74	3	0	3	2	0	1.00	9	.221	.329	.380
1997 St. Louis NL		17	34	11	0	0	2	(0	2)	17	6	2	3	0	10	0	0	0	0	0	.00	0	.324	.378	.500

John Frascatore

Pitches: Right **Bats:** Right **Pos:** RP-59   **Ht:** 6'1" **Wt:** 210 **Born:** 2/4/70 **Age:** 28

Year Team	Lg	G	GS	CG	GF	IP	BFP	H	R	ER	HR	SH	SF	HB	TBB	IBB	SO	WP	Bk	W	L	Pct.	ShO	Sv-Op	Hld	ERA
1991 Hamilton A-		30	1	0	7	30.1	162	44	38	31	3	3	1	2	22	1	18	1	2	2	7	.222	0	1- --	—	9.20
1992 Savannah A		50	0	0	44	58.2	266	49	32	25	4	8	1	3	29	2	56	4	5	2	3	.400	0	23- --	—	3.84
1993 Springfield A		27	26	2	1	157.1	654	157	84	66	6	7	5	3	33	0	126	2	3	7	12	.368	1	0- --	—	3.78
1994 Arkansas AA		12	12	4	0	78.1	324	76	37	27	3	1	2	3	15	0	63	3	0	7	3	.700	1	0- --	—	3.10
Louisville AAA		13	12	2	0	85	366	82	34	32	3	6	4	2	33	2	58	2	0	8	3	.727	1	0- --	—	3.39
1995 Louisville AAA		28	10	1	15	82	370	89	54	36	5	5	2	3	34	3	55	5	0	2	8	.200	0	5- --	—	3.95
1996 Louisville AAA		36	21	3	5	156.1	692	180	106	90	22	7	6	7	42	2	95	5	0	6	13	.316	0	0- --	—	5.18
1994 St. Louis NL		1	1	0	0	3.1	18	7	6	6	2	0	0	0	2	0	2	1	0	0	1	.000	0	0-0	0	16.20
1995 St. Louis NL		14	4	0	3	32.2	151	39	19	16	3	1	1	2	16	1	21	0	0	1	1	.500	0	0-0	0	4.41
1997 St. Louis NL		59	0	0	17	80	348	74	25	22	5	5	5	6	33	5	58	1	0	5	2	.714	0	0-4	3	2.48
3 ML YEARS		74	5	0	20	116	517	120	50	44	10	6	6	8	51	6	81	5	0	6	4	.600	0	0-4	3	3.41

Hanley Frias

Bats: Both **Throws:** Right **Pos:** SS-12; PH-4; 2B-1   **Ht:** 6'0" **Wt:** 160 **Born:** 12/5/73 **Age:** 24

Year Team	Lg	G	AB	H	2B	3B	HR	(Hm	Rd)	TB	R	RBI	TBB	IBB	SO	HBP	SH	SF	SB	CS	SB%	GDP	Avg	OBP	SLG
1992 Rangers R		58	205	50	9	2	0	—	—	63	37	28	27	0	30	2	2	2	28	6	.82	1	.244	.335	.307
1993 Chston-SC A		132	474	109	20	4	4	—	—	149	61	37	40	0	108	3	4	4	27	14	.66	8	.230	.292	.315
1994 High Desert A+		124	452	115	17	6	3	—	—	153	70	59	41	1	74	2	5	3	37	12	.76	9	.254	.317	.338
1995 Charlotte A+		33	120	40	6	3	0	—	—	52	23	14	15	0	11	1	3	1	8	6	.57	0	.333	.409	.433
Tulsa AA		93	360	101	18	4	0	—	—	127	44	27	45	0	53	1	8	2	14	12	.54	6	.281	.360	.353
1996 Tulsa AA		134	505	145	24	12	2	—	—	199	73	41	30	2	73	0	5	3	9	9	.50	19	.287	.325	.394
1997 Okla City AAA		132	484	128	17	4	5	—	—	168	64	46	56	2	72	1	8	3	35	15	.70	8	.264	.340	.347
1997 Texas AL		14	26	5	1	0	0	(0	0)	6	4	1	1	0	4	0	0	0	0	0	.00	1	.192	.222	.231

Jeff Frye

B: R **T:** R **Pos:** 2B-80; PH-21; 3B-18; DH-11; LF-5; CF-5; SS-3; RF-3; 1B-1   **Ht:** 5'9" **Wt:** 165 **Born:** 8/31/66 **Age:** 31

Year Team	Lg	G	AB	H	2B	3B	HR	(Hm	Rd)	TB	R	RBI	TBB	IBB	SO	HBP	SH	SF	SB	CS	SB%	GDP	Avg	OBP	SLG
1992 Texas AL		67	199	51	9	1	1	(0	1)	65	24	12	16	0	27	3	11	1	1	3	.25	2	.256	.320	.327
1994 Texas AL		57	205	67	20	3	0	(0	0)	93	37	18	29	0	23	1	6	1	6	1	.86	1	.327	.408	.454
1995 Texas AL		90	313	87	15	2	4	(2	2)	118	38	29	24	0	45	5	8	4	3	3	.50	7	.278	.335	.377
1996 Boston AL		105	419	120	27	2	4	(3	1)	163	74	41	54	0	57	5	5	3	18	4	.82	6	.286	.372	.389
1997 Boston AL		127	404	126	36	2	3	(2	1)	175	56	51	27	1	44	2	2	7	19	8	.70	12	.312	.352	.433
5 ML YEARS		446	1540	451	107	10	12	(7	5)	614	229	151	150	1	196	16	31	18	47	19	.71	28	.293	.358	.399

Travis Fryman

Bats: Right **Throws:** Right **Pos:** 3B-153; PH-1   **Ht:** 6'1" **Wt:** 195 **Born:** 3/25/69 **Age:** 29

Year Team	Lg	G	AB	H	2B	3B	HR	(Hm	Rd)	TB	R	RBI	TBB	IBB	SO	HBP	SH	SF	SB	CS	SB%	GDP	Avg	OBP	SLG
1990 Detroit AL		66	232	69	11	1	9	(5	4)	109	32	27	17	0	51	1	1	0	3	5	.50	3	.297	.348	.470
1991 Detroit AL		149	557	144	36	3	21	(8	13)	249	65	91	40	0	149	3	6	6	12	5	.71	13	.259	.309	.447
1992 Detroit AL		161	659	175	31	4	20	(9	11)	274	87	96	45	1	144	6	5	6	8	4	.67	13	.266	.316	.416
1993 Detroit AL		151	607	182	37	5	22	(13	9)	295	98	97	77	1	128	4	1	6	9	4	.69	8	.300	.379	.486
1994 Detroit AL		114	464	122	34	5	18	(10	8)	220	66	85	45	1	128	5	1	13	2	2	.50	6	.263	.326	.474
1995 Detroit AL		144	567	156	21	5	15	(9	6)	232	79	81	63	4	100	3	0	7	4	3	.57	18	.275	.347	.409
1996 Detroit AL		157	616	165	32	3	22	(10	12)	269	90	100	57	2	118	4	1	10	16	3	.84	15	.268	.329	.437
1997 Detroit AL		154	595	163	27	3	22	(13	9)	262	90	102	46	5	113	5	0	11	16	3	.84	15	.274	.326	.440
8 ML YEARS		1096	4297	1176	229	29	149	(77	72)	1910	607	679	390	14	931	31	15	59	58	26	.69	94	.274	.334	.444

Brad Fullmer

Bats: Left **Throws:** Right **Pos:** PH-11; 1B-8; LF-2   **Ht:** 6'1" **Wt:** 190 **Born:** 1/17/75 **Age:** 23

Year Team	Lg	G	AB	H	2B	3B	HR	(Hm	Rd)	TB	R	RBI	TBB	IBB	SO	HBP	SH	SF	SB	CS	SB%	GDP	Avg	OBP	SLG
1995 Albany A		123	468	151	38	4	8	—	—	221	69	67	36	4	33	17	0	9	10	10	.50	9	.323	.387	.472
1996 Wst Plm Bch A+		102	380	115	29	1	5	—	—	161	52	63	32	2	43	11	0	8	4	6	.40	9	.303	.367	.424
Harrisburg AA		24	98	27	4	1	4	—	—	45	11	14	3	0	8	2	0	0	0	0	.00	3	.276	.311	.459
1997 Harrisburg AA		94	357	111	24	2	19	—	—	196	60	62	30	5	25	7	0	4	6	4	.60	11	.311	.372	.549
Ottawa AAA		24	91	27	7	0	3	—	—	43	13	17	3	0	10	2	0	5	1	1	.50	3	.297	.317	.473
1997 Montreal NL		19	40	12	2	0	3	(1	2)	23	4	8	2	1	7	1	0	0	0	0	.00	0	.300	.349	.575

Gary Gaetti

Bats: R **Throws:** R **Pos:** 3B-132; 1B-20; PH-14; P-1 | **Ht:** 6'0" **Wt:** 200 **Born:** 8/19/58 **Age:** 39

Year Team	Lg	G	AB	H	2B	3B	HR	(Hm	Rd)	TB	R	RBI	TBB	IBB	SO	HBP	SH	SF	SB	CS	SB%	GDP	Avg	OBP	SLG
1981 Minnesota	AL	9	26	5	0	0	2	(1	1)	11	4	3	0	0	6	0	0	0	0	0	.00	1	.192	.192	.423
1982 Minnesota	AL	145	508	117	25	4	25	(15	10)	225	59	84	37	2	107	3	4	13	0	4	.00	16	.230	.280	.443
1983 Minnesota	AL	157	584	143	30	3	21	(7	14)	242	81	78	54	2	121	4	0	8	7	1	.88	18	.245	.309	.414
1984 Minnesota	AL	162	588	154	29	4	5	(2	3)	206	55	65	44	1	81	4	3	5	11	5	.69	9	.262	.315	.350
1985 Minnesota	AL	160	560	138	31	0	20	(10	10)	229	71	63	37	3	89	7	3	1	13	5	.72	15	.246	.301	.409
1986 Minnesota	AL	157	596	171	34	1	34	(16	18)	309	91	108	52	4	108	6	1	6	14	15	.48	18	.287	.347	.518
1987 Minnesota	AL	154	584	150	36	2	31	(18	13)	283	95	109	37	7	92	3	1	3	10	7	.59	25	.257	.303	.485
1988 Minnesota	AL	133	468	141	29	2	28	(9	19)	258	66	88	36	5	85	5	1	6	7	4	.64	10	.301	.353	.551
1989 Minnesota	AL	130	498	125	11	4	19	(10	9)	201	63	75	25	5	87	3	1	9	6	2	.75	12	.251	.286	.404
1990 Minnesota	AL	154	577	132	27	5	16	(7	9)	217	61	85	36	1	101	3	1	8	6	1	.86	22	.229	.274	.376
1991 California	AL	152	586	144	22	1	18	(12	6)	222	58	66	33	3	104	8	2	5	5	5	.50	13	.246	.293	.379
1992 California	AL	130	456	103	13	2	12	(8	4)	156	41	48	21	4	79	6	0	3	1	1	.75	9	.226	.267	.342
1993 Cal-KC	AL	102	331	81	20	1	14	(6	8)	145	40	50	21	0	87	8	2	7	1	3	.25	5	.245	.300	.438
1994 Kansas City	AL	90	327	94	15	3	12	(5	7)	151	53	57	19	3	63	2	1	3	0	2	.00	9	.287	.328	.462
1995 Kansas City	AL	137	514	134	27	0	35	(16	19)	266	76	96	47	6	91	8	3	6	3	3	.50	7	.261	.329	.518
1996 St. Louis	NL	141	522	143	27	4	23	(13	10)	247	71	80	35	6	97	4	5	2	2	2	.50	10	.274	.326	.473
1997 St. Louis	NL	148	502	126	24	1	17	(7	10)	203	63	69	36	3	88	6	4	6	7	3	.70	20	.251	.305	.404
1993 California	AL	20	50	9	2	0	0	(0	0)	11	3	4	5	0	12	0	0	1	1	0	1.00	3	.180	.250	.220
Kansas City	AL	82	281	72	18	1	14	(6	8)	134	37	46	16	0	75	8	2	6	0	3	.00	2	.256	.309	.477
17 ML YEARS		2261	8227	2101	400	37	332	(162	170)	3571	1048	1224	570	55	1486	84	31	94	95	63	.60	219	.255	.307	.434

Greg Gagne

Bats: Right **Throws:** Right **Pos:** SS-143; PH-1 | **Ht:** 5'11" **Wt:** 180 **Born:** 11/12/61 **Age:** 36

Year Team	Lg	G	AB	H	2B	3B	HR	(Hm	Rd)	TB	R	RBI	TBB	IBB	SO	HBP	SH	SF	SB	CS	SB%	GDP	Avg	OBP	SLG
1983 Minnesota	AL	10	27	3	1	0	0	(0	0)	4	2	3	0	0	6	0	0	2	0	0	.00	0	.111	.103	.148
1984 Minnesota	AL	2	1	0	0	0	0	(0	0)	0	0	0	0	0	0	0	0	0	0	0	.00	0	.000	.000	.000
1985 Minnesota	AL	114	293	66	15	3	2	(0	2)	93	37	23	20	0	57	3	3	3	10	4	.71	5	.225	.279	.317
1986 Minnesota	AL	156	472	118	22	6	12	(10	2)	188	63	54	30	0	108	6	13	3	12	10	.55	4	.250	.301	.398
1987 Minnesota	AL	137	437	116	28	7	10	(7	3)	188	68	40	25	0	84	4	10	2	6	6	.50	3	.265	.310	.430
1988 Minnesota	AL	149	461	109	20	6	14	(5	9)	183	70	48	27	2	110	7	11	1	15	7	.68	13	.236	.288	.397
1989 Minnesota	AL	149	460	125	29	7	9	(5	4)	195	69	48	17	0	80	2	7	5	11	4	.73	10	.272	.298	.424
1990 Minnesota	AL	138	388	91	22	3	7	(3	4)	140	38	38	24	0	76	1	8	2	8	8	.50	5	.235	.280	.361
1991 Minnesota	AL	139	408	108	23	3	8	(3	5)	161	52	42	26	0	72	3	5	5	11	9	.55	15	.265	.310	.395
1992 Minnesota	AL	146	439	108	23	0	7	(1	6)	152	53	39	19	0	83	2	12	1	6	7	.46	11	.246	.280	.346
1993 Kansas City	AL	159	540	151	32	3	10	(3	7)	219	66	57	33	1	93	0	4	4	10	12	.45	7	.280	.319	.406
1994 Kansas City	AL	107	375	97	23	3	7	(2	5)	147	39	51	27	0	79	4	2	1	10	17	.37	8	.259	.314	.392
1995 Kansas City	AL	120	430	110	25	4	6	(2	4)	161	58	49	38	2	60	2	7	5	3	5	.38	11	.256	.316	.374
1996 Los Angeles	NL	128	428	109	13	2	10	(3	7)	156	48	55	50	11	93	2	4	3	4	2	.67	6	.255	.333	.364
1997 Los Angeles	NL	144	514	129	20	3	9	(2	7)	182	49	57	31	4	120	4	3	1	2	5	.29	13	.251	.298	.354
15 ML YEARS		1798	5673	1440	296	50	111	(46	65)	2169	712	604	367	20	1121	40	89	38	108	96	.53	111	.254	.302	.382

Eddie Gaillard

Pitches: Right **Bats:** Right **Pos:** RP-16 | **Ht:** 6'1" **Wt:** 180 **Born:** 8/13/70 **Age:** 27

Year Team	Lg	G	GS	CG	GF	IP	BFP	H	R	ER	HR	SH	SF	HB	TBB	IBB	SO	WP	Bk	W	L	Pct.	ShO	Sv-Op	Hld	ERA
1993 Niagara Fal	A-	3	3	0	0	14.2	63	15	6	6	0	1	1	0	4	0	12	0	0	1	2	.333	0	0- -	-	3.68
Fayetteville	A	11	11	0	0	61.2	261	64	30	28	8	2	0	4	20	0	41	1	1	5	2	.714	0	0- -	-	4.09
1994 Lakeland	A+	30	9	0	8	92	389	82	37	29	3	1	2	10	29	0	51	3	1	6	1	.857	0	2- -	-	2.84
1995 Jacksnville	AA	8	0	0	2	8	42	11	5	5	0	2	1	0	5	1	4	0	0	1	0	1.000	0	0- -	-	5.63
Lakeland	A+	43	0	0	38	55	227	48	13	8	1	1	3	0	18	2	51	2	1	2	4	.333	0	25- -	-	1.31
1996 Jacksnville	AA	56	0	0	24	88	389	82	40	33	8	4	3	5	50	7	76	10	0	9	6	.600	0	1- -	-	3.38
1997 Toledo	AAA	55	0	0	46	53	235	52	27	25	7	3	1	2	24	2	54	4	1	1	4	.200	0	28- -	-	4.25
1997 Detroit	AL	16	0	0	5	20.1	88	16	12	12	2	0	2	0	10	2	12	0	0	1	0	1.000	0	1-2	0	5.31

Andres Galarraga

Bats: Right **Throws:** Right **Pos:** 1B-154; PH-1 | **Ht:** 6'3" **Wt:** 235 **Born:** 6/18/61 **Age:** 37

Year Team	Lg	G	AB	H	2B	3B	HR	(Hm	Rd)	TB	R	RBI	TBB	IBB	SO	HBP	SH	SF	SB	CS	SB%	GDP	Avg	OBP	SLG
1985 Montreal	NL	24	75	14	1	0	2	(0	2)	21	9	4	3	0	18	1	0	0	1	2	.33	0	.187	.228	.280
1986 Montreal	NL	105	321	87	13	0	10	(4	6)	130	39	42	30	5	79	3	1	1	6	5	.55	8	.271	.338	.405
1987 Montreal	NL	147	551	168	40	3	13	(6	7)	253	72	90	41	13	127	10	0	4	7	10	.41	11	.305	.361	.459
1988 Montreal	NL	157	609	184	42	8	29	(14	15)	329	99	92	39	9	153	10	0	3	13	4	.76	12	.302	.352	.540
1989 Montreal	NL	152	572	147	30	1	23	(10	13)	248	76	85	48	10	158	13	0	3	12	5	.71	12	.257	.327	.434
1990 Montreal	NL	155	579	148	29	0	20	(6	14)	237	65	87	40	8	169	4	0	5	10	1	.91	14	.256	.306	.409
1991 Montreal	NL	107	375	82	13	2	9	(3	6)	126	34	33	23	5	86	2	0	0	5	6	.45	6	.219	.268	.336
1992 St. Louis	NL	95	325	79	14	2	10	(4	6)	127	38	39	11	0	69	8	0	3	5	4	.56	8	.243	.282	.391
1993 Colorado	NL	120	470	174	35	4	22	(13	9)	283	71	98	24	12	73	6	0	6	2	4	.33	9	.370	.403	.602
1994 Colorado	NL	103	417	133	21	0	31	(18	13)	247	77	85	19	8	93	8	0	3	8	3	.73	10	.319	.356	.592
1995 Colorado	NL	143	554	155	29	3	31	(18	13)	283	89	106	32	6	146	13	0	5	12	2	.86	14	.280	.331	.511
1996 Colorado	NL	159	626	190	39	3	47	(32	15)	376	119	150	40	4	157	17	0	7	18	6	.69	6	.304	.357	.601
1997 Colorado	NL	154	600	191	31	3	41	(21	20)	351	120	140	54	2	141	17	0	3	15	8	.65	16	.318	.389	.585
13 ML YEARS		1621	6074	1752	337	29	288	(151	137)	3011	908	1051	908	81	1469	112	1	46	114	62	.65	126	.288	.342	.496

Mike Gallego

Bats: R **Throws:** R **Pos:** 2B-11; SS-10; 3B-7; PH-7   **Ht:** 5'8"   **Wt:** 175   **Born:** 10/31/60   **Age:** 37

							BATTING											BASERUNNING				PERCENTAGES		
Year Team	Lg	G	AB	H	2B	3B	HR	(Hm | Rd)	TB	R	RBI	TBB	IBB	SO	HBP	SH	SF	SB	CS	SB%	GDP	Avg	OBP	SLG
1997 Louisville *	AAA	6	18	5	1	0	0	—	—	6	0	1	3	1	5	1	0	1	1	1	.50	1	.278	.391	.333
1985 Oakland	AL	76	77	16	5	1	1	(0 | 1)	26	13	9	12	0	14	1	2	1	1	1	.50	2	.208	.319	.338
1986 Oakland	AL	20	37	10	2	0	0	(0 | 0)	12	2	4	1	0	6	0	2	0	0	2	.00	0	.270	.289	.324
1987 Oakland	AL	72	124	31	6	0	2	(0 | 2)	43	18	14	12	0	21	1	5	1	0	1	.00	5	.250	.319	.347
1988 Oakland	AL	129	277	58	8	0	2	(2 | 0)	72	38	20	34	0	53	1	8	0	2	3	.40	6	.209	.298	.260
1989 Oakland	AL	133	357	90	14	2	3	(2 | 1)	117	45	30	35	0	43	6	8	3	7	5	.58	10	.252	.327	.328
1990 Oakland	AL	140	389	80	13	2	3	(1 | 2)	106	36	34	35	0	50	4	17	2	5	5	.50	13	.206	.277	.272
1991 Oakland	AL	159	482	119	15	4	12	(6 | 6)	178	67	49	67	3	84	5	10	3	6	9	.40	8	.247	.343	.369
1992 New York	AL	53	173	44	7	1	3	(1 | 2)	62	24	14	20	0	22	4	3	1	0	1	.00	5	.254	.343	.358
1993 New York	AL	119	403	114	20	1	10	(5 | 5)	166	63	54	50	0	65	4	3	5	3	2	.60	16	.283	.364	.412
1994 New York	AL	89	306	73	17	1	6	(2 | 4)	110	39	41	38	1	46	4	5	4	0	1	.00	5	.239	.327	.359
1995 Oakland	AL	43	120	28	0	0	0	(0 | 0)	28	11	8	9	0	24	1	2	0	0	1	.00	3	.233	.292	.233
1996 St. Louis	NL	51	143	30	2	0	0	(0 | 0)	32	12	4	12	1	31	1	3	0	0	0	.00	0	.210	.276	.224
1997 St. Louis	NL	27	43	7	2	0	0	(0 | 0)	9	6	1	1	0	6	0	1	1	0	0	.00	1	.163	.178	.209
13 ML YEARS		1111	2931	700	111	12	42	(19 | 23)	961	374	282	326	5	465	32	69	21	24	31	.44	72	.239	.320	.328

Ron Gant

Bats: Right **Throws:** Right **Pos:** LF-128; PH-13; DH-1   **Ht:** 6'0"   **Wt:** 200   **Born:** 3/2/65   **Age:** 33

							BATTING											BASERUNNING				PERCENTAGES		
Year Team	Lg	G	AB	H	2B	3B	HR	(Hm	Rd)	TB	R	RBI	TBB	IBB	SO	HBP	SH	SF	SB	CS	SB%	GDP	Avg	OBP	SLG
1987 Atlanta	NL	21	83	22	4	0	2	(1	1)	32	9	9	1	0	11	0	1	1	4	2	.67	3	.265	.271	.386
1988 Atlanta	NL	146	563	146	28	8	19	(7	12)	247	85	60	46	4	118	3	2	4	19	10	.66	7	.259	.317	.439
1989 Atlanta	NL	75	260	46	8	3	9	(5	4)	87	26	25	20	0	63	1	2	2	9	6	.60	0	.177	.237	.335
1990 Atlanta	NL	152	575	174	34	3	32	(18	14)	310	107	84	50	0	86	1	1	4	33	16	.67	8	.303	.357	.539
1991 Atlanta	NL	154	561	141	35	3	32	(18	14)	278	101	105	71	8	104	5	0	5	34	15	.69	6	.251	.338	.496
1992 Atlanta	NL	153	544	141	22	6	17	(10	7)	226	74	80	45	5	101	7	0	6	32	10	.76	10	.259	.321	.415
1993 Atlanta	NL	157	606	166	27	4	36	(17	19)	309	113	117	67	2	117	2	0	7	26	9	.74	14	.274	.345	.510
1995 Cincinnati	NL	119	410	113	19	4	29	(12	17)	227	79	88	74	5	108	3	1	5	23	8	.74	11	.276	.386	.554
1996 St. Louis	NL	122	419	103	14	2	30	(17	13)	211	74	82	73	5	98	3	1	4	13	4	.76	9	.246	.359	.504
1997 St. Louis	NL	139	502	115	21	4	17	(11	6)	195	68	62	58	3	162	1	0	1	14	6	.70	2	.229	.310	.388
10 ML YEARS		1238	4523	1167	212	37	223	(116	107)	2122	736	712	505	32	968	26	8	39	207	86	.71	70	.258	.333	.469

Rich Garces

Pitches: Right **Bats:** Right **Pos:** RP-12   **Ht:** 6'0"   **Wt:** 215   **Born:** 5/18/71   **Age:** 27

		HOW MUCH HE PITCHED						WHAT HE GAVE UP												THE RESULTS					
Year Team	Lg	G	GS	CG	GF	IP	BFP	H	R	ER	HR	SH	SF	HB	TBB	IBB	SO	WP	Bk	W	L	Pct.	ShO	Sv-Op	Hld	ERA
1997 Pawtucket *	AAA	26	0	0	16	31	126	24	5	5	0	3	0	1	13	3	42	4	0	2	1	.667	0	5--	—	1.45
1990 Minnesota	AL	5	0	0	3	5.2	24	4	2	1	0	0	0	0	4	0	-1	0	0	0	0	.000	0	2-2	0	1.59
1993 Minnesota	AL	3	0	0	1	4	18	4	2	0	0	0	0	0	2	0	3	0	0	0	0	.000	0	0-0	0	0.00
1995 ChN-Fla	NL	18	0	0	7	24.1	108	25	15	12	1	1	0	0	11	2	22	0	0	0	2	.000	0	0-1	1	4.44
1996 Boston	AL	37	0	0	9	44	205	42	26	24	5	0	5	0	33	5	55	0	0	3	2	.600	0	0-2	4	4.91
1997 Boston	AL	12	0	0	4	13.2	66	14	9	7	2	0	1	1	9	0	12	0	0	0	1	.000	0	0-2	1	4.61
1995 Chicago	NL	7	0	0	4	11	46	11	6	4	0	0	0	0	3	0	6	0	0	0	0	.000	0	0-0	0	3.27
Florida	NL	11	0	0	3	13.1	62	14	9	8	1	1	0	0	8	2	16	0	0	0	2	.000	0	0-1	1	5.40
5 ML YEARS		75	0	0	24	91.2	421	89	54	44	8	1	6	1	59	7	93	0	0	3	5	.375	0	2-7	6	4.32

Carlos Garcia

Bats: R **Throws:** R **Pos:** 2B-96; SS-5; 3B-4; PH-3   **Ht:** 6'1"   **Wt:** 205   **Born:** 10/15/67   **Age:** 30

							BATTING											BASERUNNING				PERCENTAGES		
Year Team	Lg	G	AB	H	2B	3B	HR	(Hm	Rd)	TB	R	RBI	TBB	IBB	SO	HBP	SH	SF	SB	CS	SB%	GDP	Avg	OBP	SLG
1990 Pittsburgh	NL	4	4	2	0	0	0	(0	0)	2	1	0	0	0	2	0	0	0	0	0	.00	0	.500	.500	.500
1991 Pittsburgh	NL	12	24	6	0	2	0	(0	0)	10	2	1	1	0	8	0	0	0	0	0	.00	1	.250	.280	.417
1992 Pittsburgh	NL	22	39	8	1	0	0	(0	0)	9	4	4	0	0	9	0	1	2	0	0	.00	1	.205	.195	.231
1993 Pittsburgh	NL	141	546	147	25	5	12	(7	5)	218	77	47	31	2	67	9	6	5	18	11	.62	9	.269	.316	.399
1994 Pittsburgh	NL	98	412	114	15	2	6	(4	2)	151	49	28	16	2	67	4	1	1	18	9	.67	6	.277	.309	.367
1995 Pittsburgh	NL	104	367	108	24	2	6	(4	2)	154	41	50	25	5	55	2	5	3	8	4	.67	4	.294	.340	.420
1996 Pittsburgh	NL	101	390	111	18	4	6	(3	3)	155	66	44	23	3	58	4	3	2	16	6	.73	3	.285	.329	.397
1997 Toronto	AL	103	350	77	18	2	3	(0	3)	108	29	23	15	0	60	2	10	4	11	3	.79	7	.220	.253	.309
8 ML YEARS		585	2132	573	101	17	33	(18	15)	807	269	197	111	12	326	21	26	17	71	33	.68	31	.269	.309	.379

Freddy Garcia

Bats: Right **Throws:** Right **Pos:** 3B-10; PH-9; 1B-2   **Ht:** 6'2"   **Wt:** 205   **Born:** 8/1/72   **Age:** 25

							BATTING											BASERUNNING				PERCENTAGES		
Year Team	Lg	G	AB	H	2B	3B	HR	(Hm	Rd)	TB	R	RBI	TBB	IBB	SO	HBP	SH	SF	SB	CS	SB%	GDP	Avg	OBP	SLG
1993 Medicne Hat	R+	72	264	63	8	2	11	—	—	108	47	42	31	1	71	2	1	4	4	5	.44	3	.239	.319	.409
1994 St. Cathrns	A-	73	260	74	10	2	13	—	—	127	46	40	33	1	57	2	1	3	1	3	.25	6	.285	.366	.488
1996 Lynchburg	A+	129	474	145	39	3	21	—	—	253	79	86	44	2	86	1	0	12	4	2	.67	10	.306	.358	.534
1997 Calgary	AAA	35	121	29	6	0	5	—	—	50	21	17	9	3	20	1	0	2	0	0	.00	8	.240	.293	.413
Carolina	AA	73	282	82	17	4	19	—	—	164	47	57	18	2	56	6	0	1	0	1	.00	11	.291	.342	.582
1995 Pittsburgh	NL	42	57	8	1	1	0	(0	0)	11	5	1	8	0	17	0	1	0	0	1	.00	0	.140	.246	.193
1997 Pittsburgh	NL	20	40	6	1	0	3	(0	3)	16	4	5	2	0	17	0	0	0	0	0	.00	0	.150	.190	.400

Year Team	Lg	G	AB	H	2B	3B	HR	(Hm	Rd)	TB	R	RBI	TBB	IBB	SO	HBP	SH	SF	SB	CS	SB%	GDP	Avg	OBP	SLG
2 ML YEARS		62	97	14	2	1	3	(0	3)	27	9	6	10	0	34	0	1	0	0	1	.00	0	.144	.224	.278

Karim Garcia

Bats: Left **Throws:** Left **Pos:** LF-12; PH-5; RF-2 **Ht:** 6'0" **Wt:** 172 **Born:** 10/29/75 **Age:** 22

Year Team	Lg	G	AB	H	2B	3B	HR	(Hm	Rd)	TB	R	RBI	TBB	IBB	SO	HBP	SH	SF	SB	CS	SB%	GDP	Avg	OBP	SLG
1993 Bakersfield	A+	123	460	111	20	9	19	—	—	206	61	54	37	4	109	2	0	2	5	3	.63	5	.241	.299	.448
1994 Vero Beach	A+	121	452	120	28	10	21	—	—	231	72	84	37	8	112	1	0	6	8	3	.73	7	.265	.319	.511
1995 Albuquerque	AAA	124	474	151	26	10	20	—	—	257	88	91	38	5	102	2	2	3	12	6	.67	12	.319	.369	.542
1996 San Antonio	AA	35	129	32	6	1	5	—	—	55	21	22	9	0	38	0	0	0	1	1	.50	1	.248	.297	.426
Albuquerque	AAA	84	327	97	17	10	13	—	—	173	54	58	29	8	67	1	0	3	6	4	.60	9	.297	.353	.529
1997 Albuquerque	AAA	71	262	80	17	6	20	—	—	169	53	66	23	4	70	0	1	0	11	5	.69	4	.305	.361	.645
1995 Los Angeles	NL	13	20	4	0	0	0	(0	0)	4	1	0	0	0	4	0	0	0	0	0	.00	0	.200	.200	.200
1996 Los Angeles	NL	1	1	0	0	0	0	(0	0)	0	0	0	0	0	1	0	0	0	0	0	.00	0	.000	.000	.000
1997 Los Angeles	NL	15	39	5	0	0	1	(0	1)	8	5	8	6	1	14	0	0	1	0	0	.00	0	.128	.239	.205
3 ML YEARS		29	60	9	0	0	1	(0	1)	12	6	8	6	1	19	0	0	1	0	0	.00	0	.150	.224	.200

Ramon Garcia

Pitches: Right **Bats:** Right **Pos:** RP-22; SP-20 **Ht:** 6'2" **Wt:** 200 **Born:** 12/9/69 **Age:** 28

Year Team	Lg	G	GS	CG	GF	IP	BFP	H	R	ER	HR	SH	SF	HB	TBB	IBB	SO	WP	Bk	W	L	Pct.	ShO	Sv-Op	Hld	ERA
1991 Chicago	AL	16	15	0	0	78.1	332	79	50	47	13	3	2	2	31	2	40	0	2	4	4	.500	0	0-0	0	5.40
1996 Milwaukee	AL	37	2	0	14	75.2	326	84	58	56	17	1	5	6	21	3	40	2	1	4	4	.500	0	4-7	6	6.66
1997 Houston	NL	42	20	1	5	158.2	665	155	71	65	20	10	2	9	52	1	120	3	2	9	8	.529	1	1-1	1	3.69
3 ML YEARS		95	37	1	19	312.2	1323	318	179	168	50	14	9	17	104	6	200	5	5	17	16	.515	1	5-8	7	4.84

Nomar Garciaparra

Bats: Right **Throws:** Right **Pos:** SS-153; PH-1 **Ht:** 6'0" **Wt:** 167 **Born:** 7/23/73 **Age:** 24

Year Team	Lg	G	AB	H	2B	3B	HR	(Hm	Rd)	TB	R	RBI	TBB	IBB	SO	HBP	SH	SF	SB	CS	SB%	GDP	Avg	OBP	SLG
1994 Sarasota	A+	28	105	31	8	1	1	—	—	44	20	16	10	0	6	1	3	2	5	2	.71	2	.295	.356	.419
1995 Trenton	AA	125	513	137	20	8	8	—	—	197	77	47	50	3	42	8	4	6	35	12	.74	10	.267	.338	.384
1996 Red Sox	R	5	14	4	2	1	0	—	—	8	4	5	1	1	0	1	0	0	0	0	.00	1	.286	.375	.571
Pawtucket	AAA	43	172	59	15	2	16	—	—	126	40	46	14	0	21	1	0	4	3	1	.75	6	.343	.387	.733
1996 Boston	AL	24	87	21	2	3	4	(3	1)	41	11	16	4	0	14	0	1	1	5	0	1.00	0	.241	.272	.471
1997 Boston	AL	153	684	209	44	11	30	(11	19)	365	122	98	35	2	92	6	2	7	22	9	.71	9	.306	.342	.534
2 ML YEARS		177	771	230	46	14	34	(14	20)	406	133	114	39	2	106	6	3	8	27	9	.75	9	.298	.334	.527

Mark Gardner

Pitches: Right **Bats:** Right **Pos:** SP-30 **Ht:** 6'1" **Wt:** 205 **Born:** 3/1/62 **Age:** 36

Year Team	Lg	G	GS	CG	GF	IP	BFP	H	R	ER	HR	SH	SF	HB	TBB	IBB	SO	WP	Bk	W	L	Pct.	ShO	Sv-Op	Hld	ERA
1989 Montreal	NL	7	4	0	1	26.1	117	26	16	15	2	0	0	2	11	1	21	0	0	0	3	.000	0	0-0	0	5.13
1990 Montreal	NL	27	26	3	1	152.2	642	129	62	58	13	4	7	9	61	5	135	2	4	7	9	.438	3	0-0	0	3.42
1991 Montreal	NL	27	27	0	0	168.1	692	139	78	72	17	7	2	4	75	1	107	2	1	9	11	.450	0	0-0	0	3.85
1992 Montreal	NL	33	30	0	1	179.2	778	179	91	87	15	12	7	9	60	2	132	2	0	12	10	.545	0	0-0	0	4.36
1993 Kansas City	AL	17	16	0	0	91.2	387	92	65	63	17	1	7	4	36	0	54	2	0	4	6	.400	0	0-0	0	6.19
1994 Florida	NL	20	14	0	3	92.1	391	97	53	50	14	4	5	1	30	2	57	3	1	4	4	.500	0	0-0	0	4.87
1995 Florida	NL	39	11	1	7	102.1	456	109	60	51	14	7	0	5	43	5	87	3	1	5	5	.500	1	1-1	4	4.49
1996 San Francisco	NL	30	28	4	0	179.1	782	200	105	88	28	6	5	8	57	3	145	2	0	12	7	.632	1	0-0	1	4.42
1997 San Francisco	NL	30	30	2	0	180.1	764	188	92	86	28	10	6	1	57	6	136	3	3	12	9	.571	0	0-0	0	4.29
9 ML YEARS		230	186	10	13	1173	5009	1159	622	570	148	51	39	43	430	25	874	19	10	65	64	.504	6	1-1	5	4.37

Brent Gates

Bats: B **Throws:** R **Pos:** 3B-32; 2B-21; PH-17; SS-5; DH-1; 1B-1; LF-1 **Ht:** 6'1" **Wt:** 180 **Born:** 3/14/70 **Age:** 28

Year Team	Lg	G	AB	H	2B	3B	HR	(Hm	Rd)	TB	R	RBI	TBB	IBB	SO	HBP	SH	SF	SB	CS	SB%	GDP	Avg	OBP	SLG
1997 Tacoma *	AAA	7	33	15	3	0	0	—	—	18	7	6	4	0	2	0	0	0	0	0	.00	0	.455	.514	.545
1993 Oakland	AL	139	535	155	29	2	7	(4	3)	209	64	69	56	4	75	4	6	8	7	3	.70	17	.290	.357	.391
1994 Oakland	AL	64	233	66	11	1	2	(0	2)	85	29	24	21	1	32	1	3	6	3	0	1.00	8	.283	.337	.365
1995 Oakland	AL	136	524	133	24	4	5	(3	2)	180	60	56	46	2	84	0	4	11	3	3	.50	15	.254	.308	.344
1996 Oakland	AL	64	247	65	19	2	2	(1	1)	94	26	30	18	0	35	2	5	2	1	1	.50	9	.263	.316	.381
1997 Seattle	AL	65	151	36	8	0	3	(1	2)	53	18	20	14	0	21	0	2	3	0	0	.00	6	.238	.298	.351
5 ML YEARS		468	1690	455	91	9	19	(9	10)	621	197	199	155	7	247	7	20	30	14	7	.67	55	.269	.328	.367

Jason Giambi

Bats: L **Throws:** R **Pos:** LF-68; 1B-51; DH-25; PH-5 **Ht:** 6'2" **Wt:** 200 **Born:** 1/8/71 **Age:** 27

Year Team	Lg	G	AB	H	2B	3B	HR	(Hm	Rd)	TB	R	RBI	TBB	IBB	SO	HBP	SH	SF	SB	CS	SB%	GDP	Avg	OBP	SLG
1995 Oakland	AL	54	176	45	7	0	6	(3	3)	70	27	25	28	0	31	3	1	2	2	1	.67	4	.256	.364	.398

BATTING / BASERUNNING / PERCENTAGES

Year Team	Lg	G	AB	H	2B	3B	HR	(Hm Rd)	TB	R	RBI	TBB	IBB	SO	HBP	SH	SF	SB	CS	SB%	GDP	Avg	OBP	SLG
1996 Oakland	AL	140	536	156	40	1	20	(6 14)	258	84	79	51	3	95	5	1	5	0	1	.00	15	.291	.355	.481
1997 Oakland	AL	142	519	152	41	2	20	(14 6)	257	66	81	55	3	89	6	0	8	0	1	.00	11	.293	.362	.495
3 ML YEARS		336	1231	353	88	3	46	(23 23)	585	177	185	134	6	215	14	2	15	2	3	.40	30	.287	.359	.475

Benji Gil

Bats: Right Throws: Right Pos: SS-106; PH-6; DH-3

Ht: 6'2" Wt: 182 Born: 10/6/72 Age: 25

Year Team	Lg	G	AB	H	2B	3B	HR	(Hm Rd)	TB	R	RBI	TBB	IBB	SO	HBP	SH	SF	SB	CS	SB%	GDP	Avg	OBP	SLG
1993 Texas	AL	22	57	7	0	0	0	(0 0)	7	3	2	5	0	22	0	4	0	1	2	.33	0	.123	.194	.123
1995 Texas	AL	130	415	91	20	3	9	(5 4)	144	36	46	26	0	147	1	10	2	2	4	.33	5	.219	.266	.347
1996 Texas	AL	5	5	2	0	0	0	(0 0)	2	0	1	1	0	1	0	1	0	0	1	.00	0	.400	.500	.400
1997 Texas	AL	110	317	71	13	2	5	(3 2)	103	35	31	17	0	96	1	6	4	1	2	.33	3	.224	.263	.325
4 ML YEARS		267	794	171	33	5	14	(8 6)	256	74	80	49	0	266	2	21	6	4	9	.31	8	.215	.261	.322

Shawn Gilbert

Bats: R Throws: R Pos: PH-18; 2B-8; SS-6; 3B-3; LF-1

Ht: 5'9" Wt: 185 Born: 3/12/68 Age: 30

Year Team	Lg	G	AB	H	2B	3B	HR	(Hm Rd)	TB	R	RBI	TBB	IBB	SO	HBP	SH	SF	SB	CS	SB%	GDP	Avg	OBP	SLG
1987 Visalia	A+	82	272	61	5	0	5	— —	81	39	27	34	0	59	1	4	4	6	4	.60	8	.224	.322	.298
1988 Visalia	A+	14	43	16	3	2	0	— —	23	10	8	10	0	7	1	0	1	1	1	.50	0	.372	.500	.535
Kenosha	A	108	402	112	21	2	3	— —	146	80	44	63	2	61	2	0	5	49	10	.83	6	.279	.375	.363
1989 Visalia	A+	125	453	113	17	1	2	— —	138	52	43	54	1	70	3	6	3	42	16	.72	11	.249	.331	.305
1990 Orlando	AA	138	529	135	12	5	3	— —	144	68	44	61	0	69	5	4	3	31	9	.78	10	.255	.332	.314
1991 Orlando	AA	123	433	110	18	2	4	— —	166	69	38	53	1	70	11	6	6	43	19	.69	10	.255	.332	.314
1992 Portland	AAA	138	444	109	17	2	3	— —	139	60	52	36	2	55	4	5	2	31	8	.79	10	.245	.307	.313
1993 Nashville	AAA	104	278	63	17	2	0	— —	84	28	17	12	0	41	2	2	1	6	2	.75	4	.227	.263	.302
1994 Scranton-WB	AAA	141	547	139	33	4	7	— —	201	81	52	66	3	86	7	3	3	20	15	.57	9	.254	.340	.367
1995 Scranton-WB	AAA	136	536	141	26	2	2	— —	177	84	42	64	0	102	6	4	4	17	9	.65	10	.263	.346	.330
1996 Norfolk	AAA	131	493	126	28	1	9	— —	183	76	50	46	0	97	5	14	4	17	9	.65	15	.256	.323	.371
1997 Norfolk	AAA	78	288	76	13	1	8	— —	115	53	33	43	1	64	2	3	1	16	4	.80	5	.264	.362	.399
1997 New York	NL	29	22	3	0	0	1	(1 0)	6	3	1	1	0	8	0	0	0	1	0	1.00	0	.136	.174	.273

Brian Giles

Bats: L Throws: L Pos: LF-82; RF-25; CF-20; PH-19; DH-9

Ht: 5'11" Wt: 195 Born: 1/21/71 Age: 27

Year Team	Lg	G	AB	H	2B	3B	HR	(Hm Rd)	TB	R	RBI	TBB	IBB	SO	HBP	SH	SF	SB	CS	SB%	GDP	Avg	OBP	SLG
1995 Cleveland	AL	6	9	5	0	0	1	(0 1)	8	6	3	0	0	1	0	0	0	0	0	.00	0	.556	.556	.889
1996 Cleveland	AL	51	121	43	14	1	5	(2 3)	74	26	27	19	4	13	0	0	3	3	0	1.00	6	.355	.434	.612
1997 Cleveland	AL	130	377	101	15	3	17	(7 10)	173	62	61	63	2	50	1	3	7	13	3	.81	10	.268	.368	.459
3 ML YEARS		187	507	149	29	4	23	(9 14)	255	94	91	82	6	64	1	3	10	16	3	.84	16	.294	.387	.503

Bernard Gilkey

Bats: R Throws: R Pos: LF-136; PH-9; DH-2; CF-1

Ht: 6'0" Wt: 200 Born: 9/24/66 Age: 31

Year Team	Lg	G	AB	H	2B	3B	HR	(Hm Rd)	TB	R	RBI	TBB	IBB	SO	HBP	SH	SF	SB	CS	SB%	GDP	Avg	OBP	SLG
1990 St. Louis	NL	18	64	19	5	2	1	(0 1)	31	11	3	8	0	5	0	0	0	6	1	.86	1	.297	.375	.484
1991 St. Louis	NL	81	268	58	7	2	5	(2 3)	84	28	20	39	0	33	1	1	2	14	8	.64	14	.216	.316	.313
1992 St. Louis	NL	131	384	116	19	4	7	(3 4)	164	56	43	39	1	52	1	3	4	18	12	.60	5	.302	.364	.427
1993 St. Louis	NL	137	557	170	40	5	16	(7 9)	268	99	70	56	2	66	4	0	5	15	8	.65	6	.305	.370	.481
1994 St. Louis	NL	105	380	96	22	1	6	(1 5)	138	52	45	39	2	65	10	0	2	15	8	.65	6	.253	.336	.363
1995 St. Louis	NL	121	480	143	33	4	17	(5 12)	235	73	69	42	3	70	5	1	3	12	6	.67	17	.298	.358	.490
1996 New York	NL	153	571	181	44	3	30	(14 16)	321	108	117	73	7	125	4	0	7	17	9	.65	18	.317	.393	.562
1997 New York	NL	145	518	129	31	1	18	(7 11)	216	85	78	70	1	111	6	0	12	7	11	.39	9	.249	.338	.417
8 ML YEARS		891	3222	912	201	22	100	(38 62)	1457	512	445	366	16	527	31	5	36	104	65	.62	86	.283	.358	.452

Ed Giovanola

Bats: Left Throws: Right Pos: 3B-8; PH-7; 2B-1; SS-1

Ht: 5'10" Wt: 170 Born: 3/4/69 Age: 29

Year Team	Lg	G	AB	H	2B	3B	HR	(Hm Rd)	TB	R	RBI	TBB	IBB	SO	HBP	SH	SF	SB	CS	SB%	GDP	Avg	OBP	SLG
1990 Idaho Falls	R+	25	98	38	6	0	0	— —	44	25	13	17	0	9	0	2	1	6	2	.75	0	.388	.474	.449
Sumter	A	35	119	29	4	0	0	— —	33	20	8	34	1	17	0	3	0	8	6	.57	0	.244	.412	.277
1991 Durham	A+	101	299	76	9	0	6	— —	103	50	27	57	1	39	2	0	3	18	11	.62	6	.254	.374	.344
1992 Greenville	AA	75	270	72	5	0	5	— —	92	39	30	29	2	40	0	1	2	4	1	.80	1	.267	.336	.341
1993 Greenville	AA	120	384	108	21	5	5	— —	154	70	43	84	3	49	2	4	6	6	7	.46	11	.281	.408	.401
1994 Greenville	AA	25	84	20	6	1	4	— —	40	13	16	10	1	12	0	1	0	2	0	1.00	0	.238	.319	.476
Richmond	AAA	98	344	97	16	2	6	— —	135	48	30	31	5	49	3	5	2	4	2	.64	5	.282	.345	.392
1995 Richmond	AAA	99	321	103	18	2	4	— —	137	45	36	55	3	37	1	4	4	6	2	.75	10	.321	.417	.427
1996 Richmond	AAA	62	210	62	15	1	3	— —	88	29	16	37	3	34	1	4	0	2	2	.50	8	.295	.385	.390
1997 Richmond	AAA	116	395	115	23	5	2	— —	154	65	46	64	0	56	1	11	7	2	2	.50	8	.291	.385	.390
1995 Atlanta	NL	13	14	1	0	0	0	(0 0)	1	2	0	3	0	5	0	0	0	1	0	1.00	3	.071	.235	.071
1996 Atlanta	NL	43	82	19	2	0	0	(0 0)	21	10	7	8	0	13	0	0	0	1	0	1.00	2	.232	.304	.256
1997 Atlanta	NL	14	8	2	0	0	0	(0 0)	2	0	0	2	1	1	0	0	0	0	0		2	.250	.400	.250

Year Team	Lg	G	AB	H	2B	3B	HR	(Hm	Rd)	TB	R	RBI	TBB	IBB	SO	HBP	SH	SF	SB	CS	SB%	GDP	Avg	OBP	SLG
3 ML YEARS		70	104	22	2	0	0	(0	0)	24	12	7	13	1	19	1	2	1	1	0	1.00	6	.212	.303	.231

Joe Girardi

Bats: Right **Throws:** Right **Pos:** C-111; PH-1 **Ht:** 5'11" **Wt:** 195 **Born:** 10/14/64 **Age:** 33

Year Team	Lg	G	AB	H	2B	3B	HR	(Hm	Rd)	TB	R	RBI	TBB	IBB	SO	HBP	SH	SF	SB	CS	SB%	GDP	Avg	OBP	SLG
1989 Chicago	NL	59	157	39	10	0	1	(0	1)	52	15	14	11	5	26	2	1	1	2	1	.67	4	.248	.304	.331
1990 Chicago	NL	133	419	113	24	2	1	(1	0)	144	36	38	17	11	50	3	4	4	8	3	.73	13	.270	.300	.344
1991 Chicago	NL	21	47	9	2	0	0	(0	0)	11	3	6	6	1	6	0	1	0	0	0	.00	0	.191	.283	.234
1992 Chicago	NL	91	270	73	3	1	1	(1	0)	81	19	12	19	3	38	1	0	1	0	2	.00	8	.270	.320	.300
1993 Colorado	NL	86	310	90	14	5	3	(2	1)	123	35	31	24	0	41	3	12	1	6	6	.50	6	.290	.346	.397
1994 Colorado	NL	93	330	91	9	4	4	(1	3)	120	47	34	21	1	48	2	6	2	3	3	.50	13	.276	.321	.364
1995 Colorado	NL	125	462	121	17	2	8	(6	2)	166	63	55	29	0	76	2	12	1	3	3	.50	13	.262	.308	.359
1996 New York	AL	124	422	124	22	3	2	(1	1)	158	55	45	30	1	55	5	11	3	13	4	.76	11	.294	.346	.374
1997 New York	AL	112	398	105	23	1	1	(1	0)	133	38	50	26	1	53	2	5	2	2	3	.40	15	.264	.311	.334
9 ML YEARS		844	2815	765	124	18	21	(13	8)	988	311	285	183	23	393	20	52	15	37	25	.60	85	.272	.319	.351

Doug Glanville

Bats: R **Throws:** R **Pos:** LF-120; CF-30; PH-23; RF-1 **Ht:** 6'2" **Wt:** 170 **Born:** 8/25/70 **Age:** 27

Year Team	Lg	G	AB	H	2B	3B	HR	(Hm	Rd)	TB	R	RBI	TBB	IBB	SO	HBP	SH	SF	SB	CS	SB%	GDP	Avg	OBP	SLG
1991 Geneva	A-	36	152	46	8	0	2	—	—	60	29	12	11	0	25	1	3	1	17	3	.85	1	.303	.352	.395
1992 Winston-Sal	A+	120	485	125	18	4	4	—	—	163	72	36	40	1	78	4	9	2	32	9	.78	6	.258	.318	.336
1993 Daytona	A+	61	239	70	10	1	2	—	—	88	47	21	28	0	24	3	4	0	18	15	.55	2	.293	.374	.368
Orlando	AA	73	295	78	14	4	9	—	—	127	42	40	12	0	40	2	6	5	15	7	.68	1	.264	.293	.431
1994 Orlando	AA	130	483	127	22	2	5	—	—	168	53	52	24	4	49	5	10	7	26	20	.57	7	.263	.301	.348
1995 Iowa	AAA	112	419	113	16	2	4	—	—	145	48	37	16	0	64	3	7	4	13	9	.59	4	.270	.299	.346
1996 Iowa	AAA	90	373	115	23	3	3	—	—	153	53	34	12	1	35	2	7	3	15	10	.60	2	.308	.331	.410
1996 Chicago	NL	49	83	20	5	1	1	(1	0)	30	10	10	3	0	11	0	2	1	2	0	1.00	0	.241	.264	.361
1997 Chicago	NL	146	474	142	22	5	4	(2	2)	186	79	35	24	0	46	1	9	2	19	11	.63	9	.300	.333	.392
2 ML YEARS		195	557	162	27	6	5	(3	2)	216	89	45	27	0	57	1	11	3	21	11	.66	9	.291	.323	.388

Tom Glavine

Pitches: Left **Bats:** Left **Pos:** SP-33 **Ht:** 6'1" **Wt:** 185 **Born:** 3/25/66 **Age:** 32

Year Team	Lg	G	GS	CG	GF	IP	BFP	H	R	ER	HR	SH	SF	HB	TBB	IBB	SO	WP	Bk	W	L	Pct.	ShO	Sv-Op	Hld	ERA
1987 Atlanta	NL	9	9	0	0	50.1	238	55	34	31	5	2	3	3	33	4	20	1	1	2	4	.333	0	0-0	0	5.54
1988 Atlanta	NL	34	34	1	0	195.1	844	201	111	99	12	17	11	8	63	7	84	2	2	7	17	.292	0	0-0	0	4.56
1989 Atlanta	NL	29	29	6	0	186	766	172	88	76	20	11	4	2	40	3	90	2	0	14	8	.636	4	0-0	0	3.68
1990 Atlanta	NL	33	33	1	0	214.1	929	232	111	91	18	21	7	1	78	10	129	8	1	10	12	.455	0	0-0	0	4.28
1991 Atlanta	NL	34	34	9	0	246.2	989	201	83	70	17	7	6	2	69	6	192	10	2	20	11	.645	1	0-0	0	2.55
1992 Atlanta	NL	33	33	7	0	225	919	197	81	69	6	2	6	2	70	7	129	5	0	20	8	.714	5	0-0	0	2.76
1993 Atlanta	NL	36	36	4	0	239.1	1014	236	91	85	16	10	2	2	90	7	120	4	0	22	6	.786	2	0-0	0	3.20
1994 Atlanta	NL	25	25	2	0	165.1	731	173	76	73	10	9	6	1	70	10	140	8	1	13	9	.591	0	0-0	0	3.97
1995 Atlanta	NL	29	29	3	0	198.2	822	182	76	68	9	7	5	5	66	0	127	3	0	16	7	.696	1	0-0	0	3.08
1996 Atlanta	NL	36	36	1	0	235.1	994	222	91	78	14	15	2	0	85	7	181	4	0	15	10	.600	1	0-0	0	2.98
1997 Atlanta	NL	33	33	5	0	240	970	197	86	79	20	11	6	4	79	9	152	3	0	14	7	.667	2	0-0	0	2.96
11 ML YEARS		331	331	39	0	2196.1	9216	2068	928	830	147	112	53	30	743	70	1364	50	7	153	99	.607	15	0-0	0	3.40

Wayne Gomes

Pitches: Right **Bats:** Right **Pos:** RP-37 **Ht:** 6'2" **Wt:** 226 **Born:** 1/15/73 **Age:** 25

Year Team	Lg	G	GS	CG	GF	IP	BFP	H	R	ER	HR	SH	SF	HB	TBB	IBB	SO	WP	Bk	W	L	Pct.	ShO	Sv-Op	Hld	ERA
1993 Batavia	A-	5	0	0	3	7.1	32	1	1	1	0	0	0	0	8	0	11	0	1	1	0	1.000	0	4--	—	1.23
Clearwater	A+	9	0	0	8	7.2	37	1	1	1	0	0	0	0	9	0	13	2	0	0	0	.000	0	4--	—	1.17
1994 Clearwater	A+	23	21	1	0	104.1	474	85	63	55	5	2	4	3	82	1	102	27	4	6	8	.429	1	0--	—	4.74
1995 Reading	AA	22	22	1	0	104.2	462	89	54	46	8	3	1	1	70	2	102	6	6	7	4	.636	1	0--	—	3.96
1996 Reading	AA	67	0	0	55	64.1	291	53	35	32	7	1	3	1	48	3	79	14	0	0	4	.000	0	24--	—	4.48
1997 Scranton-WB	AAA	26	0	0	15	38	166	31	11	10	2	1	1	0	24	2	36	2	0	3	1	.750	0	7--	—	2.37
1997 Philadelphia	NL	37	0	0	13	42.2	191	45	26	25	4	2	0	1	24	0	24	2	0	5	1	.833	0	0-1	3	5.27

Chris Gomez

Bats: Right **Throws:** Right **Pos:** SS-150; PH-1 **Ht:** 6'1" **Wt:** 188 **Born:** 6/16/71 **Age:** 27

Year Team	Lg	G	AB	H	2B	3B	HR	(Hm	Rd)	TB	R	RBI	TBB	IBB	SO	HBP	SH	SF	SB	CS	SB%	GDP	Avg	OBP	SLG
1993 Detroit	AL	46	128	32	7	1	0	(0	0)	41	11	11	9	0	17	1	3	0	2	2	.50	2	.250	.304	.320
1994 Detroit	AL	84	296	76	19	0	8	(5	3)	119	32	53	33	0	64	3	3	1	5	3	.63	8	.257	.336	.402
1995 Detroit	AL	123	431	96	20	2	11	(5	6)	153	49	50	41	0	96	3	3	4	4	1	.80	13	.223	.292	.355
1996 Det-SD		137	456	117	21	4	1	(2	2)	152	53	45	57	1	84	7	6	2	3	3	.50	16	.257	.347	.333
1997 San Diego	NL	150	522	132	19	2	5	(2	3)	170	62	54	53	1	114	5	3	3	3	5	.38	16	.253	.326	.326
1996 Detroit	AL	48	128	31	5	0	1	(1	0)	39	21	16	18	0	20	1	3	0	1	1	.50	5	.242	.340	.305
San Diego	NL	89	328	86	16	1	3	(1	2)	113	32	29	39	1	64	6	3	2	2	2	.50	11	.262	.349	.345

		BATTING																BASERUNNING				PERCENTAGES		
Year Team	Lg	G	AB	H	2B	3B	HR	(Hm | Rd)	TB	R	RBI	TBB	IBB	SO	HBP	SH	SF	SB	CS	SB%	GDP	Avg	OBP	SLG
5 ML YEARS		540	1833	453	86	6	28	(14 | 14)	635	207	213	193	2	375	19	18	10	19	17	.53	55	.247	.324	.346

Rene Gonzales

Bats: Right **Throws:** Right **Pos:** PH-2; 3B-1   **Ht:** 6'3" **Wt:** 220 **Born:** 9/3/61 **Age:** 36

		BATTING																	BASERUNNING				PERCENTAGES		
Year Team	Lg	G	AB	H	2B	3B	HR	(Hm	Rd)	TB	R	RBI	TBB	IBB	SO	HBP	SH	SF	SB	CS	SB%	GDP	Avg	OBP	SLG
1997 Las Vegas *	AAA	13	43	8	1	0	0	—	—	9	2	3	6	0	6	1	0	0	0	0	.00	4	.186	.300	.209
Colo Sprngs *	AAA	85	296	88	20	1	3	—	—	119	48	39	37	0	43	3	4	5	2	4	.33	6	.297	.375	.402
1984 Montreal	NL	29	30	7	1	0	0	(0	0)	8	5	2	2	0	5	1	0	0	0	0	.00	0	.233	.303	.267
1986 Montreal	NL	11	26	3	0	0	0	(0	0)	3	1	0	2	0	7	0	0	0	0	2	.00	0	.115	.179	.115
1987 Baltimore	AL	37	60	16	2	1	1	(1	0)	23	14	7	3	0	11	0	2	0	1	0	1.00	2	.267	.302	.383
1988 Baltimore	AL	92	237	51	6	0	1	(1	0)	63	13	15	13	0	32	3	5	2	2	0	1.00	5	.215	.263	.266
1989 Baltimore	AL	71	166	36	4	0	1	(0	1)	43	16	11	12	0	30	0	6	1	5	3	.63	6	.217	.268	.259
1990 Baltimore	AL	67	103	22	3	1	1	(1	0)	30	13	12	12	0	14	0	6	0	1	2	.33	3	.214	.296	.291
1991 Toronto	AL	71	118	23	3	0	1	(1	0)	29	16	6	12	0	22	4	6	1	0	0	.00	5	.195	.289	.246
1992 California	AL	104	329	91	17	1	7	(6	1)	131	47	38	41	1	46	4	5	1	7	4	.64	17	.277	.363	.398
1993 California	AL	118	335	84	17	0	2	(1	1)	107	34	31	49	2	45	1	2	1	5	5	.50	12	.251	.346	.319
1994 Cleveland	AL	22	23	8	1	1	1	(0	1)	14	6	5	5	0	3	0	1	1	2	0	1.00	1	.348	.448	.609
1995 California	AL	30	18	6	1	0	1	(0	1)	10	1	3	0	0	4	0	0	0	0	0	.00	1	.333	.333	.556
1996 Texas	AL	51	92	20	4	0	2	(1	1)	30	19	5	10	0	11	0	0	0	0	0	.00	3	.217	.288	.326
1997 Colorado	NL	2	2	1	0	0	0	(0	0)	1	0	1	0	0	0	0	0	0	0	0	.00	0	.500	.500	.500
13 ML YEARS		705	1539	368	59	4	19	(12	7)	492	185	136	161	3	230	13	33	10	23	16	.59	54	.239	.315	.320

Alex Gonzalez

Bats: Right **Throws:** Right **Pos:** SS-125; PH-1   **Ht:** 6'0" **Wt:** 182 **Born:** 4/8/73 **Age:** 25

		BATTING																	BASERUNNING				PERCENTAGES		
Year Team	Lg	G	AB	H	2B	3B	HR	(Hm	Rd)	TB	R	RBI	TBB	IBB	SO	HBP	SH	SF	SB	CS	SB%	GDP	Avg	OBP	SLG
1994 Toronto	AL	15	53	8	3	1	0	(0	0)	13	7	1	4	0	17	1	1	0	3	0	1.00	2	.151	.224	.245
1995 Toronto	AL	111	367	89	19	4	10	(8	2)	146	51	42	44	1	114	1	9	4	4	4	.50	7	.243	.322	.398
1996 Toronto	AL	147	527	124	30	5	14	(3	11)	206	64	64	45	0	127	5	7	3	16	6	.73	12	.235	.300	.391
1997 Toronto	AL	126	426	102	23	2	12	(4	8)	165	46	35	34	1	94	5	11	2	15	6	.71	9	.239	.302	.387
4 ML YEARS		399	1373	323	75	12	36	(15	21)	530	168	142	127	2	352	12	28	9	38	16	.70	30	.235	.304	.386

Jeremi Gonzalez

Pitches: Right **Bats:** Right **Pos:** SP-23   **Ht:** 6'2" **Wt:** 200 **Born:** 1/8/75 **Age:** 23

		HOW MUCH HE PITCHED						WHAT HE GAVE UP											THE RESULTS						
Year Team	Lg	G	GS	CG	GF	IP	BFP	H	R	ER	HR	SH	SF	HB	TBB	IBB	SO	WP	Bk	W	L	Pct.	ShO	Sv-Op	Hld	ERA
1992 Rockies/Cub	R	14	7	0	1	45	238	65	59	39	0	0	6	10	22	0	39	11	1	0	5	.000	0	0--	—	7.80
1993 Huntington	R+	12	12	1	0	67.2	319	82	59	47	6	1	2	5	38	0	42	5	2	1	7	.125	0	0--	—	6.25
1994 Peoria	A	13	13	1	0	71.1	325	86	53	44	4	2	3	7	32	0	39	5	2	1	6	.400	1	1--	—	5.55
Williamsprt	A-	16	12	1	2	80.2	357	83	46	38	6	3	3	10	29	0	64	4	1	4	6	.400	1	1--	—	4.24
1995 Rockford	A	12	12	1	0	65.1	297	63	43	37	4	1	4	8	28	0	36	8	1	4	4	.500	0	0--	—	5.10
Daytona	A+	19	2	0	7	44.1	178	34	15	6	0	1	2	1	13	1	30	4	2	5	1	.833	0	4--	—	1.22
1996 Orlando	AA	17	14	0	2	97	415	95	39	36	6	1	2	4	28	1	85	2	0	6	3	.667	0	0--	—	3.34
1997 Iowa	AAA	10	10	1	0	62	249	47	27	24	8	1	1	1	21	0	58	2	0	2	2	.500	1	0--	—	3.48
1997 Chicago	NL	23	23	1	0	144	613	126	73	68	16	4	5	2	69	5	93	1	1	11	9	.550	1	0-0	0	4.25

Juan Gonzalez

Bats: Right **Throws:** Right **Pos:** DH-69; RF-64   **Ht:** 6'3" **Wt:** 220 **Born:** 10/16/69 **Age:** 28

		BATTING																	BASERUNNING				PERCENTAGES		
Year Team	Lg	G	AB	H	2B	3B	HR	(Hm	Rd)	TB	R	RBI	TBB	IBB	SO	HBP	SH	SF	SB	CS	SB%	GDP	Avg	OBP	SLG
1989 Texas	AL	24	60	9	3	0	1	(1	0)	15	6	7	6	0	17	0	2	0	0	0	.00	4	.150	.227	.250
1990 Texas	AL	25	90	26	7	1	4	(3	1)	47	11	12	2	0	18	2	0	1	0	1	.00	2	.289	.316	.522
1991 Texas	AL	142	545	144	34	1	27	(7	20)	261	78	102	42	7	118	5	0	3	4	4	.50	10	.264	.321	.479
1992 Texas	AL	155	584	152	24	2	43	(19	24)	309	77	109	35	1	143	5	0	8	0	1	.00	16	.260	.304	.529
1993 Texas	AL	140	536	166	33	1	46	(24	22)	339	105	118	37	7	99	13	0	1	4	1	.80	12	.310	.368	.632
1994 Texas	AL	107	422	116	18	4	19	(6	13)	199	57	85	30	10	66	7	0	4	6	4	.60	18	.275	.330	.472
1995 Texas	AL	90	352	104	20	2	27	(15	12)	209	57	82	17	3	66	0	0	0	0	0	1.00	15	.295	.324	.594
1996 Texas	AL	134	541	170	33	2	47	(23	24)	348	89	144	45	12	82	3	0	3	2	0	.00	12	.314	.368	.643
1997 Texas	AL	133	533	158	24	3	42	(18	24)	314	87	131	33	7	107	3	0	10	0	0	.00	12	.296	.335	.589
9 ML YEARS		950	3663	1045	196	16	256	(116	140)	2041	567	790	247	47	716	38	2	35	16	11	.59	99	.285	.334	.557

Luis Gonzalez

Bats: Left **Throws:** Right **Pos:** LF-146; PH-7; 1B-1   **Ht:** 6'2" **Wt:** 185 **Born:** 9/3/67 **Age:** 30

		BATTING																	BASERUNNING				PERCENTAGES		
Year Team	Lg	G	AB	H	2B	3B	HR	(Hm	Rd)	TB	R	RBI	TBB	IBB	SO	HBP	SH	SF	SB	CS	SB%	GDP	Avg	OBP	SLG
1990 Houston	NL	12	21	4	2	0	0	(0	0)	6	1	0	2	1	5	0	0	0	0	0	.00	0	.190	.261	.286
1991 Houston	NL	137	473	120	28	9	13	(4	9)	205	51	69	40	4	101	6	1	4	10	7	.59	9	.254	.320	.433
1992 Houston	NL	122	387	94	19	3	10	(4	6)	149	40	55	24	3	52	2	1	2	7	7	.50	6	.243	.289	.385
1993 Houston	NL	154	540	162	34	3	15	(8	7)	247	82	72	47	7	83	10	3	10	20	9	.69	9	.300	.361	.457
1994 Houston	NL	112	392	107	29	4	8	(3	5)	168	57	67	49	6	57	1	0	6	15	13	.54	10	.273	.353	.429
1995 Hou-ChN	NL	133	471	130	29	8	13	(6	7)	214	69	69	57	8	63	6	1	6	6	8	.43	16	.276	.357	.454

77

Year Team	Lg	G	AB	H	2B	3B	HR	(Hm	Rd)	TB	R	RBI	TBB	IBB	SO	HBP	SH	SF	SB	CS	SB%	GDP	Avg	OBP	SLG
																				BASERUNNING				PERCENTAGES		
1996 Chicago	NL	146	483	131	30	4	15	(6	9)	214	70	79	61	8	49	4	1	6	9	6	.60	13	.271	.354	.443
1997 Houston	NL	152	550	142	31	2	10	(4	6)	207	78	68	71	7	67	5	0	5	10	7	.59	12	.258	.345	.376
1995 Houston	NL	56	209	54	10	4	6	(1	5)	90	35	35	18	3	30	3	1	3	1	3	.25	8	.258	.322	.431
Chicago	NL	77	262	76	19	4	7	(5	2)	124	34	34	39	5	33	3	0	3	5	5	.50	8	.290	.384	.473
8 ML YEARS		968	3317	890	202	33	84	(35	49)	1410	448	479	351	44	477	38	7	39	77	57	.57	75	.268	.342	.425

Dwight Gooden

Pitches: Right **Bats:** Right **Pos:** SP-19; RP-1 **Ht:** 6'3" **Wt:** 210 **Born:** 11/16/64 **Age:** 33

Year Team	Lg	G	GS	CG	GF	IP	BFP	H	R	ER	HR	SH	SF	HB	TBB	IBB	SO	WP	Bk	W	L	Pct.	ShO	Sv-Op	Hld	ERA
			HOW MUCH HE PITCHED							WHAT HE GAVE UP											THE RESULTS				
1997 Norwich *	AA	3	3	0	0	18	74	13	6	6	3	0	0	2	5	0	14	0	0	3	0	1.000	0	0- -	—	3.00
Columbus *	AAA	2	2	0	0	12	50	7	5	5	1	0	0	4	4	0	10	2	0	1	1	.500	0	0- -	—	3.75
1984 New York	NL	31	31	7	0	218	879	161	72	63	7	3	2	2	73	2	276	3	7	17	9	.654	3	0-0	0	2.60
1985 New York	NL	35	35	16	0	276.2	1065	198	51	47	13	6	2	2	69	4	268	6	2	24	4	.857	8	0-0	0	1.53
1986 New York	NL	33	33	12	0	250	1020	197	92	79	17	10	8	4	80	3	200	4	4	17	6	.739	2	0-0	0	2.84
1987 New York	NL	25	25	7	0	179.2	730	162	68	64	11	5	5	2	53	2	148	1	1	15	7	.682	3	0-0	0	3.21
1988 New York	NL	34	34	10	0	248.1	1024	242	98	88	8	10	6	6	57	4	175	5	5	18	9	.667	3	0-0	0	3.19
1989 New York	NL	19	17	0	1	118.1	497	93	42	38	9	4	3	2	47	2	101	7	5	9	4	.692	0	1-1	0	2.89
1990 New York	NL	34	34	2	0	232.2	983	229	106	99	10	10	7	7	70	3	223	6	3	19	7	.731	1	0-0	0	3.83
1991 New York	NL	27	27	3	0	190	789	185	80	76	12	5	4	3	56	2	150	5	2	13	7	.650	1	0-0	0	3.60
1992 New York	NL	31	31	3	0	206	863	197	93	84	11	10	7	3	70	7	145	3	1	10	13	.435	0	0-0	0	3.67
1993 New York	NL	29	29	7	0	208.2	866	188	89	86	16	11	7	9	61	1	149	5	2	12	15	.444	2	0-0	0	3.45
1994 New York	NL	7	7	0	0	41.1	182	46	32	29	4	3	0	1	15	1	40	2	0	3	4	.429	2	0-0	0	6.31
1996 New York	AL	29	29	1	0	170.2	756	169	101	95	19	1	5	9	88	4	126	9	1	11	7	.611	1	0-0	0	5.01
1997 New York	AL	20	19	0	0	106.1	472	116	61	58	14	0	2	7	53	1	66	8	0	9	5	.643	0	0-0	0	4.91
13 ML YEARS		354	351	68	1	2446.2	10126	2183	985	900	156	78	58	57	792	36	2067	64	33	177	97	.646	24	1-1	1	3.31

Curtis Goodwin

Bats: L **Throws:** L **Pos:** CF-41; LF-32; PH-19; RF-1 **Ht:** 5'11" **Wt:** 180 **Born:** 9/30/72 **Age:** 25

Year Team	Lg	G	AB	H	2B	3B	HR	(Hm	Rd)	TB	R	RBI	TBB	IBB	SO	HBP	SH	SF	SB	CS	SB%	GDP	Avg	OBP	SLG
					BATTING															BASERUNNING				PERCENTAGES	
1997 Indianapolis *	AAA	30	116	32	4	1	1			41	14	7	15	0	20	0	1	0	11	8	.58	0	.276	.359	.353
1995 Baltimore	AL	87	289	76	11	3	1	(0	1)	96	40	24	15	0	53	2	7	3	22	4	.85	5	.263	.301	.332
1996 Cincinnati	NL	49	136	31	3	0	0	(0	0)	34	20	5	19	0	34	0	1	0	15	6	.71	1	.228	.323	.250
1997 Cincinnati	NL	85	265	67	11	0	1	(1	0)	81	27	12	24	0	53	1	6	1	22	13	.63	6	.253	.316	.306
3 ML YEARS		221	690	174	25	3	2	(1	1)	211	87	41	58	0	140	3	14	4	59	23	.72	12	.252	.311	.306

Tom Goodwin

Bats: Left **Throws:** Right **Pos:** CF-145; PH-8; LF-5 **Ht:** 6'1" **Wt:** 175 **Born:** 7/27/68 **Age:** 29

Year Team	Lg	G	AB	H	2B	3B	HR	(Hm	Rd)	TB	R	RBI	TBB	IBB	SO	HBP	SH	SF	SB	CS	SB%	GDP	Avg	OBP	SLG
					BATTING															BASERUNNING				PERCENTAGES	
1991 Los Angeles	NL	16	7	1	0	0	0	(0	0)	1	3	0	0	0	0	0	0	0	1	1	.50	0	.143	.143	.143
1992 Los Angeles	NL	57	73	17	1	1	0	(0	0)	20	15	3	6	0	10	0	0	0	7	3	.70	0	.233	.291	.274
1993 Los Angeles	NL	30	17	5	1	0	0	(0	0)	6	6	1	1	0	4	0	0	0	1	2	.33	1	.294	.333	.353
1994 Kansas City	AL	2	2	0	0	0	0	(0	0)	0	0	0	0	0	0	0	0	0	0	0	.00	0	.000	.000	.000
1995 Kansas City	AL	133	480	138	16	3	4	(2	2)	172	72	28	38	0	72	5	14	0	50	18	.74	0	.288	.346	.358
1996 Kansas City	AL	143	524	148	14	4	1	(0	1)	173	80	35	39	0	79	2	21	1	66	22	.75	3	.282	.334	.330
1997 KC-Tex	AL	150	574	149	26	6	2	(0	2)	193	90	39	44	1	88	3	11	6	50	16	.76	7	.260	.314	.336
1997 Kansas City	AL	97	367	100	13	4	2	(0	2)	127	51	22	19	0	51	2	11	1	34	10	.77	5	.272	.311	.346
Texas	AL	53	207	49	13	2	0	(0	0)	66	39	17	25	1	37	1	0	2	16	6	.73	2	.237	.319	.319
7 ML YEARS		531	1677	458	58	14	7	(2	5)	565	266	106	128	1	254	10	46	4	175	62	.74	18	.273	.328	.337

Tom Gordon

Pitches: Right **Bats:** Right **Pos:** SP-25; RP-17 **Ht:** 5'9" **Wt:** 180 **Born:** 11/18/67 **Age:** 30

Year Team	Lg	G	GS	CG	GF	IP	BFP	H	R	ER	HR	SH	SF	HB	TBB	IBB	SO	WP	Bk	W	L	Pct.	ShO	Sv-Op	Hld	ERA
			HOW MUCH HE PITCHED							WHAT HE GAVE UP											THE RESULTS				
1988 Kansas City	AL	5	2	0	0	15.2	72	16	9	9	1	0	0	0	7	0	18	0	0	0	2	.000	0	0-0	2	5.17
1989 Kansas City	AL	49	16	1	16	163	677	122	67	66	10	4	4	1	86	4	153	12	0	17	9	.654	1	1-7	3	3.64
1990 Kansas City	AL	32	32	6	0	195.1	858	192	99	81	17	8	2	3	99	1	175	11	0	12	11	.522	1	0-0	0	3.73
1991 Kansas City	AL	45	14	1	11	158	684	129	76	68	16	5	3	4	87	6	167	5	0	9	14	.391	0	1-4	4	3.87
1992 Kansas City	AL	40	11	0	13	117.2	516	116	67	60	9	2	6	4	55	4	98	5	2	6	10	.375	0	0-2	0	4.59
1993 Kansas City	AL	48	14	2	18	155.2	651	125	65	62	11	6	6	1	77	5	143	17	0	12	6	.667	0	1-6	2	3.58
1994 Kansas City	AL	24	24	0	0	155.1	675	136	79	75	15	3	8	2	87	3	126	12	1	11	7	.611	0	0-0	0	4.35
1995 Kansas City	AL	31	31	2	0	189	843	204	110	93	12	7	11	4	89	4	119	9	0	12	12	.500	0	0-0	0	4.43
1996 Boston	AL	34	34	4	0	215.2	998	249	143	134	28	2	11	4	105	5	171	6	1	12	9	.571	1	0-0	0	5.59
1997 Boston	AL	42	25	2	16	182.2	774	155	85	76	10	3	4	3	78	1	159	5	0	6	10	.375	1	11-13	0	3.74
10 ML YEARS		350	203	18	74	1548	6743	1444	800	724	129	40	55	27	770	33	1329	82	4	97	90	.519	4	14-32	11	4.21

Rick Gorecki

Pitches: Right **Bats:** Right **Pos:** RP-3; SP-1 **Ht:** 6'3" **Wt:** 167 **Born:** 8/27/73 **Age:** 24

		HOW MUCH HE PITCHED					WHAT HE GAVE UP										THE RESULTS					
Year Team	Lg	G	GS	CG	GF	IP	BFP	H	R	ER	HR	SH	SF	HB	TBB	IBB	SO	WP	Bk	W	L	Pct.	ShO	Sv-Op	Hld	ERA
1991 Great Falls	R+	13	10	0	0	51	219	44	34	25	3	2	0	1	27	0	56	4	5	0	3	.000	0	0--	—	4.41
1992 Bakersfield	A+	25	24	0	1	129	580	122	68	58	11	0	2	7	90	2	115	17	0	11	7	.611	0	0--	—	4.05
1993 San Antonio	AA	26	26	1	0	156	653	136	76	58	6	3	5	5	62	2	118	5	1	6	9	.400	0	0--	—	3.35
1994 Albuquerque	AAA	22	21	0	0	103	481	119	65	58	11	2	3	7	60	1	73	11	0	8	6	.571	0	0--	—	5.07
1995 Vero Beach	A+	6	5	0	0	27	110	19	6	2	0	1	4	9	0	24	1	0	1	2	.333	0	0--	—	0.67
1997 San Berndno	A+	14	14	0	0	51	215	38	22	22	4	0	2	2	32	0	58	4	0	2	3	.400	0	0--	—	3.88
San Antonio	AA	7	7	0	0	45.1	174	26	8	7	3	3	1	1	15	0	33	2	0	4	2	.667	0	0--	—	1.39
1997 Los Angeles	NL	4	1	0	2	6	32	9	10	10	3	0	0	0	6	1	6	0	0	1	0	1.000	0	0-0	0	15.00

Mark Grace

Bats: Left **Throws:** Left **Pos:** 1B-148; PH-3 **Ht:** 6'2" **Wt:** 190 **Born:** 6/28/64 **Age:** 34

		BATTING																	BASERUNNING				PERCENTAGES		
Year Team	Lg	G	AB	H	2B	3B	HR	(Hm	Rd)	TB	R	RBI	TBB	IBB	SO	HBP	SH	SF	SB	CS	SB%	GDP	Avg	OBP	SLG
1988 Chicago	NL	134	486	144	23	4	7	(0	7)	196	65	57	60	5	43	0	0	4	3	3	.50	12	.296	.371	.403
1989 Chicago	NL	142	510	160	28	3	13	(8	5)	233	74	79	80	13	42	0	3	3	14	7	.67	13	.314	.405	.457
1990 Chicago	NL	157	589	182	32	1	9	(4	5)	243	72	82	59	5	54	5	1	8	15	6	.71	10	.309	.372	.413
1991 Chicago	NL	160	**619**	169	28	5	8	(5	3)	231	87	58	70	7	53	3	4	7	3	4	.43	6	.273	.346	.373
1992 Chicago	NL	158	603	185	37	5	9	(5	4)	259	72	79	72	8	36	4	2	8	6	1	.86	14	.307	.380	.430
1993 Chicago	NL	155	594	193	39	4	14	(5	9)	282	86	98	71	14	32	1	1	9	8	4	.67	25	.325	.393	.475
1994 Chicago	NL	106	403	120	23	3	6	(5	1)	167	55	44	48	5	41	0	0	3	0	1	.00	10	.298	.370	.414
1995 Chicago	NL	143	552	180	51	3	16	(4	12)	285	97	92	65	9	46	2	1	7	6	5	.55	17	.326	.395	.516
1996 Chicago	NL	142	547	181	39	1	9	(4	5)	249	88	75	62	8	41	1	0	6	2	3	.40	18	.331	.396	.455
1997 Chicago	NL	151	555	177	32	5	13	(6	7)	258	87	78	88	3	45	2	1	8	2	4	.33	18	.319	.409	.465
10 ML YEARS		1448	5458	1691	332	34	104	(46	58)	2403	783	742	675	77	433	18	13	63	59	35	.63	136	.310	.384	.440

Mike Grace

Pitches: Right **Bats:** Right **Pos:** SP-6 **Ht:** 6'4" **Wt:** 220 **Born:** 6/20/70 **Age:** 28

		HOW MUCH HE PITCHED						WHAT HE GAVE UP											THE RESULTS					
Year Team	Lg	G	GS	CG	GF	IP	BFP	H	R	ER	HR	SF	SH	HB	TBB	IBB	SO	WP	Bk	W	L	Pct.	ShO	Sv-Op	Hld	ERA
1997 Reading *	AA	4	4	0	0	20.1	93	28	17	13	4	1	0	0	6	0	10	1	0	1	3	.250	0	0--	—	5.75
Scrnton-WB *	AAA	12	12	4	0	75	331	84	43	38	0	3	5	3	27	1	55	1	0	5	6	.455	0	0--	—	4.56
1995 Philadelphia	NL	2	2	0	0	11.1	47	10	4	4	0	1	0	0	4	0	7	0	0	1	1	.500	0	0-0	0	3.18
1996 Philadelphia	NL	12	12	1	0	80	323	72	33	31	9	4	0	1	16	1	49	0	1	7	2	.778	1	0-0	0	3.49
1997 Philadelphia	NL	6	6	1	0	39	151	32	16	15	3	0	1	1	10	1	26	2	0	3	2	.600	1	0-0	0	3.46
3 ML YEARS		20	20	2	0	130.1	521	114	53	50	12	5	1	2	30	2	82	2	1	11	5	.688	2	0-0	0	3.45

Tony Graffanino

Bats: R **Throws:** R **Pos:** 2B-75; PH-40; 3B-2; SS-2; 1B-1 **Ht:** 6'1" **Wt:** 175 **Born:** 6/6/72 **Age:** 26

		BATTING																	BASERUNNING				PERCENTAGES		
Year Team	Lg	G	AB	H	2B	3B	HR	(Hm	Rd)	TB	R	RBI	TBB	IBB	SO	HBP	SH	SF	SB	CS	SB%	GDP	Avg	OBP	SLG
1990 Pulaski	R+	42	131	27	5	1	0	—	—	34	23	11	26	0	17	2	1	1	6	3	.67	3	.206	.344	.260
1991 Idaho Falls	R+	66	274	95	16	4	4	—	—	131	53	57	27	0	37	3	2	2	19	4	.83	2	.347	.408	.478
1992 Macon	A	112	400	96	15	5	10	—	—	151	50	31	50	1	84	8	4	4	9	6	.60	6	.240	.333	.378
1993 Durham	A+	123	459	126	30	5	15	—	—	211	78	69	45	1	78	4	2	4	24	11	.69	10	.275	.342	.460
1994 Greenville	AA	124	440	132	28	3	7	—	—	187	66	52	50	7	53	2	7	3	29	7	.81	6	.300	.372	.425
1995 Richmond	AAA	50	179	34	6	0	4	—	—	52	20	17	15	0	49	1	1	2	2	2	.50	4	.190	.254	.291
1996 Richmond	AAA	96	353	100	22	2	7	—	—	154	57	33	34	2	72	3	5	1	11	7	.61	3	.283	.350	.436
1996 Atlanta	NL	22	46	8	1	1	0	(0	0)	11	7	2	4	0	13	1	0	1	0	0	.00	0	.174	.250	.239
1997 Atlanta	NL	104	186	48	9	1	8	(5	3)	83	33	20	26	1	46	1	3	5	6	4	.60	3	.258	.344	.446
2 ML YEARS		126	232	56	10	2	8	(5	3)	94	40	22	30	1	59	2	3	6	6	4	.60	3	.241	.326	.405

Jeff Granger

Pitches: Left **Bats:** Right **Pos:** RP-9 **Ht:** 6'4" **Wt:** 200 **Born:** 12/16/71 **Age:** 26

		HOW MUCH HE PITCHED						WHAT HE GAVE UP											THE RESULTS					
Year Team	Lg	G	GS	CG	GF	IP	BFP	H	R	ER	HR	SH	SF	HB	TBB	IBB	SO	WP	Bk	W	L	Pct.	ShO	Sv-Op	Hld	ERA
1993 Eugene	A-	8	7	0	0	36	146	28	17	12	2	1	0	1	10	1	56	1	0	3	3	.500	0	0--	—	3.00
1994 Memphis	AA	25	25	0	0	139.2	615	155	74	60	8	3	3	0	61	0	112	14	3	7	7	.500	0	0--	—	3.87
1995 Wichita	AA	18	18	0	0	95.2	439	122	76	63	9	3	4	1	40	0	81	10	0	4	7	.364	0	0--	—	5.93
1996 Omaha	AAA	45	0	0	25	77	314	65	24	20	10	2	2	2	29	2	68	3	0	5	3	.625	0	4--	—	2.34
1997 Calgary	AAA	30	12	0	7	82.2	387	111	63	51	7	3	1	3	33	5	68	6	0	1	7	.125	0	1--	—	5.55
1993 Kansas City	AL	1	0	0	0	1	8	3	3	3	0	0	0	0	2	0	1	0	0	0	0	.000	0	0-0	0	27.00
1994 Kansas City	AL	2	2	0	0	9.1	47	13	8	7	2	0	1	0	6	0	3	0	0	1	0	1.000	0	0-0	0	6.75
1996 Kansas City	AL	15	0	0	5	16.1	80	21	13	12	3	0	1	2	10	0	11	2	0	0	1	.000	0	0-0	1	6.61
1997 Pittsburgh	NL	9	0	0	1	5	32	10	10	10	3	0	0	0	8	1	4	2	0	0	0	.000	0	0-0	0	18.00
4 ML YEARS		27	2	0	6	31.2	167	47	34	32	8	0	2	2	26	1	19	4	0	0	1	.000	0	0-0	1	9.09

Danny Graves

Pitches: Right **Bats:** Right **Pos:** RP-15   **Ht:** 5'11" **Wt:** 200 **Born:** 8/7/73 **Age:** 24

		HOW MUCH HE PITCHED						WHAT HE GAVE UP										THE RESULTS					
Year Team	Lg	G	GS	CG	GF	IP	BFP	H	R	ER	HR	SH	SF	HB	TBB	IBB	SO	WP	Bk	W	L	Pct.	ShO	Sv-Op	Hld	ERA
1995 Kinston	A+	38	0	0	37	44	177	30	11	4	0	1	0	0	12	2	46	0	0	3	1	.750	0	21- --	---	0.82
Canton-Akrn	AA	17	0	0	17	23.1	82	10	1	0	0	4	0	1	2	0	11	0	0	1	0	1.000	0	10- --	---	0.00
Buffalo	AAA	3	0	0	3	3	16	5	4	1	0	0	0	0	1	0	2	1	0	0	0	.000	0	0- --	---	3.00
1996 Buffalo	AAA	43	0	0	32	79	308	57	14	13	1	5	3	2	24	2	46	1	0	4	3	.571	0	19- --	---	1.48
1997 Buffalo	AAA	19	3	0	6	43	178	45	21	20	3	0	2	2	11	0	21	0	0	2	3	.400	0	2- --	---	4.19
Indianapols	AAA	11	0	0	8	11.2	47	7	4	4	1	1	1	2	5	0	5	1	0	1	0	1.000	0	5- --	---	3.09
1996 Cleveland	AL	15	0	0	5	29.2	129	29	18	15	2	0	1	0	10	0	22	1	0	2	0	1.000	0	0-1	0	4.55
1997 Cle-Cin		15	0	0	3	26	134	41	22	16	2	3	2	0	20	1	11	1	0	0	0	.000	0	0-0	1	5.54
1997 Cleveland	AL	5	0	0	2	11.1	56	15	8	6	2	0	1	0	9	0	4	0	0	0	0	.000	0	0-0	0	4.76
Cincinnati	NL	10	0	0	1	14.2	78	26	14	10	0	3	1	0	11	1	7	1	0	0	0	.000	0	0-0	1	6.14
2 ML YEARS		30	0	0	8	55.2	263	70	40	31	4	3	3	0	30	1	33	2	0	2	0	1.000	0	0-1	1	5.01

Craig Grebeck

Bats: R **Throws:** R **Pos:** 2B-26; SS-20; 3B-15; PH-12; LF-3   **Ht:** 5'7" **Wt:** 150 **Born:** 12/29/64 **Age:** 33

		BATTING																BASERUNNING				PERCENTAGES		
Year Team	Lg	G	AB	H	2B	3B	HR	(Hm	Rd)	TB	R	RBI	TBB	IBB	SO	HBP	SH	SF	SB	CS	SB%	GDP	Avg	OBP	SLG
1990 Chicago	AL	59	119	20	3	1	1	(1	0)	28	7	9	8	0	24	2	3	3	0	0	.00	2	.168	.227	.235
1991 Chicago	AL	107	224	63	16	3	6	(3	3)	103	37	31	38	0	40	1	4	1	1	3	.25	3	.281	.386	.460
1992 Chicago	AL	88	287	77	21	2	3	(2	1)	111	24	35	30	0	34	3	10	3	0	3	.00	5	.268	.341	.387
1993 Chicago	AL	72	190	43	5	0	1	(0	1)	51	25	12	26	0	26	0	7	0	1	2	.33	4	.226	.319	.268
1994 Chicago	AL	35	97	30	5	0	0	(0	0)	35	17	5	12	0	5	1	3	0	0	0	.00	1	.309	.391	.361
1995 Chicago	AL	53	154	40	12	0	1	(0	1)	55	19	18	21	0	23	3	4	0	0	0	.00	4	.260	.360	.357
1996 Florida	NL	50	95	20	1	0	1	(0	1)	24	8	9	4	1	14	1	1	2	0	0	.00	2	.211	.245	.253
1997 Anaheim	AL	63	126	34	9	0	1	(1	0)	46	12	6	18	1	11	0	5	1	0	1	.00	6	.270	.359	.365
8 ML YEARS		527	1292	327	72	6	14	(7	7)	453	149	125	157	2	177	11	37	10	2	9	.18	32	.253	.337	.351

Scarborough Green

Bats: Right **Throws:** Right **Pos:** CF-12; LF-7; PH-7   **Ht:** 5'10" **Wt:** 170 **Born:** 6/9/74 **Age:** 24

		BATTING																BASERUNNING				PERCENTAGES		
Year Team	Lg	G	AB	H	2B	3B	HR	(Hm	Rd)	TB	R	RBI	TBB	IBB	SO	HBP	SH	SF	SB	CS	SB%	GDP	Avg	OBP	SLG
1993 Cardinals	R	33	95	21	3	1	0	--	--	26	16	11	7	0	17	3	1	0	3	2	.60	1	.221	.295	.274
1994 Johnson Cty	R+	54	199	48	5	0	0	--	--	53	32	11	25	1	61	0	4	2	22	7	.76	0	.241	.323	.266
1995 Savannah	A	132	429	98	7	6	1	--	--	120	48	25	55	0	101	3	9	1	26	9	.74	6	.228	.320	.280
1996 St. Pete	A+	36	140	41	4	1	1	--	--	50	26	11	21	1	22	2	2	0	13	9	.59	1	.293	.393	.357
Arkansas	AA	92	300	60	6	3	3	--	--	81	45	24	38	1	58	3	3	1	21	8	.72	3	.200	.295	.270
1997 Arkansas	AA	76	251	77	14	4	2	--	--	105	45	29	36	4	48	2	3	1	11	5	.69	2	.307	.397	.418
Louisville	AAA	52	209	53	11	2	3	--	--	77	26	13	22	0	55	0	1	0	10	7	.59	3	.254	.325	.368
1997 St. Louis	NL	20	31	3	0	0	0	(0	0)	3	5	1	2	0	5	0	0	0	0	0	.00	0	.097	.152	.097

Shawn Green

Bats: L **Throws:** L **Pos:** RF-46; LF-45; DH-35; PH-17   **Ht:** 6'4" **Wt:** 190 **Born:** 11/10/72 **Age:** 25

		BATTING																BASERUNNING				PERCENTAGES		
Year Team	Lg	G	AB	H	2B	3B	HR	(Hm	Rd)	TB	R	RBI	TBB	IBB	SO	HBP	SH	SF	SB	CS	SB%	GDP	Avg	OBP	SLG
1993 Toronto	AL	3	6	0	0	0	0	(0	0)	0	0	0	0	0	1	0	0	0	0	0	.00	0	.000	.000	.000
1994 Toronto	AL	14	33	3	1	0	0	(0	0)	4	1	1	1	0	8	0	0	0	1	0	1.00	1	.091	.118	.121
1995 Toronto	AL	121	379	109	31	4	15	(5	10)	193	52	54	20	3	68	3	0	3	1	2	.33	4	.288	.326	.509
1996 Toronto	AL	132	422	118	32	3	11	(7	4)	189	52	45	33	3	75	8	0	2	5	1	.83	9	.280	.342	.448
1997 Toronto	AL	135	429	123	22	4	16	(10	6)	201	57	53	36	4	99	1	1	4	14	3	.82	4	.287	.340	.469
5 ML YEARS		405	1269	353	86	11	42	(22	20)	587	162	153	90	10	251	12	1	9	21	6	.78	18	.278	.330	.463

Tyler Green

Pitches: Right **Bats:** Right **Pos:** SP-14   **Ht:** 6'5" **Wt:** 204 **Born:** 2/18/70 **Age:** 28

		HOW MUCH HE PITCHED						WHAT HE GAVE UP										THE RESULTS					
Year Team	Lg	G	GS	CG	GF	IP	BFP	H	R	ER	HR	SH	SF	HB	TBB	IBB	SO	WP	Bk	W	L	Pct.	ShO	Sv-Op	Hld	ERA
1997 Scrnton-WB *	AAA	12	12	3	0	72.1	322	80	54	49	13	1	0	1	29	3	40	4	0	4	8	.333	0	0- --	---	6.10
1993 Philadelphia	NL	3	2	0	1	7.1	41	9	6	6	1	0	0	0	5	0	7	2	0	0	0	.000	0	0-0	0	7.36
1995 Philadelphia	NL	26	25	4	0	140.2	623	157	86	83	15	5	6	4	66	3	85	9	2	8	9	.471	2	0-0	0	5.31
1997 Philadelphia	NL	14	14	0	0	76.2	340	72	50	42	8	0	3	1	45	4	58	7	0	4	4	.500	0	0-0	0	4.93
3 ML YEARS		43	41	4	1	224.2	1004	245	145	131	24	5	9	5	116	7	150	18	2	12	13	.480	2	0-0	0	5.25

Charlie Greene

Bats: Right **Throws:** Right **Pos:** C-4; PH-1   **Ht:** 6'1" **Wt:** 177 **Born:** 1/23/71 **Age:** 27

		BATTING																BASERUNNING				PERCENTAGES		
Year Team	Lg	G	AB	H	2B	3B	HR	(Hm	Rd)	TB	R	RBI	TBB	IBB	SO	HBP	SH	SF	SB	CS	SB%	GDP	Avg	OBP	SLG
1991 Padres	R	49	183	52	15	1	5	--	--	84	27	39	16	0	23	3	2	6	6	1	.86	7	.284	.341	.459
1992 Chston-SC	A	98	298	55	9	1	1	--	--	69	22	24	11	0	60	5	3	2	1	2	.33	7	.185	.225	.232
1993 Waterloo	A	84	213	38	8	0	2	--	--	52	19	20	13	0	33	3	6	3	0	0	.00	5	.178	.233	.244
1994 Binghamton	AA	30	106	18	4	0	0	--	--	22	13	2	6	1	18	1	0	1	0	0	.00	3	.170	.219	.208
St. Lucie	A+	69	224	57	4	0	0	--	--	61	23	21	9	0	31	4	4	1	0	1	.00	3	.254	.294	.272

Year Team	Lg	G	AB	H	2B	3B	HR	(Hm	Rd)	TB	R	RBI	TBB	IBB	SO	HBP	SH	SF	SB	CS	SB%	GDP	Avg	OBP	SLG
1995 Binghamton	AA	100	346	82	13	0	2	—	—	101	26	34	15	4	47	5	3	4	2	1	.67	10	.237	.276	.292
Norfolk	AAA	27	88	17	3	0	0	—	—	20	6	4	3	0	28	0	1	0	0	1	.00	1	.193	.220	.227
1996 Binghamton	AA	100	336	82	17	0	2	—	—	105	35	27	17	0	52	0	2	4	2	0	1.00	8	.244	.277	.313
1997 Norfolk	AAA	76	238	49	7	0	8	—	—	80	27	28	9	0	54	2	0	2	1	0	1.00	4	.206	.239	.336
1996 New York	NL	2	1	0	0	0	0	(0	0)	0	0	0	0	0	0	0	0	0	0	0	.00	0	.000	.000	.000
1997 Baltimore	AL	5	2	0	0	0	0	(0	0)	0	0	1	0	0	1	0	0	0	0	0	.00	0	.000	.000	.000
2 ML YEARS		7	3	0	0	0	0	(0	0)	0	0	1	0	0	1	0	0	0	0	0	.00	0	.000	.000	.000

Todd Greene

Bats: Right **Throws:** Right **Pos:** C-26; DH-8; PH-1   **Ht:** 5'10" **Wt:** 200 **Born:** 5/8/71 **Age:** 27

Year Team	Lg	G	AB	H	2B	3B	HR	(Hm	Rd)	TB	R	RBI	TBB	IBB	SO	HBP	SH	SF	SB	CS	SB%	GDP	Avg	OBP	SLG
1993 Boise	A-	76	305	82	15	3	15	—	—	148	55	71	34	6	44	9	0	3	4	3	.57	3	.269	.356	.485
1994 Lk Elsinore	A+	133	524	158	39	2	35	—	—	306	98	124	64	12	96	4	0	6	10	3	.77	12	.302	.378	.584
1995 Midland	AA	82	318	104	19	1	26	—	—	203	59	57	17	4	55	5	1	5	1	5	.38	6	.327	.365	.638
Vancouver	AAA	43	168	42	3	1	14	—	—	89	28	35	11	2	36	4	0	2	1	0	1.00	3	.250	.308	.530
1996 Vancouver	AAA	60	223	68	18	0	5	—	—	101	27	33	16	0	36	1	0	5	2	0	.00	6	.305	.347	.453
1997 Vancouver	AAA	64	260	92	22	0	25	—	—	189	51	75	20	8	31	5	0	2	5	1	.83	6	.354	.408	.727
1996 California	AL	29	79	15	1	0	2	(1	1)	22	9	9	4	0	11	1	0	0	2	0	1.00	4	.190	.238	.278
1997 Anaheim	AL	34	124	36	6	0	9	(5	4)	69	24	24	7	1	25	0	0	0	2	0	1.00	1	.290	.328	.556
2 ML YEARS		63	203	51	7	0	11	(6	5)	91	33	33	11	1	36	1	0	0	4	0	1.00	5	.251	.293	.448

Tommy Greene

Pitches: Right **Bats:** Right **Pos:** SP-2   **Ht:** 6'5" **Wt:** 222 **Born:** 4/6/67 **Age:** 31

Year Team	Lg	G	GS	CG	GF	IP	BFP	H	R	ER	HR	SH	SF	HB	TBB	IBB	SO	WP	Bk	W	L	Pct.	ShO	Sv-Op	Hld	ERA
1997 New Orleans *		13	13	0	0	74.2	305	59	30	28	12	2	3	2	25	0	75	1	0	5	3	.625	0	0--	—	3.38
1989 Atlanta	NL	4	4	1	0	26.1	103	22	12	12	5	1	2	0	6	1	17	1	0	1	2	.333	1	0-0	0	4.10
1990 Atl-Phi	NL	15	9	0	1	51.1	227	50	31	29	8	5	0	1	26	1	21	1	0	3	3	.500	0	0-0	0	5.08
1991 Philadelphia	NL	36	27	3	3	207.2	857	177	85	78	19	9	11	3	66	4	154	9	1	13	7	.650	2	0-0	0	3.38
1992 Philadelphia	NL	13	12	0	0	64.1	298	75	39	38	5	4	2	0	34	2	39	1	0	3	3	.500	0	0-0	0	5.32
1993 Philadelphia	NL	31	30	7	0	200	834	175	84	76	12	9	9	3	62	3	167	15	0	16	4	.800	2	0-0	0	3.42
1994 Philadelphia	NL	7	7	0	0	35.2	164	37	20	18	5	5	1	0	22	0	28	2	0	2	0	1.000	0	0-0	0	4.54
1995 Philadelphia	NL	11	6	0	3	33.2	167	45	32	31	6	2	1	3	20	0	24	3	1	0	5	.000	0	0-0	0	8.29
1997 Houston	NL	2	2	0	0	9	40	10	7	7	2	0	0	0	5	0	11	0	0	1	0	1.000	0	0-0	0	7.00
1990 Atlanta	NL	5	2	0	0	12.1	61	14	11	11	3	2	0	1	9	0	4	0	0	1	0	1.000	0	0-0	0	8.03
Philadelphia	NL	10	7	0	1	39	166	36	20	18	5	3	0	0	17	1	17	1	0	2	3	.400	0	0-0	0	4.15
8 ML YEARS		119	97	11	7	628	2690	591	310	289	62	35	26	10	241	11	461	32	2	38	25	.603	5	0-0	0	4.14

Willie Greene

Bats: L **Throws:** R **Pos:** 3B-103; RF-33; PH-12; 1B-7; LF-6; SS-3   **Ht:** 5'11" **Wt:** 192 **Born:** 9/23/71 **Age:** 26

Year Team	Lg	G	AB	H	2B	3B	HR	(Hm	Rd)	TB	R	RBI	TBB	IBB	SO	HBP	SH	SF	SB	CS	SB%	GDP	Avg	OBP	SLG
1992 Cincinnati	NL	29	93	25	5	2	2	(2	0)	40	10	13	10	0	23	0	0	1	0	2	.00	1	.269	.337	.430
1993 Cincinnati	NL	15	50	8	1	1	2	(2	0)	17	7	5	2	0	19	0	0	1	0	0	.00	1	.160	.189	.340
1994 Cincinnati	NL	16	37	8	2	0	0	(0	0)	10	5	3	6	1	14	0	0	1	0	0	.00	1	.216	.318	.270
1995 Cincinnati	NL	8	19	2	0	0	0	(0	0)	2	1	0	3	0	7	0	0	0	0	0	.00	0	.105	.227	.105
1996 Cincinnati	NL	115	287	70	5	5	19	(11	8)	142	48	63	36	6	88	0	1	1	0	1	.00	5	.244	.327	.495
1997 Cincinnati	NL	151	495	125	22	1	26	(13	13)	227	62	91	78	5	111	1	1	3	6	0	1.00	10	.253	.354	.459
6 ML YEARS		334	981	238	35	9	49	(28	21)	438	133	175	135	12	262	1	2	7	6	3	.67	19	.243	.333	.446

Rusty Greer

Bats: L **Throws:** L **Pos:** LF-148; CF-19; PH-3; DH-2; RF-1   **Ht:** 6'0" **Wt:** 190 **Born:** 1/21/69 **Age:** 29

Year Team	Lg	G	AB	H	2B	3B	HR	(Hm	Rd)	TB	R	RBI	TBB	IBB	SO	HBP	SH	SF	SB	CS	SB%	GDP	Avg	OBP	SLG
1994 Texas	AL	80	277	87	16	1	10	(3	7)	135	36	46	46	2	46	2	2	4	0	0	.00	3	.314	.410	.487
1995 Texas	AL	131	417	113	21	2	13	(7	6)	177	58	61	55	1	66	1	2	3	3	1	.75	9	.271	.355	.424
1996 Texas	AL	139	542	180	41	6	18	(9	9)	287	96	100	62	4	86	3	0	10	9	0	1.00	9	.332	.397	.530
1997 Texas	AL	157	601	193	42	3	26	(18	8)	319	112	87	83	4	87	3	1	2	9	5	.64	11	.321	.405	.531
4 ML YEARS		507	1837	573	120	12	67	(37	30)	918	302	294	246	11	285	9	5	19	21	6	.78	32	.312	.392	.500

Tommy Gregg

Bats: Left **Throws:** Left **Pos:** PH-8; LF-5; 1B-1; RF-1   **Ht:** 6'1" **Wt:** 190 **Born:** 7/29/63 **Age:** 34

Year Team	Lg	G	AB	H	2B	3B	HR	(Hm	Rd)	TB	R	RBI	TBB	IBB	SO	HBP	SH	SF	SB	CS	SB%	GDP	Avg	OBP	SLG
1997 Richmond *	AAA	115	385	128	36	1	9	—	—	193	52	54	46	6	64	1	0	3	3	3	.50	7	.332	.402	.501
1987 Pittsburgh	NL	10	8	2	1	0	0	(0	0)	3	3	0	0	0	2	0	0	0	0	0	.00	2	.250	.250	.375
1988 Pit-Atl	NL	25	44	13	4	0	1	(0	1)	20	5	7	3	1	6	0	0	1	0	1	.00	0	.295	.333	.455
1989 Atlanta	NL	102	276	67	8	0	6	(2	4)	93	24	23	18	2	45	0	3	1	3	4	.43	4	.243	.288	.337
1990 Atlanta	NL	124	239	63	13	1	5	(2	3)	93	18	32	20	4	39	1	0	1	4	3	.57	1	.264	.322	.389
1991 Atlanta	NL	72	107	20	8	1	1	(1	0)	33	13	4	12	2	24	1	0	0	2	2	.50	1	.187	.275	.308
1992 Atlanta	NL	18	19	5	0	0	1	(1	0)	8	1	0	1	0	7	0	0	0	2	0	1.00	1	.263	.300	.421

Year Team	Lg	G	AB	H	2B	3B	HR	(Hm	Rd)	TB	R	RBI	TBB	IBB	SO	HBP	SH	SF	SB	CS	SB%	GDP	Avg	OBP	SLG
1993 Cincinnati	NL	10	12	2	0	0	0	(0	0)	2	1	1	0	0	0	0	0	1	0	0	.00	0	.167	.154	.167
1995 Florida	NL	72	156	37	5	0	6	(2	4)	60	20	20	16	1	33	2	0	2	3	1	.75	3	.237	.313	.385
1997 Atlanta	NL	13	19	5	2	0	0	(0	0)	7	1	0	1	0	2	0	0	0	1	1	.50	3	.263	.300	.368
1988 Pittsburgh	NL	14	15	3	1	0	1	(0	1)	7	4	3	1	0	4	0	0	1	0	1	1.00	0	.200	.235	.467
Atlanta	NL	11	29	10	3	0	0	(0	0)	13	1	4	2	1	0	0	0	0	0	0	.00	1	.345	.387	.448
9 ML YEARS		446	880	214	41	2	20	(8	12)	319	86	88	71	10	158	4	3	6	14	12	.54	13	.243	.301	.363

Ben Grieve

Bats: Left **Throws:** Right **Pos:** RF-24; PH-2 **Ht:** 6'4" **Wt:** 200 **Born:** 5/4/76 **Age:** 22

Year Team	Lg	G	AB	H	2B	3B	HR	(Hm	Rd)	TB	R	RBI	TBB	IBB	SO	HBP	SH	SF	SB	CS	SB%	GDP	Avg	OBP	SLG
1994 Sou. Oregon	A-	72	252	83	13	0	7	—	—	117	44	50	51	7	48	10	0	3	2	2	.50	0	.329	.456	.464
1995 W Michigan	A	102	371	97	16	1	4	—	—	127	53	62	60	6	75	8	0	6	11	3	.79	10	.261	.371	.342
Modesto	A+	28	107	28	5	0	2	—	—	39	17	14	15	1	22	0	0	2	2	0	1.00	3	.262	.347	.364
1996 Modesto	A+	72	281	100	20	1	11	—	—	155	61	51	38	2	52	1	1	3	8	7	.53	5	.356	.430	.552
Huntsville	AA	63	232	55	8	1	8	—	—	89	34	32	35	5	53	2	0	3	0	3	.00	3	.237	.338	.384
1997 Huntsville	AA	100	372	122	29	2	24	—	—	227	100	88	81	0	75	9	0	4	5	1	.83	8	.328	.455	.610
Edmonton	AAA	27	108	46	11	1	7	—	—	80	27	28	12	0	16	1	1	1	0	1	.00	4	.426	.484	.741
1997 Oakland	AL	24	93	29	6	0	3	(3	0)	44	12	24	13	1	25	1	1	0	0	0	.00	1	.312	.402	.473

Ken Griffey Jr

Bats: Left **Throws:** Left **Pos:** CF-153; DH-4; LF-1 **Ht:** 6'3" **Wt:** 205 **Born:** 11/21/69 **Age:** 28

Year Team	Lg	G	AB	H	2B	3B	HR	(Hm	Rd)	TB	R	RBI	TBB	IBB	SO	HBP	SH	SF	SB	CS	SB%	GDP	Avg	OBP	SLG
1989 Seattle	AL	127	455	120	23	0	16	(10	6)	191	61	61	44	8	83	2	1	4	16	7	.70	4	.264	.329	.420
1990 Seattle	AL	155	597	179	28	7	22	(8	14)	287	91	80	63	12	81	2	0	4	16	11	.59	12	.300	.366	.481
1991 Seattle	AL	154	548	179	42	1	22	(16	6)	289	76	100	71	21	82	1	4	9	18	6	.75	10	.327	.399	.527
1992 Seattle	AL	142	565	174	39	4	27	(16	11)	302	83	103	44	15	67	5	0	3	10	5	.67	15	.308	.361	.535
1993 Seattle	AL	156	582	180	38	3	45	(21	24)	359	113	109	96	25	91	6	0	7	17	9	.65	14	.309	.408	.617
1994 Seattle	AL	111	433	140	24	4	40	(18	22)	292	94	90	56	19	73	2	0	2	11	3	.79	9	.323	.402	.674
1995 Seattle	AL	72	260	67	7	0	17	(13	4)	125	52	42	52	6	53	0	0	2	4	2	.67	4	.258	.379	.481
1996 Seattle	AL	140	545	165	26	2	49	(26	23)	342	125	140	78	13	104	7	1	7	16	1	.94	7	.303	.392	.628
1997 Seattle	AL	157	608	185	34	3	56	(27	29)	393	125	147	76	23	121	8	0	12	15	4	.79	12	.304	.382	**.646**
9 ML YEARS		1214	4593	1389	261	24	294	(155	139)	2580	820	872	580	142	755	33	6	50	123	48	.72	87	.302	.381	.562

Marquis Grissom

Bats: Right **Throws:** Right **Pos:** CF-144 **Ht:** 5'11" **Wt:** 190 **Born:** 4/17/67 **Age:** 31

Year Team	Lg	G	AB	H	2B	3B	HR	(Hm	Rd)	TB	R	RBI	TBB	IBB	SO	HBP	SH	SF	SB	CS	SB%	GDP	Avg	OBP	SLG
1989 Montreal	NL	26	74	19	2	0	1	(0	1)	24	16	2	12	0	21	0	1	0	1	0	1.00	1	.257	.360	.324
1990 Montreal	NL	98	288	74	14	2	3	(2	1)	101	42	29	27	2	40	0	4	1	22	2	.92	8	.257	.320	.351
1991 Montreal	NL	148	558	149	23	9	6	(3	3)	208	73	39	34	0	89	1	4	0	76	17	.82	8	.267	.310	.373
1992 Montreal	NL	159	653	180	39	6	14	(8	6)	273	99	66	42	6	81	5	3	4	78	13	.86	12	.276	.322	.418
1993 Montreal	NL	157	630	188	27	2	19	(9	10)	276	104	95	52	6	76	3	0	8	53	10	.84	9	.298	.351	.438
1994 Montreal	NL	110	475	137	25	4	11	(4	7)	203	96	45	41	4	66	1	0	4	36	6	.86	10	.288	.344	.427
1995 Atlanta	NL	139	551	142	23	3	12	(5	7)	207	80	42	47	4	61	3	1	4	29	9	.76	8	.258	.317	.376
1996 Atlanta	NL	158	671	207	32	10	23	(11	12)	328	106	74	41	6	73	3	4	4	28	11	.72	12	.308	.349	.489
1997 Cleveland	AL	144	558	146	27	6	12	(5	7)	221	74	66	43	1	89	6	6	9	22	13	.63	12	.262	.317	.396
9 ML YEARS		1139	4458	1242	212	42	101	(47	54)	1841	690	458	339	29	596	22	23	34	345	81	.81	75	.279	.330	.413

Buddy Groom

Pitches: Left **Bats:** Left **Pos:** RP-78 **Ht:** 6'2" **Wt:** 200 **Born:** 7/10/65 **Age:** 32

Year Team	Lg	G	GS	CG	GF	IP	BFP	H	R	ER	HR	SH	SF	HB	TBB	IBB	SO	WP	Bk	W	L	Pct.	ShO	Sv-Op	Hld	ERA
1992 Detroit	AL	12	7	0	3	38.2	177	48	28	25	4	3	2	0	22	4	15	0	1	0	5	.000	0	1-2	0	5.82
1993 Detroit	AL	19	3	0	8	36.2	170	48	25	25	4	2	4	2	13	5	15	2	1	0	2	.000	0	0-0	1	6.14
1994 Detroit	AL	40	0	0	10	32	139	31	14	14	4	0	3	2	13	2	27	0	0	1	1	.000	0	1-1	11	3.94
1995 Det-Fla		37	4	0	11	55.2	274	81	47	46	8	2	2	2	32	4	35	3	0	2	5	.286	0	1-3	0	7.44
1996 Oakland	AL	72	1	0	16	77.1	341	85	37	33	8	2	0	3	34	3	57	5	0	5	0	1.000	0	2-4	10	3.84
1997 Oakland	AL	78	0	0	7	64.2	285	75	38	37	9	0	4	0	24	1	45	3	0	2	2	.500	0	3-5	12	5.15
1995 Detroit	AL	23	4	0	6	40.2	203	55	35	34	6	2	2	2	26	4	23	3	0	1	3	.250	0	1-3	0	7.52
Florida	NL	14	0	0	5	15	71	26	12	12	2	0	0	0	6	0	12	0	0	1	2	.333	0	0-0	0	7.20
6 ML YEARS		258	15	0	55	305	1386	368	189	180	37	9	15	9	138	19	194	13	2	9	15	.375	0	8-15	34	5.31

Kevin Gross

Pitches: Right **Bats:** Right **Pos:** RP-9; SP-3 **Ht:** 6'5" **Wt:** 227 **Born:** 6/8/61 **Age:** 37

Year Team	Lg	G	GS	CG	GF	IP	BFP	H	R	ER	HR	SH	SF	HB	TBB	IBB	SO	WP	Bk	W	L	Pct.	ShO	Sv-Op	Hld	ERA
1997 Okla City *	AAA	6	6	0	0	31.2	134	35	18	17	4	0	1	1	6	0	26	0	0	2	3	.400	0	0--	—	4.83
Vancouver *	AAA	2	2	0	0	11	38	7	2	2	1	0	0	0	5	0	5	0	0	1	0	1.000	0	0--	—	1.64
1983 Philadelphia	NL	17	17	1	0	96	418	100	46	38	13	2	1	3	35	3	66	4	1	4	6	.400	1	0-0	0	3.56
1984 Philadelphia	NL	44	14	1	9	129	566	140	66	59	8	9	3	5	44	4	84	4	4	8	5	.615	0	1--	—	4.12

			HOW MUCH HE PITCHED						WHAT HE GAVE UP												THE RESULTS						
Year Team	Lg	G	GS	CG	GF	IP	BFP	H	R	ER	HR	SH	SF	HB	TBB	IBB	SO	WP	Bk	W	L	Pct.	ShO	Sv-Op	Hld	ERA
1985 Philadelphia	NL	38	31	6	0	205.2	873	194	86	78	11	7	5	7	81	6	151	2	0	15	13	.536	2	0- -	—	3.41
1986 Philadelphia	NL	37	36	7	0	241.2	1040	240	115	108	28	8	5	8	94	2	154	2	1	12	12	.500	2	0- -	—	4.02
1987 Philadelphia	NL	34	33	3	1	200.2	878	205	107	97	26	8	6	10	87	7	110	3	7	9	16	.360	1	0-0	0	4.35
1988 Philadelphia	NL	33	33	5	0	231.2	989	209	101	95	18	9	4	11	89	5	162	5	7	12	14	.462	1	0-0	0	3.69
1989 Montreal	NL	31	31	4	0	201.1	867	188	105	98	20	10	3	6	88	6	158	5	5	11	12	.478	3	0-0	0	4.38
1990 Montreal	NL	31	26	2	3	163.1	712	171	86	83	9	6	9	4	65	7	111	4	1	9	12	.429	1	0-0	0	4.57
1991 Los Angeles	NL	46	10	0	16	115.2	509	123	55	46	10	6	4	2	50	6	95	3	0	10	11	.476	0	3-6	4	3.58
1992 Los Angeles	NL	34	30	4	0	204.2	856	182	82	72	11	14	6	3	77	10	158	4	2	8	13	.381	3	0-0	2	3.17
1993 Los Angeles	NL	33	32	3	1	202.1	892	224	110	93	15	11	6	5	74	7	150	2	5	13	13	.500	0	0-0	0	4.14
1994 Los Angeles	NL	25	23	1	2	157.1	665	162	64	63	11	4	1	2	43	2	124	4	1	9	7	.563	0	1-1	0	3.60
1995 Texas	AL	31	30	4	0	183.2	825	200	124	113	27	5	7	8	89	8	106	5	0	9	15	.375	0	0-0	0	5.54
1996 Texas	AL	28	19	1	4	129.1	580	151	78	75	19	3	8	4	50	2	78	4	0	11	8	.579	0	0-0	2	5.22
1997 Anaheim	AL	12	3	0	2	25.1	121	30	20	19	4	2	2	1	20	1	20	2	1	2	1	.667	0	0-0	0	6.75
15 ML YEARS		474	368	42	38	2487.2	10791	2519	1245	1137	230	104	70	79	986	76	1727	53	35	142	158	.473	14	5- -	—	4.11

Mark Grudzielanek

Bats: Right **Throws:** Right **Pos:** SS-156 **Ht:** 6'1" **Wt:** 185 **Born:** 6/30/70 **Age:** 28

				BATTING													BASERUNNING			PERCENTAGES		
Year Team	Lg	G	AB	H	2B	3B	HR	(Hm | Rd)	TB	R	RBI	TBB	IBB	SO	HBP	SH	SF	SB	CS	SB%	GDP	Avg	OBP	SLG
1995 Montreal	NL	78	269	66	12	2	1	(1 | 0)	85	27	20	14	4	47	7	3	0	8	3	.73	7	.245	.300	.316
1996 Montreal	NL	153	657	201	34	4	6	(5 | 1)	261	99	49	26	3	83	9	1	3	25	7	.78	10	.306	.340	.397
1997 Montreal	NL	156	649	177	54	3	4	(1 | 3)	249	76	51	23	0	76	10	3	3	25	9	.74	13	.273	.307	.384
3 ML YEARS		387	1575	444	100	9	11	(7 | 4)	595	202	120	63	7	206	26	7	6	66	19	.78	30	.282	.319	.378

Ken Grundt

Pitches: Left **Bats:** Left **Pos:** RP-2 **Ht:** 6'4" **Wt:** 195 **Born:** 8/26/69 **Age:** 28

			HOW MUCH HE PITCHED						WHAT HE GAVE UP												THE RESULTS						
Year Team	Lg	G	GS	CG	GF	IP	BFP	H	R	ER	HR	SH	SF	HB	TBB	IBB	SO	WP	Bk	W	L	Pct.	ShO	Sv-Op	Hld	ERA
1991 Everett	A-	29	0	0	15	54	231	55	27	14	3	3	0	3	16	5	58	3	0	4	5	.444	0	4- -	—	2.33
1992 Clinton	A	40	0	0	28	57.2	226	39	11	4	2	3	0	1	11	2	59	1	0	5	3	.625	0	16- -	—	0.62
San Jose	A+	11	0	0	5	17.2	70	9	3	2	1	2	0	2	7	1	17	0	0	1	0	1.000	0	3- -	—	1.02
1993 Giants	R	4	0	0	4	4	17	5	1	1	0	0	0	0	0	0	5	0	0	0	0	.000	0	0- -	—	2.25
1994 Sioux Falls	IND	26	0	0	10	44	189	44	15	8	2	0	0	1	21	0	35	1	0	3	3	.500	0	2- -	—	1.64
1995 Asheville	A	20	0	0	11	30.1	111	18	1	1	0	1	1	1	7	1	38	2	0	0	1	.000	0	1- -	—	0.30
New Haven	AA	28	0	0	8	38	146	26	14	9	1	2	0	1	10	2	27	2	0	2	2	.500	0	2- -	—	2.13
Colo Sprngs	AAA	9	0	0	1	5.2	30	9	5	3	0	0	0	0	4	0	5	0	0	0	0	.000	0	0- -	—	4.76
1996 Trenton	AA	12	0	0	3	12.2	48	6	0	0	0	1	0	0	6	0	13	1	0	1	0	1.000	0	0- -	—	0.00
Pawtucket	AAA	44	0	0	16	64.1	274	72	32	30	4	3	2	1	16	0	46	5	0	9	4	.692	0	2- -	—	4.20
1997 Pawtucket	AAA	49	1	0	15	47.1	224	59	30	28	5	3	2	5	22	5	28	0	0	4	2	.667	0	3- -	—	5.32
1996 Boston	AL	1	0	0	0	0.1	2	1	1	1	0	0	0	0	0	0	0	0	0	0	0	.000	0	0-0	0	27.00
1997 Boston	AL	2	0	0	0	3	14	5	3	3	0	0	0	0	0	0	0	0	1	0	0	.000	0	0-0	0	9.00
2 ML YEARS		3	0	0	0	3.1	16	6	4	4	0	0	0	0	0	0	0	0	1	0	0	.000	0	0-0	0	10.80

Eddie Guardado

Pitches: Left **Bats:** Right **Pos:** RP-69 **Ht:** 6'0" **Wt:** 193 **Born:** 10/2/70 **Age:** 27

			HOW MUCH HE PITCHED						WHAT HE GAVE UP												THE RESULTS						
Year Team	Lg	G	GS	CG	GF	IP	BFP	H	R	ER	HR	SH	SF	HB	TBB	IBB	SO	WP	Bk	W	L	Pct.	ShO	Sv-Op	Hld	ERA
1993 Minnesota	AL	19	16	0	2	94.2	426	123	68	65	13	1	3	1	36	2	46	0	0	3	8	.273	0	0-0	0	6.18
1994 Minnesota	AL	4	4	0	0	17	81	26	16	16	3	1	2	0	4	0	8	0	0	0	2	.000	0	0-0	0	8.47
1995 Minnesota	AL	51	5	0	10	91.1	410	99	54	52	13	6	5	0	45	2	71	5	1	4	9	.308	0	2-5	5	5.12
1996 Minnesota	AL	83	0	0	17	73.2	313	61	45	43	12	6	4	3	33	4	74	3	0	6	5	.545	0	4-7	18	5.25
1997 Minnesota	AL	69	0	0	20	46	201	45	23	20	7	2	1	2	17	2	54	2	0	0	4	.000	0	1-1	13	3.91
5 ML YEARS		226	25	0	49	322.2	1431	354	206	196	48	16	15	6	135	10	253	10	1	13	28	.317	0	7-13	36	5.47

Mark Gubicza

Pitches: Right **Bats:** Right **Pos:** SP-2 **Ht:** 6'5" **Wt:** 230 **Born:** 8/14/62 **Age:** 35

			HOW MUCH HE PITCHED						WHAT HE GAVE UP												THE RESULTS						
Year Team	Lg	G	GS	CG	GF	IP	BFP	H	R	ER	HR	SH	SF	HB	TBB	IBB	SO	WP	Bk	W	L	Pct.	ShO	Sv-Op	Hld	ERA
1997 Lk Elsinore *	A+	2	2	0	0	4	22	12	7	7	1	0	0	0	1	0	1	0	0	0	1	.000	0	0- -	—	15.75
1984 Kansas City	AL	29	29	4	0	189	800	172	90	85	13	4	9	5	75	0	111	3	1	10	14	.417	2	0-0	0	4.05
1985 Kansas City	AL	29	28	0	0	177.1	760	160	88	80	14	1	6	5	77	0	99	12	0	14	10	.583	0	0- -	—	4.06
1986 Kansas City	AL	35	24	3	2	180.2	765	155	77	73	8	4	8	5	84	2	118	15	0	12	6	.667	2	0- -	—	3.64
1987 Kansas City	AL	35	35	10	0	241.2	1036	231	114	107	18	6	11	6	120	3	166	14	1	13	18	.419	2	0-0	0	3.98
1988 Kansas City	AL	35	35	8	0	269.2	1111	237	94	81	11	3	6	6	83	3	183	12	4	20	8	.714	4	0-0	0	2.70
1989 Kansas City	AL	36	36	8	0	255	1060	252	100	86	10	11	8	5	63	8	173	9	0	15	11	.577	2	0-0	0	3.04
1990 Kansas City	AL	16	16	2	0	94	409	101	48	47	5	6	4	4	38	4	71	2	1	4	7	.364	0	0-0	0	4.50
1991 Kansas City	AL	26	26	0	0	133	601	168	90	84	10	3	5	6	42	1	89	5	0	9	12	.429	0	0-0	0	5.68
1992 Kansas City	AL	18	18	2	0	111.1	470	110	47	46	8	5	3	1	36	3	81	5	1	7	6	.538	1	0-0	0	3.72
1993 Kansas City	AL	49	6	0	12	104.1	474	128	61	54	2	6	6	2	43	8	80	12	0	5	8	.385	0	2-3	8	4.66
1994 Kansas City	AL	22	22	0	0	130	561	158	74	65	11	5	6	2	26	5	59	9	2	7	9	.438	0	0-0	0	4.50
1995 Kansas City	AL	33	33	3	0	213.1	898	222	97	89	21	9	6	6	62	2	81	4	1	12	14	.462	2	0-0	0	3.75
1996 Kansas City	AL	19	19	2	0	119.1	512	132	70	68	22	2	5	7	34	0	55	0	0	4	12	.250	1	0-0	0	5.13
1997 Anaheim	AL	2	2	0	0	4.2	30	13	13	13	2	0	0	0	3	0	1	0	0	0	1	.000	0	0- -	—	25.07
14 ML YEARS		384	329	42	14	2223.1	9487	2239	1063	978	155	65	82	58	786	39	1371	107	11	132	136	.493	16	2- -	—	3.96

Vladimir Guerrero

Bats: Right **Throws:** Right **Pos:** RF-84; PH-5; CF-1   **Ht:** 6'2" **Wt:** 195 **Born:** 2/9/76 **Age:** 22

Year Team	Lg	G	AB	H	2B	3B	HR	(Hm	Rd)	TB	R	RBI	TBB	IBB	SO	HBP	SH	SF	SB	CS	SB%	GDP	Avg	OBP	SLG
1994 Expos	R	37	137	43	13	3	5	—	—	77	24	25	11	0	18	2	0	3	0	7	.00	0	.314	.366	.562
1995 Albany	A	110	421	140	21	10	16	—	—	229	77	63	30	3	45	7	0	4	12	7	.63	8	.333	.383	.544
1996 Wst Plm Bch	A+	20	80	29	8	0	5	—	—	52	16	18	3	0	10	1	0	1	2	2	.50	1	.363	.388	.650
Harrisburg	AA	118	417	150	32	8	19	—	—	255	84	78	51	13	42	9	0	2	17	10	.63	8	.360	.438	.612
1997 Wst Plm Bch	A+	3	10	4	2	0	0	—	—	6	0	2	1	0	0	0	0	0	1	0	1.00	1	.400	.455	.600
1996 Montreal	NL	9	27	5	0	0	1	(0	1)	8	2	1	0	0	3	0	0	0	0	0	.00	0	.185	.185	.296
1997 Montreal	NL	90	325	98	22	2	11	(5	6)	157	44	40	19	2	39	7	0	3	3	4	.43	11	.302	.350	.483
2 ML YEARS		99	352	103	22	2	12	(5	7)	165	46	41	19	2	42	7	0	3	3	4	.43	12	.293	.339	.469

Wilton Guerrero

Bats: Both **Throws:** Right **Pos:** 2B-90; PH-19; SS-5   **Ht:** 5'11" **Wt:** 155 **Born:** 10/24/74 **Age:** 23

Year Team	Lg	G	AB	H	2B	3B	HR	(Hm	Rd)	TB	R	RBI	TBB	IBB	SO	HBP	SH	SF	SB	CS	SB%	GDP	Avg	OBP	SLG
1993 Great Falls	R+	66	256	76	5	1	0	—	—	83	44	21	24	1	33	3	5	0	20	8	.71	5	.297	.364	.324
1994 Vero Beach	A+	110	402	118	11	4	1	—	—	140	55	32	29	0	71	1	10	2	23	20	.53	2	.294	.341	.348
1995 San Antonio	AA	95	382	133	13	6	0	—	—	158	53	26	26	3	63	1	4	1	21	22	.49	10	.348	.390	.414
Albuquerque	AAA	14	49	16	1	1	0	—	—	19	10	2	1	1	7	0	2	0	2	3	.40	1	.327	.340	.388
1996 Albuquerque	AAA	98	425	146	17	12	2	—	—	193	79	38	26	2	48	1	11	0	26	15	.63	6	.344	.383	.454
1997 Albuquerque	AAA	10	45	18	0	1	0	—	—	20	9	5	2	1	3	0	0	1	3	0	1.00	1	.400	.417	.444
1996 Los Angeles	NL	5	2	0	0	0	0	(0	0)	0	1	0	0	0	2	0	0	0	0	0	.00	0	.000	.000	.000
1997 Los Angeles	NL	111	357	104	10	9	4	(2	2)	144	39	32	8	1	52	0	13	2	6	5	.55	7	.291	.305	.403
2 ML YEARS		116	359	104	10	9	4	(2	2)	144	40	32	8	1	54	0	13	2	6	5	.55	7	.290	.304	.401

Giomar Guevara

Bats: Right **Throws:** Right **Pos:** DH-2; 2B-2; PH-2; SS-1   **Ht:** 5'8" **Wt:** 150 **Born:** 10/23/72 **Age:** 25

Year Team	Lg	G	AB	H	2B	3B	HR	(Hm	Rd)	TB	R	RBI	TBB	IBB	SO	HBP	SH	SF	SB	CS	SB%	GDP	Avg	OBP	SLG
1993 Bellingham	A-	62	211	48	8	3	1	—	—	65	31	23	34	2	46	2	4	0	4	7	.36	3	.227	.340	.308
1994 Appleton	A	110	385	116	23	3	8	—	—	169	57	46	42	1	77	2	5	1	9	16	.36	6	.301	.372	.439
Jacksnville	AA	7	20	4	2	0	1	—	—	9	2	3	2	0	9	0	1	0	0	0	.00	0	.200	.273	.450
1995 Riverside	A+	83	292	71	12	3	2	—	—	95	53	34	30	1	71	1	6	6	7	4	.64	4	.243	.310	.325
1996 Port City	AA	119	414	110	18	2	2	—	—	138	60	41	54	1	102	4	9	4	21	7	.75	12	.266	.353	.333
1997 Tacoma	AAA	54	176	43	5	1	2	—	—	56	29	13	5	0	39	1	5	0	3	7	.30	2	.244	.269	.318
Memphis	AA	65	228	60	10	4	4	—	—	90	30	28	20	0	42	0	0	1	5	5	.50	3	.263	.321	.395
1997 Seattle	AL	5	4	0	0	0	0	(0	0)	0	0	0	0	0	2	0	0	0	1	0	1.00	0	.000	.000	.000

Jose Guillen

Bats: Right **Throws:** Right **Pos:** RF-134; PH-8; CF-4   **Ht:** 5'11" **Wt:** 185 **Born:** 5/17/76 **Age:** 22

Year Team	Lg	G	AB	H	2B	3B	HR	(Hm	Rd)	TB	R	RBI	TBB	IBB	SO	HBP	SH	SF	SB	CS	SB%	GDP	Avg	OBP	SLG
1994 Pirates	R	30	110	29	4	1	4	—	—	47	17	11	7	0	15	6	0	0	2	1	.67	0	.264	.341	.427
1995 Erie	A-	66	258	81	17	1	12	—	—	136	41	46	10	0	44	12	0	1	1	5	.17	5	.314	.367	.527
Augusta	A	10	34	8	1	1	2	—	—	17	6	6	2	0	9	2	0	0	0	0	.00	0	.235	.316	.500
1996 Lynchburg	A+	136	528	170	30	0	21	—	—	263	78	94	20	1	73	13	1	8	24	13	.65	16	.322	.357	.498
1997 Pittsburgh	NL	143	498	133	20	5	14	(5	9)	205	58	70	17	0	88	8	0	3	1	2	.33	16	.267	.300	.412

Ozzie Guillen

Bats: Left **Throws:** Right **Pos:** SS-139; PH-5   **Ht:** 5'11" **Wt:** 164 **Born:** 1/20/64 **Age:** 34

Year Team	Lg	G	AB	H	2B	3B	HR	(Hm	Rd)	TB	R	RBI	TBB	IBB	SO	HBP	SH	SF	SB	CS	SB%	GDP	Avg	OBP	SLG
1985 Chicago	AL	150	491	134	21	9	1	(1	0)	176	71	33	12	1	36	1	8	1	7	4	.64	5	.273	.291	.358
1986 Chicago	AL	159	547	137	19	4	2	(1	1)	170	58	47	12	1	52	1	12	5	8	4	.67	14	.250	.265	.311
1987 Chicago	AL	149	560	156	22	7	2	(2	0)	198	64	51	22	2	52	1	13	8	25	8	.76	10	.279	.303	.354
1988 Chicago	AL	156	566	148	16	7	0	(0	0)	178	58	39	25	3	40	2	10	3	25	13	.66	14	.261	.294	.314
1989 Chicago	AL	155	597	151	20	8	1	(0	1)	190	63	54	15	3	48	0	11	3	36	17	.68	8	.253	.270	.318
1990 Chicago	AL	160	516	144	21	4	1	(1	0)	176	61	58	26	8	37	1	15	5	13	17	.43	6	.279	.312	.341
1991 Chicago	AL	154	524	143	20	3	3	(1	2)	178	52	49	11	1	38	1	13	7	21	15	.58	7	.273	.284	.340
1992 Chicago	AL	12	40	8	4	0	0	(0	0)	12	5	7	1	0	5	0	1	1	1	0	1.00	1	.200	.214	.300
1993 Chicago	AL	134	457	128	23	4	4	(3	1)	171	44	50	10	0	41	0	13	6	5	4	.56	6	.280	.292	.374
1994 Chicago	AL	100	365	105	9	5	1	(0	1)	127	46	39	14	2	35	0	7	4	5	4	.56	5	.288	.311	.348
1995 Chicago	AL	122	415	103	20	3	1	(1	0)	132	50	41	13	1	25	0	4	1	6	7	.46	11	.248	.270	.318
1996 Chicago	AL	150	499	131	24	8	4	(0	4)	183	62	45	10	0	27	0	12	7	6	5	.55	10	.263	.273	.367
1997 Chicago	AL	142	490	120	21	6	4	(1	3)	165	59	52	22	1	24	0	11	4	5	3	.63	7	.245	.275	.337
13 ML YEARS		1743	6067	1608	240	68	24	(11	13)	2056	693	565	193	23	460	6	130	55	163	101	.62	104	.265	.286	.339

84

Mike Gulan

Bats: Right **Throws:** Right **Pos:** PH-4; 3B-3   **Ht:** 6'1" **Wt:** 195 **Born:** 12/18/70 **Age:** 27

Year Team	Lg	G	AB	H	2B	3B	HR	(Hm	Rd)	TB	R	RBI	TBB	IBB	SO	HBP	SH	SF	SB	CS	SB%	GDP	Avg	OBP	SLG
1992 Hamilton	A-	62	242	66	8	4	7	—	—	103	33	36	23	0	53	1	0	4	12	4	.75	7	.273	.333	.426
1993 Springfield	A	132	455	118	28	4	23	—	—	223	81	76	34	0	135	9	3	3	8	4	.67	4	.259	.321	.490
1994 St. Pete	A+	120	466	113	30	2	8	—	—	171	39	56	26	2	108	2	0	6	2	8	.20	8	.242	.282	.367
1995 Arkansas	AA	64	242	76	16	3	12	—	—	134	47	48	11	1	52	6	0	1	4	2	.67	4	.314	.358	.554
Louisville	AAA	58	195	46	10	4	5	—	—	79	21	27	10	1	53	3	0	2	2	2	.50	6	.236	.281	.405
1996 Louisville	AAA	123	419	107	27	4	17	—	—	193	47	55	26	1	119	7	1	2	7	2	.78	10	.255	.308	.461
1997 Louisville	AAA	116	412	110	20	6	14	—	—	184	50	61	28	0	121	3	1	3	5	2	.71	12	.267	.316	.447
1997 St. Louis	NL	5	9	0	0	0	0	(0	0)	0	2	1	1	0	5	0	0	0	0	0	.00	0	.000	.100	.000

Eric Gunderson

Pitches: Left **Bats:** Right **Pos:** RP-60   **Ht:** 6'0" **Wt:** 190 **Born:** 3/29/66 **Age:** 32

Year Team	Lg	G	GS	CG	GF	IP	BFP	H	R	ER	HR	SH	SF	HB	TBB	IBB	SO	WP	Bk	W	L	Pct.	ShO	Sv-Op	Hld	ERA
1990 San Francisco	NL	7	4	0	1	19.2	94	24	14	12	2	1	0	0	11	1	14	0	0	1	2	.333	0	0-0	0	5.49
1991 San Francisco	NL	2	0	0	1	3.1	18	6	4	2	0	0	0	0	1	0	2	0	0	0	0	.000	0	1-1	0	5.40
1992 Seattle	AL	9	0	0	4	9.1	45	12	12	9	1	0	2	1	5	3	2	0	2	2	1	.667	0	0-0	0	8.68
1994 New York	NL	14	0	0	3	9	31	5	0	0	0	0	0	0	4	0	4	0	0	0	0	.000	0	0-0	2	0.00
1995 NYN-Bos		49	0	0	8	36.2	161	38	17	17	2	2	2	3	17	4	28	1	0	3	2	.600	0	0-3	6	4.17
1996 Boston	AL	28	0	0	2	17.1	82	21	17	16	5	0	2	2	8	2	7	3	0	1	0	1.000	0	0-0	3	8.31
1997 Texas	AL	60	0	0	11	49.2	209	45	19	18	5	2	3	2	15	3	31	2	1	2	1	.667	0	1-4	12	3.26
1995 New York	NL	30	0	0	7	24.1	103	25	10	10	2	0	1	1	8	3	19	1	0	1	1	.500	0	0-3	6	3.70
Boston	AL	19	0	0	1	12.1	58	13	7	7	0	2	1	2	9	1	9	0	0	2	1	.667	0	0-0	6	5.11
7 ML YEARS		169	4	0	30	145	640	151	83	74	15	5	9	8	61	13	88	6	3	8	7	.533	0	2-8	23	4.59

Mark Guthrie

Pitches: Left **Bats:** Right **Pos:** RP-62   **Ht:** 6'4" **Wt:** 207 **Born:** 9/22/65 **Age:** 32

Year Team	Lg	G	GS	CG	GF	IP	BFP	H	R	ER	HR	SH	SF	HB	TBB	IBB	SO	WP	Bk	W	L	Pct.	ShO	Sv-Op	Hld	ERA
1989 Minnesota	AL	13	8	0	2	57.1	254	66	32	29	7	1	5	1	21	1	38	1	0	2	4	.333	0	0-0	0	4.55
1990 Minnesota	AL	24	21	3	0	144.2	603	154	65	61	8	6	0	1	39	3	101	9	0	7	9	.438	1	0-0	0	3.79
1991 Minnesota	AL	41	12	0	13	98	432	116	52	47	11	4	3	1	41	2	72	7	0	7	5	.583	0	2-2	5	4.32
1992 Minnesota	AL	54	0	0	15	75	303	59	27	24	7	4	2	0	23	7	76	2	0	2	3	.400	0	5-7	19	2.88
1993 Minnesota	AL	22	0	0	2	21	94	20	11	11	2	1	2	0	16	2	15	1	3	2	1	.667	0	0-1	8	4.71
1994 Minnesota	AL	50	2	0	13	51.1	234	65	43	35	8	2	6	2	18	2	38	7	0	4	2	.667	0	1-3	12	6.14
1995 Min-LA		60	0	0	14	62	272	66	33	29	6	4	0	2	25	5	67	5	1	5	5	.500	0	0-2	15	4.21
1996 Los Angeles	NL	66	0	0	16	73	302	65	21	18	3	4	4	1	22	2	56	1	0	2	3	.400	0	1-3	12	2.22
1997 Los Angeles	NL	62	0	0	18	69.1	305	71	44	41	12	10	3	0	30	6	42	2	1	1	4	.200	0	1-4	13	5.32
1995 Minnesota	AL	36	0	0	7	42.1	181	47	22	21	5	2	0	1	16	3	48	3	1	5	3	.625	0	0-2	10	4.46
Los Angeles	NL	24	0	0	7	19.2	91	19	11	8	1	2	0	1	9	2	19	2	0	0	2	.000	0	0-0	5	3.66
9 ML YEARS		392	43	3	93	651.2	2799	682	328	295	64	36	25	8	235	30	505	35	5	32	36	.471	1	10-22	84	4.07

Ricky Gutierrez

Bats: R **Throws:** R **Pos:** SS-64; 3B-22; PH-17; 2B-9   **Ht:** 6'1" **Wt:** 175 **Born:** 5/23/70 **Age:** 28

Year Team	Lg	G	AB	H	2B	3B	HR	(Hm	Rd)	TB	R	RBI	TBB	IBB	SO	HBP	SH	SF	SB	CS	SB%	GDP	Avg	OBP	SLG
1997 New Orleans *	AAA	7	27	5	1	0	0	—	—	6	2	4	2	0	4	0	0	1	0	1	.00	1	.185	.233	.222
1993 San Diego	NL	133	438	110	10	5	5	(5	0)	145	76	26	50	2	97	1	4	3	4	3	.57	7	.251	.334	.331
1994 San Diego	NL	90	275	66	11	2	1	(1	0)	84	27	28	32	1	54	2	2	3	2	6	.25	8	.240	.321	.305
1995 Houston	NL	52	156	43	6	0	0	(0	0)	49	22	12	10	3	33	1	1	1	5	0	1.00	4	.276	.321	.314
1996 Houston	NL	89	218	62	8	1	1	(1	0)	75	28	15	23	3	42	3	4	1	6	1	.86	6	.284	.359	.344
1997 Houston	NL	102	303	79	14	4	3	(0	3)	110	33	34	21	2	50	3	0	1	5	2	.71	17	.261	.315	.363
5 ML YEARS		466	1390	360	49	12	10	(7	3)	463	186	115	136	11	276	14	8	6	22	12	.65	40	.259	.330	.333

Juan Guzman

Pitches: Right **Bats:** Right **Pos:** SP-13   **Ht:** 5'11" **Wt:** 195 **Born:** 10/28/66 **Age:** 31

Year Team	Lg	G	GS	CG	GF	IP	BFP	H	R	ER	HR	SH	SF	HB	TBB	IBB	SO	WP	Bk	W	L	Pct.	ShO	Sv-Op	Hld	ERA
1997 Dunedin *	A+	2	2	0	0	4	15	3	0	0	0	0	0	0	1	0	3	0	0	0	0	.000	0	0-	—	0.00
1991 Toronto	AL	23	23	1	0	138.2	574	98	53	46	6	2	5	4	66	0	123	10	0	10	3	.769	0	0-0	0	2.99
1992 Toronto	AL	28	28	1	0	180.2	733	135	56	53	6	5	3	3	72	2	165	14	2	16	5	.762	0	0-0	0	2.64
1993 Toronto	AL	33	33	2	0	221	963	211	107	98	17	5	9	3	110	2	194	26	1	14	3	.824	1	0-0	0	3.99
1994 Toronto	AL	25	25	2	0	147.1	671	165	102	93	20	1	6	3	76	1	124	13	1	12	11	.522	0	0-0	0	5.68
1995 Toronto	AL	24	24	3	0	135.1	619	151	101	95	13	3	2	3	73	6	94	8	0	4	14	.222	0	0-0	0	6.32
1996 Toronto	AL	27	27	4	0	187.2	756	158	68	61	20	2	2	7	53	3	165	7	0	11	8	.579	1	0-0	0	2.93
1997 Toronto	AL	13	13	0	0	60	261	48	42	33	14	1	2	2	31	0	52	4	0	3	6	.333	0	0-0	0	4.95
7 ML YEARS		173	173	13	0	1070.2	4577	966	529	479	96	19	29	23	481	14	917	82	4	70	50	.583	2	0-0	0	4.03

Tony Gwynn

Bats: Left **Throws:** Left **Pos:** RF-143; DH-3; PH-3 **Ht:** 5'11" **Wt:** 220 **Born:** 5/9/60 **Age:** 38

Year Team	Lg	G	AB	H	2B	3B	HR	(Hm	Rd)	TB	R	RBI	TBB	IBB	SO	HBP	SH	SF	SB	CS	SB%	GDP	Avg	OBP	SLG
1982 San Diego	NL	54	190	55	12	2	1	(0	1)	74	33	17	14	0	16	0	4	1	8	3	.73	5	.289	.337	.389
1983 San Diego	NL	86	304	94	12	2	1	(0	1)	113	34	37	23	5	21	0	4	3	7	4	.64	9	.309	.355	.372
1984 San Diego	NL	158	606	213	21	10	5	(3	2)	269	88	71	59	13	23	2	6	2	33	18	.65	15	.351	.410	.444
1985 San Diego	NL	154	622	197	29	5	6	(3	3)	254	90	46	45	4	33	2	1	1	14	11	.56	17	.317	.364	.408
1986 San Diego	NL	160	642	211	33	7	14	(8	6)	300	107	59	52	11	35	3	2	2	37	9	.80	20	.329	.381	.467
1987 San Diego	NL	157	589	218	36	13	7	(5	2)	301	119	54	82	26	35	3	2	4	56	12	.82	13	.370	.447	.511
1988 San Diego	NL	133	521	163	22	5	7	(3	4)	216	64	70	51	13	40	0	4	2	26	11	.70	11	.313	.373	.415
1989 San Diego	NL	158	604	203	27	7	4	(1	3)	256	82	62	56	16	30	1	11	7	40	16	.71	12	.336	.389	.424
1990 San Diego	NL	141	573	177	29	10	4	(2	2)	238	79	72	44	20	23	1	7	4	17	8	.68	13	.309	.357	.415
1991 San Diego	NL	134	530	168	27	11	4	(1	3)	229	69	62	34	8	19	0	0	5	8	8	.50	11	.317	.355	.432
1992 San Diego	NL	128	520	165	27	3	6	(4	2)	216	77	41	46	12	16	0	0	3	3	6	.33	13	.317	.371	.415
1993 San Diego	NL	122	489	175	41	3	7	(4	3)	243	70	59	36	11	19	1	1	7	14	1	.93	18	.358	.398	.497
1994 San Diego	NL	110	419	165	35	1	12	(4	8)	238	79	64	48	16	19	2	1	5	5	0	1.00	20	.394	.454	.568
1995 San Diego	NL	135	535	197	33	1	9	(5	4)	259	82	90	35	10	15	1	0	6	17	5	.77	20	.368	.404	.484
1996 San Diego	NL	116	451	159	27	2	3	(2	1)	199	67	50	39	12	17	1	1	6	11	4	.73	17	.353	.400	.441
1997 San Diego	NL	149	592	220	49	2	17	(8	9)	324	97	119	43	12	28	3	1	12	12	5	.71	12	.372	.409	.547
16 ML YEARS		2095	8187	2780	460	84	107	(55	52)	3729	1237	973	707	189	389	20	45	70	308	121	.72	226	.340	.390	.455

Chip Hale

Bats: Left **Throws:** Right **Pos:** PH-13; 3B-2 **Ht:** 5'11" **Wt:** 186 **Born:** 12/2/64 **Age:** 33

Year Team	Lg	G	AB	H	2B	3B	HR	(Hm	Rd)	TB	R	RBI	TBB	IBB	SO	HBP	SH	SF	SB	CS	SB%	GDP	Avg	OBP	SLG
1997 Albuquerque *	AAA	88	247	66	16	0	2	—	—	88	43	30	58	0	26	2	4	2	3	3	.50	9	.267	.408	.356
1989 Minnesota	AL	28	67	14	3	0	0	(0	0)	17	6	4	1	0	6	0	1	2	0	0	.00	0	.209	.214	.254
1990 Minnesota	AL	1	2	0	0	0	0	(0	0)	0	0	2	0	0	1	0	0	0	0	0	.00	0	.000	.000	.000
1993 Minnesota	AL	69	186	62	6	1	3	(1	2)	79	25	27	18	0	17	6	2	1	2	1	.67	3	.333	.408	.425
1994 Minnesota	AL	67	118	31	9	0	1	(0	1)	43	13	11	16	1	14	1	1	2	0	2	.00	2	.263	.350	.364
1995 Minnesota	AL	69	103	27	4	0	2	(0	2)	37	10	18	11	1	20	0	0	0	0	0	.00	6	.262	.333	.359
1996 Minnesota	AL	85	87	24	5	0	1	(0	1)	32	8	16	10	2	6	0	0	1	0	0	.00	3	.276	.347	.368
1997 Los Angeles	NL	14	12	1	0	0	0	(0	0)	1	0	0	2	0	4	0	0	0	0	0	.00	0	.083	.214	.083
7 ML YEARS		333	575	159	27	1	7	(1	6)	209	62	78	58	4	68	7	4	8	2	3	.40	14	.277	.346	.363

Darren Hall

Pitches: Right **Bats:** Right **Pos:** RP-63 **Ht:** 6'3" **Wt:** 205 **Born:** 7/14/64 **Age:** 33

Year Team	Lg	G	GS	CG	GF	IP	BFP	H	R	ER	HR	SF	HB	TBB	IBB	SO	WP	Bk	W	L	Pct.	ShO	Sv-Op	Hld	ERA
1994 Toronto	AL	30	0	0	28	31.2	131	26	12	12	3	1	0	1	14	1	28	1	0	2	3	.400	0	17-20	1	3.41
1995 Toronto	AL	17	0	0	11	16.1	77	21	9	8	2	0	0	0	9	0	11	0	0	0	2	.000	0	3-4	2	4.41
1996 Los Angeles	NL	9	0	0	3	12	53	13	9	8	2	0	0	0	5	0	12	0	0	0	1	.000	0	0-1	2	6.00
1997 Los Angeles	NL	63	0	0	20	54.2	233	58	15	14	3	1	1	0	26	7	39	0	0	3	2	.600	0	2-5	15	2.30
4 ML YEARS		119	0	0	62	114.2	494	118	45	42	10	2	1	1	54	8	90	1	0	5	9	.357	0	22-30	20	3.30

Joe Hall

Bats: Right **Throws:** Right **Pos:** RF-1; PH-1 **Ht:** 6'0" **Wt:** 180 **Born:** 3/6/66 **Age:** 32

Year Team	Lg	G	AB	H	2B	3B	HR	(Hm	Rd)	TB	R	RBI	TBB	IBB	SO	HBP	SH	SF	SB	CS	SB%	GDP	Avg	OBP	SLG
1988 Hamilton	A-	70	274	78	9	1	2	—	—	95	46	37	30	1	37	5	1	2	30	8	.79	6	.285	.363	.347
Springfield	A	1	1	0	0	0	0	—	—	0	0	0	0	0	1	0	0	0	0	0	.00	0	.000	.000	.000
1989 St. Pete	A+	134	504	147	9	3	0	—	—	162	72	54	60	2	57	8	3	9	45	28	.62	11	.292	.370	.321
1990 Arkansas	AA	115	399	108	14	4	4	—	—	142	44	44	35	4	41	3	2	4	21	14	.60	7	.271	.330	.356
1991 Vancouver	AAA	118	427	106	16	1	4	—	—	136	41	39	23	2	45	4	3	4	11	11	.50	18	.248	.290	.319
1992 Vancouver	AAA	112	367	104	19	7	6	—	—	155	46	56	60	1	44	4	10	3	11	5	.69	15	.283	.387	.422
1993 Nashville	AAA	116	424	123	33	5	10	—	—	196	66	58	52	3	56	4	1	2	10	9	.53	14	.290	.371	.462
1994 Birmingham	AA	19	67	14	6	0	0	—	—	20	9	6	15	0	11	1	0	1	0	0	.00	4	.209	.357	.299
Nashville	AAA	22	72	21	7	0	4	—	—	40	14	21	16	1	10	2	0	2	0	0	.00	1	.292	.424	.556
1995 Toledo	AAA	91	316	102	19	2	11	—	—	158	52	47	36	1	50	2	1	2	4	1	.80	7	.320	.390	.495
1996 Rochester	AAA	131	479	138	26	10	19	—	—	241	96	95	67	3	69	2	0	6	15	9	.63	8	.288	.374	.503
1997 Toledo	AAA	75	271	68	18	2	6	—	—	108	35	30	22	0	48	2	0	4	2	1	.67	10	.251	.308	.399
1994 Chicago	AL	17	28	11	3	0	1	(1	0)	17	6	5	2	0	4	1	0	0	0	0	.00	2	.393	.452	.607
1995 Detroit	AL	7	15	2	0	0	0	(0	0)	2	2	0	2	0	3	0	0	0	0	0	.00	0	.133	.235	.133
1997 Detroit	AL	2	4	2	1	0	0	(0	0)	3	1	3	0	0	0	0	0	0	0	0	.00	0	.500	.500	.750
3 ML YEARS		26	47	15	4	0	1	(1	0)	22	9	8	4	0	7	1	0	0	0	0	.00	3	.319	.385	.468

Shane Halter

B: R **T:** R **Pos:** PH-22; 2B-18; RF-17; 3B-12; LF-10; CF-9; SS-5; DH-4 **Ht:** 5'10" **Wt:** 160 **Born:** 11/8/69 **Age:** 28

Year Team	Lg	G	AB	H	2B	3B	HR	(Hm	Rd)	TB	R	RBI	TBB	IBB	SO	HBP	SH	SF	SB	CS	SB%	GDP	Avg	OBP	SLG
1991 Eugene	A-	64	236	55	9	1	1	—	—	69	41	18	49	0	59	3	2	1	12	6	.67	3	.233	.370	.292
1992 Appleton	A	80	313	83	22	3	3	—	—	120	50	33	41	1	54	1	5	3	21	6	.78	4	.265	.349	.383
Baseball Cy	A+	44	117	28	1	0	1	—	—	32	11	14	24	0	31	0	5	4	5	5	.50	4	.239	.359	.274
1993 Wilmington	A+	54	211	63	8	5	5	—	—	96	44	32	21	2	55	2	12	1	5	4	.56	3	.299	.377	.455

Year Team	Lg	G	AB	H	2B	3B	HR	(Hm	Rd)	TB	R	RBI	TBB	IBB	SO	HBP	SH	SF	SB	CS	SB%	GDP	Avg	OBP	SLG
Memphis	AA	81	306	79	7	0	4	—	—	98	50	20	30	1	74	2	10	3	4	7	.36	3	.258	.326	.320
1994 Memphis	AA	129	494	111	23	1	6	—	—	154	61	35	39	0	102	3	15	6	10	14	.42	10	.225	.282	.312
1995 Omaha	AAA	124	392	90	19	3	8	—	—	139	42	39	40	0	97	0	19	1	2	3	.40	6	.230	.300	.355
1996 Charlotte	AAA	16	41	12	1	0	0	—	—	13	3	4	2	0	8	0	0	2	0	0	.00	0	.293	.311	.317
Omaha	AAA	93	299	77	24	0	3	—	—	110	43	33	31	0	49	2	8	1	7	2	.78	6	.258	.330	.368
1997 Omaha	AAA	14	49	13	1	1	2	—	—	22	10	9	6	0	10	1	0	2	0	0	.00	1	.265	.345	.449
1997 Kansas City	AL	74	123	34	5	1	2	(1	1)	47	16	10	10	0	28	2	4	0	4	3	.57	1	.276	.341	.382

Bob Hamelin

Bats: Left **Throws:** Left **Pos:** DH-95; PH-15; 1B-7 **Ht:** 6'0" **Wt:** 235 **Born:** 11/29/67 **Age:** 30

Year Team	Lg	G	AB	H	2B	3B	HR	(Hm	Rd)	TB	R	RBI	TBB	IBB	SO	HBP	SH	SF	SB	CS	SB%	GDP	Avg	OBP	SLG
1997 Toledo *	AAA	27	91	22	7	0	6	—	—	47	14	24	27	2	24	0	0	0	0	0	.00	1	.242	.415	.516
1993 Kansas City	AL	16	49	11	3	0	2	(1	1)	20	2	5	6	0	15	0	0	0	0	0	.00	2	.224	.309	.408
1994 Kansas City	AL	101	312	88	25	1	24	(13	11)	187	64	65	56	3	62	1	0	5	4	3	.57	4	.282	.388	.599
1995 Kansas City	AL	72	208	35	7	1	7	(3	4)	65	20	25	26	1	56	6	0	1	0	1	.00	6	.168	.278	.313
1996 Kansas City	AL	89	239	61	14	1	9	(2	7)	104	31	40	54	2	58	2	0	4	5	2	.71	7	.255	.391	.435
1997 Detroit	AL	110	318	86	15	0	18	(10	8)	155	47	52	48	3	72	1	0	2	2	1	.67	8	.270	.366	.487
5 ML YEARS		388	1126	281	64	3	60	(29	31)	531	164	187	190	9	263	10	0	12	11	7	.61	27	.250	.359	.472

Darryl Hamilton

Bats: Left **Throws:** Right **Pos:** CF-119; PH-8 **Ht:** 6'1" **Wt:** 185 **Born:** 12/3/64 **Age:** 33

Year Team	Lg	G	AB	H	2B	3B	HR	(Hm	Rd)	TB	R	RBI	TBB	IBB	SO	HBP	SH	SF	SB	CS	SB%	GDP	Avg	OBP	SLG
1997 Phoenix *	AAA	3	14	4	1	0	1	—	—	8	1	2	2	0	2	0	0	0	0	0	.00	0	.286	.286	.571
1988 Milwaukee	AL	44	103	19	4	0	1	(1	0)	26	14	11	12	0	9	1	0	1	7	3	.70	2	.184	.274	.252
1990 Milwaukee	AL	89	156	46	5	0	1	(1	0)	54	27	18	9	0	12	0	3	0	10	3	.77	2	.295	.333	.346
1991 Milwaukee	AL	122	405	126	15	6	1	(0	1)	156	64	57	33	2	38	0	7	3	16	6	.73	10	.311	.361	.385
1992 Milwaukee	AL	128	470	140	19	7	5	(1	4)	188	67	62	45	0	42	1	4	7	41	14	.75	10	.298	.356	.400
1993 Milwaukee	AL	135	520	161	21	1	9	(5	4)	211	74	48	45	5	62	3	4	1	21	13	.62	9	.310	.367	.406
1994 Milwaukee	AL	36	141	37	10	1	1	(0	1)	52	23	13	15	1	17	0	2	1	3	0	1.00	2	.262	.331	.369
1995 Milwaukee	AL	112	398	108	20	6	5	(3	2)	155	54	44	47	3	35	3	8	3	11	1	.92	9	.271	.350	.389
1996 Texas	AL	148	627	184	29	4	6	(2	4)	239	94	51	54	4	66	2	7	6	15	5	.75	15	.293	.348	.381
1997 San Francisco	NL	125	460	124	23	3	5	(1	4)	168	78	43	61	1	61	0	6	2	15	10	.60	6	.270	.354	.365
9 ML YEARS		939	3280	945	146	28	34	(14	20)	1249	495	347	321	16	342	10	41	24	139	55	.72	65	.288	.351	.381

Joey Hamilton

Pitches: Right **Bats:** Right **Pos:** SP-29; RP-2 **Ht:** 6'4" **Wt:** 230 **Born:** 9/9/70 **Age:** 27

Year Team	Lg	G	GS	CG	GF	IP	BFP	H	R	ER	HR	SH	SF	HB	TBB	IBB	SO	WP	Bk	W	L	Pct.	ShO	Sv-Op	Hld	ERA
1994 San Diego	NL	16	16	1	0	108.2	447	98	40	36	7	4	2	6	29	3	61	6	0	9	6	.600	1	0-0	0	2.98
1995 San Diego	NL	31	30	2	1	204.1	850	189	89	70	17	12	4	11	56	5	123	2	0	6	9	.400	2	0-0	0	3.08
1996 San Diego	NL	34	33	3	0	211.2	908	206	100	98	19	6	5	9	83	3	184	14	1	15	9	.625	1	0-0	1	4.17
1997 San Diego	NL	31	29	1	1	192.2	831	199	100	91	22	8	8	12	69	2	124	7	0	12	7	.632	0	0-0	0	4.25
4 ML YEARS		112	108	7	2	717.1	3036	692	329	295	65	30	19	38	237	13	492	29	1	42	31	.575	4	0-0	1	3.70

Chris Hammond

Pitches: Left **Bats:** Left **Pos:** RP-21; SP-8 **Ht:** 6'1" **Wt:** 195 **Born:** 1/21/66 **Age:** 32

Year Team	Lg	G	GS	CG	GF	IP	BFP	H	R	ER	HR	SH	SF	HB	TBB	IBB	SO	WP	Bk	W	L	Pct.	ShO	Sv-Op	Hld	ERA
1990 Cincinnati	NL	3	3	0	0	11.1	56	13	9	8	2	1	0	0	12	1	4	1	3	0	2	.000	0	0-0	0	6.35
1991 Cincinnati	NL	20	18	0	0	99.2	425	92	51	45	4	6	1	2	48	3	50	3	0	7	7	.500	0	0-0	0	4.06
1992 Cincinnati	NL	28	26	0	1	147.1	627	149	75	69	13	5	3	3	55	6	79	6	0	7	10	.412	0	0-0	0	4.21
1993 Florida	NL	32	32	1	0	191	826	207	106	99	18	10	2	1	66	2	108	10	5	11	12	.478	1	0-0	0	4.66
1994 Florida	NL	13	13	1	0	73.1	312	79	30	25	5	5	2	1	23	1	40	3	0	4	4	.500	1	0-0	0	3.07
1995 Florida	NL	25	24	3	0	161	683	157	73	68	17	7	7	9	47	2	126	3	1	9	6	.600	2	0-0	0	3.80
1996 Florida	NL	38	9	0	5	81	368	104	65	59	14	3	4	4	27	3	50	1	0	5	8	.385	0	0-0	5	6.56
1997 Boston	AL	29	8	0	6	65.1	293	81	45	43	5	0	3	2	27	4	48	2	0	3	4	.429	0	1-2	4	5.92
8 ML YEARS		188	133	5	12	830	3590	882	454	416	78	37	22	22	305	22	505	29	9	46	53	.465	3	1-2	9	4.51

Jeffrey Hammonds

Bats: R **Throws:** R **Pos:** RF-54; CF-40; LF-31; PH-13; DH-4 **Ht:** 6'0" **Wt:** 195 **Born:** 3/5/71 **Age:** 27

Year Team	Lg	G	AB	H	2B	3B	HR	(Hm	Rd)	TB	R	RBI	TBB	IBB	SO	HBP	SH	SF	SB	CS	SB%	GDP	Avg	OBP	SLG
1993 Baltimore	AL	33	105	32	8	0	3	(2	1)	49	10	19	2	1	16	0	1	2	4	0	1.00	3	.305	.312	.467
1994 Baltimore	AL	68	250	74	18	2	8	(6	2)	120	45	31	17	1	39	2	0	5	5	0	1.00	3	.296	.339	.480
1995 Baltimore	AL	57	178	43	9	1	4	(2	2)	66	18	23	9	0	30	1	1	2	4	2	.67	3	.242	.279	.371
1996 Baltimore	AL	71	248	56	10	1	9	(3	6)	95	38	27	23	1	53	4	6	1	3	3	.50	7	.226	.301	.383
1997 Baltimore	AL	118	397	105	19	3	21	(9	12)	193	71	55	32	1	73	3	0	2	15	1	.94	6	.264	.323	.486
5 ML YEARS		347	1178	310	64	7	45	(22	23)	523	182	155	83	4	211	10	8	12	31	6	.84	22	.263	.314	.444

Mike Hampton

Pitches: Left Bats: Right Pos: SP-34   Ht: 5'10" Wt: 180 Born: 9/9/72 Age: 25

Year Team	Lg	G	GS	CG	GF	IP	BFP	H	R	ER	HR	SH	SF	HB	TBB	IBB	SO	WP	Bk	W	L	Pct.	ShO	Sv-Op	Hld	ERA
1993 Seattle	AL	13	3	0	2	17	95	28	20	18	3	1	1	0	17	3	8	1	1	1	3	.250	0	1-1	2	9.53
1994 Houston	NL	44	0	0	7	41.1	181	46	19	17	4	0	0	2	16	1	24	5	1	2	1	.667	0	0-1	10	3.70
1995 Houston	NL	24	24	0	0	150.2	641	141	73	56	13	11	5	4	49	3	115	3	1	9	8	.529	0	0-0	0	3.35
1996 Houston	NL	27	27	2	0	160.1	691	175	79	64	12	10	3	3	49	1	101	7	2	10	10	.500	1	0-0	0	3.59
1997 Houston	NL	34	34	7	0	223	941	217	105	95	16	11	7	2	77	2	139	6	1	15	10	.600	2	0-0	0	3.83
5 ML YEARS		142	88	9	9	592.1	2549	607	296	250	48	33	16	11	208	10	387	22	6	37	32	.536	3	1-2	12	3.80

Chris Haney

Pitches: Left Bats: Left Pos: RP-5; SP-3   Ht: 6'3" Wt: 195 Born: 11/16/68 Age: 29

Year Team	Lg	G	GS	CG	GF	IP	BFP	H	R	ER	HR	SH	SF	HB	TBB	IBB	SO	WP	Bk	W	L	Pct.	ShO	Sv-Op	Hld	ERA
1997 Omaha *	AAA	4	3	0	0	19	82	16	12	8	3	0	0	2	6	0	7	1	0	1	0	1.000	0	0--	—	3.79
Wichita *	AA	2	2	0	0	6.2	24	5	3	2	1	0	1	0	0	0	2	0	0	0	1	.000	0	0--	—	2.70
1991 Montreal	NL	16	16	0	0	84.2	387	94	49	38	6	6	1	1	43	1	51	9	0	3	7	.300	0	0-0	0	4.04
1992 Mon-KC		16	13	2	2	80	339	75	43	41	11	0	6	4	26	2	54	5	1	4	6	.400	2	0-0	0	4.61
1993 Kansas City	AL	23	23	1	0	124	556	141	87	83	13	3	4	3	53	2	65	6	1	9	9	.500	1	0-0	0	6.02
1994 Kansas City	AL	6	6	0	0	28.1	127	36	25	23	2	3	4	1	11	1	18	2	0	2	2	.500	0	0-0	0	7.31
1995 Kansas City	AL	16	13	1	0	81.1	338	78	35	33	7	1	4	2	33	0	31	2	0	3	4	.429	0	0-0	2	3.65
1996 Kansas City	AL	35	35	4	0	228	988	267	136	119	29	5	8	6	51	0	115	8	0	10	14	.417	1	0-0	0	4.70
1997 Kansas City	AL	8	3	0	1	24.2	110	29	16	12	1	7	1	2	5	2	16	1	0	1	2	.333	0	0-0	0	4.38
1992 Montreal	NL	9	6	1	2	38	165	40	25	23	6	0	3	4	10	0	27	5	1	2	3	.400	1	0-0	0	5.45
Kansas City	AL	7	7	1	0	42	174	35	18	18	5	0	3	0	16	2	27	0	0	2	3	.400	1	0-0	0	3.86
7 ML YEARS		120	109	8	3	651	2845	720	391	349	69	20	28	19	222	8	350	33	2	32	44	.421	4	0-0	3	4.82

Greg Hansell

Pitches: Right Bats: Right Pos: RP-3   Ht: 6'5" Wt: 215 Born: 3/12/71 Age: 27

Year Team	Lg	G	GS	CG	GF	IP	BFP	H	R	ER	HR	SH	SF	HB	TBB	IBB	SO	WP	Bk	W	L	Pct.	ShO	Sv-Op	Hld	ERA
1997 Tucson *	AAA	40	9	0	13	87.1	378	99	52	45	15	1	2	6	27	2	76	4	0	2	3	.400	0	2--	—	4.64
1995 Los Angeles	NL	20	0	0	7	19.1	93	29	17	16	5	1	1	2	6	1	13	0	0	0	1	.000	0	0-1	1	7.45
1996 Minnesota	AL	50	0	0	23	74.1	329	83	48	47	14	3	2	2	31	1	46	9	1	3	0	1.000	0	3-4	3	5.69
1997 Milwaukee	AL	3	0	0	1	4.2	21	5	5	5	1	0	0	1	1	0	5	0	0	0	0	.000	0	0-0	0	9.64
3 ML YEARS		73	0	0	31	98.1	443	117	70	68	20	4	3	5	38	2	64	9	1	3	1	.750	0	3-5	4	6.22

Dave Hansen

Bats: L Throws: R Pos: 3B-51; PH-45; 1B-4; 2B-1   Ht: 6'0" Wt: 195 Born: 11/24/68 Age: 29

Year Team	Lg	G	AB	H	2B	3B	HR	(Hm	Rd)	TB	R	RBI	TBB	IBB	SO	HBP	SH	SF	SB	CS	SB%	GDP	Avg	OBP	SLG
1990 Los Angeles	NL	5	7	1	0	0	0	(0	0)	1	0	1	0	0	3	0	0	0	0	0	.00	0	.143	.143	.143
1991 Los Angeles	NL	53	56	15	4	0	1	(0	1)	22	3	5	2	0	12	0	0	0	1	0	1.00	0	.268	.293	.393
1992 Los Angeles	NL	132	341	73	11	0	6	(1	5)	102	30	22	34	3	49	1	0	2	0	2	.00	9	.214	.286	.299
1993 Los Angeles	NL	84	105	38	3	0	4	(2	2)	53	13	30	21	3	13	0	0	1	0	1	.00	0	.362	.465	.505
1994 Los Angeles	NL	40	44	15	3	0	0	(0	0)	18	3	5	5	0	5	0	0	0	0	0	.00	0	.341	.408	.409
1995 Los Angeles	NL	100	181	52	10	0	1	(0	1)	65	19	14	28	4	28	1	0	1	0	0	.00	4	.287	.384	.359
1996 Los Angeles	NL	80	104	23	1	0	0	(0	0)	24	7	6	11	1	22	0	0	1	0	0	.00	4	.221	.293	.231
1997 Chicago	NL	90	151	47	8	2	3	(1	2)	68	19	21	31	1	32	1	2	1	1	2	.33	2	.311	.429	.450
8 ML YEARS		584	989	264	40	2	15	(4	11)	353	94	104	132	12	164	3	2	6	2	5	.29	19	.267	.353	.357

Jed Hansen

Bats: Right Throws: Right Pos: 2B-31; PH-7   Ht: 6'1" Wt: 195 Born: 8/19/72 Age: 25

Year Team	Lg	G	AB	H	2B	3B	HR	(Hm	Rd)	TB	R	RBI	TBB	IBB	SO	HBP	SH	SF	SB	CS	SB%	GDP	Avg	OBP	SLG
1994 Eugene	A-	66	235	57	8	2	3	—	—	78	26	17	24	2	56	8	2	1	6	4	.60	1	.243	.332	.332
1995 Springfield	A	122	414	107	27	7	9	—	—	175	86	50	78	0	73	7	6	1	44	10	.81	9	.258	.384	.423
1996 Wichita	AA	99	405	116	27	4	12	—	—	187	60	50	29	0	72	4	4	2	14	8	.64	6	.286	.339	.462
Omaha	AAA	29	99	23	4	0	3	—	—	36	14	9	12	0	22	3	1	1	2	0	1.00	1	.232	.330	.364
1997 Omaha	AAA	114	380	102	20	2	11	—	—	159	43	44	32	0	78	2	5	2	8	1	.89	9	.268	.327	.418
1997 Kansas City	AL	34	94	29	6	1	1	(1	0)	40	11	14	13	0	29	1	2	1	3	2	.60	2	.309	.394	.426

Erik Hanson

Pitches: Right Bats: Right Pos: SP-2; RP-1   Ht: 6'6" Wt: 215 Born: 5/18/65 Age: 33

Year Team	Lg	G	GS	CG	GF	IP	BFP	H	R	ER	HR	SH	SF	HB	TBB	IBB	SO	WP	Bk	W	L	Pct.	ShO	Sv-Op	Hld	ERA
1997 Dunedin *	A+	2	2	0	0	7	28	5	1	1	0	0	0	1	0	5	0	0	0	0	0	.000	0	0--	—	1.29
1988 Seattle	AL	6	6	0	0	41.2	168	35	17	15	4	3	0	1	12	1	36	2	2	2	3	.400	0	0-0	0	3.24
1989 Seattle	AL	17	17	1	0	113.1	465	103	44	40	7	4	1	5	32	1	75	3	0	9	5	.643	0	0-0	0	3.18
1990 Seattle	AL	33	33	5	0	236	964	205	88	85	15	5	6	2	68	6	211	10	1	18	9	.667	1	0-0	0	3.24
1991 Seattle	AL	27	27	2	0	174.2	744	182	82	74	16	2	8	2	56	2	143	14	1	8	8	.500	1	0-0	0	3.81
1992 Seattle	AL	31	30	6	0	186.2	809	209	110	100	14	8	9	7	57	1	112	6	0	8	17	.320	1	0-0	0	4.82

			HOW MUCH HE PITCHED						WHAT HE GAVE UP										THE RESULTS				
Year Team	Lg	G	GS	CG	GF	IP	BFP	H	R	ER	HR	SH	SF	HB	TBB	IBB	SO	WP	Bk	W	L	Pct.	ShO	Sv-Op	Hld	ERA
1993 Seattle	AL	31	30	7	0	215	898	215	91	83	17	10	4	5	60	6	163	8	0	11	12	.478	0	0-0	0	3.47
1994 Cincinnati	NL	22	21	0	1	122.2	519	137	60	56	10	4	4	3	23	3	101	8	1	5	5	.500	0	0-0	0	4.11
1995 Boston	AL	29	29	1	0	186.2	800	187	94	88	17	6	8	1	59	0	139	5	0	15	5	.750	1	0-0	0	4.24
1996 Toronto	AL	35	35	4	0	214.2	955	243	143	129	26	4	5	2	102	2	156	13	0	13	17	.433	1	0-0	0	5.41
1997 Toronto	AL	3	2	0	1	15	65	15	13	13	3	0	0	0	6	0	18	1	0	0	2	.000	0	0-0	0	7.80
10 ML YEARS		234	230	26	2	1506.1	6387	1531	742	683	129	47	45	28	475	22	1154	70	5	89	81	.524	5	0-0	0	4.08

Jason Hardtke

Bats: Both **Throws:** Right **Pos:** 2B-21; PH-11; 3B-1   **Ht:** 5'10" **Wt:** 175 **Born:** 9/15/71 **Age:** 26

							BATTING												BASERUNNING				PERCENTAGES		
Year Team	Lg	G	AB	H	2B	3B	HR	(Hm	Rd)	TB	R	RBI	TBB	IBB	SO	HBP	SH	SF	SB	CS	SB%	GDP	Avg	OBP	SLG
1990 Burlington	R+	39	142	38	7	0	4	—	—	57	18	16	23	0	19	2	0	0	11	1	.92	3	.268	.377	.401
1991 Columbus	A	139	534	155	26	8	12	—	—	233	104	81	75	5	48	1	7	6	22	4	.85	6	.290	.381	.436
1992 Kinston	A+	6	19	4	0	0	0	—	—	4	3	1	4	0	4	0	0	0	0	0	.00	0	.211	.348	.211
Waterloo	A	110	411	125	27	4	8	—	—	184	75	47	38	3	33	5	1	5	9	7	.56	9	.304	.366	.448
High Desert	A+	10	41	11	1	0	2	—	—	18	9	8	4	0	4	1	0	1	1	1	.50	1	.268	.340	.439
1993 Rancho Cuca	A+	130	523	167	38	7	11	—	—	252	98	85	61	2	54	2	2	6	7	8	.47	12	.319	.389	.482
1994 Wichita	AA	75	255	60	15	1	5	—	—	92	26	29	21	1	44	0	2	4	1	2	.33	4	.235	.289	.361
Rancho Cuca	A+	4	13	4	0	0	0	—	—	4	2	0	3	0	2	0	0	0	1	1	.50	0	.308	.438	.308
1995 Norfolk	AAA	4	7	2	1	0	0	—	—	3	1	0	2	0	0	0	0	0	1	1	.50	0	.286	.444	.429
Binghamton	AA	121	455	130	42	4	4	—	—	192	65	52	66	1	58	4	2	9	6	8	.43	7	.286	.375	.422
1996 Binghamton	AA	35	137	36	11	0	3	—	—	56	23	16	16	1	16	0	1	0	0	1	.00	3	.263	.340	.409
Norfolk	AAA	71	257	77	17	2	9	—	—	125	49	35	29	1	29	0	4	2	4	6	.40	4	.300	.368	.486
1997 Norfolk	AAA	97	388	107	23	3	11	—	—	169	46	45	40	1	54	0	4	1	3	6	.33	9	.276	.343	.436
Binghamton	AA	6	26	10	2	0	1	—	—	15	3	4	2	0	2	0	0	0	0	0	.00	1	.385	.429	.577
1996 New York	NL	19	57	11	5	0	0	(0	0)	16	3	6	2	0	12	1	0	0	0	0	.00	1	.193	.233	.281
1997 New York	NL	30	56	15	2	0	2	(0	2)	23	9	8	4	1	6	1	0	1	1	1	.50	3	.268	.323	.411
2 ML YEARS		49	113	26	7	0	2	(0	2)	39	12	14	6	1	18	2	0	1	1	1	.50	4	.230	.279	.345

Mike Harkey

Pitches: Right **Bats:** Right **Pos:** RP-10   **Ht:** 6'5" **Wt:** 235 **Born:** 10/25/66 **Age:** 31

			HOW MUCH HE PITCHED						WHAT HE GAVE UP										THE RESULTS					
Year Team	Lg	G	GS	CG	GF	IP	BFP	H	R	ER	HR	SH	SF	HB	TBB	IBB	SO	WP	Bk	W	L	Pct.	ShO	Sv-Op	Hld	ERA
1997 Albuquerque *	AAA	47	0	0	33	55.2	222	50	14	13	4	2	3	2	11	1	57	0	0	2	2	.500	0	15--	—	2.10
1988 Chicago	NL	5	5	0	0	34.2	155	33	14	10	0	5	0	2	15	3	18	2	1	0	3	.000	0	0-0	0	2.60
1990 Chicago	NL	27	27	2	0	173.2	728	153	71	63	14	5	4	7	59	8	94	8	1	12	6	.667	1	0-0	0	3.26
1991 Chicago	NL	4	4	0	0	18.2	84	21	11	11	3	0	1	0	6	1	15	1	0	0	2	.000	0	0-0	0	5.30
1992 Chicago	NL	7	7	0	0	38	159	34	13	8	4	1	2	1	15	0	21	3	1	4	0	1.000	0	0-0	0	1.89
1993 Chicago	NL	28	28	1	0	157.1	676	187	100	92	17	8	8	3	43	4	67	1	3	10	10	.500	0	0-0	0	5.26
1994 Colorado	NL	24	13	0	3	91.2	415	125	61	59	10	5	2	1	35	4	39	0	2	1	6	.143	0	0-0	0	5.79
1995 Oak-Cal	AL	26	20	1	1	127.1	573	155	78	77	24	4	4	4	47	2	56	2	0	8	9	.471	0	0-0	0	5.44
1997 Los Angeles	NL	10	0	0	5	14.2	62	12	8	7	3	0	0	0	5	0	6	0	1	1	0	1.000	0	0-0	0	4.30
1995 Oakland	AL	14	12	0	1	66	296	75	46	46	12	3	2	3	31	0	28	2	0	4	6	.400	0	0-0	0	6.27
California	AL	12	8	1	0	61.1	277	80	32	31	12	1	2	1	16	2	28	0	0	4	3	.571	0	0-0	0	4.55
8 ML YEARS		131	104	4	9	656	2852	720	356	327	75	28	21	18	225	22	316	17	8	36	36	.500	1	0-0	0	4.49

Pete Harnisch

Pitches: Right **Bats:** Right **Pos:** SP-8; RP-2   **Ht:** 6'0" **Wt:** 207 **Born:** 9/23/66 **Age:** 31

			HOW MUCH HE PITCHED						WHAT HE GAVE UP										THE RESULTS					
Year Team	Lg	G	GS	CG	GF	IP	BFP	H	R	ER	HR	SH	SF	HB	TBB	IBB	SO	WP	Bk	W	L	Pct.	ShO	Sv-Op	Hld	ERA
1997 Mets *	R	1	1	0	0	3	16	7	4	4	1	0	0	0	0	0	5	2	0	0	0	.000	0	0--	—	12.00
St. Lucie *	A+	2	2	0	0	12	45	5	5	4	1	0	1	0	4	0	7	0	0	1	0	1.000	0	0--	—	3.00
Norfolk *	AAA	3	3	0	0	16.2	74	16	12	10	4	0	0	0	10	0	16	1	0	1	1	.500	0	0--	—	5.40
1988 Baltimore	AL	2	2	0	0	13	61	13	8	8	1	2	0	0	9	1	10	1	0	0	2	.000	0	0-0	0	5.54
1989 Baltimore	AL	18	17	2	1	103.1	468	97	55	53	10	4	5	5	64	3	70	5	1	5	9	.357	0	0-0	0	4.62
1990 Baltimore	AL	31	31	3	0	188.2	821	189	96	91	17	6	5	1	86	5	122	2	2	11	11	.500	0	0-0	0	4.34
1991 Houston	NL	33	33	4	0	216.2	900	169	71	65	14	9	7	5	83	3	172	5	2	12	9	.571	2	0-0	0	2.70
1992 Houston	NL	34	34	0	0	206.2	859	182	92	85	18	5	5	6	64	3	164	4	1	9	10	.474	0	0-0	0	3.70
1993 Houston	NL	33	33	5	0	217.2	896	171	84	72	20	9	4	6	79	5	185	3	1	16	9	.640	4	0-0	0	2.98
1994 Houston	NL	17	17	1	0	95	419	100	59	57	13	3	2	3	39	1	62	2	0	8	5	.615	0	0-0	0	5.40
1995 New York	NL	18	18	0	0	110	462	111	55	45	13	4	6	3	24	4	82	0	1	2	8	.200	0	0-0	0	3.68
1996 New York	NL	31	31	2	0	194.2	839	195	91	90	30	13	9	7	61	5	114	7	3	8	12	.400	1	0-0	0	4.21
1997 NYN-Mil		10	8	0	0	39.2	186	48	33	31	6	0	2	1	23	1	22	2	0	1	2	.333	0	0-0	0	7.03
1997 New York	NL	6	5	0	0	25.2	121	35	24	23	5	0	2	1	11	1	12	1	0	0	1	.000	0	0-0	0	8.06
Milwaukee	AL	4	3	0	0	14	65	13	9	8	1	0	0	0	12	0	10	1	0	1	1	.500	0	0-0	0	5.14
10 ML YEARS		227	224	17	1	1385.1	5911	1275	656	598	142	55	45	36	532	31	1003	31	11	72	77	.483	7	0-0	0	3.88

Lenny Harris

Bats: L **Throws:** R **Pos:** PH-53; LF-26; 2B-20; RF-17; 3B-13; 1B-11   **Ht:** 5'10" **Wt:** 210 **Born:** 10/28/64 **Age:** 33

							BATTING												BASERUNNING				PERCENTAGES		
Year Team	Lg	G	AB	H	2B	3B	HR	(Hm	Rd)	TB	R	RBI	TBB	IBB	SO	HBP	SH	SF	SB	CS	SB%	GDP	Avg	OBP	SLG
1988 Cincinnati	NL	16	43	16	1	0	0	(0	0)	17	7	8	5	0	4	0	1	2	4	1	.80	0	.372	.420	.395
1989 Cin-LA	NL	115	335	79	10	1	3	(1	2)	100	36	26	20	0	33	2	1	0	14	9	.61	14	.236	.283	.299
1990 Los Angeles	NL	137	431	131	16	4	2	(0	2)	161	61	29	29	2	31	1	3	1	15	10	.60	8	.304	.348	.374

					BATTING															BASERUNNING				PERCENTAGES		
Year Team	Lg	G	AB	H	2B	3B	HR	(Hm	Rd)	TB	R	RBI	TBB	IBB	SO	HBP	SH	SF	SB	CS	SB%	GDP	Avg	OBP	SLG
1991 Los Angeles	NL	145	429	123	16	1	3	(1	2)	150	59	38	37	5	32	5	12	2	12	3	.80	16	.287	.349	.350
1992 Los Angeles	NL	135	347	94	11	0	0	(0	0)	105	28	30	24	3	24	1	6	2	19	7	.73	10	.271	.318	.303
1993 Los Angeles	NL	107	160	38	6	1	2	(0	2)	52	20	11	15	4	15	0	1	0	3	1	.75	4	.238	.303	.325
1994 Cincinnati	NL	66	100	31	3	1	0	(0	0)	36	13	14	5	0	13	0	0	1	7	2	.78	0	.310	.340	.360
1995 Cincinnati	NL	101	197	41	8	3	2	(0	2)	61	32	16	14	0	20	0	3	1	10	1	.91	6	.208	.259	.310
1996 Cincinnati	NL	125	302	86	17	2	5	(2	3)	122	33	32	21	1	31	1	6	3	14	6	.70	3	.285	.330	.404
1997 Cincinnati	NL	120	238	65	13	1	3	(2	1)	89	32	28	18	1	18	2	3	2	3	5	.57	10	.273	.327	.374
1989 Cincinnati	NL	61	188	42	4	0	2	(0	2)	52	17	11	9	0	20	1	1	0	10	6	.63	5	.223	.263	.277
Los Angeles		54	147	37	6	1	1	(1	0)	48	19	15	11	0	13	1	0	0	4	3	.57	9	.252	.308	.327
10 ML YEARS		1067	2582	704	101	14	20	(6	14)	893	321	232	188	16	221	12	36	14	102	43	.70	71	.273	.323	.346

Pep Harris

Pitches: Right **Bats:** Right **Pos:** RP-61   **Ht:** 6'2" **Wt:** 185 **Born:** 9/23/72 **Age:** 25

		HOW MUCH HE PITCHED						WHAT HE GAVE UP										THE RESULTS						
Year Team	Lg	G	GS	CG	GF	IP	BFP	H	R	ER	HR	SH	SF	HB	TBB	IBB	SO	WP	Bk	W	L	Pct.	ShO	Sv-Op	Hld	ERA
1991 Burlington	R+	13	13	0	0	65.2	292	67	30	24	7	4	2	3	31	0	47	5	0	4	3	.571	0	0- -	—	3.29
1992 Columbus	A	18	17	0	0	90.2	400	88	51	37	10	3	6	2	51	1	57	11	0	7	4	.636	0	0- -	—	3.67
1993 Columbus	A	26	17	0	4	119	510	113	67	56	7	4	1	4	44	0	82	6	0	7	8	.467	0	0- -	—	4.24
1994 Kinston	A+	27	0	0	20	32.2	140	21	14	7	1	0	0	2	16	0	37	2	0	4	1	.800	0	8- -	—	1.93
Canton-Akrn	AA	24	0	0	22	20.1	86	9	5	5	0	1	0	2	13	2	15	1	0	2	0	1.000	0	12- -	—	2.21
1995 Buffalo	AAA	14	0	0	3	32.2	141	32	11	9	2	0	0	0	15	0	18	0	0	2	1	.667	0	0- -	—	2.48
Canton-Akrn	AA	32	7	0	20	83	346	78	34	22	4	8	4	4	23	3	40	2	2	3	3	.667	0	10- -	—	2.39
1996 Midland	AA	6	6	1	0	39	177	47	27	23	2	1	0	2	9	1	28	0	1	2	2	.500	0	0- -	—	5.31
Vancouver	AAA	18	18	1	0	118.1	517	135	67	60	12	6	2	3	46	0	61	2	2	9	3	.750	0	0- -	—	4.56
1996 California	AL	11	3	0	0	32.1	146	31	16	14	4	0	4	3	17	2	20	4	0	2	0	1.000	0	0-0	2	3.90
1997 Anaheim	AL	61	0	0	17	79.2	346	82	33	32	7	3	4	2	38	6	56	3	0	5	4	.556	0	0-3	10	3.62
2 ML YEARS		72	3	0	17	112	492	113	49	46	11	3	8	5	55	8	76	7	0	7	4	.636	0	0-3	12	3.70

Reggie Harris

Pitches: Right **Bats:** Right **Pos:** RP-50   **Ht:** 6'1" **Wt:** 190 **Born:** 8/12/68 **Age:** 29

		HOW MUCH HE PITCHED						WHAT HE GAVE UP										THE RESULTS						
Year Team	Lg	G	GS	CG	GF	IP	BFP	H	R	ER	HR	SH	SF	HB	TBB	IBB	SO	WP	Bk	W	L	Pct.	ShO	Sv-Op	Hld	ERA
1990 Oakland	AL	16	1	0	9	41.1	168	25	16	16	5	1	2	2	21	1	31	2	0	1	0	1.000	0	0-0	0	3.48
1991 Oakland	AL	2	0	0	1	3	15	5	4	4	0	0	1	0	3	1	2	2	0	0	0	.000	0	0-0	0	12.00
1996 Boston	AL	4	0	0	1	4.1	24	7	6	6	2	0	0	1	5	0	4	0	0	0	0	.000	0	0-1	0	12.46
1997 Philadelphia	NL	50	0	0	13	54.1	264	55	33	32	1	3	4	5	43	1	45	5	1	1	3	.250	0	0-1	1	5.30
4 ML YEARS		72	1	0	24	103	471	92	59	58	8	4	7	8	72	3	82	9	1	2	3	.400	0	0-1	1	5.07

Shigetoshi Hasegawa

Pitches: Right **Bats:** Right **Pos:** RP-43; SP-7   **Ht:** 5'11" **Wt:** 160 **Born:** 8/1/68 **Age:** 29

		HOW MUCH HE PITCHED						WHAT HE GAVE UP										THE RESULTS						
Year Team	Lg	G	GS	CG	GF	IP	BFP	H	R	ER	HR	SH	SF	HB	TBB	IBB	SO	WP	Bk	W	L	Pct.	ShO	Sv-Op	Hld	ERA
1997 Anaheim	AL	50	7	0	17	116.2	497	118	60	51	14	5	5	3	46	6	83	2	1	3	7	.300	0	0-1	3	3.93

Bill Haselman

Bats: Right **Throws:** Right **Pos:** C-66   **Ht:** 6'3" **Wt:** 223 **Born:** 5/25/66 **Age:** 32

					BATTING															BASERUNNING				PERCENTAGES		
Year Team	Lg	G	AB	H	2B	3B	HR	(Hm	Rd)	TB	R	RBI	TBB	IBB	SO	HBP	SH	SF	SB	CS	SB%	GDP	Avg	OBP	SLG
1997 Red Sox *	R	4	16	2	0	0	0	—	—	2	2	1	0	0	1	0	0	0	0	1	1.00	0	.125	.125	.125
Trenton *	AA	7	26	6	1	0	2	—	—	13	3	3	2	0	2	0	0	0	0	0	.00	0	.231	.286	.500
1990 Texas	AL	7	13	2	0	0	0	(0	0)	2	0	3	1	0	5	0	0	0	0	0	.00	0	.154	.214	.154
1992 Seattle	AL	8	19	5	0	0	0	(0	0)	5	1	0	0	0	7	0	0	0	0	0	.00	1	.263	.263	.263
1993 Seattle	AL	58	137	35	8	0	5	(3	2)	58	21	16	12	0	19	1	2	2	2	1	.67	5	.255	.316	.423
1994 Seattle	AL	38	83	16	7	1	1	(1	0)	28	11	8	3	0	11	1	1	0	1	0	1.00	3	.193	.230	.337
1995 Boston	AL	64	152	37	6	1	5	(3	2)	60	22	23	17	0	30	2	0	3	0	2	.00	4	.243	.322	.395
1996 Boston	AL	77	237	65	13	1	8	(5	3)	104	33	34	19	3	52	1	0	0	4	2	.67	13	.274	.331	.439
1997 Boston	AL	67	212	50	15	0	6	(3	3)	83	22	26	15	2	44	2	1	2	0	2	.00	6	.236	.290	.392
7 ML YEARS		319	853	210	49	3	25	(15	10)	340	110	110	67	5	168	7	4	7	7	7	.50	33	.246	.304	.399

Scott Hatteberg

Bats: Left **Throws:** Right **Pos:** C-106; PH-14; DH-1   **Ht:** 6'1" **Wt:** 195 **Born:** 12/14/69 **Age:** 28

					BATTING															BASERUNNING				PERCENTAGES		
Year Team	Lg	G	AB	H	2B	3B	HR	(Hm	Rd)	TB	R	RBI	TBB	IBB	SO	HBP	SH	SF	SB	CS	SB%	GDP	Avg	OBP	SLG
1991 Winter Havn	A+	56	191	53	7	3	1	—	—	69	21	24	22	4	22	0	2	2	1	2	.33	6	.277	.349	.361
Lynchburg	A+	8	25	5	1	0	0	—	—	6	4	3	7	0	6	0	0	0	0	0	.00	0	.200	.375	.240
1992 New Britain	AA	103	297	69	13	2	1	—	—	89	28	30	41	2	49	2	1	3	1	3	.25	6	.232	.327	.300
1993 New Britain	AA	68	227	63	10	2	7	—	—	98	35	28	42	3	38	1	1	0	1	3	.25	6	.278	.393	.432
Pawtucket	AAA	18	53	10	0	0	1	—	—	13	6	2	6	0	12	1	2	0	0	0	.00	5	.189	.283	.245
1994 New Britain	AA	20	68	18	4	1	1	—	—	27	6	9	7	1	9	0	0	0	2	0	.00	2	.265	.329	.397
Pawtucket	AAA	78	238	56	14	0	7	—	—	91	26	19	32	1	49	3	2	1	2	1	.67	14	.235	.332	.382
1995 Pawtucket	AAA	85	251	68	15	1	7	—	—	106	36	27	40	2	39	4	1	3	2	0	1.00	8	.271	.376	.422
1996 Pawtucket	AAA	90	287	77	16	0	12	—	—	129	52	49	58	0	66	1	1	3	1	1	.50	6	.268	.391	.449

Year Team	Lg	G	AB	H	2B	3B	HR	(Hm	Rd)	TB	R	RBI	TBB	IBB	SO	HBP	SH	SF	SB	CS	SB%	GDP	Avg	OBP	SLG
1995 Boston	AL	2	2	1	0	0	0	(0	0)	1	1	0	0	0	0	0	0	0	0	0	.00	1	.500	.500	.500
1996 Boston	AL	10	11	2	1	0	0	(0	0)	3	3	0	3	0	2	0	0	0	0	0	.00	2	.182	.357	.273
1997 Boston	AL	114	350	97	23	1	10	(5	5)	152	46	44	40	2	70	2	2	1	0	1	.00	11	.277	.354	.434
3 ML YEARS		126	363	100	24	1	10	(5	5)	156	50	44	43	2	72	2	2	1	0	1	.00	14	.275	.355	.430

Gary Haught

Pitches: Right **Bats:** Both **Pos:** RP-6   **Ht:** 6'1" **Wt:** 180 **Born:** 9/29/70 **Age:** 27

		HOW MUCH HE PITCHED						WHAT HE GAVE UP											THE RESULTS						
Year Team	Lg	G	GS	CG	GF	IP	BFP	H	R	ER	HR	SH	SF	HB	TBB	IBB	SO	WP	Bk	W	L	Pct.	ShO	Sv-Op	Hld	ERA
1992 Sou. Oregon	A-	19	4	0	9	68.1	266	58	18	15	3	1	1	2	14	0	69	1	2	8	2	.800	0	2--	—	1.98
1993 Madison	A	17	12	2	1	83.2	333	62	27	24	8	3	1	2	29	2	75	1	2	7	1	.875	0	0--	—	2.58
Modesto	A+	12	0	0	4	23	106	25	14	13	3	0	2	1	17	2	15	0	0	0	0	.000	0	0--	—	5.09
1994 Modesto	A+	39	1	0	13	70.2	292	66	35	34	8	6	1	2	26	0	52	2	0	4	3	.571	0	2--	—	4.33
1995 Modesto	A+	34	4	0	6	86.2	355	76	29	25	10	10	0	6	24	1	81	0	0	9	5	.643	0	4--	—	2.60
Huntsville	AA	9	3	0	3	23	97	23	14	11	4	1	0	1	8	1	20	0	0	1	1	.500	0	0--	—	4.30
1996 Huntsville	AA	45	0	0	18	67	295	67	33	29	4	2	1	7	24	4	52	2	0	3	2	.600	0	4--	—	3.90
1997 Huntsville	AA	6	0	0	0	9.2	44	15	6	6	2	0	0	0	2	1	6	0	0	0	1	.000	0	0--	—	5.59
Edmonton	AAA	30	2	0	21	42.2	174	37	20	17	7	0	1	5	13	1	35	1	1	1	1	.500	0	11--	—	3.59
1997 Oakland	AL	6	0	0	2	11.1	52	12	9	9	3	0	1	2	6	0	11	1	0	0	0	.000	0	0-0	—	7.15

LaTroy Hawkins

Pitches: Right **Bats:** Right **Pos:** SP-20   **Ht:** 6'5" **Wt:** 193 **Born:** 12/21/72 **Age:** 25

		HOW MUCH HE PITCHED						WHAT HE GAVE UP											THE RESULTS						
Year Team	Lg	G	GS	CG	GF	IP	BFP	H	R	ER	HR	SH	SF	HB	TBB	IBB	SO	WP	Bk	W	L	Pct.	ShO	Sv-Op	Hld	ERA
1997 Salt Lake *	AAA	14	13	2	1	76	346	100	53	46	4	2	2	4	16	1	53	8	1	9	4	.692	1	0--	—	5.45
1995 Minnesota	AL	6	6	1	0	27	131	39	29	26	3	0	3	1	12	0	9	1	1	2	3	.400	0	0-0	0	8.67
1996 Minnesota	AL	7	6	0	0	26.1	124	42	24	24	8	1	1	0	9	0	24	1	1	1	1	.500	0	0-0	0	8.20
1997 Minnesota	AL	20	20	0	0	103.1	478	134	71	67	19	2	2	4	47	0	58	6	3	6	12	.333	0	0-0	0	5.84
3 ML YEARS		33	32	1	1	156.2	733	215	124	117	30	3	6	5	68	0	91	8	5	9	16	.360	0	0-0	0	6.72

Charlie Hayes

Bats: Right **Throws:** Right **Pos:** 3B-98; PH-8; 2B-5   **Ht:** 6'0" **Wt:** 224 **Born:** 5/29/65 **Age:** 33

		BATTING																	BASERUNNING				PERCENTAGES		
Year Team	Lg	G	AB	H	2B	3B	HR	(Hm	Rd)	TB	R	RBI	TBB	IBB	SO	HBP	SH	SF	SB	CS	SB%	GDP	Avg	OBP	SLG
1988 San Francisco	NL	7	11	1	0	0	0	(0	0)	1	0	0	0	0	3	0	0	0	0	0	.00	0	.091	.091	.091
1989 SF-Phi	NL	87	304	78	15	1	8	(3	5)	119	26	43	11	1	50	0	2	3	3	1	.75	6	.257	.280	.391
1990 Philadelphia	NL	152	561	145	20	0	10	(3	7)	195	56	57	28	3	91	2	0	6	4	4	.50	12	.258	.293	.348
1991 Philadelphia	NL	142	460	106	23	1	12	(6	6)	167	34	53	16	3	75	1	2	1	3	3	.50	13	.230	.257	.363
1992 New York	AL	142	509	131	19	2	18	(7	11)	208	52	66	28	0	100	3	3	6	3	5	.38	12	.257	.297	.409
1993 Colorado	NL	157	573	175	45	2	25	(17	8)	299	89	98	43	6	82	5	1	8	11	6	.65	25	.305	.355	.522
1994 Colorado	NL	113	423	122	23	4	10	(4	6)	183	46	50	36	4	71	3	0	1	3	6	.33	11	.288	.348	.433
1995 Philadelphia	NL	141	529	146	30	3	11	(5	6)	215	58	85	50	2	88	4	0	6	5	1	.83	22	.276	.340	.406
1996 Pit-NYA		148	526	133	24	2	12	(5	7)	197	58	75	37	4	90	0	3	3	6	0	1.00	17	.253	.300	.375
1997 New York	AL	100	353	91	16	0	11	(5	6)	140	39	53	40	2	66	1	0	4	3	2	.60	13	.258	.332	.397
1989 San Francisco	NL	3	5	1	0	0	0	(0	0)	1	0	0	0	0	1	0	0	0	0	0	.00	0	.200	.200	.200
Philadelphia	NL	84	299	77	15	1	8	(3	5)	118	26	43	11	1	49	0	2	3	3	1	.75	6	.258	.281	.395
1996 Pittsburgh	NL	128	459	114	21	2	10	(5	5)	169	51	62	36	4	78	0	2	3	6	0	1.00	16	.248	.301	.368
New York	AL	20	67	19	3	0	2	(0	2)	28	7	13	1	0	12	0	1	0	0	0	.00	1	.284	.294	.418
10 ML YEARS		1189	4249	1128	215	15	117	(56	61)	1724	458	580	289	25	716	19	11	38	41	28	.59	131	.265	.313	.406

Jimmy Haynes

Pitches: Right **Bats:** Right **Pos:** SP-13   **Ht:** 6'3" **Wt:** 180 **Born:** 9/5/72 **Age:** 25

		HOW MUCH HE PITCHED						WHAT HE GAVE UP											THE RESULTS						
Year Team	Lg	G	GS	CG	GF	IP	BFP	H	R	ER	HR	SH	SF	HB	TBB	IBB	SO	WP	Bk	W	L	Pct.	ShO	Sv-Op	Hld	ERA
1997 Rochester *	AAA	16	16	2	0	102	435	89	49	39	9	4	3	1	55	0	113	8	1	5	4	.556	1	0--	—	3.44
Edmonton *	AAA	5	5	0	0	29.2	135	36	22	16	4	2	0	1	11	0	24	4	0	0	2	.000	0	0--	—	4.85
1995 Baltimore	AL	4	3	0	0	24	94	11	6	6	2	1	0	0	12	1	22	0	0	2	1	.667	0	0-0	0	2.25
1996 Baltimore	AL	26	11	0	8	89	435	122	84	82	14	4	5	2	58	1	65	5	0	3	6	.333	0	1-1	0	8.29
1997 Oakland	AL	13	13	0	0	73.1	329	74	38	36	7	1	4	2	40	1	65	4	1	3	6	.333	0	0-0	0	4.42
3 ML YEARS		43	27	0	8	186.1	858	207	128	124	23	6	9	4	110	3	152	9	1	8	13	.381	0	1-1	0	5.99

Rick Helling

Pitches: Right **Bats:** Right **Pos:** RP-25; SP-16   **Ht:** 6'3" **Wt:** 215 **Born:** 12/15/70 **Age:** 27

		HOW MUCH HE PITCHED						WHAT HE GAVE UP											THE RESULTS						
Year Team	Lg	G	GS	CG	GF	IP	BFP	H	R	ER	HR	SH	SF	HB	TBB	IBB	SO	WP	Bk	W	L	Pct.	ShO	Sv-Op	Hld	ERA
1994 Texas	AL	9	9	1	0	52	228	62	34	34	14	0	0	0	18	0	25	4	1	3	2	.600	0	0-0	0	5.88
1995 Texas	AL	3	3	0	0	12.1	62	17	11	9	2	0	2	2	8	0	5	0	0	0	2	.000	0	0-0	0	6.57
1996 Tex-Fla		11	6	0	2	48	198	37	23	23	9	1	1	0	16	0	42	1	1	3	3	.500	0	0-0	1	4.31
1997 Fla-Tex		41	16	0	9	131	550	108	67	65	17	3	9	6	69	2	99	3	0	5	9	.357	0	0-1	6	4.47
1996 Texas	AL	6	2	0	2	20.1	92	23	17	17	7	0	1	0	9	0	16	1	0	1	2	.333	0	0-0	1	7.52
Florida	NL	5	4	0	0	27.2	106	14	6	6	2	1	0	0	7	0	26	0	1	2	1	.667	0	0-0	0	1.95
1997 Florida	NL	31	8	0	8	76	324	61	38	37	12	2	7	4	48	2	53	0	0	2	6	.250	0	0-1	6	4.38

		HOW MUCH HE PITCHED						WHAT HE GAVE UP											THE RESULTS						
Year Team	Lg	G	GS	CG	GF	IP	BFP	H	R	ER	HR	SH	SF	HB	TBB	IBB	SO	WP	Bk	W	L	Pct.	ShO	Sv-Op	Hld	ERA
Texas	AL	10	8	0	1	55	226	47	29	28	5	1	2	2	21	0	46	3	0	3	3	.500	0	0-0	0	4.58
4 ML YEARS		64	34	1	11	243.1	1038	224	135	131	42	4	12	8	111	2	171	8	2	11	16	.407	1	0-1	7	4.85

Todd Helton

Bats: L **Throws:** L **Pos:** LF-13; PH-13; 1B-8; RF-2   **Ht:** 6'2" **Wt:** 190 **Born:** 8/20/73 **Age:** 24

					BATTING													BASERUNNING				PERCENTAGES		
Year Team	Lg	G	AB	H	2B	3B	HR	(Hm	Rd)	TB	R	RBI	TBB	IBB	SO	HBP	SH	SF	SB	CS	SB%	GDP	Avg	OBP	SLG
1995 Asheville	A	54	201	51	11	1	1	—	—	67	24	15	25	1	32	1	0	0	1	1	.50	7	.254	.339	.333
1996 New Haven	AA	93	319	106	24	2	7	—	—	155	46	51	51	5	37	1	3	1	2	5	.29	8	.332	.425	.486
Colo Sprngs	AAA	21	71	25	4	1	2	—	—	37	13	13	11	0	12	0	0	0	0	0	.00	3	.352	.439	.521
1997 Colo Sprngs	AAA	99	392	138	31	2	16	—	—	221	87	88	61	4	68	0	1	6	3	1	.75	10	.352	.434	.564
1997 Colorado	NL	35	93	26	2	1	5	(3	2)	45	13	11	8	0	11	0	0	0	0	1	.00	1	.280	.337	.484

Rickey Henderson

Bats: R **Throws:** L **Pos:** LF-66; DH-21; CF-19; PH-10; RF-8   **Ht:** 5'10" **Wt:** 190 **Born:** 12/25/58 **Age:** 39

					BATTING													BASERUNNING				PERCENTAGES		
Year Team	Lg	G	AB	H	2B	3B	HR	(Hm	Rd)	TB	R	RBI	TBB	IBB	SO	HBP	SH	SF	SB	CS	SB%	GDP	Avg	OBP	SLG
1979 Oakland	AL	89	351	96	13	3	1	(1	0)	118	49	26	34	0	39	2	8	3	33	11	.75	4	.274	.338	.336
1980 Oakland	AL	158	591	179	22	4	9	(3	6)	236	111	53	117	7	54	5	6	3	100	26	.79	6	.303	.420	.399
1981 Oakland	AL	108	423	135	18	7	6	(5	1)	185	89	35	64	4	68	2	0	4	56	22	.72	7	.319	.408	.437
1982 Oakland	AL	149	536	143	24	4	10	(5	5)	205	119	51	116	1	94	2	0	4	130	42	.76	5	.267	.398	.382
1983 Oakland	AL	145	513	150	25	7	9	(5	4)	216	105	48	103	8	80	4	1	1	108	19	.85	11	.292	.414	.421
1984 Oakland	AL	142	502	147	27	4	16	(7	9)	230	113	58	86	1	81	5	1	3	66	18	.79	7	.293	.399	.458
1985 New York	AL	143	547	172	28	5	24	(8	16)	282	146	72	99	1	65	3	0	5	80	10	.89	8	.314	.419	.516
1986 New York	AL	153	608	160	31	5	28	(13	15)	285	130	74	89	2	81	2	0	2	87	18	.83	12	.263	.358	.469
1987 New York	AL	95	358	104	17	3	17	(10	7)	178	78	37	80	1	52	2	0	0	41	8	.84	10	.291	.423	.497
1988 New York	AL	140	554	169	30	2	6	(2	4)	221	118	50	82	1	54	3	2	6	93	13	.88	6	.305	.394	.399
1989 NYA-Oak	AL	150	541	148	26	3	12	(7	5)	216	113	57	126	5	68	3	0	4	77	14	.85	8	.274	.411	.399
1990 Oakland	AL	136	489	159	33	3	28	(8	20)	282	119	61	97	2	60	4	2	2	65	10	.87	13	.325	.439	.577
1991 Oakland	AL	134	470	126	17	1	18	(8	10)	199	105	57	98	7	73	7	0	3	58	18	.76	7	.268	.400	.423
1992 Oakland	AL	117	396	112	18	3	15	(10	5)	181	77	46	95	5	56	6	0	3	48	11	.81	5	.283	.426	.457
1993 Oak-Tor	AL	134	481	139	22	2	21	(10	11)	228	114	59	120	7	65	4	1	4	53	8	.87	9	.289	.432	.474
1994 Oakland	AL	87	296	77	13	0	6	(4	2)	108	66	20	72	1	45	5	1	2	22	7	.76	0	.260	.411	.365
1995 Oakland	AL	112	407	122	31	1	9	(3	6)	182	67	54	72	2	66	4	1	3	32	10	.76	8	.300	.407	.447
1996 San Diego	NL	148	465	112	17	2	9	(6	3)	160	110	29	125	2	90	10	0	2	37	15	.71	5	.241	.410	.344
1997 SD-Ana		120	403	100	14	0	8	(6	2)	138	84	34	97	2	85	6	1	2	45	8	.85	10	.248	.400	.342
1989 New York	AL	65	235	58	13	1	3	(1	2)	82	41	22	56	0	29	1	0	1	25	8	.76	0	.247	.392	.349
Oakland		85	306	90	13	2	9	(6	3)	134	72	35	70	5	39	2	0	3	52	6	.90	8	.294	.425	.438
1993 Oakland	AL	90	318	104	19	1	17	(8	9)	176	77	47	85	6	46	2	0	2	31	6	.84	8	.327	.469	.553
Toronto		44	163	35	3	1	4	(2	2)	52	37	12	35	1	19	2	1	2	22	2	.92	1	.215	.356	.319
1997 San Diego	NL	88	288	79	11	0	6	(5	1)	108	63	27	71	2	62	4	0	2	29	4	.88	7	.274	.422	.375
Anaheim	AL	32	115	21	3	0	2	(1	1)	30	21	7	26	0	23	2	1	0	16	4	.80	3	.183	.343	.261
19 ML YEARS		2460	8931	2550	426	59	252	(121	131)	3850	1913	921	1772	59	1276	79	24	54	1231	288	.81	141	.286	.406	.431

Oscar Henriquez

Pitches: Right **Bats:** Right **Pos:** RP-4   **Ht:** 6'6" **Wt:** 220 **Born:** 1/28/74 **Age:** 24

				HOW MUCH HE PITCHED						WHAT HE GAVE UP								THE RESULTS						
Year Team	Lg	G	GS	CG	GF	IP	BFP	H	R	ER	HR	SH	SF	HB	TBB	IBB	SO	WP	Bk	W	L	Pct.	ShO	Sv-Op	Hld	ERA
1993 Asheville	A	27	26	2	0	150	679	154	95	74	12	6	5	10	70	2	117	7	3	9	10	.474	1	0--	—	4.44
1995 Kissimmee	A+	20	0	0	7	44.2	207	40	29	25	2	2	2	6	30	0	36	3	0	3	4	.429	0	1--	—	5.04
1996 Kissimmee	A+	37	0	0	33	34	162	28	18	15	0	1	1	3	29	2	40	4	0	0	0	.000	0	15--	—	3.97
1997 New Orleans	AAA	60	0	0	37	74	313	65	28	23	4	6	3	5	27	3	80	7	1	4	5	.444	0	12--	—	2.80
1997 Houston	NL	4	0	0	1	4	17	2	2	2	0	1	0	1	3	0	3	0	0	0	1	.000	0	0-0	1	4.50

Butch Henry

Pitches: Left **Bats:** Left **Pos:** RP-31; SP-5   **Ht:** 6'1" **Wt:** 205 **Born:** 10/7/68 **Age:** 29

				HOW MUCH HE PITCHED						WHAT HE GAVE UP								THE RESULTS						
Year Team	Lg	G	GS	CG	GF	IP	BFP	H	R	ER	HR	SH	SF	HB	TBB	IBB	SO	WP	Bk	W	L	Pct.	ShO	Sv-Op	Hld	ERA
1997 Sarasota *	A+	2	2	0	0	8.1	33	8	5	5	1	0	0	0	0	0	7	0	0	1	0	.000	0	0--	—	5.40
1992 Houston	NL	28	28	2	0	165.2	710	185	81	74	16	12	7	1	41	7	96	2	2	6	9	.400	1	0-0	0	4.02
1993 Col-Mon	NL	30	16	1	4	103	467	135	76	70	15	6	6	1	28	2	47	1	0	3	9	.250	0	0-0	0	6.12
1994 Montreal	NL	24	15	0	1	107.1	433	97	30	29	10	5	3	2	20	1	70	1	0	8	3	.727	0	1-1	2	2.43
1995 Montreal	NL	21	11	0	0	126.2	524	133	47	40	11	7	3	2	28	3	60	0	1	7	9	.438	1	0-0	0	2.84
1997 Boston	AL	36	5	0	13	84.1	345	89	36	33	6	2	3	2	19	2	51	0	0	7	3	.700	0	6-8	4	3.52
1993 Colorado	NL	20	15	1	1	84.2	390	117	66	62	14	6	5	1	24	2	39	1	0	2	8	.200	0	0-0	0	6.59
Montreal	NL	10	1	0	3	18.1	77	18	10	8	1	0	1	0	4	0	8	0	0	1	1	.500	0	0-0	0	3.93
5 ML YEARS		139	85	4	18	587	2479	639	270	246	58	32	22	6	136	15	324	4	3	31	33	.484	2	7-9	6	3.77

Doug Henry

Pitches: Right **Bats:** Right **Pos:** RP-75 **Ht:** 6'4" **Wt:** 205 **Born:** 12/10/63 **Age:** 34

Year Team	Lg	G	GS	CG	GF	IP	BFP	H	R	ER	HR	SH	SF	HB	TBB	IBB	SO	WP	Bk	W	L	Pct.	ShO	Sv-Op	Hld	ERA
1991 Milwaukee	AL	32	0	0	25	36	137	16	4	4	1	1	2	0	14	1	28	0	0	2	1	.667	0	15-16	3	1.00
1992 Milwaukee	AL	68	0	0	56	65	277	64	34	29	6	1	2	0	24	4	52	4	0	1	4	.200	0	29-33	1	4.02
1993 Milwaukee	AL	54	0	0	41	55	260	67	37	34	7	5	4	3	25	8	38	4	0	4	4	.500	0	17-24	0	5.56
1994 Milwaukee	AL	25	0	0	7	31.1	143	32	17	16	7	1	0	1	23	1	20	3	0	2	3	.400	0	0-0	4	4.60
1995 New York	NL	51	0	0	20	67	273	48	23	22	7	3	2	1	25	6	62	6	1	3	6	.333	0	4-7	6	2.96
1996 New York	NL	58	0	0	33	75	343	82	48	39	7	3	3	1	36	6	58	6	1	2	8	.200	0	9-14	8	4.68
1997 San Francisco	NL	75	0	0	25	70.2	317	70	45	37	5	4	3	1	41	6	69	3	0	4	5	.444	0	3-6	21	4.71
7 ML YEARS		363	0	0	207	400	1750	379	208	181	40	18	16	7	188	32	327	26	2	18	31	.367	0	77-100	43	4.07

Pat Hentgen

Pitches: Right **Bats:** Right **Pos:** SP-35 **Ht:** 6'2" **Wt:** 200 **Born:** 11/13/68 **Age:** 29

Year Team	Lg	G	GS	CG	GF	IP	BFP	H	R	ER	HR	SH	SF	HB	TBB	IBB	SO	WP	Bk	W	L	Pct.	ShO	Sv-Op	Hld	ERA
1991 Toronto	AL	3	1	0	1	7.1	30	5	2	2	1	1	0	2	3	0	3	1	0	0	0	.000	0	0-0	0	2.45
1992 Toronto	AL	28	2	0	10	50.1	229	49	30	30	7	2	2	0	32	5	39	2	1	5	2	.714	0	0-1	1	5.36
1993 Toronto	AL	34	32	3	0	216.1	926	215	103	93	27	6	5	7	74	0	122	11	1	19	9	.679	0	0-0	0	3.87
1994 Toronto	AL	24	24	6	0	174.2	728	158	74	66	21	6	3	3	59	1	147	5	1	13	8	.619	3	0-0	0	3.40
1995 Toronto	AL	30	30	2	0	200.2	913	236	129	114	24	2	1	5	90	6	135	7	2	10	14	.417	0	0-0	0	5.11
1996 Toronto	AL	35	35	10	0	265.2	1100	238	105	95	20	5	8	5	94	3	177	8	0	20	10	.667	3	0-0	0	3.22
1997 Toronto	AL	35	35	9	0	264	1085	253	116	108	31	9	3	7	71	2	160	6	2	15	10	.600	3	0-0	0	3.68
7 ML YEARS		189	159	30	11	1179	5011	1154	559	508	131	31	22	29	423	17	783	40	7	82	53	.607	9	0-1	1	3.88

Felix Heredia

Pitches: Left **Bats:** Left **Pos:** RP-56 **Ht:** 6'0" **Wt:** 165 **Born:** 6/18/76 **Age:** 22

Year Team	Lg	G	GS	CG	GF	IP	BFP	H	R	ER	HR	SH	SF	HB	TBB	IBB	SO	WP	Bk	W	L	Pct.	ShO	Sv-Op	Hld	ERA
1993 Marlins	R	11	11	0	0	57	225	48	18	17	0	2	0	2	9	0	47	1	1	4	1	.800	0	0--	—	2.68
1994 Kane County	A	24	8	1	11	68	306	86	55	43	7	3	4	3	14	0	65	6	0	4	5	.444	0	3--	—	5.69
1995 Brevard Cty	A+	34	8	0	3	95.2	420	101	52	38	6	0	7	4	36	1	76	6	1	6	4	.600	0	1--	—	3.57
1996 Portland	AA	55	0	0	17	60	236	48	11	10	3	4	1	1	15	2	42	1	1	8	1	.889	0	5--	—	1.50
1996 Florida	NL	21	0	0	5	16.2	78	21	8	8	1	0	1	0	10	1	10	2	0	1	1	.500	0	0-0	4	4.32
1997 Florida	NL	56	0	0	10	56.2	259	53	30	27	3	2	2	5	30	1	54	2	0	5	3	.625	0	0-1	7	4.29
2 ML YEARS		77	0	0	15	73.1	337	74	38	35	4	2	3	5	40	2	64	4	0	6	4	.600	0	0-1	9	4.30

Wilson Heredia

Pitches: Right **Bats:** Right **Pos:** RP-10 **Ht:** 6'0" **Wt:** 175 **Born:** 3/30/72 **Age:** 26

Year Team	Lg	G	GS	CG	GF	IP	BFP	H	R	ER	HR	SH	SF	HB	TBB	IBB	SO	WP	Bk	W	L	Pct.	ShO	Sv-Op	Hld	ERA
1991 Rangers	R	17	0	0	8	33.2	153	25	18	8	1	0	2	4	20	0	22	1	1	2	4	.333	0	4--	—	2.14
1992 Gastonia	A	39	1	0	22	63.1	301	71	45	36	4	8	2	5	30	2	64	11	7	1	2	.333	0	5--	—	5.12
1993 Charlotte	A+	34	0	0	29	38.2	165	30	17	16	0	2	4	1	20	1	26	4	0	1	5	.167	0	15--	—	3.72
1994 Tulsa	AA	18	1	0	5	43	171	35	23	18	6	4	1	0	8	0	53	5	2	3	2	.600	0	0--	—	3.77
1995 Okla City	AAA	8	7	0	0	31.2	158	40	26	24	3	1	1	5	25	1	21	1	0	1	4	.200	0	0--	—	6.82
Tulsa	AA	8	7	1	1	45.1	194	42	19	16	4	3	1	2	21	3	34	1	3	4	2	.667	1	1--	—	3.18
Portland	AA	4	4	0	0	27	115	22	7	6	2	1	1	1	14	0	19	0	0	4	0	1.000	0	0--	—	2.00
1997 Okla City	AAA	27	26	2	0	168.1	733	167	106	93	22	3	6	7	70	1	113	10	2	7	12	.368	0	0--	—	4.97
1995 Texas	AL	6	0	0	0	12	58	9	5	5	2	2	1	0	15	2	6	0	0	1	0	1.000	0	0-0	0	3.75
1997 Texas	AL	10	0	0	3	19.2	89	14	9	7	2	0	2	0	16	0	8	0	0	0	1	.000	0	0-0	0	3.20
2 ML YEARS		16	0	0	3	31.2	147	23	14	12	4	2	3	0	31	2	14	0	0	1	1	.500	0	0-0	0	3.41

Dustin Hermanson

Pitches: Right **Bats:** Right **Pos:** SP-28; RP-4 **Ht:** 6'2" **Wt:** 195 **Born:** 12/21/72 **Age:** 25

Year Team	Lg	G	GS	CG	GF	IP	BFP	H	R	ER	HR	SH	SF	HB	TBB	IBB	SO	WP	Bk	W	L	Pct.	ShO	Sv-Op	Hld	ERA
1995 San Diego	NL	26	0	0	6	31.2	151	35	26	24	8	3	0	2	22	1	19	3	0	3	1	.750	0	0-0	1	6.82
1996 San Diego	NL	8	0	0	4	13.2	62	18	15	13	3	2	3	0	4	0	11	0	1	1	0	1.000	0	0-0	0	8.56
1997 Montreal	NL	32	28	1	0	158.1	656	134	68	65	15	10	6	1	66	2	136	4	1	8	8	.500	1	0-0	0	3.69
3 ML YEARS		66	28	1	10	203.2	869	187	109	102	26	15	9	2	92	3	166	7	2	12	9	.571	1	0-0	1	4.51

Carlos Hernandez

Bats: Right **Throws:** Right **Pos:** C-44; PH-5; 1B-4 **Ht:** 5'11" **Wt:** 215 **Born:** 5/24/67 **Age:** 31

Year Team	Lg	G	AB	H	2B	3B	HR	(Hm	Rd)	TB	R	RBI	TBB	IBB	SO	HBP	SH	SF	SB	CS	SB%	GDP	Avg	OBP	SLG
1997 Rncho Cuca *	A+	1	4	1	0	0	0	—	—	1	0	0	0	0	1	0	0	0	0	0	.00	1	.250	.250	.250
Las Vegas *	AAA	3	10	4	0	0	1	—	—	7	1	5	1	0	3	0	0	1	0	0	.00	0	.400	.417	.700
1990 Los Angeles	NL	10	20	4	1	0	0	(0	0)	5	2	1	0	0	2	0	0	0	0	0	.00	0	.200	.200	.250
1991 Los Angeles	NL	15	14	3	1	0	0	(0	0)	4	1	1	0	0	5	1	0	1	1	0	1.00	2	.214	.250	.286
1992 Los Angeles	NL	69	173	45	4	0	3	(1	2)	58	11	17	11	1	21	0	1	2	0	1	.00	8	.260	.316	.335
1993 Los Angeles	NL	50	99	25	5	0	2	(1	1)	36	6	7	2	0	11	0	1	0	0	0	.00	0	.253	.267	.364

Year Team	Lg	G	AB	H	2B	3B	HR	(Hm	Rd)	TB	R	RBI	TBB	IBB	SO	HBP	SH	SF	SB	CS	SB%	GDP	Avg	OBP	SLG
								BATTING											BASERUNNING				PERCENTAGES		
1994 Los Angeles	NL	32	64	14	2	0	2	(0	2)	22	6	6	1	0	14	0	0	0	0	0	.00	0	.219	.231	.344
1995 Los Angeles	NL	45	94	14	1	0	2	(1	1)	21	3	8	7	0	25	1	1	0	0	0	.00	5	.149	.216	.223
1996 Los Angeles	NL	13	14	4	0	0	0	(0	0)	4	1	0	2	0	2	0	0	0	0	0	.00	0	.286	.375	.286
1997 San Diego	NL	50	134	42	7	1	3	(2	1)	60	15	14	3	0	27	0	1	0	0	2	.00	5	.313	.328	.448
8 ML YEARS		284	612	151	21	1	12	(5	7)	210	45	54	26	1	107	6	3	3	1	3	.25	20	.247	.283	.343

Fernando Hernandez

Pitches: Right **Bats:** Right **Pos:** RP-2 **Ht:** 6'2" **Wt:** 185 **Born:** 6/16/71 **Age:** 27

Year Team	Lg	G	GS	CG	GF	IP	BFP	H	R	ER	HR	SH	SF	HB	TBB	IBB	SO	WP	Bk	W	L	Pct.	ShO	Sv-Op	Hld	ERA
		HOW MUCH HE PITCHED						WHAT HE GAVE UP												THE RESULTS						
1990 Indians	R	11	11	2	0	69.2	289	61	36	31	3	2	2	1	30	0	43	2	7	4	4	.500	0	0- -	-	4.00
1991 Burlington	R+	14	13	0	1	77	326	74	33	25	4	2	0	7	19	0	86	12	1	4	4	.500	0	0- -	-	2.92
1992 Columbus	A	11	11	1	0	68.2	268	42	16	12	4	1	0	6	33	1	70	4	1	4	5	.444	1	0- -	-	1.57
Kinston	A+	8	8	1	0	41.2	177	36	23	21	2	3	3	1	22	0	32	3	0	1	3	.250	0	0- -	-	4.54
1993 Kinston	A+	8	8	0	0	51	200	34	15	10	1	2	1	2	18	0	53	1	0	2	3	.400	0	0- -	-	1.76
Canton-Akrn	AA	2	2	0	0	7.2	40	14	11	10	1	0	1	1	5	0	8	0	0	1	0	1.000	0	0- -	-	11.74
Rancho Cuca	A+	17	17	1	0	99.2	441	90	54	46	8	3	4	2	67	0	121	4	1	7	5	.583	0	0- -	-	4.15
1994 Wichita	AA	23	23	1	0	131.1	595	124	82	70	12	8	9	10	77	6	95	8	0	7	9	.438	1	0- -	-	4.80
1995 Las Vegas	AAA	8	8	0	0	37.2	186	43	32	32	3	0	2	3	31	3	40	4	0	1	6	.143	0	0- -	-	7.65
Memphis	AA	12	12	0	0	66.1	303	72	46	38	4	0	0	3	42	1	74	8	1	4	6	.400	0	0- -	-	5.16
1996 Memphis	AA	27	27	0	0	147.1	655	128	83	76	8	3	8	8	85	4	161	11	1	11	10	.524	0	0- -	-	4.64
1997 Toledo	AAA	55	1	0	18	76.2	350	71	44	35	5	4	2	1	51	1	98	1	1	6	5	.545	0	4- -	-	4.11
1997 Detroit	AL	2	0	0	0	1.1	13	5	6	6	0	0	0	1	3	1	2	0	0	0	0	.000	0	0-0	0	40.50

Jose Hernandez

Bats: R **Throws:** R **Pos:** PH-51; 3B-47; SS-21; 2B-20; LF-6; DH-1; 1B-1 **Ht:** 6'1" **Wt:** 180 **Born:** 7/14/69 **Age:** 28

Year Team	Lg	G	AB	H	2B	3B	HR	(Hm	Rd)	TB	R	RBI	TBB	IBB	SO	HBP	SH	SF	SB	CS	SB%	GDP	Avg	OBP	SLG
								BATTING											BASERUNNING				PERCENTAGES		
1991 Texas	AL	45	98	18	2	1	0	(0	0)	22	8	4	3	0	31	0	6	0	0	1	.00	2	.184	.208	.224
1992 Cleveland	AL	3	4	0	0	0	0	(0	0)	0	0	0	0	0	2	0	0	0	0	0	.00	0	.000	.000	.000
1994 Chicago	NL	56	132	32	2	3	1	(0	1)	43	18	9	8	0	29	1	5	0	2	2	.50	4	.242	.291	.326
1995 Chicago	NL	93	245	60	11	4	13	(6	7)	118	37	40	13	3	69	0	8	2	1	0	1.00	5	.245	.281	.482
1996 Chicago	NL	131	331	80	14	1	10	(4	6)	126	52	41	24	4	97	1	5	2	4	0	1.00	10	.242	.293	.381
1997 Chicago	NL	121	183	50	8	5	7	(4	3)	89	33	26	14	2	42	0	1	1	2	5	.29	5	.273	.323	.486
6 ML YEARS		449	993	240	37	14	31	(14	17)	398	148	120	62	9	270	2	25	5	9	8	.53	29	.242	.286	.401

Livan Hernandez

Pitches: Right **Bats:** Right **Pos:** SP-17 **Ht:** 6'2" **Wt:** 220 **Born:** 2/20/75 **Age:** 23

Year Team	Lg	G	GS	CG	GF	IP	BFP	H	R	ER	HR	SH	SF	HB	TBB	IBB	SO	WP	Bk	W	L	Pct.	ShO	Sv-Op	Hld	ERA
		HOW MUCH HE PITCHED						WHAT HE GAVE UP												THE RESULTS						
1996 Charlotte	AAA	10	10	0	0	49	239	61	32	28	3	2	4	1	34	1	45	2	4	2	4	.333	0	0- -	-	5.14
Portland	AA	15	15	0	0	93.1	380	81	48	45	14	3	0	3	34	1	95	3	1	9	2	.818	0	0- -	-	4.34
1997 Portland	AA	1	1	0	0	4	21	2	1	1	0	0	0	1	7	0	2	0	0	0	0	.000	0	0- -	-	2.25
Charlotte	AAA	14	14	0	0	81.1	352	76	39	36	5	2	1	3	38	2	58	1	1	5	3	.625	0	0- -	-	3.98
1996 Florida	NL	1	0	0	0	3	13	3	0	0	0	0	0	0	2	0	2	0	0	0	0	.000	0	0-0	0	0.00
1997 Florida	NL	17	17	0	0	96.1	405	81	39	34	5	4	7	3	38	1	72	0	0	9	3	.750	0	0-0	0	3.18
2 ML YEARS		18	17	0	0	99.1	418	84	39	34	5	4	7	3	40	1	74	0	0	9	3	.750	0	0-0	0	3.08

Roberto Hernandez

Pitches: Right **Bats:** Right **Pos:** RP-74 **Ht:** 6'4" **Wt:** 235 **Born:** 11/11/64 **Age:** 33

Year Team	Lg	G	GS	CG	GF	IP	BFP	H	R	ER	HR	SH	SF	HB	TBB	IBB	SO	WP	Bk	W	L	Pct.	ShO	Sv-Op	Hld	ERA
		HOW MUCH HE PITCHED						WHAT HE GAVE UP												THE RESULTS						
1991 Chicago	AL	9	3	0	1	15	69	18	15	13	1	0	0	0	7	0	6	1	0	1	0	1.000	0	0-0	0	7.80
1992 Chicago	AL	43	0	0	27	71	277	45	15	13	4	0	3	4	20	1	68	2	0	7	3	.700	0	12-16	6	1.65
1993 Chicago	AL	70	0	0	67	78.2	314	66	21	20	6	2	2	0	20	1	71	2	0	3	4	.429	0	38-44	0	2.29
1994 Chicago	AL	45	0	0	43	47.2	206	44	29	26	5	0	1	1	19	1	50	1	0	4	4	.500	0	14-20	0	4.91
1995 Chicago	AL	60	0	0	57	59.2	272	63	30	26	9	4	0	3	28	4	84	1	0	3	7	.300	0	32-42	0	3.92
1996 Chicago	AL	72	0	0	61	84.2	355	65	21	18	2	2	2	0	38	5	85	6	0	6	5	.545	0	38-46	0	1.91
1997 ChA-SF		74	0	0	50	80.2	340	67	24	22	7	2	1	1	38	5	82	3	0	10	3	.769	0	31-39	9	2.45
1997 Chicago	AL	46	0	0	43	48	203	38	15	13	5	1	1	1	24	4	47	2	0	5	1	.833	0	27-31	0	2.44
San Francisco	NL	28	0	0	7	32.2	137	29	9	9	2	1	0	0	14	1	35	1	0	5	2	.714	0	4-8	9	2.48
7 ML YEARS		373	3	0	306	437.1	1833	368	155	138	34	10	9	9	170	17	446	16	0	34	26	.567	0	165-207	15	2.84

Xavier Hernandez

Pitches: Right **Bats:** Left **Pos:** RP-44 **Ht:** 6'2" **Wt:** 195 **Born:** 8/16/65 **Age:** 32

Year Team	Lg	G	GS	CG	GF	IP	BFP	H	R	ER	HR	SH	SF	HB	TBB	IBB	SO	WP	Bk	W	L	Pct.	ShO	Sv-Op	Hld	ERA
		HOW MUCH HE PITCHED						WHAT HE GAVE UP												THE RESULTS						
1989 Toronto	AL	7	0	0	2	22.2	101	25	15	12	2	0	2	1	8	0	7	1	0	1	0	1.000	0	0-0	1	4.76
1990 Houston	NL	34	1	0	10	62.1	268	60	34	32	8	2	4	4	24	5	24	6	0	2	1	.667	0	0-1	1	4.62
1991 Houston	NL	32	6	0	8	63	285	66	34	33	6	1	1	0	32	7	55	0	0	2	7	.222	0	3-6	5	4.71
1992 Houston	NL	77	0	0	25	111	454	81	31	26	5	3	2	3	42	7	96	5	0	9	1	.900	0	7-10	8	2.11
1993 Houston	NL	72	0	0	29	96.2	389	75	37	28	6	3	3	1	28	3	101	6	0	4	5	.444	0	9-17	22	2.61

94

Year Team	Lg	G	GS	CG	GF	IP	BFP	H	R	ER	HR	SH	SF	HB	TBB	IBB	SO	WP	Bk	W	L	Pct.	ShO	Sv-Op	Hld	ERA
		HOW MUCH HE PITCHED						WHAT HE GAVE UP												THE RESULTS						
1994 New York	AL	31	0	0	14	40	187	48	27	26	7	2	2	2	21	3	37	3	0	4	4	.500	0	6-8	1	5.85
1995 Cincinnati	NL	59	0	0	19	90	391	95	47	46	8	6	2	4	31	1	84	7	0	7	2	.778	0	3-4	6	4.60
1996 Cin-Hou	NL	61	0	0	27	78	340	77	45	40	13	8	3	2	28	5	81	9	0	5	5	.500	0	6-10	7	4.62
1997 Texas	AL	44	0	0	20	49.1	221	51	27	25	7	1	1	2	22	4	36	5	0	0	4	.000	0	0-1	13	4.56
1996 Cincinnati	NL	3	0	0	0	3.1	19	8	6	5	2	0	0	0	2	0	3	0	0	0	0	.000	0	0-0	0	13.50
Houston	NL	58	0	0	27	74.2	321	69	39	35	11	8	3	2	26	5	78	9	0	5	5	.500	0	6-10	7	4.22
9 ML YEARS		417	7	0	154	613	2636	578	297	268	62	26	20	19	236	35	521	42	0	34	29	.540	0	34-57	64	3.93

Orel Hershiser

Pitches: Right **Bats:** Right **Pos:** SP-32   **Ht:** 6'3" **Wt:** 195 **Born:** 9/16/58 **Age:** 39

Year Team	Lg	G	GS	CG	GF	IP	BFP	H	R	ER	HR	SH	SF	HB	TBB	IBB	SO	WP	Bk	W	L	Pct.	ShO	Sv-Op	Hld	ERA
		HOW MUCH HE PITCHED						WHAT HE GAVE UP												THE RESULTS						
1983 Los Angeles	NL	8	0	0	4	8	37	7	6	3	1	0	0	0	6	0	5	1	0	0	0	.000	0	1- -	—	3.38
1984 Los Angeles	NL	45	20	8	10	189.2	771	160	65	56	9	2	3	4	50	8	150	8	1	11	8	.579	4	2- -	—	2.66
1985 Los Angeles	NL	36	34	9	1	239.2	953	179	72	54	8	5	4	6	68	5	157	5	0	19	3	.864	5	0- -	—	2.03
1986 Los Angeles	NL	35	35	8	0	231.1	988	213	112	99	13	14	6	5	86	11	153	12	3	14	14	.500	1	0-0	0	3.85
1987 Los Angeles	NL	37	35	10	2	264.2	1093	247	105	90	17	8	2	9	74	5	190	11	2	16	16	.500	1	1-1	0	3.06
1988 Los Angeles	NL	35	34	15	1	267	1068	208	73	67	18	9	6	4	73	10	178	6	5	23	8	.742	8	1-1	0	2.26
1989 Los Angeles	NL	35	33	8	0	256.2	1047	226	75	66	9	19	6	3	77	14	178	8	4	15	15	.500	4	0-0	0	2.31
1990 Los Angeles	NL	4	4	0	0	25.1	106	26	12	12	1	1	0	1	4	0	16	0	1	1	1	.500	0	0-0	0	4.26
1991 Los Angeles	NL	21	21	0	0	112	473	112	43	43	3	2	1	5	32	6	73	2	4	7	2	.778	0	0-0	0	3.46
1992 Los Angeles	NL	33	33	1	0	210.2	910	209	101	86	15	15	6	8	69	13	130	10	0	10	15	.400	1	0-0	0	3.67
1993 Los Angeles	NL	33	33	5	0	215.2	913	201	106	86	17	12	4	7	72	13	141	7	0	12	14	.462	1	0-0	0	3.59
1994 Los Angeles	NL	21	21	1	0	135.1	575	146	67	57	15	4	3	2	42	6	72	6	2	6	6	.500	0	0-0	0	3.79
1995 Cleveland	AL	26	26	1	0	167.1	683	151	76	72	21	3	4	5	51	1	111	3	0	16	6	.727	1	0-0	0	3.87
1996 Cleveland	AL	33	33	1	0	206	908	238	115	97	21	5	4	4	58	4	125	11	1	15	9	.625	0	0-0	0	4.24
1997 Cleveland	AL	32	32	1	0	195.1	826	199	105	97	26	6	8	11	69	2	107	11	0	14	6	.700	0	0-0	0	4.47
15 ML YEARS		434	394	68	18	2724.2	11351	2522	1133	985	194	106	57	82	831	98	1786	101	23	179	123	.593	25	5- -	—	3.25

Richard Hidalgo

Bats: R **Throws:** R **Pos:** CF-17; PH-3; LF-1; RF-1   **Ht:** 6'3" **Wt:** 190 **Born:** 7/2/75 **Age:** 22

Year Team	Lg	G	AB	H	2B	3B	HR	(Hm	Rd)	TB	R	RBI	TBB	IBB	SO	HBP	SH	SF	SB	CS	SB%	GDP	Avg	OBP	SLG
		BATTING																	BASERUNNING				PERCENTAGES		
1992 Astros	R	51	184	57	7	3	1	—	—	73	20	27	13	0	27	3	1	5	14	5	.74	1	.310	.360	.397
1993 Asheville	A	111	403	109	23	3	10	—	—	168	49	55	30	0	76	4	2	5	21	13	.62	3	.270	.324	.417
1994 Quad City	A	124	476	139	47	6	12	—	—	234	68	76	23	1	80	7	1	4	12	12	.50	6	.292	.331	.492
1995 Jackson	AA	133	489	130	28	6	14	—	—	212	59	59	32	1	76	2	0	7	9	9	.47	11	.266	.309	.434
1996 Jackson	AA	130	513	151	34	2	14	—	—	231	66	78	29	2	55	11	1	7	11	7	.61	24	.294	.341	.450
1997 New Orleans	AAA	134	526	147	37	5	11	—	—	227	74	78	35	3	57	8	0	7	6	10	.38	16	.279	.330	.432
1997 Houston	NL	19	62	19	5	0	2	(0	2)	30	8	6	4	0	18	1	0	0	1	0	1.00	0	.306	.358	.484

Bob Higginson

Bats: L **Throws:** R **Pos:** LF-105; RF-57; PH-4; CF-2; DH-1   **Ht:** 5'11" **Wt:** 195 **Born:** 8/18/70 **Age:** 27

Year Team	Lg	G	AB	H	2B	3B	HR	(Hm	Rd)	TB	R	RBI	TBB	IBB	SO	HBP	SH	SF	SB	CS	SB%	GDP	Avg	OBP	SLG
		BATTING																	BASERUNNING				PERCENTAGES		
1995 Detroit	AL	131	410	92	17	5	14	(10	4)	161	61	43	62	3	107	5	2	7	6	4	.60	5	.224	.329	.393
1996 Detroit	AL	130	440	141	35	0	26	(15	11)	254	75	81	65	7	66	1	3	6	6	3	.67	1	.320	.404	.577
1997 Detroit	AL	146	546	163	30	5	27	(16	11)	284	94	101	70	2	85	3	0	4	12	7	.63	10	.299	.379	.520
3 ML YEARS		407	1396	396	82	10	67	(41	26)	699	230	225	197	12	258	9	5	17	24	14	.63	22	.284	.372	.501

Glenallen Hill

Bats: Right **Throws:** Right **Pos:** RF-97; PH-28; DH-7   **Ht:** 6'2" **Wt:** 220 **Born:** 3/22/65 **Age:** 33

Year Team	Lg	G	AB	H	2B	3B	HR	(Hm	Rd)	TB	R	RBI	TBB	IBB	SO	HBP	SH	SF	SB	CS	SB%	GDP	Avg	OBP	SLG
		BATTING																	BASERUNNING				PERCENTAGES		
1989 Toronto	AL	19	52	15	0	0	1	(1	0)	18	4	7	3	0	12	0	0	0	2	1	.67	0	.288	.327	.346
1990 Toronto	AL	84	260	60	11	3	12	(7	5)	113	47	32	18	0	62	0	0	0	8	3	.73	5	.231	.281	.435
1991 Tor-Cle	AL	72	221	57	8	2	8	(3	5)	93	29	25	23	0	54	0	1	3	6	4	.60	7	.258	.324	.421
1992 Cleveland	AL	102	369	89	16	1	18	(7	11)	161	38	49	20	0	73	4	0	1	9	6	.60	11	.241	.287	.436
1993 Cle-ChN		97	261	69	14	2	15	(5	10)	132	33	47	17	1	71	1	1	4	8	3	.73	4	.264	.307	.506
1994 Chicago	NL	89	269	80	12	1	10	(5	5)	124	48	38	29	0	57	0	0	1	19	6	.76	5	.297	.365	.461
1995 San Francisco	NL	132	497	131	29	4	24	(13	11)	240	71	86	39	4	98	1	0	2	25	5	.83	11	.264	.317	.483
1996 San Francisco	NL	98	379	106	26	0	19	(9	10)	189	56	67	33	3	95	6	0	3	6	3	.67	6	.280	.344	.499
1997 San Francisco	NL	128	398	104	28	4	11	(3	8)	173	47	64	19	0	87	4	0	7	7	4	.64	9	.261	.297	.435
1991 Toronto	AL	35	99	25	5	2	3	(2	1)	43	14	11	7	0	24	0	0	2	2	2	.50	2	.253	.296	.434
Cleveland	AL	37	122	32	3	0	5	(1	4)	50	15	14	16	0	30	0	1	1	4	2	.67	5	.262	.345	.410
1993 Cleveland	AL	66	174	39	7	2	5	(0	5)	65	19	25	11	1	50	1	1	4	7	3	.70	3	.224	.268	.374
Chicago	NL	31	87	30	7	0	10	(5	5)	67	14	22	6	0	21	0	0	0	1	0	1.00	1	.345	.387	.770
9 ML YEARS		821	2706	711	144	17	118	(51	67)	1243	373	415	201	8	609	16	2	21	90	35	.72	57	.263	.315	.459

Ken Hill

Pitches: Right **Bats:** Right **Pos:** SP-31   **Ht:** 6'2" **Wt:** 205 **Born:** 12/14/65 **Age:** 32

Year Team	Lg	G	GS	CG	GF	IP	BFP	H	R	ER	HR	SH	SF	HB	TBB	IBB	SO	WP	Bk	W	L	Pct.	ShO	Sv-Op	Hld	ERA
1997 Tulsa *	AA	1	1	0	0	5	16	2	0	0	0	1	0	0	1	0	3	0	0	0	0	.000	0	0--	0	0.00
1988 St. Louis	NL	4	1	0	0	14	62	16	9	8	0	0	0	0	6	0	6	1	0	0	1	.000	0	0-0	0	5.14
1989 St. Louis	NL	33	33	2	0	196.2	862	186	92	83	9	14	5	5	99	6	112	11	2	7	15	.318	1	0-0	0	3.80
1990 St. Louis	NL	17	14	1	1	78.2	343	79	49	48	7	5	5	1	33	1	58	5	0	5	6	.455	0	0-0	1	5.49
1991 St. Louis	NL	30	30	0	0	181.1	743	147	76	72	15	7	7	6	67	4	121	7	1	11	10	.524	0	0-0	0	3.57
1992 Montreal	NL	33	33	3	0	218	908	187	76	65	13	15	3	3	75	4	150	11	4	16	9	.640	3	0-0	0	2.68
1993 Montreal	NL	28	28	2	0	183.2	780	163	84	66	7	9	7	6	74	7	90	6	2	9	7	.563	0	0-0	0	3.23
1994 Montreal	NL	23	23	2	0	154.2	647	145	61	57	12	6	6	6	44	7	85	3	0	16	5	.762	1	0-0	0	3.32
1995 StL-Cle		30	29	1	0	185	817	202	107	95	21	12	3	1	77	4	98	6	0	10	8	.556	0	0-0	0	4.62
1996 Texas	AL	35	35	7	0	250.2	1061	250	110	101	19	4	7	6	95	3	170	5	4	16	10	.615	3	0-0	0	3.63
1997 Tex-Ana	AL	31	31	1	0	190	833	194	103	96	19	3	7	3	95	3	106	7	0	9	12	.429	0	0-0	0	4.55
1995 St. Louis	NL	18	18	0	0	110.1	493	125	71	62	16	9	2	0	45	4	50	3	0	6	7	.462	0	0-0	0	5.06
Cleveland	AL	12	11	1	0	74.2	324	77	36	33	5	3	1	1	32	0	48	3	0	4	1	.800	0	0-0	0	3.98
1997 Texas	AL	19	19	0	0	111	499	129	69	64	11	2	6	2	56	3	68	5	0	5	8	.385	0	0-0	0	5.19
Anaheim	AL	12	12	1	0	79	334	65	34	32	8	1	1	1	39	0	38	2	0	4	4	.500	0	0-0	0	3.65
10 ML YEARS		264	257	19	1	1652.2	7056	1569	767	691	122	75	50	37	665	39	996	62	13	99	83	.544	8	0-0	1	3.76

Sterling Hitchcock

Pitches: Left **Bats:** Left **Pos:** SP-28; RP-4   **Ht:** 6'1" **Wt:** 192 **Born:** 4/29/71 **Age:** 27

Year Team	Lg	G	GS	CG	GF	IP	BFP	H	R	ER	HR	SH	SF	HB	TBB	IBB	SO	WP	Bk	W	L	Pct.	ShO	Sv-Op	Hld	ERA
1992 New York	AL	3	3	0	0	13	68	23	12	12	2	0	1	0	6	0	6	0	0	0	2	.000	0	0-0	0	8.31
1993 New York	AL	6	6	0	0	31	135	32	18	16	4	0	2	1	14	1	26	3	2	1	2	.333	0	0-0	0	4.65
1994 New York	AL	23	5	1	4	49.1	218	48	24	23	3	1	7	0	29	1	37	5	0	4	1	.800	0	2-2	0	4.20
1995 New York	AL	27	27	4	0	168.1	719	155	91	88	22	5	9	5	68	1	121	5	2	11	10	.524	1	0-0	0	4.70
1996 Seattle	AL	35	35	0	0	196.2	885	245	131	117	27	3	8	7	73	4	132	4	1	13	9	.591	0	0-0	0	5.35
1997 San Diego	NL	32	28	1	1	161	693	172	102	93	24	7	4	4	55	2	106	6	2	10	11	.476	0	0-0	0	5.20
6 ML YEARS		126	104	6	5	619.1	2718	675	378	349	82	16	30	18	245	9	428	23	7	39	35	.527	1	2-2	3	5.07

Denny Hocking

B: B **T:** R **Pos:** SS-44; 3B-39; PH-34; 2B-15; RF-12; LF-7; CF-2; DH-1; 1B-1   **Ht:** 5'10" **Wt:** 174 **Born:** 4/2/70 **Age:** 28

Year Team	Lg	G	AB	H	2B	3B	HR	(Hm	Rd)	TB	R	RBI	TBB	IBB	SO	HBP	SH	SF	SB	CS	SB%	GDP	Avg	OBP	SLG
1993 Minnesota	AL	15	36	5	1	0	0	(0	0)	6	7	0	6	0	8	0	0	0	1	0	1.00	1	.139	.262	.167
1994 Minnesota	AL	11	31	10	3	0	0	(0	0)	13	3	2	0	0	4	0	0	0	2	0	1.00	1	.323	.323	.419
1995 Minnesota	AL	9	25	5	0	2	0	(0	0)	9	4	3	2	1	2	0	1	0	1	0	1.00	1	.200	.259	.360
1996 Minnesota	AL	49	127	25	6	0	1	(0	1)	34	16	10	8	0	24	0	1	1	3	3	.50	3	.197	.243	.268
1997 Minnesota	AL	115	253	65	12	4	2	(0	2)	91	28	25	18	0	51	1	5	1	3	5	.38	6	.257	.308	.360
5 ML YEARS		199	472	110	22	6	3	(0	3)	153	58	40	34	1	89	1	7	2	10	8	.56	12	.233	.285	.324

Trevor Hoffman

Pitches: Right **Bats:** Right **Pos:** RP-70   **Ht:** 6'0" **Wt:** 205 **Born:** 10/13/67 **Age:** 30

Year Team	Lg	G	GS	CG	GF	IP	BFP	H	R	ER	HR	SH	SF	HB	TBB	IBB	SO	WP	Bk	W	L	Pct.	ShO	Sv-Op	Hld	ERA
1993 Fla-SD	NL	67	0	0	26	90	391	80	43	39	10	4	5	1	39	13	79	5	0	4	6	.400	0	5-8	15	3.90
1994 San Diego	NL	47	0	0	41	56	225	39	16	16	4	1	2	0	20	6	68	3	0	4	4	.500	0	20-23	1	2.57
1995 San Diego	NL	55	0	0	51	53.1	218	48	25	23	10	0	0	0	14	3	52	1	0	7	4	.636	0	31-38	0	3.88
1996 San Diego	NL	70	0	0	62	88	348	50	23	22	6	2	2	2	31	5	111	2	0	9	5	.643	0	42-49	0	2.25
1997 San Diego	NL	70	0	0	59	81.1	322	59	25	24	9	2	1	0	24	4	111	7	0	6	4	.600	0	37-44	0	2.66
1993 Florida	NL	28	0	0	13	35.2	152	24	13	13	5	2	1	0	19	7	26	3	0	2	2	.500	0	2-3	8	3.28
San Diego	NL	39	0	0	13	54.1	239	56	30	26	5	2	4	1	20	6	53	2	0	2	4	.333	0	3-5	7	4.31
5 ML YEARS		309	0	0	239	368.2	1504	276	132	124	39	9	10	3	128	31	421	18	0	30	23	.566	0	135-162	16	3.03

Chris Hoiles

Bats: R **Throws:** R **Pos:** C-87; DH-8; 1B-4; 3B-1; PH-1   **Ht:** 6'0" **Wt:** 215 **Born:** 3/20/65 **Age:** 33

Year Team	Lg	G	AB	H	2B	3B	HR	(Hm	Rd)	TB	R	RBI	TBB	IBB	SO	HBP	SH	SF	SB	CS	SB%	GDP	Avg	OBP	SLG
1997 Bowie *	AA	3	7	1	1	0	0	—	—	2	1	2	3	0	2	0	0	0	0	0	.00	0	.143	.400	.286
1989 Baltimore	AL	6	9	1	1	0	0	(0	0)	2	0	1	1	0	3	0	0	0	0	0	.00	0	.111	.200	.222
1990 Baltimore	AL	23	63	12	3	0	1	(1	0)	18	7	6	5	1	12	0	0	0	0	0	.00	0	.190	.250	.286
1991 Baltimore	AL	107	341	83	15	0	11	(5	6)	131	36	31	29	1	61	1	0	1	0	2	.00	11	.243	.304	.384
1992 Baltimore	AL	96	310	85	10	1	20	(8	12)	157	49	40	55	2	60	2	1	3	0	2	.00	8	.274	.384	.506
1993 Baltimore	AL	126	419	130	28	0	29	(16	13)	245	80	82	69	4	94	9	3	3	1	1	.50	10	.310	.416	.585
1994 Baltimore	AL	99	332	82	10	0	19	(11	8)	149	45	53	63	2	73	5	1	4	2	0	1.00	6	.247	.371	.449
1995 Baltimore	AL	114	352	88	15	1	19	(9	10)	162	53	58	67	3	80	4	0	3	1	0	1.00	11	.250	.373	.460
1996 Baltimore	AL	127	407	105	13	0	25	(13	12)	193	64	73	57	1	97	9	1	7	0	1	.00	7	.258	.356	.474
1997 Baltimore	AL	99	320	83	15	0	12	(9	3)	134	45	49	51	3	86	10	0	3	1	0	1.00	7	.259	.375	.419
9 ML YEARS		797	2553	669	110	2	136	(72	64)	1191	379	393	397	17	566	40	6	24	5	6	.45	60	.262	.367	.467

Todd Hollandsworth

Bats: L **Throws:** L **Pos:** LF-80; CF-30; PH-22; RF-4   **Ht:** 6'2" **Wt:** 193 **Born:** 4/20/73 **Age:** 25

						BATTING												BASERUNNING				PERCENTAGES		
Year Team	Lg	G	AB	H	2B	3B	HR	(Hm | Rd)	TB	R	RBI	TBB	IBB	SO	HBP	SH	SF	SB	CS	SB%	GDP	Avg	OBP	SLG
1997 Albuquerque *	AAA	13	56	24	4	3	1	—	—	37	13	14	4	0	4	0	0	0	2	3	.40	0	.429	.467	.661
San Berndno *	A+	2	8	2	0	1	0	—	—	4	1	2	1	1	2	0	0	0	0	0	.00	0	.250	.333	.500
1995 Los Angeles	NL	41	103	24	2	0	5	(3 | 2)	41	16	13	10	2	29	1	0	1	2	1	.67	1	.233	.304	.398
1996 Los Angeles	NL	149	478	139	26	4	12	(2 | 10)	209	64	59	41	1	93	2	3	2	21	6	.78	2	.291	.348	.437
1997 Los Angeles	NL	106	296	73	20	2	4	(1 | 3)	109	39	31	17	2	60	0	2	2	5	5	.50	8	.247	.286	.368
3 ML YEARS		296	877	236	48	6	21	(6 | 15)	359	119	103	68	5	182	3	5	5	28	12	.70	11	.269	.322	.409

Dave Hollins

Bats: Both **Throws:** Right **Pos:** 3B-135; 1B-14; PH-3   **Ht:** 6'1" **Wt:** 210 **Born:** 5/25/66 **Age:** 32

						BATTING												BASERUNNING				PERCENTAGES		
Year Team	Lg	G	AB	H	2B	3B	HR	(Hm	Rd)	TB	R	RBI	TBB	IBB	SO	HBP	SH	SF	SB	CS	SB%	GDP	Avg	OBP	SLG
1990 Philadelphia	NL	72	114	21	0	0	5	(2	3)	36	14	15	10	3	28	1	0	2	0	0	.00	1	.184	.252	.316
1991 Philadelphia	NL	56	151	45	10	2	6	(3	3)	77	18	21	17	1	26	3	0	1	1	1	.50	2	.298	.378	.510
1992 Philadelphia	NL	156	586	158	28	4	27	(14	13)	275	104	93	76	4	110	19	0	4	9	6	.60	8	.270	.369	.469
1993 Philadelphia	NL	143	543	148	30	4	18	(9	9)	240	104	93	85	5	109	5	0	7	2	3	.40	15	.273	.372	.442
1994 Philadelphia	NL	44	162	36	7	1	4	(1	3)	57	28	26	23	0	32	4	0	3	1	0	1.00	6	.222	.328	.352
1995 Phi-Bos		70	218	49	12	2	7	(5	2)	86	48	26	57	4	45	5	0	4	1	1	.50	4	.225	.391	.394
1996 Min-Sea	AL	149	516	135	29	0	16	(7	9)	212	88	78	84	7	117	13	1	2	6	6	.50	11	.262	.377	.411
1997 Anaheim	AL	149	572	165	29	2	16	(15	1)	246	101	85	62	2	124	8	1	5	16	6	.73	12	.288	.363	.430
1995 Philadelphia	NL	65	205	47	12	2	7	(5	2)	84	46	25	53	4	38	5	0	4	1	1	.50	4	.229	.393	.410
Boston	AL	5	13	2	0	0	0	(0	0)	2	2	1	4	0	7	0	0	0	0	0	.00	0	.154	.353	.154
1996 Minnesota	AL	121	422	102	26	0	13	(6	7)	167	71	53	71	5	102	10	0	0	6	4	.60	9	.242	.364	.396
Seattle	AL	28	94	33	3	0	3	(1	2)	45	17	25	13	2	15	3	1	2	0	2	.00	2	.351	.438	.479
8 ML YEARS		839	2862	757	145	15	99	(56	43)	1229	505	437	414	26	591	58	2	28	36	23	.61	59	.265	.366	.429

Darren Holmes

Pitches: Right **Bats:** Right **Pos:** RP-36; SP-6   **Ht:** 6'0" **Wt:** 202 **Born:** 4/25/66 **Age:** 32

		HOW MUCH HE PITCHED						WHAT HE GAVE UP										THE RESULTS					
Year Team	Lg	G	GS	CG	GF	IP	BFP	H	R	ER	HR	SH	SF	HB	TBB	IBB	SO	WP	Bk	W	L	Pct.	ShO	Sv-Op	Hld	ERA
1990 Los Angeles	AL	14	0	0	1	17.1	77	15	10	10	1	1	2	0	11	3	19	1	0	0	1	.000	0	0-0	0	5.19
1991 Milwaukee	AL	40	0	0	9	76.1	344	90	43	40	6	8	3	1	27	1	59	6	0	1	4	.200	0	3-6	3	4.72
1992 Milwaukee	AL	41	0	0	25	42.1	173	35	12	12	1	4	0	2	11	4	31	0	0	4	4	.500	0	6-8	2	2.55
1993 Colorado	NL	62	0	0	51	66.2	274	56	31	30	6	0	0	2	20	1	60	2	1	3	3	.500	0	25-29	4	4.05
1994 Colorado	NL	29	0	0	14	28.1	142	35	25	20	5	4	1	1	24	4	33	2	0	0	3	.000	0	3-8	3	6.35
1995 Colorado	NL	68	0	0	33	66.2	286	59	26	24	3	5	3	3	28	3	61	7	1	6	1	.857	0	14-18	13	3.24
1996 Colorado	NL	62	0	0	21	77	333	78	41	34	8	2	1	1	28	2	73	2	0	5	4	.556	0	1-8	7	3.97
1997 Colorado	NL	42	6	0	10	89.1	406	113	58	53	12	6	4	0	36	3	70	4	0	9	2	.818	0	3-4	5	5.34
8 ML YEARS		358	6	0	164	464	2035	481	246	223	42	30	14	8	185	21	406	24	2	28	22	.560	0	55-81	35	4.33

Chris Holt

Pitches: Right **Bats:** Right **Pos:** SP-32; RP-1   **Ht:** 6'4" **Wt:** 205 **Born:** 9/18/71 **Age:** 26

		HOW MUCH HE PITCHED						WHAT HE GAVE UP										THE RESULTS					
Year Team	Lg	G	GS	CG	GF	IP	BFP	H	R	ER	HR	SH	SF	HB	TBB	IBB	SO	WP	Bk	W	L	Pct.	ShO	Sv-Op	Hld	ERA
1992 Auburn	A-	14	14	0	0	83	353	75	48	41	9	4	2	7	24	0	81	11	4	2	5	.286	0	0- -	—	4.45
1993 Quad City	A	26	26	10	0	186.1	775	162	70	47	10	8	2	3	54	1	176	9	3	11	10	.524	3	0- -	—	2.27
1994 Jackson	AA	26	25	5	0	167	679	169	78	64	11	6	4	9	22	2	111	5	1	10	9	.526	2	0- -	—	3.45
1995 Jackson	AA	5	5	1	0	32.1	126	27	8	6	2	1	0	0	5	1	24	1	0	2	2	.500	1	0- -	—	1.67
Tucson	AAA	20	19	0	0	118.2	524	155	65	54	5	7	3	7	32	1	69	6	0	5	8	.385	0	0- -	—	4.10
1996 Tucson	AAA	28	27	4	0	186.1	782	208	87	75	11	11	0	5	38	1	137	6	1	9	6	.600	0	0- -	—	3.62
1996 Houston	NL	4	0	0	3	4.2	22	5	3	3	0	0	0	0	3	1	0	1	0	1	0	1.000	0	0-0	0	5.79
1997 Houston	NL	33	32	0	0	209.2	883	211	98	82	17	7	5	8	61	4	95	1	0	8	12	.400	0	0-0	0	3.52
2 ML YEARS		37	32	0	3	214.1	905	216	101	85	17	7	5	8	64	5	95	2	0	8	13	.381	0	0-0	0	3.57

Mike Holtz

Pitches: Left **Bats:** Left **Pos:** RP-66   **Ht:** 5'9" **Wt:** 175 **Born:** 10/10/72 **Age:** 25

		HOW MUCH HE PITCHED						WHAT HE GAVE UP										THE RESULTS					
Year Team	Lg	G	GS	CG	GF	IP	BFP	H	R	ER	HR	SH	SF	HB	TBB	IBB	SO	WP	Bk	W	L	Pct.	ShO	Sv-Op	Hld	ERA
1994 Boise	A-	35	0	0	16	35	143	22	4	2	0	0	1	2	12	1	59	3	1	0	0	.000	0	11- -	—	0.51
1995 Lk Elsinore	A+	56	0	0	19	82.2	341	70	26	21	7	5	4	5	23	3	101	2	0	4	4	.500	0	3- -	—	2.29
1996 Midland	AA	33	0	0	13	41	188	52	34	19	6	1	1	9	14	1	41	4	0	1	2	.333	0	2- -	—	4.17
1996 California	AL	30	0	0	8	29.1	127	21	11	8	1	1	1	3	19	2	31	1	0	3	3	.500	0	0-0	5	2.45
1997 Anaheim	AL	66	0	0	11	43.1	187	38	21	16	7	1	2	2	15	4	40	1	0	3	4	.429	0	2-8	14	3.32
2 ML YEARS		96	0	0	19	72.2	314	59	32	24	8	2	3	5	34	6	71	2	0	6	7	.462	0	2-8	19	2.97

Mark Holzemer

Pitches: Left **Bats:** Left **Pos:** RP-14   **Ht:** 6'0" **Wt:** 165 **Born:** 8/20/69 **Age:** 28

		HOW MUCH HE PITCHED						WHAT HE GAVE UP										THE RESULTS					
Year Team	Lg	G	GS	CG	GF	IP	BFP	H	R	ER	HR	SH	SF	HB	TBB	IBB	SO	WP	Bk	W	L	Pct.	ShO	Sv-Op	Hld	ERA
1997 Tacoma *	AAA	37	0	0	26	41	165	32	10	10	1	0	2	0	10	3	38	1	0	1	0	1.000	0	13- -	—	2.20

Year Team	Lg	G	GS	CG	GF	IP	BFP	H	R	ER	HR	SH	SF	HB	TBB	IBB	SO	WP	Bk	W	L	Pct.	ShO	Sv-Op	Hld	ERA
1993 California	AL	5	4	0	1	23.1	117	34	24	23	2	1	0	3	13	0	10	1	0	0	3	.000	0	0-0	0	8.87
1995 California	AL	12	0	0	5	8.1	45	11	6	5	1	1	0	1	7	1	5	0	0	0	0	.000	0	0-0	0	5.40
1996 California	AL	25	0	0	3	24.2	119	35	28	24	7	0	1	3	8	1	20	0	0	1	0	1.000	0	0-0	1	8.76
1997 Seattle	AL	14	0	0	2	9	44	9	6	6	0	0	0	0	8	0	7	0	0	0	0	.000	0	1-1	1	6.00
4 ML YEARS		56	4	0	11	65.1	325	89	64	58	10	2	1	7	36	2	42	1	0	1	4	.200	0	1-1	2	7.99

Rick Honeycutt

Pitches: Left **Bats:** Left **Pos:** RP-2   **Ht:** 6'1" **Wt:** 195 **Born:** 6/29/54 **Age:** 44

Year Team	Lg	G	GS	CG	GF	IP	BFP	H	R	ER	HR	SH	SF	HB	TBB	IBB	SO	WP	Bk	W	L	Pct.	ShO	Sv-Op	Hld	ERA
1977 Seattle	AL	10	3	0	3	29	125	26	16	14	7	0	2	3	11	2	17	2	1	0	1	.000	0	0- -	—	4.34
1978 Seattle	AL	26	24	4	0	134.1	594	150	81	73	12	9	7	3	49	5	50	3	0	5	11	.313	1	0- -	—	4.89
1979 Seattle	AL	33	28	8	2	194	839	201	103	87	22	11	6	6	67	7	83	5	1	11	12	.478	1	0- -	—	4.04
1980 Seattle	AL	30	30	9	0	203.1	871	221	99	89	22	11	7	3	60	7	79	4	0	10	17	.370	1	0-0	0	3.94
1981 Texas	AL	20	20	8	0	127.2	509	120	49	47	12	5	0	0	17	1	40	1	0	11	6	.647	2	0-0	0	3.31
1982 Texas	AL	30	26	4	3	164	728	201	103	96	20	4	8	3	54	4	64	3	1	5	17	.227	1	0- -	—	5.27
1983 Tex-LA	AL	34	32	6	0	213.2	865	214	85	72	15	5	6	8	50	6	71	1	1	16	11	.593	2	0-0	0	3.03
1984 Los Angeles	NL	29	28	6	0	183.2	762	180	72	58	11	6	5	2	51	11	75	1	2	10	9	.526	2	0- -	—	2.84
1985 Los Angeles	NL	31	25	1	2	142	600	141	71	54	9	5	4	1	49	7	67	2	0	8	12	.400	0	1- -	—	3.42
1986 Los Angeles	NL	32	28	0	2	171	713	164	71	63	9	6	1	3	45	4	100	4	1	11	9	.550	0	0- -	—	3.32
1987 LA-Oak	AL	34	24	1	1	139.1	631	158	91	73	13	1	3	4	54	4	102	5	1	3	16	.158	1	0-0	1	4.72
1988 Oakland	AL	55	0	0	17	79.2	330	74	36	31	6	3	6	3	25	2	47	3	8	3	2	.600	0	7-9	19	3.50
1989 Oakland	AL	64	0	0	24	76.2	305	56	26	20	5	5	2	1	26	3	52	6	1	2	2	.500	0	12-16	24	2.35
1990 Oakland	AL	63	0	0	13	63.1	256	46	23	19	2	2	6	1	22	2	38	1	1	2	2	.500	0	7-10	27	2.70
1991 Oakland	AL	43	0	0	7	37.2	167	37	16	15	3	2	1	2	20	3	26	0	0	2	4	.333	0	0-4	14	3.58
1992 Oakland	AL	54	0	0	7	39	169	41	19	16	2	4	1	3	10	3	32	2	0	1	4	.200	0	3-7	18	3.69
1993 Oakland	AL	52	0	0	7	41.2	174	30	18	13	2	7	4	1	20	6	21	0	0	1	4	.200	0	1-3	20	2.81
1994 Texas	AL	42	0	0	9	25	122	37	21	20	4	5	0	2	9	1	18	0	0	1	2	.333	0	1-2	11	7.20
1995 Oak-NYA	AL	52	0	0	6	45.2	180	39	16	15	6	3	1	1	10	0	21	0	0	5	1	.833	0	2-5	12	2.96
1996 St. Louis	NL	61	0	0	13	47.1	190	42	15	15	3	5	3	0	7	3	30	1	0	2	1	.667	0	4-7	19	2.85
1997 St. Louis	NL	2	0	0	2	2	11	5	3	3	0	0	0	0	1	0	2	1	1	0	0	.000	0	0-0	0	13.50
1983 Texas	AL	25	25	5	0	174.2	693	168	59	47	9	3	6	6	37	2	56	1	2	14	8	.636	2	0-0	0	2.42
Los Angeles	NL	9	7	1	0	39	172	46	26	25	6	2	0	2	13	4	18	0	1	2	3	.400	0	0- -	—	5.77
1987 Los Angeles	NL	27	20	1	0	115.2	525	133	74	59	10	0	0	2	45	4	92	4	0	2	12	.143	1	0-0	1	4.59
Oakland	AL	7	4	0	1	23.2	106	25	17	14	3	1	3	2	9	0	10	1	1	1	4	.200	0	0-0	0	5.32
1995 Oakland	AL	49	0	0	6	44.2	174	37	13	12	5	3	1	1	9	0	21	0	0	5	0	.833	0	2-5	12	2.42
New York	AL	3	0	0	0	1	6	2	3	3	1	0	0	0	1	0	0	0	0	0	1	.000	0	0-0	0	27.00
21 ML YEARS		797	268	47	118	2160	9141	2183	1034	893	185	99	73	50	657	81	1038	45	23	109	143	.433	11	38- -	—	3.72

Tyler Houston

Bats: L **Throws:** R **Pos:** C-41; PH-21; 3B-12; 1B-2; 2B-1; SS-1   **Ht:** 6'2" **Wt:** 210 **Born:** 1/17/71 **Age:** 27

Year Team	Lg	G	AB	H	2B	3B	HR	(Hm	Rd)	TB	R	RBI	TBB	IBB	SO	HBP	SH	SF	SB	CS	SB%	GDP	Avg	OBP	SLG
1989 Idaho Falls	R+	50	176	43	11	0	4	—	—	66	30	24	25	1	41	1	0	0	4	0	1.00	4	.244	.342	.375
1990 Sumter	A	117	442	93	14	3	7	—	—	152	58	56	49	1	101	2	2	7	6	2	.75	15	.210	.288	.344
1991 Macon	A	107	351	81	16	3	8	—	—	127	41	47	39	0	70	1	1	3	10	2	.83	8	.231	.307	.362
1992 Durham	A+	117	402	91	17	1	7	—	—	131	39	38	20	0	89	1	3	5	5	6	.45	5	.226	.262	.326
1993 Greenville	AA	84	262	73	14	1	5	—	—	104	27	33	13	4	50	2	3	4	5	3	.63	12	.279	.313	.397
Richmond	AAA	13	36	5	1	1	1	—	—	11	4	3	1	0	8	0	0	0	0	0	.00	1	.139	.162	.306
1994 Richmond	AAA	97	312	76	15	2	4	—	—	107	33	33	16	1	44	0	0	5	3	3	.50	12	.244	.276	.343
1995 Richmond	AAA	103	349	89	10	3	12	—	—	141	41	42	18	3	62	4	1	2	3	5	.38	6	.255	.298	.404
1997 Iowa	AAA	6	23	5	2	0	0	—	—	7	0	4	0	0	2	0	0	0	0	0	.00	0	.217	.217	.304
Rockford	A	2	6	3	1	0	0	—	—	4	1	1	0	0	0	0	0	0	0	0	.00	0	.500	.500	.667
1996 Atl-ChN	NL	79	142	45	9	1	3	(1	2)	65	21	27	9	1	27	0	0	0	3	2	.60	5	.317	.358	.458
1997 Chicago	NL	72	196	51	10	0	2	(0	2)	67	15	28	9	1	35	0	0	2	1	0	1.00	3	.260	.290	.342
1996 Atlanta	NL	33	27	6	2	1	1	(1	0)	13	3	8	1	0	9	0	0	0	0	0	.00	1	.222	.250	.481
Chicago	NL	46	115	39	7	0	2	(0	2)	52	18	19	8	1	18	0	0	0	3	2	.60	4	.339	.382	.452
2 ML YEARS		151	338	96	19	1	5	(1	4)	132	36	55	18	2	62	0	0	2	4	2	.67	9	.284	.318	.391

David Howard

Bats: B **Throws:** R **Pos:** 2B-34; PH-19; RF-17; SS-9; 3B-7; DH-5; LF-5; CF-2 **Ht:** 6'0" **Wt:** 175 **Born:** 2/26/67 **Age:** 31

Year Team	Lg	G	AB	H	2B	3B	HR	(Hm	Rd)	TB	R	RBI	TBB	IBB	SO	HBP	SH	SF	SB	CS	SB%	GDP	Avg	OBP	SLG
1991 Kansas City	AL	94	236	51	7	0	1	(0	1)	61	20	17	16	0	45	1	9	2	3	2	.60	1	.216	.267	.258
1992 Kansas City	AL	74	219	49	6	2	1	(1	0)	62	19	18	15	0	43	0	8	2	3	4	.43	3	.224	.271	.283
1993 Kansas City	AL	15	24	8	0	1	0	(0	0)	10	5	2	2	0	5	0	2	1	1	0	1.00	0	.333	.370	.417
1994 Kansas City	AL	46	83	19	4	0	1	(0	1)	26	9	13	11	0	23	0	3	3	3	2	.60	1	.229	.309	.313
1995 Kansas City	AL	95	255	62	13	4	0	(0	0)	83	23	19	24	1	41	1	6	1	3	5	.38	6	.243	.310	.325
1996 Kansas City	AL	143	420	92	14	5	4	(3	1)	128	51	48	40	0	74	4	17	4	5	6	.45	6	.219	.291	.305
1997 Kansas City	AL	80	162	39	8	1	1	(0	1)	52	24	13	10	1	31	1	3	1	2	2	.50	1	.241	.287	.321
7 ML YEARS		547	1399	320	52	13	8	(4	4)	422	151	130	118	2	262	7	48	14	23	17	.58	19	.229	.289	.302

Thomas Howard

Bats: L Throws: R Pos: PH-52; CF-41; RF-18; LF-10   Ht: 6'2" Wt: 205 Born: 12/11/64 Age: 33

							BATTING										BASERUNNING				PERCENTAGES		
Year Team	Lg	G	AB	H	2B	3B	HR	(Hm | Rd)	TB	R	RBI	TBB	IBB	SO	HBP	SH	SF	SB	CS	SB%	GDP	Avg	OBP	SLG
1990 San Diego	NL	20	44	12	2	0	0	(0 | 0)	14	4	0	0	0	11	0	1	0	0	1	.00	1	.273	.273	.318
1991 San Diego	NL	106	281	70	12	3	4	(4 | 0)	100	30	22	24	4	57	1	2	1	10	7	.59	4	.249	.309	.356
1992 SD-Cle		122	361	100	15	2	2	(1 | 1)	125	37	32	17	1	60	0	11	2	15	8	.65	4	.277	.308	.346
1993 Cle-Cin		112	319	81	15	3	7	(5 | 2)	123	48	36	24	0	63	0	0	5	10	7	.59	9	.254	.302	.386
1994 Cincinnati	NL	83	178	47	11	0	5	(4 | 1)	73	24	24	10	1	30	0	3	1	4	2	.67	2	.264	.302	.410
1995 Cincinnati	NL	113	281	85	15	2	3	(1 | 2)	113	42	26	20	0	37	1	1	1	17	8	.68	3	.302	.350	.402
1996 Cincinnati	NL	121	360	98	19	10	6	(1 | 5)	155	50	42	17	3	51	3	2	4	6	5	.55	5	.272	.307	.431
1997 Houston	NL	107	255	63	16	1	3	(0 | 3)	90	24	22	26	1	48	3	1	1	2	2	.33	3	.247	.323	.353
1992 San Diego	NL	5	3	1	0	0	0	(0 | 0)	1	1	0	0	0	0	0	1	0	0	0	.00	0	.333	.333	.333
Cleveland	AL	117	358	99	15	2	2	(1 | 1)	124	36	32	17	1	60	0	10	2	15	8	.65	4	.277	.308	.346
1993 Cleveland	AL	74	178	42	7	0	3	(3 | 0)	58	26	23	12	0	42	0	0	4	5	1	.83	5	.236	.278	.326
Cincinnati	NL	38	141	39	8	3	4	(2 | 2)	65	22	13	12	0	21	0	0	1	5	6	.45	4	.277	.331	.461
8 ML YEARS		784	2079	556	105	21	30	(16 | 14)	793	259	204	138	10	357	8	21	15	63	40	.61	31	.267	.313	.381

Jack Howell

Bats: L Throws: R Pos: PH-27; 3B-24; DH-22; 1B-12   Ht: 6'0" Wt: 190 Born: 8/18/61 Age: 36

							BATTING										BASERUNNING				PERCENTAGES		
Year Team	Lg	G	AB	H	2B	3B	HR	(Hm | Rd)	TB	R	RBI	TBB	IBB	SO	HBP	SH	SF	SB	CS	SB%	GDP	Avg	OBP	SLG
1985 California	AL	43	137	27	4	0	5	(2 | 3)	46	19	18	16	2	33	0	4	1	1	1	.50	1	.197	.279	.336
1986 California	AL	63	151	41	14	2	4	(1 | 3)	71	26	21	19	0	28	0	3	2	2	0	1.00	1	.272	.349	.470
1987 California	AL	138	449	110	18	5	23	(15 | 8)	207	64	64	57	4	118	2	1	2	4	3	.57	7	.245	.331	.461
1988 California	AL	154	500	127	32	2	16	(9 | 7)	211	59	63	46	8	130	6	4	2	2	6	.25	8	.254	.323	.422
1989 California	AL	144	474	108	19	4	20	(9 | 11)	195	56	52	52	9	125	3	3	1	0	3	.00	8	.228	.308	.411
1990 California	AL	105	316	72	19	1	8	(3 | 5)	117	35	33	46	5	61	1	1	2	3	0	1.00	3	.228	.326	.370
1991 Cal-SD		90	241	50	5	1	8	(3 | 5)	81	35	23	29	1	44	0	1	1	1	1	.50	2	.207	.293	.336
1996 California	AL	66	126	34	4	1	8	(4 | 4)	64	20	21	10	0	30	0	0	0	1	0	1.00	3	.270	.324	.508
1997 Anaheim	AL	77	174	45	7	0	14	(5 | 9)	94	25	34	13	2	36	0	1	3	1	1	.50	1	.259	.305	.540
1991 Anaheim	AL	32	81	17	2	0	2	(0 | 2)	25	11	7	11	0	11	0	0	0	1	1	.50	1	.210	.304	.309
San Diego	NL	58	160	33	3	1	6	(3 | 3)	56	24	16	18	1	33	0	1	1	0	0	.00	1	.206	.287	.350
9 ML YEARS		880	2568	614	122	16	106	(51 | 55)	1086	339	329	288	31	605	12	18	13	14	15	.48	37	.239	.317	.423

Mike Hubbard

Bats: Right Throws: Right Pos: C-20; PH-10; 3B-1   Ht: 6'1" Wt: 195 Born: 2/16/71 Age: 27

							BATTING										BASERUNNING				PERCENTAGES		
Year Team	Lg	G	AB	H	2B	3B	HR	(Hm | Rd)	TB	R	RBI	TBB	IBB	SO	HBP	SH	SF	SB	CS	SB%	GDP	Avg	OBP	SLG
1997 Iowa *	AAA	50	186	52	15	1	6	—	—	87	24	26	11	0	23	0	1	2	2	0	1.00	2	.280	.317	.468
1995 Chicago	NL	15	23	4	0	0	0	(0 | 0)	4	2	1	2	0	2	0	0	1	0	0	.00	1	.174	.240	.174
1996 Chicago	NL	21	38	4	0	0	1	(1 | 0)	7	1	4	0	0	15	0	0	1	0	0	.00	0	.105	.103	.184
1997 Chicago	NL	29	64	13	0	0	1	(0 | 1)	16	4	2	2	1	21	0	0	0	0	0	.00	1	.203	.227	.250
3 ML YEARS		65	125	21	0	0	2	(1 | 1)	27	7	7	4	1	38	0	0	1	0	0	.00	2	.168	.192	.216

Trent Hubbard

Bats: Right Throws: Right Pos: LF-5; PH-2; CF-1   Ht: 5'8" Wt: 180 Born: 5/11/66 Age: 32

							BATTING										BASERUNNING				PERCENTAGES		
Year Team	Lg	G	AB	H	2B	3B	HR	(Hm | Rd)	TB	R	RBI	TBB	IBB	SO	HBP	SH	SF	SB	CS	SB%	GDP	Avg	OBP	SLG
1997 Buffalo *	AAA	103	375	117	22	1	16	—	—	189	71	60	57	0	52	3	0	6	26	10	.72	10	.312	.401	.504
1994 Colorado	NL	18	25	7	1	1	1	(1 | 0)	13	3	3	3	0	4	0	0	0	0	0	.00	1	.280	.357	.520
1995 Colorado	NL	24	58	18	4	0	3	(2 | 1)	31	13	9	8	0	6	0	1	0	2	1	.67	3	.310	.394	.534
1996 Col-SF	NL	55	89	19	5	2	2	(2 | 0)	34	15	14	11	0	27	1	0	0	2	0	1.00	3	.213	.307	.382
1997 Cleveland	AL	7	12	3	1	0	0	(0 | 0)	4	3	0	1	0	3	0	0	0	2	0	1.00	0	.250	.308	.333
1996 Colorado	NL	45	60	13	5	1	1	(1 | 0)	23	12	12	9	0	22	1	0	0	0	0	.00	2	.217	.329	.383
San Francisco	NL	10	29	6	0	1	1	(1 | 0)	11	3	2	2	0	5	0	0	0	2	0	1.00	1	.207	.258	.379
4 ML YEARS		104	184	47	11	3	6	(5 | 1)	82	34	26	23	0	40	1	1	0	6	1	.86	6	.255	.341	.446

John Hudek

Pitches: Right Bats: Both Pos: RP-40   Ht: 6'1" Wt: 200 Born: 8/8/66 Age: 31

		HOW MUCH HE PITCHED						WHAT HE GAVE UP										THE RESULTS					
Year Team	Lg	G	GS	CG	GF	IP	BFP	H	R	ER	HR	SH	SF	HB	TBB	IBB	SO	WP	Bk	W	L	Pct.	ShO	Sv-Op	Hld	ERA
1997 New Orleans *	AAA	19	0	0	16	20.2	67	3	1	1	0	1	0	0	3	0	26	0	0	0	0	.000	0	7- -		0.44
1994 Houston	NL	42	0	0	33	39.1	159	24	14	13	5	0	2	1	18	2	39	0	0	0	2	.000	0	16-18	1	2.97
1995 Houston	NL	20	0	0	16	20	83	19	12	12	3	1	0	0	5	0	29	2	0	2	2	.500	0	7-9	0	5.40
1996 Houston	NL	15	0	0	6	16	65	12	5	5	2	2	0	0	5	2	14	1	1	2	0	1.000	0	2-2	1	2.81
1997 Houston	NL	40	0	0	20	40.2	188	38	27	27	8	1	0	3	33	2	36	4	0	1	3	.250	0	4-8	2	5.98
4 ML YEARS		116	0	0	75	116	495	93	58	57	18	4	2	4	61	6	118	7	1	5	7	.417	0	29-37	4	4.42

Rex Hudler

Bats: R **Throws:** R **Pos:** PH-17; CF-16; LF-11; RF-8; 2B-6   **Ht:** 6'0" **Wt:** 195 **Born:** 9/2/60 **Age:** 37

Year Team	Lg	G	AB	H	2B	3B	HR	(Hm	Rd)	TB	R	RBI	TBB	IBB	SO	HBP	SH	SF	SB	CS	SB%	GDP	Avg	OBP	SLG
1997 Reading *	AA	6	23	8	2	0	1	—	—	13	5	5	1	0	2	0	0	0	0	0	.00	0	.348	.375	.565
Clearwater *	A+	9	34	11	2	1	3	—	—	24	8	6	0	0	8	0	0	1	1	0	1.00	0	.324	.314	.706
Scrnton-WB *	AAA	3	9	3	0	0	0	—	—	3	0	0	0	0	0	0	0	0	0	0	.00	0	.333	.333	.333
1984 New York	AL	9	7	1	1	0	0	(0	0)	2	2	0	1	0	5	1	0	0	0	0	.00	0	.143	.333	.286
1985 New York	AL	20	51	8	0	1	0	(0	0)	10	4	1	1	0	9	0	5	0	0	1	.00	1	.157	.173	.196
1986 Baltimore	AL	14	1	0	0	0	0	(0	0)	0	1	0	0	0	0	0	0	0	1	0	1.00	0	.000	.000	.000
1988 Montreal	NL	77	216	59	14	2	4	(1	3)	89	38	14	10	6	34	0	1	2	29	7	.81	2	.273	.303	.412
1989 Montreal	NL	92	155	38	7	0	6	(3	3)	63	21	13	6	2	23	1	0	0	15	4	.79	2	.245	.278	.406
1990 Mon-StL	NL	93	220	62	11	2	7	(2	5)	98	31	22	12	1	32	2	2	1	18	10	.64	3	.282	.323	.445
1991 St. Louis	NL	101	207	47	10	2	1	(1	0)	64	21	15	10	1	29	0	2	2	12	8	.60	1	.227	.260	.309
1992 St. Louis	NL	61	98	24	4	0	3	(2	1)	37	17	5	2	0	23	1	1	1	2	6	.25	0	.245	.265	.378
1994 California	AL	56	124	37	8	0	8	(4	4)	69	17	20	6	0	28	0	4	2	2	2	.50	7	.298	.326	.556
1995 California	AL	84	223	59	16	0	6	(4	2)	93	30	27	10	1	48	5	2	1	13	0	1.00	2	.265	.310	.417
1996 California	AL	92	302	90	20	3	16	(6	10)	168	60	40	9	0	54	3	2	1	14	5	.74	7	.311	.337	.556
1997 Philadelphia	NL	50	122	27	4	0	5	(5	0)	46	17	10	6	1	28	1	1	0	1	0	1.00	2	.221	.264	.377
1990 Montreal	NL	4	3	1	0	0	0	(0	0)	1	1	0	0	0	1	0	0	0	0	0	.00	0	.333	.333	.333
St. Louis	NL	89	217	61	11	2	7	(2	5)	97	30	22	12	1	31	2	2	1	18	10	.64	3	.281	.323	.447
12 ML YEARS		749	1726	456	95	10	56	(28	28)	739	259	167	73	12	313	14	20	10	107	43	.71	26	.264	.298	.428

Joe Hudson

Pitches: Right **Bats:** Right **Pos:** RP-26   **Ht:** 6'1" **Wt:** 180 **Born:** 9/29/70 **Age:** 27

Year Team	Lg	G	GS	CG	GF	IP	BFP	H	R	ER	HR	SH	SF	HB	TBB	IBB	SO	WP	Bk	W	L	Pct.	ShO	Sv-Op	Hld	ERA
1997 Pawtucket *	AAA	29	0	0	17	32	148	25	8	8	1	2	2	3	23	3	14	3	0	2	1	.667	0	7- -		2.25
1995 Boston	AL	39	0	0	11	46	205	53	21	21	2	3	1	2	23	1	29	6	0	0	1	.000	0	1-4	8	4.11
1996 Boston	AL	36	0	0	16	45	214	57	35	27	4	1	2	0	32	4	19	0	0	3	5	.375	0	1-5	5	5.40
1997 Boston	AL	26	0	0	9	35.2	154	39	16	14	1	1	0	4	14	2	14	1	0	3	1	.750	0	0-0	0	3.53
3 ML YEARS		101	0	0	36	126.2	573	149	72	62	7	5	3	6	69	7	62	7	0	6	7	.462	0	2-9	11	4.41

Todd Hundley

Bats: Both **Throws:** Right **Pos:** C-122; PH-13; DH-2   **Ht:** 5'11" **Wt:** 185 **Born:** 5/27/69 **Age:** 29

Year Team	Lg	G	AB	H	2B	3B	HR	(Hm	Rd)	TB	R	RBI	TBB	IBB	SO	HBP	SH	SF	SB	CS	SB%	GDP	Avg	OBP	SLG
1990 New York	NL	36	67	14	6	0	0	(0	0)	20	8	2	6	0	18	0	1	0	0	0	.00	1	.209	.274	.299
1991 New York	NL	21	60	8	0	1	1	(1	0)	13	5	7	6	0	14	1	1	0	0	0	.00	3	.133	.221	.217
1992 New York	NL	123	358	75	17	0	7	(2	5)	113	32	32	19	4	76	4	7	2	3	0	1.00	8	.209	.256	.316
1993 New York	NL	130	417	95	17	2	11	(5	6)	149	40	53	23	7	62	2	2	4	1	1	.50	10	.228	.269	.357
1994 New York	NL	91	291	69	10	1	16	(8	8)	129	45	42	25	4	73	3	3	1	2	1	.67	9	.237	.303	.443
1995 New York	NL	90	275	77	11	0	15	(9	6)	133	39	51	42	5	64	5	1	3	1	0	1.00	4	.280	.382	.484
1996 New York	NL	153	540	140	32	1	41	(20	21)	297	85	112	79	15	146	3	0	2	1	3	.25	9	.259	.356	.550
1997 New York	NL	132	417	114	21	2	30	(14	16)	229	78	86	83	16	116	3	0	5	2	3	.40	10	.273	.394	.549
8 ML YEARS		776	2425	592	114	7	121	(56	65)	1083	332	385	283	51	569	21	15	18	10	8	.56	48	.244	.326	.447

Brian L. Hunter

Bats: Right **Throws:** Right **Pos:** CF-162   **Ht:** 6'4" **Wt:** 180 **Born:** 3/5/71 **Age:** 27

Year Team	Lg	G	AB	H	2B	3B	HR	(Hm	Rd)	TB	R	RBI	TBB	IBB	SO	HBP	SH	SF	SB	CS	SB%	GDP	Avg	OBP	SLG
1994 Houston	NL	6	24	6	1	0	0	(0	0)	7	2	0	1	0	6	0	1	0	2	1	.67	1	.250	.280	.292
1995 Houston	NL	78	321	97	14	5	2	(0	2)	127	52	28	21	0	52	2	2	3	24	7	.77	5	.302	.346	.396
1996 Houston	NL	132	526	145	27	2	5	(1	4)	191	74	35	17	0	92	2	1	7	35	9	.80	6	.276	.297	.363
1997 Detroit	AL	162	658	177	29	7	4	(2	2)	232	112	45	66	1	121	1	8	5	74	18	.80	13	.269	.334	.353
4 ML YEARS		378	1529	425	71	14	11	(3	8)	557	240	108	105	1	271	5	12	15	135	35	.79	21	.278	.323	.364

Torii Hunter

Bats: Right **Throws:** Right **Pos:** PH-1   **Ht:** 6'2" **Wt:** 201 **Born:** 7/18/75 **Age:** 22

Year Team	Lg	G	AB	H	2B	3B	HR	(Hm	Rd)	TB	R	RBI	TBB	IBB	SO	HBP	SH	SF	SB	CS	SB%	GDP	Avg	OBP	SLG
1993 Twins	R	28	100	19	3	0	0	—	—	22	6	8	4	0	23	9	1	0	4	2	.67	1	.190	.283	.220
1994 Ft. Wayne	A	91	335	98	17	1	10	—	—	147	57	50	25	1	80	10	0	2	8	10	.44	5	.293	.358	.439
1995 Ft. Myers	A+	113	391	96	15	2	7	—	—	136	64	36	38	1	77	12	5	1	7	4	.64	8	.246	.330	.348
1996 Ft. Myers	A+	4	16	3	0	0	0	—	—	3	1	1	2	0	5	0	0	0	1	1	.50	0	.188	.278	.188
Hardware City	AA	99	342	90	20	3	7	—	—	137	49	33	28	1	60	7	9	1	7	7	.50	7	.263	.331	.401
1997 New Britain	AA	127	471	109	22	2	8	—	—	159	57	56	47	1	94	3	6	1	8	8	.50	6	.231	.305	.338
1997 Minnesota	AL	1	0	0	0	0	0	(0	0)	0	0	0	0	0	0	0	0	0	0	0	.00	0	.000	.000	.000

Jimmy Hurst

Bats: R **Throws:** R **Pos:** RF-10; PH-2; DH-1; LF-1; CF-1 **Ht:** 6'6" **Wt:** 225 **Born:** 3/1/72 **Age:** 26

							BATTING											BASERUNNING				PERCENTAGES		
Year Team	Lg	G	AB	H	2B	3B	HR	(Hm | Rd)	TB	R	RBI	TBB	IBB	SO	HBP	SH	SF	SB	CS	SB%	GDP	Avg	OBP	SLG
1991 White Sox	R	36	121	31	4	0	0	—	—	35	14	12	13	0	32	1	0	0	6	1	.86	3	.256	.333	.289
1992 Utica	A-	68	220	50	8	5	6	—	—	86	31	35	27	1	78	4	2	5	11	3	.79	4	.227	.316	.391
1993 South Bend	A	123	464	113	26	0	20	—	—	199	79	79	37	3	141	8	0	5	15	2	.88	9	.244	.307	.429
1994 Pr William	A+	127	455	126	31	6	25	—	—	244	90	91	72	4	128	4	0	5	15	8	.65	9	.277	.377	.536
1995 Birmingham	AA	91	301	57	11	0	12	—	—	104	47	34	33	0	95	1	0	2	12	5	.71	5	.189	.270	.346
1996 Birmingham	AA	126	472	125	23	1	18	—	—	204	62	88	53	2	128	3	0	8	19	11	.63	10	.265	.338	.432
Nashville	AAA	3	6	2	1	0	1	—	—	6	2	2	1	0	3	0	0	0	0	0	.00	0	.333	.429	1.000
1997 Jacksnville	AA	5	17	8	2	0	2	—	—	16	5	6	3	0	6	0	0	1	0	0	.00	0	.471	.524	.941
Toledo	AAA	110	377	102	11	3	18	—	—	173	51	51	47	1	115	0	1	4	14	5	.74	11	.271	.348	.459
1997 Detroit	AL	13	17	3	1	0	1	(1 | 0)	7	1	1	2	0	6	0	0	0	0	0	.00	0	.176	.263	.412

Edwin Hurtado

Pitches: Right **Bats:** Right **Pos:** RP-12; SP-1 **Ht:** 6'3" **Wt:** 215 **Born:** 2/1/70 **Age:** 28

		HOW MUCH HE PITCHED						WHAT HE GAVE UP										THE RESULTS						
Year Team	Lg	G	GS	CG	GF	IP	BFP	H	R	ER	HR	SH	SF	HB	TBB	IBB	SO	WP	Bk	W	L	Pct.	ShO	Sv-Op	Hld	ERA
1997 Tacoma *	AAA	20	20	5	0	132.1	567	139	60	57	9	2	5	3	37	1	100	7	0	10	6	.625	3	0- -	—	3.88
1995 Toronto	AL	14	10	1	0	77.2	345	81	50	47	11	2	3	5	40	3	33	11	0	5	2	.714	0	0-0	1	5.45
1996 Seattle	AL	16	4	0	6	47.2	223	61	42	41	10	0	5	0	30	3	36	2	0	2	5	.286	0	2-3	0	7.74
1997 Seattle	AL	13	1	0	2	19	94	25	19	19	5	0	1	2	15	0	10	2	0	1	2	.333	0	0-0	1	9.00
3 ML YEARS		43	15	1	8	144.1	662	167	111	107	26	2	9	7	85	6	79	15	0	8	9	.471	0	2-3	2	6.67

Butch Huskey

Bats: R **Throws:** R **Pos:** RF-72; LF-30; 1B-22; PH-18; 3B-15; DH-4 **Ht:** 6'3" **Wt:** 244 **Born:** 11/10/71 **Age:** 26

							BATTING											BASERUNNING				PERCENTAGES		
Year Team	Lg	G	AB	H	2B	3B	HR	(Hm	Rd)	TB	R	RBI	TBB	IBB	SO	HBP	SH	SF	SB	CS	SB%	GDP	Avg	OBP	SLG
1993 New York	NL	13	41	6	1	0	0	(0	0)	7	2	3	1	1	13	0	0	2	0	0	.00	0	.146	.159	.171
1995 New York	NL	28	90	17	1	0	3	(2	1)	27	8	11	10	0	16	0	1	1	1	0	1.00	3	.189	.267	.300
1996 New York	NL	118	414	115	16	2	15	(9	6)	180	43	60	27	3	77	0	0	4	1	2	.33	10	.278	.319	.435
1997 New York	NL	142	471	135	26	2	24	(7	17)	237	61	81	25	5	84	1	0	8	8	5	.62	21	.287	.319	.503
4 ML YEARS		301	1016	273	44	4	42	(18	24)	451	114	155	63	9	190	1	1	15	10	7	.59	34	.269	.308	.444

Jeff Huson

Bats: L **Throws:** R **Pos:** PH-41; 2B-32; 1B-21; LF-8; DH-4; 3B-2; RF-1 **Ht:** 6'1" **Wt:** 185 **Born:** 8/15/64 **Age:** 33

							BATTING											BASERUNNING				PERCENTAGES		
Year Team	Lg	G	AB	H	2B	3B	HR	(Hm	Rd)	TB	R	RBI	TBB	IBB	SO	HBP	SH	SF	SB	CS	SB%	GDP	Avg	OBP	SLG
1997 Colo Sprngs *	AAA	9	20	7	3	0	1	—	—	13	3	5	2	0	2	0	0	0	2	1	.67	1	.350	.409	.650
1988 Montreal	NL	20	42	13	2	0	0	(0	0)	15	7	3	4	2	3	0	0	0	2	1	.67	0	.310	.370	.357
1989 Montreal	NL	32	74	12	5	0	0	(0	0)	17	1	2	6	3	6	0	3	0	3	0	1.00	6	.162	.225	.230
1990 Texas	AL	145	396	95	12	2	0	(0	0)	111	57	28	46	0	54	2	7	3	12	4	.75	8	.240	.320	.280
1991 Texas	AL	119	268	57	8	3	2	(1	1)	77	36	26	39	0	32	0	9	1	8	3	.73	6	.213	.312	.287
1992 Texas	AL	123	318	83	14	3	4	(0	4)	115	49	24	41	2	43	1	8	6	18	6	.75	7	.261	.342	.362
1993 Texas	AL	23	45	6	1	1	0	(0	0)	9	3	2	0	0	10	0	1	0	0	0	.00	0	.133	.133	.200
1995 Baltimore	AL	66	161	40	4	2	1	(0	1)	51	24	19	15	1	20	1	2	1	5	4	.56	4	.248	.315	.317
1996 Baltimore	AL	17	28	9	1	0	0	(0	0)	10	5	2	1	0	3	0	1	0	0	0	.00	0	.321	.333	.357
1997 Milwaukee	AL	84	143	29	3	0	0	(0	0)	32	12	11	5	0	15	2	1	1	3	0	1.00	7	.203	.238	.224
9 ML YEARS		629	1475	344	50	11	7	(1	6)	437	194	117	157	8	186	6	32	13	51	18	.74	40	.233	.307	.296

Mark Hutton

Pitches: Right **Bats:** Right **Pos:** RP-39; SP-1 **Ht:** 6'6" **Wt:** 240 **Born:** 2/6/70 **Age:** 28

		HOW MUCH HE PITCHED						WHAT HE GAVE UP										THE RESULTS						
Year Team	Lg	G	GS	CG	GF	IP	BFP	H	R	ER	HR	SH	SF	HB	TBB	IBB	SO	WP	Bk	W	L	Pct.	ShO	Sv-Op	Hld	ERA
1993 New York	AL	7	4	0	2	22	104	24	17	14	2	2	2	1	17	0	12	0	0	1	1	.500	0	0-0	0	5.73
1994 New York	AL	2	0	0	1	3.2	16	4	3	2	0	0	0	0	1	0	1	0	0	0	0	.000	0	0-0	0	4.91
1996 NYA-Fla		25	11	0	5	86.2	374	79	42	40	9	0	3	4	36	1	56	2	0	5	3	.625	0	0-0	1	4.15
1997 Fla-Col	NL	40	1	0	9	60.1	272	72	34	30	10	7	4	6	26	3	39	3	1	3	2	.600	0	0-3	4	4.48
1996 New York	AL	12	2	0	5	30.1	140	32	19	17	3	0	2	1	18	1	25	0	0	0	2	.000	0	0-0	0	5.04
Florida	NL	13	9	0	0	56.1	234	47	23	23	6	0	1	3	18	0	31	2	0	5	1	.833	0	0-0	0	3.67
1997 Florida	NL	32	0	0	9	47.2	204	50	24	20	7	5	3	2	19	3	29	3	1	3	1	.750	0	0-2	3	3.78
Colorado	NL	8	1	0	0	12.2	68	22	10	10	3	2	1	4	7	0	10	0	0	0	1	.000	0	0-1	1	7.11
4 ML YEARS		74	16	0	17	172.2	766	179	96	86	21	9	9	11	79	4	108	5	1	9	6	.600	0	0-3	5	4.48

Raul Ibanez

Bats: Left **Throws:** Right **Pos:** RF-6; PH-4; LF-2; DH-1 **Ht:** 6'2" **Wt:** 200 **Born:** 6/2/72 **Age:** 26

							BATTING											BASERUNNING				PERCENTAGES		
Year Team	Lg	G	AB	H	2B	3B	HR	(Hm	Rd)	TB	R	RBI	TBB	IBB	SO	HBP	SH	SF	SB	CS	SB%	GDP	Avg	OBP	SLG
1992 Mariners	R	33	120	37	8	2	1	—	—	52	16	9	9	1	18	2	0	1	4	8	.33	4	.308	.366	.433
1993 Appleton	A	52	157	43	9	0	5	—	—	67	26	21	24	2	31	1	1	2	0	2	.00	2	.274	.370	.427
Bellingham	A-	43	134	38	5	2	0	—	—	47	16	15	21	1	23	0	0	1	0	3	.00	3	.284	.378	.351
1994 Appleton	A	91	327	102	30	3	7	—	—	159	55	59	32	3	37	2	0	2	10	5	.67	3	.312	.375	.486

Year Team	Lg	G	AB	H	2B	3B	HR	(Hm Rd)	TB	R	RBI	TBB	IBB	SO	HBP	SH	SF	SB	CS	SB%	GDP	Avg	OBP	SLG
1995 Riverside	A+	95	361	120	23	9	20	— —	221	59	108	41	1	49	2	1	9	4	3	.57	7	.332	.395	.612
1996 Port City	AA	19	76	28	8	1	1	— —	41	12	13	8	1	7	0	0	1	3	2	.60	1	.368	.424	.539
Tacoma	AAA	111	405	115	20	3	11	— —	174	59	47	44	2	56	2	0	5	7	7	.50	4	.284	.353	.430
1997 Tacoma	AAA	111	438	133	30	5	15	— —	218	84	84	32	1	75	1	3	4	7	5	.58	12	.304	.349	.498
1996 Seattle	AL	4	5	0	0	0	0	(0 0)	0	0	0	0	0	1	1	0	0	0	0	.00	0	.000	.167	.000
1997 Seattle	AL	11	26	4	0	1	1	(1 0)	9	3	4	0	0	6	0	0	0	0	0	.00	0	.154	.154	.346
2 ML YEARS		15	31	4	0	1	1	(1 0)	9	3	4	0	0	7	1	0	0	0	0	.00	0	.129	.156	.290

Pete Incaviglia

Bats: R **Throws:** R **Pos:** DH-31; PH-15; RF-14; LF-4 **Ht:** 6'1" **Wt:** 225 **Born:** 4/2/64 **Age:** 34

Year Team	Lg	G	AB	H	2B	3B	HR	(Hm Rd)	TB	R	RBI	TBB	IBB	SO	HBP	SH	SF	SB	CS	SB%	GDP	Avg	OBP	SLG
1997 Columbus *	AAA	3	13	4	1	0	0	— —	5	1	2	0	0	4	0	0	0	0	0	.00	0	.308	.308	.385
1986 Texas	AL	153	540	135	21	2	30	(17 13)	250	82	88	55	2	185	4	0	7	3	2	.60	9	.250	.320	.463
1987 Texas	AL	139	509	138	26	4	27	(11 16)	253	85	80	48	1	168	1	0	5	9	3	.75	8	.271	.332	.497
1988 Texas	AL	116	418	104	19	3	22	(12 10)	195	59	54	39	3	153	7	0	3	6	4	.60	6	.249	.321	.467
1989 Texas	AL	133	453	107	27	4	21	(13 8)	205	48	81	32	0	136	6	0	4	5	7	.42	12	.236	.293	.453
1990 Texas	AL	153	529	123	27	0	24	(15 9)	222	59	85	45	5	146	9	0	4	3	4	.43	18	.233	.302	.420
1991 Detroit	AL	97	337	72	12	1	11	(6 5)	119	38	38	36	0	92	1	1	2	1	3	.25	6	.214	.290	.353
1992 Houston	NL	113	349	93	22	1	11	(6 5)	150	31	44	25	2	99	3	0	2	2	2	.50	6	.266	.319	.430
1993 Philadelphia	NL	116	368	101	16	3	24	(15 9)	195	60	89	21	1	82	6	0	7	1	1	.50	9	.274	.318	.530
1994 Philadelphia	NL	80	244	56	10	1	13	(6 7)	107	28	32	16	3	71	1	0	7	1	0	1.00	3	.230	.278	.439
1997 Bal-NYA	AL	53	154	38	4	0	5	(2 3)	57	19	12	11	2	46	3	0	1	0	0	.00	1	.247	.308	.370
1996 Phi-Bal		111	302	73	9	2	18	(6 12)	140	37	50	30	2	89	4	0	1	2	0	1.00	3	.242	.318	.439
1996 Philadelphia	NL	99	269	63	7	2	16	(6 10)	122	33	42	30	2	82	3	0	0	2	0	1.00	6	.234	.318	.454
Baltimore	AL	12	33	10	2	0	2	(0 2)	18	4	8	0	0	7	1	0	1	0	0	.00	0	.303	.314	.545
1997 Baltimore	AL	48	154	34	4	0	5	(2 3)	53	18	12	11	2	43	3	0	1	0	0	.00	1	.246	.314	.384
New York	AL	5	16	4	0	0	0	(0 0)	4	1	0	0	0	3	0	0	0	0	0	.00		.250	.250	.250
11 ML YEARS		1264	4203	1040	193	21	206	(109 97)	1893	546	653	358	21	1267	45	1	38	33	26	.56	84	.247	.311	.450

Garey Ingram

Bats: Right **Throws:** Right **Pos:** LF-6; PH-5; CF-1 **Ht:** 5'11" **Wt:** 185 **Born:** 7/25/70 **Age:** 27

Year Team	Lg	G	AB	H	2B	3B	HR	(Hm Rd)	TB	R	RBI	TBB	IBB	SO	HBP	SH	SF	SB	CS	SB%	GDP	Avg	OBP	SLG
1997 San Antonio *	AA	92	348	104	28	7	12	— —	182	68	62	37	1	50	4	1	2	16	6	.73	5	.299	.371	.523
1994 Los Angeles	NL	26	78	22	1	0	3	(1 2)	32	10	8	7	3	22	0	1	0	0	0	.00	0	.282	.341	.410
1995 Los Angeles	NL	44	55	11	2	0	0	(0 0)	13	5	3	9	0	8	0	2	0	3	0	1.00	0	.200	.313	.236
1997 Los Angeles	NL	12	9	4	0	0	0	(0 0)	4	2	1	1	0	3	0	0	0	1	0	1.00	0	.444	.500	.444
3 ML YEARS		82	142	37	3	0	3	(1 2)	49	17	12	17	3	33	0	3	0	4	0	1.00	3	.261	.340	.345

Hideki Irabu

Pitches: Right **Bats:** Right **Pos:** SP-9; RP-4 **Ht:** 6'4" **Wt:** 240 **Born:** 5/5/69 **Age:** 29

Year Team	Lg	G	GS	CG	GF	IP	BFP	H	R	ER	HR	SH	SF	HB	TBB	IBB	SO	WP	Bk	W	L	Pct.	ShO	Sv-Op	Hld	ERA
1997 Tampa	A+	2	2	0	0	9	29	4	0	0	0	0	0	0	0	0	12	0	3	1	0	1.000	0	0--	—	0.00
Norwich	AA	2	2	0	0	10	41	13	5	5	1	0	0	0	0	0	9	0	2	1	1	.500	0	0--	—	4.50
Columbus	AAA	4	4	1	0	27	101	19	7	5	1	1	1	0	5	0	28	2	3	2	0	1.000	1	0--	—	1.67
1997 New York	AL	13	9	0	0	53.1	246	69	47	42	15	2	1	1	20	0	56	4	3	5	4	.556	0	0-0	1	7.09

Jason Isringhausen

Pitches: Right **Bats:** Right **Pos:** SP-6 **Ht:** 6'3" **Wt:** 196 **Born:** 9/7/72 **Age:** 25

Year Team	Lg	G	GS	CG	GF	IP	BFP	H	R	ER	HR	SH	SF	HB	TBB	IBB	SO	WP	Bk	W	L	Pct.	ShO	Sv-Op	Hld	ERA
1997 Mets *	R	1	0	0	0	4.2	17	2	1	1	0	0	0	0	1	0	7	0	0	1	0	1.000	0	0--	—	1.93
St. Lucie *	A+	2	2	0	0	12	47	8	1	0	0	0	0	0	1	0	15	1	0	1	0	1.000	0	0--	—	0.00
Norfolk *	AAA	3	3	0	0	20	87	20	10	9	4	1	1	0	8	0	17	1	0	0	2	.000	0	0--	—	4.05
1995 New York	NL	14	14	1	0	93	385	88	29	29	6	3	3	2	31	2	55	4	1	9	2	.818	1	0-0	0	2.81
1996 New York	NL	27	27	2	0	171.2	766	190	103	91	13	7	9	8	73	5	114	14	0	6	14	.300	1	0-0	0	4.77
1997 New York	NL	6	6	0	0	29.2	145	40	27	25	3	1	2	1	22	0	25	3	0	2	2	.500	0	0-0	0	7.58
3 ML YEARS		47	47	3	0	294.1	1296	318	159	145	22	11	14	11	126	7	194	21	1	17	18	.486	1	0-0	0	4.43

Damian Jackson

Bats: Right **Throws:** Right **Pos:** SS-11; PH-6; 2B-4 **Ht:** 5'10" **Wt:** 160 **Born:** 8/16/73 **Age:** 24

Year Team	Lg	G	AB	H	2B	3B	HR	(Hm Rd)	TB	R	RBI	TBB	IBB	SO	HBP	SH	SF	SB	CS	SB%	GDP	Avg	OBP	SLG
1992 Burlington	R+	62	226	56	12	1	0	— —	70	32	23	32	0	31	6	6	3	29	5	.85	1	.248	.352	.310
1993 Columbus	A	108	350	94	19	3	6	— —	137	70	45	45	0	61	6	5	5	27	7	.79	1	.269	.353	.391
1994 Canton-Akrn	AA	138	531	143	29	5	5	— —	197	85	46	60	2	121	5	10	5	37	16	.70	8	.269	.346	.371
1995 Canton-Akrn	AA	131	484	120	20	2	3	— —	153	67	34	65	0	103	9	7	0	40	22	.65	6	.248	.348	.316
1996 Buffalo	AAA	133	452	116	15	1	12	— —	169	77	49	48	0	78	7	8	6	24	7	.77	7	.257	.333	.374
1997 Buffalo	AAA	73	266	78	12	0	4	— —	102	51	13	37	2	45	3	3	2	20	8	.71	2	.293	.383	.383
Indianapolis	AAA	19	71	19	6	1	0	— —	27	12	7	10	0	17	1	0	1	4	1	.80	1	.268	.361	.380

			BATTING																	BASERUNNING				PERCENTAGES		
Year Team	Lg	G	AB	H	2B	3B	HR	(Hm Rd)	TB	R	RBI	TBB	IBB	SO	HBP	SH	SF	SB	CS	SB%	GDP	Avg	OBP	SLG
1996 Cleveland	AL	5	10	3	2	0	0	(0 0)	5	2	1	1	0	4	0	0	0	0	0	.00	0	.300	.364	.500
1997 Cle-Cin		20	36	7	2	1	1	(0 1)	14	8	2	4	1	8	1	1	0	2	1	.67	0	.194	.293	.389
1997 Cleveland	AL	8	9	1	0	0	0	(0 0)	1	2	0	0	0	1	1	0	0	1	0	1.00	0	.111	.200	.111
Cincinnati	NL	12	27	6	2	1	1	(0 1)	13	6	2	4	1	7	0	1	0	1	1	.50	0	.222	.323	.481
2 ML YEARS		25	46	10	4	1	1	(0 1)	19	10	3	5	1	12	1	1	0	2	1	.67	0	.217	.308	.413

Danny Jackson

Pitches: Left   Bats: Right   Pos: SP-13; RP-4   Ht: 6'0"   Wt: 220   Born: 1/5/62   Age: 36

		HOW MUCH HE PITCHED						WHAT HE GAVE UP												THE RESULTS						
Year Team	Lg	G	GS	CG	GF	IP	BFP	H	R	ER	HR	SH	SF	HB	TBB	IBB	SO	WP	Bk	W	L	Pct.	ShO	Sv-Op	Hld	ERA
1997 Louisville *	AAA	4	4	0	0	25	100	20	6	5	3	2	0	0	8	0	14	0	0	1	0	1.000	0	0--	—	1.80
1983 Kansas City	AL	4	3	0	0	19	87	26	12	11	1	1	0	0	6	0	9	0	0	1	1	.500	0	0--	—	5.21
1984 Kansas City	AL	15	11	1	3	76	338	84	41	36	4	3	0	5	35	0	40	3	2	2	6	.250	0	0--	—	4.26
1985 Kansas City	AL	32	32	4	0	208	893	209	94	79	7	5	4	6	76	2	114	4	2	14	12	.538	3	0-0	0	3.42
1986 Kansas City	AL	32	27	4	3	185.2	789	177	83	66	13	10	4	4	79	1	115	7	0	11	12	.478	1	1--	0	3.20
1987 Kansas City	AL	36	34	11	1	224	981	219	115	100	11	8	7	7	109	1	152	5	0	9	18	.333	2	0-1	0	4.02
1988 Cincinnati	NL	35	35	15	0	260.2	1034	206	86	79	13	13	5	2	71	6	161	5	2	23	8	.742	6	0-0	0	2.73
1989 Cincinnati	NL	20	20	1	0	115.2	519	122	78	72	10	6	4	1	57	7	70	3	2	6	11	.353	0	0-0	0	5.60
1990 Cincinnati	NL	22	21	0	1	117.1	499	119	54	47	11	4	5	2	40	4	76	3	1	6	6	.500	0	0-0	0	3.61
1991 Chicago	NL	17	14	0	0	70.2	347	89	59	53	8	8	2	1	48	1	31	1	1	1	5	.167	0	0-0	0	6.75
1992 ChN-Pit	NL	34	34	0	0	201.1	883	211	99	86	6	17	10	4	77	6	97	2	2	8	13	.381	0	0-0	0	3.84
1993 Philadelphia	NL	32	32	2	0	210.1	919	214	105	88	12	14	8	4	80	2	120	4	0	12	11	.522	1	0-0	0	3.77
1994 Philadelphia	NL	25	25	4	0	179.1	755	183	71	65	13	14	6	2	46	1	129	2	0	14	6	.700	1	0-0	0	3.26
1995 St. Louis	NL	19	19	2	0	100.2	467	120	82	66	10	10	7	6	48	1	52	6	0	2	12	.143	1	0-0	0	5.90
1996 St. Louis	NL	13	4	0	3	36.1	154	33	18	18	3	0	1	1	16	1	27	0	1	1	1	.500	0	0-0	0	4.46
1997 Stl-SD	NL	17	13	0	0	67.2	321	98	64	57	11	4	5	5	28	3	32	2	0	2	9	.182	0	0-0	0	7.58
1992 Chicago	NL	19	19	0	0	113	501	117	59	53	5	11	5	3	48	3	51	1	2	4	9	.308	0	0-0	0	4.22
Pittsburgh		15	15	0	0	88.1	382	94	40	33	1	6	5	1	29	3	46	1	0	4	4	.500	0	0-0	0	3.36
1997 St. Louis	NL	4	4	0	0	18.2	88	26	17	16	3	1	2	1	8	1	13	0	0	1	2	.333	0	0-0	0	7.71
San Diego	NL	13	9	0	0	49	233	72	47	41	8	3	3	3	20	2	19	2	0	1	7	.125	0	0-0	0	7.53
15 ML YEARS		353	324	44	11	2072.2	8986	2110	1061	923	133	117	68	50	816	39	1225	47	12	112	131	.461	15	1--	—	4.01

Darrin Jackson

Bats: R   Throws: R   Pos: CF-53; LF-21; PH-10; RF-3   Ht: 6'0"   Wt: 185   Born: 8/22/63   Age: 34

			BATTING																	BASERUNNING				PERCENTAGES		
Year Team	Lg	G	AB	H	2B	3B	HR	(Hm Rd)	TB	R	RBI	TBB	IBB	SO	HBP	SH	SF	SB	CS	SB%	GDP	Avg	OBP	SLG
1997 Salt Lake *	AAA	19	80	24	3	3	1	(— —)	36	14	12	5	0	17	1	0	0	3	0	1.00	0	.300	.349	.450
1985 Chicago	NL	5	11	1	0	0	0	(0 0)	1	0	0	0	0	3	0	0	0	0	0	.00	0	.091	.091	.091
1987 Chicago	NL	7	5	4	1	0	0	(0 0)	5	2	0	0	0	0	0	0	0	0	0	.00	0	.800	.800	1.000
1988 Chicago	NL	100	188	50	11	3	6	(3 3)	85	29	20	5	1	28	1	2	1	4	1	.80	3	.266	.287	.452
1989 ChN-SD	NL	70	170	37	7	0	4	(1 3)	56	17	20	15	5	34	0	0	2	3	1	.00	1	.218	.270	.329
1990 San Diego	NL	58	113	29	3	0	3	(1 2)	41	10	9	5	1	24	0	1	3	5	3	.63	1	.257	.286	.363
1991 San Diego	NL	122	359	94	12	1	21	(12 9)	171	51	49	27	2	66	2	3	3	14	3	.82	21	.249	.283	.392
1992 San Diego	NL	155	587	146	23	5	17	(11 6)	230	72	70	26	4	106	4	6	5	5	1	.83	9	.249	.283	.392
1993 Tor-NYN		77	263	55	9	0	6	(4 2)	82	19	26	10	0	75	0	6	1	0	2	.00	9	.209	.237	.312
1994	AL	104	369	115	17	3	10	(4 6)	168	43	51	27	3	56	3	2	2	7	1	.88	5	.312	.362	.455
1997 Min-Mil	AL	75	211	55	9	1	5	(4 1)	81	26	36	6	3	31	0	5	2	4	1	.80	5	.261	.279	.384
1989 Chicago	NL	45	83	19	4	0	1	(0 1)	26	7	8	6	1	17	0	0	1	2	.33		2	.229	.281	.313
San Diego		25	87	18	3	0	3	(1 2)	30	10	12	7	4	17	0	0	1	2	.00		2	.207	.260	.345
1993 Toronto	AL	46	176	38	8	0	5	(4 1)	61	15	19	8	0	53	0	5	0	0	0	.00	9	.195	.211	.241
New York	NL	31	87	17	1	0	1	(0 1)	21	4	7	2	0	22	0	1	1	0	2	.00	0	.195	.211	.241
1997 Minnesota	AL	49	130	33	2	1	3	(3 0)	46	19	21	4	0	21	0	3	2	2	1	.67	3	.254	.289	.354
Milwaukee	AL	26	81	22	7	0	2	(1 1)	35	7	15	2	0	10	0	2	0	2	1	.67	2	.272	.289	.432
10 ML YEARS		773	2276	586	92	13	72	(40 32)	920	269	281	119	16	423	10	25	17	38	15	.72	51	.257	.295	.404

Mike Jackson

Pitches: Right   Bats: Right   Pos: RP-71   Ht: 6'2"   Wt: 225   Born: 12/22/64   Age: 33

		HOW MUCH HE PITCHED						WHAT HE GAVE UP												THE RESULTS						
Year Team	Lg	G	GS	CG	GF	IP	BFP	H	R	ER	HR	SH	SF	HB	TBB	IBB	SO	WP	Bk	W	L	Pct.	ShO	Sv-Op	Hld	ERA
1986 Philadelphia	NL	9	0	0	4	13.1	54	12	5	5	2	0	0	2	4	1	3	0	0	0	0	.000	0	0--	—	3.38
1987 Philadelphia	NL	55	7	0	8	109.1	468	88	55	51	16	3	4	3	56	6	93	6	8	3	10	.231	0	1-2	6	4.20
1988 Seattle	AL	62	0	0	29	99.1	412	74	37	29	10	3	10	2	43	10	76	6	6	6	5	.545	0	4-11	10	2.63
1989 Seattle	AL	65	0	0	27	99.1	431	81	43	35	8	6	2	6	54	6	94	1	2	6	6	.500	0	7-10	9	3.17
1990 Seattle	AL	63	0	0	28	77.1	338	64	42	39	8	8	5	2	44	12	69	9	2	5	7	.417	0	3-12	13	4.54
1991 Seattle	AL	72	0	0	35	88.2	363	64	35	32	5	4	0	6	34	11	74	3	0	7	7	.500	0	14-22	9	3.25
1992 San Francisco	NL	67	0	0	24	82	346	76	35	34	7	5	2	4	33	10	80	1	0	6	6	.500	0	2-3	9	3.73
1993 San Francisco	NL	81	0	0	17	77.1	317	58	28	26	7	4	2	3	24	6	70	2	2	6	6	.500	0	1-6	34	3.03
1994 San Francisco	NL	36	0	0	12	42.1	158	23	8	7	4	1	2	1	11	0	51	0	0	1	1	.500	0	4-6	9	1.49
1995 Cincinnati	NL	40	0	0	10	49	200	38	13	13	5	1	1	1	19	1	41	1	1	6	1	.857	0	2-4	9	2.39
1996 Seattle	AL	73	0	0	23	72	302	61	32	29	11	0	1	9	29	5	74	2	0	1	2	.333	0	6-8	15	3.63
1997 Cleveland	AL	71	0	0	38	75	313	59	33	27	3	3	3	4	29	5	74	2	0	2	5	.286	0	15-17	14	3.24
12 ML YEARS		694	7	0	255	885	3702	698	366	327	86	41	31	41	375	71	795	33	21	49	56	.467	0	59--	—	3.33

Jason Jacome

Pitches: Left **Bats:** Left **Pos:** RP-24; SP-4 **Ht:** 6'0" **Wt:** 180 **Born:** 11/24/70 **Age:** 27

Year Team	Lg	G	GS	CG	GF	IP	BFP	H	R	ER	HR	SH	SF	HB	TBB	IBB	SO	WP	Bk	W	L	Pct.	ShO	Sv-Op	Hld	ERA
1997 Buffalo *	AAA	7	7	1	0	37	151	41	14	13	7	1	3	1	10	0	23	0	1	3	1	.750	0	0- -	—	3.16
1994 New York	NL	8	8	1	0	54	222	54	17	16	3	3	1	0	17	2	30	2	0	4	3	.571	1	0-0	0	2.67
1995 NYN-KC		20	19	1	0	105	474	134	76	74	18	3	4	2	36	2	50	1	0	4	10	.286	0	0-0	0	6.34
1996 Kansas City	AL	49	2	0	21	47.2	226	67	27	25	5	3	0	2	22	5	32	1	0	0	4	.000	0	1-4	6	4.72
1997 KC-Cle	AL	28	4	0	2	49.1	218	58	33	32	10	0	1	1	20	5	27	2	0	2	0	1.000	0	0-1	1	5.84
1995 New York	NL	5	5	0	0	21	110	33	24	24	3	1	1	1	15	0	11	1	0	0	4	.000	0	0-0	0	10.29
Kansas City	AL	15	14	1	0	84	364	101	52	50	15	2	3	1	21	2	39	0	0	4	6	.400	0	0-0	0	5.36
1997 Kansas City	AL	7	0	0	0	6.2	35	13	7	7	2	0	0	1	5	1	3	0	0	0	0	.000	0	0-0	0	9.45
Cleveland	AL	21	4	0	2	42.2	183	45	26	25	8	0	1	0	15	4	24	2	0	2	0	1.000	0	0-1	1	5.27
4 ML YEARS		105	33	2	23	256	1140	313	153	147	36	9	6	5	95	14	139	6	1	10	17	.370	1	1-5	7	5.17

John Jaha

Bats: Right **Throws:** Right **Pos:** 1B-27; DH-20; PH-1 **Ht:** 6'1" **Wt:** 222 **Born:** 5/27/66 **Age:** 32

Year Team	Lg	G	AB	H	2B	3B	HR	(Hm	Rd)	TB	R	RBI	TBB	IBB	SO	HBP	SH	SF	SB	CS	SB%	GDP	Avg	OBP	SLG
1992 Milwaukee	AL	47	133	30	3	1	2	(1	1)	41	17	10	12	1	30	2	1	4	10	0	1.00	1	.226	.291	.308
1993 Milwaukee	AL	153	515	136	21	0	19	(5	14)	214	78	70	51	4	109	8	4	4	13	9	.59	6	.264	.337	.416
1994 Milwaukee	AL	84	291	70	14	0	12	(5	7)	120	45	39	32	3	75	10	1	4	3	3	.50	8	.241	.332	.412
1995 Milwaukee	AL	88	316	99	20	2	20	(8	12)	183	59	65	36	0	66	4	0	1	2	1	.67	8	.313	.389	.579
1996 Milwaukee	AL	148	543	163	28	1	34	(17	17)	295	108	118	85	1	118	5	0	3	3	1	.75	16	.300	.398	.543
1997 Milwaukee	AL	46	162	40	7	0	11	(1	10)	80	25	26	25	1	40	3	0	2	1	0	1.00	6	.247	.354	.494
6 ML YEARS		566	1960	538	93	4	98	(37	61)	933	332	328	241	10	438	32	6	18	32	14	.70	45	.274	.360	.476

Mike James

Pitches: Right **Bats:** Right **Pos:** RP-58 **Ht:** 6'3" **Wt:** 185 **Born:** 8/15/67 **Age:** 30

Year Team	Lg	G	GS	CG	GF	IP	BFP	H	R	ER	HR	SH	SF	HB	TBB	IBB	SO	WP	Bk	W	L	Pct.	ShO	Sv-Op	Hld	ERA
1995 California	AL	46	0	0	11	55.2	237	49	27	24	6	2	0	3	26	2	36	1	0	3	0	1.000	0	1-2	3	3.88
1996 California	AL	69	0	0	23	81	353	62	27	24	7	6	5	10	42	7	65	5	0	5	5	.500	0	1-6	18	2.67
1997 Anaheim	AL	58	0	0	22	62.2	284	69	32	30	3	6	1	5	28	4	57	1	0	5	5	.500	0	7-13	12	4.31
3 ML YEARS		173	0	0	56	199.1	874	180	86	78	16	14	6	18	96	13	158	7	0	13	10	.565	0	9-21	33	3.52

Marty Janzen

Pitches: Right **Bats:** Right **Pos:** RP-12 **Ht:** 6'3" **Wt:** 200 **Born:** 5/31/73 **Age:** 25

Year Team	Lg	G	GS	CG	GF	IP	BFP	H	R	ER	HR	SH	SF	HB	TBB	IBB	SO	WP	Bk	W	L	Pct.	ShO	Sv-Op	Hld	ERA
1992 Yankees	R	12	11	0	0	68.2	277	55	21	18	0	3	2	5	15	0	73	3	3	7	2	.778	0	0- -	—	2.36
Greensboro	A	2	0	0	2	5	20	5	2	2	0	0	0	1	1	0	5	2	0	0	0	.000	0	1- -	—	3.60
1993 Yankees	R	5	5	0	0	22.1	93	20	5	3	0	0	0	1	3	0	19	0	0	1	1	.000	0	0- -	—	1.21
1994 Greensboro	A	17	17	0	0	104	431	98	57	45	8	0	0	2	25	1	92	2	2	3	7	.300	0	0- -	—	3.89
1995 Tampa	A+	18	18	1	0	113.2	461	102	38	33	4	1	2	4	30	0	104	3	4	10	3	.769	0	0- -	—	2.61
Norwich	AA	3	3	0	0	20	85	17	11	11	2	0	0	2	7	0	16	2	0	1	2	.333	0	0- -	—	4.95
Knoxville	AA	7	7	2	0	48	188	35	14	14	2	0	2	1	14	0	44	1	1	5	1	.833	1	0- -	—	2.63
1996 Syracuse	AAA	10	10	0	0	55.2	257	74	54	48	12	1	4	2	24	2	34	2	0	3	4	.429	0	0- -	—	7.76
1997 Syracuse	AAA	22	9	0	6	65	304	76	58	52	12	3	3	3	36	0	56	8	0	0	5	.000	0	1- -	—	7.20
1996 Toronto	AL	15	11	0	3	73.2	344	95	65	60	16	1	3	2	38	1	47	7	0	4	6	.400	0	0-0	0	7.33
1997 Toronto	AL	12	0	0	6	25	105	23	11	10	4	0	0	0	13	2	17	0	0	2	1	.667	0	0-0	0	3.60
2 ML YEARS		27	11	0	9	98.2	449	118	76	70	20	1	3	2	51	3	64	7	0	6	7	.462	0	0-0	0	6.39

Kevin Jarvis

Pitches: Right **Bats:** Left **Pos:** RP-27; SP-5 **Ht:** 6'2" **Wt:** 200 **Born:** 8/1/69 **Age:** 28

Year Team	Lg	G	GS	CG	GF	IP	BFP	H	R	ER	HR	SH	SF	HB	TBB	IBB	SO	WP	Bk	W	L	Pct.	ShO	Sv-Op	Hld	ERA
1997 Toledo *	AAA	2	2	0	0	8	36	7	6	6	0	0	0	0	4	0	5	0	0	0	1	.000	0	0- -	—	6.75
1994 Cincinnati	NL	6	3	0	0	17.2	79	22	14	14	4	1	0	0	5	0	10	1	0	1	1	.500	0	0-0	0	7.13
1995 Cincinnati	NL	19	11	1	2	79	354	91	56	50	13	2	5	3	32	2	33	2	0	3	4	.429	1	0-0	0	5.70
1996 Cincinnati	NL	24	20	2	2	120.1	552	152	93	80	17	6	2	2	43	5	63	3	0	8	9	.471	1	0-0	0	5.98
1997 Cin-Min-Det		32	5	0	13	68	329	99	62	58	17	2	1	1	29	0	48	4	0	0	4	.000	0	1-1	0	7.68
1997 Cincinnati	NL	9	0	0	3	13.1	70	21	16	15	4	1	0	1	7	0	12	2	0	0	1	.000	0	1-1	0	10.13
Minnesota	AL	6	2	0	1	13	70	23	18	18	4	0	0	0	8	0	9	2	0	0	0	.000	0	0-0	0	12.46
Detroit	AL	17	3	0	9	41.2	189	55	28	25	9	1	1	0	14	0	27	0	0	0	3	.000	0	0-0	0	5.40
4 ML YEARS		81	39	3	17	285	1314	364	225	202	51	11	8	6	109	7	154	10	0	12	18	.400	2	1-1	0	6.38

Stan Javier

Bats: B **Throws:** R **Pos:** RF-95; CF-46; PH-18; LF-5; 1B-3 **Ht:** 6'0" **Wt:** 185 **Born:** 1/9/64 **Age:** 34

Year Team	Lg	G	AB	H	2B	3B	HR	(Hm	Rd)	TB	R	RBI	TBB	IBB	SO	HBP	SH	SF	SB	CS	SB%	GDP	Avg	OBP	SLG
1984 New York	AL	7	7	1	0	0	0	(0	0)	1	1	0	0	0	1	0	0	0	0	0	.00	0	.143	.143	.143
1986 Oakland	AL	59	114	23	8	0	0	(0	0)	31	13	8	16	0	27	1	0	0	8	0	1.00	2	.202	.305	.272

Year Team	Lg	G	AB	H	2B	3B	HR	(Hm	Rd)	TB	R	RBI	TBB	IBB	SO	HBP	SH	SF	SB	CS	SB%	GDP	Avg	OBP	SLG
1987 Oakland	AL	81	151	28	3	1	2	(1	1)	39	22	9	19	3	33	0	6	0	3	2	.60	2	.185	.276	.258
1988 Oakland	AL	125	397	102	13	3	2	(0	2)	127	49	35	32	1	63	2	6	3	20	1	.95	13	.257	.313	.320
1989 Oakland	AL	112	310	77	12	3	1	(1	0)	98	42	28	31	1	45	1	4	2	12	2	.86	6	.248	.317	.316
1990 Oak-LA	AL	123	309	92	9	6	3	(1	2)	122	60	27	40	2	50	0	6	2	15	7	.68	6	.298	.376	.395
1991 Los Angeles	NL	121	176	36	5	3	1	(0	1)	50	21	11	16	0	36	0	3	2	7	1	.88	4	.205	.268	.284
1992 LA-Phi	NL	130	334	83	11	1	1	(1	0)	105	42	29	37	2	54	3	3	2	18	3	.86	4	.249	.327	.314
1993 California	AL	92	237	69	10	4	3	(0	3)	96	33	28	27	1	33	1	1	3	12	2	.86	7	.291	.362	.405
1994 Oakland	AL	109	419	114	23	0	10	(1	9)	167	75	44	49	1	76	2	7	3	24	7	.77	7	.272	.349	.399
1995 Oakland	AL	130	442	123	20	2	8	(3	5)	171	81	56	49	3	63	4	5	4	36	5	.88	8	.278	.353	.387
1996 San Francisco	NL	71	274	74	25	0	2	(1	1)	105	44	22	25	0	51	2	5	0	14	2	.88	4	.270	.336	.383
1997 San Francisco	NL	142	440	126	16	4	8	(6	2)	174	69	50	56	1	70	5	2	7	25	3	.89	5	.286	.368	.395
1990 Oakland	AL	19	33	8	0	2	0	(0	0)	12	4	3	3	0	6	0	0	0	0	0	.00	0	.242	.306	.364
Los Angeles	NL	104	276	84	9	4	3	(1	2)	110	56	24	37	2	44	0	6	2	15	7	.68	6	.304	.384	.399
1992 Los Angeles	NL	56	58	11	3	0	1	(1	0)	17	6	5	6	2	11	1	1	0	1	2	.33	0	.190	.277	.293
Philadelphia	NL	74	276	72	14	1	0	(0	0)	88	36	24	31	0	43	2	2	2	17	1	.94	4	.261	.338	.319
13 ML YEARS		1302	3610	948	161	27	41	(15	26)	1286	552	347	397	15	602	21	48	28	194	35	.85	68	.263	.337	.356

Gregg Jefferies

Bats: Both **Throws:** Right **Pos:** LF-124; PH-7 **Ht:** 5'10" **Wt:** 184 **Born:** 8/1/67 **Age:** 30

Year Team	Lg	G	AB	H	2B	3B	HR	(Hm	Rd)	TB	R	RBI	TBB	IBB	SO	HBP	SH	SF	SB	CS	SB%	GDP	Avg	OBP	SLG
1987 New York	NL	6	6	3	1	0	0	(0	0)	4	0	2	0	0	0	0	0	0	0	0	.00	0	.500	.500	.667
1988 New York	NL	29	109	35	8	2	6	(3	3)	65	19	17	8	0	10	0	0	1	5	1	.83	1	.321	.364	.596
1989 New York	NL	141	508	131	28	2	12	(7	5)	199	72	56	39	8	46	5	2	5	21	6	.78	16	.258	.314	.392
1990 New York	NL	153	604	171	40	3	15	(9	6)	262	96	68	46	2	40	5	0	4	11	2	.85	12	.283	.337	.434
1991 New York	NL	136	486	132	19	2	9	(5	4)	182	59	62	47	2	38	2	1	3	26	5	.84	12	.272	.336	.374
1992 Kansas City	AL	152	604	172	36	3	10	(3	7)	244	66	75	43	4	29	1	0	9	19	9	.68	24	.285	.329	.404
1993 St. Louis	NL	142	544	186	24	3	16	(10	6)	264	89	83	62	7	32	2	0	4	46	9	.84	15	.342	.408	.485
1994 St. Louis	NL	103	397	129	27	1	12	(7	5)	194	52	55	45	12	26	1	0	4	12	5	.71	9	.325	.391	.489
1995 Philadelphia	NL	114	480	147	31	2	11	(4	7)	215	69	56	35	5	26	0	0	6	9	5	.64	15	.306	.349	.448
1996 Philadelphia	NL	104	404	118	17	3	7	(4	3)	162	59	51	36	6	21	1	0	5	20	6	.77	9	.292	.348	.401
1997 Philadelphia	NL	130	476	122	25	3	11	(2	9)	186	68	48	53	7	27	2	0	0	12	6	.67	9	.256	.333	.391
11 ML YEARS		1210	4618	1346	256	24	109	(54	55)	1977	649	573	414	53	295	19	3	41	181	54	.77	121	.291	.349	.428

Reggie Jefferson

Bats: Left **Throws:** Left **Pos:** DH-119; 1B-12; PH-12 **Ht:** 6'4" **Wt:** 215 **Born:** 9/25/68 **Age:** 29

Year Team	Lg	G	AB	H	2B	3B	HR	(Hm	Rd)	TB	R	RBI	TBB	IBB	SO	HBP	SH	SF	SB	CS	SB%	GDP	Avg	OBP	SLG
1991 Cin-Cle		31	108	21	3	0	3	(2	1)	33	11	13	4	0	24	0	0	1	0	0	.00	1	.194	.221	.306
1992 Cleveland	AL	24	89	30	6	2	1	(1	0)	43	8	6	1	0	17	1	0	0	0	0	.00	0	.337	.352	.483
1993 Cleveland	AL	113	366	91	11	2	10	(4	6)	136	35	34	28	7	78	5	3	1	1	3	.25	7	.249	.310	.372
1994 Seattle	AL	63	162	53	11	0	8	(4	4)	88	24	32	17	5	32	1	0	1	0	0	.00	6	.327	.392	.543
1995 Boston	AL	46	121	35	8	0	5	(1	4)	58	21	26	9	1	24	0	0	0	0	0	.00	3	.289	.333	.479
1996 Boston	AL	122	386	134	30	4	19	(12	7)	229	67	74	25	5	89	3	0	4	0	0	.00	11	.347	.388	.593
1997 Boston	AL	136	489	156	33	1	13	(6	7)	230	74	67	24	5	93	7	1	3	1	2	.33	17	.319	.358	.470
1991 Cincinnati	NL	5	7	1	0	0	1	(1	0)	4	1	1	1	0	2	0	0	0	0	0	.00	0	.143	.250	.571
Cleveland	AL	26	101	20	3	0	2	(1	1)	29	10	12	3	0	22	0	0	1	0	0	.00	1	.198	.219	.287
7 ML YEARS		535	1721	520	102	9	59	(30	29)	817	240	252	108	23	357	17	4	12	2	5	.29	47	.302	.347	.475

Robin Jennings

Bats: Left **Throws:** Left **Pos:** PH-6; LF-4; CF-2 **Ht:** 6'2" **Wt:** 205 **Born:** 4/11/72 **Age:** 26

Year Team	Lg	G	AB	H	2B	3B	HR	(Hm	Rd)	TB	R	RBI	TBB	IBB	SO	HBP	SH	SF	SB	CS	SB%	GDP	Avg	OBP	SLG
1992 Geneva	A-	72	275	82	12	2	1	—	—	119	39	47	20	5	43	2	0	0	10	3	.77	7	.298	.350	.433
1993 Peoria	A	132	474	146	29	5	3	—	—	194	65	65	46	2	73	4	5	3	11	11	.50	6	.308	.372	.409
1994 Daytona	A+	128	476	133	24	5	8	—	—	191	54	60	45	4	54	4	4	4	2	10	.17	13	.279	.344	.401
1995 Orlando	AA	132	490	145	27	7	17	—	—	237	71	79	44	5	61	4	0	5	7	14	.33	11	.296	.355	.484
1996 Iowa	AAA	86	334	91	15	6	18	—	—	175	56	56	32	1	53	1	0	2	2	0	1.00	6	.284	.346	.529
1997 Iowa	AAA	126	464	128	25	5	20	—	—	223	67	71	56	5	73	5	0	2	5	3	.63	7	.276	.359	.481
1996 Chicago	NL	31	58	13	5	0	0	(0	0)	18	7	4	3	0	9	1	0	0	1	0	1.00	1	.224	.274	.310
1997 Chicago	NL	9	18	3	1	0	0	(0	0)	4	1	2	0	0	2	0	0	1	0	0	.00	0	.167	.158	.222
2 ML YEARS		40	76	16	6	0	0	(0	0)	22	8	6	3	0	11	1	0	1	1	0	1.00	1	.211	.247	.289

Marcus Jensen

Bats: Both **Throws:** Right **Pos:** C-36; PH-3 **Ht:** 6'4" **Wt:** 195 **Born:** 12/14/72 **Age:** 25

Year Team	Lg	G	AB	H	2B	3B	HR	(Hm	Rd)	TB	R	RBI	TBB	IBB	SO	HBP	SH	SF	SB	CS	SB%	GDP	Avg	OBP	SLG
1990 Everett	A-	51	171	29	3	0	2	—	—	38	21	12	24	0	60	0	0	0	1	1	.50	3	.170	.290	.222
1991 Giants	R	48	155	44	8	3	2	—	—	64	28	30	34	3	22	5	0	4	4	2	.67	4	.284	.419	.413
1992 Clinton	A	86	264	62	14	0	4	—	—	88	35	33	54	3	87	4	1	2	4	2	.67	5	.235	.370	.333
1993 Clinton	A	104	324	85	24	2	11	—	—	146	53	56	65	5	98	4	0	4	1	2	.33	5	.262	.389	.451
1994 San Jose	A+	118	418	101	18	0	7	—	—	140	56	47	61	5	100	8	2	6	1	1	.50	4	.242	.345	.335
1995 Shreveport	AA	95	321	91	22	8	4	—	—	141	55	45	41	1	68	3	5	8	0	0	.00	4	.283	.362	.439
1996 Phoenix	AAA	120	405	107	22	4	5	—	—	152	41	53	44	4	95	3	2	1	1	1	.50	10	.264	.338	.375

BATTING | | | | | | | | | | | | | | | | | | | **BASERUNNING** | | | | **PERCENTAGES**

Year Team	Lg	G	AB	H	2B	3B	HR	(Hm	Rd)	TB	R	RBI	TBB	IBB	SO	HBP	SH	SF	SB	CS	SB%	GDP	Avg	OBP	SLG
1997 Toledo	AAA	24	80	14	5	0	0	—	—	19	5	9	9	0	25	0	2	0	0	0	.00	0	.175	.258	.238
1996 San Francisco	NL	9	19	4	1	0	0	(0	0)	5	4	4	8	0	7	0	0	0	0	0	.00	1	.211	.444	.263
1997 SF-Det		38	85	13	2	0	1	(1	0)	18	6	4	8	1	28	0	0	0	0	0	.00	2	.153	.226	.212
1997 San Francisco	NL	30	74	11	2	0	1	(1	0)	16	5	3	7	1	23	0	0	0	0	0	.00	2	.149	.222	.216
Detroit	AL	8	11	2	0	0	0	(0	0)	2	1	1	1	0	5	0	0	0	0	0	.00	0	.182	.250	.182
2 ML YEARS		47	104	17	3	0	1	(1	0)	23	10	8	16	1	35	0	0	0	0	0	.00	3	.163	.275	.221

Derek Jeter

Bats: Right **Throws:** Right **Pos:** SS-159 **Ht:** 6'3" **Wt:** 185 **Born:** 6/26/74 **Age:** 24

Year Team	Lg	G	AB	H	2B	3B	HR	(Hm	Rd)	TB	R	RBI	TBB	IBB	SO	HBP	SH	SF	SB	CS	SB%	GDP	Avg	OBP	SLG
1995 New York	AL	15	48	12	4	1	0	(0	0)	18	5	7	3	0	11	0	0	0	0	0	.00	0	.250	.294	.375
1996 New York	AL	157	582	183	25	6	10	(3	7)	250	104	78	48	1	102	9	6	9	14	7	.67	13	.314	.370	.430
1997 New York	AL	159	654	190	31	7	10	(5	5)	265	116	70	74	0	125	10	8	2	23	12	.66	14	.291	.370	.405
3 ML YEARS		331	1284	385	60	14	20	(8	12)	533	225	155	125	1	238	19	14	11	37	19	.66	27	.300	.368	.415

Brian Johnson

Bats: Right **Throws:** Right **Pos:** C-98; PH-3; DH-2; 1B-2 **Ht:** 6'2" **Wt:** 210 **Born:** 1/8/68 **Age:** 30

Year Team	Lg	G	AB	H	2B	3B	HR	(Hm	Rd)	TB	R	RBI	TBB	IBB	SO	HBP	SH	SF	SB	CS	SB%	GDP	Avg	OBP	SLG
1997 Toledo *	AAA	7	21	3	2	0	0	—	—	5	0	1	0	0	2	0	0	1	0	0	.00	0	.143	.136	.238
1994 San Diego	NL	36	93	23	4	1	3	(3	0)	38	7	16	5	0	21	0	2	1	0	0	.00	4	.247	.283	.409
1995 San Diego	NL	68	207	52	9	0	3	(1	2)	70	20	29	11	2	39	1	1	4	0	0	.00	2	.251	.287	.338
1996 San Diego	NL	82	243	66	13	1	8	(3	5)	105	18	35	4	2	36	4	2	4	0	0	.00	8	.272	.290	.432
1997 Det-SF		101	318	83	13	3	13	(8	5)	141	32	45	19	8	45	2	5	4	1	1	.50	11	.261	.303	.443
1997 Detroit	AL	45	139	33	6	1	2	(2	0)	47	13	18	5	1	19	0	2	1	1	0	1.00	3	.237	.262	.338
San Francisco	NL	56	179	50	7	2	11	(6	5)	94	19	27	14	7	26	2	3	3	0	1	.00	8	.279	.333	.525
4 ML YEARS		287	861	224	39	5	27	(15	12)	354	77	125	39	12	141	7	10	13	1	1	.50	25	.260	.293	.411

Charles Johnson

Bats: Right **Throws:** Right **Pos:** C-123; PH-1 **Ht:** 6'2" **Wt:** 215 **Born:** 7/20/71 **Age:** 26

Year Team	Lg	G	AB	H	2B	3B	HR	(Hm	Rd)	TB	R	RBI	TBB	IBB	SO	HBP	SH	SF	SB	CS	SB%	GDP	Avg	OBP	SLG
1994 Florida	NL	4	11	5	1	0	1	(1	0)	9	5	4	1	0	4	0	0	1	0	0	.00	1	.455	.462	.818
1995 Florida	NL	97	315	79	15	1	11	(8	3)	129	40	39	46	2	71	4	4	2	0	0	.00	11	.251	.351	.410
1996 Florida	NL	120	386	84	13	1	13	(9	4)	138	34	37	40	6	91	2	2	4	1	0	1.00	20	.218	.292	.358
1997 Florida	NL	124	416	104	26	1	19	(7	12)	189	43	63	60	6	109	3	3	2	0	2	.00	13	.250	.347	.454
4 ML YEARS		345	1128	272	55	3	44	(20	24)	465	122	143	147	14	275	9	9	9	1	4	.20	45	.241	.331	.412

Dane Johnson

Pitches: Right **Bats:** Right **Pos:** RP-38 **Ht:** 6'5" **Wt:** 205 **Born:** 2/10/63 **Age:** 35

		HOW MUCH HE PITCHED						**WHAT HE GAVE UP**												**THE RESULTS**						
Year Team	Lg	G	GS	CG	GF	IP	BFP	H	R	ER	HR	SH	SF	HB	TBB	IBB	SO	WP	Bk	W	L	Pct.	ShO	Sv-Op	Hld	ERA
1997 Edmonton *	AAA	14	0	0	11	16	72	17	11	10	1	1	0	0	8	1	13	0	0	1	1	.500	0	6- -	-	5.63
1994 Chicago	AL	15	0	0	4	12.1	61	16	9	9	2	0	1	0	11	1	7	0	0	2	1	.667	0	0-0	2	6.57
1996 Toronto	AL	10	0	0	2	9	36	5	3	3	0	0	0	0	5	0	7	0	0	0	0	.000	0	0-0	2	3.00
1997 Oakland	AL	38	0	0	12	45.2	217	49	28	23	4	0	4	2	31	4	43	4	1	4	1	.800	0	2-4	2	4.53
3 ML YEARS		63	0	0	18	67	314	70	40	35	6	0	5	2	47	5	57	4	1	6	2	.750	0	2-4	6	4.70

Jason Johnson

Pitches: Right **Bats:** Right **Pos:** RP-3 **Ht:** 6'6" **Wt:** 216 **Born:** 10/27/73 **Age:** 24

		HOW MUCH HE PITCHED						**WHAT HE GAVE UP**												**THE RESULTS**						
Year Team	Lg	G	GS	CG	GF	IP	BFP	H	R	ER	HR	SH	SF	HB	TBB	IBB	SO	WP	Bk	W	L	Pct.	ShO	Sv-Op	Hld	ERA
1992 Pirates	R	5	0	0	4	7.1	32	6	3	3	0	0	0	0	6	0	3	1	0	2	0	1.000	0	0- -	—	3.68
1993 Pirates	R	9	9	0	0	54	217	48	22	14	0	0	1	1	14	0	39	1	0	1	4	.200	0	0- -	—	2.33
Welland	A-	6	6	1	0	35	152	33	24	18	0	4	1	2	9	0	19	1	0	1	5	.167	0	0- -	—	4.63
1994 Augusta	A	20	19	1	0	102.2	465	119	67	46	5	4	4	7	32	0	69	12	2	2	12	.143	0	0- -	—	4.03
1995 Augusta	A	11	11	1	0	53.2	233	57	32	26	2	1	1	4	17	0	42	3	0	3	5	.375	0	0- -	—	4.36
Lynchburg	A+	10	10	0	0	55	236	58	37	30	9	1	3	2	20	0	41	2	0	1	4	.200	0	0- -	—	4.91
1996 Lynchburg	A+	15	5	0	1	44.1	204	56	37	32	6	5	1	1	12	0	27	0	0	1	4	.200	0	0- -	—	6.50
Augusta	A	14	14	1	0	84	359	82	40	29	2	5	3	6	25	0	83	5	2	4	4	.500	1	0- -	—	3.11
1997 Lynchburg	A+	17	17	0	0	99.1	411	98	43	41	4	4	2	6	30	1	92	7	0	8	4	.667	0	0- -	—	3.71
Carolina	AA	9	9	1	0	57.1	244	56	31	26	1	1	1	1	16	0	63	1	0	3	3	.500	0	0- -	—	4.08
1997 Pittsburgh	NL	3	0	0	0	6	27	10	4	4	2	0	1	0	1	0	3	0	0	0	0	.000	0	0-0	0	6.00

Lance Johnson

Bats: Left **Throws:** Left **Pos:** CF-105; PH-12; DH-1 **Ht:** 5'11" **Wt:** 160 **Born:** 7/6/63 **Age:** 34

Year Team	Lg	G	AB	H	2B	3B	HR	(Hm	Rd)	TB	R	RBI	TBB	IBB	SO	HBP	SH	SF	SB	CS	SB%	GDP	Avg	OBP	SLG
1987 St. Louis	NL	33	59	13	2	1	0	(0	0)	17	4	7	4	1	6	0	0	0	6	1	.86	2	.220	.270	.288

Year Team	Lg	G	AB	H	2B	3B	HR	Hm	Rd	TB	R	RBI	TBB	IBB	SO	HBP	SH	SF	SB	CS	SB%	GDP	Avg	OBP	SLG
1988 Chicago	AL	33	124	23	4	1	0	(0	0)	29	11	6	6	0	11	0	2	0	6	2	.75	1	.185	.223	.234
1989 Chicago	AL	50	180	54	8	2	0	(0	0)	66	28	16	17	0	24	0	2	0	16	3	.84	1	.300	.360	.367
1990 Chicago	AL	151	541	154	18	9	1	(0	1)	193	76	51	33	2	45	1	8	4	36	22	.62	12	.285	.325	.357
1991 Chicago	AL	160	588	161	14	13	0	(0	0)	201	72	49	26	2	58	1	6	3	26	11	.70	14	.274	.304	.342
1992 Chicago	AL	157	567	158	15	12	3	(2	1)	206	67	47	34	4	33	1	4	5	41	14	.75	20	.279	.318	.363
1993 Chicago	AL	147	540	168	18	14	0	(0	0)	214	75	47	36	1	33	0	3	0	35	7	.83	10	.311	.354	.396
1994 Chicago	AL	106	412	114	11	14	3	(1	2)	162	56	54	26	5	23	2	0	3	26	6	.81	8	.277	.321	.393
1995 Chicago	AL	142	607	186	18	12	10	(2	8)	258	98	57	32	2	31	1	2	8	40	6	.87	7	.306	.341	.425
1996 New York	NL	160	682	227	31	21	9	(1	8)	327	117	69	33	8	40	1	3	5	50	12	.81	8	.333	.362	.479
1997 NYN-ChN	NL	111	410	126	16	8	5	(4	1)	173	60	39	42	3	31	0	0	2	20	12	.63	8	.307	.370	.422
1997 New York	NL	72	265	82	10	6	1	(1	0)	107	43	24	33	2	21	0	0	1	15	10	.60	6	.309	.385	.404
Chicago	NL	39	145	44	6	2	4	(3	1)	66	17	15	9	1	10	0	0	1	5	2	.71	2	.303	.342	.455
11 ML YEARS		1250	4710	1384	155	107	31	(10	21)	1846	664	442	289	28	335	7	30	25	302	96	.76	91	.294	.334	.392

Mark Johnson

Bats: Left **Throws:** Left **Pos:** 1B-63; PH-17; DH-1   **Ht:** 6'4" **Wt:** 230 **Born:** 10/17/67 **Age:** 30

Year Team	Lg	G	AB	H	2B	3B	HR	Hm	Rd	TB	R	RBI	TBB	IBB	SO	HBP	SH	SF	SB	CS	SB%	GDP	Avg	OBP	SLG
1997 Calgary *	AAA	34	115	39	11	1	6	—	—	70	28	16	4		28	1	0	1	4	2	.67	2	.339	.446	.609
Indianapols *	AAA	3	4	0	0	0	0	—	—	0	0	0	2		2	0	0	0	0	1	.00	0	.000	.333	.000
1995 Pittsburgh	NL	79	221	46	6	1	13	(7	6)	93	32	28	37	2	66	2	0	1	5	2	.71	2	.208	.326	.421
1996 Pittsburgh	NL	127	343	94	18	0	13	(10	3)	157	55	47	44	3	64	5	0	4	6	4	.60	5	.274	.361	.458
1997 Pittsburgh	NL	78	219	47	10	0	4	(2	2)	69	30	29	43	1	78	2	0	3	1	1	.50	1	.215	.345	.315
3 ML YEARS		284	783	187	40	1	30	(19	11)	319	117	104	124	6	208	9	0	8	12	7	.63	8	.239	.346	.407

Mike Johnson

Pitches: Right **Bats:** Left **Pos:** SP-16; RP-9   **Ht:** 6'2" **Wt:** 175 **Born:** 10/3/75 **Age:** 22

Year Team	Lg	G	GS	CG	GF	IP	BFP	H	R	ER	HR	SH	SF	HB	TBB	IBB	SO	WP	Bk	W	L	Pct.	ShO	Sv-Op	Hld	ERA
1993 Blue Jays	R	16	1	0	7	44.1	208	51	40	24	4	1	3	2	22	0	31	4	2	0	2	.000	0	1--	—	4.87
1994 Medicne Hat	R+	9	9	0	0	36.1	170	48	31	18	2	2	0	1	22	0	8	8	1	1	3	.250	0	0--	—	4.46
1995 Blue Jays	R	3	3	0	0	15	74	20	15	12	1	0	0	3	8	0	13	7	0	2		.000	0	0--	—	7.20
Medicne Hat	R+	19	0	0	0	49	217	46	26	21	2	2	0		25	1	32	6	0	4	1	.800	0	3--	—	3.86
1996 Hagerstown	A	29	23	5	1	162.2	671	157	74	57	6	5	5	8	39	0	155	12	1	11	8	.579	3	0--	—	3.15
1997 Bal-Mon		25	16	0	5	89.2	403	106	70	68	20	2	4	1	37	4	57	5	0	2	6	.250	0	2-2	0	6.83
1997 Baltimore	AL	14	5	0	5	39.2	183	52	36	35	12	0	2	1	16	2	29	1	0	0	1	.000	0	2-2	0	7.94
Montreal	NL	11	11	0	0	50	220	54	34	33	8	2	2	0	21	2	28	4	0	2	5	.286	0	0-0	0	5.94

Randy Johnson

Pitches: Left **Bats:** Right **Pos:** SP-29; RP-1   **Ht:** 6'10" **Wt:** 230 **Born:** 9/10/63 **Age:** 34

Year Team	Lg	G	GS	CG	GF	IP	BFP	H	R	ER	HR	SH	SF	HB	TBB	IBB	SO	WP	Bk	W	L	Pct.	ShO	Sv-Op	Hld	ERA
1988 Montreal	NL	4	4	1	0	26	109	23	8	7	3	0	0	0	7	0	25	3	0	3	0	1.000	0	0-0	0	2.42
1989 Mon-Sea		29	28	2	1	160.2	715	147	100	86	13	10	13	3	96	2	130	7	7	7	13	.350	0	0-0	0	4.82
1990 Seattle	AL	33	33	5	0	219.2	944	174	103	89	26	7	5	12	120	2	194	4	2	14	11	.560	2	0-0	0	3.65
1991 Seattle	AL	33	33	2	0	201.1	889	151	96	89	15	9	8	12	152	0	228	12	2	13	10	.565	1	0-0	0	3.98
1992 Seattle	AL	31	31	6	0	210.1	922	154	104	88	13	3	8	18	144	1	241	13	1	12	14	.462	2	0-0	0	3.77
1993 Seattle	AL	35	34	10	1	255.1	1043	185	97	92	22	8	7	16	99	1	308	8	2	19	8	.704	3	1-1	0	3.24
1994 Seattle	AL	23	23	9	0	172	694	132	65	61	14	3	1	6	72	2	204	5	0	13	6	.684	4	0-0	0	3.19
1995 Seattle	AL	30	30	6	0	214.1	866	159	65	59	12	2	1	6	65	1	294	5	2	18	2	.900	3	0-0	0	2.48
1996 Seattle	AL	14	8	0	2	61.1	256	48	27	25	8	1	0	2	25	0	85	3	1	5	0	1.000	0	1-2	0	3.67
1997 Seattle	AL	30	29	5	0	213	850	147	60	54	20	4	1	10	77	2	291	4	0	20	4	.833	2	0-0	0	2.28
1989 Montreal	NL	7	6	0	1	29.2	142	29	25	22	2	3	4	0	26	1	26	2	2	0	4	.000	0	0-0	0	4.40
Seattle	AL	22	22	2	0	131	572	118	75	64	11	7	9	3	70	1	104	5	5	7	9	.438	0	0-0	0	4.40
10 ML YEARS		262	253	46	4	1734	7288	1320	725	650	146	47	45	78	857	11	2000	64	17	124	68	.646	17	2-3	0	3.37

Russ Johnson

Bats: Right **Throws:** Right **Pos:** 3B-14; PH-7; 2B-3   **Ht:** 5'10" **Wt:** 180 **Born:** 2/22/73 **Age:** 25

Year Team	Lg	G	AB	H	2B	3B	HR	Hm	Rd	TB	R	RBI	TBB	IBB	SO	HBP	SH	SF	SB	CS	SB%	GDP	Avg	OBP	SLG
1995 Jackson	AA	132	475	118	16	2	9	—	—	165	65	53	50	1	60	0	2	5	10	5	.67	11	.248	.329	.347
1996 Jackson	AA	132	496	154	24	5	15	—	—	233	86	74	56	1	50	3	5	3	9	4	.69	16	.310	.382	.470
1997 New Orleans	AAA	122	445	123	16	6	4	—	—	163	72	49	66	1	78	1	2	2	7	4	.64	10	.276	.370	.366
1997 Houston	NL	21	60	18	1	0	2	(2	0)	25	7	9	6	0	14	0	1	0	1	1	.50	2	.300	.364	.417

John Johnstone

Pitches: Right **Bats:** Right **Pos:** RP-18   **Ht:** 6'3" **Wt:** 195 **Born:** 11/25/68 **Age:** 29

Year Team	Lg	G	GS	CG	GF	IP	BFP	H	R	ER	HR	SH	SF	HB	TBB	IBB	SO	WP	Bk	W	L	Pct.	ShO	Sv-Op	Hld	ERA
1997 Phoenix *	AAA	38	0	0	34	38	161	34	17	17	3	0	0	1	15	3	30	4	0	0	3	.000	0	24--	—	4.03
1993 Florida	NL	7	0	0	3	10.2	54	16	8	7	1	0	0	0	7	0	5	1	0	0	2	.000	0	0-0	0	5.91
1994 Florida	NL	17	0	0	7	21.1	105	23	20	14	4	0	0	1	16	5	23	0	0	1	1	.333	0	0-0	3	5.91

Year Team	Lg	G	GS	CG	GF	IP	BFP	H	R	ER	HR	SH	SF	HB	TBB	IBB	SO	WP	Bk	W	L	Pct.	ShO	Sv-Op	Hld	ERA
1995 Florida	NL	4	0	0	0	4.2	23	7	2	2	1	0	0	0	2	1	3	0	0	0	0	.000	0	0-0	0	3.86
1996 Houston	NL	9	0	0	6	13	60	17	8	8	2	0	2	0	5	0	5	0	0	0	1	1.000	0	0-0	0	5.54
1997 SF-Oak		18	0	0	3	25	112	22	9	9	1	2	4	4	14	0	19	0	0	0	0	.000	0	0-0	1	3.24
1997 San Francisco	NL	13	0	0	2	18.2	80	15	7	7	1	2	3	4	7	0	15	0	0	0	0	.000	0	0-0	1	3.38
Oakland	AL	5	0	0	1	6.1	32	7	2	2	0	0	1	0	7	0	4	0	0	0	0	.000	0	0-0	0	2.84
5 ML YEARS		55	0	0	19	74.2	354	85	47	40	9	3	6	5	44	6	55	1	0	2	4	.333	0	0-0	4	4.82

Andruw Jones

Bats: R **Throws:** R **Pos:** RF-95; CF-57; PH-34; LF-2 **Ht:** 6'1" **Wt:** 185 **Born:** 4/23/77 **Age:** 21

Year Team	Lg	G	AB	H	2B	3B	HR	(Hm	Rd)	TB	R	RBI	TBB	IBB	SO	HBP	SH	SF	SB	CS	SB%	GDP	Avg	OBP	SLG
1994 Braves	R	27	95	21	5	1	2	—	—	34	22	10	16	2	19	2	0	0	5	2	.71	3	.221	.345	.358
Danville	R+	36	143	48	9	2	1	—	—	64	20	16	9	0	25	3	0	1	16	9	.64	0	.336	.385	.448
1995 Macon	A	139	537	149	41	5	25	—	—	275	104	100	70	7	122	16	0	9	56	11	.84	9	.277	.372	.512
1996 Durham	A+	66	243	76	14	3	17	—	—	147	65	43	42	3	54	3	0	1	16	4	.80	5	.313	.419	.605
Greenville	AA	38	157	58	10	1	12	—	—	106	39	37	17	0	34	1	0	1	12	4	.75	3	.369	.432	.675
Richmond	AAA	12	45	17	3	1	5	—	—	37	11	12	1	0	9	0	0	1	2	2	.50	0	.378	.391	.822
1996 Atlanta	NL	31	106	23	7	1	5	(3	2)	47	11	13	7	0	29	0	0	0	3	0	1.00	1	.217	.265	.443
1997 Atlanta	NL	153	399	92	18	1	18	(5	13)	166	60	70	56	2	107	4	5	3	20	11	.65	11	.231	.329	.416
2 ML YEARS		184	505	115	25	2	23	(8	15)	213	71	83	63	2	136	4	5	3	23	11	.68	12	.228	.317	.422

Bobby Jones

Pitches: Right **Bats:** Right **Pos:** SP-30 **Ht:** 6'4" **Wt:** 225 **Born:** 2/10/70 **Age:** 28

Year Team	Lg	G	GS	CG	GF	IP	BFP	H	R	ER	HR	SH	SF	HB	TBB	IBB	SO	WP	Bk	W	L	Pct.	ShO	Sv-Op	Hld	ERA
1993 New York	NL	9	9	0	0	61.2	265	61	35	25	6	5	3	2	22	3	35	1	0	2	4	.333	0	0-0	0	3.65
1994 New York	NL	24	24	1	0	160	685	157	75	56	10	11	4	4	56	9	80	1	3	12	7	.632	1	0-0	0	3.15
1995 New York	NL	30	30	3	0	195.2	839	209	107	91	20	11	6	7	53	6	127	2	1	10	10	.500	1	0-0	0	4.19
1996 New York	NL	31	31	3	0	195.2	826	219	102	96	26	12	5	3	46	6	116	2	0	12	8	.600	1	0-0	0	4.42
1997 New York	NL	30	30	2	0	193.1	806	177	88	78	24	6	4	2	63	3	125	3	1	15	9	.625	1	0-0	0	3.63
5 ML YEARS		124	124	9	0	806.1	3421	823	407	346	86	45	22	18	240	27	483	9	5	51	38	.573	4	0-0	0	3.86

Bobby M. Jones

Pitches: Left **Bats:** Right **Pos:** SP-4 **Ht:** 6'0" **Wt:** 175 **Born:** 4/11/72 **Age:** 26

Year Team	Lg	G	GS	CG	GF	IP	BFP	H	R	ER	HR	SH	SF	HB	TBB	IBB	SO	WP	Bk	W	L	Pct.	ShO	Sv-Op	Hld	ERA
1992 Helena	R+	14	13	1	0	76.1	341	93	51	37	7	4	2	1	23	0	53	6	5	5	4	.556	0	0- —	—	4.36
1993 Beloit	A	25	25	4	0	144.2	661	159	82	66	9	1	6	9	65	1	115	4	4	10	10	.500	0	0- —	—	4.11
1994 Stockton	A+	26	26	2	0	147.2	638	131	90	69	12	4	4	4	64	0	147	5	2	6	12	.333	0	0- —	—	4.21
1995 Colo Sprngs	AAA	11	8	0	0	40.2	204	50	38	33	5	4	1	2	30	3	48	4	1	2	2	.333	0	0- —	—	7.30
New Haven	AA	27	8	0	9	73.1	315	61	27	21	4	3	3	8	36	2	70	7	0	5	2	.714	0	3- —	—	2.58
1996 Colo Sprngs	AAA	57	0	0	17	88.2	410	88	54	49	8	5	2	4	63	4	78	7	2	2	8	.200	0	3- —	—	4.97
1997 Colo Sprngs	AAA	25	21	0	2	133	593	135	89	76	16	1	5	12	71	2	104	2	0	7	11	.389	0	0- —	—	5.14
1997 Colorado	NL	4	4	0	0	19.1	96	30	18	18	2	2	3	0	12	0	5	0	0	1	1	.500	0	0-0	0	8.38

Chipper Jones

Bats: B **Throws:** R **Pos:** 3B-152; LF-3; RF-3; PH-3 **Ht:** 6'3" **Wt:** 200 **Born:** 4/24/72 **Age:** 26

Year Team	Lg	G	AB	H	2B	3B	HR	(Hm	Rd)	TB	R	RBI	TBB	IBB	SO	HBP	SH	SF	SB	CS	SB%	GDP	Avg	OBP	SLG
1993 Atlanta	NL	8	3	2	1	0	0	(0	0)	3	2	0	1	0	1	0	0	0	0	0	.00	0	.667	.750	1.000
1995 Atlanta	NL	140	524	139	22	3	23	(15	8)	236	87	86	73	1	99	0	1	4	8	4	.67	10	.265	.353	.450
1996 Atlanta	NL	157	598	185	32	5	30	(18	12)	317	114	110	87	0	88	0	1	7	14	1	.93	14	.309	.393	.530
1997 Atlanta	NL	157	597	176	41	3	21	(7	14)	286	100	111	76	8	88	0	0	6	20	5	.80	19	.295	.371	.479
4 ML YEARS		462	1722	502	96	11	74	(40	34)	842	303	307	237	9	276	0	2	17	42	10	.81	43	.292	.374	.489

Chris Jones

Bats: R **Throws:** R **Pos:** PH-41; RF-25; LF-24; CF-19 **Ht:** 6'2" **Wt:** 210 **Born:** 12/16/65 **Age:** 32

Year Team	Lg	G	AB	H	2B	3B	HR	(Hm	Rd)	TB	R	RBI	TBB	IBB	SO	HBP	SH	SF	SB	CS	SB%	GDP	Avg	OBP	SLG
1991 Cincinnati	NL	52	89	26	1	2	2	(0	2)	37	14	6	2	0	31	0	0	1	2	1	.67	2	.292	.304	.416
1992 Houston	NL	54	63	12	2	1	1	(1	0)	19	7	4	7	0	21	0	3	0	3	0	1.00	1	.190	.271	.302
1993 Colorado	NL	86	209	57	11	4	6	(2	4)	94	29	31	10	1	48	0	5	1	9	4	.69	6	.273	.305	.450
1994 Colorado	NL	21	40	12	2	1	0	(0	0)	16	6	2	2	1	14	0	0	0	1	0	1.00	1	.300	.333	.400
1995 New York	NL	79	182	51	6	2	8	(4	4)	85	33	31	13	1	45	1	2	3	2	1	.67	0	.280	.327	.467
1996 New York	NL	89	149	36	7	0	4	(2	2)	55	22	18	12	1	42	2	0	0	1	0	1.00	3	.242	.307	.369
1997 San Diego	NL	92	152	37	9	0	7	(4	3)	67	24	25	16	0	45	2	1	1	7	2	.78	1	.243	.322	.441
7 ML YEARS		473	884	231	38	10	28	(13	15)	373	135	117	62	4	246	5	11	6	24	9	.73	19	.261	.311	.422

Doug Jones

Pitches: Right **Bats:** Right **Pos:** RP-75

Ht: 6'2" **Wt:** 205 **Born:** 6/24/57 **Age:** 41

Year Team	Lg	HOW MUCH HE PITCHED						WHAT HE GAVE UP											THE RESULTS					
		G	GS	CG	GF	IP	BFP	H	R	ER	HR	SH	SF	HB	TBB	IBB	SO	WP	Bk	W	L	Pct.	ShO	Sv-Op	Hld	ERA
1982 Milwaukee	AL	4	0	0	2	2.2	14	5	3	3	1	0	0	0	1	0	1	0	0	0	0	.000	0	0--	—	10.13
1986 Cleveland	AL	11	0	0	5	18	79	18	5	5	0	1	1	1	6	1	12	0	0	1	0	1.000	0	1--	—	2.50
1987 Cleveland	AL	49	0	0	29	91.1	400	101	45	32	4	5	5	6	24	5	87	0	0	6	5	.545	0	8-12	1	3.15
1988 Cleveland	AL	51	0	0	46	83.1	338	69	26	21	4	1	3	0	16	3	72	2	3	3	4	.429	0	37-43	0	2.27
1989 Cleveland	AL	59	0	0	53	80.2	331	76	25	21	4	8	6	1	13	4	65	1	1	7	10	.412	0	32-41	0	2.34
1990 Cleveland	AL	66	0	0	64	84.1	331	66	26	24	5	2	2	2	22	4	55	2	0	5	5	.500	0	43-51	0	2.56
1991 Cleveland	AL	36	4	0	29	63.1	293	87	42	39	7	2	2	0	17	5	48	1	0	4	8	.333	0	7-12	0	5.54
1992 Houston	NL	80	0	0	70	111.2	440	96	29	23	5	9	0	5	17	5	93	2	1	11	8	.579	0	36-42	0	1.85
1993 Houston	NL	71	0	0	60	85.1	381	102	46	43	7	9	4	5	21	6	66	3	0	4	10	.286	0	26-34	1	4.54
1994 Philadelphia	NL	47	0	0	42	54	226	55	14	13	2	4	0	0	6	0	38	1	0	2	4	.333	0	27-29	0	2.17
1995 Baltimore	AL	52	0	0	47	46.2	211	55	30	26	6	1	0	2	16	2	42	0	0	0	4	.000	0	22-25	0	5.01
1996 ChN-Mil		52	0	0	21	64	282	72	33	30	7	1	2	3	20	6	60	1	0	7	2	.778	0	3-11	2	4.22
1997 Milwaukee	AL	75	0	0	73	80.1	307	62	20	18	4	1	5	3	9	1	82	2	0	6	6	.500	0	36-38	0	2.02
1996 Chicago	NL	28	0	0	13	32.1	143	41	20	18	4	1	0	1	7	4	26	0	0	2	2	.500	0	2-7	0	5.01
Milwaukee	AL	24	0	0	8	31.2	139	31	13	12	3	0	2	2	13	2	34	1	0	5	0	1.000	0	1-4	2	3.41
13 ML YEARS		653	4	0	541	865.2	3633	864	344	298	53	46	27	30	188	42	721	15	5	56	66	.459	0	278--	—	3.10

Todd Jones

Pitches: Right **Bats:** Left **Pos:** RP-68

Ht: 6'3" **Wt:** 200 **Born:** 4/24/68 **Age:** 30

Year Team	Lg	HOW MUCH HE PITCHED						WHAT HE GAVE UP											THE RESULTS					
		G	GS	CG	GF	IP	BFP	H	R	ER	HR	SH	SF	HB	TBB	IBB	SO	WP	Bk	W	L	Pct.	ShO	Sv-Op	Hld	ERA
1993 Houston	NL	27	0	0	8	37.1	150	28	14	13	4	2	1	1	15	2	25	1	1	1	2	.333	0	2-3	6	3.13
1994 Houston	NL	48	0	0	20	72.2	288	52	23	22	3	3	1	1	26	4	63	1	0	5	2	.714	0	5-9	8	2.72
1995 Houston	NL	68	0	0	40	99.2	442	89	38	34	8	5	4	6	52	17	96	5	0	6	5	.545	0	15-20	8	3.07
1996 Houston	NL	51	0	0	37	57.1	263	61	30	28	5	2	1	5	32	6	44	3	0	6	3	.667	0	17-23	1	4.40
1997 Detroit	AL	68	0	0	51	70	301	60	29	24	3	1	4	1	35	2	70	7	0	5	4	.556	0	31-36	5	3.09
5 ML YEARS		262	0	0	156	337	1444	290	134	121	23	13	11	14	160	31	298	17	1	23	16	.590	0	70-91	28	3.23

Brian Jordan

Bats: Right **Throws:** Right **Pos:** RF-30; CF-14; PH-5

Ht: 6'1" **Wt:** 215 **Born:** 3/29/67 **Age:** 31

Year Team	Lg	BATTING															BASERUNNING				PERCENTAGES		
		G	AB	H	2B	3B	HR	(Hm	Rd)	TB	R	RBI	TBB	IBB	SO	HBP	SH	SF	SB	CS	SB%	GDP	Avg	OBP	SLG
1997 Louisville *	AAA	6	20	3	0	0	0	—	—	3	1	2	1	0	2	1	0	0	0	1	.00	0	.150	.227	.150
1992 St. Louis	NL	55	193	40	9	4	5	(3	2)	72	17	22	10	1	48	1	0	0	7	2	.78	6	.207	.250	.373
1993 St. Louis	NL	67	223	69	10	6	10	(4	6)	121	33	44	12	0	35	4	0	3	6	6	.50	6	.309	.351	.543
1994 St. Louis	NL	53	178	46	8	2	5	(4	1)	73	14	15	16	0	40	1	0	2	4	3	.57	6	.258	.320	.410
1995 St. Louis	NL	131	490	145	20	4	22	(14	8)	239	83	81	22	4	79	11	0	2	24	9	.73	6	.296	.339	.488
1996 St. Louis	NL	140	513	159	36	1	17	(3	14)	248	82	104	29	4	84	7	2	9	22	5	.81	6	.310	.349	.483
1997 St. Louis	NL	47	145	34	5	0	0	(0	0)	39	17	10	10	1	21	6	0	0	6	1	.86	4	.234	.311	.269
6 ML YEARS		493	1742	493	88	17	59	(28	31)	792	246	276	99	10	307	30	2	16	69	26	.73	33	.283	.330	.455

Kevin Jordan

Bats: R **Throws:** R **Pos:** PH-47; 1B-25; 3B-12; 2B-6; DH-1

Ht: 6'1" **Wt:** 194 **Born:** 10/9/69 **Age:** 28

Year Team	Lg	BATTING															BASERUNNING				PERCENTAGES		
		G	AB	H	2B	3B	HR	(Hm	Rd)	TB	R	RBI	TBB	IBB	SO	HBP	SH	SF	SB	CS	SB%	GDP	Avg	OBP	SLG
1997 Scrnton-WB *	AAA	7	30	9	2	2	0	—	—	15	5	2	2	0	6	0	0	0	2	0	1.00	1	.300	.344	.500
1995 Philadelphia	NL	24	54	10	1	0	2	(1	1)	17	6	6	2	1	9	1	0	0	0	0	.00	0	.185	.228	.315
1996 Philadelphia	NL	43	131	37	10	0	3	(2	1)	56	15	12	5	0	20	1	3	2	2	1	.67	3	.282	.309	.427
1997 Philadelphia	NL	84	177	47	8	0	6	(4	2)	73	19	30	3	0	26	0	0	3	0	1	.00	5	.266	.273	.412
3 ML YEARS		151	362	94	19	0	11	(7	4)	146	40	48	10	1	55	2	3	5	2	2	.50	8	.260	.280	.403

Ricardo Jordan

Pitches: Left **Bats:** Left **Pos:** RP-22

Ht: 6'0" **Wt:** 180 **Born:** 6/27/70 **Age:** 28

Year Team	Lg	HOW MUCH HE PITCHED						WHAT HE GAVE UP											THE RESULTS					
		G	GS	CG	GF	IP	BFP	H	R	ER	HR	SH	SF	HB	TBB	IBB	SO	WP	Bk	W	L	Pct.	ShO	Sv-Op	Hld	ERA
1997 Norfolk *	AAA	34	0	0	10	29	128	20	11	9	1	0	1	2	24	2	34	1	0	0	1	.000	0	1--	—	2.79
1995 Toronto	AL	15	0	0	3	15	76	18	11	11	3	0	2	2	13	1	10	1	0	1	0	1.000	0	1-1	1	6.60
1996 Philadelphia	NL	15	0	0	2	25	103	18	6	5	0	1	0	0	12	0	17	1	0	2	2	.500	0	0-0	4	1.80
1997 New York	NL	22	0	0	4	27	123	31	17	16	1	2	2	2	15	2	19	0	0	1	2	.333	0	0-0	1	5.33
3 ML YEARS		63	0	0	9	67	302	67	34	32	4	3	5	4	40	3	46	2	0	4	4	.500	0	1-1	6	4.30

Wally Joyner

Bats: Left **Throws:** Left **Pos:** 1B-131; PH-11

Ht: 6'2" **Wt:** 200 **Born:** 6/16/62 **Age:** 36

Year Team	Lg	BATTING															BASERUNNING				PERCENTAGES		
		G	AB	H	2B	3B	HR	(Hm	Rd)	TB	R	RBI	TBB	IBB	SO	HBP	SH	SF	SB	CS	SB%	GDP	Avg	OBP	SLG
1997 Las Vegas *	AAA	3	8	2	0	0	0	—	—	2	0	1	1	0	1	0	0	0	0	0	.00	1	.250	.250	.250
1986 California	AL	154	593	172	27	3	22	(11	11)	271	82	100	57	8	58	2	10	12	5	2	.71	11	.290	.348	.457
1987 California	AL	149	564	161	33	1	34	(19	15)	298	100	117	72	12	64	5	2	10	8	2	.80	14	.285	.366	.528
1988 California	AL	158	597	176	31	2	13	(6	7)	250	81	85	55	14	51	5	0	16	8	2	.80	16	.295	.356	.419

Year Team	Lg	G	AB	H	2B	3B	HR	(Hm	Rd)	TB	R	RBI	TBB	IBB	SO	HBP	SH	SF	SB	CS	SB%	GDP	Avg	OBP	SLG
1989 California	AL	159	593	167	30	2	16	(8	8)	249	78	79	46	7	58	6	1	8	3	2	.60	15	.282	.335	.420
1990 California	AL	83	310	83	15	0	8	(5	3)	122	35	41	41	4	34	1	1	5	2	1	.67	10	.268	.350	.394
1991 California	AL	143	551	166	34	3	21	(10	11)	269	79	96	52	4	66	1	2	5	2	0	1.00	11	.301	.360	.488
1992 Kansas City	AL	149	572	154	36	2	9	(1	8)	221	66	66	55	4	50	4	0	2	11	5	.69	19	.269	.336	.386
1993 Kansas City	AL	141	497	145	36	3	15	(4	11)	232	83	65	66	13	67	3	2	5	5	9	.36	6	.292	.375	.467
1994 Kansas City	AL	97	363	113	20	3	8	(2	6)	163	52	57	47	3	43	0	2	5	3	2	.60	12	.311	.386	.449
1995 Kansas City	AL	131	465	144	28	0	12	(6	6)	208	69	83	69	10	65	2	5	9	3	2	.60	10	.310	.394	.447
1996 San Diego	NL	121	433	120	29	1	8	(5	3)	175	59	65	69	8	71	3	1	4	5	3	.63	6	.277	.377	.404
1997 San Diego	NL	135	455	149	29	2	13	(6	7)	221	59	83	51	5	51	2	0	10	3	5	.38	14	.327	.390	.486
12 ML YEARS		1620	5993	1750	348	22	179	(83	96)	2679	843	937	680	92	678	34	26	81	58	35	.62	144	.292	.363	.447

Mike Judd

Pitches: Right **Bats:** Right **Pos:** RP-1   **Ht:** 6'1" **Wt:** 200 **Born:** 6/30/75 **Age:** 23

Year Team	Lg	G	GS	CG	GF	IP	BFP	H	R	ER	HR	SH	SF	HB	TBB	IBB	SO	WP	Bk	W	L	Pct.	ShO	Sv-Op	Hld	ERA
1995 Yankees	R	21	0	0	18	32.1	123	18	5	4	0	0	0	4	6	0	30	4	0	1	1	.500	0	8- -	-	1.11
Greensboro	A	1	0	0	1	2.2	11	2	0	0	0	0	0	0	0	0	0	0	0	0	0	.000	0	0- -	-	0.00
1996 Greensboro	A	29	0	0	26	28.1	119	22	14	12	2	2	0	2	8	3	36	2	1	2	2	.500	0	10- -	-	3.81
Savannah	A	15	8	1	7	55.1	220	40	21	15	2	2	0	2	15	0	62	9	0	5	0	1.000	0	3- -	-	2.44
1997 Vero Beach	A+	14	14	1	0	86.2	361	67	37	34	4	3	3	1	39	1	104	4	1	6	5	.545	0	0- -	-	3.53
San Antonio	AA	12	12	0	0	79	323	69	27	24	0	0	2	3	33	0	65	8	2	4	2	.667	0	0- -	-	2.73
1997 Los Angeles	NL	1	0	0	0	2.2	11	4	0	0	0	0	0	0	0	0	4	0	0	0	0	.000	0	0-0	0	0.00

Jeff Juden

Pitches: Right **Bats:** Both **Pos:** SP-27; RP-3   **Ht:** 6'8" **Wt:** 265 **Born:** 1/19/71 **Age:** 27

Year Team	Lg	G	GS	CG	GF	IP	BFP	H	R	ER	HR	SH	SF	HB	TBB	IBB	SO	WP	Bk	W	L	Pct.	ShO	Sv-Op	Hld	ERA
1991 Houston	NL	4	3	0	0	18	81	19	14	12	3	2	3	0	7	1	11	0	1	0	2	.000	0	0-0		6.00
1993 Houston	NL	2	0	0	1	5	23	4	3	3	1	0	1	0	4	1	7	0	0	0	1	.000	0	0-0		5.40
1994 Philadelphia	NL	6	5	0	0	27.2	121	29	25	19	4	1	2	1	12	0	22	0	2	1	4	.200	0	0-0		6.18
1995 Philadelphia	NL	13	10	1	0	62.2	271	53	31	28	6	5	4	5	31	0	47	4	1	2	4	.333	0	0-0		4.02
1996 SF-Mon	NL	58	0	0	16	74.1	318	61	35	27	8	3	3	4	34	2	61	5	0	5	0	1.000	0	0-0	3	3.27
1997 Mon-Cle		30	27	3	0	161.1	706	157	85	80	23	7	6	10	72	2	136	8	1	11	6	.647	0	0-0		4.46
1996 San Francisco	NL	36	0	0	9	41.2	180	39	23	19	7	1	2	1	20	2	35	3	0	4	0	1.000	0	0-0	3	4.10
Montreal	NL	22	0	0	7	32.2	138	22	12	8	1	2	1	4	14	0	26	2	0	1	0	1.000	0	0-0		2.20
1997 Montreal	NL	22	22	3	0	130	565	125	64	61	17	5	4	9	57	2	107	7	1	11	5	.688	0	0-0		4.22
Cleveland	AL	8	5	0	0	31.1	141	32	21	19	6	2	2	1	15	0	29	1	0	0	1	.000	0	0-0		5.46
6 ML YEARS		113	45	4	17	349	1520	323	193	169	45	18	19	21	160	6	284	17	5	19	17	.528	0	0-0	3	4.36

David Justice

Bats: L **Throws:** L **Pos:** LF-74; DH-61; RF-5; PH-4   **Ht:** 6'3" **Wt:** 200 **Born:** 4/14/66 **Age:** 32

Year Team	Lg	G	AB	H	2B	3B	HR	(Hm	Rd)	TB	R	RBI	TBB	IBB	SO	HBP	SH	SF	SB	CS	SB%	GDP	Avg	OBP	SLG
1989 Atlanta	NL	16	51	12	3	0	1	(1	0)	18	7	3	3	1	9	1	1	0	2	1	.67	1	.235	.291	.353
1990 Atlanta	NL	127	439	124	23	2	28	(19	9)	235	76	78	64	4	92	0	0	1	11	6	.65	2	.282	.373	.535
1991 Atlanta	NL	109	396	109	25	1	21	(11	10)	199	67	87	65	9	81	3	0	5	8	8	.50	4	.275	.377	.503
1992 Atlanta	NL	144	484	124	19	5	21	(10	11)	216	78	72	79	8	85	2	0	6	2	4	.33	1	.256	.359	.446
1993 Atlanta	NL	157	585	158	15	4	40	(18	22)	301	90	120	78	12	90	3	0	4	3	5	.38	9	.270	.357	.515
1994 Atlanta	NL	104	352	110	16	2	19	(9	10)	187	61	59	69	5	45	2	0	1	2	4	.33	8	.313	.427	.531
1995 Atlanta	NL	120	411	104	17	2	24	(15	9)	197	73	78	73	5	68	2	0	5	4	2	.67	5	.253	.365	.479
1996 Atlanta	NL	40	140	45	9	0	6	(5	1)	72	23	25	21	1	22	1	0	2	1	1	.50	5	.321	.409	.514
1997 Cleveland	AL	139	495	163	31	1	33	(17	16)	295	84	101	80	11	79	0	0	7	3	5	.38	12	.329	.418	.596
9 ML YEARS		956	3353	949	158	17	193	(105	88)	1720	559	623	532	56	571	14	1	31	36	36	.50	47	.283	.380	.513

Scott Kamieniecki

Pitches: Right **Bats:** Right **Pos:** SP-30   **Ht:** 6'0" **Wt:** 195 **Born:** 4/19/64 **Age:** 34

Year Team	Lg	G	GS	CG	GF	IP	BFP	H	R	ER	HR	SH	SF	HB	TBB	IBB	SO	WP	Bk	W	L	Pct.	ShO	Sv-Op	Hld	ERA
1991 New York	AL	9	9	0	0	55.1	239	54	24	24	8	2	1	3	22	1	34	1	0	4	4	.500	0	0-0	0	3.90
1992 New York	AL	28	28	4	0	188	804	193	100	91	13	3	5	5	74	9	88	9	1	6	14	.300	0	0-0	0	4.36
1993 New York	AL	30	20	2	4	154.1	659	163	73	70	17	3	5	3	59	7	72	2	0	10	7	.588	0	1-1	0	4.08
1994 New York	AL	22	16	1	2	117.1	509	115	53	49	13	4	3	3	59	5	71	4	0	8	6	.571	0	0-0	1	3.76
1995 New York	AL	17	16	1	1	89.2	391	83	43	40	8	1	0	3	49	1	43	4	0	7	6	.538	0	0-0	0	4.01
1996 New York	AL	7	5	0	0	22.2	120	36	30	28	6	0	0	2	19	1	15	1	0	1	2	.333	0	0-1	0	11.12
1997 Baltimore	AL	30	30	0	0	179.1	764	179	83	80	20	1	6	4	67	2	109	5	0	10	6	.625	0	0-0	0	4.01
7 ML YEARS		143	124	8	7	806.2	3486	823	406	382	85	14	20	23	349	26	432	26	1	46	45	.505	0	1-2	1	4.26

Matt Karchner

Pitches: Right **Bats:** Right **Pos:** RP-52   **Ht:** 6'4" **Wt:** 210 **Born:** 6/28/67 **Age:** 31

Year Team	Lg	G	GS	CG	GF	IP	BFP	H	R	ER	HR	SH	SF	HB	TBB	IBB	SO	WP	Bk	W	L	Pct.	ShO	Sv-Op	Hld	ERA
1997 Nashville *	AAA	13	0	0	8	18.2	78	12	5	4	1	2	1	1	6	0	11	1	0	2	1	.667	0	3- -	—	1.93

			HOW MUCH HE PITCHED					WHAT HE GAVE UP												THE RESULTS						
Year Team	Lg	G	GS	CG	GF	IP	BFP	H	R	ER	HR	SH	SF	HB	TBB	IBB	SO	WP	Bk	W	L	Pct.	ShO	Sv-Op	Hld	ERA
1995 Chicago	AL	31	0	0	10	32	137	33	8	6	2	0	4	1	12	2	24	1	0	4	2	.667	0	0-0	13	1.69
1996 Chicago	AL	50	0	0	13	59.1	278	61	42	38	10	2	4	2	41	8	46	4	0	7	4	.636	0	1-9	13	5.76
1997 Chicago	AL	52	0	0	25	52.2	224	50	18	17	4	3	1	0	26	4	30	6	0	3	1	.750	0	15-16	12	2.91
3 ML YEARS		133	0	0	48	144	639	144	68	61	16	5	9	3	79	14	100	11	0	14	7	.667	0	16-25	38	3.81

Ron Karkovice

Bats: Right **Throws:** Right **Pos:** C-51   Ht: 6'1" **Wt:** 219 **Born:** 8/8/63 **Age:** 34

							BATTING												BASERUNNING			PERCENTAGES		
Year Team	Lg	G	AB	H	2B	3B	HR	(Hm	Rd)	TB	R	RBI	TBB	IBB	SO	HBP	SH	SF	SB	CS	SB%	GDP	Avg	OBP	SLG
1986 Chicago	AL	37	97	24	7	0	4	(1	3)	43	13	13	9	0	37	1	1	1	1	0	1.00	3	.247	.315	.443
1987 Chicago	AL	39	85	6	0	0	2	(1	1)	12	7	7	7	0	40	2	1	0	3	0	1.00	2	.071	.160	.141
1988 Chicago	AL	46	115	20	4	0	3	(1	2)	33	10	9	7	0	30	1	3	0	4	2	.67	1	.174	.228	.287
1989 Chicago	AL	71	182	48	9	2	3	(0	3)	70	21	24	10	0	56	2	7	2	0	0	.00	0	.264	.306	.385
1990 Chicago	AL	68	183	45	10	0	6	(0	6)	73	30	20	16	1	52	1	7	1	2	0	1.00	1	.246	.308	.399
1991 Chicago	AL	75	167	41	13	0	5	(0	5)	69	25	22	15	1	42	1	9	1	0	0	.00	2	.246	.310	.413
1992 Chicago	AL	123	342	81	12	1	13	(5	8)	134	39	50	30	1	89	3	4	2	10	4	.71	3	.237	.302	.392
1993 Chicago	AL	128	403	92	17	1	20	(6	14)	171	60	54	29	1	126	6	11	4	2	2	.50	12	.228	.287	.424
1994 Chicago	AL	77	207	44	9	1	11	(6	5)	88	33	29	36	2	68	0	2	3	0	3	.00	0	.213	.325	.425
1995 Chicago	AL	113	323	70	14	1	13	(5	8)	125	44	51	39	0	84	5	9	6	2	3	.40	5	.217	.306	.387
1996 Chicago	AL	111	355	78	22	0	10	(5	5)	130	44	38	24	2	93	1	7	2	0	0	.00	7	.220	.270	.366
1997 Chicago	AL	51	138	25	3	0	6	(4	2)	46	10	18	11	0	32	3	4	5	0	0	.00	3	.181	.248	.333
12 ML YEARS		939	2597	574	120	6	96	(34	62)	994	336	335	233	8	749	26	65	27	24	14	.63	39	.221	.289	.383

Scott Karl

Pitches: Left **Bats:** Left **Pos:** SP-32   Ht: 6'2" **Wt:** 195 **Born:** 8/9/71 **Age:** 26

				HOW MUCH HE PITCHED					WHAT HE GAVE UP												THE RESULTS						
Year Team	Lg	G	GS	CG	GF	IP	BFP	H	R	ER	HR	SH	SF	HB	TBB	IBB	SO	WP	Bk	W	L	Pct.	ShO	Sv-Op	Hld	ERA
1995 Milwaukee	AL	25	18	1	3	124	548	141	65	57	10	3	3	3	50	6	59	0	0	6	7	.462	1	0-0	1	4.14
1996 Milwaukee	AL	32	32	3	0	207.1	905	220	124	112	29	2	7	11	72	0	121	5	1	13	9	.591	1	0-0	0	4.86
1997 Milwaukee	AL	32	32	1	0	193.1	839	212	103	96	23	5	2	4	67	1	119	6	0	10	13	.435	0	0-0	0	4.47
3 ML YEARS		89	82	5	3	524.2	2292	573	292	265	62	10	12	18	189	7	299	11	1	29	29	.500	1	0-0	1	4.55

Ryan Karp

Pitches: Left **Bats:** Left **Pos:** RP-14; SP-1   Ht: 6'4" **Wt:** 214 **Born:** 4/5/70 **Age:** 28

				HOW MUCH HE PITCHED					WHAT HE GAVE UP												THE RESULTS						
Year Team	Lg	G	GS	CG	GF	IP	BFP	H	R	ER	HR	SH	SF	HB	TBB	IBB	SO	WP	Bk	W	L	Pct.	ShO	Sv-Op	Hld	ERA
1992 Oneonta	A-	14	13	1	0	70.1	300	66	38	32	2	1	1	3	30	0	58	2	0	6	4	.600	1	0- -	—	4.09
1993 Greensboro	A	17	17	0	0	109.1	436	73	26	22	2	0	2	2	40	0	132	6	1	13	1	.929	0	0- -	—	1.81
Pr William	A+	8	8	1	0	49	189	35	17	12	4	2	2	2	12	0	34	5	1	3	2	.600	0	0- -	—	2.20
Albany-Colo	AA	3	3	0	0	13	60	13	7	6	1	0	1	0	9	0	10	1	0	0	0	.000	0	0- -	—	4.15
1994 Reading	AA	21	21	0	0	121.1	528	123	67	60	12	0	4	3	54	3	96	4	0	4	11	.267	0	0- -	—	4.45
1995 Reading	AA	7	7	0	0	47	190	44	18	16	4	3	0	0	15	0	37	1	2	1	2	.333	0	0- -	—	3.06
Scranton-WB	AAA	13	13	0	0	81.1	357	81	43	38	6	2	2	4	31	0	73	2	0	7	1	.875	0	0- -	—	4.20
1996 Scranton-WB	AAA	7	7	0	0	41	168	35	14	14	1	1	0	0	14	1	30	3	0	1	1	.500	0	0- -	—	3.07
1997 Scranton-WB	AAA	32	5	0	6	73	326	72	35	34	9	4	1	2	42	6	55	5	0	4	3	.571	0	1- -	—	4.19
1995 Philadelphia	NL	1	0	0	0	2	10	1	1	1	0	0	0	0	3	0	2	1	0	0	0	.000	0	0-0	0	4.50
1997 Philadelphia	NL	15	1	0	1	15	67	12	12	9	2	1	0	2	9	0	18	1	0	1	1	.500	0	0-1	5	5.40
2 ML YEARS		16	1	0	1	17	77	13	13	10	2	1	0	2	12	0	20	2	0	1	1	.500	0	0-1	5	5.29

Eric Karros

Bats: Right **Throws:** Right **Pos:** 1B-162   Ht: 6'4" **Wt:** 222 **Born:** 11/4/67 **Age:** 30

							BATTING												BASERUNNING			PERCENTAGES		
Year Team	Lg	G	AB	H	2B	3B	HR	(Hm	Rd)	TB	R	RBI	TBB	IBB	SO	HBP	SH	SF	SB	CS	SB%	GDP	Avg	OBP	SLG
1991 Los Angeles	NL	14	14	1	0	0	0	(0	0)	2	0	1	1	0	6	0	0	0	0	0	.00	0	.071	.133	.143
1992 Los Angeles	NL	149	545	140	30	1	20	(6	14)	232	63	88	37	3	103	2	0	5	2	4	.33	15	.257	.304	.426
1993 Los Angeles	NL	158	619	153	27	2	23	(13	10)	253	74	80	34	1	82	2	0	3	0	1	.00	17	.247	.287	.409
1994 Los Angeles	NL	111	406	108	21	1	14	(5	9)	173	51	46	29	1	53	0	2	11	2	0	1.00	13	.266	.310	.426
1995 Los Angeles	NL	143	551	164	29	3	32	(19	13)	295	83	105	61	4	115	4	0	4	4	4	.50	14	.298	.369	.535
1996 Los Angeles	NL	154	608	158	29	1	34	(16	18)	291	84	111	53	2	121	1	0	8	8	0	1.00	27	.260	.316	.479
1997 Los Angeles	NL	162	628	167	28	0	31	(13	18)	288	86	104	61	2	116	2	0	9	15	7	.68	10	.266	.329	.459
7 ML YEARS		891	3371	891	165	8	154	(72	82)	1534	441	535	276	13	596	13	0	40	31	16	.66	96	.264	.319	.455

Steve Karsay

Pitches: Right **Bats:** Right **Pos:** SP-24   Ht: 6'3" **Wt:** 205 **Born:** 3/24/72 **Age:** 26

				HOW MUCH HE PITCHED					WHAT HE GAVE UP												THE RESULTS						
Year Team	Lg	G	GS	CG	GF	IP	BFP	H	R	ER	HR	SH	SF	HB	TBB	IBB	SO	WP	Bk	W	L	Pct.	ShO	Sv-Op	Hld	ERA
1993 Oakland	AL	8	8	0	0	49	210	49	23	22	4	2	2	.16	1	33	1	0	3	3	.500	0	0-0	0	4.04
1994 Oakland	AL	4	4	1	0	28	115	26	8	8	1	2	1	1	8	0	15	0	0	1	1	.500	0	0-0	0	2.57
1997 Oakland	AL	24	24	0	0	132.2	609	166	92	85	20	2	5	9	47	3	92	7	0	3	12	.200	0	0-0	0	5.77
3 ML YEARS		36	36	1	0	209.2	934	241	123	115	25	4	8	12	71	4	140	8	0	7	16	.304	0	0-0	0	4.94

111

Takashi Kashiwada

Pitches: Left Bats: Left Pos: RP-35 Ht: 5'11" Wt: 165 Born: 5/14/71 Age: 27

Year Team	Lg	G	GS	CG	GF	IP	BFP	H	R	ER	HR	SH	SF	HB	TBB	IBB	SO	WP	Bk	W	L	Pct.	ShO	Sv-Op	Hld	ERA
1997 Norfolk	AAA	14	0	0	7	13.1	58	11	9	7	0	4	1	2	5	0	12	1	1	0	1	.000	0	0- -	—	4.73
1997 New York	NL	35	0	0	11	31.1	145	35	15	15	4	1	2	3	18	0	19	4	0	3	1	.750	0	0-2	3	4.31

Greg Keagle

Pitches: Right Bats: Right Pos: SP-10; RP-1 Ht: 6'2" Wt: 195 Born: 6/28/71 Age: 27

Year Team	Lg	G	GS	CG	GF	IP	BFP	H	R	ER	HR	SH	SF	HB	TBB	IBB	SO	WP	Bk	W	L	Pct.	ShO	Sv-Op	Hld	ERA
1993 Spokane	A-	15	15	1	0	83	368	80	37	30	2	4	4	7	40	2	77	4	4	3	3	.500	0	0- -	—	3.25
1994 Rancho Cuca	A+	14	14	1	0	92	377	62	23	21	2	1	3	5	41	1	91	1	0	11	1	.917	1	0- -	—	2.05
Wichita	AA	13	13	0	0	70.1	321	84	53	49	5	5	2	2	32	1	57	3	1	3	9	.250	0	0- -	—	6.27
1995 Memphis	AA	15	15	1	0	81	365	82	52	46	11	1	3	6	41	2	82	8	3	4	9	.308	0	0- -	—	5.11
Rancho Cuca	A+	2	2	0	0	14	59	14	9	7	1	0	1	2	2	0	11	1	0	0	0	.000	0	0- -	—	4.50
Las Vegas	AAA	14	13	0	1	75.2	351	76	47	36	3	6	5	6	42	2	49	2	0	7	6	.538	0	0- -	—	4.28
1996 Toledo	AAA	6	6	0	0	27	135	42	32	30	7	1	2	4	11	0	24	0	1	2	3	.400	0	0- -	—	10.00
1997 Toledo	AAA	23	23	3	0	151.1	645	136	68	64	8	4	2	10	61	0	140	4	1	11	7	.611	1	0- -	—	3.81
1996 Detroit	AL	26	6	0	5	87.2	435	104	76	72	13	2	7	9	68	5	70	2	0	3	6	.333	0	0-0	—	7.39
1997 Detroit	AL	11	10	0	0	45.1	214	58	33	33	9	2	1	5	18	0	33	1	0	3	5	.375	0	0-0	—	6.55
2 ML YEARS		37	16	0	5	133	649	162	109	105	22	4	8	14	86	5	103	3	0	6	11	.353	0	0-0	0	7.11

Mike Kelly

Bats: R Throws: R Pos: PH-36; RF-31; LF-17; CF-11 Ht: 6'4" Wt: 195 Born: 6/2/70 Age: 28

Year Team	Lg	G	AB	H	2B	3B	HR	(Hm	Rd)	TB	R	RBI	TBB	IBB	SO	HBP	SH	SF	SB	CS	SB%	GDP	Avg	OBP	SLG
1997 Chattanooga *	AA	15	60	21	7	0	3	—	—	37	14	12	3	0	16	0	0	1	3	2	.60	0	.350	.375	.617
Indianapolis *	AAA	27	92	32	8	0	7	—	—	61	28	18	23	2	23	0	0	0	7	1	.88	0	.348	.478	.663
1994 Atlanta	NL	30	77	21	10	1	2	(0	2)	39	14	9	2	0	17	1	0	0	0	1	.00	1	.273	.300	.506
1995 Atlanta	NL	97	137	26	6	1	3	(0	3)	43	26	17	11	0	49	2	2	1	7	3	.70	2	.190	.258	.314
1996 Cincinnati	NL	19	49	9	4	0	1	(0	1)	16	5	7	9	0	11	2	0	0	4	0	1.00	0	.184	.333	.327
1997 Cincinnati	NL	73	140	41	13	2	6	(3	3)	76	27	19	10	0	30	0	0	1	6	1	.86	3	.293	.338	.543
4 ML YEARS		219	403	97	33	4	12	(3	9)	174	72	52	32	0	107	5	2	2	17	5	.77	8	.241	.303	.432

Pat Kelly

Bats: Right Throws: Right Pos: 2B-48; PH-31; DH-16 Ht: 6'0" Wt: 182 Born: 10/14/67 Age: 30

Year Team	Lg	G	AB	H	2B	3B	HR	(Hm	Rd)	TB	R	RBI	TBB	IBB	SO	HBP	SH	SF	SB	CS	SB%	GDP	Avg	OBP	SLG
1997 Columbus *	AAA	11	44	15	4	0	2	—	—	25	8	6	4	1	6	0	0	0	1	1	.50	1	.341	.396	.568
1991 New York	AL	96	298	72	12	4	3	(3	0)	101	35	23	15	0	52	5	2	2	12	1	.92	5	.242	.288	.339
1992 New York	AL	106	318	72	22	2	7	(3	4)	119	38	27	25	1	72	10	6	3	8	5	.62	6	.226	.301	.374
1993 New York	AL	127	406	111	24	1	7	(4	3)	158	49	51	24	0	68	5	10	6	14	11	.56	9	.273	.317	.389
1994 New York	AL	93	286	80	21	2	3	(1	2)	114	35	41	19	1	51	5	14	5	6	5	.55	10	.280	.330	.399
1995 New York	AL	89	270	64	12	1	4	(1	3)	90	32	29	23	0	65	5	10	2	8	3	.73	5	.237	.307	.333
1996 New York	AL	13	21	3	0	0	0	(0	0)	3	4	2	2	0	9	0	0	0	0	1	.00	1	.143	.217	.143
1997 New York	AL	67	120	29	6	1	2	(1	1)	43	25	10	14	1	37	1	2	1	8	1	.89	4	.242	.324	.358
7 ML YEARS		591	1719	431	97	11	26	(13	13)	628	218	183	122	3	354	31	44	19	56	27	.67	40	.251	.309	.365

Roberto Kelly

Bats: R Throws: R Pos: RF-57; LF-29; PH-17; DH-13; CF-2 Ht: 6'2" Wt: 202 Born: 10/1/64 Age: 33

Year Team	Lg	G	AB	H	2B	3B	HR	(Hm	Rd)	TB	R	RBI	TBB	IBB	SO	HBP	SH	SF	SB	CS	SB%	GDP	Avg	OBP	SLG
1997 Ft. Myers *	A+	4	11	4	0	0	1	—	—	7	2	3	4	0	1	0	0	0	0	0	.00	0	.364	.533	.636
1987 New York	AL	23	52	14	3	0	1	(0	1)	20	12	7	5	0	15	0	1	1	9	3	.75	0	.269	.328	.385
1988 New York	AL	38	77	19	4	1	1	(1	0)	28	9	7	3	0	15	0	3	1	5	2	.71	0	.247	.272	.364
1989 New York	AL	137	441	133	18	3	9	(2	7)	184	65	48	41	3	89	6	8	0	35	12	.74	9	.302	.369	.417
1990 New York	AL	162	641	183	32	4	15	(5	10)	268	85	61	33	0	148	4	4	4	42	17	.71	7	.285	.323	.418
1991 New York	AL	126	486	130	22	2	20	(11	9)	216	68	69	45	2	77	5	2	5	32	9	.78	14	.267	.333	.444
1992 New York	AL	152	580	158	31	2	10	(6	4)	223	81	66	41	4	96	4	1	6	28	5	.85	19	.272	.322	.384
1993 Cincinnati	NL	78	320	102	17	3	9	(4	5)	152	44	35	17	0	43	2	0	3	21	5	.81	10	.319	.354	.475
1994 Cin-Atl	NL	110	434	127	23	3	9	(4	5)	183	73	45	35	1	71	3	0	3	19	11	.63	8	.293	.347	.422
1995 Mon-LA	NL	136	504	140	23	2	7	(2	5)	188	58	57	22	6	79	6	0	7	19	10	.66	14	.278	.312	.373
1996 Minnesota	AL	98	322	104	17	4	6	(3	3)	147	41	47	23	0	53	7	0	5	10	2	.83	17	.323	.375	.457
1997 Min-Sea	AL	105	368	107	26	2	12	(8	4)	173	58	59	22	0	67	3	2	3	9	5	.64	6	.291	.333	.470
1994 Cincinnati	NL	47	179	54	8	0	3	(1	2)	71	29	21	11	1	35	0	0	1	9	8	.53	3	.302	.351	.397
Atlanta	NL	63	255	73	15	3	6	(3	3)	112	44	24	24	0	36	0	0	2	10	3	.77	5	.286	.345	.439
1995 Mon-LA	NL	24	95	26	4	0	1	(0	1)	33	11	9	7	1	14	2	0	0	4	3	.57	4	.274	.337	.347
Los Angeles	NL	112	409	114	19	2	6	(2	4)	155	47	48	15	5	65	4	0	7	15	7	.68	10	.279	.306	.379
1997 Minnesota	AL	75	247	71	19	2	5	(5	0)	109	39	37	17	0	50	2	1	2	7	4	.64	4	.287	.336	.441
Seattle	AL	30	121	36	7	0	7	(3	4)	64	19	22	5	0	17	1	1	1	2	1	.67	2	.298	.328	.529
11 ML YEARS		1165	4225	1217	216	26	99	(46	53)	1782	594	501	287	16	753	40	21	38	229	81	.74	104	.288	.336	.422

112

Jason Kendall

Bats: Right **Throws:** Right **Pos:** C-142; PH-2 **Ht:** 6'0" **Wt:** 181 **Born:** 6/26/74 **Age:** 24

								BATTING												BASERUNNING				PERCENTAGES		
Year Team	Lg	G	AB	H	2B	3B	HR	(Hm	Rd)	TB	R	RBI	TBB	IBB	SO	HBP	SH	SF		SB	CS	SB%	GDP	Avg	OBP	SLG
1992 Pirates	R	33	111	29	2	0	0	—	—	31	7	10	8	1	9	2	0	2		2	2	.50	3	.261	.317	.279
1993 Augusta	A	102	366	101	17	4	1	—	—	129	43	40	22	1	30	7	0	5		8	5	.62	17	.276	.325	.352
1994 Salem	A+	101	371	118	19	2	7	—	—	162	68	66	47	1	21	13	0	7		14	3	.82	15	.318	.406	.437
Carolina	AA	13	47	11	2	0	0	—	—	13	6	6	2	0	3	2	0	0		0	0	.00	0	.234	.294	.277
1995 Carolina	AA	117	429	140	26	1	8	—	—	192	87	71	56	5	22	14	1	8		10	7	.59	10	.326	.414	.448
1996 Pittsburgh	NL	130	414	124	23	5	3	(2	1)	166	54	42	35	11	30	15	3	4		5	2	.71	7	.300	.372	.401
1997 Pittsburgh	NL	144	486	143	36	4	8	(5	3)	211	71	49	49	2	53	31	1	5		18	6	.75	11	.294	.391	.434
2 ML YEARS		274	900	267	59	9	11	(7	4)	377	125	91	84	13	83	46	4	9		23	8	.74	18	.297	.382	.419

Jeff Kent

Bats: Right **Throws:** Right **Pos:** 2B-148; 1B-13; PH-2 **Ht:** 6'1" **Wt:** 185 **Born:** 3/7/68 **Age:** 30

								BATTING												BASERUNNING				PERCENTAGES		
Year Team	Lg	G	AB	H	2B	3B	HR	(Hm	Rd)	TB	R	RBI	TBB	IBB	SO	HBP	SH	SF		SB	CS	SB%	GDP	Avg	OBP	SLG
1992 Tor-NYN		102	305	73	21	2	11	(4	7)	131	52	50	27	0	76	7	0	4		2	3	.40	5	.239	.312	.430
1993 New York	NL	140	496	134	24	0	21	(9	12)	221	65	80	30	2	88	8	6	4		4	4	.50	11	.270	.320	.446
1994 New York	NL	107	415	121	24	5	14	(10	4)	197	53	68	23	3	84	10	1	3		1	4	.20	7	.292	.341	.475
1995 New York	NL	125	472	131	22	3	20	(11	9)	219	65	65	29	3	89	8	1	4		3	3	.50	9	.278	.327	.464
1996 NYN-Cle		128	437	124	27	1	12	(4	8)	189	61	55	31	1	78	2	1	6		6	4	.60	8	.284	.330	.432
1997 San Francisco	NL	155	580	145	38	2	29	(13	16)	274	90	121	48	6	133	13	0	10		11	3	.79	14	.250	.316	.472
1992 Toronto	AL	65	192	46	13	1	8	(2	6)	85	36	35	20	0	47	6	0	4		2	1	.67	3	.240	.324	.443
New York	NL	37	113	27	8	1	3	(2	1)	46	16	15	7	0	29	1	0	0		0	2	.00	2	.239	.289	.407
1996 New York	NL	89	335	97	20	1	9	(2	7)	146	45	39	21	1	56	1	1	3		4	3	.57	7	.290	.331	.436
Cleveland	AL	39	102	27	7	0	3	(2	1)	43	16	16	10	0	22	1	0	3		2	1	.67	1	.265	.328	.422
6 ML YEARS		757	2705	728	156	13	107	(51	56)	1231	386	439	188	15	548	48	9	31		27	21	.56	54	.269	.324	.455

Jimmy Key

Pitches: Left **Bats:** Right **Pos:** SP-34 **Ht:** 6'1" **Wt:** 185 **Born:** 4/22/61 **Age:** 37

		HOW MUCH HE PITCHED						WHAT HE GAVE UP										THE RESULTS						
Year Team	Lg	G	GS	CG	GF	IP	BFP	H	R	ER	HR	SH	SF	HB	TBB	IBB	SO	WP	Bk	W	L	Pct.	ShO	Sv-Op Hld	ERA
1984 Toronto	AL	63	0	0	24	62	285	70	37	32	8	6	1	1	32	8	44	3	1	4	5	.444	0	10- —	4.65
1985 Toronto	AL	35	32	3	0	212.2	856	188	77	71	22	5	5	2	50	1	85	6	1	14	6	.700	0	0- —	3.00
1986 Toronto	AL	36	35	4	0	232	959	222	98	92	24	10	6	3	74	1	141	3	0	14	11	.560	2	0- —	3.57
1987 Toronto	AL	36	36	8	0	261	1033	210	93	80	24	11	3	2	66	6	161	8	5	17	8	.680	1	0-0 0	2.76
1988 Toronto	AL	21	21	2	0	131.1	551	127	55	48	13	4	3	5	30	2	65	1	0	12	5	.706	2	0-0 0	3.29
1989 Toronto	AL	33	33	5	0	216	886	226	99	93	18	9	9	3	27	2	118	4	1	13	14	.481	1	0-0 0	3.88
1990 Toronto	AL	27	27	0	0	154.2	636	169	79	73	20	5	6	1	22	2	88	0	1	13	7	.650	0	0-0 0	4.25
1991 Toronto	AL	33	33	2	0	209.1	877	207	84	71	12	10	5	3	44	3	125	1	0	16	12	.571	2	0-0 0	3.05
1992 Toronto	AL	33	33	4	0	216.2	900	205	88	85	24	2	7	4	59	0	117	5	0	13	13	.500	2	0-0 0	3.53
1993 New York	AL	34	34	4	0	236.2	948	219	84	79	26	6	9	1	43	1	173	3	0	18	6	.750	2	0-0 0	3.00
1994 New York	AL	25	25	1	0	168	710	177	68	61	10	4	2	3	52	0	97	8	1	17	4	.810	0	0-0 0	3.27
1995 New York	AL	5	5	0	0	30.1	134	40	20	19	3	3	1	0	6	1	14	1	0	1	2	.333	0	0-0 0	5.64
1996 New York	AL	30	30	0	0	169.1	715	171	93	88	21	7	5	2	58	1	116	2	0	12	11	.522	0	0-0 0	4.68
1997 Baltimore	AL	34	34	1	0	212.1	902	210	90	81	24	5	6	5	82	1	141	4	1	16	10	.615	1	0-0 0	3.43
14 ML YEARS		445	378	34	24	2512.1	10392	2441	1065	973	249	87	68	35	645	29	1485	49	11	180	114	.612	13	10- —	3.49

Brooks Kieschnick

Bats: Left **Throws:** Right **Pos:** LF-26; PH-12; RF-1 **Ht:** 6'4" **Wt:** 225 **Born:** 6/6/72 **Age:** 26

								BATTING												BASERUNNING				PERCENTAGES		
Year Team	Lg	G	AB	H	2B	3B	HR	(Hm	Rd)	TB	R	RBI	TBB	IBB	SO	HBP	SH	SF		SB	CS	SB%	GDP	Avg	OBP	SLG
1993 Cubs	R	3	9	2	1	0	0	—	—	3	0	0	0	0	1	0	0	0		0	0	.00	0	.222	.222	.333
Daytona	A+	6	22	4	2	0	0	—	—	6	1	2	1	0	4	0	0	0		0	1	.00	1	.182	.217	.273
Orlando	AA	25	91	31	6	0	2	—	—	45	12	10	7	1	19	0	0	0		1	2	.33	0	.341	.388	.495
1994 Orlando	AA	126	468	132	25	3	14	—	—	205	57	55	33	3	78	4	0	4		3	5	.38	10	.282	.332	.438
1995 Iowa	AAA	138	505	149	30	1	23	—	—	250	61	73	58	7	91	4	0	3		2	3	.40	11	.295	.370	.495
1996 Iowa	AAA	117	441	114	20	1	18	—	—	190	47	64	37	4	108	0	0	2		0	1	.00	8	.259	.315	.431
1997 Iowa	AAA	97	360	93	21	0	21	—	—	177	57	66	36	4	89	1	0	5		0	2	.00	6	.258	.323	.492
1996 Chicago	NL	25	29	10	2	0	1	(0	1)	15	6	6	3	0	8	0	0	0		0	0	.00	0	.345	.406	.517
1997 Chicago	NL	39	90	18	2	0	4	(3	1)	32	9	12	12	0	21	0	0	0		1	0	1.00	2	.200	.294	.356
2 ML YEARS		64	119	28	4	0	5	(3	2)	47	15	18	15	0	29	0	0	0		1	0	1.00	2	.235	.321	.395

Darryl Kile

Pitches: Right **Bats:** Right **Pos:** SP-34 **Ht:** 6'5" **Wt:** 185 **Born:** 12/2/68 **Age:** 29

		HOW MUCH HE PITCHED						WHAT HE GAVE UP										THE RESULTS						
Year Team	Lg	G	GS	CG	GF	IP	BFP	H	R	ER	HR	SH	SF	HB	TBB	IBB	SO	WP	Bk	W	L	Pct.	ShO	Sv-Op Hld	ERA
1991 Houston	NL	37	22	0	5	153.2	689	144	81	63	16	9	5	6	84	4	100	5	4	7	11	.389	0	0-1 0	3.69
1992 Houston	NL	22	22	2	0	125.1	554	124	61	55	8	5	6	4	63	4	90	3	4	5	10	.333	0	0-0 0	3.95
1993 Houston	NL	32	26	4	0	171.2	733	152	73	67	12	5	7	15	69	1	141	9	3	15	8	.652	2	0-0 0	3.51
1994 Houston	NL	24	24	0	0	147.2	664	153	84	75	13	14	2	9	82	6	105	10	0	9	6	.600	0	0-0 0	4.57
1995 Houston	NL	25	21	0	1	127	570	114	81	70	5	7	3	12	73	2	113	11	1	4	12	.250	0	0-0 0	4.96
1996 Houston	NL	35	33	4	1	219	975	233	113	102	16	10	9	16	97	8	219	13	3	12	11	.522	0	0-0 0	4.19
1997 Houston	NL	34	34	6	0	255.2	1056	208	87	73	19	17	10	10	94	2	205	7	1	19	7	.731	4	0-0 0	2.57

Year Team	Lg	G	GS	CG	GF	IP	BFP	H	R	ER	HR	SH	SF	HB	TBB	IBB	SO	WP	Bk	W	L	Pct.	ShO	Sv-Op	Hld	ERA
		HOW MUCH HE PITCHED						WHAT HE GAVE UP										THE RESULTS					
7 ML YEARS		209	182	16	7	1200	5241	1128	580	505	89	67	42	72	562	27	973	58	16	71	65	.522	6	0-1	0	3.79

Curtis King

Pitches: Right **Bats:** Right **Pos:** RP-30 **Ht:** 6'5" **Wt:** 205 **Born:** 10/25/70 **Age:** 27

Year Team	Lg	G	GS	CG	GF	IP	BFP	H	R	ER	HR	SH	SF	HB	TBB	IBB	SO	WP	Bk	W	L	Pct.	ShO	Sv-Op	Hld	ERA
1994 New Jersey	A-	5	4	0	0	20.2	92	19	7	6	0	1	0	1	11	0	14	2	1	1	0	1.000	0	0- --	--	2.61
Savannah	A	8	8	2	0	53	202	37	14	11	4	2	1	4	9	0	40	1	0	4	1	.800	2	0- --	--	1.87
1995 St. Pete	A+	28	21	3	1	136	567	117	49	39	3	4	2	11	49	2	65	6	0	7	8	.467	0	0- --	--	2.58
1996 Arkansas	AA	5	0	0	3	5	37	15	12	11	1	0	0	0	6	1	5	0	0	0	1	.000	0	1- --	--	19.80
St. Pete	A+	48	0	0	46	55.2	232	41	20	17	0	5	2	5	24	4	27	2	0	3	3	.500	0	30- --	--	2.75
1997 Arkansas	AA	32	0	0	27	36.1	154	38	19	18	7	2	0	1	10	1	29	1	0	2	3	.400	0	16- --	--	4.46
Louisville	AAA	16	0	0	9	22	89	19	5	5	1	5	0	0	6	1	9	0	0	2	1	.667	0	3- --	--	2.05
1997 St. Louis	NL	30	0	0	8	29.1	136	38	14	9	0	4	3	1	11	0	13	2	0	4	2	.667	0	0-3	10	2.76

Jeff King

Bats: Right **Throws:** Right **Pos:** 1B-150; PH-5; DH-2 **Ht:** 6'1" **Wt:** 184 **Born:** 12/26/64 **Age:** 33

Year Team	Lg	G	AB	H	2B	3B	HR	(Hm	Rd)	TB	R	RBI	TBB	IBB	SO	HBP	SH	SF	SB	CS	SB%	GDP	Avg	OBP	SLG
		BATTING																	BASERUNNING				PERCENTAGES		
1989 Pittsburgh	NL	75	215	42	13	3	5	(3	2)	76	31	19	20	1	34	2	2	4	4	2	.67	3	.195	.266	.353
1990 Pittsburgh	NL	127	371	91	17	1	14	(9	5)	152	46	53	21	1	50	1	2	7	3	3	.50	12	.245	.283	.410
1991 Pittsburgh	NL	33	109	26	1	1	4	(3	1)	41	16	18	14	3	15	1	0	1	3	1	.75	3	.239	.328	.376
1992 Pittsburgh	NL	130	480	111	21	2	14	(6	8)	178	56	65	27	3	56	2	8	5	4	6	.40	8	.231	.272	.371
1993 Pittsburgh	NL	158	611	180	35	3	9	(4	5)	248	82	98	59	4	54	4	1	8	8	6	.57	17	.295	.356	.406
1994 Pittsburgh	NL	94	339	89	23	0	5	(2	3)	127	36	42	30	1	38	0	2	7	3	2	.60	7	.263	.316	.375
1995 Pittsburgh	NL	122	445	118	27	2	18	(7	11)	203	61	87	55	5	63	1	0	8	7	4	.64	10	.265	.342	.456
1996 Pittsburgh	NL	155	591	160	36	4	30	(14	16)	294	91	111	70	3	95	2	1	8	15	1	.94	17	.271	.346	.497
1997 Kansas City	AL	155	543	129	30	1	28	(11	17)	245	84	112	89	4	96	2	1	12	16	5	.76	9	.238	.341	.451
9 ML YEARS		1049	3704	946	203	17	127	(59	68)	1564	503	605	385	25	501	15	17	60	63	30	.68	86	.255	.323	.422

Wayne Kirby

Bats: L **Throws:** R **Pos:** PH-23; CF-16; LF-9; RF-2 **Ht:** 5'10" **Wt:** 190 **Born:** 1/22/64 **Age:** 34

Year Team	Lg	G	AB	H	2B	3B	HR	(Hm	Rd)	TB	R	RBI	TBB	IBB	SO	HBP	SH	SF	SB	CS	SB%	GDP	Avg	OBP	SLG
		BATTING																	BASERUNNING				PERCENTAGES		
1997 Albuquerque *	AAA	68	269	90	16	5	10	---	---	146	57	43	26	0	33	1	1	2	18	5	.78	5	.335	.393	.543
1991 Cleveland	AL	21	43	9	2	0	0	(0	0)	11	4	5	2	0	6	0	1	1	1	2	.33	2	.209	.239	.256
1992 Cleveland	AL	21	18	3	1	0	1	(0	1)	7	9	1	3	0	2	0	0	0	0	3	.00	1	.167	.286	.389
1993 Cleveland	AL	131	458	123	19	5	6	(4	2)	170	71	60	37	2	58	3	7	6	17	5	.77	8	.269	.323	.371
1994 Cleveland	AL	78	191	56	6	0	5	(3	2)	77	33	23	13	0	30	1	2	0	11	4	.73	1	.293	.341	.403
1995 Cleveland	AL	101	188	39	10	2	1	(0	1)	56	29	14	13	0	32	1	1	2	10	3	.77	4	.207	.260	.298
1996 Cle-LA		92	204	55	11	1	1	(0	0)	71	26	12	19	1	19	1	1	1	4	3	.57	4	.270	.333	.348
1997 Los Angeles	NL	46	65	11	2	0	0	(0	0)	13	6	4	10	0	12	0	0	0	0	0	.00	1	.169	.280	.200
1996 Cleveland	AL	27	16	4	1	0	0	(0	0)	5	3	1	2	0	2	0	0	0	0	1	.00	1	.250	.333	.313
Los Angeles	NL	65	188	51	10	1	1	(0	1)	66	23	11	17	1	17	1	1	1	4	2	.67	3	.271	.333	.351
7 ML YEARS		490	1167	296	51	8	14	(7	7)	405	178	119	97	3	159	6	12	10	43	20	.68	21	.254	.312	.347

Ryan Klesko

Bats: Left **Throws:** Left **Pos:** LF-130; 1B-22; PH-9 **Ht:** 6'3" **Wt:** 220 **Born:** 6/12/71 **Age:** 27

Year Team	Lg	G	AB	H	2B	3B	HR	(Hm	Rd)	TB	R	RBI	TBB	IBB	SO	HBP	SH	SF	SB	CS	SB%	GDP	Avg	OBP	SLG
		BATTING																	BASERUNNING				PERCENTAGES		
1992 Atlanta	NL	13	14	0	0	0	0	(0	0)	0	1	0	0	0	5	1	0	0	0	0	.00	0	.000	.067	.000
1993 Atlanta	NL	22	17	6	1	0	2	(2	0)	13	3	5	3	1	4	0	0	0	0	0	.00	0	.353	.450	.765
1994 Atlanta	NL	92	245	68	13	3	17	(7	10)	138	42	47	26	3	48	1	0	4	1	0	1.00	6	.278	.344	.563
1995 Atlanta	NL	107	329	102	25	2	23	(15	8)	200	48	70	47	10	72	2	0	3	5	4	.56	8	.310	.396	.608
1996 Atlanta	NL	153	528	149	21	4	34	(20	14)	280	90	93	68	10	129	2	0	4	6	3	.67	10	.282	.364	.530
1997 Atlanta	NL	143	467	122	23	6	24	(10	14)	229	67	84	48	5	130	4	1	2	4	4	.50	12	.261	.334	.490
6 ML YEARS		530	1600	447	83	15	100	(54	46)	860	250	300	192	29	388	10	1	13	16	11	.59	38	.279	.358	.538

Steve Kline

Pitches: Left **Bats:** Both **Pos:** RP-45; SP-1 **Ht:** 6'2" **Wt:** 200 **Born:** 8/22/72 **Age:** 25

Year Team	Lg	G	GS	CG	GF	IP	BFP	H	R	ER	HR	SH	SF	HB	TBB	IBB	SO	WP	Bk	W	L	Pct.	ShO	Sv-Op	Hld	ERA
		HOW MUCH HE PITCHED						WHAT HE GAVE UP										THE RESULTS					
1993 Burlington	R+	2	1	0	0	7.1	34	11	4	4	0	1	0	0	2	1	4	0	0	1	1	.500	0	0- --	--	4.91
Watertown	A-	13	13	2	0	79	332	77	36	28	3	3	2	4	12	0	45	5	0	5	4	.556	1	0- --	--	3.19
1994 Columbus	A	28	28	2	0	185.2	744	175	67	62	14	1	2	7	36	0	174	6	1	18	5	.783	1	0- --	--	3.01
1995 Canton-Akrn	AA	14	14	0	0	89.1	377	86	34	24	6	4	1	1	30	3	45	1	1	2	3	.400	0	0- --	--	2.42
1996 Canton-Akrn	AA	25	24	0	0	146.2	658	168	98	89	16	10	4	6	55	2	107	5	1	8	12	.400	0	0- --	--	5.46
1997 Buffalo	AAA	20	4	0	5	51.1	219	53	26	23	4	3	0	3	13	1	41	1	1	3	3	.500	0	1- --	--	4.03
1997 Cle-Mon		46	1	0	7	52.2	248	73	37	35	10	4	2	2	23	4	37	4	1	4	4	.500	0	0-3	5	5.98
1997 Cleveland	AL	20	1	0	0	26.1	130	42	19	17	6	1	0	1	13	1	17	3	1	3	1	.750	0	0-2	4	5.81
Montreal	NL	26	0	0	7	26.1	118	31	18	18	4	3	2	1	10	3	20	1	0	1	3	.250	0	0-1	1	6.15

114

Chuck Knoblauch

Bats: Right **Throws:** Right **Pos:** 2B-154; DH-1; SS-1　　**Ht:** 5'9" **Wt:** 181 **Born:** 7/7/68 **Age:** 29

Year Team	Lg	G	AB	H	2B	3B	HR	(Hm	Rd)	TB	R	RBI	TBB	IBB	SO	HBP	SH	SF	SB	CS	SB%	GDP	Avg	OBP	SLG
1991 Minnesota	AL	151	565	159	24	6	1	(1	0)	198	78	50	59	0	40	4	1	5	25	5	.83	8	.281	.351	.350
1992 Minnesota	AL	155	600	178	19	6	2	(0	2)	215	104	56	88	1	60	5	2	12	34	13	.72	8	.297	.384	.358
1993 Minnesota	AL	153	602	167	27	4	2	(2	0)	208	82	41	65	1	44	9	4	5	29	11	.73	11	.277	.354	.346
1994 Minnesota	AL	109	445	139	45	3	5	(1	4)	205	85	51	41	2	56	10	0	3	35	6	.85	13	.312	.381	.461
1995 Minnesota	AL	136	538	179	34	8	11	(4	7)	262	107	63	78	3	95	10	0	3	46	18	.72	15	.333	.424	.487
1996 Minnesota	AL	153	578	197	35	14	13	(7	6)	299	140	72	98	6	74	19	0	6	45	14	.76	9	.341	.448	.517
1997 Minnesota	AL	156	611	178	26	10	9	(2	7)	251	117	58	84	6	84	17	0	4	62	10	.86	11	.291	.390	.411
7 ML YEARS		1013	3939	1197	210	51	43	(17	26)	1638	713	391	513	19	453	74	7	38	276	77	.78	75	.304	.391	.416

Randy Knorr

Bats: Right **Throws:** Right **Pos:** C-3; 1B-2　　**Ht:** 6'2" **Wt:** 215 **Born:** 11/12/68 **Age:** 29

Year Team	Lg	G	AB	H	2B	3B	HR	(Hm	Rd)	TB	R	RBI	TBB	IBB	SO	HBP	SH	SF	SB	CS	SB%	GDP	Avg	OBP	SLG
1997 New Orleans *	AAA	72	244	58	10	0	5	—	—	83	22	27	22	3	38	0	1	1	0	0	.00	13	.238	.300	.340
1991 Toronto	AL	3	1	0	0	0	0	(0	0)	0	0	0	1	0	1	0	0	0	0	0	.00	0	.000	.500	.000
1992 Toronto	AL	8	19	5	0	0	1	(0	1)	8	1	2	1	1	5	0	0	0	0	0	.00	0	.263	.300	.421
1993 Toronto	AL	39	101	25	3	2	4	(2	2)	44	11	20	9	0	29	0	2	0	0	0	.00	2	.248	.309	.436
1994 Toronto	AL	40	124	30	2	0	7	(4	3)	53	20	19	10	0	35	1	0	1	0	0	.00	7	.242	.301	.427
1995 Toronto	AL	45	132	28	8	0	3	(2	1)	45	18	16	11	0	28	0	1	0	0	0	.00	5	.212	.273	.341
1996 Houston	NL	37	87	17	5	0	1	(1	0)	25	7	7	5	2	18	1	0	1	0	1	.00	1	.195	.245	.287
1997 Houston	NL	4	8	3	0	0	1	(1	0)	6	1	1	0	0	2	0	0	0	0	0	.00	0	.375	.375	.750
7 ML YEARS		176	472	108	18	2	17	(10	7)	181	58	65	37	3	118	2	3	2	0	1	.00	15	.229	.287	.383

Paul Konerko

Bats: Right **Throws:** Right **Pos:** PH-4; 1B-1; 3B-1　　**Ht:** 6'3" **Wt:** 205 **Born:** 3/5/76 **Age:** 22

Year Team	Lg	G	AB	H	2B	3B	HR	(Hm	Rd)	TB	R	RBI	TBB	IBB	SO	HBP	SH	SF	SB	CS	SB%	GDP	Avg	OBP	SLG
1994 Yakima	A-	67	257	74	15	2	6	—	—	111	25	58	36	4	52	6	0	7	1	0	1.00	6	.288	.379	.432
1995 San Berndno	A+	118	448	124	21	1	19	—	—	204	77	77	59	2	88	4	2	6	3	1	.75	12	.277	.362	.455
1996 San Antonio	AA	133	470	141	23	2	29	—	—	255	78	86	72	6	85	8	0	7	1	3	.25	7	.300	.397	.543
Albuquerque	AAA	4	14	6	0	0	1	—	—	9	2	2	1	0	2	0	0	0	0	1	.00	0	.429	.467	.643
1997 Albuquerque	AAA	130	483	156	31	1	37	—	—	300	97	127	64	3	61	8	0	5	2	3	.40	16	.323	.407	.621
1997 Los Angeles	NL	6	7	1	0	0	0	(0	0)	1	0	1	0	1	2	0	0	0	0	0	.00	1	.143	.250	.143

Mark Kotsay

Bats: Left **Throws:** Left **Pos:** CF-14　　**Ht:** 6'0" **Wt:** 180 **Born:** 12/2/75 **Age:** 22

Year Team	Lg	G	AB	H	2B	3B	HR	(Hm	Rd)	TB	R	RBI	TBB	IBB	SO	HBP	SH	SF	SB	CS	SB%	GDP	Avg	OBP	SLG
1996 Kane County	A	17	60	17	5	0	2	—	—	28	16	8	16	0	8	1	0	1	3	0	1.00	3	.283	.436	.467
1997 Portland	AA	114	438	134	27	2	20	—	—	225	103	77	75	3	65	0	0	3	17	5	.77	16	.306	.405	.514
1997 Florida	NL	14	52	10	1	1	0	(0	0)	13	5	4	4	0	7	0	1	0	3	0	1.00	1	.192	.250	.250

Chad Kreuter

Bats: B **Throws:** R **Pos:** C-80; PH-12; DH-2; 1B-2　　**Ht:** 6'2" **Wt:** 200 **Born:** 8/26/64 **Age:** 33

Year Team	Lg	G	AB	H	2B	3B	HR	(Hm	Rd)	TB	R	RBI	TBB	IBB	SO	HBP	SH	SF	SB	CS	SB%	GDP	Avg	OBP	SLG
1988 Texas	AL	16	51	14	2	1	1	(0	1)	21	3	5	7	0	13	0	0	0	0	0	.00	1	.275	.362	.412
1989 Texas	AL	87	158	24	3	0	5	(2	3)	42	16	9	27	0	40	0	6	1	0	1	.00	4	.152	.274	.266
1990 Texas	AL	22	22	1	1	0	0	(0	0)	2	2	2	8	0	9	0	1	1	0	0	.00	0	.045	.290	.091
1991 Texas	AL	3	4	0	0	0	0	(0	0)	0	0	0	0	0	1	0	0	0	0	0	.00	0	.000	.000	.000
1992 Detroit	AL	67	190	48	9	0	2	(2	0)	63	22	16	20	1	38	0	3	2	0	1	.00	8	.253	.321	.332
1993 Detroit	AL	119	374	107	23	3	15	(9	6)	181	59	51	49	4	92	3	2	3	2	1	.67	5	.286	.371	.484
1994 Detroit	AL	65	170	38	8	0	1	(1	0)	49	17	19	28	0	36	0	2	4	0	1	.00	3	.224	.327	.288
1995 Seattle	AL	26	75	17	5	0	1	(0	1)	25	12	8	5	0	22	2	1	0	0	0	.00	2	.227	.293	.333
1996 Chicago	AL	46	114	25	8	0	3	(2	1)	42	14	18	13	0	29	2	2	1	0	0	.00	7	.219	.308	.368
1997 ChA-Ana	AL	89	255	59	9	2	5	(3	2)	87	25	21	29	0	66	0	1	1	0	3	.00	7	.231	.310	.341
1997 Chicago	AL	19	37	8	2	1	1	(1	0)	15	6	3	8	0	9	0	1	0	0	1	.00	0	.216	.356	.405
Anaheim	AL	70	218	51	7	1	4	(2	2)	72	19	18	21	0	57	0	0	1	0	2	.00	7	.234	.301	.330
10 ML YEARS		540	1413	333	68	6	33	(19	14)	512	170	149	186	5	346	7	18	12	2	7	.22	30	.236	.325	.362

Rick Krivda

Pitches: Left **Bats:** Right **Pos:** SP-10　　**Ht:** 6'1" **Wt:** 180 **Born:** 1/19/70 **Age:** 28

	HOW MUCH HE PITCHED						WHAT HE GAVE UP											THE RESULTS						
Year Team	Lg	G	GS	CG	GF	IP	BFP	H	R	ER	HR	SH	SF	HB	TBB	IBB	SO	WP	Bk	W	L	Pct.	ShO	Sv-Op	Hld	ERA
1997 Rochester *	AAA	22	21	6	0	146	589	122	61	55	13	0	2	5	34	0	128	2	2	14	2	.875	3	0- -	—	3.39
1995 Baltimore	AL	13	13	1	0	75.1	319	76	40	38	9	0	4	4	25	1	53	2	2	2	7	.222	0	0-0	0	4.54
1996 Baltimore	AL	22	11	0	4	81.2	359	89	48	45	14	2	0	1	39	2	54	3	1	3	5	.375	0	0-0	1	4.96
1997 Baltimore	AL	10	10	0	0	50	225	67	36	35	7	1	2	0	18	1	29	0	2	4	2	.667	0	0-0	0	6.30
3 ML YEARS		45	34	1	4	207	903	232	124	118	30	3	6	5	82	4	136	5	5	9	14	.391	0	0-0	1	5.13

Marc Kroon

Pitches: Right **Bats:** Right **Pos:** RP-12   **Ht:** 6'2" **Wt:** 195 **Born:** 4/2/73 **Age:** 25

Year Team	Lg	G	GS	CG	GF	IP	BFP	H	R	ER	HR	SH	SF	HB	TBB	IBB	SO	WP	Bk	W	L	Pct.	ShO	Sv-Op	Hld	ERA
1991 Mets	R	12	10	1	2	47.2	208	39	33	24	1	0	1	4	22	0	39	10	5	2	3	.400	0	0- --	—	4.53
1992 Kingsport	R+	12	12	0	0	68	307	52	41	31	3	0	3	1	57	0	60	13	2	3	5	.375	0	0- --	—	4.10
1993 Capital Cty	A	29	19	0	8	124.1	542	123	65	48	6	1	8	5	70	0	122	10	2	2	11	.154	0	2- --	—	3.47
1994 Rancho Cuca	A+	26	26	0	0	143.1	655	143	86	77	14	4	9	11	81	1	153	9	3	11	6	.647	0	0- --	—	4.83
1995 Memphis	AA	22	19	0	2	115.1	497	90	49	45	12	2	2	6	61	1	123	16	1	7	5	.583	0	2- --	—	3.51
1996 Memphis	AA	44	0	0	43	46.2	208	33	19	15	4	1	4	3	28	1	56	6	1	2	4	.333	0	22- --	—	2.89
1997 Las Vegas	AAA	46	0	0	33	41.2	175	34	22	21	5	2	2	3	22	0	53	6	0	1	3	.250	0	15- --	—	4.54
1995 San Diego	NL	2	0	0	1	1.2	7	1	2	2	0	0	0	0	2	0	2	0	0	0	1	.000	0	0-0	0	10.80
1997 San Diego	NL	12	0	0	2	11.1	56	14	9	9	2	0	1	0	5	0	12	1	0	0	1	.000	0	0-0	1	7.15
2 ML YEARS		14	0	0	3	13	63	15	11	11	2	0	1	0	7	0	14	1	0	0	2	.000	0	0-0	1	7.62

Tim Kubinski

Pitches: Left **Bats:** Left **Pos:** RP-11   **Ht:** 6'4" **Wt:** 205 **Born:** 1/20/72 **Age:** 26

Year Team	Lg	G	GS	CG	GF	IP	BFP	H	R	ER	HR	SH	SF	HB	TBB	IBB	SO	WP	Bk	W	L	Pct.	ShO	Sv-Op	Hld	ERA
1993 Athletics	R	1	1	0	0	3	13	5	2	2	1	0	0	0	0	0	3	0	0	1	0	1.000	0	0- --	—	6.00
Sou. Oregon	A-	12	12	1	0	70	294	67	36	22	4	2	2	6	18	0	51	2	2	5	5	.500	0	0- --	—	2.83
1994 W Michigan	A	30	23	1	4	158.2	677	168	82	64	8	13	4	7	36	0	126	8	10	14	6	.700	0	0- --	—	3.63
1995 Edmonton	AAA	6	5	0	0	32	136	34	18	17	4	0	4	0	10	0	12	0	4	1	2	.333	0	0- --	—	4.78
Modesto	A+	25	17	0	4	109	485	126	73	60	12	6	5	8	24	0	83	10	1	6	10	.375	0	2- --	—	4.95
1996 Huntsville	AA	43	3	0	15	102	418	84	41	27	7	4	3	3	36	6	78	8	3	8	7	.533	0	3- --	—	2.38
Edmonton	AAA	1	0	0	1	1	4	1	0	0	0	0	0	1	0	0	0	0	0	0	0	.000	0	0- --	—	0.00
1997 Edmonton	AAA	47	0	0	17	76	315	64	39	38	8	6	1	1	34	4	53	7	2	4	4	.500	0	7- --	—	4.50
1997 Oakland	AL	11	0	0	3	12.2	56	12	9	8	2	0	1	1	6	1	10	0	0	0	0	.000	0	0-0	1	5.68

Kerry Lacy

Pitches: Right **Bats:** Right **Pos:** RP-33   **Ht:** 6'2" **Wt:** 215 **Born:** 8/7/72 **Age:** 25

Year Team	Lg	G	GS	CG	GF	IP	BFP	H	R	ER	HR	SH	SF	HB	TBB	IBB	SO	WP	Bk	W	L	Pct.	ShO	Sv-Op	Hld	ERA
1991 Butte	R+	24	2	0	6	48	221	47	34	30	5	0	2	6	36	0	45	15	4	2	1	.667	0	1- --	—	5.63
1992 Gastonia	A	49	1	0	32	55.2	262	55	35	24	2	2	0	1	42	2	57	9	2	3	7	.300	0	17- --	—	3.88
1993 Chston-SC	A	58	0	0	57	60	267	49	25	21	1	3	5	5	32	5	54	6	2	0	6	.000	0	36- --	—	3.15
Charlotte	A+	4	0	0	3	4.2	21	2	2	1	0	0	0	1	3	0	3	1	0	0	0	.000	0	2- --	—	1.93
1994 Tulsa	AA	41	0	0	35	63.2	270	49	30	26	4	3	2	3	37	4	46	3	1	2	6	.250	0	12- --	—	3.68
1995 Tulsa	AA	28	7	0	16	82	363	94	47	39	5	3	3	3	39	7	49	7	0	2	7	.222	0	9- --	—	4.28
Okla City	AAA	1	0	0	1	2.1	7	0	0	0	0	0	0	0	0	0	1	0	0	0	0	.000	0	1- --	—	0.00
1996 Tulsa	AA	2	0	0	2	4	15	4	0	0	0	1	0	2	0	0	1	0	0	0	0	.000	0	1- --	—	0.00
Okla City	AAA	37	0	0	28	56	232	48	21	18	2	2	0	0	15	2	31	2	0	3	3	.500	0	6- --	—	2.89
Pawtucket	AAA	7	0	0	6	8	26	1	0	0	0	0	0	0	2	0	8	0	0	0	0	.000	0	4- --	—	0.00
1997 Pawtucket	AAA	23	0	0	19	32.1	144	36	18	17	4	1	0	2	11	1	21	1	0	5	3	.625	0	8- --	—	4.73
1996 Boston	AL	11	0	0	3	10.2	54	15	5	4	2	0	0	1	8	0	9	0	0	2	0	1.000	0	0-2	1	3.38
1997 Boston	AL	33	0	0	12	45.2	215	60	34	31	7	0	2	0	22	4	18	0	0	1	1	.500	0	3-3	5	6.11
2 ML YEARS		44	0	0	15	56.1	269	75	39	35	9	0	2	1	30	4	27	0	0	3	1	.750	0	3-5	6	5.59

Tim Laker

Bats: Right **Throws:** Right **Pos:** C-7   **Ht:** 6'3" **Wt:** 200 **Born:** 11/27/69 **Age:** 28

Year Team	Lg	G	AB	H	2B	3B	HR	(Hm	Rd)	TB	R	RBI	TBB	IBB	SO	HBP	SH	SF	SB	CS	SB%	GDP	Avg	OBP	SLG
1997 Rochester *	AAA	79	290	75	11	1	11	—	—	121	45	37	34	1	49	5	0	4	1	2	.33	4	.259	.342	.417
1992 Montreal	NL	28	46	10	3	0	0	(0	0)	13	8	4	2	0	14	0	0	0	1	1	.50	1	.217	.250	.283
1993 Montreal	NL	43	86	17	2	1	0	(0	0)	21	3	7	2	0	16	1	3	1	2	0	1.00	2	.198	.222	.244
1995 Montreal	NL	64	141	33	8	1	3	(1	2)	52	17	20	14	4	38	1	1	1	0	1	.00	5	.234	.306	.369
1997 Baltimore	AL	7	14	0	0	0	0	(0	0)	0	0	1	2	0	9	0	1	0	0	0	.00	0	.000	.118	.000
4 ML YEARS		142	287	60	13	2	3	(1	2)	86	28	32	20	4	77	2	5	3	3	2	.60	8	.209	.263	.300

Tom Lampkin

Bats: Left **Throws:** Right **Pos:** C-86; PH-41   **Ht:** 5'11" **Wt:** 185 **Born:** 3/4/64 **Age:** 34

Year Team	Lg	G	AB	H	2B	3B	HR	(Hm	Rd)	TB	R	RBI	TBB	IBB	SO	HBP	SH	SF	SB	CS	SB%	GDP	Avg	OBP	SLG
1988 Cleveland	AL	4	4	0	0	0	0	(0	0)	0	0	0	1	0	0	0	0	0	0	0	.00	1	.000	.200	.000
1990 San Diego	NL	26	63	14	0	1	1	(1	0)	19	4	4	4	1	9	0	0	0	0	1	.00	2	.222	.269	.302
1991 San Diego	NL	38	58	11	3	1	0	(0	0)	16	4	3	3	0	9	0	0	0	0	0	.00	2	.190	.230	.276
1992 San Diego	NL	9	17	4	0	0	0	(0	0)	4	3	0	6	0	1	1	0	0	2	0	1.00	0	.235	.458	.235
1993 Milwaukee	AL	73	162	32	8	0	4	(1	3)	52	22	25	20	3	26	0	2	1	7	3	.70	2	.198	.280	.321
1995 San Francisco	NL	65	76	21	2	0	1	(1	0)	26	8	9	9	1	8	1	0	0	2	0	1.00	1	.276	.360	.342
1996 San Francisco	NL	66	177	41	8	0	6	(1	5)	67	26	29	20	2	22	5	0	2	1	5	.17	2	.232	.324	.379
1997 St. Louis	NL	108	229	56	8	1	7	(2	5)	87	28	22	28	5	30	4	4	2	2	1	.67	8	.245	.335	.380
8 ML YEARS		389	786	179	29	3	19	(10	9)	271	95	92	91	12	105	11	6	8	14	10	.58	16	.228	.314	.345

Mark Langston

Pitches: Left **Bats:** Right **Pos:** SP-9   **Ht:** 6'2" **Wt:** 184 **Born:** 8/20/60 **Age:** 37

		HOW MUCH HE PITCHED					WHAT HE GAVE UP										THE RESULTS						
Year Team	Lg	G	GS	CG	GF	IP	BFP	H	R	ER	HR	SH	SF	HB	TBB	IBB	SO	WP	Bk	W	L	Pct.	ShO	Sv-Op Hld	ERA
1997 Lk Elsinore *	A+	3	3	0	0	14	53	11	7	5	1	0	0	1	2	0	10	0	0	0	2	.000	0	0- --	3.21
1984 Seattle	AL	35	33	5	0	225	965	188	99	85	16	13	7	8	118	5	204	4	2	17	10	.630	2	0- --	3.40
1985 Seattle	AL	24	24	2	0	126.2	577	122	85	77	22	3	2	2	91	2	72	3	3	7	14	.333	0	0-0 0	5.47
1986 Seattle	AL	37	36	9	1	239.1	1057	234	142	129	30	5	8	4	123	1	245	10	3	12	14	.462	0	0- --	4.85
1987 Seattle	AL	35	35	14	0	272	1152	242	132	116	30	12	6	5	114	0	262	9	2	19	13	.594	3	0-0 0	3.84
1988 Seattle	AL	35	35	9	0	261.1	1078	222	108	97	32	6	5	3	110	2	235	7	4	15	11	.577	3	0-0 0	3.34
1989 Sea-Mon		34	34	8	0	250	1037	198	87	76	16	9	7	4	112	6	235	6	4	16	14	.533	5	0-0 0	2.74
1990 California	AL	33	33	5	0	223	950	215	120	109	13	6	6	5	104	1	195	8	0	10	17	.370	1	0-0 0	4.40
1991 California	AL	34	34	7	0	246.1	992	190	89	82	30	4	6	2	96	3	183	6	0	19	8	.704	0	0-0 0	3.00
1992 California	AL	32	32	9	0	229	941	206	103	93	14	4	5	6	74	2	174	5	0	13	14	.481	2	0-0 0	3.66
1993 California	AL	35	35	7	0	256.1	1039	220	100	91	22	3	8	1	85	2	196	10	2	16	11	.593	0	0-0 0	3.20
1994 California	AL	18	18	2	0	119.1	517	121	67	62	19	3	8	0	54	1	109	6	0	7	8	.467	1	0-0 0	4.68
1995 California	AL	31	31	2	0	200.1	859	212	109	103	21	11	3	3	64	1	142	5	1	15	7	.682	1	0-0 0	4.63
1996 California	AL	18	18	2	0	123.1	518	116	68	66	18	0	2	2	45	0	83	4	0	6	5	.545	0	0-0 0	4.82
1997 Anaheim	AL	9	9	0	0	47.2	226	61	34	31	8	2	2	0	29	1	30	1	0	2	4	.333	0	0-0 0	5.85
1989 Seattle		10	10	2	0	73.1	297	60	30	29	3	0	3	4	19	0	60	1	2	4	5	.444	1	0-0 0	3.56
Montreal	NL	24	24	6	0	176.2	740	138	57	47	13	9	4	0	93	6	175	5	2	12	9	.571	4	0-0 0	2.39
14 ML YEARS		410	407	81	1	2819.2	11908	2547	1343	1217	291	81	75	45	1219	27	2365	84	21	174	150	.537	18	0- --	3.88

Ray Lankford

Bats: Left **Throws:** Left **Pos:** CF-132; PH-2   **Ht:** 5'11" **Wt:** 200 **Born:** 6/5/67 **Age:** 31

		BATTING																	BASERUNNING				PERCENTAGES		
Year Team	Lg	G	AB	H	2B	3B	HR	(Hm	Rd)	TB	R	RBI	TBB	IBB	SO	HBP	SH	SF	SB	CS	SB%	GDP	Avg	OBP	SLG
1997 Pr William *	A+	4	13	4	1	0	0	—		5	3	4	4	0	5	0	0	1	1	1	.50	0	.308	.444	.385
1990 St. Louis	NL	39	126	36	10	1	3	(2	1)	57	12	12	13	0	27	0	0	0	8	2	.80	1	.286	.353	.452
1991 St. Louis	NL	151	566	142	23	15	9	(4	5)	222	83	69	41	1	114	1	4	3	44	20	.69	4	.251	.301	.392
1992 St. Louis	NL	153	598	175	40	6	20	(13	7)	287	87	86	72	6	147	5	2	5	42	24	.64	5	.293	.371	.480
1993 St. Louis	NL	127	407	97	17	3	7	(6	1)	141	64	45	81	7	111	3	1	3	14	14	.50	5	.238	.366	.346
1994 St. Louis	NL	109	416	111	25	5	19	(8	11)	203	89	57	58	3	113	4	0	4	11	10	.52	0	.267	.359	.488
1995 St. Louis	NL	132	483	134	35	2	25	(16	9)	248	81	82	63	6	110	2	0	5	24	8	.75	10	.277	.360	.513
1996 St. Louis	NL	149	545	150	36	8	21	(8	13)	265	100	86	79	10	133	3	1	7	35	7	.83	12	.275	.366	.486
1997 St. Louis	NL	133	465	137	36	3	31	(10	21)	272	94	98	95	10	125	0	0	5	21	11	.66	9	.295	.411	.585
8 ML YEARS		993	3606	982	222	43	135	(67	68)	1695	610	535	502	43	880	18	8	32	199	96	.67	46	.272	.361	.470

Mike Lansing

Bats: Right **Throws:** Right **Pos:** 2B-144   **Ht:** 6'0" **Wt:** 180 **Born:** 4/3/68 **Age:** 30

		BATTING																	BASERUNNING				PERCENTAGES		
Year Team	Lg	G	AB	H	2B	3B	HR	(Hm	Rd)	TB	R	RBI	TBB	IBB	SO	HBP	SH	SF	SB	CS	SB%	GDP	Avg	OBP	SLG
1993 Montreal	NL	141	491	141	29	1	3	(1	2)	181	64	45	46	2	56	5	10	3	23	5	.82	16	.287	.352	.369
1994 Montreal	NL	106	394	105	21	2	5	(3	2)	145	44	35	30	3	37	7	2	2	12	8	.60	10	.266	.328	.368
1995 Montreal	NL	127	467	119	30	2	10	(4	6)	183	47	62	28	2	65	3	1	3	27	4	.87	14	.255	.299	.392
1996 Montreal	NL	159	641	183	40	2	11	(3	8)	260	99	53	44	1	85	10	9	1	23	8	.74	19	.285	.341	.406
1997 Montreal	NL	144	572	161	45	2	20	(11	9)	270	86	70	45	2	92	5	6	3	11	5	.69	9	.281	.338	.472
5 ML YEARS		677	2565	709	165	9	49	(22	27)	1039	340	265	193	10	335	30	28	12	96	30	.76	68	.276	.333	.405

Barry Larkin

Bats: Right **Throws:** Right **Pos:** SS-63; PH-8; DH-2   **Ht:** 6'0" **Wt:** 195 **Born:** 4/28/64 **Age:** 34

		BATTING																	BASERUNNING				PERCENTAGES		
Year Team	Lg	G	AB	H	2B	3B	HR	(Hm	Rd)	TB	R	RBI	TBB	IBB	SO	HBP	SH	SF	SB	CS	SB%	GDP	Avg	OBP	SLG
1986 Cincinnati	NL	41	159	45	4	3	3	(3	0)	64	27	19	9	1	21	0	0	1	8	0	1.00	6	.283	.320	.403
1987 Cincinnati	NL	125	439	107	16	2	12	(6	6)	163	64	43	36	3	52	5	5	3	21	6	.78	8	.244	.306	.371
1988 Cincinnati	NL	151	588	174	32	5	12	(9	3)	252	91	56	41	3	24	8	10	5	40	7	.85	7	.296	.347	.429
1989 Cincinnati	NL	97	325	111	14	4	4	(1	3)	145	47	36	20	5	23	2	2	9	10	5	.67	7	.342	.375	.446
1990 Cincinnati	NL	158	614	185	25	6	7	(4	3)	243	85	67	49	3	49	7	7	4	30	5	.86	14	.301	.358	.396
1991 Cincinnati	NL	123	464	140	27	4	20	(16	4)	235	88	69	55	1	64	3	3	2	24	6	.80	7	.302	.378	.506
1992 Cincinnati	NL	140	533	162	32	6	12	(8	4)	242	76	78	63	8	58	4	2	7	15	4	.79	13	.304	.377	.454
1993 Cincinnati	NL	100	384	121	20	3	8	(4	4)	171	57	51	51	6	33	1	1	3	14	1	.93	13	.315	.394	.445
1994 Cincinnati	NL	110	427	119	23	5	9	(3	6)	179	78	52	64	3	58	0	5	5	26	2	.93	6	.279	.369	.419
1995 Cincinnati	NL	131	496	158	29	6	15	(7	8)	244	98	66	61	2	49	3	3	4	51	5	.91	5	.319	.394	.492
1996 Cincinnati	NL	152	517	154	32	4	33	(14	19)	293	117	89	96	3	52	7	0	7	36	10	.78	20	.298	.410	.567
1997 Cincinnati	NL	73	224	71	17	3	4	(0	4)	106	34	20	47	6	24	3	1	1	14	3	.82	3	.317	.440	.473
12 ML YEARS		1401	5170	1547	271	51	139	(76	63)	2337	862	646	592	44	507	43	39	50	289	54	.84	106	.299	.373	.452

Chris Latham

Bats: Both **Throws:** Right **Pos:** PH-10; CF-8; RF-3   **Ht:** 6'0" **Wt:** 185 **Born:** 5/26/73 **Age:** 25

		BATTING																	BASERUNNING				PERCENTAGES		
Year Team	Lg	G	AB	H	2B	3B	HR	(Hm	Rd)	TB	R	RBI	TBB	IBB	SO	HBP	SH	SF	SB	CS	SB%	GDP	Avg	OBP	SLG
1991 Dodgers	R	43	109	26	2	1	0	—		30	17	11	16	0	45	0	0	1	14	4	.78	0	.239	.333	.275
1992 Great Falls	R+	17	37	12	2	0	0	—		14	8	3	8	0	8	0	0	0	1	1	.50	0	.324	.444	.378
Dodgers	R	14	48	11	2	0	0	—		13	4	2	5	1	17	0	1	1	2	3	.40	0	.229	.296	.271
1993 Yakima	A-	54	192	50	2	6	4	—		76	46	17	39	0	53	1	0	1	24	9	.73	2	.260	.388	.396

Year Team	Lg	G	AB	H	2B	3B	HR	(Hm	Rd)	TB	R	RBI	TBB	IBB	SO	HBP	SH	SF	SB	CS	SB%	GDP	Avg	OBP	SLG
Bakersfield	A+	6	27	5	1	0	0	—	—	6	1	3	4	0	5	0	0	0	2	2	.50	2	.185	.290	.222
1994 Bakersfield	A+	52	191	41	5	2	2	—	—	56	29	15	28	1	49	2	4	0	28	7	.80	2	.215	.321	.293
Yakima	A-	71	288	98	19	8	5	—	—	148	69	32	55	7	66	2	3	0	33	20	.62	1	.340	.449	.514
1995 Vero Beach	A+	71	259	74	13	4	6	—	—	113	53	39	56	4	54	2	2	3	42	11	.79	2	.286	.413	.470
San Antonio	AA	58	214	64	14	5	9	—	—	115	38	37	33	0	59	2	1	1	11	11	.50	2	.299	.396	.537
Albuquerque	AAA	5	18	3	0	1	0	—	—	5	2	3	1	0	4	0	0	1	1	0	1.00	0	.167	.200	.278
1996 Salt Lake	AAA	115	376	103	16	6	9	—	—	158	59	50	36	1	91	2	4	3	26	9	.74	5	.274	.338	.420
1997 Salt Lake	AAA	118	492	152	22	5	8	—	—	208	78	58	58	0	110	4	4	1	21	19	.53	8	.309	.386	.423
1997 Minnesota	AL	15	22	4	1	0	0	(0	0)	5	4	1	0	0	8	0	0	0	0	0	.00	0	.182	.182	.227

Matt Lawton

Bats: L **Throws:** R **Pos:** RF-67; LF-58; CF-23; PH-15   **Ht:** 5'10" **Wt:** 196 **Born:** 11/3/71 **Age:** 26

Year Team	Lg	G	AB	H	2B	3B	HR	(Hm	Rd)	TB	R	RBI	TBB	IBB	SO	HBP	SH	SF	SB	CS	SB%	GDP	Avg	OBP	SLG
1995 Minnesota	AL	21	60	19	4	1	1	(1	0)	28	11	12	7	0	11	3	0	0	1	1	.50	1	.317	.414	.467
1996 Minnesota	AL	79	252	65	7	1	6	(1	5)	92	34	42	28	1	28	4	0	2	4	4	.50	6	.258	.339	.365
1997 Minnesota	AL	142	460	114	29	3	14	(8	6)	191	74	60	76	3	81	10	1	1	7	4	.64	7	.248	.366	.415
3 ML YEARS		242	772	198	40	5	21	(10	11)	311	119	114	111	4	120	17	1	3	12	9	.57	14	.256	.361	.403

Aaron Ledesma

Bats: R **Throws:** R **Pos:** 2B-22; 3B-11; PH-7; 1B-5; SS-4   **Ht:** 6'2" **Wt:** 200 **Born:** 6/3/71 **Age:** 27

Year Team	Lg	G	AB	H	2B	3B	HR	(Hm	Rd)	TB	R	RBI	TBB	IBB	SO	HBP	SH	SF	SB	CS	SB%	GDP	Avg	OBP	SLG
1990 Kingsport	R+	66	243	81	11	1	5	—	—	109	50	38	30	2	28	8	0	4	23	6	.79	4	.333	.418	.449
1991 Columbia	A	33	115	39	8	0	1	—	—	50	19	14	8	0	16	4	3	3	3	2	.60	1	.339	.392	.435
1992 St. Lucie	A+	134	456	120	17	2	2	—	—	147	51	50	46	1	66	11	2	7	20	12	.63	13	.263	.340	.322
1993 Binghamton	AA	66	206	55	12	0	5	—	—	82	23	22	14	0	43	2	4	1	2	1	.67	6	.267	.318	.398
1994 Norfolk	AAA	119	431	118	20	1	3	—	—	149	49	56	28	0	41	6	9	6	18	8	.69	16	.274	.323	.346
1995 Norfolk	AAA	56	201	60	12	1	0	—	—	74	26	28	10	1	22	1	1	0	6	3	.67	5	.299	.335	.368
1996 Vancouver	AAA	109	440	134	27	4	1	—	—	172	60	51	32	2	59	7	2	1	2	3	.40	18	.305	.360	.391
1997 Rochester	AAA	85	326	106	26	1	3	—	—	143	40	43	35	3	48	3	2	7	12	2	.86	10	.325	.388	.439
1995 New York	NL	21	33	8	0	0	0	(0	0)	8	4	3	6	1	7	0	0	0	0	0	.00	2	.242	.359	.242
1997 Baltimore	AL	43	88	31	5	1	2	(1	1)	44	24	11	13	0	9	1	1	1	1	0	1.00	1	.352	.437	.500
2 ML YEARS		64	121	39	5	1	2	(1	1)	52	28	14	19	1	16	1	1	1	1	0	1.00	3	.322	.415	.430

Derrek Lee

Bats: Right **Throws:** Right **Pos:** 1B-21; PH-6   **Ht:** 6'5" **Wt:** 205 **Born:** 9/6/75 **Age:** 22

Year Team	Lg	G	AB	H	2B	3B	HR	(Hm	Rd)	TB	R	RBI	TBB	IBB	SO	HBP	SH	SF	SB	CS	SB%	GDP	Avg	OBP	SLG
1993 Padres	R	15	52	17	1	1	2	—	—	26	11	5	6	1	7	0	0	0	4	0	1.00	1	.327	.397	.500
Rancho Cuca	A+	20	73	20	5	1	1	—	—	30	13	10	10	0	20	1	0	0	0	2	.00	1	.274	.369	.411
1994 Rancho Cuca	A+	126	442	118	19	2	8	—	—	165	66	53	42	2	95	7	0	6	18	14	.56	11	.267	.336	.373
1995 Rancho Cuca	A+	128	502	151	25	2	23	—	—	249	82	95	49	2	130	7	0	7	14	7	.67	8	.301	.366	.496
Memphis	AA	2	9	1	0	0	0	—	—	1	0	1	0	0	2	0	0	0	0	0	.00	0	.111	.111	.111
1996 Memphis	AA	134	500	140	39	2	34	—	—	285	98	104	65	3	170	2	0	8	13	6	.68	8	.280	.360	.570
1997 Las Vegas	AAA	125	472	153	29	2	13	—	—	225	86	64	60	4	116	0	0	2	17	3	.85	9	.324	.399	.477
1997 San Diego	NL	22	54	14	3	0	1	(0	1)	20	9	4	9	0	24	0	0	0	0	0	.00	1	.259	.365	.370

Al Leiter

Pitches: Left **Bats:** Left **Pos:** SP-27   **Ht:** 6'3" **Wt:** 215 **Born:** 10/12/65 **Age:** 32

		HOW MUCH HE PITCHED						WHAT HE GAVE UP												THE RESULTS						
Year Team	Lg	G	GS	CG	GF	IP	BFP	H	R	ER	HR	SH	SF	HB	TBB	IBB	SO	WP	Bk	W	L	Pct.	ShO	Sv-Op	Hld	ERA
1987 New York	AL	4	4	0	0	22.2	104	24	16	16	2	1	0	1	15	0	28	4	0	2	2	.500	0	0-0	0	6.35
1988 New York	AL	14	14	0	0	57.1	251	49	27	25	7	1	0	5	33	0	60	1	4	4	4	.500	0	0-0	0	3.92
1989 NYA-Tor	AL	5	5	0	0	33.1	154	32	23	21	1	1	2	23	0	26	2	1	1	2	.333	0	0-0	0	5.67	
1990 Toronto	AL	4	0	0	2	6.1	22	1	0	0	0	1	0	0	2	0	5	0	0	0	0	.000	0	0-0	0	0.00
1991 Toronto	AL	3	0	0	1	1.2	13	3	5	5	0	1	0	0	5	0	1	0	0	0	0	.000	0	0-0	0	27.00
1992 Toronto	AL	1	0	0	0	1	7	1	1	1	0	0	0	0	2	0	0	0	0	0	0	.000	0	0-0	0	9.00
1993 Toronto	AL	34	12	1	4	105	454	93	52	48	8	3	3	4	56	2	66	2	2	9	6	.600	1	2-3	3	4.11
1994 Toronto	AL	20	20	1	0	111.2	516	125	68	63	6	3	8	2	65	3	100	7	5	6	7	.462	0	0-0	0	5.08
1995 Toronto	AL	28	28	2	0	183	805	162	80	74	15	6	4	6	108	1	153	14	0	11	11	.500	1	0-0	0	3.64
1996 Florida	NL	33	33	2	0	215.1	896	153	74	70	14	7	3	11	119	3	200	5	0	16	12	.571	1	0-0	0	2.93
1997 Florida	NL	27	27	0	0	151.1	668	133	78	73	13	10	3	12	91	4	132	2	0	11	9	.550	0	0-0	0	4.34
1989 New York	AL	4	4	0	0	26.2	123	23	20	18	1	1	1	2	21	0	22	1	1	2	.333	0	0-0	0	6.08	
Toronto	AL	1	1	0	0	6.2	31	9	3	3	1	0	0	0	2	0	4	1	0	0	0	.000	0	0-0	0	4.05
11 ML YEARS		173	143	6	7	888.2	3890	776	424	396	67	33	22	42	519	13	771	37	12	60	53	.531	3	2-3	3	4.01

Mark Leiter

Pitches: Right **Bats:** Right **Pos:** SP-31   **Ht:** 6'3" **Wt:** 210 **Born:** 4/13/63 **Age:** 35

		HOW MUCH HE PITCHED						WHAT HE GAVE UP												THE RESULTS						
Year Team	Lg	G	GS	CG	GF	IP	BFP	H	R	ER	HR	SH	SF	HB	TBB	IBB	SO	WP	Bk	W	L	Pct.	ShO	Sv-Op	Hld	ERA
1990 New York	AL	8	3	0	2	26.1	119	33	20	20	5	2	1	2	9	0	21	0	0	1	1	.500	0	0-0	0	6.84

Year Team	Lg	G	GS	CG	GF	IP	BFP	H	R	ER	HR	SH	SF	HB	TBB	IBB	SO	WP	Bk	W	L	Pct.	ShO	Sv-Op	Hld	ERA
1991 Detroit	AL	38	15	1	7	134.2	578	125	66	63	16	5	6	6	50	4	103	2	0	9	7	.563	0	1-2	2	4.21
1992 Detroit	AL	35	14	1	7	112	475	116	57	52	9	2	8	3	43	5	75	3	0	8	5	.615	0	0-0	3	4.18
1993 Detroit	AL	27	13	1	4	106.2	471	111	61	56	17	3	5	3	44	5	70	5	0	6	6	.500	0	0-1	1	4.73
1994 California	AL	40	7	0	15	95.1	425	99	56	50	13	4	4	9	35	6	71	2	0	4	7	.364	0	2-3	3	4.72
1995 San Francisco	NL	30	29	7	0	195.2	817	185	91	83	19	10	6	17	55	4	129	9	3	10	12	.455	1	0-0	0	3.82
1996 SF-Mon	NL	35	34	2	0	205	904	219	128	112	37	12	6	16	69	8	164	6	4	8	12	.400	0	0-0	0	4.92
1997 Philadelphia	NL	31	31	3	0	182.2	832	216	132	115	25	11	8	9	64	4	148	11	2	10	17	.370	0	0-0	0	5.67
1996 San Francisco	NL	23	22	1	0	135.1	602	151	93	78	25	7	3	9	50	7	118	2	3	4	10	.286	0	0-0	0	5.19
Montreal	NL	12	12	1	0	69.2	302	68	35	34	12	5	3	7	19	1	46	4	1	4	2	.667	0	0-0	0	4.39
8 ML YEARS		244	146	15	35	1058.1	4621	1104	611	551	141	49	44	65	369	36	781	38	9	56	67	.455	1	3-6	9	4.69

Mark Lemke

Bats: Both **Throws:** Right **Pos:** 2B-104; PH-5 **Ht:** 5'9" **Wt:** 167 **Born:** 8/13/65 **Age:** 32

								BATTING											BASERUNNING				PERCENTAGES		
Year Team	Lg	G	AB	H	2B	3B	HR	(Hm	Rd)	TB	R	RBI	TBB	IBB	SO	HBP	SH	SF	SB	CS	SB%	GDP	Avg	OBP	SLG
1988 Atlanta	NL	16	58	13	4	0	0	(0	0)	17	8	2	4	0	5	0	2	0	0	2	.00	1	.224	.274	.293
1989 Atlanta	NL	14	55	10	2	1	2	(1	1)	20	4	10	5	0	7	0	0	0	0	1	.00	1	.182	.250	.364
1990 Atlanta	NL	102	239	54	13	0	0	(0	0)	67	22	21	21	3	22	0	4	2	0	1	.00	6	.226	.286	.280
1991 Atlanta	NL	136	269	63	11	2	2	(2	0)	84	36	23	29	2	27	0	6	4	1	2	.33	6	.234	.305	.312
1992 Atlanta	NL	155	427	97	7	4	6	(4	2)	130	38	26	50	11	39	0	12	2	0	3	.00	9	.227	.307	.304
1993 Atlanta	NL	151	493	124	19	2	7	(3	4)	168	52	49	65	13	50	0	5	6	1	2	.33	11	.252	.335	.341
1994 Atlanta	NL	104	350	103	15	0	3	(2	1)	127	40	31	38	12	37	0	6	0	0	3	.00	11	.294	.363	.363
1995 Atlanta	NL	116	399	101	16	5	5	(3	2)	142	42	38	44	4	40	0	7	3	2	2	.50	17	.253	.325	.356
1996 Atlanta	NL	135	498	127	17	0	5	(3	2)	159	64	37	53	1	48	0	5	6	5	2	.71	9	.255	.323	.319
1997 Atlanta	NL	109	351	86	17	1	2	(2	0)	111	33	26	33	2	51	0	8	5	2	0	1.00	10	.245	.306	.316
10 ML YEARS		1038	3139	778	121	15	32	(20	12)	1025	339	263	342	48	326	0	55	28	11	18	.38	94	.248	.319	.327

Patrick Lennon

Bats: R **Throws:** R **Pos:** LF-23; PH-21; DH-17; RF-12; CF-1 **Ht:** 6'2" **Wt:** 200 **Born:** 4/27/68 **Age:** 30

								BATTING											BASERUNNING				PERCENTAGES		
Year Team	Lg	G	AB	H	2B	3B	HR	(Hm	Rd)	TB	R	RBI	TBB	IBB	SO	HBP	SH	SF	SB	CS	SB%	GDP	Avg	OBP	SLG
1986 Bellingham	A-	51	169	41	5	2	3	—	—	59	35	27	36	0	50	0	1	1	8	6	.57	3	.243	.374	.349
1987 Wausau	A	98	319	80	21	3	7	—	—	128	54	34	46	1	82	1	1	2	25	8	.76	10	.251	.345	.401
1988 Vermont	AA	95	321	83	9	3	9	—	—	125	44	40	21	1	87	3	3	4	15	6	.71	9	.259	.307	.389
1989 Williamsprt	AA	66	248	65	14	2	3	—	—	92	32	31	23	2	53	0	0	5	7	4	.64	9	.262	.319	.371
1990 San Berndno	A+	44	163	47	6	2	8	—	—	81	29	30	15	1	51	0	0	1	6	0	1.00	4	.288	.346	.497
Williamsprt	AA	49	167	49	6	4	5	—	—	78	24	22	10	0	37	2	0	3	10	4	.71	2	.293	.335	.467
1991 Calgary	AAA	112	416	137	29	5	15	—	—	221	75	74	46	4	68	4	1	1	12	5	.71	9	.329	.400	.531
1992 Calgary	AAA	13	48	17	3	0	1	—	—	23	8	9	6	0	10	0	0	0	4	1	.80	1	.354	.426	.479
1993 Canton-Akrn	AA	45	152	39	7	1	4	—	—	60	24	22	30	1	45	1	0	2	4	2	.67	4	.257	.378	.395
1994 New Britain	AA	114	429	140	30	5	17	—	—	231	80	67	48	1	96	5	0	1	13	9	.59	10	.326	.400	.538
1995 Pawtucket	AAA	40	128	35	6	2	3	—	—	54	20	20	16	0	42	1	0	1	6	4	.60	6	.273	.356	.422
Trenton	AA	27	98	39	7	0	1	—	—	49	19	8	14	0	22	1	0	0	7	2	.78	3	.398	.478	.500
Salt Lake	AAA	34	115	46	15	0	6	—	—	79	26	29	12	2	29	1	0	1	2	1	.67	1	.400	.457	.687
1996 Edmonton	AAA	68	251	82	16	2	12	—	—	138	37	42	28	2	82	2	0	0	3	3	.50	5	.327	.399	.550
1997 Edmonton	AAA	39	134	46	7	0	9	—	—	80	28	35	22	4	34	2	0	2	0	0	.00	5	.343	.438	.597
Modesto	A+	5	16	3	1	0	1	—	—	7	3	4	3	1	5	0	0	0	0	0	.00	0	.188	.316	.438
1991 Seattle	AL	9	8	1	1	0	0	(0	0)	2	2	1	3	0	1	0	0	0	0	0	.00	0	.125	.364	.250
1992 Seattle	AL	1	2	0	0	0	0	(0	0)	0	0	0	0	0	1	0	0	0	0	0	.00	0	.000	.000	.000
1996 Kansas City	AL	14	30	7	3	0	0	(0	0)	10	5	1	7	0	10	0	0	0	0	0	.00	0	.233	.378	.333
1997 Oakland	AL	56	116	34	6	1	1	(1	0)	45	14	14	15	0	35	0	0	1	0	1	.00	3	.293	.374	.388
4 ML YEARS		80	156	42	10	1	1	(1	0)	57	21	16	25	0	46	0	0	1	0	1	.00	3	.269	.370	.365

John LeRoy

Pitches: Right **Bats:** Right **Pos:** RP-1 **Ht:** 6'3" **Wt:** 175 **Born:** 4/19/75 **Age:** 23

								WHAT HE GAVE UP											THE RESULTS						
Year Team	Lg	G	GS	CG	GF	IP	BFP	H	R	ER	HR	SH	SF	HB	TBB	IBB	SO	WP	Bk	W	L	Pct.	ShO	Sv-Op	Hld	ERA
1993 Braves	R	10	2	0	4	26.1	107	21	9	6	1	1	1	0	8	1	32	2	0	2	2	.500	0	1--	—	2.05
1994 Macon	A	10	9	0	0	40.1	173	36	21	20	4	2	1	0	20	0	44	1	5	3	3	.500	0	0--	—	4.46
1995 Durham	A+	24	22	1	0	125.2	545	128	82	76	17	2	5	5	57	1	77	5	1	9	6	.400	0	0--	—	5.44
1996 Durham	A+	19	19	0	0	110.2	463	91	47	43	6	4	5	2	52	0	94	10	2	7	4	.636	0	0--	—	3.50
Greenville	AA	8	8	0	0	45.1	193	43	18	15	5	2	2	2	18	1	38	4	1	1	1	.500	0	1--	—	2.98
1997 Greenville	AA	29	14	0	9	98.1	444	105	59	55	20	1	2	5	43	1	84	15	1	5	5	.500	0	1--	—	5.03
1997 Atlanta	NL	1	0	0	0	2	10	1	0	0	0	0	0	0	3	1	3	0	0	1	0	1.000	0	0-0	0	0.00

Brian Lesher

Bats: R **Throws:** L **Pos:** LF-31; PH-13; DH-3; 1B-3; RF-3 **Ht:** 6'5" **Wt:** 205 **Born:** 3/5/71 **Age:** 27

								BATTING											BASERUNNING				PERCENTAGES		
Year Team	Lg	G	AB	H	2B	3B	HR	(Hm	Rd)	TB	R	RBI	TBB	IBB	SO	HBP	SH	SF	SB	CS	SB%	GDP	Avg	OBP	SLG
1992 Sou. Oregon	A-	46	136	26	7	1	3	—	—	44	21	14	12	0	35	2	0	1	3	7	.30	3	.191	.265	.324
1993 Madison	A	119	394	108	13	5	5	—	—	146	63	47	46	1	102	9	6	6	20	9	.69	13	.274	.358	.371
1994 Modesto	A+	117	393	114	21	0	14	—	—	177	76	68	81	5	84	8	0	8	11	11	.50	8	.290	.414	.450
1995 Huntsville	AA	127	471	123	23	2	19	—	—	207	78	71	64	2	110	2	0	1	7	8	.47	7	.261	.351	.439
1996 Edmonton	AAA	109	414	119	29	2	18	—	—	206	57	75	36	0	77	2	3	1	6	5	.55	9	.287	.352	.498

119

Year Team	Lg	G	AB	H	2B	3B	HR	(Hm	Rd)	TB	R	RBI	TBB	IBB	SO	HBP	SH	SF	SB	CS	SB%	GDP	Avg	OBP	SLG
1997 Edmonton	AAA	110	415	134	27	5	21	—	—	234	85	78	64	3	86	3	0	2	14	3	.82	14	.323	.415	.564
1996 Oakland	AL	26	82	19	3	0	5	(2	3)	37	11	16	5	0	17	1	1	1	0	0	.00	2	.232	.281	.451
1997 Oakland	AL	46	131	30	4	1	4	(2	2)	48	17	16	9	0	30	0	0	2	4	1	.80	4	.229	.275	.366
2 ML YEARS		72	213	49	7	1	9	(4	5)	85	28	32	14	0	47	1	1	3	4	1	.80	6	.230	.277	.399

Curt Leskanic

Pitches: Right **Bats:** Right **Pos:** RP-55   **Ht:** 6'0" **Wt:** 180 **Born:** 4/2/68 **Age:** 30

| | | | HOW MUCH HE PITCHED | | | | WHAT HE GAVE UP | | | | | | | | | | | THE RESULTS | | | | | | |
Year Team	Lg	G	GS	CG	GF	IP	BFP	H	R	ER	HR	SH	SF	HB	TBB	IBB	SO	WP	Bk	W	L	Pct.	ShO	Sv-Op	Hld	ERA
1997 Salem *	A+	2	1	0	0	2.1	12	5	2	1	0	0	0	0	1	0	3	0	0	0	0	.000	0	0- -	—	3.86
Colo Sprngs *	AAA	10	3	0	6	19	81	11	9	8	1	0	0	0	18	0	20	1	0	0	0	.000	0	2- -	—	3.79
1993 Colorado	NL	18	8	0	1	57	260	59	40	34	7	5	4	2	27	1	30	8	2	1	5	.167	0	0-0	0	5.37
1994 Colorado	NL	8	3	0	2	22.1	98	27	14	14	2	2	0	0	10	0	17	2	0	1	1	.500	0	0-0	0	5.64
1995 Colorado	NL	76	0	0	27	98	406	83	38	37	7	3	2	0	33	1	107	6	1	6	3	.667	0	10-16	19	3.40
1996 Colorado	NL	70	0	0	32	73.2	334	82	51	51	12	3	3	2	38	1	76	6	2	7	5	.583	0	6-10	9	6.23
1997 Colorado	NL	55	0	0	23	58.1	248	59	36	36	8	2	4	0	24	0	53	4	0	4	0	1.000	0	2-4	6	5.55
5 ML YEARS		227	11	0	85	309.1	1346	310	179	172	36	15	13	4	132	3	283	26	5	19	14	.576	0	18-30	34	5.00

Al Levine

Pitches: Right **Bats:** Left **Pos:** RP-25   **Ht:** 6'3" **Wt:** 180 **Born:** 5/22/68 **Age:** 30

| | | | HOW MUCH HE PITCHED | | | | WHAT HE GAVE UP | | | | | | | | | | | THE RESULTS | | | | | | |
Year Team	Lg	G	GS	CG	GF	IP	BFP	H	R	ER	HR	SH	SF	HB	TBB	IBB	SO	WP	Bk	W	L	Pct.	ShO	Sv-Op	Hld	ERA
1991 Utica	A-	16	12	2	3	85	361	75	43	30	2	4	2	4	26	0	83	8	1	6	4	.600	1	1- -	—	3.18
1992 South Bend	A	23	23	2	0	156.2	650	151	67	49	6	6	2	8	36	1	131	9	1	9	5	.643	0	0- -	—	2.81
Sarasota	A+	3	2	0	0	15.2	68	17	11	7	1	3	2	0	5	1	11	0	1	0	2	.000	0	0- -	—	4.02
1993 Sarasota	A+	27	26	5	0	161.1	696	169	87	66	6	11	3	7	50	3	129	11	3	11	8	.579	1	0- -	—	3.68
1994 Birmingham	AA	18	18	1	0	114.1	501	117	50	42	7	2	3	14	44	1	94	3	0	5	9	.357	0	0- -	—	3.31
Nashville	AAA	8	4	0	1	24	116	34	23	21	2	1	3	2	11	0	24	0	0	0	2	.000	0	0- -	—	7.88
1995 Nashville	AAA	3	3	0	0	14	69	20	10	8	1	0	0	0	7	0	14	3	0	0	2	.000	0	0- -	—	5.14
Birmingham	AA	43	1	0	31	73	305	61	22	19	2	2	2	2	25	5	68	7	1	4	3	.571	0	7- -	—	2.34
1996 Nashville	AAA	43	0	0	28	61.2	267	58	27	25	4	2	2	3	24	6	45	1	0	4	5	.444	0	12- -	—	3.65
1997 Nashville	AAA	26	0	0	0	35.1	171	58	32	28	3	1	1	2	11	1	29	5	0	1	1	.500	0	2- -	—	7.13
1996 Chicago	AL	16	0	0	5	18.1	85	22	14	11	1	0	1	1	7	1	12	0	0	0	1	.000	0	0-1	0	5.40
1997 Chicago	AL	25	0	0	6	27.1	133	35	22	21	4	1	2	2	16	1	22	2	0	2	1	.500	0	0-1	3	6.91
2 ML YEARS		41	0	0	11	45.2	218	57	36	32	5	1	3	3	23	2	34	2	0	2	2	.400	0	0-2	3	6.31

Jesse Levis

Bats: Left **Throws:** Right **Pos:** C-78; PH-49; DH-8   **Ht:** 5'9" **Wt:** 180 **Born:** 4/14/68 **Age:** 30

| | | | | | BATTING | | | | | | | | | | | | | | BASERUNNING | | | | PERCENTAGES | | |
Year Team	Lg	G	AB	H	2B	3B	HR	(Hm	Rd)	TB	R	RBI	TBB	IBB	SO	HBP	SH	SF	SB	CS	SB%	GDP	Avg	OBP	SLG
1992 Cleveland	AL	28	43	12	4	0	1	(0	1)	19	2	3	0	0	5	0	0	0	0	0	.00	1	.279	.279	.442
1993 Cleveland	AL	31	63	11	2	0	0	(0	0)	13	7	4	2	0	10	0	1	1	0	0	.00	0	.175	.197	.206
1994 Cleveland	AL	1	1	1	0	0	0	(0	0)	1	0	0	0	0	0	0	0	0	0	0	.00	0	1.000	1.000	1.000
1995 Cleveland	AL	12	18	6	2	0	0	(0	0)	8	1	3	1	0	0	0	0	2	0	0	.00	1	.333	.333	.444
1996 Milwaukee	AL	104	233	55	6	1	1	(0	1)	66	27	21	38	0	15	2	1	0	0	0	.00	7	.236	.348	.283
1997 Milwaukee	AL	99	200	57	7	0	1	(1	0)	67	19	19	24	0	17	1	5	2	1	0	1.00	4	.285	.361	.335
6 ML YEARS		275	558	142	21	1	3	(1	2)	174	56	50	65	0	47	3	8	5	1	0	1.00	13	.254	.333	.312

Darren Lewis

Bats: R **Throws:** R **Pos:** CF-66; PH-36; LF-23; DH-6; RF-1   **Ht:** 6'0" **Wt:** 189 **Born:** 8/28/67 **Age:** 30

| | | | | | BATTING | | | | | | | | | | | | | | BASERUNNING | | | | PERCENTAGES | | |
Year Team	Lg	G	AB	H	2B	3B	HR	(Hm	Rd)	TB	R	RBI	TBB	IBB	SO	HBP	SH	SF	SB	CS	SB%	GDP	Avg	OBP	SLG
1990 Oakland	AL	25	35	8	0	0	0	(0	0)	8	4	1	7	0	4	1	3	0	2	0	1.00	2	.229	.372	.229
1991 San Francisco	NL	72	222	55	5	3	1	(0	1)	69	41	15	36	0	30	2	7	0	13	7	.65	1	.248	.358	.311
1992 San Francisco	NL	100	320	74	8	1	1	(1	0)	87	38	18	29	0	46	1	10	2	28	8	.78	3	.231	.295	.272
1993 San Francisco	NL	136	522	132	17	7	2	(2	0)	169	84	48	30	0	40	7	12	1	46	15	.75	4	.253	.302	.324
1994 San Francisco	NL	114	451	116	15	9	4	(4	0)	161	70	29	53	0	50	4	4	1	30	13	.70	6	.257	.340	.357
1995 SF-Cin	NL	132	472	118	13	3	1	(1	0)	140	66	24	34	0	57	8	12	1	32	18	.64	9	.250	.311	.297
1996 Chicago	AL	141	337	77	12	2	4	(0	4)	105	55	53	45	1	40	3	15	5	21	5	.81	9	.228	.321	.312
1997 ChA-LA		107	154	41	4	1	1	(0	1)	50	22	15	17	0	31	0	7	0	14	6	.70	3	.266	.339	.325
1995 San Francisco	NL	74	309	78	10	3	1	(1	0)	97	47	16	17	0	37	6	7	1	21	7	.75	6	.252	.303	.314
Cincinnati	NL	58	163	40	3	0	0	(0	0)	43	19	8	17	0	20	2	5	0	11	11	.50	3	.245	.324	.264
1997 Chicago	AL	81	77	18	1	0	0	(0	0)	19	15	5	11	0	14	0	5	0	11	4	.73	2	.234	.330	.247
Los Angeles	NL	26	77	23	3	1	1	(0	1)	31	7	10	6	0	17	0	2	0	3	2	.60	1	.299	.349	.403
8 ML YEARS		827	2513	621	74	26	14	(8	6)	789	380	203	251	1	298	26	70	10	186	72	.72	37	.247	.321	.314

Mark Lewis

Bats: R **Throws:** R **Pos:** 3B-69; 2B-29; PH-25; DH-1   **Ht:** 6'1" **Wt:** 185 **Born:** 11/30/69 **Age:** 28

| | | | | | BATTING | | | | | | | | | | | | | | BASERUNNING | | | | PERCENTAGES | | |
Year Team	Lg	G	AB	H	2B	3B	HR	(Hm	Rd)	TB	R	RBI	TBB	IBB	SO	HBP	SH	SF	SB	CS	SB%	GDP	Avg	OBP	SLG
1991 Cleveland	AL	84	314	83	15	1	0	(0	0)	100	29	30	15	0	45	0	2	5	2	2	.50	12	.264	.293	.318
1992 Cleveland	AL	122	413	109	21	0	5	(2	3)	145	44	30	25	1	69	3	1	4	4	5	.44	12	.264	.308	.351

Year Team	Lg	G	AB	H	2B	3B	HR	(Hm	Rd)	TB	R	RBI	TBB	IBB	SO	HBP	SH	SF	SB	CS	SB%	GDP	Avg	OBP	SLG
1993 Cleveland	AL	14	52	13	2	0	1	(1	0)	18	6	5	0	0	7	0	1	0	3	0	1.00	1	.250	.250	.346
1994 Cleveland	AL	20	73	15	5	0	1	(1	0)	23	6	8	2	0	13	0	1	0	1	0	1.00	2	.205	.227	.315
1995 Cincinnati	NL	81	171	58	13	1	3	(1	2)	82	25	30	21	2	33	0	0	2	0	3	.00	1	.339	.407	.480
1996 Detroit	AL	145	545	147	30	3	11	(8	3)	216	69	55	42	0	109	5	4	3	6	1	.86	12	.270	.326	.396
1997 San Francisco	NL	118	341	91	14	6	10	(4	6)	147	50	42	23	2	62	4	1	3	3	2	.60	8	.267	.318	.431
7 ML YEARS		584	1909	516	100	11	31	(17	14)	731	229	200	128	5	338	12	10	17	19	13	.59	48	.270	.318	.383

Richie Lewis

Pitches: Right **Bats:** Right **Pos:** RP-18   **Ht:** 5'10" **Wt:** 175 **Born:** 1/25/66 **Age:** 32

Year Team	Lg	G	GS	CG	GF	IP	BFP	H	R	ER	HR	SH	SF	HB	TBB	IBB	SO	WP	Bk	W	L	Pct.	ShO	Sv-Op	Hld	ERA
1997 Edmonton *	AAA	11	1	0	4	20	96	24	13	13	2	1	1	1	14	1	25	3	0	1	1	.500	0	1- --	---	5.85
Indianapolis *	AAA	27	0	0	17	29.2	120	22	7	5	0	1	2	2	7	2	33	3	0	0	1	.000	0	9- --	---	1.52
1992 Baltimore	AL	2	2	0	0	6.2	40	13	8	8	1	0	1	0	7	0	4	0	0	1	1	.500	0	0-0	0	10.80
1993 Florida	NL	57	0	0	14	77.1	341	68	37	28	7	8	4	1	43	6	65	9	1	6	3	.667	0	0-2	3	3.26
1994 Florida	NL	45	0	0	9	54	261	62	44	34	7	3	1	1	38	9	45	10	1	1	4	.200	0	0-0	4	5.67
1995 Florida	NL	21	1	0	6	36	152	30	15	15	9	2	0	1	15	5	32	1	2	0	1	.000	0	0-0	1	3.75
1996 Detroit	AL	72	0	0	19	90.1	412	78	45	42	9	5	10	4	65	9	78	14	2	4	6	.400	0	2-6	6	4.18
1997 Oak-Cin		18	0	0	5	24.1	119	28	26	24	10	3	1	1	18	0	16	2	0	2	0	1.000	0	0-0	0	8.88
1997 Oakland	AL	14	0	0	5	18.2	94	24	21	20	7	1	1	1	15	0	12	2	0	2	0	1.000	0	0-0	0	9.64
Cincinnati	NL	4	0	0	0	5.2	25	4	5	4	3	2	0	0	3	0	4	0	0	0	0	.000	0	0-0	0	6.35
6 ML YEARS		215	3	0	53	288.2	1325	279	175	151	43	21	17	8	186	29	240	36	6	14	15	.483	0	2-8	13	4.71

Jim Leyritz

Bats: R **Throws:** R **Pos:** C-69; 1B-24; DH-22; PH-13   **Ht:** 6'0" **Wt:** 195 **Born:** 12/27/63 **Age:** 34

Year Team	Lg	G	AB	H	2B	3B	HR	(Hm	Rd)	TB	R	RBI	TBB	IBB	SO	HBP	SH	SF	SB	CS	SB%	GDP	Avg	OBP	SLG
1990 New York	AL	92	303	78	13	1	5	(1	4)	108	28	25	27	1	51	7	1	1	2	3	.40	11	.257	.331	.356
1991 New York	AL	32	77	14	3	0	0	(0	0)	17	8	4	13	0	15	0	1	0	0	1	.00	0	.182	.300	.221
1992 New York	AL	63	144	37	6	0	7	(3	4)	64	17	26	14	1	22	6	0	3	0	1	.00	2	.257	.341	.444
1993 New York	AL	95	259	80	14	0	14	(6	8)	136	43	53	37	3	59	8	0	1	0	0	.00	12	.309	.410	.525
1994 New York	AL	75	249	66	12	0	17	(4	13)	129	47	58	35	1	61	6	0	3	0	0	.00	9	.265	.365	.518
1995 New York	AL	77	264	71	12	0	7	(3	4)	104	37	37	37	2	73	8	0	1	1	1	.50	4	.269	.374	.394
1996 New York	AL	88	265	70	10	0	7	(3	4)	101	23	40	30	3	68	9	2	3	2	0	1.00	8	.264	.355	.381
1997 Ana-Tex	AL	121	379	105	11	0	11	(3	8)	149	58	64	60	2	78	6	4	6	2	1	.67	13	.277	.379	.393
1997 Anaheim	AL	84	294	81	7	0	11	(3	8)	121	47	50	37	2	56	3	3	5	1	1	.50	11	.276	.357	.412
Texas	AL	37	85	24	4	0	0	(0	0)	28	11	14	23	0	22	3	1	1	1	0	1.00	2	.282	.446	.329
8 ML YEARS		643	1940	521	81	1	68	(23	45)	808	261	307	253	13	427	50	8	18	7	7	.50	62	.269	.364	.416

Cory Lidle

Pitches: Right **Bats:** Right **Pos:** RP-52; SP-2   **Ht:** 5'11" **Wt:** 180 **Born:** 3/22/72 **Age:** 26

Year Team	Lg	G	GS	CG	GF	IP	BFP	H	R	ER	HR	SH	SF	HB	TBB	IBB	SO	WP	Bk	W	L	Pct.	ShO	Sv-Op	Hld	ERA
1991 Twins	R	4	0	0	1	4.2	19	5	3	3	0	0	0	0	0	0	5	1	2	1	1	.500	0	0- --	---	5.79
1992 Elizabethtn	R+	19	2	0	11	43.2	190	40	29	18	2	0	2	0	21	0	32	3	1	2	1	.667	0	6- --	---	3.71
1993 Pocatello	R+	17	16	3	1	106.2	463	104	59	49	6	1	4	5	54	0	91	14	1	8	4	.667	0	1- --	---	4.13
1994 Stockton	A+	25	1	0	12	42.2	200	60	32	21	2	0	0	1	13	1	38	1	0	1	2	.333	0	4- --	---	4.43
Beloit	A	13	9	1	0	69	279	65	24	20	4	1	0	2	11	0	62	6	0	3	4	.429	1	0- --	---	2.61
1995 El Paso	AA	45	9	0	12	109.2	480	126	52	41	6	6	1	6	36	3	78	6	0	5	4	.556	0	2- --	---	3.36
1996 Binghamton	AA	27	27	6	0	190.1	779	186	78	70	13	6	2	3	49	4	141	14	3	14	10	.583	1	0- --	---	3.31
1997 Norfolk	AAA	7	7	1	0	42	181	46	20	17	1	4	1	1	10	0	34	0	0	4	2	.667	0	0- --	---	3.64
1997 New York	NL	54	2	0	20	81.2	345	86	38	32	7	4	4	3	20	4	54	2	0	7	2	.778	0	2-3	9	3.53

Jon Lieber

Pitches: Right **Bats:** Left **Pos:** SP-32; RP-1   **Ht:** 6'3" **Wt:** 220 **Born:** 4/2/70 **Age:** 28

Year Team	Lg	G	GS	CG	GF	IP	BFP	H	R	ER	HR	SH	SF	HB	TBB	IBB	SO	WP	Bk	W	L	Pct.	ShO	Sv-Op	Hld	ERA
1994 Pittsburgh	NL	17	17	1	0	108.2	460	116	62	45	12	3	3	1	25	3	71	2	3	6	7	.462	0	0-0	0	3.73
1995 Pittsburgh	NL	21	12	0	3	72.2	327	103	56	51	7	5	6	4	14	0	45	0	0	4	7	.364	0	0-1	3	6.32
1996 Pittsburgh	NL	51	15	0	6	142	600	156	70	63	19	7	2	3	28	2	94	0	0	9	5	.643	0	1-4	9	3.99
1997 Pittsburgh	NL	33	32	1	0	188.1	799	193	102	94	23	6	7	1	51	8	160	3	1	11	14	.440	0	0-0	0	4.49
4 ML YEARS		122	76	2	9	511.2	2186	568	290	253	61	21	18	9	118	13	370	8	4	30	33	.476	0	1-5	12	4.45

Mike Lieberthal

Bats: Right **Throws:** Right **Pos:** C-129; PH-10; DH-1   **Ht:** 6'0" **Wt:** 178 **Born:** 1/18/72 **Age:** 26

Year Team	Lg	G	AB	H	2B	3B	HR	(Hm	Rd)	TB	R	RBI	TBB	IBB	SO	HBP	SH	SF	SB	CS	SB%	GDP	Avg	OBP	SLG
1994 Philadelphia	NL	24	79	21	3	1	1	(1	0)	29	6	5	3	0	5	1	1	0	0	0	.00	4	.266	.301	.367
1995 Philadelphia	NL	16	47	12	2	0	0	(0	0)	14	1	4	5	0	5	0	2	0	0	0	.00	1	.255	.327	.298
1996 Philadelphia	NL	50	166	42	8	0	7	(4	3)	71	21	23	10	0	30	2	0	4	0	0	.00	4	.253	.297	.428
1997 Philadelphia	NL	134	455	112	27	1	20	(11	9)	201	59	77	44	1	76	4	0	7	3	4	.43	10	.246	.314	.442
4 ML YEARS		224	747	187	40	2	28	(16	12)	315	87	109	62	1	116	7	3	11	3	4	.43	19	.250	.310	.422

Kerry Ligtenberg

Pitches: Right **Bats:** Right **Pos:** RP-15   **Ht:** 6'2" **Wt:** 205 **Born:** 5/11/71 **Age:** 27

		HOW MUCH HE PITCHED						WHAT HE GAVE UP										THE RESULTS					
Year Team	Lg	G	GS	CG	GF	IP	BFP	H	R	ER	HR	SH	SF	HB	TBB	IBB	SO	WP	Bk	W	L	Pct.	ShO	Sv-Op Hld	ERA
1994 Minneapolis	IND	19	19	2	0	114.1	487	103	47	42	11	5	3	3	44	4	94	6	0	5	5	.500	0	0-- —	3.31
1996 Durham	A+	49	0	0	42	59.2	255	58	20	16	3	2	3	6	16	3	76	4	1	7	4	.636	0	20-- —	2.41
1997 Greenville	AA	31	0	0	27	35.1	140	20	8	8	3	0	0	1	14	1	43	1	0	3	1	.750	0	16-- —	2.04
Richmond	AAA	14	0	0	6	25	94	21	13	12	3	1	2	0	2	0	35	3	0	0	3	.000	0	1-- —	4.32
1997 Atlanta	NL	15	0	0	9	15	61	12	5	5	4	0	0	0	4	2	19	0	0	1	0	1.000	0	1-1 0	3.00

Jose Lima

Pitches: Right **Bats:** Right **Pos:** RP-51; SP-1   **Ht:** 6'2" **Wt:** 205 **Born:** 9/30/72 **Age:** 25

		HOW MUCH HE PITCHED						WHAT HE GAVE UP										THE RESULTS					
Year Team	Lg	G	GS	CG	GF	IP	BFP	H	R	ER	HR	SH	SF	HB	TBB	IBB	SO	WP	Bk	W	L	Pct.	ShO	Sv-Op Hld	ERA
1994 Detroit	AL	3	1	0	1	6.2	34	11	10	10	2	0	0	3	1	1	7	1	0	0	1	.000	0	0-0 0	13.50
1995 Detroit	AL	15	15	0	0	73.2	320	85	52	50	10	2	1	4	18	4	37	5	0	3	9	.250	0	0-0 0	6.11
1996 Detroit	AL	39	4	0	15	72.2	329	87	48	46	13	5	3	5	22	4	59	3	0	5	6	.455	0	3-7 6	5.70
1997 Houston	NL	52	1	0	15	75	321	79	45	44	9	6	3	5	16	2	63	2	0	1	6	.143	0	2-2 3	5.28
4 ML YEARS		109	21	0	31	228	1004	262	155	150	34	13	7	14	59	11	166	11	0	9	22	.290	0	5-9 9	5.92

Felipe Lira

Pitches: Right **Bats:** Right **Pos:** SP-18; RP-10   **Ht:** 6'0" **Wt:** 170 **Born:** 4/26/72 **Age:** 26

		HOW MUCH HE PITCHED						WHAT HE GAVE UP										THE RESULTS					
Year Team	Lg	G	GS	CG	GF	IP	BFP	H	R	ER	HR	SH	SF	HB	TBB	IBB	SO	WP	Bk	W	L	Pct.	ShO	Sv-Op Hld	ERA
1997 Everett *	A-	1	1	0	0	5	24	6	3	2	0	0	1	0	2	0	9	0	0	1	0	1.000	0	0-- —	3.60
Tacoma *	AAA	3	3	0	0	21	87	21	8	8	1	1	0	0	5	1	17	0	0	2	0	1.000	0	0-- —	3.43
1995 Detroit	AL	37	22	0	7	146.1	635	151	74	70	17	4	9	8	56	7	89	5	1	9	13	.409	0	1-3 1	4.31
1996 Detroit	AL	32	32	3	0	194.2	850	204	123	113	30	5	11	10	66	2	113	7	0	6	14	.300	2	0-0 0	5.22
1997 Det-Sea	AL	28	18	1	3	110.2	516	132	82	78	18	2	4	6	55	2	73	7	0	5	11	.313	1	0-0 1	6.34
1997 Detroit	AL	20	15	1	1	92	415	101	61	59	15	2	2	2	45	2	64	7	0	5	7	.417	1	0-0 0	5.77
Seattle	AL	8	3	0	2	18.2	101	31	21	19	3	0	2	4	10	0	9	0	0	0	4	.000	0	0-0 1	9.16
3 ML YEARS		97	72	4	10	451.2	2001	487	279	261	65	11	24	24	177	11	275	19	1	20	38	.345	3	1-3 2	5.20

Nelson Liriano

Bats: B **Throws:** R **Pos:** PH-61; 2B-17; 1B-2; 3B-1; SS-1   **Ht:** 5'10" **Wt:** 181 **Born:** 6/3/64 **Age:** 34

		BATTING																	BASERUNNING				PERCENTAGES		
Year Team	Lg	G	AB	H	2B	3B	HR	(Hm	Rd)	TB	R	RBI	TBB	IBB	SO	HBP	SH	SF	SB	CS	SB%	GDP	Avg	OBP	SLG
1987 Toronto	AL	37	158	38	6	2	2	(1	1)	54	29	10	16	2	22	0	2	0	13	2	.87	3	.241	.310	.342
1988 Toronto	AL	99	276	73	6	2	3	(0	3)	92	36	23	11	0	40	2	5	1	12	5	.71	4	.264	.297	.333
1989 Toronto	AL	132	418	110	26	3	5	(3	2)	157	51	53	43	0	51	2	10	5	16	7	.70	10	.263	.331	.376
1990 Tor-Min	AL	103	355	83	12	9	1	(1	0)	116	46	28	38	0	44	1	4	2	8	7	.53	8	.234	.308	.327
1991 Kansas City	AL	10	22	9	0	0	0	(0	0)	9	5	1	0	0	2	0	1	0	0	1	.00	0	.409	.409	.409
1993 Colorado	NL	48	151	46	6	3	2	(0	2)	64	28	15	18	2	22	0	5	1	6	4	.60	6	.305	.376	.424
1994 Colorado	NL	87	255	65	17	5	3	(2	1)	101	39	31	42	5	44	0	3	3	0	2	.00	4	.255	.357	.396
1995 Pittsburgh	NL	107	259	74	12	1	5	(2	3)	103	29	38	24	3	34	2	1	3	2	2	.50	2	.286	.347	.398
1996 Pittsburgh	NL	112	217	58	14	2	3	(0	3)	85	23	30	14	2	22	0	0	3	2	0	1.00	3	.267	.308	.392
1997 Los Angeles	NL	76	88	20	6	0	1	(0	1)	29	10	11	6	1	12	0	2	1	0	0	.00	1	.227	.274	.330
1990 Detroit	AL	50	170	36	7	2	1	(1	0)	50	16	15	16	0	20	1	1	1	3	5	.38	5	.212	.282	.294
Minnesota	AL	53	185	47	5	7	0	(0	0)	66	30	13	22	0	24	0	3	1	5	2	.71	3	.254	.332	.357
10 ML YEARS		811	2199	576	105	27	25	(9	16)	810	296	240	212	15	293	7	33	19	59	30	.66	39	.262	.326	.368

Pat Listach

Bats: B **Throws:** R **Pos:** SS-31; PH-18; CF-4; LF-1; RF-1   **Ht:** 5'9" **Wt:** 180 **Born:** 9/12/67 **Age:** 30

		BATTING																	BASERUNNING				PERCENTAGES		
Year Team	Lg	G	AB	H	2B	3B	HR	(Hm	Rd)	TB	R	RBI	TBB	IBB	SO	HBP	SH	SF	SB	CS	SB%	GDP	Avg	OBP	SLG
1997 Buffalo *	AAA	25	73	19	1	1	0	—	—	22	3	2	12	1	10	2	0	1	6	3	.67	1	.260	.375	.301
1992 Milwaukee	AL	149	579	168	19	6	1	(0	1)	202	93	47	55	0	124	1	12	2	54	18	.75	3	.290	.352	.349
1993 Milwaukee	AL	98	356	87	15	1	3	(0	3)	113	50	30	37	0	70	3	5	2	18	9	.67	7	.244	.319	.317
1994 Milwaukee	AL	16	54	16	3	0	0	(0	0)	19	8	2	3	0	8	0	0	0	2	1	.67	1	.296	.333	.352
1995 Milwaukee	AL	101	334	73	8	2	0	(0	0)	85	35	25	25	0	61	2	7	1	13	3	.81	6	.219	.276	.254
1996 Milwaukee	AL	87	317	76	16	2	1	(1	0)	99	51	33	36	0	51	1	6	2	25	5	.83	2	.240	.317	.312
1997 Houston	NL	52	132	24	2	2	0	(0	0)	30	13	6	11	2	24	1	5	2	4	2	.67	7	.182	.247	.227
6 ML YEARS		503	1772	444	63	13	5	(1	4)	548	250	143	167	2	338	8	35	9	116	38	.75	26	.251	.316	.309

Scott Livingstone

Bats: L **Throws:** R **Pos:** PH-56; 3B-5; 1B-2; DH-1; 2B-1; RF-1   **Ht:** 6'0" **Wt:** 190 **Born:** 7/15/65 **Age:** 32

		BATTING																	BASERUNNING				PERCENTAGES		
Year Team	Lg	G	AB	H	2B	3B	HR	(Hm	Rd)	TB	R	RBI	TBB	IBB	SO	HBP	SH	SF	SB	CS	SB%	GDP	Avg	OBP	SLG
1997 Rncho Cuca *	A+	3	8	2	0	0	0	—	—	2	2	0	3	0	0	0	0	0	0	1	.00	0	.250	.455	.250
Louisville *	AAA	9	25	9	1	0	0	—	—	10	4	2	2	0	3	0	1	1	0	0	.00	0	.360	.393	.400
1991 Detroit	AL	44	127	37	5	0	2	(1	1)	48	19	11	10	0	25	0	1	1	2	1	.67	0	.291	.341	.378
1992 Detroit	AL	117	354	100	21	0	4	(2	2)	133	43	46	21	1	36	0	3	4	1	3	.25	8	.282	.319	.376

Year Team	Lg	G	AB	H	2B	3B	HR	(Hm	Rd)	TB	R	RBI	TBB	IBB	SO	HBP	SH	SF	SB	CS	SB%	GDP	Avg	OBP	SLG
1993 Detroit	AL	98	304	89	10	2	2	(1	1)	109	39	39	19	1	32	0	1	6	1	3	.25	4	.293	.328	.359
1994 Det-SD		72	203	54	13	1	2	(1	1)	75	11	11	7	0	26	0	0	1	2	2	.50	5	.266	.289	.369
1995 San Diego	NL	99	196	66	15	0	5	(1	4)	96	26	32	15	1	22	0	0	2	2	1	.67	3	.337	.380	.490
1996 San Diego	NL	102	172	51	4	1	2	(0	2)	63	20	20	9	0	22	0	0	0	0	1	.00	6	.297	.331	.366
1997 SD-StL	NL	65	67	11	2	0	0	(0	0)	13	4	6	3	0	11	0	0	2	1	0	1.00	1	.164	.194	.194
1994 Detroit	AL	15	23	5	1	0	0	(0	0)	6	0	1	1	0	4	0	0	0	0	0	.00	0	.217	.250	.261
San Diego	NL	57	180	49	12	1	2	(1	1)	69	11	10	6	0	22	0	0	1	2	2	.50	5	.272	.294	.383
1997 San Diego	NL	23	26	4	1	0	0	(0	0)	5	1	3	2	0	1	0	0	0	0	0	.00	0	.154	.214	.192
St. Louis	NL	42	41	7	1	0	0	(0	0)	8	3	3	1	0	10	0	0	2	1	0	1.00	1	.171	.182	.195
7 ML YEARS		597	1423	408	70	4	17	(6	11)	537	162	165	84	3	174	0	5	16	9	11	.45	27	.287	.323	.377

Graeme Lloyd

Pitches: Left **Bats:** Left **Pos:** RP-46   **Ht:** 6'7" **Wt:** 234 **Born:** 4/9/67 **Age:** 31

Year Team	Lg	G	GS	CG	GF	IP	BFP	H	R	ER	HR	SH	SF	HB	TBB	IBB	SO	WP	Bk	W	L	Pct.	ShO	Sv-Op	Hld	ERA
1993 Milwaukee	AL	55	0	0	12	63.2	269	64	24	20	5	1	2	3	13	3	31	4	0	3	4	.429	0	0-4	6	2.83
1994 Milwaukee	AL	43	0	0	21	47	203	49	28	27	4	1	2	3	15	6	31	2	0	2	3	.400	0	3-6	3	5.17
1995 Milwaukee	AL	33	0	0	14	32	127	28	16	16	4	1	4	0	8	2	13	3	0	0	5	.000	0	4-6	9	4.50
1996 Mil-NYA	AL	65	0	0	15	56.2	252	61	30	27	4	5	3	1	22	4	30	4	0	2	6	.250	0	0-5	17	4.29
1997 New York	AL	46	0	0	17	49	217	55	24	18	6	3	5	1	20	7	26	3	0	1	1	.500	0	1-1	2	3.31
1996 Milwaukee	AL	52	0	0	15	51	217	49	19	16	3	5	1	1	17	3	24	0	0	2	4	.333	0	0-3	15	2.82
New York	AL	13	0	0	0	5.2	35	12	11	11	1	0	2	0	5	1	6	4	0	0	2	.000	0	0-2	2	17.47
5 ML YEARS		242	0	0	79	248.1	1068	257	122	108	23	11	16	8	78	22	131	16	0	8	19	.296	0	8-22	37	3.91

Esteban Loaiza

Pitches: Right **Bats:** Right **Pos:** SP-32; RP-1   **Ht:** 6'4" **Wt:** 190 **Born:** 12/31/71 **Age:** 26

Year Team	Lg	G	GS	CG	GF	IP	BFP	H	R	ER	HR	SH	SF	HB	TBB	IBB	SO	WP	Bk	W	L	Pct.	ShO	Sv-Op	Hld	ERA
1995 Pittsburgh	NL	32	31	1	0	172.2	762	205	115	99	17	9	5	5	53	3	85	6	1	8	9	.471	0	0-0	0	5.16
1996 Pittsburgh	NL	10	10	1	0	52.2	236	65	32	29	11	3	1	2	19	2	32	0	0	2	3	.400	1	0-0	0	4.96
1997 Pittsburgh	NL	33	32	1	0	196.1	851	214	99	90	17	10	7	12	56	9	122	2	3	11	11	.500	0	0-0	0	4.13
3 ML YEARS		75	73	3	0	421.2	1849	484	246	218	49	23	17	19	130	14	239	8	4	21	23	.477	1	0-0	0	4.65

Keith Lockhart

Bats: L **Throws:** R **Pos:** PH-70; 2B-20; 3B-11; DH-4   **Ht:** 5'10" **Wt:** 170 **Born:** 11/10/64 **Age:** 33

Year Team	Lg	G	AB	H	2B	3B	HR	(Hm	Rd)	TB	R	RBI	TBB	IBB	SO	HBP	SH	SF	SB	CS	SB%	GDP	Avg	OBP	SLG
1994 San Diego	NL	27	43	9	0	0	2	(2	0)	15	4	6	4	0	10	1	1	1	1	0	1.00	2	.209	.286	.349
1995 Kansas City	AL	94	274	88	19	3	6	(3	3)	131	41	33	14	2	21	4	1	7	8	1	.89	2	.321	.355	.478
1996 Kansas City	AL	138	433	118	33	3	7	(4	3)	178	49	55	30	4	40	2	1	5	11	6	.65	7	.273	.319	.411
1997 Atlanta	NL	96	147	41	5	3	6	(3	3)	70	25	32	14	0	17	1	3	4	0	0	.00	4	.279	.337	.476
4 ML YEARS		355	897	256	57	9	21	(12	9)	394	119	126	62	6	88	8	6	17	20	7	.74	15	.285	.331	.439

Kenny Lofton

Bats: Left **Throws:** Left **Pos:** CF-122   **Ht:** 6'0" **Wt:** 180 **Born:** 5/31/67 **Age:** 31

Year Team	Lg	G	AB	H	2B	3B	HR	(Hm	Rd)	TB	R	RBI	TBB	IBB	SO	HBP	SH	SF	SB	CS	SB%	GDP	Avg	OBP	SLG
1991 Houston	NL	20	74	15	1	0	0	(0	0)	16	9	0	5	0	19	0	0	0	2	1	.67	0	.203	.253	.216
1992 Cleveland	AL	148	576	164	15	8	5	(3	2)	210	96	42	68	3	54	2	4	1	66	12	.85	7	.285	.362	.365
1993 Cleveland	AL	148	569	185	28	8	1	(1	0)	232	116	42	81	6	83	1	2	4	70	14	.83	8	.325	.408	.408
1994 Cleveland	AL	112	459	160	32	9	12	(10	2)	246	105	57	52	5	56	2	4	6	60	12	.83	5	.349	.412	.536
1995 Cleveland	AL	118	481	149	22	13	7	(5	2)	218	93	53	40	6	49	1	4	3	54	15	.78	6	.310	.362	.453
1996 Cleveland	AL	154	662	210	35	4	14	(7	7)	295	132	67	61	3	82	0	7	6	75	17	.82	7	.317	.372	.446
1997 Atlanta	NL	122	493	164	20	6	5	(3	2)	211	90	48	64	5	83	2	2	3	27	20	.57	10	.333	.409	.428
7 ML YEARS		822	3314	1047	153	48	44	(29	15)	1428	641	309	371	28	426	8	23	23	354	91	.80	43	.316	.384	.431

Rich Loiselle

Pitches: Right **Bats:** Right **Pos:** RP-72   **Ht:** 6'5" **Wt:** 225 **Born:** 1/12/72 **Age:** 26

Year Team	Lg	G	GS	CG	GF	IP	BFP	H	R	ER	HR	SH	SF	HB	TBB	IBB	SO	WP	Bk	W	L	Pct.	ShO	Sv-Op	Hld	ERA
1991 Padres	R	12	12	0	0	61.1	285	72	40	24	1	1	3	3	26	0	47	4	3	2	3	.400	0	0- -	—	3.52
1992 Chston-SC	A	19	19	2	0	97	407	93	51	40	2	0	1	3	42	0	64	2	0	4	8	.333	2	0- -	—	3.71
1993 Waterloo	A	10	10	1	0	59.1	254	55	28	26	3	2	1	4	29	1	47	6	0	1	5	.167	1	0- -	—	3.94
Rancho Cuca	A+	14	14	1	0	82.2	380	109	64	53	5	3	3	5	34	1	53	1	0	5	8	.385	0	0- -	—	5.77
1994 Rancho Cuca	A+	27	27	0	0	156.2	704	189	83	69	12	7	6	11	76	2	120	12	0	9	10	.474	0	0- -	—	3.96
1995 Memphis	AA	13	13	1	0	78.2	357	82	46	31	5	1	1	6	33	2	48	3	1	6	3	.667	1	0- -	—	3.55
Las Vegas	AAA	8	7	1	0	27.1	131	36	27	22	5	1	0	2	9	0	16	0	0	2	2	.500	0	0- -	—	7.24
Tucson	AAA	2	1	0	0	10.1	44	8	4	3	0	0	0	4	4	0	10	1	0	0	0	—	0	0- -	—	2.61
1996 Jackson	AA	16	16	2	0	98.2	429	107	46	38	6	0	1	4	27	0	65	3	0	7	4	.636	1	0- -	—	3.47
Tucson	AAA	5	5	1	0	33.1	145	28	20	9	1	0	1	1	11	0	31	0	0	2	2	.500	1	0- -	—	2.43
Calgary	AAA	8	8	0	0	50.2	234	64	29	23	1	4	3	2	16	1	41	0	0	2	2	.500	0	0- -	—	4.09
1996 Pittsburgh	NL	5	3	0	0	20.2	90	22	8	7	3	0	0	0	8	1	9	3	0	1	0	1.000	0	0-0	1	3.05

	HOW MUCH HE PITCHED			WHAT HE GAVE UP			THE RESULTS		
Year Team	Lg	G GS CG GF	IP	BFP	H R ER HR SH SF HB	TBB IBB	SO	WP	Bk	W L Pct.	ShO Sv-Op Hld	ERA
1997 Pittsburgh	NL	72 0 0 58	72.2	312	76 29 25 7 2 2 1	24 3	66	4	0	1 5 .167	0 29-34 5	3.10
2 ML YEARS		77 3 0 58	93.1	402	98 37 32 10 2 2 1	32 4	75	7	0	2 5 .286	0 29-34 6	3.09

Joey Long

Pitches: Left **Bats:** Right **Pos:** RP-10   **Ht:** 6'2" **Wt:** 220 **Born:** 7/15/70 **Age:** 27

		HOW MUCH HE PITCHED			WHAT HE GAVE UP				THE RESULTS		
Year Team	Lg	G GS CG GF	IP	BFP	H R ER HR SH SF HB	TBB IBB	SO	WP	Bk	W L Pct.	ShO Sv-Op Hld	ERA
1991 Spokane	A-	13 11 0 0	56.2	282	78 57 44 2 1 3 2	39 0	40	8	4	1 9 .100	0 0- - —	6.99
1993 Waterloo	A	33 7 0 7	96.1	415	96 56 52 7 3 1 3	36 2	90	8	3	4 3 .571	0 0- - —	4.86
1994 Rancho Cuca	A+	46 0 0 17	52	248	69 36 27 3 6 2 1	22 1	52	8	0	2 4 .333	0 3- - —	4.67
1995 Las Vegas	AAA	25 0 0 9	31.1	143	38 22 16 1 0 4 0	16 2	13	0	0	1 3 .250	0 0- - —	4.60
Memphis	AA	25 0 0 3	21.2	104	28 15 8 0 1 1 1	10 2	18	0	0	0 2 .000	0 0- - —	3.32
1996 Memphis	AA	10 0 0 1	18	79	16 4 4 0 1 0 0	11 1	14	3	0	2 0 1.000	0 0- - —	2.00
Las Vegas	AAA	32 0 0 13	34	156	39 21 16 2 2 3 0	23 3	23	5	0	3 3 .500	0 1- - —	4.24
1997 Las Vegas	AAA	16 0 0 2	18.2	83	17 10 10 3 0 0 0	12 2	13	2	0	0 0 .000	0 0- - —	4.82
1997 San Diego	NL	10 0 0 4	11	60	17 11 10 1 1 0 1	8 1	8	1	0	0 0 .000	0 0-0 0	8.18

Ryan Long

Bats: Right **Throws:** Right **Pos:** RF-4; DH-1; LF-1; PH-1   **Ht:** 6'2" **Wt:** 215 **Born:** 2/3/73 **Age:** 25

		BATTING		BASERUNNING	PERCENTAGES
Year Team	Lg	G AB H 2B 3B HR (Hm Rd) TB R RBI TBB IBB SO HBP SH SF		SB CS SB% GDP	Avg OBP SLG
1991 Royals	R	48 177 54 2 2 0 — — 60 17 20 10 0 20 2 0 1		4 4 .56 3	.305 .347 .339
1992 Eugene	A-	54 183 42 5 2 0 — — 51 19 18 3 0 33 4 2 1		7 5 .58 4	.230 .257 .279
1993 Rockford	A	107 396 115 27 6 8 — — 178 46 68 16 3 76 18 2 5		16 6 .73 6	.290 .343 .449
1994 Wilmington	A+	123 494 130 25 5 11 — — 198 69 68 16 0 72 8 3 3		7 3 .70 4	.263 .296 .401
1995 Wichita	AA	102 342 79 26 0 5 — — 120 36 34 10 1 48 5 1 0		4 4 .50 9	.231 .263 .351
1996 Wichita	AA	122 442 125 29 1 20 — — 216 64 78 17 0 71 5 1 2		6 5 .55 9	.283 .315 .489
1997 Omaha	AAA	113 411 109 26 0 19 — — 192 48 56 18 2 98 7 3 3		2 4 .33 14	.265 .305 .467
1997 Kansas City	AL	6 9 2 0 0 0 (0 0) 2 2 2 0 0 3 1 0 0		0 0 .00 0	.222 .300 .222

Albie Lopez

Pitches: Right **Bats:** Right **Pos:** RP-31; SP-6   **Ht:** 6'2" **Wt:** 185 **Born:** 8/18/71 **Age:** 26

		HOW MUCH HE PITCHED			WHAT HE GAVE UP				THE RESULTS		
Year Team	Lg	G GS CG GF	IP	BFP	H R ER HR SH SF HB	TBB IBB	SO	WP	Bk	W L Pct.	ShO Sv-Op Hld	ERA
1997 Akron *	AA	1 0 0 0	1	5	2 0 0 0 0 0 0	0 0	2	0	0	0 0 .000	0 0- - —	0.00
Buffalo *	AAA	7 0 0 6	11.1	43	6 0 0 0 0 0 1	2 0	13	2	0	1 0 1.000	0 1- - —	0.00
1993 Cleveland	AL	9 9 0 0	49.2	222	49 34 33 7 1 1 1	32 1	25	0	0	3 1 .750	0 0-0 0	5.98
1994 Cleveland	AL	4 4 1 0	17	76	20 11 8 3 0 1 1	6 0	18	3	0	1 2 .333	1 0-0 0	4.24
1995 Cleveland	AL	6 2 0 0	23	92	17 8 8 4 0 1 1	7 1	22	2	0	0 0 .000	0 0-0 0	3.13
1996 Cleveland	AL	13 10 0 0	62	282	80 47 44 14 0 1 2	22 1	45	2	0	5 4 .556	0 0-0 0	6.39
1997 Cleveland	AL	37 6 0 10	76.2	364	101 61 59 11 3 2 4	40 9	63	5	0	3 7 .300	0 0-1 4	6.93
5 ML YEARS		69 31 1 10	228.1	1036	267 161 152 39 4 5 9	107 12	173	12	0	12 14 .462	1 0-1 4	5.99

Javy Lopez

Bats: Right **Throws:** Right **Pos:** C-117; PH-15   **Ht:** 6'3" **Wt:** 200 **Born:** 11/5/70 **Age:** 27

		BATTING		BASERUNNING	PERCENTAGES
Year Team	Lg	G AB H 2B 3B HR (Hm Rd) TB R RBI TBB IBB SO HBP SH SF		SB CS SB% GDP	Avg OBP SLG
1992 Atlanta	NL	9 16 6 2 0 0 (0 0) 8 3 2 0 0 1 0 0 0		0 0 .00 0	.375 .375 .500
1993 Atlanta	NL	8 16 6 1 1 1 (0 1) 12 1 2 0 0 2 1 0 0		0 0 .00 0	.375 .412 .750
1994 Atlanta	NL	80 277 68 9 0 13 (4 9) 116 27 35 17 0 61 5 2 2		0 2 .00 12	.245 .299 .419
1995 Atlanta	NL	100 333 105 11 4 14 (8 6) 166 37 51 14 0 57 2 0 3		1 .00 13	.315 .344 .498
1996 Atlanta	NL	138 489 138 19 1 23 (10 13) 228 56 69 28 5 84 3 1 5		1 6 .14 17	.282 .322 .466
1997 Atlanta	NL	123 414 122 28 1 23 (11 12) 221 52 68 40 10 82 5 1 4		1 1 .50 9	.295 .361 .534
6 ML YEARS		458 1545 445 70 7 74 (33 41) 751 176 227 99 15 287 16 4 14		2 10 .17 51	.288 .335 .486

Luis Lopez

Bats: B **Throws:** R **Pos:** SS-45; PH-26; 2B-20; 3B-4   **Ht:** 5'11" **Wt:** 175 **Born:** 9/4/70 **Age:** 27

		BATTING		BASERUNNING	PERCENTAGES
Year Team	Lg	G AB H 2B 3B HR (Hm Rd) TB R RBI TBB IBB SO HBP SH SF		SB CS SB% GDP	Avg OBP SLG
1997 Norfolk *	AAA	48 203 67 12 1 4 — — 93 32 19 9 2 29 1 2 2		2 6 .25 1	.330 .358 .458
1993 San Diego	NL	17 43 5 1 0 0 (0 0) 6 1 1 0 0 8 0 0 1		0 0 .00 0	.116 .114 .140
1994 San Diego	NL	77 235 65 16 1 2 (2 0) 89 29 20 15 2 39 3 2 2		3 2 .60 7	.277 .325 .379
1996 San Diego	NL	63 139 25 3 0 2 (1 1) 34 10 11 9 1 35 1 1 1		0 0 .00 7	.180 .233 .245
1997 New York	NL	78 178 48 12 1 0 (1 0) 65 19 19 12 2 42 4 2 0		2 4 .33 2	.270 .330 .365
4 ML YEARS		235 595 143 32 2 5 (4 1) 194 59 51 36 5 124 8 5 4		5 6 .45 16	.240 .291 .326

Mark Loretta

Bats: R **Throws:** R **Pos:** 2B-63; SS-44; 1B-19; 3B-15; PH-11   **Ht:** 6'0" **Wt:** 175 **Born:** 8/14/71 **Age:** 26

Year Team	Lg	G	AB	H	2B	3B	HR	(Hm	Rd)	TB	R	RBI	TBB	IBB	SO	HBP	SH	SF	SB	CS	SB%	GDP	Avg	OBP	SLG
1995 Milwaukee	AL	19	50	13	3	0	1	(0	1)	19	13	3	4	0	7	1	1	0	1	1	.50	1	.260	.327	.380
1996 Milwaukee	AL	73	154	43	3	0	1	(0	1)	49	20	13	14	0	15	0	2	0	2	1	.67	7	.279	.339	.318
1997 Milwaukee	AL	132	418	120	17	5	5	(2	3)	162	56	47	47	2	60	2	5	10	5	5	.50	15	.287	.354	.388
3 ML YEARS		224	622	176	23	5	7	(2	5)	230	89	63	65	2	82	3	8	10	8	7	.53	23	.283	.349	.370

Andrew Lorraine

Pitches: Left **Bats:** Left **Pos:** SP-6; RP-6   **Ht:** 6'3" **Wt:** 195 **Born:** 8/11/72 **Age:** 25

Year Team	Lg	G	GS	CG	GF	IP	BFP	H	R	ER	HR	SH	SF	HB	TBB	IBB	SO	WP	Bk	W	L	Pct.	ShO	Sv-Op	Hld	ERA
1997 Edmonton *	AAA	23	20	2	2	117.2	520	143	72	62	12	3	7	2	34	1	75	3	0	8	6	.571	2	0- —	—	4.74
1994 California	AL	4	3	0	0	18.2	96	30	23	22	7	2	1	0	11	0	10	0	0	0	2	.000	0	0-0	0	10.61
1995 Chicago	AL	5	0	0	2	8	30	3	3	3	0	0	0	1	2	0	5	0	0	0	0	.000	0	0-0	1	3.38
1997 Oakland	AL	12	6	0	1	29.2	146	45	22	21	2	0	3	1	15	0	18	0	0	3	1	.750	0	0-0	0	6.37
3 ML YEARS		21	9	0	3	56.1	272	78	48	46	9	2	4	2	28	0	33	0	0	3	3	.500	0	0-0	1	7.35

Derek Lowe

Pitches: Right **Bats:** Right **Pos:** RP-11; SP-9   **Ht:** 6'6" **Wt:** 170 **Born:** 6/1/73 **Age:** 25

Year Team	Lg	G	GS	CG	GF	IP	BFP	H	R	ER	HR	SH	SF	HB	TBB	IBB	SO	WP	Bk	W	L	Pct.	ShO	Sv-Op	Hld	ERA
1991 Mariners	R	12	12	0	0	71	295	58	26	19	2	1	4	2	21	0	60	4	6	5	3	.625	0	0- —	—	2.41
1992 Bellingham	A-	14	13	2	1	85.2	349	69	34	23	2	3	1	4	22	0	66	5	4	7	3	.700	1	0- —	—	2.42
1993 Riverside	A+	27	26	3	1	154	687	189	104	90	9	2	2	2	60	0	80	12	9	12	9	.571	2	0- —	—	5.26
1994 Jacksnville	AA	26	26	0	0	151.1	676	177	92	83	7	6	3	9	50	1	75	11	0	7	10	.412	0	0- —	—	4.94
1995 Mariners	R	2	2	0	0	9.2	35	5	1	1	0	0	0	0	2	0	11	0	0	1	0	1.000	0	0- —	—	0.93
Port City	AA	10	10	1	0	53.1	244	70	41	36	8	3	2	3	22	1	30	2	0	1	6	.143	0	0- —	—	6.08
1996 Port City	AA	10	10	0	0	65	258	56	27	22	7	0	2	1	17	0	33	0	0	5	3	.625	0	0- —	—	3.05
Tacoma	AAA	17	16	1	0	105	463	118	64	53	7	4	5	3	37	1	54	1	2	6	9	.400	1	0- —	—	4.54
1997 Tacoma	AAA	10	9	1	0	57.1	242	53	26	22	3	0	1	2	20	0	49	1	0	3	4	.429	0	0- —	—	3.45
Pawtucket	AAA	6	5	0	1	30.1	121	23	8	8	3	1	0	1	11	0	21	0	0	4	0	1.000	0	0- —	—	2.37
1997 Sea-Bos	AL	20	9	0	1	69	298	74	49	47	11	4	2	4	23	3	52	2	0	6	2	.250	0	0-2	1	6.13
1997 Seattle	AL	12	9	0	1	53	234	59	43	41	11	2	1	2	20	2	39	2	0	2	4	.333	0	0-0	0	6.96
Boston	AL	8	0	0	0	16	64	15	6	6	0	2	1	2	3	1	13	0	0	0	2	.000	0	0-2	1	3.38

Sean Lowe

Pitches: Right **Bats:** Right **Pos:** SP-4; RP-2   **Ht:** 6'2" **Wt:** 205 **Born:** 3/29/71 **Age:** 27

Year Team	Lg	G	GS	CG	GF	IP	BFP	H	R	ER	HR	SH	SF	HB	TBB	IBB	SO	WP	Bk	W	L	Pct.	ShO	Sv-Op	Hld	ERA
1992 Hamilton	A-	5	5	0	0	28	109	14	8	5	0	0	0	1	14	0	22	1	1	2	0	1.000	0	0- —	—	1.61
1993 St. Pete	A+	25	25	0	0	132.2	594	152	80	63	6	2	5	6	62	1	87	4	5	6	11	.353	0	0- —	—	4.27
1994 St. Pete	A+	21	21	0	0	114	488	119	51	44	6	3	2	5	37	0	92	3	0	5	6	.455	0	0- —	—	3.47
Arkansas	AA	3	3	0	0	19.1	76	13	3	3	0	2	0	0	8	0	11	0	0	2	1	.667	0	0- —	—	1.40
1995 Arkansas	AA	24	24	0	0	129	578	143	84	70	2	5	4	5	64	0	77	9	0	9	8	.529	0	0- —	—	4.88
1996 Arkansas	AA	6	6	0	0	33	150	32	24	22	1	2	1	2	15	1	25	1	0	2	3	.400	0	0- —	—	6.00
Louisville	AAA	25	18	0	1	115	515	127	72	60	7	4	6	7	51	7	76	6	0	8	9	.471	0	0- —	—	4.70
1997 Louisville	AAA	26	23	1	2	131.2	581	142	74	64	13	3	3	10	53	4	117	5	2	6	10	.375	0	1- —	—	4.37
1997 St. Louis	NL	6	4	0	1	17.1	89	27	21	18	2	1	2	1	10	0	8	0	0	0	2	.000	0	0-0	0	9.35

Terrell Lowery

Bats: Right **Throws:** Right **Pos:** PH-6; LF-5; CF-2   **Ht:** 6'3" **Wt:** 180 **Born:** 10/25/70 **Age:** 27

Year Team	Lg	G	AB	H	2B	3B	HR	(Hm	Rd)	TB	R	RBI	TBB	IBB	SO	HBP	SH	SF	SB	CS	SB%	GDP	Avg	OBP	SLG
1991 Butte	R+	54	214	64	10	7	3	—	—	97	38	33	29	0	44	1	0	2	23	12	.66	2	.299	.382	.453
1993 Charlotte	A+	65	257	77	7	9	3	—	—	111	46	36	46	2	47	2	1	1	14	15	.48	2	.300	.408	.432
Tulsa	AA	66	258	62	5	1	3	—	—	78	29	14	28	1	50	1	1	1	10	12	.45	5	.240	.316	.302
1994 Tulsa	AA	129	496	142	34	8	8	—	—	216	89	54	59	0	113	5	5	5	33	15	.69	7	.286	.365	.435
1995 Rangers	R	10	34	9	3	1	3	—	—	23	10	7	6	0	7	0	0	0	1	0	1.00	1	.265	.375	.676
Charlotte	A+	11	35	9	2	2	0	—	—	15	4	4	6	0	6	1	0	0	1	0	1.00	0	.257	.381	.429
1996 Binghamton	AA	62	211	58	13	4	7	—	—	100	34	32	44	2	44	2	2	3	5	6	.45	4	.275	.400	.474
Norfolk	AAA	62	193	45	7	2	4	—	—	68	25	21	22	0	44	1	3	2	6	3	.67	1	.233	.312	.352
1997 Iowa	AAA	110	386	116	28	3	17	—	—	201	69	71	65	2	97	1	1	2	9	8	.53	8	.301	.401	.521
1997 Chicago	NL	9	14	4	0	0	0	(0	0)	4	2	0	3	0	3	0	0	0	1	0	1.00	0	.286	.412	.286

Eric Ludwick

Pitches: Right   **Bats:** Right   **Pos:** RP-6; SP-5   **Ht:** 6'5"   **Wt:** 220   **Born:** 12/14/71   **Age:** 26

Year Team	Lg		HOW MUCH HE PITCHED							WHAT HE GAVE UP										THE RESULTS					
		G	GS	CG	GF	IP	BFP	H	R	ER	HR	SH	SF	HB	TBB	IBB	SO	WP	Bk	W	L	Pct.	ShO	Sv-Op	Hld	ERA
1993 Pittsfield	A-	10	10	1	0	51	219	51	27	18	0	3	1	0	18	0	40	4	2	4	4	.500	0	0- -	—	3.18
1994 St. Lucie	A+	27	27	3	0	150.1	671	162	102	76	6	1	12	6	77	1	77	3	5	7	13	.350	0	0- -	—	4.55
1995 Binghamton	AA	23	22	3	0	143.1	590	108	52	47	9	4	6	2	68	1	131	6	0	12	5	.706	2	0- -	—	2.95
Norfolk	AAA	4	3	0	0	20	88	22	15	13	3	0	0	1	7	0	9	1	0	1	1	.500	0	0- -	—	5.85
1996 Louisville	AAA	11	11	0	0	60.1	253	55	24	19	4	2	1	1	24	2	73	2	0	3	4	.429	0	0- -	—	2.83
1997 Louisville	AAA	24	11	1	12	80	325	67	31	26	7	1	1	4	26	0	85	4	0	6	8	.429	0	4- -	—	2.93
Edmonton	AAA	6	3	0	0	19	84	22	7	7	1	1	1	1	4	0	20	2	0	1	1	.500	0	0- -	—	3.32
1996 St. Louis	NL	6	1	0	2	10	45	11	11	10	4	0	1	1	3	0	12	0	0	0	1	.000	0	0-0	0	9.00
1997 Stl-Oak		11	5	0	3	30.2	152	44	31	29	8	2	0	1	22	1	21	0	0	1	5	.167	0	0-0	0	8.51
1997 St. Louis	NL	5	0	0	3	6.2	36	12	7	7	1	0	0	0	6	0	7	0	0	0	1	.000	0	0-0	0	9.45
Oakland	AL	6	5	0	0	24	116	32	24	22	7	2	0	1	16	1	14	0	0	1	4	.200	0	0-0	0	8.25
2 ML YEARS		17	6	0	5	40.2	197	55	42	39	12	2	1	2	25	1	33	0	0	1	6	.143	0	0-0	0	8.63

John Mabry

Bats: L   **Throws:** R   **Pos:** RF-71; 1B-49; CF-6; PH-6; LF-4; 3B-1   **Ht:** 6'4"   **Wt:** 205   **Born:** 10/17/70   **Age:** 27

Year Team	Lg		BATTING															BASERUNNING				PERCENTAGES		
		G	AB	H	2B	3B	HR	(Hm	Rd)	TB	R	RBI	TBB	IBB	SO	HBP	SH	SF	SB	CS	SB%	GDP	Avg	OBP	SLG
1994 St. Louis	NL	6	23	7	3	0	0	(0	0)	10	2	3	2	0	4	0	0	0	0	0	.00	0	.304	.360	.435
1995 St. Louis	NL	129	388	119	21	1	5	(2	3)	157	35	41	24	5	45	2	0	4	0	3	.00	6	.307	.347	.405
1996 St. Louis	NL	151	543	161	30	2	13	(3	10)	234	63	74	37	11	84	3	3	5	3	2	.60	21	.297	.342	.431
1997 St. Louis	NL	116	388	110	19	0	5	(5	0)	144	40	36	39	9	77	3	2	2	0	1	.00	11	.284	.352	.371
4 ML YEARS		402	1342	397	73	3	23	(10	13)	545	140	154	102	25	210	8	5	11	3	6	.33	38	.296	.347	.406

Mike Macfarlane

Bats: Right   **Throws:** Right   **Pos:** C-81; PH-3   **Ht:** 6'1"   **Wt:** 210   **Born:** 4/12/64   **Age:** 34

Year Team	Lg		BATTING															BASERUNNING				PERCENTAGES		
		G	AB	H	2B	3B	HR	(Hm	Rd)	TB	R	RBI	TBB	IBB	SO	HBP	SH	SF	SB	CS	SB%	GDP	Avg	OBP	SLG
1987 Kansas City	AL	8	19	4	1	0	0	(0	0)	5	0	3	2	0	2	0	0	0	0	0	.00	1	.211	.286	.263
1988 Kansas City	AL	70	211	56	15	0	4	(2	2)	83	25	26	21	2	37	1	1	2	0	0	.00	5	.265	.332	.393
1989 Kansas City	AL	69	157	35	6	0	2	(0	2)	47	13	19	7	0	27	2	0	1	0	0	.00	8	.223	.263	.299
1990 Kansas City	AL	124	400	102	24	4	6	(1	5)	152	37	58	25	2	69	7	1	6	1	0	1.00	9	.255	.306	.380
1991 Kansas City	AL	84	267	74	18	2	13	(6	7)	135	34	41	17	0	52	6	1	4	1	0	1.00	4	.277	.330	.506
1992 Kansas City	AL	129	402	94	28	3	17	(7	10)	179	51	48	30	2	89	15	1	2	1	5	.17	8	.234	.310	.445
1993 Kansas City	AL	117	388	106	27	0	20	(7	13)	193	55	67	40	2	83	16	1	6	2	5	.29	8	.273	.360	.497
1994 Kansas City	AL	92	314	80	17	3	14	(9	5)	145	53	47	35	1	71	18	0	3	1	0	1.00	9	.255	.359	.462
1995 Boston	AL	115	364	82	18	1	15	(7	8)	147	45	51	38	0	78	14	0	4	2	1	.67	9	.225	.319	.404
1996 Kansas City	AL	112	379	104	24	2	19	(9	10)	189	58	54	31	5	57	7	0	2	3	3	.50	4	.274	.339	.499
1997 Kansas City	AL	82	257	61	14	2	8	(5	3)	103	34	35	24	3	47	6	3	1	0	2	.00	4	.237	.316	.401
11 ML YEARS		1002	3158	798	192	17	118	(53	65)	1378	405	449	270	17	612	92	8	31	11	16	.41	69	.253	.327	.436

Robert Machado

Bats: Right   **Throws:** Right   **Pos:** C-10; PH-2   **Ht:** 6'1"   **Wt:** 205   **Born:** 6/3/73   **Age:** 25

Year Team	Lg		BATTING															BASERUNNING				PERCENTAGES		
		G	AB	H	2B	3B	HR	(Hm	Rd)	TB	R	RBI	TBB	IBB	SO	HBP	SH	SF	SB	CS	SB%	GDP	Avg	OBP	SLG
1991 White Sox	R	38	126	31	4	1	0	—	—	37	11	15	6	0	21	6	0	1	2	1	.67	2	.246	.309	.294
1992 Utica	A-	45	161	44	13	1	2	—	—	65	16	20	5	0	26	0	0	1	1	5	.17	3	.273	.293	.404
1993 South Bend	A	75	281	86	14	3	2	—	—	112	34	33	19	0	59	4	2	4	2	1	.33	6	.306	.354	.399
1994 Pr William	A+	93	312	81	17	1	11	—	—	133	45	47	27	0	68	4	2	1	0	1	.00	10	.260	.326	.426
1995 Nashville	AAA	16	49	7	3	0	1	—	—	13	7	5	7	0	12	0	0	0	0	1	.00	1	.143	.250	.265
Pr William	A+	83	272	69	14	0	6	—	—	101	37	31	40	5	47	7	2	1	0	0	.00	6	.254	.363	.371
1996 Birmingham	AA	87	309	74	16	0	6	—	—	108	35	28	20	1	56	3	10	1	1	4	.20	9	.239	.291	.350
1997 Nashville	AAA	84	308	83	18	0	8	—	—	125	43	30	12	0	61	1	5	2	5	0	1.00	6	.269	.297	.406
1996 Chicago	AL	4	6	4	1	0	0	(0	0)	5	1	2	0	0	0	0	0	0	0	0	.00	1	.667	.667	.833
1997 Chicago	AL	10	15	3	0	1	0	(0	0)	5	1	2	1	0	6	0	1	0	0	0	.00	0	.200	.250	.333
2 ML YEARS		14	21	7	1	1	0	(0	0)	10	2	4	1	0	6	0	1	0	0	0	.00	1	.333	.364	.476

Shane Mack

Bats: R   **Throws:** R   **Pos:** CF-43; PH-21; DH-5; LF-3   **Ht:** 6'0"   **Wt:** 190   **Born:** 12/7/63   **Age:** 34

Year Team	Lg		BATTING															BASERUNNING				PERCENTAGES		
		G	AB	H	2B	3B	HR	(Hm	Rd)	TB	R	RBI	TBB	IBB	SO	HBP	SH	SF	SB	CS	SB%	GDP	Avg	OBP	SLG
1987 San Diego	NL	105	238	57	11	3	4	(2	2)	86	28	25	18	0	47	3	6	2	4	6	.40	11	.239	.299	.361
1988 San Diego	NL	56	119	29	3	0	0	(0	0)	32	13	12	14	0	21	3	3	1	5	1	.83	2	.244	.336	.269
1990 Minnesota	AL	125	313	102	10	4	8	(5	3)	144	50	44	29	1	69	5	6	0	13	4	.76	7	.326	.392	.460
1991 Minnesota	AL	143	442	137	27	8	18	(4	14)	234	79	74	34	1	79	6	2	5	13	9	.59	11	.310	.363	.529
1992 Minnesota	AL	156	600	189	31	6	16	(10	6)	280	101	75	64	1	106	15	11	2	26	14	.65	8	.315	.394	.467
1993 Minnesota	AL	128	503	139	30	4	10	(3	7)	207	66	61	41	1	76	4	3	2	15	5	.75	13	.276	.335	.412
1994 Minnesota	AL	81	303	101	21	3	15	(8	7)	171	55	61	32	1	51	6	1	5	4	1	.80	11	.333	.402	.564
1997 Boston	AL	60	130	41	7	0	3	(2	1)	57	13	17	9	1	24	3	2	2	2	1	.67	3	.315	.368	.438
8 ML YEARS		854	2648	795	140	27	74	(34	40)	1211	405	369	241	6	473	45	34	19	82	41	.67	66	.300	.366	.457

Greg Maddux

Pitches: Right **Bats:** Right **Pos:** SP-33   **Ht:** 6'0" **Wt:** 175 **Born:** 4/14/66 **Age:** 32

		HOW MUCH HE PITCHED						WHAT HE GAVE UP												THE RESULTS					
Year Team	Lg	G	GS	CG	GF	IP	BFP	H	R	ER	HR	SH	SF	HB	TBB	IBB	SO	WP	Bk	W	L	Pct.	ShO	Sv-Op	Hld	ERA
1986 Chicago	NL	6	5	1	1	31	144	44	20	19	3	1	0	1	11	2	20	2	0	2	4	.333	0	0-0	0	5.52
1987 Chicago	NL	30	27	1	2	155.2	701	181	111	97	17	7	1	4	74	13	101	4	7	6	14	.300	1	0-0	0	5.61
1988 Chicago	NL	34	34	9	0	249	1047	230	97	88	13	11	2	9	81	16	140	3	6	18	8	.692	3	0-0	0	3.18
1989 Chicago	NL	35	35	7	0	238.1	1002	222	90	78	13	18	6	6	82	13	135	5	3	19	12	.613	1	0-0	0	2.95
1990 Chicago	NL	35	35	8	0	237	1011	242	116	91	11	18	5	4	71	10	144	3	3	15	15	.500	2	0-0	0	3.46
1991 Chicago	NL	37	37	7	0	263	1070	232	113	98	18	16	3	6	66	9	198	6	3	15	11	.577	2	0-0	0	3.35
1992 Chicago	NL	35	35	9	0	268	1061	201	68	65	7	15	3	14	70	7	199	5	0	20	11	.645	4	0-0	0	2.18
1993 Atlanta	NL	36	36	8	0	267	1064	228	85	70	14	15	7	6	52	7	197	5	1	20	10	.667	1	0-0	0	2.36
1994 Atlanta	NL	25	25	10	0	202	774	150	44	35	4	6	5	6	31	3	156	3	1	16	6	.727	3	0-0	0	1.56
1995 Atlanta	NL	28	28	10	0	209.2	785	147	39	38	8	9	1	4	23	3	181	1	0	19	2	.905	3	0-0	0	1.63
1996 Atlanta	NL	35	35	5	0	245	978	225	85	74	11	8	5	3	28	11	172	4	0	15	11	.577	1	0-0	0	2.72
1997 Atlanta	NL	33	33	5	0	232.2	893	200	58	57	9	11	7	6	20	6	177	0	0	19	4	.826	2	0-0	0	2.20
12 ML YEARS		369	365	80	3	2598.1	10530	2302	926	810	128	135	45	69	609	100	1820	41	24	184	108	.630	23	0-0	0	2.81

Mike Maddux

Pitches: Right **Bats:** Left **Pos:** RP-6   **Ht:** 6'2" **Wt:** 185 **Born:** 8/27/61 **Age:** 36

		HOW MUCH HE PITCHED						WHAT HE GAVE UP												THE RESULTS					
Year Team	Lg	G	GS	CG	GF	IP	BFP	H	R	ER	HR	SH	SF	HB	TBB	IBB	SO	WP	Bk	W	L	Pct.	ShO	Sv-Op	Hld	ERA
1997 Tacoma *	AAA	1	1	0	0	5	18	1	0	0	0	0	0	1	2	0	5	0	0	0	0	.000	0	0- --		0.00
Las Vegas *	AAA	3	3	0	0	16	77	23	11	10	0	1	2	0	9	1	13	0	0	0	2	.000	0	0- --	--	5.63
1986 Philadelphia	NL	16	16	0	0	78	351	88	56	47	6	3	3	3	34	4	44	4	2	3	7	.300	0	0-0	0	5.42
1987 Philadelphia	NL	7	2	0	0	17	72	17	5	5	0	0	0	0	5	0	15	1	0	2	0	1.000	0	0-0	0	2.65
1988 Philadelphia	NL	25	11	0	4	88.2	380	91	41	37	6	7	3	5	34	4	59	4	2	4	3	.571	0	0-0	0	3.76
1989 Philadelphia	NL	16	4	2	1	43.2	191	52	29	25	3	3	1	2	14	3	26	3	1	1	3	.250	1	1-1	2	5.15
1990 Los Angeles	NL	11	2	0	3	20.2	88	24	15	15	3	0	1	1	4	0	11	2	0	0	1	.000	0	0-0	1	6.53
1991 San Diego	NL	64	1	0	27	98.2	388	78	30	27	4	5	2	1	27	3	57	5	0	7	2	.778	0	5-7	9	2.46
1992 San Diego	NL	50	1	0	14	79.2	330	71	25	21	2	2	3	0	24	4	60	4	1	2	2	.500	0	5-9	8	2.37
1993 New York	NL	58	0	0	31	75	320	67	34	30	3	7	6	4	27	7	57	4	1	3	8	.273	0	5-11	3	3.60
1994 New York	NL	27	0	0	12	44	186	45	25	25	7	0	2	0	13	4	32	2	0	2	1	.667	0	2-4	1	5.11
1995 Pit-Bos		44	4	0	7	98.2	409	100	49	45	5	1	1	2	18	4	69	6	0	5	1	.833	0	1-1	6	4.10
1996 Boston	AL	23	7	0	2	64.1	295	76	37	32	12	3	2	5	27	2	32	1	0	3	2	.600	0	0-0	2	4.48
1997 Seattle	AL	6	0	0	1	10.2	59	20	12	12	1	0	0	1	8	2	7	1	0	1	0	1.000	0	0-0	0	10.13
1995 Pittsburgh	NL	8	0	0	1	9	42	14	9	9	0	0	0	0	3	1	4	1	0	1	0	1.000	0	0-0	2	9.00
Boston	AL	36	4	0	6	89.2	367	86	40	36	5	1	1	2	15	3	65	5	0	4	1	.800	0	1-1	4	3.61
12 ML YEARS		347	48	2	102	719	3069	729	358	321	52	31	24	24	235	37	469	37	7	33	30	.524	1	19-33	32	4.02

Calvin Maduro

Pitches: Right **Bats:** Right **Pos:** SP-13; RP-2   **Ht:** 6'0" **Wt:** 175 **Born:** 9/5/74 **Age:** 23

		HOW MUCH HE PITCHED						WHAT HE GAVE UP												THE RESULTS					
Year Team	Lg	G	GS	CG	GF	IP	BFP	H	R	ER	HR	SH	SF	HB	TBB	IBB	SO	WP	Bk	W	L	Pct.	ShO	Sv-Op	Hld	ERA
1992 Orioles	R	13	12	1	0	71.1	289	56	29	18	2	2	3	1	26	0	66	4	3	1	4	.200	1	0- --		2.27
1993 Bluefield	R+	14	14	3	0	91	378	90	46	40	4	0	2	3	17	0	83	4	1	9	4	.692	0	0- --	--	3.96
1994 Frederick	A+	27	26	0	1	152.1	636	132	86	72	18	3	3	4	59	0	137	10	4	9	8	.529	0	0- --	--	4.25
1995 Frederick	A+	20	20	2	0	122.1	499	109	43	40	16	3	2	6	34	0	120	2	0	8	5	.615	2	0- --	--	2.94
Bowie	AA	7	7	0	0	35.1	165	39	28	20	3	1	2	0	27	0	26	3	0	0	6	.000	0	0- --	--	5.09
1996 Bowie	AA	19	19	4	0	124.1	507	116	50	45	8	4	1	2	36	0	87	4	2	9	7	.563	3	0- --	--	3.26
Rochester	AAA	8	8	0	0	43.2	197	49	25	23	8	1	1	3	18	0	40	2	0	3	5	.375	0	0- --	--	4.74
1997 Scranton-WB	AAA	13	13	2	0	79.1	354	71	48	44	10	5	2	1	57	1	53	6	0	6	4	.600	0	0- --	--	4.99
1996 Philadelphia	NL	4	2	0	0	15.1	62	13	6	6	1	1	0	2	3	0	11	1	0	0	1	.000	0	0-0	0	3.52
1997 Philadelphia	NL	15	13	0	0	71	331	83	59	57	12	1	4	3	41	5	31	6	2	3	7	.300	0	0-0	0	7.23
2 ML YEARS		19	15	0	0	86.1	393	96	65	63	13	2	4	5	44	5	42	7	2	3	8	.273	0	0-0	0	6.57

Dave Magadan

Bats: L **Throws:** R **Pos:** PH-58; 3B-49; 1B-30; DH-25   **Ht:** 6'3" **Wt:** 210 **Born:** 9/30/62 **Age:** 35

		BATTING																	BASERUNNING			PERCENTAGES		
Year Team	Lg	G	AB	H	2B	3B	HR	(Hm	Rd)	TB	R	RBI	TBB	IBB	SO	HBP	SH	SF	SB	CS	SB%	GDP	Avg	OBP	SLG
1986 New York	NL	10	18	8	0	0	0	(0	0)	8	3	3	3	0	1	0	0	0	0	0	.00	1	.444	.524	.444
1987 New York	NL	85	192	61	13	1	3	(2	1)	85	21	24	22	2	22	0	1	1	0	0	.00	5	.318	.386	.443
1988 New York	NL	112	314	87	15	0	1	(1	0)	105	39	35	60	4	39	2	1	3	0	1	.00	9	.277	.393	.334
1989 New York	NL	127	374	107	22	3	4	(3	1)	147	47	41	49	6	37	1	1	4	1	0	1.00	2	.286	.367	.393
1990 New York	NL	144	451	148	28	6	6	(2	4)	206	74	72	74	4	55	2	4	10	2	1	.67	11	.328	.417	.457
1991 New York	NL	124	418	108	23	0	4	(2	2)	143	58	51	83	3	50	2	7	7	1	1	.50	5	.258	.378	.342
1992 New York	NL	99	321	91	9	1	3	(2	1)	111	33	28	56	3	44	0	2	0	1	0	1.00	6	.283	.390	.346
1993 Fla-Sea		137	455	124	23	0	5	(3	2)	162	49	50	80	7	63	1	2	6	2	1	.67	12	.273	.378	.356
1994 Florida	NL	74	211	58	7	0	1	(1	0)	68	30	17	39	0	25	1	0	3	0	0	.00	8	.275	.386	.322
1995 Houston	NL	127	348	109	24	0	2	(0	2)	139	44	51	71	9	56	0	1	2	2	1	.67	9	.313	.428	.399
1996 Chicago	NL	78	169	43	10	0	3	(2	1)	62	23	17	29	3	23	0	1	2	0	0	.00	3	.254	.360	.367
1997 Oakland	AL	128	271	82	10	1	4	(2	2)	106	38	30	50	1	40	2	4	1	1	0	1.00	3	.303	.414	.391
1993 Florida	NL	66	227	65	12	0	4	(3	1)	89	22	29	44	4	30	1	0	3	0	1	.00	3	.286	.400	.392
Seattle	AL	71	228	59	11	0	1	(0	1)	73	27	21	36	3	33	0	2	3	2	0	1.00	9	.259	.356	.320
12 ML YEARS		1245	3542	1026	184	12	36	(20	16)	1342	459	419	616	42	455	11	24	39	10	7	.59	78	.290	.393	.379

Wendell Magee

Bats: Right **Throws:** Right **Pos:** CF-38; PH-1 **Ht:** 6'0" **Wt:** 220 **Born:** 8/3/72 **Age:** 25

Year Team	Lg	G	AB	H	2B	3B	HR	(Hm	Rd)	TB	R	RBI	TBB	IBB	SO	HBP	SH	SF	SB	CS	SB%	GDP	Avg	OBP	SLG
1994 Batavia	A-	63	229	64	12	4	2	—	—	90	42	35	16	1	24	4	1	2	10	2	.83	5	.279	.335	.393
1995 Clearwater	A+	96	388	137	24	5	6	—	—	189	67	46	33	3	40	4	1	5	7	10	.41	15	.353	.405	.487
Reading	AA	39	136	40	9	1	3	—	—	60	17	21	21	1	17	0	0	4	3	4	.43	3	.294	.379	.441
1996 Reading	AA	71	270	79	15	5	6	—	—	122	38	30	24	1	40	1	0	0	10	6	.63	8	.293	.353	.452
Scranton-WB	AAA	44	155	44	9	2	10	—	—	87	31	32	21	0	31	0	0	2	3	1	.75	2	.284	.365	.561
1997 Scranton-WB	AAA	83	294	72	20	1	10	—	—	124	39	39	30	1	56	0	0	5	4	7	.36	10	.245	.310	.422
1996 Philadelphia	NL	38	142	29	7	0	2	(2	0)	42	9	14	9	0	33	0	0	0	0	0	.00	2	.204	.252	.296
1997 Philadelphia	NL	38	115	23	4	0	1	(0	1)	30	7	9	9	1	20	0	0	2	1	4	.20	8	.200	.254	.261
2 ML YEARS		76	257	52	11	0	3	(2	1)	72	16	23	18	1	53	0	0	2	1	4	.20	10	.202	.253	.280

Mike Magnante

Pitches: Left **Bats:** Left **Pos:** RP-40 **Ht:** 6'1" **Wt:** 195 **Born:** 6/17/65 **Age:** 33

Year Team	Lg	G	GS	CG	GF	IP	BFP	H	R	ER	HR	SH	SF	HB	TBB	IBB	SO	WP	Bk	W	L	Pct.	ShO	Sv-Op	Hld	ERA
1997 New Orleans *	AAA	17	0	0	6	24	107	31	14	12	0	5	0	23	2	0	1	—	—			.400	0	1- --	—	4.50
1991 Kansas City	AL	38	0	0	10	55	236	55	19	15	3	2	1	0	23	3	42	1	0	0	1	.000	0	0-0	2	2.45
1992 Kansas City	AL	44	12	0	11	89.1	403	115	53	49	5	5	7	2	35	5	31	2	0	4	9	.308	0	0-3	4	4.94
1993 Kansas City	AL	7	6	0	0	35.1	145	37	16	16	3	1	1	1	11	1	16	1	0	1	2	.333	0	0-0	0	4.08
1994 Kansas City	AL	36	1	0	10	47	211	55	27	24	5	2	3	0	16	1	21	3	0	2	3	.400	0	0-0	6	4.60
1995 Kansas City	AL	28	0	0	7	44.2	190	45	23	21	6	2	2	2	16	1	28	2	0	1	1	.500	0	0-1	5	4.23
1996 Kansas City	AL	38	0	0	9	54	238	58	38	34	5	0	4	4	24	1	32	3	0	2	2	.500	0	0-1	5	5.67
1997 Houston	NL	40	0	0	14	47.2	191	39	16	12	2	3	2	0	11	2	43	2	2	3	1	.750	0	1-5	3	2.27
7 ML YEARS		231	19	0	61	373	1614	404	192	171	29	15	20	9	136	14	213	14	2	13	19	.406	0	1-10	25	4.13

Ron Mahay

Pitches: Left **Bats:** Left **Pos:** RP-28 **Ht:** 6'2" **Wt:** 189 **Born:** 6/28/71 **Age:** 27

Year Team	Lg	G	GS	CG	GF	IP	BFP	H	R	ER	HR	SH	SF	HB	TBB	IBB	SO	WP	Bk	W	L	Pct.	ShO	Sv-Op	Hld	ERA
1996 Sarasota	A+	31	4	0	13	70.2	295	61	33	30	5	1	0	0	35	0	68	4	1	2	2	.500	0	2- --	—	3.82
Trenton	AA	1	1	0	0	3.2	29	12	13	12	1	0	0	0	6	0	0	1	0	0	1	.000	0	0- --	—	29.45
1997 Trenton	AA	17	4	0	9	40.2	165	29	16	14	0	0	0	1	13	0	47	2	0	3	3	.500	0	5- --	—	3.10
Pawtucket	AAA	2	0	0	0	4.2	18	3	0	0	0	0	0	0	1	0	6	0	0	1	0	1.000	0	0- --	—	0.00
1997 Boston	AL	28	0	0	7	25	105	19	7	7	3	1	0	0	11	0	22	3	0	3	1	1.000	0	0-1	5	2.52

Pat Mahomes

Pitches: Right **Bats:** Right **Pos:** RP-10 **Ht:** 6'4" **Wt:** 212 **Born:** 8/9/70 **Age:** 27

Year Team	Lg	G	GS	CG	GF	IP	BFP	H	R	ER	HR	SH	SF	HB	TBB	IBB	SO	WP	Bk	W	L	Pct.	ShO	Sv-Op	Hld	ERA
1997 Pawtucket *	AAA	18	1	0	10	31.2	129	22	11	10	2	1	0	0	17	0	40	3	0	5	1	.833	0	7- --	—	2.84
1992 Minnesota	AL	14	13	0	1	69.2	302	73	41	39	5	0	3	0	37	0	44	2	1	3	4	.429	0	0-0	0	5.04
1993 Minnesota	AL	12	5	0	4	37.1	173	47	34	32	8	1	1	0	16	0	23	3	0	1	5	.167	0	0-0	0	7.71
1994 Minnesota	AL	21	21	0	0	120	517	121	68	63	22	1	4	1	62	1	53	3	0	9	5	.643	0	0-0	0	4.73
1995 Minnesota	AL	47	7	0	16	94.2	423	100	74	67	22	3	2	2	47	1	67	6	0	4	10	.286	0	3-7	9	6.37
1996 Min-Bos	AL	31	5	0	10	57.1	271	72	46	44	13	2	2	0	33	0	36	2	0	3	4	.429	0	2-2	4	6.91
1997 Boston	AL	10	0	0	2	10	54	15	10	9	2	0	1	2	10	1	5	1	0	1	0	1.000	0	0-0	1	8.10
1996 Minnesota	AL	20	5	0	5	45	220	63	38	36	10	0	2	0	27	0	30	2	0	1	4	.200	0	0-0	3	7.20
Boston	AL	11	0	0	5	12.1	51	9	8	8	3	2	0	0	6	0	6	0	0	2	0	1.000	0	2-2	1	5.84
6 ML YEARS		135	51	0	33	389	1740	428	273	254	72	7	15	6	205	3	228	17	1	21	28	.429	0	5-9	14	5.88

Jose Malave

Bats: Right **Throws:** Right **Pos:** LF-4 **Ht:** 6'2" **Wt:** 212 **Born:** 5/31/71 **Age:** 27

Year Team	Lg	G	AB	H	2B	3B	HR	(Hm	Rd)	TB	R	RBI	TBB	IBB	SO	HBP	SH	SF	SB	CS	SB%	GDP	Avg	OBP	SLG
1990 Elmira	A-	13	29	4	1	0	0	—	—	5	4	3	2	0	12	0	0	1	1	0	1.00	0	.138	.188	.172
1991 Red Sox	R	37	146	47	4	2	2	—	—	61	24	28	10	0	23	1	0	3	6	0	1.00	3	.322	.363	.418
1992 Winter Havn	A+	8	25	4	0	0	0	—	—	4	1	0	0	0	11	0	1	0	0	0	.00	0	.160	.160	.160
Elmira	A-	65	268	87	9	1	12	—	—	134	44	46	14	3	48	3	0	5	8	3	.73	2	.325	.364	.500
1993 Lynchburg	A+	82	312	94	27	1	8	—	—	147	42	54	36	3	54	3	0	5	2	3	.40	8	.301	.374	.471
1994 New Britain	AA	122	465	139	37	7	24	—	—	262	87	92	52	1	81	4	0	7	4	7	.36	12	.299	.369	.563
1995 Pawtucket	AAA	91	318	86	12	1	23	—	—	169	55	57	30	1	67	2	0	5	0	1	.00	4	.270	.337	.531
1996 Pawtucket	AAA	41	155	42	6	0	8	—	—	72	30	29	12	1	37	2	0	1	2	1	.67	5	.271	.329	.465
1997 Pawtucket	AAA	115	427	127	24	2	17	—	—	206	87	70	55	1	78	2	0	5	12	4	.75	12	.297	.376	.482
1996 Boston	AL	41	102	24	3	0	4	(1	3)	39	12	17	2	0	25	1	0	0	0	0	.00	0	.235	.257	.382
1997 Boston	AL	4	4	0	0	0	0	(0	0)	0	0	0	0	0	2	0	0	1	0	0	.00	1	.000	.000	.000
2 ML YEARS		45	106	24	3	0	4	(1	3)	39	12	17	2	0	27	1	0	1	0	0	.00	1	.226	.248	.368

Sean Maloney

Pitches: Right **Bats:** Right **Pos:** RP-3   **Ht:** 6'7" **Wt:** 230 **Born:** 5/25/71 **Age:** 27

Year Team	Lg	G	GS	CG	GF	IP	BFP	H	R	ER	HR	SH	SF	HB	TBB	IBB	SO	WP	Bk	W	L	Pct.	ShO	Sv-Op	Hld	ERA
1993 Helena	R+	17	3	1	10	47.2	209	55	31	23	2	3	2	2	11	1	35	3	0	2	2	.500	0	0--	—	4.34
1994 Beloit	A	51	0	0	41	59	272	73	42	36	3	2	5	4	10	5	53	6	1	2	6	.250	0	22--	—	5.49
1995 El Paso	AA	43	0	0	27	64.2	292	69	41	30	4	4	4	3	28	9	54	5	0	7	5	.583	0	15--	—	4.18
1996 El Paso	AA	51	0	0	49	56.2	230	49	11	9	1	2	1	1	12	1	57	6	1	3	2	.600	0	38--	—	1.43
1997 Tucson	AAA	15	0	0	10	18.2	82	24	10	10	3	5	0	0	3	3	21	1	0	0	2	.000	0	5--	—	4.82
1997 Milwaukee	AL	3	0	0	2	7	29	7	4	4	1	0	2	2	2	0	5	2	0	0	0	.000	0	0-0	0	5.14

Jeff Manto

Bats: Right **Throws:** Right **Pos:** 3B-7; 1B-6; PH-5; LF-1   **Ht:** 6'3" **Wt:** 210 **Born:** 8/23/64 **Age:** 33

Year Team	Lg	G	AB	H	2B	3B	HR	(Hm	Rd)	TB	R	RBI	TBB	IBB	SO	HBP	SH	SF	SB	CS	SB%	GDP	Avg	OBP	SLG
1997 Syracuse *	AAA	40	132	27	5	1	3	—	—	43	18	11	22	1	30	1	1	0	1	2	.33	3	.205	.323	.326
Buffalo *	AAA	54	187	60	11	0	20	—	—	131	37	54	31	2	43	2	0	1	0	2	.00	6	.321	.421	.701
1990 Cleveland	AL	30	76	17	5	1	2	(1	1)	30	12	14	21	1	18	0	0	0	0	1	.00	0	.224	.392	.395
1991 Cleveland	AL	47	128	27	7	0	2	(0	2)	40	15	13	14	0	22	4	1	1	2	0	1.00	3	.211	.306	.313
1993 Philadelphia	NL	8	18	1	0	0	0	(0	0)	1	0	0	0	0	3	1	0	0	0	0	.00	0	.056	.105	.056
1995 Baltimore	AL	89	254	65	9	0	17	(12	5)	125	31	38	24	0	69	2	0	0	0	3	.00	6	.256	.325	.492
1996 Bos-Sea	AL	43	102	20	6	1	3	(3	0)	37	15	10	17	0	24	1	0	0	0	1	.00	2	.196	.317	.363
1997 Cleveland	AL	16	30	8	3	0	2	(2	0)	17	3	7	1	0	10	0	0	0	0	0	.00	0	.267	.290	.567
1996 Boston	AL	22	48	10	3	1	2	(2	0)	21	8	6	8	0	12	1	0	0	0	0	.00	0	.208	.333	.438
Seattle	AL	21	54	10	3	0	1	(1	0)	16	7	4	9	0	12	0	0	0	0	1	.00	2	.185	.302	.296
6 ML YEARS		233	608	138	30	2	26	(18	8)	250	76	82	77	1	146	8	1	1	2	5	.29	13	.227	.321	.411

Barry Manuel

Pitches: Right **Bats:** Right **Pos:** RP-19   **Ht:** 5'11" **Wt:** 185 **Born:** 8/12/65 **Age:** 32

Year Team	Lg	G	GS	CG	GF	IP	BFP	H	R	ER	HR	SH	SF	HB	TBB	IBB	SO	WP	Bk	W	L	Pct.	ShO	Sv-Op	Hld	ERA
1997 Norfolk *	AAA	19	8	0	4	61	259	60	36	33	9	0	2	6	21	1	52	5	1	2	5	.286	0	0--	—	4.87
1991 Texas	AL	8	0	0	5	16	58	7	2	2	0	0	3	0	6	0	5	2	0	1	0	1.000	0	0-0	0	1.13
1992 Texas	AL	3	0	0	0	5.2	25	6	3	3	2	0	1	1	1	0	9	0	0	1	0	1.000	0	0-0	0	4.76
1996 Montreal	NL	53	0	0	7	86	360	70	34	31	10	6	2	7	26	4	62	4	0	4	1	.800	0	0-0	2	3.24
1997 New York	NL	19	0	0	6	25.2	123	35	18	15	6	1	0	1	13	1	21	0	1	0	1	.000	0	0-0	1	5.26
4 ML YEARS		83	0	0	18	133.1	566	118	57	51	18	7	5	9	46	5	97	6	1	6	2	.750	0	0-0	3	3.44

Kirt Manwaring

Bats: Right **Throws:** Right **Pos:** C-100; PH-4   **Ht:** 5'11" **Wt:** 203 **Born:** 7/15/65 **Age:** 32

Year Team	Lg	G	AB	H	2B	3B	HR	(Hm	Rd)	TB	R	RBI	TBB	IBB	SO	HBP	SH	SF	SB	CS	SB%	GDP	Avg	OBP	SLG
1987 San Francisco	NL	6	7	1	0	0	0	(0	0)	1	0	0	0	0	1	1	0	0	0	0	.00	1	.143	.250	.143
1988 San Francisco	NL	40	116	29	7	0	1	(0	1)	39	12	15	2	0	21	3	1	1	0	1	.00	1	.250	.279	.336
1989 San Francisco	NL	85	200	42	4	2	0	(0	0)	50	14	18	11	1	28	4	7	1	2	1	.67	5	.210	.264	.250
1990 San Francisco	NL	8	13	2	0	1	0	(0	0)	4	0	1	0	0	3	0	0	0	0	0	.00	0	.154	.154	.308
1991 San Francisco	NL	67	178	40	9	0	0	(0	0)	49	16	19	9	0	22	3	7	2	1	1	.50	2	.225	.271	.275
1992 San Francisco	NL	109	349	85	10	5	4	(1	3)	117	24	26	29	0	42	5	6	7	2	1	.67	12	.244	.311	.335
1993 San Francisco	NL	130	432	119	15	1	5	(3	2)	151	48	49	41	13	76	6	5	2	1	3	.25	14	.275	.345	.350
1994 San Francisco	NL	97	316	79	17	1	1	(0	1)	101	30	29	25	3	50	3	4	3	1	1	.50	10	.250	.308	.320
1995 San Francisco	NL	118	379	95	15	2	4	(4	0)	126	21	36	27	6	72	10	4	4	1	0	1.00	8	.251	.314	.332
1996 SF-Hou	NL	86	227	52	9	0	1	(1	0)	64	14	18	19	1	40	5	2	2	0	1	.00	4	.229	.300	.282
1997 Colorado	NL	104	337	76	6	4	1	(1	0)	93	22	37	30	0	78	2	4	2	1	5	.17	10	.226	.291	.276
1996 San Francisco	NL	49	145	34	6	0	1	(1	0)	43	9	14	16	1	24	3	1	0	0	1	.00	2	.234	.319	.297
Houston	NL	37	82	18	3	0	0	(0	0)	21	5	4	3	0	16	2	1	2	0	0	.00	2	.220	.264	.256
11 ML YEARS		850	2554	620	92	16	17	(10	7)	795	201	238	193	24	433	42	40	17	9	14	.39	67	.243	.305	.311

Josias Manzanillo

Pitches: Right **Bats:** Right **Pos:** RP-16   **Ht:** 6'0" **Wt:** 190 **Born:** 10/16/67 **Age:** 30

Year Team	Lg	G	GS	CG	GF	IP	BFP	H	R	ER	HR	SH	SF	HB	TBB	IBB	SO	WP	Bk	W	L	Pct.	ShO	Sv-Op	Hld	ERA
1997 Memphis *	AA	2	0	0	1	3	10	1	1	1	1	0	0	0	0	0	6	0	0	0	0	.000	0	0--	—	3.00
Tacoma *	AAA	11	0	0	4	14	65	16	10	10	4	0	1	0	8	0	15	0	0	0	0	.000	0	1--	—	6.43
New Orleans *	AAA	11	0	0	5	14.1	63	17	7	7	3	0	0	1	6	0	11	0	0	0	0	.000	0	0--	—	4.40
1991 Boston	AL	1	0	0	1	1	8	2	2	2	0	0	0	0	3	0	1	0	0	0	0	.000	0	0-0	0	18.00
1993 Mil-NYN		16	1	0	6	29	140	30	27	22	2	3	3	2	19	3	21	1	0	1	1	.500	0	1-2	0	6.83
1994 New York	NL	37	0	0	14	47.1	186	34	15	14	4	0	0	3	13	2	48	2	0	3	2	.600	0	2-5	11	2.66
1995 NYN-NYA		23	0	0	8	33.1	154	37	19	18	4	2	1	2	15	4	25	6	0	1	2	.333	0	0-0	0	4.86
1997 Seattle	AL	15	0	0	4	18.1	88	19	13	11	3	0	2	0	11	0	18	2	0	0	1	.000	0	0-1	1	5.40
1993 Milwaukee	AL	10	1	0	4	17	86	22	20	18	1	2	2	2	10	3	10	1	0	1	1	.500	0	1-2	0	9.53
New York	NL	6	0	0	2	12	54	8	7	4	1	1	1	0	9	0	11	0	0	0	0	.000	0	0-0	0	3.00
1995 New York	NL	4	0	0	4	16	73	18	15	14	3	0	1	0	6	2	14	5	0	0	2	.000	0	0-0	0	7.88
New York	AL	11	0	0	4	17.1	81	19	4	4	1	2	0	2	9	2	11	1	0	0	0	.000	0	0-0	0	2.08
5 ML YEARS		93	1	0	33	129	576	122	76	67	13	5	6	7	67	10	113	11	0	5	6	.455	0	3-8	12	4.67

Eli Marrero

Bats: Right **Throws:** Right **Pos:** C-17; PH-1   **Ht:** 6'1" **Wt:** 180 **Born:** 11/17/73 **Age:** 24

							BATTING										BASERUNNING				PERCENTAGES		
Year Team	Lg	G	AB	H	2B	3B	HR	(Hm | Rd)	TB	R	RBI	TBB	IBB	SO	HBP	SH	SF	SB	CS	SB%	GDP	Avg	OBP	SLG
1993 Johnson Cty	R+	18	61	22	8	0	2	—	—	36	10	14	12	0	9	1	0	1	1	2	.33	0	.361	.467	.590
1994 Savannah	A	116	421	110	16	3	21	—	—	195	71	79	39	3	92	5	2	5	5	4	.56	6	.261	.328	.463
1995 St. Pete	A+	107	383	81	16	1	10	—	—	129	43	55	23	2	55	1	0	7	9	4	.69	10	.211	.254	.337
1996 Arkansas	AA	116	374	101	17	3	19	—	—	181	65	65	32	1	55	6	0	2	9	6	.60	7	.270	.336	.484
1997 Louisville	AAA	112	395	108	21	7	20	—	—	203	60	68	25	2	53	3	1	5	4	4	.50	8	.273	.318	.514
1997 St. Louis	NL	17	45	11	2	0	2	(0 | 2)	19	4	7	2	1	13	0	0	1	4	0	1.00	1	.244	.271	.422

Al Martin

Bats: Left **Throws:** Left **Pos:** LF-110; PH-3   **Ht:** 6'2" **Wt:** 210 **Born:** 11/24/67 **Age:** 30

							BATTING										BASERUNNING				PERCENTAGES		
Year Team	Lg	G	AB	H	2B	3B	HR	(Hm | Rd)	TB	R	RBI	TBB	IBB	SO	HBP	SH	SF	SB	CS	SB%	GDP	Avg	OBP	SLG
1997 Carolina *	AA	3	9	1	0	0	0	—	—	1	0	0	0	0	0	0	0	0	0	0	.00	0	.111	.111	.111
1992 Pittsburgh	NL	12	12	2	0	1	0	(0 | 0)	4	1	2	0	0	5	0	0	1	0	0	.00	0	.167	.154	.333
1993 Pittsburgh	NL	143	480	135	26	8	18	(15 | 3)	231	85	64	42	5	122	1	2	3	16	9	.64	5	.281	.338	.481
1994 Pittsburgh	NL	82	276	79	12	4	9	(6 | 3)	126	48	33	34	3	56	2	0	1	15	6	.71	3	.286	.367	.457
1995 Pittsburgh	NL	124	439	124	25	3	13	(8 | 5)	194	70	41	44	6	92	2	1	0	20	11	.65	5	.282	.351	.442
1996 Pittsburgh	NL	155	630	189	40	1	18	(8 | 10)	285	101	72	54	2	116	2	1	7	38	12	.76	9	.300	.354	.452
1997 Pittsburgh	NL	113	423	123	24	7	13	(8 | 5)	200	64	59	45	7	83	3	1	5	23	7	.77	7	.291	.359	.473
6 ML YEARS		629	2260	652	127	24	71	(45 | 26)	1040	369	271	219	23	474	10	5	17	112	45	.71	29	.288	.352	.460

Norberto Martin

Bats: R **Throws:** R **Pos:** SS-28; PH-21; 3B-17; 2B-9; DH-6   **Ht:** 5'10" **Wt:** 164 **Born:** 12/10/66 **Age:** 31

							BATTING										BASERUNNING				PERCENTAGES		
Year Team	Lg	G	AB	H	2B	3B	HR	(Hm | Rd)	TB	R	RBI	TBB	IBB	SO	HBP	SH	SF	SB	CS	SB%	GDP	Avg	OBP	SLG
1993 Chicago	AL	8	14	5	0	0	0	(0 | 0)	5	3	2	1	0	1	0	0	0	0	0	.00	0	.357	.400	.357
1994 Chicago	AL	45	131	36	7	1	1	(0 | 1)	48	19	16	9	0	16	0	3	2	4	2	.67	2	.275	.317	.366
1995 Chicago	AL	72	160	43	7	4	2	(1 | 1)	64	17	17	3	0	25	1	2	3	5	0	1.00	5	.269	.281	.400
1996 Chicago	AL	70	140	49	7	0	1	(0 | 1)	59	30	14	6	0	17	0	4	1	10	2	.83	4	.350	.374	.421
1997 Chicago	AL	71	213	64	7	1	2	(1 | 1)	79	24	27	6	0	31	0	0	0	1	4	.20	2	.300	.320	.371
5 ML YEARS		266	658	197	28	6	6	(2 | 4)	255	93	76	25	0	90	1	9	6	20	8	.71	13	.299	.323	.388

Tom Martin

Pitches: Left **Bats:** Left **Pos:** RP-55   **Ht:** 6'1" **Wt:** 185 **Born:** 5/21/70 **Age:** 28

			HOW MUCH HE PITCHED						WHAT HE GAVE UP									THE RESULTS					
Year Team	Lg	G	GS	CG	GF	IP	BFP	H	R	ER	HR	SH	SF	HB	TBB	IBB	SO	WP	Bk	W	L	Pct.	ShO	Sv-Op	Hld	ERA
1989 Bluefield	R+	8	8	0	0	39	176	36	28	20	3	1	1	0	25	0	31	2	1	3	3	.500	0	0- -	—	4.62
Erie	A-	7	7	0	0	40.2	190	42	39	30	2	0	2	1	25	0	44	11	2	0	5	.000	0	0- -	—	6.64
1990 Wausau	A	9	9	0	0	40	183	31	25	11	1	3	0	5	27	0	45	4	0	2	3	.400	0	0- -	—	2.48
1991 Kane County	A	38	10	0	19	99	442	92	50	40	4	6	4	3	56	3	106	13	0	4	10	.286	0	6- -	—	3.64
1992 High Desert	A+	11	0	0	8	16.1	85	23	19	17	4	0	0	0	16	0	10	2	0	0	2	.000	0	0- -	—	9.37
Waterloo	A	39	2	0	11	55	248	62	38	26	3	5	1	4	22	4	57	5	0	2	6	.250	0	3- -	—	4.25
1993 Rancho Cuca	A+	47	1	0	16	59.1	290	72	41	37	4	1	7	7	39	2	53	9	0	1	4	.200	0	0- -	—	5.61
1994 Greenville	AA	36	6	0	9	74	324	82	40	38	6	7	1	4	27	3	51	3	0	5	6	.455	0	0- -	—	4.62
1995 Richmond	AAA	7	0	0	2	9	45	10	9	9	4	0	0	0	10	2	3	0	0	0	0	.000	0	0- -	—	9.00
1996 Tucson	AAA	5	0	0	3	6	25	6	0	0	0	0	0	0	2	2	1	0	0	0	0	.000	0	0- -	—	0.00
Jackson	AA	57	0	0	18	75	338	71	35	27	8	5	3	4	42	4	58	4	0	6	2	.750	0	3- -	—	3.24
1997 Houston	NL	55	0	0	18	56	236	52	13	13	2	6	1	1	23	2	36	3	0	5	3	.625	0	2-3	7	2.09

Dave Martinez

Bats: L **Throws:** L **Pos:** RF-75; 1B-52; CF-45; PH-14; LF-4   **Ht:** 5'10" **Wt:** 175 **Born:** 9/26/64 **Age:** 33

							BATTING										BASERUNNING				PERCENTAGES		
Year Team	Lg	G	AB	H	2B	3B	HR	(Hm | Rd)	TB	R	RBI	TBB	IBB	SO	HBP	SH	SF	SB	CS	SB%	GDP	Avg	OBP	SLG
1986 Chicago	NL	53	108	15	1	1	1	(1 | 0)	21	13	7	6	0	22	1	0	1	4	2	.67	1	.139	.190	.194
1987 Chicago	NL	142	459	134	18	8	8	(5 | 3)	192	70	36	57	4	96	2	1	1	16	8	.67	4	.292	.372	.418
1988 ChN-Mon	NL	138	447	114	13	6	6	(2 | 4)	157	51	46	38	8	94	2	2	5	23	9	.72	3	.255	.313	.351
1989 Montreal	NL	126	361	99	16	7	3	(1 | 2)	138	41	27	27	2	57	0	7	1	23	4	.85	1	.274	.324	.382
1990 Montreal	NL	118	391	109	13	5	11	(5 | 6)	165	60	39	24	2	48	1	3	2	13	11	.54	8	.279	.321	.422
1991 Montreal	NL	124	396	117	18	5	7	(3 | 4)	166	47	42	20	3	54	3	5	3	16	7	.70	3	.295	.332	.419
1992 Cincinnati	NL	135	393	100	20	5	3	(3 | 0)	139	47	31	42	4	54	0	6	4	12	8	.60	6	.254	.323	.354
1993 San Francisco	NL	91	241	58	12	1	5	(1 | 4)	87	28	27	27	3	39	0	0	0	6	3	.67	5	.241	.317	.361
1994 San Francisco	NL	97	235	58	9	3	4	(1 | 3)	85	23	27	21	1	22	2	2	0	3	4	.43	6	.247	.314	.362
1995 Chicago	AL	118	303	93	16	4	5	(2 | 3)	132	49	37	32	2	41	1	9	4	8	2	.80	6	.307	.371	.436
1996 Chicago	AL	146	440	140	20	8	10	(3 | 7)	206	85	53	52	1	52	3	2	1	15	7	.68	4	.318	.393	.468
1997 Chicago	AL	145	504	144	16	6	12	(5 | 7)	208	78	55	55	7	69	3	6	4	12	6	.67	4	.286	.356	.413
1988 Chicago	NL	75	256	65	10	1	4	(2 | 2)	89	27	34	21	5	46	2	0	4	7	3	.70	2	.254	.311	.348
Montreal	NL	63	191	49	3	5	2	(0 | 2)	68	24	12	17	3	48	0	2	1	16	6	.73	1	.257	.316	.356
12 ML YEARS		1433	4278	1181	172	59	75	(32 | 43)	1696	592	427	401	37	648	18	42	28	151	71	.68	51	.276	.339	.396

Dennis Martinez

Pitches: Right Bats: Right Pos: SP-9
Ht: 6'1" Wt: 180 Born: 5/14/55 Age: 43

			HOW MUCH HE PITCHED				WHAT HE GAVE UP										THE RESULTS					
Year Team	Lg	G	GS	CG	GF	IP	BFP	H	R	ER	HR	SH	SF	HB	TBB	IBB	SO	WP	Bk	W	L	Pct.	ShO	Sv-Op	Hld	ERA
1976 Baltimore	AL	4	2	1	1	27.2	106	23	8	8	1	1	0	0	8	0	18	1	0	1	2	.333	0	0- --	—	2.60
1977 Baltimore	AL	42	13	5	19	166.2	709	157	86	76	10	8	8	8	64	5	107	5	0	14	7	.667	0	4- --	—	4.10
1978 Baltimore	AL	40	38	15	0	276.1	1140	257	121	108	20	8	7	3	93	4	142	8	0	16	11	.593	2	0- --	—	3.52
1979 Baltimore	AL	40	39	18	0	292.1	1206	279	129	119	28	12	12	1	78	1	132	9	2	15	16	.484	3	0- --	—	3.66
1980 Baltimore	AL	25	12	2	8	99.2	428	103	44	44	12	1	3	2	44	6	42	0	1	6	4	.600	0	1- --	—	3.97
1981 Baltimore	AL	25	24	9	0	179	753	173	84	66	10	2	5	2	62	1	88	4	1	14	5	.737	2	0- --	—	3.32
1982 Baltimore	AL	40	39	10	0	252	1093	262	123	118	30	11	7	7	87	2	111	7	1	16	12	.571	2	0- --	—	4.21
1983 Baltimore	AL	32	25	4	3	153	688	209	108	94	21	3	5	2	45	0	71	2	0	7	16	.304	0	0- --	—	5.53
1984 Baltimore	AL	34	20	2	4	141.2	599	145	81	79	26	0	5	5	37	2	77	13	0	6	9	.400	1	0- --	—	5.02
1985 Baltimore	AL	33	31	3	1	180	789	203	110	103	29	0	11	9	63	3	68	4	1	13	11	.542	1	0- --	—	5.15
1986 Bal-Mon		23	15	1	2	104.2	449	114	57	55	11	8	2	3	30	4	65	3	2	3	6	.333	1	0- --	—	4.73
1987 Montreal	NL	22	22	2	0	144.2	599	133	59	53	9	4	3	6	40	2	84	4	2	11	4	.733	1	0-0	0	3.30
1988 Montreal	NL	34	34	9	0	235.1	968	215	94	71	21	2	6	6	55	3	120	5	10	15	13	.536	2	0-0	0	2.72
1989 Montreal	NL	34	33	5	1	232	950	227	88	82	21	8	2	7	49	4	142	5	2	16	7	.696	2	0-0	0	3.18
1990 Montreal	NL	32	32	7	0	226	908	191	80	74	16	11	3	6	49	9	156	1	1	10	11	.476	2	0-0	0	2.95
1991 Montreal	NL	31	31	9	0	222	905	187	70	59	9	7	3	4	62	3	123	3	0	14	11	.560	5	0-0	0	2.39
1992 Montreal	NL	32	32	6	0	226.1	900	172	75	62	12	12	5	9	60	3	147	2	0	16	11	.593	0	0-0	0	2.47
1993 Montreal	NL	35	34	2	1	224.2	945	211	110	96	27	10	4	11	64	7	138	2	4	15	9	.625	0	1-1	0	3.85
1994 Cleveland	AL	24	24	7	0	176.2	730	166	75	69	14	3	5	7	44	2	92	4	3	11	6	.647	3	0-0	0	3.52
1995 Cleveland	AL	28	28	3	0	187	771	174	71	64	17	4	4	12	46	2	99	3	0	12	5	.706	2	0-0	0	3.08
1996 Cleveland	AL	20	20	1	0	112	483	122	63	56	12	2	3	2	37	2	48	0	0	9	6	.600	1	0-0	0	4.50
1997 Seattle	AL	9	9	0	0	49	239	65	46	42	8	1	3	7	29	1	17	0	0	1	5	.167	0	0- --	—	7.71
1986 Baltimore	AL	4	0	0	1	6.2	33	11	5	5	0	0	1	0	2	0	2	1	0	0	0	.000	0	0- --	—	6.75
Montreal	NL	19	15	1	1	98	416	103	52	50	11	8	1	3	28	4	63	2	2	3	6	.333	1	0- --	—	4.59
22 ML YEARS		639	557	121	40	3908.2	16358	3788	1782	1598	364	118	106	119	1146	66	2087	87	30	241	187	.563	29	6- --	—	3.68

Edgar Martinez

Bats: R Throws: R Pos: DH-144; 1B-7; PH-3; 3B-1
Ht: 5'11" Wt: 200 Born: 1/2/63 Age: 35

								BATTING										BASERUNNING				PERCENTAGES		
Year Team	Lg	G	AB	H	2B	3B	HR	(Hm	Rd)	TB	R	RBI	TBB	IBB	SO	HBP	SH	SF	SB	CS	SB%	GDP	Avg	OBP	SLG
1987 Seattle	AL	13	43	16	5	2	0	(0	0)	25	6	5	2	0	5	1	0	0	0	0	.00	0	.372	.413	.581
1988 Seattle	AL	14	32	9	4	0	0	(0	0)	13	0	5	4	0	7	0	1	1	0	0	.00	0	.281	.351	.406
1989 Seattle	AL	65	171	41	5	0	2	(0	2)	52	20	20	17	1	26	3	2	3	2	1	.67	3	.240	.314	.304
1990 Seattle	AL	144	487	147	27	2	11	(3	8)	211	71	49	74	3	62	5	1	3	1	4	.20	13	.302	.397	.433
1991 Seattle	AL	150	544	167	35	1	14	(8	6)	246	98	52	84	9	72	8	2	4	0	3	.00	19	.307	.405	.452
1992 Seattle	AL	135	528	181	46	3	18	(11	7)	287	100	73	54	2	61	4	1	5	14	4	.78	15	.343	.404	.544
1993 Seattle	AL	42	135	32	7	0	4	(1	3)	51	20	13	28	1	19	0	1	1	0	0	.00	4	.237	.366	.378
1994 Seattle	AL	89	326	93	23	1	13	(4	9)	157	47	51	53	3	42	3	2	3	6	2	.75	2	.285	.387	.482
1995 Seattle	AL	145	511	182	52	0	29	(16	13)	321	121	113	116	19	87	8	0	4	4	3	.57	11	.356	.479	.628
1996 Seattle	AL	139	499	163	52	2	26	(14	12)	297	121	103	123	12	84	8	0	4	3	3	.50	15	.327	.464	.595
1997 Seattle	AL	155	542	179	35	1	28	(12	16)	300	104	108	119	11	86	11	0	6	2	4	.33	21	.330	.456	.554
11 ML YEARS		1091	3818	1210	291	12	145	(69	76)	1960	708	592	674	61	551	51	10	34	32	24	.57	103	.317	.423	.513

Felix Martinez

Bats: Both Throws: Right Pos: SS-12; PH-5
Ht: 6'0" Wt: 180 Born: 5/18/74 Age: 24

								BATTING										BASERUNNING				PERCENTAGES		
Year Team	Lg	G	AB	H	2B	3B	HR	(Hm	Rd)	TB	R	RBI	TBB	IBB	SO	HBP	SH	SF	SB	CS	SB%	GDP	Avg	OBP	SLG
1993 Royals	R	57	165	42	5	1	0	—	—	49	23	12	17	0	26	3	1	0	22	5	.81	5	.255	.335	.297
1994 Wilmington	A+	117	400	107	16	4	2	—	—	137	65	43	30	0	91	3	12	2	19	8	.70	10	.268	.322	.343
1995 Wichita	AA	127	426	112	15	3	3	—	—	142	53	30	31	0	71	6	4	1	44	20	.69	5	.263	.321	.333
1996 Omaha	AAA	118	395	93	13	3	5	—	—	127	54	35	44	0	79	5	10	0	18	10	.64	11	.235	.320	.322
1997 Omaha	AAA	112	410	104	19	4	2	—	—	137	55	36	29	0	86	7	5	1	21	11	.66	11	.254	.313	.334
1997 Kansas City	AL	16	31	7	1	1	0	(0	0)	10	3	3	6	0	8	0	1	0	0	0	.00	1	.226	.351	.323

Pedro Martinez

Pitches: Right Bats: Right Pos: SP-31
Ht: 5'11" Wt: 170 Born: 10/25/71 Age: 26

			HOW MUCH HE PITCHED				WHAT HE GAVE UP										THE RESULTS					
Year Team	Lg	G	GS	CG	GF	IP	BFP	H	R	ER	HR	SH	SF	HB	TBB	IBB	SO	WP	Bk	W	L	Pct.	ShO	Sv-Op	Hld	ERA
1992 Los Angeles	NL	2	1	0	1	8	31	6	2	2	0	0	0	0	1	0	8	0	0	0	1	.000	0	0-0	0	2.25
1993 Los Angeles	NL	65	2	0	20	107	444	76	34	31	5	0	5	4	57	4	119	3	1	10	5	.667	0	2-3	14	2.61
1994 Montreal	NL	24	23	1	1	144.2	584	115	58	55	11	2	3	11	45	3	142	6	0	11	5	.688	1	1-1	0	3.42
1995 Montreal	NL	30	30	2	0	194.2	784	158	79	76	21	7	3	11	66	1	174	5	2	14	10	.583	2	0-0	0	3.51
1996 Montreal	NL	33	33	4	0	216.2	901	189	100	89	19	9	6	3	70	3	222	6	0	13	10	.565	1	0-0	0	3.70
1997 Montreal	NL	31	31	13	0	241.1	947	158	65	51	16	9	1	9	67	5	305	3	1	17	8	.680	4	0-0	0	1.90
6 ML YEARS		185	120	20	22	912.1	3691	702	338	304	72	27	18	38	306	16	970	23	4	65	39	.625	8	3-4	14	3.00

Pedro A. Martinez

Pitches: Left Bats: Right Pos: RP-8
Ht: 6'2" Wt: 185 Born: 9/29/68 Age: 29

			HOW MUCH HE PITCHED				WHAT HE GAVE UP										THE RESULTS					
Year Team	Lg	G	GS	CG	GF	IP	BFP	H	R	ER	HR	SH	SF	HB	TBB	IBB	SO	WP	Bk	W	L	Pct.	ShO	Sv-Op	Hld	ERA
1997 Indianapls *	AAA	28	11	1	2	80.1	341	70	37	31	9	3	1	0	35	0	36	1	0	4	3	.571	1	0- --	—	3.47

			HOW MUCH HE PITCHED					WHAT HE GAVE UP												THE RESULTS				
Year Team	Lg	G	GS	CG	GF	IP	BFP	H	R	ER	HR	SH	SF	HB	TBB	IBB	SO	WP	Bk	W	L	Pct.	ShO	Sv-Op	Hld	ERA
1993 San Diego	NL	32	0	0	9	37	148	23	11	10	4	0	0	1	13	1	32	0	0	3	1	.750	0	0-1	3	2.43
1994 San Diego	NL	48	1	0	18	68.1	308	52	31	22	4	9	1	1	49	9	52	2	1	3	2	.600	0	3-5	3	2.90
1995 Houston	NL	25	0	0	3	20.2	109	29	18	17	3	2	1	2	16	1	17	0	1	0	0	.000	0	0-0	3	7.40
1996 NYN-Cin	NL	9	0	0	0	10	51	13	9	7	2	1	1	0	8	4	9	0	0	0	0	.000	0	0-0	1	6.30
1997 Cincinnati	NL	8	0	0	1	6.2	37	8	9	7	1	0	1	1	7	0	4	0	0	1	1	.500	0	0-0	0	9.45
1996 New York	NL	5	0	0	0	7	36	8	7	5	1	1	1	0	7	4	6	0	0	0	0	.000	0	0-0	3	6.43
Cincinnati	NL	4	0	0	0	3	15	5	2	2	1	0	0	0	1	0	3	0	0	0	0	.000	0	0-0	1	6.00
5 ML YEARS		122	1	0	31	142.2	653	125	78	63	14	12	4	5	93	15	114	2	2	7	4	.636	0	3-6	13	3.97

Ramon Martinez

Pitches: Right **Bats:** Right **Pos:** SP-22 **Ht:** 6'4" **Wt:** 186 **Born:** 3/22/68 **Age:** 30

			HOW MUCH HE PITCHED					WHAT HE GAVE UP												THE RESULTS				
Year Team	Lg	G	GS	CG	GF	IP	BFP	H	R	ER	HR	SH	SF	HB	TBB	IBB	SO	WP	Bk	W	L	Pct.	ShO	Sv-Op	Hld	ERA
1988 Los Angeles	NL	9	6	0	0	35.2	151	27	17	15	0	4	0	0	22	1	23	1	0	1	3	.250	0	0-0	1	3.79
1989 Los Angeles	NL	15	15	2	0	98.2	410	79	39	35	11	4	0	5	41	1	89	1	0	6	4	.600	2	0-0	0	3.19
1990 Los Angeles	NL	33	33	12	0	234.1	950	191	89	76	22	7	5	4	67	5	223	3	3	20	6	.769	3	0-0	0	2.92
1991 Los Angeles	NL	33	33	6	0	220.1	916	190	89	80	18	8	4	7	69	4	150	6	0	17	13	.567	4	0-0	0	3.27
1992 Los Angeles	NL	25	25	1	0	150.2	662	141	82	67	11	12	1	5	69	4	101	9	0	8	11	.421	1	0-0	0	4.00
1993 Los Angeles	NL	32	32	4	0	211.2	918	202	88	81	15	12	5	4	104	9	127	2	2	10	12	.455	3	0-0	0	3.44
1994 Los Angeles	NL	24	24	4	0	170	718	160	83	75	18	6	8	6	56	2	119	2	0	12	7	.632	3	0-0	0	3.97
1995 Los Angeles	NL	30	30	4	0	206.1	859	176	95	84	19	7	5	5	81	5	138	3	0	17	7	.708	0	0-0	0	3.66
1996 Los Angeles	NL	28	27	2	1	168.2	732	153	76	64	12	7	6	8	86	5	133	2	1	15	6	.714	2	0-0	0	3.42
1997 Los Angeles	NL	22	22	1	0	133.2	590	123	64	54	14	5	4	6	68	1	120	1	1	10	5	.667	0	0-0	1	3.64
10 ML YEARS		251	247	36	1	1630	6906	1442	722	631	140	72	38	50	663	37	1223	30	7	116	74	.611	20	0-0	1	3.48

Sandy Martinez

Bats: Left **Throws:** Right **Pos:** C-3; PH-1 **Ht:** 6'2" **Wt:** 200 **Born:** 10/3/72 **Age:** 25

					BATTING														BASERUNNING				PERCENTAGES		
Year Team	Lg	G	AB	H	2B	3B	HR	(Hm	Rd)	TB	R	RBI	TBB	IBB	SO	HBP	SH	SF	SB	CS	SB%	GDP	Avg	OBP	SLG
1997 Syracuse *	AAA	96	322	72	12	1	4	—	—	98	28	29	27	2	76	5	3	2	7	2	.78	9	.224	.292	.304
1995 Toronto	AL	62	191	46	12	0	2	(1	1)	64	12	25	7	0	45	1	0	1	0	0	.00	1	.241	.270	.335
1996 Toronto	AL	76	229	52	9	3	3	(2	1)	76	17	18	16	0	58	4	1	1	0	0	.00	4	.227	.288	.332
1997 Toronto	AL	3	2	0	0	0	0	(0	0)	0	1	0	1	0	1	0	0	0	0	0	.00	0	.000	.333	.000
3 ML YEARS		141	422	98	21	3	5	(3	2)	140	30	43	24	0	104	5	1	2	0	0	.00	5	.232	.280	.332

Tino Martinez

Bats: Left **Throws:** Right **Pos:** 1B-150; DH-7; PH-2 **Ht:** 6'2" **Wt:** 210 **Born:** 12/7/67 **Age:** 30

					BATTING														BASERUNNING				PERCENTAGES		
Year Team	Lg	G	AB	H	2B	3B	HR	(Hm	Rd)	TB	R	RBI	TBB	IBB	SO	HBP	SH	SF	SB	CS	SB%	GDP	Avg	OBP	SLG
1990 Seattle	AL	24	68	15	4	0	0	(0	0)	19	4	5	9	0	9	0	0	1	0	0	.00	0	.221	.308	.279
1991 Seattle	AL	36	112	23	2	0	4	(3	1)	37	11	9	11	0	24	0	0	2	0	0	.00	2	.205	.272	.330
1992 Seattle	AL	136	460	118	19	2	16	(10	6)	189	53	66	42	9	77	2	1	8	2	1	.67	24	.257	.316	.411
1993 Seattle	AL	109	408	108	25	1	17	(8	9)	186	48	60	45	9	56	5	3	3	0	3	.00	7	.265	.343	.456
1994 Seattle	AL	97	329	86	21	0	20	(8	12)	167	42	61	29	2	52	1	4	3	1	2	.33	9	.261	.320	.508
1995 Seattle	AL	141	519	152	35	3	31	(14	17)	286	92	111	62	15	91	4	2	6	0	0	.00	10	.293	.369	.551
1996 New York	AL	155	595	174	28	0	25	(9	16)	277	82	117	68	4	85	2	1	5	2	1	.67	18	.292	.364	.466
1997 New York	AL	158	594	176	31	2	44	(18	26)	343	96	141	75	14	75	3	0	13	3	1	.75	15	.296	.371	.577
8 ML YEARS		856	3085	852	165	8	157	(71	86)	1504	428	570	341	53	469	17	11	41	8	8	.50	85	.276	.347	.488

John Marzano

Bats: Right **Throws:** Right **Pos:** C-37; PH-5; DH-1 **Ht:** 5'11" **Wt:** 195 **Born:** 2/14/63 **Age:** 35

					BATTING														BASERUNNING				PERCENTAGES		
Year Team	Lg	G	AB	H	2B	3B	HR	(Hm	Rd)	TB	R	RBI	TBB	IBB	SO	HBP	SH	SF	SB	CS	SB%	GDP	Avg	OBP	SLG
1987 Boston	AL	52	168	41	11	0	5	(4	1)	67	20	24	7	0	41	3	2	2	0	1	.00	3	.244	.283	.399
1988 Boston	AL	10	29	4	1	0	0	(0	0)	5	3	1	1	0	3	0	0	0	0	0	.00	0	.138	.167	.172
1989 Boston	AL	7	18	8	3	0	1	(1	0)	14	5	3	0	0	2	0	1	1	0	0	.00	1	.444	.421	.778
1990 Boston	AL	32	83	20	4	0	0	(0	0)	24	8	6	5	0	10	0	2	1	0	0	.00	0	.241	.281	.289
1991 Boston	AL	49	114	30	8	0	0	(0	0)	38	10	9	1	0	16	1	1	2	0	0	.00	0	.263	.271	.333
1992 Boston	AL	19	50	4	2	1	0	(0	0)	8	4	1	2	0	12	1	1	0	0	0	.00	0	.080	.132	.160
1995 Texas	AL	2	6	2	0	0	0	(0	0)	2	1	0	0	0	0	0	0	0	0	0	.00	0	.333	.333	.333
1996 Seattle	AL	41	106	26	6	0	0	(0	0)	32	8	6	7	0	15	4	3	0	0	0	.00	2	.245	.316	.302
1997 Seattle	AL	39	87	25	3	0	1	(1	0)	31	7	10	7	0	15	0	2	0	0	0	.00	2	.287	.340	.356
9 ML YEARS		251	661	160	38	1	7	(6	1)	221	66	60	30	0	114	9	12	6	0	2	.00	14	.242	.282	.334

Damon Mashore

Bats: R **Throws:** R **Pos:** CF-71; LF-28; PH-11; RF-6 **Ht:** 5'11" **Wt:** 195 **Born:** 10/31/69 **Age:** 28

					BATTING														BASERUNNING				PERCENTAGES		
Year Team	Lg	G	AB	H	2B	3B	HR	(Hm	Rd)	TB	R	RBI	TBB	IBB	SO	HBP	SH	SF	SB	CS	SB%	GDP	Avg	OBP	SLG
1991 Sou. Oregon	A-	73	264	72	17	6	6	—	—	119	48	31	34	1	94	2	2	3	15	5	.75	6	.273	.356	.451
1992 Modesto	A+	124	471	133	22	3	18	—	—	215	91	64	73	3	136	6	5	1	29	17	.63	6	.282	.385	.456
1993 Huntsville	AA	70	253	59	7	2	3	—	—	79	35	20	25	0	64	4	1	2	18	4	.82	5	.233	.310	.312
1994 Athletics	R	11	34	14	2	0	0	—	—	16	6	6	4	0	3	1	0	1	1	1	.50	3	.412	.475	.471

Year Team	Lg	G	AB	H	2B	3B	HR	(Hm	Rd)	TB	R	RBI	TBB	IBB	SO	HBP	SH	SF	SB	CS	SB%	GDP	Avg	OBP	SLG
Huntsville	AA	59	210	47	11	2	3	—	—	71	24	21	13	1	53	0	1	3	6	1	.86	3	.224	.265	.338
1995 Edmonton	AAA	117	337	101	19	5	1	—	—	133	50	37	42	0	77	5	3	3	17	5	.77	9	.300	.382	.395
1996 Edmonton	AAA	50	183	49	9	1	8	—	—	84	32	29	19	0	48	5	2	2	6	2	.75	3	.268	.349	.459
1996 Oakland	AL	50	105	28	7	1	3	(1	2)	46	20	12	16	0	31	1	1	1	4	0	1.00	2	.267	.366	.438
1997 Oakland	AL	92	279	69	10	2	3	(1	2)	92	55	18	50	1	82	5	7	1	5	4	.56	5	.247	.370	.330
2 ML YEARS		142	384	97	17	3	6	(2	4)	138	75	30	66	1	113	6	8	2	9	4	.69	7	.253	.369	.359

Mike Matheny

Bats: Right **Throws:** Right **Pos:** C-121; 1B-2; PH-1   **Ht:** 6'3" **Wt:** 205 **Born:** 9/22/70 **Age:** 27

Year Team	Lg	G	AB	H	2B	3B	HR	(Hm	Rd)	TB	R	RBI	TBB	IBB	SO	HBP	SH	SF	SB	CS	SB%	GDP	Avg	OBP	SLG
1994 Milwaukee	AL	28	53	12	3	0	1	(1	0)	18	3	2	3	0	13	2	1	0	0	1	.00	1	.226	.293	.340
1995 Milwaukee	AL	80	166	41	9	1	0	(0	0)	52	13	21	12	0	28	2	1	0	2	1	.67	3	.247	.306	.313
1996 Milwaukee	AL	106	313	64	15	2	8	(5	3)	107	31	46	14	0	80	3	7	4	3	2	.60	9	.204	.243	.342
1997 Milwaukee	AL	123	320	78	16	1	4	(2	2)	108	29	32	17	0	68	7	9	3	0	1	.00	9	.244	.294	.338
4 ML YEARS		337	852	195	43	4	13	(8	5)	285	76	101	46	0	189	14	18	7	5	5	.50	22	.229	.277	.335

T.J. Mathews

Pitches: Right **Bats:** Right **Pos:** RP-64   **Ht:** 6'2" **Wt:** 200 **Born:** 1/19/70 **Age:** 28

		HOW MUCH HE PITCHED						WHAT HE GAVE UP										THE RESULTS					
Year Team	Lg	G	GS	CG	GF	IP	BFP	H	R	ER	HR	SH	SF	HB	TBB	IBB	SO	WP	Bk	W	L	Pct.	ShO	Sv-Op	Hld	ERA
1995 St. Louis	NL	23	0	0	12	29.2	120	21	7	5	1	4	0	0	11	1	28	2	0	1	1	.500	0	2-2	7	1.52
1996 St. Louis	NL	67	0	0	23	83.2	345	62	32	28	8	5	0	2	32	4	80	1	0	2	6	.250	0	6-11	9	3.01
1997 Stl-Oak		64	0	0	26	74.2	329	75	32	25	9	8	1	2	30	4	70	1	0	10	6	.625	0	3-9	12	3.01
1997 St. Louis	NL	40	0	0	12	46	197	41	14	11	4	6	0	1	18	3	46	1	0	4	4	.500	0	0-3	8	2.15
Oakland	AL	24	0	0	14	28.2	132	34	18	14	5	2	1	1	12	1	24	0	0	6	2	.750	0	3-6	4	4.40
3 ML YEARS		154	0	0	61	188	794	158	71	58	18	17	1	4	73	9	178	4	0	13	13	.500	0	11-22	28	2.78

Terry Mathews

Pitches: Right **Bats:** Left **Pos:** RP-57   **Ht:** 6'2" **Wt:** 225 **Born:** 10/5/64 **Age:** 33

		HOW MUCH HE PITCHED						WHAT HE GAVE UP										THE RESULTS					
Year Team	Lg	G	GS	CG	GF	IP	BFP	H	R	ER	HR	SH	SF	HB	TBB	IBB	SO	WP	Bk	W	L	Pct.	ShO	Sv-Op	Hld	ERA
1991 Texas	AL	34	2	0	8	57.1	236	54	24	23	5	2	0	1	18	3	51	5	0	4	0	1.000	0	1-3	2	3.61
1992 Texas	AL	40	0	0	11	42.1	199	48	29	28	4	1	3	1	31	3	26	2	1	2	4	.333	0	0-4	6	5.95
1994 Florida	NL	24	2	0	5	43	179	45	16	16	4	1	0	1	9	1	21	1	0	2	1	.667	0	0-1	3	3.35
1995 Florida	NL	57	0	0	14	82.2	332	70	32	31	9	5	1	1	27	4	72	3	0	4	4	.500	0	3-7	11	3.38
1996 Fla-Bal		71	0	0	24	73.2	326	79	40	37	10	3	1	1	34	5	62	0	0	4	6	.400	0	4-6	15	4.52
1997 Baltimore	AL	57	0	0	19	63.1	285	63	35	31	8	9	4	0	36	2	39	3	0	4	4	.500	0	1-2	8	4.41
1996 Florida	NL	57	0	0	19	55	247	59	33	30	7	2	1	0	27	5	49	0	0	4	4	.333	0	4-5	11	4.91
Baltimore	AL	14	0	0	5	18.2	79	20	7	7	3	1	0	0	7	0	13	0	0	2	2	.500	0	0-1	4	3.38
6 ML YEARS		283	4	0	81	362.1	1557	359	176	166	40	21	9	5	155	18	271	14	1	20	19	.513	0	9-23	45	4.12

Darrell May

Pitches: Left **Bats:** Left **Pos:** RP-27; SP-2   **Ht:** 6'2" **Wt:** 170 **Born:** 6/13/72 **Age:** 26

		HOW MUCH HE PITCHED						WHAT HE GAVE UP										THE RESULTS					
Year Team	Lg	G	GS	CG	GF	IP	BFP	H	R	ER	HR	SH	SF	HB	TBB	IBB	SO	WP	Bk	W	L	Pct.	ShO	Sv-Op	Hld	ERA
1992 Braves	R	12	7	0	4	53	204	34	13	8	0	2	0	2	13	0	61	2	1	4	3	.571	0	1--	—	1.36
1993 Macon	A	17	17	0	0	104.1	404	81	29	26	6	0	0	1	22	1	111	3	0	10	4	.714	0	0--	—	2.24
Durham	A+	9	9	0	0	51.2	213	44	18	12	4	4	2	1	16	0	47	2	1	5	2	.714	0	0--	—	2.09
1994 Durham	A+	12	12	1	0	74.2	307	74	29	25	6	0	1	3	17	1	73	3	0	4	2	.800	0	0--	—	3.01
Greenville	AA	11	11	1	0	63.2	265	61	25	22	4	1	2	2	17	0	42	6	0	5	3	.625	0	0--	—	3.11
1995 Greenville	AA	15	15	0	0	91.1	377	81	44	36	18	2	5	3	20	0	79	4	0	2	8	.200	0	0--	—	3.55
Richmond	AAA	9	9	0	0	51	216	53	21	21	1	1	3	0	16	1	42	2	0	4	2	.667	0	0--	—	3.71
1996 Calgary	AAA	23	22	1	0	131.2	558	146	64	60	17	3	5	0	36	6	75	3	1	7	6	.538	1	0--	—	4.10
1997 Vancouver	AAA	13	12	2	0	80	330	65	31	29	10	2	4	1	31	0	62	0	1	7	5	.583	2	0--	—	3.26
1995 Atlanta	NL	2	0	0	1	4	21	10	5	5	0	0	1	0	1	0	1	0	0	0	0	.000	0	0-0	0	11.25
1996 Pit-Cal		10	2	0	2	11.1	60	18	13	12	6	0	2	1	6	0	6	0	0	0	1	.000	0	0-0	1	9.53
1997 Anaheim	AL	29	2	0	7	51.2	234	56	31	30	6	3	4	0	25	2	42	2	0	2	1	.667	0	0-1	2	5.23
1996 Pittsburgh	NL	5	2	0	0	8.2	47	15	10	9	5	0	0	1	4	0	5	0	0	0	1	.000	0	0-0	0	9.35
California	AL	5	0	0	2	2.2	13	3	3	3	1	0	2	0	2	0	1	0	0	0	0	.000	0	0-0	0	10.13
3 ML YEARS		41	4	0	10	67	315	84	49	47	12	3	7	1	31	2	49	2	0	2	2	.500	0	0-1	3	6.31

Derrick May

Bats: Left **Throws:** Right **Pos:** RF-49; PH-33; LF-7   **Ht:** 6'4" **Wt:** 225 **Born:** 7/14/68 **Age:** 29

Year Team	Lg	G	AB	H	2B	3B	HR	(Hm	Rd)	TB	R	RBI	TBB	IBB	SO	HBP	SH	SF	SB	CS	SB%	GDP	Avg	OBP	SLG
1990 Chicago	NL	17	61	15	3	0	1	(1	0)	21	8	11	2	0	7	0	0	0	1	0	1.00	1	.246	.270	.344
1991 Chicago	NL	15	22	5	2	0	1	(1	0)	10	4	2	1	0	5	0	0	0	0	0	.00	2	.227	.280	.455
1992 Chicago	NL	124	351	96	11	0	8	(3	5)	131	33	45	14	4	40	3	2	1	5	3	.63	10	.274	.306	.373
1993 Chicago	NL	128	465	137	25	2	10	(3	7)	196	62	77	31	6	41	1	0	6	10	3	.77	15	.295	.336	.422
1994 Chicago	NL	100	345	98	19	2	8	(5	3)	145	43	51	30	4	34	0	0	1	3	2	.60	11	.284	.340	.420
1995 Mil-Hou		110	319	90	18	2	9	(4	5)	139	44	50	24	0	42	2	0	3	1	1	.83	5	.282	.333	.436

Year Team	Lg	G	AB	H	2B	3B	HR	(Hm	Rd)	TB	R	RBI	TBB	IBB	SO	HBP	SH	SF	SB	CS	SB%	GDP	Avg	OBP	SLG
1996 Houston	NL	109	259	65	12	3	5	(2	3)	98	24	33	30	8	33	2	0	3	2	2	.50	3	.251	.330	.378
1997 Philadelphia	NL	83	149	34	5	1	1	(0	1)	44	8	13	8	3	26	0	0	1	4	1	.80	4	.228	.266	.295
1995 Milwaukee	AL	32	113	28	3	1	1	(1	0)	36	15	9	5	0	18	1	0	0	0	1	.00	1	.248	.286	.319
Houston	NL	78	206	62	15	1	8	(3	5)	103	29	41	19	0	24	1	0	3	5	0	1.00	4	.301	.358	.500
8 ML YEARS		686	1971	540	95	10	43	(19	24)	784	226	283	141	25	224	8	3	17	30	12	.71	50	.274	.322	.398

Brent Mayne

Bats: Left **Throws:** Right **Pos:** C-83; PH-8   **Ht:** 6'1" **Wt:** 190 **Born:** 4/19/68 **Age:** 30

Year Team	Lg	G	AB	H	2B	3B	HR	(Hm	Rd)	TB	R	RBI	TBB	IBB	SO	HBP	SH	SF	SB	CS	SB%	GDP	Avg	OBP	SLG
1997 Edmonton *	AAA	2	3	0	0	0	0	—	—	0	0	0	0	0	1	0	0	0	0	0	.00	0	.000	.000	.000
1990 Kansas City	AL	5	13	3	0	0	0	(0	0)	3	2	1	3	0	3	0	0	0	0	1	.00	0	.231	.375	.231
1991 Kansas City	AL	85	231	58	8	0	3	(2	1)	75	22	31	23	4	42	0	2	3	2	4	.33	6	.251	.315	.325
1992 Kansas City	AL	82	213	48	10	0	0	(0	0)	58	16	18	11	0	26	0	2	3	0	4	.00	5	.225	.260	.272
1993 Kansas City	AL	71	205	52	9	1	2	(0	2)	69	22	22	18	7	31	1	3	0	3	2	.60	6	.254	.317	.337
1994 Kansas City	AL	46	144	37	5	1	2	(1	1)	50	19	20	14	1	27	0	0	0	1	0	1.00	3	.257	.323	.347
1995 Kansas City	AL	110	307	77	18	1	1	(1	0)	100	23	27	25	1	41	3	11	1	1	1	.00	16	.251	.313	.326
1996 New York	AL	70	99	26	6	0	1	(0	1)	35	9	6	12	1	22	0	2	0	0	1	.00	4	.263	.342	.354
1997 Oakland	AL	85	256	74	12	0	6	(4	2)	104	29	22	18	1	33	4	2	2	1	0	1.00	6	.289	.343	.406
8 ML YEARS		554	1468	375	68	3	15	(8	7)	494	142	147	124	15	225	8	22	9	7	13	.35	46	.255	.315	.337

Jamie McAndrew

Pitches: Right **Bats:** Right **Pos:** SP-4; RP-1   **Ht:** 6'2" **Wt:** 190 **Born:** 9/2/67 **Age:** 30

Year Team	Lg	G	GS	CG	GF	IP	BFP	H	R	ER	HR	SH	SF	HB	TBB	IBB	SO	WP	Bk	W	L	Pct.	ShO	Sv-Op	Hld	ERA
1997 Tucson *	AAA	22	21	0	0	108.2	512	132	87	82	10	2	3	0	65	1	63	8	4	7	8	.467	0	0--	—	6.79
1995 Milwaukee	AL	10	4	0	0	36.1	153	37	21	19	2	1	0	1	12	2	19	0	0	2	3	.400	0	0-0	1	4.71
1997 Milwaukee	AL	5	4	0	0	19.1	104	24	19	18	1	0	0	2	23	0	8	2	0	1	1	.500	0	0-0	0	8.38
2 ML YEARS		15	8	0	2	55.2	257	61	40	37	3	1	0	3	35	2	27	2	0	3	4	.429	0	0-0	1	5.98

Greg McCarthy

Pitches: Left **Bats:** Left **Pos:** RP-37   **Ht:** 6'2" **Wt:** 215 **Born:** 10/30/68 **Age:** 29

Year Team	Lg	G	GS	CG	GF	IP	BFP	H	R	ER	HR	SH	SF	HB	TBB	IBB	SO	WP	Bk	W	L	Pct.	ShO	Sv-Op	Hld	ERA
1987 Utica	A-	20	0	0	13	29.2	130	14	9	3	0	2	1	2	23	2	40	1	2	4	1	.800	0	3--	—	0.91
1988 Spartanburg	A	34	1	0	20	64.2	297	52	36	29	3	3	3	10	52	0	65	8	3	4	2	.667	0	2--	—	4.04
1989 Spartanburg	A	24	15	2	4	112	499	90	58	52	3	3	5	9	80	0	115	8	2	5	8	.385	1	0--	—	4.18
1990 Clearwater	A+	42	1	0	19	59.2	265	47	32	22	4	2	2	1	38	1	67	5	2	1	3	.250	0	5--	—	3.32
1992 Kinston	A+	23	0	0	21	27.1	105	14	0	0	0	1	0	5	9	0	37	8	0	3	0	1.000	0	12--	—	0.00
1993 Kinston	A+	9	0	0	6	10.2	51	8	4	2	0	0	0	0	13	0	14	2	0	0	0	.000	0	2--	—	1.69
Canton-Akrn	AA	33	0	0	19	34.1	156	28	18	18	1	0	3	2	37	2	39	5	0	2	3	.400	0	6--	—	4.72
1994 Canton-Akrn	AA	22	0	0	19	32	133	19	12	8	0	0	0	1	23	2	39	2	0	2	3	.400	0	9--	—	2.25
Charlotte	AAA	18	0	0	11	23.1	118	17	22	18	1	1	2	6	28	1	21	5	0	1	0	1.000	0	0--	—	6.94
1995 Birmingham	AA	38	0	0	13	44.2	195	37	28	25	4	4	2	2	29	3	48	3	1	3	3	.500	0	3--	—	5.04
1996 Tacoma	AAA	39	0	0	14	68.1	317	58	31	25	2	3	1	5	53	2	90	11	2	4	2	.667	0	4--	—	3.29
1997 Tacoma	AAA	22	0	0	10	22	103	21	8	8	3	1	0	2	16	2	34	1	0	2	1	.667	0	3--	—	3.27
1996 Seattle	AL	10	0	0	1	9.2	45	8	2	2	0	1	1	4	4	0	7	0	0	0	0	.000	0	0-0	1	1.86
1997 Seattle	AL	37	0	0	4	29.2	130	26	21	18	4	0	0	1	16	0	34	4	0	1	1	.500	0	0-0	8	5.46
2 ML YEARS		47	0	0	5	39.1	175	34	23	20	4	1	1	5	20	0	41	4	0	1	1	.500	0	0-0	9	4.58

Quinton McCracken

Bats: Both **Throws:** Right **Pos:** CF-133; PH-32   **Ht:** 5'7" **Wt:** 173 **Born:** 3/16/70 **Age:** 28

Year Team	Lg	G	AB	H	2B	3B	HR	(Hm	Rd)	TB	R	RBI	TBB	IBB	SO	HBP	SH	SF	SB	CS	SB%	GDP	Avg	OBP	SLG
1995 Colorado	NL	3	1	0	0	0	0	(0	0)	0	0	0	0	0	1	0	0	0	0	0	.00	0	.000	.000	.000
1996 Colorado	NL	124	283	82	13	6	3	(2	1)	116	50	40	32	0	62	1	12	1	17	6	.74	5	.290	.363	.410
1997 Colorado	NL	147	325	95	11	1	3	(1	2)	117	69	36	42	0	62	1	6	1	28	11	.72	6	.292	.374	.360
3 ML YEARS		274	609	177	24	7	6	(3	3)	233	119	76	74	4	125	2	18	2	45	17	.73	11	.291	.368	383

Jeff McCurry

Pitches: Right **Bats:** Right **Pos:** RP-33   **Ht:** 6'6" **Wt:** 215 **Born:** 1/21/70 **Age:** 28

Year Team	Lg	G	GS	CG	GF	IP	BFP	H	R	ER	HR	SH	SF	HB	TBB	IBB	SO	WP	Bk	W	L	Pct.	ShO	Sv-Op	Hld	ERA
1997 Colo Sprngs *	AAA	16	0	0	8	17.2	77	17	12	10	2	1	1	2	6	1	13	4	0	1	1	.500	0	3--	—	5.09
1995 Pittsburgh	NL	55	0	0	10	61	282	82	38	34	9	4	0	5	30	4	27	2	0	1	4	.200	0	1-2	5	5.02
1996 Detroit	AL	2	0	0	1	3.1	21	9	9	9	3	0	0	0	2	0	0	0	0	0	0	.000	0	0-0	0	24.30
1997 Colorado	NL	33	0	0	14	40.2	179	43	22	20	7	3	1	0	20	0	19	2	0	1	4	.200	0	0-2	4	4.43
3 ML YEARS		90	0	0	25	105	482	134	69	63	19	7	1	5	52	4	46	4	0	2	8	.200	0	1-4	9	5.40

Allen McDill

Pitches: Left **Bats:** Left **Pos:** RP-3   **Ht:** 6'0" **Wt:** 155 **Born:** 8/23/71 **Age:** 26

Year Team	Lg	G	GS	CG	GF	IP	BFP	H	R	ER	HR	SH	SF	HB	TBB	IBB	SO	WP	Bk	W	L	Pct.	ShO	Sv-Op	Hld	ERA
1992 Kingsport	R+	1	0	0	0	0.1	3	0	0	0	0	0	0	0	2	0	0	0	0	0	0	.000	0	0--	—	0.00
Mets	R	10	9	0	0	53.1	216	36	23	16	3	0	0	4	15	0	60	3	0	3	4	.429	0	0--	—	2.70
1993 Kingsport	R+	9	9	0	0	53.1	224	52	19	13	1	1	2	0	14	0	42	2	2	5	2	.714	0	0--	—	2.19
Pittsfield	A-	5	5	0	0	28.1	132	31	22	17	0	2	2	1	15	0	24	3	0	2	3	.400	0	0--	—	5.40
1994 Capital city	A	19	19	1	0	111.2	461	101	52	44	11	5	2	4	38	2	102	9	0	9	6	.600	0	0--	—	3.55
1995 St. Lucie	A+	7	7	1	0	49.1	190	36	11	9	2	1	0	1	13	0	28	3	0	4	2	.667	1	0--	—	1.64
Binghamton	AA	12	12	1	0	73	324	69	42	37	5	1	4	3	38	2	44	3	1	3	5	.375	0	0--	—	4.56
Wichita	AA	12	1	0	5	21.1	85	16	7	5	2	0	0	1	5	0	20	1	0	1	0	1.000	0	1--	—	2.11
1996 Omaha	AAA	2	0	0	0	0.1	5	3	2	2	0	0	0	0	1	0	1	2	0	0	0	.000	0	0--	—	54.00
Wichita	AA	54	0	0	30	65	288	79	43	40	10	2	4	4	21	3	62	7	0	1	5	.167	0	11--	—	5.54
1997 Omaha	AAA	23	6	0	5	64.1	295	80	42	42	10	2	1	5	26	2	51	2	0	5	2	.714	0	2--	—	5.88
Wichita	AA	16	0	0	7	17.1	72	18	7	6	0	1	0	0	7	1	14	1	0	0	1	.000	0	3--	—	3.12
1997 Kansas City	AL	3	0	0	1	4	24	3	6	6	1	1	0	1	8	0	2	0	0	0	0	.000	0	0-0	0	13.50

Ben McDonald

Pitches: Right **Bats:** Right **Pos:** SP-21   **Ht:** 6'7" **Wt:** 214 **Born:** 11/24/67 **Age:** 30

Year Team	Lg	G	GS	CG	GF	IP	BFP	H	R	ER	HR	SH	SF	HB	TBB	IBB	SO	WP	Bk	W	L	Pct.	ShO	Sv-Op	Hld	ERA
1989 Baltimore	AL	6	0	0	2	7.1	33	8	7	7	2	0	1	0	4	0	3	1	1	1	0	1.000	0	0-0	0	8.59
1990 Baltimore	AL	21	15	3	2	118.2	472	88	36	32	9	3	5	0	35	0	65	5	0	8	5	.615	2	0-0	0	2.43
1991 Baltimore	AL	21	21	1	0	126.1	532	126	71	68	16	2	3	1	43	2	85	3	0	6	8	.429	0	0-0	0	4.84
1992 Baltimore	AL	35	35	4	0	227	958	213	113	107	32	6	6	9	74	5	158	3	2	13	13	.500	2	0-0	0	4.24
1993 Baltimore	AL	34	34	7	0	220.1	914	185	92	83	17	7	4	5	86	4	171	7	1	13	14	.481	1	0-0	0	3.39
1994 Baltimore	AL	24	24	5	0	157.1	655	151	75	71	14	6	1	2	54	2	94	3	1	14	7	.667	1	0-0	0	4.06
1995 Baltimore	AL	14	13	1	1	80	342	67	40	37	10	0	2	3	38	3	62	4	2	3	6	.333	0	0-0	0	4.16
1996 Milwaukee	AL	35	35	2	0	221.1	951	228	104	96	25	8	7	6	67	0	146	4	0	12	10	.545	0	0-0	0	3.90
1997 Milwaukee	AL	21	21	1	0	133	551	120	68	60	13	3	1	5	36	2	110	3	0	8	7	.533	0	0-0	0	4.06
9 ML YEARS		211	198	24	5	1291.1	5408	1186	606	561	138	35	30	31	437	18	894	33	7	78	70	.527	6	0-0	0	3.91

Jason McDonald

Bats: Both **Throws:** Right **Pos:** CF-66; LF-18; PH-16   **Ht:** 5'8" **Wt:** 185 **Born:** 3/20/72 **Age:** 26

Year Team	Lg	G	AB	H	2B	3B	HR	(Hm	Rd)	TB	R	RBI	TBB	IBB	SO	HBP	SH	SF	SB	CS	SB%	GDP	Avg	OBP	SLG
1993 Sou. Oregon	A-	35	112	33	5	2	0	—	—	42	26	8	31	2	17	0	2	0	22	4	.85	0	.295	.448	.375
1994 W Michigan	A	116	404	96	11	9	2	—	—	131	67	31	81	1	87	4	9	1	52	23	.69	5	.238	.369	.324
1995 Modesto	A+	133	493	129	25	7	6	—	—	186	109	50	110	0	84	6	8	2	70	20	.78	6	.262	.401	.377
1996 Edmonton	AAA	137	479	114	7	5	8	—	—	155	71	46	63	0	82	15	10	6	33	13	.72	8	.238	.341	.324
1997 Edmonton	AAA	79	276	73	14	6	4	—	—	111	74	30	74	0	58	7	8	1	31	9	.78	4	.264	.430	.402
1997 Oakland	AL	78	236	62	11	4	4	(1	3)	93	47	14	36	0	49	1	2	1	13	8	.62	0	.263	.361	.394

Jack McDowell

Pitches: Right **Bats:** Right **Pos:** SP-6; RP-2   **Ht:** 6'5" **Wt:** 188 **Born:** 1/16/66 **Age:** 32

Year Team	Lg	G	GS	CG	GF	IP	BFP	H	R	ER	HR	SH	SF	HB	TBB	IBB	SO	WP	Bk	W	L	Pct.	ShO	Sv-Op	Hld	ERA
1987 Chicago	AL	4	4	0	0	28	103	16	6	6	1	0	0	2	6	0	15	0	0	3	0	1.000	0	0-0	0	1.93
1988 Chicago	AL	26	26	1	0	158.2	687	147	85	70	12	6	7	7	68	5	84	11	1	5	10	.333	0	0-0	0	3.97
1990 Chicago	AL	33	33	4	0	205	866	189	93	87	20	1	5	7	77	0	165	7	1	14	9	.609	4	0-0	0	3.82
1991 Chicago	AL	35	35	15	0	253.2	1028	212	97	96	19	8	4	4	82	2	191	10	1	17	10	.630	3	0-0	0	3.41
1992 Chicago	AL	34	34	13	0	260.2	1079	247	95	92	21	8	6	7	75	9	178	6	0	20	10	.667	1	0-0	0	3.18
1993 Chicago	AL	34	34	10	0	256.2	1067	261	104	96	20	8	6	3	69	6	158	8	1	22	10	.688	4	0-0	0	3.37
1994 Chicago	AL	25	25	6	0	181	755	186	82	75	12	4	4	5	42	2	127	4	0	10	9	.526	2	0-0	0	3.73
1995 New York	AL	30	30	8	0	217.2	927	211	106	95	25	8	6	5	78	1	157	9	1	15	10	.600	1	0-0	0	3.93
1996 Cleveland	AL	30	30	5	0	192	846	214	119	109	22	10	5	4	67	2	141	5	0	13	9	.591	1	0-0	0	5.11
1997 Cleveland	AL	8	6	0	0	40.2	181	44	25	23	6	4	2	1	18	1	38	1	0	3	3	.500	0	0-0	0	5.09
10 ML YEARS		259	257	62	0	1794	7539	1727	812	749	158	57	45	45	582	28	1254	61	5	122	80	.604	13	0-0	0	3.76

Roger McDowell

Pitches: Right **Bats:** Both **Pos:** RP   **Ht:** 6'1" **Wt:** 195 **Born:** 12/21/60 **Age:** 37

Year Team	Lg	G	GS	CG	GF	IP	BFP	H	R	ER	HR	SH	SF	HB	TBB	IBB	SO	WP	Bk	W	L	Pct.	ShO	Sv-Op	Hld	ERA
1985 New York	NL	62	2	0	36	127.1	516	108	43	40	9	6	2	1	37	8	70	6	2	6	5	.545	0	17--	—	2.83
1986 New York	NL	75	0	0	52	128	524	107	48	43	4	7	3	4	42	6	65	3	3	14	9	.609	0	22--	—	3.02
1987 New York	NL	56	0	0	45	88.2	384	95	41	41	7	5	5	2	28	4	32	3	1	7	5	.583	0	25-32	1	4.16
1988 New York	NL	62	0	0	41	89	378	80	31	26	1	3	5	3	31	7	46	6	1	5	5	.500	0	16-20	7	2.63
1989 NYN-Phi	NL	69	0	0	56	92	387	79	36	20	3	6	1	3	38	8	47	3	1	4	8	.333	0	23-28	2	1.96
1990 Philadelphia	NL	72	0	0	60	86.1	373	92	41	37	2	10	4	2	35	9	39	1	0	6	8	.429	0	22-28	1	3.86
1991 Phi-LA	NL	71	0	0	34	101.1	445	100	40	33	4	11	3	2	48	20	50	2	0	9	9	.500	0	10-15	10	2.93
1992 Los Angeles	NL	65	0	0	39	83.2	393	103	46	38	3	10	3	1	42	13	50	4	1	6	10	.375	0	14-22	5	4.09
1993 Los Angeles	NL	54	0	0	19	68	300	76	32	17	2	3	1	0	30	10	27	5	0	5	3	.625	0	2-3	3	2.25
1994 Los Angeles	NL	32	0	0	11	41.1	193	50	25	24	3	5	0	1	22	6	29	3	0	0	3	.000	0	0-1	0	5.23
1995 Texas	AL	64	0	0	26	85	362	86	39	38	5	6	5	6	34	7	49	1	1	7	4	.636	0	4-8	9	4.02

Year Team	Lg	G	GS	CG	GF	IP	BFP	H	R	ER	HR	SH	SF	HB	TBB	IBB	SO	WP	Bk	W	L	Pct.	ShO	Sv-Op	Hld	ERA
		HOW MUCH HE PITCHED						**WHAT HE GAVE UP**												**THE RESULTS**						
1996 Baltimore	AL	41	0	0	11	59.1	262	69	32	28	7	3	1	2	23	1	20	0	0	1	1	.500	0	4-6	9	4.25
1989 New York	NL	25	0	0	15	35.1	156	34	21	13	1	3	1	2	16	3	15	3	1	1	5	.167	0	4-5	2	3.31
Philadelphia	NL	44	0	0	41	56.2	231	45	15	7	2	3	0	1	22	5	32	0	0	3	3	.500	0	19-23	0	1.11
1991 Philadelphia	NL	38	0	0	16	59	271	61	28	21	1	7	1	2	32	12	28	1	0	3	6	.333	0	3-6	6	3.20
Los Angeles	NL	33	0	0	18	42.1	174	39	12	12	3	4	2	0	16	8	22	1	0	6	3	.667	0	7-9	4	2.55
12 ML YEARS		723	2	0	430	1050	4517	1045	454	385	50	75	33	28	410	98	524	37	11	70	70	.500	0	159- –	—	3.30

Chuck McElroy

Pitches: Left **Bats:** Left **Pos:** RP-61 **Ht:** 6'0" **Wt:** 195 **Born:** 10/1/67 **Age:** 30

Year Team	Lg	G	GS	CG	GF	IP	BFP	H	R	ER	HR	SH	SF	HB	TBB	IBB	SO	WP	Bk	W	L	Pct.	ShO	Sv-Op	Hld	ERA
		HOW MUCH HE PITCHED						**WHAT HE GAVE UP**												**THE RESULTS**						
1989 Philadelphia	NL	11	0	0	4	10.1	46	12	2	2	1	0	0	0	4	1	8	0	0	0	0	.000	0	0-0	0	1.74
1990 Philadelphia	NL	16	0	0	8	14	76	24	13	12	0	1	0	0	10	2	16	0	0	0	1	.000	0	0-0	0	7.71
1991 Chicago	NL	71	0	0	12	101.1	419	73	33	22	7	9	6	0	57	7	92	1	0	6	2	.750	0	3-6	10	1.95
1992 Chicago	NL	72	0	0	30	83.2	369	73	40	33	5	5	5	0	51	10	83	3	0	4	7	.364	0	6-11	3	3.55
1993 Chicago	NL	49	0	0	11	47.1	214	51	30	24	4	5	1	1	25	5	31	3	0	2	2	.500	0	0-0	4	4.56
1994 Cincinnati	NL	52	0	0	13	57.2	230	52	15	15	3	2	0	0	15	2	38	4	0	1	2	.333	0	5-11	10	2.34
1995 Cincinnati	NL	44	0	0	11	40.1	178	46	29	27	5	1	3	1	15	3	27	1	0	3	4	.429	0	0-3	3	6.02
1996 Cin-Cal		52	0	0	12	49	210	45	22	21	4	1	1	2	23	3	45	1	0	7	1	.875	0	0-2	7	3.86
1997 Ana-ChA	AL	61	0	0	16	75	320	73	36	32	5	3	3	2	22	1	62	1	0	1	3	.250	0	1-6	15	3.84
1996 Cincinnati	NL	12	0	0	1	12.1	59	13	10	9	2	0	0	0	10	1	13	0	0	2	0	1.000	0	0-0	1	6.57
California	AL	40	0	0	11	36.2	151	32	12	12	2	1	1	2	13	2	32	1	0	5	1	.833	0	0-2	6	2.95
1997 Anaheim	AL	13	0	0	3	15.2	66	17	7	6	2	0	0	0	3	0	18	0	0	0	0	.000	0	0-2	4	3.45
Chicago	AL	48	0	0	13	59.1	254	56	29	26	3	3	3	2	19	1	44	1	0	1	3	.250	0	1-4	11	3.94
9 ML YEARS		428	0	0	117	478.2	2062	449	220	188	34	26	20	6	222	34	402	14	0	24	22	.522	0	15-39	54	3.53

Willie McGee

Bats: B **Throws:** R **Pos:** PH-59; RF-53; LF-18; CF-18; DH-3 **Ht:** 6'1" **Wt:** 185 **Born:** 11/2/58 **Age:** 39

Year Team	Lg	G	AB	H	2B	3B	HR	(Hm	Rd)	TB	R	RBI	TBB	IBB	SO	HBP	SH	SF	SB	CS	SB%	GDP	Avg	OBP	SLG
		BATTING																	**BASERUNNING**				**PERCENTAGES**		
1982 St. Louis	NL	123	422	125	12	8	4	(2	2)	165	43	56	12	2	58	2	2	1	24	12	.67	9	.296	.318	.391
1983 St. Louis	NL	147	601	172	22	8	5	(4	1)	225	75	75	26	2	98	0	1	3	39	8	.83	8	.286	.314	.374
1984 St. Louis	NL	145	571	166	19	11	6	(2	4)	225	82	50	29	2	80	1	0	3	43	10	.81	12	.291	.325	.394
1985 St. Louis	NL	152	612	216	26	18	10	(3	7)	308	114	82	34	2	86	0	1	5	56	16	.78	3	.353	.384	.503
1986 St. Louis	NL	124	497	127	22	7	7	(7	0)	184	65	48	37	7	82	1	0	4	19	16	.54	8	.256	.306	.370
1987 St. Louis	NL	153	620	177	37	11	11	(6	5)	269	76	105	24	5	90	2	1	5	16	4	.80	24	.285	.312	.434
1988 St. Louis	NL	137	562	164	24	6	3	(1	2)	209	73	50	32	5	84	1	2	3	41	6	.87	10	.292	.329	.372
1989 St. Louis	NL	58	199	47	10	2	3	(1	2)	70	23	17	10	0	34	1	0	1	8	6	.57	2	.236	.275	.352
1990 StL-Oak		154	614	199	35	7	3	(1	2)	257	99	77	48	6	104	1	0	2	31	9	.78	13	.324	.373	.419
1991 San Francisco	NL	131	497	155	30	3	4	(2	2)	203	67	43	34	3	74	2	8	2	17	9	.65	11	.312	.357	.408
1992 San Francisco	NL	138	474	141	20	2	1	(0	1)	168	56	36	29	3	88	1	5	1	13	4	.76	7	.297	.339	.354
1993 San Francisco	NL	130	475	143	28	1	4	(3	1)	185	53	46	38	7	67	1	3	2	10	9	.53	12	.301	.353	.389
1994 San Francisco	NL	45	156	44	3	0	5	(2	3)	62	19	23	15	2	24	0	1	4	3	0	1.00	8	.282	.337	.397
1995 Boston	AL	67	200	57	11	3	2	(1	1)	80	32	15	9	0	41	0	5	3	5	2	.71	5	.285	.311	.400
1996 San Francisco	NL	123	309	95	15	2	5	(2	3)	129	52	41	18	2	60	2	1	1	5	2	.71	8	.307	.348	.417
1997 St. Louis	NL	122	300	90	19	4	3	(2	1)	126	29	38	22	2	59	0	0	1	8	2	.80	6	.300	.347	.420
1990 St. Louis	NL	125	501	168	32	5	3	(1	2)	219	76	62	38	6	86	1	0	2	28	9	.76	9	.335	.382	.437
Oakland	AL	29	113	31	3	2	0	(0	0)	38	23	15	10	0	18	0	0	0	3	0	1.00	4	.274	.333	.336
16 ML YEARS		1949	7109	2118	333	93	76	(36	40)	2865	958	802	417	50	1129	15	30	41	338	115	.75	146	.298	.336	.403

Tom McGraw

Pitches: Left **Bats:** Left **Pos:** RP-2 **Ht:** 6'2" **Wt:** 195 **Born:** 12/8/67 **Age:** 30

Year Team	Lg	G	GS	CG	GF	IP	BFP	H	R	ER	HR	SH	SF	HB	TBB	IBB	SO	WP	Bk	W	L	Pct.	ShO	Sv-Op	Hld	ERA
		HOW MUCH HE PITCHED						**WHAT HE GAVE UP**												**THE RESULTS**						
1990 Beloit	A	12	12	1	0	70	299	49	33	15	1	2	1	1	34	0	61	4	4	7	3	.700	1	0- —		1.93
1991 El Paso	AA	9	7	0	2	35.2	163	43	28	23	1	2	1	1	21	0	28	0	0	1	1	.500	0	1- —		5.80
Stockton	A+	11	7	0	1	47	183	35	15	12	2	2	1	2	13	0	39	3	1	3	0	1.000	0	0- —		2.30
1992 Stockton	A+	15	15	1	0	97.1	414	97	44	29	1	4	3	2	31	5	70	5	0	4	6	.400	0	0- —		2.68
El Paso	AA	11	10	1	1	69.1	299	75	24	21	2	2	0	0	26	1	53	2	0	6	0	1.000	0	0- —		2.73
1993 High Desert	A+	6	6	1	0	38	153	38	17	15	3	1	2	1	7	0	31	1	0	2	3	.400	0	0- —		3.55
Edmonton	AAA	5	2	0	1	9.2	45	12	7	6	1	0	1	0	4	0	8	1	0	2	0	1.000	0	0- —		5.59
1994 Portland	AA	37	7	0	11	74	327	81	44	38	9	3	1	5	35	3	56	6	0	3	5	.375	0	2- —		4.62
1995 Portland	AA	51	0	0	11	74.2	322	69	21	15	2	7	3	4	31	3	60	4	0	3	0	1.000	0	2- —		1.81
1996 Trenton	AA	30	0	0	12	34	149	34	15	12	1	3	0	0	19	7	32	1	0	3	4	.429	0	2- —		3.18
1997 Louisville	AAA	45	0	0	18	49	226	55	34	29	3	4	2	0	26	2	39	3	0	1	4	.200	0	0- —		5.33
1997 St. Louis	NL	2	0	0	2	1.2	8	2	0	0	0	0	1	0	1	0	0	1	0	0	0	.000	0	0-0	0	0.00

Fred McGriff

Bats: Left **Throws:** Left **Pos:** 1B-149; PH-3 **Ht:** 6'3" **Wt:** 215 **Born:** 10/31/63 **Age:** 34

Year Team	Lg	G	AB	H	2B	3B	HR	(Hm	Rd)	TB	R	RBI	TBB	IBB	SO	HBP	SH	SF	SB	CS	SB%	GDP	Avg	OBP	SLG
		BATTING																	**BASERUNNING**				**PERCENTAGES**		
1986 Toronto	AL	3	5	1	0	0	0	(0	0)	1	1	0	0	0	2	0	0	0	0	0	.00	0	.200	.200	.200
1987 Toronto	AL	107	295	73	16	0	20	(7	13)	149	58	43	60	4	104	1	0	0	3	2	.60	3	.247	.376	.505
1988 Toronto	AL	154	536	151	35	4	34	(18	16)	296	100	82	79	3	149	4	0	4	6	1	.86	15	.282	.376	.552

Year Team	Lg	G	AB	H	2B	3B	HR	(Hm	Rd)	TB	R	RBI	TBB	IBB	SO	HBP	SH	SF	SB	CS	SB%	GDP	Avg	OBP	SLG
1989 Toronto	AL	161	551	148	27	3	36	(18	18)	289	98	92	119	12	132	4	1	5	7	4	.64	14	.269	.399	.525
1990 Toronto	AL	153	557	167	21	1	35	(14	21)	295	91	88	94	12	108	2	1	4	5	3	.63	7	.300	.400	.530
1991 San Diego	NL	153	528	147	19	1	31	(18	13)	261	84	106	105	26	135	2	0	7	4	1	.80	14	.286	.394	.494
1992 San Diego	NL	152	531	152	30	4	35	(21	14)	295	79	104	96	23	108	1	0	4	8	6	.57	14	.286	.394	.556
1993 SD-Atl	NL	151	557	162	29	2	37	(15	22)	306	111	101	76	6	106	2	0	5	5	3	.63	14	.291	.375	.549
1994 Atlanta	NL	113	424	135	25	1	34	(13	21)	264	81	94	50	8	76	1	0	3	7	3	.70	8	.318	.389	.623
1995 Atlanta	NL	144	528	148	27	1	27	(15	12)	258	85	93	65	6	99	5	0	6	3	6	.33	19	.280	.361	.489
1996 Atlanta	NL	159	617	182	37	1	28	(17	11)	305	81	107	68	12	116	2	0	4	7	3	.70	20	.295	.365	.494
1997 Atlanta	NL	152	564	156	25	1	22	(8	14)	249	77	97	68	4	112	4	0	5	5	0	1.00	22	.277	.356	.441
1993 San Diego	NL	83	302	83	11	1	18	(7	11)	150	52	46	42	4	55	1	0	4	4	3	.57	9	.275	.361	.497
Atlanta	NL	68	255	79	18	1	19	(8	11)	156	59	55	34	2	51	1	0	1	1	0	1.00	5	.310	.392	.612
12 ML YEARS		1602	5693	1622	291	19	339	(164	175)	2968	946	1007	880	116	1247	28	2	47	60	32	.65	150	.285	.381	.521

Ryan McGuire

Bats: L Throws: L Pos: 1B-30; RF-22; LF-21; PH-13; DH-3; CF-2   Ht: 6'2" Wt: 210 Born: 11/23/71 Age: 26

Year Team	Lg	G	AB	H	2B	3B	HR	(Hm	Rd)	TB	R	RBI	TBB	IBB	SO	HBP	SH	SF	SB	CS	SB%	GDP	Avg	OBP	SLG
1993 Ft. Laud	A+	58	213	69	12	2	4	—	—	97	23	38	27	3	34	2	1	3	2	4	.33	11	.324	.400	.455
1994 Lynchburg	A+	137	489	133	29	0	10	—	—	192	70	73	79	2	77	2	4	7	10	9	.53	19	.272	.371	.393
1995	AA	109	414	138	29	1	7	—	—	190	59	59	58	5	51	0	4	1	11	8	.58	10	.333	.414	.459
1996 Ottawa	AAA	134	451	116	21	2	12	—	—	177	62	60	59	4	80	2	1	3	11	4	.73	12	.257	.344	.392
1997 Ottawa	AAA	50	184	55	11	1	3	—	—	77	37	15	36	2	29	0	0	2	5	2	.71	4	.299	.410	.418
1997 Montreal	NL	84	199	51	15	2	3	(2	1)	79	27	17	19	1	34	0	3	1	1	4	.20	3	.256	.320	.397

Mark McGwire

Bats: Right Throws: Right Pos: 1B-151; PH-6   Ht: 6'5" Wt: 250 Born: 10/1/63 Age: 34

Year Team	Lg	G	AB	H	2B	3B	HR	(Hm	Rd)	TB	R	RBI	TBB	IBB	SO	HBP	SH	SF	SB	CS	SB%	GDP	Avg	OBP	SLG
1986 Oakland	AL	18	53	10	1	0	3	(1	2)	20	10	9	4	0	18	1	0	0	0	1	.00	0	.189	.259	.377
1987 Oakland	AL	151	557	161	28	4	49	(21	28)	344	97	118	71	18	131	5	0	8	1	1	.50	6	.289	.370	.618
1988 Oakland	AL	155	550	143	22	1	32	(12	20)	263	87	99	76	4	117	4	1	4	0	0	.00	15	.260	.352	.478
1989 Oakland	AL	143	490	113	17	0	33	(12	21)	229	74	95	83	5	94	3	0	11	1	1	.50	23	.231	.339	.467
1990 Oakland	AL	156	523	123	16	0	39	(14	25)	256	87	108	110	9	116	7	1	9	2	1	.67	13	.235	.370	.489
1991 Oakland	AL	154	483	97	22	0	22	(15	7)	185	62	75	93	3	116	3	1	5	2	1	.67	13	.201	.330	.383
1992 Oakland	AL	139	467	125	22	0	42	(24	18)	273	87	104	90	12	105	5	0	9	0	1	.00	10	.268	.385	.585
1993 Oakland	AL	27	84	28	6	0	9	(5	4)	61	16	24	21	5	19	1	0	1	0	0	.00	3	.333	.467	.726
1994 Oakland	AL	47	135	34	3	0	9	(6	3)	64	26	25	37	3	40	0	0	0	0	0	.00	3	.252	.413	.474
1995 Oakland	AL	104	317	87	13	0	39	(15	24)	217	75	90	88	5	77	11	0	6	1	1	.50	9	.274	.441	.685
1996 Oakland	AL	130	423	132	21	0	52	(24	28)	309	104	113	116	16	112	8	0	1	0	0	.00	14	.312	.467	.730
1997 Oak-StL		156	540	148	27	0	58	(30	28)	349	86	123	101	16	159	9	0	7	3	0	1.00	9	.274	.393	.646
1997 Oakland	AL	105	366	104	24	0	34	(17	17)	230	48	81	58	8	98	4	0	5	1	0	1.00	6	.284	.383	.628
St. Louis	NL	51	174	44	3	0	24	(13	11)	119	38	42	43	8	61	5	0	2	2	0	1.00	3	.253	.411	.684
12 ML YEARS		1380	4622	1201	198	5	387	(179	208)	2570	811	983	890	86	1104	57	3	61	10	8	.56	115	.260	.382	.556

Walt McKeel

Bats: Right Throws: Right Pos: C-4; 1B-1; PH-1   Ht: 6'0" Wt: 200 Born: 1/17/72 Age: 26

Year Team	Lg	G	AB	H	2B	3B	HR	(Hm	Rd)	TB	R	RBI	TBB	IBB	SO	HBP	SH	SF	SB	CS	SB%	GDP	Avg	OBP	SLG
1990 Red Sox	R	13	44	11	3	0	0	—	—	14	2	6	3	0	8	0	0	1	0	2	.00	2	.250	.292	.318
1991 Red Sox	R	35	113	15	0	1	2	—	—	23	10	12	17	0	20	1	0	4	0	0	.00	5	.133	.244	.204
1992 Lynchburg	A+	96	288	64	11	0	12	—	—	111	33	33	22	0	77	3	5	1	2	1	.67	6	.222	.283	.385
1993 Lynchburg	A+	80	247	59	17	2	5	—	—	95	28	32	26	0	40	3	6	3	0	1	.00	6	.239	.315	.385
1994 Sarasota	A+	37	137	38	8	1	2	—	—	54	15	15	8	1	19	1	0	0	1	0	1.00	1	.277	.322	.394
New Britain	AA	50	164	30	6	1	1	—	—	41	10	17	7	1	35	3	1	2	0	0	.00	1	.183	.227	.250
1995 Trenton	AA	29	84	20	3	1	2	—	—	31	11	11	8	0	15	0	0	2	2	1	.67	1	.238	.298	.369
Sarasota	A+	62	198	66	14	0	8	—	—	104	26	35	25	0	28	3	0	5	6	3	.67	13	.333	.407	.525
1996 Trenton	AA	128	464	140	19	1	16	—	—	209	86	78	60	3	52	7	5	7	2	4	.33	13	.302	.385	.450
1997 Pawtucket	AAA	66	237	60	15	0	6	—	—	93	34	30	34	3	39	1	1	2	0	1	.00	8	.253	.347	.392
Trenton	AA	7	25	4	2	0	0	—	—	6	0	4	1	0	2	0	0	0	0	0	.00	0	.160	.192	.240
1996 Boston	AL	1	0	0	0	0	0	(0	0)	0	0	0	0	0	0	0	0	0	0	0	.00	0	.000	.000	.000
1997 Boston	AL	5	3	0	0	0	0	(0	0)	0	0	0	0	0	1	0	0	0	0	0	.00	0	.000	.000	.000
2 ML YEARS		6	3	0	0	0	0	(0	0)	0	0	0	0	0	1	0	0	0	0	0	.00	0	.000	.000	.000

Mark McLemore

Bats: Both Throws: Right Pos: 2B-89; PH-2; LF-1   Ht: 5'11" Wt: 207 Born: 10/4/64 Age: 33

Year Team	Lg	G	AB	H	2B	3B	HR	(Hm	Rd)	TB	R	RBI	TBB	IBB	SO	HBP	SH	SF	SB	CS	SB%	GDP	Avg	OBP	SLG
1997 Charlotte *	A+	2	7	4	1	0	0	—	—	5	1	3	2	0	1	0	0	0	1	1	.50	0	.571	.667	.714
Okla City *	AAA	3	10	1	0	0	0	—	—	1	0	1	0	0	2	0	0	0	1	0	1.00	0	.100	.167	.100
1986 California	AL	5	4	0	0	0	0	(0	0)	0	0	0	1	0	2	0	1	0	0	1	.00	0	.000	.200	.000
1987 California	AL	138	433	102	13	3	3	(3	0)	130	61	41	48	0	72	0	15	3	25	8	.76	7	.236	.310	.300
1988 California	AL	77	233	56	11	2	2	(1	1)	77	38	16	25	0	28	0	5	2	13	7	.65	0	.240	.312	.330
1989 California	AL	32	103	25	3	1	0	(0	0)	30	12	14	7	0	19	1	3	1	6	1	.86	5	.243	.295	.291
1990 Cal-Cle	AL	28	60	9	2	0	0	(0	0)	11	6	2	4	0	15	0	1	0	0	1	1.00	0	.150	.203	.183

Year Team	Lg	G	AB	H	2B	3B	HR	(Hm	Rd)	TB	R	RBI	TBB	IBB	SO	HBP	SH	SF	SB	CS	SB%	GDP	Avg	OBP	SLG
1991 Houston	NL	21	61	9	1	0	0	(0	0)	10	6	2	6	0	13	0	0	1	0	1	.00	1	.148	.221	.164
1992 Baltimore	AL	101	228	56	7	2	0	(0	0)	67	40	27	21	1	26	0	6	1	11	5	.69	6	.246	.308	.294
1993 Baltimore	AL	148	581	165	27	5	4	(2	2)	214	81	72	64	4	92	1	11	6	21	15	.58	21	.284	.353	.368
1994 Baltimore	AL	104	343	88	11	1	3	(2	1)	110	44	29	51	3	50	1	4	1	20	5	.80	7	.257	.354	.321
1995 Texas	AL	129	467	122	20	5	5	(3	2)	167	73	41	59	6	71	3	10	3	21	11	.66	10	.261	.346	.358
1996 Texas	AL	147	517	150	23	4	5	(3	2)	196	84	46	87	5	69	0	2	5	27	10	.73	16	.290	.389	.379
1997 Texas	AL	89	349	91	17	2	1	(0	1)	115	47	25	40	1	54	2	6	2	7	5	.58	5	.261	.338	.330
1990 California	AL	20	48	7	2	0	0	(0	0)	9	4	2	4	0	9	0	1	0	1	0	1.00	1	.146	.212	.188
Cleveland	AL	8	12	2	0	0	0	(0	0)	2	2	0	0	0	6	0	0	0	0	0	.00	0	.167	.167	.167
12 ML YEARS		1019	3379	873	135	25	23	(14	9)	1127	492	315	413	20	511	8	64	25	152	69	.69	82	.258	.338	.334

Greg McMichael

Pitches: Right **Bats:** Right **Pos:** RP-73   **Ht:** 6'3" **Wt:** 215 **Born:** 12/1/66 **Age:** 31

Year Team	Lg	G	GS	CG	GF	IP	BFP	H	R	ER	HR	SH	SF	HB	TBB	IBB	SO	WP	Bk	W	L	Pct.	ShO	Sv-Op	Hld	ERA
1993 Atlanta	NL	74	0	0	40	91.2	365	68	22	21	3	4	2	0	29	4	89	6	1	2	3	.400	0	19-21	12	2.06
1994 Atlanta	NL	51	0	0	41	58.2	259	66	29	25	1	3	1	0	19	6	47	3	1	4	6	.400	0	21-31	1	3.84
1995 Atlanta	NL	67	0	0	16	80.2	337	64	27	25	8	5	0	0	32	9	74	3	0	7	2	.778	0	2-4	20	2.79
1996 Atlanta	NL	73	0	0	14	86.2	366	84	37	31	4	3	3	1	27	7	78	4	1	5	3	.625	0	2-8	18	3.22
1997 New York	NL	73	0	0	23	87.2	355	73	34	29	8	9	4	2	27	6	81	5	0	7	10	.412	0	7-18	19	2.98
5 ML YEARS		338	0	0	134	405.1	1682	355	149	131	24	24	10	3	134	32	369	21	3	25	24	.510	0	51-82	70	2.91

Billy McMillon

Bats: Left **Throws:** Left **Pos:** LF-21; PH-15; RF-2   **Ht:** 5'11" **Wt:** 172 **Born:** 11/17/71 **Age:** 26

Year Team	Lg	G	AB	H	2B	3B	HR	(Hm	Rd)	TB	R	RBI	TBB	IBB	SO	HBP	SH	SF	SB	CS	SB%	GDP	Avg	OBP	SLG
1993 Elmira	A-	57	227	69	14	2	6	—	—	105	38	35	30	4	44	4	0	0	5	4	.56	3	.304	.395	.463
1994 Kane County	A	137	496	125	25	3	17	—	—	207	88	101	84	2	99	10	1	9	7	3	.70	13	.252	.366	.417
1995 Portland	AA	141	518	162	29	3	14	—	—	239	92	93	96	5	90	7	1	5	15	9	.63	10	.313	.423	.461
1996 Charlotte	AAA	97	347	122	32	2	17	—	—	209	72	70	86	0	76	5	0	2	5	3	.63	8	.352	.418	.602
1997 Charlotte	AAA	57	204	57	18	0	8	—	—	99	34	26	32	1	51	1	0	1	8	0	1.00	3	.279	.378	.485
Scranton-WB	AAA	26	92	27	8	1	4	—	—	49	18	21	12	0	24	0	0	0	2	0	1.00	1	.293	.375	.533
1996 Florida	NL	28	51	11	0	0	0	(0	0)	11	4	4	5	1	14	0	0	0	0	0	.00	1	.216	.286	.216
1997 Fla-Phi	NL	37	90	23	5	1	2	(2	0)	36	10	14	6	0	24	0	0	3	2	1	.67	1	.256	.293	.400
1997 Florida	NL	13	18	2	1	0	0	(0	0)	3	0	1	0	0	7	0	0	0	0	1	.00	0	.111	.111	.167
Philadelphia	NL	24	72	21	4	1	2	(2	0)	33	10	13	6	0	17	0	0	3	2	1	.67	1	.292	.333	.458
2 ML YEARS		65	141	34	5	1	2	(2	0)	47	14	18	11	1	38	0	0	3	2	1	.67	2	.241	.290	.333

Brian McRae

Bats: Both **Throws:** Right **Pos:** CF-148; PH-9   **Ht:** 6'0" **Wt:** 196 **Born:** 8/27/67 **Age:** 30

Year Team	Lg	G	AB	H	2B	3B	HR	(Hm	Rd)	TB	R	RBI	TBB	IBB	SO	HBP	SH	SF	SB	CS	SB%	GDP	Avg	OBP	SLG
1990 Kansas City	AL	46	168	48	8	3	2	(1	1)	68	21	23	9	0	29	0	3	2	4	3	.57	5	.286	.318	.405
1991 Kansas City	AL	152	629	164	28	9	8	(3	5)	234	86	64	24	1	99	2	3	5	20	11	.65	12	.261	.288	.372
1992 Kansas City	AL	149	533	119	23	5	4	(2	2)	164	63	52	42	1	88	6	7	4	18	5	.78	10	.223	.285	.308
1993 Kansas City	AL	153	627	177	28	9	12	(5	7)	259	78	69	37	1	105	4	14	3	23	14	.62	8	.282	.325	.413
1994 Kansas City	AL	114	436	119	22	6	4	(2	2)	165	71	40	54	3	67	6	6	3	28	8	.78	3	.273	.359	.378
1995 Chicago	NL	137	580	167	38	7	12	(6	6)	255	92	48	47	1	92	7	3	1	27	8	.77	12	.288	.348	.440
1996 Chicago	NL	157	624	172	32	5	17	(9	8)	265	111	66	73	6	84	12	2	5	37	9	.80	11	.276	.360	.425
1997 ChN-NYN	NL	153	562	136	32	7	11	(6	5)	215	86	43	65	2	84	6	4	2	17	10	.63	13	.242	.326	.383
1997 Chicago	NL	108	417	100	27	5	6	(4	2)	155	63	28	52	2	62	4	3	1	14	6	.70	11	.240	.329	.372
New York	NL	45	145	36	5	2	5	(2	3)	60	23	15	13	0	22	2	1	1	3	4	.43	2	.248	.317	.414
8 ML YEARS		1061	4159	1102	211	51	70	(34	36)	1625	608	405	351	15	648	43	42	25	174	68	.72	74	.265	.327	.391

Pat Meares

Bats: Right **Throws:** Right **Pos:** SS-134; PH-3   **Ht:** 6'0" **Wt:** 188 **Born:** 9/6/68 **Age:** 29

Year Team	Lg	G	AB	H	2B	3B	HR	(Hm	Rd)	TB	R	RBI	TBB	IBB	SO	HBP	SH	SF	SB	CS	SB%	GDP	Avg	OBP	SLG
1993 Minnesota	AL	111	346	87	14	3	0	(0	0)	107	33	33	7	0	52	1	4	3	4	5	.44	11	.251	.266	.309
1994 Minnesota	AL	80	229	61	12	1	2	(0	2)	81	29	24	14	0	50	2	6	3	5	1	.83	3	.266	.310	.354
1995 Minnesota	AL	116	390	105	19	4	12	(3	9)	168	57	49	15	0	68	11	4	1	10	4	.71	17	.269	.311	.431
1996 Minnesota	AL	152	517	138	26	7	8	(3	5)	202	66	67	17	1	90	9	4	7	9	4	.69	19	.267	.298	.391
1997 Minnesota	AL	134	439	121	23	3	10	(5	5)	180	63	60	18	0	86	16	3	7	7	7	.50	9	.276	.323	.410
5 ML YEARS		593	1921	512	94	18	32	(11	21)	738	248	233	71	1	346	39	21	25	35	21	.63	59	.267	.303	.384

Jim Mecir

Pitches: Right **Bats:** Both **Pos:** RP-25   **Ht:** 6'1" **Wt:** 195 **Born:** 5/16/70 **Age:** 28

Year Team	Lg	G	GS	CG	GF	IP	BFP	H	R	ER	HR	SH	SF	HB	TBB	IBB	SO	WP	Bk	W	L	Pct.	ShO	Sv-Op	Hld	ERA
1997 Columbus *	AAA	24	0	0	17	27	98	14	4	3	0	1	0	2	6	0	34	0	0	0	0	.500	0	11--	—	1.00
1995 Seattle	AL	2	0	0	1	4.2	21	5	1	0	0	0	0	0	2	0	3	0	0	0	0	.000	0	0-0	0	0.00
1996 New York	AL	26	0	0	10	40.1	185	42	24	23	6	5	4	0	23	4	38	6	0	1	1	.500	0	0-0	0	5.13

			HOW MUCH HE PITCHED					WHAT HE GAVE UP											THE RESULTS					
Year Team	Lg	G	GS	CG	GF	IP	BFP	H	R	ER	HR	SH	SF	HB	TBB	IBB	SO	WP	Bk	W	L	Pct.	ShO	Sv-Op	Hld	ERA
1997 New York	AL	25	0	0	11	33.2	142	36	23	22	5	0	1	2	10	1	25	1	0	0	4	.000	0	0-1	1	5.88
3 ML YEARS		53	0	0	22	78.2	348	83	48	45	11	5	5	2	35	5	66	7	0	1	5	.167	0	0-1	1	5.15

Roberto Mejia

Bats: Right **Throws:** Right **Pos:** 2B-3; PH-3; LF-1; RF-1 **Ht:** 5'11" **Wt:** 165 **Born:** 4/14/72 **Age:** 26

								BATTING											BASERUNNING				PERCENTAGES		
Year Team	Lg	G	AB	H	2B	3B	HR	(Hm	Rd)	TB	R	RBI	TBB	IBB	SO	HBP	SH	SF	SB	CS	SB%	GDP	Avg	OBP	SLG
1997 Louisville *	AAA	6	21	7	1	0	1	—	—	11	3	2	0	0	4	1	0	0	0	2	.00	0	.333	.364	.524
1993 Colorado	NL	65	229	53	14	5	5	(3	2)	92	31	20	13	1	63	1	4	1	4	1	.80	2	.231	.275	.402
1994 Colorado	NL	38	116	28	8	1	4	(1	3)	50	11	14	15	2	33	0	0	1	3	1	.75	1	.241	.326	.431
1995 Colorado	NL	23	52	8	1	0	1	(1	0)	12	5	4	0	0	17	0	1	1	0	1	.00	1	.154	.167	.231
1997 St. Louis	NL	7	14	1	1	0	0	(0	0)	2	0	2	0	0	5	0	1	1	0	0	.00	0	.071	.067	.143
4 ML YEARS		133	411	90	24	6	10	(5	5)	156	47	40	28	3	118	2	5	4	7	3	.70	4	.219	.270	.380

Carlos Mendoza

Bats: Left **Throws:** Left **Pos:** PH-12; CF-3; LF-2 **Ht:** 5'11" **Wt:** 165 **Born:** 11/14/74 **Age:** 23

								BATTING											BASERUNNING				PERCENTAGES		
Year Team	Lg	G	AB	H	2B	3B	HR	(Hm	Rd)	TB	R	RBI	TBB	IBB	SO	HBP	SH	SF	SB	CS	SB%	GDP	Avg	OBP	SLG
1995 Kingsport	R+	51	192	63	9	0	1	—	—	75	26	24	27	0	24	3	4	2	28	6	.82	3	.328	.415	.391
1996 Capital City	A	85	300	101	10	2	0	—	—	115	61	37	57	1	46	8	11	2	31	13	.70	2	.337	.452	.383
1997 Binghamton	AA	59	228	87	12	2	1	—	—	106	36	13	14	1	25	4	7	0	14	12	.54	4	.382	.427	.465
Devil Rays	R	9	0	0	0	0	0	—	—	0	0	0	0	0	0	0	0	0	0	0	.00	0	.000	.000	.000
Norfolk	AAA	10	35	5	0	1	0	—	—	7	3	0	3	0	4	1	1	0	1	0	1.00	1	.143	.231	.200
1997 New York	NL	15	12	3	0	0	0	(0	0)	3	6	1	4	0	2	2	0	0	0	0	.00	0	.250	.500	.250

Ramiro Mendoza

Pitches: Right **Bats:** Right **Pos:** RP-24; SP-15 **Ht:** 6'2" **Wt:** 154 **Born:** 6/15/72 **Age:** 26

			HOW MUCH HE PITCHED					WHAT HE GAVE UP											THE RESULTS					
Year Team	Lg	G	GS	CG	GF	IP	BFP	H	R	ER	HR	SH	SF	HB	TBB	IBB	SO	WP	Bk	W	L	Pct.	ShO	Sv-Op	Hld	ERA
1993 Yankees	R	15	9	0	3	67.2	275	59	26	21	3	0	1	4	7	0	61	3	0	4	5	.444	0	1--	—	2.79
Greensboro	A	2	0	0	1	3.2	18	3	1	1	0	0	0	0	5	0	3	0	0	0	1	.000	0	0--	—	2.45
1994 Tampa	A+	22	21	1	1	134.1	560	133	54	45	7	5	3	2	35	1	110	2	3	12	6	.667	0	0--	—	3.01
1995 Norwich	AA	19	19	2	0	89.2	380	87	39	32	4	1	0	2	33	0	68	2	1	5	6	.455	0	0--	—	3.21
Columbus	AAA	2	2	0	0	14	51	10	4	4	0	0	1	0	2	0	13	1	0	1	0	1.000	0	0--	—	2.57
1996 Columbus	AAA	15	15	0	0	97	392	96	30	27	2	3	4	5	19	0	61	1	0	6	2	.750	0	0--	—	2.51
1997 Columbus	AAA	1	1	0	0	6.1	31	7	6	4	1	0	0	0	1	0	4	0	0	0	1	.000	0	0--	—	5.68
1996 New York	AL	12	11	0	0	53	249	80	43	40	5	1	4	1	10	1	34	2	1	4	5	.444	0	0-0	0	6.79
1997 New York	AL	39	15	0	9	133.2	578	157	67	63	15	3	5	5	28	2	82	2	1	8	6	.571	0	2-4	4	4.24
2 ML YEARS		51	26	0	9	186.2	827	237	110	103	20	4	6	9	38	3	116	4	2	12	11	.522	0	2-4	4	4.97

Paul Menhart

Pitches: Right **Bats:** Right **Pos:** SP-8; RP-1 **Ht:** 6'2" **Wt:** 190 **Born:** 3/25/69 **Age:** 29

			HOW MUCH HE PITCHED					WHAT HE GAVE UP											THE RESULTS					
Year Team	Lg	G	GS	CG	GF	IP	BFP	H	R	ER	HR	SH	SF	HB	TBB	IBB	SO	WP	Bk	W	L	Pct.	ShO	Sv-Op	Hld	ERA
1997 Tacoma *	AAA	15	10	0	2	61.1	285	76	46	42	11	2	1	4	34	1	51	4	1	4	7	.364	0	1--	—	6.16
Las Vegas *	AAA	11	11	1	0	66.1	294	78	46	44	7	7	3	2	21	1	44	2	1	7	0	.000	0	0--	—	5.97
1995 Toronto	AL	21	9	1	6	78.2	350	72	49	43	9	3	4	6	47	4	50	6	0	1	4	.200	0	0-0	0	4.92
1996 Seattle	AL	11	6	0	4	42	196	55	36	34	9	1	0	2	25	0	18	1	0	2	2	.500	0	0-0	0	7.29
1997 San Diego	NL	9	8	0	0	44	180	42	23	23	6	2	1	0	13	0	22	4	0	2	3	.400	0	0-0	0	4.70
3 ML YEARS		41	23	1	10	164.2	726	169	108	100	24	6	5	8	85	4	90	11	0	5	9	.357	0	0-0	0	5.47

Orlando Merced

Bats: L **Throws:** R **Pos:** RF-96; PH-3; DH-1; 1B-1 **Ht:** 5'11" **Wt:** 183 **Born:** 11/2/66 **Age:** 31

								BATTING											BASERUNNING				PERCENTAGES		
Year Team	Lg	G	AB	H	2B	3B	HR	(Hm	Rd)	TB	R	RBI	TBB	IBB	SO	HBP	SH	SF	SB	CS	SB%	GDP	Avg	OBP	SLG
1990 Pittsburgh	NL	25	24	5	1	0	0	(0	0)	6	3	0	1	0	9	0	0	0	0	0	.00	1	.208	.240	.250
1991 Pittsburgh	NL	120	411	113	17	2	10	(5	5)	164	83	50	64	4	81	1	1	1	8	4	.67	6	.275	.373	.399
1992 Pittsburgh	NL	134	405	100	28	5	6	(4	2)	156	50	60	52	8	63	2	1	5	5	4	.56	6	.247	.332	.385
1993 Pittsburgh	NL	137	447	140	26	4	8	(3	5)	198	68	70	77	10	64	1	0	2	3	3	.50	9	.313	.414	.443
1994 Pittsburgh	NL	108	386	105	21	3	9	(4	5)	159	48	51	42	5	58	1	0	1	4	1	.80	17	.272	.343	.412
1995 Pittsburgh	NL	132	487	146	29	4	15	(8	7)	228	75	83	52	9	74	1	0	5	7	2	.78	9	.300	.365	.468
1996 Pittsburgh	NL	120	453	130	24	1	17	(9	8)	207	69	80	51	5	74	0	0	3	8	4	.67	9	.287	.357	.457
1997 Toronto	AL	98	368	98	23	2	9	(3	6)	152	45	40	47	1	62	3	0	2	7	3	.70	6	.266	.352	.413
8 ML YEARS		874	2981	837	169	21	74	(36	38)	1270	441	434	386	42	485	9	2	20	42	21	.67	63	.281	.363	.426

Henry Mercedes

Bats: Right **Throws:** Right **Pos:** C-23; PH-1 **Ht:** 6'1" **Wt:** 210 **Born:** 7/23/69 **Age:** 28

								BATTING											BASERUNNING				PERCENTAGES		
Year Team	Lg	G	AB	H	2B	3B	HR	(Hm	Rd)	TB	R	RBI	TBB	IBB	SO	HBP	SH	SF	SB	CS	SB%	GDP	Avg	OBP	SLG
1997 Okla City *	AAA	16	57	14	3	0	1	—	—	20	6	4	9	0	12	0	0	0	0	0	.00	3	.246	.348	.351

139

Year Team	Lg	G	AB	H	2B	3B	HR	(Hm	Rd)	TB	R	RBI	TBB	IBB	SO	HBP	SH	SF	SB	CS	SB%	GDP	Avg	OBP	SLG
1992 Oakland	AL	9	5	4	0	1	0	(0	0)	6	1	1	0	0	1	0	0	0	0	0	.00	0	.800	.800	1.200
1993 Oakland	AL	20	47	10	2	0	0	(0	0)	12	5	3	2	0	15	1	0	1	1	1	.50	0	.213	.260	.255
1995 Kansas City	AL	23	43	11	2	0	0	(0	0)	13	7	9	8	0	13	1	1	2	0	0	.00	0	.256	.370	.302
1996 Kansas City	AL	4	4	1	0	0	0	(0	0)	1	1	0	0	0	1	0	0	0	0	0	.00	0	.250	.250	.250
1997 Texas	AL	23	47	10	4	0	0	(0	0)	14	4	4	6	0	25	0	3	0	0	0	.00	0	.213	.302	.298
5 ML YEARS		79	146	36	8	1	0	(0	0)	46	18	17	16	0	55	2	4	2	1	1	.50	0	.247	.325	.315

Jose Mercedes

Pitches: Right **Bats:** Right **Pos:** SP-23; RP-6   **Ht:** 6'1" **Wt:** 199 **Born:** 3/5/71 **Age:** 27

Year Team	Lg	G	GS	CG	GF	IP	BFP	H	R	ER	HR	SH	SF	HB	TBB	IBB	SO	WP	Bk	W	L	Pct.	ShO	Sv-Op	Hld	ERA
1994 Milwaukee	AL	19	0	0	5	31	120	22	9	8	4	0	0	2	16	1	11	0	1	2	0	1.000	0	0-1	3	2.32
1995 Milwaukee	AL	5	0	0	0	7.1	42	12	9	8	1	0	2	0	8	0	6	1	0	0	1	.000	0	0-2	1	9.82
1996 Milwaukee	AL	11	0	0	4	16.2	74	20	18	17	6	0	1	0	5	0	6	2	0	0	2	.000	0	0-1	2	9.18
1997 Milwaukee	AL	29	23	2	1	159	653	146	76	67	24	3	4	5	53	2	80	1	1	7	10	.412	1	0-0	1	3.79
4 ML YEARS		64	23	2	10	214	889	200	112	100	35	3	7	7	82	3	103	4	2	9	13	.409	1	0-4	7	4.21

Kent Mercker

Pitches: Left **Bats:** Left **Pos:** SP-25; RP-3   **Ht:** 6'2" **Wt:** 195 **Born:** 2/1/68 **Age:** 30

Year Team	Lg	G	GS	CG	GF	IP	BFP	H	R	ER	HR	SH	SF	HB	TBB	IBB	SO	WP	Bk	W	L	Pct.	ShO	Sv-Op	Hld	ERA
1989 Atlanta	NL	2	1	0	1	4.1	26	8	6	6	0	0	0	0	6	0	4	0	0	0	0	.000	0	0-0	0	12.46
1990 Atlanta	NL	36	0	0	28	48.1	211	43	22	17	6	1	2	2	24	3	39	2	0	4	7	.364	0	7-10	0	3.17
1991 Atlanta	NL	50	4	0	28	73.1	306	56	23	21	5	2	2	1	35	3	62	4	1	5	3	.625	0	6-8	3	2.58
1992 Atlanta	NL	53	0	0	18	68.1	289	51	27	26	4	4	1	3	35	1	49	6	0	3	2	.600	0	6-9	6	3.42
1993 Atlanta	NL	43	6	0	9	66	283	52	24	21	2	0	0	2	36	3	59	5	1	3	1	.750	0	0-3	4	2.86
1994 Atlanta	NL	20	17	2	0	112.1	461	90	46	43	16	4	3	0	45	3	111	4	1	9	4	.692	1	0-0	0	3.45
1995 Atlanta	NL	29	26	0	1	143	622	140	73	66	16	8	7	3	61	2	102	6	2	7	8	.467	0	0-0	0	4.15
1996 Bal-Cle	AL	24	12	0	2	69.2	329	83	60	54	13	3	6	3	38	2	29	3	1	4	6	.400	0	0-0	2	6.98
1997 Cincinnati	NL	28	25	0	0	144.2	616	135	65	63	16	8	4	2	62	6	75	2	1	8	11	.421	0	0-0	0	3.92
1996 Baltimore	AL	14	12	0	0	58	283	73	56	50	12	3	4	3	35	1	22	3	1	3	6	.333	0	0-0	0	7.76
Cleveland	AL	10	0	0	2	11.2	46	10	4	4	1	0	2	0	3	1	7	0	0	1	0	1.000	0	0-0	2	3.09
9 ML YEARS		285	91	2	87	730	3143	658	346	317	78	30	25	16	342	23	530	32	7	43	42	.506	1	19-30	15	3.91

Jose Mesa

Pitches: Right **Bats:** Right **Pos:** RP-66   **Ht:** 6'3" **Wt:** 225 **Born:** 5/22/66 **Age:** 32

Year Team	Lg	G	GS	CG	GF	IP	BFP	H	R	ER	HR	SH	SF	HB	TBB	IBB	SO	WP	Bk	W	L	Pct.	ShO	Sv-Op	Hld	ERA
1987 Baltimore	AL	6	5	0	0	31.1	143	38	23	21	7	0	0	0	15	0	17	4	0	1	3	.250	0	0-0	1	6.03
1990 Baltimore	AL	7	7	0	0	46.2	202	37	20	20	2	2	2	1	27	2	24	1	1	3	2	.600	0	0-0	0	3.86
1991 Baltimore	AL	23	23	0	0	123.2	566	151	86	82	11	5	4	3	62	2	64	3	0	6	11	.353	1	0-0	0	5.97
1992 Bal-Cle	AL	28	27	1	1	160.2	700	169	86	82	14	2	5	4	70	1	62	2	0	7	12	.368	1	0-0	0	4.59
1993 Cleveland	AL	34	33	3	0	208.2	897	232	122	114	21	9	9	7	62	2	118	8	2	10	12	.455	0	0-0	0	4.92
1994 Cleveland	AL	51	0	0	22	73	315	71	33	31	3	3	4	3	26	7	63	3	0	7	5	.583	0	2-6	8	3.82
1995 Cleveland	AL	62	0	0	57	64	250	49	9	8	3	4	2	0	17	2	58	5	0	3	0	1.000	0	46-48	0	1.13
1996 Cleveland	AL	69	0	0	60	72.1	304	69	32	30	6	2	3	2	28	4	64	4	0	2	7	.222	0	39-44	0	3.73
1997 Cleveland	AL	66	0	0	38	82.1	356	83	28	22	7	2	2	3	28	3	69	1	0	4	4	.500	0	16-21	9	2.40
1992 Baltimore	AL	13	12	0	1	67.2	300	77	41	39	9	0	3	2	27	1	22	2	0	3	8	.273	0	0-0	0	5.19
Cleveland	AL	15	15	1	0	93	400	92	45	43	5	2	2	2	43	0	40	0	0	4	4	.500	1	0-0	0	4.16
9 ML YEARS		346	95	6	178	862.2	3733	899	439	410	74	29	30	24	335	23	539	31	3	43	56	.434	2	103-119	18	4.28

Hensley Meulens

Bats: Right **Throws:** Right **Pos:** LF-8; PH-8; 1B-3   **Ht:** 6'3" **Wt:** 212 **Born:** 6/23/67 **Age:** 31

Year Team	Lg	G	AB	H	2B	3B	HR	(Hm	Rd)	TB	R	RBI	TBB	IBB	SO	HBP	SH	SF	SB	CS	SB%	GDP	Avg	OBP	SLG
1997 Wst Plm Bch *	A+	1	4	1	1	0	0	—	—	2	0	0	0	0	2	0	0	0	0	0	.00	0	.250	.250	.500
Ottawa *	AAA	121	423	116	20	2	24	—	—	212	81	75	62	4	119	5	0	5	19	5	.79	11	.274	.370	.501
1989 New York	AL	8	28	5	0	0	0	(0	0)	5	2	1	2	0	8	0	0	0	0	1	.00	2	.179	.233	.179
1990 New York	AL	23	83	20	7	0	3	(2	1)	36	12	10	9	0	25	3	0	0	1	0	1.00	3	.241	.337	.434
1991 New York	AL	96	288	64	8	1	6	(4	2)	92	37	29	18	1	97	4	1	2	3	0	1.00	5	.222	.276	.319
1992 New York	AL	2	5	3	0	0	1	(1	0)	6	1	1	1	0	0	0	0	0	0	0	.00	1	.600	.667	1.200
1993 New York	AL	30	53	9	1	1	2	(1	1)	18	8	5	8	0	19	0	0	0	0	1	.00	1	.170	.279	.340
1997 Montreal	NL	16	24	7	1	0	2	(1	1)	14	6	6	4	0	10	0	0	1	0	0	.00	0	.292	.379	.583
6 ML YEARS		175	481	108	17	2	14	(9	5)	171	66	52	42	1	159	7	1	3	4	3	.57	15	.225	.295	.356

Dan Miceli

Pitches: Right **Bats:** Right **Pos:** RP-71   **Ht:** 6'0" **Wt:** 216 **Born:** 9/9/70 **Age:** 27

Year Team	Lg	G	GS	CG	GF	IP	BFP	H	R	ER	HR	SH	SF	HB	TBB	IBB	SO	WP	Bk	W	L	Pct.	ShO	Sv-Op	Hld	ERA
1993 Pittsburgh	NL	9	0	0	1	5.1	25	6	3	3	0	0	0	0	3	0	4	0	1	0	0	.000	0	0-0	0	5.06
1994 Pittsburgh	NL	28	0	0	9	27.1	121	28	19	18	5	1	2	2	11	2	27	2	0	2	1	.667	0	2-3	4	5.93
1995 Pittsburgh	NL	58	0	0	51	58	264	61	30	30	7	2	4	4	28	5	56	4	0	4	4	.500	0	21-27	2	4.66

Year Team	Lg	HOW MUCH HE PITCHED						WHAT HE GAVE UP												THE RESULTS						
		G	GS	CG	GF	IP	BFP	H	R	ER	HR	SH	SF	HB	TBB	IBB	SO	WP	Bk	W	L	Pct.	ShO	Sv-Op	Hld	ERA
1996 Pittsburgh	NL	44	9	0	17	85.2	398	99	65	55	15	3	7	3	45	5	66	9	0	2	10	.167	0	1-1	4	5.78
1997 Detroit	AL	71	0	0	24	82.2	357	77	49	46	13	5	3	1	38	4	79	3	0	3	2	.600	0	3-8	11	5.01
5 ML YEARS		210	9	0	102	259	1165	271	166	152	40	11	16	10	125	16	232	18	1	11	17	.393	0	27-39	21	5.28

Matt Mieske

Bats: R **Throws:** R **Pos:** RF-52; LF-26; PH-15; DH-5   **Ht:** 6'0" **Wt:** 192 **Born:** 2/13/68 **Age:** 30

Year Team	Lg	BATTING																	BASERUNNING				PERCENTAGES		
		G	AB	H	2B	3B	HR	(Hm	Rd)	TB	R	RBI	TBB	IBB	SO	HBP	SH	SF	SB	CS	SB%	GDP	Avg	OBP	SLG
1993 Milwaukee	AL	23	58	14	0	0	3	(1	2)	23	9	7	4	0	14	0	1	0	0	2	.00	2	.241	.290	.397
1994 Milwaukee	AL	84	259	67	13	1	10	(7	3)	112	39	38	21	0	62	1	0	5	3	5	.38	6	.259	.320	.432
1995 Milwaukee	AL	117	267	67	13	1	12	(3	9)	118	42	48	27	0	45	4	0	5	2	4	.33	8	.251	.323	.442
1996 Milwaukee	AL	127	374	104	24	3	14	(9	5)	176	46	64	26	2	76	2	1	6	1	5	.17	9	.278	.324	.471
1997 Milwaukee	AL	84	253	63	15	3	5	(1	4)	99	39	21	19	2	50	0	0	1	1	0	1.00	12	.249	.300	.391
5 ML YEARS		435	1211	315	65	8	44	(21	23)	528	175	178	97	4	247	9	4	13	7	16	.30	37	.260	.317	.436

Damian Miller

Bats: Right **Throws:** Right **Pos:** C-20; DH-3; PH-2   **Ht:** 6'3" **Wt:** 202 **Born:** 10/13/69 **Age:** 28

Year Team	Lg	BATTING																	BASERUNNING				PERCENTAGES		
		G	AB	H	2B	3B	HR	(Hm	Rd)	TB	R	RBI	TBB	IBB	SO	HBP	SH	SF	SB	CS	SB%	GDP	Avg	OBP	SLG
1990 Elizabethtn	R+	14	45	10	1	0	1	—	—	14	7	6	9	0	3	0	0	0	1	0	1.00	2	.222	.352	.311
1991 Kenosha	A	80	267	62	11	1	3	—	—	84	28	34	24	1	53	2	2	3	3	2	.60	4	.232	.297	.315
1992 Kenosha	A	115	377	110	27	2	5	—	—	156	53	56	53	1	66	7	2	4	6	1	.86	13	.292	.385	.414
1993 Ft. Myers	A+	87	325	69	12	1	1	—	—	86	31	26	31	0	44	0	1	0	0	0	.00	6	.212	.281	.265
Nashville	AA	4	13	3	0	0	0	—	—	3	0	0	2	0	4	0	0	0	0	0	.00	0	.231	.333	.231
1994 Nashville	AA	103	328	88	10	0	8	—	—	122	36	35	35	2	51	1	2	5	4	6	.40	11	.268	.336	.372
1995 Salt Lake	AAA	83	295	84	23	1	3	—	—	118	39	41	15	1	39	3	5	2	2	4	.33	11	.285	.324	.400
1996 Salt Lake	AAA	104	385	110	27	1	7	—	—	160	54	55	25	2	58	6	2	4	1	4	.20	13	.286	.336	.416
1997 Salt Lake	AAA	85	314	106	19	3	11	—	—	164	48	82	29	0	62	3	1	3	6	1	.86	7	.338	.395	.522
1997 Minnesota	AL	25	66	18	1	0	2	(1	1)	25	5	13	2	0	12	0	0	3	0	0	.00	2	.273	.282	.379

Kurt Miller

Pitches: Right **Bats:** Right **Pos:** RP-7   **Ht:** 6'5" **Wt:** 205 **Born:** 8/24/72 **Age:** 25

Year Team	Lg	HOW MUCH HE PITCHED						WHAT HE GAVE UP												THE RESULTS						
		G	GS	CG	GF	IP	BFP	H	R	ER	HR	SH	SF	HB	TBB	IBB	SO	WP	Bk	W	L	Pct.	ShO	Sv-Op	Hld	ERA
1997 Brevard Cty *	A+	2	2	0	0	5	22	6	1	1	1	0	0	0	2	0	7	0	0	0	0	.000	0	0--	—	1.80
Charlotte *	AAA	21	0	0	2	27.2	129	25	12	11	2	1	1	2	22	0	31	5	0	2	1	.667	0	0--	—	3.58
1994 Florida	NL	4	4	0	0	20	92	26	18	18	3	0	1	2	7	0	11	0	0	1	3	.250	0	0-0	0	8.10
1996 Florida	NL	26	5	0	6	46.1	222	57	41	35	5	4	1	2	33	8	30	1	1	1	3	.250	0	0-2	0	6.80
1997 Florida	NL	7	0	0	1	7.1	41	12	8	8	2	0	0	1	7	0	7	0	0	0	1	.000	0	0-0	0	9.82
3 ML YEARS		37	9	0	7	73.2	355	95	67	61	10	4	2	5	47	8	48	1	1	2	7	.222	0	0-2	0	7.45

Orlando Miller

Bats: R **Throws:** R **Pos:** SS-31; DH-11; PH-9; 3B-4; 1B-3   **Ht:** 6'1" **Wt:** 180 **Born:** 1/13/69 **Age:** 29

Year Team	Lg	BATTING																	BASERUNNING				PERCENTAGES		
		G	AB	H	2B	3B	HR	(Hm	Rd)	TB	R	RBI	TBB	IBB	SO	HBP	SH	SF	SB	CS	SB%	GDP	Avg	OBP	SLG
1997 Lakeland *	A+	5	21	4	1	1	0	—	—	7	1	0	1	0	4	0	0	0	0	0	.00	1	.190	.227	.333
Jacksonville *	AA	3	11	4	1	0	1	—	—	8	2	3	1	0	1	1	0	0	0	0	.00	0	.364	.462	.727
Toledo *	AAA	8	30	8	1	0	1	—	—	12	3	5	2	0	5	0	0	0	2	1	.67	1	.267	.313	.400
1994 Houston	NL	16	40	13	0	1	2	(0	2)	21	3	9	2	2	12	2	0	0	3	0	1.00	7	.325	.386	.525
1995 Houston	NL	92	324	85	20	1	5	(1	4)	122	36	36	22	8	71	5	4	0	3	4	.43	7	.262	.319	.377
1996 Houston	NL	139	468	120	26	2	15	(7	8)	195	43	58	14	4	116	10	1	3	3	7	.30	14	.256	.291	.417
1997 Detroit	AL	50	111	26	7	1	2	(2	0)	41	13	10	5	0	24	4	1	1	0	1	1.00	1	.234	.289	.369
4 ML YEARS		297	943	244	53	5	24	(10	14)	379	95	113	43	14	223	21	6	4	8	11	.42	22	.259	.305	.402

Travis Miller

Pitches: Left **Bats:** Right **Pos:** SP-7; RP-6   **Ht:** 6'3" **Wt:** 200 **Born:** 11/2/72 **Age:** 25

Year Team	Lg	HOW MUCH HE PITCHED						WHAT HE GAVE UP												THE RESULTS						
		G	GS	CG	GF	IP	BFP	H	R	ER	HR	SH	SF	HB	TBB	IBB	SO	WP	Bk	W	L	Pct.	ShO	Sv-Op	Hld	ERA
1994 Ft. Wayne	A	11	9	1	0	55.1	223	52	17	16	2	1	3	2	12	0	50	5	2	4	1	.800	0	0--	—	2.60
Nashville	AA	1	1	0	0	6.1	23	3	3	2	0	0	0	0	2	0	4	1	0	0	0	.000	0	0--	—	2.84
1995 Hardware City	AA	28	27	1	1	162.2	723	172	93	79	17	6	3	4	65	2	151	5	0	7	9	.438	1	0--	—	4.37
1996 Salt Lake	AAA	27	27	1	0	160.1	709	187	97	86	17	2	6	7	57	1	143	6	1	8	10	.444	0	0--	—	4.83
1997 Salt Lake	AAA	21	21	0	0	125.2	558	140	73	66	11	5	2	4	57	0	86	5	0	10	6	.625	0	0--	—	4.73
1996 Minnesota	AL	7	7	0	0	26.1	126	45	29	27	7	1	0	0	9	0	15	0	0	1	2	.333	0	0-0	0	9.23
1997 Minnesota	AL	13	7	0	1	48.1	227	64	49	41	8	1	2	1	23	2	26	5	0	1	5	.167	0	0-0	0	7.63
2 ML YEARS		20	14	0	1	74.2	353	109	78	68	15	2	2	1	32	2	41	5	0	2	7	.222	0	0-0	0	8.20

Ralph Milliard

Bats: Right **Throws:** Right **Pos:** 2B-8 **Ht:** 5'11" **Wt:** 170 **Born:** 12/30/73 **Age:** 24

Year Team	Lg	G	AB	H	2B	3B	HR	(Hm	Rd)	TB	R	RBI	TBB	IBB	SO	HBP	SH	SF	SB	CS	SB%	GDP	Avg	OBP	SLG
1993 Marlins	R	53	192	45	15	0	0	—	—	60	35	25	30	0	17	6	0	1	11	5	.69	8	.234	.354	.313
1994 Kane County	A	133	515	153	34	2	8	—	—	215	97	67	68	2	63	9	4	7	10	10	.50	6	.297	.384	.417
1995 Portland	AA	128	464	124	22	3	11	—	—	185	104	40	85	3	83	14	13	4	22	10	.69	5	.267	.393	.399
1996 Charlotte	AAA	69	250	69	15	2	6	—	—	106	47	26	38	0	43	5	1	1	8	4	.67	5	.276	.381	.424
Portland	A	6	20	4	0	1	0	—	—	6	2	2	1	0	5	0	0	0	1	0	1.00	0	.200	.238	.300
1997 Charlotte	AAA	33	132	35	5	1	4	—	—	54	19	9	9	0	21	3	4	0	5	3	.63	1	.265	.326	.409
Portland	AA	19	69	19	1	2	0	—	—	24	13	5	7	0	8	1	3	0	3	2	.60	2	.275	.351	.348
1996 Florida	NL	24	62	10	2	0	0	(0	0)	12	7	1	14	1	16	0	0	1	2	0	1.00	1	.161	.312	.194
1997 Florida	NL	8	30	6	0	0	0	(0	0)	6	2	2	3	0	3	2	1	0	1	1	.50	2	.200	.314	.200
2 ML YEARS		32	92	16	2	0	0	(0	0)	18	9	3	17	1	19	2	1	1	3	1	.75	3	.174	.313	.196

Alan Mills

Pitches: Right **Bats:** Both **Pos:** RP-39 **Ht:** 6'1" **Wt:** 195 **Born:** 10/18/66 **Age:** 31

Year Team	Lg	G	GS	CG	GF	IP	BFP	H	R	ER	HR	SH	SF	HB	TBB	IBB	SO	WP	Bk	W	L	Pct.	ShO	Sv-Op	Hld	ERA
1990 New York	AL	36	0	0	18	41.2	200	48	21	19	4	4	1		33	6	24	3	0	1	5	.167	0	0-2	3	4.10
1991 New York	AL	6	2	0	3	16.1	72	16	9	8	1	0	1		8	0	11	2	0	1	1	.500	0	0-0	0	4.41
1992 Baltimore	AL	35	3	0	12	103.1	428	78	33	30	5	6	5		54	10	60	2	0	10	4	.714	0	2-3	2	2.61
1993 Baltimore	AL	45	0	0	18	100.1	421	80	39	36	14	4	6		51	5	68	3	0	5	4	.556	0	4-7	4	3.23
1994 Baltimore	AL	47	0	0	16	45.1	199	43	26	26	7	1	1		24	2	44	2	0	3	3	.500	0	2-4	14	5.16
1995 Baltimore	AL	21	0	0	1	23	118	30	20	19	4	2	1		18	4	16	1	0	3	0	1.000	0	0-1	1	7.43
1996 Baltimore	AL	49	0	0	23	54.2	233	40	26	26	10	3	2		35	2	50	6	0	3	2	.600	0	3-8	9	4.28
1997 Baltimore	AL	39	0	0	11	38.2	192	41	23	21	5	4	1		33	1	32	2	0	2	3	.400	0	0-0	7	4.89
8 ML YEARS		278	5	0	102	423.1	1863	376	197	185	50	22	18	12	256	30	305	21	0	28	22	.560	0	11-25	40	3.93

Kevin Millwood

Pitches: Right **Bats:** Right **Pos:** SP-8; RP-4 **Ht:** 6'4" **Wt:** 205 **Born:** 12/24/74 **Age:** 23

Year Team	Lg	G	GS	CG	GF	IP	BFP	H	R	ER	HR	SH	SF	HB	TBB	IBB	SO	WP	Bk	W	L	Pct.	ShO	Sv-Op	Hld	ERA
1993 Braves	R	12	9	0	1	50	219	36	27	17	3	2	1	4	28	0	49	5	1	3	3	.500	0	0--	—	3.06
1994 Macon	A	12	4	0	4	32.2	165	31	31	21	4	2	1	2	32	1	24	4	0	0	5	.000	0	1--	—	5.79
Danville	R+	13	5	0	2	46	211	42	25	19	4	4	1	2	34	2	56	1	0	3	3	.500	0	1--	—	3.72
1995 Macon	A	29	12	0	5	103	458	86	65	53	10	3	1	5	57	0	89	10	0	5	6	.455	0	0--	—	4.63
1996 Durham	A+	33	20	1	3	149.1	638	138	77	71	17	9	6	8	58	0	139	8	3	6	9	.400	0	1--	—	4.28
1997 Greenville	AA	11	11	0	0	61.1	264	59	37	28	8	2	0	2	24	0	61	7	0	3	5	.375	0	0--	—	4.11
Richmond	AAA	9	9	1	0	60.2	232	38	13	13	2	2	0	1	16	0	46	2	0	7	0	1.000	0	0--	—	1.93
1997 Atlanta	NL	12	8	0	2	51.1	227	55	36	23	1	3	5	2	21	1	42	1	0	5	3	.625	0	0--	0	4.03

Michael Mimbs

Pitches: Left **Bats:** Left **Pos:** RP-16; SP-1 **Ht:** 6'2" **Wt:** 190 **Born:** 2/13/69 **Age:** 29

Year Team	Lg	G	GS	CG	GF	IP	BFP	H	R	ER	HR	SH	SF	HB	TBB	IBB	SO	WP	Bk	W	L	Pct.	ShO	Sv-Op	Hld	ERA
1997 Scranton-WB *	AAA	11	8	1	2	43.2	199	52	33	29	8	1	2	1	20	0	41	5	1	4	2	.667	0	0--	—	5.98
1995 Philadelphia	NL	35	19	2	6	136.2	603	127	70	63	10	6	8	6	75	2	93	9	0	9	7	.563	1	1-1	0	4.15
1996 Philadelphia	NL	21	17	0	0	99.1	448	116	66	61	13	8	3	2	41	1	56	7	0	3	9	.250	0	0-0	0	5.53
1997 Philadelphia	NL	17	1	0	2	28.2	146	31	27	24	6	2	0	3	27	1	29	4	0	0	3	.000	0	0-0	0	7.53
3 ML YEARS		73	37	2	8	264.2	1197	274	163	148	29	16	11	11	143	4	178	20	0	12	19	.387	1	1-1	0	5.03

Nate Minchey

Pitches: Right **Bats:** Right **Pos:** RP-2 **Ht:** 6'7" **Wt:** 215 **Born:** 8/31/69 **Age:** 28

Year Team	Lg	G	GS	CG	GF	IP	BFP	H	R	ER	HR	SH	SF	HB	TBB	IBB	SO	WP	Bk	W	L	Pct.	ShO	Sv-Op	Hld	ERA
1997 Colo Sprngs *	AAA	27	21	3	0	157.2	678	172	87	79	17	5	3	6	53	1	107	4	0	15	6	.714	0	0--	—	4.51
1993 Boston	AL	5	5	1	0	33	141	35	16	13	5	1	0	0	8	2	18	2	0	1	2	.333	0	0-0	0	3.55
1994 Boston	AL	6	5	0	0	23	121	44	26	22	1	1	3	0	14	2	15	3	1	2	3	.400	0	0-0	0	8.61
1996 Boston	AL	2	2	0	0	6	36	16	11	10	1	0	1	0	5	0	4	1	0	0	2	.000	0	0-0	0	15.00
1997 Colorado	NL	2	0	0	0	2	12	5	3	3	0	2	0	1	1	0	1	0	0	0	0	.000	0	0-0	0	13.50
4 ML YEARS		15	12	1	0	64	310	100	56	48	7	4	4	0	28	4	38	6	1	3	7	.300	0	0-0	0	6.75

Blas Minor

Pitches: Right **Bats:** Right **Pos:** RP-11 **Ht:** 6'3" **Wt:** 203 **Born:** 3/20/66 **Age:** 32

Year Team	Lg	G	GS	CG	GF	IP	BFP	H	R	ER	HR	SH	SF	HB	TBB	IBB	SO	WP	Bk	W	L	Pct.	ShO	Sv-Op	Hld	ERA
1997 New Orleans *	AAA	23	0	0	15	31.2	122	20	8	8	1	3	2	0	9	3	27	3	0	3	3	.500	0	6--	—	2.27
Tucson *	AAA	12	3	0	2	29	137	36	21	13	3	1	0	2	15	1	21	2	0	2	2	.500	0	1--	—	4.03
1992 Pittsburgh	NL	1	0	0	0	2	9	3	2	1	0	0	0	0	0	0	0	1	0	0	0	.000	0	0-0	0	4.50
1993 Pittsburgh	NL	65	0	0	18	94.1	398	94	43	43	8	6	4	4	26	3	84	5	0	8	6	.571	0	2-3	7	4.10
1994 Pittsburgh	NL	17	0	0	2	19	90	27	17	17	4	2	1	1	9	2	17	0	0	0	1	.000	0	1-1	2	8.05

Year Team	Lg	G	GS	CG	GF	IP	BFP	H	R	ER	HR	SH	SF	HB	TBB	IBB	SO	WP	Bk	W	L	Pct.	ShO	Sv-Op	Hld	ERA
1995 New York	NL	35	0	0	10	46.2	192	44	21	19	6	4	0	1	13	1	43	3	0	4	2	.667	0	1-1	2	3.66
1996 NYN-Sea		28	0	0	10	51	213	50	25	24	10	0	1	0	17	2	34	3	0	0	1	.000	0	0-1	1	4.24
1997 Houston	NL	11	0	0	5	12	55	13	7	6	1	1	1	1	5	0	6	4	0	1	0	1.000	0	1-3	2	4.50
1996 New York	NL	17	0	0	4	25.2	104	23	11	10	4	0	1	0	6	2	20	1	0	0	0	.000	0	0-1	1	3.51
Seattle	AL	11	0	0	6	25.1	109	27	14	14	6	0	0	0	11	0	14	2	0	0	1	.000	0	0-0	1	4.97
6 ML YEARS		157	0	0	45	225	957	231	115	110	29	13	7	7	70	8	184	16	0	13	10	.565	0	5-9	14	4.40

Doug Mirabelli

Bats: Right **Throws:** Right **Pos:** C-6   **Ht:** 6'0" **Wt:** 210 **Born:** 10/18/70 **Age:** 27

Year Team	Lg	G	AB	H	2B	3B	HR	(Hm	Rd)	TB	R	RBI	TBB	IBB	SO	HBP	SH	SF	SB	CS	SB%	GDP	Avg	OBP	SLG
1992 San Jose	A+	53	177	41	11	1	0	—	—	54	30	21	24	0	18	4	2	2	1	3	.25	7	.232	.333	.305
1993 San Jose	A+	113	371	100	19	2	1	—	—	126	58	48	72	1	55	4	2	4	0	4	.00	7	.270	.390	.340
1994 Shreveport	AA	85	255	56	8	0	4	—	—	76	23	24	36	5	48	0	1	2	3	1	.75	6	.220	.316	.298
1995 Phoenix	AAA	23	66	11	0	1	0	—	—	13	3	7	12	1	10	1	0	2	1	0	1.00	5	.167	.296	.197
Shreveport	AA	40	126	38	13	0	0	—	—	51	14	16	20	1	14	0	2	0	1	0	1.00	3	.302	.397	.405
1996 Phoenix	AAA	14	47	14	7	0	0	—	—	21	10	7	4	0	7	1	0	0	0	0	.00	1	.298	.365	.447
Shreveport	AA	115	380	112	23	0	21	—	—	198	60	70	76	0	49	6	1	1	1	1	.50	9	.295	.419	.521
1997 Phoenix	AAA	100	332	88	23	2	8	—	—	139	49	48	58	2	69	7	3	1	1	2	.33	9	.265	.384	.419
1996 San Francisco	NL	9	18	4	1	0	0	(0	0)	5	2	1	3	0	4	0	0	0	0	0	.00	0	.222	.333	.278
1997 San Francisco	NL	6	7	1	0	0	0	(0	0)	1	0	0	1	0	3	0	0	0	0	0	.00	0	.143	.250	.143
2 ML YEARS		15	25	5	1	0	0	(0	0)	6	2	1	4	0	7	0	0	0	0	0	.00	0	.200	.310	.240

Angel Miranda

Pitches: Left **Bats:** Left **Pos:** RP-10   **Ht:** 6'1" **Wt:** 195 **Born:** 11/9/69 **Age:** 28

Year Team	Lg	G	GS	CG	GF	IP	BFP	H	R	ER	HR	SH	SF	HB	TBB	IBB	SO	WP	Bk	W	L	Pct.	ShO	Sv-Op	Hld	ERA
1997 Stockton *	A+	1	1	0	0	2	8	0	0	0	0	0	0	0	2	0	2	0	0	0	0	.000	0	0-—	—	0.00
Buffalo *	AAA	9	0	0	3	11.2	58	20	14	13	3	0	1	0	5	0	9	2	0	0	2	.000	0	0-—	—	10.03
Okla City *	AAA	2	0	0	0	2.2	13	4	5	5	0	0	0	1	1	0	2	0	0	0	1	.000	0	0-—	—	16.88
1993 Milwaukee	AL	22	17	2	0	120	502	100	53	44	12	3	3	2	52	4	88	4	2	4	5	.444	0	0-0	0	3.30
1994 Milwaukee	AL	8	8	1	0	46	196	39	28	27	8	1	1	0	27	0	24	1	1	2	5	.286	0	0-0	0	5.28
1995 Milwaukee	AL	30	10	0	5	74	339	83	47	43	8	1	4	0	49	2	45	5	1	4	5	.444	0	1-3	3	5.23
1996 Milwaukee	AL	46	12	0	5	109.1	503	116	68	60	12	5	8	2	69	4	78	10	0	7	6	.538	0	1-2	6	4.94
1997 Milwaukee	AL	10	0	0	1	14	68	17	6	6	1	1	0	3	9	2	8	2	0	0	0	.000	0	0-0	2	3.86
5 ML YEARS		116	47	3	11	363.1	1608	355	202	180	41	11	16	7	206	12	243	22	4	17	21	.447	0	2-5	11	4.46

Mike Misuraca

Pitches: Right **Bats:** Right **Pos:** RP-5   **Ht:** 6'0" **Wt:** 188 **Born:** 8/21/68 **Age:** 29

Year Team	Lg	G	GS	CG	GF	IP	BFP	H	R	ER	HR	SH	SF	HB	TBB	IBB	SO	WP	Bk	W	L	Pct.	ShO	Sv-Op	Hld	ERA
1989 Kenosha	A	9	9	0	0	46	204	47	32	27	9	3	0	5	15	0	30	1	4	1	5	.167	0	0-—	—	5.28
Elizabethtn	R+	13	13	9	0	103	424	92	34	29	3	4	4	5	33	0	89	8	6	10	3	.769	0	0-—	—	2.53
1990 Kenosha	A	26	26	1	0	167.1	718	164	81	62	6	5	4	12	57	1	116	6	8	9	9	.500	0	0-—	—	3.33
1991 Visalia	A+	21	19	2	0	116	512	131	65	55	7	3	8	9	39	1	82	13	0	7	9	.438	0	0-—	—	4.27
1992 Miracle	A+	28	28	3	0	157	687	163	84	63	7	7	4	9	63	1	107	4	0	7	14	.333	1	0-—	—	3.61
1993 Nashville	AA	25	17	2	2	113	483	103	57	48	9	6	1	5	40	0	80	7	1	6	6	.500	1	0-—	—	3.82
1994 Nashville	AA	17	17	0	0	106.2	450	115	56	43	10	1	2	5	22	0	80	4	0	8	4	.667	0	0-—	—	3.63
Salt Lake	AAA	10	10	1	0	65.2	295	88	43	38	5	2	2	4	13	0	51	6	0	3	5	.375	0	0-—	—	5.21
1995 Salt Lake	AAA	31	19	1	2	143.1	628	174	93	85	15	0	6	8	36	1	67	7	0	9	6	.600	0	0-—	—	5.34
1996 Salt Lake	AAA	18	2	0	0	37.1	173	50	33	26	4	1	3	0	16	2	25	3	1	1	2	.333	0	1-—	—	6.27
New Orleans	AAA	23	12	0	5	80.2	358	93	42	37	11	4	0	3	31	3	57	5	1	2	7	.222	0	2-—	—	4.13
1997 Tucson	AAA	33	10	0	8	108.1	472	119	68	60	15	1	8	5	39	3	62	2	1	8	7	.533	0	1-—	—	4.98
1997 Milwaukee	AL	5	0	0	2	10.1	52	15	13	13	5	0	0	1	7	1	10	1	0	0	0	.000	0	0-0	2	11.32

Kevin Mitchell

Bats: Right **Throws:** Right **Pos:** DH-16; PH-4; LF-1   **Ht:** 5'11" **Wt:** 244 **Born:** 1/13/62 **Age:** 36

Year Team	Lg	G	AB	H	2B	3B	HR	(Hm	Rd)	TB	R	RBI	TBB	IBB	SO	HBP	SH	SF	SB	CS	SB%	GDP	Avg	OBP	SLG
1984 New York	NL	7	14	3	0	0	0	(0	0)	3	0	1	0	0	3	0	0	0	0	1	.00	0	.214	.214	.214
1986 New York	NL	108	328	91	22	2	12	(4	8)	153	51	43	33	0	61	1	1	1	3	3	.50	6	.277	.344	.466
1987 SD-SF	NL	131	464	130	20	2	22	(9	13)	220	68	70	48	4	88	2	0	1	9	6	.60	10	.280	.350	.474
1988 San Francisco	NL	148	505	127	25	7	19	(10	9)	223	60	80	48	7	85	5	1	7	5	5	.50	9	.251	.319	.442
1989 San Francisco	NL	154	543	158	34	6	47	(22	25)	345	100	125	87	32	115	3	0	7	3	4	.43	6	.291	.388	.635
1990 San Francisco	NL	140	524	152	24	2	35	(15	20)	285	90	93	58	9	87	2	0	5	4	7	.36	8	.290	.360	.544
1991 San Francisco	NL	113	371	95	13	1	27	(9	18)	191	52	69	43	8	57	5	0	4	2	3	.40	6	.256	.338	.515
1992 Seattle	AL	99	360	103	24	0	9	(5	4)	154	48	67	35	4	46	3	0	4	0	2	.00	4	.286	.351	.428
1993 Cincinnati	NL	93	323	110	21	3	19	(10	9)	194	56	64	25	4	48	1	0	3	2	0	1.00	14	.341	.385	.601
1994 Cincinnati	NL	95	310	101	18	1	30	(18	12)	211	57	77	59	15	62	3	0	8	2	0	1.00	12	.326	.429	.681
1996 Bos-Cin		64	206	65	15	0	8	(6	2)	104	27	39	37	2	30	1	0	1	0	0	.00	8	.316	.420	.505
1997 Cleveland	AL	20	59	9	1	0	4	(1	3)	22	7	11	9	2	11	1	0	0	0	1	1.00	0	.153	.275	.373
1987 San Diego	NL	62	196	48	7	1	7	(2	5)	78	19	26	20	3	38	0	0	1	2	2	.50	5	.245	.333	.398
San Francisco	NL	69	268	82	13	1	15	(7	8)	142	49	44	28	1	50	2	0	0	7	4	.64	5	.306	.376	.530
1996 Boston	AL	27	92	28	4	0	2	(1	1)	38	9	13	11	0	14	1	0	0	0	0	.00	3	.304	.385	.413

Year Team	Lg	G	AB	H	2B	3B	HR	(Hm	Rd)	TB	R	RBI	TBB	IBB	SO	HBP	SH	SF	SB	CS	SB%	GDP	Avg	OBP	SLG
								BATTING											BASERUNNING				PERCENTAGES		
Cincinnati	NL	37	114	37	11	0	6	(5	1)	66	18	26	26	2	16	0	0	1	0	0	.00	5	.325	.447	.579
12 ML YEARS		1172	4007	1144	217	24	232	(109	123)	2105	616	739	482	87	693	27	2	42	30	31	49	85	.286	.363	.525

Dave Mlicki

Pitches: Right **Bats:** Right **Pos:** SP-32   **Ht:** 6'4" **Wt:** 205 **Born:** 6/8/68 **Age:** 30

Year Team	Lg	G	GS	CG	GF	IP	BFP	H	R	ER	HR	SH	SF	HB	TBB	IBB	SO	WP	Bk	W	L	Pct.	ShO	Sv-Op	Hld	ERA
			HOW MUCH HE PITCHED							WHAT HE GAVE UP												THE RESULTS				
1992 Cleveland	AL	4	4	0	0	21.2	101	23	14	12	3	2	0	1	16	0	16	1	0	0	2	.000	0	0-0	0	4.98
1993 Cleveland	AL	3	3	0	0	13.1	58	11	6	5	2	0	0	2	6	0	7	2	0	0	0	.000	0	0-0	0	3.38
1995 New York	NL	29	25	0	1	160.2	696	160	82	76	23	8	5	4	54	2	123	5	1	9	7	.563	0	0-0	0	4.26
1996 New York	NL	51	2	0	16	90	393	95	46	33	9	8	3	6	33	8	83	7	0	6	7	.462	0	1-3	8	3.30
1997 New York	NL	32	32	1	0	193.2	838	194	89	86	21	3	6	5	76	7	157	5	1	8	12	.400	1	0-0	0	4.00
5 ML YEARS		119	66	1	17	479.1	2086	483	237	212	58	21	14	18	185	17	386	20	2	23	28	.451	1	1-3	8	3.98

Brian Moehler

Pitches: Right **Bats:** Right **Pos:** SP-31   **Ht:** 6'3" **Wt:** 220 **Born:** 12/31/71 **Age:** 26

Year Team	Lg	G	GS	CG	GF	IP	BFP	H	R	ER	HR	SH	SF	HB	TBB	IBB	SO	WP	Bk	W	L	Pct.	ShO	Sv-Op	Hld	ERA
			HOW MUCH HE PITCHED							WHAT HE GAVE UP												THE RESULTS				
1993 Niagara Fal	A-	12	11	0	0	58.2	262	51	33	21	3	1	3	4	27	0	38	8	2	6	5	.545	0	0- --	--	3.22
1994 Lakeland	A+	26	25	5	0	164.2	687	153	66	55	3	7	7	6	65	0	92	8	3	12	12	.500	2	0- --	--	3.01
1995 Jacksonville	AA	28	27	0	1	162.1	696	176	94	87	14	3	5	6	52	1	89	15	0	8	10	.444	0	0- --	--	4.82
1996 Jacksonville	AA	28	28	1	0	173.1	744	186	80	67	9	3	2	4	50	2	120	11	2	15	6	.714	0	0- --	--	3.48
1996 Detroit	AL	2	2	0	0	10.1	51	11	10	5	1	1	0	0	8	1	2	1	0	0	1	.000	0	0-0	0	4.35
1997 Detroit	AL	31	31	2	0	175.1	770	198	97	91	22	1	8	5	61	1	97	3	0	11	12	.478	1	0-0	0	4.67
2 ML YEARS		33	33	2	0	185.2	821	209	107	96	23	2	8	5	69	2	99	4	0	11	13	.458	1	0-0	0	4.65

Mike Mohler

Pitches: Left **Bats:** Right **Pos:** RP-52; SP-10   **Ht:** 6'2" **Wt:** 195 **Born:** 7/26/68 **Age:** 29

Year Team	Lg	G	GS	CG	GF	IP	BFP	H	R	ER	HR	SH	SF	HB	TBB	IBB	SO	WP	Bk	W	L	Pct.	ShO	Sv-Op	Hld	ERA
			HOW MUCH HE PITCHED							WHAT HE GAVE UP												THE RESULTS				
1993 Oakland	AL	42	9	0	4	64.1	290	57	45	40	10	5	2	2	44	4	42	0	1	1	6	.143	0	0-1	1	5.60
1994 Oakland	AL	1	1	0	0	2.1	14	2	3	2	1	0	0	0	2	0	4	0	0	0	1	.000	0	0-0	0	7.71
1995 Oakland	AL	28	0	0	6	23.2	100	16	8	8	0	1	0	0	18	1	15	1	0	1	1	.500	0	1-2	4	3.04
1996 Oakland	AL	72	0	0	30	81	352	79	36	33	9	6	4	1	41	6	64	9	0	6	3	.667	0	7-13	13	3.67
1997 Oakland	AL	62	10	0	16	101.2	462	116	65	58	11	9	7	7	54	8	66	4	0	1	10	.091	0	1-4	11	5.13
5 ML YEARS		205	20	0	56	273	1218	270	157	141	31	21	13	10	159	19	191	14	1	9	21	.300	0	9-20	29	4.65

Izzy Molina

Bats: Right **Throws:** Right **Pos:** C-48; PH-3   **Ht:** 6'1" **Wt:** 200 **Born:** 6/3/71 **Age:** 27

Year Team	Lg	G	AB	H	2B	3B	HR	(Hm	Rd)	TB	R	RBI	TBB	IBB	SO	HBP	SH	SF	SB	CS	SB%	GDP	Avg	OBP	SLG
								BATTING											BASERUNNING				PERCENTAGES		
1990 Athletics	R	38	122	43	12	2	0	—	—	59	19	18	9	1	21	2	1	3	5	0	1.00	0	.352	.397	.484
1991 Madison	A	95	316	89	16	1	3	—	—	116	35	45	15	1	40	6	1	4	6	4	.60	9	.282	.323	.367
1992 Reno	A+	116	436	113	17	2	10	—	—	164	71	75	39	0	57	7	7	6	8	7	.53	20	.259	.326	.376
Tacoma	AAA	10	36	7	0	1	0	—	—	9	3	5	2	0	6	0	0	0	1	0	1.00	1	.194	.237	.250
1993 Modesto	A+	125	444	116	26	5	6	—	—	170	61	69	44	0	85	3	4	11	2	8	.20	11	.261	.325	.383
1994 Huntsville	AA	116	388	84	17	2	8	—	—	129	31	50	16	0	47	5	7	7	5	1	.83	10	.216	.252	.332
1995 Edmonton	AAA	2	6	1	0	0	0	—	—	1	0	0	0	0	2	0	0	0	0	0	.00	0	.167	.167	.167
Huntsville	AA	83	301	78	16	1	8	—	—	120	38	26	26	0	62	8	0	2	3	4	.43	9	.259	.332	.399
1996 Edmonton	AAA	98	342	90	12	3	12	—	—	144	45	56	25	4	55	3	5	2	2	5	.29	9	.263	.317	.421
1997 Edmonton	AAA	61	218	57	11	3	6	—	—	92	33	34	12	0	27	0	1	0	2	0	1.00	4	.261	.300	.422
1996 Oakland	AL	14	25	5	2	0	0	(0	0)	7	0	1	1	0	3	0	0	0	0	0	.00	0	.200	.231	.280
1997 Oakland	AL	48	111	22	3	1	3	(1	2)	36	6	7	3	0	17	0	1	0	0	0	.00	1	.198	.219	.324
2 ML YEARS		62	136	27	5	1	3	(1	2)	43	6	8	4	0	20	0	1	0	0	0	.00	1	.199	.221	.316

Paul Molitor

Bats: Right **Throws:** Right **Pos:** DH-122; 1B-12; PH-2   **Ht:** 6'0" **Wt:** 190 **Born:** 8/22/56 **Age:** 41

Year Team	Lg	G	AB	H	2B	3B	HR	(Hm	Rd)	TB	R	RBI	TBB	IBB	SO	HBP	SH	SF	SB	CS	SB%	GDP	Avg	OBP	SLG
								BATTING											BASERUNNING				PERCENTAGES		
1978 Milwaukee	AL	125	521	142	26	4	6	(4	2)	194	73	45	19	2	54	4	7	5	30	12	.71	6	.273	.301	.372
1979 Milwaukee	AL	140	584	188	27	16	9	(3	6)	274	88	62	48	5	48	2	6	5	33	13	.72	9	.322	.372	.469
1980 Milwaukee	AL	111	450	137	29	2	9	(2	7)	197	81	37	48	4	48	3	6	5	34	7	.83	5	.304	.372	.438
1981 Milwaukee	AL	64	251	67	11	0	2	(1	1)	84	45	19	25	1	29	3	5	0	10	6	.63	3	.267	.341	.335
1982 Milwaukee	AL	160	666	201	26	8	19	(9	10)	300	136	71	69	1	93	1	10	5	41	9	.82	9	.302	.366	.450
1983 Milwaukee	AL	152	608	164	28	6	15	(9	6)	249	95	47	59	4	74	2	7	6	41	8	.84	12	.270	.333	.410
1984 Milwaukee	AL	13	46	10	1	0	0	(0	0)	11	3	6	2	0	8	0	0	1	1	0	1.00	0	.217	.245	.239
1985 Milwaukee	AL	140	576	171	28	3	10	(6	4)	235	93	48	54	6	80	1	7	4	21	7	.75	12	.297	.356	.408
1986 Milwaukee	AL	105	437	123	24	6	9	(5	4)	186	62	55	40	0	81	0	2	3	20	5	.80	9	.281	.340	.426
1987 Milwaukee	AL	118	465	164	41	5	16	(7	9)	263	114	75	69	2	67	2	5	1	45	10	.82	5	.353	.438	.566
1988 Milwaukee	AL	154	609	190	34	6	13	(9	4)	275	115	60	71	8	54	2	5	3	41	10	.80	10	.312	.384	.452
1989 Milwaukee	AL	155	615	194	35	4	11	(6	5)	270	84	56	64	4	67	4	4	9	27	11	.71	11	.315	.379	.439
1990 Milwaukee	AL	103	418	119	27	6	12	(6	6)	194	64	45	37	4	51	1	0	2	18	3	.86	7	.285	.343	.464

144

				BATTING																BASERUNNING				PERCENTAGES		
Year Team	Lg	G	AB	H	2B	3B	HR	(Hm	Rd)	TB	R	RBI	TBB	IBB	SO	HBP	SH	SF	SB	CS	SB%	GDP	Avg	OBP	SLG
1991 Milwaukee	AL	158	665	216	32	13	17	(7	10)	325	133	75	77	16	62	6	0	1	19	8	.70	11	.325	.399	.489
1992 Milwaukee	AL	158	609	195	36	7	12	(4	8)	281	89	89	73	12	66	3	4	11	31	6	.84	13	.320	.389	.461
1993 Toronto	AL	160	636	211	37	5	22	(13	9)	324	121	111	77	3	71	3	1	8	22	4	.85	13	.332	.402	.509
1994 Toronto	AL	115	454	155	30	4	14	(8	6)	235	86	75	55	4	48	1	0	5	20	0	1.00	13	.341	.410	.518
1995 Toronto	AL	130	525	142	31	2	15	(6	9)	222	63	60	61	1	57	5	3	4	12	0	1.00	10	.270	.350	.423
1996 Minnesota	AL	161	660	225	41	8	9	(6	3)	309	99	113	56	10	72	3	0	9	18	6	.75	21	.341	.390	.468
1997 Minnesota	AL	135	538	164	32	4	10	(6	9)	234	63	89	45	8	73	0	2	12	11	4	.73	8	.305	.351	.435
20 ML YEARS		2557	10333	3178	576	109	230	(116	114)	4662	1707	1238	1049	95	1203	46	74	99	495	129	.79	190	.308	.371	.451

Raul Mondesi

Bats: Right **Throws:** Right **Pos:** RF-159; PH-1 **Ht:** 5'11" **Wt:** 212 **Born:** 3/12/71 **Age:** 27

				BATTING																BASERUNNING				PERCENTAGES		
Year Team	Lg	G	AB	H	2B	3B	HR	(Hm	Rd)	TB	R	RBI	TBB	IBB	SO	HBP	SH	SF	SB	CS	SB%	GDP	Avg	OBP	SLG
1993 Los Angeles	NL	42	86	25	3	1	4	(2	2)	42	13	10	4	0	16	0	1	0	4	1	.80	1	.291	.322	.488
1994 Los Angeles	NL	112	434	133	27	8	16	(10	6)	224	63	56	16	5	78	2	0	2	11	8	.58	9	.306	.333	.516
1995 Los Angeles	NL	139	536	153	23	6	26	(13	13)	266	91	88	33	4	96	4	0	7	27	4	.87	7	.285	.328	.496
1996 Los Angeles	NL	157	634	188	40	7	24	(11	13)	314	98	88	32	9	122	5	0	2	14	7	.67	6	.297	.334	.495
1997 Los Angeles	NL	159	616	191	42	5	30	(16	14)	333	95	87	44	7	105	6	1	3	32	15	.68	11	.310	.360	.541
5 ML YEARS		609	2306	690	135	27	100	(52	48)	1179	360	329	129	25	417	17	2	14	88	35	.72	34	.299	.339	.511

Jeff Montgomery

Pitches: Right **Bats:** Right **Pos:** RP-55 **Ht:** 5'11" **Wt:** 180 **Born:** 1/7/62 **Age:** 36

		HOW MUCH HE PITCHED						WHAT HE GAVE UP												THE RESULTS						
Year Team	Lg	G	GS	CG	GF	IP	BFP	H	R	ER	HR	SH	SF	HB	TBB	IBB	SO	WP	Bk	W	L	Pct.	ShO	Sv-Op	Hld	ERA
1997 Omaha *	AAA	2	0	0	1	2	8	1	0	0	0	0	0	0	1	0	2	0	0	0	0	.000	0	0--		0.00
1987 Cincinnati	NL	14	1	0	6	19.1	89	25	15	14	2	0	0	0	9	1	13	1	1	2	2	.500	0	0-0	1	6.52
1988 Kansas City	AL	45	0	0	13	62.2	271	54	25	24	6	3	2	2	30	1	47	3	6	7	2	.778	0	1-3	9	3.45
1989 Kansas City	AL	63	0	0	39	92	363	66	16	14	3	1	1	2	25	4	94	6	1	7	3	.700	0	18-24	11	1.37
1990 Kansas City	AL	73	0	0	59	94.1	400	81	36	25	6	2	2	5	34	8	94	3	0	6	5	.545	0	24-34	7	2.39
1991 Kansas City	AL	67	0	0	55	90	376	83	32	29	6	6	2	2	28	2	77	6	0	4	4	.500	0	33-39	3	2.90
1992 Kansas City	AL	65	0	0	62	82.2	333	61	23	20	5	4	2	3	27	2	69	2	0	1	6	.143	0	39-46	0	2.18
1993 Kansas City	AL	69	0	0	63	87.1	347	65	22	22	3	5	1	2	23	4	66	3	0	7	5	.583	0	45-51	0	2.27
1994 Kansas City	AL	42	0	0	38	44.2	193	48	21	20	5	2	1	1	15	1	50	2	0	2	3	.400	0	27-32	0	4.03
1995 Kansas City	AL	54	0	0	46	65.2	275	60	27	25	7	5	5	2	25	4	49	1	1	2	3	.400	0	31-38	0	3.43
1996 Kansas City	AL	48	0	0	41	63.1	261	59	31	30	14	3	1	3	19	3	45	0	0	4	6	.400	0	24-34	0	4.26
1997 Kansas City	AL	55	0	0	37	59.1	245	53	24	23	9	4	2	0	18	5	48	5	0	1	4	.200	0	14-17	3	3.49
11 ML YEARS		595	1	0	459	761.1	3153	655	272	246	66	35	19	22	253	35	652	32	9	43	43	.500	0	256-318	34	2.91

Ray Montgomery

Bats: R **Throws:** R **Pos:** RF-15; PH-13; LF-2; CF-2 **Ht:** 6'3" **Wt:** 195 **Born:** 8/8/69 **Age:** 28

				BATTING																BASERUNNING				PERCENTAGES		
Year Team	Lg	G	AB	H	2B	3B	HR	(Hm	Rd)	TB	R	RBI	TBB	IBB	SO	HBP	SH	SF	SB	CS	SB%	GDP	Avg	OBP	SLG
1990 Auburn	A-	61	193	45	8	1	0	—		55	19	13	23	1	32	1	4	1	11	5	.69	5	.233	.317	.285
1991 Burlington	A	120	433	109	24	3	3	—		148	60	57	37	1	66	8	11	2	17	14	.55	10	.252	.321	.342
1992 Jackson	AA	51	148	31	4	1	1	—		40	13	10	7	2	27	0	1	1	4	1	.80	5	.209	.244	.270
1993 Tucson	AAA	15	50	17	3	1	2	—		28	9	6	5	0	7	1	1	0	1	2	.33	1	.340	.411	.560
Jackson	AA	100	338	95	16	3	10	—		147	50	59	36	1	54	6	1	6	12	6	.67	7	.281	.355	.435
1994 Tucson	AAA	103	332	85	19	6	7	—		137	51	51	35	6	54	2	2	3	5	3	.63	9	.256	.328	.413
1995 Jackson	AA	35	127	38	8	1	10	—		78	24	24	13	2	13	5	0	1	6	3	.67	3	.299	.384	.614
Tucson	AAA	88	291	88	19	0	11	—		140	48	68	24	1	58	2	1	8	5	3	.63	5	.302	.351	.481
1996 Tucson	AAA	100	360	110	20	0	22	—		196	70	75	59	7	54	3	0	1	7	1	.88	12	.306	.407	.544
1997 New Orleans	AAA	20	73	21	5	0	6	—		44	17	13	11	0	15	0	0	0	1	1	.50	2	.288	.381	.603
1996 Houston	NL	12	14	3	1	0	1	(1	0)	7	4	4	1	0	5	0	0	0	0	0	.00	0	.214	.267	.500
1997 Houston	NL	29	68	16	4	1	0	(0	0)	22	8	4	5	0	18	0	0	3	0	0	.00	0	.235	.276	.324
2 ML YEARS		41	82	19	5	1	1	(1	0)	29	12	8	6	0	23	0	0	3	0	0	.00	2	.232	.275	.354

Steve Montgomery

Pitches: Right **Bats:** Right **Pos:** RP-4 **Ht:** 6'4" **Wt:** 208 **Born:** 12/25/70 **Age:** 27

		HOW MUCH HE PITCHED						WHAT HE GAVE UP												THE RESULTS						
Year Team	Lg	G	GS	CG	GF	IP	BFP	H	R	ER	HR	SH	SF	HB	TBB	IBB	SO	WP	Bk	W	L	Pct.	ShO	Sv-Op	Hld	ERA
1993 St. Pete	A+	14	5	0	7	40.2	161	33	14	12	2	1	2	0	9	0	34	1	0	3	1	.667	0	3--	—	2.66
Arkansas	AA	6	6	0	0	32	140	34	17	14	2	2	0	0	12	2	19	2	0	3	3	.500	0	0--	—	3.94
1994 Arkansas	AA	50	9	0	19	107	447	97	43	39	10	4	4	3	33	3	73	5	0	4	5	.444	0	2--	—	3.28
1995 Arkansas	AA	55	0	0	53	61	259	52	22	22	6	7	1	4	22	6	56	5	1	5	2	.714	0	36--	—	3.25
1996 Edmonton	AAA	37	0	0	15	56	230	51	19	18	7	2	0	1	12	1	40	1	0	2	0	1.000	0	1--	—	2.89
1997 Edmonton	AAA	30	0	0	13	46.2	216	61	30	30	6	1	1	1	17	2	38	4	0	2	1	.667	0	3--	—	5.79
Buffalo	AAA	7	0	0	0	8	37	12	6	5	2	1	0	0	3	0	5	0	0		1	.333	0	1--	—	5.63
1996 Oakland	AL	8	0	0	0	13.2	71	18	14	14	5	0	0	0	13	2	8	3	0	1	0	1.000	0	0-0	0	9.22
1997 Oakland	AL	4	0	0	0	6.1	35	10	7	7	2	0	1	0	8	2	1	0	0	0	1	.000	0	0-0	0	9.95
2 ML YEARS		12	0	0	0	20	106	28	21	21	7	0	1	0	21	4	9	3	0	1	1	.500	0	0-0	1	9.45

Eric Moody

Pitches: Right **Bats:** Right **Pos:** RP-9; SP-1   **Ht:** 6'6" **Wt:** 185 **Born:** 1/6/71 **Age:** 27

		HOW MUCH HE PITCHED						WHAT HE GAVE UP											THE RESULTS						
Year Team	Lg	G	GS	CG	GF	IP	BFP	H	R	ER	HR	SH	SF	HB	TBB	IBB	SO	WP	Bk	W	L	Pct.	ShO	Sv-Op	Hld	ERA
1993 Erie	A-	17	7	0	4	54	229	54	30	23	3	0	1	2	13	1	33	3	1	3	3	.500	0	0- -	-	3.83
1994 Hudson Vall	A-	15	12	1	1	89	355	82	32	28	2	2	3	2	18	1	68	3	4	7	3	.700	0	0- -	-	2.83
1995 Charlotte	A+	13	13	2	0	88.1	353	84	30	27	2	3	1	5	13	0	57	0	0	5	5	.500	2	0- -	-	2.75
1996 Tulsa	AA	44	5	0	29	95.2	395	92	40	38	4	1	3	1	23	2	80	4	0	8	4	.667	0	16- -	-	3.57
1997 Okla City	AAA	35	10	1	10	112	469	114	49	43	13	5	1	4	21	1	72	1	0	5	6	.455	1	1- -	-	3.46
1997 Texas	AL	10	1	0	3	19	82	26	10	9	4	0	1	0	2	0	12	0	0	0	1	.000	0	0-1	0	4.26

Mickey Morandini

Bats: Left **Throws:** Right **Pos:** 2B-146; PH-4; SS-1   **Ht:** 5'11" **Wt:** 176 **Born:** 4/22/66 **Age:** 32

		BATTING																BASERUNNING				PERCENTAGES		
Year Team	Lg	G	AB	H	2B	3B	HR	(Hm	Rd)	TB	R	RBI	TBB	IBB	SO	HBP	SH	SF	SB	CS	SB%	GDP	Avg	OBP	SLG
1990 Philadelphia	NL	25	79	19	4	0	1	(1	0)	26	9	3	6	0	19	0	2	0	3	0	1.00	1	.241	.294	.329
1991 Philadelphia	NL	98	325	81	11	4	1	(1	0)	103	38	20	29	0	45	0	2	6	13	2	.87	7	.249	.313	.317
1992 Philadelphia	NL	127	422	112	8	8	3	(2	1)	145	47	30	25	2	64	0	6	2	8	3	.73	4	.265	.305	.344
1993 Philadelphia	NL	120	425	105	19	9	3	(2	1)	151	57	33	34	2	73	5	4	2	13	2	.87	7	.247	.309	.355
1994 Philadelphia	NL	87	274	80	16	5	2	(1	1)	112	40	26	34	5	33	4	4	0	10	5	.67	4	.292	.378	.409
1995 Philadelphia	NL	127	494	140	34	7	6	(3	3)	206	65	49	42	3	80	9	4	1	9	6	.60	11	.283	.350	.417
1996 Philadelphia	NL	140	539	135	24	6	3	(2	1)	180	64	32	49	0	87	9	5	4	26	5	.84	15	.250	.321	.334
1997 Philadelphia	NL	150	553	163	40	2	1	(1	0)	210	83	39	62	0	91	8	12	5	16	13	.55	8	.295	.371	.380
8 ML YEARS		874	3111	835	156	41	20	(13	7)	1133	403	232	281	12	492	37	43	16	98	36	.73	57	.268	.335	.364

Mike Mordecai

Bats: R **Throws:** R **Pos:** PH-43; 3B-19; 2B-4; SS-4; 1B-3; DH-1; RF-1   **Ht:** 5'11" **Wt:** 175 **Born:** 12/13/67 **Age:** 30

		BATTING																BASERUNNING				PERCENTAGES		
Year Team	Lg	G	AB	H	2B	3B	HR	(Hm	Rd)	TB	R	RBI	TBB	IBB	SO	HBP	SH	SF	SB	CS	SB%	GDP	Avg	OBP	SLG
1997 Richmond *	AAA	31	122	38	10	0	3	—	—	57	23	15	9	0	17	1	2	1	0	1	.00	0	.311	.361	.467
1994 Atlanta	NL	4	4	1	0	0	1	(1	0)	4	1	3	1	0	0	0	0	0	0	0	.00	0	.250	.400	1.000
1995 Atlanta	NL	69	75	21	6	0	3	(1	2)	36	10	11	9	0	16	0	2	1	0	0	.00	0	.280	.353	.480
1996 Atlanta	NL	66	108	26	5	0	2	(0	2)	37	12	8	9	1	24	0	4	1	1	0	1.00	1	.241	.297	.343
1997 Atlanta	NL	61	81	14	2	1	0	(0	0)	18	8	3	6	0	16	0	1	1	0	0	.00	4	.173	.227	.222
4 ML YEARS		200	268	62	13	1	6	(2	4)	95	31	25	25	1	56	0	7	3	1	1	.50	5	.231	.294	.354

Ramon Morel

Pitches: Right **Bats:** Right **Pos:** RP-8   **Ht:** 6'2" **Wt:** 193 **Born:** 8/15/74 **Age:** 23

		HOW MUCH HE PITCHED						WHAT HE GAVE UP											THE RESULTS						
Year Team	Lg	G	GS	CG	GF	IP	BFP	H	R	ER	HR	SH	SF	HB	TBB	IBB	SO	WP	Bk	W	L	Pct.	ShO	Sv-Op	Hld	ERA
1997 Calgary *	AAA	27	18	0	3	101.2	466	131	71	65	13	3	2	4	42	1	72	4	2	6	7	.462	0	0- -	—	5.75
1995 Pittsburgh	NL	5	0	0	0	6.1	23	6	2	2	1	0	0	0	2	1	3	0	0	0	1	.000	0	0-1	0	2.84
1996 Pittsburgh	NL	29	0	0	4	42	198	57	27	25	4	1	1	1	19	5	22	1	1	2	1	.667	0	0-0	2	5.36
1997 Pit-ChN	NL	8	0	0	2	11.1	53	14	6	6	3	0	0	0	7	1	7	0	0	0	0	.000	0	0-0	0	4.76
1997 Pittsburgh	NL	5	0	0	2	7.2	36	11	4	4	2	0	0	0	4	1	4	0	0	0	0	.000	0	0-0	0	4.70
Chicago	NL	3	0	0	3	3.2	17	3	2	2	1	0	0	0	3	0	3	0	0	0	0	.000	0	0-0	0	4.91
3 ML YEARS		42	0	0	9	59.2	274	77	35	33	7	2	1	1	28	7	32	1	1	2	2	.500	0	0-1	2	4.98

Kevin Morgan

Bats: Right **Throws:** Right **Pos:** 3B-1; PH-1   **Ht:** 6'1" **Wt:** 170 **Born:** 12/3/69 **Age:** 28

		BATTING																BASERUNNING				PERCENTAGES		
Year Team	Lg	G	AB	H	2B	3B	HR	(Hm	Rd)	TB	R	RBI	TBB	IBB	SO	HBP	SH	SF	SB	CS	SB%	GDP	Avg	OBP	SLG
1991 Niagara Fal	A-	70	252	60	13	0	0	—	—	73	23	26	21	0	49	3	4	4	8	6	.57	2	.238	.300	.290
1992 Fayetteville	A	123	466	106	19	2	0	—	—	129	55	37	49	2	61	6	6	4	15	19	.44	10	.227	.307	.277
1993 Lakeland	A+	112	417	99	12	2	2	—	—	121	45	34	32	2	84	2	3	4	9	6	.60	9	.237	.292	.290
1994 St. Lucie	A+	132	448	122	8	3	1	—	—	139	63	47	37	0	62	7	9	3	7	7	.50	5	.272	.335	.310
1995 Binghamton	AA	114	430	119	21	1	4	—	—	154	63	51	44	4	52	5	7	2	9	9	.50	2	.277	.349	.358
Norfolk	AAA	19	62	20	1	0	0	—	—	21	10	8	4	0	8	1	0	0	1	3	.25	1	.323	.373	.339
1996 Norfolk	AAA	29	82	11	3	0	0	—	—	14	7	5	9	0	14	2	4	1	3	1	.75	0	.134	.234	.171
Binghamton	AA	107	409	103	11	2	6	—	—	136	61	35	53	2	59	3	10	3	13	4	.76	15	.252	.340	.333
1997 Binghamton	AA	51	191	37	7	0	1	—	—	47	16	10	19	1	25	3	0	3	11	2	.85	3	.194	.277	.246
Norfolk	AAA	71	256	70	11	1	2	—	—	89	34	20	27	1	26	0	0	0	6	5	.55	5	.273	.343	.348
1997 New York	NL	1	1	0	0	0	0	(0	0)	0	0	0	0	0	0	0	0	0	0	0	.00	0	.000	.000	.000

Mike Morgan

Pitches: Right **Bats:** Right **Pos:** SP-30; RP-1   **Ht:** 6'2" **Wt:** 220 **Born:** 10/8/59 **Age:** 38

		HOW MUCH HE PITCHED						WHAT HE GAVE UP											THE RESULTS						
Year Team	Lg	G	GS	CG	GF	IP	BFP	H	R	ER	HR	SH	SF	HB	TBB	IBB	SO	WP	Bk	W	L	Pct.	ShO	Sv-Op	Hld	ERA
1978 Oakland	AL	3	3	1	0	12.1	60	19	12	10	1	1	0	0	8	0	0	0	0	0	3	.000	0	0-0	0	7.30
1979 Oakland	AL	13	13	2	0	77.1	368	102	57	51	7	4	4	3	50	0	17	7	0	2	10	.167	0	0-0	0	5.94
1982 New York	AL	30	23	2	2	150.1	661	167	77	73	15	2	4	2	67	5	71	6	0	7	11	.389	0	0- -	-	4.37
1983 Toronto	AL	16	4	0	2	45.1	198	48	26	26	6	0	1	0	21	0	22	3	0	0	3	.000	0	0- -	-	5.16
1985 Seattle	AL	2	2	0	0	6	33	11	8	8	0	0	0	0	5	0	2	1	0	1	0	.500	0	0-0	0	12.00

		HOW MUCH HE PITCHED						WHAT HE GAVE UP											THE RESULTS					
Year Team	Lg	G	GS	CG	GF	IP	BFP	H	R	ER	HR	SH	SF	HB	TBB	IBB	SO	WP	Bk	W	L	Pct.	ShO	Sv-Op	Hld	ERA
1986 Seattle	AL	37	33	9	2	216.1	951	243	122	109	24	7	3	4	86	3	116	8	1	11	17	.393	1	1- -	—	4.53
1987 Seattle	AL	34	31	8	2	207	898	245	117	107	25	8	5	5	53	3	85	11	0	12	17	.414	2	0-0	0	4.65
1988 Baltimore	AL	22	10	2	6	71.1	299	70	45	43	6	1	0	1	23	1	29	5	0	1	6	.143	0	1-1	0	5.43
1989 Los Angeles	NL	40	19	0	7	152.2	604	130	51	43	6	8	6	2	33	8	72	6	0	8	11	.421	0	0-1	1	2.53
1990 Los Angeles	NL	33	33	6	0	211	891	216	100	88	19	11	4	5	60	5	106	4	1	11	15	.423	4	0-0	0	3.75
1991 Los Angeles	NL	34	33	5	1	236.1	949	197	85	73	12	10	4	3	61	10	140	6	0	14	10	.583	1	1-1	0	2.78
1992 Chicago	NL	34	34	6	0	240	966	203	80	68	14	10	5	3	79	10	123	11	0	16	8	.667	1	0-0	0	2.55
1993 Chicago	NL	32	32	1	0	207.2	883	206	100	93	15	11	5	7	74	8	111	8	2	10	15	.400	1	0-0	0	4.03
1994 Chicago	NL	15	15	1	0	80.2	380	111	65	60	12	7	6	4	35	2	57	5	0	2	10	.167	0	0-0	0	6.69
1995 ChN-StL	NL	21	21	1	0	131.1	548	133	56	52	12	12	5	6	34	2	61	6	0	7	7	.500	0	0-0	0	3.56
1996 StL-Cin	NL	23	23	0	0	130.1	567	146	72	67	16	6	7	1	47	0	74	2	0	6	11	.353	0	0-0	0	4.63
1997 Cincinnati	NL	31	30	1	0	162	688	165	91	86	13	9	2	8	49	6	103	7	0	9	12	.429	0	0-0	1	4.78
1995 Chicago	NL	4	4	0	0	24.2	100	19	8	6	2	2	0	1	9	1	15	0	0	2	1	.667	0	0-0	0	2.19
St. Louis	NL	17	17	1	0	106.2	448	114	48	46	10	10	5	5	25	1	46	6	0	5	6	.455	0	0-0	0	3.88
1996 St. Louis	NL	18	18	0	0	103	452	118	63	60	14	5	6	0	40	0	55	2	0	4	8	.333	0	0-0	0	5.24
Cincinnati	NL	5	5	0	0	27.1	115	28	9	7	2	1	1	1	7	0	19	0	0	2	3	.400	0	0-0	0	2.30
17 ML YEARS		420	359	45	22	2338	9944	2412	1164	1057	205	107	61	54	785	63	1189	96	4	117	167	.412	10	3- -	—	4.07

Alvin Morman

Pitches: Left **Bats:** Right **Pos:** RP-34   **Ht:** 6'3" **Wt:** 210 **Born:** 1/6/69 **Age:** 29

		HOW MUCH HE PITCHED						WHAT HE GAVE UP											THE RESULTS					
Year Team	Lg	G	GS	CG	GF	IP	BFP	H	R	ER	HR	SH	SF	HB	TBB	IBB	SO	WP	Bk	W	L	Pct.	ShO	Sv-Op	Hld	ERA
1991 Astros	R	11	0	0	3	16.2	71	15	7	4	0	1	0	0	5	0	24	0	4	1	0	1.000	0	1- -	—	2.16
Osceola	A+	3	0	0	0	6	25	5	3	1	0	0	0	0	2	0	3	1	0	0	0	.000	0	0- -	—	1.50
1992 Asheville	A	57	0	0	37	75.1	313	60	17	13	3	3	1	3	26	2	70	2	0	8	0	1.000	0	15- -	—	1.55
1993 Jackson	AA	19	19	0	0	97.1	392	77	35	32	7	3	2	5	28	0	101	5	1	8	2	.800	0	0- -	—	2.96
1994 Tucson	AAA	58	0	0	23	74	327	84	51	42	7	5	9	2	26	4	49	3	0	3	7	.300	0	5- -	—	5.11
1995 Tucson	AAA	45	0	0	10	48.1	211	50	26	21	6	5	8	0	20	1	36	2	0	5	1	.833	0	3- -	—	3.91
1997 New Orleans	AAA	8	0	0	1	10	42	11	5	5	1	1	1	0	2	1	14	1	0	0	1	.000	0	0- -	—	4.50
Buffalo	AAA	3	0	0	1	3.1	12	2	0	0	0	0	0	0	0	0	3	0	0	0	0	.000	0	0- -	—	0.00
1996 Houston	NL	53	0	0	9	42	192	43	24	23	8	2	1	0	24	6	31	3	1	4	1	.800	0	0-2	7	4.93
1997 Cleveland	AL	34	0	0	7	18.1	86	19	13	12	2	0	0	1	14	3	13	1	0	0	0	.000	0	2-2	5	5.89
2 ML YEARS		87	0	0	16	60.1	278	62	37	35	10	2	1	1	38	9	44	4	1	4	1	.800	0	2-4	12	5.22

Russ Morman

Bats: Right **Throws:** Right **Pos:** RF-2; PH-2; 1B-1   **Ht:** 6'4" **Wt:** 225 **Born:** 4/28/62 **Age:** 36

		BATTING																BASERUNNING				PERCENTAGES		
Year Team	Lg	G	AB	H	2B	3B	HR	(Hm	Rd)	TB	R	RBI	TBB	IBB	SO	HBP	SH	SF	SB	CS	SB%	GDP	Avg	OBP	SLG
1997 Charlotte *	AAA	117	395	126	17	2	33	—	—	246	82	99	58	11	89	4	0	5	3	2	.60	6	.319	.407	.623
1986 Chicago	AL	49	159	40	5	0	4	(1	3)	57	18	17	16	0	36	2	1	2	1	0	1.00	5	.252	.324	.358
1988 Chicago	AL	40	75	18	2	0	0	(0	0)	20	8	3	3	0	17	0	2	0	0	0	.00	5	.240	.269	.267
1989 Chicago	AL	37	58	13	2	0	0	(0	0)	15	5	8	6	1	16	0	2	1	1	0	1.00	1	.224	.292	.259
1990 Kansas City	AL	12	37	10	4	2	1	(0	1)	21	5	3	3	0	3	0	0	1	0	0	.00	1	.270	.317	.568
1991 Kansas City	AL	12	23	6	0	0	0	(0	0)	6	1	1	1	1	5	0	0	0	0	0	.00	0	.261	.292	.261
1994 Florida	NL	13	33	7	0	1	1	(0	1)	12	2	2	2	0	9	1	0	0	0	0	.00	1	.212	.278	.364
1995 Florida	NL	34	72	20	2	1	3	(1	2)	33	9	7	3	0	12	1	0	0	0	0	.00	5	.278	.316	.458
1996 Florida	NL	6	6	1	1	0	0	(0	0)	2	0	0	1	0	2	0	0	0	0	0	.00	0	.167	.286	.333
1997 Florida	NL	4	7	2	1	0	1	(0	1)	6	3	2	0	0	0	0	0	0	1	0	1.00	0	.286	.286	.857
9 ML YEARS		207	470	117	17	4	10	(2	8)	172	51	43	35	2	102	4	5	4	3	0	1.00	17	.249	.304	.366

Hal Morris

Bats: Left **Throws:** Left **Pos:** 1B-89; PH-11   **Ht:** 6'4" **Wt:** 210 **Born:** 4/9/65 **Age:** 33

		BATTING																BASERUNNING				PERCENTAGES		
Year Team	Lg	G	AB	H	2B	3B	HR	(Hm	Rd)	TB	R	RBI	TBB	IBB	SO	HBP	SH	SF	SB	CS	SB%	GDP	Avg	OBP	SLG
1988 New York	AL	15	20	2	0	0	0	(0	0)	2	1	0	0	0	9	0	0	0	0	0	.00	0	.100	.100	.100
1989 New York	AL	15	18	5	0	0	0	(0	0)	5	2	4	1	0	4	0	0	0	0	0	.00	2	.278	.316	.278
1990 Cincinnati	NL	107	309	105	22	3	7	(3	4)	154	50	36	21	4	32	1	3	2	9	3	.75	12	.340	.381	.498
1991 Cincinnati	NL	136	478	152	33	1	14	(9	5)	229	72	59	46	7	61	1	5	7	10	4	.71	4	.318	.374	.479
1992 Cincinnati	NL	115	395	107	21	3	6	(3	3)	152	41	53	45	8	53	2	2	2	6	6	.50	12	.271	.347	.385
1993 Cincinnati	NL	101	379	120	18	0	7	(2	5)	159	48	49	34	4	51	2	0	6	2	2	.50	5	.317	.371	.420
1994 Cincinnati	NL	112	436	146	30	4	10	(5	5)	214	60	78	34	8	62	5	2	6	6	2	.75	16	.335	.385	.491
1995 Cincinnati	NL	101	359	100	25	2	11	(6	5)	162	53	51	29	7	58	1	1	1	1	1	.50	10	.279	.333	.451
1996 Cincinnati	NL	142	528	165	32	4	16	(7	9)	253	82	80	50	5	76	5	5	6	7	5	.58	12	.313	.374	.479
1997 Cincinnati	NL	96	333	92	20	1	1	(1	0)	117	42	33	23	2	43	3	4	1	3	1	.75	10	.276	.328	.351
10 ML YEARS		940	3255	994	201	18	72	(36	36)	1447	451	443	283	45	449	20	22	31	44	24	.65	83	.305	.361	.445

Matt Morris

Pitches: Right **Bats:** Right **Pos:** SP-33   **Ht:** 6'5" **Wt:** 210 **Born:** 8/9/74 **Age:** 23

		HOW MUCH HE PITCHED						WHAT HE GAVE UP											THE RESULTS					
Year Team	Lg	G	GS	CG	GF	IP	BFP	H	R	ER	HR	SH	SF	HB	TBB	IBB	SO	WP	Bk	W	L	Pct.	ShO	Sv-Op	Hld	ERA
1995 New Jersey	A-	2	2	0	0	11	45	12	3	2	1	0	0	0	3	0	13	0	3	1	0	1.000	0	0- -	—	1.64
St. Pete	A+	6	6	1	0	34	134	22	16	9	1	2	0	0	11	0	31	0	2	3	2	.600	1	0- -	—	2.38
1996 Arkansas	AA	27	27	4	0	167	711	178	79	72	14	8	4	2	48	1	120	9	0	12	12	.500	4	0- -	—	3.88
Louisville	AAA	1	1	0	0	8	32	8	3	3	0	0	0	0	1	0	9	0	0	0	1	.000	0	0- -	—	3.38

147

		HOW MUCH HE PITCHED		WHAT HE GAVE UP			THE RESULTS		
Year Team	Lg	G GS CG GF	IP	BFP	H R ER HR SH SF HB	TBB IBB	SO WP Bk	W L	Pct.	ShO Sv-Op Hld	ERA
1997 St. Louis	NL	33 33 3 0	217	900	208 88 77 12 11 7 7	69 2	149 5 3	12 9	.571	0 0-0 0	3.19

Julio Mosquera

Bats: Right **Throws:** Right **Pos:** C-3   **Ht:** 6'0" **Wt:** 190 **Born:** 1/29/72 **Age:** 26

		BATTING														BASERUNNING				PERCENTAGES		
Year Team	Lg	G	AB	H	2B	3B	HR	(Hm	Rd)	TB	R	RBI	TBB	IBB	SO	HBP	SH	SF	SB	CS	SB%	GDP	Avg	OBP	SLG
1993 Blue Jays	R	35	108	28	3	2	0	—	—	35	9	15	8	0	16	1	2	1	3	2	.60	3	.259	.314	.324
1994 Medicne Hat	R+	59	229	78	17	1	2	—	—	103	33	44	18	3	35	3	0	2	3	3	.50	4	.341	.393	.450
1995 Hagerstown	A	108	406	118	22	5	3	—	—	159	64	46	29	2	53	13	3	5	5	5	.50	13	.291	.353	.392
1996 Knoxville	AA	92	318	73	17	0	2	—	—	96	36	31	29	1	55	4	3	1	6	5	.55	16	.230	.301	.302
Syracuse	AAA	23	72	18	1	0	0	—	—	19	6	5	6	0	14	1	0	0	0	0	.00	1	.250	.316	.264
1997 Syracuse	AAA	10	35	8	1	0	0	—	—	9	5	1	2	0	5	1	0	0	0	0	.00	2	.229	.289	.257
Knoxville	AA	87	309	90	23	1	5	—	—	130	47	50	22	0	56	5	2	3	3	4	.43	10	.291	.345	.421
1996 Toronto	AL	8	22	5	2	0	0	(0	0)	7	2	2	0	0	3	1	0	0	0	1	.00	0	.227	.261	.318
1997 Toronto	AL	3	8	2	1	0	0	(0	0)	3	0	0	0	0	2	0	0	0	0	0	.00	0	.250	.250	.375
2 ML YEARS		11	30	7	3	0	0	(0	0)	10	2	2	0	0	5	1	0	0	0	1	.00	0	.233	.258	.333

James Mouton

Bats: R **Throws:** R **Pos:** CF-39; PH-35; RF-14; LF-9   **Ht:** 5'9" **Wt:** 175 **Born:** 12/29/68 **Age:** 29

		BATTING														BASERUNNING				PERCENTAGES		
Year Team	Lg	G	AB	H	2B	3B	HR	(Hm | Rd)	TB	R	RBI	TBB	IBB	SO	HBP	SH	SF	SB	CS	SB%	GDP	Avg	OBP	SLG
1994 Houston	NL	99	310	76	11	0	5	(1 | 4)	93	43	16	27	0	69	5	2	1	24	5	.83	6	.245	.315	.300
1995 Houston	NL	104	298	78	18	2	4	(2 | 2)	112	42	27	25	1	59	4	3	1	25	8	.76	5	.262	.326	.376
1996 Houston	NL	122	300	79	15	1	3	(2 | 1)	105	40	34	38	2	55	0	2	3	21	9	.70	9	.263	.343	.350
1997 Houston	NL	86	180	38	9	1	3	(1 | 2)	58	24	23	18	0	30	2	2	2	9	7	.56	3	.211	.287	.322
4 ML YEARS		411	1088	271	53	4	12	(6 | 6)	368	149	100	108	3	213	11	9	7	79	29	.73	23	.249	.321	.338

Lyle Mouton

Bats: R **Throws:** R **Pos:** RF-55; PH-18; LF-16; DH-11   **Ht:** 6'4" **Wt:** 240 **Born:** 5/13/69 **Age:** 29

		BATTING														BASERUNNING				PERCENTAGES		
Year Team	Lg	G	AB	H	2B	3B	HR	(Hm	Rd)	TB	R	RBI	TBB	IBB	SO	HBP	SH	SF	SB	CS	SB%	GDP	Avg	OBP	SLG
1997 Birmingham *	AA	3	11	2	0	0	1	—	—	5	1	1	1	0	4	0	0	0	0	0	.00	0	.182	.250	.455
1995 Chicago	AL	58	179	54	16	0	5	(4	1)	85	23	27	19	0	46	2	0	1	0	1	.00	1	.302	.373	.475
1996 Chicago	AL	87	214	63	8	1	7	(4	3)	94	25	39	22	4	50	2	0	3	3	0	1.00	3	.294	.361	.439
1997 Chicago	AL	88	242	65	9	0	5	(4	1)	89	26	23	14	1	66	1	0	3	4	4	.50	8	.269	.308	.368
3 ML YEARS		233	635	182	33	1	17	(12	5)	268	74	89	55	5	162	5	0	7	8	4	.67	18	.287	.345	.422

Jamie Moyer

Pitches: Left **Bats:** Left **Pos:** SP-30   **Ht:** 6'0" **Wt:** 170 **Born:** 11/18/62 **Age:** 35

		HOW MUCH HE PITCHED			WHAT HE GAVE UP												THE RESULTS					
Year Team	Lg	G	GS	CG	GF	IP	BFP	H	R	ER	HR	SH	SF	HB	TBB	IBB	SO	WP	Bk	W	L	Pct.	ShO	Sv-Op	Hld	ERA
1997 Tacoma *	AAA	1	1	0	0	5	16	1	0	0	0	0	0	0	0	0	6	0	0	1	0	1.000	0	0--	—	0.00
1986 Chicago	NL	16	16	1	0	87.1	395	107	52	49	10	3	3	3	42	1	45	3	3	7	4	.636	1	0-0	0	5.05
1987 Chicago	NL	35	33	1	1	201	899	210	127	114	28	14	7	5	97	9	147	11	2	12	15	.444	0	0-0	0	5.10
1988 Chicago	NL	34	30	3	1	202	855	212	84	78	20	14	4	4	55	7	121	4	0	9	15	.375	1	0-2	0	3.48
1989 Texas	AL	15	15	1	0	76	337	84	51	41	10	1	4	2	33	0	44	1	0	4	9	.308	0	0-0	0	4.86
1990 Texas	AL	33	10	1	6	102.1	447	115	59	53	6	1	7	4	39	4	58	1	0	2	6	.250	0	0-0	0	4.66
1991 St. Louis	NL	8	7	0	1	31.1	142	38	21	20	5	4	2	1	16	0	20	2	1	0	5	.000	0	0-0	0	5.74
1993 Baltimore	AL	25	25	3	0	152	630	154	63	58	11	3	1	6	38	2	90	1	1	12	9	.571	1	0-0	0	3.43
1994 Baltimore	AL	23	23	0	0	149	631	158	81	79	23	5	2	2	38	3	87	1	1	5	7	.417	0	0-0	0	4.77
1995 Baltimore	AL	27	18	0	3	115.2	483	117	70	67	18	5	3	3	30	0	65	0	0	8	6	.571	0	0-0	1	5.21
1996 Bos-Sea	AL	34	21	0	1	160.2	703	177	86	71	23	7	6	2	46	5	79	3	1	13	3	.813	0	0-0	1	3.98
1997 Seattle	AL	30	30	2	0	188.2	787	187	82	81	21	6	1	7	43	2	113	3	0	17	5	.773	0	0-0	0	3.86
1996 Boston	AL	23	10	0	1	90	405	111	50	45	14	4	3	1	27	2	50	2	1	7	1	.875	0	0-0	1	4.50
Seattle	AL	11	11	0	0	70.2	298	66	36	26	9	3	3	1	19	3	29	1	0	6	2	.750	0	0-0	0	3.31
11 ML YEARS		280	228	12	13	1466	6309	1559	776	711	175	63	40	39	477	33	869	30	8	89	84	.514	3	0-2	2	4.36

Bill Mueller

Bats: Both **Throws:** Right **Pos:** 3B-122; PH-10   **Ht:** 5'11" **Wt:** 175 **Born:** 3/17/71 **Age:** 27

		BATTING														BASERUNNING				PERCENTAGES		
Year Team	Lg	G	AB	H	2B	3B	HR	(Hm	Rd)	TB	R	RBI	TBB	IBB	SO	HBP	SH	SF	SB	CS	SB%	GDP	Avg	OBP	SLG
1993 Everett	A-	58	200	60	8	2	1	—	—	75	31	24	42	1	17	3	6	2	13	6	.68	3	.300	.425	.375
1994 San Jose	A+	120	431	130	20	9	5	—	—	183	79	72	103	11	47	3	1	6	4	8	.33	15	.302	.435	.425
1995 Shreveport	AA	88	330	102	16	2	1	—	—	125	56	39	53	2	36	4	1	5	6	5	.55	9	.309	.406	.379
Phoenix	AAA	41	172	51	13	6	2	—	—	82	23	19	19	0	31	0	6	1	0	0	.00	7	.297	.365	.477
1996 Phoenix	AAA	106	440	133	14	6	4	—	—	171	73	36	44	4	40	1	0	3	2	5	.29	11	.302	.365	.389
1996 San Francisco	NL	55	200	66	15	1	0	(0	0)	83	31	19	24	0	26	1	1	2	0	0	.00	2	.330	.401	.415
1997 San Francisco	NL	128	390	114	26	3	7	(5	2)	167	51	44	48	1	71	3	6	6	4	3	.57	10	.292	.369	.428
2 ML YEARS		183	590	180	41	4	7	(5	2)	250	82	63	72	1	97	4	7	8	4	3	.57	11	.305	.380	.424

Terry Mulholland

Pitches: Left   **Bats:** Right   **Pos:** SP-27; RP-13   **Ht:** 6'3"   **Wt:** 212   **Born:** 3/9/63   **Age:** 35

Year Team	Lg	G	GS	CG	GF	IP	BFP	H	R	ER	HR	SH	SF	HB	TBB	IBB	SO	WP	Bk	W	L	Pct.	ShO	Sv-Op	Hld	ERA
1986 San Francisco	NL	15	10	0	1	54.2	245	51	33	30	3	5	1	1	35	2	27	6	0	1	7	.125	0	0- -	—	4.94
1988 San Francisco	NL	9	6	2	1	46	191	50	20	19	3	5	0	1	7	0	18	1	0	2	1	.667	1	0-0	1	3.72
1989 SF-Phi	NL	25	18	2	4	115.1	513	137	66	63	8	7	1	4	36	3	66	3	0	4	7	.364	1	0-0	1	4.92
1990 Philadelphia	NL	33	26	6	2	180.2	746	172	78	67	15	7	12	2	42	7	75	7	2	9	10	.474	1	0-1	0	3.34
1991 Philadelphia	NL	34	34	8	0	232	956	231	100	93	15	11	6	3	49	2	142	3	0	16	13	.552	3	0-0	0	3.61
1992 Philadelphia	NL	32	32	12	0	229	937	227	101	97	14	10	7	3	46	3	125	3	0	13	11	.542	2	0-0	0	3.81
1993 Philadelphia	NL	29	28	7	0	191	786	177	80	69	20	5	4	3	40	2	116	5	0	12	9	.571	2	0-0	0	3.25
1994 New York	AL	24	19	2	4	120.2	542	150	94	87	24	3	4	3	37	1	72	5	0	6	7	.462	0	0-0	0	6.49
1995 San Francisco	NL	29	24	2	2	149	666	190	112	96	25	11	6	4	38	1	65	4	0	5	13	.278	0	0-0	0	5.80
1996 Phi-Sea	NL	33	33	3	0	202.2	871	232	112	105	22	11	8	5	49	4	86	6	0	13	11	.542	0	0-0	0	4.66
1997 ChN-SF	NL	40	27	1	5	186.2	794	190	100	88	24	14	4	11	51	3	99	3	0	6	13	.316	0	0-0	1	4.24
1989 San Francisco	NL	5	1	0	2	11	51	15	5	5	0	0	0	0	4	0	6	0	0	0	0	.000	0	0-0	1	4.09
Philadelphia	NL	20	17	2	2	104.1	462	122	61	58	8	7	1	4	32	3	60	3	0	4	7	.364	1	0-0	0	5.00
1996 Philadelphia	NL	21	21	3	0	133.1	571	157	74	69	17	6	5	3	21	1	52	5	0	8	7	.533	0	0-0	0	4.66
Seattle	AL	12	12	0	0	69.1	300	75	38	36	5	5	3	2	28	3	34	1	0	5	4	.556	0	0-0	0	4.67
1997 Chicago	NL	25	25	1	0	157	668	162	79	71	20	13	3	9	45	2	74	2	0	6	12	.333	0	0-0	0	4.07
San Francisco	NL	15	2	0	5	29.2	126	28	21	17	4	4	1	2	6	1	25	1	0	0	1	.000	0	0-0	1	5.16
11 ML YEARS		303	257	45	19	1707.2	7247	1807	896	814	173	92	53	40	430	28	891	46	2	87	102	.460	10	0- -	—	4.29

Bobby Munoz

Pitches: Right   **Bats:** Right   **Pos:** SP-7; RP-1   **Ht:** 6'8"   **Wt:** 259   **Born:** 3/3/68   **Age:** 30

Year Team	Lg	G	GS	CG	GF	IP	BFP	H	R	ER	HR	SH	SF	HB	TBB	IBB	SO	WP	Bk	W	L	Pct.	ShO	Sv-Op	Hld	ERA
1997 Las Vegas *	AAA	17	1	0	6	22.2	108	30	26	25	2	0	2	0	11	0	13	1	0	0	2	.000	0	0- -	—	9.93
Albuquerque *	AAA	18	0	0	6	31	145	43	17	15	2	0	1	0	15	3	20	1	0	0	3	.000	0	0- -	—	4.35
1993 New York	AL	38	0	0	12	45.2	208	48	27	27	1	1	3	0	26	5	33	2	0	3	3	.500	0	0-2	6	5.32
1994 Philadelphia	NL	21	14	1	1	104.1	447	101	40	31	8	5	5	1	35	0	59	5	1	7	5	.583	0	1-2	0	2.67
1995 Philadelphia	NL	3	3	0	0	15.2	70	15	13	10	2	0	2	3	9	0	6	0	0	0	2	.000	0	0-0	0	5.74
1996 Philadelphia	NL	6	6	0	0	25.1	123	42	28	22	5	2	1	1	7	1	8	0	0	0	3	.000	0	0-0	0	7.82
1997 Philadelphia	NL	8	7	0	1	33.1	161	47	35	33	4	2	3	2	15	1	20	3	1	1	5	.167	0	0-0	0	8.91
5 ML YEARS		76	30	1	14	224.1	1009	253	143	123	20	10	14	7	92	7	126	10	2	11	18	.379	0	1-4	6	4.93

Mike Munoz

Pitches: Left   **Bats:** Left   **Pos:** RP-64   **Ht:** 6'2"   **Wt:** 192   **Born:** 7/12/65   **Age:** 32

Year Team	Lg	G	GS	CG	GF	IP	BFP	H	R	ER	HR	SH	SF	HB	TBB	IBB	SO	WP	Bk	W	L	Pct.	ShO	Sv-Op	Hld	ERA
1989 Los Angeles	NL	3	0	0	1	2.2	14	5	5	5	1	0	0	0	2	0	3	0	0	0	0	.000	0	0-0	0	16.88
1990 Los Angeles	NL	8	0	0	3	5.2	24	6	2	2	0	1	0	0	3	0	2	0	0	0	1	.000	0	0-1	2	3.18
1991 Detroit	AL	6	0	0	4	9.1	46	14	10	10	0	0	1	0	5	0	3	1	0	0	0	.000	0	0-0	0	9.64
1992 Detroit	AL	65	0	0	15	48	210	44	16	16	3	4	2	0	25	6	23	2	0	1	2	.333	0	2-3	15	3.00
1993 Det-Col		29	0	0	10	21	101	25	14	11	2	3	2	0	15	4	17	2	0	2	2	.500	0	0-2	4	4.71
1994 Colorado	NL	57	0	0	8	45.2	200	37	22	19	3	2	1	0	31	5	32	2	0	4	2	.667	0	1-2	12	3.74
1995 Colorado	NL	64	0	0	19	43.2	208	54	38	36	9	2	2	1	27	0	37	5	0	2	4	.333	0	2-4	12	7.42
1996 Colorado	NL	54	0	0	7	44.2	203	55	33	33	4	3	1	1	16	2	45	0	0	2	2	.500	0	0-3	13	6.65
1997 Colorado	NL	64	0	0	16	45.2	192	52	25	23	4	0	2	0	13	0	26	3	0	3	3	.500	0	2-2	19	4.53
1993 Detroit	AL	8	0	0	3	3	19	4	2	2	1	0	0	0	6	1	1	0	0	0	1	.000	0	0-0	1	6.00
Colorado	NL	21	0	0	7	18	82	21	12	9	1	3	2	0	9	3	16	2	0	2	1	.667	0	0-2	1	4.50
9 ML YEARS		350	0	0	83	266.1	1198	292	165	155	26	15	11	2	137	17	188	15	0	14	16	.467	0	7-17	75	5.24

Eddie Murray

Bats: Both   **Throws:** Right   **Pos:** DH-45; PH-12   **Ht:** 6'2"   **Wt:** 220   **Born:** 2/24/56   **Age:** 42

																		BASERUNNING				PERCENTAGES		
Year Team	Lg	G	AB	H	2B	3B	HR	(Hm	Rd)	TB	R	RBI	TBB	IBB	SO	HBP	SH	SF	SB	CS	SB%	GDP	Avg	OBP	SLG
1997 Lk Elsinore *	A+	2	8	4	0	0	1	—	—	7	1	2	0	0	0	0	0	0	0	0	.00	0	.500	.500	.875
Albuquerque *	AAA	9	26	8	1	0	2	—	—	15	4	9	3	0	3	0	0	0	0	0	.00	0	.308	.379	.577
1977 Baltimore	AL	160	611	173	29	2	27	(14	13)	287	81	88	48	6	104	1	0	6	0	1	.00	22	.283	.333	.470
1978 Baltimore	AL	161	610	174	32	3	27	(10	17)	293	85	95	70	7	97	1	1	8	6	5	.55	15	.285	.356	.480
1979 Baltimore	AL	159	606	179	30	2	25	(10	15)	288	90	99	72	9	78	2	1	6	10	2	.83	16	.295	.369	.475
1980 Baltimore	AL	158	621	186	36	2	32	(10	22)	322	100	116	54	10	71	2	0	6	7	2	.78	18	.300	.354	.519
1981 Baltimore	AL	99	378	111	21	2	22	(12	10)	202	57	78	40	10	43	1	0	3	2	3	.40	10	.294	.360	.534
1982 Baltimore	AL	151	550	174	30	1	32	(16	16)	302	87	110	70	18	82	1	0	6	7	2	.78	17	.316	.391	.549
1983 Baltimore	AL	156	582	178	30	3	33	(16	17)	313	115	111	86	13	90	3	0	9	5	1	.83	13	.306	.393	.538
1984 Baltimore	AL	162	588	180	26	3	29	(18	11)	299	97	110	107	25	87	2	0	8	10	2	.83	9	.306	.410	.509
1985 Baltimore	AL	156	583	173	37	1	31	(16	15)	305	111	124	84	12	68	2	0	8	5	2	.71	8	.297	.383	.523
1986 Baltimore	AL	137	495	151	25	1	17	(9	8)	229	61	84	78	7	49	0	0	5	3	0	1.00	17	.305	.396	.463
1987 Baltimore	AL	160	618	171	28	3	30	(14	16)	295	89	91	73	6	80	0	0	3	1	2	.33	15	.277	.352	.477
1988 Baltimore	AL	161	603	171	27	2	28	(14	14)	286	75	84	75	8	78	0	0	4	5	2	.71	20	.284	.361	.474
1989 Los Angeles	NL	160	594	147	29	1	20	(4	16)	238	66	88	87	24	85	2	0	7	7	2	.78	12	.247	.342	.401
1990 Los Angeles	NL	155	558	184	22	3	26	(12	14)	290	96	95	82	21	64	1	0	4	8	5	.62	19	.330	.414	.520
1991 Los Angeles	NL	153	576	150	23	1	19	(11	8)	232	69	96	55	17	74	0	0	6	10	3	.77	17	.260	.321	.403
1992 New York	NL	156	551	144	37	2	16	(7	9)	233	64	93	66	8	74	0	0	8	4	2	.67	15	.261	.336	.423
1993 New York	NL	154	610	174	28	1	27	(15	12)	285	77	100	40	4	61	0	0	9	2	2	.50	24	.285	.325	.467

Year Team	Lg	G	AB	H	2B	3B	HR	(Hm	Rd)	TB	R	RBI	TBB	IBB	SO	HBP	SH	SF	SB	CS	SB%	GDP	Avg	OBP	SLG
1994 Cleveland	AL	108	433	110	21	1	17	(7	10)	184	57	76	31	6	53	0	0	3	8	4	.67	8	.254	.302	.425
1995 Cleveland	AL	113	436	141	21	0	21	(11	10)	225	68	82	39	5	65	0	0	5	5	1	.83	12	.323	.375	.516
1996 Cle-Bal	AL	152	566	147	21	1	22	(13	9)	236	69	79	61	6	87	0	0	10	4	0	1.00	19	.260	.327	.417
1997 Ana-LA	AL	55	167	37	7	0	3	(2	1)	53	13	18	15	0	26	0	0	3	1	0	1.00	10	.222	.281	.317
1996 Cleveland	AL	88	336	88	9	1	12	(7	5)	135	33	45	34	2	45	0	0	4	3	0	1.00	13	.262	.326	.402
Baltimore	AL	64	230	59	12	0	10	(6	4)	101	36	34	27	4	42	0	0	6	1	0	1.00	6	.257	.327	.439
1997 Anaheim	AL	46	160	35	7	0	3	(2	1)	51	13	15	13	0	24	0	0	3	1	0	1.00	8	.219	.273	.319
Los Angeles	NL	9	7	2	0	0	0	(0	0)	2	0	3	2	0	2	0	0	0	0	0	.00	2	.286	.444	.286
21 ML YEARS		3026	11336	3255	560	35	504	(242	262)	5397	1627	1917	1333	222	1516	18	2	128	110	43	.72	316	.287	.359	.476

Heath Murray

Pitches: Left **Bats:** Left **Pos:** RP-14; SP-3 **Ht:** 6'4" **Wt:** 205 **Born:** 4/19/73 **Age:** 25

Year Team	Lg	G	GS	CG	GF	IP	BFP	H	R	ER	HR	SH	SF	HB	TBB	IBB	SO	WP	Bk	W	L	Pct.	ShO	Sv-Op	Hld	ERA
1994 Spokane	A-	15	15	2	0	99.1	408	101	46	32	6	6	2	5	18	0	78	4	3	5	6	.455	1	0- —	—	2.90
1995 Rancho Cuca	A+	14	14	4	0	92.1	381	80	37	32	5	3	2	4	38	1	81	6	3	9	4	.692	2	0- —	—	3.12
Memphis	AA	14	14	0	0	77.1	363	83	36	29	1	3	3	4	42	1	71	7	1	5	4	.556	0	0- —	—	3.38
1996 Memphis	AA	27	27	1	0	174	728	154	83	62	13	4	3	6	60	2	156	7	3	13	9	.591	1	0- —	—	3.21
1997 Las Vegas	AAA	19	19	2	0	109	493	142	72	66	10	1	2	5	41	1	99	8	1	6	8	.429	1	0- —	—	5.45
1997 San Diego	NL	17	3	0	1	33.1	162	50	25	25	3	3	1	4	21	3	16	1	1	1	2	.333	0	0-0	1	6.75

Mike Mussina

Pitches: Right **Bats:** Left **Pos:** SP-33 **Ht:** 6'1" **Wt:** 180 **Born:** 12/8/68 **Age:** 29

Year Team	Lg	G	GS	CG	GF	IP	BFP	H	R	ER	HR	SH	SF	HB	TBB	IBB	SO	WP	Bk	W	L	Pct.	ShO	Sv-Op	Hld	ERA
1991 Baltimore	AL	12	12	2	0	87.2	349	77	31	28	7	3	7	2	21	0	52	3	1	4	5	.444	0	0-0	0	2.87
1992 Baltimore	AL	32	32	8	0	241	957	212	70	68	16	13	6	2	48	2	130	6	0	18	5	.783	4	0-0	0	2.54
1993 Baltimore	AL	25	25	3	0	167.2	693	163	84	83	20	6	4	3	44	2	117	5	0	14	6	.700	2	0-0	0	4.46
1994 Baltimore	AL	24	24	3	0	176.1	712	163	63	60	19	3	9	1	42	1	99	0	0	16	5	.762	0	0-0	0	3.06
1995 Baltimore	AL	32	32	7	0	221.2	882	187	86	81	24	2	2	1	50	4	158	2	0	19	9	.679	4	0-0	0	3.29
1996 Baltimore	AL	36	36	4	0	243.1	1039	264	137	130	31	4	4	3	69	0	204	3	0	19	11	.633	1	0-0	0	4.81
1997 Baltimore	AL	33	33	4	0	224.2	905	197	87	80	27	3	2	3	54	3	218	5	0	15	8	.652	1	0-0	0	3.20
7 ML YEARS		194	194	31	0	1362.1	5537	1263	558	530	144	34	29	14	328	12	978	24	1	105	49	.682	12	0-0	0	3.50

Greg Myers

Bats: Left **Throws:** Right **Pos:** C-40; PH-25; DH-10 **Ht:** 6'2" **Wt:** 215 **Born:** 4/14/66 **Age:** 32

Year Team	Lg	G	AB	H	2B	3B	HR	(Hm	Rd)	TB	R	RBI	TBB	IBB	SO	HBP	SH	SF	SB	CS	SB%	GDP	Avg	OBP	SLG
1987 Toronto	AL	7	9	1	0	0	0	(0	0)	1	1	0	0	0	3	0	0	0	0	0	.00	2	.111	.111	.111
1989 Toronto	AL	17	44	5	2	0	0	(0	0)	7	0	1	2	0	9	0	0	1	0	1	.00	2	.114	.152	.159
1990 Toronto	AL	87	250	59	7	1	5	(3	2)	83	33	22	22	0	33	0	1	4	0	1	.00	12	.236	.293	.332
1991 Toronto	AL	107	309	81	22	0	8	(5	3)	127	25	36	21	4	45	0	0	3	0	0	.00	13	.262	.306	.411
1992 Tor-Cal	AL	30	78	18	7	0	1	(0	1)	28	4	13	5	0	11	0	1	2	0	0	.00	2	.231	.271	.359
1993 California	AL	108	290	74	10	0	7	(4	3)	105	27	40	17	2	47	2	3	3	3	3	.50	8	.255	.298	.362
1994 California	AL	45	126	31	6	0	2	(1	1)	43	10	8	10	3	27	0	5	1	0	2	.00	3	.246	.299	.341
1995 California	AL	85	273	71	12	2	9	(6	3)	114	35	38	17	3	49	1	1	2	0	1	.00	4	.260	.304	.418
1996 Minnesota	AL	97	329	94	22	3	6	(3	3)	140	37	47	19	3	52	0	0	5	0	0	.00	11	.286	.320	.426
1997 Min-Atl	AL	71	174	45	11	1	5	(3	2)	73	24	29	17	2	32	0	0	4	0	0	.00	4	.259	.321	.420
1992 Toronto	AL	22	61	14	6	0	1	(0	1)	23	4	13	5	0	5	0	0	2	0	0	.00	2	.230	.279	.377
California	AL	8	17	4	1	0	0	(0	0)	5	0	0	0	0	6	0	1	0	0	0	.00	0	.235	.235	.294
1997 Minnesota	AL	62	165	44	11	1	5	(3	2)	72	24	28	16	2	29	0	0	4	0	0	.00	4	.267	.328	.436
Atlanta	NL	9	9	1	0	0	0	(0	0)	1	0	1	1	0	3	0	0	0	0	0	.00	0	.111	.200	.111
10 ML YEARS		654	1882	479	99	7	43	(25	18)	721	196	234	130	17	308	3	11	22	3	8	.27	61	.255	.300	.383

Mike Myers

Pitches: Left **Bats:** Left **Pos:** RP-88 **Ht:** 6'4" **Wt:** 197 **Born:** 6/26/69 **Age:** 29

Year Team	Lg	G	GS	CG	GF	IP	BFP	H	R	ER	HR	SH	SF	HB	TBB	IBB	SO	WP	Bk	W	L	Pct.	ShO	Sv-Op	Hld	ERA
1995 Fla-Det		13	0	0	5	8.1	42	11	7	7	1	0	1	2	7	0	4	0	2	1	0	1.000	0	0-1	1	7.56
1996 Detroit		83	0	0	25	64.2	298	70	41	36	6	2	1	4	34	8	69	2	0	1	5	.167	0	6-8	17	5.01
1997 Detroit	AL	88	0	0	23	53.2	246	58	36	34	12	3	2	3	25	2	50	0	0	0	4	.000	0	2-5	18	5.70
1995 Florida	NL	2	0	0	2	2	9	1	0	0	0	0	0	0	3	0	0	0	0	0	0	.000	0	0-0	0	0.00
Detroit	AL	11	0	0	3	6.1	33	10	7	7	1	0	1	2	4	0	4	0	0	1	0	1.000	0	0-1	1	9.95
3 ML YEARS		184	0	0	53	126.2	586	139	84	77	19	6	5	8	66	10	123	2	0	2	9	.182	0	8-14	36	5.47

Randy Myers

Pitches: Left **Bats:** Left **Pos:** RP-61 **Ht:** 6'1" **Wt:** 225 **Born:** 9/19/62 **Age:** 35

Year Team	Lg	G	GS	CG	GF	IP	BFP	H	R	ER	HR	SH	SF	HB	TBB	IBB	SO	WP	Bk	W	L	Pct.	ShO	Sv-Op	Hld	ERA
1985 New York	NL	1	0	0	1	2	7	0	0	0	0	0	0	0	1	0	2	0	0	0	0	.000	0	0-0	0	0.00
1986 New York	NL	10	0	0	5	10.2	53	11	5	5	1	0	0	1	9	1	13	0	0	0	0	.000	0	0-0	0	4.22
1987 New York	NL	54	0	0	18	75	314	61	36	33	6	7	6	0	30	5	92	3	0	3	6	.333	0	6-9	7	3.96

Year Team	Lg	G	GS	CG	GF	IP	BFP	H	R	ER	HR	SH	SF	HB	TBB	IBB	SO	WP	Bk	W	L	Pct.	ShO	Sv-Op	Hld	ERA
1988 New York	NL	55	0	0	44	68	261	45	15	13	5	3	2	2	17	2	69	2	0	7	3	.700	0	26-29	3	1.72
1989 New York	NL	65	0	0	47	84.1	349	62	23	22	4	6	2	0	40	4	88	3	0	7	4	.636	0	24-29	2	2.35
1990 Cincinnati	NL	66	0	0	59	86.2	353	59	24	20	6	4	2	3	38	8	98	2	1	4	6	.400	0	31-37	0	2.08
1991 Cincinnati	NL	58	12	1	18	132	575	116	61	52	8	8	6	1	80	5	108	2	1	6	13	.316	0	6-10	8	3.55
1992 San Diego	NL	66	0	0	57	79.2	348	84	38	38	7	7	5	1	34	3	66	5	0	3	6	.333	0	38-46	0	4.29
1993 Chicago	NL	73	0	0	69	75.1	313	65	26	26	7	1	2	1	26	2	86	3	0	2	4	.333	0	53-59	0	3.11
1994 Chicago	NL	38	0	0	34	40.1	174	40	18	17	3	3	1	0	16	1	32	2	0	1	5	.167	0	21-26	0	3.79
1995 Chicago	NL	57	0	0	47	55.2	240	49	25	24	7	2	3	0	28	1	59	0	0	1	2	.333	0	38-44	0	3.88
1996 Baltimore	AL	62	0	0	50	58.2	262	60	24	23	7	3	3	1	29	4	74	3	0	4	4	.500	0	31-38	2	3.53
1997 Baltimore	AL	61	0	0	57	59.2	241	47	12	10	2	2	0	0	22	2	56	3	0	2	3	.400	0	45-46	1	1.51
13 ML YEARS		666	12	1	506	828	3490	699	307	283	63	46	32	10	370	38	843	28	2	40	56	.417	0	319-373	24	3.08

Rod Myers

Bats: L **Throws:** L **Pos:** LF-12; RF-10; CF-9; PH-7 **Ht:** 6'0" **Wt:** 190 **Born:** 1/14/73 **Age:** 25

Year Team	Lg	G	AB	H	2B	3B	HR	(Hm	Rd)	TB	R	RBI	TBB	IBB	SO	HBP	SH	SF	SB	CS	SB%	GDP	Avg	OBP	SLG
1991 Royals	R	44	133	37	2	3	1	—	—	48	14	18	6	1	27	5	0	1	12	2	.86	1	.278	.331	.361
Baseball Cy	A+	4	11	2	0	0	0	—	—	2	1	0	0	0	5	0	0	0	1	1	.50	1	.182	.182	.182
1992 Appleton	A	71	218	48	10	2	4	—	—	74	31	30	39	1	67	2	4	4	25	6	.81	3	.220	.338	.339
1993 Rockford	A	129	474	123	24	5	9	—	—	184	69	68	58	6	117	5	6	4	49	16	.75	7	.259	.344	.388
1994 Wilmington	A+	126	457	120	20	4	12	—	—	184	76	65	67	3	93	6	12	1	31	11	.74	4	.263	.363	.403
1995 Wichita	AA	131	499	153	22	6	7	—	—	208	71	62	34	3	77	4	8	3	29	16	.64	7	.307	.354	.417
1996 Omaha	AAA	112	411	120	27	1	16	—	—	197	68	54	49	6	106	9	9	3	37	8	.82	6	.292	.377	.479
1997 Wichita	AA	4	16	5	2	0	0	—	—	7	3	3	3	0	3	0	0	0	0	1	.00	0	.313	.421	.438
Omaha	AAA	38	142	36	10	0	2	—	—	52	21	10	15	0	37	0	4	1	6	4	.60	0	.254	.323	.366
1996 Kansas City	AL	22	63	18	7	0	1	(1	0)	28	9	11	7	0	16	0	0	0	3	2	.60	1	.286	.357	.444
1997 Kansas City	AL	31	101	26	7	0	2	(1	1)	39	14	9	17	0	22	1	2	0	4	0	1.00	2	.257	.370	.386
2 ML YEARS		53	164	44	14	0	3	(2	1)	67	23	20	24	0	38	1	2	0	7	2	.78	3	.268	.365	.409

Rodney Myers

Pitches: Right **Bats:** Right **Pos:** RP-4; SP-1 **Ht:** 6'1" **Wt:** 200 **Born:** 6/26/69 **Age:** 29

Year Team	Lg	G	GS	CG	GF	IP	BFP	H	R	ER	HR	SH	SF	HB	TBB	IBB	SO	WP	Bk	W	L	Pct.	ShO	Sv-Op	Hld	ERA
1990 Eugene	A-	6	4	0	0	22.2	98	19	9	3	2	0	1	0	13	0	17	1	1	0	2	.000	0	0- -	—	1.19
1991 Appleton	A	9	4	0	1	27.2	127	22	9	8	0	1	1	1	26	0	29	1	1	1	1	.500	0	0- -	—	2.60
1992 Lethbridge	R+	15	15	5	0	103.1	452	93	57	46	3	4	2	5	61	1	76	14	2	5	8	.385	0	0- -	—	4.01
1993 Rockford	A	12	12	5	0	85.1	322	65	22	17	3	2	2	1	18	0	65	3	1	7	3	.700	2	0- -	—	1.79
Memphis	AA	12	12	1	0	65.2	294	73	46	41	8	2	2	10	32	0	42	3	3	3	6	.333	1	0- -	—	5.62
1994 Wilmington	A+	4	0	0	2	9.1	37	9	6	5	1	0	0	1	0	0	9	1	0	1	1	.500	0	1- -	—	4.82
Memphis	AA	42	0	0	30	69.2	284	45	20	8	3	2	4	5	29	2	53	3	0	5	1	.833	0	9- -	—	1.03
1995 Omaha	AAA	38	0	0	17	48.1	212	52	26	22	5	2	3	0	19	1	38	1	1	4	5	.444	0	2- -	—	4.10
1997 Iowa	AAA	24	23	1	0	140.2	590	140	76	64	18	2	7	6	38	1	79	3	0	7	8	.467	0	0- -	—	4.09
1996 Chicago	NL	45	0	0	8	67.1	298	61	38	35	6	1	5	3	38	3	50	4	1	2	1	.667	0	0-0	1	4.68
1997 Chicago	NL	5	1	0	2	9	44	12	6	6	1	0	0	1	7	1	6	0	0	0	0	.000	0	0-0	0	6.00
2 ML YEARS		50	1	0	10	76.1	342	73	44	41	7	1	5	4	45	4	56	4	1	2	1	.667	0	0-0	1	4.83

Tim Naehring

Bats: Right **Throws:** Right **Pos:** 3B-68; PH-2; DH-1 **Ht:** 6'2" **Wt:** 203 **Born:** 2/1/67 **Age:** 31

Year Team	Lg	G	AB	H	2B	3B	HR	(Hm	Rd)	TB	R	RBI	TBB	IBB	SO	HBP	SH	SF	SB	CS	SB%	GDP	Avg	OBP	SLG
1990 Boston	AL	24	85	23	6	0	2	(2	0)	35	10	12	8	1	15	0	0	0	0	0	.00	2	.271	.333	.412
1991 Boston	AL	20	55	6	1	0	0	(0	0)	7	1	3	6	0	15	0	4	0	0	0	.00	0	.109	.197	.127
1992 Boston	AL	72	186	43	8	0	3	(0	3)	60	12	14	18	0	31	3	6	1	0	0	.00	1	.231	.308	.323
1993 Boston	AL	39	127	42	10	0	1	(0	1)	55	14	17	10	0	26	0	3	1	1	0	1.00	0	.331	.377	.433
1994 Boston	AL	80	297	82	18	1	7	(4	3)	123	41	42	30	1	56	4	7	1	1	3	.25	11	.276	.349	.414
1995 Boston	AL	126	433	133	27	2	10	(5	5)	194	61	57	77	5	66	4	4	2	0	2	.00	16	.307	.415	.448
1996 Boston	AL	116	430	124	16	0	17	(9	8)	191	77	65	49	4	63	4	2	4	2	1	.67	16	.288	.363	.444
1997 Boston	AL	70	259	74	18	1	9	(4	5)	121	38	40	38	0	40	1	0	3	1	1	.50	10	.286	.375	.467
8 ML YEARS		547	1872	527	104	4	49	(24	25)	786	254	250	236	11	312	16	26	12	5	7	.42	57	.282	.365	.420

Charles Nagy

Pitches: Right **Bats:** Left **Pos:** SP-34 **Ht:** 6'3" **Wt:** 200 **Born:** 5/5/67 **Age:** 31

Year Team	Lg	G	GS	CG	GF	IP	BFP	H	R	ER	HR	SH	SF	HB	TBB	IBB	SO	WP	Bk	W	L	Pct.	ShO	Sv-Op	Hld	ERA
1990 Cleveland	AL	9	8	0	1	45.2	208	58	31	30	7	1	1	1	21	1	26	1	1	2	4	.333	0	0-0	0	5.91
1991 Cleveland	AL	33	33	6	0	211.1	914	228	103	97	15	5	9	6	66	7	109	6	2	10	15	.400	1	0-0	0	4.13
1992 Cleveland	AL	33	33	10	0	252	1018	245	91	83	11	6	9	2	57	1	169	7	0	17	10	.630	3	0-0	0	2.96
1993 Cleveland	AL	9	9	1	0	48.2	223	66	38	34	6	2	1	2	13	1	30	2	0	2	6	.250	0	0-0	0	6.29
1994 Cleveland	AL	23	23	3	0	169.1	717	175	76	65	15	2	2	5	48	1	108	5	1	10	8	.556	0	0-0	0	3.45
1995 Cleveland	AL	29	29	2	0	178	771	194	95	90	20	2	5	6	61	0	139	2	1	16	6	.727	1	0-0	0	4.55
1996 Cleveland	AL	32	32	5	0	222	921	217	88	84	21	2	4	3	61	2	167	7	0	17	5	.773	0	0-0	0	3.41
1997 Cleveland	AL	34	34	1	0	227	991	253	115	108	27	5	6	7	77	4	149	5	0	15	11	.577	1	0-0	0	4.28
8 ML YEARS		202	201	28	1	1354	5763	1436	638	591	122	25	37	32	404	17	897	35	4	89	65	.578	6	0-0	0	3.93

Bob Natal

Bats: Right **Throws:** Right **Pos:** C-4 **Ht:** 5'11" **Wt:** 190 **Born:** 11/13/65 **Age:** 32

Year Team	Lg	G	AB	H	2B	3B	HR	(Hm	Rd)	TB	R	RBI	TBB	IBB	SO	HBP	SH	SF	SB	CS	SB%	GDP	Avg	OBP	SLG
1997 Charlotte *	AAA	78	251	67	17	2	11	—	—	121	34	49	19	0	37	1	0	2	2	2	.50	9	.267	.319	.482
1992 Montreal	NL	5	6	0	0	0	0	(0	0)	0	0	0	1	0	1	0	0	0	0	0	.00	1	.000	.143	.000
1993 Florida	NL	41	117	25	4	1	1	(0	1)	34	3	6	6	0	22	4	3	1	1	0	1.00	6	.214	.273	.291
1994 Florida	NL	10	29	8	2	0	0	(0	0)	10	2	2	5	0	5	0	0	0	1	0	1.00	1	.276	.382	.345
1995 Florida	NL	16	43	10	2	1	2	(2	0)	20	2	6	1	0	9	0	1	1	0	0	.00	0	.233	.244	.465
1996 Florida	NL	44	90	12	1	1	0	(0	0)	15	4	2	15	5	31	0	0	0	0	1	.00	3	.133	.257	.167
1997 Florida	NL	4	4	2	1	0	1	(1	0)	6	2	3	2	0	0	0	0	0	0	0	.00	0	.500	.571	1.500
6 ML YEARS		120	289	57	10	3	4	(3	1)	85	13	19	30	5	68	4	4	3	2	1	.67	11	.197	.279	.294

Dan Naulty

Pitches: Right **Bats:** Right **Pos:** RP-29 **Ht:** 6'6" **Wt:** 211 **Born:** 1/6/70 **Age:** 28

Year Team	Lg	G	GS	CG	GF	IP	BFP	H	R	ER	HR	SH	SF	HB	TBB	IBB	SO	WP	Bk	W	L	Pct.	ShO	Sv-Op	Hld	ERA
1992 Kenosha	A	6	2	0	1	18	83	22	12	11	3	1	0	1	7	0	14	1	1	0	1	.000	0	0- -	—	5.50
1993 Ft. Myers	A+	7	6	0	0	30	148	41	22	19	4	1	1	6	14	1	20	3	0	0	0	.000	0	0- -	—	5.70
Ft. Wayne	A	18	18	3	0	116	478	101	45	42	5	3	1	2	48	0	96	7	5	6	8	.429	2	0- -	—	3.26
1994 Ft. Myers	A+	16	15	1	1	88.1	380	78	35	29	6	1	5	3	32	2	83	5	0	8	4	.667	0	0- -	—	2.95
Nashville	AA	9	9	0	0	47.1	208	48	32	31	4	2	5	1	22	1	29	3	0	0	7	.000	0	0- -	—	5.89
1995 Salt Lake	AAA	42	8	0	19	90.1	393	92	55	52	10	2	1	2	47	2	76	6	0	2	6	.250	0	4- -	—	5.18
1997 Twins	R	2	2	0	0	4	15	2	1	1	0	1	0	3	0	3	0	0	0	0	.000	0	0- -	—	2.25
Salt Lake	AAA	6	0	0	2	6.1	34	11	10	8	4	1	0	0	2	0	5	2	0	0	1	.000	0	0- -	—	11.37
1996 Minnesota	AL	49	0	0	15	57	245	43	26	24	5	2	0	0	35	3	56	2	0	3	2	.600	0	4-9	4	3.79
1997 Minnesota	AL	29	0	0	8	30.2	128	29	20	20	8	0	4	0	10	0	23	3	0	1	1	.500	0	1-3	8	5.87
2 ML YEARS		78	0	0	23	87.2	373	72	46	44	13	2	4	0	45	3	79	5	0	4	3	.571	0	5-12	12	4.52

Jaime Navarro

Pitches: Right **Bats:** Right **Pos:** SP-33 **Ht:** 6'4" **Wt:** 230 **Born:** 3/27/68 **Age:** 30

Year Team	Lg	G	GS	CG	GF	IP	BFP	H	R	ER	HR	SH	SF	HB	TBB	IBB	SO	WP	Bk	W	L	Pct.	ShO	Sv-Op	Hld	ERA
1989 Milwaukee	AL	19	17	1	1	109.2	470	119	47	38	6	5	2	1	32	3	56	3	0	7	8	.467	0	0-0	0	3.12
1990 Milwaukee	AL	32	22	3	2	149.1	654	176	83	74	11	4	5	4	41	3	75	6	5	8	7	.533	0	1-2	3	4.46
1991 Milwaukee	AL	34	34	10	0	234	1002	237	117	102	18	7	8	6	73	3	114	10	0	15	12	.556	2	0-0	0	3.92
1992 Milwaukee	AL	34	34	5	0	246	1004	224	98	91	14	9	6	1	64	4	100	6	0	17	11	.607	3	0-0	0	3.33
1993 Milwaukee	AL	35	34	5	0	214.1	955	254	135	127	21	6	17	11	73	4	114	11	0	11	12	.478	1	0-0	0	5.33
1994 Milwaukee	AL	29	10	0	7	89.2	411	115	71	66	10	2	4	4	35	4	65	3	0	4	9	.308	0	0-0	0	6.62
1995 Chicago	NL	29	29	1	0	200.1	837	194	79	73	19	2	3	3	56	7	128	1	0	14	6	.700	1	0-0	0	3.28
1996 Chicago	NL	35	35	4	0	236.2	1007	244	116	103	25	10	7	10	72	5	158	10	0	15	12	.556	1	0-0	0	3.92
1997 Chicago	AL	33	33	2	0	209.2	957	267	155	135	22	2	14	3	73	6	142	14	1	9	14	.391	0	0-0	0	5.79
9 ML YEARS		280	248	31	10	1689.2	7297	1830	901	809	146	47	73	48	519	39	952	64	6	100	91	.524	8	1-2	3	4.31

Denny Neagle

Pitches: Left **Bats:** Left **Pos:** SP-34 **Ht:** 6'2" **Wt:** 216 **Born:** 9/13/68 **Age:** 29

Year Team	Lg	G	GS	CG	GF	IP	BFP	H	R	ER	HR	SH	SF	HB	TBB	IBB	SO	WP	Bk	W	L	Pct.	ShO	Sv-Op	Hld	ERA
1991 Minnesota	AL	7	3	0	2	20	92	28	9	9	3	0	0	0	7	2	14	1	0	0	1	.000	0	0-0	0	4.05
1992 Pittsburgh	NL	55	6	0	8	86.1	380	81	46	43	9	4	3	2	43	8	77	3	2	4	6	.400	0	2-4	5	4.48
1993 Pittsburgh	NL	50	7	0	13	81.1	360	82	49	48	10	1	1	3	37	3	73	5	0	3	5	.375	0	1-1	6	5.31
1994 Pittsburgh	NL	24	24	2	0	137	587	135	80	78	18	7	6	3	49	3	122	2	0	9	10	.474	0	0-0	0	5.12
1995 Pittsburgh	NL	31	31	5	0	209.2	876	221	91	80	20	13	6	3	45	3	150	6	0	13	8	.619	1	0-0	0	3.43
1996 Pit-Atl	NL	33	33	2	0	221.1	910	226	93	86	26	10	4	3	48	2	149	3	1	16	9	.640	0	0-0	0	3.50
1997 Atlanta	NL	34	34	4	0	233.1	947	204	87	77	18	12	6	6	49	5	172	3	0	20	5	.800	4	0-0	0	2.97
1996 Pittsburgh	NL	27	27	1	0	182.2	745	186	67	62	21	9	3	3	34	2	131	2	1	14	6	.700	0	0-0	0	3.05
Atlanta	NL	6	6	1	0	38.2	165	40	26	24	5	1	1	0	14	0	18	1	0	2	3	.400	0	0-0	0	5.59
7 ML YEARS		234	138	13	23	989	4152	977	455	421	104	47	26	20	278	26	757	23	3	65	44	.596	5	3-5	11	3.83

Jeff Nelson

Pitches: Right **Bats:** Right **Pos:** RP-77 **Ht:** 6'8" **Wt:** 235 **Born:** 11/17/66 **Age:** 31

Year Team	Lg	G	GS	CG	GF	IP	BFP	H	R	ER	HR	SH	SF	HB	TBB	IBB	SO	WP	Bk	W	L	Pct.	ShO	Sv-Op	Hld	ERA
1992 Seattle	AL	66	0	0	27	81	352	71	34	31	7	9	3	6	44	12	46	2	0	1	7	.125	0	6-14	6	3.44
1993 Seattle	AL	71	0	0	13	60	269	57	30	29	5	2	4	8	34	10	61	2	0	5	3	.625	0	1-11	17	4.35
1994 Seattle	AL	28	0	0	7	42.1	185	35	18	13	3	1	1	8	20	4	44	2	0	0	0	.000	0	0-0	2	2.76
1995 Seattle	AL	62	0	0	24	78.2	318	58	21	19	4	5	3	6	27	5	96	1	0	7	3	.700	0	2-4	14	2.17
1996 New York	AL	73	0	0	27	74.1	328	75	38	36	6	3	1	2	36	1	91	4	0	4	4	.500	0	2-4	10	4.36
1997 New York	AL	77	0	0	22	78.2	327	53	32	25	7	7	2	4	37	12	81	4	0	3	7	.300	0	2-8	22	2.86
6 ML YEARS		377	0	0	120	415	1779	349	173	153	32	27	14	34	198	44	419	15	0	20	24	.455	0	13-41	71	3.32

152

Robb Nen

Pitches: Right **Bats:** Right **Pos:** RP-73   **Ht:** 6'4" **Wt:** 190 **Born:** 11/28/69 **Age:** 28

		HOW MUCH HE PITCHED						WHAT HE GAVE UP										THE RESULTS						
Year Team	Lg	G	GS	CG	GF	IP	BFP	H	R	ER	HR	SH	SF	HB	TBB	IBB	SO	WP	Bk	W	L	Pct.	ShO	Sv-Op Hld	ERA
1993 Tex-Fla		24	4	0	5	56	272	63	45	42	6	1	2	0	46	0	39	6	1	2	1	.667	0	0-0 0	6.75
1994 Florida	NL	44	0	0	28	58	228	46	20	19	6	3	1	0	17	2	60	3	2	5	5	.500	0	15-15 1	2.95
1995 Florida	NL	62	0	0	54	65.2	279	62	26	24	6	0	1	1	23	3	68	2	0	0	7	.000	0	23-29 0	3.29
1996 Florida	NL	75	0	0	66	83	326	67	21	18	2	5	1	1	21	6	92	4	0	5	1	.833	0	35-42 0	1.95
1997 Florida	NL	73	0	0	65	74	332	72	35	32	7	1	3	0	40	7	81	5	0	9	3	.750	0	35-42 0	3.89
1993 Texas	AL	9	3	0	3	22.2	113	28	17	16	1	0	1	0	26	0	12	2	1	1	1	.500	0	0-0 0	6.35
Florida	NL	15	1	0	2	33.1	159	35	28	26	5	1	1	0	20	0	27	4	0	1	0	1.000	0	0-0 0	7.02
5 ML YEARS		278	4	0	218	336.2	1437	310	147	135	27	10	8	2	147	18	340	20	3	21	17	.553	0	108-128 1	3.61

Phil Nevin

Bats: R **Throws:** R **Pos:** LF-40; DH-30; PH-20; 3B-17; 1B-7; C-1   **Ht:** 6'2" **Wt:** 210 **Born:** 1/19/71 **Age:** 27

					BATTING														BASERUNNING				PERCENTAGES		
Year Team	Lg	G	AB	H	2B	3B	HR	(Hm	Rd)	TB	R	RBI	TBB	IBB	SO	HBP	SH	SF	SB	CS	SB%	GDP	Avg	OBP	SLG
1997 Lakeland *	A+	3	9	5	1	0	1	—	—	9	3	4	3	0	2	0	0	0	0	0	.00	0	.556	.667	1.000
Toledo *	AAA	5	19	3	0	0	1	—	—	6	1	3	2	1	9	0	0	0	0	0	.00	0	.158	.238	.316
1995 Hou-Det		47	156	28	4	1	2	(2	0)	40	13	13	18	1	40	4	1	0	1	0	1.00	5	.179	.281	.256
1996 Detroit	AL	38	120	35	5	0	8	(3	5)	64	15	19	8	0	39	1	0	1	1	0	1.00	1	.292	.338	.533
1997 Detroit	AL	93	251	59	16	1	9	(4	5)	104	32	35	25	1	68	1	0	1	0	1	.00	5	.235	.306	.414
1995 Houston	NL	18	60	7	1	0	0	(0	0)	8	4	1	7	1	13	1	1	0	1	0	1.00	1	.117	.221	.133
Detroit	AL	29	96	21	3	1	2	(2	0)	32	9	12	11	0	27	3	0	0	0	0	.00	3	.219	.318	.333
3 ML YEARS		178	527	122	25	2	19	(9	10)	208	60	67	51	2	147	6	1	2	2	1	.67	11	.231	.305	.395

Marc Newfield

Bats: Right **Throws:** Right **Pos:** LF-28; DH-18; PH-5   **Ht:** 6'4" **Wt:** 205 **Born:** 10/19/72 **Age:** 25

					BATTING														BASERUNNING				PERCENTAGES		
Year Team	Lg	G	AB	H	2B	3B	HR	(Hm	Rd)	TB	R	RBI	TBB	IBB	SO	HBP	SH	SF	SB	CS	SB%	GDP	Avg	OBP	SLG
1997 Tucson *	AAA	8	31	10	1	0	1	—	—	14	4	3	4	1	6	0	0	0	0	0	.00	1	.323	.400	.452
1993 Seattle	AL	22	66	15	3	0	1	(1	0)	21	5	7	2	0	8	1	0	1	0	1	.00	2	.227	.257	.318
1994 Seattle	AL	12	38	7	1	0	1	(0	1)	11	3	4	2	0	4	0	0	0	0	0	.00	1	.184	.225	.289
1995 Sea-SD		45	140	33	8	1	4	(1	3)	55	13	21	5	1	24	1	0	0	0	0	.00	5	.236	.267	.393
1996 SD-Mil		133	370	103	26	0	12	(5	7)	165	48	57	27	2	70	6	0	7	1	2	.33	8	.278	.332	.446
1997 Milwaukee	AL	50	157	36	8	0	1	(0	1)	47	14	18	14	0	27	2	0	3	0	0	.00	3	.229	.295	.299
1995 Seattle	AL	24	85	16	3	0	3	(0	3)	28	7	14	3	1	16	1	0	0	0	0	.00	4	.188	.225	.329
San Diego	NL	21	55	17	5	1	1	(1	0)	27	6	7	2	0	8	0	0	0	0	0	.00	1	.309	.333	.491
1996 San Diego	NL	84	191	48	11	0	5	(1	4)	74	27	26	16	1	44	2	0	3	1	1	.50	7	.251	.311	.387
Milwaukee	AL	49	179	55	15	0	7	(4	3)	91	21	31	11	1	26	4	0	4	0	1	.00	1	.307	.354	.508
5 ML YEARS		262	771	194	46	1	19	(7	12)	299	83	107	50	3	133	10	0	11	1	3	.25	21	.252	.302	.388

Warren Newson

Bats: L **Throws:** L **Pos:** RF-44; PH-34; LF-20; DH-9   **Ht:** 5'7" **Wt:** 202 **Born:** 7/3/64 **Age:** 33

					BATTING														BASERUNNING				PERCENTAGES		
Year Team	Lg	G	AB	H	2B	3B	HR	(Hm	Rd)	TB	R	RBI	TBB	IBB	SO	HBP	SH	SF	SB	CS	SB%	GDP	Avg	OBP	SLG
1997 Tulsa *	AA	2	7	1	0	0	1	—	—	4	1	2	2	0	1	0	0	0	0	0	.00	0	.143	.333	.571
1991 Chicago	AL	71	132	39	5	0	4	(1	3)	56	20	25	28	1	34	0	0	0	2	2	.50	4	.295	.419	.424
1992 Chicago	AL	63	136	30	3	0	1	(1	0)	36	19	11	37	2	38	0	0	0	3	0	1.00	4	.221	.387	.265
1993 Chicago	AL	26	40	12	0	0	2	(2	0)	18	9	6	9	1	12	0	0	0	0	0	.00	2	.300	.429	.450
1994 Chicago	AL	63	102	26	5	0	2	(2	0)	37	16	7	14	1	23	0	2	0	1	0	1.00	1	.255	.345	.363
1995 ChA-Sea	AL	84	157	41	2	2	5	(4	1)	62	34	15	39	0	45	1	0	0	2	1	.67	3	.261	.411	.395
1996 Texas	AL	91	235	60	14	1	10	(5	5)	106	34	31	37	1	82	0	0	1	3	0	1.00	4	.255	.355	.451
1997 Texas	AL	81	169	36	10	1	10	(2	8)	78	23	23	31	2	53	0	0	1	3	0	1.00	4	.213	.333	.462
1995 Chicago	AL	51	85	20	0	2	3	(3	0)	33	19	9	23	0	27	1	0	0	1	1	.50	2	.235	.404	.388
Seattle	AL	33	72	21	2	0	2	(1	1)	29	15	6	16	0	18	0	0	0	1	0	1.00	1	.292	.420	.403
7 ML YEARS		479	971	244	39	4	34	(17	17)	393	155	118	195	8	287	1	2	2	14	3	.82	23	.251	.376	.405

Melvin Nieves

Bats: B **Throws:** R **Pos:** RF-101; PH-19; DH-12; CF-2   **Ht:** 6'2" **Wt:** 210 **Born:** 12/28/71 **Age:** 26

					BATTING														BASERUNNING				PERCENTAGES		
Year Team	Lg	G	AB	H	2B	3B	HR	(Hm	Rd)	TB	R	RBI	TBB	IBB	SO	HBP	SH	SF	SB	CS	SB%	GDP	Avg	OBP	SLG
1992 Atlanta	NL	12	19	4	1	0	0	(0	0)	5	0	1	2	0	7	0	0	0	0	0	.00	0	.211	.286	.263
1993 San Diego	NL	19	47	9	0	0	2	(2	0)	15	4	3	3	0	21	1	0	0	0	0	.00	0	.191	.255	.319
1994 San Diego	NL	10	19	5	1	0	1	(0	1)	9	2	4	3	0	10	0	0	0	0	0	.00	0	.263	.364	.474
1995 San Diego	NL	98	234	48	6	1	14	(5	9)	98	32	38	19	0	88	5	1	3	2	3	.40	9	.205	.276	.419
1996 Detroit	AL	120	431	106	23	4	24	(10	14)	209	71	60	44	2	158	6	0	3	1	2	.33	10	.246	.322	.485
1997 Detroit	AL	116	359	82	18	1	20	(7	13)	162	46	64	39	6	157	5	0	2	1	7	.13	3	.228	.311	.451
6 ML YEARS		375	1109	254	49	6	61	(24	37)	498	155	170	110	8	441	17	1	8	4	12	.25	22	.229	.306	.449

153

Dave Nilsson

Bats: L **Throws:** R **Pos:** 1B-74; DH-59; LF-22; PH-5   **Ht:** 6'3"   **Wt:** 231   **Born:** 12/14/69   **Age:** 28

							BATTING												BASERUNNING				PERCENTAGES		
Year Team	Lg	G	AB	H	2B	3B	HR	(Hm	Rd)	TB	R	RBI	TBB	IBB	SO	HBP	SH	SF	SB	CS	SB%	GDP	Avg	OBP	SLG
1992 Milwaukee	AL	51	164	38	8	0	4	(1	3)	58	15	25	17	1	18	0	2	0	2	2	.50	1	.232	.304	.354
1993 Milwaukee	AL	100	296	76	10	2	7	(5	2)	111	35	40	37	5	36	0	4	3	3	6	.33	10	.257	.336	.375
1994 Milwaukee	AL	109	397	109	28	3	12	(4	8)	179	51	69	34	9	61	0	1	8	1	0	1.00	7	.275	.326	.451
1995 Milwaukee	AL	81	263	73	12	1	12	(7	5)	123	41	53	24	4	41	2	0	5	2	0	1.00	9	.278	.337	.468
1996 Milwaukee	AL	123	453	150	33	2	17	(3	14)	238	81	84	57	6	68	3	0	3	2	3	.40	4	.331	.407	.525
1997 Milwaukee	AL	156	554	154	33	0	20	(5	15)	247	71	81	65	8	88	2	1	7	2	3	.40	7	.278	.352	.446
6 ML YEARS		620	2127	600	124	8	72	(25	47)	956	294	352	234	33	312	7	8	26	12	14	.46	38	.282	.351	.449

Otis Nixon

Bats: Both **Throws:** Right **Pos:** CF-144; DH-1; PH-1   **Ht:** 6'2"   **Wt:** 180   **Born:** 1/9/59   **Age:** 39

							BATTING												BASERUNNING				PERCENTAGES		
Year Team	Lg	G	AB	H	2B	3B	HR	(Hm	Rd)	TB	R	RBI	TBB	IBB	SO	HBP	SH	SF	SB	CS	SB%	GDP	Avg	OBP	SLG
1983 New York	AL	13	14	2	0	0	0	(0	0)	2	2	0	1	0	5	0	0	0	2	0	1.00	0	.143	.200	.143
1984 Cleveland	AL	49	91	14	0	0	0	(0	0)	14	16	1	8	0	11	0	3	1	12	6	.67	2	.154	.220	.154
1985 Cleveland	AL	104	162	38	4	0	3	(1	2)	51	34	9	8	0	27	0	4	0	20	11	.65	2	.235	.271	.315
1986 Cleveland	AL	105	95	25	4	1	0	(0	0)	31	33	8	13	0	12	0	2	0	23	6	.79	1	.263	.352	.326
1987 Cleveland	AL	19	17	1	0	0	0	(0	0)	1	2	1	3	0	4	0	0	0	2	3	.40	0	.059	.200	.059
1988 Montreal	NL	90	271	66	8	2	0	(0	0)	78	47	15	28	0	42	0	4	2	46	13	.78	0	.244	.312	.288
1989 Montreal	NL	126	258	56	7	2	0	(0	0)	67	41	21	33	1	36	0	2	0	37	12	.76	4	.217	.306	.260
1990 Montreal	NL	119	231	58	6	2	1	(0	1)	71	46	20	28	0	33	0	3	1	50	13	.79	2	.251	.331	.307
1991 Atlanta	NL	124	401	119	10	1	0	(0	0)	131	81	26	47	3	40	2	7	3	72	21	.77	5	.297	.371	.327
1992 Atlanta	NL	120	456	134	14	2	2	(1	1)	158	79	22	39	0	54	0	5	2	41	18	.69	4	.294	.348	.346
1993 Atlanta	NL	134	461	124	12	3	1	(1	0)	145	77	24	61	2	63	0	5	5	47	13	.78	10	.269	.351	.315
1994 Boston	AL	103	398	109	15	1	0	(0	0)	126	60	25	55	1	65	0	6	2	42	10	.81	0	.274	.360	.317
1995 Texas	AL	139	589	174	21	2	0	(0	0)	199	87	45	58	1	85	0	6	3	50	21	.70	6	.295	.357	.338
1996 Toronto	AL	125	496	142	15	1	1	(1	0)	162	87	29	71	1	68	1	7	0	54	13	.81	9	.286	.377	.327
1997 Tor-LA		145	576	153	18	3	2	(0	1)	183	84	44	65	0	78	0	8	6	59	12	.83	12	.266	.337	.318
1997 Toronto	AL	103	401	105	12	1	1	(0	1)	122	54	26	52	0	54	0	6	5	47	10	.82	10	.262	.343	.304
Los Angeles	NL	42	175	48	6	2	0	(0	0)	61	30	18	13	0	24	0	2	1	12	2	.86	2	.274	.323	.349
15 ML YEARS		1515	4516	1215	134	20	10	(4	6)	1419	776	290	518	9	623	3	62	25	557	172	.76	57	.269	.343	.314

Hideo Nomo

Pitches: Right **Bats:** Right **Pos:** SP-33   **Ht:** 6'2"   **Wt:** 210   **Born:** 8/31/68   **Age:** 29

		HOW MUCH HE PITCHED						WHAT HE GAVE UP											THE RESULTS						
Year Team	Lg	G	GS	CG	GF	IP	BFP	H	R	ER	HR	SH	SF	HB	TBB	IBB	SO	WP	Bk	W	L	Pct.	ShO	Sv-Op	Hld	ERA
1995 Los Angeles	NL	28	28	4	0	191.1	780	124	63	54	14	11	4	5	78	2	236	19	5	13	6	.684	3	0-0	0	2.54
1996 Los Angeles	NL	33	33	3	0	228.1	932	180	93	81	23	12	6	2	85	6	234	11	3	16	11	.593	2	0-0	0	3.19
1997 Los Angeles	NL	33	33	1	0	207.1	904	193	104	98	23	7	1	9	92	2	233	10	4	14	12	.538	0	0-0	0	4.25
3 ML YEARS		94	94	8	0	627	2616	497	260	233	60	30	11	16	255	10	703	40	12	43	29	.597	5	0-0	0	3.34

Greg Norton

Bats: Both **Throws:** Right **Pos:** 3B-11; PH-9; DH-2   **Ht:** 6'1"   **Wt:** 190   **Born:** 7/6/72   **Age:** 25

							BATTING												BASERUNNING				PERCENTAGES		
Year Team	Lg	G	AB	H	2B	3B	HR	(Hm	Rd)	TB	R	RBI	TBB	IBB	SO	HBP	SH	SF	SB	CS	SB%	GDP	Avg	OBP	SLG
1993 White Sox	R	3	9	2	0	0	0	—	—	2	1	2	1	0	1	0	0	0	0	0	.00	0	.222	.300	.222
Hickory	A	71	254	62	12	2	4	—	—	90	36	36	41	1	44	1	1	4	0	2	.00	6	.244	.347	.354
1994 South Bend	A	127	477	137	22	2	6	—	—	181	73	64	62	4	71	2	2	3	5	3	.63	7	.287	.369	.379
1995 Birmingham	AA	133	469	117	23	2	6	—	—	162	65	60	64	7	90	5	3	10	19	12	.61	10	.249	.339	.345
1996 Birmingham	AA	76	287	81	14	3	8	—	—	125	40	44	33	5	55	1	1	1	5	5	.50	5	.282	.357	.436
Nashville	AAA	43	164	47	14	2	7	—	—	86	28	26	17	3	42	0	0	2	2	3	.40	1	.287	.350	.524
1997 Nashville	AAA	114	414	114	27	1	26	—	—	221	82	76	57	2	101	4	1	3	3	5	.38	9	.275	.366	.534
1996 Chicago	AL	11	23	5	0	0	2	(0	2)	11	4	3	4	0	6	0	0	0	0	1	.00	0	.217	.333	.478
1997 Chicago	AL	18	34	9	2	2	0	(0	0)	15	5	1	2	0	8	0	1	0	0	0	.00	0	.265	.306	.441
2 ML YEARS		29	57	14	2	2	2	(0	2)	26	9	4	6	0	14	0	1	0	0	1	.00	0	.246	.317	.456

Abraham Nunez

Bats: Both **Throws:** Right **Pos:** SS-12; 2B-9; PH-4   **Ht:** 5'11"   **Wt:** 170   **Born:** 3/16/76   **Age:** 22

							BATTING												BASERUNNING				PERCENTAGES		
Year Team	Lg	G	AB	H	2B	3B	HR	(Hm	Rd)	TB	R	RBI	TBB	IBB	SO	HBP	SH	SF	SB	CS	SB%	GDP	Avg	OBP	SLG
1996 St. Cathrns	A-	75	297	83	6	4	3	—	—	106	43	26	31	0	43	4	8	2	37	14	.73	2	.279	.353	.357
1997 Lynchburg	A+	78	304	79	9	4	3	—	—	105	45	32	23	0	47	1	9	1	29	14	.67	5	.260	.313	.345
Carolina	AA	47	198	65	6	1	1	—	—	76	31	14	20	1	28	0	2	3	10	5	.67	2	.328	.385	.384
1997 Pittsburgh	NL	19	40	9	2	2	0	(0	0)	15	3	6	3	0	10	1	0	1	1	0	1.00	1	.225	.289	.375

Jon Nunnally

Bats: L **Throws:** R **Pos:** CF-46; RF-19; PH-16; LF-15   **Ht:** 5'10"   **Wt:** 190   **Born:** 11/9/71   **Age:** 26

							BATTING												BASERUNNING				PERCENTAGES		
Year Team	Lg	G	AB	H	2B	3B	HR	(Hm	Rd)	TB	R	RBI	TBB	IBB	SO	HBP	SH	SF	SB	CS	SB%	GDP	Avg	OBP	SLG
1997 Omaha *	AAA	68	230	64	11	1	15	—	—	122	35	33	39	2	67	3	0	2	8	3	.73	3	.278	.387	.530

Year Team	Lg	G	AB	H	2B	3B	HR	(Hm	Rd)	TB	R	RBI	TBB	IBB	SO	HBP	SH	SF	SB	CS	SB%	GDP	Avg	OBP	SLG
1995 Kansas City	AL	119	303	74	15	6	14	(6	8)	143	51	42	51	5	86	2	4	0	6	4	.60	4	.244	.357	.472
1996 Kansas City	AL	35	90	19	5	1	5	(2	3)	41	16	17	13	2	25	0	0	1	0	0	.00	0	.211	.308	.456
1997 KC-Cin		78	230	71	12	4	14	(7	7)	133	46	39	31	0	58	2	1	1	7	3	.70	2	.309	.394	.578
1997 Kansas City	AL	13	29	7	0	1	1	(1	0)	12	8	4	5	0	7	0	0	0	0	0	.00	0	.241	.353	.414
Cincinnati	NL	65	201	64	12	3	13	(6	7)	121	38	35	26	0	51	2	1	1	7	3	.70	2	.318	.400	.602
3 ML YEARS		232	623	164	32	11	33	(15	18)	317	113	98	95	7	169	4	5	2	13	7	.65	6	.263	.363	.509

Ryan Nye

Pitches: Right **Bats:** Right **Pos:** SP-2; RP-2   **Ht:** 6'2" **Wt:** 195 **Born:** 6/24/73 **Age:** 25

			HOW MUCH HE PITCHED				WHAT HE GAVE UP										THE RESULTS					
Year Team	Lg	G	GS	CG	GF	IP	BFP	H	R	ER	HR	SH	SF	HB	TBB	IBB	SO	WP	Bk	W	L	Pct.	ShO	Sv-Op	Hld	ERA
1994 Batavia	A-	13	12	1	0	71.2	301	64	27	21	3	1	0	6	15	0	71	2	1	7	2	.778	0	0- -	—	2.64
1995 Clearwater	A+	27	27	5	0	167	681	164	71	63	8	5	5	6	33	1	116	4	3	12	7	.632	1	0- -	—	3.40
1996 Reading	AA	14	14	0	0	86.2	365	76	41	37	9	1	3	6	30	1	90	3	1	8	2	.800	0	0- -	—	3.84
Scranton-WB	AAA	14	14	0	0	80.2	362	97	52	45	10	0	2	3	30	0	51	1	1	5	2	.714	0	0- -	—	5.02
1997 Scranton-WB	AAA	17	17	0	0	109.1	465	117	70	67	20	2	2	2	32	1	85	2	1	4	10	.286	0	0- -	—	5.52
1997 Philadelphia	NL	4	2	0	1	12	65	20	11	11	2	1	2	2	9	0	7	0	0	0	2	.000	0	0-0	0	8.25

Sherman Obando

Bats: R **Throws:** R **Pos:** PH-27; RF-14; DH-2; LF-1   **Ht:** 6'4" **Wt:** 215 **Born:** 1/23/70 **Age:** 28

Year Team	Lg	G	AB	H	2B	3B	HR	(Hm	Rd)	TB	R	RBI	TBB	IBB	SO	HBP	SH	SF	SB	CS	SB%	GDP	Avg	OBP	SLG
1997 Ottawa *	AAA	7	21	5	0	0	3	—	—	14	5	8	5	0	7	1	0	0	0	0	.00	3	.238	.407	.667
1993 Baltimore	AL	31	92	25	2	0	3	(2	1)	36	8	15	4	0	26	1	0	0	0	0	.00	1	.272	.309	.391
1995 Baltimore	AL	16	38	10	1	0	0	(0	0)	11	0	3	2	0	12	0	0	1	1	0	1.00	0	.263	.293	.289
1996 Montreal	NL	89	178	44	9	0	8	(6	2)	77	30	22	22	1	48	1	0	1	2	0	1.00	2	.247	.332	.433
1997 Montreal	NL	41	47	6	1	0	2	(0	2)	13	3	9	6	0	14	1	0	0	0	0	.00	0	.128	.241	.277
4 ML YEARS		177	355	85	13	0	13	(8	5)	137	41	49	34	1	100	3	0	2	3	0	1.00	3	.239	.310	.386

Charlie O'Brien

Bats: Right **Throws:** Right **Pos:** C-69   **Ht:** 6'2" **Wt:** 205 **Born:** 5/1/61 **Age:** 37

Year Team	Lg	G	AB	H	2B	3B	HR	(Hm	Rd)	TB	R	RBI	TBB	IBB	SO	HBP	SH	SF	SB	CS	SB%	GDP	Avg	OBP	SLG
1985 Oakland	AL	16	11	3	1	0	0	(0	0)	4	3	1	3	0	3	0	0	0	0	0	.00	0	.273	.429	.364
1987 Milwaukee	AL	10	35	7	3	1	0	(0	0)	12	2	0	4	0	4	0	1	0	0	1	.00	0	.200	.282	.343
1988 Milwaukee	AL	40	118	26	6	0	2	(2	0)	38	12	9	5	0	16	0	4	0	0	1	.00	3	.220	.252	.322
1989 Milwaukee	AL	62	188	44	10	0	6	(4	2)	72	22	35	21	1	11	9	8	0	0	0	.00	11	.234	.339	.383
1990 Mil-NYN		74	213	38	10	2	0	(0	0)	52	17	20	21	3	34	3	10	2	0	0	.00	4	.178	.259	.244
1991 New York	NL	69	168	31	6	0	2	(1	1)	43	16	14	17	1	25	4	0	2	0	2	.00	5	.185	.272	.256
1992 New York	NL	68	156	33	12	0	2	(1	1)	51	15	13	16	1	18	1	4	0	0	1	.00	4	.212	.289	.327
1993 New York	NL	67	188	48	11	0	4	(1	3)	71	15	23	14	1	14	2	3	1	1	1	.50	4	.255	.312	.378
1994 Atlanta	NL	51	152	37	11	0	8	(6	2)	72	24	28	15	2	24	3	1	1	0	0	.00	5	.243	.322	.474
1995 Atlanta	NL	67	198	45	7	0	9	(4	5)	79	18	23	29	2	40	6	0	0	0	1	.00	5	.227	.343	.399
1996 Toronto	AL	109	324	77	17	0	13	(8	5)	133	33	44	29	1	68	17	3	2	0	1	.00	8	.238	.331	.410
1997 Toronto	AL	69	225	49	15	1	4	(2	2)	78	22	27	22	1	45	11	3	6	0	2	.00	6	.218	.311	.347
1990 Milwaukee	AL	46	145	27	7	2	0	(0	0)	38	11	11	11	1	26	2	8	0	0	0	.00	3	.186	.253	.262
New York	NL	28	68	11	3	0	0	(0	0)	14	6	9	10	2	8	1	2	2	0	0	.00	1	.162	.272	.206
12 ML YEARS		702	1976	438	109	4	50	(29	21)	705	199	237	196	13	302	56	37	14	1	10	.09	58	.222	.308	.357

Alex Ochoa

Bats: R **Throws:** R **Pos:** RF-84; PH-34; CF-4; DH-1   **Ht:** 6'0" **Wt:** 185 **Born:** 3/29/72 **Age:** 26

Year Team	Lg	G	AB	H	2B	3B	HR	(Hm	Rd)	TB	R	RBI	TBB	IBB	SO	HBP	SH	SF	SB	CS	SB%	GDP	Avg	OBP	SLG
1995 New York	NL	11	37	11	1	0	0	(0	0)	12	7	0	2	0	10	0	0	0	1	0	1.00	1	.297	.333	.324
1996 New York	NL	82	282	83	19	3	4	(1	3)	120	37	33	17	0	30	2	0	3	4	3	.57	2	.294	.336	.426
1997 New York	NL	113	238	58	14	1	3	(1	2)	83	31	22	18	0	32	2	2	2	3	4	.43	7	.244	.300	.349
3 ML YEARS		206	557	152	34	4	7	(2	5)	215	75	55	37	0	72	4	2	5	8	7	.53	10	.273	.320	.386

Jose Offerman

Bats: Both **Throws:** Right **Pos:** 2B-101; PH-5; DH-1   **Ht:** 6'0" **Wt:** 190 **Born:** 11/8/68 **Age:** 29

Year Team	Lg	G	AB	H	2B	3B	HR	(Hm	Rd)	TB	R	RBI	TBB	IBB	SO	HBP	SH	SF	SB	CS	SB%	GDP	Avg	OBP	SLG
1990 Los Angeles	NL	29	58	9	0	0	1	(1	0)	12	7	7	4	1	14	0	1	0	1	0	1.00	0	.155	.210	.207
1991 Los Angeles	NL	52	113	22	2	0	0	(0	0)	24	10	3	25	2	32	1	1	0	3	2	.60	5	.195	.345	.212
1992 Los Angeles	NL	149	534	139	20	8	1	(1	0)	178	67	30	57	4	98	0	5	2	23	16	.59	5	.260	.331	.333
1993 Los Angeles	NL	158	590	159	21	6	1	(1	0)	195	77	62	71	7	75	2	25	8	30	13	.70	12	.269	.346	.331
1994 Los Angeles	NL	72	243	51	8	4	1	(0	1)	70	27	25	38	4	38	0	6	2	2	1	.67	6	.210	.314	.288
1995 Los Angeles	NL	119	429	123	14	6	4	(2	2)	161	69	33	69	0	67	3	10	4	2	7	.22	5	.287	.389	.375
1996 Kansas City	AL	151	561	170	33	8	5	(1	4)	234	85	47	74	3	98	1	7	2	24	10	.71	9	.303	.384	.417
1997 Kansas City	AL	106	424	126	23	6	2	(2	0)	167	59	39	41	3	64	0	6	0	9	10	.47	5	.297	.359	.394
8 ML YEARS		836	2952	799	121	38	15	(8	7)	1041	401	246	379	24	486	7	61	14	94	59	.61	47	.271	.354	.353

155

Chad Ogea

Pitches: Right **Bats:** Right **Pos:** SP-21   **Ht:** 6'2" **Wt:** 200 **Born:** 11/9/70 **Age:** 27

Year Team	Lg	G	GS	CG	GF	IP	BFP	H	R	ER	HR	SH	SF	HB	TBB	IBB	SO	WP	Bk	W	L	Pct.	ShO	Sv-Op	Hld	ERA
1997 Buffalo *	AAA	4	4	0	0	21	88	24	10	10	2	0	0	0	6	0	11	0	0	1	1	.500	0	0- -	—	4.29
1994 Cleveland	AL	4	1	0	0	16.1	80	21	11	11	2	0	0	1	10	2	11	0	0	0	1	.000	0	0-0	0	6.06
1995 Cleveland	AL	20	14	1	3	106.1	442	95	38	36	11	0	5	1	29	0	57	3	1	8	3	.727	0	0-0	0	3.05
1996 Cleveland	AL	29	21	1	2	146.2	620	151	82	78	22	3	3	5	42	3	101	2	1	10	6	.625	1	0-0	0	4.79
1997 Cleveland	AL	21	21	1	0	126.1	552	139	79	70	13	3	5	5	47	4	80	4	2	8	9	.471	0	0-0	0	4.99
4 ML YEARS		74	57	3	5	395.2	1694	406	210	195	48	6	13	12	128	9	249	9	3	26	19	.578	1	0-0	0	4.44

Kirt Ojala

Pitches: Left **Bats:** Left **Pos:** SP-5; RP-2   **Ht:** 6'2" **Wt:** 210 **Born:** 12/24/68 **Age:** 29

Year Team	Lg	G	GS	CG	GF	IP	BFP	H	R	ER	HR	SH	SF	HB	TBB	IBB	SO	WP	Bk	W	L	Pct.	ShO	Sv-Op	Hld	ERA
1990 Oneonta	A-	14	14	1	0	79	353	75	28	19	2	5	2	3	43	0	87	1	2	7	2	.778	0	0- -	—	2.16
1991 Pr William	A+	25	23	1	0	156.2	636	120	52	44	5	3	4	4	61	1	112	3	1	8	7	.533	0	0- -	—	2.53
1992 Albany-Colo	AA	24	23	2	0	151.2	642	130	71	61	10	3	7	0	80	0	116	10	0	12	8	.600	1	0- -	—	3.62
1993 Albany-Colo	AA	1	1	0	0	6.1	26	5	0	0	0	0	0	0	2	0	6	2	0	1	0	1.000	0	0- -	—	0.00
Columbus	AAA	31	20	0	3	126	575	145	85	77	13	4	5	3	71	2	83	13	1	8	9	.471	0	0- -	—	5.50
1994 Columbus	AAA	25	23	1	0	148	638	157	78	63	12	2	2	4	46	1	81	10	1	11	7	.611	1	0- -	—	3.83
1995 Columbus	AAA	32	20	0	5	145.2	619	138	74	64	15	6	2	3	54	3	107	7	1	8	7	.533	0	1- -	—	3.95
1996 Indianapolis	AAA	22	21	3	0	133.2	569	143	67	56	15	2	2	6	31	0	92	3	0	7	7	.500	0	0- -	—	3.77
1997 Charlotte	AAA	25	24	0	1	149	627	148	74	58	13	4	1	3	55	2	119	4	0	8	7	.533	0	0- -	—	3.50
1997 Florida	NL	7	5	0	1	28.2	130	28	10	10	4	0	1	0	18	0	19	0	0	1	2	.333	0	0-0	0	3.14

Troy O'Leary

Bats: L **Throws:** L **Pos:** RF-119; LF-24; PH-15; DH-1   **Ht:** 6'0" **Wt:** 198 **Born:** 8/4/69 **Age:** 28

Year Team	Lg	G	AB	H	2B	3B	HR	(Hm	Rd)	TB	R	RBI	TBB	IBB	SO	HBP	SH	SF	SB	CS	SB%	GDP	Avg	OBP	SLG
1993 Milwaukee	AL	19	41	12	3	0	0	(0	0)	15	3	3	5	0	9	0	3	0	1	1	.00	1	.293	.370	.366
1994 Milwaukee	AL	27	66	18	1	1	2	(0	2)	27	9	7	5	0	12	1	0	1	1	1	.50	0	.273	.329	.409
1995 Boston	AL	112	399	123	31	6	10	(5	5)	196	60	49	29	4	64	1	3	2	5	3	.63	8	.308	.355	.491
1996 Boston	AL	149	497	129	28	5	15	(10	5)	212	68	81	47	3	80	2	1	4	3	2	.60	13	.260	.327	.427
1997 Boston	AL	146	499	154	32	4	15	(5	10)	239	65	80	39	7	70	2	1	4	0	5	.00	13	.309	.358	.479
5 ML YEARS		453	1502	436	95	16	42	(20	22)	689	205	220	125	14	235	8	8	10	9	11	.45	35	.290	.346	.459

John Olerud

Bats: Left **Throws:** Left **Pos:** 1B-146; PH-10   **Ht:** 6'5" **Wt:** 220 **Born:** 8/5/68 **Age:** 29

Year Team	Lg	G	AB	H	2B	3B	HR	(Hm	Rd)	TB	R	RBI	TBB	IBB	SO	HBP	SH	SF	SB	CS	SB%	GDP	Avg	OBP	SLG
1989 Toronto	AL	6	8	3	0	0	0	(0	0)	3	2	0	0	0	1	0	0	0	0	0	.00	0	.375	.375	.375
1990 Toronto	AL	111	358	95	15	1	14	(11	3)	154	43	48	57	6	75	1	1	4	0	2	.00	5	.265	.364	.430
1991 Toronto	AL	139	454	116	30	1	17	(10	7)	199	64	68	68	9	84	1	1	6	0	3	.00	12	.256	.353	.438
1992 Toronto	AL	138	458	130	28	0	16	(4	12)	206	68	66	70	11	61	1	1	7	1	0	1.00	15	.284	.375	.450
1993 Toronto	AL	158	551	200	54	2	24	(9	15)	330	109	107	114	33	65	7	0	7	0	2	.00	12	.363	.473	.599
1994 Toronto	AL	108	384	114	29	2	12	(6	6)	183	47	67	61	12	53	3	0	5	1	2	.33	11	.297	.393	.477
1995 Toronto	AL	135	492	143	32	0	8	(1	7)	199	72	54	84	10	54	4	0	1	0	0	.00	17	.291	.398	.404
1996 Toronto	AL	125	398	109	25	0	18	(8	10)	188	59	61	60	6	37	10	0	1	0	1	1.00	10	.274	.382	.472
1997 New York	NL	154	524	154	34	1	22	(13	9)	256	90	102	85	5	67	13	0	8	0	0	.00	19	.294	.400	.489
9 ML YEARS		1074	3627	1064	247	7	131	(60	71)	1718	554	573	599	92	497	45	5	43	3	8	.27	101	.293	.396	.474

Omar Olivares

Pitches: Right **Bats:** Right **Pos:** SP-31; RP-1   **Ht:** 6'1" **Wt:** 190 **Born:** 7/6/67 **Age:** 30

Year Team	Lg	G	GS	CG	GF	IP	BFP	H	R	ER	HR	SH	SF	HB	TBB	IBB	SO	WP	Bk	W	L	Pct.	ShO	Sv-Op	Hld	ERA
1990 St. Louis	NL	9	6	0	0	49.1	201	45	17	16	2	1	0	2	17	0	20	1	1	1	1	.500	0	0-0	1	2.92
1991 St. Louis	NL	28	24	0	2	167.1	688	148	72	69	13	11	2	5	61	1	91	3	1	11	7	.611	0	1-1	0	3.71
1992 St. Louis	NL	32	30	1	1	197	818	189	84	84	20	8	7	4	63	5	124	2	0	9	9	.500	0	0-0	0	3.84
1993 St. Louis	NL	58	9	0	11	118.2	537	134	60	55	10	4	4	9	54	7	63	4	3	5	3	.625	0	1-5	2	4.17
1994 St. Louis	NL	14	12	1	2	73.2	333	84	53	47	10	3	3	4	37	0	26	5	0	3	4	.429	0	1-1	0	5.74
1995 Col-Phi	NL	16	6	0	4	41.2	195	55	34	32	5	2	2	2	23	0	22	4	0	1	4	.200	0	0-0	0	6.91
1996 Detroit	AL	25	25	4	0	160	708	169	90	87	16	3	6	9	75	4	81	4	1	7	11	.389	0	0-0	0	4.89
1997 Det-Sea	AL	32	31	3	0	177.1	794	191	109	98	18	2	7	13	81	4	103	5	0	6	10	.375	2	0-0	0	4.97
1995 Colorado	NL	11	6	0	1	31.2	151	44	28	26	4	1	1	2	21	0	15	4	0	1	3	.250	0	0-0	0	7.39
Philadelphia	NL	5	0	0	3	10	44	11	6	6	1	1	1	0	2	0	7	0	0	0	1	.000	0	0-0	0	5.40
1997 Detroit	AL	19	19	3	0	115	502	110	68	60	8	2	4	9	53	1	74	5	0	5	6	.455	2	0-0	0	4.70
Seattle	AL	13	12	0	0	62.1	292	81	41	38	10	0	3	4	28	3	29	0	0	1	4	.200	0	0-0	0	5.49
8 ML YEARS		214	143	9	20	985	4274	1015	519	488	94	34	31	49	411	21	530	28	6	43	49	.467	2	3-7	3	4.46

Darren Oliver

Pitches: Left **Bats:** Right **Pos:** SP-32 **Ht:** 6'2" **Wt:** 200 **Born:** 10/6/70 **Age:** 27

Year Team	Lg	G	GS	CG	GF	IP	BFP	H	R	ER	HR	SH	SF	HB	TBB	IBB	SO	WP	Bk	W	L	Pct.	ShO	Sv-Op	Hld	ERA
1993 Texas	AL	2	0	0	0	3.1	14	2	1	1	0	0	0	1	1	1	4	0	0	0	0	.000	0	0-0	0	2.70
1994 Texas	AL	43	0	0	10	50	226	40	24	19	4	6	0	6	35	4	50	2	2	4	0	1.000	0	2-3	9	3.42
1995 Texas	AL	17	7	0	2	49	222	47	25	23	3	5	1	1	32	1	39	4	0	4	2	.667	0	0-0	0	4.22
1996 Texas	AL	30	30	1	0	173.2	777	190	97	90	20	2	7	10	76	3	112	5	1	14	6	.700	1	0-0	0	4.66
1997 Texas	AL	32	32	3	0	201.1	887	213	111	94	29	2	5	11	82	3	104	7	0	13	12	.520	1	0-0	0	4.20
5 ML YEARS		124	69	4	12	477.1	2126	492	258	227	57	15	13	28	226	12	309	18	3	35	20	.636	2	2-3	9	4.28

Joe Oliver

Bats: Right **Throws:** Right **Pos:** C-106; PH-8; 1B-4 **Ht:** 6'3" **Wt:** 220 **Born:** 7/24/65 **Age:** 32

								BATTING											BASERUNNING				PERCENTAGES		
Year Team	Lg	G	AB	H	2B	3B	HR	(Hm	Rd)	TB	R	RBI	TBB	IBB	SO	HBP	SH	SF	SB	CS	SB%	GDP	Avg	OBP	SLG
1997 Indianapolis *	AAA	2	9	3	0	0	1	—	—	6	1	1	0	0	1	0	0	0	0	0	.00	0	.333	.333	.667
1989 Cincinnati	NL	49	151	41	8	0	3	(1	2)	58	13	23	6	1	28	1	1	2	0	0	.00	3	.272	.300	.384
1990 Cincinnati	NL	121	364	84	23	0	8	(3	5)	131	34	52	37	15	75	2	5	1	1	1	.50	6	.231	.304	.360
1991 Cincinnati	NL	94	269	58	11	0	11	(7	4)	102	21	41	18	5	53	0	4	0	0	0	.00	14	.216	.265	.379
1992 Cincinnati	NL	143	485	131	25	1	10	(3	7)	188	42	57	35	19	75	1	6	7	2	3	.40	12	.270	.316	.388
1993 Cincinnati	NL	139	482	115	28	0	14	(7	7)	185	40	75	27	2	91	1	2	9	0	0	.00	13	.239	.276	.384
1994 Cincinnati	NL	6	19	4	0	0	1	(1	0)	7	1	5	2	1	3	0	0	0	0	0	.00	1	.211	.286	.368
1995 Milwaukee	AL	97	337	92	20	0	12	(4	8)	148	43	51	27	1	66	3	2	0	2	4	.33	11	.273	.332	.439
1996 Cincinnati	NL	106	289	70	12	1	11	(6	5)	117	31	46	28	6	54	2	3	3	2	0	1.00	8	.242	.311	.405
1997 Cincinnati	NL	111	349	90	13	0	14	(7	7)	145	28	43	25	1	58	5	2	5	1	3	.25	7	.258	.313	.415
9 ML YEARS		866	2745	685	140	2	84	(43	41)	1081	253	393	205	51	503	15	25	27	8	11	.42	75	.250	.302	.394

Gregg Olson

Pitches: Right **Bats:** Right **Pos:** RP-45 **Ht:** 6'4" **Wt:** 212 **Born:** 10/11/66 **Age:** 31

Year Team	Lg	G	GS	CG	GF	IP	BFP	H	R	ER	HR	SH	SF	HB	TBB	IBB	SO	WP	Bk	W	L	Pct.	ShO	Sv-Op	Hld	ERA
1997 Omaha *	AAA	9	5	0	2	35.1	140	30	13	13	4	0	0	0	10	0	20	1	0	3	1	.750	0	0- -	—	3.31
1988 Baltimore	AL	10	0	0	4	11	51	10	4	4	1	0	0	0	10	1	9	0	1	1	1	.500	0	0-1	1	3.27
1989 Baltimore	AL	64	0	0	52	85	356	57	17	16	1	4	1	1	46	10	90	9	3	5	2	.714	0	27-33	1	1.69
1990 Baltimore	AL	64	0	0	58	74.1	305	57	20	20	3	1	2	3	31	3	74	5	0	6	5	.545	0	37-42	0	2.42
1991 Baltimore	AL	72	0	0	62	73.2	319	74	28	26	1	5	1	1	29	5	72	8	1	4	6	.400	0	31-39	1	3.18
1992 Baltimore	AL	60	0	0	56	61.1	244	46	14	14	3	0	2	0	24	0	58	4	0	1	5	.167	0	36-44	0	2.05
1993 Baltimore	AL	50	0	0	45	45	188	37	9	8	1	2	2	0	18	3	44	5	0	0	2	.000	0	29-35	0	1.60
1994 Atlanta	NL	16	0	0	6	14.2	77	19	15	15	1	2	1	1	13	3	10	0	2	0	2	.000	0	1-1	0	9.20
1995 Cle-KC	AL	23	0	0	12	33	141	28	15	15	4	1	2	0	19	2	21	1	0	3	3	.500	0	3-5	2	4.09
1996 Det-Hou		52	0	0	30	52.1	243	55	30	29	7	1	1	1	35	6	37	6	0	4	0	1.000	0	8-10	1	4.99
1997 Min-KC	AL	45	0	0	18	50	226	58	35	31	3	1	1	1	28	4	34	1	0	4	3	.571	0	1-4	5	5.58
1995 Cleveland	AL	3	0	0	2	2.2	14	5	4	4	1	0	0	0	2	0	0	0	0	0	0	.000	0	0-0	0	13.50
	Kansas City	AL	20	0	0	10	30.1	127	23	11	11	3	1	2	0	17	2	21	1	0	3	3	.500	0	3-5	2	3.26
1996 Detroit	AL	43	0	0	28	43	196	43	25	24	6	1	0	1	28	4	29	5	0	3	0	1.000	0	8-10	1	5.02
Houston	NL	9	0	0	2	9.1	47	12	5	5	1	0	1	0	7	2	8	1	0	1	0	1.000	0	0-0	0	4.82
1997 Minnesota	AL	11	0	0	5	8.1	55	19	17	17	0	0	0	0	11	1	6	0	0	0	0	.000	0	0-0	1	18.36
Kansas City	AL	34	0	0	13	41.2	171	39	18	14	3	2	1	1	17	3	28	1	0	4	3	.571	0	1-4	4	3.02
10 ML YEARS		456	0	0	343	500.1	2150	441	187	178	25	18	13	8	253	37	449	39	7	28	29	.491	0	173-214	12	3.20

Paul O'Neill

Bats: L **Throws:** L **Pos:** RF-146; PH-4; DH-2; 1B-2 **Ht:** 6'4" **Wt:** 215 **Born:** 2/25/63 **Age:** 35

								BATTING											BASERUNNING				PERCENTAGES		
Year Team	Lg	G	AB	H	2B	3B	HR	(Hm	Rd)	TB	R	RBI	TBB	IBB	SO	HBP	SH	SF	SB	CS	SB%	GDP	Avg	OBP	SLG
1985 Cincinnati	NL	5	12	4	1	0	0	(0	0)	5	1	1	0	0	2	0	0	0	0	0	.00	0	.333	.333	.417
1986 Cincinnati	NL	3	2	0	0	0	0	(0	0)	0	0	0	1	0	1	0	0	0	0	0	.00	0	.000	.333	.000
1987 Cincinnati	NL	84	160	41	14	1	7	(4	3)	78	24	28	18	1	29	0	0	0	2	1	.67	3	.256	.331	.488
1988 Cincinnati	NL	145	485	122	25	3	16	(12	4)	201	58	73	38	5	65	2	3	5	8	6	.57	7	.252	.306	.414
1989 Cincinnati	NL	117	428	118	24	2	15	(11	4)	191	49	74	46	8	64	2	0	4	20	5	.80	7	.276	.346	.446
1990 Cincinnati	NL	145	503	136	28	0	16	(10	6)	212	59	78	53	13	103	2	1	5	13	11	.54	12	.270	.339	.421
1991 Cincinnati	NL	152	532	136	36	0	28	(20	8)	256	71	91	73	14	107	1	0	1	12	7	.63	8	.256	.346	.481
1992 Cincinnati	NL	148	496	122	19	1	14	(6	8)	185	59	66	77	15	85	2	1	3	6	3	.67	10	.246	.346	.373
1993 New York	AL	141	498	155	34	1	20	(8	12)	251	71	75	44	5	69	2	0	3	2	4	.33	13	.311	.367	.504
1994 New York	AL	103	368	132	25	1	21	(10	11)	222	68	83	72	13	56	0	0	3	5	4	.56	16	.359	.460	.603
1995 New York	AL	127	460	138	30	4	22	(12	10)	242	82	96	71	8	76	1	0	11	1	2	.33	25	.300	.387	.526
1996 New York	AL	150	546	165	35	1	19	(7	12)	259	89	91	102	8	76	4	0	8	0	1	.00	21	.302	.411	.474
1997 New York	AL	149	553	179	42	0	21	(10	11)	284	89	117	75	8	92	0	0	9	10	7	.59	16	.324	.399	.514
13 ML YEARS		1469	5043	1448	313	14	199	(110	89)	2386	720	873	670	98	825	16	7	55	79	51	.61	138	.287	.369	.473

Mike Oquist

Pitches: Right **Bats:** Right **Pos:** SP-17; RP-2 **Ht:** 6'2" **Wt:** 170 **Born:** 5/30/68 **Age:** 30

Year Team	Lg	G	GS	CG	GF	IP	BFP	H	R	ER	HR	SH	SF	HB	TBB	IBB	SO	WP	Bk	W	L	Pct.	ShO	Sv-Op	Hld	ERA
1997 Edmonton *	AAA	9	9	1	0	52.2	225	57	23	19	3	2	1	0	16	0	37	0	0	6	1	.857	0	0- -	—	3.25
Modesto *	A+	2	2	0	0	3.2	17	5	2	2	1	0	0	0	1	0	5	0	0	0	0	.000	0	0- -	—	4.91

		HOW MUCH HE PITCHED						WHAT HE GAVE UP												THE RESULTS						
Year Team	Lg	G	GS	CG	GF	IP	BFP	H	R	ER	HR	SH	SF	HB	TBB	IBB	SO	WP	Bk	W	L	Pct.	ShO	Sv-Op	Hld	ERA
1993 Baltimore	AL	5	0	0	2	11.2	50	12	5	5	0	0	0	0	4	1	8	0	0	0	0	.000	0	0-0	0	3.86
1994 Baltimore	AL	15	9	0	3	58.1	278	75	41	40	7	3	4	6	30	4	39	3	0	3	3	.500	0	0-0	0	6.17
1995 Baltimore	AL	27	0	0	2	54	255	51	27	25	6	1	4	2	41	3	27	2	0	2	1	.667	0	0-1	0	4.17
1996 San Diego	NL	8	0	0	3	7.2	30	6	2	2	0	0	0	0	4	2	4	1	0	0	0	.000	0	0-0	0	2.35
1997 Oakland	AL	19	17	1	0	107.2	473	111	62	60	15	3	3	6	43	3	72	2	0	4	6	.400	0	0-0	0	5.02
5 ML YEARS		74	26	1	10	239.1	1086	255	137	132	28	7	11	14	122	13	150	8	0	9	10	.474	0	0-1	0	4.96

Luis Ordaz

Bats: Right **Throws:** Right **Pos:** SS-11; PH-1   **Ht:** 5'11" **Wt:** 170 **Born:** 8/12/75 **Age:** 22

		BATTING															BASERUNNING				PERCENTAGES		
Year Team	Lg	G	AB	H	2B	3B	HR	(Hm | Rd)	TB	R	RBI	TBB	IBB	SO	HBP	SH	SF	SB	CS	SB%	GDP	Avg	OBP	SLG
1993 Princeton	R+	57	217	65	9	7	2	—	—	94	28	39	7	2	32	2	0	5	3	1	.75	2	.300	.320	.433
1994 Chston-WV	A	9	31	7	0	0	0	—	—	7	3	0	1	0	4	1	1	0	1	0	1.00	1	.226	.273	.226
Princeton	R+	60	211	52	12	3	0	—	—	70	33	12	10	1	27	2	5	1	7	5	.58	2	.246	.286	.332
1995 Chston-WV	A	112	359	83	14	7	2	—	—	117	43	42	13	1	47	6	8	4	12	5	.71	10	.231	.267	.326
1996 St. Pete	A+	126	423	115	13	3	3	—	—	143	46	49	30	0	53	1	7	6	10	5	.67	10	.272	.317	.338
1997 Arkansas	AA	115	390	112	20	6	4	—	—	156	44	58	22	1	39	2	7	6	11	10	.52	19	.287	.324	.400
1997 St. Louis	NL	12	22	6	1	0	0	(0 | 0)	7	3	1	1	0	2	0	0	0	3	0	1.00	1	.273	.304	.318

Magglio Ordonez

Bats: Right **Throws:** Right **Pos:** RF-19; PH-3   **Ht:** 5'11" **Wt:** 170 **Born:** 1/28/74 **Age:** 24

		BATTING															BASERUNNING				PERCENTAGES		
Year Team	Lg	G	AB	H	2B	3B	HR	(Hm	Rd)	TB	R	RBI	TBB	IBB	SO	HBP	SH	SF	SB	CS	SB%	GDP	Avg	OBP	SLG
1992 White Sox	R	38	111	20	10	2	1	—	—	37	17	14	13	0	26	2	0	1	6	4	.60	2	.180	.276	.333
1993 Hickory	A	84	273	59	14	4	3	—	—	90	32	20	26	0	66	0	2	0	5	5	.50	6	.216	.284	.330
1994 Hickory	A	132	490	144	24	5	11	—	—	211	86	69	45	1	57	1	7	3	16	7	.70	11	.294	.353	.431
1995 Pr William	A+	131	487	116	24	2	12	—	—	180	61	65	41	0	71	3	0	4	11	5	.69	16	.238	.299	.370
1996 Birmingham	AA	130	479	126	41	0	18	—	—	221	66	67	39	1	74	9	1	0	9	10	.47	16	.263	.330	.461
1997 Nashville	AAA	135	523	172	29	3	14	—	—	249	65	90	32	5	61	2	2	9	14	10	.58	18	.329	.364	.476
1997 Chicago	AL	21	69	22	6	0	4	(2	2)	40	12	11	2	0	8	0	1	0	1	2	.33	1	.319	.338	.580

Rey Ordonez

Bats: Right **Throws:** Right **Pos:** SS-118; PH-5   **Ht:** 5'9" **Wt:** 159 **Born:** 11/11/72 **Age:** 25

		BATTING															BASERUNNING				PERCENTAGES		
Year Team	Lg	G	AB	H	2B	3B	HR	(Hm	Rd)	TB	R	RBI	TBB	IBB	SO	HBP	SH	SF	SB	CS	SB%	GDP	Avg	OBP	SLG
1994 St. Lucie	A+	79	314	97	21	2	2	—	—	128	47	40	14	0	28	0	6	2	11	6	.65	8	.309	.336	.408
Binghamton	AA	48	191	50	10	2	1	—	—	67	22	20	4	0	18	1	1	1	4	3	.57	2	.262	.279	.351
1995 Norfolk	AAA	125	439	94	21	4	2	—	—	129	49	50	27	2	50	3	10	7	11	13	.46	12	.214	.261	.294
1996 New York	NL	151	502	129	12	4	1	(0	1)	152	51	30	22	12	53	1	4	1	1	3	.25	12	.257	.289	.303
1997 New York	NL	120	356	77	5	3	1	(1	0)	91	35	33	18	3	36	1	14	2	11	5	.69	10	.216	.255	.256
2 ML YEARS		271	858	206	17	7	2	(1	1)	243	86	63	40	15	89	2	18	3	12	8	.60	22	.240	.275	.283

Kevin Orie

Bats: Right **Throws:** Right **Pos:** 3B-112; PH-4; SS-3   **Ht:** 6'4" **Wt:** 210 **Born:** 9/1/72 **Age:** 25

		BATTING															BASERUNNING				PERCENTAGES		
Year Team	Lg	G	AB	H	2B	3B	HR	(Hm	Rd)	TB	R	RBI	TBB	IBB	SO	HBP	SH	SF	SB	CS	SB%	GDP	Avg	OBP	SLG
1993 Peoria	A	65	238	64	17	1	7	—	—	104	28	45	21	1	51	10	2	2	3	5	.38	7	.269	.351	.437
1994 Daytona	A+	6	17	7	3	1	1	—	—	15	4	5	8	1	4	1	0	0	1	0	1.00	1	.412	.615	.882
1995 Daytona	A+	119	409	100	17	4	9	—	—	152	54	51	42	2	71	15	0	6	5	4	.56	11	.244	.333	.372
1996 Orlando	AA	82	296	93	25	0	8	—	—	142	42	58	48	3	52	0	0	6	2	0	1.00	7	.314	.403	.480
Iowa	AAA	14	48	10	1	0	2	—	—	17	5	6	6	1	10	0	0	0	0	0	.00	1	.208	.296	.354
1997 Orlando	AA	3	13	5	2	0	2	—	—	13	3	6	2	1	1	0	0	0	0	0	.00	1	.385	.467	1.000
Iowa	AAA	9	32	12	4	0	1	—	—	19	7	8	5	0	5	0	0	0	0	0	.00	0	.375	.459	.594
1997 Chicago	NL	114	364	100	23	5	8	(6	2)	157	40	44	39	3	57	5	3	4	2	2	.50	13	.275	.350	.431

Jesse Orosco

Pitches: Left **Bats:** Right **Pos:** RP-71   **Ht:** 6'2" **Wt:** 205 **Born:** 4/21/57 **Age:** 41

		HOW MUCH HE PITCHED						WHAT HE GAVE UP												THE RESULTS						
Year Team	Lg	G	GS	CG	GF	IP	BFP	H	R	ER	HR	SH	SF	HB	TBB	IBB	SO	WP	Bk	W	L	Pct.	ShO	Sv-Op	Hld	ERA
1979 New York	NL	18	2	0	6	35	154	33	20	19	4	3	0	2	22	0	22	0	0	1	2	.333	0	0- -	—	4.89
1981 New York	NL	8	0	0	4	17.1	69	13	4	3	2	2	0	0	6	2	18	0	1	0	0	.000	0	1- -	—	1.56
1982 New York	NL	54	2	0	22	109.1	451	92	37	33	7	5	4	2	40	2	89	3	2	4	10	.286	0	4- -	—	2.72
1983 New York	NL	62	0	0	42	110	432	76	27	18	3	4	3	1	38	7	84	1	2	13	7	.650	0	17- -	—	1.47
1984 New York	NL	60	0	0	52	87	355	58	29	25	7	3	3	2	34	6	85	1	1	10	6	.625	0	31- -	—	2.59
1985 New York	NL	54	0	0	39	79	331	66	26	24	6	1	1	0	34	7	68	4	0	8	6	.571	0	17- -	—	2.73
1986 New York	NL	58	0	0	40	81	338	64	23	21	6	2	3	3	35	3	62	2	0	8	6	.571	0	21- -	—	2.33
1987 New York	NL	58	0	0	41	77	335	78	41	38	5	5	4	2	31	9	78	2	0	3	9	.250	0	16-22	4	4.44
1988 Los Angeles	NL	55	0	0	21	53	229	41	18	16	4	3	3	2	30	3	43	1	0	3	2	.600	0	9-15	14	2.72
1989 Cleveland	AL	69	0	0	29	78	312	54	20	18	7	8	3	2	26	4	79	0	0	3	4	.429	0	3-7	12	2.08
1990 Cleveland	AL	55	0	0	28	64.2	289	58	35	28	9	5	3	0	38	7	55	1	0	5	4	.556	0	2-3	2	3.90
1991 Cleveland	AL	47	0	0	20	45.2	202	52	20	19	4	1	3	1	15	8	36	1	1	2	0	1.000	0	0-0	3	3.74
1992 Milwaukee	AL	59	0	0	14	39	158	33	15	14	5	0	2	1	13	1	40	2	0	3	1	.750	0	1-2	11	3.23

Year Team	Lg	G	GS	CG	GF	IP	BFP	H	R	ER	HR	SH	SF	HB	TBB	IBB	SO	WP	Bk	W	L	Pct.	ShO	Sv-Op	Hld	ERA
1993 Milwaukee	AL	57	0	0	27	56.2	233	47	25	20	2	1	2	3	17	3	67	3	1	3	5	.375	0	8-13	11	3.18
1994 Milwaukee	AL	40	0	0	5	39	174	32	26	22	4	0	2	2	26	2	36	0	0	3	1	.750	0	0-4	8	5.08
1995 Baltimore	AL	65	0	0	23	49.2	200	28	19	18	4	2	4	1	27	7	58	2	1	2	4	.333	0	3-6	15	3.26
1996 Baltimore	AL	66	0	0	10	55.2	236	42	22	21	5	2	1	2	28	4	52	2	0	3	1	.750	0	0-3	19	3.40
1997 Baltimore	AL	71	0	0	12	50.1	205	29	13	13	6	1	2	0	30	0	46	1	1	6	3	.667	0	0-4	21	2.32
18 ML YEARS		956	4	0	435	1127.1	4703	896	420	370	90	48	43	26	490	75	1018	26	10	80	72	.526	0	133- -	—	2.95

Joe Orsulak

Bats: L **Throws:** L **Pos:** LF-37; PH-33; RF-26; 1B-15; DH-1 **Ht:** 6'1" **Wt:** 205 **Born:** 5/31/62 **Age:** 36

Year Team	Lg	G	AB	H	2B	3B	HR	(Hm	Rd)	TB	R	RBI	TBB	IBB	SO	HBP	SH	SF	SB	CS	SB%	GDP	Avg	OBP	SLG
1983 Pittsburgh	NL	7	11	2	0	0	0	(0	0)	2	0	1	0	0	2	0	0	1	0	1	.00	0	.182	.167	.182
1984 Pittsburgh	NL	32	67	17	1	2	0	(0	0)	22	12	3	1	0	7	1	3	1	3	1	.75	0	.254	.271	.328
1985 Pittsburgh	NL	121	397	119	14	6	0	(0	0)	145	54	21	26	3	27	1	9	3	24	11	.69	5	.300	.342	.365
1986 Pittsburgh	NL	138	401	100	19	6	2	(0	2)	137	60	19	28	2	38	1	6	1	24	11	.69	4	.249	.299	.342
1988 Baltimore	AL	125	379	109	21	3	8	(3	5)	160	48	27	23	2	30	3	8	3	9	8	.53	7	.288	.331	.422
1989 Baltimore	AL	123	390	111	22	5	7	(0	7)	164	59	55	41	6	35	2	7	6	5	3	.63	8	.285	.351	.421
1990 Baltimore	AL	124	413	111	14	3	11	(9	2)	164	49	57	46	9	48	1	4	1	6	8	.43	7	.269	.343	.397
1991 Baltimore	AL	143	486	135	22	1	5	(3	2)	174	57	43	28	1	45	4	0	3	6	2	.75	9	.278	.321	.358
1992 Baltimore	AL	117	391	113	18	3	4	(2	2)	149	45	39	28	5	34	4	4	1	5	4	.56	3	.289	.342	.381
1993 New York	NL	134	409	116	15	4	8	(5	3)	163	59	35	28	1	25	2	0	2	5	4	.56	6	.284	.331	.399
1994 New York	NL	96	292	76	3	0	8	(4	4)	103	39	42	16	2	21	3	0	7	4	2	.67	11	.260	.299	.353
1995 New York	NL	108	290	82	19	2	1	(1	0)	108	41	37	19	2	35	1	1	6	1	3	.25	3	.283	.323	.372
1996 Florida	NL	120	217	48	6	1	2	(2	0)	62	23	19	16	1	38	0	0	1	1	1	.50	4	.221	.274	.286
1997 Montreal	NL	106	150	34	12	1	1	(0	1)	51	13	7	18	0	17	0	2	0	0	1	.00	2	.227	.310	.340
14 ML YEARS		1494	4293	1173	186	37	57	(29	28)	1604	559	405	318	34	402	23	44	36	93	60	.61	69	.273	.324	.374

David Ortiz

Bats: Left **Throws:** Left **Pos:** 1B-11 **Ht:** 6'4" **Wt:** 230 **Born:** 11/18/75 **Age:** 22

Year Team	Lg	G	AB	H	2B	3B	HR	(Hm	Rd)	TB	R	RBI	TBB	IBB	SO	HBP	SH	SF	SB	CS	SB%	GDP	Avg	OBP	SLG
1994 Mariners	R	53	167	41	10	1	2	—	—	59	14	20	14	2	46	2	1	4	1	4	.20	2	.246	.305	.353
1995 Mariners	R	48	184	61	18	4	4	—	—	99	30	37	23	1	52	1	0	3	2	0	1.00	2	.332	.403	.538
1996 Wisconsin	A	130	487	156	34	2	18	—	—	248	89	93	52	8	108	5	2	4	3	4	.43	5	.320	.389	.509
1997 Ft. Myers	A+	61	239	79	15	0	13	—	—	133	45	58	22	3	53	1	0	3	2	1	.67	3	.331	.385	.556
New Britain	AA	69	258	83	22	2	14	—	—	151	40	56	21	1	78	4	0	2	2	6	.25	6	.322	.379	.585
Salt Lake	AAA	10	42	9	1	0	4	—	—	22	5	10	2	0	11	0	0	0	0	1	.00	4	.214	.250	.524
1997 Minnesota	AL	15	49	16	3	0	1	(0	1)	22	10	6	2	0	19	0	0	0	0	0	.00	1	.327	.353	.449

Donovan Osborne

Pitches: Left **Bats:** Left **Pos:** SP-14 **Ht:** 6'2" **Wt:** 195 **Born:** 6/21/69 **Age:** 29

Year Team	Lg	G	GS	CG	GF	IP	BFP	H	R	ER	HR	SH	SF	HB	TBB	IBB	SO	WP	Bk	W	L	Pct.	ShO	Sv-Op	Hld	ERA
1997 Louisville *	AAA	3	3	0	0	13.1	58	13	7	7	2	1	1	0	5	1	13	1	0	0	1	.000	0	0- -	—	4.73
1992 St. Louis	NL	34	29	0	2	179	754	193	91	75	14	7	4	2	38	2	104	6	0	11	9	.550	0	0-0	1	3.77
1993 St. Louis	NL	26	26	1	0	155.2	657	153	73	65	18	6	2	7	47	4	83	4	0	10	7	.588	0	0-0	0	3.76
1995 St. Louis	NL	19	19	0	0	113.1	477	112	58	48	17	8	3	2	34	2	82	0	0	4	6	.400	0	0-0	0	3.81
1996 St. Louis	NL	30	30	2	0	198.2	822	191	87	78	22	7	4	1	57	5	134	6	1	13	9	.591	1	0-0	0	3.53
1997 St. Louis	NL	14	14	0	0	80.1	337	84	46	44	10	3	3	1	23	2	51	1	0	3	7	.300	0	0-0	0	4.93
5 ML YEARS		123	118	3	2	727	3047	733	355	310	81	31	16	13	199	15	454	17	1	41	38	.519	1	0-0	1	3.84

Keith Osik

Bats: R **Throws:** R **Pos:** C-32; PH-14; 2B-4; 1B-1; 3B-1 **Ht:** 6'0" **Wt:** 185 **Born:** 10/22/68 **Age:** 29

Year Team	Lg	G	AB	H	2B	3B	HR	(Hm	Rd)	TB	R	RBI	TBB	IBB	SO	HBP	SH	SF	SB	CS	SB%	GDP	Avg	OBP	SLG
1990 Welland	A-	29	97	27	4	0	1	—	—	34	13	20	11	1	12	2	1	3	6	6	.25	1	.278	.354	.351
1991 Carolina	AA	17	43	13	3	1	0	—	—	18	9	5	5	0	5	0	0	0	0	0	.00	1	.302	.375	.419
Salem	A+	87	300	81	13	1	6	—	—	114	31	35	38	0	48	3	3	2	2	3	.40	13	.270	.356	.380
1992 Carolina	AA	129	425	110	17	1	5	—	—	144	41	45	52	1	69	15	0	4	2	9	.18	12	.259	.357	.339
1993 Carolina	AA	103	371	105	21	2	10	—	—	160	47	47	30	1	47	9	4	1	0	2	.00	13	.283	.350	.431
1994 Buffalo	AAA	83	260	55	16	0	5	—	—	86	27	33	28	0	41	3	0	2	1	0	1.00	5	.212	.294	.331
1995 Calgary	AAA	90	301	101	25	1	10	—	—	158	40	59	21	2	42	5	0	4	2	2	.50	5	.336	.384	.525
1996 Erie	A-	3	10	3	1	0	0	—	—	4	1	2	1	0	2	1	0	0	0	0	.00	0	.300	.417	.400
1996 Pittsburgh	NL	48	140	41	14	1	1	(0	1)	60	18	14	14	1	22	1	1	0	1	0	1.00	3	.293	.361	.429
1997 Pittsburgh	NL	49	105	27	9	1	0	(0	0)	38	10	7	9	1	21	1	2	0	0	1	.00	1	.257	.322	.362
2 ML YEARS		97	245	68	23	2	1	(0	1)	98	28	21	23	2	43	2	3	0	1	1	.50	4	.278	.344	.400

Antonio Osuna

Pitches: Right **Bats:** Right **Pos:** RP-48 **Ht:** 5'11" **Wt:** 160 **Born:** 4/12/73 **Age:** 25

Year Team	Lg	G	GS	CG	GF	IP	BFP	H	R	ER	HR	SH	SF	HB	TBB	IBB	SO	WP	Bk	W	L	Pct.	ShO	Sv-Op	Hld	ERA
1997 Albuquerque *	AAA	13	0	0	12	14	55	9	3	3	0	0	0	0	4	0	26	1	0	1	1	.500	0	6- -	—	1.93

Year Team	Lg	G	GS	CG	GF	IP	BFP	H	R	ER	HR	SH	SF	HB	TBB	IBB	SO	WP	Bk	W	L	Pct.	ShO	Sv-Op	Hld	ERA
						HOW MUCH HE PITCHED						WHAT HE GAVE UP											THE RESULTS				
1995 Los Angeles	NL	39	0	0	8	44.2	186	39	22	22	5	2	1	1	20	2	46	1	0	2	4	.333	0	0-2	11	4.43
1996 Los Angeles	NL	73	0	0	21	84	342	65	33	28	6	7	5	2	32	12	85	3	2	9	6	.600	0	4-9	16	3.00
1997 Los Angeles	NL	48	0	0	18	61.2	245	46	15	15	6	4	1	1	19	2	68	2	0	3	4	.429	0	0-0	10	2.19
3 ML YEARS		160	0	0	47	190.1	773	150	70	65	17	13	7	4	71	16	199	6	2	14	14	.500	0	4-11	37	3.07

Ricky Otero

Bats: B **Throws:** R **Pos:** CF-40; PH-12; LF-1; RF-1   **Ht:** 5'5" **Wt:** 150 **Born:** 4/15/72 **Age:** 26

Year Team	Lg	G	AB	H	2B	3B	HR	(Hm	Rd)	TB	R	RBI	TBB	IBB	SO	HBP	SH	SF	SB	CS	SB%	GDP	Avg	OBP	SLG
							BATTING												BASERUNNING				PERCENTAGES		
1997 Scrnton-WB *	AAA	38	160	53	10	5	1	—	—	76	24	15	13	0	13	0	0	3	5	4	.56	1	.331	.375	.475
1995 New York	NL	35	51	7	2	0	0	(0	0)	9	5	1	3	0	10	0	1	0	2	1	.67	1	.137	.185	.176
1996 Philadelphia	NL	104	411	112	11	7	2	(0	2)	143	54	32	34	0	30	2	0	2	16	10	.62	3	.273	.330	.348
1997 Philadelphia	NL	50	151	38	6	2	0	(0	0)	48	20	3	19	0	15	1	3	0	0	3	.00	2	.252	.339	.318
3 ML YEARS		189	613	157	19	9	2	(0	2)	200	79	36	56	0	55	3	4	2	18	14	.56	6	.256	.320	.326

Eric Owens

Bats: R **Throws:** R **Pos:** LF-9; PH-9; CF-8; 2B-2; RF-1   **Ht:** 6'1" **Wt:** 185 **Born:** 2/3/71 **Age:** 27

Year Team	Lg	G	AB	H	2B	3B	HR	(Hm	Rd)	TB	R	RBI	TBB	IBB	SO	HBP	SH	SF	SB	CS	SB%	GDP	Avg	OBP	SLG
							BATTING												BASERUNNING				PERCENTAGES		
1997 Indianaplis *	AAA	104	391	112	15	4	11	—	—	168	56	44	42	0	55	3	1	4	23	10	.70	8	.286	.357	.430
1995 Cincinnati	NL	2	2	2	0	0	0	(0	0)	2	0	1	0	0	0	0	1	0	0	0	.00	0	1.000	1.000	1.000
1996 Cincinnati	NL	88	205	41	6	0	0	(0	0)	47	26	9	23	1	38	1	1	2	16	2	.89	2	.200	.281	.229
1997 Cincinnati	NL	27	57	15	0	0	0	(0	0)	15	8	3	4	0	11	0	0	0	3	2	.60	2	.263	.311	.263
3 ML YEARS		117	264	58	6	0	0	(0	0)	64	34	13	27	1	49	1	2	2	19	4	.83	4	.220	.293	.242

Jayhawk Owens

Bats: Right **Throws:** Right **Pos:** C/PH   **Ht:** 6'1" **Wt:** 213 **Born:** 2/10/69 **Age:** 29

Year Team	Lg	G	AB	H	2B	3B	HR	(Hm	Rd)	TB	R	RBI	TBB	IBB	SO	HBP	SH	SF	SB	CS	SB%	GDP	Avg	OBP	SLG
							BATTING												BASERUNNING				PERCENTAGES		
1993 Colorado	NL	33	86	18	5	0	3	(2	1)	32	12	6	6	1	30	2	0	0	1	0	1.00	1	.209	.277	.372
1994 Colorado	NL	6	12	3	0	1	0	(0	0)	5	4	1	3	0	3	0	0	0	0	0	.00	1	.250	.400	.417
1995 Colorado	NL	18	45	11	2	0	4	(3	1)	25	7	12	2	0	15	1	0	1	0	0	.00	0	.244	.286	.556
1996 Colorado	NL	73	180	43	9	1	4	(3	1)	66	31	17	27	0	56	1	3	2	4	1	.80	1	.239	.338	.367
4 ML YEARS		130	323	75	16	2	11	(8	3)	128	54	36	38	1	104	4	3	3	5	1	.83	3	.232	.318	.396

Tom Pagnozzi

Bats: R **Throws:** R **Pos:** C-13; PH-11; 1B-2; 3B-1   **Ht:** 6'1" **Wt:** 195 **Born:** 7/30/62 **Age:** 35

Year Team	Lg	G	AB	H	2B	3B	HR	(Hm	Rd)	TB	R	RBI	TBB	IBB	SO	HBP	SH	SF	SB	CS	SB%	GDP	Avg	OBP	SLG
							BATTING												BASERUNNING				PERCENTAGES		
1997 Louisville *	AAA	3	5	0	0	0	0	—	—	0	0	0	0	0	1	0	0	0	0	0	.00	0	.000	.000	.000
Arkansas *	AA	21	63	20	0	0	5	—	—	35	8	17	4	0	8	0	0	1	0	0	.00	0	.317	.353	.556
1987 St. Louis	NL	27	48	9	1	0	2	(2	0)	16	8	9	4	2	13	0	1	0	1	0	1.00	0	.188	.250	.333
1988 St. Louis	NL	81	195	55	9	0	0	(0	0)	64	17	15	11	1	32	0	2	1	0	0	.00	5	.282	.319	.328
1989 St. Louis	NL	52	80	12	2	0	0	(0	0)	14	3	3	6	2	19	1	0	1	0	0	.00	7	.150	.216	.175
1990 St. Louis	NL	69	220	61	15	0	2	(2	0)	82	20	23	14	1	37	1	0	2	1	1	.50	0	.277	.321	.373
1991 St. Louis	NL	140	459	121	24	5	2	(2	0)	161	38	57	36	6	63	4	6	5	9	13	.41	10	.264	.319	.351
1992 St. Louis	NL	139	485	121	26	3	7	(3	4)	174	33	44	28	9	64	1	6	3	2	5	.29	15	.249	.290	.359
1993 St. Louis	NL	92	330	85	15	1	7	(1	6)	123	31	41	19	6	30	1	0	5	1	0	1.00	7	.258	.296	.373
1994 St. Louis	NL	70	243	66	12	1	7	(2	5)	101	21	40	21	5	39	0	0	2	0	0	.00	3	.272	.327	.416
1995 St. Louis	NL	62	219	47	14	1	2	(1	1)	69	17	15	11	0	31	1	0	1	0	1	.00	9	.215	.254	.315
1996 St. Louis	NL	119	407	110	23	0	13	(9	4)	172	48	55	24	2	78	2	3	4	4	1	.80	9	.270	.311	.423
1997 St. Louis	NL	25	50	11	3	0	1	(1	0)	17	4	8	1	0	7	0	0	0	0	0	.00	2	.220	.235	.340
11 ML YEARS		876	2736	698	144	11	43	(23	20)	993	240	310	175	34	413	11	18	24	18	21	.46	67	.255	.300	.363

Lance Painter

Pitches: Left **Bats:** Left **Pos:** RP-14   **Ht:** 6'1" **Wt:** 197 **Born:** 7/21/67 **Age:** 30

Year Team	Lg	G	GS	CG	GF	IP	BFP	H	R	ER	HR	SH	SF	HB	TBB	IBB	SO	WP	Bk	W	L	Pct.	ShO	Sv-Op	Hld	ERA
						HOW MUCH HE PITCHED						WHAT HE GAVE UP											THE RESULTS				
1997 Louisville *	AAA	18	2	0	7	20.2	85	18	14	12	2	2	1	4	0	22	0	1	1	0	1.000	0	0--	—	5.23
1993 Colorado	NL	10	6	1	2	39	166	52	26	26	5	1	0	0	9	0	16	2	0	2	2	.500	0	0-0	0	6.00
1994 Colorado	NL	15	14	0	1	73.2	336	91	51	50	9	3	5	1	26	2	41	3	1	4	6	.400	0	0-0	0	6.11
1995 Colorado	NL	33	1	0	7	45.1	198	55	23	22	9	0	0	2	10	0	36	4	1	3	0	1.000	0	1-1	4	4.37
1996 Colorado	NL	34	1	0	4	50.2	234	56	37	33	12	3	3	3	25	3	48	1	0	4	2	.667	0	0-1	4	5.86
1997 St. Louis	NL	14	0	0	4	17	69	13	9	9	1	0	0	0	8	2	11	0	0	1	1	.500	0	0-0	3	4.76
5 ML YEARS		106	22	1	18	225.2	1003	267	146	140	36	7	8	6	78	7	152	10	2	14	11	.560	0	1-2	11	5.58

160

Donn Pall

Pitches: Right **Bats:** Right **Pos:** RP-2   **Ht:** 6'1" **Wt:** 180 **Born:** 1/11/62 **Age:** 36

		HOW MUCH HE PITCHED						WHAT HE GAVE UP											THE RESULTS						
Year Team	Lg	G	GS	CG	GF	IP	BFP	H	R	ER	HR	SH	SF	HB	TBB	IBB	SO	WP	Bk	W	L	Pct.	ShO	Sv-Op	Hld	ERA
1997 Charlotte *	AAA	59	0	0	28	79.2	334	82	40	30	10	2	1	5	11	2	70	3	0	4	7	.364	0	8- -	—	3.39
1988 Chicago	AL	17	0	0	6	28.2	130	39	11	11	1	2	1	0	8	1	16	1	0	0	2	.000	0	0-0	4	3.45
1989 Chicago	AL	53	0	0	27	87	370	90	35	32	9	8	2	8	19	3	58	4	1	4	5	.444	0	6-10	5	3.31
1990 Chicago	AL	56	0	0	11	76	306	63	33	28	7	4	2	4	24	8	39	2	0	3	5	.375	0	2-3	13	3.32
1991 Chicago	AL	51	0	0	7	71	282	59	22	19	7	4	0	3	20	3	40	2	0	7	2	.778	0	0-1	12	2.41
1992 Chicago	AL	39	0	0	12	73	323	79	43	40	9	1	3	2	27	8	27	1	2	5	2	.714	0	1-2	2	4.93
1993 ChA-Phi		47	0	0	11	76.1	320	77	32	26	6	7	1	2	14	3	40	3	1	3	3	.500	0	1-2	9	3.07
1994 NYA-ChN		28	0	0	7	39	176	51	20	16	4	0	1	1	10	0	23	2	0	1	2	.333	0	0-0	3	3.69
1996 Florida	NL	12	0	0	2	18.2	80	16	15	12	3	1	1	0	9	1	9	1	0	1	1	.500	0	0-0	1	5.79
1997 Florida	NL	2	0	0	0	2.1	11	3	1	1	1	0	0	0	1	0	0	0	0	0	0	.000	0	0-1	0	3.86
1993 Chicago	AL	39	0	0	9	58.2	251	62	25	21	5	6	1	2	11	3	29	3	0	2	3	.400	0	1-2	8	3.22
Philadelphia	NL	8	0	0	2	17.2	69	15	7	5	1	1	0	0	3	0	11	0	1	1	0	1.000	0	0-0	1	2.55
1994 New York	AL	26	0	0	7	35	157	43	18	14	3	0	1	1	9	0	21	2	0	1	2	.333	0	0-0	3	3.60
Chicago	NL	2	0	0	0	4	19	8	2	2	1	0	0	0	1	0	2	0	0	0	0	.000	0	0-0	0	4.50
9 ML YEARS		305	0	0	83	472	1998	477	212	185	47	27	11	20	132	27	252	16	4	24	22	.522	0	10-19	49	3.53

Orlando Palmeiro

Bats: L **Throws:** R **Pos:** CF-45; PH-30; DH-11; LF-4; RF-4   **Ht:** 5'11" **Wt:** 160 **Born:** 1/19/69 **Age:** 29

		BATTING															BASERUNNING				PERCENTAGES		
Year Team	Lg	G	AB	H	2B	3B	HR	(Hm | Rd)	TB	R	RBI	TBB	IBB	SO	HBP	SH	SF	SB	CS	SB%	GDP	Avg	OBP	SLG
1995 California	AL	15	20	7	0	0	0	(0 | 0)	7	3	1	1	0	1	0	0	0	0	0	.00	0	.350	.381	.350
1996 California	AL	50	87	25	6	1	0	(0 | 0)	33	6	6	8	1	13	2	1	0	0	1	.00	1	.287	.361	.379
1997 Anaheim	AL	74	134	29	2	2	0	(0 | 0)	35	19	8	17	1	11	1	3	1	2	2	.50	4	.216	.307	.261
3 ML YEARS		139	241	61	8	3	0	(0 | 0)	75	28	15	26	2	25	3	4	1	2	3	.40	5	.253	.332	.311

Rafael Palmeiro

Bats: Left **Throws:** Left **Pos:** 1B-155; PH-4; DH-3   **Ht:** 6'0" **Wt:** 190 **Born:** 9/24/64 **Age:** 33

		BATTING															BASERUNNING				PERCENTAGES		
Year Team	Lg	G	AB	H	2B	3B	HR	(Hm | Rd)	TB	R	RBI	TBB	IBB	SO	HBP	SH	SF	SB	CS	SB%	GDP	Avg	OBP	SLG
1986 Chicago	NL	22	73	18	4	0	3	(1 | 2)	31	9	12	4	0	6	1	0	0	1	1	.50	4	.247	.295	.425
1987 Chicago	NL	84	221	61	15	1	14	(5 | 9)	120	32	30	20	1	26	1	0	2	2	2	.50	4	.276	.336	.543
1988 Chicago	NL	152	580	178	41	5	8	(8 | 0)	253	75	53	38	6	34	3	2	6	12	2	.86	11	.307	.349	.436
1989 Texas	AL	156	559	154	23	4	8	(4 | 4)	209	76	64	63	3	48	6	2	4	4	3	.57	18	.275	.354	.374
1990 Texas	AL	154	598	191	35	6	14	(9 | 5)	280	72	89	40	6	59	3	2	8	3	3	.50	24	.319	.361	.468
1991 Texas	AL	159	631	203	49	3	26	(12 | 14)	336	115	88	68	10	72	6	2	7	4	3	.57	17	.322	.389	.532
1992 Texas	AL	159	608	163	27	4	22	(8 | 14)	264	84	85	72	8	83	10	5	6	2	3	.40	10	.268	.352	.434
1993 Texas	AL	160	597	176	40	2	37	(22 | 15)	331	124	105	73	22	85	5	2	9	22	3	.88	8	.295	.371	.554
1994 Baltimore	AL	111	436	139	32	0	23	(11 | 12)	240	82	76	54	1	63	2	0	6	7	3	.70	11	.319	.392	.550
1995 Baltimore	AL	143	554	172	30	2	39	(21 | 18)	323	89	104	62	5	65	3	0	5	3	1	.75	12	.310	.380	.583
1996 Baltimore	AL	162	626	181	40	2	39	(21 | 18)	342	110	142	95	12	96	3	0	8	8	0	1.00	9	.289	.381	.546
1997 Baltimore	AL	158	614	156	24	2	38	(20 | 18)	298	95	110	67	7	109	5	0	6	5	2	.71	14	.254	.329	.485
12 ML YEARS		1620	6097	1792	360	31	271	(142 | 129)	3027	963	958	656	81	746	48	15	65	73	26	.74	142	.294	.364	.496

Dean Palmer

Bats: Right **Throws:** Right **Pos:** 3B-141; PH-3; DH-1   **Ht:** 6'1" **Wt:** 210 **Born:** 12/27/68 **Age:** 29

		BATTING															BASERUNNING				PERCENTAGES		
Year Team	Lg	G	AB	H	2B	3B	HR	(Hm | Rd)	TB	R	RBI	TBB	IBB	SO	HBP	SH	SF	SB	CS	SB%	GDP	Avg	OBP	SLG
1989 Texas	AL	16	19	2	2	0	0	(0 | 0)	4	0	1	0	0	12	0	0	1	0	0	.00	0	.105	.100	.211
1991 Texas	AL	81	268	50	9	2	15	(6 | 9)	108	38	37	32	0	98	3	1	0	0	2	.00	4	.187	.281	.403
1992 Texas	AL	152	541	124	25	0	26	(11 | 15)	227	74	72	62	2	154	4	2	4	10	4	.71	9	.229	.311	.420
1993 Texas	AL	148	519	127	31	2	33	(12 | 21)	261	88	96	53	4	154	8	0	5	11	10	.52	5	.245	.321	.503
1994 Texas	AL	93	342	84	14	2	19	(11 | 8)	159	50	59	26	0	89	2	0	1	3	4	.43	7	.246	.302	.465
1995 Texas	AL	36	119	40	6	0	9	(5 | 4)	73	30	24	21	1	21	4	0	1	1	1	.50	2	.336	.448	.613
1996 Texas	AL	154	582	163	26	2	38	(19 | 19)	307	98	107	59	4	145	5	0	6	2	0	1.00	15	.280	.348	.527
1997 Tex-KC	AL	143	542	139	31	1	23	(10 | 13)	241	70	86	41	2	134	5	1	5	2	2	.50	7	.256	.310	.445
1997 Texas	AL	94	355	87	21	0	14	(6 | 8)	150	47	55	26	2	84	1	1	3	1	0	1.00	4	.245	.296	.423
Kansas City	AL	49	187	52	10	1	9	(4 | 5)	91	23	31	15	0	50	2	0	2	1	2	.33	3	.278	.335	.487
8 ML YEARS		823	2932	729	144	9	163	(74 | 89)	1380	448	482	294	13	807	29	4	23	29	23	.56	49	.249	.321	.471

Jose Paniagua

Pitches: Right **Bats:** Right **Pos:** RP-6; SP-3   **Ht:** 6'2" **Wt:** 185 **Born:** 8/20/73 **Age:** 24

		HOW MUCH HE PITCHED						WHAT HE GAVE UP											THE RESULTS						
Year Team	Lg	G	GS	CG	GF	IP	BFP	H	R	ER	HR	SH	SF	HB	TBB	IBB	SO	WP	Bk	W	L	Pct.	ShO	Sv-Op	Hld	ERA
1993 Expos	R	4	4	1	0	27	100	13	2	2	0	0	0	2	5	0	25	1	1	3	0	1.000	0	0- -	—	0.67
1994 Wst Plm Bch	A+	26	26	1	0	141	606	131	66	57	6	5	4	6	54	2	110	13	2	9	9	.500	0	0- -	—	3.64
1995 Harrisburg	AA	25	25	0	0	126.1	575	140	84	75	9	5	5	12	62	0	89	8	0	7	12	.368	1	0- -	—	5.34
1996 Harrisburg	AA	3	3	0	0	18	66	12	1	0	0	1	0	1	2	0	16	1	0	3	0	1.000	0	0- -	—	0.00
Ottawa	AAA	15	14	2	0	85	352	72	39	30	7	2	4	3	23	0	61	4	0	9	5	.643	1	0- -	—	3.18
1997 Wst Plm Bch	A+	2	2	0	0	10	36	5	0	0	0	0	0	0	2	0	11	0	0	1	0	1.000	0	0- -	—	0.00
Ottawa	AAA	22	22	1	0	137.2	618	164	79	71	13	5	6	7	44	1	87	5	0	8	10	.444	0	0- -	—	4.64
1996 Montreal	NL	13	11	0	0	51	223	55	24	20	7	1	1	3	23	0	27	2	2	2	4	.333	0	0-0	0	3.53

		HOW MUCH HE PITCHED				WHAT HE GAVE UP											THE RESULTS					
Year Team	Lg	G GS CG GF	IP	BFP	H	R	ER	HR SH SF HB	TBB	IBB	SO WP Bk	W	L	Pct.	ShO	Sv-Op	Hld	ERA
1997 Montreal	NL	9 3 0 0	18	100	29	24	24	2 1 1 4	16	1	8 1 0	1	2	.333	0	0-0	0	12.00
2 ML YEARS		22 14 0 0	69	323	84	48	44	9 2 2 7	39	1	35 3 2	3	6	.333	0	0-0	0	5.74

Craig Paquette

Bats: Right **Throws:** Right **Pos:** 3B-72; PH-7; LF-4   **Ht:** 6'0" **Wt:** 190 **Born:** 3/28/69 **Age:** 29

		BATTING																	BASERUNNING				PERCENTAGES		
Year Team	Lg	G	AB	H	2B	3B	HR	(Hm Rd)	TB	R	RBI	TBB	IBB	SO	HBP	SH	SF	SB	CS	SB%	GDP	Avg	OBP	SLG
1997 Omaha *	AAA	23	91	28	6	0	3	— —	43	9	20	6	0	26	0	0	2	0	2	.00	6	.308	.343	.473
1993 Oakland	AL	105	393	86	20	4	12	(8 4)	150	35	46	14	2	108	0	1	1	4	2	.67	7	.219	.245	.382
1994 Oakland	AL	14	49	7	2	0	0	(0 0)	9	0	0	0	0	14	0	1	0	1	0	1.00	0	.143	.143	.184
1995 Oakland	AL	105	283	64	13	1	13	(8 5)	118	42	49	12	0	88	1	3	5	5	2	.71	5	.226	.256	.417
1996 Kansas City	AL	118	429	111	15	1	22	(12 10)	194	61	67	23	2	101	2	3	5	5	3	.63	11	.259	.296	.452
1997 Kansas City	AL	77	252	58	15	1	8	(7 1)	99	26	33	10	0	57	2	1	2	2	2	.50	13	.230	.263	.393
5 ML YEARS		419	1406	326	65	7	55	(35 20)	570	164	195	59	4	368	5	9	13	17	9	.65	36	.232	.263	.405

Mark Parent

Bats: Right **Throws:** Right **Pos:** C-38; PH-1   **Ht:** 6'5" **Wt:** 245 **Born:** 9/16/61 **Age:** 36

		BATTING																	BASERUNNING				PERCENTAGES		
Year Team	Lg	G	AB	H	2B	3B	HR	(Hm Rd)	TB	R	RBI	TBB	IBB	SO	HBP	SH	SF	SB	CS	SB%	GDP	Avg	OBP	SLG
1986 San Diego	NL	8	14	2	0	0	0	(0 0)	2	1	0	1	0	3	0	0	0	0	0	.00	1	.143	.200	.143
1987 San Diego	NL	12	25	2	0	0	0	(0 0)	2	0	2	0	0	9	0	0	0	0	0	.00	0	.080	.080	.080
1988 San Diego	NL	41	118	23	3	0	6	(4 2)	44	9	15	6	0	23	0	0	1	0	0	.00	1	.195	.232	.373
1989 San Diego	NL	52	141	27	4	0	7	(6 1)	52	12	21	8	2	34	0	1	4	1	0	1.00	5	.191	.229	.369
1990 San Diego	NL	65	189	42	11	0	3	(1 2)	62	13	16	16	3	29	0	3	0	1	0	1.00	2	.222	.283	.328
1991 Texas	AL	3	1	0	0	0	0	(0 0)	0	0	0	0	0	1	0	0	0	0	0	.00	0	.000	.000	.000
1992 Baltimore	AL	17	34	8	1	0	2	(0 2)	15	4	4	3	0	7	1	2	0	0	0	.00	0	.235	.316	.441
1993 Baltimore	AL	22	54	14	2	0	4	(1 3)	28	7	12	3	0	14	0	3	1	0	0	.00	1	.259	.293	.519
1994 Chicago	AL	44	99	26	4	0	3	(0 3)	39	8	16	13	1	24	1	1	2	0	1	.00	5	.263	.348	.394
1995 Pit-ChN	NL	81	265	62	11	0	18	(7 11)	127	30	38	26	2	69	0	1	0	0	0	.00	6	.234	.302	.479
1996 Det-Bal	AL	56	137	31	7	0	9	(4 5)	65	17	23	5	0	37	0	1	1	0	0	.00	3	.226	.252	.474
1997 Philadelphia	NL	39	113	17	3	0	0	(0 0)	20	4	8	7	0	39	0	1	0	0	1	.00	3	.150	.198	.177
1995 Pittsburgh	NL	69	233	54	9	0	15	(5 10)	108	25	33	23	2	62	0	1	0	0	0	.00	1	.232	.301	.464
Chicago	NL	12	32	8	2	0	3	(2 1)	19	5	5	3	0	7	0	0	0	0	0	.00	1	.250	.314	.594
1996 Detroit	AL	38	104	25	6	0	7	(4 3)	52	13	17	3	0	27	0	0	1	0	0	.00	2	.240	.259	.500
Baltimore	AL	18	33	6	1	0	2	(0 2)	13	4	6	2	0	10	0	1	0	0	0	.00	1	.182	.229	.394
12 ML YEARS		440	1190	254	46	0	52	(23 29)	456	105	155	88	8	289	2	12	10	2	2	.50	27	.213	.267	.383

Chan Ho Park

Pitches: Right **Bats:** Right **Pos:** SP-29; RP-3   **Ht:** 6'2" **Wt:** 195 **Born:** 6/30/73 **Age:** 25

		HOW MUCH HE PITCHED				WHAT HE GAVE UP											THE RESULTS					
Year Team	Lg	G GS CG GF	IP	BFP	H	R	ER	HR SH SF HB	TBB	IBB	SO WP Bk	W	L	Pct.	ShO	Sv-Op	Hld	ERA
1994 Los Angeles	NL	2 0 0 1	4	23	5	5	5	1 0 0 1	5	0	6 0 0	0	0	.000	0	0-0	0	11.25
1995 Los Angeles	NL	2 1 0 0	4	16	2	2	2	1 0 0 0	2	0	7 1 0	0	0	.000	0	0-0	0	4.50
1996 Los Angeles	NL	48 10 0 7	108.2	477	82	48	44	7 8 1 4	71	3	119 4 3	5	5	.500	0	0-0	4	3.64
1997 Los Angeles	NL	32 29 2 1	192	792	149	80	72	24 9 5 8	70	1	166 4 1	14	8	.636	0	0-0	4	3.38
4 ML YEARS		84 40 2 9	308.2	1308	238	135	123	33 17 6 13	148	4	298 8 5	19	13	.594	0	0-0	4	3.59

Bob Patterson

Pitches: Left **Bats:** Right **Pos:** RP-76   **Ht:** 6'2" **Wt:** 195 **Born:** 5/16/59 **Age:** 39

		HOW MUCH HE PITCHED				WHAT HE GAVE UP											THE RESULTS					
Year Team	Lg	G GS CG GF	IP	BFP	H	R	ER	HR SH SF HB	TBB	IBB	SO WP Bk	W	L	Pct.	ShO	Sv-Op	Hld	ERA
1985 San Diego	NL	3 0 0 2	4	26	13	11	11	2 0 0 0	3	0	1 0 1	0	0	.000	0	0--	—	24.75
1986 Pittsburgh	NL	11 5 0 2	36.1	159	49	20	20	1 1 1 0	5	2	20 0 1	2	3	.400	0	0--	—	4.95
1987 Pittsburgh	NL	15 7 0 2	43	201	49	34	32	5 6 3 1	22	4	27 1 0	1	4	.200	0	0-0	—	6.70
1989 Pittsburgh	NL	12 3 0 2	26.2	109	23	13	12	3 1 1 0	8	2	20 0 0	4	3	.571	0	1-1	0	4.05
1990 Pittsburgh	NL	55 0 0 19	94.2	386	88	33	31	9 5 3 3	21	7	70 1 2	8	5	.615	0	5-8	8	2.95
1991 Pittsburgh	NL	54 1 0 19	65.2	270	67	32	30	7 2 2 0	15	1	57 0 0	4	3	.571	0	2-3	13	4.11
1992 Pittsburgh	NL	60 0 0 26	64.2	268	59	22	21	7 3 2 0	23	6	43 3 0	6	3	.667	0	9-13	10	2.92
1993 Texas	AL	52 0 0 29	52.2	224	59	28	28	8 1 2 1	11	0	46 0 0	2	4	.333	0	1-2	6	4.78
1994 California	AL	47 0 0 11	42	170	35	21	19	6 0 0 2	15	2	30 1 0	2	3	.400	0	1-1	10	4.07
1995 California	AL	62 0 0 20	53.1	212	48	18	18	6 2 1 1	13	3	41 0 1	5	2	.714	0	0-1	12	3.04
1996 Chicago	NL	79 0 0 27	54.2	230	46	19	19	6 2 4 0	22	7	53 1 1	3	3	.500	0	8-10	15	3.13
1997 Chicago	NL	76 0 0 12	59.1	231	47	23	22	9 5 4 0	10	1	58 1 0	1	6	.143	0	0-3	22	3.34
12 ML YEARS		526 21 0 171	597	2486	583	274	263	68 28 23 9	168	35	466 8 6	38	39	.494	0	27--	—	3.96

Danny Patterson

Pitches: Right **Bats:** Right **Pos:** RP-54   **Ht:** 6'0" **Wt:** 185 **Born:** 2/17/71 **Age:** 27

		HOW MUCH HE PITCHED				WHAT HE GAVE UP											THE RESULTS					
Year Team	Lg	G GS CG GF	IP	BFP	H	R	ER	HR SH SF HB	TBB	IBB	SO WP Bk	W	L	Pct.	ShO	Sv-Op	Hld	ERA
1990 Butte	R+	13 3 0 2	28.1	135	36	23	20	3 0 3 1	14	1	18 3 1	0	3	.000	0	1--	—	6.35
1991 Rangers	R	11 9 0 0	50	201	43	21	18	1 1 0 3	12	0	46 2 3	5	3	.625	0	0--	—	3.24
1992 Gastonia	A	23 21 3 0	105.1	447	106	47	42	9 2 2 4	33	3	84 5 13	4	6	.400	1	0--	—	3.59

		HOW MUCH HE PITCHED						WHAT HE GAVE UP												THE RESULTS						
Year Team	Lg	G	GS	CG	GF	IP	BFP	H	R	ER	HR	SH	SF	HB	TBB	IBB	SO	WP	Bk	W	L	Pct.	ShO	Sv-Op	Hld	ERA
1993 Charlotte	A+	47	0	0	24	68	286	55	22	19	2	5	1	1	28	4	41	5	0	5	6	.455	0	7- -	—	2.51
1994 Charlotte	A+	7	0	0	4	13.2	57	13	7	7	1	0	1	0	5	0	9	1	0	1	0	1.000	0	0- -	—	4.61
Tulsa	AA	30	1	0	19	44	181	35	13	8	2	3	3	1	17	1	33	5	2	1	4	.200	0	6- -	—	1.64
1995 Tulsa	AA	26	0	0	22	36.1	163	45	27	25	2	0	1	2	13	2	24	5	0	2	2	.500	0	5- -	—	6.19
Okla City	AAA	14	0	0	3	27.1	111	23	8	5	0	3	2	1	9	2	9	4	0	1	0	1.000	0	2- -	—	1.65
1996 Okla City	AAA	44	0	0	34	80.1	334	79	22	15	5	2	0	7	15	3	53	5	0	6	2	.750	0	10- -	—	1.68
1997 Tulsa	AA	2	2	0	0	2	13	5	4	1	0	0	0	1	0	0	0	0	0	0	0	.000	0	0- -	—	4.50
1996 Texas	AL	7	0	0	5	8.2	38	10	4	0	0	0	0	0	3	1	5	0	0	0	0	.000	0	0-0	—	0.00
1997 Texas	AL	54	0	0	17	71	296	70	29	27	3	4	3	0	23	4	69	7	1	10	6	.625	0	1-8	9	3.42
2 ML YEARS		61	0	0	22	79.2	334	80	33	27	3	4	3	0	26	5	74	7	1	10	6	.625	0	1-8	9	3.05

Roger Pavlik

Pitches: Right **Bats:** Right **Pos:** SP-11   **Ht:** 6'2" **Wt:** 220 **Born:** 10/4/67 **Age:** 30

		HOW MUCH HE PITCHED						WHAT HE GAVE UP												THE RESULTS						
Year Team	Lg	G	GS	CG	GF	IP	BFP	H	R	ER	HR	SH	SF	HB	TBB	IBB	SO	WP	Bk	W	L	Pct.	ShO	Sv-Op	Hld	ERA
1997 Rangers *	R	2	2	0	0	7	29	8	1	1	1	0	0	0	0	0	5	0	0	0	0	.000	0	0- -	—	1.29
Tulsa *	AA	1	1	0	0	5	19	3	2	2	0	2	0	0	2	0	4	0	0	0	0	.000	0	0- -	—	3.60
Okla City *	AAA	1	1	0	0	6	21	2	0	0	0	0	0	0	0	0	4	0	0	0	0	.000	0	0- -	—	0.00
1992 Texas	AL	13	13	2	0	62	275	66	32	29	3	0	2	3	34	0	45	9	0	4	4	.500	0	0-0	0	4.21
1993 Texas	AL	26	26	2	0	166.1	712	151	67	63	18	6	4	5	80	3	131	6	0	12	6	.667	0	0-0	0	3.41
1994 Texas	AL	11	11	0	0	50.1	245	61	45	43	8	4	4	4	30	1	31	5	1	2	5	.286	0	0-0	0	7.69
1995 Texas	AL	31	31	2	0	191.2	819	174	96	93	19	4	5	4	90	5	149	10	1	10	10	.500	1	0-0	0	4.37
1996 Texas	AL	34	34	7	0	201	877	216	120	116	28	3	4	5	81	5	127	8	0	15	8	.652	0	0-0	0	5.19
1997 Texas	AL	11	11	0	0	57.2	256	59	29	28	7	2	1	1	31	1	35	0	0	3	5	.375	0	0-0	0	4.37
6 ML YEARS		126	125	12	0	729	3184	727	389	372	83	19	20	22	346	15	518	38	2	46	38	.548	1	0-0	0	4.59

Rudy Pemberton

Bats: Right **Throws:** Right **Pos:** RF-23; PH-9   **Ht:** 6'1" **Wt:** 185 **Born:** 12/17/69 **Age:** 28

		BATTING																		BASERUNNING				PERCENTAGES		
Year Team	Lg	G	AB	H	2B	3B	HR	(Hm	Rd)	TB	R	RBI	TBB	IBB	SO	HBP	SH	SF		SB	CS	SB%	GDP	Avg	OBP	SLG
1988 Bristol	R+	6	5	0	0	0	0	—	—	0	2	0	1	0	3	2	0	0		0	0	.00	1	.000	.375	.000
1989 Bristol	R+	56	214	58	9	2	6	—	—	89	40	39	14	0	43	4	0	1		19	3	.86	3	.271	.326	.416
1990 Fayetteville	A	127	454	126	14	5	6	—	—	168	60	61	42	1	91	12	1	9		12	9	.57	12	.278	.348	.370
1991 Lakeland	A+	111	375	86	15	2	3	—	—	114	40	36	25	2	51	9	6	2		25	15	.63	5	.229	.292	.304
1992 Lakeland	A+	104	343	91	16	5	3	—	—	126	41	43	21	2	37	13	2	3		25	10	.71	4	.265	.329	.367
1993 London	AA	124	471	130	22	4	15	—	—	205	70	67	24	1	80	12	0	3		14	12	.54	11	.276	.325	.435
1994 Toledo	AAA	99	360	109	13	3	12	—	—	164	49	58	18	3	62	6	0	6		30	9	.77	8	.303	.341	.456
1995 Toledo	AAA	67	224	77	15	3	7	—	—	119	31	23	15	2	36	5	0	3		8	4	.67	5	.344	.393	.531
1996 Okla City	AAA	17	71	18	3	0	2	—	—	27	6	11	1	0	10	1	0	1		1	4	.20	0	.254	.270	.380
Pawtucket	AAA	102	396	129	28	3	27	—	—	244	77	92	18	0	63	14	0	1		16	7	.70	12	.326	.375	.616
1995 Detroit	AL	12	30	9	3	1	0	(0	0)	14	3	3	1	0	5	1	0	0		0	0	.00	3	.300	.344	.467
1996 Boston	AL	13	41	21	8	0	1	(1	0)	32	14	10	2	0	4	2	0	0		3	1	.75	0	.512	.556	.780
1997 Boston	AL	27	63	15	2	0	2	(1	1)	23	8	10	4	0	13	3	0	0		0	0	.00	0	.238	.314	.365
3 ML YEARS		52	134	45	13	1	3	(2	1)	69	22	23	7	0	22	6	0	0		3	1	.75	3	.336	.395	.515

Tony Pena

Bats: Right **Throws:** Right **Pos:** C-38; PH-2; 3B-1   **Ht:** 6'0" **Wt:** 185 **Born:** 6/4/57 **Age:** 41

		BATTING																		BASERUNNING				PERCENTAGES		
Year Team	Lg	G	AB	H	2B	3B	HR	(Hm	Rd)	TB	R	RBI	TBB	IBB	SO	HBP	SH	SF		SB	CS	SB%	GDP	Avg	OBP	SLG
1980 Pittsburgh	NL	8	21	9	1	1	0	(0	0)	12	1	1	0	0	4	0	0	0		0	1	.00	1	.429	.429	.571
1981 Pittsburgh	NL	66	210	63	9	1	2	(1	1)	80	16	17	8	2	23	1	2	2		1	2	.33	4	.300	.326	.381
1982 Pittsburgh	NL	138	497	147	28	4	11	(5	6)	216	53	63	17	3	57	4	3	2		2	5	.29	17	.296	.323	.435
1983 Pittsburgh	NL	151	542	163	22	3	15	(8	7)	236	51	70	31	8	73	0	6	1		6	7	.46	13	.301	.338	.435
1984 Pittsburgh	NL	147	546	156	27	2	15	(7	8)	232	77	78	36	5	79	4	4	2		12	8	.60	14	.286	.333	.425
1985 Pittsburgh	NL	147	546	136	27	2	10	(5	5)	197	53	59	29	4	67	0	7	5		12	8	.60	19	.249	.284	.361
1986 Pittsburgh	NL	144	510	147	26	2	10	(5	5)	207	56	52	53	6	69	1	0	1		9	10	.47	21	.288	.356	.406
1987 St. Louis	NL	116	384	82	13	4	5	(1	4)	118	40	44	36	9	54	1	2	2		6	1	.86	19	.214	.281	.307
1988 St. Louis	NL	149	505	133	23	1	10	(4	6)	188	55	51	33	11	60	1	3	4		6	2	.75	12	.263	.308	.372
1989 St. Louis	NL	141	424	110	17	2	4	(3	1)	143	36	37	35	19	33	2	2	1		5	3	.63	19	.259	.318	.337
1990 Boston	AL	143	491	129	19	1	7	(3	4)	171	62	56	43	3	71	1	2	3		8	6	.57	23	.263	.322	.348
1991 Boston	AL	141	464	107	23	2	5	(2	3)	149	45	48	37	1	53	4	4	3		8	3	.73	23	.231	.291	.321
1992 Boston	AL	133	410	99	21	1	1	(1	0)	125	39	38	24	0	61	1	13	2		3	2	.60	11	.241	.284	.305
1993 Boston	AL	126	304	55	11	0	4	(1	1)	78	20	19	25	0	46	2	13	3		1	3	.25	12	.181	.246	.257
1994 Cleveland	AL	40	112	33	8	1	2	(1	1)	49	18	10	9	0	11	0	3	1		0	1	.00	6	.295	.341	.438
1995 Cleveland	AL	91	263	69	15	0	5	(1	4)	99	25	28	14	1	44	1	1	0		1	0	1.00	9	.262	.302	.376
1996 Cleveland	AL	67	174	34	4	0	1	(0	0)	41	14	27	15	0	25	0	3	0		0	0	.00	8	.195	.255	.236
1997 ChA-Hou		40	86	15	4	0	0	(0	0)	19	6	10	10	0	16	0	0	2		0	0	.00	3	.174	.255	.221
1997 Chicago	AL	31	67	11	1	0	0	(0	0)	12	4	8	8	0	13	0	0	2		0	0	.00	3	.164	.250	.179
Houston	NL	9	19	4	3	0	0	(0	0)	7	2	2	2	0	3	0	0	0		0	0	.00	0	.211	.273	.368
18 ML YEARS		1988	6489	1687	298	27	107	(46	61)	2360	667	708	455	72	846	23	68	38		80	63	.56	234	.260	.309	.364

Terry Pendleton

Bats: Both **Throws:** Right **Pos:** 3B-32; PH-24 **Ht:** 5'9" **Wt:** 195 **Born:** 7/16/60 **Age:** 37

							BATTING												BASERUNNING				PERCENTAGES		
Year Team	Lg	G	AB	H	2B	3B	HR	(Hm	Rd)	TB	R	RBI	TBB	IBB	SO	HBP	SH	SF	SB	CS	SB%	GDP	Avg	OBP	SLG
1997 Indianapols *	AAA	4	12	2	0	0	0	—	—	2	2	2	4	1	1	0	0	0	0	0	.00	1	.167	.353	.167
1984 St. Louis	NL	67	262	85	16	3	1	(0	1)	110	37	33	16	3	32	0	0	5	20	5	.80	7	.324	.357	.420
1985 St. Louis	NL	149	559	134	16	3	5	(3	2)	171	56	69	37	4	75	0	3	3	17	12	.59	18	.240	.285	.306
1986 St. Louis	NL	159	578	138	26	5	1	(0	1)	177	56	59	34	10	59	1	6	7	24	6	.80	12	.239	.279	.306
1987 St. Louis	NL	159	583	167	29	4	12	(5	7)	240	82	96	70	6	74	2	3	9	19	12	.61	18	.286	.360	.412
1988 St. Louis	NL	110	391	99	20	2	6	(3	3)	141	44	53	21	4	51	2	4	3	3	3	.50	9	.253	.293	.361
1989 St. Louis	NL	162	613	162	28	5	13	(8	5)	239	83	74	44	3	81	0	2	2	9	5	.64	16	.264	.313	.390
1990 St. Louis	NL	121	447	103	20	2	6	(6	0)	145	46	58	30	8	58	1	0	6	7	5	.58	12	.230	.277	.324
1991 Atlanta	NL	153	586	187	34	8	22	(13	9)	303	94	86	43	8	70	1	7	7	10	2	.83	16	.319	.363	.517
1992 Atlanta	NL	160	640	199	39	1	21	(13	8)	303	98	105	37	8	67	0	5	7	5	2	.71	16	.311	.345	.473
1993 Atlanta	NL	161	633	172	33	1	17	(9	8)	258	81	84	36	5	97	3	1	8	5	1	.83	18	.272	.311	.408
1994 Atlanta	NL	77	309	78	18	3	7	(3	4)	123	25	30	12	3	57	0	3	0	2	0	1.00	8	.252	.280	.398
1995 Florida	NL	133	513	149	32	1	14	(8	6)	225	70	78	38	7	84	2	0	4	1	2	.33	7	.290	.339	.439
1996 Fla-Atl	NL	153	568	135	26	1	11	(6	5)	196	51	75	41	6	111	3	1	5	2	3	.40	18	.238	.290	.345
1997 Cincinnati	NL	50	113	28	9	0	1	(1	0)	40	11	17	12	1	14	0	0	0	2	1	.67	1	.248	.320	.354
1996 Florida	NL	111	406	102	20	1	7	(4	3)	145	30	58	26	5	75	3	1	5	0	2	.00	10	.251	.298	.357
Atlanta	NL	42	162	33	6	0	4	(2	2)	51	21	17	15	1	36	0	0	0	2	1	.67	8	.204	.271	.315
14 ML YEARS		1814	6795	1836	346	39	137	(78	59)	2671	834	917	471	76	930	15	37	65	126	59	.68	176	.270	.316	.393

Troy Percival

Pitches: Right **Bats:** Right **Pos:** RP-55 **Ht:** 6'3" **Wt:** 200 **Born:** 8/9/69 **Age:** 28

		HOW MUCH HE PITCHED						WHAT HE GAVE UP											THE RESULTS						
Year Team	Lg	G	GS	CG	GF	IP	BFP	H	R	ER	HR	SH	SF	HB	TBB	IBB	SO	WP	Bk	W	L	Pct.	ShO	Sv-Op	Hld	ERA
1997 Lk Elsinore *	A+	2	1	0	0	2	7	1	0	0	0	0	0	0	3	0	3	0	0	0	0	.000	0	0- —		0.00
1995 California	AL	62	0	0	16	74	284	37	19	16	6	4	1	1	26	2	94	2	2	3	2	.600	0	3-6	29	1.95
1996 California	AL	62	0	0	52	74	291	38	20	19	8	2	1	2	31	4	100	2	0	0	2	.000	0	36-39	2	2.31
1997 Anaheim	AL	55	0	0	46	52	224	40	20	20	6	1	2	4	22	2	72	5	0	5	5	.500	0	27-31	0	3.46
3 ML YEARS		179	0	0	114	200	799	115	59	55	20	7	4	7	79	8	266	9	2	8	9	.471	0	66-76	31	2.48

Carlos Perez

Pitches: Left **Bats:** Left **Pos:** SP-32; RP-1 **Ht:** 6'3" **Wt:** 195 **Born:** 1/14/71 **Age:** 27

		HOW MUCH HE PITCHED						WHAT HE GAVE UP											THE RESULTS						
Year Team	Lg	G	GS	CG	GF	IP	BFP	H	R	ER	HR	SH	SF	HB	TBB	IBB	SO	WP	Bk	W	L	Pct.	ShO	Sv-Op	Hld	ERA
1990 Expos	R	13	2	0	6	35.2	145	24	14	10	0	1	1	1	15	0	38	1	0	3	1	.750	0	2- —		2.52
1991 Sumter	A	16	12	0	2	73.2	306	57	29	20	3	0	7	0	32	0	69	3	1	2	2	.500	0	0- —		2.44
1992 Rockford	A	7	1	0	2	9.1	43	12	7	6	3	1	0	1	5	0	8	1	0	0	1	.000	0	1- —		5.79
1993 Burlington	A	12	1	0	5	16.2	69	13	6	6	0	3	0	0	9	0	21	0	1	1	0	1.000	0	0- —		3.24
San Berndno	A+	20	18	3	0	131	550	120	57	50	12	3	2	0	44	0	98	9	6	8	7	.533	0	0- —		3.44
1994 Harrisburg	AA	12	11	2	1	79	307	55	27	17	5	3	0	2	18	0	69	5	0	7	2	.778	2	1- —		1.94
Ottawa	AAA	17	17	3	0	119	511	130	50	44	8	5	3	3	41	2	82	4	1	7	5	.583	0	0- —		3.33
1995 Montreal	NL	28	23	2	2	141.1	592	142	61	58	18	6	1	5	28	2	106	8	4	10	8	.556	1	0-0	1	3.69
1997 Montreal	NL	33	32	8	0	206.2	857	206	109	89	21	5	7	4	48	1	110	2	1	12	13	.480	5	0-0	0	3.88
2 ML YEARS		61	55	10	2	348	1449	348	170	147	39	11	8	9	76	3	216	10	5	22	21	.512	6	0-0	1	3.80

Eddie Perez

Bats: Right **Throws:** Right **Pos:** C-64; 1B-6; PH-5 **Ht:** 6'1" **Wt:** 175 **Born:** 5/4/68 **Age:** 30

							BATTING												BASERUNNING				PERCENTAGES		
Year Team	Lg	G	AB	H	2B	3B	HR	(Hm	Rd)	TB	R	RBI	TBB	IBB	SO	HBP	SH	SF	SB	CS	SB%	GDP	Avg	OBP	SLG
1995 Atlanta	NL	7	13	4	1	0	1	(0	1)	8	1	4	0	0	2	0	0	0	0	0	.00	0	.308	.308	.615
1996 Atlanta	NL	68	156	40	9	1	4	(2	2)	63	19	17	8	0	19	1	0	2	0	0	.00	6	.256	.293	.404
1997 Atlanta	NL	73	191	41	5	0	6	(4	2)	64	20	18	10	0	35	2	1	2	0	1	.00	8	.215	.259	.335
3 ML YEARS		148	360	85	15	1	11	(6	5)	135	40	39	18	0	56	3	1	4	0	1	.00	14	.236	.275	.375

Eduardo Perez

Bats: R **Throws:** R **Pos:** 1B-67; PH-27; LF-11; 3B-8; DH-1; RF-1 **Ht:** 6'4" **Wt:** 215 **Born:** 9/11/69 **Age:** 28

							BATTING												BASERUNNING				PERCENTAGES		
Year Team	Lg	G	AB	H	2B	3B	HR	(Hm	Rd)	TB	R	RBI	TBB	IBB	SO	HBP	SH	SF	SB	CS	SB%	GDP	Avg	OBP	SLG
1993 California	AL	52	180	45	6	2	4	(2	2)	67	16	30	9	0	39	2	0	1	5	4	.56	4	.250	.292	.372
1994 California	AL	38	129	27	7	0	5	(3	2)	49	10	16	12	1	29	0	1	1	3	0	1.00	5	.209	.275	.380
1995 California	AL	29	71	12	4	1	1	(0	1)	21	9	7	12	0	9	2	0	1	0	2	.00	3	.169	.302	.296
1996 Cincinnati	NL	18	36	8	0	0	3	(3	0)	17	8	5	5	1	9	0	0	0	0	0	.00	2	.222	.317	.472
1997 Cincinnati	NL	106	297	75	18	0	16	(7	9)	141	44	52	29	1	76	2	0	2	5	1	.83	6	.253	.321	.475
5 ML YEARS		243	713	167	35	3	29	(15	14)	295	87	110	67	3	162	6	1	5	13	7	.65	20	.234	.303	.414

Mike Perez

Pitches: Right **Bats:** Right **Pos:** RP-16 **Ht:** 6'0" **Wt:** 200 **Born:** 10/19/64 **Age:** 33

		HOW MUCH HE PITCHED						WHAT HE GAVE UP											THE RESULTS						
Year Team	Lg	G	GS	CG	GF	IP	BFP	H	R	ER	HR	SH	SF	HB	TBB	IBB	SO	WP	Bk	W	L	Pct.	ShO	Sv-Op	Hld	ERA
1997 Omaha *	AAA	34	0	0	22	36.1	166	38	22	19	4	2	1	2	18	3	29	2	0	4	1	.800	0	8- —		4.71

Year Team	Lg	G	GS	CG	GF	IP	BFP	H	R	ER	HR	SH	SF	HB	TBB	IBB	SO	WP	Bk	W	L	Pct.	ShO	Sv-Op	Hld	ERA
1990 St. Louis	NL	13	0	0	7	13.2	55	12	6	6	0	0	2	0	3	0	5	0	0	1	0	1.000	0	1-2	2	3.95
1991 St. Louis	NL	14	0	0	2	17	75	19	11	11	1	1	0	1	7	2	7	0	1	0	2	.000	0	0-0	2	5.82
1992 St. Louis	NL	77	0	0	22	93	377	70	23	19	4	7	4	1	32	9	46	4	0	9	3	.750	0	0-3	9	1.84
1993 St. Louis	NL	65	0	0	25	72.2	298	65	24	20	4	5	5	1	20	1	58	2	0	7	2	.778	0	7-10	13	2.48
1994 St. Louis	NL	36	0	0	18	31	155	52	32	30	5	4	5	3	10	1	20	0	0	2	3	.400	0	12-14	6	8.71
1995 Chicago	NL	68	0	0	18	71.1	308	72	30	29	8	5	3	4	27	8	49	4	0	1	6	.250	0	2-3	16	3.66
1996 Chicago	NL	24	0	0	4	27	127	29	14	14	2	1	0	3	13	1	22	1	0	1	0	1.000	0	0-0	1	4.67
1997 Kansas City	AL	16	0	0	4	20.1	80	15	8	8	2	1	0	1	8	0	17	1	0	2	0	1.000	0	0-0	1	3.54
8 ML YEARS		313	0	0	100	346	1475	334	148	137	26	24	19	14	120	22	224	12	1	24	16	.600	0	22-32	50	3.56

Neifi Perez

Bats: B Throws: R Pos: SS-45; 2B-41; PH-3; 3B-2 Ht: 6'0" Wt: 173 Born: 2/2/75 Age: 23

Year Team	Lg	G	AB	H	2B	3B	HR	(Hm	Rd)	TB	R	RBI	TBB	IBB	SO	HBP	SH	SF	SB	CS	SB%	GDP	Avg	OBP	SLG
1993 Bend	A-	75	296	77	11	4	3	—	—	105	35	32	19	2	43	2	4	3	19	14	.58	3	.260	.306	.355
1994 Central Val	A+	134	506	121	16	7	1	—	—	154	64	35	32	1	79	2	19	5	9	7	.56	6	.239	.284	.304
1995 Colo Spmgs	AAA	11	36	10	4	0	0	—	—	14	4	2	0	0	5	0	1	0	1	1	.50	0	.278	.278	.389
New Haven	AA	116	427	108	28	3	5	—	—	157	59	43	24	2	52	2	4	1	5	2	.71	6	.253	.295	.368
1996 Colo Spmgs	AAA	133	570	180	28	12	7	—	—	253	77	72	21	4	48	2	4	10	16	13	.55	13	.316	.337	.444
1997 Colo Spmgs	AAA	68	303	110	24	3	8	—	—	164	68	46	17	0	27	0	0	3	8	2	.80	3	.363	.393	.541
1996 Colorado	NL	17	45	7	2	0	0	(0	0)	9	4	3	0	0	8	0	1	0	2	2	.50	2	.156	.156	.200
1997 Colorado	NL	83	313	91	13	10	5	(3	2)	139	46	31	21	4	43	1	5	4	4	3	.57	3	.291	.333	.444
2 ML YEARS		100	358	98	15	10	5	(3	2)	148	50	34	21	4	51	1	6	4	6	5	.55	5	.274	.313	.413

Robert Perez

Bats: R Throws: R Pos: LF-17; PH-12; RF-9; DH-7 Ht: 6'3" Wt: 205 Born: 6/4/69 Age: 29

Year Team	Lg	G	AB	H	2B	3B	HR	(Hm	Rd)	TB	R	RBI	TBB	IBB	SO	HBP	SH	SF	SB	CS	SB%	GDP	Avg	OBP	SLG
1994 Toronto	AL	4	8	1	0	0	0	(0	0)	1	0	0	0	0	1	0	0	0	0	0	.00	1	.125	.125	.125
1995 Toronto	AL	17	48	9	2	0	1	(1	0)	14	2	3	0	0	5	0	0	0	0	0	.00	1	.188	.188	.292
1996 Toronto	AL	86	202	66	10	0	2	(0	2)	82	30	21	8	0	17	1	4	1	3	0	1.00	6	.327	.354	.406
1997 Toronto	AL	37	78	15	4	1	2	(0	2)	27	4	6	0	0	16	0	0	0	0	0	.00	2	.192	.192	.346
4 ML YEARS		144	336	91	16	1	5	(1	4)	124	36	30	8	0	39	1	4	1	3	0	1.00	10	.271	.289	.369

Tomas Perez

Bats: Both Throws: Right Pos: SS-32; 2B-8 Ht: 5'11" Wt: 165 Born: 12/29/73 Age: 24

Year Team	Lg	G	AB	H	2B	3B	HR	(Hm	Rd)	TB	R	RBI	TBB	IBB	SO	HBP	SH	SF	SB	CS	SB%	GDP	Avg	OBP	SLG
1997 Syracuse *	AAA	89	303	68	13	0	1	—	—	84	32	20	37	1	67	0	14	1	3	4	.43	9	.224	.308	.277
1995 Toronto	AL	41	98	24	3	1	1	(1	0)	32	12	8	7	0	18	0	0	1	0	1	.00	2	.245	.292	.327
1996 Toronto	AL	91	295	74	13	4	1	(1	0)	98	24	19	25	0	29	1	6	1	1	2	.33	10	.251	.311	.332
1997 Toronto	AL	40	123	24	3	2	0	(0	0)	31	9	9	11	0	28	1	3	0	1	1	.50	2	.195	.267	.252
3 ML YEARS		172	516	122	19	7	2	(2	0)	161	45	36	43	0	75	2	9	2	2	4	.33	18	.236	.297	.312

Yorkis Perez

Pitches: Left Bats: Left Pos: RP-9 Ht: 6'0" Wt: 180 Born: 9/30/67 Age: 30

Year Team	Lg	G	GS	CG	GF	IP	BFP	H	R	ER	HR	SH	SF	HB	TBB	IBB	SO	WP	Bk	W	L	Pct.	ShO	Sv-Op	Hld	ERA
1997 Binghamton *	AA	12	3	0	4	27.1	104	15	4	2	1	1	0	0	12	1	39	1	0	2	1	.667	0	0- —		0.66
Norfolk *	AAA	17	0	0	8	20.2	89	22	9	8	2	2	2	0	7	0	24	0	0	1	0	1.000	0	3- —		3.48
1991 Chicago	NL	3	0	0	0	4.1	16	2	1	1	0	0	2	0	2	0	3	2	0	1	0	1.000	0	0-1	0	2.08
1994 Florida	NL	44	0	0	11	40.2	167	33	18	16	4	2	0	1	14	3	41	4	1	3	0	1.000	0	0-2	15	3.54
1995 Florida	NL	69	0	0	11	46.2	205	35	29	27	6	2	1	2	28	4	47	2	0	6	6	.250	0	1-4	16	5.21
1996 Florida	NL	64	0	0	15	47.2	222	51	28	28	2	2	1	0	31	4	47	0	0	3	4	.429	0	0-2	10	5.29
1997 New York	NL	9	0	0	1	8.2	45	15	8	8	2	0	1	0	4	0	7	1	0	0	1	.000	0	0-1	1	8.31
5 ML YEARS		189	0	0	38	148	655	136	84	80	14	6	6	4	79	11	145	11	1	9	11	.450	0	1-10	42	4.86

Matt Perisho

Pitches: Left Bats: Left Pos: SP-8; RP-3 Ht: 6'0" Wt: 175 Born: 6/8/75 Age: 23

Year Team	Lg	G	GS	CG	GF	IP	BFP	H	R	ER	HR	SH	SF	HB	TBB	IBB	SO	WP	Bk	W	L	Pct.	ShO	Sv-Op	Hld	ERA
1993 Angels	R	11	11	1	0	64	266	58	32	26	1	1	3	2	23	0	65	2	2	7	3	.700	0	0- —		3.66
1994 Cedar Rapds	A	27	27	0	0	147.2	689	165	90	71	11	7	7	4	88	0	107	8	3	12	9	.571	0	0- —		4.33
1995 Lk Elsinore	A+	24	22	0	0	115.1	541	137	91	81	10	0	8	6	60	0	68	7	0	8	9	.471	0	0- —		6.32
1996 Lk Elsinore	A+	21	18	1	1	128.2	565	131	72	60	9	8	7	7	58	0	97	5	4	7	5	.583	0	0- —		4.20
Midland	AA	8	8	0	0	53.1	222	48	22	19	4	4	1	2	20	0	50	1	0	3	2	.600	0	0- —		3.21
1997 Midland	AA	10	10	3	0	73	299	60	26	24	5	0	1	0	26.	0	62	1	2	5	2	.714	0	0- —		2.96
Vancouver	AAA	9	9	1	0	52.1	254	68	42	31	3	3	2	3	29	0	47	5	3	4	4	.500	0	0- —		5.33
1997 Anaheim	AL	11	8	0	2	45	217	59	34	30	2	2	3		28	0	35	5	2	0	2	.000	0	0-0	0	6.00

Robert Person

Pitches: Right Bats: Right Pos: SP-22; RP-1   Ht: 6'0" Wt: 185 Born: 10/6/69 Age: 28

Year Team	Lg	G	GS	CG	GF	IP	BFP	H	R	ER	HR	SH	SF	HB	TBB	IBB	SO	WP	Bk	W	L	Pct.	ShO	Sv-Op	Hld	ERA
1997 Syracuse *	AAA	1	1	0	0	7	26	4	1	0	0	0	0	0	2	0	5	0	0	1	0	1.000	0	0--	--	0.00
1995 New York	NL	3	1	0	0	12	44	5	1	1	1	0	0	0	2	0	10	0	0	1	0	1.000	0	0-0	0	0.75
1996 New York	NL	27	13	0	1	89.2	390	86	50	45	16	1	4	2	35	3	76	3	0	4	5	.444	0	0-0	1	4.52
1997 Toronto	AL	23	22	0	0	128.1	566	125	86	80	19	4	6	5	60	2	99	7	0	5	10	.333	0	0-0	0	5.61
3 ML YEARS		53	36	0	1	230	1000	216	137	126	36	5	10	7	97	5	185	10	0	10	15	.400	0	0-0	1	4.93

Roberto Petagine

Bats: Left Throws: Left Pos: PH-7; 1B-6; LF-1   Ht: 6'1" Wt: 170 Born: 6/2/71 Age: 27

Year Team	Lg	G	AB	H	2B	3B	HR	(Hm	Rd)	TB	R	RBI	TBB	IBB	SO	HBP	SH	SF	SB	CS	SB%	GDP	Avg	OBP	SLG
1997 Norfolk *	AAA	129	441	140	32	1	31	--	--	267	90	100	85	3	92	8	1	8	0	1	.00	6	.317	.430	.605
1994 Houston	NL	8	7	0	0	0	0	(0	0)	0	0	0	1	0	3	0	0	0	0	0	.00	0	.000	.125	.000
1995 San Diego	NL	89	124	29	8	0	3	(2	1)	46	15	17	26	2	41	0	2	0	0	0	.00	2	.234	.367	.371
1996 New York	NL	50	99	23	3	0	4	(2	2)	38	10	17	9	1	27	3	1	1	0	2	.00	4	.232	.313	.384
1997 New York	NL	12	15	1	0	0	0	(0	0)	1	2	2	3	0	6	0	0	0	0	0	.00	0	.067	.222	.067
4 ML YEARS		159	245	53	11	0	7	(4	3)	85	27	36	39	3	77	3	3	1	0	2	.00	6	.216	.330	.347

Chris Peters

Pitches: Left Bats: Left Pos: RP-30; SP-1   Ht: 6'1" Wt: 162 Born: 1/28/72 Age: 26

Year Team	Lg	G	GS	CG	GF	IP	BFP	H	R	ER	HR	SH	SF	HB	TBB	IBB	SO	WP	Bk	W	L	Pct.	ShO	Sv-Op	Hld	ERA
1993 Welland	A-	16	0	0	4	27.2	137	33	16	14	0	0	1	2	20	1	25	5	1	1	0	1.000	0	0--	--	4.55
1994 Salem	A+	3	0	0	1	3.1	16	5	5	5	2	0	0	1	1	0	2	1	0	1	0	1.000	0	0--	--	13.50
Augusta	A	54	0	0	29	60.2	268	51	34	29	1	5	2	2	33	2	83	7	0	4	5	.444	0	4--	--	4.30
1995 Lynchburg	A+	24	24	3	0	144.2	586	126	57	39	5	7	4	5	35	2	132	12	1	11	5	.688	3	0--	--	2.43
Carolina	AA	2	2	0	0	14	56	9	2	2	0	0	1	0	2	0	7	2	0	2	0	1.000	0	0--	--	1.29
1996 Carolina	AA	14	14	0	0	92	378	73	37	27	4	4	2	0	34	2	69	4	0	7	3	.700	0	0--	--	2.64
Calgary	AAA	4	4	0	0	27.2	102	18	3	3	0	1	1	0	8	1	16	1	0	1	1	.500	0	0--	--	0.98
1997 Calgary	AAA	14	9	0	1	51.1	243	52	32	25	5	0	2	5	30	1	55	2	0	2	4	.333	0	1--	--	4.38
1996 Pittsburgh	NL	16	10	0	5	64	283	72	43	40	9	3	3	1	25	0	28	4	0	2	4	.333	0	0-0	2	5.63
1997 Pittsburgh	NL	31	1	0	5	37.1	167	38	23	19	6	5	1	3	21	4	17	4	0	2	2	.500	0	0-1	2	4.58
2 ML YEARS		47	11	0	5	101.1	450	110	66	59	15	8	4	4	46	4	45	8	0	4	6	.400	0	0-1	4	5.24

Mark Petkovsek

Pitches: Right Bats: Right Pos: RP-53; SP-2   Ht: 6'0" Wt: 195 Born: 11/18/65 Age: 32

Year Team	Lg	G	GS	CG	GF	IP	BFP	H	R	ER	HR	SH	SF	HB	TBB	IBB	SO	WP	Bk	W	L	Pct.	ShO	Sv-Op	Hld	ERA
1991 Texas	AL	4	1	0	1	9.1	53	21	16	15	4	0	1	0	4	0	6	2	0	0	0	.000	0	0-0	0	14.46
1993 Pittsburgh	NL	26	0	0	8	32.1	145	43	25	25	7	4	1	0	9	2	14	4	0	3	0	1.000	0	0-0	0	6.96
1995 St. Louis	NL	26	21	1	1	137.1	569	136	71	61	11	4	4	6	35	3	71	1	1	6	6	.500	1	0-0	0	4.00
1996 St. Louis	NL	48	6	0	7	88.2	377	83	37	35	9	5	1	5	35	2	45	2	1	11	4	.846	0	0-3	10	3.55
1997 St. Louis	NL	55	2	0	19	96	414	109	61	54	14	2	2	6	31	4	51	2	0	4	7	.364	0	2-2	5	5.06
5 ML YEARS		159	30	1	36	363.2	1558	392	210	190	45	15	9	17	114	11	187	11	2	24	16	.600	1	2-5	15	4.70

Andy Pettitte

Pitches: Left Bats: Left Pos: SP-35   Ht: 6'5" Wt: 235 Born: 6/15/72 Age: 26

Year Team	Lg	G	GS	CG	GF	IP	BFP	H	R	ER	HR	SH	SF	HB	TBB	IBB	SO	WP	Bk	W	L	Pct.	ShO	Sv-Op	Hld	ERA
1995 New York	AL	31	26	3	1	175	745	183	86	81	15	4	5	1	63	3	114	8	1	12	9	.571	0	0-0	0	4.17
1996 New York	AL	35	34	2	1	221	929	229	105	95	23	7	3	3	72	2	162	6	1	21	8	.724	0	0-0	0	3.87
1997 New York	AL	35	35	4	0	240.1	986	233	86	77	7	6	2	3	65	0	166	7	0	18	7	.720	1	0-0	0	2.88
3 ML YEARS		101	95	9	2	636.1	2660	645	277	253	45	17	10	7	200	5	442	21	2	51	24	.680	1	0-0	0	3.58

J.R. Phillips

Bats: Left Throws: Left Pos: PH-9; 1B-3; RF-3   Ht: 6'1" Wt: 185 Born: 4/29/70 Age: 28

Year Team	Lg	G	AB	H	2B	3B	HR	(Hm	Rd)	TB	R	RBI	TBB	IBB	SO	HBP	SH	SF	SB	CS	SB%	GDP	Avg	OBP	SLG
1997 New Orleans *	AAA	104	411	119	28	0	21	--	--	210	59	71	39	3	112	0	0	4	0	1	.00	11	.290	.348	.511
1993 San Francisco	NL	11	16	5	1	1	1	(0	1)	11	1	4	0	0	5	0	0	0	0	0	.00	0	.313	.313	.688
1994 San Francisco	NL	15	38	5	0	0	1	(0	1)	8	1	3	1	0	13	0	0	1	1	0	1.00	0	.132	.150	.211
1995 San Francisco	NL	92	231	45	9	0	9	(5	4)	81	27	28	19	2	69	0	2	0	1	1	.50	3	.195	.256	.351
1996 SF-Phi	NL	50	104	17	5	0	7	(4	3)	43	12	15	11	1	51	1	0	0	0	0	.00	1	.163	.250	.413
1997 Houston	NL	13	15	2	0	0	1	(1	0)	5	2	4	0	0	7	0	0	1	0	0	.00	1	.133	.125	.333
1996 San Francisco	NL	15	25	5	0	0	2	(0	2)	11	3	5	1	0	13	0	0	0	0	0	.00	0	.200	.231	.440
Philadelphia	NL	35	79	12	5	0	5	(4	1)	32	9	10	10	1	38	1	0	0	0	0	.00	1	.152	.256	.405
5 ML YEARS		181	404	74	15	1	19	(10	9)	148	43	54	31	3	145	1	2	2	2	1	.67	5	.183	.242	.366

Tony Phillips

Bats: B Throws: R Pos: 2B-43; LF-31; RF-31; DH-26; 3B-10; PH-4; CF-2   Ht: 5'10" Wt: 175 Born: 4/25/59 Age: 39

Year Team	Lg	G	AB	H	2B	3B	HR	(Hm	Rd)	TB	R	RBI	TBB	IBB	SO	HBP	SH	SF	SB	CS	SB%	GDP	Avg	OBP	SLG
1982 Oakland	AL	40	81	17	2	2	0	(0	0)	23	11	8	12	0	26	2	5	0	2	3	.40	0	.210	.326	.284
1983 Oakland	AL	148	412	102	12	3	4	(1	3)	132	54	35	48	1	70	2	11	3	16	5	.76	5	.248	.327	.320
1984 Oakland	AL	154	451	120	24	3	4	(2	2)	162	62	37	42	1	86	0	7	1	10	6	.63	5	.266	.325	.359
1985 Oakland	AL	42	161	45	12	2	4	(2	2)	73	23	17	13	0	34	0	3	1	3	2	.60	1	.280	.331	.453
1986 Oakland	AL	118	441	113	14	5	5	(3	2)	152	76	52	76	0	82	3	9	3	15	10	.60	2	.256	.367	.345
1987 Oakland	AL	111	379	91	20	0	10	(5	5)	141	48	46	57	1	76	0	2	3	7	6	.54	9	.240	.337	.372
1988 Oakland	AL	79	212	43	8	4	2	(2	0)	65	32	17	36	0	50	1	1	1	0	2	.00	6	.203	.320	.307
1989 Oakland	AL	143	451	118	15	6	4	(2	2)	157	48	47	58	2	66	3	5	7	3	8	.27	11	.262	.345	.348
1990 Detroit	AL	152	573	144	23	5	8	(4	4)	201	97	55	99	0	85	4	9	2	19	9	.68	10	.251	.364	.351
1991 Detroit	AL	146	564	160	28	4	17	(9	8)	247	87	72	79	5	95	3	3	6	10	5	.67	8	.284	.371	.438
1992 Detroit	AL	159	606	167	32	3	10	(3	7)	235	114	64	114	2	93	1	5	7	12	10	.55	13	.276	.387	.388
1993 Detroit	AL	151	566	177	27	0	7	(3	4)	225	113	57	132	5	102	4	1	4	16	11	.59	11	.313	.443	.398
1994 Detroit	AL	114	438	123	19	3	19	(12	7)	205	91	61	95	3	105	2	0	3	13	5	.72	8	.281	.409	.468
1995 California	AL	139	525	137	21	1	27	(13	14)	241	119	61	113	6	135	3	1	1	13	10	.57	5	.261	.394	.459
1996 Chicago	AL	153	581	161	29	3	12	(6	6)	232	119	63	125	9	132	4	1	8	13	8	.62	6	.277	.404	.399
1997 ChA-Ana	AL	141	534	147	34	2	8	(5	3)	209	96	57	102	5	118	3	5	4	13	10	.57	11	.275	.392	.391
1997 Chicago	AL	36	129	40	6	0	2	(1	1)	52	23	9	29	0	29	1	2	0	4	1	.80	3	.310	.440	.403
Anaheim	AL	105	405	107	28	2	6	(4	2)	157	73	48	73	5	89	2	3	4	9	9	.50	8	.264	.376	.388
16 ML YEARS		1990	6975	1865	320	46	141	(72	69)	2700	1190	749	1201	40	1355	35	68	58	165	110	.60	117	.267	.375	.387

Mike Piazza

Bats: Right Throws: Right Pos: C-139; DH-7; PH-6   Ht: 6'3" Wt: 215 Born: 9/4/68 Age: 29

Year Team	Lg	G	AB	H	2B	3B	HR	(Hm	Rd)	TB	R	RBI	TBB	IBB	SO	HBP	SH	SF	SB	CS	SB%	GDP	Avg	OBP	SLG
1992 Los Angeles	NL	21	69	16	3	0	1	(1	0)	22	5	7	4	0	12	1	0	0	0	0	.00	1	.232	.284	.319
1993 Los Angeles	NL	149	547	174	24	2	35	(21	14)	307	81	112	46	6	86	3	0	6	3	4	.43	10	.318	.370	.561
1994 Los Angeles	NL	107	405	129	18	0	24	(13	11)	219	64	92	33	10	65	1	0	2	1	3	.25	11	.319	.370	.541
1995 Los Angeles	NL	112	434	150	17	0	32	(9	23)	263	82	93	39	10	80	1	0	1	1	0	1.00	10	.346	.400	.606
1996 Los Angeles	NL	148	547	184	16	0	36	(14	22)	308	87	105	81	21	93	1	0	2	0	3	.00	21	.336	.422	.563
1997 Los Angeles	NL	152	556	201	32	1	40	(22	18)	355	104	124	69	11	77	3	0	5	5	1	.83	19	.362	.431	.638
6 ML YEARS		689	2558	854	110	3	168	(80	88)	1474	423	533	272	58	413	10	0	16	10	11	.48	72	.334	.398	.576

Hipolito Pichardo

Pitches: Right Bats: Right Pos: RP-47   Ht: 6'1" Wt: 185 Born: 8/22/69 Age: 28

Year Team	Lg	G	GS	CG	GF	IP	BFP	H	R	ER	HR	SH	SF	HB	TBB	IBB	SO	WP	Bk	W	L	Pct.	ShO	Sv-Op	Hld	ERA
1997 Omaha *	AAA	5	1	0	2	4.2	22	5	3	3	1	0	0	0	3	0	3	0	1	0	0	.000	0	1- --	--	5.79
1992 Kansas City	AL	31	24	1	0	143.2	615	148	71	63	9	4	5	3	49	1	59	3	1	9	6	.600	1	0-0	0	3.95
1993 Kansas City	AL	30	25	2	2	165	720	183	85	74	10	3	8	6	53	2	70	5	3	7	8	.467	0	0-0	1	4.04
1994 Kansas City	AL	45	0	0	19	67.2	303	82	42	37	4	4	2	7	24	5	36	3	0	5	3	.625	0	3-5	6	4.92
1995 Kansas City	AL	44	0	0	16	64	287	66	34	31	4	3	1	4	30	7	43	4	1	8	4	.667	0	1-2	7	4.36
1996 Kansas City	AL	57	0	0	28	68	294	74	41	41	5	3	2	2	26	5	43	4	0	3	5	.375	0	3- 5	15	5.43
1997 Kansas City	AL	47	0	0	26	49	215	51	24	23	7	2	0	1	24	8	34	2	1	3	5	.375	0	11-13	4	4.22
6 ML YEARS		254	49	3	91	557.1	2434	604	297	269	39	19	18	23	206	28	285	21	6	35	31	.530	1	18-25	33	4.34

Marc Pisciotta

Pitches: Right Bats: Right Pos: RP-24   Ht: 6'5" Wt: 225 Born: 8/7/70 Age: 27

Year Team	Lg	G	GS	CG	GF	IP	BFP	H	R	ER	HR	SH	SF	HB	TBB	IBB	SO	WP	Bk	W	L	Pct.	ShO	Sv-Op	Hld	ERA
1991 Welland	A-	24	0	0	21	34	143	16	4	1	0	2	1	3	20	1	47	7	1	1	1	.500	0	8- --	--	0.26
1992 Augusta	A	20	12	1	0	79.1	372	91	51	40	4	5	1	10	43	2	54	12	2	4	5	.444	0	1- --	--	4.54
1993 Augusta	A	34	0	0	28	43.2	188	31	18	13	0	5	0	5	17	1	49	5	0	5	2	.714	0	12- --	--	2.68
Salem	A+	20	0	0	18	18.1	88	23	13	6	0	1	1	0	13	0	13	2	0	0	0	.000	0	12- --	--	2.95
1994 Carolina	AA	26	0	0	17	25.2	127	32	21	16	2	6	2	3	15	2	21	1	1	3	4	.429	0	5- --	--	5.61
Salem	A+	31	0	0	30	29.1	134	24	14	5	1	2	1	3	13	1	23	4	0	1	4	.200	0	19- --	--	1.53
1995 Carolina	AA	56	0	0	27	69.1	313	60	37	32	2	7	3	6	45	8	57	4	0	6	4	.600	0	9- --	--	4.15
1996 Calgary	AAA	57	0	0	27	65.2	308	71	38	30	4	9	2	2	46	8	46	7	0	2	7	.222	0	1- --	--	4.11
1997 Iowa	AAA	42	0	0	38	45.2	194	29	12	12	2	4	2	2	24	3	48	6	0	6	2	.750	0	22- --	--	2.36
1997 Chicago	NL	24	0	0	7	28.1	119	20	10	10	1	1	1	1	16	0	21	2	0	3	1	.750	0	0-1	10	3.18

Jim Pittsley

Pitches: Right Bats: Right Pos: SP-21   Ht: 6'7" Wt: 215 Born: 4/3/74 Age: 24

Year Team	Lg	G	GS	CG	GF	IP	BFP	H	R	ER	HR	SH	SF	HB	TBB	IBB	SO	WP	Bk	W	L	Pct.	ShO	Sv-Op	Hld	ERA
1992 Royals	R	9	9	0	0	43.1	175	27	16	16	0	0	2	5	15	0	47	2	2	4	1	.800	0	0- --	--	3.32
Baseball Cy	A+	1	1	0	0	3	11	2	0	0	0	0	0	0	1	0	4	0	0	0	0	.000	0	0- --	--	0.00
1993 Rockford	A	15	15	2	0	80.1	344	76	43	38	3	2	4	5	32	0	87	5	3	5	5	.500	1	0- --	--	4.26
1994 Wilmington	A+	27	27	1	0	161.2	673	154	73	57	15	3	9	4	42	0	171	2	1	11	5	.688	1	0- --	--	3.17
1995 Omaha	AAA	8	8	0	0	47.2	189	38	20	17	5	0	0	2	16	0	39	0	2	4	1	.800	0	0- --	--	3.21
1996 Wilmington	A+	2	2	0	0	9	42	13	12	11	4	0	0	0	5	1	10	0	0	0	1	.000	0	0- --	--	11.00
Wichita	AA	3	3	0	0	22	78	13	1	1	0	1	0	0	5	0	7	0	0	3	0	1.000	0	0- --	--	0.41

Year Team	Lg	HOW MUCH HE PITCHED						WHAT HE GAVE UP												THE RESULTS						
		G	GS	CG	GF	IP	BFP	H	R	ER	HR	SH	SF	HB	TBB	IBB	SO	WP	Bk	W	L	Pct.	ShO	Sv-Op	Hld	ERA
Omaha	AAA	13	13	0	0	70.1	312	74	34	31	8	3	2	1	39	0	53	0	0	7	1	.875	0	0- --	--	3.97
1997 Omaha	AAA	7	7	0	0	38.2	173	36	21	19	3	0	1	2	20	0	30	2	0	1	2	.333	0	0- --	--	4.42
1995 Kansas City	AL	1	1	0	0	3.1	17	7	5	5	3	0	0	0	1	0	0	0	0	0	0	.000	0	0- --	--	13.50
1997 Kansas City	AL	21	21	0	0	112	501	120	72	68	15	2	6	6	54	1	52	3	0	5	8	.385	0	0-0	0	5.46
2 ML YEARS		22	22	0	0	115.1	518	127	77	73	18	2	6	6	55	1	52	3	0	5	8	.385	0	0-0	0	5.70

Erik Plantenberg

Pitches: Left **Bats:** Right **Pos:** RP-35 **Ht:** 6'1" **Wt:** 180 **Born:** 10/30/68 **Age:** 29

Year Team	Lg	HOW MUCH HE PITCHED						WHAT HE GAVE UP												THE RESULTS						
		G	GS	CG	GF	IP	BFP	H	R	ER	HR	SH	SF	HB	TBB	IBB	SO	WP	Bk	W	L	Pct.	ShO	Sv-Op	Hld	ERA
1990 Elmira	A-	16	5	0	4	40.1	186	44	26	18	2	6	1	0	19	0	36	4	1	2	3	.400	0	1- --	--	4.02
1991 Lynchburg	A+	20	20	0	0	103	461	116	59	43	3	4	2	4	51	1	73	8	0	11	5	.688	0	0- --	--	3.76
1992 Lynchburg	A+	21	12	0	4	81.2	384	112	69	47	7	2	4	5	36	0	62	6	0	3	3	.400	0	0- --	--	5.18
1993 Jacksnville	AA	34	0	0	13	44.2	182	38	11	10	0	1	0	0	14	1	49	1	0	2	1	.667	0	1- --	--	2.01
1994 Jacksnville	AA	14	0	0	7	20.1	85	19	6	3	0	1	1	0	8	2	23	0	0	0	1	.000	0	4- --	--	1.33
Calgary	AAA	19	19	1	0	101.2	480	122	82	66	10	2	3	2	62	1	69	14	0	6	7	.462	1	0- --	--	5.84
1995 Las Vegas	AAA	2	0	0	0	0.1	5	3	3	3	0	0	0	1	0	0	1	0	0	0	0	.000	0	0- --	--	81.00
Memphis	AA	20	0	0	9	21.2	80	19	4	4	2	1	0	1	2	1	16	1	0	2	0	1.000	0	2- --	--	1.66
1996 Canton-Akrn	AA	19	0	0	9	21	84	21	7	7	3	1	0	0	2	1	26	2	0	0	0	.000	0	0- --	--	3.00
Buffalo	AAA	17	1	0	7	33.2	148	35	16	14	2	0	1	0	14	0	29	0	0	2	2	.500	0	1- --	--	3.74
1997 Scranton-WB	AAA	18	0	0	8	14.1	74	22	12	12	1	1	1	0	9	2	12	1	0	0	0	.000	0	0- --	--	7.53
1993 Seattle	AL	20	0	0	4	9.2	53	11	7	7	0	1	0	0	12	1	3	1	0	0	0	.000	0	1-1	6	6.52
1994 Seattle	AL	6	0	0	2	7	31	4	0	0	0	0	0	1	7	0	1	0	0	0	0	.000	0	0-0	1	0.00
1997 Philadelphia	NL	35	0	0	9	25.2	113	25	14	14	1	1	1	1	12	0	12	2	0	0	0	.000	0	0-0	3	4.91
3 ML YEARS		61	0	0	15	42.1	197	40	21	21	1	2	1	3	31	1	16	3	0	0	0	.000	0	1-1	10	4.46

Phil Plantier

Bats: Left **Throws:** Right **Pos:** RF-23; PH-17; LF-13 **Ht:** 5'11" **Wt:** 195 **Born:** 1/27/69 **Age:** 29

Year Team	Lg	BATTING																	BASERUNNING				PERCENTAGES		
		G	AB	H	2B	3B	HR	(Hm	Rd)	TB	R	RBI	TBB	IBB	SO	HBP	SH	SF	SB	CS	SB%	GDP	Avg	OBP	SLG
1997 Las Vegas *	AAA	15	56	24	6	0	5	—	—	45	13	9	4	0	8	0	0	0	1	1	.50	0	.429	.467	.804
Rncho Cuca *	A+	4	17	4	1	1	0	—	—	7	1	3	0	0	1	0	0	0	1	0	1.00	0	.235	.235	.412
Louisville *	AAA	9	31	8	3	0	1	—	—	14	6	10	6	1	3	0	0	2	0	0	.00	1	.258	.359	.452
1990 Boston	AL	14	15	2	1	0	0	(0	0)	3	1	3	4	0	6	1	0	1	0	0	.00	1	.133	.333	.200
1991 Boston	AL	53	148	49	7	1	11	(6	5)	91	27	35	23	2	38	1	0	2	1	0	1.00	2	.331	.420	.615
1992 Boston	AL	108	349	86	19	0	7	(5	2)	126	46	30	44	8	83	2	2	2	2	3	.40	9	.246	.332	.361
1993 San Diego	NL	138	462	111	20	1	34	(16	18)	235	67	100	61	7	124	7	1	5	4	5	.44	4	.240	.335	.509
1994 San Diego	NL	96	341	75	21	0	18	(7	11)	150	44	41	36	6	91	5	1	2	3	1	.75	8	.220	.302	.440
1995 Hou-SD	NL	76	216	55	6	0	9	(1	8)	88	33	34	28	3	48	1	0	3	1	1	.50	3	.255	.339	.407
1996 Oakland	AL	73	231	49	8	1	7	(3	4)	80	29	31	28	0	56	3	0	1	2	2	.50	5	.212	.304	.346
1997 SD-StL	NL	52	121	30	8	0	5	(2	3)	53	13	18	13	1	30	3	0	2	0	3	.00	5	.248	.331	.438
1995 Houston	NL	22	68	17	2	0	4	(0	4)	31	12	15	11	1	19	1	0	0	0	0	.00	0	.250	.349	.456
San Diego	NL	54	148	38	4	0	5	(1	4)	57	21	19	17	2	29	0	0	3	1	1	.50	3	.257	.333	.385
1997 San Diego	NL	10	8	1	0	0	0	(0	0)	1	0	0	2	0	3	0	0	0	0	0	.00	0	.125	.300	.125
St. Louis	NL	42	113	29	8	0	5	(2	3)	52	13	18	11	1	27	3	0	2	0	3	.00	5	.257	.333	.460
8 ML YEARS		610	1883	457	90	3	91	(40	51)	826	260	292	237	27	476	23	4	18	13	15	.46	37	.243	.332	.439

Dan Plesac

Pitches: Left **Bats:** Left **Pos:** RP-73 **Ht:** 6'5" **Wt:** 215 **Born:** 2/4/62 **Age:** 36

Year Team	Lg	HOW MUCH HE PITCHED						WHAT HE GAVE UP												THE RESULTS						
		G	GS	CG	GF	IP	BFP	H	R	ER	HR	SH	SF	HB	TBB	IBB	SO	WP	Bk	W	L	Pct.	ShO	Sv-Op	Hld	ERA
1986 Milwaukee	AL	51	0	0	33	91	377	81	34	30	5	6	5	0	29	1	75	4	0	10	7	.588	0	14- --	--	2.97
1987 Milwaukee	AL	57	0	0	44	79.1	325	63	30	23	8	1	2	3	23	1	89	6	0	5	6	.455	0	23-36	0	2.61
1988 Milwaukee	AL	50	0	0	48	52.1	211	46	14	14	2	2	0	0	12	2	52	4	6	1	2	.333	0	30-35	0	2.41
1989 Milwaukee	AL	52	0	0	51	61.1	242	47	16	16	6	0	4	0	17	1	52	0	0	3	4	.429	0	33-40	0	2.35
1990 Milwaukee	AL	66	0	0	52	69	299	67	36	34	5	2	2	3	31	6	65	2	0	3	7	.300	0	24-34	2	4.43
1991 Milwaukee	AL	45	10	0	25	92.1	402	92	49	44	12	3	7	3	39	1	61	2	1	2	7	.222	0	8-12	1	4.29
1992 Milwaukee	AL	44	4	0	13	79	330	64	28	26	5	8	4	3	35	5	54	3	1	5	4	.556	0	1-3	1	2.96
1993 Chicago	NL	57	0	0	12	62.2	276	74	37	33	10	4	3	0	21	6	47	5	2	2	1	.667	0	0-2	12	4.74
1994 Chicago	NL	54	0	0	14	54.2	235	61	30	28	9	1	1	1	13	0	53	0	0	2	3	.400	0	1-3	14	4.61
1995 Pittsburgh	NL	58	0	0	16	60.1	259	53	26	24	3	4	3	1	27	7	57	1	0	4	4	.500	0	3-5	11	3.58
1996 Pittsburgh	NL	73	0	0	30	70.1	300	67	35	32	4	2	3	0	24	6	76	4	0	6	5	.545	0	11-17	11	4.09
1997 Toronto	AL	73	0	0	18	50.1	215	47	22	20	8	2	1	0	19	4	61	2	0	2	4	.333	0	1-5	27	3.58
12 ML YEARS		680	14	0	359	822.2	3471	762	357	324	77	35	35	14	290	40	742	33	10	45	54	.455	0	149- --	--	3.54

Eric Plunk

Pitches: Right **Bats:** Right **Pos:** RP-55 **Ht:** 6'6" **Wt:** 220 **Born:** 9/3/63 **Age:** 34

Year Team	Lg	HOW MUCH HE PITCHED						WHAT HE GAVE UP												THE RESULTS						
		G	GS	CG	GF	IP	BFP	H	R	ER	HR	SH	SF	HB	TBB	IBB	SO	WP	Bk	W	L	Pct.	ShO	Sv-Op	Hld	ERA
1986 Oakland	AL	26	15	0	2	120.1	537	91	75	71	14	2	3	5	102	2	98	9	6	4	7	.364	0	0- --	--	5.31
1987 Oakland	AL	32	11	0	11	95	432	91	53	50	8	3	5	2	62	3	90	5	2	4	6	.400	0	2-5	1	4.74
1988 Oakland	AL	49	0	0	22	78	331	62	27	26	6	3	2	1	39	4	79	4	7	7	2	.778	0	5-9	5	3.00
1989 Oak-NYA	AL	50	7	0	17	104.1	445	82	43	38	10	3	4	1	64	2	85	10	3	8	6	.571	0	1-3	7	3.28
1990 New York	AL	47	0	0	16	72.2	310	58	27	22	6	7	0	2	43	4	67	4	2	6	3	.667	0	0-1	3	2.72

Year Team	Lg	G	GS	CG	GF	IP	BFP	H	R	ER	HR	SH	SF	HB	TBB	IBB	SO	WP	Bk	W	L	Pct.	ShO	Sv-Op	Hld	ERA
						HOW MUCH HE PITCHED					**WHAT HE GAVE UP**												**THE RESULTS**			
1991 New York	AL	43	8	0	6	111.2	521	128	69	59	18	6	4	1	62	1	103	6	2	2	5	.286	0	0-0	2	4.76
1992 Cleveland	AL	58	0	0	20	71.2	309	61	31	29	5	3	2	0	38	2	50	5	0	9	6	.600	0	4-8	7	3.64
1993 Cleveland	AL	70	0	0	40	71	306	61	29	22	5	4	2	0	30	4	77	6	0	4	5	.444	0	15-18	16	2.79
1994 Cleveland	AL	41	0	0	18	71	306	61	25	20	3	2	1	2	37	5	73	7	0	7	2	.778	0	3-7	8	2.54
1995 Cleveland	AL	56	0	0	22	64	263	48	19	19	5	2	2	4	27	2	71	3	0	6	2	.750	0	2-5	10	2.67
1996 Cleveland	AL	56	0	0	12	77.2	318	56	21	21	6	1	4	3	34	2	85	4	1	3	2	.600	0	2-3	15	2.43
1997 Cleveland	AL	55	0	0	22	65.2	293	62	37	34	12	1	2	1	36	7	66	6	0	4	5	.444	0	0-2	10	4.66
1989 Oakland	AL	23	0	0	12	28.2	113	17	7	7	1	1	0	1	12	0	24	4	0	1	1	.500	0	1-3	5	2.20
New York	AL	27	7	0	5	75.2	332	65	36	31	9	2	4	0	52	2	61	6	3	7	5	.583	0	0-0	2	3.69
12 ML YEARS		583	41	0	208	1003	4371	861	456	411	98	37	31	22	574	38	944	69	:23	64	51	.557	0	34- —	—	3.69

Kevin Polcovich

Bats: R Throws: R Pos: SS-80; PH-3; 2B-2; 3B-1   Ht: 5'9" Wt: 168 Born: 6/28/70 Age: 28

Year Team	Lg	G	AB	H	2B	3B	HR	(Hm	Rd)	TB	R	RBI	TBB	IBB	SO	HBP	SH	SF	SB	CS	SB%	GDP	Avg	OBP	SLG
							BATTING												**BASERUNNING**				**PERCENTAGES**		
1992 Carolina	AA	13	35	6	0	0	0	—	—	6	1	1	4	0	4	2	0	0	0	2	.00	1	.171	.293	.171
Augusta	A	46	153	40	6	2	0	—	—	50	24	10	18	0	30	8	3	0	7	7	.50	1	.261	.369	.327
1993 Augusta	A	14	48	13	2	0	0	—	—	15	9	4	7	0	8	0	2	1	2	1	.67	1	.271	.357	.313
Carolina	AA	4	11	3	0	0	0	—	—	3	1	1	1	0	1	0	2	0	0	0	.00	1	.273	.333	.273
Salem	A+	94	282	72	10	3	1	—	—	91	44	25	49	0	42	12	6	3	13	6	.68	7	.255	.384	.323
1994 Carolina	AA	125	406	95	14	2	2	—	—	119	46	33	38	4	70	11	10	8	9	4	.69	6	.234	.311	.293
1995 Carolina	AA	64	221	70	8	0	3	—	—	87	27	18	14	1	29	5	3	1	10	5	.67	3	.317	.369	.394
Calgary	AAA	62	213	60	8	1	3	—	—	79	31	27	11	0	32	8	2	3	5	6	.45	7	.282	.336	.371
1996 Carolina	AAA	104	336	92	21	3	1	—	—	122	53	46	18	3	49	14	5	2	7	6	.54	9	.274	.335	.363
1997 Carolina	AA	17	50	16	5	0	3	—	—	30	13	7	10	0	4	2	2	0	4	2	.67	1	.320	.452	.600
Calgary	AAA	17	62	19	4	0	1	—	—	26	7	9	1	0	7	1	0	1	0	0	.00	1	.306	.323	.419
1997 Pittsburgh	NL	84	245	67	16	1	4	(0	4)	97	37	21	21	4	45	9	2	2	2	5	.50	11	.273	.350	.396

Jim Poole

Pitches: Left Bats: Left Pos: RP-63   Ht: 6'2" Wt: 203 Born: 4/28/66 Age: 32

Year Team	Lg	G	GS	CG	GF	IP	BFP	H	R	ER	HR	SH	SF	HB	TBB	IBB	SO	WP	Bk	W	L	Pct.	ShO	Sv-Op	Hld	ERA
						HOW MUCH HE PITCHED					**WHAT HE GAVE UP**												**THE RESULTS**			
1990 Los Angeles	NL	16	0	0	4	10.2	46	7	5	5	1	0	0	0	8	4	6	1	0	0	0	.000	0	0-0	2	4.22
1991 Tex-Bal	AL	29	0	0	5	42	166	29	14	11	3	3	3	0	12	2	38	2	0	3	2	.600	0	1-1	4	2.36
1992 Baltimore	AL	6	0	0	1	3.1	14	3	3	0	0	0	0	0	1	0	3	0	0	0	0	.000	0	0-1	0	0.00
1993 Baltimore	AL	55	0	0	11	50.1	197	30	18	12	2	3	2	0	21	5	29	0	0	2	1	.667	0	2-3	14	2.15
1994 Baltimore	AL	38	0	0	10	20.1	100	32	15	15	4	0	3	0	11	2	18	1	0	1	0	1.000	0	0-2	10	6.64
1995 Cleveland	AL	42	0	0	9	50.1	206	40	22	21	7	1	2	2	17	0	41	2	1	3	3	.500	0	0-0	6	3.75
1996 Cle-SF		67	0	0	13	50.1	218	44	22	16	5	3	1	1	27	7	38	3	0	1	6	.143	0	0-4	10	2.86
1997 San Francisco	NL	63	0	0	11	49.1	242	73	44	39	6	4	2	4	25	4	26	5	0	3	1	.750	0	0-0	9	7.11
1991 Texas	AL	5	0	0	2	6	31	10	4	3	0	0	1	0	3	0	4	0	0	0	0	.000	0	1-1	0	4.50
Baltimore	AL	24	0	0	3	36	135	19	10	8	3	3	2	0	9	2	34	2	0	3	2	.600	0	0-0	4	2.00
1996 Cleveland	AL	32	0	0	8	26.2	121	29	15	9	3	0	1	0	14	4	19	2	0	4	0	1.000	0	0-1	5	3.04
San Francisco	NL	35	0	0	5	23.2	97	15	7	7	2	3	0	1	13	3	19	1	0	2	1	.667	0	0-3	5	2.66
8 ML YEARS		316	0	0	64	276.2	1189	258	143	119	28	14	13	7	122	24	199	14	1	18	8	.692	0	3-11	55	3.87

Mark Portugal

Pitches: Right Bats: Right Pos: SP-3   Ht: 6'0" Wt: 190 Born: 10/30/62 Age: 35

Year Team	Lg	G	GS	CG	GF	IP	BFP	H	R	ER	HR	SH	SF	HB	TBB	IBB	SO	WP	Bk	W	L	Pct.	ShO	Sv-Op	Hld	ERA
						HOW MUCH HE PITCHED					**WHAT HE GAVE UP**												**THE RESULTS**			
1985 Minnesota	AL	6	4	0	0	24.1	105	24	16	15	3	0	2	0	14	0	12	1	1	1	3	.250	0	0- —	—	5.55
1986 Minnesota	AL	27	15	3	7	112.2	481	112	56	54	10	5	3	1	50	1	67	5	0	6	10	.375	0	1- —	—	4.31
1987 Minnesota	AL	13	7	0	3	44	204	58	40	38	13	0	1	1	24	1	28	2	0	1	3	.250	0	0-1	0	7.77
1988 Minnesota	AL	26	0	0	9	57.2	242	60	30	29	11	2	3	1	17	1	31	2	2	3	3	.500	0	3-4	0	4.53
1989 Houston	NL	20	15	2	1	108	440	91	34	33	7	8	1	2	37	0	86	3	0	7	1	.875	1	0-0	1	2.75
1990 Houston	NL	32	32	1	0	196.2	831	187	90	79	21	7	6	4	67	4	136	6	0	11	10	.524	0	0-0	0	3.62
1991 Houston	NL	32	27	1	3	168.1	710	163	91	84	19	6	6	2	59	5	120	4	1	10	12	.455	0	1-2	1	4.49
1992 Houston	NL	18	16	1	0	101.1	405	76	32	30	7	5	1	1	41	3	62	1	1	6	3	.667	1	0-0	0	2.66
1993 Houston	NL	33	33	1	0	208	876	194	75	64	10	11	3	4	77	3	131	9	2	18	4	.818	1	0-0	0	2.77
1994 San Francisco	NL	21	21	1	0	137.1	580	135	68	60	17	6	4	6	45	2	87	5	0	10	8	.556	0	0-0	0	3.93
1995 SF-Cin	NL	31	31	1	0	181.2	775	185	91	81	17	9	1	4	56	2	96	7	0	11	10	.524	0	0-0	0	4.01
1996 Cincinnati	NL	27	26	1	0	156	646	146	77	69	20	7	6	2	42	2	93	6	0	8	9	.471	0	0-0	0	3.98
1997 Philadelphia	NL	3	3	0	0	13.2	60	17	8	7	0	1	1	0	5	0	2	0	0	2	0	.000	0	0-0	0	4.61
1995 San Francisco	NL	17	17	1	0	104	445	106	56	48	10	5	0	2	34	2	63	2	0	5	5	.500	0	0-0	0	4.15
Cincinnati	NL	14	14	0	0	77.2	330	79	35	33	7	4	1	2	22	0	33	5	0	6	5	.545	0	0-0	0	3.82
13 ML YEARS		289	230	12	23	1509.2	6355	1448	708	643	155	67	38	28	534	24	951	51	7	92	78	.541	4	5- —	—	3.83

Jorge Posada

Bats: Both Throws: Right Pos: C-60   Ht: 6'2" Wt: 205 Born: 8/17/71 Age: 26

Year Team	Lg	G	AB	H	2B	3B	HR	(Hm	Rd)	TB	R	RBI	TBB	IBB	SO	HBP	SH	SF	SB	CS	SB%	GDP	Avg	OBP	SLG
							BATTING												**BASERUNNING**				**PERCENTAGES**		
1991 Oneonta	A-	71	217	51	5	5	4	—	—	78	34	33	51	0	49	4	8	1	6	4	.60	3	.235	.388	.359
1992 Greensboro	A	101	339	94	22	4	12	—	—	160	60	58	58	2	87	6	0	3	11	6	.65	8	.277	.389	.472
1993 Pr William	A+	118	410	106	27	2	17	—	—	188	71	61	67	4	90	6	1	6	17	5	.77	7	.259	.366	.459

Year Team	Lg	G	AB	H	2B	3B	HR	(Hm	Rd)	TB	R	RBI	TBB	IBB	SO	HBP	SH	SF	SB	CS	SB%	GDP	Avg	OBP	SLG
Albany-Colo	AA	7	25	7	0	0	0	—	—	7	3	0	2	0	7	0	0	0	0	0	.00	1	.280	.333	.280
1994 Columbus	AAA	92	313	75	13	3	11	—	—	127	46	48	32	1	81	1	4	5	5	5	.50	3	.240	.308	.406
1995 Columbus	AAA	108	368	94	32	5	8	—	—	160	60	51	54	2	101	1	6	3	4	4	.50	14	.255	.350	.435
1996 Columbus	AAA	106	354	96	22	6	11	—	—	163	76	62	79	3	86	3	1	3	3	3	.50	13	.271	.405	.460
1995 New York	AL	1	0	0	0	0	0	(0	0)	0	0	0	0	0	0	0	0	0	0	0	.00	0	.000	.000	.000
1996 New York	AL	8	14	1	0	0	0	(0	0)	1	1	0	1	0	6	0	0	0	0	0	.00	1	.071	.133	.071
1997 New York	AL	60	188	47	12	0	6	(2	4)	77	29	25	30	2	33	3	1	2	1	2	.33	3	.250	.359	.410
3 ML YEARS		69	202	48	12	0	6	(2	4)	78	30	25	31	2	39	3	1	2	1	2	.33	4	.238	.345	.386

Scott Pose

Bats: L Throws: R Pos: LF-28; PH-24; RF-17; DH-5; CF-3   Ht: 5'11" Wt: 165 Born: 2/11/67 Age: 31

Year Team	Lg	G	AB	H	2B	3B	HR	(Hm	Rd)	TB	R	RBI	TBB	IBB	SO	HBP	SH	SF	SB	CS	SB%	GDP	Avg	OBP	SLG
1989 Billings	R+	60	210	74	7	2	0	—	—	85	52	25	54	3	31	1	1	1	26	3	.90	2	.352	.485	.405
1990 Chston-WV	A	135	480	143	13	5	0	—	—	166	106	46	114	8	56	7	5	6	49	21	.70	5	.298	.435	.346
1991 Nashville	AAA	15	52	10	0	0	0	—	—	10	7	3	2	0	9	2	2	0	3	1	.75	0	.192	.250	.192
Chattanooga	AA	117	402	110	8	5	1	—	—	131	61	31	69	3	50	2	7	3	17	13	.57	7	.274	.380	.326
1992 Chattanooga	AA	136	526	180	22	8	2	—	—	224	87	45	63	5	66	4	4	3	21	27	.44	8	.342	.414	.426
1993 Edmonton	AAA	109	398	113	8	6	0	—	—	133	61	27	42	3	36	1	5	1	19	9	.68	8	.284	.353	.334
1994 New Orleans	AAA	124	429	121	13	7	0	—	—	148	60	52	47	2	52	2	9	4	20	8	.71	7	.282	.353	.345
1995 Albuquerque	AAA	7	16	3	1	0	0	—	—	4	5	1	2	0	0	0	0	0	2	0	1.00	0	.188	.278	.250
Salt Lake	AAA	70	203	63	9	1	0	—	—	74	41	19	29	2	28	1	3	3	13	4	.76	2	.310	.394	.365
1996 Syracuse	AAA	113	419	114	11	6	0	—	—	137	71	39	58	0	71	3	9	4	30	16	.65	3	.272	.362	.327
1997 Columbus	AAA	57	227	70	10	7	2	—	—	100	50	32	32	0	29	5	2	0	13	5	.72	2	.308	.405	.441
1993 Florida	NL	15	41	8	2	0	0	(0	0)	10	0	3	2	0	4	0	0	0	0	2	.00	1	.195	.233	.244
1997 New York	AL	54	87	19	2	1	0	(0	0)	23	19	5	9	0	11	0	0	0	3	1	.75	1	.218	.292	.264
2 ML YEARS		69	128	27	4	1	0	(0	0)	33	19	8	11	0	15	0	0	0	3	3	.50	1	.211	.273	.258

Dante Powell

Bats: Right Throws: Right Pos: CF-20; PH-8; RF-2   Ht: 6'2" Wt: 180 Born: 8/25/73 Age: 24

Year Team	Lg	G	AB	H	2B	3B	HR	(Hm	Rd)	TB	R	RBI	TBB	IBB	SO	HBP	SH	SF	SB	CS	SB%	GDP	Avg	OBP	SLG
1994 Everett	A-	41	165	51	15	1	5	—	—	83	31	25	19	1	47	4	0	2	27	1	.96	1	.309	.389	.503
San Jose	A+	1	4	2	0	1	0	—	—	4	0	0	0	1	1	0	0	0	0	0	.00	0	.500	.500	1.000
1995 San Jose	A+	135	505	125	23	8	10	—	—	194	74	70	46	2	131	3	1	4	43	12	.78	8	.248	.312	.384
1996 Shreveport	AA	135	508	142	27	2	21	—	—	236	92	78	72	4	92	3	1	2	43	23	.65	6	.280	.371	.465
Phoenix	AAA	2	8	2	0	1	0	—	—	4	0	0	2	0	3	0	0	0	0	1	.00	0	.250	.400	.500
1997 Phoenix	AAA	108	452	109	24	4	11	—	—	174	91	42	52	1	105	3	3	0	34	10	.77	9	.241	.323	.385
1997 San Francisco	NL	27	39	12	1	0	1	(1	0)	16	8	3	4	0	11	0	1	0	1	1	.50	0	.308	.372	.410

Jay Powell

Pitches: Right Bats: Right Pos: RP-74   Ht: 6'4" Wt: 225 Born: 1/19/72 Age: 26

Year Team	Lg	G	GS	CG	GF	IP	BFP	H	R	ER	HR	SH	SF	HB	TBB	IBB	SO	WP	Bk	W	L	Pct.	ShO	Sv-Op	Hld	ERA
1995 Florida	NL	9	0	0	1	8.1	38	7	2	1	0	1	0	2	6	1	4	0	0	0	0	.000	0	0-0	2	1.08
1996 Florida	NL	67	0	0	16	71.1	321	71	41	36	5	2	1	4	36	1	52	3	0	4	3	.571	0	2-5	10	4.54
1997 Florida	NL	74	0	0	23	79.2	337	71	35	29	3	6	4	4	30	3	65	3	0	7	2	.778	0	2-4	24	3.28
3 ML YEARS		150	0	0	40	159.1	696	149	78	66	8	9	5	10	72	5	121	6	0	11	5	.688	0	4-9	36	3.73

Arquimedez Pozo

Bats: Right Throws: Right Pos: 3B-4   Ht: 5'10" Wt: 160 Born: 8/24/73 Age: 24

Year Team	Lg	G	AB	H	2B	3B	HR	(Hm	Rd)	TB	R	RBI	TBB	IBB	SO	HBP	SH	SF	SB	CS	SB%	GDP	Avg	OBP	SLG
1992 San Berndno	A+	54	199	52	8	4	3	—	—	77	33	19	20	0	41	2	1	0	13	8	.62	2	.261	.335	.387
Bellingham	A-	39	149	48	12	0	7	—	—	81	37	21	20	0	24	2	1	1	9	5	.64	1	.322	.407	.544
1993 Riverside	A+	127	515	176	44	6	13	—	—	271	98	63	56	4	56	2	1	5	10	10	.50	22	.342	.405	.526
1994 Jacksnville	AA	119	447	129	31	1	14	—	—	204	70	54	32	0	43	7	3	6	11	8	.58	8	.289	.341	.456
1995 Tacoma	AAA	122	450	135	19	6	10	—	—	196	57	62	26	1	31	3	1	4	3	3	.50	15	.300	.340	.436
1996 Tacoma	AAA	95	365	102	12	5	15	—	—	169	55	64	39	1	40	6	1	8	3	3	.50	11	.279	.352	.463
Pawtucket	AAA	11	37	9	1	0	1	—	—	13	6	3	3	0	6	2	0	0	0	0	.00	1	.243	.333	.351
1997 Pawtucket	AAA	101	377	107	18	4	21	—	—	193	61	70	37	4	55	7	0	1	4	4	.50	9	.284	.358	.512
1995 Seattle	AL	1	1	0	0	0	0	(0	0)	0	0	0	0	0	0	0	0	0	0	0	.00	0	.000	.000	.000
1996 Boston	AL	21	58	10	3	1	1	(0	1)	18	4	11	2	0	10	1	0	1	1	0	1.00	1	.172	.210	.310
1997 Boston	AL	4	15	4	1	0	0	(0	0)	5	0	3	0	0	5	0	1	0	0	0	.00	1	.267	.250	.333
3 ML YEARS		26	74	14	4	1	1	(0	1)	23	4	14	2	0	15	1	1	1	1	0	1.00	1	.189	.215	.311

Todd Pratt

Bats: Right Throws: Right Pos: C-36; PH-3   Ht: 6'3" Wt: 220 Born: 2/9/67 Age: 31

Year Team	Lg	G	AB	H	2B	3B	HR	(Hm	Rd)	TB	R	RBI	TBB	IBB	SO	HBP	SH	SF	SB	CS	SB%	GDP	Avg	OBP	SLG
1997 Norfolk *	AAA	59	206	62	8	3	9	—	—	103	42	34	26	1	48	2	2	1	1	2	.33	8	.301	.383	.500
1992 Philadelphia	NL	16	46	13	1	0	2	(2	0)	20	6	10	4	0	12	0	0	0	0	0	.00	2	.283	.340	.435

Year Team	Lg	G	AB	H	2B	3B	HR	(Hm	Rd)	TB	R	RBI	TBB	IBB	SO	HBP	SH	SF	SB	CS	SB%	GDP	Avg	OBP	SLG
																		BASERUNNING					PERCENTAGES		
1993 Philadelphia	NL	33	87	25	6	0	5	(4	1)	46	8	13	5	0	19	1	1	1	0	0	.00	2	.287	.330	.529
1994 Philadelphia	NL	28	102	20	6	1	2	(1	1)	34	10	9	12	0	29	0	0	0	0	1	.00	3	.196	.281	.333
1995 Chicago	NL	25	60	8	2	0	0	(0	0)	10	3	4	6	1	21	0	0	1	0	0	.00	1	.133	.209	.167
1997 New York	NL	39	106	30	6	0	2	(1	1)	42	12	19	13	0	32	2	0	0	0	1	.00	1	.283	.372	.396
5 ML YEARS		141	401	96	21	1	11	(8	3)	152	39	55	40	1	113	3	1	2	0	2	.00	9	.239	.312	.379

Curtis Pride

Bats: L **Throws:** R **Pos:** PH-37; LF-34; DH-23; RF-3   **Ht:** 6'0" **Wt:** 200 **Born:** 12/17/68 **Age:** 29

Year Team	Lg	G	AB	H	2B	3B	HR	(Hm	Rd)	TB	R	RBI	TBB	IBB	SO	HBP	SH	SF	SB	CS	SB%	GDP	Avg	OBP	SLG
1997 Pawtucket *	AAA	1	3	0	0	0	0	—	—	0	0	0	0	0	2	0	0	0	0	0	.00	0	.000	.000	.000
1993 Montreal	NL	10	9	4	1	1	1	(0	1)	10	3	5	0	0	3	0	0	0	1	0	1.00	0	.444	.444	1.111
1995 Montreal	NL	48	63	11	1	0	0	(0	0)	12	10	2	5	0	16	0	1	0	3	2	.60	2	.175	.235	.190
1996 Detroit	AL	95	267	80	17	5	10	(5	5)	137	52	31	31	1	63	0	3	0	11	6	.65	2	.300	.372	.513
1997 Bos-Det	AL	81	164	35	4	4	3	(3	0)	56	22	20	24	1	46	1	2	1	6	4	.60	4	.213	.316	.341
1997 Boston	AL	2	2	1	0	0	1	(1	0)	4	1	1	0	0	1	0	0	0	0	0	.00	0	.500	.500	2.000
Detroit	AL	79	162	34	4	4	2	(2	0)	52	21	19	24	1	45	1	2	1	6	4	.60	4	.210	.314	.321
4 ML YEARS		234	503	130	23	10	14	(8	6)	215	87	58	60	2	128	1	6	1	21	12	.64	8	.258	.338	.427

Ariel Prieto

Pitches: Right **Bats:** Right **Pos:** SP-22   **Ht:** 6'3" **Wt:** 225 **Born:** 10/22/69 **Age:** 28

Year Team	Lg	G	GS	CG	GF	IP	BFP	H	R	ER	HR	SH	SF	HB	TBB	IBB	SO	WP	Bk	W	L	Pct.	ShO	Sv-Op	Hld	ERA
1997 Edmonton *	AAA	2	2	0	0	6	22	4	1	1	0	0	0	0	1	0	7	1	0	0	0	.000	0	0--	—	1.50
1995 Oakland	AL	14	9	1	1	58	258	57	35	32	4	3	2	5	32	1	37	4	1	2	6	.250	0	0-0	0	4.97
1996 Oakland	AL	21	21	2	0	125.2	547	130	66	58	9	5	5	7	54	2	75	6	2	6	7	.462	0	0-0	0	4.15
1997 Oakland	AL	22	22	0	0	125	588	155	84	70	16	3	4	5	70	3	90	7	1	6	8	.429	0	0-0	0	5.04
3 ML YEARS		57	52	3	1	308.2	1393	342	185	160	29	11	11	17	156	6	202	17	4	14	21	.400	0	0-0	0	4.67

Tom Prince

Bats: Right **Throws:** Right **Pos:** C-45; PH-8   **Ht:** 5'11" **Wt:** 202 **Born:** 8/13/64 **Age:** 33

Year Team	Lg	G	AB	H	2B	3B	HR	(Hm	Rd)	TB	R	RBI	TBB	IBB	SO	HBP	SH	SF	SB	CS	SB%	GDP	Avg	OBP	SLG
1987 Pittsburgh	NL	4	9	2	1	0	1	(0	1)	6	1	2	0	0	2	0	0	0	0	0	.00	0	.222	.222	.667
1988 Pittsburgh	NL	29	74	13	2	0	0	(0	0)	15	3	6	4	0	15	0	2	0	0	0	.00	5	.176	.218	.203
1989 Pittsburgh	NL	21	52	7	4	0	0	(0	0)	11	1	5	6	1	12	0	0	1	1	1	.50	1	.135	.220	.212
1990 Pittsburgh	NL	4	10	1	0	0	0	(0	0)	1	1	0	1	0	2	0	0	0	0	0	.00	0	.100	.182	.100
1991 Pittsburgh	NL	26	34	9	3	0	1	(0	1)	15	4	2	7	0	3	1	0	0	0	0	.00	3	.265	.405	.441
1992 Pittsburgh	NL	27	44	4	2	0	0	(0	0)	6	1	5	6	0	9	0	2	0	1	1	.50	2	.091	.192	.136
1993 Pittsburgh	NL	66	179	35	14	0	2	(2	0)	55	14	24	13	2	38	7	2	3	1	1	.50	5	.196	.272	.307
1994 Los Angeles	NL	3	6	2	0	0	0	(0	0)	2	2	1	1	0	3	0	0	0	0	0	.00	0	.333	.429	.333
1995 Los Angeles	NL	18	40	8	2	1	1	(0	1)	15	3	4	4	0	10	0	0	0	0	0	.00	0	.200	.273	.375
1996 Los Angeles	NL	40	64	19	6	0	1	(0	1)	28	6	11	6	2	15	2	3	2	0	0	.00	0	.297	.365	.438
1997 Los Angeles	NL	47	100	22	5	0	3	(2	1)	36	17	14	5	0	15	3	4	1	0	0	.00	2	.220	.275	.360
11 ML YEARS		285	612	122	39	1	9	(4	5)	190	53	74	53	5	124	13	11	9	3	4	.43	18	.199	.274	.310

Tim Pugh

Pitches: Right **Bats:** Right **Pos:** SP-2   **Ht:** 6'6" **Wt:** 225 **Born:** 1/26/67 **Age:** 31

Year Team	Lg	G	GS	CG	GF	IP	BFP	H	R	ER	HR	SH	SF	HB	TBB	IBB	SO	WP	Bk	W	L	Pct.	ShO	Sv-Op	Hld	ERA
1997 Toledo *	AAA	19	17	0	1	109	460	115	60	52	18	2	3	5	28	0	97	4	0	3	5	.375	0	0--	—	4.29
1992 Cincinnati	NL	7	7	0	0	45.1	187	47	15	13	2	2	1	1	13	3	18	0	0	4	2	.667	0	0-0	0	2.58
1993 Cincinnati	NL	31	27	3	1	164.1	738	200	102	96	19	6	5	7	59	1	94	3	2	10	15	.400	1	0-0	0	5.26
1994 Cincinnati	NL	10	9	1	0	47.2	227	60	37	32	5	2	5	3	26	0	24	4	0	3	3	.500	0	0-0	1	6.04
1995 Cincinnati	NL	28	12	0	4	98.1	413	100	46	42	13	2	2	5	32	2	38	3	1	6	5	.545	0	0-0	3	3.84
1997 Detroit	AL	2	2	0	0	9	37	6	5	5	0	0	0	0	5	0	4	0	0	1	1	.500	0	0-0	0	5.00
1996 Cin-KC	NL	29	1	0	8	52	247	66	44	42	12	2	2	3	23	3	36	3	0	1	2	.333	0	0-0	3	7.27
1996 Cincinnati	NL	10	0	0	0	15.2	83	24	20	20	3	2	1	1	11	2	9	1	0	1	1	.500	0	0-0	3	11.49
Kansas City	AL	19	1	0	8	36.1	164	42	24	22	9	0	1	2	12	1	27	2	0	0	1	.000	0	0-0	0	5.45
6 ML YEARS		107	58	4	15	416.2	1849	479	249	230	51	14	15	15	158	9	214	13	3	25	28	.472	1	0-0	4	4.97

Harvey Pulliam

Bats: R **Throws:** R **Pos:** PH-31; LF-24; RF-10; CF-1   **Ht:** 6'0" **Wt:** 205 **Born:** 10/20/67 **Age:** 30

Year Team	Lg	G	AB	H	2B	3B	HR	(Hm	Rd)	TB	R	RBI	TBB	IBB	SO	HBP	SH	SF	SB	CS	SB%	GDP	Avg	OBP	SLG
1997 Colo Spmgs *	AAA	40	137	55	10	2	12	—	—	105	44	43	21	3	19	4	0	0	1	0	1.00	1	.401	.494	.766
1991 Kansas City	AL	18	33	9	1	0	3	(2	1)	19	4	4	3	1	9	0	1	0	0	0	.00	1	.273	.333	.576
1992 Kansas City	AL	4	5	1	1	0	0	(0	0)	2	2	0	1	0	3	0	0	0	0	0	.00	0	.200	.333	.400
1993 Kansas City	AL	27	62	16	5	0	1	(0	1)	24	7	6	2	0	14	1	0	0	0	0	.00	3	.258	.292	.387
1995 Colorado	NL	5	5	2	1	0	1	(1	0)	6	1	3	0	0	2	0	0	0	0	0	.00	0	.400	.400	1.200
1996 Colorado	NL	10	15	2	0	0	0	(0	0)	2	2	0	2	0	6	0	0	0	0	0	.00	0	.133	.235	.133
1997 Colorado	NL	59	67	19	3	0	3	(2	1)	31	15	9	5	0	15	0	0	0	0	0	.00	2	.284	.333	.463

BATTING																		BASERUNNING				PERCENTAGES		
Year Team	Lg	G	AB	H	2B	3B	HR	(Hm | Rd)	TB	R	RBI	TBB	IBB	SO	HBP	SH	SF	SB	CS	SB%	GDP	Avg	OBP	SLG
6 ML YEARS		123	187	49	11	0	8	(5 | 3)	84	31	22	13	1	49	1	1	0	0	1	.00	7	.262	.313	.449

Bill Pulsipher

Pitches: Left **Bats:** Left **Pos:** SP   **Ht:** 6'3" **Wt:** 208 **Born:** 10/9/73 **Age:** 24

		HOW MUCH HE PITCHED						WHAT HE GAVE UP										THE RESULTS					
Year Team	Lg	G	GS	CG	GF	IP	BFP	H	R	ER	HR	SH	SF	HB	TBB	IBB	SO	WP	Bk	W	L	Pct.	ShO	Sv-Op	Hld	ERA
1995 New York	NL	17	17	2	0	126.2	530	122	58	56	11	2	1	4	45	0	81	2	1	5	7	.417	0	0-0	0	3.98

Paul Quantrill

Pitches: Right **Bats:** Left **Pos:** RP-77   **Ht:** 6'1" **Wt:** 185 **Born:** 11/3/68 **Age:** 29

		HOW MUCH HE PITCHED						WHAT HE GAVE UP										THE RESULTS					
Year Team	Lg	G	GS	CG	GF	IP	BFP	H	R	ER	HR	SH	SF	HB	TBB	IBB	SO	WP	Bk	W	L	Pct.	ShO	Sv-Op	Hld	ERA
1992 Boston	AL	27	0	0	10	49.1	213	55	18	12	1	4	2	1	15	5	24	1	0	2	3	.400	0	1-5	3	2.19
1993 Boston	AL	49	14	1	8	138	594	151	73	60	13	4	2	2	44	14	66	0	1	6	12	.333	1	1-2	3	3.91
1994 Bos-Phi		35	1	0	9	53	236	64	31	29	7	5	3	5	15	4	28	0	2	3	3	.500	0	1-4	3	4.92
1995 Philadelphia	NL	33	29	0	1	179.1	784	212	102	93	20	9	6	6	44	3	103	0	3	11	12	.478	0	0-0	0	4.67
1996 Toronto	AL	38	20	0	7	134.1	609	172	90	81	27	5	7	2	51	3	86	1	1	5	14	.263	0	0-2	1	5.43
1997 Toronto	AL	77	0	0	29	88	373	103	25	19	5	5	3	1	17	3	56	1	0	6	7	.462	0	5-10	16	1.94
1994 Boston	AL	17	0	0	4	23	101	25	10	9	4	2	2	2	5	1	15	0	0	1	1	.500	0	0-2	2	3.52
Philadelphia	NL	18	1	0	5	30	135	39	21	20	3	3	1	3	10	3	13	0	2	2	2	.500	0	1-2	1	6.00
6 ML YEARS		259	64	1	64	642	2809	757	339	294	73	32	23	17	186	32	363	3	7	33	51	.393	1	8-23	26	4.12

Brian Raabe

Bats: Right **Throws:** Right **Pos:** 2B-2; 3B-2; PH-2   **Ht:** 5'9" **Wt:** 177 **Born:** 11/5/67 **Age:** 30

BATTING																		BASERUNNING				PERCENTAGES		
Year Team	Lg	G	AB	H	2B	3B	HR	(Hm	Rd)	TB	R	RBI	TBB	IBB	SO	HBP	SH	SF	SB	CS	SB%	GDP	Avg	OBP	SLG
1990 Visalia	A+	42	138	34	3	2	0	—	—	41	11	17	10	0	9	1	1	0	5	1	.83	6	.246	.302	.297
1991 Visalia	A+	85	311	80	3	1	1	—	—	88	36	22	40	0	14	4	3	2	15	5	.75	8	.257	.347	.283
1992 Miracle	A+	102	361	104	16	2	2	—	—	130	52	32	48	1	17	8	1	3	7	6	.54	3	.288	.381	.360
Orlando	AA	32	108	30	6	0	2	—	—	42	12	6	2	0	2	0	3	0	0	4	.00	2	.278	.291	.389
1993 Nashville	AA	134	524	150	23	2	6	—	—	195	80	52	56	1	28	10	10	4	18	8	.69	9	.286	.364	.372
1994 Salt Lake	AAA	123	474	152	26	3	3	—	—	193	78	49	50	1	11	1	0	8	9	8	.53	19	.321	.381	.407
1995 Salt Lake	AAA	112	440	134	32	6	3	—	—	187	88	60	45	2	14	3	2	7	15	0	1.00	12	.305	.368	.425
1996 Salt Lake	AAA	116	482	169	39	4	18	—	—	270	103	69	47	2	19	4	2	4	8	8	.50	12	.351	.410	.560
1997 Tacoma	AAA	135	543	191	35	4	14	—	—	276	101	80	38	5	20	16	1	9	1	6	.14	12	.352	.404	.508
1995 Minnesota	AL	6	14	3	0	0	0	(0	0)	3	4	1	1	0	0	0	0	0	0	0	.00	0	.214	.267	.214
1996 Minnesota	AL	7	9	2	0	0	0	(0	0)	2	0	1	0	0	1	0	0	1	0	0	.00	0	.222	.200	.222
1997 Sea-Col		4	6	1	0	0	0	(0	0)	1	0	0	1	0	3	0	1	0	0	0	.00	0	.167	.286	.167
1997 Seattle	AL	2	3	0	0	0	0	(0	0)	0	0	0	1	0	2	0	0	0	0	0	.00	0	.000	.250	.000
Colorado	NL	2	3	1	0	0	0	(0	0)	1	0	0	0	0	1	0	1	0	0	0	.00	0	.333	.333	.333
3 ML YEARS		17	29	6	0	0	0	(0	0)	6	4	2	2	0	4	0	1	1	0	0	.00	0	.207	.250	.207

Scott Radinsky

Pitches: Left **Bats:** Left **Pos:** RP-75   **Ht:** 6'3" **Wt:** 204 **Born:** 3/3/68 **Age:** 30

		HOW MUCH HE PITCHED						WHAT HE GAVE UP										THE RESULTS					
Year Team	Lg	G	GS	CG	GF	IP	BFP	H	R	ER	HR	SH	SF	HB	TBB	IBB	SO	WP	Bk	W	L	Pct.	ShO	Sv-Op	Hld	ERA
1990 Chicago	AL	62	0	0	18	52.1	237	47	29	28	4	2	2	2	36	1	46	2	1	6	1	.857	0	4-5	10	4.82
1991 Chicago	AL	67	0	0	19	71.1	289	53	18	16	4	4	4	2	23	2	49	0	0	5	5	.500	0	8-15	15	2.02
1992 Chicago	AL	68	0	0	33	59.1	261	54	21	18	3	2	1	2	34	5	48	3	0	3	7	.300	0	15-23	16	2.73
1993 Chicago	AL	73	0	0	24	54.2	250	61	33	26	3	2	0	1	19	3	44	0	4	8	2	.800	0	4-5	12	4.28
1995 Chicago	AL	46	0	0	10	38	171	46	23	23	7	1	4	0	17	4	14	0	0	2	1	.667	0	1-3	5	5.45
1996 Los Angeles	NL	58	0	0	19	52.1	221	52	19	14	2	4	3	0	17	5	48	0	3	5	1	.833	0	1-4	7	2.41
1997 Los Angeles	NL	75	0	0	14	62.1	258	54	22	20	4	3	4	1	21	5	44	0	0	5	1	.833	0	3-5	26	2.89
7 ML YEARS		449	0	0	137	390.1	1687	367	165	145	24	18	18	7	167	25	293	5	8	34	18	.654	0	36-60	94	3.34

Brad Radke

Pitches: Right **Bats:** Right **Pos:** SP-35   **Ht:** 6'2" **Wt:** 186 **Born:** 10/27/72 **Age:** 25

		HOW MUCH HE PITCHED						WHAT HE GAVE UP										THE RESULTS					
Year Team	Lg	G	GS	CG	GF	IP	BFP	H	R	ER	HR	SH	SF	HB	TBB	IBB	SO	WP	Bk	W	L	Pct.	ShO	Sv-Op	Hld	ERA
1995 Minnesota	AL	29	28	2	0	181	772	195	112	107	32	2	9	4	47	0	75	4	0	11	14	.440	1	0-0	0	5.32
1996 Minnesota	AL	35	35	3	0	232	973	231	125	115	40	5	6	4	57	2	148	1	0	11	16	.407	0	0-0	0	4.46
1997 Minnesota	AL	35	35	4	0	239.2	989	238	114	103	28	2	9	3	48	1	174	1	1	20	10	.667	1	0-0	0	3.87
3 ML YEARS		99	98	9	0	652.2	2734	664	351	325	100	9	24	11	152	3	397	6	1	42	40	.512	2	0-0	0	4.48

Brady Raggio

Pitches: Right **Bats:** Right **Pos:** RP-11; SP-4   **Ht:** 6'4" **Wt:** 210 **Born:** 9/17/72 **Age:** 25

		HOW MUCH HE PITCHED						WHAT HE GAVE UP										THE RESULTS					
Year Team	Lg	G	GS	CG	GF	IP	BFP	H	R	ER	HR	SH	SF	HB	TBB	IBB	SO	WP	Bk	W	L	Pct.	ShO	Sv-Op	Hld	ERA
1992 Cardinals	R	14	6	3	4	48.1	207	51	26	19	1	2	2	3	7	1	48	5	0	4	3	.571	0	1--	—	3.54
1994 New Jersey	A-	4	4	0	0	27	115	28	7	5	0	0	1	0	4	0	20	1	0	3	0	1.000	0	0--	—	1.67

Year Team	Lg	G	GS	CG	GF	IP	BFP	H	R	ER	HR	SH	SF	HB	TBB	IBB	SO	WP	Bk	W	L	Pct.	ShO	Sv-Op	Hld	ERA
Madison	A	11	11	1	0	67.1	277	63	31	24	8	3	2	3	14	1	66	3	0	4	3	.571	2	0--	—	3.21
1995 Peoria	A	8	8	3	0	48.2	181	42	13	10	1	1	1	0	2	0	34	0	0	3	0	1.000	2	0--	—	1.85
St. Pete	A+	20	3	0	4	47.1	195	43	24	20	2	3	1	1	13	2	35	2	1	2	3	.400	0	0--	—	3.80
1996 Arkansas	AA	26	24	4	0	162.1	667	160	68	58	17	8	2	3	40	2	123	3	2	9	10	.474	1	0--	—	3.22
1997 Louisville	AAA	22	22	2	0	138	576	145	68	64	18	5	3	6	32	0	91	3	1	8	11	.421	0	0--	—	4.17
1997 St. Louis	NL	15	4	0	5	31.1	151	44	24	24	1	1	2	1	16	0	21	3	0	1	2	.333	0	0-0	—	6.89

Tim Raines

Bats: Both **Throws:** Right **Pos:** LF-57; DH-13; PH-7 **Ht:** 5'8" **Wt:** 186 **Born:** 9/16/59 **Age:** 38

Year Team	Lg	G	AB	H	2B	3B	HR	(Hm	Rd)	TB	R	RBI	TBB	IBB	SO	HBP	SH	SF	SB	CS	SB%	GDP	Avg	OBP	SLG
1997 Yankees *	R	1	4	1	0	0	0	—	—	1	0	2	1	0	1	0	0	0	0	0	.00	0	.250	.400	.250
Norwich *	AA	2	7	2	1	0	0	—	—	3	0	2	0	0	2	0	0	0	0	0	.00	0	.286	.286	.429
Tampa *	A+	11	35	12	0	0	2	—	—	18	8	5	11	2	1	0	0	0	1	0	1.00	0	.343	.500	.514
Columbus *	AAA	4	13	2	0	0	0	—	—	2	1	0	3	0	2	0	0	0	0	0	.00	0	.154	.313	.154
1979 Montreal	NL	6	0	0	0	0	0	(0	0)	0	3	0	0	0	0	0	0	0	2	0	1.00	0	.000	.000	.000
1980 Montreal	NL	15	20	1	0	0	0	(0	0)	1	5	0	6	0	3	0	1	0	5	0	1.00	0	.050	.269	.050
1981 Montreal	NL	88	313	95	13	7	5	(3	2)	137	61	37	45	5	31	2	0	3	71	11	.87	7	.304	.391	.438
1982 Montreal	NL	156	647	179	32	8	4	(1	3)	239	90	43	75	9	83	2	6	1	78	16	.83	6	.277	.353	.369
1983 Montreal	NL	156	615	183	32	8	11	(5	6)	264	133	71	97	9	70	2	2	4	90	14	.87	12	.298	.393	.429
1984 Montreal	NL	160	622	192	38	9	8	(2	6)	272	106	60	87	7	69	2	3	4	75	10	.88	7	.309	.393	.437
1985 Montreal	NL	150	575	184	30	13	11	(4	7)	273	115	41	81	13	60	3	3	3	70	9	.89	9	.320	.405	.475
1986 Montreal	NL	151	580	194	35	10	9	(4	5)	276	91	62	78	9	52	4	0	3	70	9	.89	6	.334	.413	.476
1987 Montreal	NL	139	530	175	34	8	18	(9	9)	279	123	68	90	26	52	4	0	3	50	5	.91	9	.330	.429	.526
1988 Montreal	NL	109	429	116	19	7	12	(5	7)	185	66	48	53	14	44	2	0	4	33	7	.83	8	.270	.350	.431
1989 Montreal	NL	145	517	148	29	6	9	(6	3)	216	76	60	93	18	48	3	0	5	41	9	.82	6	.286	.395	.418
1990 Montreal	NL	130	457	131	11	5	9	(6	3)	179	65	62	70	8	43	3	0	3	49	16	.75	9	.287	.379	.392
1991 Chicago	AL	155	609	163	20	6	5	(1	4)	210	102	50	83	9	68	5	9	3	51	15	.77	7	.294	.380	.405
1992 Chicago	AL	144	551	162	22	9	7	(4	3)	223	102	54	81	4	48	0	4	8	45	6	.88	5	.294	.380	.405
1993 Chicago	AL	115	415	127	16	4	16	(7	9)	199	75	54	64	4	35	3	2	2	21	7	.75	7	.306	.401	.480
1994 Chicago	AL	101	384	102	15	5	10	(5	5)	157	80	52	61	3	43	1	4	3	13	0	1.00	10	.266	.365	.409
1995 Chicago	AL	133	502	143	25	4	12	(6	6)	212	81	67	70	3	52	3	3	3	13	2	.87	8	.285	.374	.422
1996 New York	AL	59	201	57	10	0	9	(7	2)	94	45	33	34	1	29	1	0	4	10	1	.91	5	.284	.383	.468
1997 New York	AL	74	271	87	20	2	4	(3	1)	123	56	38	41	0	34	0	0	6	8	5	.62	4	.321	.403	.454
19 ML YEARS		2186	8238	2439	401	111	159	(78	81)	3539	1475	900	1209	142	872	38	38	67	795	142	.85	127	.296	.386	.430

Manny Ramirez

Bats: Right **Throws:** Right **Pos:** RF-146; DH-4 **Ht:** 6'0" **Wt:** 190 **Born:** 5/30/72 **Age:** 26

Year Team	Lg	G	AB	H	2B	3B	HR	(Hm	Rd)	TB	R	RBI	TBB	IBB	SO	HBP	SH	SF	SB	CS	SB%	GDP	Avg	OBP	SLG
1993 Cleveland	AL	22	53	9	1	0	2	(0	2)	16	5	5	2	0	8	-0	0	0	0	0	.00	3	.170	.200	.302
1994 Cleveland	AL	91	290	78	22	0	17	(9	8)	151	51	60	42	4	72	0	0	4	4	2	.67	6	.269	.357	.521
1995 Cleveland	AL	137	484	149	26	1	31	(12	19)	270	85	107	75	6	112	5	2	5	6	6	.50	13	.308	.402	.558
1996 Cleveland	AL	152	550	170	45	3	33	(19	14)	320	94	112	85	8	104	3	0	9	8	5	.62	18	.309	.399	.582
1997 Cleveland	AL	150	561	184	40	0	26	(14	12)	302	99	88	79	5	115	7	0	4	2	3	.40	19	.328	.415	.538
5 ML YEARS		552	1938	590	134	4	109	(54	55)	1059	334	372	283	23	411	15	2	22	20	16	.56	59	.304	.393	.546

Edgar Ramos

Pitches: Right **Bats:** Right **Pos:** SP-2; RP-2 **Ht:** 6'4" **Wt:** 190 **Born:** 3/6/75 **Age:** 23

Year Team	Lg	G	GS	CG	GF	IP	BFP	H	R	ER	HR	SH	SF	HB	TBB	IBB	SO	WP	Bk	W	L	Pct.	ShO	Sv-Op	Hld	ERA
1993 Astros	R	14	12	0	1	75	297	59	23	18	0	0	2	3	15	0	70	4	2	5	2	.714	0	0--	—	2.16
1994 Quad City	A	22	16	1	4	98.2	429	110	59	49	3	2	1	3	30	1	92	6	0	2	8	.200	0	1--	—	4.47
1995 Quad City	A	2	2	0	0	4.2	27	5	9	8	0	0	0	1	7	0	5	1	0	0	1	.000	0	0--	—	15.43
Astros	R	5	5	0	0	14.2	62	14	6	3	0	1	0	2	5	0	16	1	0	1	0	1.000	0	0--	—	1.84
Kissimmee	A+	4	4	0	0	22	80	11	4	1	1	0	0	1	1	0	16	0	0	4	0	1.000	0	0--	—	0.41
1996 Kissimmee	A+	11	11	1	0	77.2	298	51	17	13	4	3	1	6	15	0	81	4	0	9	0	1.000	1	0--	—	1.51
Jackson	AA	12	11	1	0	66.1	293	63	41	36	2	3	1	11	29	0	52	7	0	4	5	.444	0	0--	—	4.88
1997 Clearwater	A+	2	2	0	0	5	19	3	3	2	0	0	0	0	2	0	3	0	0	0	0	.000	0	0--	—	3.60
Jackson	AA	4	3	0	0	18.2	88	24	12	10	0	2	0	1	7	1	12	3	0	0	2	.000	0	0--	—	4.82
1997 Philadelphia	NL	4	2	0	0	14	60	15	9	8	3	1	0	1	6	0	4	1	0	0	2	.000	0	0-0	—	5.14

Ken Ramos

Bats: Left **Throws:** Left **Pos:** PH-14; LF-1; RF-1 **Ht:** 6'1" **Wt:** 185 **Born:** 6/6/67 **Age:** 31

Year Team	Lg	G	AB	H	2B	3B	HR	(Hm	Rd)	TB	R	RBI	TBB	IBB	SO	HBP	SH	SF	SB	CS	SB%	GDP	Avg	OBP	SLG
1989 Indians	R	54	193	60	7	2	1	—	—	74	41	14	39	1	18	3	3	2	17	7	.71	4	.311	.430	.383
Kinston	A+	8	21	3	0	0	0	—	—	3	6	0	5	0	2	0	1	0	2	0	1.00	0	.143	.308	.143
1990 Kinston	A+	96	339	117	16	6	0	—	—	145	71	31	48	4	34	1	5	2	18	14	.56	4	.345	.426	.428
Canton-Akrn	AA	19	73	24	2	2	0	—	—	30	12	11	8	0	10	0	4	1	2	1	.67	1	.329	.390	.411
1991 Canton-Akrn	AA	74	257	62	6	3	2	—	—	80	41	13	28	0	22	1	4	1	8	4	.67	8	.241	.317	.311
1992 Canton-Akrn	AA	125	442	150	23	5	5	—	—	198	93	42	82	6	37	0	5	1	14	11	.56	8	.339	.442	.448
1993 Charlotte	AAA	132	480	140	16	11	3	—	—	187	77	41	47	4	41	0	7	3	12	8	.60	10	.292	.353	.390
1994 Tucson	AAA	121	393	118	19	7	1	—	—	154	81	32	74	5	27	0	3	5	22	12	.65	8	.300	.407	.392

Year Team	Lg	G	AB	H	2B	3B	HR	(Hm	Rd)	TB	R	RBI	TBB	IBB	SO	HBP	SH	SF	SB	CS	SB%	GDP	Avg	OBP	SLG
1995 Tucson	AAA	112	327	103	24	8	3	—	—	152	57	47	51	3	27	3	4	5	14	5	.74	3	.315	.407	.465
1996 Tucson	AAA	104	385	104	22	3	4	—	—	144	54	34	41	2	41	0	3	4	6	9	.40	2	.270	.337	.374
1997 New Orleans	AAA	92	253	73	9	1	0	—	—	84	32	22	45	5	15	1	4	1	2	7	.22	6	.289	.397	.332
1997 Houston	NL	14	12	0	0	0	0	(0	0)	0	0	1	2	0	0	0	0	1	0	0	.00	1	.000	.133	.000

Joe Randa

Bats: Right **Throws:** Right **Pos:** 3B-120; 2B-13; PH-1 **Ht:** 5'11" **Wt:** 190 **Born:** 12/18/69 **Age:** 28

Year Team	Lg	G	AB	H	2B	3B	HR	(Hm	Rd)	TB	R	RBI	TBB	IBB	SO	HBP	SH	SF	SB	CS	SB%	GDP	Avg	OBP	SLG
1997 Calgary *	AAA	3	11	4	1	0	1	—	—	8	4	4	3	0	4	0	0	0	0	0	.00		.364	.500	.727
1995 Kansas City	AL	34	70	12	2	0	1	(1	0)	17	6	5	6	0	17	0	0	0	0	1	.00	2	.171	.237	.243
1996 Kansas City	AL	110	337	102	24	1	6	(2	4)	146	36	47	26	4	47	1	2	4	0	1	.00	2	.303	.351	.433
1997 Pittsburgh	NL	126	443	134	27	9	7	(5	2)	200	58	60	41	1	64	6	4	5	4	2	.67	10	.302	.366	.451
3 ML YEARS		270	850	248	53	10	14	(8	6)	363	100	112	73	5	128	7	6	9	17	7	.71	22	.292	.349	.427

Pat Rapp

Pitches: Right **Bats:** Right **Pos:** SP-25; RP-2 **Ht:** 6'3" **Wt:** 215 **Born:** 7/13/67 **Age:** 30

Year Team	Lg	G	GS	CG	GF	IP	BFP	H	R	ER	HR	SH	SF	HB	TBB	IBB	SO	WP	Bk	W	L	Pct.	ShO	Sv-Op	Hld	ERA
1997 Phoenix *	AAA	3	3	0	0	15	69	16	6	6	2	0	0	1	9	0	6	0	0	2	0	1.000	0	0--	0	3.60
1992 San Francisco	NL	3	2	0	1	10	43	8	8	8	0	2	0	1	6	1	3	0	0	0	2	.000	0	0-0	0	7.20
1993 Florida	NL	16	16	1	0	94	412	101	49	42	7	3	4	2	39	1	57	6	0	4	6	.400	0	0-0	0	4.02
1994 Florida	NL	24	23	2	1	133.1	584	132	67	57	13	8	4	7	69	3	75	5	1	7	8	.467	1	0-0	0	3.85
1995 Florida	NL	28	28	3	0	167.1	716	158	72	64	10	8	0	7	76	2	102	7	0	14	7	.667	2	0-0	0	3.44
1996 Florida	NL	30	29	0	1	162.1	728	184	95	92	12	15	8	3	91	6	86	13	0	8	16	.333	0	0-0	0	5.10
1997 Fla-SF	NL	27	25	1	0	141.2	638	158	83	76	16	6	6	5	72	4	92	8	0	5	8	.385	1	0-0	0	4.83
1997 Florida	NL	19	19	1	0	108.2	484	121	59	54	11	4	3	3	51	3	64	5	0	4	6	.400	1	0-0	0	4.47
San Francisco	NL	8	6	0	0	33	154	37	24	22	5	2	3	2	21	1	28	3	0	1	2	.333	0	0-0	0	6.00
6 ML YEARS		128	123	7	3	708.2	3121	741	374	339	58	47	22	25	353	17	415	39	1	38	47	.447	4	0-0	0	4.31

Jeff Reboulet

Bats: R **Throws:** R **Pos:** 2B-63; SS-22; PH-21; 3B-12; RF-1 **Ht:** 6'0" **Wt:** 171 **Born:** 4/30/64 **Age:** 34

Year Team	Lg	G	AB	H	2B	3B	HR	(Hm	Rd)	TB	R	RBI	TBB	IBB	SO	HBP	SH	SF	SB	CS	SB%	GDP	Avg	OBP	SLG
1992 Minnesota	AL	73	137	26	7	1	1	(1	0)	38	15	16	23	0	26	1	7	0	3	2	.60	0	.190	.311	.277
1993 Minnesota	AL	109	240	62	8	0	1	(0	1)	73	33	15	35	0	37	2	5	1	5	5	.50	6	.258	.356	.304
1994 Minnesota	AL	74	189	49	11	1	3	(2	1)	71	28	23	18	0	23	1	2	0	0	0	.00	6	.259	.327	.376
1995 Minnesota	AL	87	216	63	11	0	4	(1	3)	86	39	23	27	0	34	1	2	3	1	2	.33	3	.292	.373	.398
1996 Minnesota	AL	107	234	52	9	0	0	(0	0)	61	20	23	25	1	34	1	4	2	4	2	.67	10	.222	.298	.261
1997 Baltimore	AL	99	228	54	9	0	4	(2	2)	75	26	27	23	0	44	1	11	2	3	0	1.00	3	.237	.307	.329
6 ML YEARS		549	1244	306	55	2	13	(6	7)	404	161	127	151	1	198	7	31	5	16	11	.59	28	.246	.330	.325

Jeff Reed

Bats: Left **Throws:** Right **Pos:** C-78; PH-18 **Ht:** 6'2" **Wt:** 190 **Born:** 11/12/62 **Age:** 35

Year Team	Lg	G	AB	H	2B	3B	HR	(Hm	Rd)	TB	R	RBI	TBB	IBB	SO	HBP	SH	SF	SB	CS	SB%	GDP	Avg	OBP	SLG
1984 Minnesota	AL	18	21	3	3	0	0	(0	0)	6	3	1	2	0	6	0	1	0	0	0	.00	0	.143	.217	.286
1985 Minnesota	AL	7	10	2	0	0	0	(0	0)	2	2	0	0	0	3	0	0	0	0	0	.00	0	.200	.200	.200
1986 Minnesota	AL	68	165	39	6	1	2	(1	1)	53	13	9	16	0	19	1	3	0	1	0	1.00	0	.236	.308	.321
1987 Montreal	NL	75	207	44	11	0	1	(1	0)	58	15	21	12	1	20	1	4	4	0	1	.00	2	.213	.254	.280
1988 Mon-Cin	NL	92	265	60	9	2	1	(1	0)	76	20	16	28	1	41	0	1	1	1	0	1.00	5	.226	.299	.287
1989 Cincinnati	NL	102	287	64	11	0	3	(1	2)	84	16	23	34	5	46	2	3	4	0	0	.00	5	.223	.306	.293
1990 Cincinnati	NL	72	175	44	8	1	3	(1	2)	63	12	16	24	5	26	0	5	1	0	0	.00	4	.251	.340	.360
1991 Cincinnati	NL	91	270	72	15	2	3	(1	2)	100	20	31	23	3	38	1	1	5	0	1	.00	4	.267	.321	.370
1992 Cincinnati	NL	15	25	4	0	0	0	(0	0)	4	2	2	1	1	4	0	0	1	0	0	.00	1	.160	.192	.160
1993 San Francisco	NL	66	119	31	3	0	6	(5	1)	52	10	12	16	4	22	0	0	2	0	1	.00	2	.261	.346	.437
1994 San Francisco	NL	50	103	18	3	0	1	(0	1)	24	11	7	11	4	21	0	0	0	0	0	.00	3	.175	.254	.233
1995 San Francisco	NL	66	113	30	2	0	0	(0	1)	32	12	9	20	3	17	0	1	0	0	0	.00	3	.265	.376	.283
1996 Colorado	NL	116	341	97	20	1	8	(7	1)	143	34	37	43	8	65	2	6	3	2	2	.50	8	.284	.365	.419
1997 Colorado	NL	90	256	76	10	0	17	(9	8)	137	43	47	35	1	55	2	5	2	2	1	.67	8	.297	.386	.535
1988 Montreal	NL	43	123	27	3	2	0	(0	0)	34	10	9	13	1	22	0	1	1	1	0	1.00	3	.220	.292	.276
Cincinnati	NL	49	142	33	6	0	1	(1	0)	42	10	7	15	0	19	0	0	0	0	0	.00	2	.232	.306	.296
14 ML YEARS		928	2357	584	101	7	45	(28	17)	834	213	231	265	36	383	9	30	19	6	6	.50	56	.248	.324	.354

Jody Reed

Bats: Right **Throws:** Right **Pos:** 2B-41; PH-17; DH-5 **Ht:** 5'9" **Wt:** 165 **Born:** 7/26/62 **Age:** 35

Year Team	Lg	G	AB	H	2B	3B	HR	(Hm	Rd)	TB	R	RBI	TBB	IBB	SO	HBP	SH	SF	SB	CS	SB%	GDP	Avg	OBP	SLG
1987 Boston	AL	9	30	9	1	1	0	(0	0)	12	4	8	4	0	0	0	1		1	1	.50	0	.300	.382	.400
1988 Boston	AL	109	338	99	23	1	1	(1	0)	127	60	28	45	1	21	4	11	2	1	3	.25	5	.293	.380	.376
1989 Boston	AL	146	524	151	42	2	3	(2	1)	206	76	40	73	0	44	4	13	5	4	5	.44	12	.288	.376	.393
1990 Boston	AL	155	598	173	45	0	5	(3	2)	233	70	51	75	4	65	4	11	3	4	4	.50	19	.289	.371	.390

BATTING																		BASERUNNING				PERCENTAGES		
Year Team	Lg	G	AB	H	2B	3B	HR	(Hm Rd)	TB	R	RBI	TBB	IBB	SO	HBP	SH	SF	SB	CS	SB%	GDP	Avg	OBP	SLG
1991 Boston	AL	153	618	175	42	2	5	(3 2)	236	87	60	60	2	53	4	11	3	6	5	.55	15	.283	.349	.382
1992 Boston	AL	143	550	136	27	1	3	(2 1)	174	64	40	62	2	44	0	10	4	7	8	.47	17	.247	.321	.316
1993 Los Angeles	NL	132	445	123	21	2	2	(0 2)	154	48	31	38	10	40	1	17	3	1	3	.25	16	.276	.333	.346
1994 Milwaukee	AL	108	399	108	22	0	2	(1 1)	136	48	37	57	1	34	2	4	3	5	4	.56	8	.271	.362	.341
1995 San Diego	NL	131	445	114	18	1	4	(4 0)	146	58	40	59	1	38	5	3	3	6	4	.60	9	.256	.348	.328
1996 San Diego	NL	146	495	121	20	0	2	(1 1)	147	45	49	59	8	53	3	5	6	2	5	.29	15	.244	.325	.297
1997 Detroit	AL	52	112	22	2	0	0	(0 0)	24	6	8	10	0	15	3	3	1	3	2	.60	2	.196	.278	.214
11 ML YEARS		1284	4554	1231	263	10	27	(17 10)	1595	566	392	542	29	407	30	89	33	40	44	.48	118	.270	.349	.350

Rick Reed

Pitches: Right Bats: Right Pos: SP-31; RP-2 Ht: 6'1" Wt: 195 Born: 8/16/65 Age: 32

HOW MUCH HE PITCHED							WHAT HE GAVE UP												THE RESULTS						
Year Team	Lg	G	GS	CG	GF	IP	BFP	H	R	ER	HR	SH	SF	HB	TBB	IBB	SO	WP	Bk	W	L	Pct.	ShO	Sv-Op	Hld	ERA
1988 Pittsburgh	NL	2	2	0	0	12	47	10	4	4	1	2	0	0	2	0	6	0	0	1	0	1.000	0	0-0	0	3.00
1989 Pittsburgh	NL	15	7	0	2	54.2	232	62	35	34	5	2	3	2	11	3	34	0	3	1	4	.200	0	0-0	0	5.60
1990 Pittsburgh	NL	13	8	1	2	53.2	238	62	32	26	6	2	1	1	12	6	27	0	0	2	3	.400	1	1-1	1	4.36
1991 Pittsburgh	NL	1	1	0	0	4.1	21	8	6	5	1	0	0	0	1	0	2	0	0	0	0	.000	0	0-0	0	10.38
1992 Kansas City	AL	19	18	1	0	100.1	419	105	47	41	10	2	5	5	20	3	49	0	0	3	7	.300	1	0-0	0	3.68
1993 KC-Tex	AL	3	0	0	0	7.2	36	12	5	5	1	0	0	2	2	0	5	0	0	1	0	1.000	0	0-0	0	5.87
1994 Texas	AL	4	3	0	0	16.2	75	17	13	11	3	0	0	1	7	0	12	0	0	1	1	.500	0	0-0	0	5.94
1995 Cincinnati	NL	4	3	0	1	17	70	18	12	11	5	1	0	0	3	0	10	0	0	0	0	.000	0	0-0	0	5.82
1997 New York	NL	33	31	2	0	208.1	824	186	76	67	19	7	3	5	31	4	113	0	1	13	9	.591	0	0-0	0	2.89
1993 Kansas City	AL	1	0	0	0	3.2	18	6	4	4	0	0	0	1	1	0	3	0	0	0	0	.000	0	0-0	0	9.82
Texas	AL	2	0	0	0	4	18	6	1	1	0	0	1	0	1	0	2	0	0	1	0	1.000	0	0-0	0	2.25
9 ML YEARS		94	73	4	5	474.2	1962	480	230	204	51	16	12	16	89	16	258	0	3	22	24	.478	2	1-1	1	3.87

Steve Reed

Pitches: Right Bats: Right Pos: RP-63 Ht: 6'2" Wt: 212 Born: 3/11/66 Age: 32

HOW MUCH HE PITCHED							WHAT HE GAVE UP												THE RESULTS						
Year Team	Lg	G	GS	CG	GF	IP	BFP	H	R	ER	HR	SH	SF	HB	TBB	IBB	SO	WP	Bk	W	L	Pct.	ShO	Sv-Op	Hld	ERA
1992 San Francisco	NL	18	0	0	2	15.2	63	13	5	4	2	0	0	1	3	0	11	0	0	1	0	1.000	0	0-0	1	2.30
1993 Colorado	NL	64	0	0	14	84.1	347	80	47	42	13	2	3	3	30	5	51	1	0	9	5	.643	0	3-6	9	4.48
1994 Colorado	NL	61	0	0	11	64	297	79	33	28	9	0	7	6	26	3	51	1	0	3	2	.600	0	3-10	14	3.94
1995 Colorado	NL	71	0	0	15	84	327	61	24	20	8	3	1	1	21	3	79	0	2	5	2	.714	0	3-6	11	2.14
1996 Colorado	NL	70	0	0	7	75	307	66	38	33	11	2	4	6	19	0	51	1	0	4	3	.571	0	0-6	22	3.96
1997 Colorado	NL	63	0	0	23	62.1	260	49	28	28	10	3	1	5	27	1	43	0	0	4	6	.400	0	6-13	10	4.04
6 ML YEARS		347	0	0	72	385.1	1601	348	175	155	53	10	16	22	126	12	286	3	2	26	18	.591	0	15-41	67	3.62

Pokey Reese

Bats: R Throws: R Pos: SS-110; PH-10; 2B-8; 3B-8 Ht: 5'11" Wt: 180 Born: 6/10/73 Age: 25

BATTING																		BASERUNNING				PERCENTAGES		
Year Team	Lg	G	AB	H	2B	3B	HR	(Hm Rd)	TB	R	RBI	TBB	IBB	SO	HBP	SH	SF	SB	CS	SB%	GDP	Avg	OBP	SLG
1991 Princeton	R+	62	231	55	8	3	3	— —	78	30	27	23	0	44	0	0	2	10	8	.56	4	.238	.305	.338
1992 Chston-WV	A	106	380	102	19	3	6	— —	145	50	53	24	0	75	5	4	7	19	8	.70	2	.268	.315	.382
1993 Chattanooga	AA	102	345	73	17	4	3	— —	107	35	37	23	1	77	1	3	7	8	5	.62	2	.212	.258	.310
1994 Chattanooga	AA	134	484	130	23	4	12	— —	197	77	49	43	1	75	7	6	1	21	4	.84	6	.269	.336	.407
1995 Indianapolis	AAA	89	343	82	21	1	10	— —	135	51	46	36	0	81	4	1	3	8	5	.62	3	.239	.316	.394
1996 Indianapolis	AAA	79	280	65	16	0	1	— —	84	26	23	21	0	46	5	4	3	5	2	.71	10	.232	.294	.300
1997 Indianapolis	AAA	17	72	17	2	0	4	— —	31	12	11	9	0	12	0	0	0	4	0	1.00	2	.236	.321	.431
1997 Cincinnati	NL	128	397	87	15	0	4	(3 1)	114	48	26	31	2	82	5	4	0	25	7	.78	1	.219	.284	.287

Bryan Rekar

Pitches: Right Bats: Right Pos: SP-2 Ht: 6'3" Wt: 210 Born: 6/3/72 Age: 26

HOW MUCH HE PITCHED							WHAT HE GAVE UP												THE RESULTS						
Year Team	Lg	G	GS	CG	GF	IP	BFP	H	R	ER	HR	SH	SF	HB	TBB	IBB	SO	WP	Bk	W	L	Pct.	ShO	Sv-Op	Hld	ERA
1997 Colo Sprngs *	AAA	28	25	0	0	145	636	169	96	88	21	1	3	10	39	2	116	7	0	10	9	.526	0	0-	—	5.46
1995 Colorado	NL	15	14	1	0	85	375	95	51	47	11	7	4	3	24	2	60	3	2	4	6	.400	0	0-0	1	4.98
1996 Colorado	NL	14	11	0	0	58.1	289	87	61	58	11	3	3	5	26	1	25	4	0	2	4	.333	0	0-1	0	8.95
1997 Colorado	NL	2	2	0	0	9.1	46	11	7	6	3	1	0	0	6	0	4	0	0	1	0	1.000	0	0-0	0	5.79
3 ML YEARS		31	27	1	0	152.2	710	193	119	111	25	11	7	8	56	3	89	7	2	7	10	.412	0	0-1	1	6.54

Desi Relaford

Bats: Both Throws: Right Pos: SS-12; PH-3 Ht: 5'8" Wt: 155 Born: 9/16/73 Age: 24

BATTING																		BASERUNNING				PERCENTAGES		
Year Team	Lg	G	AB	H	2B	3B	HR	(Hm Rd)	TB	R	RBI	TBB	IBB	SO	HBP	SH	SF	SB	CS	SB%	GDP	Avg	OBP	SLG
1991 Mariners	R	46	163	43	7	3	0	— —	56	36	18	22	1	24	1	1	5	15	3	.83	0	.264	.346	.344
1992 Peninsula	A+	130	445	96	18	1	3	— —	125	53	34	39	1	88	1	4	6	27	7	.79	7	.216	.277	.281
1993 Jacksnville	AA	133	472	115	16	4	8	— —	163	64	47	50	1	103	7	6	4	16	12	.57	4	.244	.323	.345
1994 Jacksnville	AA	37	143	29	7	3	3	— —	51	24	11	22	0	28	0	2	1	10	1	.91	2	.203	.305	.357
Riverside	A+	99	374	116	27	5	5	— —	168	95	59	78	6	78	4	3	6	27	6	.82	7	.310	.429	.449
1995 Port City	AA	90	352	101	11	2	7	— —	137	51	27	41	2	58	2	2	0	25	9	.74	4	.287	.365	.389
Tacoma	AAA	30	113	27	5	1	2	— —	40	20	7	13	2	24	0	0	2	6	1	1.00	2	.239	.313	.354

Year Team	Lg	G	AB	H	2B	3B	HR	(Hm	Rd)	TB	R	RBI	TBB	IBB	SO	HBP	SH	SF	SB	CS	SB%	GDP	Avg	OBP	SLG
1996 Tacoma	AAA	93	317	65	12	0	4	—	—	89	27	32	23	0	58	1	4	3	10	6	.63	7	.205	.259	.281
Scranton-WB	AAA	21	85	20	4	1	1	—	—	29	12	11	8	0	19	1	1	1	7	1	.88	0	.235	.305	.341
1997 Scranton-WB	AAA	131	517	138	34	4	9	—	—	207	82	53	43	0	77	7	4	5	29	8	.78	12	.267	.329	.400
1996 Philadelphia	NL	15	40	7	2	0	0	(0	0)	9	2	1	3	0	9	0	1	0	1	0	1.00	1	.175	.233	.225
1997 Philadelphia	NL	15	38	7	1	2	0	(0	0)	12	3	6	5	0	6	0	1	0	3	0	1.00	0	.184	.279	.316
2 ML YEARS		30	78	14	3	2	0	(0	0)	21	5	7	8	0	15	0	2	0	4	0	1.00	1	.179	.256	.269

Mike Remlinger

Pitches: Left **Bats:** Left **Pos:** RP-57; SP-12 **Ht:** 6'0" **Wt:** 195 **Born:** 3/23/66 **Age:** 32

Year Team	Lg	G	GS	CG	GF	IP	BFP	H	R	ER	HR	SH	SF	HB	TBB	IBB	SO	WP	Bk	W	L	Pct.	ShO	Sv-Op	Hld	ERA
1991 San Francisco	NL	8	6	1	1	35	155	36	17	17	5	1	1	0	20	1	19	2	1	1	2	.667	1	0-0	0	4.37
1994 New York	NL	10	9	0	0	54.2	252	55	30	28	9	2	3	1	35	4	33	3	0	1	5	.167	0	0-0	1	4.61
1995 NYN-Cin	NL	7	0	0	4	6.2	34	9	6	5	1	1	0	0	5	0	7	0	0	0	1	.000	0	0-1	0	6.75
1996 Cincinnati	NL	19	4	0	2	27.1	125	24	17	17	4	3	1	3	19	2	19	2	2	0	1	.000	0	0-0	0	5.60
1997 Cincinnati	NL	69	12	2	10	124	525	100	61	57	11	6	4	7	60	6	145	12	2	8	8	.500	0	2-2	14	4.14
1995 New York	NL	5	0	0	4	5.2	27	7	5	4	1	1	0	0	2	0	6	0	0	0	1	.000	0	0-1	0	6.35
Cincinnati	NL	2	0	0	0	1	7	2	1	1	0	0	0	0	3	0	1	0	0	0	0	.000	0	0-0	0	9.00
5 ML YEARS		113	31	3	17	247.2	1091	224	131	124	30	13	9	11	139	13	223	19	5	11	16	.407	1	2-3	16	4.51

Edgar Renteria

Bats: Right **Throws:** Right **Pos:** SS-153; PH-2 **Ht:** 6'1" **Wt:** 172 **Born:** 8/7/75 **Age:** 22

Year Team	Lg	G	AB	H	2B	3B	HR	(Hm	Rd)	TB	R	RBI	TBB	IBB	SO	HBP	SH	SF	SB	CS	SB%	GDP	Avg	OBP	SLG
1992 Marlins	R	43	163	47	8	1	0	—	—	57	25	9	8	0	29	2	2	0	10	6	.63	1	.288	.329	.350
1993 Kane County	A	116	384	78	8	0	1	—	—	89	40	35	35	0	94	0	6	3	7	8	.47	3	.203	.268	.232
1994 Brevard Cty	A+	128	439	111	15	1	0	—	—	128	46	36	35	2	56	0	2	2	6	11	.35	14	.253	.307	.292
1995 Portland	AA	135	508	147	15	7	7	—	—	197	70	68	32	2	85	2	8	8	30	11	.73	10	.289	.329	.388
1996 Charlotte	AAA	35	132	37	8	0	2	—	—	51	17	16	9	0	17	0	2	0	10	4	.71	5	.280	.326	.386
1996 Florida	NL	106	431	133	18	3	5	(2	3)	172	68	31	33	0	68	2	2	3	16	2	.89	12	.309	.358	.399
1997 Florida	NL	154	617	171	21	3	4	(3	1)	210	90	52	45	1	108	4	19	6	32	15	.68	17	.277	.327	.340
2 ML YEARS		260	1048	304	39	6	9	(5	4)	382	158	83	78	1	176	6	21	9	48	17	.74	29	.290	.340	.365

Al Reyes

Pitches: Right **Bats:** Right **Pos:** RP-19 **Ht:** 6'1" **Wt:** 193 **Born:** 4/10/71 **Age:** 27

Year Team	Lg	G	GS	CG	GF	IP	BFP	H	R	ER	HR	SH	SF	HB	TBB	IBB	SO	WP	Bk	W	L	Pct.	ShO	Sv-Op	Hld	ERA
1997 Tucson *	AAA	38	0	0	17	57.1	262	52	39	32	12	4	3	7	34	2	70	1	0	2	4	.333	0	7--	5	5.02
1995 Milwaukee	AL	27	0	0	13	33.1	138	19	9	9	3	1	2	3	18	2	29	0	1	1	1	.500	0	1-1	0	2.43
1996 Milwaukee	AL	5	0	0	2	5.2	27	8	5	5	1	0	0	0	2	0	2	2	0	1	0	1.000	0	0-0	0	7.94
1997 Milwaukee	AL	19	0	0	7	29.2	131	32	19	18	4	2	0	3	9	0	28	1	0	1	2	.333	0	1-1	1	5.46
3 ML YEARS		51	0	0	22	68.2	296	59	33	32	8	3	2	6	29	2	59	3	0	3	3	.500	0	2-2	5	4.19

Carlos Reyes

Pitches: Right **Bats:** Both **Pos:** RP-31; SP-6 **Ht:** 6'1" **Wt:** 190 **Born:** 4/4/69 **Age:** 29

Year Team	Lg	G	GS	CG	GF	IP	BFP	H	R	ER	HR	SH	SF	HB	TBB	IBB	SO	WP	Bk	W	L	Pct.	ShO	Sv-Op	Hld	ERA
1997 Columbus *	AAA	1	1	0	0	2	12	5	4	4	0	0	0	1	0	0	2	0	0	0	0	.000	0	0--	0	18.00
Edmonton *	AAA	5	4	1	0	31	123	30	14	12	2	0	2	0	3	1	23	0	0	2	0	1.000	0	0--	0	3.48
1994 Oakland	AL	27	9	0	8	78	344	71	38	36	10	2	3	2	44	1	57	3	0		3	.000	0	1-1	0	4.15
1995 Oakland	AL	40	1	0	19	66.2	306	71	43	39	10	4	0	5	28	4	48	5	0	4	6	.400	0	0-1	4	5.09
1996 Oakland	AL	46	10	0	14	122.1	550	134	71	65	19	2	8	2	61	8	78	2	1	7	10	.412	0	0-0	1	4.78
1997 Oakland	AL	37	6	0	9	77.1	352	101	52	50	13	3	2	2	25	2	43	2	1	3	4	.429	0	0-1	1	5.82
4 ML YEARS		150	26	0	50	346.2	1552	377	204	190	52	11	13	11	158	15	226	12	2	14	23	.378	0	1-3	6	4.93

Dennis Reyes

Pitches: Left **Bats:** Right **Pos:** RP-9; SP-5 **Ht:** 6'3" **Wt:** 246 **Born:** 4/19/77 **Age:** 21

Year Team	Lg	G	GS	CG	GF	IP	BFP	H	R	ER	HR	SH	SF	HB	TBB	IBB	SO	WP	Bk	W	L	Pct.	ShO	Sv-Op	Hld	ERA
1994 Vero Beach	A+	9	9	0	0	41.2	199	58	37	31	6	1	1	0	18	0	25	1	1	2	4	.333	0	0--	—	6.70
Great Falls	R+	14	9	0	2	66.2	294	71	37	28	0	0	0	2	25	0	70	10	1	7	1	.875	0	0--	—	3.78
1995 Vero Beach	A+	3	2	0	0	10	43	8	2	2	0	1	0	0	6	0	9	1	0	1	0	1.000	0	0--	—	1.80
1996 San Berndno	A+	29	28	0	0	166	731	166	106	77	11	4	2	6	77	0	176	9	3	11	12	.478	0	0--	—	4.17
1997 San Antonio	AA	12	12	1	0	80.1	335	79	33	27	6	3	1	1	28	1	66	2	2	8	1	.889	0	0--	—	3.02
Albuquerque	AAA	10	10	1	0	57.1	271	70	40	36	4	1	5	1	33	0	45	5	0	6	3	.667	0	0--	—	5.65
1997 Los Angeles	NL	14	5	0	0	47	207	51	21	20	4	5	1	1	18	3	36	2	1	2	3	.400	0	0-0	0	3.83

Shane Reynolds

Pitches: Right **Bats:** Right **Pos:** SP-30 **Ht:** 6'3" **Wt:** 210 **Born:** 3/26/68 **Age:** 30

Year Team	Lg	G	GS	CG	GF	IP	BFP	H	R	ER	HR	SH	SF	HB	TBB	IBB	SO	WP	Bk	W	L	Pct.	ShO	Sv-Op	Hld	ERA
1997 New Orleans *	AAA	1	1	0	0	5	19	3	0	0	0	0	0	1	1	0	6	0	0	1	0	1.000	0	0--	—	0.00
1992 Houston	NL	8	5	0	0	25.1	122	42	22	20	2	6	1	0	6	1	10	1	1	1	3	.250	0	0-0	0	7.11
1993 Houston	NL	5	1	0	0	11	49	11	4	1	0	0	0	0	6	1	10	0	0	0	0	.000	0	0-0	0	0.82
1994 Houston	NL	33	14	1	5	124	517	128	46	42	10	4	0	6	21	3	110	3	2	8	5	.615	1	0-0	5	3.05
1995 Houston	NL	30	30	3	0	189.1	792	196	87	73	15	8	0	2	37	6	175	7	1	10	11	.476	2	0-0	0	3.47
1996 Houston	NL	35	35	4	0	239	981	227	103	97	20	11	7	8	44	3	204	5	1	16	10	.615	1	0-0	0	3.65
1997 Houston	NL	30	30	2	0	181	773	189	92	85	19	9	5	3	47	5	152	5	2	9	10	.474	0	0-0	0	4.23
6 ML YEARS		141	115	10	5	769.2	3234	793	354	318	66	38	13	19	161	19	661	21	7	44	39	.530	4	0-0	5	3.72

Armando Reynoso

Pitches: Right **Bats:** Right **Pos:** SP-16 **Ht:** 6'0" **Wt:** 204 **Born:** 5/1/66 **Age:** 32

Year Team	Lg	G	GS	CG	GF	IP	BFP	H	R	ER	HR	SH	SF	HB	TBB	IBB	SO	WP	Bk	W	L	Pct.	ShO	Sv-Op	Hld	ERA
1997 St. Lucie *	A+	2	2	0	0	10	38	9	3	3	0	0	0	1	0	0	6	0	0	1	1	.500	0	0--	—	2.70
1991 Atlanta	NL	6	5	0	1	23.1	103	26	18	16	4	3	0	3	10	1	10	2	0	2	1	.667	0	0-0	0	6.17
1992 Atlanta	NL	3	1	0	1	7.2	32	11	4	4	2	1	0	1	2	1	2	0	0	1	0	1.000	0	1-1	0	4.70
1993 Colorado	NL	30	30	4	0	189	830	206	101	84	22	5	8	9	63	7	117	7	6	12	11	.522	1	0-0	0	4.00
1994 Colorado	NL	9	9	1	0	52.1	226	54	30	28	5	2	2	6	22	1	25	2	2	3	4	.429	1	0-0	0	4.82
1995 Colorado	NL	20	18	0	0	93	418	116	61	55	12	8	2	5	36	3	40	2	0	7	7	.500	0	0-0	0	5.32
1996 Colorado	NL	30	30	0	0	168.2	733	195	97	93	27	3	3	9	49	0	88	4	3	8	9	.471	0	0-0	0	4.96
1997 New York	NL	16	16	1	0	91.1	388	95	47	46	7	3	5	6	29	4	47	4	1	6	3	.667	1	0-0	0	4.53
7 ML YEARS		114	109	6	2	625.1	2730	703	358	326	79	25	20	39	211	17	329	21	12	39	35	.527	3	1-1	0	4.69

Arthur Rhodes

Pitches: Left **Bats:** Left **Pos:** RP-53 **Ht:** 6'2" **Wt:** 205 **Born:** 10/24/69 **Age:** 28

Year Team	Lg	G	GS	CG	GF	IP	BFP	H	R	ER	HR	SH	SF	HB	TBB	IBB	SO	WP	Bk	W	L	Pct.	ShO	Sv-Op	Hld	ERA
1991 Baltimore	AL	8	8	0	0	36	174	47	35	32	4	1	3	0	23	0	23	2	0	0	3	.000	0	0-0	0	8.00
1992 Baltimore	AL	15	15	2	0	94.1	394	87	39	38	6	5	1	1	38	2	77	2	1	7	5	.583	1	0-0	0	3.63
1993 Baltimore	AL	17	17	0	0	85.2	387	91	62	62	16	2	3	1	49	1	49	2	0	5	6	.455	0	0-0	0	6.51
1994 Baltimore	AL	10	10	3	0	52.2	238	51	34	34	8	2	3	2	30	1	47	3	0	3	5	.375	2	0-0	0	5.81
1995 Baltimore	AL	19	9	0	3	75.1	336	68	53	52	13	4	0	0	48	1	77	3	1	2	5	.286	0	0-1	0	6.21
1996 Baltimore	AL	28	2	0	5	53	224	48	28	24	6	1	1	0	23	3	62	0	0	9	1	.900	0	1-1	2	4.08
1997 Baltimore	AL	53	0	0	6	95.1	378	75	32	32	9	0	4	4	26	5	102	2	0	10	3	.769	0	1-2	9	3.02
7 ML YEARS		150	61	5	14	492.1	2131	467	283	274	62	15	15	8	237	13	437	14	2	36	28	.563	3	2-4	11	5.01

Brad Rigby

Pitches: Right **Bats:** Right **Pos:** SP-14 **Ht:** 6'6" **Wt:** 195 **Born:** 5/14/73 **Age:** 25

Year Team	Lg	G	GS	CG	GF	IP	BFP	H	R	ER	HR	SH	SF	HB	TBB	IBB	SO	WP	Bk	W	L	Pct.	ShO	Sv-Op	Hld	ERA
1994 Modesto	A+	11	1	0	3	23.2	101	20	10	10	0	1	1	2	10	1	28	1	0	2	1	.667	0	2--	—	3.80
1995 Modesto	A+	31	15	2	4	154.2	653	135	79	66	5	2	7	12	48	0	145	8	2	11	8	.733	0	2--	—	3.84
1996 Huntsville	AA	26	26	3	0	159.1	682	161	89	70	13	3	3	7	59	8	127	13	2	9	12	.429	0	0--	—	3.95
1997 Edmonton	AAA	15	15	0	0	82.1	370	95	49	40	10	3	3	3	26	4	49	5	0	8	4	.667	0	0--	—	4.37
1997 Oakland	AL	14	14	0	0	77.2	339	92	44	42	14	2	8	2	22	2	34	3	0	1	7	.125	0	0-0	0	4.87

Adam Riggs

Bats: Right **Throws:** Right **Pos:** 2B-8; PH-2 **Ht:** 6'0" **Wt:** 194 **Born:** 10/4/72 **Age:** 25

Year Team	Lg	G	AB	H	2B	3B	HR	(Hm	Rd)	TB	R	RBI	TBB	IBB	SO	HBP	SH	SF	SB	CS	SB%	GDP	Avg	OBP	SLG
1994 Great Falls	R+	62	234	73	20	3	5	—	—	114	55	44	31	1	38	4	2	2	19	8	.70	2	.312	.399	.487
Yakima	A-	4	7	2	1	0	0	—	—	3	1	0	0	0	1	0	0	0	0	0	.00	0	.286	.286	.429
1995 San Berndno	A+	134	542	196	39	5	24	—	—	317	111	106	59	1	93	10	7	4	31	10	.76	9	.362	.431	.585
1996 San Antonio	AA	134	506	143	31	6	14	—	—	228	68	66	37	1	82	9	5	5	16	6	.73	13	.283	.339	.451
1997 Albuquerque	AAA	57	227	69	8	3	13	—	—	122	59	28	29	1	39	3	0	0	12	2	.86	2	.304	.390	.537
1997 Los Angeles	NL	9	20	4	1	0	0	(0	0)	5	3	1	4	1	3	0	0	0	1	0	1.00	0	.200	.333	.250

Ricardo Rincon

Pitches: Left **Bats:** Left **Pos:** RP-62 **Ht:** 6'0" **Wt:** 190 **Born:** 4/13/70 **Age:** 28

Year Team	Lg	G	GS	CG	GF	IP	BFP	H	R	ER	HR	SH	SF	HB	TBB	IBB	SO	WP	Bk	W	L	Pct.	ShO	Sv-Op	Hld	ERA
1997 Pittsburgh	NL	62	0	0	23	60	254	51	26	23	5	5	1	2	24	6	71	2	3	4	8	.333	0	4-6	18	3.45

Danny Rios

Pitches: Right **Bats:** Right **Pos:** RP-2   **Ht:** 6'2" **Wt:** 192 **Born:** 11/11/72 **Age:** 25

Year Team	Lg	G	GS	CG	GF	IP	BFP	H	R	ER	HR	SH	SF	HB	TBB	IBB	SO	WP	Bk	W	L	Pct.	ShO	Sv-Op	Hld	ERA
1993 Yankees	R	24	0	0	17	38.1	170	34	18	15	0	2	1	5	16	0	29	9	3	2	1	.667	0	6- -	—	3.52
1994 Greensboro	A	37	0	0	34	41.1	164	32	4	4	1	2	0	3	13	1	36	3	0	3	2	.600	0	17- -	—	0.87
Tampa	A+	9	0	0	8	10.1	41	6	2	0	0	0	1	1	4	0	11	0	0	0	0	.000	0	2- -	—	0.00
1995 Tampa	A+	57	0	0	52	67.1	296	67	24	15	1	5	2	8	20	4	72	2	0	0	4	.000	0	24- -	—	2.00
1996 Norwich	AA	38	0	0	29	43	183	34	14	10	0	2	0	3	21	1	38	3	2	3	1	.750	0	17- -	—	2.09
Columbus	AAA	24	0	0	6	27.2	111	22	7	6	1	0	2	4	6	0	22	1	0	4	1	.800	0	0- -	—	1.95
1997 Columbus	AAA	58	0	0	14	84.2	351	73	37	29	8	3	4	1	31	1	53	5	0	7	4	.636	0	3- -	—	3.08
1997 New York	AL	2	0	0	0	2.1	19	9	5	5	3	0	0	1	2	0	1	0	0	0	0	.000	0	0-0	0	19.29

Billy Ripken

Bats: R **Throws:** R **Pos:** SS-31; 2B-25; 3B-13; 1B-9; PH-3   **Ht:** 6'1" **Wt:** 190 **Born:** 12/16/64 **Age:** 33

Year Team	Lg	G	AB	H	2B	3B	HR	(Hm	Rd)	TB	R	RBI	TBB	IBB	SO	HBP	SH	SF	SB	CS	SB%	GDP	Avg	OBP	SLG
1987 Baltimore	AL	58	234	72	9	0	2	(0	2)	87	27	20	21	0	23	0	1	1	4	1	.80	3	.308	.363	.372
1988 Baltimore	AL	150	512	106	18	1	2	(0	2)	132	52	34	33	0	63	5	6	3	8	2	.80	14	.207	.260	.258
1989 Baltimore	AL	115	318	76	11	2	2	(0	2)	97	31	26	22	0	53	0	19	5	1	2	.33	12	.239	.284	.305
1990 Baltimore	AL	129	406	118	28	1	3	(2	1)	157	48	38	28	2	43	4	17	1	5	2	.71	7	.291	.342	.387
1991 Baltimore	AL	104	287	62	11	1	0	(0	0)	75	24	14	15	0	31	0	11	2	0	1	.00	14	.216	.253	.261
1992 Baltimore	AL	111	330	76	15	0	4	(3	1)	103	35	36	18	1	26	3	10	2	2	3	.40	10	.230	.275	.312
1993 Texas	AL	50	132	25	4	0	0	(0	0)	29	12	11	11	0	19	4	5	1	0	2	.00	6	.189	.270	.220
1994 Texas	AL	32	81	25	5	0	0	(0	0)	30	9	6	3	0	11	0	1	0	2	0	1.00	2	.309	.333	.370
1995 Cleveland	AL	8	17	7	0	0	2	(1	1)	13	4	3	0	0	3	0	0	0	0	0	.00	0	.412	.412	.765
1996 Baltimore	AL	57	135	31	8	0	2	(1	1)	45	19	12	9	0	18	1	1	1	0	0	.00	4	.230	.281	.333
1997 Texas	AL	71	203	56	9	1	3	(1	2)	76	18	24	9	0	32	0	1	5	0	1	.00	7	.276	.300	.374
11 ML YEARS		885	2655	654	118	6	20	(8	12)	844	279	224	169	3	322	17	72	21	22	14	.61	79	.246	.294	.318

Cal Ripken

Bats: Right **Throws:** Right **Pos:** 3B-162; SS-3   **Ht:** 6'4" **Wt:** 220 **Born:** 8/24/60 **Age:** 37

Year Team	Lg	G	AB	H	2B	3B	HR	(Hm	Rd)	TB	R	RBI	TBB	IBB	SO	HBP	SH	SF	SB	CS	SB%	GDP	Avg	OBP	SLG
1981 Baltimore	AL	23	39	5	0	0	0	(0	0)	5	1	0	1	0	8	0	0	0	0	0	.00	4	.128	.150	.128
1982 Baltimore	AL	160	598	158	32	5	28	(11	17)	284	90	93	46	3	95	3	2	6	3	3	.50	16	.264	.317	.475
1983 Baltimore	AL	162	663	211	47	2	27	(12	15)	343	121	102	58	0	97	0	0	5	0	4	.00	24	.318	.371	.517
1984 Baltimore	AL	162	641	195	37	7	27	(16	11)	327	103	86	71	1	89	2	0	2	2	1	.67	16	.304	.374	.510
1985 Baltimore	AL	161	642	181	32	5	26	(15	11)	301	116	110	67	1	68	1	0	8	2	3	.40	32	.282	.347	.469
1986 Baltimore	AL	162	627	177	35	1	25	(10	15)	289	98	81	70	5	60	4	0	6	4	2	.67	19	.282	.355	.461
1987 Baltimore	AL	162	624	157	28	3	27	(17	10)	272	97	98	81	0	77	1	0	11	3	5	.38	19	.252	.333	.436
1988 Baltimore	AL	161	575	152	25	1	23	(11	12)	248	87	81	102	7	69	2	0	10	2	2	.50	10	.264	.372	.431
1989 Baltimore	AL	162	646	166	30	0	21	(13	8)	259	80	93	57	5	72	3	0	6	3	2	.60	22	.257	.317	.401
1990 Baltimore	AL	161	600	150	28	4	21	(8	13)	249	78	84	82	18	66	5	1	7	3	1	.75	12	.250	.341	.415
1991 Baltimore	AL	162	650	210	46	5	34	(16	18)	368	99	114	53	15	46	5	0	9	6	1	.86	19	.323	.374	.566
1992 Baltimore	AL	162	637	160	29	1	14	(6	9)	233	73	72	64	14	50	7	0	7	4	3	.57	13	.251	.323	.366
1993 Baltimore	AL	162	641	165	26	3	24	(14	10)	269	87	90	65	19	58	6	0	6	1	4	.20	17	.257	.329	.420
1994 Baltimore	AL	112	444	140	19	3	13	(5	8)	204	71	75	32	3	41	4	0	4	1	0	1.00	17	.315	.364	.459
1995 Baltimore	AL	144	550	144	33	2	17	(10	7)	232	71	88	52	6	59	2	1	8	0	1	.00	15	.262	.324	.422
1996 Baltimore	AL	163	640	178	40	1	26	(10	16)	298	94	102	59	2	78	4	0	4	1	2	.33	28	.278	.341	.466
1997 Baltimore	AL	162	615	166	30	0	17	(10	7)	247	79	84	56	3	73	5	0	10	1	0	1.00	19	.270	.331	.402
17 ML YEARS		2543	9832	2715	517	43	370	(183	187)	4428	1445	1453	1016	103	1106	54	4	109	36	34	.51	302	.276	.344	.450

Bill Risley

Pitches: Right **Bats:** Right **Pos:** RP-3   **Ht:** 6'2" **Wt:** 230 **Born:** 5/29/67 **Age:** 31

Year Team	Lg	G	GS	CG	GF	IP	BFP	H	R	ER	HR	SH	SF	HB	TBB	IBB	SO	WP	Bk	W	L	Pct.	ShO	Sv-Op	Hld	ERA
1997 Dunedin *	A+	8	6	0	0	12	49	9	9	6	0	1	0	1	3	0	11	0	1	0	2	.000	0	0- -	—	4.50
Syracuse *	AAA	11	1	0	4	15.1	78	19	15	14	5	0	0	3	10	0	20	2	0	1	2	.333	0	0- -	—	8.22
1992 Montreal	NL	1	1	0	0	5	19	4	1	1	0	1	0	1	1	0	2	0	0	1	0	1.000	0	0-0	0	1.80
1993 Montreal	NL	2	0	0	1	3	14	2	3	2	1	1	0	1	2	0	2	0	0	0	0	.000	0	0-0	0	6.00
1994 Seattle	AL	37	0	0	7	52.1	203	31	20	20	7	0	2	0	19	4	61	2	0	9	6	.600	0	0-2	5	3.44
1995 Seattle	AL	45	0	0	5	60.1	249	55	21	21	7	2	3	1	18	1	65	0	0	2	1	.667	0	1-7	13	3.13
1996 Toronto	AL	25	0	0	11	41.2	177	33	20	18	7	1	2	0	25	0	29	1	0	0	1	.000	0	0-2	4	3.89
1997 Toronto	AL	3	0	0	1	4.1	18	3	4	4	2	0	0	0	2	0	2	0	0	0	1	.000	0	0-1	0	8.31
6 ML YEARS		113	1	0	25	166.2	680	128	69	66	24	5	7	2	67	5	161	5	0	12	9	.571	0	1-12	22	3.56

Todd Ritchie

Pitches: Right **Bats:** Right **Pos:** RP-42   **Ht:** 6'3" **Wt:** 205 **Born:** 11/7/71 **Age:** 26

Year Team	Lg	G	GS	CG	GF	IP	BFP	H	R	ER	HR	SH	SF	HB	TBB	IBB	SO	WP	Bk	W	L	Pct.	ShO	Sv-Op	Hld	ERA
1990 Elizabethtn	R+	11	11	1	0	65	261	45	22	14	5	2	2	6	24	0	49	2	3	5	2	.714	0	0- -	—	1.94
1991 Kenosha	A	21	21	0	0	116.2	498	113	53	46	3	4	1	7	50	1	101	10	1	7	6	.538	0	0- -	—	3.55
1992 Visalia	A+	28	28	3	0	172.2	763	193	113	97	13	6	6	7	65	2	129	16	1	11	9	.550	1	0- -	—	5.06
1993 Nashville	AA	12	10	0	0	46.2	194	46	21	24	2	1	1	0	15	0	41	5	1	3	2	.600	0	0- -	—	3.66

Year Team	Lg	G	GS	CG	GF	IP	BFP	H	R	ER	HR	SH	SF	HB	TBB	IBB	SO	WP	Bk	W	L	Pct.	ShO	Sv-Op	Hld	ERA
HOW MUCH HE PITCHED								**WHAT HE GAVE UP**												**THE RESULTS**						
1994 Nashville	AA	4	4	0	0	17	74	24	10	8	1	1	0	0	7	0	9	2	0	0	2	.000	0	0- --	-	4.24
1995 Hardware City	AA	24	21	0	0	113	515	135	78	72	12	4	5	6	54	0	60	8	0	4	9	.308	0	0- --	-	5.73
1996 Hardware City	AA	29	10	0	14	82.2	376	101	55	50	6	3	4	5	30	1	53	4	0	3	7	.300	0	4- --	-	5.44
Salt Lake	AAA	16	0	0	4	24.2	113	27	15	15	5	2	1	1	11	0	19	4	0	0	4	.000	0	0- --	-	5.47
1997 Minnesota	AL	42	0	0	19	74.2	331	87	41	38	11	0	1	2	28	0	44	11	0	2	3	.400	0	0-2	3	4.58

Kevin Ritz

Pitches: Right **Bats:** Right **Pos:** SP-18   **Ht:** 6'4" **Wt:** 222 **Born:** 6/8/65 **Age:** 33

Year Team	Lg	G	GS	CG	GF	IP	BFP	H	R	ER	HR	SH	SF	HB	TBB	IBB	SO	WP	Bk	W	L	Pct.	ShO	Sv-Op	Hld	ERA
HOW MUCH HE PITCHED								**WHAT HE GAVE UP**												**THE RESULTS**						
1989 Detroit	AL	12	12	1	0	74	334	75	41	36	2	1	5	1	44	5	56	6	0	4	6	.400	0	0-0	0	4.38
1990 Detroit	AL	4	4	0	0	7.1	52	14	12	9	0	3	0	0	14	2	3	3	0	0	4	.000	0	0-0	0	11.05
1991 Detroit	AL	11	5	0	3	15.1	86	17	22	20	1	1	2	2	22	1	9	0	0	0	3	.000	0	0-1	0	11.74
1992 Detroit	AL	23	11	0	4	80.1	368	88	52	50	4	1	4	3	44	4	57	7	1	2	5	.286	0	0-0	0	5.60
1994 Colorado	NL	15	15	0	0	73.2	335	88	49	46	5	4	2	4	35	4	53	6	1	5	6	.455	0	0-0	0	5.62
1995 Colorado	NL	31	28	0	3	173.1	743	171	91	81	16	8	5	6	65	3	120	6	1	11	11	.500	0	2-2	0	4.21
1996 Colorado	NL	35	35	2	0	213	966	236	135	125	24	8	4	12	105	3	105	10	1	17	11	.607	0	0-0	0	5.28
1997 Colorado	NL	18	18	1	0	107.1	486	142	72	70	16	4	5	1	46	3	56	7	0	6	8	.429	0	0-0	0	5.87
8 ML YEARS		149	128	4	10	744.1	3370	831	474	437	68	30	27	29	375	25	459	45	3	45	54	.455	0	2-3	0	5.28

Luis Rivera

Bats: Right **Throws:** Right **Pos:** SS-6; PH-2; 2B-1   **Ht:** 5'10" **Wt:** 175 **Born:** 1/3/64 **Age:** 34

Year Team	Lg	G	AB	H	2B	3B	HR	(Hm	Rd)	TB	R	RBI	TBB	IBB	SO	HBP	SH	SF	SB	CS	SB%	GDP	Avg	OBP	SLG
BATTING																			**BASERUNNING**				**PERCENTAGES**		
1997 New Orleans *	AAA	124	382	91	23	4	3			131	46	45	34	2	51	3	5	8	5	4	.56	12	.238	.300	.343
1986 Montreal	NL	55	166	34	11	1	0	(0	0)	47	20	13	17	0	33	2	1	1	1	1	.50	1	.205	.285	.283
1987 Montreal	NL	18	32	5	2	0	0	(0	0)	7	0	1	1	0	8	0	0	0	0	0	.00	0	.156	.182	.219
1988 Montreal	NL	123	371	83	17	3	4	(2	2)	118	35	30	24	4	69	1	3	3	3	4	.43	9	.224	.271	.318
1989 Boston	AL	93	323	83	17	1	5	(4	1)	117	35	29	20	1	60	1	4	1	2	3	.40	7	.257	.301	.362
1990 Boston	AL	118	346	78	20	0	7	(4	3)	119	38	45	25	0	58	1	12	1	4	3	.57	10	.225	.279	.344
1991 Boston	AL	129	414	107	22	3	8	(4	4)	159	64	40	35	0	86	3	12	4	4	4	.50	10	.258	.318	.384
1992 Boston	AL	102	288	62	11	1	0	(0	0)	75	17	29	26	0	56	3	5	0	4	3	.57	5	.215	.287	.260
1993 Boston	AL	62	130	27	8	1	1	(1	0)	40	13	7	11	0	36	1	2	1	1	2	.33	2	.208	.273	.308
1994 New York	NL	32	43	12	2	1	3	(2	1)	25	11	5	4	0	14	2	0	0	0	1	.00	1	.279	.367	.581
1997 Houston	NL	7	13	3	0	1	0	(0	0)	5	2	3	1	0	6	0	1	0	0	0	.00	0	.231	.286	.385
10 ML YEARS		739	2126	494	110	12	28	(17	11)	712	235	202	164	5	426	14	40	11	19	21	.48	45	.232	.290	.335

Mariano Rivera

Pitches: Right **Bats:** Right **Pos:** RP-66   **Ht:** 6'2" **Wt:** 168 **Born:** 11/29/69 **Age:** 28

Year Team	Lg	G	GS	CG	GF	IP	BFP	H	R	ER	HR	SH	SF	HB	TBB	IBB	SO	WP	Bk	W	L	Pct.	ShO	Sv-Op	Hld	ERA
HOW MUCH HE PITCHED								**WHAT HE GAVE UP**												**THE RESULTS**						
1995 New York	AL	19	10	0	2	67	301	71	43	41	11	0	2	2	30	0	51	0	1	5	3	.625	0	0-0	0	5.51
1996 New York	AL	61	0	0	14	107.2	425	73	25	25	1	2	1	2	34	3	130	1	0	8	3	.727	0	5-8	27	2.09
1997 New York	AL	66	0	0	56	71.2	301	65	17	15	5	3	4	0	20	6	68	2	0	6	4	.600	0	43-52	0	1.88
3 ML YEARS		146	10	0	72	246.1	1027	209	85	81	17	5	7	4	84	9	249	3	1	19	10	.655	0	48-61	27	2.96

Ruben Rivera

Bats: R **Throws:** R **Pos:** PH-12; CF-4; RF-4; LF-2   **Ht:** 6'3" **Wt:** 200 **Born:** 11/14/73 **Age:** 24

Year Team	Lg	G	AB	H	2B	3B	HR	(Hm	Rd)	TB	R	RBI	TBB	IBB	SO	HBP	SH	SF	SB	CS	SB%	GDP	Avg	OBP	SLG
BATTING																			**BASERUNNING**				**PERCENTAGES**		
1992 Yankees	R	53	194	53	10	3	1	—	—	72	37	20	42	0	49	6	2	0	21	6	.78	2	.273	.417	.371
1993 Oneonta	A-	55	199	55	7	6	13	—	—	113	45	47	32	1	66	5	1	3	11	5	.69	2	.276	.385	.568
1994 Greensboro	A	105	400	115	24	3	28	—	—	229	83	81	47	1	125	8	0	2	36	5	.88	6	.288	.372	.573
Tampa	A+	34	134	35	4	3	5	—	—	60	18	20	8	0	38	1	0	0	12	5	.71	7	.261	.308	.448
1995 Norwich	AA	71	256	75	16	8	9	—	—	134	49	39	37	2	77	11	0	2	16	8	.67	4	.293	.402	.523
Columbus	AAA	48	174	47	8	2	15	—	—	104	37	35	26	0	62	3	0	1	8	4	.67	5	.270	.373	.598
1996 Columbus	AAA	101	362	85	20	4	10	—	—	143	59	46	40	4	96	8	1	1	15	10	.60	4	.235	.324	.395
1997 Rancho Cuca	A+	6	23	4	1	0	1	—	—	8	6	3	3	0	9	0	0	1	1	0	1.00	0	.174	.259	.348
Las Vegas	AAA	12	48	12	5	1	1	—	—	22	6	6	1	0	20	1	0	0	1	0	1.00	0	.250	.280	.458
1995 New York	AL	5	1	0	0	0	0	(0	0)	0	0	0	0	0	1	0	0	0	0	0	.00	0	.000	.000	.000
1996 New York	AL	46	88	25	6	1	2	(0	2)	39	17	16	13	0	26	2	1	2	6	2	.75	1	.284	.381	.443
1997 San Diego	NL	17	20	5	1	0	0	(0	0)	6	2	1	2	0	9	0	0	0	2	1	.67	0	.250	.318	.300
3 ML YEARS		68	109	30	7	1	2	(0	2)	45	19	17	15	0	36	2	1	2	8	3	.73	1	.275	.367	.413

Joe Roa

Pitches: Right **Bats:** Right **Pos:** RP-25; SP-3   **Ht:** 6'1" **Wt:** 194 **Born:** 10/11/71 **Age:** 26

Year Team	Lg	G	GS	CG	GF	IP	BFP	H	R	ER	HR	SH	SF	HB	TBB	IBB	SO	WP	Bk	W	L	Pct.	ShO	Sv-Op	Hld	ERA
HOW MUCH HE PITCHED								**WHAT HE GAVE UP**												**THE RESULTS**						
1989 Braves	R	13	4	0	4	37.1	156	40	18	12	2	1	0	10	1	21	3	0	2	2	.500	2	0- --	—	2.89
1990 Pulaski	R+	14	11	3	1	75.2	313	55	29	25	3	2	1	2	26	0	49	2	2	4	2	.667	1	0- --	—	2.97
1991 Macon	A	30	18	4	2	141	556	106	46	33	6	0	3	5	33	4	96	3	0	13	3	.813	2	1- --	—	2.11
1992 St. Lucie	A+	26	24	2	0	156.1	647	176	80	63	9	6	6	6	15	1	61	0	1	9	7	.563	1	0- --	—	3.63

179

Year Team	Lg	G	GS	CG	GF	IP	BFP	H	R	ER	HR	SH	SF	HB	TBB	IBB	SO	WP	Bk	W	L	Pct.	ShO	Sv-Op	Hld	ERA
1993 Binghamton	AA	32	23	2	0	167.1	693	190	80	72	9	2	4	10	24	0	73	3	2	12	7	.632	1	0- -	—	3.87
1994 Binghamton	AA	3	3	0	0	20	82	18	6	4	0	2	2	1	1	0	11	1	2	2	1	.667	0	0- -	—	1.80
Norfolk	AAA	25	25	5	0	167.2	703	184	82	65	16	3	12	4	34	1	74	4	0	8	8	.500	0	0- -	—	3.49
1995 Buffalo	AAA	25	24	3	1	164.2	678	168	71	64	9	2	5	7	28	1	93	1	2	11	8	.579	0	0- -	—	3.50
1996 Buffalo	AAA	26	24	5	0	165.1	676	161	66	60	19	5	3	6	36	0	82	6	1	11	8	.579	0	0- -	—	3.27
1997 Phoenix	AAA	6	5	0	0	36	158	43	21	19	4	1	0	1	11	0	16	0	0	3	1	.750	0	0- -	—	4.75
1995 Cleveland	AL	1	1	0	0	6	28	9	4	4	1	1	0	0	2	0	0	0	0	0	1	.000	0	0-0	0	6.00
1996 Cleveland	AL	1	0	0	0	1.2	11	4	2	2	0	0	0	0	3	0	0	0	0	0	0	.000	0	0-0	0	10.80
1997 San Francisco	NL	28	3	0	4	65.2	289	86	40	38	8	5	4	2	20	5	34	0	1	2	5	.286	0	0-0	2	5.21
3 ML YEARS		30	4	0	4	73.1	328	99	46	44	9	6	4	2	25	5	34	0	1	2	6	.250	0	0-0	2	5.40

Bip Roberts

Bats: B **Throws:** R **Pos:** LF-92; PH-14; 2B-13; 3B-10; CF-2   **Ht:** 5'7" **Wt:** 165 **Born:** 10/27/63 **Age:** 34

Year Team	Lg	G	AB	H	2B	3B	HR	(Hm	Rd)	TB	R	RBI	TBB	IBB	SO	HBP	SH	SF	SB	CS	SB%	GDP	Avg	OBP	SLG
1986 San Diego	NL	101	241	61	5	2	1	(0	1)	73	34	12	14	1	29	0	2	1	14	12	.54	2	.253	.293	.303
1988 San Diego	NL	5	9	3	0	0	0	(0	0)	3	1	0	1	0	2	0	0	0	0	2	.00	0	.333	.400	.333
1989 San Diego	NL	117	329	99	15	8	3	(2	1)	139	81	25	49	0	45	1	6	2	21	11	.66	3	.301	.391	.422
1990 San Diego	NL	149	556	172	36	3	9	(4	5)	241	104	44	55	1	65	6	8	4	46	12	.79	8	.309	.375	.433
1991 San Diego	NL	117	424	119	13	3	3	(3	0)	147	66	32	37	0	71	4	4	3	26	11	.70	6	.281	.342	.347
1992 Cincinnati	NL	147	532	172	34	6	4	(3	1)	230	92	45	62	4	54	2	1	4	44	16	.73	7	.323	.393	.432
1993 Cincinnati	NL	83	292	70	13	0	1	(0	1)	86	46	18	38	1	46	3	0	3	26	6	.81	2	.240	.330	.295
1994 San Diego	NL	105	403	129	15	5	2	(1	1)	160	52	31	39	1	57	3	2	2	21	7	.75	7	.320	.383	.397
1995 San Diego	NL	73	296	90	14	0	2	(2	0)	110	40	25	17	1	36	2	1	0	20	2	.91	2	.304	.346	.372
1996 Kansas City	AL	90	339	96	21	2	0	(0	0)	121	39	52	25	8	38	2	0	6	12	9	.57	8	.283	.331	.357
1997 KC-Cle	AL	120	431	130	20	2	4	(1	3)	166	63	44	28	2	67	3	1	5	18	3	.86	7	.302	.345	.385
1997 Kansas City	AL	97	346	107	17	2	1	(0	1)	131	44	36	21	2	53	1	1	3	15	3	.83	6	.309	.348	.379
Cleveland	AL	23	85	23	3	0	3	(1	2)	35	19	8	7	0	14	2	0	2	3	0	1.00	1	.271	.333	.412
11 ML YEARS		1107	3852	1141	186	31	29	(16	13)	1476	618	328	365	19	510	26	25	30	248	91	.73	52	.296	.359	.383

Mike Robertson

Bats: L **Throws:** L **Pos:** PH-13; 1B-5; LF-4; DH-1; RF-1   **Ht:** 6'0" **Wt:** 180 **Born:** 10/9/70 **Age:** 27

Year Team	Lg	G	AB	H	2B	3B	HR	(Hm	Rd)	TB	R	RBI	TBB	IBB	SO	HBP	SH	SF	SB	CS	SB%	GDP	Avg	OBP	SLG
1991 Utica	A-	13	54	9	2	1	0	—	—	13	6	8	5	0	10	0	0	0	2	1	.67	0	.167	.237	.241
South Bend	A	54	210	69	16	2	1	—	—	92	30	26	18	3	24	3	3	3	7	6	.54	5	.329	.385	.438
1992 Sarasota	A+	106	395	99	21	3	10	—	—	156	50	59	50	3	55	7	1	3	5	7	.42	8	.251	.343	.395
Birmingham	AA	27	90	17	8	1	1	—	—	30	6	9	10	1	19	0	1	1	1	1	.00	2	.189	.267	.333
1993 Birmingham	AA	138	511	138	31	3	11	—	—	208	73	73	59	4	97	3	0	8	10	5	.67	10	.270	.344	.407
1994 Birmingham	AA	53	196	62	20	2	3	—	—	95	32	30	31	4	34	2	0	2	6	3	.67	5	.316	.411	.485
Nashville	AAA	67	213	48	8	1	8	—	—	82	21	21	15	4	27	3	0	0	0	2	.00	4	.225	.286	.385
1995 Nashville	AAA	139	499	124	17	4	19	—	—	206	55	52	50	7	72	11	3	2	2	4	.33	8	.248	.329	.413
1995 Nashville	AAA	138	450	116	16	4	21	—	—	203	64	74	38	4	83	5	9	2	1	2	.33	10	.258	.321	.451
1997 Scranton-WB	AAA	121	416	124	17	3	12	—	—	183	61	72	58	4	67	4	1	6	0	2	.00	6	.298	.384	.440
1996 Chicago	AL	6	7	1	0	0	0	(0	0)	1	0	0	0	0	1	0	0	0	0	0	.00	0	.143	.143	.286
1997 Philadelphia	NL	22	38	8	2	1	0	(0	0)	12	3	4	0	0	6	3	0	0	1	0	1.00	0	.211	.268	.316
2 ML YEARS		28	45	9	3	1	0	(0	0)	14	3	4	0	0	7	3	0	0	1	0	1.00	0	.200	.250	.311

Rich Robertson

Pitches: Left **Bats:** Left **Pos:** SP-26; RP-5   **Ht:** 6'4" **Wt:** 175 **Born:** 9/15/68 **Age:** 29

Year Team	Lg	G	GS	CG	GF	IP	BFP	H	R	ER	HR	SH	SF	HB	TBB	IBB	SO	WP	Bk	W	L	Pct.	ShO	Sv-Op	Hld	ERA
1993 Pittsburgh	NL	9	0	0	2	9	44	15	6	6	0	1	0	0	4	0	5	0	0	0	1	.000	0	0-1	0	6.00
1994 Pittsburgh	NL	8	0	0	1	15.2	76	20	12	12	2	1	1	0	10	4	8	0	0	0	0	.000	0	0-0	0	6.89
1995 Minnesota	AL	25	4	1	8	51.2	228	48	28	22	4	5	2	0	31	4	38	0	1	2	0	1.000	0	0-0	0	3.83
1996 Minnesota	AL	36	31	5	1	186.1	853	197	113	106	22	2	4	9	116	2	114	7	0	7	17	.292	3	0-1	1	5.12
1997 Minnesota	AL	31	26	0	2	147	666	169	105	93	19	3	8	6	70	3	69	10	0	8	12	.400	0	0-0	0	5.69
5 ML YEARS		109	61	6	14	409.2	1867	449	264	239	47	12	15	15	231	13	234	17	1	17	30	.362	3	0-2	2	5.25

Ken Robinson

Pitches: Right **Bats:** Right **Pos:** RP-3   **Ht:** 5'9" **Wt:** 170 **Born:** 11/3/69 **Age:** 28

Year Team	Lg	G	GS	CG	GF	IP	BFP	H	R	ER	HR	SH	SF	HB	TBB	IBB	SO	WP	Bk	W	L	Pct.	ShO	Sv-Op	Hld	ERA
1997 Syracuse *	AAA	56	0	0	41	81	319	44	24	23	6	4	2	0	36	1	96	5	0	7	7	.500	0	17- -	—	2.56
1995 Toronto	AL	21	0	0	9	39	167	25	21	16	7	1	2	2	22	1	31	1	0	1	2	.333	0	0-0	1	3.69
1996 Kansas City	AL	5	0	0	2	6	30	9	4	4	0	0	1	0	3	1	5	1	0	1	0	1.000	0	0-0	0	6.00
1997 Toronto	AL	3	0	0	2	3.1	11	1	1	1	1	0	0	0	1	0	4	0	0	0	0	.000	0	0-1	0	2.70
3 ML YEARS		29	0	0	13	48.1	208	35	26	21	8	1	3	2	26	2	40	2	0	2	2	.500	0	0-1	1	3.91

Alex Rodriguez

Bats: Right **Throws:** Right **Pos:** SS-140; DH-1 **Ht:** 6'3" **Wt:** 195 **Born:** 7/27/75 **Age:** 22

							BATTING											BASERUNNING				PERCENTAGES		
Year Team	Lg	G	AB	H	2B	3B	HR	(Hm | Rd)	TB	R	RBI	TBB	IBB	SO	HBP	SH	SF	SB	CS	SB%	GDP	Avg	OBP	SLG
1994 Seattle	AL	17	54	11	0	0	0	(0 | 0)	11	4	2	3	0	20	0	1	1	3	0	1.00	0	.204	.241	.204
1995 Seattle	AL	48	142	33	6	2	5	(1 | 4)	58	15	19	6	0	42	0	1	0	4	2	.67	1	.232	.264	.408
1996 Seattle	AL	146	601	215	54	1	36	(18 | 18)	379	141	123	59	1	104	4	6	7	15	4	.79	15	.358	.414	.631
1997 Seattle	AL	141	587	176	40	3	23	(16 | 7)	291	100	84	41	1	99	5	4	1	29	6	.83	14	.300	.350	.496
4 ML YEARS		352	1384	435	100	6	64	(35 | 29)	739	260	228	109	2	265	9	12	9	51	12	.81	29	.314	.366	.534

Felix Rodriguez

Pitches: Right **Bats:** Right **Pos:** RP-25; SP-1 **Ht:** 6'1" **Wt:** 180 **Born:** 12/5/72 **Age:** 25

		HOW MUCH HE PITCHED						WHAT HE GAVE UP										THE RESULTS					
Year Team	Lg	G	GS	CG	GF	IP	BFP	H	R	ER	HR	SH	SF	HB	TBB	IBB	SO	WP	Bk	W	L	Pct.	ShO	Sv-Op	Hld	ERA
1993 Vero Beach	A+	32	20	2	1	132	570	109	71	55	15	6	3	6	71	1	80	9	6	8	8	.500	1	0- -		3.75
1994 San Antonio	AA	26	26	0	0	136.1	588	106	70	61	8	6	7	4	88	3	126	4	5	6	8	.429	0	0- -		4.03
1995 Albuquerque	AAA	14	11	0	0	51	224	52	29	24	5	4	1	0	26	0	46	0	1	3	2	.600	0	0- -		4.24
1996 Albuquerque	AAA	27	19	0	1	107.1	476	111	70	66	17	7	4	9	60	1	65	5	4	3	9	.250	0	0- -		5.53
1997 Indianapolis	AAA	23	0	0	7	26.2	124	22	10	3	0	2	0	2	16	1	26	1	3	3	3	.500	0	1- -		1.01
1995 Los Angeles	NL	11	0	0	5	10.2	45	11	3	3	2	0	0	0	5	0	5	0	0	1	1	.500	0	0-1	0	2.53
1997 Cincinnati	NL	26	1	0	13	46	212	48	23	22	2	0	1	6	28	2	34	4	1	0	0	.000	0	0-0	1	4.30
2 ML YEARS		37	1	0	18	56.2	257	59	26	25	4	0	1	6	33	2	39	4	1	1	1	.500	0	0-1	1	3.97

Frank Rodriguez

Pitches: Right **Bats:** Right **Pos:** RP-28; SP-15 **Ht:** 6'0" **Wt:** 195 **Born:** 12/11/72 **Age:** 25

		HOW MUCH HE PITCHED						WHAT HE GAVE UP										THE RESULTS					
Year Team	Lg	G	GS	CG	GF	IP	BFP	H	R	ER	HR	SH	SF	HB	TBB	IBB	SO	WP	Bk	W	L	Pct.	ShO	Sv-Op	Hld	ERA
1995 Bos-Min	AL	25	18	0	1	105.2	478	114	83	72	11	1	4	5	57	1	59	9	0	5	8	.385	0	0-0	1	6.13
1996 Minnesota	AL	38	33	3	4	206.2	899	218	129	116	27	6	8	5	78	1	110	2	0	13	14	.481	0	2-2	0	5.05
1997 Minnesota	AL	43	15	0	5	142.1	613	147	82	73	12	4	2	4	60	9	65	6	0	3	6	.333	0	0-4	4	4.62
1995 Boston	AL	9	2	0	1	15.1	75	21	19	18	3	0	0	0	10	1	14	4	0	0	2	.000	0	0-0	1	10.57
Minnesota	AL	16	16	0	0	90.1	403	93	64	54	8	1	4	5	47	0	45	5	0	5	6	.455	0	0-0	0	5.38
3 ML YEARS		106	66	3	10	454.2	1990	479	294	261	50	11	14	14	195	11	234	17	0	21	28	.429	0	2-4	5	5.17

Henry Rodriguez

Bats: L **Throws:** L **Pos:** LF-126; PH-5; 1B-3; RF-1 **Ht:** 6'1" **Wt:** 205 **Born:** 11/8/67 **Age:** 30

							BATTING											BASERUNNING				PERCENTAGES		
Year Team	Lg	G	AB	H	2B	3B	HR	(Hm	Rd)	TB	R	RBI	TBB	IBB	SO	HBP	SH	SF	SB	CS	SB%	GDP	Avg	OBP	SLG
1992 Los Angeles	NL	53	146	32	7	0	3	(2	1)	48	11	14	8	0	30	0	1	1	0	0	.00	2	.219	.258	.329
1993 Los Angeles	NL	76	176	39	10	0	8	(5	3)	73	20	23	11	2	39	0	1	1	1	0	1.00	1	.222	.266	.415
1994 Los Angeles	NL	104	306	82	14	2	8	(5	3)	124	33	49	17	2	58	2	1	4	0	1	.00	5	.268	.307	.405
1995 LA-Mon	NL	45	138	33	4	1	2	(1	1)	45	13	15	11	2	28	0	0	1	0	1	.00	5	.239	.293	.326
1996 Montreal	NL	145	532	147	42	1	36	(20	16)	299	81	103	37	7	160	3	0	4	2	0	1.00	10	.276	.325	.562
1997 Montreal	NL	132	476	116	28	3	26	(14	12)	228	55	83	42	5	149	2	0	3	3	3	.50	6	.244	.306	.479
1995 Los Angeles	NL	21	80	21	4	1	1	(0	1)	30	6	10	5	2	17	0	0	0	0	1	.00	3	.263	.306	.375
Montreal	NL	24	58	12	0	0	1	(1	0)	15	7	5	6	0	11	0	0	1	0	0	.00	2	.207	.277	.259
6 ML YEARS		555	1774	449	105	7	83	(47	36)	817	213	287	126	18	464	7	2	14	6	5	.55	33	.253	.303	.461

Ivan Rodriguez

Bats: Right **Throws:** Right **Pos:** C-143; DH-5; PH-5 **Ht:** 5'9" **Wt:** 205 **Born:** 11/30/71 **Age:** 26

							BATTING											BASERUNNING				PERCENTAGES		
Year Team	Lg	G	AB	H	2B	3B	HR	(Hm	Rd)	TB	R	RBI	TBB	IBB	SO	HBP	SH	SF	SB	CS	SB%	GDP	Avg	OBP	SLG
1991 Texas	AL	88	280	74	16	0	3	(3	0)	99	24	27	5	0	42	0	2	1	0	1	.00	10	.264	.276	.354
1992 Texas	AL	123	420	109	16	1	8	(4	4)	151	39	37	24	2	73	1	7	2	0	0	.00	15	.260	.300	.360
1993 Texas	AL	137	473	129	28	4	10	(7	3)	195	56	66	29	3	70	4	5	8	8	7	.53	16	.273	.315	.412
1994 Texas	AL	99	363	108	19	1	16	(7	9)	177	56	57	31	5	42	7	0	4	6	3	.67	10	.298	.360	.488
1995 Texas	AL	130	492	149	32	2	12	(5	7)	221	56	67	16	2	48	4	0	5	0	2	.00	11	.303	.327	.449
1996 Texas	AL	153	639	192	47	3	19	(10	9)	302	116	86	38	7	55	4	0	4	5	0	1.00	15	.300	.342	.473
1997 Texas	AL	150	597	187	34	4	20	(12	8)	289	98	77	38	7	89	8	1	4	7	3	.70	18	.313	.360	.484
7 ML YEARS		880	3264	948	192	15	88	(48	40)	1434	445	417	181	26	419	28	15	28	26	16	.62	95	.290	.330	.439

Nerio Rodriguez

Pitches: Right **Bats:** Right **Pos:** RP-4; SP-2 **Ht:** 6'0" **Wt:** 165 **Born:** 3/22/73 **Age:** 25

		HOW MUCH HE PITCHED						WHAT HE GAVE UP										THE RESULTS					
Year Team	Lg	G	GS	CG	GF	IP	BFP	H	R	ER	HR	SH	SF	HB	TBB	IBB	SO	WP	Bk	W	L	Pct.	ShO	Sv-Op	Hld	ERA
1995 High Desert	A+	7	0	0	3	10	44	8	2	2	0	0	0	0	7	0	10	0	0	0	0	.000	0	0- -	—	1.80
1996 Frederick	A+	24	17	1	7	111.1	462	83	42	28	10	5	0	4	40	0	114	6	1	8	7	.533	0	2- -	—	2.26
Rochester	AAA	2	2	0	0	15	58	10	3	3	0	0	0	0	2	0	6	2	0	1	0	1.000	0	0- -	—	1.80
1997 Rochester	AAA	27	27	1	0	168.1	688	124	82	73	23	6	0	8	62	0	160	4	3	11	10	.524	1	0- -	—	3.90
1996 Baltimore	AL	8	1	0	2	16.2	77	18	11	8	2	0	1	0	7	0	12	0	0	1	0	.000	0	0-0	—	4.32
1997 Baltimore	AL	6	2	0	1	22	98	21	15	12	2	1	4	1	8	0	11	1	0	2	1	.667	0	0-1	—	4.91
2 ML YEARS		14	3	0	3	38.2	175	39	26	20	4	1	5	1	15	0	23	1	0	2	2	.500	0	0-1	0	4.66

Rich Rodriguez

Pitches: Left **Bats:** Left **Pos:** RP-71   **Ht:** 6'0" **Wt:** 200 **Born:** 3/1/63 **Age:** 35

		HOW MUCH HE PITCHED						WHAT HE GAVE UP										THE RESULTS					
Year Team	Lg	G	GS	CG	GF	IP	BFP	H	R	ER	HR	SH	SF	HB	TBB	IBB	SO	WP	Bk	W	L	Pct.	ShO	Sv-Op Hld	ERA
1990 San Diego	NL	32	0	0	15	47.2	201	52	17	15	2	2	1	1	16	4	22	1	1	1	1	.500	0	1-1 3	2.83
1991 San Diego	NL	64	1	0	19	80	335	66	31	29	8	7	2	0	44	8	40	4	1	3	1	.750	0	0-2 8	3.26
1992 San Diego	NL	61	1	0	15	91	369	77	28	24	4	2	2	0	29	4	64	1	1	6	3	.667	0	0-1 5	2.37
1993 SD-Fla	NL	70	0	0	21	76	331	73	38	32	10	5	0	2	33	8	43	3	0	2	4	.333	0	3-7 10	3.79
1994 St. Louis	NL	56	0	0	15	60.1	260	62	30	27	6	2	1	1	26	4	43	4	0	3	5	.375	0	0-3 15	4.03
1995 St. Louis	NL	1	0	0	0	1.2	4	0	0	0	0	0	0	0	0	0	0	0	0	0	0	.000	0	0-0 0	0.00
1997 San Francisco	NL	71	0	0	15	65.1	271	65	24	23	7	3	0	1	21	4	32	0	0	4	3	.571	0	1-5 14	3.17
1993 San Diego	NL	34	0	0	10	30	133	34	15	11	2	2	0	1	9	3	22	1	0	2	3	.400	0	2-5 8	3.30
Florida	NL	36	0	0	11	46	198	39	23	21	8	3	0	1	24	5	21	2	0	0	1	.000	0	1-2 2	4.11
7 ML YEARS		355	2	0	100	422	1771	395	168	150	37	21	6	5	169	32	244	13	3	19	17	.528	0	5-19 55	3.20

Kenny Rogers

Pitches: Left **Bats:** Left **Pos:** SP-22; RP-9   **Ht:** 6'1" **Wt:** 205 **Born:** 11/10/64 **Age:** 33

		HOW MUCH HE PITCHED						WHAT HE GAVE UP										THE RESULTS					
Year Team	Lg	G	GS	CG	GF	IP	BFP	H	R	ER	HR	SH	SF	HB	TBB	IBB	SO	WP	Bk	W	L	Pct.	ShO	Sv-Op Hld	ERA
1989 Texas	AL	73	0	0	24	73.2	314	60	28	24	2	6	3	4	42	9	63	6	0	3	4	.429	0	2-5 16	2.93
1990 Texas	AL	69	3	0	46	97.2	428	93	40	34	6	7	4	1	42	5	74	5	0	10	6	.625	0	15-23 6	3.13
1991 Texas	AL	63	9	0	20	109.2	511	121	80	66	14	9	5	6	61	7	73	3	1	10	10	.500	0	5-6 11	5.42
1992 Texas	AL	81	0	0	38	78.2	337	80	32	27	7	4	1	0	26	8	70	4	1	3	6	.333	0	6-10 16	3.09
1993 Texas	AL	35	33	5	0	208.1	885	210	108	95	18	7	5	4	71	2	140	6	5	16	10	.615	0	0-0 1	4.10
1994 Texas	AL	24	24	6	0	167.1	714	169	93	83	24	3	6	3	52	1	120	3	1	11	8	.579	2	0-0 0	4.46
1995 Texas	AL	31	31	3	0	208	877	192	87	78	26	3	5	2	76	1	140	8	1	17	7	.708	1	0-0 0	3.38
1996 New York	AL	30	30	2	0	179	786	179	97	93	16	6	3	8	83	2	92	5	0	12	8	.600	1	0-0 0	4.68
1997 New York	AL	31	22	1	4	145	651	161	100	91	18	2	4	1	62	1	78	2	2	6	7	.462	0	0-0 1	5.65
9 ML YEARS		437	152	17	132	1267.1	5503	1265	665	591	131	47	36	35	515	36	850	42	11	88	66	.571	4	28-44 51	4.20

Dan Rohrmeier

Bats: Right **Throws:** Right **Pos:** PH-5; DH-4; 1B-3   **Ht:** 6'0" **Wt:** 195 **Born:** 1/27/65 **Age:** 33

		BATTING																		BASERUNNING				PERCENTAGES		
Year Team	Lg	G	AB	H	2B	3B	HR	(Hm	Rd)	TB	R	RBI	TBB	IBB	SO	HBP	SH	SF	SB	CS	SB%	GDP	Avg	OBP	SLG
1987 Peninsula	A+	68	243	80	13	2	5	—	—	112	43	34	29	0	37	2	2	3	2	3	.40	3	.329	.401	.461
1988 Tampa	A+	114	421	109	28	8	5	—	—	168	53	50	27	2	58	1	1	5	11	7	.61	4	.259	.302	.399
1989 Sarasota	A+	25	74	16	2	0	1	—	—	21	11	4	12	0	15	0	1	1	1	0	1.00	2	.216	.322	.284
Charlotte	A+	18	65	20	3	1	1	—	—	28	9	11	7	0	8	1	0	1	0	1	.00	1	.308	.378	.431
Tulsa	AA	57	210	67	3	4	5	—	—	93	24	27	11	0	20	1	4	0	5	8	.38	5	.319	.356	.443
1990 Tulsa	AA	119	453	138	24	7	10	—	—	206	76	62	37	0	51	0	1	4	13	11	.54	14	.305	.354	.455
1991 Tulsa	AA	121	418	122	20	2	5	—	—	161	67	62	60	1	57	4	4	7	3	2	.60	14	.292	.380	.385
1992 Memphis	AA	123	433	140	33	2	6	—	—	195	54	69	26	2	46	4	0	4	3	7	.30	11	.323	.364	.450
Omaha	AAA	8	29	7	1	0	1	—	—	11	4	5	3	0	4	0	0	0	0	1	.00	0	.241	.313	.379
1993 Omaha	AAA	118	432	107	23	3	17	—	—	187	51	70	23	0	59	3	1	7	2	1	.67	10	.248	.286	.433
1994 Memphis	AA	112	436	118	34	0	18	—	—	206	64	72	31	3	80	6	0	3	2	2	.50	15	.271	.326	.472
Chattanooga	AA	17	66	22	7	0	0	—	—	29	9	10	5	0	5	0	0	1	0	1	.00	5	.333	.375	.439
1995 Indianapolis	AAA	10	34	6	3	1	0	—	—	11	5	3	0	0	4	0	0	0	0	0	.00	1	.176	.176	.324
Chattanooga	AA	118	426	139	31	0	17	—	—	221	77	76	41	5	63	7	1	7	0	1	.00	9	.326	.389	.519
1996 Memphis	AA	134	471	162	29	2	28	—	—	279	98	95	77	10	76	2	0	4	2	5	.29	12	.344	.435	.592
1997 Tacoma	AAA	125	471	140	43	4	33	—	—	290	86	120	45	2	81	0	0	6	1	0	1.00	14	.297	.354	.616
1997 Seattle	AL	7	9	3	0	0	0	(0	0)	3	4	2	2	0	4	0	0	0	0	0	.00	0	.333	.455	.333

Mel Rojas

Pitches: Right **Bats:** Right **Pos:** RP-77   **Ht:** 5'11" **Wt:** 195 **Born:** 12/10/66 **Age:** 31

		HOW MUCH HE PITCHED						WHAT HE GAVE UP										THE RESULTS					
Year Team	Lg	G	GS	CG	GF	IP	BFP	H	R	ER	HR	SH	SF	HB	TBB	IBB	SO	WP	Bk	W	L	Pct.	ShO	Sv-Op Hld	ERA
1990 Montreal	NL	23	0	0	5	40	173	34	17	16	5	2	0	2	24	4	26	2	0	3	1	.750	0	1-2 1	3.60
1991 Montreal	NL	37	0	0	13	48	200	42	21	20	4	0	2	1	13	1	37	3	0	3	3	.500	0	6-9 7	3.75
1992 Montreal	NL	68	0	0	26	100.2	399	71	17	16	2	4	2	2	34	8	70	2	0	7	1	.875	0	10-11 13	1.43
1993 Montreal	NL	66	0	0	25	88.1	378	80	39	29	6	8	6	4	30	3	48	5	0	5	8	.385	0	10-19 14	2.95
1994 Montreal	NL	58	0	0	27	84	341	71	35	31	11	2	1	4	21	0	84	3	0	3	2	.600	0	16-18 19	3.32
1995 Montreal	NL	59	0	0	48	67.2	302	69	32	31	2	2	1	7	29	4	61	6	0	1	4	.200	0	30-39 3	4.12
1996 Montreal	NL	74	0	0	64	81	326	56	30	29	5	2	4	2	28	3	92	3	0	7	4	.636	0	36-40 5	3.22
1997 ChN-NYN	NL	77	0	0	50	85.1	370	78	47	44	15	2	2	7	36	2	93	3	0	0	6	.000	0	15-22 7	4.64
1997 Chicago	NL	54	0	0	38	59	259	54	30	29	11	2	1	5	30	1	61	2	0	0	4	.000	0	13-19 2	4.42
New York	NL	23	0	0	12	26.1	111	24	17	15	4	0	1	2	6	1	32	1	0	0	2	.000	0	2-3 5	5.13
8 ML YEARS		462	0	0	258	595	2489	501	238	216	50	22	18	29	215	25	511	27	0	29	29	.500	0	124-160 65	3.27

Scott Rolen

Bats: Right **Throws:** Right **Pos:** 3B-155; PH-1   **Ht:** 6'4" **Wt:** 195 **Born:** 4/4/75 **Age:** 23

		BATTING																		BASERUNNING				PERCENTAGES		
Year Team	Lg	G	AB	H	2B	3B	HR	(Hm	Rd)	TB	R	RBI	TBB	IBB	SO	HBP	SH	SF	SB	CS	SB%	GDP	Avg	OBP	SLG
1993 Martinsville	R+	25	80	25	5	0	0	—	—	30	8	12	10	0	15	7	0	1	3	4	.43	3	.313	.429	.375
1994 Spartanburg	A	138	513	151	34	5	14	—	—	237	83	72	55	4	90	4	1	7	6	8	.43	8	.294	.363	.462
1995 Clearwater	A+	66	238	69	13	2	10	—	—	116	45	39	37	1	46	5	0	3	4	0	1.00	4	.290	.392	.487

Year Team	Lg	G	AB	H	2B	3B	HR	(Hm	Rd)	TB	R	RBI	TBB	IBB	SO	HBP	SH	SF	SB	CS	SB%	GDP	Avg	OBP	SLG
Reading	AA	20	76	22	3	0	3	—	—	34	16	15	7	0	14	1	1	1	1	0	1.00	2	.289	.353	.447
1996 Reading	AA	61	230	83	22	2	9	—	—	136	44	42	34	3	32	5	0	5	8	3	.73	5	.361	.445	.591
Scranton-WB	AAA	45	168	46	17	0	2	—	—	69	23	19	28	0	28	0	0	1	4	5	.44	9	.274	.376	.411
1996 Philadelphia	NL	37	130	33	7	0	4	(2	2)	52	10	18	13	0	27	1	0	2	0	2	.00	4	.254	.322	.400
1997 Philadelphia	NL	156	561	159	35	3	21	(11	10)	263	93	92	76	4	138	13	0	7	16	6	.73	6	.283	.377	.469
2 ML YEARS		193	691	192	42	3	25	(13	12)	315	103	110	89	4	165	14	0	9	16	8	.67	10	.278	.367	.456

Mandy Romero

Bats: Both **Throws:** Right **Pos:** C-19; PH-6 **Ht:** 6'0" **Wt:** 180 **Born:** 10/29/67 **Age:** 30

Year Team	Lg	G	AB	H	2B	3B	HR	(Hm	Rd)	TB	R	RBI	TBB	IBB	SO	HBP	SH	SF	SB	CS	SB%	GDP	Avg	OBP	SLG
1988 Princeton	R+	30	71	22	6	0	2	—	—	34	7	11	13	0	15	1	0	0	1	0	1.00	0	.310	.424	.479
1989 Augusta	A	121	388	87	26	3	4	—	—	131	58	55	67	4	74	6	3	6	8	5	.62	10	.224	.343	.338
1990 Salem	A+	124	460	134	31	3	17	—	—	222	62	90	55	3	68	5	2	4	0	2	.00	10	.291	.370	.483
1991 Carolina	AA	98	323	70	12	0	3	—	—	91	28	31	45	4	53	1	2	2	1	2	.33	9	.217	.313	.282
1992 Carolina	AA	80	269	58	16	0	3	—	—	83	28	27	29	0	39	1	1	2	0	3	.00	5	.216	.292	.309
1993 Buffalo	AAA	42	136	31	6	1	2	—	—	45	11	14	6	1	12	0	1	1	1	0	1.00	5	.228	.259	.331
1994 Buffalo	AAA	7	23	3	0	0	0	—	—	3	3	1	2	0	1	0	1	0	0	0	.00	2	.130	.200	.130
1995 Wichita	AA	121	440	133	32	1	21	—	—	230	73	82	69	10	60	5	0	1	1	3	.25	15	.302	.402	.523
1996 Memphis	AA	88	297	80	15	0	10	—	—	125	40	46	41	2	52	1	1	2	3	1	.75	15	.269	.358	.421
1997 Mobile	AA	61	222	71	22	0	13	—	—	132	50	52	38	3	31	2	0	1	0	1	.00	4	.320	.422	.595
Las Vegas	AAA	33	91	28	4	1	3	—	—	43	19	13	11	1	19	1	0	1	0	0	.00	4	.308	.385	.473
1997 San Diego	NL	21	48	10	0	0	2	(1	1)	16	7	4	2	0	18	0	0	0	1	0	1.00	1	.208	.240	.333

Jose Rosado

Pitches: Left **Bats:** Left **Pos:** SP-33 **Ht:** 6'0" **Wt:** 175 **Born:** 11/9/74 **Age:** 23

Year Team	Lg	G	GS	CG	GF	IP	BFP	H	R	ER	HR	SH	SF	HB	TBB	IBB	SO	WP	Bk	W	L	Pct.	ShO	Sv-Op	Hld	ERA
1994 Royals	R	14	12	0	2	64.2	246	45	14	9	0	3	2	2	7	0	56	0	0	6	2	.750	0	0- -	—	1.25
1995 Wilmington	A+	25	25	0	0	138	562	128	53	48	9	2	7	3	30	6	117	1	5	10	7	.588	0	0- -	—	3.13
1996 Wichita	AA	2	2	0	0	13	48	10	0	0	0	1	0	0	1	0	12	0	0	2	0	1.000	0	0- -	—	0.00
Omaha	AAA	15	15	1	0	96.2	399	80	38	34	16	3	1	2	38	0	82	4	1	8	3	.727	0	0- -	—	3.17
1996 Kansas City	AL	16	16	2	0	106.2	441	101	39	38	7	1	4	4	26	1	64	5	1	8	6	.571	1	0-0	—	3.21
1997 Kansas City	AL	33	33	2	0	203.1	881	208	117	106	26	6	11	4	73	3	129	4	2	9	12	.429	0	0-0	—	4.69
2 ML YEARS		49	49	4	0	310	1322	309	156	144	33	7	15	8	99	4	193	9	3	17	18	.486	1	0-0	—	4.18

Mel Rosario

Bats: Both **Throws:** Right **Pos:** C-4 **Ht:** 6'0" **Wt:** 200 **Born:** 5/25/73 **Age:** 25

Year Team	Lg	G	AB	H	2B	3B	HR	(Hm	Rd)	TB	R	RBI	TBB	IBB	SO	HBP	SH	SF	SB	CS	SB%	GDP	Avg	OBP	SLG
1992 Spokane	A-	66	237	54	13	1	10	—	—	99	38	40	20	2	62	4	0	4	5	3	.63	6	.228	.294	.418
1993 Waterloo	A	32	105	22	6	2	5	—	—	47	15	15	7	1	37	2	0	0	5	2	.71	0	.210	.272	.448
Spokane	A-	41	140	32	5	0	4	—	—	49	17	19	8	2	36	0	0	0	2	1	.67	1	.229	.270	.350
1995 South Bend	A	118	450	123	30	6	15	—	—	210	58	57	30	7	109	4	1	3	1	8	.11	0	.273	.322	.467
1996 Rancho Cuca	A+	10	33	9	3	0	3	—	—	21	7	10	3	0	8	0	0	0	1	0	1.00	0	.273	.333	.636
High Desert	A+	42	163	52	9	1	10	—	—	93	35	34	21	0	45	9	0	0	4	0	1.00	3	.319	.425	.571
Bowie	AA	47	162	34	10	0	2	—	—	50	14	17	6	1	43	5	1	2	3	2	.60	4	.210	.257	.309
Rochester	AAA	3	2	0	0	0	0	—	—	0	0	0	0	0	1	0	0	0	0	0	.00	0	.000	.000	.000
1997 Bowie	AA	123	430	113	26	1	12	—	—	177	68	60	27	2	106	9	1	4	4	7	.36	5	.263	.317	.412
1997 Baltimore	AL	4	3	0	0	0	0	(0	0)	0	0	0	0	0	1	0	0	0	0	0	.00	0	.000	.000	.000

Brian Rose

Pitches: Right **Bats:** Right **Pos:** SP-1 **Ht:** 6'3" **Wt:** 212 **Born:** 2/13/76 **Age:** 22

Year Team	Lg	G	GS	CG	GF	IP	BFP	H	R	ER	HR	SH	SF	HB	TBB	IBB	SO	WP	Bk	W	L	Pct.	ShO	Sv-Op	Hld	ERA
1995 Michigan	A	21	20	2	0	136	561	127	63	52	5	3	1	9	31	0	105	4	0	8	5	.615	0	0- -	—	3.44
1996 Trenton	AA	27	27	4	0	163.2	687	157	82	73	21	6	4	13	45	3	115	1	1	12	7	.632	2	0- -	—	4.01
1997 Pawtucket	AAA	27	26	3	0	190.2	787	188	74	64	21	1	5	7	46	2	116	5	0	17	5	.773	0	0- -	—	3.02
1997 Boston	AL	1	1	0	0	3	16	5	4	4	0	0	0	0	2	0	3	0	0	0	0	.000	0	0-0	0	12.00

Pete Rose Jr

Bats: Left **Throws:** Right **Pos:** PH-10; 3B-2; 1B-1 **Ht:** 6'1" **Wt:** 180 **Born:** 11/16/69 **Age:** 28

Year Team	Lg	G	AB	H	2B	3B	HR	(Hm	Rd)	TB	R	RBI	TBB	IBB	SO	HBP	SH	SF	SB	CS	SB%	GDP	Avg	OBP	SLG
1989 Frederick	A+	24	67	12	3	0	0	—	—	15	3	7	0	0	15	1	0	0	1	1	.50	1	.179	.191	.224
Erie	A-	58	228	63	13	5	2	—	—	92	30	26	12	1	34	1	2	0	1	2	.33	4	.276	.315	.404
1990 Frederick	A+	97	323	75	14	2	1	—	—	96	32	41	26	0	33	1	7	5	0	3	.00	6	.232	.287	.297
1991 Sarasota	A+	99	323	70	12	2	0	—	—	86	31	35	36	3	35	2	8	3	5	6	.45	3	.217	.297	.266
1992 Columbus	A	131	510	129	24	6	9	—	—	192	67	54	48	2	53	6	8	3	3	4	.57	9	.253	.323	.376
1993 Kinston	A+	74	284	62	10	1	7	—	—	95	33	30	25	0	34	2	6	1	1	3	.25	5	.218	.285	.335
1994 Hickory	A	32	114	25	4	1	0	—	—	31	14	12	13	2	18	2	3	2	0	0	.00	3	.219	.305	.272
White Sox	R	2	4	2	0	0	0	—	—	2	1	1	0	0	0	0	0	0	0	0	.00	0	.500	.500	.500

183

Year Team	Lg	G	AB	H	2B	3B	HR	(Hm Rd)	TB	R	RBI	TBB	IBB	SO	HBP	SH	SF	SB	CS	SB%	GDP	Avg	OBP	SLG
Pr William	A+	45	146	41	3	1	4	— —	58	18	22	18	0	15	0	2	3	0	1	.00	2	.281	.353	.397
1995 Birmingham	AA	5	13	5	1	0	0	— —	6	1	2	3	0	3	0	0	0	0	0	.00	2	.385	.500	.462
South Bend	A	116	423	117	24	6	4	— —	165	56	65	54	0	45	5	2	7	2	0	1.00	6	.277	.360	.390
1996 Birmingham	AA	108	399	97	13	1	3	— —	121	40	44	32	1	54	2	5	3	1	3	.25	9	.243	.300	.303
1997 Indianapolis	AAA	12	40	9	2	0	0	— —	11	2	1	2	0	11	0	0	0	0	0	.00	1	.225	.262	.275
Chattanooga	AA	112	445	137	31	0	25	— —	243	75	98	34	1	63	3	1	3	0	1	.00	5	.308	.359	.546
1997 Cincinnati	NL	11	14	2	0	0	0	(0 0)	2	2	0	2	0	9	0	0	0	0	0	.00	0	.143	.250	.143

Matt Ruebel

Pitches: Left Bats: Left Pos: RP-44   Ht: 6'2" Wt: 180 Born: 10/16/69 Age: 28

Year Team	Lg	G	GS	CG	GF	IP	BFP	H	R	ER	HR	SH	SF	HB	TBB	IBB	SO	WP	Bk	W	L	Pct.	ShO	Sv-Op	Hld	ERA
1991 Welland	A-	6	6	0	0	27.2	113	16	9	6	3	0	1	4	11	0	27	2	3	1	1	.500	0	0- -	—	1.95
Augusta	A	8	8	2	0	47	202	43	26	20	2	1	0	2	25	0	35	3	0	3	4	.429	1	0- -	—	3.83
1992 Augusta	A	12	10	1	1	64.2	268	53	26	20	1	3	0	5	19	0	65	2	1	5	2	.714	0	0- -	—	2.78
Salem	A+	13	13	1	0	78.1	344	77	49	41	13	6	5	3	43	0	46	6	1	1	6	.143	0	0- -	—	4.71
1993 Salem	A+	19	1	0	4	33.1	168	34	31	22	6	3	0	3	32	3	29	8	2	1	4	.200	0	0- -	—	5.94
Augusta	A	23	7	1	6	63.1	276	51	28	17	2	1	3	5	34	4	50	1	0	5	5	.500	1	0- -	—	2.42
1994 Carolina	AA	6	3	0	0	16.1	78	28	15	12	3	1	1	1	3	0	14	0	0	1	1	.500	0	0- -	—	6.61
Salem	A+	21	13	0	0	86.1	374	87	49	33	9	2	3	7	27	0	72	4	1	6	6	.500	0	0- -	—	3.44
1995 Carolina	AA	27	27	4	0	169.1	699	150	68	52	7	4	7	7	45	1	136	7	1	13	5	.722	3	0- -	—	2.76
1996 Calgary	AAA	13	13	1	0	76.1	338	89	43	39	8	4	3	3	28	2	48	0	0	5	3	.625	0	0- -	—	4.60
1996 Pittsburgh	NL	26	7	0	3	58.2	265	64	38	30	7	0	3	6	25	0	22	2	0	1	1	.500	0	1-1	4	4.60
1997 Pittsburgh	NL	44	0	0	9	62.2	296	77	50	44	8	3	5	5	27	3	50	4	0	3	2	.600	0	0-1	8	6.32
2 ML YEARS		70	7	0	12	121.1	561	141	88	74	15	3	8	11	52	3	72	6	0	4	3	.571	0	1-2	12	5.49

Kirk Rueter

Pitches: Left Bats: Left Pos: SP-32   Ht: 6'3" Wt: 195 Born: 12/1/70 Age: 27

Year Team	Lg	G	GS	CG	GF	IP	BFP	H	R	ER	HR	SH	SF	HB	TBB	IBB	SO	WP	Bk	W	L	Pct.	ShO	Sv-Op	Hld	ERA
1993 Montreal	NL	14	14	1	0	85.2	341	85	33	26	5	1	0	0	18	1	31	0	0	8	0	1.000	0	0-0	0	2.73
1994 Montreal	NL	20	20	0	0	92.1	397	106	60	53	11	6	6	2	23	1	50	2	0	7	3	.700	0	0-0	0	5.17
1995 Montreal	NL	9	9	1	0	47.1	184	38	17	17	3	4	0	1	9	0	28	0	0	5	3	.625	1	0-0	0	3.23
1996 Mon-SF	NL	20	19	0	0	102	430	109	50	45	12	4	1	2	27	0	46	2	0	6	8	.429	0	0-0	0	3.97
1997 San Francisco	NL	32	32	0	0	190.2	802	194	83	73	17	10	6	1	51	8	115	3	0	13	6	.684	0	0-0	0	3.45
1996 Montreal	NL	16	16	0	0	78.2	338	91	44	40	12	4	1	2	22	0	30	1	0	5	6	.455	0	0-0	0	4.58
San Francisco	NL	4	3	0	0	23.1	92	18	6	5	0	0	0	0	5	0	16	2	0	1	2	.333	0	0-0	0	1.93
5 ML YEARS		95	94	2	0	518	2154	532	243	214	48	25	13	6	128	10	270	7	0	39	20	.661	1	0-0	0	3.72

Scott Ruffcorn

Pitches: Right Bats: Right Pos: RP-14; SP-4   Ht: 6'4" Wt: 210 Born: 12/29/69 Age: 28

Year Team	Lg	G	GS	CG	GF	IP	BFP	H	R	ER	HR	SH	SF	HB	TBB	IBB	SO	WP	Bk	W	L	Pct.	ShO	Sv-Op	Hld	ERA
1991 White Sox	R	4	2	0	1	11.1	49	8	7	4	0	0	0	0	5	0	15	1	1	0	0	.000	0	0- -	—	3.18
South Bend	A	9	9	0	0	43.2	193	35	26	19	1	2	1	2	25	0	45	1	2	1	3	.250	0	0- -	—	3.92
1992 Sarasota	A+	25	24	2	0	160.1	642	122	53	39	7	4	5	3	39	0	140	3	1	14	5	.737	2	0- -	—	2.19
1993 Birmingham	AA	20	20	3	0	135	563	108	47	41	6	5	0	4	52	0	141	7	0	9	4	.692	3	0- -	—	2.73
Nashville	AAA	7	6	1	0	45	172	30	16	14	5	2	1	1	8	1	44	3	0	2	2	.500	0	0- -	—	2.80
1994 Nashville	AAA	24	24	3	0	165.2	672	139	57	50	5	3	6	6	40	1	144	6	0	15	3	.833	3	0- -	—	2.72
1995 Nashville	AAA	2	2	0	0	0.1	9	3	4	4	0	0	0	2	3	0	1	0	1	0	0	.000	0	0- -	—	108.00
Birmingham	AA	3	3	0	0	16	71	11	11	10	0	0	0	0	10	0	13	2	0	0	2	.000	0	0- -	—	5.63
White Sox	R	3	3	0	0	10	46	7	4	1	0	1	0	0	5	0	7	1	0	0	2	.000	0	0- -	—	0.90
1996 Nashville	AAA	24	24	2	0	149	649	142	71	64	18	6	4	5	61	1	129	7	0	13	4	.765	1	0- -	—	3.87
1997 Scranton-WB	AAA	5	5	2	0	31	126	22	6	4	0	2	0	1	10	0	20	0	0	2	0	1.000	2	0- -	—	1.16
1993 Chicago	AL	3	2	0	1	10	46	9	11	9	2	1	1	0	10	0	2	1	0	0	2	.000	0	0-0	0	8.10
1994 Chicago	AL	2	2	0	0	6.1	39	15	11	9	1	0	1	0	5	0	3	2	0	0	2	.000	0	0-0	0	12.79
1995 Chicago	AL	4	0	0	0	8	46	10	7	7	0	1	0	2	13	0	5	0	0	0	0	.000	0	0-0	0	7.88
1996 Chicago	AL	3	1	0	1	6.1	34	10	8	8	1	1	0	0	6	0	3	2	0	0	0	.000	0	0-0	0	11.37
1997 Philadelphia	NL	18	4	0	3	39.2	202	42	40	34	4	1	5	7	36	1	33	6	1	0	3	.000	0	0-0	0	7.71
5 ML YEARS		30	9	0	5	70.1	367	86	77	67	8	4	7	9	70	1	46	9	1	0	8	.000	0	0-0	0	8.57

Bruce Ruffin

Pitches: Left Bats: Both Pos: RP-23   Ht: 6'2" Wt: 215 Born: 10/4/63 Age: 34

Year Team	Lg	G	GS	CG	GF	IP	BFP	H	R	ER	HR	SH	SF	HB	TBB	IBB	SO	WP	Bk	W	L	Pct.	ShO	Sv-Op	Hld	ERA
1997 Colo Spngs *	AAA	2	0	0	0	2.2	9	1	1	1	1	0	0	0	0	2	0	0	0	0	0	.000	0	0- -	—	3.38
1986 Philadelphia	NL	21	21	6	0	146.1	600	138	53	40	6	2	4	1	44	6	70	0	1	9	4	.692	0	0-0	0	2.46
1987 Philadelphia	NL	35	35	3	0	204.2	884	236	118	99	17	8	10	2	73	4	93	6	0	11	14	.440	1	0-0	0	4.35
1988 Philadelphia	NL	55	15	3	14	144.1	646	151	86	71	7	10	3	3	80	6	82	12	0	6	10	.375	0	3-5	0	4.43
1989 Philadelphia	NL	24	23	1	0	125.2	576	152	69	62	10	8	1	0	62	6	70	8	0	6	10	.375	0	0-0	0	4.44
1990 Philadelphia	NL	32	25	2	1	149	678	178	99	89	14	10	6	1	62	7	79	3	2	6	13	.316	1	0-0	0	5.38
1991 Philadelphia	NL	31	15	1	2	119	508	125	52	50	6	6	4	1	38	3	85	6	1	4	7	.364	0	0-0	5	3.78
1992 Milwaukee	AL	25	6	1	6	58	272	66	43	43	7	3	3	0	41	3	45	2	0	1	6	.143	0	0-2	1	6.67
1993 Colorado	NL	59	12	0	8	139.2	619	145	71	60	10	4	5	1	69	8	126	8	0	6	5	.545	0	2-3	3	3.87

Year Team	Lg	G	GS	CG	GF	IP	BFP	H	R	ER	HR	SH	SF	HB	TBB	IBB	SO	WP	Bk	W	L	Pct.	ShO	Sv-Op	Hld	ERA
1994 Colorado	NL	56	0	0	39	55.2	252	55	28	25	6	1	3	1	30	2	65	5	0	4	5	.444	0	16-21	5	4.04
1995 Colorado	NL	37	0	0	19	34	140	26	8	8	1	4	0	0	19	1	23	1	0	0	1	.000	0	11-12	6	2.12
1996 Colorado	NL	71	0	0	56	69.2	292	55	35	31	5	0	3	0	29	3	74	10	0	7	5	.583	0	24-29	6	4.00
1997 Colorado	NL	23	0	0	15	22	102	18	15	13	3	2	0	0	18	0	31	2	0	0	2	.000	0	7-9	2	5.32
12 ML YEARS		469	152	17	160	1268	5569	1345	677	591	92	58	42	10	565	50	843	61	3	60	82	.423	3	63-81	36	4.19

Glendon Rusch

Pitches: Left **Bats:** Left **Pos:** SP-27; RP-3 **Ht:** 6'1" **Wt:** 195 **Born:** 11/7/74 **Age:** 23

Year Team	Lg	G	GS	CG	GF	IP	BFP	H	R	ER	HR	SH	SF	HB	TBB	IBB	SO	WP	Bk	W	L	Pct.	ShO	Sv-Op	Hld	ERA
1993 Royals	R	11	10	0	0	62	234	43	14	11	0	3	1	1	11	0	48	2	1	4	2	.667	0	0--	—	1.60
Rockford	A	2	2	0	0	8	40	10	6	3	0	0	1	0	7	0	8	1	0	1	0	1.000	0	0--	—	3.38
1994 Rockford	A	28	17	1	5	114	485	111	61	59	5	6	5	6	34	2	122	7	1	8	5	.615	1	1--	—	4.66
1995 Wilmington	A+	26	26	1	0	165.2	629	110	41	32	5	4	3	4	34	3	147	3	1	14	6	.700	1	0--	—	1.74
1996 Omaha	AAA	28	28	1	0	169.2	723	177	88	75	15	7	8	6	40	3	117	3	0	11	9	.550	0	0--	—	3.98
1997 Omaha	AAA	1	1	0	0	6	25	7	3	3	3	0	0	0	1	0	2	1	0	0	1	.000	0	0--	—	4.50
1997 Kansas City	AL	30	27	1	0	170.1	758	206	111	104	28	8	7	7	52	0	116	0	1	6	9	.400	0	0-0	0	5.50

Ken Ryan

Pitches: Right **Bats:** Right **Pos:** RP-22 **Ht:** 6'3" **Wt:** 230 **Born:** 10/24/68 **Age:** 29

Year Team	Lg	G	GS	CG	GF	IP	BFP	H	R	ER	HR	SH	SF	HB	TBB	IBB	SO	WP	Bk	W	L	Pct.	ShO	Sv-Op	Hld	ERA
1997 Reading *	AA	2	2	0	0	2	7	1	0	0	0	0	0	0	1	0	0	0	0	0	0	.000	0	0--	—	0.00
Scrnton-WB *	AAA	3	0	0	1	4	18	5	2	2	0	0	0	0	3	0	3	0	0	1	0	1.000	0	1--	—	4.50
1992 Boston	AL	7	0	0	6	7	30	4	5	5	2	1	1	0	5	0	5	0	0	0	0	.000	0	1-1		6.43
1993 Boston	AL	47	0	0	26	50	223	43	23	20	2	4	4	3	29	5	49	3	0	7	2	.778	0	1-4	3	3.60
1994 Boston	AL	42	0	0	26	48	202	46	14	13	1	4	0	1	17	3	32	2	0	2	3	.400	0	13-16	5	2.44
1995 Boston	AL	28	0	0	20	32.2	153	34	20	18	4	1	0	1	24	6	34	1	0	0	4	.000	0	7-10	0	4.96
1996 Philadelphia	NL	62	0	0	26	89	370	71	32	24	4	5	0	1	45	8	70	4	3	3	5	.375	0	8-13	15	2.43
1997 Philadelphia	NL	22	0	0	10	20.2	108	31	23	22	5	1	2	2	13	1	10	0	0	1	0	1.000	0	0-0	2	9.58
6 ML YEARS		208	0	0	114	247.1	1086	229	117	102	18	16	7	8	133	23	200	10	3	13	14	.481	0	30-44	25	3.71

Bret Saberhagen

Pitches: Right **Bats:** Right **Pos:** SP-6 **Ht:** 6'1" **Wt:** 200 **Born:** 4/11/64 **Age:** 34

Year Team	Lg	G	GS	CG	GF	IP	BFP	H	R	ER	HR	SH	SF	HB	TBB	IBB	SO	WP	Bk	W	L	Pct.	ShO	Sv-Op	Hld	ERA
1997 Lowell *	A-	1	1	0	0	3	10	1	0	0	0	0	0	0	0	0	2	0	0	0	0	.000	0	0--	—	0.00
Trenton *	AA	2	2	0	0	8	27	2	0	0	0	0	0	1	1	0	9	0	0	0	0	.000	0	0--	—	0.00
Pawtucket *	AAA	2	2	0	0	11	45	11	4	4	1	0	0	1	1	0	9	0	0	0	1	.000	0	0--	—	3.27
1984 Kansas City	AL	38	18	2	9	157.2	634	138	71	61	13	8	5	2	36	4	73	7	1	10	11	.476	1	1--	—	3.48
1985 Kansas City	AL	32	32	10	0	235.1	931	211	79	75	19	9	7	1	38	1	158	1	1	20	6	.769	1	0-0	0	2.87
1986 Kansas City	AL	30	25	4	4	156	652	165	77	72	15	3	3	2	29	1	112	1	1	7	12	.368	2	0--	—	4.15
1987 Kansas City	AL	33	33	15	0	257	1048	246	99	96	27	8	5	6	53	2	163	6	1	18	10	.643	4	0-0	0	3.36
1988 Kansas City	AL	35	35	9	0	260.2	1089	271	122	110	18	8	10	4	59	5	171	9	0	14	16	.467	0	0-0	0	3.80
1989 Kansas City	AL	36	35	12	0	262.1	1021	209	74	63	13	9	6	2	43	6	193	8	1	23	6	.793	4	0-0	0	2.16
1990 Kansas City	AL	20	20	5	0	135	561	146	52	49	9	4	4	1	28	1	87	1	0	5	9	.357	0	0-0	0	3.27
1991 Kansas City	AL	28	28	7	0	196.1	789	165	76	67	12	8	3	0	45	5	136	8	1	13	8	.619	2	0-0	0	3.07
1992 New York	NL	17	15	1	0	97.2	397	84	39	38	6	3	3	4	27	1	81	1	2	3	5	.375	1	0-1	0	3.50
1993 New York	NL	19	19	4	0	139.1	556	131	55	51	11	6	6	3	17	4	93	2	2	7	7	.500	1	0-0	0	3.29
1994 New York	NL	24	24	4	0	177.1	696	169	58	54	13	9	5	4	13	0	143	0	0	14	4	.778	0	0-0	0	2.74
1995 NYN-Col	NL	25	25	3	0	153	658	165	78	71	21	7	3	10	33	3	100	3	0	7	6	.538	0	0-0	0	4.18
1997 Boston	AL	6	6	0	0	26	120	30	20	19	5	1	3	2	10	0	14	1	0	0	6	.000	0	0-0	0	6.58
1995 New York	NL	16	16	3	0	110	452	105	45	41	13	5	3	5	20	2	71	2	0	5	5	.500	0	0-0	0	3.35
Colorado	NL	9	9	0	0	43	206	60	33	30	8	2	0	5	13	1	29	1	0	2	1	.667	0	0-0	0	6.28
13 ML YEARS		343	315	76	13	2253.2	9152	2130	900	826	182	83	63	50	431	33	1524	48	12	141	101	.583	16	1--	—	3.30

A.J. Sager

Pitches: Right **Bats:** Right **Pos:** RP-37; SP-1 **Ht:** 6'4" **Wt:** 220 **Born:** 3/3/65 **Age:** 33

Year Team	Lg	G	GS	CG	GF	IP	BFP	H	R	ER	HR	SH	SF	HB	TBB	IBB	SO	WP	Bk	W	L	Pct.	ShO	Sv-Op	Hld	ERA
1994 San Diego	NL	22	3	0	4	46.2	217	62	34	31	4	6	2	2	16	5	26	0	0	1	4	.200	0	0-0	0	5.98
1995 Colorado	NL	10	0	0	2	14.2	70	19	16	12	1	2	0	0	7	1	10	0	0	0	0	.000	0	0-1	0	7.36
1996 Detroit	AL	22	9	0	1	79	347	91	46	44	10	3	3	2	29	2	52	1	0	4	5	.444	0	0-0	1	5.01
1997 Detroit	AL	38	1	0	8	84	350	81	43	39	10	5	6	1	24	6	53	0	0	3	4	.429	0	3-4	10	4.18
4 ML YEARS		92	13	0	15	224.1	984	253	139	126	25	16	11	5	76	14	141	1	0	8	13	.381	0	3-5	11	5.05

Marc Sagmoen

Bats: L **Throws:** L **Pos:** RF-16; PH-5; LF-2; 1B-1 **Ht:** 5'11" **Wt:** 185 **Born:** 4/16/71 **Age:** 27

Year Team	Lg	G	AB	H	2B	3B	HR	(Hm	Rd)	TB	R	RBI	TBB	IBB	SO	HBP	SH	SF	SB	CS	SB%	GDP	Avg	OBP	SLG
1993 Erie	A-	6	23	7	1	1	0	--	--	10	6	2	3	0	7	1	0	1	0	0	.00	0	.304	.393	.435
Chston-SC	A	63	234	69	13	4	6	--	--	108	44	34	23	0	39	3	3	3	16	4	.80	2	.295	.361	.462

	BATTING																	BASERUNNING				PERCENTAGES		
Year Team	Lg	G	AB	H	2B	3B	HR	(Hm | Rd)	TB	R	RBI	TBB	IBB	SO	HBP	SH	SF	SB	CS	SB%	GDP	Avg	OBP	SLG
1994 Charlotte	A+	122	475	139	25	10	3	—	—	193	74	47	37	2	56	3	1	3	15	10	.60	15	.293	.346	.406
1995 Okla City	AAA	56	188	42	11	3	3	—	—	68	20	25	16	0	31	2	1	4	5	2	.71	2	.223	.286	.362
Tulsa	AA	63	242	56	8	5	6	—	—	92	36	22	23	0	23	4	1	2	5	4	.56	2	.231	.306	.380
1996 Tulsa	AA	96	387	109	21	6	10	—	—	172	58	62	33	4	58	2	0	7	5	8	.38	7	.282	.336	.444
Okla City	AAA	32	116	34	6	0	5	—	—	55	16	16	4	0	20	1	0	1	1	0	1.00	0	.293	.320	.474
1997 Okla City	AAA	111	418	110	32	6	5	—	—	169	47	44	26	4	95	1	1	2	4	3	.57	10	.263	.306	.404
1997 Texas	AL	21	43	6	2	0	1	(0 | 1)	11	2	4	2	0	13	0	0	1	0	0	.00	1	.140	.174	.256

Tim Salmon

Bats: Right **Throws:** Right **Pos:** RF-153; DH-4   **Ht:** 6'3" **Wt:** 220 **Born:** 8/24/68 **Age:** 29

	BATTING																	BASERUNNING				PERCENTAGES		
Year Team	Lg	G	AB	H	2B	3B	HR	(Hm | Rd)	TB	R	RBI	TBB	IBB	SO	HBP	SH	SF	SB	CS	SB%	GDP	Avg	OBP	SLG
1992 California	AL	23	79	14	1	0	2	(1 | 1)	21	8	6	11	1	23	1	0	1	1	1	.50	1	.177	.283	.266
1993 California	AL	142	515	146	35	1	31	(23 | 8)	276	93	95	82	5	135	5	0	8	5	6	.45	6	.283	.382	.536
1994 California	AL	100	373	107	18	2	23	(12 | 11)	198	67	70	54	2	102	5	0	3	1	3	.25	3	.287	.382	.531
1995 California	AL	143	537	177	34	3	34	(15 | 19)	319	111	105	91	2	111	6	0	4	5	5	.50	9	.330	.429	.594
1996 California	AL	156	581	166	27	4	30	(18 | 12)	291	90	98	93	7	125	4	0	3	4	2	.67	8	.286	.386	.501
1997 Anaheim	AL	157	582	172	28	1	33	(17 | 16)	301	95	129	95	5	142	7	0	11	9	12	.43	7	.296	.394	.517
6 ML YEARS		721	2667	782	143	11	153	(86 | 67)	1406	464	503	426	22	638	28	0	30	25	29	.46	34	.293	.392	.527

Juan Samuel

Bats: R **Throws:** R **Pos:** DH-16; PH-15; 3B-9; 1B-7; 2B-4; RF-2   **Ht:** 5'11" **Wt:** 180 **Born:** 12/9/60 **Age:** 37

	BATTING																	BASERUNNING				PERCENTAGES		
Year Team	Lg	G	AB	H	2B	3B	HR	(Hm | Rd)	TB	R	RBI	TBB	IBB	SO	HBP	SH	SF	SB	CS	SB%	GDP	Avg	OBP	SLG
1983 Philadelphia	NL	18	65	18	1	2	2	(1 | 1)	29	14	5	4	1	16	1	0	1	3	2	.60	1	.277	.324	.446
1984 Philadelphia	NL	160	701	191	36	19	15	(8 | 7)	310	105	69	28	2	168	7	0	1	72	15	.83	6	.272	.307	.442
1985 Philadelphia	NL	161	663	175	31	13	19	(8 | 11)	289	101	74	33	2	141	6	2	5	53	19	.74	8	.264	.303	.436
1986 Philadelphia	NL	145	591	157	36	12	16	(10 | 6)	265	90	78	26	3	142	8	1	7	42	14	.75	8	.266	.302	.448
1987 Philadelphia	NL	160	655	178	37	15	28	(15 | 13)	329	113	100	60	5	162	5	0	6	35	15	.70	12	.272	.335	.502
1988 Philadelphia	NL	157	629	153	32	9	12	(7 | 5)	239	68	67	39	6	151	12	0	5	33	10	.77	7	.243	.298	.380
1989 Phi-NYN	NL	137	532	125	16	2	11	(5 | 6)	178	69	48	42	2	120	11	2	2	42	12	.78	7	.235	.303	.335
1990 Los Angeles	NL	143	492	119	24	3	13	(6 | 7)	188	62	52	51	5	126	5	5	5	38	20	.66	8	.242	.316	.382
1991 Los Angeles	NL	153	594	161	22	6	12	(4 | 8)	231	74	58	49	4	133	3	10	3	23	8	.74	8	.271	.328	.389
1992 LA-KC		76	224	61	8	4	0	(0 | 0)	77	22	23	14	4	49	2	4	2	8	3	.73	2	.272	.318	.344
1993 Cincinnati	NL	103	261	60	10	4	4	(1 | 3)	90	31	26	23	3	53	3	0	2	9	7	.56	2	.230	.298	.345
1994 Detroit	AL	59	136	42	9	5	5	(4 | 1)	76	32	21	10	0	26	3	0	2	5	2	.71	4	.309	.364	.559
1995 Det-KC	AL	91	205	54	10	1	12	(6 | 6)	102	31	39	29	1	49	2	1	0	6	4	.60	3	.263	.360	.498
1996 Toronto	AL	69	188	48	8	3	8	(4 | 4)	86	34	26	15	0	65	3	0	1	9	1	.90	2	.255	.319	.457
1997 Toronto	AL	45	95	27	5	4	3	(2 | 1)	49	13	15	10	0	28	2	1	0	5	3	.63	2	.284	.364	.516
1989 Philadelphia	NL	51	199	49	3	1	8	(3 | 5)	78	32	20	18	1	45	1	0	1	11	3	.79	2	.246	.311	.392
New York	NL	86	333	76	13	1	3	(2 | 1)	100	37	28	24	1	75	10	2	1	31	9	.78	5	.228	.299	.300
1992 Los Angeles	NL	47	122	32	3	1	0	(0 | 0)	37	7	15	7	3	22	1	4	2	2	2	.50	0	.262	.303	.303
Kansas City	AL	29	102	29	5	3	0	(0 | 0)	40	15	8	7	1	27	1	0	0	6	1	.86	2	.284	.336	.392
1995 Detroit	AL	76	171	48	10	1	10	(6 | 4)	90	28	34	24	0	38	2	1	0	5	4	.56	3	.281	.376	.526
Kansas City	AL	15	34	6	0	0	2	(0 | 2)	12	3	5	5	1	11	0	0	0	1	0	1.00	0	.176	.282	.353
15 ML YEARS		1677	6031	1569	285	102	160	(81 | 79)	2538	859	701	433	38	1429	73	26	42	383	135	.74	81	.260	.315	.421

Rey Sanchez

Bats: R **Throws:** R **Pos:** 2B-69; SS-69; PH-14; 3B-1   **Ht:** 5'9" **Wt:** 175 **Born:** 10/5/67 **Age:** 30

	BATTING																	BASERUNNING				PERCENTAGES		
Year Team	Lg	G	AB	H	2B	3B	HR	(Hm | Rd)	TB	R	RBI	TBB	IBB	SO	HBP	SH	SF	SB	CS	SB%	GDP	Avg	OBP	SLG
1991 Chicago	NL	13	23	6	0	0	0	(0 | 0)	6	1	2	4	0	3	0	0	0	0	0	.00	0	.261	.370	.261
1992 Chicago	NL	74	255	64	14	3	1	(1 | 0)	87	24	19	10	1	17	3	5	2	2	1	.67	7	.251	.285	.341
1993 Chicago	NL	105	344	97	11	2	0	(0 | 0)	112	35	28	15	7	22	3	9	2	1	1	.50	8	.282	.316	.326
1994 Chicago	NL	96	291	83	13	1	0	(0 | 0)	98	26	24	20	4	29	7	4	1	2	5	.29	9	.285	.345	.337
1995 Chicago	NL	114	428	119	22	2	3	(0 | 3)	154	57	27	14	2	48	1	8	2	6	4	.60	9	.278	.301	.360
1996 Chicago	NL	95	289	61	9	0	1	(1 | 0)	73	28	12	22	6	42	3	8	2	7	1	.88	6	.211	.272	.253
1997 ChN-NYA		135	343	94	21	0	2	(1 | 1)	121	35	27	16	2	47	1	9	4	4	6	.40	8	.274	.307	.353
1997 Chicago	NL	97	205	51	9	0	1	(1 | 0)	63	14	12	11	2	26	0	4	0	4	2	.67	7	.249	.287	.307
New York	AL	38	138	43	12	0	1	(0 | 1)	58	21	15	5	0	21	1	5	1	0	4	.00	1	.312	.338	.420
7 ML YEARS		632	1973	524	90	8	7	(3 | 4)	651	206	139	101	22	208	18	43	10	22	18	.55	47	.266	.306	.330

Ryne Sandberg

Bats: Right **Throws:** Right **Pos:** 2B-126; PH-10; DH-1   **Ht:** 6'2" **Wt:** 190 **Born:** 9/18/59 **Age:** 38

	BATTING																	BASERUNNING				PERCENTAGES		
Year Team	Lg	G	AB	H	2B	3B	HR	(Hm | Rd)	TB	R	RBI	TBB	IBB	SO	HBP	SH	SF	SB	CS	SB%	GDP	Avg	OBP	SLG
1981 Philadelphia	NL	13	6	1	0	0	0	(0 | 0)	1	2	0	0	0	1	0	0	0	0	0	.00	0	.167	.167	.167
1982 Chicago	NL	156	635	172	33	5	7	(5 | 2)	236	103	54	36	3	90	4	7	5	32	12	.73	7	.271	.312	.372
1983 Chicago	NL	158	633	165	25	4	8	(4 | 4)	222	94	48	51	3	79	3	7	5	37	11	.77	6	.261	.316	.351
1984 Chicago	NL	156	636	200	36	19	19	(11 | 8)	331	114	84	52	3	101	3	5	4	32	7	.82	7	.314	.367	.520
1985 Chicago	NL	153	609	186	31	6	26	(17 | 9)	307	113	83	57	5	97	1	2	4	54	11	.83	4	.305	.364	.504
1986 Chicago	NL	154	627	178	28	5	14	(8 | 6)	258	68	76	46	6	79	0	3	6	34	11	.76	11	.284	.330	.411
1987 Chicago	NL	132	523	154	25	2	16	(8 | 8)	231	81	59	59	4	79	2	1	2	21	2	.91	11	.294	.367	.442
1988 Chicago	NL	155	618	163	23	8	19	(10 | 9)	259	77	69	54	3	91	1	1	5	25	10	.71	14	.264	.322	.419

BATTING																			BASERUNNING				PERCENTAGES		
Year Team	Lg	G	AB	H	2B	3B	HR	(Hm	Rd)	TB	R	RBI	TBB	IBB	SO	HBP	SH	SF	SB	CS	SB%	GDP	Avg	OBP	SLG
1989 Chicago	NL	157	606	176	25	5	30	(16	14)	301	104	76	59	8	85	4	1	2	15	5	.75	9	.290	.356	.497
1990 Chicago	NL	155	615	188	30	3	40	(25	15)	344	116	100	50	8	84	1	0	9	25	7	.78	8	.306	.354	.559
1991 Chicago	NL	158	585	170	32	2	26	(15	11)	284	104	100	87	4	89	2	1	9	22	8	.73	9	.291	.379	.485
1992 Chicago	NL	158	612	186	32	8	26	(16	10)	312	100	87	68	4	73	1	0	6	17	6	.74	13	.304	.371	.510
1993 Chicago	NL	117	456	141	20	0	9	(5	4)	188	67	45	37	1	62	2	2	6	9	2	.82	12	.309	.359	.412
1994 Chicago	NL	57	223	53	9	5	5	(3	2)	87	36	24	23	0	40	1	0	0	2	3	.40	6	.238	.312	.390
1996 Chicago	NL	150	554	135	28	4	25	(12	13)	246	85	92	54	4	116	7	1	5	12	8	.60	9	.244	.316	.444
1997 Chicago	NL	135	447	118	26	0	12	(9	3)	180	54	64	28	3	94	2	0	3	7	4	.64	5	.264	.308	.403
16 ML YEARS		2164	8385	2386	403	76	282	(164	118)	3787	1318	1061	761	59	1260	34	31	71	344	107	.76	139	.285	.344	.452

Deion Sanders

Bats: Left **Throws:** Left **Pos:** CF-77; LF-37; PH-5 **Ht:** 6'1" **Wt:** 195 **Born:** 8/9/67 **Age:** 30

BATTING																			BASERUNNING				PERCENTAGES		
Year Team	Lg	G	AB	H	2B	3B	HR	(Hm	Rd)	TB	R	RBI	TBB	IBB	SO	HBP	SH	SF	SB	CS	SB%	GDP	Avg	OBP	SLG
1989 New York	AL	14	47	11	2	0	2	(0	2)	19	7	7	3	1	8	0	0	0	1	0	1.00	1	.234	.280	.404
1990 New York	AL	57	133	21	2	2	3	(1	2)	36	24	9	13	0	27	1	1	1	8	2	.80	2	.158	.236	.271
1991 Atlanta	NL	54	110	21	1	2	4	(2	2)	38	16	13	12	0	23	0	0	0	11	3	.79	1	.191	.270	.345
1992 Atlanta	NL	97	303	92	6	14	8	(5	3)	150	54	28	18	0	52	2	1	1	26	9	.74	5	.304	.346	.495
1993 Atlanta	NL	95	272	75	18	6	6	(1	5)	123	42	28	16	3	42	3	1	2	19	7	.73	3	.276	.321	.452
1994 Atl-Cin	NL	92	375	106	17	4	4	(2	2)	143	58	28	32	1	63	3	2	2	38	16	.70	5	.283	.342	.381
1995 Cin-SF	NL	85	343	92	11	8	6	(3	3)	137	48	28	27	0	60	4	3	2	24	9	.73	1	.268	.327	.399
1997 Cincinnati	NL	115	465	127	13	7	5	(0	5)	169	53	23	34	2	67	6	2	2	56	13	.81	4	.273	.329	.363
1994 Atlanta	NL	46	191	55	10	0	4	(2	2)	77	32	21	16	1	28	1	1	2	19	7	.73	4	.288	.343	.403
Cincinnati	NL	46	184	51	7	4	0	(0	0)	66	26	7	16	0	35	2	1	0	19	9	.68	1	.277	.342	.359
1995 Cincinnati	NL	33	129	31	2	3	1	(1	0)	42	19	10	9	0	18	2	2	2	16	3	.84	0	.240	.296	.326
San Francisco	NL	52	214	61	9	5	5	(2	3)	95	29	18	18	0	42	2	1	0	8	6	.57	1	.285	.346	.444
8 ML YEARS		609	2048	545	70	43	38	(14	24)	815	302	164	155	7	342	19	10	10	183	59	.76	21	.266	.322	.398

Reggie Sanders

Bats: Right **Throws:** Right **Pos:** RF-85; PH-1 **Ht:** 6'1" **Wt:** 185 **Born:** 12/1/67 **Age:** 30

BATTING																			BASERUNNING				PERCENTAGES		
Year Team	Lg	G	AB	H	2B	3B	HR	(Hm	Rd)	TB	R	RBI	TBB	IBB	SO	HBP	SH	SF	SB	CS	SB%	GDP	Avg	OBP	SLG
1997 Chattanooga *	AA	3	11	6	1	1	1	—	—	12	3	3	1	0	2	1	0	0	0	0	.00	0	.545	.615	1.091
Indianapols *	AAA	5	19	4	0	0	0	—	—	4	1	1	1	0	6	0	0	0	0	0	.00	0	.211	.250	.211
1991 Cincinnati	NL	9	40	8	0	0	1	(0	1)	11	6	3	0	0	9	0	0	0	1	1	.50	1	.200	.200	.275
1992 Cincinnati	NL	116	385	104	26	6	12	(6	6)	178	62	36	48	2	98	4	0	1	16	7	.70	6	.270	.356	.462
1993 Cincinnati	NL	138	496	136	16	4	20	(8	12)	220	90	83	51	7	118	5	3	8	27	10	.73	10	.274	.343	.444
1994 Cincinnati	NL	107	400	105	20	8	17	(10	7)	192	66	62	41	1	114	2	1	3	21	9	.70	2	.263	.332	.480
1995 Cincinnati	NL	133	484	148	36	6	28	(9	19)	280	91	99	69	4	122	8	0	6	36	12	.75	9	.306	.397	.579
1996 Cincinnati	NL	81	287	72	17	1	14	(7	7)	133	49	33	44	4	86	2	0	1	24	8	.75	8	.251	.353	.463
1997 Cincinnati	NL	86	312	79	19	2	8	(11	8)	159	52	56	42	3	93	3	1	0	13	7	.65	9	.253	.347	.510
7 ML YEARS		670	2404	652	134	27	111	(51	60)	1173	416	372	295	21	640	24	5	19	138	54	.72	45	.271	.354	.488

Scott Sanders

Pitches: Right **Bats:** Right **Pos:** RP-27; SP-20 **Ht:** 6'4" **Wt:** 220 **Born:** 3/25/69 **Age:** 29

HOW MUCH HE PITCHED							WHAT HE GAVE UP												THE RESULTS						
Year Team	Lg	G	GS	CG	GF	IP	BFP	H	R	ER	HR	SH	SF	HB	TBB	IBB	SO	WP	Bk	W	L	Pct.	ShO	Sv-Op	Hld	ERA
1993 San Diego	NL	9	9	0	0	52.1	231	54	32	24	4	1	2	1	23	1	37	0	1	3	3	.500	0	0-0	0	4.13
1994 San Diego	NL	23	20	0	2	111	485	103	63	59	10	6	5	5	48	4	109	10	1	4	8	.333	0	1-1	1	4.78
1995 San Diego	NL	17	15	1	0	90	383	79	46	43	14	2	2	2	31	4	88	6	1	5	5	.500	0	0-0	1	4.30
1996 San Diego	NL	46	16	0	6	144	594	117	58	54	10	7	7	2	48	5	157	7	0	9	5	.643	0	0-0	3	3.38
1997 Sea-Det	AL	47	20	1	15	139.2	626	152	92	91	30	3	10	4	62	6	120	8	0	6	14	.300	1	2-4	4	5.86
1997 Seattle	AL	33	6	0	15	65.1	309	73	48	47	16	2	5	3	38	5	62	4	0	3	6	.333	0	2-4	4	6.47
Detroit	AL	14	14	1	0	74.1	317	79	44	44	14	1	5	1	24	1	58	4	0	3	8	.273	1	0-0	0	5.33
5 ML YEARS		142	80	2	23	537	2319	505	291	271	68	19	26	14	212	20	511	31	3	27	35	.435	1	3-5	9	4.54

Julio Santana

Pitches: Right **Bats:** Right **Pos:** RP-16; SP-14 **Ht:** 6'0" **Wt:** 185 **Born:** 1/20/73 **Age:** 25

HOW MUCH HE PITCHED							WHAT HE GAVE UP												THE RESULTS						
Year Team	Lg	G	GS	CG	GF	IP	BFP	H	R	ER	HR	SH	SF	HB	TBB	IBB	SO	WP	Bk	W	L	Pct.	ShO	Sv-Op	Hld	ERA
1993 Rangers	R	26	0	0	12	39	153	31	9	6	0	0	0	1	7	0	50	1	0	4	1	.800	0	7- —	—	1.38
1994 Chston-SC	A	16	16	0	0	91.1	383	65	38	25	3	0	4	7	44	0	103	7	1	6	7	.462	0	0- —	—	2.46
Tulsa	AA	11	11	2	0	71.1	290	50	26	23	1	1	2	2	41	0	45	2	0	7	2	.778	0	0- —	—	2.90
1995 Okla City	AAA	2	2	0	0	3	25	9	14	13	3	0	0	0	7	0	6	1	1	0	2	.000	0	0- —	—	39.00
Charlotte	A+	5	5	1	0	31.1	136	32	16	13	1	1	1	0	16	0	27	7	2	3	3	.000	0	0- —	—	3.73
Tulsa	AA	15	15	3	0	103	438	91	40	36	8	2	4	0	52	2	71	8	1	6	4	.600	0	0- —	—	3.15
1996 Okla City	AAA	29	29	4	0	185.2	787	171	102	83	12	5	9	5	66	1	113	12	1	11	12	.478	1	0- —	—	4.02
1997 Okla City	AAA	1	1	0	0	3	20	9	6	5	0	0	0	0	2	0	1	0	0	0	0	.000	0	0- —	—	15.00
1997 Texas	AL	30	14	0	3	104	496	141	86	78	16	1	5	4	49	2	64	8	1	4	6	.400	0	0-1	1	6.75

F.P. Santangelo

Bats: B **Throws:** R **Pos:** RF-51; LF-40; 3B-32; PH-18; CF-13; 2B-7; SS-1   **Ht:** 5'10"   **Wt:** 168   **Born:** 10/24/67   **Age:** 30

							BATTING											BASERUNNING				PERCENTAGES		
Year Team	Lg	G	AB	H	2B	3B	HR	(Hm | Rd)	TB	R	RBI	TBB	IBB	SO	HBP	SH	SF	SB	CS	SB%	GDP	Avg	OBP	SLG
1995 Montreal	NL	35	98	29	5	1	1	(1 | 0)	39	11	9	12	0	9	2	1	0	1	1	.50	0	.296	.384	.398
1996 Montreal	NL	152	393	109	20	5	7	(5 | 2)	160	54	56	49	4	61	11	9	5	5	2	.71	6	.277	.369	.407
1997 Montreal	NL	130	350	87	19	5	5	(5 | 0)	131	56	31	50	1	73	25	12	3	8	5	.62	1	.249	.379	.374
3 ML YEARS		317	841	225	44	11	13	(11 | 2)	330	121	96	111	5	143	38	22	8	14	8	.64	7	.268	.375	.392

Benito Santiago

Bats: Right **Throws:** Right **Pos:** C-95; DH-1; PH-1   **Ht:** 6'1"   **Wt:** 185   **Born:** 3/9/65   **Age:** 33

							BATTING											BASERUNNING				PERCENTAGES		
Year Team	Lg	G	AB	H	2B	3B	HR	(Hm | Rd)	TB	R	RBI	TBB	IBB	SO	HBP	SH	SF	SB	CS	SB%	GDP	Avg	OBP	SLG
1986 San Diego	NL	17	62	18	2	0	3	(2 | 1)	29	10	6	2	0	12	0	0	1	0	0	1.00	0	.290	.308	.468
1987 San Diego	NL	146	546	164	33	2	18	(11 | 7)	255	64	79	16	2	112	5	1	4	21	12	.64	12	.300	.324	.467
1988 San Diego	NL	139	492	122	22	2	10	(3 | 7)	178	49	46	24	2	82	1	5	5	15	7	.68	18	.248	.282	.362
1989 San Diego	NL	129	462	109	16	3	16	(8 | 8)	179	50	62	26	6	89	1	3	2	11	6	.65	9	.236	.277	.387
1990 San Diego	NL	100	344	93	8	5	11	(5 | 6)	144	42	53	27	2	55	3	1	7	5	5	.50	4	.270	.323	.419
1991 San Diego	NL	152	580	155	22	3	17	(6 | 11)	234	60	87	23	5	114	4	0	7	8	10	.44	21	.267	.296	.403
1992 San Diego	NL	106	386	97	21	0	10	(2 | 8)	148	37	42	21	1	52	0	0	4	2	5	.29	14	.251	.287	.383
1993 Florida	NL	139	469	108	19	6	13	(6 | 7)	178	49	50	37	2	88	5	0	4	10	7	.59	9	.230	.291	.380
1994 Florida	NL	101	337	92	14	2	11	(4 | 7)	143	35	41	25	1	57	1	2	4	1	2	.33	11	.273	.322	.424
1995 Cincinnati	NL	81	266	76	20	0	11	(7 | 4)	129	40	44	24	1	48	4	0	2	2	2	.50	7	.286	.351	.485
1996 Philadelphia	NL	136	481	127	21	2	30	(8 | 22)	242	71	85	49	7	104	1	0	2	2	0	1.00	8	.264	.332	.503
1997 Toronto	AL	97	341	83	10	0	13	(6 | 7)	132	31	42	17	1	80	2	1	5	1	0	1.00	10	.243	.279	.387
12 ML YEARS		1343	4766	1244	208	25	163	(75 | 88)	1991	538	637	291	30	893	27	13	47	78	57	.58	123	.261	.304	.418

Jose Santiago

Pitches: Right **Bats:** Right **Pos:** RP-4   **Ht:** 6'3"   **Wt:** 215   **Born:** 11/5/74   **Age:** 23

		HOW MUCH HE PITCHED						WHAT HE GAVE UP											THE RESULTS						
Year Team	Lg	G	GS	CG	GF	IP	BFP	H	R	ER	HR	SH	SF	HB	TBB	IBB	SO	WP	Bk	W	L	Pct.	ShO	Sv-Op	Hld	ERA
1994 Royals	R	10	1	0	7	19	84	17	7	5	1	0	0	1	7	0	10	2	1	1	0	1.000	0	2--	—	2.37
1995 Spokane	A-	22	0	0	10	48.2	227	60	26	17	1	1	2	5	20	4	32	3	0	2	4	.333	0	1--	—	3.14
1996 Lansing	A	54	0	0	46	77	331	78	34	22	4	7	1	5	21	3	55	3	1	7	6	.538	0	19--	—	2.57
1997 Wilmington	A+	4	0	0	4	3.2	18	3	3	2	0	1	0	1	1	0	1	0	0	1	1	.500	0	2--	—	4.91
Lansing	A	9	0	0	6	13	57	10	6	3	0	0	1	0	6	1	8	0	0	1	0	1.000	0	1--	—	2.08
Wichita	AA	22	0	0	8	27	120	32	13	12	1	1	2	2	8	1	12	0	0	2	1	.667	0	3--	—	4.00
1997 Kansas City	AL	4	0	0	3	4.2	24	7	2	1	0	0	0	1	1	0	0	0	0	0	0	.000	0	0-0	0	1.93

Tony Saunders

Pitches: Left **Bats:** Left **Pos:** SP-21; RP-1   **Ht:** 6'2"   **Wt:** 205   **Born:** 4/29/74   **Age:** 24

		HOW MUCH HE PITCHED						WHAT HE GAVE UP											THE RESULTS						
Year Team	Lg	G	GS	CG	GF	IP	BFP	H	R	ER	HR	SH	SF	HB	TBB	IBB	SO	WP	Bk	W	L	Pct.	ShO	Sv-Op	Hld	ERA
1992 Marlins	R	24	0	0	16	45.2	180	29	10	6	0	2	3	1	13	2	37	4	0	4	1	.800	0	7--	—	1.18
1993 Kane County	A	23	10	2	1	83.1	344	72	23	21	3	6	0	2	32	3	87	2	1	6	1	.857	0	1--	—	2.27
1994 Brevard Cty	A+	10	10	1	0	60	237	54	24	21	4	2	1	2	9	0	46	2	0	5	5	.500	0	0--	—	3.15
1995 Brevard Cty	A+	13	13	0	0	71	275	60	29	24	6	1	4	7	15	0	54	3	0	6	5	.545	0	0--	—	3.04
1996 Portland	AA	26	26	2	0	167.2	669	121	51	49	10	8	4	0	62	3	156	8	1	13	4	.765	0	0--	—	2.63
1997 Portland	AA	1	1	0	0	2	10	3	2	2	0	0	0	1	1	0	3	0	0	0	0	.000	0	0--	—	9.00
Charlotte	AAA	3	3	0	0	13	50	9	4	4	1	1	0	0	6	0	9	0	0	1	0	1.000	0	0--	—	2.77
1997 Florida	NL	22	21	0	0	111.1	483	99	62	57	12	8	4	2	64	1	102	2	1	4	6	.400	0	0-0	0	4.61

Steve Scarsone

Bats: R **Throws:** R **Pos:** 2B-2; 3B-1; LF-1; CF-1; PH-1   **Ht:** 6'2"   **Wt:** 195   **Born:** 4/11/66   **Age:** 32

							BATTING											BASERUNNING				PERCENTAGES		
Year Team	Lg	G	AB	H	2B	3B	HR	(Hm	Rd)	TB	R	RBI	TBB	IBB	SO	HBP	SH	SF	SB	CS	SB%	GDP	Avg	OBP	SLG
1997 Louisville *	AAA	10	26	4	0	0	1	(Hm	Rd)	7	5	3	7	0	10	2	0	0	0	0	.00	0	.154	.371	.269
Las Vegas *	AAA	82	251	58	13	1	11	—	—	106	37	35	38	0	78	3	2	2	2	2	.50	1	.231	.337	.422
1992 Phi-Bal		18	30	5	0	0	0	(0	0)	5	3	0	2	0	12	0	1	0	0	0	.00	0	.167	.219	.167
1993 San Francisco	NL	44	103	26	9	0	2	(1	1)	41	16	15	4	0	32	0	0	0	0	1	.00	0	.252	.278	.398
1994 San Francisco	NL	52	103	28	8	0	2	(0	2)	42	21	13	10	1	20	0	3	2	0	2	.00	1	.272	.330	.408
1995 San Francisco	NL	80	233	62	10	3	11	(7	4)	111	33	29	18	0	82	6	3	1	3	2	.60	2	.266	.333	.476
1996 San Francisco	NL	105	283	62	12	1	5	(4	1)	91	28	23	25	0	91	2	8	1	2	3	.40	6	.219	.286	.322
1997 St. Louis	NL	5	10	1	0	0	0	(0	0)	1	0	0	2	0	5	0	0	0	1	0	1.00	0	.100	.250	.100
1992 Philadelphia	NL	7	13	2	0	0	0	(0	0)	2	1	0	6	0	6	0	0	0	0	0	.00	0	.154	.214	.154
Baltimore	AL	11	17	3	0	0	0	(0	0)	3	2	0	1	0	6	0	1	0	0	0	.00	0	.176	.222	.176
6 ML YEARS		304	762	184	39	4	20	(12	8)	291	101	80	61	1	242	8	19	5	6	8	.43	9	.241	.303	.382

Curt Schilling

Pitches: Right **Bats:** Right **Pos:** SP-35   **Ht:** 6'4"   **Wt:** 226   **Born:** 11/14/66   **Age:** 31

		HOW MUCH HE PITCHED						WHAT HE GAVE UP											THE RESULTS						
Year Team	Lg	G	GS	CG	GF	IP	BFP	H	R	ER	HR	SH	SF	HB	TBB	IBB	SO	WP	Bk	W	L	Pct.	ShO	Sv-Op	Hld	ERA
1988 Baltimore	AL	4	4	0	0	14.2	76	22	19	16	3	0	3	1	10	1	4	2	0	0	3	.000	0	0-0	0	9.82

Year Team	Lg	G	GS	CG	GF	IP	BFP	H	R	ER	HR	SH	SF	HB	TBB	IBB	SO	WP	Bk	W	L	Pct.	ShO	Sv-Op	Hld	ERA
1989 Baltimore	AL	5	1	0	0	8.2	38	10	6	6	2	0	0	0	3	0	6	1	0	0	1	.000	0	0-0	0	6.23
1990 Baltimore	AL	35	0	0	16	46	191	38	13	13	1	2	4	0	19	0	32	0	0	1	2	.333	0	3-9	5	2.54
1991 Houston	NL	56	0	0	34	75.2	336	79	35	32	2	5	1	0	39	7	71	4	1	3	5	.375	0	8-11	5	3.81
1992 Philadelphia	NL	42	26	10	10	226.1	895	165	67	59	11	7	8	1	59	4	147	4	0	14	11	.560	4	2-3	0	2.35
1993 Philadelphia	NL	34	34	7	0	235.1	982	234	114	105	23	9	7	4	57	6	186	9	3	16	7	.696	2	0-0	0	4.02
1994 Philadelphia	NL	13	13	1	0	82.1	360	87	42	41	10	6	1	3	28	3	58	3	1	2	8	.200	0	0-0	0	4.48
1995 Philadelphia	NL	17	17	1	0	116	473	96	52	46	12	5	2	3	26	2	114	0	1	7	5	.583	0	0-0	0	3.57
1996 Philadelphia	NL	26	26	8	0	183.1	732	149	69	65	16	6	4	3	50	5	182	5	0	9	10	.474	2	0-0	0	3.19
1997 Philadelphia	NL	35	35	7	0	254.1	1009	208	96	84	25	8	8	5	58	3	319	5	1	17	11	.607	2	0-0	0	2.97
10 ML YEARS		267	156	34	60	1242.2	5092	1088	513	467	105	48	38	20	349	31	1119	33	7	69	63	.523	10	13-23	10	3.38

Jason Schmidt

Pitches: Right **Bats:** Right **Pos:** SP-32　　**Ht:** 6'5" **Wt:** 185 **Born:** 1/29/73 **Age:** 25

Year Team	Lg	G	GS	CG	GF	IP	BFP	H	R	ER	HR	SH	SF	HB	TBB	IBB	SO	WP	Bk	W	L	Pct.	ShO	Sv-Op	Hld	ERA
1995 Atlanta	NL	9	2	0	1	25	119	27	17	16	2	2	4	1	18	3	19	1	0	2	2	.500	0	0-1	0	5.76
1996 Atl-Pit	NL	19	17	1	0	96.1	445	108	67	61	10	4	9	2	53	0	74	8	1	5	6	.455	0	0-0	0	5.70
1997 Pittsburgh	NL	32	32	2	0	187.2	825	193	106	96	16	10	3	9	76	2	136	8	0	10	9	.526	0	0-0	0	4.60
1996 Atlanta	NL	13	11	0	0	58.2	274	69	48	44	8	3	6	0	32	0	48	5	1	3	4	.429	0	0-0	0	6.75
Pittsburgh	NL	6	6	1	0	37.2	171	39	19	17	2	1	3	2	21	0	26	3	0	2	2	.500	0	0-0	0	4.06
3 ML YEARS		60	51	3	1	309	1389	328	190	173	28	16	16	12	147	5	229	17	1	17	17	.500	0	0-1	0	5.04

Pete Schourek

Pitches: Left **Bats:** Left **Pos:** SP-17; RP-1　　**Ht:** 6'5" **Wt:** 205 **Born:** 5/10/69 **Age:** 29

Year Team	Lg	G	GS	CG	GF	IP	BFP	H	R	ER	HR	SH	SF	HB	TBB	IBB	SO	WP	Bk	W	L	Pct.	ShO	Sv-Op	Hld	ERA
1991 New York	NL	35	8	1	7	86.1	385	82	49	41	7	5	4	2	43	4	67	1	0	5	4	.556	1	2-3	3	4.27
1992 New York	NL	22	21	0	0	136	578	137	60	55	9	4	4	2	44	6	60	4	2	6	8	.429	0	0-0	0	3.64
1993 New York	NL	41	18	0	6	128.1	586	168	90	85	13	3	8	3	45	7	72	1	2	5	12	.294	0	0-1	2	5.96
1994 Cincinnati	NL	22	10	0	3	81.1	354	90	39	37	11	6	2	3	29	4	69	0	0	7	2	.778	0	0-0	0	4.09
1995 Cincinnati	NL	29	29	2	0	190.1	754	158	72	68	17	4	4	8	45	3	160	1	1	18	7	.720	0	0-0	0	3.22
1996 Cincinnati	NL	12	12	0	0	67.1	304	79	48	45	7	3	4	3	24	1	54	3	0	4	5	.444	0	0-0	0	6.01
1997 Cincinnati	NL	18	17	0	0	84.2	371	78	59	51	18	4	1	4	38	0	59	2	0	5	8	.385	0	0-0	0	5.42
7 ML YEARS		179	115	3	16	774.1	3332	792	417	382	82	29	27	25	268	25	541	12	5	50	46	.521	1	2-4	5	4.44

Tim Scott

Pitches: Right **Bats:** Right **Pos:** RP-17　　**Ht:** 6'2" **Wt:** 205 **Born:** 11/16/66 **Age:** 31

Year Team	Lg	G	GS	CG	GF	IP	BFP	H	R	ER	HR	SH	SF	HB	TBB	IBB	SO	WP	Bk	W	L	Pct.	ShO	Sv-Op	Hld	ERA
1997 Colo Spngs *	AAA	12	0	0	9	14.2	52	7	2	2	1	1	1	0	3	0	18	1	1	0	0	.000	0	3- -	—	1.23
1991 San Diego	NL	2	0	0	0	1	5	2	2	1	0	0	0	0	0	0	1	1	0	0	0	.000	0	0-0	0	9.00
1992 San Diego	NL	34	0	0	16	37.2	173	39	24	22	4	4	1	1	21	6	30	0	1	4	1	.800	0	0-1	4	5.26
1993 SD-Mon	NL	56	0	0	18	71.2	317	69	28	24	4	3	2	4	34	2	65	2	1	7	2	.778	0	1-4	3	3.01
1994 Montreal	NL	40	0	0	8	53.1	223	51	17	16	0	0	0	2	18	3	37	1	1	5	2	.714	0	1-1	7	2.70
1995 Montreal	NL	62	0	0	15	63.1	268	52	30	28	6	4	1	6	23	2	57	4	0	2	0	1.000	0	2-5	19	3.98
1996 Mon-SF	NL	65	0	0	16	66	288	65	36	34	8	4	3	3	30	2	47	3	0	5	7	.417	0	1-5	10	4.64
1997 SD-Col	NL	17	0	0	2	21	101	30	20	19	2	1	1	3	7	0	16	0	0	1	1	.500	0	0-1	1	8.14
1993 San Diego	NL	24	0	0	2	37.2	169	38	13	10	1	2	2	4	15	0	30	1	1	2	0	1.000	0	0-2	0	2.39
Montreal	NL	32	0	0	16	34	148	31	15	14	3	1	0	0	19	2	35	1	0	5	2	.714	0	1-2	3	3.71
1996 Montreal	NL	45	0	0	14	46.1	198	41	18	16	3	1	2	2	21	2	37	1	0	3	5	.375	0	1-3	8	3.11
San Francisco	NL	20	0	0	2	19.2	90	24	18	18	5	3	1	1	9	0	10	2	0	2	2	.500	0	0-2	2	8.24
1997 San Diego	NL	14	0	0	2	18.1	87	25	17	16	2	0	1	3	5	0	14	0	0	1	1	.500	0	0-1	1	7.85
Colorado	NL	3	0	0	0	2.2	14	5	3	3	0	1	0	0	2	0	2	0	0	0	0	.000	0	0-0	0	10.13
7 ML YEARS		276	0	0	75	314	1375	308	157	144	24	16	8	19	133	15	253	10	3	24	13	.649	0	5-17	44	4.13

Kevin Sefcik

Bats: R **Throws:** R **Pos:** PH-32; 2B-22; SS-10; 3B-4　　**Ht:** 5'10" **Wt:** 175 **Born:** 2/10/71 **Age:** 27

Year Team	Lg	G	AB	H	2B	3B	HR	(Hm	Rd)	TB	R	RBI	TBB	IBB	SO	HBP	SH	SF	SB	CS	SB%	GDP	Avg	OBP	SLG
1997 Scrnton-WB *	AAA	29	123	41	11	2	1	—	—	59	19	7	9	0	11	0	2	0	5	1	.83	1	.333	.379	.480
1995 Philadelphia	NL	5	4	0	0	0	0	(0	0)	0	1	0	0	0	2	0	0	0	0	0	.00	0	.000	.000	.000
1996 Philadelphia	NL	44	116	33	5	3	0	(0	0)	44	10	9	9	3	16	2	1	2	3	0	1.00	4	.284	.341	.379
1997 Philadelphia	NL	61	119	32	3	0	2	(2	0)	41	11	6	4	0	9	1	7	0	1	2	.33	4	.269	.298	.345
3 ML YEARS		110	239	65	8	3	2	(2	0)	85	22	15	13	3	27	3	8	2	4	2	.67	8	.272	.315	.356

David Segui

Bats: Both **Throws:** Left **Pos:** 1B-125　　**Ht:** 6'1" **Wt:** 202 **Born:** 7/19/66 **Age:** 31

Year Team	Lg	G	AB	H	2B	3B	HR	(Hm	Rd)	TB	R	RBI	TBB	IBB	SO	HBP	SH	SF	SB	CS	SB%	GDP	Avg	OBP	SLG
1990 Baltimore	AL	40	123	30	7	0	2	(1	1)	43	14	15	11	2	15	1	1	0	0	0	.00	12	.244	.311	.350
1991 Baltimore	AL	86	212	59	7	0	2	(1	1)	72	15	22	12	2	19	0	3	1	1	1	.50	7	.278	.316	.340

Year Team	Lg	G	AB	H	2B	3B	HR	(Hm	Rd)	TB	R	RBI	TBB	IBB	SO	HBP	SH	SF	SB	CS	SB%	GDP	Avg	OBP	SLG
1992 Baltimore	AL	115	189	44	9	0	1	(1	0)	56	21	17	20	3	23	0	2	0	1	0	1.00	4	.233	.306	.296
1993 Baltimore	AL	146	450	123	27	0	10	(6	4)	180	54	60	58	4	53	0	3	8	2	1	.67	18	.273	.351	.400
1994 New York	NL	92	336	81	17	1	10	(5	5)	130	46	43	33	6	43	1	1	3	0	0	.00	6	.241	.308	.387
1995 NYN-Mon	NL	130	456	141	25	4	12	(6	6)	210	68	68	40	5	47	3	8	3	2	7	.22	10	.309	.367	.461
1996 Montreal	NL	115	416	119	30	1	11	(6	5)	184	69	58	60	4	54	0	0	1	4	4	.50	8	.286	.375	.442
1997 Montreal	NL	125	459	141	22	3	21	(10	11)	232	75	68	57	12	66	1	0	6	1	0	1.00	9	.307	.380	.505
1995 New York	NL	33	73	24	3	1	2	(2	0)	35	9	11	12	1	9	1	4	2	1	3	.25	2	.329	.420	.479
Montreal	NL	97	383	117	22	3	10	(4	6)	175	59	57	28	4	38	2	4	1	1	4	.20	8	.305	.355	.457
8 ML YEARS		849	2641	738	144	9	69	(36	33)	1107	362	351	291	38	320	6	18	22	11	13	46	74	.279	.350	.419

Kevin Seitzer

Bats: R Throws: R Pos: DH-24; 1B-19; 3B-13; PH-12   Ht: 5'11" Wt: 193 Born: 3/26/62 Age: 36

Year Team	Lg	G	AB	H	2B	3B	HR	(Hm	Rd)	TB	R	RBI	TBB	IBB	SO	HBP	SH	SF	SB	CS	SB%	GDP	Avg	OBP	SLG
1986 Kansas City	AL	28	96	31	4	1	2	(1	1)	43	16	11	19	0	14	1	0	0	0	0	.00	0	.323	.440	.448
1987 Kansas City	AL	161	641	207	33	8	15	(7	8)	301	105	83	80	0	85	2	1	1	12	7	.63	18	.323	.399	.470
1988 Kansas City	AL	149	559	170	32	5	5	(4	1)	227	90	60	72	4	64	6	3	3	10	8	.56	15	.304	.388	.406
1989 Kansas City	AL	160	597	168	17	2	4	(2	2)	201	78	48	102	7	76	5	4	7	17	8	.68	16	.281	.387	.337
1990 Kansas City	AL	158	622	171	31	5	6	(5	1)	230	91	38	67	2	66	2	4	2	7	5	.58	11	.275	.346	.370
1991 Kansas City	AL	85	234	62	11	3	1	(0	1)	82	28	25	29	3	21	2	1	1	4	1	.80	4	.265	.350	.350
1992 Milwaukee	AL	148	540	146	35	1	5	(2	3)	198	74	71	57	4	44	2	7	9	13	11	.54	16	.270	.337	.367
1993 Oak-Mil	AL	120	417	112	16	2	11	(6	5)	165	45	57	44	1	48	2	3	5	7	7	.50	14	.269	.338	.396
1994 Milwaukee	AL	80	309	97	24	2	5	(4	1)	140	44	49	30	1	38	2	4	3	2	1	.67	7	.314	.375	.453
1995 Milwaukee	AL	132	492	153	33	3	5	(1	4)	207	56	69	64	2	57	6	5	3	2	0	1.00	13	.311	.395	.421
1996 Mil-Cle	AL	154	573	187	35	3	13	(5	8)	267	85	78	87	7	79	5	5	5	6	1	.86	13	.326	.416	.466
1997 Cleveland	AL	64	198	53	14	0	2	(1	1)	73	27	24	18	0	25	0	2	2	0	0	.00	6	.268	.326	.369
1993 Oakland	AL	73	255	65	10	2	4	(2	2)	91	24	27	27	1	33	1	2	4	4	7	.36	7	.255	.324	.357
Milwaukee	AL	47	162	47	6	0	7	(4	3)	74	21	30	17	0	15	1	1	1	3	0	1.00	7	.290	.359	.457
1996 Milwaukee	AL	132	490	155	25	3	12	(5	7)	222	74	62	73	6	68	4	5	5	6	1	.86	11	.316	.406	.453
Cleveland	AL	22	83	32	10	0	1	(0	1)	45	11	16	14	1	11	1	0	0	0	0	.00	2	.386	.480	.542
12 ML YEARS		1439	5278	1557	285	35	74	(38	36)	2134	739	613	669	31	617	35	39	41	80	49	62	133	.295	.375	.404

Aaron Sele

Pitches: Right Bats: Right Pos: SP-33   Ht: 6'5" Wt: 215 Born: 6/25/70 Age: 28

Year Team	Lg	G	GS	CG	GF	IP	BFP	H	R	ER	HR	SH	SF	HB	TBB	IBB	SO	WP	Bk	W	L	Pct.	ShO	Sv-Op	Hld	ERA
1993 Boston	AL	18	18	0	0	111.2	484	100	42	34	5	2	5	7	48	2	93	5	0	7	2	.778	0	0-0	0	2.74
1994 Boston	AL	22	22	2	0	143.1	615	140	68	61	13	4	5	9	60	2	105	4	0	8	7	.533	0	0-0	0	3.83
1995 Boston	AL	6	6	0	0	32.1	146	32	14	11	3	1	1	3	14	0	21	3	0	3	1	.750	0	0-0	0	3.06
1996 Boston	AL	29	29	1	0	157.1	722	192	110	93	14	6	7	8	67	2	137	2	0	7	11	.389	0	0-0	0	5.32
1997 Boston	AL	33	33	1	0	177.1	810	196	115	106	25	5	7	15	80	4	122	7	0	13	12	.520	0	0-0	0	5.38
5 ML YEARS		108	108	4	0	622	2777	660	349	305	60	18	25	42	269	10	478	21	0	38	33	.535	0	0-0	0	4.41

Dan Serafini

Pitches: Left Bats: Both Pos: SP-4; RP-2   Ht: 6'1" Wt: 180 Born: 1/25/74 Age: 24

Year Team	Lg	G	GS	CG	GF	IP	BFP	H	R	ER	HR	SH	SF	HB	TBB	IBB	SO	WP	Bk	W	L	Pct.	ShO	Sv-Op	Hld	ERA
1992 Twins	R	8	6	0	0	29.2	130	27	16	12	0	1	1	15	0	33	3	1	1	0	1.000	0	0--	--	3.64
1993 Ft. Wayne	A	27	27	1	0	140.2	606	117	72	57	5	2	2	6	83	0	147	12	2	10	8	.556	1	0--	--	3.65
1994 Ft. Myers	A+	23	23	2	0	136.2	600	149	84	70	11	7	5	6	57	1	130	7	1	9	9	.500	1	0--	--	4.61
1995 Hardware City	AA	27	27	1	0	162.2	692	155	74	61	7	3	4	12	72	0	123	3	4	12	9	.571	1	0--	--	3.38
Salt Lake	AAA	1	0	0	1	4	17	4	3	3	2	0	0	0	1	0	4	0	0	0	0	.000	0	1--	--	6.75
1996 Salt Lake	AAA	25	23	1	1	130.2	588	164	84	81	20	5	6	2	58	1	109	9	2	7	7	.500	0	0--	--	5.58
1997 Salt Lake	AAA	28	24	2	1	152	660	166	87	84	18	4	3	8	55	0	118	3	0	9	7	.563	0	0--	--	4.97
1996 Minnesota	AL	1	1	0	0	4.1	23	5	5	5	1	0	1	1	2	0	1	0	0	0	1	.000	0	0-0	0	10.38
1997 Minnesota	AL	6	4	1	1	26.1	111	27	11	10	1	1	0	0	11	0	15	1	0	2	1	.667	0	0-0	0	3.42
2 ML YEARS		7	5	1	1	30.2	134	34	16	15	2	1	1	1	13	0	16	1	0	2	2	.500	0	0-0	0	4.40

Scott Servais

Bats: R Throws: R Pos: C-118; PH-7; DH-2; 1B-1   Ht: 6'2" Wt: 205 Born: 6/4/67 Age: 31

Year Team	Lg	G	AB	H	2B	3B	HR	(Hm	Rd)	TB	R	RBI	TBB	IBB	SO	HBP	SH	SF	SB	CS	SB%	GDP	Avg	OBP	SLG
1991 Houston	NL	16	37	6	3	0	0	(0	0)	9	0	6	4	0	8	0	1	0	0	0	.00	0	.162	.244	.243
1992 Houston	NL	77	205	49	9	0	0	(0	0)	58	12	15	11	2	25	5	6	0	0	0	.00	7	.239	.294	.283
1993 Houston	NL	85	258	63	11	0	11	(5	6)	107	24	32	22	2	45	5	3	3	0	0	.00	6	.244	.313	.415
1994 Houston	NL	78	251	49	15	1	9	(3	6)	93	27	41	10	0	44	4	7	3	0	0	.00	6	.195	.235	.371
1995 Hou-ChN	NL	80	264	70	22	0	13	(8	5)	131	38	47	32	8	52	3	2	3	2	2	.50	9	.265	.348	.496
1996 Chicago	NL	129	445	118	20	0	11	(6	5)	171	42	63	30	1	75	14	3	7	0	2	.00	18	.265	.327	.384
1997 Chicago	NL	122	385	100	21	0	6	(4	2)	139	36	45	24	7	56	6	7	3	0	1	.00	7	.260	.311	.361
1995 Houston	NL	28	89	20	10	0	1	(1	0)	33	7	12	9	2	15	1	1	0	0	1	.00	4	.225	.300	.371
Chicago	NL	52	175	50	12	0	12	(7	5)	98	31	35	23	6	37	2	1	2	2	1	.67	5	.286	.371	.560
7 ML YEARS		587	1845	455	101	1	50	(26	24)	708	179	249	133	20	305	37	29	19	2	5	.29	53	.247	.307	.384

Scott Service

Pitches: Right **Bats:** Right **Pos:** RP-16   Ht: 6'6"   Wt: 226   Born: 2/26/67   Age: 31

Year Team	Lg	G	GS	CG	GF	IP	BFP	H	R	ER	HR	SH	SF	HB	TBB	IBB	SO	WP	Bk	W	L	Pct.	ShO	Sv-Op	Hld	ERA
1997 Indianapolis *	AAA	33	0	0	28	34	148	30	15	14	5	4	0	2	12	1	53	2	0	3	2	.600	0	15- -	—	3.71
Omaha *	AAA	16	0	0	14	14.2	57	9	0	0	0	0	0	0	4	0	16	0	0	0	0	.000	0	9- -	—	0.00
1988 Philadelphia	NL	5	0	0	1	5.1	23	7	1	1	0	0	0	1	1	0	6	0	0	0	0	.000	0	0-0	0	1.69
1992 Montreal	NL	5	0	0	0	7	41	15	11	11	1	0	0	0	5	0	11	0	0	0	0	.000	0	0-0	1	14.14
1993 Col-Cin	NL	29	0	0	7	46	197	44	24	22	6	2	4	2	16	4	43	0	0	2	2	.500	0	2-2	3	4.30
1994 Cincinnati	NL	6	0	0	2	7.1	35	8	9	6	2	2	0	0	3	0	5	0	0	1	2	.333	0	0-0	0	7.36
1995 San Francisco	NL	28	0	0	6	31	129	18	11	11	4	3	2	2	20	4	30	3	0	3	1	.750	0	0-0	7	3.19
1996 Cincinnati	NL	34	1	0	5	48	213	51	21	21	7	4	1	6	18	4	46	5	0	1	0	1.000	0	0-0	3	3.94
1997 Cin-KC	NL	16	0	0	3	22.1	95	28	16	16	2	2	1	0	6	0	22	2	0	0	3	.000	0	0-1	3	6.45
1993 Colorado	NL	3	0	0	0	4.2	24	8	5	5	1	0	2	1	1	0	3	0	0	0	0	.000	0	0-0	0	9.64
Cincinnati	NL	26	0	0	7	41.1	173	36	19	17	5	2	2	1	15	4	40	0	0	2	2	.500	0	2-2	3	3.70
1997 Cincinnati	NL	4	0	0	2	5.1	26	11	7	7	1	1	0	0	1	0	3	2	0	0	0	.000	0	0-0	1	11.81
Kansas City	AL	12	0	0	1	17	69	17	9	9	1	1	1	0	5	0	19	0	0	0	3	.000	0	0-1	2	4.76
7 ML YEARS		123	1	0	24	167	733	171	93	88	22	13	8	11	69	12	163	10	0	7	8	.467	0	2-3	17	4.74

Richie Sexson

Bats: Right **Throws:** Right **Pos:** PH-3; 1B-2; DH-1   Ht: 6'6"   Wt: 206   Born: 12/29/74   Age: 23

Year Team	Lg	G	AB	H	2B	3B	HR	(Hm	Rd)	TB	R	RBI	TBB	IBB	SO	HBP	SH	SF	SB	CS	SB%	GDP	Avg	OBP	SLG
1993 Burlington	R+	40	97	18	3	0	1	—	—	24	11	5	18	2	21	1	2	1	1	1	.50	1	.186	.316	.247
1994 Columbus	A	130	488	133	25	2	14	—	—	204	88	77	37	2	87	14	0	5	7	3	.70	5	.273	.338	.418
1995 Kinston	A+	131	494	151	34	0	22	—	—	251	80	85	43	5	115	10	0	7	4	6	.40	8	.306	.368	.508
1996 Canton-Akrn	AA	133	518	143	33	3	16	—	—	230	85	76	39	5	118	6	0	5	2	1	.67	13	.276	.331	.444
1997 Buffalo	AAA	115	434	113	20	2	31	—	—	230	57	88	27	1	87	4	3	4	5	1	.83	11	.260	.307	.530
1997 Cleveland	AL	5	11	3	0	0	0	(0	0)	3	1	0	0	0	2	0	0	0	0	0	.00	2	.273	.273	.273

Jeff Shaw

Pitches: Right **Bats:** Right **Pos:** RP-78   Ht: 6'2"   Wt: 200   Born: 7/7/66   Age: 31

Year Team	Lg	G	GS	CG	GF	IP	BFP	H	R	ER	HR	SH	SF	HB	TBB	IBB	SO	WP	Bk	W	L	Pct.	ShO	Sv-Op	Hld	ERA
1990 Cleveland	AL	12	9	0	0	48.2	229	73	38	36	11	1	3	0	20	0	25	3	0	3	4	.429	0	0-0	0	6.66
1991 Cleveland	AL	29	1	0	9	72.1	311	72	34	27	6	1	4	4	27	5	31	6	0	0	5	.000	0	1-4	0	3.36
1992 Cleveland	AL	2	1	0	1	7.2	33	7	7	7	2	2	0	0	4	0	3	0	0	0	1	.000	0	0-0	0	8.22
1993 Montreal	NL	55	8	0	13	95.2	404	91	47	44	12	5	2	7	32	2	50	2	0	2	7	.222	0	0-1	4	4.14
1994 Montreal	NL	46	0	0	15	67.1	287	67	32	29	8	2	4	2	15	2	47	5	0	5	2	.714	0	1-2	10	3.88
1995 Mon-ChA		59	0	0	18	72	309	70	42	39	6	7	1	4	27	4	51	0	0	1	6	.143	0	3-5	6	4.88
1996 Cincinnati	NL	78	0	0	24	104.2	434	99	34	29	8	5	5	2	29	11	69	0	0	8	6	.571	0	4-11	22	2.49
1997 Cincinnati	NL	78	0	0	62	94.2	367	79	26	25	7	3	3	1	12	3	74	1	0	4	2	.667	0	42-49	5	2.38
1995 Montreal	NL	50	0	0	17	62.1	268	58	35	32	4	6	1	3	26	4	45	0	0	1	6	.143	0	3-5	5	4.62
Chicago	AL	9	0	0	1	9.2	41	12	7	7	2	1	0	1	1	0	6	0	0	0	0	.000	0	0-0	1	6.52
8 ML YEARS		359	19	0	142	563	2374	558	260	236	60	26	22	20	166	27	350	17	0	23	33	.411	0	51-72	47	3.77

Danny Sheaffer

Bats: R **Throws:** R **Pos:** 3B-30; PH-28; LF-13; C-9; RF-9; 2B-3; CF-2   Ht: 6'0"   Wt: 195   Born: 8/2/61   Age: 36

Year Team	Lg	G	AB	H	2B	3B	HR	(Hm	Rd)	TB	R	RBI	TBB	IBB	SO	HBP	SH	SF	SB	CS	SB%	GDP	Avg	OBP	SLG
1987 Boston	AL	25	66	8	1	0	1	(0	1)	12	5	5	0	0	14	0	1	1	0	0	.00	2	.121	.119	.182
1989 Cleveland	AL	7	16	1	0	0	0	(0	0)	1	1	0	2	0	2	0	1	0	0	0	.00	0	.063	.167	.063
1993 Colorado	NL	82	216	60	9	1	4	(2	2)	83	26	32	8	0	15	1	2	6	2	3	.40	9	.278	.299	.384
1994 Colorado	NL	44	110	24	4	0	1	(0	1)	31	11	12	10	0	11	0	0	0	0	2	.00	2	.218	.283	.282
1995 St. Louis	NL	76	208	48	10	1	5	(2	3)	75	24	30	23	2	38	0	0	1	0	0	.00	8	.231	.306	.361
1996 St. Louis	NL	79	198	45	9	3	2	(1	1)	66	10	20	9	0	25	3	4	0	3	3	.50	13	.227	.271	.333
1997 St. Louis	NL	76	132	33	5	0	0	(0	0)	38	10	11	8	0	17	1	4	1	1	0	1.00	10	.250	.296	.288
7 ML YEARS		389	946	219	38	5	13	(5	8)	306	87	110	60	2	122	5	12	9	6	8	.43	44	.232	.278	.323

Andy Sheets

Bats: R **Throws:** R **Pos:** 3B-21; SS-9; 2B-2; PH-1   Ht: 6'2"   Wt: 180   Born: 11/19/71   Age: 26

Year Team	Lg	G	AB	H	2B	3B	HR	(Hm	Rd)	TB	R	RBI	TBB	IBB	SO	HBP	SH	SF	SB	CS	SB%	GDP	Avg	OBP	SLG
1993 Riverside	A+	52	176	34	9	1	1	—	—	48	23	12	17	1	51	0	6	4	2	2	.50	4	.193	.259	.273
Appleton	A	69	259	68	10	4	1	—	—	89	32	25	20	1	59	3	4	2	7	7	.50	3	.263	.320	.344
1994 Riverside	A+	31	100	27	5	1	2	—	—	40	17	10	16	0	22	0	1	0	6	1	.86	1	.270	.371	.400
Calgary	AAA	26	93	32	8	1	2	—	—	48	22	16	11	0	20	1	0	1	1	1	.50	1	.344	.415	.516
Jacksnville	AA	70	232	51	12	0	0	—	—	63	26	17	20	0	54	2	6	1	3	5	.38	4	.220	.286	.272
1995 Tacoma	AAA	132	437	128	29	9	2	—	—	181	57	47	32	2	83	0	10	4	8	3	.73	9	.293	.338	.414
1996 Tacoma	AAA	62	232	83	16	5	5	—	—	124	44	33	25	0	56	0	4	6	6	4	.60	6	.358	.415	.534
1997 Tacoma	AAA	113	401	104	23	0	14	—	—	169	57	53	46	1	97	2	5	2	7	2	.78	9	.259	.337	.421
1996 Seattle	AL	47	110	21	8	0	0	(0	0)	29	18	9	10	0	41	1	2	1	2	0	1.00	2	.191	.262	.264
1997 Seattle	AL	32	89	22	3	0	4	(2	2)	37	18	9	7	0	34	0	5	1	2	0	1.00	1	.247	.299	.416
2 ML YEARS		79	199	43	11	0	4	(2	2)	66	36	18	17	0	75	1	7	2	4	0	1.00	3	.216	.279	.332

Gary Sheffield

Bats: Right **Throws:** Right **Pos:** RF-132; PH-2; DH-1   **Ht:** 5'11" **Wt:** 190 **Born:** 11/18/68 **Age:** 29

Year Team	Lg	G	AB	H	2B	3B	HR	(Hm	Rd)	TB	R	RBI	TBB	IBB	SO	HBP	SH	SF	SB	CS	SB%	GDP	Avg	OBP	SLG
1988 Milwaukee	AL	24	80	19	1	0	4	(1	3)	32	12	12	7	0	7	0	1	1	3	1	.75	5	.238	.295	.400
1989 Milwaukee	AL	95	368	91	18	0	5	(2	3)	124	34	32	27	0	33	4	3	3	10	6	.63	4	.247	.303	.337
1990 Milwaukee	AL	125	487	143	18	0	10	(3	7)	205	67	67	44	1	41	3	4	9	25	10	.71	11	.294	.350	.421
1991 Milwaukee	AL	50	175	34	12	2	2	(2	0)	56	25	22	19	1	15	3	1	5	5	5	.50	3	.194	.277	.320
1992 San Diego	NL	146	557	184	34	3	33	(23	10)	323	87	100	48	5	40	6	0	7	5	6	.45	19	.330	.385	.580
1993 SD-Fla	NL	140	494	145	20	5	20	(10	10)	235	67	73	47	6	64	9	0	7	17	5	.77	11	.294	.361	.476
1994 Florida	NL	87	322	89	16	1	27	(15	12)	188	61	78	51	11	50	6	0	5	12	6	.67	10	.276	.380	.584
1995 Florida	NL	63	213	69	8	0	16	(4	12)	125	46	46	55	8	45	4	0	2	19	4	.83	3	.324	.467	.587
1996 Florida	NL	161	519	163	33	1	42	(19	23)	324	118	120	142	19	66	10	0	6	16	9	.64	16	.314	.465	.624
1997 Florida	NL	135	444	111	22	1	21	(13	8)	198	86	71	121	11	79	15	0	2	11	7	.61	7	.250	.424	.446
1993 San Diego	NL	68	258	76	12	2	10	(6	4)	122	34	36	18	0	30	3	0	3	5	1	.83	9	.295	.344	.473
Florida	NL	72	236	69	8	3	10	(4	6)	113	33	37	29	6	34	6	0	4	12	4	.75	2	.292	.378	.479
10 ML YEARS		1026	3659	1048	194	14	180	(92	88)	1810	603	621	561	62	440	60	9	47	123	59	.68	89	.286	.386	.495

Scott Sheldon

Bats: R **Throws:** R **Pos:** SS-12; PH-2; 2B-1; 3B-1   **Ht:** 6'3" **Wt:** 185 **Born:** 11/28/68 **Age:** 29

Year Team	Lg	G	AB	H	2B	3B	HR	(Hm	Rd)	TB	R	RBI	TBB	IBB	SO	HBP	SH	SF	SB	CS	SB%	GDP	Avg	OBP	SLG
1991 Sou. Oregon	A-	65	229	58	10	3	0	—	—	74	34	24	23	0	44	2	3	1	9	5	.64	5	.253	.325	.323
1992 Madison	A	74	279	76	16	0	6	—	—	110	41	24	32	1	78	1	3	4	5	4	.56	2	.272	.345	.394
1993 Madison	A	131	428	91	22	1	8	—	—	139	67	67	49	3	121	8	3	8	8	7	.53	8	.213	.300	.325
1994 Huntsville	AA	91	268	62	10	1	0	—	—	74	31	28	28	1	69	7	7	3	7	1	.88	4	.231	.317	.276
1995 Edmonton	AAA	45	128	33	7	1	4	—	—	54	21	12	15	0	15	2	4	1	4	2	.67	0	.258	.342	.422
Huntsville	AA	66	235	51	10	2	4	—	—	77	25	15	23	0	60	1	3	1	5	0	1.00	7	.217	.288	.328
1996 Edmonton	AAA	98	350	105	27	3	10	—	—	168	61	60	43	3	83	4	3	4	5	3	.63	8	.300	.379	.480
1997 Edmonton	AAA	118	422	133	39	6	19	—	—	241	89	77	59	4	104	6	3	3	5	2	.71	11	.315	.404	.571
1997 Oakland	AL	13	24	6	0	0	1	(1	0)	9	2	2	1	0	6	1	1	0	0	0	.00	0	.250	.308	.375

Craig Shipley

Bats: R **Throws:** R **Pos:** PH-26; SS-21; 2B-16; 1B-4; 3B-2   **Ht:** 6'1" **Wt:** 190 **Born:** 1/7/63 **Age:** 35

Year Team	Lg	G	AB	H	2B	3B	HR	(Hm	Rd)	TB	R	RBI	TBB	IBB	SO	HBP	SH	SF	SB	CS	SB%	GDP	Avg	OBP	SLG
1997 Las Vegas *	AAA	6	19	6	3	0	0	(Hm	Rd)	9	0	1	0	0	5	0	0	0	0	0	.00	0	.316	.316	.474
1986 Los Angeles	NL	12	27	3	1	0	0	(0	0)	4	3	4	2	1	5	1	1	0	0	0	.00	1	.111	.200	.148
1987 Los Angeles	NL	26	35	9	1	0	0	(0	0)	10	3	2	0	0	6	0	0	0	0	0	.00	0	.257	.257	.286
1989 New York	NL	4	7	1	0	0	0	(0	0)	1	3	0	0	0	1	0	0	0	0	0	.00	0	.143	.143	.143
1991 San Diego	NL	37	91	25	3	0	1	(0	1)	31	6	6	2	0	14	1	1	0	0	0	.00	1	.275	.298	.341
1992 San Diego	NL	52	105	26	6	0	0	(0	0)	32	7	7	2	1	21	0	1	0	1	1	.50	2	.248	.262	.305
1993 San Diego	NL	105	230	54	9	0	4	(2	2)	75	25	22	10	0	31	3	1	1	12	3	.80	3	.235	.275	.326
1994 San Diego	NL	81	240	80	14	4	4	(2	2)	114	32	30	9	1	28	3	4	2	6	6	.50	3	.333	.362	.475
1995 Houston	NL	92	232	61	8	1	3	(1	2)	80	23	24	8	3	28	2	1	2	6	1	.86	13	.263	.291	.345
1996 San Diego	NL	33	92	29	5	0	1	(0	1)	37	13	7	2	1	15	2	1	2	7	0	1.00	1	.315	.337	.402
1997 San Diego	NL	63	139	38	9	0	5	(3	2)	62	22	19	7	0	20	1	1	1	1	1	.50	1	.273	.306	.372
10 ML YEARS		505	1198	326	56	5	18	(8	10)	446	137	121	42	7	169	12	11	8	33	13	.72	26	.272	.302	.372

Paul Shuey

Pitches: Right **Bats:** Right **Pos:** RP-40   **Ht:** 6'3" **Wt:** 215 **Born:** 9/16/70 **Age:** 27

Year Team	Lg	G	GS	CG	GF	IP	BFP	H	R	ER	HR	SH	SF	HB	TBB	IBB	SO	WP	Bk	W	L	Pct.	ShO	Sv-Op	Hld	ERA
1997 Buffalo *	AAA	2	0	0	0	5	23	4	2	2	0	1	0		4	0	6	0	0	0	0	.000	0	0--	--	3.60
Akron *	AA	3	0	0	1	8	32	10	3	3	1	0	0	0	9	1		0	0	0	0	.000	0	0--	--	3.38
1994 Cleveland	AL	14	0	0	11	11.2	62	14	11	11	1	0	0	0	12	1	16	4	0	0	1	.000	0	5-5	1	8.49
1995 Cleveland	AL	7	0	0	3	6.1	28	5	4	3	0	0	0	0	5	0	5	1	0	0	0	.000	0	0-0	0	4.26
1996 Cleveland	AL	42	0	0	18	53.2	225	45	19	17	6	1	3	0	26	3	44	3	1	5	2	.714	0	4-7	7	2.85
1997 Cleveland	AL	40	0	0	16	45	212	52	31	31	5	4	2	1	28	3	46	2	0	4	2	.667	0	2-3	4	6.20
4 ML YEARS		103	0	0	48	116.2	527	116	65	62	12	5	5	1	71	7	111	10	1	9	7	.563	0	11-15	12	4.78

Terry Shumpert

Bats: R **Throws:** R **Pos:** 2B-7; PH-3; 3B-2; LF-2; RF-1   **Ht:** 5'11" **Wt:** 185 **Born:** 8/16/66 **Age:** 31

Year Team	Lg	G	AB	H	2B	3B	HR	(Hm	Rd)	TB	R	RBI	TBB	IBB	SO	HBP	SH	SF	SB	CS	SB%	GDP	Avg	OBP	SLG
1997 Las Vegas *	AAA	32	109	31	8	1	1	—	—	44	18	16	9	1	20	3	1	2	3	0	1.00	1	.284	.350	.404
New Haven *	AA	5	17	4	0	0	0	—	—	7	2	1	0	0	2	0	0	0	0	0	.00	0	.235	.235	.412
Colo Spmgs *	AAA	10	37	11	3	0	1	—	—	17	8	2	2	0	7	0	0	0	0	0	.00	1	.297	.333	.459
1990 Kansas City	AL	32	91	25	6	1	0	(0	0)	33	7	8	2	0	17	1	0	2	3	3	.50	4	.275	.292	.363
1991 Kansas City	AL	144	369	80	16	4	5	(1	4)	119	45	34	30	0	75	5	10	3	17	11	.61	10	.217	.283	.322
1992 Kansas City	AL	36	94	14	5	1	1	(1	0)	24	6	11	3	0	17	0	2	0	2	2	.50	2	.149	.175	.255
1993 Kansas City	AL	8	10	1	0	0	0	(0	0)	1	0	0	2	0	2	0	0	0	1	0	1.00	0	.100	.250	.100
1994 Kansas City	AL	64	183	44	6	2	8	(2	6)	78	28	24	13	0	39	0	5	1	18	3	.86	0	.240	.289	.426
1995 Boston	AL	21	47	11	3	0	0	(0	0)	14	6	3	4	0	13	0	0	0	3	1	.75	0	.234	.294	.298
1996 Chicago	NL	27	31	7	1	0	2	(2	0)	14	5	6	2	0	11	1	0	0	0	0	.00	0	.226	.286	.452

Year Team	Lg	G	AB	H	2B	3B	HR	(Hm	Rd)	TB	R	RBI	TBB	IBB	SO	HBP	SH	SF	SB	CS	SB%	GDP	Avg	OBP	SLG
1997 San Diego	NL	13	33	9	3	0	1	(0	1)	15	4	6	3	0	4	0	0	1	0	0	.00	1	.273	.324	.455
8 ML YEARS		345	858	191	40	8	17	(5	12)	298	101	92	59	0	178	7	17	8	44	21	.68	17	.223	.276	.347

Ruben Sierra

Bats: B **Throws:** R **Pos:** LF-18; RF-14; DH-6; PH-4 **Ht:** 6'1" **Wt:** 200 **Born:** 10/6/65 **Age:** 32

Year Team	Lg	G	AB	H	2B	3B	HR	(Hm	Rd)	TB	R	RBI	TBB	IBB	SO	HBP	SH	SF	SB	CS	SB%	GDP	Avg	OBP	SLG
1997 Syracuse *	AAA	8	32	7	2	0	1	—	—	12	5	5	2	1	6	0	0	0	0	0	.00	0	.219	.265	.375
1986 Texas	AL	113	382	101	13	10	16	(8	8)	182	50	55	22	3	65	1	1	5	7	8	.47	8	.264	.302	.476
1987 Texas	AL	158	643	169	35	4	30	(15	15)	302	97	109	39	4	114	2	0	12	16	11	.59	18	.263	.302	.470
1988 Texas	AL	156	615	156	32	2	23	(15	8)	261	77	91	44	10	91	1	0	8	18	4	.82	15	.254	.301	.424
1989 Texas	AL	162	634	194	35	14	29	(21	8)	344	101	119	43	2	82	2	0	10	8	2	.80	7	.306	.347	.543
1990 Texas	AL	159	608	170	37	2	16	(10	6)	259	70	96	49	13	86	1	0	8	9	0	1.00	15	.280	.330	.426
1991 Texas	AL	161	661	203	44	5	25	(12	13)	332	110	116	56	7	91	0	0	9	16	4	.80	17	.307	.357	.502
1992 Tex-Oak	AL	151	601	167	34	7	17	(10	7)	266	83	87	45	12	68	0	0	10	14	4	.78	11	.278	.323	.443
1993 Oakland	AL	158	630	147	23	5	22	(9	13)	246	77	101	52	16	97	0	0	10	25	5	.83	17	.233	.288	.390
1994 Oakland	AL	110	426	114	21	1	23	(11	12)	206	71	92	23	4	64	0	0	11	8	5	.62	15	.268	.298	.484
1995 Oak-NYA	AL	126	479	126	32	0	19	(8	11)	215	73	86	46	4	76	0	0	8	5	4	.56	8	.263	.323	.449
1996 NYA-Det	AL	142	518	128	26	2	12	(4	8)	194	61	72	60	12	83	0	0	9	4	4	.50	12	.247	.320	.375
1997 Cin-Tor		39	138	32	5	3	3	(3	0)	52	10	12	9	2	34	0	0	1	0	0	.00	1	.232	.277	.377
1992 Texas	AL	124	500	139	30	6	14	(8	6)	223	66	70	31	6	59	0	0	8	12	4	.75	9	.278	.315	.446
Oakland	AL	27	101	28	4	1	3	(2	1)	43	17	17	14	6	9	0	0	2	2	0	1.00	2	.277	.359	.426
1995 Oak-NYA	AL	70	264	70	17	0	12	(3	9)	123	40	42	24	2	42	0	0	3	4	4	.50	2	.265	.323	.466
New York	AL	56	215	56	15	0	7	(5	2)	92	33	44	22	2	34	0	0	5	1	0	1.00	6	.260	.322	.428
1996 New York	AL	96	360	93	17	1	11	(4	7)	145	39	52	40	11	58	0	0	7	1	3	.25	10	.258	.327	.403
Detroit	AL	46	158	35	9	1	1	(0	1)	49	22	20	20	1	25	0	0	2	3	1	.75	2	.222	.306	.310
1997 Cincinnati	NL	25	90	22	5	1	2	(2	0)	35	6	7	6	1	21	0	0	0	0	0	.00	1	.244	.292	.389
Toronto	AL	14	48	10	0	2	1	(1	0)	17	4	5	3	1	13	0	0	1	0	0	.00	0	.208	.250	.354
12 ML YEARS		1635	6335	1707	337	55	235	(126	109)	2859	880	1036	488	89	951	7	1	101	130	51	.72	144	.269	.318	.451

Jose Silva

Pitches: Right **Bats:** Right **Pos:** RP-7; SP-4 **Ht:** 6'5" **Wt:** 210 **Born:** 12/19/73 **Age:** 24

Year Team	Lg	G	GS	CG	GF	IP	BFP	H	R	ER	HR	SH	SF	HB	TBB	IBB	SO	WP	Bk	W	L	Pct.	ShO	Sv-Op	Hld	ERA
1992 Blue Jays	R	12	12	0	0	59.1	231	42	23	15	1	0	1	2	18	0	78	1	2	6	4	.600	0	0- –	—	2.28
1993 Hagerstown	A	24	24	0	0	142.2	581	103	50	40	6	0	4	4	62	0	161	9	1	12	5	.706	0	0- –	—	2.52
1994 Dunedin	A+	8	7	0	0	43	188	41	32	18	4	2	6	0	24	0	41	5	0	0	2	.000	0	0- –	—	3.77
Knoxville	AA	16	16	1	0	91.1	381	89	47	42	9	2	2	3	31	0	71	4	0	4	8	.333	1	0- –	—	4.14
1995 Knoxville	AA	3	0	0	0	2	15	3	2	2	0	1	1	0	6	0	2	0	0	0	0	.000	0	0- –	—	9.00
1996 Knoxville	AA	22	6	0	4	44	196	45	27	24	3	3	1	3	22	2	26	4	0	2	3	.400	0	0- –	—	4.91
1997 Calgary	AAA	17	11	0	1	66	288	74	27	25	3	3	1	3	22	0	54	2	1	5	1	.833	0	0- –	—	3.41
1996 Toronto	AL	2	0	0	0	2	11	5	3	3	1	0	0	0	0	0	0	0	0	0	0	.000	0	0-0	0	13.50
1997 Pittsburgh	NL	11	4	0	0	36.1	174	52	26	24	4	4	3	1	16	3	30	0	1	2	1	.667	0	0-0	0	5.94
2 ML YEARS		13	4	0	0	38.1	185	57	29	27	5	4	3	1	16	3	30	0	1	2	1	.667	0	0-0	0	6.34

Dave Silvestri

Bats: Right **Throws:** Right **Pos:** 3B-1; SS-1 **Ht:** 6'0" **Wt:** 196 **Born:** 9/29/67 **Age:** 30

Year Team	Lg	G	AB	H	2B	3B	HR	(Hm	Rd)	TB	R	RBI	TBB	IBB	SO	HBP	SH	SF	SB	CS	SB%	GDP	Avg	OBP	SLG
1997 Okla City *	AAA	124	467	112	25	3	17	—	—	194	54	68	55	1	104	0	2	6	4	6	.40	9	.240	.316	.415
1992 New York	AL	7	13	4	0	2	0	(0	0)	8	3	1	0	0	3	0	0	0	0	0	.00	1	.308	.308	.615
1993 New York	AL	7	21	6	1	0	1	(0	1)	10	4	4	5	0	3	0	0	0	0	0	.00	0	.286	.423	.476
1994 New York	AL	12	18	2	0	1	1	(1	0)	7	3	2	4	0	9	0	0	1	0	1	.00	0	.111	.261	.389
1995 NYA-Mon		56	93	21	6	0	3	(0	3)	36	16	11	13	0	36	1	1	2	2	0	1.00	3	.226	.321	.387
1996 Montreal	NL	86	162	33	4	0	1	(0	1)	40	16	17	34	6	41	0	3	1	2	1	.67	5	.204	.340	.247
1997 Texas	AL	2	4	0	0	0	0	(0	0)	0	0	0	0	0	1	0	0	0	0	0	.00	0	.000	.000	.000
1995 New York	AL	17	21	2	0	0	1	(0	1)	5	4	4	4	0	9	1	0	0	0	0	.00	1	.095	.259	.238
Montreal	NL	39	72	19	6	0	2	(0	2)	31	12	7	9	0	27	0	1	1	2	0	1.00	2	.264	.341	.431
6 ML YEARS		170	311	66	11	3	6	(1	5)	101	42	35	56	6	93	1	4	4	4	2	.67	10	.212	.331	.325

Bill Simas

Pitches: Right **Bats:** Right **Pos:** RP-40 **Ht:** 6'3" **Wt:** 220 **Born:** 11/28/71 **Age:** 26

Year Team	Lg	G	GS	CG	GF	IP	BFP	H	R	ER	HR	SH	SF	HB	TBB	IBB	SO	WP	Bk	W	L	Pct.	ShO	Sv-Op	Hld	ERA
1995 Chicago	AL	14	0	0	4	14	66	15	5	4	1	0	0	1	10	2	16	1	0	1	1	.500	0	0-0	3	2.57
1996 Chicago	AL	64	0	0	16	72.2	328	75	39	37	5	1	2	3	39	6	65	0	0	2	8	.200	0	2-8	15	4.58
1997 Chicago	AL	40	0	0	11	41.1	193	46	23	19	6	1	1	2	24	3	38	2	0	3	1	.750	0	1-2	3	4.14
3 ML YEARS		118	0	0	31	128	587	136	67	60	12	2	3	6	73	11	119	3	0	6	10	.375	0	3-10	21	4.22

Mike Simms

Bats: R **Throws:** R **Pos:** DH-28; PH-23; RF-17; 1B-2; LF-2 **Ht:** 6'4" **Wt:** 200 **Born:** 1/12/67 **Age:** 31

Year Team	Lg	G	AB	H	2B	3B	HR	(Hm	Rd)	TB	R	RBI	TBB	IBB	SO	HBP	SH	SF	SB	CS	SB%	GDP	Avg	OBP	SLG
1997 Okla City *	AAA	10	39	15	4	0	3	—	—	28	7	8	6	1	8	1	0	1	0	0	.00	2	.385	.468	.718
1990 Houston	NL	12	13	4	1	0	1	(0	1)	8	3	2	0	0	4	0	0	0	0	0	.00	1	.308	.308	.615
1991 Houston	NL	49	123	25	5	0	3	(1	2)	39	18	16	18	0	38	0	0	2	1	0	1.00	2	.203	.301	.317
1992 Houston	NL	15	24	6	1	0	1	(0	1)	10	1	3	2	0	9	1	0	0	0	0	.00	1	.250	.333	.417
1994 Houston	NL	6	12	1	1	0	0	(0	0)	2	1	0	0	0	5	0	0	0	1	0	1.00	0	.083	.083	.167
1995 Houston	NL	50	121	31	4	0	9	(5	4)	62	14	24	13	0	28	3	0	1	1	2	.33	3	.256	.341	.512
1996 Houston	NL	49	68	12	2	1	1	(1	0)	19	6	8	4	0	16	1	0	0	1	0	1.00	1	.176	.233	.279
1997 Texas	AL	59	111	28	8	0	5	(3	2)	51	13	22	8	1	27	0	0	2	0	1	.00	3	.252	.298	.459
7 ML YEARS		240	472	107	22	1	20	(10	10)	191	56	75	45	1	127	5	0	5	4	3	.57	11	.227	.298	.405

Randall Simon

Bats: Left **Throws:** Left **Pos:** PH-9; 1B-6 **Ht:** 6'0" **Wt:** 180 **Born:** 5/26/75 **Age:** 23

Year Team	Lg	G	AB	H	2B	3B	HR	(Hm	Rd)	TB	R	RBI	TBB	IBB	SO	HBP	SH	SF	SB	CS	SB%	GDP	Avg	OBP	SLG
1993 Danville	R+	61	232	59	17	1	3	—	—	87	28	31	10	2	34	2	0	1	1	1	.50	4	.254	.289	.375
1994 Macon	A	106	358	105	23	1	10	—	—	160	45	54	6	2	56	1	1	2	7	6	.54	7	.293	.305	.447
1995 Durham	A+	122	420	111	18	1	18	—	—	185	56	79	36	14	63	5	0	5	6	5	.55	15	.264	.326	.440
1996 Greenville	AA	134	498	139	26	2	18	—	—	223	74	77	37	7	61	4	0	4	4	9	.31	13	.279	.331	.448
1997 Richmond	AAA	133	519	160	45	1	14	—	—	249	62	102	17	2	76	4	1	1	1	6	.14	18	.308	.335	.480
1997 Atlanta	NL	13	14	6	1	0	0	(0	0)	7	2	1	1	0	2	0	0	0	0	0	.00	1	.429	.467	.500

Mike Sirotka

Pitches: Left **Bats:** Left **Pos:** SP-4; RP-3 **Ht:** 6'1" **Wt:** 200 **Born:** 5/13/71 **Age:** 27

Year Team	Lg	G	GS	CG	GF	IP	BFP	H	R	ER	HR	SH	SF	HB	TBB	IBB	SO	WP	Bk	W	L	Pct.	ShO	Sv-Op	Hld	ERA
1997 Nashville *	AAA	19	19	1	0	112.1	469	115	49	41	13	2	3	1	22	0	92	2	1	7	5	.583	0	0- -		3.28
1995 Chicago	AL	6	6	0	0	34.1	152	39	16	16	2	1	3	0	17	0	19	2	0	1	2	.333	0	0-0	0	4.19
1996 Chicago	AL	15	4	0	2	26.1	122	34	27	21	3	0	2	0	12	0	11	1	0	1	2	.333	0	0-0	0	7.18
1997 Chicago	AL	7	4	0	1	32	130	36	9	8	4	0	1	0	5	1	24	0	0	3	0	1.000	0	0-0	1	2.25
3 ML YEARS		28	14	0	3	92.2	404	109	52	45	9	1	5	1	34	1	54	3	0	5	4	.556	0	0-0	1	4.37

Don Slaught

Bats: Right **Throws:** Right **Pos:** PH-16; C-6 **Ht:** 6'1" **Wt:** 185 **Born:** 9/11/58 **Age:** 39

Year Team	Lg	G	AB	H	2B	3B	HR	(Hm	Rd)	TB	R	RBI	TBB	IBB	SO	HBP	SH	SF	SB	CS	SB%	GDP	Avg	OBP	SLG
1982 Kansas City	AL	43	115	32	6	0	3	(0	3)	47	14	8	9	0	12	0	2	0	0	0	.00	3	.278	.331	.409
1983 Kansas City	AL	83	276	86	13	4	0	(0	0)	107	21	28	11	0	27	0	1	2	3	1	.75	8	.312	.336	.388
1984 Kansas City	AL	124	409	108	27	4	4	(1	3)	155	48	42	20	4	55	2	8	7	0	0	.00	8	.264	.297	.379
1985 Texas	AL	102	343	96	17	4	8	(4	4)	145	34	35	20	1	41	6	1	0	4	4	.56	8	.280	.331	.423
1986 Texas	AL	95	314	83	17	1	13	(5	8)	141	39	46	16	0	59	5	3	3	3	2	.60	8	.264	.308	.449
1987 Texas	AL	95	237	53	15	2	8	(5	3)	96	25	16	24	3	51	1	4	0	0	3	.00	7	.224	.298	.405
1988 New York	AL	97	322	91	25	1	9	(7	2)	145	33	43	24	3	54	3	5	4	1	0	1.00	10	.283	.334	.450
1989 New York	AL	117	350	88	21	3	5	(3	2)	130	34	38	30	3	57	5	2	5	1	1	.50	9	.251	.315	.371
1990 Pittsburgh	NL	84	230	69	18	3	4	(1	3)	105	27	29	27	2	27	3	3	4	0	0	.00	8	.300	.375	.457
1991 Pittsburgh	NL	77	220	65	17	1	1	(0	1)	87	19	29	21	1	32	3	5	1	1	0	1.00	6	.295	.363	.395
1992 Pittsburgh	NL	87	255	88	17	3	4	(2	2)	123	26	37	17	5	23	2	6	5	2	2	.50	6	.345	.384	.482
1993 Pittsburgh	NL	116	377	113	19	2	10	(1	9)	166	34	55	29	2	56	6	4	4	2	1	.67	13	.300	.356	.440
1994 Pittsburgh	NL	76	240	69	7	0	2	(1	1)	82	21	21	34	2	31	3	1	1	0	0	.00	5	.288	.381	.342
1995 Pittsburgh	NL	35	112	34	6	0	0	(0	0)	40	13	13	9	2	8	1	1	0	0	0	.00	5	.304	.361	.357
1996 Cal-ChA	AL	76	243	76	10	0	6	(3	3)	104	25	36	15	0	22	2	1	2	0	0	.00	16	.313	.355	.428
1997 San Diego	NL	20	20	0	0	0	0	(0	0)	0	2	0	5	0	4	0	1	0	0	0	.00	1	.000	.200	.000
1996 California	AL	62	207	67	9	0	6	(3	3)	94	23	32	13	0	20	2	0	2	0	0	.00	12	.324	.366	.454
Chicago	AL	14	36	9	1	0	0	(0	0)	10	2	4	2	0	2	0	1	0	0	0	.00	4	.250	.289	.278
16 ML YEARS		1327	4063	1151	235	28	77	(33	44)	1673	415	476	311	28	559	42	48	38	18	15	.55	115	.283	.338	.412

Heathcliff Slocumb

Pitches: Right **Bats:** Right **Pos:** RP-76 **Ht:** 6'3" **Wt:** 220 **Born:** 6/7/66 **Age:** 32

Year Team	Lg	G	GS	CG	GF	IP	BFP	H	R	ER	HR	SH	SF	HB	TBB	IBB	SO	WP	Bk	W	L	Pct.	ShO	Sv-Op	Hld	ERA
1991 Chicago	NL	52	0	0	21	62.2	274	53	29	24	3	6	6	3	30	6	34	9	0	2	1	.667	0	1-3	6	3.45
1992 Chicago	NL	30	0	0	11	36	174	52	27	26	3	2	2	1	21	3	27	1	0	0	3	.000	0	1-1	1	6.50
1993 ChN-Cle		30	0	0	9	38	164	35	19	17	3	1	0	0	20	2	22	0	0	4	1	.800	0	0-2	3	4.03
1994 Philadelphia	NL	52	0	0	16	72.1	322	75	32	23	0	2	4	2	28	4	58	9	0	5	1	.833	0	0-5	18	2.86
1995 Philadelphia	NL	61	0	0	54	65.1	289	64	26	21	2	4	0	1	35	3	63	3	0	5	6	.455	0	32-38	3	2.89
1996 Boston	AL	75	0	0	60	83.1	368	68	31	28	2	1	3	3	55	5	88	10	0	5	5	.500	0	31-39	2	3.02
1997 Bos-Sea	AL	76	0	0	61	75	353	84	45	43	6	4	2	4	49	5	64	10	0	0	9	.000	0	27-33	5	5.16
1993 Chicago	NL	10	0	0	4	10.2	42	7	5	4	0	1	0	4	0	4	0	0	1	0	1.000	0	0-0	2	3.38
Cleveland	AL	20	0	0	5	27.1	122	28	14	13	3	1	2	0	16	2	18	0	0	1	1	.750	0	0-2	1	4.28
1997 Boston	AL	49	0	0	37	46.2	227	58	32	30	4	2	2	3	34	4	36	6	0	0	5	.000	0	17-22	5	5.79
Seattle	AL	27	0	0	24	28.1	126	26	13	13	2	2	0	1	15	1	28	4	0	0	4	.000	0	10-11	2	4.13
7 ML YEARS		376	0	0	232	432.2	1944	431	209	182	19	20	20	14	238	28	356	42	0	21	26	.447	0	92-121	36	3.79

Aaron Small

Pitches: Right Bats: Right Pos: RP-71   Ht: 6'5" Wt: 208 Born: 11/23/71 Age: 26

Year Team	Lg	G	GS	CG	GF	IP	BFP	H	R	ER	HR	SH	SF	HB	TBB	IBB	SO	WP	Bk	W	L	Pct.	ShO	Sv-Op	Hld	ERA
1989 Medicne Hat	R+	15	14	0	0	70.2	326	80	55	46	2	3	2	3	31	1	40	9	5	1	7	.125	0	0-	—	5.86
1990 Myrtle Bch	A	27	27	1	0	147.2	643	150	72	46	6	2	7	4	56	2	96	16	5	9	9	.500	0	0-	—	2.80
1991 Dunedin	A+	24	23	1	0	148.1	595	129	51	45	5	5	5	5	42	1	92	7	0	8	7	.533	0	0-	—	2.73
1992 Knoxville	AA	27	24	2	0	135	610	152	94	79	13	2	4	6	61	0	79	14	0	5	12	.294	1	0-	—	5.27
1993 Knoxville	AA	48	9	0	32	93	408	99	44	35	5	3	0	2	40	4	44	8	0	4	4	.500	0	16-	—	3.39
1994 Syracuse	AAA	13	0	0	6	24.1	99	19	8	6	2	2	0	1	9	2	15	2	0	3	2	.600	0	0-	—	2.22
Knoxville	AA	29	11	1	13	96.1	405	92	37	32	4	3	5	3	38	0	75	5	1	5	5	.500	1	5-	—	2.99
1995 Syracuse	AAA	1	0	0	0	1.2	9	3	1	1	1	0	0	0	1	0	2	0	0	0	0	.000	0	0-	—	5.40
Charlotte	AAA	33	0	0	17	40.2	170	36	15	13	2	0	1	2	10	1	31	3	0	2	1	.667	0	10-	—	2.88
1996 Edmonton	AAA	25	19	1	4	119.2	492	111	65	57	9	2	2	5	28	0	83	9	0	8	6	.571	1	1-	—	4.29
1997 Edmonton	AAA	1	1	0	0	5	16	1	0	0	0	0	0	0	0	0	4	0	0	1	0	1.000	0	0-	—	0.00
1994 Toronto	AL	1	0	0	1	2	13	5	2	2	1	0	1	0	2	0	0	0	0	0	0	.000	0	0-0	—	9.00
1995 Florida	NL	7	0	0	1	6.1	32	7	2	1	1	0	0	0	6	0	5	0	0	1	0	1.000	0	0-0	—	1.42
1996 Oakland	AL	12	3	0	4	28.2	144	37	28	26	3	0	1	1	22	1	17	2	0	1	3	.250	0	0-0	—	8.16
1997 Oakland	AL	71	0	0	22	96.2	425	109	50	46	6	5	6	3	40	6	57	4	0	9	5	.643	0	4-6	8	4.28
4 ML YEARS		91	3	0	28	133.2	614	158	82	75	11	5	8	4	70	7	79	6	0	11	8	.579	0	4-6	8	5.05

John Smiley

Pitches: Left Bats: Left Pos: SP-26   Ht: 6'4" Wt: 210 Born: 3/17/65 Age: 33

Year Team	Lg	G	GS	CG	GF	IP	BFP	H	R	ER	HR	SH	SF	HB	TBB	IBB	SO	WP	Bk	W	L	Pct.	ShO	Sv-Op	Hld	ERA
1986 Pittsburgh	NL	12	0	0	2	11.2	42	4	6	5	2	0	0	0	1	0	9	0	0	1	0	1.000	0	0-	—	3.86
1987 Pittsburgh	NL	63	0	0	19	75	336	69	49	48	7	0	3	0	50	8	58	5	1	5	5	.500	0	4-6	12	5.76
1988 Pittsburgh	NL	34	32	5	0	205	835	185	81	74	15	11	8	3	46	4	129	6	6	13	11	.542	1	0-0	1	3.25
1989 Pittsburgh	NL	28	28	8	0	205.1	835	174	78	64	22	5	7	4	49	5	123	5	2	12	8	.600	1	0-0	0	2.81
1990 Pittsburgh	NL	26	25	2	0	149.1	632	161	83	77	15	5	4	2	36	1	86	2	2	9	10	.474	0	0-0	0	4.64
1991 Pittsburgh	NL	33	32	2	0	207.2	836	194	78	71	17	11	4	3	44	0	129	3	1	20	8	.714	1	0-0	0	3.08
1992 Minnesota	NL	34	34	5	0	241	970	205	93	86	17	4	9	6	65	0	163	4	0	16	9	.640	2	0-0	0	3.21
1993 Cincinnati	NL	18	18	2	0	105.2	455	117	69	66	15	10	3	2	31	0	60	2	1	3	9	.250	0	0-0	0	5.62
1994 Cincinnati	NL	24	24	1	0	158.2	672	169	80	68	18	16	0	4	37	3	112	4	2	11	10	.524	1	0-0	0	3.86
1995 Cincinnati	NL	28	27	1	0	176.2	724	173	72	68	11	17	5	4	39	3	124	5	1	12	5	.706	0	0-0	0	3.46
1996 Cincinnati	NL	35	34	2	0	217.1	889	207	100	88	20	16	7	4	54	5	171	7	1	13	14	.481	2	0-1	0	3.64
1997 Cin-Cle		26	26	0	0	154.1	674	184	99	91	26	6	2	7	41	3	120	5	0	11	14	.440	0	0-0	0	5.31
1997 Cincinnati	NL	20	20	0	0	117	514	139	76	68	17	6	1	6	31	3	94	2	0	9	10	.474	0	0-0	0	5.23
Cleveland	AL	6	6	0	0	37.1	160	45	23	23	9	0	1	1	10	0	26	3	0	2	4	.333	0	0-0	0	5.54
12 ML YEARS		361	280	28	21	1907.2	7900	1842	888	806	185	101	52	39	496	32	1284	48	17	126	103	.550	8	4-	—	3.80

Lee Smith

Pitches: Right Bats: Right Pos: RP-25   Ht: 6'6" Wt: 269 Born: 12/4/57 Age: 40

Year Team	Lg	G	GS	CG	GF	IP	BFP	H	R	ER	HR	SH	SF	HB	TBB	IBB	SO	WP	Bk	W	L	Pct.	ShO	Sv-Op	Hld	ERA
1980 Chicago	NL	18	0	0	6	21.2	97	21	9	7	0	1	1	0	14	5	17	0	0	2	0	1.000	0	0-	—	2.91
1981 Chicago	NL	40	1	0	12	66.2	280	57	31	26	2	8	1	3	31	8	50	7	1	3	6	.333	0	1-	—	3.51
1982 Chicago	NL	72	5	0	38	117	480	105	38	35	5	6	5	3	37	5	99	6	1	2	5	.286	0	17-	—	2.69
1983 Chicago	NL	66	0	0	56	103.1	413	70	23	19	5	9	2	1	41	14	91	5	2	4	10	.286	0	29-	—	1.65
1984 Chicago	NL	69	0	0	59	101	428	98	42	41	6	4	5	0	35	7	86	6	0	9	7	.563	0	33-	—	3.65
1985 Chicago	NL	65	0	0	57	97.2	397	87	35	33	9	3	1	1	32	6	112	4	0	7	4	.636	0	33-	—	3.04
1986 Chicago	NL	66	0	0	59	90.1	372	69	32	31	7	6	3	0	42	11	93	2	0	9	9	.500	0	31-	—	3.09
1987 Chicago	NL	62	0	0	55	83.2	360	84	30	29	4	4	0	0	32	5	96	4	0	4	10	.286	0	36-48	0	3.12
1988 Boston	AL	64	0	0	57	83.2	363	72	34	26	7	3	2	1	37	6	96	2	0	4	5	.444	0	29-37	1	2.80
1989 Boston	AL	64	0	0	50	70.2	290	53	30	28	6	2	2	0	33	6	96	1	0	6	1	.857	0	25-30	4	3.57
1990 Bos-StL		64	0	0	53	83	344	71	24	19	3	2	3	0	29	7	87	2	0	5	5	.500	0	31-37	1	2.06
1991 St. Louis	NL	67	0	0	61	73	300	70	19	19	5	5	1	0	13	5	67	1	0	6	3	.667	0	47-53	0	2.34
1992 St. Louis	NL	70	0	0	55	75	310	62	28	26	4	2	1	0	26	4	60	2	0	4	9	.308	0	43-51	0	3.12
1993 StL-NYA		63	0	0	56	58	239	53	25	25	11	0	3	0	14	2	60	1	0	2	4	.333	0	46-53	0	3.88
1994 Baltimore	AL	41	0	0	39	38.1	160	34	16	14	6	5	2	0	11	1	42	0	0	1	4	.200	0	33-39	0	3.29
1995 California	AL	52	0	0	51	49.1	209	42	19	19	3	3	3	1	25	4	43	1	0	0	5	.000	0	37-41	0	3.47
1996 Cal-Cin		54	0	0	24	55.1	245	57	24	23	4	0	2	1	26	4	41	3	0	3	4	.429	0	2-8	8	3.74
1997 Montreal	NL	25	0	0	14	21.2	100	28	16	14	2	0	0	0	8	0	15	0	0	0	1	.000	0	5-6	2	5.82
1990 Boston	AL	11	0	0	8	14.1	64	13	4	3	0	0	0	0	9	2	17	1	0	2	1	.667	0	4-5	0	1.88
St. Louis	NL	53	0	0	45	68.2	280	58	20	16	3	2	3	0	20	5	70	1	0	3	4	.429	0	27-32	1	2.10
1993 St. Louis	NL	55	0	0	48	50	206	49	25	25	11	0	2	0	9	1	49	1	0	2	4	.333	0	43-50	0	4.50
New York	AL	8	0	0	8	8	33	4	0	0	0	0	1	0	5	1	11	0	0	0	0	.000	0	3-3	0	0.00
1996 California	AL	11	0	0	8	11	44	8	4	3	0	0	2	0	3	0	6	1	0	0	0	.000	0	0-2	0	2.45
Cincinnati	NL	43	0	0	16	44.1	201	49	20	20	4	0	0	1	23	4	35	2	0	3	4	.429	0	2-6	8	4.06
18 ML YEARS		1022	6	0	802	1289.1	5387	1133	475	434	89	63	38	10	486	100	1251	47	4	71	92	.436	0	478-	—	3.03

Mark Smith

Bats: R Throws: R Pos: RF-22; LF-21; PH-19; 1B-9; DH-5   Ht: 6'3" Wt: 205 Born: 5/7/70 Age: 28

Year Team	Lg	G	AB	H	2B	3B	HR	(Hm	Rd)	TB	R	RBI	TBB	IBB	SO	HBP	SH	SF	SB	CS	SB%	GDP	Avg	OBP	SLG
1997 Calgary *	AAA	39	137	51	14	1	14	—	—	109	37	42	21	1	15	2	0	0	2	1	.67	5	.372	.463	.796

Year Team	Lg	G	AB	H	2B	3B	HR	(Hm Rd)	TB	R	RBI	TBB	IBB	SO	HBP	SH	SF	SB	CS	SB%	GDP	Avg	OBP	SLG
						BATTING													**BASERUNNING**				**PERCENTAGES**		
1994 Carolina *	AA	3	12	5	1	0	3	— —	15	5	4	0	0	1	0	0	0	0	0	.00	0	.417	.417	1.250
1994 Baltimore	AL	3	7	1	0	0	0	(0 0)	1	0	2	0	0	2	0	0	0	0	0	.00	0	.143	.143	.143
1995 Baltimore	AL	37	104	24	5	0	3	(1 2)	38	11	15	12	2	22	1	2	1	3	0	1.00	4	.231	.314	.365
1996 Baltimore	AL	27	78	19	2	0	4	(3 1)	33	9	10	3	0	20	3	0	0	0	2	.00	4	.244	.298	.423
1997 Pittsburgh	NL	71	193	55	13	1	9	(6 3)	97	29	35	28	1	36	0	0	1	3	1	.75	3	.285	.374	.503
4 ML YEARS		138	382	99	20	1	16	(10 6)	169	49	62	43	3	80	4	2	2	6	3	.67	7	.259	.339	.442

Pete Smith

Pitches: Right **Bats:** Right **Pos:** RP-22; SP-15   **Ht:** 6'2" **Wt:** 200 **Born:** 2/27/66 **Age:** 32

Year Team	Lg	G	GS	CG	GF	IP	BFP	H	R	ER	HR	SH	SF	HB	TBB	IBB	SO	WP	Bk	W	L	Pct.	ShO	Sv-Op	Hld	ERA
				HOW MUCH HE PITCHED								**WHAT HE GAVE UP**										**THE RESULTS**				
1997 Las Vegas *	AAA	6	6	0	0	33.2	138	38	16	16	5	2	0	0	6	0	24	0	1	3	2	.600	0	0- -	—	4.28
1987 Atlanta	NL	6	6	0	0	31.2	143	39	21	17	3	0	2	0	14	0	11	3	1	1	2	.333	0	0-0	0	4.83
1988 Atlanta	NL	32	32	5	0	195.1	837	183	89	80	15	12	4	1	88	3	124	5	7	7	15	.318	3	0-0	0	3.69
1989 Atlanta	NL	28	27	1	0	142	613	144	83	75	13	4	5	0	57	2	115	3	7	5	14	.263	0	0-0	0	4.75
1990 Atlanta	NL	13	13	3	0	77	327	77	45	41	11	4	3	0	24	2	56	2	1	5	6	.455	0	0-0	0	4.79
1991 Atlanta	NL	14	10	0	2	48	211	48	33	27	5	2	4	0	22	3	29	5	1	1	3	.250	0	0-0	0	5.06
1992 Atlanta	NL	12	11	2	0	79	323	63	19	18	3	4	1	0	28	2	43	2	1	7	0	1.000	1	0-0	0	2.05
1993 Atlanta	NL	20	14	0	2	90.2	390	92	45	44	15	6	5	2	36	3	53	1	1	4	8	.333	0	0-0	0	4.37
1994 New York	NL	21	21	1	0	131.1	565	145	83	81	25	5	7	2	42	4	62	3	1	4	10	.286	0	0-0	0	5.55
1995 Cincinnati	NL	11	2	0	3	24.1	106	30	19	18	8	1	3	1	7	1	14	1	0	1	2	.333	0	0-0	0	6.66
1997 San Diego	NL	37	15	0	7	118	511	120	66	63	16	7	2	1	52	2	68	0	3	7	6	.538	0	1-1	2	4.81
10 ML YEARS		194	151	12	14	937.1	4026	941	503	464	114	45	36	7	370	22	575	21	26	42	66	.389	4	1-1	3	4.46

John Smoltz

Pitches: Right **Bats:** Right **Pos:** SP-35   **Ht:** 6'3" **Wt:** 185 **Born:** 5/15/67 **Age:** 31

Year Team	Lg	G	GS	CG	GF	IP	BFP	H	R	ER	HR	SH	SF	HB	TBB	IBB	SO	WP	Bk	W	L	Pct.	ShO	Sv-Op	Hld	ERA
				HOW MUCH HE PITCHED								**WHAT HE GAVE UP**										**THE RESULTS**				
1988 Atlanta	NL	12	12	0	0	64	297	74	40	39	10	2	0	2	33	4	37	2	1	2	7	.222	0	0-0	0	5.48
1989 Atlanta	NL	29	29	5	0	208	847	160	79	68	15	10	7	2	72	2	168	8	3	12	11	.522	0	0-0	0	2.94
1990 Atlanta	NL	34	34	6	0	231.1	966	206	109	99	20	9	8	1	90	3	170	14	3	14	11	.560	2	0-0	0	3.85
1991 Atlanta	NL	36	36	5	0	229.2	947	206	101	97	16	9	9	3	77	1	148	20	2	14	13	.519	0	0-0	0	3.80
1992 Atlanta	NL	35	35	9	0	246.2	1021	206	90	78	17	7	8	5	80	5	215	17	1	15	12	.556	3	0-0	0	2.85
1993 Atlanta	NL	35	35	3	0	243.2	1028	208	104	98	23	13	4	6	100	12	208	13	1	15	11	.577	1	0-0	0	3.62
1994 Atlanta	NL	21	21	1	0	134.2	568	120	69	62	15	7	6	4	48	4	113	7	0	6	10	.375	0	0-0	0	4.14
1995 Atlanta	NL	29	29	2	0	192.2	808	166	76	68	15	13	5	4	72	8	193	13	0	12	7	.632	1	0-0	0	3.18
1996 Atlanta	NL	35	35	6	0	253.2	995	199	93	83	19	12	4	2	55	3	276	10	1	24	8	.750	2	0-0	0	2.94
1997 Atlanta	NL	35	35	7	0	256	1043	234	97	86	21	10	3	1	63	9	241	10	1	15	12	.556	2	0-0	0	3.02
10 ML YEARS		301	301	44	0	2060.1	8520	1779	858	778	171	92	54	30	690	51	1769	114	13	129	102	.558	11	0-0	0	3.40

Chris Snopek

Bats: Right **Throws:** Right **Pos:** 3B-82; SS-4; PH-3   **Ht:** 6'1" **Wt:** 185 **Born:** 9/20/70 **Age:** 27

Year Team	Lg	G	AB	H	2B	3B	HR	(Hm Rd)	TB	R	RBI	TBB	IBB	SO	HBP	SH	SF	SB	CS	SB%	GDP	Avg	OBP	SLG
						BATTING													**BASERUNNING**				**PERCENTAGES**		
1997 Nashville *	AAA	20	73	17	4	0	3	— —	30	8	8	7	0	13	0	0	0	0	0	.00	4	.233	.300	.411
1995 Chicago	AL	22	68	22	4	0	1	(1 0)	29	12	7	9	0	12	0	0	0	1	0	1.00	2	.324	.403	.426
1996 Chicago	AL	46	104	27	6	1	6	(3 3)	53	18	18	6	0	16	1	1	1	0	1	.00	5	.260	.304	.510
1997 Chicago	AL	86	298	65	15	0	5	(3 2)	95	27	35	18	0	51	1	4	2	3	2	.60	4	.218	.263	.319
3 ML YEARS		154	470	114	25	1	12	(7 5)	177	57	60	33	0	79	2	5	3	4	3	.57	11	.243	.293	.377

J.T. Snow

Bats: Both **Throws:** Left **Pos:** 1B-156; PH-4   **Ht:** 6'2" **Wt:** 202 **Born:** 2/26/68 **Age:** 30

Year Team	Lg	G	AB	H	2B	3B	HR	(Hm Rd)	TB	R	RBI	TBB	IBB	SO	HBP	SH	SF	SB	CS	SB%	GDP	Avg	OBP	SLG
						BATTING													**BASERUNNING**				**PERCENTAGES**		
1992 New York	AL	7	14	2	1	0	0	(0 0)	3	1	2	5	1	5	0	0	0	0	0	.00	0	.143	.368	.214
1993 California	AL	129	419	101	18	2	16	(10 6)	171	60	57	55	4	88	2	7	6	3	0	1.00	10	.241	.328	.408
1994 California	AL	61	223	49	4	0	8	(1 7)	77	22	30	19	1	48	3	2	1	0	1	.00	2	.220	.289	.345
1995 California	AL	143	544	157	22	1	24	(14 10)	253	80	102	52	4	91	3	5	2	2	1	.67	16	.289	.353	.465
1996 California	AL	155	575	148	20	1	17	(8 9)	221	69	67	56	6	96	5	2	3	1	6	.14	19	.257	.327	.384
1997 San Francisco	NL	157	531	149	36	1	28	(14 14)	271	81	104	96	13	124	1	2	7	6	4	.60	8	.281	.387	.510
6 ML YEARS		652	2306	606	101	5	93	(53 40)	996	313	362	283	29	452	14	18	19	12	12	.50	55	.263	.344	.432

Clint Sodowsky

Pitches: Right **Bats:** Left **Pos:** RP-45   **Ht:** 6'4" **Wt:** 200 **Born:** 7/13/72 **Age:** 25

Year Team	Lg	G	GS	CG	GF	IP	BFP	H	R	ER	HR	SH	SF	HB	TBB	IBB	SO	WP	Bk	W	L	Pct.	ShO	Sv-Op	Hld	ERA
				HOW MUCH HE PITCHED								**WHAT HE GAVE UP**										**THE RESULTS**				
1991 Bristol	R+	14	8	0	3	55	253	49	34	23	2	3	2	1	34	0	44	8	4	0	5	.000	0	0- -	—	3.76
1992 Bristol	R+	15	6	0	2	56	243	46	35	22	3	1	2	4	29	0	48	6	1	2	2	.500	0	0- -	—	3.54
1993 Fayetteville	A	27	27	1	0	155.2	676	177	101	88	11	2	6	6	51	0	80	4	5	14	10	.583	0	0- -	—	5.09
1994 Lakeland	A+	19	18	1	0	110.1	466	111	58	47	5	2	2	6	34	0	73	12	0	6	3	.667	1	0- -	—	3.83
1995 Jacksonville	AA	19	19	5	0	123.2	497	102	46	35	4	2	2	5	50	1	77	3	0	5	5	.500	2	0- -	—	2.55
Toledo	AAA	9	9	1	0	60	247	47	21	19	5	2	0	3	30	1	32	1	0	5	1	.833	0	0- -	—	2.85

196

| | | HOW MUCH HE PITCHED | | | | | | WHAT HE GAVE UP | | | | | | THE RESULTS | | | | |

Year Team	Lg	G	GS	CG	GF	IP	BFP	H	R	ER	HR	SH	SF	HB	TBB	IBB	SO	WP	Bk	W	L	Pct.	ShO	Sv-Op	Hld	ERA
1996 Toledo	AAA	19	19	1	0	118.2	525	128	67	52	8	8	3	6	51	0	59	3	2	6	8	.429	0	0--	--	3.94
1997 Calgary	AAA	8	0	0	1	13.2	64	19	10	10	1	0	0	0	6	0	9	1	0	0	1	.000	0	1--	--	6.59
1995 Detroit	AL	6	6	0	0	23.1	112	24	15	13	4	1	0	0	18	0	14	1	1	2	2	.500	0	0-0	0	5.01
1996 Detroit	AL	7	7	0	0	24.1	132	40	34	32	5	1	0	3	20	0	9	3	0	1	3	.250	0	0-0	0	11.84
1997 Pittsburgh	NL	45	0	0	8	52	236	49	22	21	6	1	2	2	34	7	51	6	0	2	2	.500	0	0-2	5	3.63
3 ML YEARS		58	13	0	8	99.2	480	113	71	66	15	3	2	5	72	7	74	10	1	5	7	.417	0	0-2	5	5.96

Luis Sojo

Bats: R **Throws:** R **Pos:** 2B-72; SS-4; PH-4; 3B-3; 1B-2   **Ht:** 5'11" **Wt:** 175 **Born:** 1/3/66 **Age:** 32

					BATTING														BASERUNNING				PERCENTAGES		
Year Team	Lg	G	AB	H	2B	3B	HR	(Hm	Rd)	TB	R	RBI	TBB	IBB	SO	HBP	SH	SF	SB	CS	SB%	GDP	Avg	OBP	SLG
1990 Toronto	AL	33	80	18	3	0	1	(0	1)	24	14	9	5	0	5	0	0	0	1	1	.50	1	.225	.271	.300
1991 California	AL	113	364	94	14	1	3	(1	2)	119	38	20	14	0	26	5	19	0	4	2	.67	12	.258	.295	.327
1992 California	AL	106	368	100	12	3	7	(2	5)	139	37	43	14	0	24	1	7	1	7	11	.39	14	.272	.299	.378
1993 Toronto	AL	19	47	8	2	0	0	(0	0)	10	5	6	4	0	2	0	2	1	0	0	.00	3	.170	.231	.213
1994 Seattle	AL	63	213	59	9	2	6	(4	2)	90	32	22	8	0	25	2	3	1	2	1	.67	2	.277	.308	.423
1995 Seattle	AL	102	339	98	18	2	7	(4	3)	141	50	39	23	0	19	1	6	1	4	2	.67	6	.289	.335	.416
1996 Sea-NYA	AL	95	287	63	10	1	1	(1	0)	78	23	21	11	0	17	1	8	1	2	2	.50	10	.220	.250	.272
1997 New York	AL	77	215	66	6	1	2	(2	0)	80	27	25	16	0	14	1	5	2	3	1	.75	5	.307	.355	.372
1996 Seattle	AL	77	247	52	8	1	1	(1	0)	65	20	16	10	0	13	1	6	0	2	2	.50	8	.211	.244	.263
New York	AL	18	40	11	2	0	0	(0	0)	13	3	5	1	0	4	0	2	1	0	0	.00	2	.275	.286	.325
8 ML YEARS		608	1913	506	74	10	27	(14	13)	681	226	185	95	0	132	11	50	7	23	20	.53	56	.265	.302	.356

Paul Sorrento

Bats: Left **Throws:** Right **Pos:** 1B-139; PH-25; DH-1   **Ht:** 6'2" **Wt:** 220 **Born:** 11/17/65 **Age:** 32

					BATTING														BASERUNNING				PERCENTAGES		
Year Team	Lg	G	AB	H	2B	3B	HR	(Hm	Rd)	TB	R	RBI	TBB	IBB	SO	HBP	SH	SF	SB	CS	SB%	GDP	Avg	OBP	SLG
1989 Minnesota	AL	14	21	5	0	0	0	(0	0)	5	2	1	5	1	4	0	0	1	0	0	.00	0	.238	.370	.238
1990 Minnesota	AL	41	121	25	4	1	5	(2	3)	46	11	13	12	0	31	1	0	1	1	1	.50	3	.207	.281	.380
1991 Minnesota	AL	26	47	12	2	0	4	(2	2)	26	6	13	4	2	11	0	0	0	0	0	.00	3	.255	.314	.553
1992 Cleveland	AL	140	458	123	24	1	18	(11	7)	203	52	60	51	7	89	1	1	3	0	3	.00	13	.269	.341	.443
1993 Cleveland	AL	148	463	119	26	1	18	(8	10)	201	75	65	58	11	121	2	0	4	3	1	.75	10	.257	.340	.434
1994 Cleveland	AL	95	322	90	14	0	14	(8	6)	146	43	62	34	6	68	0	1	3	0	1	.00	7	.280	.345	.453
1995 Cleveland	AL	104	323	76	14	0	25	(12	13)	165	50	79	51	6	71	0	0	4	1	1	.50	10	.235	.336	.511
1996 Seattle	AL	143	471	136	32	1	23	(13	10)	239	67	93	57	10	103	7	2	5	0	2	.00	10	.289	.370	.507
1997 Seattle	AL	146	457	123	19	0	31	(18	13)	235	68	80	51	9	112	3	0	2	2	2	.00	13	.269	.345	.514
9 ML YEARS		857	2683	709	135	4	138	(74	64)	1266	374	466	323	52	610	14	4	23	5	11	.31	69	.264	.344	.472

Sammy Sosa

Bats: Right **Throws:** Right **Pos:** RF-161; PH-1   **Ht:** 6'0" **Wt:** 190 **Born:** 11/12/68 **Age:** 29

					BATTING														BASERUNNING				PERCENTAGES		
Year Team	Lg	G	AB	H	2B	3B	HR	(Hm	Rd)	TB	R	RBI	TBB	IBB	SO	HBP	SH	SF	SB	CS	SB%	GDP	Avg	OBP	SLG
1989 Tex-ChA	AL	58	183	47	8	0	4	(1	3)	67	27	13	11	2	47	2	5	2	7	5	.58	6	.257	.303	.366
1990 Chicago	AL	153	532	124	26	10	15	(10	5)	215	72	70	33	4	150	6	2	6	32	16	.67	10	.233	.282	.404
1991 Chicago	AL	116	316	64	10	1	10	(3	7)	106	39	33	14	2	98	2	5	1	13	6	.68	5	.203	.240	.335
1992 Chicago	NL	67	262	68	7	2	8	(4	4)	103	41	25	19	1	63	4	4	2	15	7	.68	4	.260	.317	.393
1993 Chicago	NL	159	598	156	25	5	33	(23	10)	290	92	93	38	6	135	4	0	1	36	11	.77	14	.261	.309	.485
1994 Chicago	NL	105	426	128	17	6	25	(11	14)	232	59	70	25	1	92	2	1	4	22	13	.63	7	.300	.339	.545
1995 Chicago	NL	144	564	151	17	3	36	(19	17)	282	89	119	58	11	134	5	0	2	34	7	.83	8	.268	.340	.500
1996 Chicago	NL	124	498	136	21	2	40	(26	14)	281	84	100	34	6	134	5	0	1	18	5	.78	14	.273	.323	.564
1997 Chicago	NL	162	642	161	31	4	36	(25	11)	308	90	119	45	9	174	2	0	5	22	12	.65	16	.251	.300	.480
1989 Texas	AL	25	84	20	3	0	1	(0	1)	26	8	3	0	0	20	0	4	0	0	2	.00	3	.238	.238	.310
Chicago	AL	33	99	27	5	0	3	(1	2)	41	19	10	11	2	27	2	1	2	7	3	.70	3	.273	.351	.414
9 ML YEARS		1088	4021	1035	162	33	207	(122	85)	1884	593	642	277	42	1027	32	17	27	199	82	.71	84	.257	.308	.469

Tim Spehr

Bats: Right **Throws:** Right **Pos:** C-24; PH-1   **Ht:** 6'2" **Wt:** 200 **Born:** 7/2/66 **Age:** 31

					BATTING														BASERUNNING				PERCENTAGES		
Year Team	Lg	G	AB	H	2B	3B	HR	(Hm	Rd)	TB	R	RBI	TBB	IBB	SO	HBP	SH	SF	SB	CS	SB%	GDP	Avg	OBP	SLG
1997 Richmond *	AAA	36	120	23	5	0	3	—	—	37	13	14	12	0	37	1	0	2	0	0	.00	1	.192	.267	.308
1991 Kansas City	AL	37	74	14	5	0	3	(1	2)	28	7	14	9	0	18	1	3	1	1	0	1.00	2	.189	.282	.378
1993 Montreal	NL	53	87	20	6	0	2	(0	2)	32	14	10	6	1	20	1	3	2	2	0	1.00	1	.230	.281	.368
1994 Montreal	NL	52	36	9	3	1	0	(0	0)	14	8	5	4	0	11	0	1	0	2	0	1.00	0	.250	.325	.389
1995 Montreal	NL	41	35	9	5	0	1	(0	1)	17	4	3	6	0	7	0	3	0	0	0	.00	0	.257	.366	.486
1996 Montreal	NL	63	44	4	1	0	1	(1	0)	8	4	3	3	0	15	1	1	0	1	0	1.00	1	.091	.167	.182
1997 KC-Atl		25	49	9	1	0	2	(1	1)	16	5	6	2	0	16	1	0	0	1	0	1.00	0	.184	.231	.327
1997 Kansas City	AL	17	35	6	0	0	1	(0	1)	9	3	2	2	0	12	1	0	0	0	0	.00	0	.171	.237	.257
Atlanta	NL	8	14	3	1	0	1	(1	0)	7	2	4	0	0	4	0	0	0	1	0	1.00	0	.214	.214	.500
6 ML YEARS		271	325	65	21	1	9	(3	6)	115	42	41	30	1	87	4	11	3	7	0	1.00	3	.200	.273	.354

Bill Spiers

Bats: L **Throws:** R **Pos:** 3B-84; PH-43; SS-28; 1B-8; 2B-4   **Ht:** 6'2" **Wt:** 190 **Born:** 6/5/66 **Age:** 32

						BATTING												BASERUNNING				PERCENTAGES		
Year Team	Lg	G	AB	H	2B	3B	HR	(Hm	Rd)	TB	R	RBI	TBB	IBB	SO	HBP	SH	SF	SB	CS	SB%	GDP	Avg	OBP	SLG
1989 Milwaukee	AL	114	345	88	9	3	4	(1	3)	115	44	33	21	1	63	1	4	2	10	2	.83	2	.255	.298	.333
1990 Milwaukee	AL	112	363	88	15	3	2	(2	0)	115	44	36	16	0	45	1	6	3	11	6	.65	12	.242	.274	.317
1991 Milwaukee	AL	133	414	117	13	6	8	(1	7)	166	71	54	34	0	55	2	10	4	14	8	.64	9	.283	.337	.401
1992 Milwaukee	AL	12	16	5	2	0	0	(0	0)	7	2	2	1	0	4	0	1	0	1	1	.50	0	.313	.353	.438
1993 Milwaukee	AL	113	340	81	8	4	2	(2	0)	103	43	36	29	2	51	4	9	4	9	8	.53	11	.238	.302	.303
1994 Milwaukee	AL	73	214	54	10	1	0	(0	0)	66	27	17	19	1	42	1	3	0	7	1	.88	5	.252	.316	.308
1995 New York	NL	63	72	15	2	1	0	(0	0)	19	5	11	12	1	15	0	1	2	0	1	.00	0	.208	.314	.264
1996 Houston	NL	122	218	55	10	1	6	(3	3)	85	27	26	20	4	34	2	1	1	7	0	1.00	3	.252	.320	.390
1997 Houston	NL	132	291	93	27	4	4	(0	4)	140	51	48	61	6	42	1	1	1	10	5	.67	4	.320	.438	.481
9 ML YEARS		874	2273	596	96	23	26	(9	17)	816	314	263	213	15	351	12	36	17	69	32	.68	46	.262	.326	.359

Scott Spiezio

Bats: Both **Throws:** Right **Pos:** 2B-146; PH-3; 3B-1   **Ht:** 6'2" **Wt:** 195 **Born:** 9/21/72 **Age:** 25

						BATTING												BASERUNNING				PERCENTAGES		
Year Team	Lg	G	AB	H	2B	3B	HR	(Hm	Rd)	TB	R	RBI	TBB	IBB	SO	HBP	SH	SF	SB	CS	SB%	GDP	Avg	OBP	SLG
1993 Sou. Oregon	A-	31	125	41	10	2	3	—	—	64	32	19	16	0	18	0	0	0	0	1	.00	1	.328	.404	.512
Modesto	A+	32	110	28	9	1	1	—	—	42	12	13	23	0	19	1	1	0	1	5	.17	4	.255	.388	.382
1994 Modesto	A+	127	453	127	32	5	14	—	—	211	84	68	88	4	72	7	3	9	5	0	1.00	15	.280	.399	.466
1995 Huntsville	AA	141	528	149	33	8	13	—	—	237	78	86	67	2	78	4	2	14	10	3	.77	10	.282	.359	.449
1996 Edmonton	AAA	140	523	137	30	4	20	—	—	235	87	91	56	6	66	4	3	5	6	5	.55	7	.262	.335	.449
1997 Sou. Oregon	A-	2	9	5	0	0	0	—	—	5	1	2	2	1	1	0	0	1	0	0	.00	0	.556	.583	.556
1996 Oakland	AL	9	29	9	2	0	2	(1	1)	17	6	8	4	1	4	0	2	0	1	0	1.00	0	.310	.394	.586
1997 Oakland	AL	147	538	131	28	4	14	(6	8)	209	58	65	44	2	75	1	3	4	9	3	.75	13	.243	.300	.388
2 ML YEARS		156	567	140	30	4	16	(7	9)	226	64	73	48	3	79	1	5	4	9	4	.69	13	.247	.305	.399

Paul Spoljaric

Pitches: Left **Bats:** Right **Pos:** RP-57   **Ht:** 6'3" **Wt:** 205 **Born:** 9/24/70 **Age:** 27

		HOW MUCH HE PITCHED						WHAT HE GAVE UP											THE RESULTS					
Year Team	Lg	G	GS	CG	GF	IP	BFP	H	R	ER	HR	SH	SF	HB	TBB	IBB	SO	WP	Bk	W	L	Pct.	ShO	Sv-Op	Hld	ERA
1997 Dunedin *	A+	4	3	0	1	10.2	43	10	3	2	1	0	0	0	2	0	10	1	0	0	0	.000	0	0- -	-	1.69
1994 Toronto	AL	2	1	0	0	2.1	21	5	10	10	3	0	0	0	9	1	2	0	0	0	1	.000	0	0-0	0	38.57
1996 Toronto	AL	28	0	0	12	38	163	30	17	13	6	1	1	2	19	1	38	0	0	2	2	.500	0	1-1	5	3.08
1997 Tor-Sea	AL	57	0	0	10	70.2	302	61	30	29	4	2	2	3	36	6	70	6	3	0	5	.000	0	3-5	10	3.69
1997 Toronto	AL	37	0	0	10	48	198	37	17	17	3	1	2	2	21	4	43	5	1	0	3	.000	0	3-3	8	3.19
Seattle	AL	20	0	0	0	22.2	104	24	13	12	1	1	0	1	15	2	27	1	2	0	2	.000	0	0-2	2	4.76
3 ML YEARS		87	1	0	22	111	486	96	57	52	13	3	3	5	64	8	110	6	3	2	6	.250	0	4-6	15	4.22

Jerry Spradlin

Pitches: Right **Bats:** Both **Pos:** RP-76   **Ht:** 6'7" **Wt:** 240 **Born:** 6/14/67 **Age:** 31

		HOW MUCH HE PITCHED						WHAT HE GAVE UP											THE RESULTS					
Year Team	Lg	G	GS	CG	GF	IP	BFP	H	R	ER	HR	SH	SF	HB	TBB	IBB	SO	WP	Bk	W	L	Pct.	ShO	Sv-Op	Hld	ERA
1993 Cincinnati	NL	37	0	0	16	49	193	44	20	19	4	3	4	0	9	0	24	3	1	2	1	.667	0	2-3	0	3.49
1994 Cincinnati	NL	6	0	0	2	8	38	12	11	9	2	0	2	0	2	0	4	0	0	0	0	.000	0	0-0	0	10.13
1996 Cincinnati	NL	1	0	0	1	0.1	1	0	0	0	0	0	0	0	0	0	0	1	0	0	0	.000	0	0-0	0	0.00
1997 Philadelphia	NL	76	0	0	23	81.2	345	86	45	43	9	1	2	1	27	3	67	5	2	4	8	.333	0	1-5	18	4.74
4 ML YEARS		120	0	0	42	139	577	142	76	71	15	4	8	1	38	3	95	9	3	6	9	.400	0	3-8	18	4.60

Ed Sprague

Bats: Right **Throws:** Right **Pos:** 3B-129; DH-8; PH-1   **Ht:** 6'2" **Wt:** 210 **Born:** 7/25/67 **Age:** 30

						BATTING												BASERUNNING				PERCENTAGES		
Year Team	Lg	G	AB	H	2B	3B	HR	(Hm	Rd)	TB	R	RBI	TBB	IBB	SO	HBP	SH	SF	SB	CS	SB%	GDP	Avg	OBP	SLG
1991 Toronto	AL	61	160	44	7	0	4	(3	1)	63	17	20	19	2	43	3	0	1	0	3	.00	2	.275	.361	.394
1992 Toronto	AL	22	47	11	2	0	1	(1	0)	16	6	7	3	0	7	0	0	0	0	0	.00	0	.234	.280	.340
1993 Toronto	AL	150	546	142	31	1	12	(8	4)	211	50	73	32	1	85	10	2	6	1	0	1.00	23	.260	.310	.386
1994 Toronto	AL	109	405	97	19	1	11	(6	5)	151	38	44	23	1	95	11	2	4	1	0	1.00	11	.240	.296	.373
1995 Toronto	AL	144	521	127	27	2	18	(12	6)	212	77	74	58	3	96	15	1	7	0	0	.00	19	.244	.333	.407
1996 Toronto	AL	159	591	146	35	2	36	(17	19)	293	88	101	60	3	146	12	0	7	0	0	.00	7	.247	.325	.496
1997 Toronto	AL	138	504	115	29	4	14	(5	9)	194	63	48	51	0	102	6	0	1	0	1	.00	10	.228	.306	.385
7 ML YEARS		783	2774	682	150	10	96	(52	44)	1140	339	367	246	10	574	57	5	26	2	4	.33	72	.246	.317	.411

Dennis Springer

Pitches: Right **Bats:** Right **Pos:** SP-28; RP-4   **Ht:** 5'10" **Wt:** 185 **Born:** 2/12/65 **Age:** 33

		HOW MUCH HE PITCHED						WHAT HE GAVE UP											THE RESULTS					
Year Team	Lg	G	GS	CG	GF	IP	BFP	H	R	ER	HR	SH	SF	HB	TBB	IBB	SO	WP	Bk	W	L	Pct.	ShO	Sv-Op	Hld	ERA
1997 Vancouver *	AAA	2	2	2	0	15	63	12	6	5	1	0	0	1	6	0	7	0	0	1	1	.500	0	0- -	-	3.00
1995 Philadelphia	NL	4	4	0	0	22.1	94	21	15	12	3	2	0	1	9	1	15	1	0	0	3	.000	0	0-0	0	4.84
1996 California	AL	20	15	2	3	94.2	413	91	65	58	24	0	1	6	43	0	64	1	0	5	6	.455	1	0-0	1	5.51
1997 Anaheim	AL	32	28	3	0	194.2	846	199	118	112	32	4	13	10	73	0	75	7	0	9	9	.500	1	0-0	0	5.18
3 ML YEARS		56	47	5	3	311.2	1353	311	198	182	59	6	14	17	125	1	154	9	0	14	18	.438	2	0-0	1	5.26

Russ Springer

Pitches: Right **Bats:** Right **Pos:** RP-54 **Ht:** 6'4" **Wt:** 205 **Born:** 11/7/68 **Age:** 29

Year Team	Lg	HOW MUCH HE PITCHED						WHAT HE GAVE UP												THE RESULTS						
		G	GS	CG	GF	IP	BFP	H	R	ER	HR	SH	SF	HB	TBB	IBB	SO	WP	Bk	W	L	Pct.	ShO	Sv-Op	Hld	ERA
1997 Jackson *	AA	1	0	0	0	1	5	2	1	1	0	0	0	0	0	0	2	0	0	0	0	.000	0	0--	—	9.00
1992 New York	AL	14	0	0	5	16	75	18	11	11	0	0	0	1	10	0	12	0	0	0	0	.000	0	0-0	2	6.19
1993 California	AL	14	9	1	3	60	278	73	48	48	11	1	1	3	32	1	31	6	0	1	6	.143	0	0-0	0	7.20
1994 California	AL	18	5	0	6	45.2	198	53	28	28	9	1	1	0	14	0	28	2	0	2	2	.500	0	2-3	1	5.52
1995 Cal-Phi		33	6	0	6	78.1	350	82	48	46	16	2	2	7	35	4	70	2	0	1	2	.333	0	1-2	0	5.29
1996 Philadelphia	NL	51	7	0	12	96.2	437	106	60	50	12	5	3	1	38	6	94	5	0	3	10	.231	0	0-3	6	4.66
1997 Houston	NL	54	0	0	13	55.1	241	48	28	26	4	1	2	4	27	2	74	4	0	3	3	.500	0	3-7	9	4.23
1995 California	AL	19	6	0	3	51.2	238	60	37	35	11	1	0	5	25	1	38	1	0	1	2	.333	0	1-2	0	6.10
Philadelphia	NL	14	0	0	3	26.2	112	22	11	11	5	1	2	2	10	3	32	1	0	0	0	.000	0	0-0	0	3.71
6 ML YEARS		184	27	1	45	352	1579	380	223	209	52	10	9	16	156	13	309	19	0	10	23	.303	0	6-15	18	5.34

Scott Stahoviak

Bats: Left **Throws:** Right **Pos:** 1B-81; PH-17; DH-5 **Ht:** 6'5" **Wt:** 222 **Born:** 3/6/70 **Age:** 28

Year Team	Lg	BATTING																	BASERUNNING				PERCENTAGES		
		G	AB	H	2B	3B	HR	Hm	Rd	TB	R	RBI	TBB	IBB	SO	HBP	SH	SF	SB	CS	SB%	GDP	Avg	OBP	SLG
1997 Salt Lake *	AAA	8	28	6	0	0	2	—	—	12	5	10	5	0	8	1	0	0	0	0	.00	1	.214	.353	.429
1993 Minnesota	AL	20	57	11	4	0	0	0	0	15	1	1	3	0	22	0	0	0	0	2	.00	1	.193	.233	.263
1995 Minnesota	AL	94	263	70	19	4	3	1	2	98	28	23	30	1	61	1	0	2	5	1	.83	3	.266	.341	.373
1996 Minnesota	AL	130	405	115	30	3	13	8	5	190	72	61	59	7	114	2	1	2	3	3	.50	9	.284	.376	.469
1997 Minnesota	AL	91	275	63	17	0	10	4	6	110	33	33	24	1	73	6	0	4	5	2	.71	7	.229	.301	.400
4 ML YEARS		335	1000	259	70	3	26	13	13	413	134	118	116	9	270	9	1	8	13	8	.62	21	.259	.339	.413

Matt Stairs

Bats: L **Throws:** R **Pos:** RF-63; PH-42; LF-28; DH-17; 1B-7 **Ht:** 5'9" **Wt:** 200 **Born:** 2/27/68 **Age:** 30

Year Team	Lg	BATTING																	BASERUNNING				PERCENTAGES		
		G	AB	H	2B	3B	HR	Hm	Rd	TB	R	RBI	TBB	IBB	SO	HBP	SH	SF	SB	CS	SB%	GDP	Avg	OBP	SLG
1992 Montreal	NL	13	30	5	2	0	0	0	0	7	2	5	7	0	7	0	0	1	0	0	.00	1	.167	.316	.233
1993 Montreal	NL	6	8	3	1	0	0	0	0	4	1	2	0	0	1	0	0	0	0	0	.00	1	.375	.375	.500
1995 Boston	AL	39	88	23	7	1	1	0	0	35	8	17	4	0	14	1	1	1	0	1	.00	4	.261	.298	.398
1996 Oakland	AL	61	137	38	5	1	10	5	5	75	21	23	19	2	23	1	0	1	1	1	.50	2	.277	.367	.547
1997 Oakland	AL	133	352	105	19	0	27	20	7	205	62	73	50	1	60	3	1	4	3	2	.60	6	.298	.386	.582
5 ML YEARS		252	615	174	34	2	38	25	13	326	94	120	80	3	105	5	2	7	4	4	.50	13	.283	.366	.530

Robby Stanifer

Pitches: Right **Bats:** Right **Pos:** RP-36 **Ht:** 6'3" **Wt:** 205 **Born:** 3/10/72 **Age:** 26

Year Team	Lg	HOW MUCH HE PITCHED						WHAT HE GAVE UP												THE RESULTS						
		G	GS	CG	GF	IP	BFP	H	R	ER	HR	SH	SF	HB	TBB	IBB	SO	WP	Bk	W	L	Pct.	ShO	Sv-Op	Hld	ERA
1994 Elmira	A-	9	8	1	0	49	211	54	17	14	2	0	1	2	12	1	38	2	3	2	1	.667	0	0--	—	2.57
Brevard Cty	A+	5	5	0	0	24.1	115	32	20	17	2	1	1	3	10	0	12	2	1	1	2	.333	0	0--	—	6.29
1995 Brevard Cty	A+	18	13	0	0	82.2	360	97	47	38	4	4	5	7	15	0	45	2	0	3	6	.333	0	0--	—	4.14
1996 Brevard Cty	A+	22	0	0	4	49	206	54	17	13	3	0	1	1	9	0	32	1	0	4	2	.667	0	0--	—	2.39
Portland	AA	18	0	0	10	34.1	137	27	15	6	3	1	2	1	7	0	33	2	0	3	1	.750	0	2--	—	1.57
1997 Charlotte	AAA	22	0	0	16	27.2	123	34	16	15	3	1	1	1	7	0	25	2	0	4	0	1.000	0	5--	—	4.88
1997 Florida	NL	36	0	0	10	45	188	43	23	23	9	4	0	3	16	0	28	1	0	1	2	.333	0	1-2	4	4.60

Andy Stankiewicz

Bats: R **Throws:** R **Pos:** PH-42; 2B-25; SS-14; 3B-3; DH-2 **Ht:** 5'9" **Wt:** 165 **Born:** 8/10/64 **Age:** 33

Year Team	Lg	BATTING																	BASERUNNING				PERCENTAGES		
		G	AB	H	2B	3B	HR	Hm	Rd	TB	R	RBI	TBB	IBB	SO	HBP	SH	SF	SB	CS	SB%	GDP	Avg	OBP	SLG
1992 New York	AL	116	400	107	22	2	2	2	0	139	52	25	38	0	42	5	7	1	9	5	.64	13	.268	.338	.348
1993 New York	AL	16	9	0	0	0	0	0	0	0	5	0	1	0	1	0	0	0	0	0	.00	0	.000	.100	.000
1994 Houston	NL	37	54	14	3	0	1	1	0	20	10	5	12	0	12	1	2	0	1	1	.50	2	.259	.403	.370
1995 Houston	NL	43	52	6	1	0	0	0	0	7	6	7	12	2	19	0	1	0	4	2	.67	1	.115	.281	.135
1996 Montreal	NL	64	77	22	5	1	0	0	0	29	12	9	6	1	12	3	1	1	1	0	1.00	1	.286	.356	.377
1997 Montreal	NL	76	107	24	9	0	1	0	1	36	11	5	4	0	22	0	7	1	1	1	.50	1	.224	.250	.336
6 ML YEARS		352	699	173	40	3	4	3	1	231	96	51	73	3	108	9	18	3	16	9	.64	18	.247	.325	.330

Mike Stanley

Bats: R **Throws:** R **Pos:** DH-69; 1B-43; PH-34; C-15 **Ht:** 6'0" **Wt:** 190 **Born:** 6/25/63 **Age:** 35

Year Team	Lg	BATTING																	BASERUNNING				PERCENTAGES		
		G	AB	H	2B	3B	HR	Hm	Rd	TB	R	RBI	TBB	IBB	SO	HBP	SH	SF	SB	CS	SB%	GDP	Avg	OBP	SLG
1986 Texas	AL	15	30	10	3	0	1	0	1	16	4	1	3	0	7	0	0	0	1	0	1.00	0	.333	.394	.533
1987 Texas	AL	78	216	59	8	1	6	3	3	87	34	37	31	0	48	1	1	6	3	0	1.00	6	.273	.361	.403
1988 Texas	AL	94	249	57	8	0	3	1	2	74	21	27	37	0	62	0	1	5	0	0	.00	6	.229	.323	.297
1989 Texas	AL	67	122	30	3	1	1	1	0	38	9	11	12	1	29	2	1	0	0	0	.00	5	.246	.324	.311
1990 Texas	AL	103	189	47	8	1	2	1	1	63	21	19	30	2	25	0	6	1	1	0	1.00	4	.249	.350	.333
1991 Texas	AL	95	181	45	13	1	3	1	1	69	25	25	34	0	44	2	5	1	0	0	.00	5	.249	.372	.381
1992 New York	AL	68	173	43	7	0	8	5	3	74	24	27	33	0	45	1	0	0	0	0	.00	6	.249	.372	.428
1993 New York	AL	130	423	129	17	1	26	17	9	226	70	84	57	1	85	5	0	6	1	0	.50	10	.305	.389	.534

Year Team	Lg	G	AB	H	2B	3B	HR	(Hm	Rd)	TB	R	RBI	TBB	IBB	SO	HBP	SH	SF	SB	CS	SB%	GDP	Avg	OBP	SLG
						BATTING														BASERUNNING				PERCENTAGES		
1994 New York	AL	82	290	87	20	0	17	(8	9)	158	54	57	39	2	56	2	0	2	0	0	.00	10	.300	.384	.545
1995 New York	AL	118	399	107	29	1	18	(13	5)	192	63	83	57	1	106	5	0	9	1	1	.50	14	.268	.360	.481
1996 Boston	AL	121	397	107	20	1	24	(10	14)	201	73	69	69	3	62	5	0	2	2	0	1.00	8	.270	.383	.506
1997 Bos-NYA	AL	125	347	103	25	0	16	(6	10)	176	61	65	54	4	72	6	0	8	0	1	.00	13	.297	.393	.507
1997 Boston	AL	97	260	78	17	0	13	(5	8)	134	45	53	39	0	50	6	0	7	0	1	.00	9	.300	.394	.515
New York	AL	28	87	25	8	0	3	(1	2)	42	16	12	15	4	22	0	0	1	0	0	.00	4	.287	.388	.483
12 ML YEARS		1096	3016	824	161	7	125	(66	59)	1374	459	505	456	17	641	29	14	38	10	3	.77	84	.273	.370	.456

Mike Stanton

Pitches: Left   Bats: Left   Pos: RP-64   Ht: 6'1"   Wt: 215   Born: 6/2/67   Age: 31

Year Team	Lg	G	GS	CG	GF	IP	BFP	H	R	ER	HR	SH	SF	HB	TBB	IBB	SO	WP	Bk	W	L	Pct.	ShO	Sv-Op	Hld	ERA
		HOW MUCH HE PITCHED						WHAT HE GAVE UP												THE RESULTS						
1989 Atlanta	NL	20	0	0	10	24	94	17	4	4	0	4	0	0	8	1	27	1	0	0	1	.000	0	7-8	2	1.50
1990 Atlanta	NL	7	0	0	4	7	42	16	16	14	1	1	0	1	4	2	7	1	0	0	3	.000	0	2-3	0	18.00
1991 Atlanta	NL	74	0	0	20	78	314	62	27	25	6	6	0	1	21	6	54	0	0	5	5	.500	0	7-10	15	2.88
1992 Atlanta	NL	65	0	0	23	63.2	264	59	32	29	6	1	2	2	20	2	44	3	0	5	4	.556	0	8-11	15	4.10
1993 Atlanta	NL	63	0	0	41	52	236	51	33	27	4	5	2	0	29	7	43	1	0	4	6	.400	0	27-33	5	4.67
1994 Atlanta	NL	49	0	0	15	45.2	197	41	18	18	2	2	1	3	26	3	35	1	0	3	1	.750	0	3-4	10	3.55
1995 Atl-Bos		48	0	0	22	40.1	178	48	23	19	6	2	1	1	14	2	23	2	1	2	1	.667	0	1-3	8	4.24
1996 Bos-Tex	AL	81	0	0	28	78.2	327	78	32	32	11	4	2	0	27	5	60	3	2	4	4	.500	0	1-6	22	3.66
1997 New York	AL	64	0	0	15	66.2	283	50	19	19	3	2	0	3	34	2	70	3	2	6	1	.857	0	3-5	26	2.57
1995 Atlanta	NL	26	0	0	10	19.1	94	31	14	12	3	2	1	1	6	2	13	1	1	1	1	.500	0	1-2	4	5.59
Boston	AL	22	0	0	12	21	84	17	9	7	3	0	0	0	8	0	10	1	0	1	0	1.000	0	0-1	4	3.00
1996 Boston	AL	59	0	0	19	56.1	239	58	24	24	8	2	0	0	23	4	46	3	2	4	3	.571	0	1-5	15	3.83
Texas	AL	22	0	0	9	22.1	88	20	8	8	2	1	0	0	4	1	14	0	0	1	0	.000	0	0-1	7	3.22
9 ML YEARS		471	0	0	178	456	1935	422	206	187	39	27	8	11	183	26	363	15	5	29	26	.527	0	59-83	103	3.69

Terry Steinbach

Bats: R   Throws: R   Pos: C-116; PH-6; 1B-2; DH-1   Ht: 6'1"   Wt: 195   Born: 3/2/62   Age: 36

Year Team	Lg	G	AB	H	2B	3B	HR	(Hm	Rd)	TB	R	RBI	TBB	IBB	SO	HBP	SH	SF	SB	CS	SB%	GDP	Avg	OBP	SLG
						BATTING														BASERUNNING				PERCENTAGES		
1986 Oakland	AL	6	15	5	0	0	2	(0	2)	11	3	4	1	0	0	0	0	0	0	0	.00	0	.333	.375	.733
1987 Oakland	AL	122	391	111	16	3	16	(6	10)	181	66	56	32	2	66	9	3	3	1	2	.33	10	.284	.349	.463
1988 Oakland	AL	104	351	93	19	1	9	(6	3)	141	42	51	33	2	47	6	3	5	3	0	1.00	13	.265	.334	.402
1989 Oakland	AL	130	454	124	13	1	7	(5	2)	160	37	42	30	2	66	2	2	3	1	2	.33	14	.273	.319	.352
1990 Oakland	AL	114	379	95	15	2	9	(3	6)	141	32	57	19	1	66	4	5	3	0	1	.00	11	.251	.291	.372
1991 Oakland	AL	129	456	125	31	1	6	(1	5)	176	50	67	22	4	70	7	0	9	2	2	.50	15	.274	.312	.386
1992 Oakland	AL	128	438	122	20	1	12	(3	9)	180	48	53	45	3	58	1	0	3	2	3	.40	20	.279	.345	.411
1993 Oakland	AL	104	389	111	19	1	10	(5	5)	162	47	43	25	1	65	3	0	1	3	3	.50	13	.285	.333	.416
1994 Oakland	AL	103	369	105	21	2	11	(5	6)	163	51	57	26	4	62	0	1	6	2	1	.67	10	.285	.327	.442
1995 Oakland	AL	114	406	113	26	1	15	(9	6)	186	43	65	25	4	74	3	1	4	1	3	.25	15	.278	.322	.458
1996 Oakland	AL	145	514	140	25	1	35	(16	19)	272	79	100	49	5	115	6	0	2	0	1	.00	16	.272	.342	.529
1997 Minnesota	AL	122	447	111	27	1	12	(6	6)	176	60	54	35	2	106	1	0	4	6	1	.86	14	.248	.302	.394
12 ML YEARS		1321	4609	1255	232	15	144	(65	79)	1949	558	649	342	30	795	42	15	43	21	19	.53	151	.272	.325	.423

Garrett Stephenson

Pitches: Right   Bats: Right   Pos: SP-18; RP-2   Ht: 6'4"   Wt: 195   Born: 1/2/72   Age: 26

Year Team	Lg	G	GS	CG	GF	IP	BFP	H	R	ER	HR	SH	SF	HB	TBB	IBB	SO	WP	Bk	W	L	Pct.	ShO	Sv-Op	Hld	ERA
		HOW MUCH HE PITCHED						WHAT HE GAVE UP												THE RESULTS						
1992 Bluefield	R+	12	3	0	0	32.1	141	35	22	17	4	0	1	1	7	0	30	4	1	3	1	.750	0	0-	—	4.73
1993 Albany	A	30	24	3	3	171.1	697	142	65	54	6	1	4	5	44	0	147	3	5	16	7	.696	2	1-	—	2.84
1994 Frederick	A+	18	17	1	0	107.1	450	91	62	48	13	2	5	5	36	2	133	2	4	7	5	.583	0	0-	—	4.02
Bowie	AA	7	7	1	0	36.2	161	47	22	21	2	0	1	0	11	1	32	3	2	3	2	.600	1	0-	—	5.15
1995 Bowie	AA	29	29	1	0	175.1	743	154	87	71	23	5	7	18	47	0	139	4	2	7	10	.412	0	0-	—	3.64
1996 Rochester	AAA	23	21	3	1	121.2	515	123	66	65	13	2	5	10	44	0	86	3	2	7	6	.538	1	0-	—	4.81
1997 Scranton-WB	AAA	7	3	0	1	29	125	27	19	19	6	0	1	0	12	0	27	2	0	3	1	.750	0	0-	—	5.90
1996 Baltimore	AL	3	0	0	2	6.1	35	13	9	9	1	1	0	1	3	1	3	0	0	0	1	.000	0	0-0	0	12.79
1997 Philadelphia	NL	20	18	2	0	117	474	104	45	41	11	2	5	3	38	0	81	1	0	8	6	.571	0	0-0	0	3.15
2 ML YEARS		23	18	2	2	123.1	509	117	54	50	12	3	5	4	41	1	84	1	0	8	7	.533	0	0-0	0	3.65

Dave Stevens

Pitches: Right   Bats: Right   Pos: RP-10; SP-6   Ht: 6'3"   Wt: 205   Born: 3/4/70   Age: 28

Year Team	Lg	G	GS	CG	GF	IP	BFP	H	R	ER	HR	SH	SF	HB	TBB	IBB	SO	WP	Bk	W	L	Pct.	ShO	Sv-Op	Hld	ERA
		HOW MUCH HE PITCHED						WHAT HE GAVE UP												THE RESULTS						
1997 Salt Lake *	AAA	16	14	1	0	90	395	93	52	43	10	1	2	4	31	0	71	4	1	9	3	.750	0	0-	—	4.30
Iowa *	AAA	6	0	0	5	7.2	34	8	4	4	0	1	0	0	5	1	8	0	0	1	1	.500	0	1-	—	4.70
1994 Minnesota	AL	24	0	0	6	45	208	55	35	34	6	2	0	1	23	2	24	3	0	5	2	.714	0	0-0	0	6.80
1995 Minnesota	AL	56	0	0	34	65.2	302	74	40	37	14	4	5	1	32	1	47	2	0	5	4	.556	0	10-12	5	5.07
1996 Minnesota	AL	49	0	0	38	58	251	58	30	30	12	3	0	2	25	2	29	1	0	3	3	.500	0	11-16	0	4.66
1997 Min-ChN		16	6	0	0	32.1	174	54	34	33	8	0	1	1	26	0	29	1	3	1	5	.167	0	0-0	0	9.19
1997 Minnesota	AL	6	6	0	0	23	124	41	23	23	8	0	0	1	17	0	16	1	2	1	3	.250	0	0-0	0	9.00
Chicago	NL	10	0	0	0	9.1	50	13	11	10	0	0	1	1	9	0	13	0	1	0	2	.000	0	0-0	0	9.64
4 ML YEARS		145	6	0	78	201	935	241	140	134	40	9	9	3	106	5	129	7	3	14	14	.500	0	21-28	6	6.00

Lee Stevens

Bats: L **Throws:** L **Pos:** 1B-62; DH-38; PH-27; RF-19; LF-3   **Ht:** 6'4" **Wt:** 219 **Born:** 7/10/67 **Age:** 30

Year Team	Lg	G	AB	H	2B	3B	HR	(Hm	Rd)	TB	R	RBI	TBB	IBB	SO	HBP	SH	SF	SB	CS	SB%	GDP	Avg	OBP	SLG
1990 California	AL	67	248	53	10	0	7	(4	3)	84	28	32	22	3	75	0	2	3	1	1	.50	8	.214	.275	.339
1991 California	AL	18	58	17	7	0	0	(0	0)	24	8	9	6	2	12	0	1	1	2	2	.33	0	.293	.354	.414
1992 California	AL	106	312	69	19	0	7	(2	5)	109	25	37	29	6	64	1	1	2	1	4	.20	4	.221	.288	.349
1996 Texas	AL	27	78	14	2	3	3	(2	1)	35	6	12	6	0	22	1	0	1	0	0	.00	2	.231	.291	.449
1997 Texas	AL	137	426	128	24	2	21	(12	9)	219	58	74	23	2	83	1	1	3	1	3	.25	18	.300	.336	.514
5 ML YEARS		355	1122	285	62	5	38	(20	18)	471	125	164	86	13	256	3	5	10	4	10	.29	32	.254	.306	.420

Andy Stewart

Bats: Right **Throws:** Right **Pos:** C-4; PH-2; DH-1   **Ht:** 5'11" **Wt:** 205 **Born:** 12/5/70 **Age:** 27

Year Team	Lg	G	AB	H	2B	3B	HR	(Hm	Rd)	TB	R	RBI	TBB	IBB	SO	HBP	SH	SF	SB	CS	SB%	GDP	Avg	OBP	SLG
1990 Royals	R	21	52	10	4	0	0	—	—	14	5	1	9	1	13	3	3	0	3	0	1.00	0	.192	.344	.269
1991 Baseball Cy	A+	78	276	64	16	1	3	—	—	91	30	36	7	1	59	4	4	2	6	4	.60	6	.232	.260	.330
1992 Baseball Cy	A+	94	283	73	13	1	4	—	—	100	31	38	21	1	45	2	4	1	3	8	.27	4	.258	.313	.353
1993 Wilmington	A+	110	361	100	20	3	8	—	—	150	54	42	26	0	88	8	0	1	7	1	.88	6	.277	.338	.416
1994 Wilmington	A+	94	360	114	24	3	17	—	—	195	53	66	30	4	56	13	2	4	0	2	.00	11	.317	.386	.542
Memphis	AA	20	72	17	1	0	0	—	—	18	10	5	3	1	5	4	1	1	0	0	.00	3	.236	.300	.250
1995 Wichita	AA	60	216	56	18	0	3	—	—	83	28	32	11	0	31	4	0	2	1	2	.33	9	.259	.305	.384
Omaha	AAA	44	156	47	11	0	3	—	—	67	24	21	12	1	18	8	0	0	0	1	.00	9	.301	.381	.429
1996 Omaha	AAA	50	181	39	10	2	2	—	—	59	23	13	15	0	25	5	0	1	0	2	.00	9	.215	.292	.326
Wichita	AA	58	202	61	17	3	3	—	—	93	29	32	14	1	25	4	2	2	3	2	.60	9	.302	.356	.460
1997 Omaha	AAA	86	288	79	10	1	6	—	—	109	38	24	18	0	43	9	5	1	1	1	.50	11	.274	.335	.378
1997 Kansas City	AL	5	8	2	1	0	0	(0	0)	3	1	0	0	0	0	0	0	0	0	0	.00	0	.250	.250	.375

Shannon Stewart

Bats: R **Throws:** R **Pos:** CF-40; PH-3; LF-2; DH-1   **Ht:** 6'1" **Wt:** 190 **Born:** 2/25/74 **Age:** 24

Year Team	Lg	G	AB	H	2B	3B	HR	(Hm	Rd)	TB	R	RBI	TBB	IBB	SO	HBP	SH	SF	SB	CS	SB%	GDP	Avg	OBP	SLG
1992 Blue Jays	R	50	172	40	1	0	1	—	—	44	44	11	24	0	27	3	4	2	32	5	.86	3	.233	.333	.256
1993 St. Cathrns	A-	75	301	84	15	2	3	—	—	112	53	29	33	1	43	2	3	3	25	10	.71	7	.279	.351	.372
1994 Hagerstown	A	56	225	73	10	5	4	—	—	105	39	25	23	1	39	1	2	2	15	11	.58	3	.324	.386	.467
1995 Knoxville	AA	138	498	143	24	6	5	—	—	194	89	55	89	3	61	6	3	5	42	16	.72	13	.287	.398	.390
1996 Syracuse	AAA	112	420	125	26	8	6	—	—	185	77	42	54	0	61	2	5	4	35	8	.81	6	.298	.377	.440
1997 Syracuse	AAA	58	208	72	13	1	5	—	—	102	41	24	36	3	26	4	1	0	9	6	.60	1	.346	.452	.490
1995 Toronto	AL	12	38	8	0	0	0	(0	0)	8	2	1	5	0	5	1	0	0	2	0	1.00	0	.211	.318	.211
1996 Toronto	AL	7	17	3	1	0	0	(0	0)	4	2	2	1	0	4	0	0	0	1	0	1.00	1	.176	.222	.235
1997 Toronto	AL	44	168	48	13	7	0	(0	0)	75	25	22	19	1	24	4	0	2	10	3	.77	3	.286	.368	.446
3 ML YEARS		63	223	59	14	7	0	(0	0)	87	29	25	25	1	33	5	0	2	13	3	.81	4	.265	.349	.390

Kelly Stinnett

Bats: Right **Throws:** Right **Pos:** C-25; PH-8; DH-1   **Ht:** 5'11" **Wt:** 195 **Born:** 2/14/70 **Age:** 28

Year Team	Lg	G	AB	H	2B	3B	HR	(Hm	Rd)	TB	R	RBI	TBB	IBB	SO	HBP	SH	SF	SB	CS	SB%	GDP	Avg	OBP	SLG
1997 Tucson *	AAA	64	209	67	15	3	10	—	—	118	50	43	42	1	46	6	0	2	1	1	.50	2	.321	.444	.565
1994 New York	NL	47	150	38	6	2	2	(0	2)	54	20	14	11	1	28	5	0	1	2	0	1.00	3	.253	.323	.360
1995 New York	NL	77	196	43	8	1	4	(1	3)	65	23	18	29	3	65	6	0	0	2	0	1.00	3	.219	.338	.332
1996 Milwaukee	AL	14	26	2	0	0	0	(0	0)	2	1	0	2	0	11	1	0	0	0	0	.00	0	.077	.172	.077
1997 Milwaukee	AL	30	36	9	4	0	0	(0	0)	13	2	3	3	0	9	0	0	0	0	0	.00	0	.250	.308	.361
4 ML YEARS		168	408	92	18	3	6	(1	5)	134	46	35	45	4	113	12	0	1	4	0	1.00	6	.225	.320	.328

Kevin Stocker

Bats: Both **Throws:** Right **Pos:** SS-147; PH-2   **Ht:** 6'1" **Wt:** 175 **Born:** 2/13/70 **Age:** 28

Year Team	Lg	G	AB	H	2B	3B	HR	(Hm	Rd)	TB	R	RBI	TBB	IBB	SO	HBP	SH	SF	SB	CS	SB%	GDP	Avg	OBP	SLG
1993 Philadelphia	NL	70	259	84	12	3	2	(1	1)	108	46	31	30	11	43	8	4	1	5	0	1.00	8	.324	.409	.417
1994 Philadelphia	NL	82	271	74	11	2	2	(2	0)	95	38	28	44	8	41	7	4	4	2	2	.50	3	.273	.383	.351
1995 Philadelphia	NL	125	412	90	14	3	1	(1	0)	113	42	32	43	9	75	9	10	3	6	1	.86	7	.218	.304	.274
1996 Philadelphia	NL	119	394	100	22	6	5	(0	5)	149	46	41	43	9	89	8	3	4	6	4	.60	6	.254	.336	.378
1997 Philadelphia	NL	149	504	134	23	5	4	(2	2)	179	51	40	51	7	91	2	3	1	11	6	.65	14	.266	.335	.355
5 ML YEARS		545	1840	482	82	19	14	(6	8)	644	223	172	211	44	339	34	23	13	30	13	.70	38	.262	.347	.350

Todd Stottlemyre

Pitches: Right **Bats:** Left **Pos:** SP-28   **Ht:** 6'3" **Wt:** 200 **Born:** 5/20/65 **Age:** 33

Year Team	Lg	G	GS	CG	GF	IP	BFP	H	R	ER	HR	SH	SF	HB	TBB	IBB	SO	WP	Bk	W	L	Pct.	ShO	Sv-Op	Hld	ERA
1988 Toronto	AL	28	16	0	2	98	443	109	70	62	15	5	3	4	46	5	67	2	3	4	8	.333	0	0-1	0	5.69
1989 Toronto	AL	27	18	0	4	127.2	545	137	56	55	11	3	4	4	44	4	63	4	1	7	7	.500	0	0-0	0	3.88
1990 Toronto	AL	33	33	4	0	203	866	214	101	98	18	3	5	8	69	4	115	6	1	13	17	.433	0	0-0	0	4.34
1991 Toronto	AL	34	34	1	0	219	921	194	97	92	21	0	8	12	75	3	116	4	0	15	8	.652	0	0-0	0	3.78

Year Team	Lg	G	GS	CG	GF	IP	BFP	H	R	ER	HR	SH	SF	HB	TBB	IBB	SO	WP	Bk	W	L	Pct.	ShO	Sv-Op	Hld	ERA
1992 Toronto	AL	28	27	6	0	174	755	175	99	87	20	2	11	10	63	4	98	7	0	12	11	.522	2	0-0	0	4.50
1993 Toronto	AL	30	28	1	0	176.2	786	204	107	95	11	5	11	3	69	5	98	7	1	11	12	.478	1	0-0	0	4.84
1994 Toronto	AL	26	19	3	5	140.2	605	149	67	66	19	4	5	7	48	2	105	0	0	7	7	.500	1	1-3	0	4.22
1995 Oakland	AL	31	31	2	0	209.2	920	228	117	106	26	4	4	6	80	7	205	11	0	14	7	.667	0	0-0	0	4.55
1996 St. Louis	NL	34	33	5	0	223.1	944	191	100	96	30	12	9	4	93	8	194	8	1	14	11	.560	2	0-0	0	3.87
1997 St. Louis	NL	28	28	0	0	181	761	155	86	78	16	8	5	12	65	3	160	6	0	12	9	.571	0	0-0	0	3.88
10 ML YEARS		299	267	22	11	1753	7546	1756	900	835	187	46	68	71	652	45	1221	55	7	109	97	.529	6	1-4	0	4.29

Doug Strange

Bats: B **Throws:** R **Pos:** 3B-105; PH-9; 2B-3; LF-2; 1B-1   **Ht:** 6'1" **Wt:** 185 **Born:** 4/13/64 **Age:** 34

Year Team	Lg	G	AB	H	2B	3B	HR	(Hm	Rd)	TB	R	RBI	TBB	IBB	SO	HBP	SH	SF	SB	CS	SB%	GDP	Avg	OBP	SLG
1997 Ottawa *	AAA	2	7	3	1	0	0	—	—	4	3	1	0	1	0	0	0	0	0	0	.00	2	.429	.500	.571
1989 Detroit	AL	64	196	42	4	1	1	(1	0)	51	16	14	17	0	36	1	3	0	3	3	.50	6	.214	.280	.260
1991 Chicago	NL	3	9	4	1	0	0	(0	0)	5	0	1	0	0	1	1	0	1	1	0	1.00	0	.444	.455	.556
1992 Chicago	NL	52	94	15	1	0	1	(0	1)	19	7	5	10	2	15	0	2	0	1	0	1.00	1	.160	.240	.202
1993 Texas	AL	145	484	124	29	0	7	(4	3)	174	58	60	43	3	69	3	8	4	6	4	.60	12	.256	.318	.360
1994 Texas	AL	73	226	48	12	1	5	(3	2)	77	26	26	15	0	38	3	4	2	1	3	.25	6	.212	.268	.341
1995 Seattle	AL	74	155	42	9	2	2	(1	1)	61	19	21	10	0	25	2	1	0	0	3	.00	5	.271	.323	.394
1996 Seattle	AL	88	183	43	7	1	3	(2	1)	61	19	23	14	0	31	1	0	2	1	0	1.00	3	.235	.290	.333
1997 Montreal	NL	118	327	84	16	2	12	(6	6)	140	40	47	36	9	76	2	5	2	0	2	.00	1	.257	.332	.428
8 ML YEARS		617	1674	402	79	7	31	(17	14)	588	185	197	145	14	291	13	23	11	13	15	.46	36	.240	.304	.351

Darryl Strawberry

Bats: Left **Throws:** Left **Pos:** DH-4; LF-4; PH-3   **Ht:** 6'6" **Wt:** 215 **Born:** 3/12/62 **Age:** 36

Year Team	Lg	G	AB	H	2B	3B	HR	(Hm	Rd)	TB	R	RBI	TBB	IBB	SO	HBP	SH	SF	SB	CS	SB%	GDP	Avg	OBP	SLG
1997 Norwich *	AA	1	2	0	0	0	0	—	—	0	0	0	0	0	1	0	0	0	0	0	.00	1	.000	.000	.000
Tampa *	A+	4	16	7	1	0	0	—	—	8	2	4	1	0	3	0	0	0	0	0	.00	1	.438	.471	.500
Columbus *	AAA	1	38	11	3	0	6			32	8	19	8	0	10	0	0	1	0	0	.00	1	.289	.404	.842
1983 New York	NL	122	420	108	15	7	26	(10	16)	215	63	74	47	9	128	4	0	2	19	6	.76	5	.257	.336	.512
1984 New York	NL	147	522	131	27	4	26	(8	18)	244	75	97	75	15	131	0	1	4	27	8	.77	9	.251	.343	.467
1985 New York	NL	111	393	109	15	4	29	(14	15)	219	78	79	73	13	96	1	0	3	26	11	.70	9	.277	.389	.557
1986 New York	NL	136	475	123	27	5	27	(11	16)	241	76	93	72	9	141	6	0	9	28	12	.70	4	.259	.358	.507
1987 New York	NL	154	532	151	32	5	39	(19	19)	310	108	104	97	13	122	7	0	4	36	12	.75	4	.284	.398	.583
1988 New York	NL	153	543	146	27	3	39	(21	18)	296	101	101	85	21	127	3	0	9	29	14	.67	6	.269	.366	.545
1989 New York	NL	134	476	107	26	1	29	(15	14)	222	69	77	61	13	105	1	0	3	11	4	.73	4	.225	.312	.466
1990 New York	NL	152	542	150	18	1	37	(24	13)	281	92	108	70	15	110	4	0	5	15	8	.65	5	.277	.361	.518
1991 Los Angeles	NL	139	505	134	22	4	28	(14	14)	248	86	99	75	4	125	3	0	5	10	8	.56	8	.265	.361	.491
1992 Los Angeles	NL	43	156	37	8	0	5	(3	2)	60	20	25	19	4	34	1	0	1	3	1	.75	2	.237	.322	.385
1993 Los Angeles	NL	32	100	14	2	0	5	(3	2)	31	12	12	16	1	19	2	0	2	1	0	1.00	1	.140	.267	.310
1994 San Francisco	NL	29	92	22	3	1	4	(2	2)	39	13	17	19	4	22	0	0	2	0	3	.00	2	.239	.363	.424
1995 New York	AL	32	87	24	4	1	3	(3	0)	39	15	13	10	1	22	2	0	0	0	0	.00	0	.276	.364	.448
1996 New York	AL	63	202	53	13	0	11	(8	3)	99	35	36	31	5	55	1	0	3	6	5	.55	3	.262	.359	.490
1997 New York	AL	11	29	3	1	0	0	(0	0)	4	1	2	3	0	9	0	0	0	0	1	.00	2	.103	.188	.138
15 ML YEARS		1458	5074	1312	240	36	308	(156	152)	2548	844	937	753	127	1246	35	1	52	211	92	.70	63	.259	.355	.502

Everett Stull

Pitches: Right **Bats:** Right **Pos:** RP-3   **Ht:** 6'3" **Wt:** 200 **Born:** 8/24/71 **Age:** 26

Year Team	Lg	G	GS	CG	GF	IP	BFP	H	R	ER	HR	SH	SF	HB	TBB	IBB	SO	WP	Bk	W	L	Pct.	ShO	Sv-Op	Hld	ERA
1992 Jamestown	A-	14	14	0	0	63.1	303	52	49	38	2	2	3	3	61	0	64	18	4	3	5	.375	0	0- -	—	5.40
1993 Burlington	A	15	15	1	0	82.1	366	68	44	35	8	2	1	3	59	0	85	11	4	4	9	.308	0	0- -	—	3.83
1994 Wst Plm Bch	A+	27	26	3	0	147	627	116	60	54	3	7	3	12	78	0	165	15	6	10	10	.500	1	0- -	—	3.31
1995 Harrisburg	AA	24	24	0	0	126.2	569	114	88	78	12	5	5	9	79	2	132	7	1	3	12	.200	0	0- -	—	5.54
1996 Harrisburg	AA	14	14	0	0	80	345	64	31	28	8	3	2	2	52	1	81	6	0	6	3	.667	0	0- -	—	3.15
Ottawa	AAA	13	13	1	0	69.2	331	87	57	49	7	3	3	3	39	1	69	5	0	2	6	.250	0	0- -	—	6.33
1997 Ottawa	AAA	27	27	1	0	159.1	710	166	110	103	25	4	4	13	86	0	130	9	0	8	10	.444	0	0- -	—	5.82
1997 Montreal	NL	3	0	0	1	3.1	21	7	7	6	1	1	0	0	4	0	2	0	0	0	1	.000	0	0-0	0	16.20

Tanyon Sturtze

Pitches: Right **Bats:** Right **Pos:** SP-5; RP-4   **Ht:** 6'5" **Wt:** 205 **Born:** 10/12/70 **Age:** 27

Year Team	Lg	G	GS	CG	GF	IP	BFP	H	R	ER	HR	SH	SF	HB	TBB	IBB	SO	WP	Bk	W	L	Pct.	ShO	Sv-Op	Hld	ERA
1990 Athletics	R	12	10	0	1	48	232	55	41	29	3	0	2	5	26	0	30	5	2	2	5	.286	0	0- -	—	5.44
1991 Madison	A	27	27	0	0	163	685	136	77	56	5	6	6	5	58	5	88	10	5	10	5	.667	0	0- -	—	3.09
1992 Modesto	A+	25	25	1	0	151	656	143	72	63	6	5	5	4	78	1	102	9	1	7	11	.389	0	0- -	—	3.75
1993 Huntsville	AA	28	28	1	0	165.2	734	169	102	88	16	3	11	6	85	2	112	11	1	5	12	.294	1	0- -	—	4.78
1994 Huntsville	AA	17	17	1	0	103.1	435	100	40	37	5	3	4	3	39	1	63	1	0	6	3	.667	0	0- -	—	3.22
Tacoma	AAA	11	9	0	2	64.2	294	73	36	29	5	0	1	2	34	2	28	6	0	4	5	.444	0	0- -	—	4.04
1995 Iowa	AAA	23	17	1	0	86	398	108	66	65	18	5	2	5	42	1	48	5	0	4	7	.364	1	0- -	—	6.80
1996 Iowa	AAA	51	1	0	18	72.1	315	80	42	39	7	3	0	3	23	2	51	6	1	4	6	.400	0	4- -	—	4.85
1997 Okla City	AAA	25	19	1	3	114.2	515	133	76	65	10	1	7	9	47	1	79	3	1	8	6	.571	0	0- -	—	5.10
1995 Chicago	NL	2	0	0	0	2	9	2	2	2	1	0	0	0	0	0	0	0	0	0	0	.000	0	0-0	0	9.00

Year Team	Lg	G	GS	CG	GF	IP	BFP	H	R	ER	HR	SH	SF	HB	TBB	IBB	SO	WP	Bk	W	L	Pct.	ShO	Sv-Op	Hld	ERA
1996 Chicago	NL	6	0	0	3	11	51	16	11	11	3	0	0	0	5	0	7	0	0	1	0	1.000	0	0-0	0	9.00
1997 Texas	AL	9	5	0	1	32.2	155	45	30	30	6	0	4	0	18	0	18	1	1	1	1	.500	0	0-0	0	8.27
3 ML YEARS		17	5	0	4	45.2	215	63	43	43	10	0	4	0	24	0	25	1	1	2	1	.667	0	0-0	0	8.47

Chris Stynes

Bats: Right **Throws:** Right **Pos:** LF-38; 2B-8; 3B-3   **Ht:** 5'9" **Wt:** 175 **Born:** 1/19/73 **Age:** 25

Year Team	Lg	G	AB	H	2B	3B	HR	(Hm	Rd)	TB	R	RBI	TBB	IBB	SO	HBP	SH	SF	SB	CS	SB%	GDP	Avg	OBP	SLG
1997 Omaha *	AAA	82	332	88	18	1	8	—	—	132	53	44	19	1	25	0	4	2	3	1	.75	7	.265	.303	.398
Indianapolis *	AAA	21	86	31	8	0	1	—	—	42	14	17	2	0	5	1	1	2	4	1	.80	3	.360	.374	.488
1995 Kansas City	AL	22	35	6	1	0	0	(0	0)	7	7	2	4	0	3	0	0	0	0	0	.00	3	.171	.256	.200
1996 Kansas City	AL	36	92	27	6	0	0	(0	0)	33	8	6	2	0	5	0	1	0	5	2	.71	1	.293	.309	.359
1997 Cincinnati	NL	49	198	69	7	1	6	(2	4)	96	31	28	11	1	13	4	2	0	11	2	.85	5	.348	.394	.485
3 ML YEARS		107	325	102	14	1	6	(2	4)	136	46	36	17	1	21	4	3	0	16	4	.80	9	.314	.355	.418

Scott Sullivan

Pitches: Right **Bats:** Right **Pos:** RP-59   **Ht:** 6'4" **Wt:** 210 **Born:** 3/13/71 **Age:** 27

Year Team	Lg	G	GS	CG	GF	IP	BFP	H	R	ER	HR	SH	SF	HB	TBB	IBB	SO	WP	Bk	W	L	Pct.	ShO	Sv-Op	Hld	ERA
1993 Billings	R+	18	7	2	9	54	224	33	13	10	1	3	0	6	25	0	79	2	5	5	0	1.000	2	5- -	—	1.67
1994 Chattanooga	AA	34	13	2	16	121.1	508	101	60	46	8	2	1	6	40	1	111	6	4	11	7	.611	0	7- -	—	3.41
1995 Indianapolis	AAA	44	0	0	21	58.2	253	51	31	23	2	3	4	2	24	4	54	3	0	4	3	.571	0	1- -	—	3.53
1996 Indianapolis	AAA	53	3	0	12	108.2	452	95	38	33	10	1	2	4	37	3	77	5	0	5	2	.714	0	1- -	—	2.73
1997 Indianapolis	AAA	19	0	0	10	27.2	96	16	4	4	0	3	2	1	4	1	23	1	0	3	1	.750	0	2- -	—	1.30
1995 Cincinnati	NL	3	0	0	1	3.2	17	4	2	2	0	1	0	0	2	0	2	0	0	0	0	.000	0	0-0	0	4.91
1996 Cincinnati	NL	7	0	0	4	8	35	7	2	2	0	1	0	1	5	0	3	1	0	0	0	.000	0	0-0	0	2.25
1997 Cincinnati	NL	59	0	0	15	97.1	402	79	36	35	12	3	7	30	8	96			5		5	3	.625	0	1-2	13	3.24
3 ML YEARS		69	0	0	20	109	454	90	40	39	12	5	3	8	37	8	101	8	1	5	3	.625	0	1-2	13	3.22

Jeff Suppan

Pitches: Right **Bats:** Right **Pos:** SP-22; RP-1   **Ht:** 6'2" **Wt:** 210 **Born:** 1/2/75 **Age:** 23

Year Team	Lg	G	GS	CG	GF	IP	BFP	H	R	ER	HR	SH	SF	HB	TBB	IBB	SO	WP	Bk	W	L	Pct.	ShO	Sv-Op	Hld	ERA
1993 Red Sox	R	10	9	2	1	57.2	239	52	20	14	0	1	0	3	16	0	64	2	0	4	3	.571	1	0- -	—	2.18
1994 Sarasota	A+	27	27	4	0	174	712	153	74	63	10	6	2	6	50	0	173	6	1	13	7	.650	2	0- -	—	3.26
1995 Trenton	AA	15	15	1	0	99	409	86	35	26	5	1	3	8	26	1	88	4	0	6	2	.750	1	0- -	—	2.36
Pawtucket	AAA	7	7	0	0	45.2	191	50	29	27	9	0	1	1	9	0	32	2	0	2	3	.400	0	0- -	—	5.32
1996 Pawtucket	AAA	22	22	7	0	145.1	593	130	66	52	16	0	3	6	25	1	142	9	1	10	6	.625	1	0- -	—	3.22
1997 Pawtucket	AAA	9	9	2	0	60.2	239	51	26	25	7	0	4	1	15	0	40	2	1	5	1	.833	1	0- -	—	3.71
1995 Boston	AL	8	3	0	1	22.2	100	29	15	15	4	1	0	5	1	19	0	0	1	2	.333	0	0-0	1	5.96
1996 Boston	AL	8	4	0	2	22.2	107	29	19	19	3	1	4	1	13	0	13	3	0	1	1	.500	0	0-0	0	7.54
1997 Boston	AL	23	22	0	1	112.1	503	140	75	71	12	0	4	4	36	1	67	5	0	7	3	.700	0	0-0	0	5.69
3 ML YEARS		39	29	0	4	157.2	710	198	109	105	19	2	9	5	54	2	99	8	0	9	6	.600	0	0-0	1	5.99

B.J. Surhoff

Bats: L **Throws:** R **Pos:** LF-133; DH-9; PH-4; 1B-3; 3B-3   **Ht:** 6'1" **Wt:** 200 **Born:** 8/4/64 **Age:** 33

Year Team	Lg	G	AB	H	2B	3B	HR	(Hm	Rd)	TB	R	RBI	TBB	IBB	SO	HBP	SH	SF	SB	CS	SB%	GDP	Avg	OBP	SLG
1987 Milwaukee	AL	115	395	118	22	3	7	(5	2)	167	50	68	36	1	30	0	5	9	11	10	.52	13	.299	.350	.423
1988 Milwaukee	AL	139	493	121	21	0	5	(2	3)	157	47	38	31	9	49	3	11	3	21	6	.78	12	.245	.292	.318
1989 Milwaukee	AL	126	436	108	17	4	5	(3	2)	148	42	55	25	1	29	3	3	10	14	12	.54	8	.248	.287	.339
1990 Milwaukee	AL	135	474	131	21	4	6	(4	2)	178	55	59	41	5	37	1	7	7	18	7	.72	8	.276	.331	.376
1991 Milwaukee	AL	143	505	146	19	4	5	(3	2)	188	57	68	26	2	33	0	13	9	5	8	.38	21	.289	.319	.372
1992 Milwaukee	AL	139	480	121	19	1	4	(3	1)	154	63	62	46	8	41	2	5	10	14	8	.64	9	.252	.314	.321
1993 Milwaukee	AL	148	552	151	38	3	7	(4	3)	216	66	79	36	5	47	2	4	5	12	9	.57	9	.274	.318	.391
1994 Milwaukee	AL	40	134	35	11	2	5	(3	2)	65	20	22	16	0	14	0	2	2	0	1	.00	5	.261	.336	.485
1995 Milwaukee	AL	117	415	133	26	3	13	(7	6)	204	72	73	37	4	43	4	2	4	7	3	.70	7	.320	.378	.492
1996 Baltimore	AL	143	537	157	27	6	21	(12	9)	259	74	82	47	8	79	3	2	1	0	1	.00	7	.292	.352	.482
1997 Baltimore	AL	147	528	150	30	4	18	(10	8)	242	80	88	49	14	60	5	3	10	1	1	.50	7	.284	.345	.458
11 ML YEARS		1392	4949	1371	251	34	96	(55	41)	1978	626	694	390	57	462	23	57	70	103	66	.61	106	.277	.328	.400

Larry Sutton

Bats: L **Throws:** L **Pos:** PH-13; 1B-12; DH-3; LF-1   **Ht:** 6'0" **Wt:** 185 **Born:** 5/14/70 **Age:** 28

Year Team	Lg	G	AB	H	2B	3B	HR	(Hm	Rd)	TB	R	RBI	TBB	IBB	SO	HBP	SH	SF	SB	CS	SB%	GDP	Avg	OBP	SLG
1992 Eugene	A-	70	238	74	17	3	15	—	—	142	45	58	48	5	33	5	0	2	3	6	.33	3	.311	.433	.597
Appleton	A	1	2	0	0	0	0	—	—	0	1	2	0	1	0	0	0	0	0	1	.00	0	.000	.500	.000
1993 Rockford	A	113	361	97	24	1	7	—	—	144	67	50	95	5	65	8	0	8	3	5	.38	3	.269	.424	.399
1994 Wilmington	A+	129	480	147	33	1	26	—	—	260	91	94	81	10	71	6	1	9	2	1	.67	7	.306	.406	.542
1995 Wichita	AA	53	197	53	11	1	5	—	—	81	31	32	26	0	33	2	0	2	1	1	.50	3	.269	.357	.411
1996 Wichita	AA	125	463	137	22	2	22	—	—	229	84	84	77	3	66	8	0	6	4	1	.80	11	.296	.401	.495
1997 Omaha	AAA	106	380	114	27	1	19	—	—	200	61	72	61	4	57	0	0	2	0	0	.00	6	.300	.395	.526

			BATTING																BASERUNNING				PERCENTAGES		
Year Team	Lg	G	AB	H	2B	3B	HR	(Hm Rd)	TB	R	RBI	TBB	IBB	SO	HBP	SH	SF	SB	CS	SB%	GDP	Avg	OBP	SLG
1997 Kansas City	AL	27	69	20	2	0	2	(1 1)	28	9	8	5	0	12	0	1	0	0	0	.00	0	.290	.338	.406

Dale Sveum

Bats: B **Throws:** R **Pos:** PH-48; 3B-47; SS-28; 1B-21; 2B-2 **Ht:** 6'3" **Wt:** 185 **Born:** 11/23/63 **Age:** 34

			BATTING																BASERUNNING				PERCENTAGES		
Year Team	Lg	G	AB	H	2B	3B	HR	(Hm Rd)	TB	R	RBI	TBB	IBB	SO	HBP	SH	SF	SB	CS	SB%	GDP	Avg	OBP	SLG
1986 Milwaukee	AL	91	317	78	13	2	7	(4 3)	116	35	35	32	0	63	1	5	1	4	3	.57	7	.246	.316	.366
1987 Milwaukee	AL	153	535	135	27	3	25	(9 16)	243	86	95	40	4	133	1	5	5	2	6	.25	11	.252	.303	.454
1988 Milwaukee	AL	129	467	113	14	4	9	(2 7)	162	41	51	21	0	122	1	3	3	1	0	1.00	6	.242	.274	.347
1990 Milwaukee	AL	48	117	23	7	0	1	(1 0)	33	15	12	12	0	30	2	0	2	0	1	.00	2	.197	.278	.282
1991 Milwaukee	AL	90	266	64	19	1	4	(3 1)	97	33	43	32	0	78	1	5	4	2	4	.33	8	.241	.320	.365
1992 Phi-ChA		94	249	49	13	0	4	(1 3)	74	28	28	28	4	68	0	2	5	1	1	.50	6	.197	.273	.297
1993 Oakland	AL	30	79	14	2	1	2	(0 2)	24	12	6	16	1	21	0	1	0	0	0	.00	2	.177	.316	.304
1994 Seattle	AL	10	27	5	0	0	1	(0 1)	8	3	2	2	0	10	0	0	0	0	0	.00	1	.185	.241	.296
1996 Pittsburgh	NL	12	34	12	5	0	1	(0 1)	20	9	5	6	0	6	0	0	0	0	0	.00	0	.353	.450	.588
1997 Pittsburgh	NL	126	306	80	20	1	12	(5 7)	138	30	47	27	2	81	0	4	2	0	3	.00	8	.261	.319	.451
1992 Philadelphia	NL	54	135	24	4	0	2	(0 2)	34	13	16	16	4	39	0	2	0	0	0	.00	5	.178	.261	.252
Chicago	AL	40	114	25	9	0	2	(1 1)	40	15	12	12	0	29	0	2	3	1	1	.50	1	.219	.287	.351
10 ML YEARS		783	2397	573	120	12	66	(25 41)	915	292	324	216	11	612	6	25	22	10	18	.36	51	.239	.301	.382

Dave Swartzbaugh

Pitches: Right **Bats:** Right **Pos:** SP-2 **Ht:** 6'2" **Wt:** 210 **Born:** 2/11/68 **Age:** 30

		HOW MUCH HE PITCHED						WHAT HE GAVE UP												THE RESULTS						
Year Team	Lg	G	GS	CG	GF	IP	BFP	H	R	ER	HR	SH	SF	HB	TBB	IBB	SO	WP	Bk	W	L	Pct.	ShO	Sv-Op	Hld	ERA
1989 Geneva	A-	18	10	0	1	75	338	81	59	41	5	0	3	1	35	1	77	8	1	2	3	.400	0	0--		4.92
1990 Peoria	A	29	29	5	0	169.2	736	147	88	72	11	1	3	7	89	1	129	10	4	8	11	.421	2	0--		3.82
1991 Peoria	A	5	5	1	0	34.1	145	21	16	7	0	2	1	2	15	1	31	2	0	5	0	.000		0--		1.83
Winston-Sal	A+	15	15	2	0	93.2	379	71	22	19	3	5	1	1	42	1	73	4	0	10	4	.714	1	0--		1.83
Charlotte	AA	1	1	0	0	5.1	25	6	7	6	1	0	0	0	3	1	5	1	0	0	1	.000	0			10.13
1992 Charlotte	AA	27	27	5	0	165	689	134	78	67	13	5	10	9	62	2	111	5	1	7	10	.412	2			3.65
1993 Iowa	AAA	26	9	0	5	86.2	385	90	57	51	16	6	4	5	44	1	69	6	0	4	6	.400	0	1--		5.30
Orlando	AA	10	9	1	0	66	268	52	33	31	5	2	1	3	18	0	59	2	0	1	3	.250	0			4.23
1994 Iowa	AAA	10	0	0	1	19.1	94	24	18	18	8	1	2	1	15	1	14	2	0	1	0	1.000	0			8.38
Orlando	AA	42	1	0	11	79	327	70	36	29	7	5	3	4	19	2	70	0	0	2	4	.333	0			3.30
1995 Orlando	AA	16	0	0	3	29	111	18	10	8	1	1	1	2	7	0	37	1	1	4	0	1.000	0			2.48
Iowa	AAA	30	0	0	9	47	187	33	10	8	1	2	0	1	18	1	38	1	0	3	0	1.000	0			1.53
1996 Iowa	AAA	44	13	0	11	118.1	491	106	61	51	22	5	4	3	33	1	103	5	0	8	11	.421	0	0--		3.88
1997 Iowa	AAA	24	20	1	1	134	561	129	55	42	12	4	5	1	48	1	97	3	1	8	7	.533	1	1--		2.82
1995 Chicago	NL	7	0	0	2	7.1	27	5	2	0	0	0	0	0	3	1	5	2	0	0	0		0	0-0	0	0.00
1996 Chicago	NL	6	5	0	0	24	110	26	17	17	3	2	0	0	14	1	13	2	0	0	2	.000	0	0-0	0	6.38
1997 Chicago	NL	2	2	0	0	8	42	12	8	8	1	0	1	1	7	0	4	0	0	0	1	.000	0	0-0	0	9.00
3 ML YEARS		15	7	0	2	39.1	179	43	27	25	4	2	1	1	24	2	22	2	0	0	3	.000	0	0-0	0	5.72

Mark Sweeney

Bats: L **Throws:** L **Pos:** PH-73; RF-28; LF-16; 1B-11; CF-1 **Ht:** 6'1" **Wt:** 195 **Born:** 10/26/69 **Age:** 28

			BATTING																BASERUNNING				PERCENTAGES		
Year Team	Lg	G	AB	H	2B	3B	HR	(Hm Rd)	TB	R	RBI	TBB	IBB	SO	HBP	SH	SF	SB	CS	SB%	GDP	Avg	OBP	SLG
1995 St. Louis	NL	37	77	21	2	0	2	(0 2)	29	5	13	10	0	15	0	1	2	*1	1	.50	3	.273	.348	.377
1996 St. Louis	NL	98	170	45	9	0	3	(0 3)	63	32	22	33	2	29	1	5	0	3	0	1.00	4	.265	.387	.371
1997 StL-SD	NL	115	164	46	7	0	2	(2 0)	59	16	23	20	1	32	1	1	2	2	3	.40	3	.280	.358	.360
1997 St. Louis	NL	44	61	13	3	0	0	(0 0)	16	5	4	9	1	14	1	1	1	0	1	.00	2	.213	.319	.262
San Diego	NL	71	103	33	4	0	2	(2 0)	43	11	19	11	0	18	0	0	1	2	2	.50	1	.320	.383	.417
3 ML YEARS		250	411	112	18	0	7	(2 5)	151	53	58	63	3	76	2	7	4	6	4	.60	10	.273	.369	.367

Mike Sweeney

Bats: Right **Throws:** Right **Pos:** C-76; PH-10; DH-3 **Ht:** 6'1" **Wt:** 195 **Born:** 7/22/73 **Age:** 24

			BATTING																BASERUNNING				PERCENTAGES		
Year Team	Lg	G	AB	H	2B	3B	HR	(Hm Rd)	TB	R	RBI	TBB	IBB	SO	HBP	SH	SF	SB	CS	SB%	GDP	Avg	OBP	SLG
1997 Omaha *	AAA	40	144	34	8	1	10	-- --	74	22	29	18	1	20	2	0	3	0	2	.00	3	.236	.323	.514
1995 Kansas City	AL	4	4	1	0	0	0	(0 0)	1	0	0	0	0	0	0	0	0	0	0	.00	0	.250	.250	.250
1996 Kansas City	AL	50	165	46	10	0	4	(1 3)	68	23	24	18	0	21	4	0	3	1	2	.33	7	.279	.358	.412
1997 Kansas City	AL	84	240	58	8	0	7	(5 2)	87	30	31	17	0	33	6	1	2	3	2	.60	8	.242	.306	.363
3 ML YEARS		138	409	105	18	0	11	(6 5)	156	54	55	35	0	54	10	1	5	4	4	.50	15	.257	.327	.381

Bill Swift

Pitches: Right **Bats:** Right **Pos:** SP-13; RP-1 **Ht:** 6'0" **Wt:** 197 **Born:** 10/27/61 **Age:** 36

		HOW MUCH HE PITCHED						WHAT HE GAVE UP												THE RESULTS						
Year Team	Lg	G	GS	CG	GF	IP	BFP	H	R	ER	HR	SH	SF	HB	TBB	IBB	SO	WP	Bk	W	L	Pct.	ShO	Sv-Op	Hld	ERA
1997 Salem *	A+	1	1	0	0	4	16	4	3	3	1	0	0	0	1	0	1	0	0	0	1	.000	0	0--	—	6.75
Colo Sprngs *	AAA	1	1	0	0	3	16	4	4	4	1	0	0	0	3	0	1	0	0	0	1	.000	0	0--	—	12.00
Rochester *	AAA	2	0	0	0	3.2	16	2	2	2	0	0	0	0	3	0	2	0	0	0	0	.000	0	0--	—	4.91
1985 Seattle	AL	23	21	0	0	120.2	532	131	71	64	8	6	3	5	48	5	55	5	3	6	10	.375	0	0--	—	4.77

		HOW MUCH HE PITCHED						WHAT HE GAVE UP												THE RESULTS						
Year Team	Lg	G	GS	CG	GF	IP	BFP	H	R	ER	HR	SH	SF	HB	TBB	IBB	SO	WP	Bk	W	L	Pct.	ShO	Sv-Op	Hld	ERA
1986 Seattle	AL	29	17	1	3	115.1	534	148	85	70	5	5	3	7	55	2	55	2	1	2	9	.182	0	0--	—	5.46
1988 Seattle	AL	38	24	6	4	174.2	757	199	99	89	10	5	3	8	65	3	47	6	2	8	12	.400	1	0-1	1	4.59
1989 Seattle	AL	37	16	0	7	130	551	140	72	64	7	4	3	2	38	4	45	4	1	7	3	.700	0	1-1	2	4.43
1990 Seattle	AL	55	8	0	18	128	533	135	46	34	4	5	4	7	21	6	42	8	3	6	4	.600	0	6-7	7	2.39
1991 Seattle	AL	71	0	0	30	90.1	359	74	22	20	3	2	0	1	26	4	48	2	1	1	2	.333	0	17-18	13	1.99
1992 San Francisco	NL	30	22	3	2	164.2	655	144	41	38	6	5	2	3	43	3	77	0	1	10	4	.714	2	1-1	3	2.08
1993 San Francisco	NL	34	34	1	0	232.2	928	195	82	73	18	4	2	6	55	5	157	4	0	21	8	.724	1	0-0	0	2.82
1994 San Francisco	NL	17	17	0	0	109.1	457	109	49	41	10	7	2	1	31	6	62	2	0	8	7	.533	0	0-0	0	3.38
1995 Colorado	NL	19	19	0	0	105.2	463	122	62	58	12	6	1	1	43	2	68	2	0	9	3	.750	0	0-0	0	4.94
1996 Colorado	NL	7	3	0	2	18.1	81	23	12	11	1	0	1	0	5	0	5	0	0	1	1	.500	0	2-2	1	5.40
1997 Colorado	NL	14	13	0	1	65.1	304	85	57	46	11	4	4	2	26	0	29	2	2	4	6	.400	0	0-0	0	6.34
12 ML YEARS		374	194	11	67	1455	6154	1505	698	608	95	53	28	43	456	40	690	37	14	83	69	.546	4	27--	—	3.76

Greg Swindell

Pitches: Left **Bats:** Right **Pos:** RP-64; SP-1 **Ht:** 6'3" **Wt:** 225 **Born:** 1/2/65 **Age:** 33

		HOW MUCH HE PITCHED						WHAT HE GAVE UP												THE RESULTS						
Year Team	Lg	G	GS	CG	GF	IP	BFP	H	R	ER	HR	SH	SF	HB	TBB	IBB	SO	WP	Bk	W	L	Pct.	ShO	Sv-Op	Hld	ERA
1986 Cleveland	AL	9	9	1	0	61.2	255	57	35	29	9	3	1	1	15	0	46	3	2	5	2	.714	0	0-0	0	4.23
1987 Cleveland	AL	16	15	4	0	102.1	441	112	62	58	18	4	3	1	37	1	97	0	1	3	8	.273	1	0-0	1	5.10
1988 Cleveland	AL	33	33	12	0	242	988	234	97	86	18	9	5	1	45	3	180	5	0	18	14	.563	4	0-0	0	3.20
1989 Cleveland	AL	28	28	5	0	184.1	749	170	71	69	16	4	4	0	51	1	129	3	1	13	6	.684	2	0-0	0	3.37
1990 Cleveland	AL	34	34	3	0	214.2	912	245	110	105	27	8	6	1	47	2	135	3	2	12	9	.571	0	0-0	0	4.40
1991 Cleveland	AL	33	33	7	0	238	971	241	112	92	21	13	8	3	31	1	169	3	1	9	16	.360	0	0-0	0	3.48
1992 Cincinnati	NL	31	30	5	0	213.2	867	210	72	64	14	9	7	2	41	4	138	3	2	12	8	.600	3	0-0	0	2.70
1993 Houston	NL	31	30	1	0	190.1	818	215	98	88	24	13	3	1	40	3	124	2	2	12	13	.480	1	0-0	0	4.16
1994 Houston	NL	24	24	1	0	148.1	623	175	80	72	20	9	7	1	26	2	74	1	1	8	9	.471	0	0-0	0	4.37
1995 Houston	NL	33	26	1	3	153	659	180	86	76	21	4	8	2	39	2	96	3	0	10	9	.526	1	0-2	0	4.47
1996 Hou-Cle		21	6	0	4	51.2	237	66	46	41	13	1	2	1	19	0	36	0	0	1	4	.200	0	0-2	1	7.14
1997 Minnesota	AL	65	1	0	12	115.2	460	102	46	46	12	2	5	0	25	3	75	0	0	7	4	.636	0	1-7	12	3.58
1996 Minnesota	NL	8	4	0	3	23	116	35	21	17	8	0	2	0	11	0	15	0	0	0	3	.000	0	0-2	0	7.83
Cleveland		13	2	0	1	28.2	121	31	21	21	8	1	1	0	8	0	21	0	0	1	1	.500	0	0-0	0	6.59
12 ML YEARS		358	269	40	19	1915.2	7980	2007	915	826	213	79	57	16	416	22	1299	26	12	110	102	.519	12	1-11	14	3.88

Jeff Tabaka

Pitches: Left **Bats:** Right **Pos:** RP-3 **Ht:** 6'2" **Wt:** 195 **Born:** 1/17/64 **Age:** 34

		HOW MUCH HE PITCHED						WHAT HE GAVE UP												THE RESULTS						
Year Team	Lg	G	GS	CG	GF	IP	BFP	H	R	ER	HR	SH	SF	HB	TBB	IBB	SO	WP	Bk	W	L	Pct.	ShO	Sv-Op	Hld	ERA
1997 Indianapolis *	AAA	58	0	0	23	57.2	228	44	19	17	5	1	2	1	19	3	68	8	0	3	2	.600	0	3--	—	2.65
1994 Pit-SD	NL	39	0	0	10	41	181	32	29	24	1	3	1	0	27	3	32	1	0	3	1	.750	0	1-1	1	5.27
1995 SD-Hou	NL	34	0	0	6	30.2	128	27	11	11	2	0	0	0	17	1	25	1	0	1	0	1.000	0	0-1	5	3.23
1996 Houston	NL	18	0	0	5	20.1	105	28	18	15	5	1	0	3	14	0	18	3	0	2	0	1.000	0	1-1	0	6.64
1997 Cincinnati	NL	3	0	0	1	2	10	1	1	1	0	0	0	2	1	0	1	0	0	0	0	.000	0	0-0	0	4.50
1994 Pittsburgh	NL	5	0	0	2	4	24	4	8	8	1	0	0	0	8	2	2	0	0	0	0	.000	0	0-0	0	18.00
San Diego		34	0	0	8	37	157	28	21	16	0	3	1	0	19	3	30	1	0	3	1	.750	0	1-1	1	3.89
1995 San Diego	NL	10	0	0	3	6.1	32	10	5	5	1	0	0	0	5	1	6	1	0	0	0	.000	0	0-1	0	7.11
Houston	NL	24	0	0	3	24.1	96	17	6	6	1	0	0	0	12	0	19	0	0	1	0	1.000	0	0-0	5	2.22
4 ML YEARS		94	0	0	22	94	424	88	59	51	9	4	1	5	59	4	76	5	0	4	3	.571	0	2-3	6	4.88

Kevin Tapani

Pitches: Right **Bats:** Right **Pos:** SP-13 **Ht:** 6'0" **Wt:** 189 **Born:** 2/18/64 **Age:** 34

		HOW MUCH HE PITCHED						WHAT HE GAVE UP												THE RESULTS						
Year Team	Lg	G	GS	CG	GF	IP	BFP	H	R	ER	HR	SH	SF	HB	TBB	IBB	SO	WP	Bk	W	L	Pct.	ShO	Sv-Op	Hld	ERA
1997 Orlando *	AA	1	1	0	0	4	16	3	2	2	2	0	0	0	2	0	2	0	0	0	0	.000	0	0--	—	4.50
Daytona *	A+	1	1	0	0	4.2	21	5	2	2	0	0	0	0	2	0	4	0	0	0	0	.000	0	0--	—	3.86
Rockford *	A	2	2	0	0	11	37	5	1	1	0	0	0	0	0	0	7	0	0	1	0	1.000	0	0--	—	0.82
Iowa *	AAA	1	1	1	0	9	32	5	4	4	1	0	0	0	1	0	4	0	0	1	0	1.000	0	0--	—	4.00
1989 NYN-Min		8	5	0	1	40	169	39	18	17	3	1	2	0	12	1	23	0	1	2	2	.500	0	0-0	0	3.83
1990 Minnesota	AL	28	28	1	0	159.1	659	164	75	72	12	3	4	2	29	2	101	1	0	12	8	.600	1	0-0	0	4.07
1991 Minnesota	AL	34	34	0	0	244	974	225	84	81	23	9	6	2	40	0	135	3	3	16	9	.640	0	0-0	0	2.99
1992 Minnesota	AL	34	34	4	0	220	911	226	103	97	17	8	11	5	48	2	138	4	0	16	11	.593	1	0-0	0	3.97
1993 Minnesota	AL	36	35	3	0	225.2	964	243	123	111	21	3	5	6	57	1	150	4	0	12	15	.444	1	0-0	0	4.43
1994 Minnesota	AL	24	24	4	0	156	672	181	86	80	13	2	5	4	39	0	91	1	0	11	7	.611	0	0-0	0	4.62
1995 Min-LA		33	31	3	0	190.2	834	227	116	105	29	6	5	8	48	4	131	4	0	10	13	.435	1	0-0	0	4.96
1996 Chicago	NL	34	34	1	0	225.1	971	236	123	115	34	6	6	3	76	5	150	13	0	13	10	.565	0	0-0	0	4.59
1997 Chicago	NL	13	13	1	0	85	352	77	33	32	7	7	2	2	23	2	55	0	2	9	3	.750	1	0-0	0	3.39
1989 New York	NL	3	0	0	1	7.1	31	5	3	3	1	1	0	0	4	0	2	0	1	0	0	.000	0	0-0	0	3.68
Minnesota	AL	5	5	0	0	32.2	138	34	15	14	2	1	1	0	8	1	21	0	0	2	2	.500	0	0-0	0	3.86
1995 Minnesota	AL	20	20	3	0	133.2	579	155	79	73	21	3	3	4	34	2	88	3	0	6	11	.353	1	0-0	0	4.92
Los Angeles	NL	13	11	0	0	57	255	72	37	32	8	3	2	1	14	2	43	1	0	4	2	.667	0	0-0	0	5.05
9 ML YEARS		244	238	21	1	1546	6506	1618	761	710	159	45	46	29	372	17	974	30	6	101	78	.564	7	0-0	0	4.13

Tony Tarasco

Bats: L **Throws:** R **Pos:** RF-68; PH-30; CF-8; LF-7; DH-2 **Ht:** 6'1" **Wt:** 205 **Born:** 12/9/70 **Age:** 27

Year Team	Lg	G	AB	H	2B	3B	HR	(Hm	Rd)	TB	R	RBI	TBB	IBB	SO	HBP	SH	SF	SB	CS	SB%	GDP	Avg	OBP	SLG
1997 Rochester *	AAA	10	35	7	0	0	2	—	—	13	4	6	7	0	7	0	0	1	0	0	.00	1	.200	.326	.371
1993 Atlanta	NL	24	35	8	2	0	0	(0	0)	10	6	2	0	0	5	1	0	1	0	1	.00	1	.229	.243	.286
1994 Atlanta	NL	87	132	36	6	0	5	(2	3)	57	16	19	9	1	17	0	0	3	5	0	1.00	5	.273	.313	.432
1995 Montreal	NL	126	438	109	18	4	14	(7	7)	177	64	40	51	12	78	2	3	1	24	3	.89	2	.249	.329	.404
1996 Baltimore	AL	31	84	20	3	0	1	(1	0)	26	14	9	7	0	15	0	1	0	5	3	.63	1	.238	.297	.310
1997 Baltimore	AL	100	166	34	8	1	7	(4	3)	65	26	26	25	1	33	1	1	0	2	2	.50	3	.205	.313	.392
5 ML YEARS		368	855	207	37	5	27	(14	13)	335	126	96	92	14	148	4	5	5	36	9	.80	12	.242	.317	.392

Danny Tartabull

Bats: Right **Throws:** Right **Pos:** RF-3 **Ht:** 6'1" **Wt:** 204 **Born:** 10/30/62 **Age:** 35

Year Team	Lg	G	AB	H	2B	3B	HR	(Hm	Rd)	TB	R	RBI	TBB	IBB	SO	HBP	SH	SF	SB	CS	SB%	GDP	Avg	OBP	SLG
1984 Seattle	AL	10	20	6	1	0	2	(1	1)	13	3	7	2	0	3	1	0	1	0	0	.00	0	.300	.375	.650
1985 Seattle	AL	19	61	20	7	1	1	(0	1)	32	8	7	8	0	14	0	0	0	1	0	1.00	1	.328	.406	.525
1986 Seattle	AL	137	511	138	25	6	25	(13	12)	250	76	96	61	2	157	1	2	3	4	8	.33	10	.270	.347	.489
1987 Kansas City	AL	158	582	180	27	3	34	(15	19)	315	95	101	79	2	136	1	0	5	9	4	.69	14	.309	.390	.541
1988 Kansas City	AL	146	507	139	38	3	26	(15	11)	261	80	102	76	4	119	4	0	6	8	5	.62	10	.274	.369	.515
1989 Kansas City	AL	133	441	118	22	0	18	(9	9)	194	54	62	69	2	123	3	0	2	4	2	.67	12	.268	.369	.440
1990 Kansas City	AL	88	313	84	19	0	15	(5	10)	148	41	60	36	0	93	0	0	3	1	1	.50	9	.268	.341	.473
1991 Kansas City	AL	132	484	153	35	3	31	(13	18)	287	78	100	65	6	121	3	0	5	6	3	.67	9	.316	.397	.593
1992 New York	AL	123	421	112	19	0	25	(11	14)	206	72	85	103	14	115	0	0	2	2	2	.50	7	.266	.409	.489
1993 New York	AL	138	513	128	33	2	31	(11	20)	258	87	102	92	9	156	2	0	4	0	0	.00	8	.250	.363	.503
1994 New York	AL	104	399	102	24	1	19	(10	9)	185	68	67	66	3	111	1	0	4	1	1	.50	11	.256	.360	.464
1995 NYA-Oak	AL	83	240	66	16	0	8	(3	5)	106	34	35	43	1	82	1	0	4	0	2	.00	9	.236	.335	.379
1996 Chicago	AL	132	472	120	23	3	27	(11	16)	230	58	101	64	4	128	0	1	2	1	2	.33	10	.254	.340	.487
1997 Philadelphia	NL	3	7	0	0	0	0	(0	0)	0	2	0	4	0	4	0	0	0	0	0	.00	0	.000	.364	.000
1995 New York	AL	59	192	43	12	0	6	(2	4)	73	25	28	33	1	54	1	0	4	0	0	.00	6	.224	.335	.380
Oakland	AL	24	88	23	4	0	2	(1	1)	33	9	7	10	0	28	0	0	0	0	2	.00	3	.261	.337	.375
14 ML YEARS		1406	5011	1366	289	22	262	(117	145)	2485	756	925	768	47	1362	17	2	44	37	30	.55	110	.273	.368	.496

Fernando Tatis

Bats: Right **Throws:** Right **Pos:** 3B-60 **Ht:** 6'1" **Wt:** 175 **Born:** 1/1/75 **Age:** 23

Year Team	Lg	G	AB	H	2B	3B	HR	(Hm	Rd)	TB	R	RBI	TBB	IBB	SO	HBP	SH	SF	SB	CS	SB%	GDP	Avg	OBP	SLG
1994 Rangers	R	60	212	70	10	2	6	—	—	102	34	32	25	4	33	3	0	2	20	4	.83	4	.330	.405	.481
1995 Chston-SC	A	131	499	151	43	4	15	—	—	247	74	84	45	4	94	7	1	4	22	19	.54	5	.303	.366	.495
1996 Charlotte	A+	85	325	93	25	0	12	—	—	154	46	53	30	4	48	6	1	4	9	3	.75	9	.286	.353	.474
Okla City	AAA	2	4	2	1	0	0	—	—	3	0	0	0	0	1	0	0	0	0	0	.00	0	.500	.500	.750
1997 Tulsa	AA	102	382	120	26	1	24	—	—	220	73	61	46	4	72	3	0	2	17	8	.68	15	.314	.390	.576
1997 Texas	AL	60	223	57	9	0	8	(6	2)	90	29	29	14	0	42	0	2	2	3	0	1.00	6	.256	.297	.404

Ramon Tatis

Pitches: Left **Bats:** Left **Pos:** RP-56 **Ht:** 6'3" **Wt:** 195 **Born:** 5/2/73 **Age:** 25

Year Team	Lg	G	GS	CG	GF	IP	BFP	H	R	ER	HR	SH	SF	HB	TBB	IBB	SO	WP	Bk	W	L	Pct.	ShO	Sv-Op	Hld	ERA
1992 Mets	R	11	5	0	0	36	184	56	40	34	2	0	1	4	15	0	25	7	1	1	3	.250	0	0- -	—	8.50
1993 Kingsport	R+	13	3	0	5	42.2	204	51	42	29	1	3	1	5	23	0	25	4	0	2	0	.000	0	1- -	—	6.12
1994 Kingsport	R+	13	4	0	8	40.2	187	35	25	15	2	2	1	2	31	0	36	5	2	1	3	.250	0	0- -	—	3.32
1995 Pittsfield	A-	13	13	1	0	79.1	341	88	40	32	2	1	1	3	27	0	69	8	3	5	4	.444	1	0- -	—	3.63
Capital City	A	18	2	0	9	32	141	34	27	20	1	2	1	1	14	0	27	5	0	2	3	.400	0	0- -	—	5.63
1996 St. Lucie	A+	46	1	0	20	74.1	325	71	35	28	4	7	2	2	38	8	46	14	1	4	2	.667	0	6- -	—	3.39
1997 Chicago	NL	56	0	0	12	55.2	255	66	36	33	13	6	3	3	29	6	33	4	2	1	1	.500	0	0-1	8	5.34

Eddie Taubensee

Bats: L **Throws:** R **Pos:** C-64; PH-38; 1B-7; LF-6; RF-5; DH-3 **Ht:** 6'4" **Wt:** 205 **Born:** 10/31/68 **Age:** 29

Year Team	Lg	G	AB	H	2B	3B	HR	(Hm	Rd)	TB	R	RBI	TBB	IBB	SO	HBP	SH	SF	SB	CS	SB%	GDP	Avg	OBP	SLG
1991 Cleveland	AL	26	66	16	2	1	0	(0	0)	20	5	8	5	1	16	0	0	2	0	0	.00	1	.242	.288	.303
1992 Houston	NL	104	297	66	15	0	5	(2	3)	96	23	28	31	3	78	2	0	1	2	1	.67	4	.222	.299	.323
1993 Houston	NL	94	288	72	11	1	9	(4	5)	112	26	42	21	5	44	0	1	2	1	0	1.00	8	.250	.299	.389
1994 Hou-Cin	NL	66	187	53	8	2	8	(2	6)	89	29	21	15	2	31	0	1	2	2	0	1.00	2	.283	.333	.476
1995 Cincinnati	NL	80	218	62	14	2	9	(4	5)	107	32	44	22	2	52	2	1	1	2	2	.50	2	.284	.354	.491
1996 Cincinnati	NL	108	327	95	20	0	12	(6	6)	151	46	48	26	5	64	0	1	5	3	4	.43	4	.291	.338	.462
1997 Cincinnati	NL	108	254	68	18	0	10	(7	3)	116	26	34	22	2	66	1	1	5	0	1	.00	2	.268	.323	.457
1994 Houston	NL	5	10	1	0	0	0	(0	0)	1	0	0	0	0	3	0	0	0	0	0	.00	1	.100	.100	.100
Cincinnati	NL	61	177	52	8	2	8	(2	6)	88	29	21	15	2	28	0	1	2	2	0	1.00	1	.294	.345	.497
7 ML YEARS		586	1637	432	88	6	53	(25	28)	691	187	225	142	20	351	5	5	18	10	8	.56	23	.264	.321	.422

Jesus Tavarez

Bats: B **Throws:** R **Pos:** CF-29; PH-11; LF-4; RF-4; DH-2 **Ht:** 6'0" **Wt:** 170 **Born:** 3/26/71 **Age:** 27

Year Team	Lg	G	AB	H	2B	3B	HR	(Hm	Rd)	TB	R	RBI	TBB	IBB	SO	HBP	SH	SF	SB	CS	SB%	GDP	Avg	OBP	SLG
1997 Pawtucket *	AAA	59	229	61	6	3	3	—	—	82	43	20	27	1	31	1	6	0	22	9	.71	3	.266	.346	.358
1994 Florida	NL	17	39	7	0	0	0	(0	0)	7	4	4	1	0	5	0	1	0	1	1	.50	0	.179	.200	.179
1995 Florida	NL	63	190	55	6	2	2	(1	1)	71	31	13	16	1	27	1	3	1	7	5	.58	1	.289	.346	.374
1996 Florida	NL	98	114	25	3	0	0	(0	0)	28	14	6	7	0	18	0	3	0	5	1	.83	2	.219	.264	.246
1997 Boston	AL	42	69	12	3	1	0	(0	0)	17	12	9	4	0	9	0	0	1	0	0	.00	2	.174	.216	.246
4 ML YEARS		220	412	99	12	3	2	(1	1)	123	61	32	28	1	59	1	7	2	13	7	.65	5	.240	.289	.299

Julian Tavarez

Pitches: Right **Bats:** Left **Pos:** RP-89 **Ht:** 6'2" **Wt:** 165 **Born:** 5/22/73 **Age:** 25

Year Team	Lg	G	GS	CG	GF	IP	BFP	H	R	ER	HR	SH	SF	HB	TBB	IBB	SO	WP	Bk	W	L	Pct.	ShO	Sv-Op	Hld	ERA
1993 Cleveland	AL	8	7	0	0	37	172	53	29	27	7	0	1	2	13	2	19	3	1	2	2	.500	0	0-0	0	6.57
1994 Cleveland	AL	1	1	0	0	1.2	14	6	8	4	1	0	1	0	1	1	0	0	0	0	1	.000	0	0-0	0	21.60
1995 Cleveland	AL	57	0	0	15	85	350	76	36	23	7	0	2	3	21	0	68	3	2	10	2	.833	0	0-4	19	2.44
1996 Cleveland	AL	51	4	0	13	80.2	353	101	49	48	9	5	4	1	22	5	46	1	0	4	7	.364	0	0-0	13	5.36
1997 San Francisco	NL	89	0	0	13	88.1	378	91	43	38	6	3	8	4	34	5	38	4	0	6	4	.600	0	0-3	26	3.87
5 ML YEARS		206	12	0	41	292.2	1267	327	165	140	30	8	16	10	91	13	171	11	3	22	16	.579	0	0-7	58	4.31

Billy Taylor

Pitches: Right **Bats:** Right **Pos:** RP-72 **Ht:** 6'8" **Wt:** 200 **Born:** 10/16/61 **Age:** 36

Year Team	Lg	G	GS	CG	GF	IP	BFP	H	R	ER	HR	SH	SF	HB	TBB	IBB	SO	WP	Bk	W	L	Pct.	ShO	Sv-Op	Hld	ERA
1994 Oakland	AL	41	0	0	11	46.1	195	38	24	18	4	1	1	2	18	5	48	0	0	1	3	.250	0	1-3	2	3.50
1996 Oakland	AL	55	0	0	30	60.1	261	52	30	29	5	4	3	4	25	4	67	1	0	6	3	.667	0	17-19	4	4.33
1997 Oakland	AL	72	0	0	45	73	320	70	32	31	3	1	2	5	36	9	66	0	0	4	4	.429	0	23-30	7	3.82
3 ML YEARS		168	0	0	86	179.2	776	160	86	78	12	6	6	11	79	18	181	1	0	10	10	.500	0	41-52	13	3.91

Miguel Tejada

Bats: Right **Throws:** Right **Pos:** SS-26; PH-1 **Ht:** 5'10" **Wt:** 170 **Born:** 5/25/76 **Age:** 22

Year Team	Lg	G	AB	H	2B	3B	HR	(Hm	Rd)	TB	R	RBI	TBB	IBB	SO	HBP	SH	SF	SB	CS	SB%	GDP	Avg	OBP	SLG
1995 Sou. Oregon	A-	74	269	66	15	5	8	—	—	115	45	44	41	2	54	2	0	3	19	2	.90	3	.245	.346	.428
1996 Modesto	A+	114	458	128	12	5	20	—	—	210	97	72	51	3	93	4	1	7	27	16	.63	9	.279	.352	.459
1997 Huntsville	AA	128	502	138	20	3	22	—	—	230	85	97	50	0	99	7	1	8	15	11	.58	9	.275	.344	.458
1997 Oakland	AL	26	99	20	3	2	2	(1	1)	33	10	10	2	0	22	3	0	0	2	0	1.00	3	.202	.240	.333

Amaury Telemaco

Pitches: Right **Bats:** Right **Pos:** SP-5; RP-5 **Ht:** 6'3" **Wt:** 210 **Born:** 1/19/74 **Age:** 24

Year Team	Lg	G	GS	CG	GF	IP	BFP	H	R	ER	HR	SH	SF	HB	TBB	IBB	SO	WP	Bk	W	L	Pct.	ShO	Sv-Op	Hld	ERA
1992 Huntington	R+	12	12	2	0	76.1	318	71	45	34	6	2	1	2	17	0	93	7	0	3	5	.375	0	0- -	—	4.01
Peoria	A	2	1	0	0	5.2	31	9	5	5	0	0	0	1	5	0	5	0	0	0	1	.000	0	0- -	—	7.94
1993 Peoria	A	23	23	3	0	143.2	602	129	69	55	9	2	6	5	54	0	133	8	0	9	12	.421	0	0- -	—	3.45
1994 Daytona	A+	11	11	2	0	76.2	313	62	35	29	4	4	2	4	23	0	59	3	3	7	3	.700	0	0- -	—	3.40
Orlando	AA	12	12	2	0	62.2	264	56	29	24	6	4	2	4	20	0	49	3	0	3	5	.375	0	0- -	—	3.45
1995 Orlando	AA	22	22	3	0	147.2	587	112	60	54	13	8	3	4	42	3	151	7	1	8	8	.500	1	0- -	—	3.29
1996 Iowa	AAA	8	8	1	0	50	205	38	19	17	5	2	2	2	18	2	42	3	0	3	1	.750	0	0- -	—	3.06
1997 Orlando	AA	1	1	0	0	8	34	9	2	2	0	0	0	0	2	0	6	1	0	1	0	1.000	0	0- -	—	2.25
Iowa	AAA	18	18	3	0	113.2	501	121	70	57	20	3	3	4	38	1	75	6	1	5	9	.357	2	0- -	—	4.51
1996 Chicago	NL	25	17	0	2	97.1	427	108	67	59	20	5	3	3	31	2	64	3	0	5	7	.417	0	0-0	0	5.46
1997 Chicago	NL	10	5	0	2	38	169	47	26	26	4	2	1	0	11	0	29	1	0	0	3	.000	0	0-0	0	6.16
2 ML YEARS		35	22	0	4	135.1	596	155	93	85	24	7	4	3	42	2	93	4	0	5	10	.333	0	0-0	0	5.65

Anthony Telford

Pitches: Right **Bats:** Right **Pos:** RP-65 **Ht:** 6'0" **Wt:** 184 **Born:** 3/6/66 **Age:** 32

Year Team	Lg	G	GS	CG	GF	IP	BFP	H	R	ER	HR	SH	SF	HB	TBB	IBB	SO	WP	Bk	W	L	Pct.	ShO	Sv-Op	Hld	ERA
1990 Baltimore	AL	8	8	0	0	36.1	168	43	22	20	4	0	2	1	19	0	20	1	0	3	3	.500	0	0-0	0	4.95
1991 Baltimore	AL	9	1	0	4	26.2	109	27	12	12	3	0	1	0	6	1	24	1	0	0	0	.000	0	0-0	0	4.05
1993 Baltimore	AL	3	0	0	2	7.1	34	11	8	8	3	0	0	1	1	0	6	1	0	0	0	.000	0	0-0	0	9.82
1997 Montreal	NL	65	0	0	17	89	369	77	34	32	11	4	1	5	33	4	61	6	0	4	6	.400	0	1-5	11	3.24
4 ML YEARS		85	9	0	23	159.1	680	158	76	72	21	4	4	7	59	5	111	9	0	7	9	.438	0	1-5	11	4.07

Dave Telgheder

Pitches: Right   **Bats:** Right   **Pos:** SP-19; RP-1   **Ht:** 6'3"   **Wt:** 212   **Born:** 11/11/66   **Age:** 31

			HOW MUCH HE PITCHED						WHAT HE GAVE UP												THE RESULTS						
Year Team	Lg	G	GS	CG	GF	IP	BFP	H	R	ER	HR	SH	SF	HB	TBB	IBB	SO	WP	Bk	W	L	Pct.	ShO	Sv-Op	Hld	ERA
1997 Modesto *	A+	2	2	0	0	5.1	21	3	2	2	0	0	0	0	2	0	4	0	0	0	0	.000	0	0- -	—	3.38
1993 New York	NL	24	7	0	7	75.2	325	82	40	40	10	2	1	4	21	2	35	1	0	6	2	.750	0	0-0	1	4.76
1994 New York	NL	6	0	0	0	10	48	11	8	8	2	1	0	0	8	2	4	0	0	0	1	.000	0	0-0	0	·7.20
1995 New York	NL	7	4	0	2	25.2	118	34	18	16	4	3	1	0	7	3	16	0	1	1	2	.333	0	0-0	0	5.61
1996 Oakland	AL	16	14	1	1	79.1	348	92	42	41	12	3	3	1	26	1	43	0	0	4	7	.364	1	0-0	0	4.65
1997 Oakland	AL	20	19	0	0	101	458	134	71	68	15	0	7	2	35	1	55	4	0	4	6	.400	0	0-0	0	6.06
5 ML YEARS		73	44	1	10	291.2	1297	353	179	173	43	9	12	7	97	9	153	7	1	15	18	.455	1	0-0	1	5.34

Mickey Tettleton

Bats: Both   **Throws:** Right   **Pos:** DH-13; PH-6   **Ht:** 6'2"   **Wt:** 212   **Born:** 9/16/60   **Age:** 37

					BATTING															BASERUNNING				PERCENTAGES		
Year Team	Lg	G	AB	H	2B	3B	HR	(Hm	Rd)	TB	R	RBI	TBB	IBB	SO	HBP	SH	SF		SB	CS	SB%	GDP	Avg	OBP	SLG
1997 Okla City *	AAA	4	9	4	1	0	0	—	—	5	4	0	6	0	1	0	0	0		0	0	.00	0	.444	.667	.556
Tulsa *	AA	3	11	2	0	0	1	—	—	5	4	2	4	0	2	0	0	0		0	0	.00	0	.182	.400	.455
1984 Oakland	AL	33	76	20	2	1	1	(1	0)	27	10	5	11	0	21	0	0	1		0	0	.00	3	.263	.352	.355
1985 Oakland	AL	78	211	53	12	0	3	(1	2)	74	23	15	28	0	59	2	5	0		2	2	.50	6	.251	.344	.351
1986 Oakland	AL	90	211	43	9	0	10	(4	6)	82	26	35	39	0	51	1	7	4		7	1	.88	3	.204	.325	.389
1987 Oakland	AL	82	211	41	3	0	8	(5	3)	68	19	26	30	0	65	0	5	2		1	1	.50	3	.194	.292	.322
1988 Baltimore	AL	86	283	74	11	1	11	(7	4)	120	31	37	28	2	70	2	1	2		0	1	.00	9	.261	.330	.424
1989 Baltimore	AL	117	411	106	21	2	26	(15	11)	209	72	65	73	4	117	1	1	3		3	2	.60	8	.258	.369	.509
1990 Baltimore	AL	135	444	99	21	2	15	(8	7)	169	68	51	106	3	160	5	0	4		2	4	.33	7	.223	.376	.381
1991 Detroit	AL	154	501	132	17	2	31	(15	16)	246	85	89	101	9	131	2	0	4		3	3	.50	12	.263	.387	.491
1992 Detroit	AL	157	525	125	25	0	32	(18	14)	246	82	83	122	18	137	1	0	6		0	6	.00	5	.238	.379	.469
1993 Detroit	AL	152	522	128	25	4	32	(16	16)	257	79	110	109	12	139	0	0	6		3	7	.30	5	.245	.372	.492
1994 Detroit	AL	107	339	84	18	2	17	(9	8)	157	57	51	97	10	98	5	0	3		0	1	.00	4	·.248	.419	.463
1995 Texas	AL	134	429	102	19	1	32	(22	10)	219	76	78	107	5	110	7 -	1	3		0	0	.00	8	.238	.396	.510
1996 Texas	AL	143	491	121	26	1	24	(14	10)	221	78	83	95	8	137	3	1	9		2	1	.67	12	.246	.366	.450
1997 Texas	AL	17	44	4	1	0	3	(2	1)	14	5	4	3	1	12	1	0	0		0	0	.00	1	.091	.167	.318
14 ML YEARS		1485	4698	1132	210	16	245	(137	108)	2109	711	732	949	72	1307	30	21	47		23	29	.44	86	.241	.369	.449

Bob Tewksbury

Pitches: Right   **Bats:** Right   **Pos:** SP-26   **Ht:** 6'4"   **Wt:** 205   **Born:** 11/30/60   **Age:** 37

				HOW MUCH HE PITCHED					WHAT HE GAVE UP											THE RESULTS						
Year Team	Lg	G	GS	CG	GF	IP	BFP	H	R	ER	HR	SH	SF	HB	TBB	IBB	SO	WP	Bk	W	L	Pct.	ShO	Sv-Op	Hld	ERA
1986 New York	AL	23	20	2	0	130.1	558	144	58	48	8	4	7	5	31	0	49	3	2	9	5	.643	0	0- -	—	3.31
1987 NYA-ChN		15	9	0	4	51.1	242	79	41	38	6	5	1	1	20	3	22	1	2	1	8	.111	0	0-1	0	6.66
1988 Chicago	NL	1	1	0	0	3.1	18	6	5	3	1	0	1	0	2	0	1	0	0	0	0	.000	0	0-0	0	8.10
1989 St. Louis	NL	7	4	1	2	30	125	25	12	11	2	1	1	2	10	3	17	0	0	1	0	1.000	1	0-0	0	3.30
1990 St. Louis	NL	28	20	3	1	145.1	595	151	67	56	7	5	7	3	15	3	50	2	0	10	9	.526	2	1-1	2	3.47
1991 St. Louis	NL	30	30	3	0	191	798	206	86	69	13	12	10	5	38	2	75	0	0	11	12	.478	0	0-0	0	3.25
1992 St. Louis	NL	33	32	5	1	233	915	217	63	56	15	9	7	3	20	0	91	2	0	16	5	.762	0	0-0	0	2.16
1993 St. Louis	NL	32	32	2	0	213.2	907	258	99	91	15	15	9	6	20	1	97	2	0	17	10	.630	0	0-0	0	3.83
1994 St. Louis	NL	24	24	4	0	155.2	667	190	97	92	19	12	4	3	22	1	79	1	0	12	10	.545	1	0-0	0	5.32
1995 Texas	AL	21	21	4	0	129.2	561	169	75	66	8	6	3	3	20	4	53	4	0	8	7	.533	0	0-0	0	4.58
1996 San Diego	NL	36	33	1	0	206.2	881	224	116	99	17	10	11	3	43	3	126	2	3	10	10	.500	0	0-0	0	4.31
1997 Minnesota	AL	26	26	5	0	168.2	721	200	83	79	12	8	7	1	31	1	92	2	0	8	13	.381	2	0-0	0	4.22
1987 New York	AL	8	6	0	0	33.1	149	47	26	25	5	2	0	1	7	0	12	0	0	1	4	.200	0	0-0	0	6.75
Chicago	NL	7	3	0	3	18	93	32	15	13	1	3	1	0	13	3	10	1	2	0	4	.000	0	0-1	0	6.50
12 ML YEARS		276	252	30	8	1658.2	6988	1869	802	708	123	87	68	35	272	21	752	19	7	103	89	.536	7	1- -	—	3.84

Frank Thomas

Bats: Right   **Throws:** Right   **Pos:** 1B-97; DH-49   **Ht:** 6'5"   **Wt:** 257   **Born:** 5/27/68   **Age:** 30

					BATTING														BASERUNNING			PERCENTAGES		
Year Team	Lg	G	AB	H	2B	3B	HR	(Hm	Rd)	TB	R	RBI	TBB	IBB	SO	HBP	SH	SF	SB	CS	SB%	GDP	Avg	OBP	SLG
1990 Chicago	AL	60	191	63	11	3	7	(2	5)	101	39	31	44	0	54	2	0	3	0	1	.00	5	.330	.454	.529
1991 Chicago	AL	158	559	178	31	2	32	(24	8)	309	104	109	138	13	112	1	0	2	1	2	.33	20	.318	.453	.553
1992 Chicago	AL	160	573	185	46	2	24	(10	14)	307	108	115	122	6	88	5	0	11	6	3	.67	19	.323	.439	.536
1993 Chicago	AL	153	549	174	36	0	41	(26	15)	333	106	128	112	23	54	2	0	13	4	2	.67	10	.317	.426	.607
1994 Chicago	AL	113	399	141	34	1	38	(22	16)	291	106	101	109	12	61	2	0	7	2	3	.40	15	.353	.487	.729
1995 Chicago	AL	145	493	152	27	0	40	(15	25)	299	102	111	136	29	74	6	0	12	3	2	.60	14	.308	.454	.606
1996 Chicago	AL	141	527	184	26	0	40	(16	24)	330	110	134	109	26	70	5	0	8	1	1	.50	25	.349	.459	.626
1997 Chicago	AL	146	530	184	35	0	35	(16	19)	324	110	125	109	9	69	3	0	7	1	1	.50	15	.347	.456	.611
8 ML YEARS		1076	3821	1261	246	8	257	(131	126)	2294	785	854	879	118	582	26	0	63	18	15	.55	123	.330	.452	.600

Larry Thomas

Pitches: Left   **Bats:** Right   **Pos:** RP-5   **Ht:** 6'1"   **Wt:** 195   **Born:** 10/25/69   **Age:** 28

				HOW MUCH HE PITCHED					WHAT HE GAVE UP											THE RESULTS						
Year Team	Lg	G	GS	CG	GF	IP	BFP	H	R	ER	HR	SH	SF	HB	TBB	IBB	SO	WP	Bk	W	L	Pct.	ShO	Sv-Op	Hld	ERA
1997 Nashville *	AAA	44	1	0	12	48	208	47	24	21	6	2	1	1	18	4	53	2	0	3	2	.600	0	2- -	5	3.94
1995 Chicago	AL	17	0	0	7	13.2	54	8	2	2	1	0	0	0	6	1	12	1	0	0	0	.000	0	0-0	2	1.32
1996 Chicago	AL	57	0	0	11	30.2	135	32	11	11	1	4	0	3	14	2	20	1	0	2	3	.400	0	0-2	7	3.23

208

			HOW MUCH HE PITCHED					WHAT HE GAVE UP											THE RESULTS				
Year Team	Lg	G	GS	CG	GF	IP	BFP	H	R	ER	HR	SH	SF	HB	TBB	IBB	SO	WP	Bk	W	L	Pct.	ShO	Sv-Op	Hld	ERA
1997 Chicago	AL	5	0	0	0	3.1	15	3	3	3	1	1	0	0	2	0	0	0	0	0	0	.000	0	0-0	0	8.10
3 ML YEARS		79	0	0	16	47.2	204	43	16	16	3	5	0	3	22	3	32	2	0	2	3	.400	0	0-2	9	3.02

Jim Thome

Bats: Left **Throws:** Right **Pos:** 1B-145; PH-7 **Ht:** 6'4" **Wt:** 220 **Born:** 8/27/70 **Age:** 27

							BATTING													BASERUNNING				PERCENTAGES		
Year Team	Lg	G	AB	H	2B	3B	HR	(Hm	Rd)	TB	R	RBI	TBB	IBB	SO	HBP	SH	SF		SB	CS	SB%	GDP	Avg	OBP	SLG
1991 Cleveland	AL	27	98	25	4	2	1	(0	1)	36	7	9	5	1	16	1	0	0		1	1	.50	4	.255	.298	.367
1992 Cleveland	AL	40	117	24	3	1	2	(1	1)	35	8	12	10	2	34	2	0	2		2	0	1.00	3	.205	.275	.299
1993 Cleveland	AL	47	154	41	11	0	7	(5	2)	73	28	22	29	1	36	4	0	5		2	1	.67	3	.266	.385	.474
1994 Cleveland	AL	98	321	86	20	1	20	(10	10)	168	58	52	46	5	84	0	1	1		3	3	.50	11	.268	.359	.523
1995 Cleveland	AL	137	452	142	29	3	25	(13	12)	252	92	73	97	3	113	5	0	3		4	3	.57	8	.314	.438	.558
1996 Cleveland	AL	151	505	157	28	5	38	(18	20)	309	122	116	123	8	141	6	0	2		2	2	.50	13	.311	.450	.612
1997 Cleveland	AL	147	496	142	25	0	40	(17	23)	287	104	102	120	9	146	3	0	8		1	1	.50	9	.286	.423	.579
7 ML YEARS		647	2143	617	120	12	133	(64	69)	1160	419	386	430	29	570	21	1	21		15	11	.58	51	.288	.408	.541

Justin Thompson

Pitches: Left **Bats:** Left **Pos:** SP-32 **Ht:** 6'4" **Wt:** 215 **Born:** 3/8/73 **Age:** 25

				HOW MUCH HE PITCHED					WHAT HE GAVE UP											THE RESULTS				
Year Team	Lg	G	GS	CG	GF	IP	BFP	H	R	ER	HR	SH	SF	HB	TBB	IBB	SO	WP	Bk	W	L	Pct.	ShO	Sv-Op	Hld	ERA
1991 Bristol	R+	10	10	0	0	50	217	45	29	20	4	0	1	2	24	1	60	7	6	2	5	.286	0	0- -	-	3.60
1992 Fayetteville	A	20	19	0	1	95	390	79	32	23	6	0	4	1	40	0	88	7	3	4	4	.500	0	0- -	-	2.18
1993 Lakeland	A+	11	11	0	0	55.2	241	65	25	22	1	3	0	1	16	0	46	3	1	4	4	.500	0	0- -	-	3.56
London	AA	14	14	1	0	83.2	376	96	51	38	9	0	4	2	37	0	72	4	1	3	6	.333	0	0- -	-	4.09
1995 Lakeland	A+	6	6	0	0	24	107	30	13	13	1	0	2	2	8	0	20	0	0	2	1	.667	0	0- -	-	4.88
Jacksnville	AA	18	18	3	0	123	502	110	55	51	7	4	2	3	38	2	98	3	0	6	7	.462	0	0- -	-	3.73
1996 Fayettevlle	A	1	1	0	0	3	10	1	1	1	0	0	0	0	0	0	5	0	0	0	0	.000	0	0- -	-	3.00
Visalia	A+	1	1	0	0	3	13	2	0	0	0	0	0	0	2	0	7	1	0	0	0	.000	0	0- -	-	0.00
Toledo	AAA	13	13	3	0	84.1	338	74	36	32	2	1	2	1	26	0	69	2	0	6	3	.667	1	0- -	-	3.42
1996 Detroit	AL	11	11	0	0	59	267	62	35	30	7	0	2	2	31	2	44	1	0	1	6	.143	0	0-0	0	4.58
1997 Detroit	AL	32	32	4	0	223.1	891	188	82	75	20	5	10	2	66	1	151	4	0	15	11	.577	2	0-0	0	3.02
2 ML YEARS		43	43	4	0	282.1	1158	250	117	105	27	5	12	4	97	3	195	5	0	16	17	.485	2	0-0	0	3.35

Mark Thompson

Pitches: Right **Bats:** Right **Pos:** SP-6 **Ht:** 6'2" **Wt:** 205 **Born:** 4/7/71 **Age:** 27

				HOW MUCH HE PITCHED					WHAT HE GAVE UP											THE RESULTS				
Year Team	Lg	G	GS	CG	GF	IP	BFP	H	R	ER	HR	SH	SF	HB	TBB	IBB	SO	WP	Bk	W	L	Pct.	ShO	Sv-Op	Hld	ERA
1997 Asheville *	A	4	4	0	0	13.1	58	11	5	4	0	0	0	2	5	0	9	0	0	0	2	.000	0	0- -	—	2.70
Colo Sprngs *	AAA	1	1	0	0	3	14	6	4	4	1	0	0	0	1	0	1	0	0	0	0	.000	0	0- -	—	12.00
1994 Colorado	NL	2	2	0	0	9	49	16	9	9	2	0	0	1	8	0	5	0	0	1	1	.500	0	0-0	0	9.00
1995 Colorado	NL	21	5	0	3	51	240	73	42	37	7	4	4	1	22	2	30	2	0	2	3	.400	0	0-0	2	6.53
1996 Colorado	NL	34	28	3	2	169.2	763	189	109	100	25	10	3	13	74	1	99	1	1	9	11	.450	1	0-1	0	5.30
1997 Colorado	NL	6	6	0	0	29.2	146	40	27	26	8	3	2	4	13	0	9	0	1	3	3	.500	0	0-0	0	7.89
4 ML YEARS		63	41	3	5	259.1	1198	318	187	172	42	17	9	19	117	3	143	3	2	15	18	.455	1	0-1	2	5.97

Robby Thompson

Bats: Right **Throws:** Right **Pos:** 2B/PH **Ht:** 5'11" **Wt:** 173 **Born:** 5/10/62 **Age:** 36

							BATTING													BASERUNNING				PERCENTAGES		
Year Team	Lg	G	AB	H	2B	3B	HR	(Hm	Rd)	TB	R	RBI	TBB	IBB	SO	HBP	SH	SF		SB	CS	SB%	GDP	Avg	OBP	SLG
1986 San Francisco	NL	149	549	149	27	3	7	(0	7)	203	73	47	42	0	112	5	18	1		12	15	.44	11	.271	.328	.370
1987 San Francisco	NL	132	420	110	26	5	10	(7	3)	176	62	44	40	3	91	8	6	0		16	11	.59	8	.262	.338	.419
1988 San Francisco	NL	138	477	126	24	6	7	(3	4)	183	66	48	40	0	111	4	14	5		14	5	.74	7	.264	.323	.384
1989 San Francisco	NL	148	547	132	26	11	13	(7	6)	219	91	50	51	0	133	13	9	0		12	2	.86	6	.241	.321	.400
1990 San Francisco	NL	144	498	122	22	3	15	(8	7)	195	67	56	34	1	96	6	8	3		14	4	.78	9	.245	.299	.392
1991 San Francisco	NL	144	492	129	24	5	19	(11	8)	220	74	48	63	2	95	6	11	5		14	7	.67	6	.262	.352	.447
1992 San Francisco	NL	128	443	115	25	1	14	(8	6)	184	54	49	43	1	75	8	7	4		5	9	.36	8	.260	.333	.415
1993 San Francisco	NL	128	494	154	30	2	19	(13	6)	245	85	65	45	0	97	7	9	4		10	4	.71	7	.312	.375	.496
1994 San Francisco	NL	35	129	27	8	2	2	(1	1)	45	13	7	15	0	32	0	5	1		3	1	.75	2	.209	.290	.349
1995 San Francisco	NL	95	336	75	15	0	8	(4	4)	114	51	23	42	1	76	4	9	0		2	4	.33	3	.223	.317	.339
1996 San Francisco	NL	63	227	48	11	1	5	(2	3)	76	35	21	24	0	69	5	3	0		2	2	.50	6	.211	.301	.335
11 ML YEARS		1304	4612	1187	238	39	119	(64	55)	1860	671	458	439	8	987	66	99	19		103	62	.62	72	.257	.329	.403

John Thomson

Pitches: Right **Bats:** Right **Pos:** SP-27 **Ht:** 6'3" **Wt:** 180 **Born:** 10/1/73 **Age:** 24

				HOW MUCH HE PITCHED					WHAT HE GAVE UP											THE RESULTS				
Year Team	Lg	G	GS	CG	GF	IP	BFP	H	R	ER	HR	SH	SF	HB	TBB	IBB	SO	WP	Bk	W	L	Pct.	ShO	Sv-Op	Hld	ERA
1993 Rockies	R	11	11	0	0	50.2	228	43	40	26	0	0	2	3	31	0	36	14	1	3	5	.375	0	0- -	—	4.62
1994 Asheville	A	19	15	1	1	88.1	361	70	34	28	3	2	1	5	33	1	79	1	0	6	6	.500	1	0- -	—	2.85
Central Val	A+	9	8	0	0	49.1	201	43	20	18	0	0	2	1	18	1	41	3	1	3	1	.750	0	0- -	—	3.28
1995 New Haven	AA	26	24	0	0	131.1	572	132	69	61	8	2	7	2	56	0	82	3	2	7	8	.467	0	0- -	—	4.18
1996 New Haven	AA	16	16	1	0	97.2	389	82	35	31	8	2	1	2	27	1	86	2	1	9	4	.692	0	0- -	—	2.86
Colo Sprngs	AAA	11	11	0	0	69.2	305	76	45	39	6	3	1	4	26	2	62	4	1	4	7	.364	0	0- -	—	5.04

209

		HOW MUCH HE PITCHED							WHAT HE GAVE UP												THE RESULTS					
Year Team	Lg	G	GS	CG	GF	IP	BFP	H	R	ER	HR	SH	SF	HB	TBB	IBB	SO	WP	Bk	W	L	Pct.	ShO	Sv-Op	Hld	ERA
1997 Colo Sprngs	AAA	7	7	0	0	42	169	36	18	16	4	1	0	0	14	1	49	2	0	4	2	.667	0	0- -	—	3.43
1997 Colorado	NL	27	27	2	0	166.1	721	193	94	87	15	10	3	5	51	0	106	2	0	7	9	.438	1	0-0	0	4.71

Gary Thurman

Bats: Right **Throws:** Right **Pos:** PH-8; CF-4; LF-3; RF-1　　　　**Ht:** 5'10" **Wt:** 180 **Born:** 11/12/64 **Age:** 33

		BATTING																BASERUNNING				PERCENTAGES		
Year Team	Lg	G	AB	H	2B	3B	HR	(Hm	Rd)	TB	R	RBI	TBB	IBB	SO	HBP	SH	SF	SB	CS	SB%	GDP	Avg	OBP	SLG
1997 Norfolk *	AAA	23	80	20	4	0	0	—	—	24	7	12	11	0	16	0	1	2	4	1	.80	2	.250	.333	.300
Ottawa *	AAA	43	104	22	4	1	0	—	—	28	16	5	18	1	28	2	3	0	8	4	.67	3	.212	.339	.269
1987 Kansas City	AL	27	81	24	2	0	0	(0	0)	26	12	5	8	0	20	0	1	0	7	2	.78	1	.296	.360	.321
1988 Kansas City	AL	35	66	11	1	0	0	(0	0)	12	6	2	4	0	20	0	0	0	5	1	.83	0	.167	.214	.182
1989 Kansas City	AL	72	87	17	2	1	0	(0	0)	21	24	5	15	0	26	0	2	1	16	0	1.00	0	.195	.311	.241
1990 Kansas City	AL	23	60	14	3	0	0	(0	0)	17	5	3	2	0	12	0	1	0	1	1	.50	2	.233	.258	.283
1991 Kansas City	AL	80	184	51	9	0	2	(1	1)	66	24	13	11	0	42	1	3	1	15	5	.75	4	.277	.320	.359
1992 Kansas City	AL	88	200	49	6	3	0	(0	0)	61	25	20	9	0	34	1	6	0	9	6	.60	3	.245	.281	.305
1993 Detroit	AL	75	89	19	2	2	0	(0	0)	25	22	13	11	0	30	0	1	1	7	0	1.00	1	.213	.297	.281
1995 Seattle	AL	13	25	8	2	0	0	(0	0)	10	3	3	1	0	3	0	0	1	5	2	.71	0	.320	.333	.400
1997 New York	NL	11	6	1	0	0	0	(0	0)	1	0	0	0	0	0	0	0	0	0	1	.00	1	.167	.167	.167
9 ML YEARS		424	798	194	27	6	2	(1	1)	239	121	64	61	0	187	2	14	4	65	18	.78	13	.243	.297	.299

Mike Thurman

Pitches: Right **Bats:** Right **Pos:** RP-3; SP-2　　　　**Ht:** 6'4" **Wt:** 210 **Born:** 7/22/73 **Age:** 24

		HOW MUCH HE PITCHED							WHAT HE GAVE UP												THE RESULTS					
Year Team	Lg	G	GS	CG	GF	IP	BFP	H	R	ER	HR	SH	SF	HB	TBB	IBB	SO	WP	Bk	W	L	Pct.	ShO	Sv-Op	Hld	ERA
1994 Vermont	A-	2	2	0	0	6.2	28	6	4	4	1	0	0	0	2	0	3	0	0	0	1	.000	0	0- -	—	5.40
1995 Albany	A	22	22	2	0	110.1	482	133	79	67	4	3	7	4	32	0	77	7	0	3	8	.273	0	0- -	—	5.47
1996 Wst Plm Bch	A+	19	19	0	0	113.2	479	122	53	43	3	2	2	5	23	0	68	7	1	6	8	.429	0	0- -	—	3.40
Harrisburg	AA	4	4	1	0	24.2	101	25	14	14	6	1	1	3	5	0	14	0	0	3	1	.750	0	0- -	—	5.11
1997 Harrisburg	AA	20	20	1	0	115.2	474	102	54	49	16	3	7	5	30	0	85	3	0	9	6	.600	0	0- -	—	3.81
Ottawa	AAA	4	4	0	0	19.2	85	17	13	12	1	0	0	1	9	0	15	2	1	1	3	.250	0	0- -	—	5.49
1997 Montreal	NL	5	2	0	1	11.2	48	8	9	7	3	0	0	1	4	0	8	0	0	1	0	1.000	0	0-0	0	5.40

Mike Timlin

Pitches: Right **Bats:** Right **Pos:** RP-64　　　　**Ht:** 6'4" **Wt:** 210 **Born:** 3/10/66 **Age:** 32

		HOW MUCH HE PITCHED							WHAT HE GAVE UP												THE RESULTS					
Year Team	Lg	G	GS	CG	GF	IP	BFP	H	R	ER	HR	SH	SF	HB	TBB	IBB	SO	WP	Bk	W	L	Pct.	ShO	Sv-Op	Hld	ERA
1991 Toronto	AL	63	3	0	17	108.1	463	94	43	38	6	6	2	1	50	11	85	5	0	11	6	.647	0	3-8	9	3.16
1992 Toronto	AL	26	0	0	14	43.2	190	45	23	20	0	2	1	1	20	5	35	0	0	0	2	.000	0	1-1	1	4.12
1993 Toronto	AL	54	0	0	27	55.2	254	63	32	29	7	1	3	1	27	3	49	1	0	4	2	.667	0	1-4	9	4.69
1994 Toronto	AL	34	0	0	16	40	179	41	25	23	5	0	0	2	20	0	38	3	0	0	1	.000	0	2-4	5	5.18
1995 Toronto	AL	31	0	0	19	42	179	38	13	10	1	3	0	2	17	5	36	3	1	4	3	.571	0	5-9	4	2.14
1996 Toronto	AL	59	0	0	56	56.2	230	47	25	23	4	2	3	2	18	4	52	3	0	1	6	.143	0	31-38	2	3.65
1997 Tor-Sea	AL	64	0	0	31	72.2	297	69	30	26	8	6	1	1	20	5	45	1	1	6	4	.600	0	10-18	9	3.22
1997 Toronto	AL	38	0	0	26	47	190	41	17	15	6	4	1	1	15	4	36	1	1	3	2	.600	0	9-13	2	2.87
Seattle	AL	26	0	0	5	25.2	107	28	13	11	2	2	0	0	5	1	9	0	0	3	2	.600	0	1-5	7	3.86
7 ML YEARS		331	3	0	180	419	1792	397	191	169	31	20	10	10	172	33	340	16	2	26	24	.520	0	53-82	39	3.63

Ozzie Timmons

Bats: Right **Throws:** Right **Pos:** PH-5; LF-1　　　　**Ht:** 6'2" **Wt:** 220 **Born:** 9/18/70 **Age:** 27

		BATTING																BASERUNNING				PERCENTAGES		
Year Team	Lg	G	AB	H	2B	3B	HR	(Hm	Rd)	TB	R	RBI	TBB	IBB	SO	HBP	SH	SF	SB	CS	SB%	GDP	Avg	OBP	SLG
1997 Indianapols *	AAA	125	407	103	14	1	14	—	—	161	46	55	60	5	100	2	0	5	1	4	.20	11	.253	.348	.396
1995 Chicago	NL	77	171	45	10	1	8	(5	3)	81	30	28	13	2	32	0	0	1	3	0	1.00	8	.263	.314	.474
1996 Chicago	NL	65	140	28	4	0	7	(6	1)	53	18	16	15	0	30	1	1	0	1	0	1.00	1	.200	.282	.379
1997 Cincinnati	NL	6	9	3	1	0	0	(0	0)	4	1	0	0	0	1	0	0	0	0	0	.00	0	.333	.333	.444
3 ML YEARS		148	320	76	15	1	15	(11	4)	138	49	44	28	2	63	1	1	1	4	0	1.00	9	.238	.300	.431

Lee Tinsley

Bats: B **Throws:** R **Pos:** LF-34; PH-13; CF-6; DH-4; RF-2　　　　**Ht:** 5'10" **Wt:** 195 **Born:** 3/4/69 **Age:** 29

		BATTING																BASERUNNING				PERCENTAGES		
Year Team	Lg	G	AB	H	2B	3B	HR	(Hm	Rd)	TB	R	RBI	TBB	IBB	SO	HBP	SH	SF	SB	CS	SB%	GDP	Avg	OBP	SLG
1997 Tacoma *	AAA	31	105	19	2	1	2	—	—	29	15	7	12	0	34	0	0	0	1	4	.20	0	.181	.265	.276
1993 Seattle	AL	11	19	3	1	0	1	(0	1)	7	2	2	2	0	9	0	0	0	0	0	.00	1	.158	.238	.368
1994 Boston	AL	78	144	32	4	0	2	(1	1)	42	27	14	19	1	36	1	3	1	13	0	1.00	2	.222	.315	.292
1995 Boston	AL	100	341	97	17	1	7	(4	3)	137	61	41	39	1	74	1	9	1	18	8	.69	8	.284	.359	.402
1996 Phi-Bos		123	244	54	6	1	3	(1	2)	71	29	16	17	0	78	2	2	1	8	12	.40	6	.221	.277	.291
1997 Seattle	AL	49	122	24	6	2	0	(0	0)	34	12	6	11	0	34	0	0	0	2	0	1.00	4	.197	.263	.279
1996 Philadelphia	NL	31	52	7	0	0	0	(0	0)	7	1	2	4	0	22	0	1	0	2	4	.33	1	.135	.196	.135
Boston	AL	92	192	47	6	1	3	(1	2)	64	28	14	13	0	56	2	1	1	6	8	.43	5	.245	.298	.333
5 ML YEARS		361	870	210	34	4	13	(6	7)	291	131	79	88	2	231	4	14	3	41	20	.67	21	.241	.313	.334

Andy Tomberlin

Bats: Left   **Throws:** Left   **Pos:** PH-4; LF-1; RF-1   **Ht:** 5'11"   **Wt:** 180   **Born:** 11/7/66   **Age:** 31

Year Team	Lg	G	AB	H	2B	3B	HR	(Hm	Rd)	TB	R	RBI	TBB	IBB	SO	HBP	SH	SF	SB	CS	SB%	GDP	Avg	OBP	SLG
1997 Mets *	R	7	22	7	0	0	2	—	—	13	6	7	3	0	7	0	0	0	1	0	1.00	1	.318	.400	.591
St. Lucie *	A+	1	3	0	0	0	0	—	—	0	0	1	1	0	2	0	0	0	0	0	.00	0	.000	.250	.000
1993 Pittsburgh	NL	27	42	12	0	1	1	(0	1)	17	4	5	2	0	14	1	0	0	0	0	.00	0	.286	.333	.405
1994 Boston	AL	17	36	7	0	1	1	(1	0)	12	1	1	6	0	12	0	0	0	1	0	1.00	0	.194	.310	.333
1995 Oakland	AL	46	85	18	0	0	4	(3	1)	30	15	10	5	0	22	0	2	0	4	1	.80	2	.212	.256	.353
1996 New York	NL	63	66	17	4	0	3	(2	1)	30	12	10	9	0	27	1	0	0	0	0	.00	0	.258	.355	.455
1997 New York	NL	6	7	2	0	0	0	(0	0)	2	0	0	1	0	3	0	0	0	0	0	.00	0	.286	.375	.286
5 ML YEARS		159	236	56	4	2	9	(6	3)	91	32	26	23	0	78	2	2	0	5	1	.83	2	.237	.310	.386

Brett Tomko

Pitches: Right   **Bats:** Right   **Pos:** SP-19; RP-3   **Ht:** 6'4"   **Wt:** 215   **Born:** 4/7/73   **Age:** 25

Year Team	Lg	G	GS	CG	GF	IP	BFP	H	R	ER	HR	SH	SF	HB	TBB	IBB	SO	WP	Bk	W	L	Pct.	ShO	Sv-Op	Hld	ERA
1995 Chston-WV	A	9	7	0	0	49	192	41	12	10	1	1	1	1	9	1	46	4	2	4	2	.667	0	0- -	—	1.84
1996 Chattanooga	AA	27	27	0	0	157.2	647	131	73	68	20	3	4	5	54	4	164	6	5	11	7	.611	0	0- -	—	3.88
1997 Indianapolis	AAA	10	10	0	0	61	239	53	21	20	7	0	1	1	9	0	60	0	0	6	3	.667	0	0- -	—	2.95
1997 Cincinnati	NL	22	19	0	1	126	519	106	50	48	14	5	9	4	47	4	95	5	0	11	7	.611	0	0-0	0	3.43

Salomon Torres

Pitches: Right   **Bats:** Right   **Pos:** RP-14   **Ht:** 5'11"   **Wt:** 165   **Born:** 3/11/72   **Age:** 26

Year Team	Lg	G	GS	CG	GF	IP	BFP	H	R	ER	HR	SH	SF	HB	TBB	IBB	SO	WP	Bk	W	L	Pct.	ShO	Sv-Op	Hld	ERA
1997 Ottawa *	AAA	2	1	0	1	5	24	7	5	3	0	0	0	0	2	0	2	0	1	0	0	.000	0	0- -	—	5.40
1993 San Francisco	NL	8	8	0	0	44.2	196	37	21	20	5	7	1	1	27	3	23	3	1	3	5	.375	0	0-0	0	4.03
1994 San Francisco	NL	16	14	1	2	84.1	378	95	55	51	10	4	8	7	34	2	42	4	1	2	8	.200	0	0-0	0	5.44
1995 SF-Sea		20	14	1	4	80	384	100	61	56	16	1	0	2	49	3	47	1	2	3	9	.250	0	0-0	0	6.30
1996 Seattle	AL	10	7	1	1	49	212	44	27	25	5	3	1	3	23	2	36	1	0	3	3	.500	1	0-0	0	4.59
1997 Sea-Mon		14	0	0	4	25.2	127	32	29	28	2	3	1	3	15	0	11	3	0	0	0	.000	0	0-0	0	9.82
1995 San Francisco	NL	4	1	0	2	8	40	13	8	8	4	0	0	0	7	0	2	0	0	0	1	.000	0	0-0	0	9.00
Seattle	AL	16	13	1	2	72	344	87	53	48	12	1	0	2	42	3	45	1	2	3	8	.273	0	0-0	0	6.00
1997 Seattle	AL	2	0	0	1	3.1	21	7	10	10	0	0	0	1	3	0	0	0	0	0	0	.000	0	0-0	0	27.00
Montreal	NL	12	0	0	3	22.1	106	25	19	18	2	3	1	2	12	0	11	3	0	0	0	.000	0	0-0	0	7.25
5 ML YEARS		68	43	3	11	283.2	1297	308	193	180	38	18	11	16	148	10	159	12	4	11	25	.306	1	0-0	0	5.71

Steve Trachsel

Pitches: Right   **Bats:** Right   **Pos:** SP-34   **Ht:** 6'4"   **Wt:** 205   **Born:** 10/31/70   **Age:** 27

Year Team	Lg	G	GS	CG	GF	IP	BFP	H	R	ER	HR	SH	SF	HB	TBB	IBB	SO	WP	Bk	W	L	Pct.	ShO	Sv-Op	Hld	ERA
1993 Chicago	NL	3	3	0	0	19.2	78	16	10	10	4	1	1	0	3	0	14	1	0	0	2	.000	0	0-0	0	4.58
1994 Chicago	NL	22	22	1	0	146	612	133	57	52	19	3	3	3	54	4	108	6	0	9	7	.563	0	0-0	0	3.21
1995 Chicago	NL	30	29	2	0	160.2	722	174	104	92	25	12	5	0	76	8	117	2	1	7	13	.350	0	0-0	0	5.15
1996 Chicago	NL	31	31	0	0	205	845	181	82	69	30	3	8	8	62	3	132	5	2	13	9	.591	2	0-0	0	3.03
1997 Chicago	NL	34	34	0	0	201.1	878	225	110	101	32	8	11	5	69	6	160	4	1	8	12	.400	0	0-0	0	4.51
5 ML YEARS		120	119	6	0	732.2	3135	729	363	324	110	27	23	16	264	21	531	18	4	37	43	.463	2	0-0	0	3.98

Bubba Trammell

Bats: R   **Throws:** R   **Pos:** RF-15; DH-14; LF-13; PH-5   **Ht:** 6'2"   **Wt:** 220   **Born:** 11/6/71   **Age:** 26

Year Team	Lg	G	AB	H	2B	3B	HR	(Hm	Rd)	TB	R	RBI	TBB	IBB	SO	HBP	SH	SF	SB	CS	SB%	GDP	Avg	OBP	SLG
1994 Jamestown	A-	65	235	70	18	6	5	—	—	115	37	41	23	0	32	4	0	4	9	7	.56	1	.298	.365	.489
1995 Lakeland	A+	122	454	129	32	3	16	—	—	215	61	72	48	2	80	4	0	4	13	3	.81	9	.284	.355	.474
1996 Jacksonville	AA	83	311	102	23	2	27	—	—	210	63	75	32	6	61	8	0	1	5	3	.60	11	.328	.403	.675
Toledo	AAA	51	180	53	14	1	6	—	—	87	32	24	22	1	44	0	0	1	5	1	.83	1	.294	.369	.483
1997 Toledo	AAA	90	319	80	15	1	28	—	—	181	56	75	38	1	91	5	0	4	2	2	.50	1	.251	.336	.567
1997 Detroit	AL	44	123	28	5	0	4	(2	2)	45	14	13	15	0	35	0	0	2	3	1	.75	2	.228	.307	.366

Ricky Trlicek

Pitches: Right   **Bats:** Right   **Pos:** RP-27   **Ht:** 6'2"   **Wt:** 200   **Born:** 4/26/69   **Age:** 29

Year Team	Lg	G	GS	CG	GF	IP	BFP	H	R	ER	HR	SH	SF	HB	TBB	IBB	SO	WP	Bk	W	L	Pct.	ShO	Sv-Op	Hld	ERA
1992 Toronto	AL	2	0	0	0	1.2	9	2	2	2	0	0	0	0	2	0	1	0	0	0	0	.000	0	0-0	0	10.80
1993 Los Angeles	NL	41	0	0	18	64	267	59	32	29	3	2	0	2	21	4	41	4	1	1	2	.333	0	1-1	1	4.08
1994 Boston	AL	12	1	0	2	22.1	113	32	21	20	5	0	0	0	16	2	7	1	2	1	1	.500	0	0-1	0	8.06
1996 New York	NL	5	0	0	2	5.1	20	3	2	2	0	2	0	1	3	1	3	0	0	0	1	.000	0	0-0	0	3.38
1997 Bos-NYN		27	0	0	12	32.1	150	36	23	20	4	2	1	1	23	4	14	4	0	3	4	.429	0	0-1	1	5.57
1997 Boston	AL	18	0	0	8	23.1	111	26	14	12	2	1	1	1	18	4	10	2	0	3	4	.429	0	0-0	1	4.63
New York	NL	9	0	0	4	9	39	10	9	8	2	1	0	0	5	0	4	2	0	0	0	.000	0	0-1	0	8.00
5 ML YEARS		87	1	0	34	125.2	559	132	80	73	12	6	1	4	65	11	66	9	3	5	8	.385	0	1-3	2	5.23

Mike Trombley

Pitches: Right   **Bats:** Right   **Pos:** RP-67   **Ht:** 6'2"   **Wt:** 206   **Born:** 4/14/67   **Age:** 31

				HOW MUCH HE PITCHED			WHAT HE GAVE UP												THE RESULTS					
Year Team	Lg	G	GS	CG	GF	IP	BFP	H	R	ER	HR	SH	SF	HB	TBB	IBB	SO	WP	Bk	W	L	Pct.	ShO	Sv-Op	Hld	ERA
1992 Minnesota	AL	10	7	0	0	46.1	194	43	20	17	5	2	0	1	17	0	38	0	0	3	2	.600	0	0-0	0	3.30
1993 Minnesota	AL	44	10	0	8	114.1	506	131	72	62	15	3	7	3	41	4	85	5	0	6	6	.500	0	2-5	8	4.88
1994 Minnesota	AL	24	0	0	8	48.1	219	56	36	34	10	1	2	3	18	2	32	3	0	2	0	1.000	0	0-1	1	6.33
1995 Minnesota	AL	20	18	0	0	97.2	442	107	68	61	18	3	2	3	42	1	68	4	0	4	8	.333	0	0-0	0	5.62
1996 Minnesota	AL	43	0	0	19	68.2	292	61	24	23	2	0	3	5	25	8	57	4	0	5	1	.833	0	6-9	4	3.01
1997 Minnesota	AL	67	0	0	21	82.1	349	77	43	40	7	2	3	2	31	4	74	5	0	2	3	.400	0	1-1	11	4.37
6 ML YEARS		208	35	0	56	457.2	2002	475	263	237	57	11	17	17	174	19	354	21	0	22	20	.524	0	9-16	24	4.66

Michael Tucker

Bats: Left   **Throws:** Right   **Pos:** RF-102; LF-53; PH-13   **Ht:** 6'2"   **Wt:** 185   **Born:** 6/25/71   **Age:** 27

						BATTING												BASERUNNING				PERCENTAGES		
Year Team	Lg	G	AB	H	2B	3B	HR	(Hm	Rd)	TB	R	RBI	TBB	IBB	SO	HBP	SH	SF	SB	CS	SB%	GDP	Avg	OBP	SLG
1995 Kansas City	AL	62	177	46	10	0	4	(1	3)	68	23	17	18	2	51	1	2	0	2	3	.40	3	.260	.332	.384
1996 Kansas City	AL	108	339	88	18	4	12	(2	10)	150	55	53	40	1	69	7	3	4	10	4	.71	7	.260	.346	.442
1997 Atlanta	NL	138	499	141	25	7	14	(5	9)	222	80	56	44	0	116	6	4	1	12	7	.63	7	.283	.347	.445
3 ML YEARS		308	1015	275	53	11	30	(8	22)	440	158	126	102	3	236	14	9	5	24	14	.63	17	.271	.344	.433

Chris Turner

Bats: R   **Throws:** R   **Pos:** C-8; PH-3; 1B-2; DH-1; RF-1   **Ht:** 6'3"   **Wt:** 200   **Born:** 3/23/69   **Age:** 29

						BATTING												BASERUNNING				PERCENTAGES		
Year Team	Lg	G	AB	H	2B	3B	HR	(Hm	Rd)	TB	R	RBI	TBB	IBB	SO	HBP	SH	SF	SB	CS	SB%	GDP	Avg	OBP	SLG
1997 Lk Elsinore *	A+	3	12	1	0	1	0	—	—	3	0	1	0	0	3	0	0	0	0	0	.00	1	.083	.083	.250
Vancouver *	AAA	37	135	50	10	0	4	—	—	72	26	22	14	0	22	2	0	0	0	0	.00	5	.370	.437	.533
1993 California	AL	25	75	21	5	0	1	(0	1)	29	9	13	9	0	16	1	0	1	1	1	.50	1	.280	.360	.387
1994 California	AL	58	149	36	7	1	1	(1	0)	48	23	12	10	0	29	1	1	2	3	0	1.00	2	.242	.290	.322
1995 California	AL	5	10	1	0	0	0	(0	0)	1	0	1	0	0	3	0	0	0	0	0	.00	0	.100	.100	.100
1996 California	AL	4	3	1	0	0	0	(0	0)	1	1	1	1	0	0	0	0	1	0	0	.00	0	.333	.400	.333
1997 Anaheim	AL	13	23	6	1	1	1	(0	1)	12	4	2	5	0	8	0	1	0	0	0	.00	0	.261	.393	.522
5 ML YEARS		105	260	65	13	2	3	(1	2)	91	37	29	25	0	56	2	2	4	4	1	.80	3	.250	.316	.350

Tim Unroe

Bats: R   **Throws:** R   **Pos:** 1B-23; PH-9; 3B-2; 2B-1; LF-1; RF-1   **Ht:** 6'3"   **Wt:** 200   **Born:** 10/7/70   **Age:** 27

						BATTING												BASERUNNING				PERCENTAGES		
Year Team	Lg	G	AB	H	2B	3B	HR	(Hm	Rd)	TB	R	RBI	TBB	IBB	SO	HBP	SH	SF	SB	CS	SB%	GDP	Avg	OBP	SLG
1992 Helena	R+	74	266	74	13	2	16	—	—	139	61	58	47	1	91	4	1	1	3	4	.43	2	.278	.393	.523
1993 Stockton	A+	108	382	96	21	6	12	—	—	165	57	63	36	0	96	7	3	4	9	10	.47	8	.251	.324	.432
1994 El Paso	AA	126	474	147	36	7	15	—	—	242	97	103	42	2	107	5	0	9	14	6	.70	6	.310	.366	.511
1995 New Orleans	AAA	102	371	97	21	2	6	—	—	140	43	45	18	1	94	7	1	5	4	3	.57	9	.261	.304	.377
1996 New Orleans	AAA	109	404	109	26	4	25	—	—	218	72	67	36	2	121	4	0	4	8	3	.73	10	.270	.333	.540
1997 Tucson	AAA	63	234	68	17	1	9	—	—	114	45	46	9	0	62	2	0	2	3	3	.50	6	.291	.320	.487
1995 Milwaukee	AL	2	4	1	0	0	0	(0	0)	1	0	0	0	0	0	0	0	0	0	0	.00	0	.250	.250	.250
1996 Milwaukee	AL	14	16	3	0	0	0	(0	0)	3	5	0	4	0	5	0	0	0	1	0	.00	0	.188	.350	.188
1997 Milwaukee	AL	32	16	4	1	0	2	(1	1)	11	3	5	2	0	9	0	0	0	2	0	1.00	0	.250	.333	.688
3 ML YEARS		48	36	8	1	0	2	(1	1)	15	8	5	6	0	14	0	0	0	2	1	.67	0	.222	.333	.417

Ugueth Urbina

Pitches: Right   **Bats:** Right   **Pos:** RP-63   **Ht:** 6'2"   **Wt:** 185   **Born:** 2/15/74   **Age:** 24

				HOW MUCH HE PITCHED			WHAT HE GAVE UP												THE RESULTS					
Year Team	Lg	G	GS	CG	GF	IP	BFP	H	R	ER	HR	SH	SF	HB	TBB	IBB	SO	WP	Bk	W	L	Pct.	ShO	Sv-Op	Hld	ERA
1995 Montreal	NL	7	4	0	0	23.1	109	26	17	16	6	2	0	0	14	1	15	2	0	2	2	.500	0	0-0	0	6.17
1996 Montreal	NL	33	17	0	2	114	484	102	54	47	18	1	3	1	44	4	108	3	1	10	5	.667	0	0-1	6	3.71
1997 Montreal	NL	63	0	0	50	64.1	276	52	29	27	9	3	0	1	29	2	84	2	0	5	8	.385	0	27-32	1	3.78
3 ML YEARS		103	21	0	52	201.2	869	180	100	90	33	6	3	2	87	7	207	7	1	17	15	.531	0	27-33	7	4.02

Ismael Valdes

Pitches: Right   **Bats:** Right   **Pos:** SP-30   **Ht:** 6'3"   **Wt:** 207   **Born:** 8/21/73   **Age:** 24

				HOW MUCH HE PITCHED			WHAT HE GAVE UP												THE RESULTS					
Year Team	Lg	G	GS	CG	GF	IP	BFP	H	R	ER	HR	SH	SF	HB	TBB	IBB	SO	WP	Bk	W	L	Pct.	ShO	Sv-Op	Hld	ERA
1994 Los Angeles	NL	21	1	0	7	28.1	115	21	10	10	2	3	0	0	10	2	28	1	2	3	1	.750	0	0-0	4	3.18
1995 Los Angeles	NL	33	27	6	1	197.2	804	168	76	67	17	10	5	1	51	5	150	1	3	13	11	.542	2	1-1	2	3.05
1996 Los Angeles	NL	33	33	0	0	225	945	219	94	83	20	7	7	3	54	10	173	1	5	15	7	.682	0	0-0	0	3.32
1997 Los Angeles	NL	30	30	0	0	196.2	795	171	68	58	16	11	3	3	47	1	140	3	2	10	11	.476	0	0-0	0	2.65
4 ML YEARS		117	91	6	8	647.2	2659	579	248	218	55	31	15	7	162	18	491	6	12	41	30	.577	2	1-1	6	3.03

Marc Valdes

Pitches: Right **Bats:** Right **Pos:** RP-41; SP-7   **Ht:** 6'0" **Wt:** 187 **Born:** 12/20/71 **Age:** 26

Year Team	Lg	G	GS	CG	GF	IP	BFP	H	R	ER	HR	SH	SF	HB	TBB	IBB	SO	WP	Bk	W	L	Pct.	ShO	Sv-Op	Hld	ERA
1995 Florida	NL	3	3	0	0	7	49	17	13	11	1	1	1	1	9	0	2	1	0	0	0	.000	0	0-0	0	14.14
1996 Florida	NL	11	8	0	0	48.2	228	63	32	26	5	1	3	1	23	0	13	3	2	1	3	.250	0	0-1	0	4.81
1997 Montreal	NL	48	7	0	9	95	407	84	36	33	2	5	5	8	39	5	54	2	0	4	4	.500	0	2-2	1	3.13
3 ML YEARS		62	18	0	9	150.2	684	164	81	70	8	7	9	10	71	5	69	6	2	5	7	.417	0	2-3	1	4.18

Mario Valdez

Bats: L **Throws:** L **Pos:** 1B-47; PH-9; DH-2; 3B-1   **Ht:** 6'2" **Wt:** 190 **Born:** 11/19/74 **Age:** 23

								BATTING											BASERUNNING				PERCENTAGES		
Year Team	Lg	G	AB	H	2B	3B	HR	(Hm	Rd)	TB	R	RBI	TBB	IBB	SO	HBP	SH	SF	SB	CS	SB%	GDP	Avg	OBP	SLG
1994 White Sox	R	53	157	37	11	2	2	—	—	58	20	25	30	0	28	2	0	1	0	6	.00	3	.236	.363	.369
1995 Hickory	A	130	441	120	30	5	11	—	—	193	65	56	67	2	107	5	0	3	9	7	.56	5	.272	.372	.438
1996 South Bend	A	61	202	76	19	0	10	—	—	125	46	43	36	2	42	6	0	2	2	4	.33	3	.376	.480	.619
Birmingham	AA	51	168	46	10	2	3	—	—	69	22	28	32	2	34	5	0	3	0	0	.00	3	.274	.399	.411
1997 Nashville	AAA	81	282	79	20	1	15	—	—	146	44	61	43	3	77	9	1	4	1	1	.50	8	.280	.388	.518
1997 Chicago	AL	54	115	28	7	0	1	(0	1)	38	11	13	17	0	39	3	0	2	1	0	1.00	3	.243	.350	.330

Javier Valentin

Bats: Both **Throws:** Right **Pos:** C-4   **Ht:** 5'10" **Wt:** 198 **Born:** 9/19/75 **Age:** 22

								BATTING											BASERUNNING				PERCENTAGES		
Year Team	Lg	G	AB	H	2B	3B	HR	(Hm	Rd)	TB	R	RBI	TBB	IBB	SO	HBP	SH	SF	SB	CS	SB%	GDP	Avg	OBP	SLG
1993 Twins	R	32	103	27	6	1	1	—	—	38	18	19	14	0	19	1	0	4	0	2	.00	1	.262	.344	.369
Elizabethtn	R+	9	24	5	1	0	0	—	—	6	3	3	4	0	2	1	0	0	0	0	.00	0	.208	.345	.250
1994 Elizabethtn	R+	54	210	44	5	0	9	—	—	76	23	27	15	0	44	2	0	5	0	1	.00	9	.210	.263	.362
1995 Ft. Wayne	A	112	383	123	26	5	19	—	—	216	59	65	47	7	75	2	1	0	0	5	.00	7	.321	.398	.564
1996 Ft. Myers	A+	87	338	89	26	1	7	—	—	138	34	54	32	4	65	4	0	5	1	0	1.00	5	.263	.330	.408
Hardware City	AA	48	165	39	8	0	3	—	—	56	22	14	16	1	35	1	3	0	0	3	.00	2	.236	.308	.339
1997 New Britain	AA	102	370	90	17	0	8	—	—	131	41	50	30	1	61	1	2	6	2	3	.40	5	.243	.297	.354
1997 Minnesota	AL	4	7	2	0	0	0	(0	0)	2	1	0	0	0	3	0	0	0	0	0	.00	0	.286	.286	.286

John Valentin

Bats: Right **Throws:** Right **Pos:** 2B-79; 3B-64; PH-1   **Ht:** 6'0" **Wt:** 180 **Born:** 2/18/67 **Age:** 31

								BATTING											BASERUNNING				PERCENTAGES		
Year Team	Lg	G	AB	H	2B	3B	HR	(Hm	Rd)	TB	R	RBI	TBB	IBB	SO	HBP	SH	SF	SB	CS	SB%	GDP	Avg	OBP	SLG
1992 Boston	AL	58	185	51	13	0	5	(1	4)	79	21	25	20	0	17	2	4	1	1	0	1.00	5	.276	.351	.427
1993 Boston	AL	144	468	130	40	3	11	(7	4)	209	50	66	49	2	77	2	16	4	3	4	.43	9	.278	.346	.447
1994 Boston	AL	84	301	95	26	2	9	(6	3)	152	53	49	42	1	38	3	5	4	3	1	.75	3	.316	.400	.505
1995 Boston	AL	135	520	155	37	2	27	(11	16)	277	108	102	81	2	67	10	4	6	20	5	.80	7	.298	.399	.533
1996 Boston	AL	131	527	156	29	3	13	(9	4)	230	84	59	63	0	59	7	2	7	9	10	.47	15	.296	.374	.436
1997 Boston	AL	143	575	176	47	5	18	(11	7)	287	95	77	58	5	66	5	1	5	7	4	.64	21	.306	.372	.499
6 ML YEARS		695	2576	763	192	15	83	(45	38)	1234	411	378	313	10	324	29	32	27	43	24	.64	60	.296	.375	.479

Jose Valentin

Bats: Both **Throws:** Right **Pos:** SS-134; DH-1; PH-1   **Ht:** 5'10" **Wt:** 166 **Born:** 10/12/69 **Age:** 28

								BATTING											BASERUNNING				PERCENTAGES		
Year Team	Lg	G	AB	H	2B	3B	HR	(Hm	Rd)	TB	R	RBI	TBB	IBB	SO	HBP	SH	SF	SB	CS	SB%	GDP	Avg	OBP	SLG
1997 Beloit *	A	2	6	3	1	0	0	—	—	4	3	1	2	0	1	0	0	0	0	0	.00	0	.500	.625	.667
1992 Milwaukee	AL	4	3	0	0	0	0	(0	0)	0	1	1	0	0	0	0	0	1	0	0	.00	0	.000	.000	.000
1993 Milwaukee	AL	19	53	13	1	2	1	(1	0)	21	10	7	7	1	16	1	2	0	1	0	1.00	1	.245	.344	.396
1994 Milwaukee	AL	97	285	68	19	0	11	(8	3)	120	47	46	38	1	75	2	4	2	12	3	.80	1	.239	.330	.421
1995 Milwaukee	AL	112	338	74	23	3	11	(8	3)	136	62	49	37	0	83	0	7	4	16	8	.67	0	.219	.293	.402
1996 Milwaukee	AL	154	552	143	33	7	24	(10	14)	262	90	95	66	9	145	0	6	4	17	4	.81	4	.259	.336	.475
1997 Milwaukee	AL	136	494	125	23	1	17	(4	13)	201	58	58	39	4	109	4	4	5	19	8	.70	5	.253	.310	.407
6 ML YEARS		522	1725	423	99	13	64	(26	38)	740	268	256	187	15	428	7	23	16	65	23	.74	11	.245	.319	.429

Fernando Valenzuela

Pitches: Left **Bats:** Left **Pos:** SP-18   **Ht:** 5'11" **Wt:** 200 **Born:** 11/1/60 **Age:** 37

Year Team	Lg	G	GS	CG	GF	IP	BFP	H	R	ER	HR	SH	SF	HB	TBB	IBB	SO	WP	Bk	W	L	Pct.	ShO	Sv-Op	Hld	ERA
1980 Los Angeles	NL	10	0	0	4	17.2	66	8	2	0	0	1	1	0	5	0	16	0	1	2	0	1.000	0	1-1	0	0.00
1981 Los Angeles	NL	25	25	11	0	192.1	758	140	55	53	11	9	3	1	61	4	180	4	0	13	7	.650	8	0-0	0	2.48
1982 Los Angeles	NL	37	37	18	0	285	1156	247	105	91	13	19	6	2	83	12	199	4	0	19	13	.594	4	0-0	0	2.87
1983 Los Angeles	NL	35	35	9	0	257	1094	245	122	107	16	27	5	3	99	10	189	12	1	15	10	.600	4	0-0	0	3.75
1984 Los Angeles	NL	34	34	12	0	261	1078	218	109	88	14	11	7	1	106	4	240	11	1	12	17	.414	2	0-0	0	3.03
1985 Los Angeles	NL	35	35	14	0	272.1	1109	211	92	74	14	13	8	1	101	5	208	10	1	17	10	.630	5	0-0	0	2.45
1986 Los Angeles	NL	34	34	20	0	269.1	1102	226	104	94	18	15	3	1	85	5	242	13	0	21	11	.656	3	0-0	0	3.14
1987 Los Angeles	NL	34	34	12	0	251	1116	254	120	111	25	18	2	4	124	4	190	14	1	14	14	.500	1	0-0	0	3.98
1988 Los Angeles	NL	23	22	3	1	142.1	626	142	71	67	11	15	5	0	76	4	64	7	1	5	8	.385	0	1-1	0	4.24
1989 Los Angeles	NL	31	31	3	0	196.2	852	185	89	75	11	7	7	2	98	6	116	6	4	10	13	.435	0	0-0	0	3.43
1990 Los Angeles	NL	33	33	5	0	204	900	223	112	104	19	11	4	0	77	4	115	13	1	13	13	.500	2	0-0	0	4.59

		HOW MUCH HE PITCHED						WHAT HE GAVE UP												THE RESULTS						
Year Team	Lg	G	GS	CG	GF	IP	BFP	H	R	ER	HR	SH	SF	HB	TBB	IBB	SO	WP	Bk	W	L	Pct.	ShO	Sv-Op	Hld	ERA
1991 California	AL	2	2	0	0	6.2	36	14	10	9	3	1	1	0	3	0	5	1	0	0	2	.000	0	0-0	0	12.15
1993 Baltimore	AL	32	31	5	0	178.2	768	179	104	98	18	4	7	4	79	2	78	8	0	8	10	.444	2	0-0	0	4.94
1994 Philadelphia	NL	8	7	0	0	45	182	42	16	15	8	3	2	0	7	1	19	1	0	1	2	.333	0	0-0	0	3.00
1995 San Diego	NL	29	15	0	5	90.1	395	101	53	50	16	10	2	0	34	2	57	4	0	8	3	.727	0	0-0	2	4.98
1996 San Diego	NL	33	31	0	0	171.2	741	177	78	69	17	11	4	0	67	2	95	7	0	13	8	.619	0	0-0	0	3.62
1997 SD-StL	NL	18	18	1	0	89	419	106	61	49	12	7	2	5	46	0	61	4	0	2	11	.143	0	0-0	0	4.96
1997 San Diego	NL	13	13	1	0	66.1	313	84	42	35	10	3	2	4	32	0	51	2	0	2	8	.200	0	0-0	0	4.75
St. Louis	NL	5	5	0	0	22.2	106	22	19	14	2	4	0	1	14	0	10	2	0	0	4	.000	0	0-0	0	5.56
17 ML YEARS		453	424	113	10	2930	12398	2718	1303	1154	226	182	69	25	1151	65	2074	119	11	173	153	.531	31	2-2	4	3.54

John Vander Wal

Bats: L **Throws:** L **Pos:** PH-61; RF-8; 1B-5; DH-2; LF-2   **Ht:** 6'2" **Wt:** 198 **Born:** 4/29/66 **Age:** 32

		BATTING																BASERUNNING				PERCENTAGES		
Year Team	Lg	G	AB	H	2B	3B	HR	(Hm	Rd)	TB	R	RBI	TBB	IBB	SO	HBP	SH	SF	SB	CS	SB%	GDP	Avg	OBP	SLG
1997 Colo Spmgs *	AAA	25	103	42	12	1	3	—	—	65	29	19	11	1	28	0	0	0	1	1	.50	1	.408	.465	.631
1991 Montreal	NL	21	61	13	4	1	1	(0	1)	22	4	8	1	0	18	0	0	1	0	0	.00	2	.213	.222	.361
1992 Montreal	NL	105	213	51	8	2	4	(2	2)	75	21	20	24	2	36	0	0	0	3	0	1.00	3	.239	.316	.352
1993 Montreal	NL	106	215	50	7	4	5	(1	4)	80	34	30	27	2	30	1	0	1	6	3	.67	1	.233	.320	.372
1994 Colorado	NL	91	110	27	3	1	5	(1	4)	47	12	15	16	0	31	0	0	1	2	1	.67	4	.245	.339	.427
1995 Colorado	NL	105	101	35	8	1	5	(2	3)	60	15	21	16	5	23	0	0	1	1	1	.50	2	.347	.432	.594
1996 Colorado	NL	104	151	38	6	2	5	(5	0)	63	20	31	19	2	38	1	0	2	2	2	.50	1	.252	.335	.417
1997 Colorado	NL	76	92	16	2	0	1	(0	1)	21	7	11	11	0	33	0	0	1	1	1	.50	2	.174	.255	.228
7 ML YEARS		608	943	230	38	11	26	(11	15)	368	113	136	113	11	209	2	0	6	15	8	.65	17	.244	.324	.390

William VanLandingham

Pitches: Right **Bats:** Right **Pos:** SP-17; RP-1   **Ht:** 6'2" **Wt:** 210 **Born:** 7/16/70 **Age:** 27

		HOW MUCH HE PITCHED						WHAT HE GAVE UP												THE RESULTS						
Year Team	Lg	G	GS	CG	GF	IP	BFP	H	R	ER	HR	SH	SF	HB	TBB	IBB	SO	WP	Bk	W	L	Pct.	ShO	Sv-Op	Hld	ERA
1997 Phoenix *	AAA	4	4	0	0	17	92	20	19	17	2	2	3	0	21	0	7	4	1	1	1	.500	0	0- —	—	9.00
1994 San Francisco	NL	16	14	0	1	84	363	70	37	33	4	3	1	2	43	4	56	3	3	8	2	.800	1	0-0	0	3.54
1995 San Francisco	NL	18	18	1	0	122.2	523	124	58	50	14	6	5	2	40	2	95	5	4	6	3	.667	1	0-0	0	3.67
1996 San Francisco	NL	32	32	0	0	181.2	810	196	120	109	17	7	5	9	78	6	97	7	2	9	14	.391	0	0-0	0	5.40
1997 San Francisco	NL	18	17	0	1	89	403	80	56	49	11	0	7	0	59	3	52	9	2	4	7	.364	0	0-0	0	4.96
4 ML YEARS		84	81	1	2	477.1	2099	470	274	241	46	16	18	13	220	15	300	24	11	27	26	.509	0	0-0	0	4.54

Jason Varitek

Bats: Both **Throws:** Right **Pos:** C-1; PH-1   **Ht:** 6'2" **Wt:** 210 **Born:** 4/11/72 **Age:** 26

		BATTING																BASERUNNING				PERCENTAGES		
Year Team	Lg	G	AB	H	2B	3B	HR	(Hm	Rd)	TB	R	RBI	TBB	IBB	SO	HBP	SH	SF	SB	CS	SB%	GDP	Avg	OBP	SLG
1995 Port City	AA	104	352	79	14	2	10	—	—	127	42	44	61	4	126	2	3	3	0	1	.00	8	.224	.337	.361
1996 Port City	AA	134	503	132	34	1	12	—	—	204	63	67	66	7	93	4	0	4	7	6	.54	14	.262	.350	.406
1997 Tacoma	AAA	87	307	78	13	0	15	—	—	136	54	48	34	2	71	2	4	4	0	1	.00	13	.254	.329	.443
Pawtucket	AAA	20	66	13	5	0	1	—	—	21	6	5	8	0	12	0	0	0	0	0	.00	4	.197	.284	.318
1997 Boston	AL	1	1	1	0	0	0	(0	0)	1	0	0	0	0	0	0	0	0	0	0	.00	0	1.000	1.000	1.000

Greg Vaughn

Bats: Right **Throws:** Right **Pos:** LF-94; PH-28; DH-3   **Ht:** 6'0" **Wt:** 202 **Born:** 7/3/65 **Age:** 32

		BATTING																BASERUNNING				PERCENTAGES		
Year Team	Lg	G	AB	H	2B	3B	HR	(Hm	Rd)	TB	R	RBI	TBB	IBB	SO	HBP	SH	SF	SB	CS	SB%	GDP	Avg	OBP	SLG
1989 Milwaukee	AL	38	113	30	3	0	5	(1	4)	48	18	23	13	0	23	0	0	2	4	1	.80	0	.265	.336	.425
1990 Milwaukee	AL	120	382	84	26	2	17	(9	8)	165	51	61	33	1	91	1	7	6	7	4	.64	11	.220	.280	.432
1991 Milwaukee	AL	145	542	132	24	5	27	(16	11)	247	81	98	62	2	125	1	2	7	2	2	.50	5	.244	.319	.456
1992 Milwaukee	AL	141	501	114	18	2	23	(11	12)	205	77	78	60	1	123	5	2	5	15	15	.50	8	.228	.313	.409
1993 Milwaukee	AL	154	569	152	28	2	30	(12	18)	274	97	97	89	14	118	5	0	5	10	7	.59	6	.267	.369	.482
1994 Milwaukee	AL	95	370	94	24	1	19	(9	10)	177	59	55	51	6	93	1	0	1	9	5	.64	6	.254	.345	.478
1995 Milwaukee	AL	108	392	88	19	1	17	(8	9)	160	67	59	55	3	89	0	0	4	10	4	.71	10	.224	.317	.408
1996 Mil-SD		145	516	134	19	1	41	(22	19)	278	98	117	82	6	130	6	0	5	9	3	.75	7	.260	.365	.539
1997 San Diego	NL	120	361	78	10	0	18	(11	7)	142	60	57	56	1	110	2	0	3	7	4	.64	7	.216	.322	.393
1996 Milwaukee	AL	102	375	105	16	0	31	(16	15)	214	78	95	58	4	99	4	0	5	5	2	.71	6	.280	.378	.571
San Diego	NL	43	141	29	3	1	10	(6	4)	64	20	22	24	2	31	2	0	0	4	1	.80	1	.206	.329	.454
9 ML YEARS		1066	3746	906	171	14	197	(99	98)	1696	608	645	501	34	902	21	11	37	73	45	.62	60	.242	.332	.453

Mo Vaughn

Bats: Left **Throws:** Right **Pos:** 1B-131; DH-9; PH-1   **Ht:** 6'1" **Wt:** 240 **Born:** 12/15/67 **Age:** 30

		BATTING																BASERUNNING				PERCENTAGES		
Year Team	Lg	G	AB	H	2B	3B	HR	(Hm	Rd)	TB	R	RBI	TBB	IBB	SO	HBP	SH	SF	SB	CS	SB%	GDP	Avg	OBP	SLG
1991 Boston	AL	74	219	57	12	0	4	(1	3)	81	21	32	26	2	43	2	0	4	2	1	.67	7	.260	.339	.370
1992 Boston	AL	113	355	83	16	2	13	(8	5)	142	42	57	47	7	67	3	0	3	3	3	.50	8	.234	.326	.400
1993 Boston	AL	152	539	160	34	1	29	(13	16)	283	86	101	79	23	130	8	0	7	4	3	.57	14	.297	.390	.525
1994 Boston	AL	111	394	122	25	1	26	(15	11)	227	65	82	57	20	112	10	0	2	4	4	.50	7	.310	.408	.576
1995 Boston	AL	140	550	165	28	3	39	(15	24)	316	98	126	68	17	150	14	0	4	11	4	.73	17	.300	.388	.575
1996 Boston	AL	161	635	207	29	1	44	(27	17)	370	118	143	95	19	154	14	0	8	2	0	1.00	17	.326	.420	.583

214

		BATTING																	BASERUNNING				PERCENTAGES		
Year Team	Lg	G	AB	H	2B	3B	HR	(Hm	Rd)	TB	R	RBI	TBB	IBB	SO	HBP	SH	SF	SB	CS	SB%	GDP	Avg	OBP	SLG
1997 Boston	AL	141	527	166	24	0	35	(20	15)	295	91	96	86	17	154	12	0	3	2	2	.50	10	.315	.420	.560
7 ML YEARS		892	3219	960	168	8	190	(99	91)	1714	521	637	458	105	810	63	0	31	28	17	.62	80	.298	.393	.532

Jorge Velandia

Bats: Right **Throws:** Right **Pos:** SS-6; 2B-5; 3B-3; PH-1 **Ht:** 5'9" **Wt:** 160 **Born:** 1/12/75 **Age:** 23

Year Team	Lg	G	AB	H	2B	3B	HR	(Hm	Rd)	TB	R	RBI	TBB	IBB	SO	HBP	SH	SF	SB	CS	SB%	GDP	Avg	OBP	SLG
1992 Bristol	R+	45	119	24	6	1	0	—	—	32	20	9	15	0	16	0	3	0	3	2	.60	1	.202	.291	.269
1993 Fayetteville	A	37	106	17	4	0	0	—	—	21	15	11	13	0	21	3	0	2	5	0	1.00	3	.160	.266	.198
Niagara Fal	A-	72	212	41	11	0	1	—	—	55	30	22	19	0	48	0	3	2	22	4	.85	2	.193	.258	.259
1994 Lakeland	A+	22	60	14	4	0	0	—	—	18	8	3	6	0	14	0	3	1	0	2	.00	0	.233	.299	.300
Springfield	A	98	290	71	14	0	4	—	—	97	42	36	21	0	46	4	6	3	5	6	.45	8	.245	.302	.334
1995 Memphis	AA	63	186	38	10	2	4	—	—	64	23	17	14	2	37	1	1	1	0	2	.00	4	.204	.262	.344
Las Vegas	AAA	66	206	54	12	3	0	—	—	72	25	25	13	1	37	2	7	2	0	0	.00	5	.262	.309	.350
1996 Memphis	AA	122	392	94	19	0	9	—	—	140	42	48	31	3	65	3	5	8	3	7	.30	10	.240	.295	.357
1997 Las Vegas	AAA	114	405	110	15	2	3	—	—	138	46	35	29	3	62	4	8	1	13	3	.81	5	.272	.326	.341
1997 San Diego	NL	14	29	3	2	0	0	(0	0)	5	0	0	1	0	7	0	0	0	0	0	.00	0	.103	.133	.172

Randy Velarde

Bats: Right **Throws:** Right **Pos:** PH-1 **Ht:** 6'0" **Wt:** 192 **Born:** 11/24/62 **Age:** 35

		BATTING																	BASERUNNING				PERCENTAGES		
Year Team	Lg	G	AB	H	2B	3B	HR	(Hm	Rd)	TB	R	RBI	TBB	IBB	SO	HBP	SH	SF	SB	CS	SB%	GDP	Avg	OBP	SLG
1987 New York	AL	8	22	4	0	0	0	(0	0)	4	1	1	0	0	6	0	0	0	0	0	.00	1	.182	.182	.182
1988 New York	AL	48	115	20	6	0	5	(2	3)	41	18	12	8	0	24	2	0	0	1	1	.50	3	.174	.240	.357
1989 New York	AL	33	100	34	4	2	2	(1	1)	48	12	11	7	0	14	1	3	0	0	3	.00	0	.340	.389	.480
1990 New York	AL	95	229	48	6	2	5	(1	4)	73	21	19	20	0	53	1	2	1	0	3	.00	6	.210	.275	.319
1991 New York	AL	80	184	45	11	1	1	(0	1)	61	19	15	18	0	43	3	5	0	3	1	.75	6	.245	.322	.332
1992 New York	AL	121	412	112	24	1	7	(2	5)	159	57	46	38	1	78	2	4	1	7	2	.78	13	.272	.333	.386
1993 New York	AL	85	226	68	13	2	7	(4	3)	106	28	24	18	2	39	4	3	2	2	2	.50	12	.301	.360	.469
1994 New York	AL	77	280	78	16	1	9	(3	6)	123	47	34	22	0	61	4	2	2	4	2	.67	7	.279	.338	.439
1995 New York	AL	111	367	102	19	1	7	(2	5)	144	60	46	55	0	64	4	3	3	5	1	.83	9	.278	.375	.392
1996 California	AL	136	530	151	27	3	14	(8	6)	226	82	54	70	0	118	5	4	2	7	7	.50	7	.285	.372	.426
1997 Anaheim	AL	1	0	0	0	0	0	(0	0)	0	0	0	0	0	0	0	0	0	0	0	.00	0	.000	.000	.000
11 ML YEARS		795	2465	662	126	13	57	(23	34)	985	345	262	256	3	500	26	26	15	29	22	.57	64	.269	.342	.400

Robin Ventura

Bats: Left **Throws:** Right **Pos:** 3B-54 **Ht:** 6'1" **Wt:** 198 **Born:** 7/14/67 **Age:** 30

		BATTING																	BASERUNNING				PERCENTAGES		
Year Team	Lg	G	AB	H	2B	3B	HR	(Hm	Rd)	TB	R	RBI	TBB	IBB	SO	HBP	SH	SF	SB	CS	SB%	GDP	Avg	OBP	SLG
1997 Nashville *	AAA	5	15	6	1	0	2	—	—	13	3	5	2	0	1	0	0	0	0	1	.00	0	.400	.471	.867
Birmingham *	AA	4	17	5	1	0	1	—	—	9	3	2	1	0	1	0	0	0	0	0	.00	2	.294	.333	.529
1989 Chicago	AL	16	45	8	3	0	0	(0	0)	11	5	7	8	0	6	1	1	3	0	0	.00	1	.178	.298	.244
1990 Chicago	AL	150	493	123	17	1	5	(2	3)	157	48	54	55	2	53	1	13	3	1	4	.20	5	.249	.324	.318
1991 Chicago	AL	157	606	172	25	1	23	(16	7)	268	92	100	80	3	67	4	8	7	2	4	.33	22	.284	.367	.442
1992 Chicago	AL	157	592	167	38	1	16	(7	9)	255	85	93	93	9	71	0	1	8	2	4	.33	14	.282	.375	.431
1993 Chicago	AL	157	554	145	27	1	22	(12	10)	240	85	94	105	6	82	1	0	6	1	6	.14	18	.262	.379	.433
1994 Chicago	AL	109	401	113	15	1	18	(8	10)	184	57	78	61	15	69	2	2	8	3	1	.75	8	.282	.373	.459
1995 Chicago	AL	135	492	145	22	0	26	(8	18)	245	79	93	75	11	98	1	1	8	4	3	.57	8	.295	.384	.498
1996 Chicago	AL	158	586	168	31	2	34	(13	21)	305	96	105	78	10	81	2	0	8	1	3	.25	18	.287	.368	.520
1997 Chicago	AL	54	183	48	10	1	6	(2	4)	78	27	26	34	5	21	0	0	3	0	0	.00	3	.262	.373	.426
9 ML YEARS		1093	3952	1089	188	8	150	(68	82)	1743	574	650	589	71	548	14	27	54	14	25	.36	97	.276	.367	.441

Dario Veras

Pitches: Right **Bats:** Right **Pos:** RP-23 **Ht:** 6'1" **Wt:** 155 **Born:** 3/13/73 **Age:** 25

		HOW MUCH HE PITCHED					WHAT HE GAVE UP											THE RESULTS					
Year Team	Lg	G	GS	CG	GF	IP	BFP	H	R	ER	HR	SH	SF	HB	TBB	IBB	SO	WP	Bk	W	L	Pct.	ShO	Sv-Op	Hld	ERA
1993 Bakersfield	A+	7	0	0	1	13.1	61	13	11	11	1	0	1	0	8	2	11	0	0	1	0	1.000	0	0- —	—	7.43
Vero Beach	A+	24	0	0	8	54.2	229	59	23	17	2	3	1	1	14	5	31	3	0	2	2	.500	0	2- —	—	2.80
1994 Rancho Cuca	A+	59	0	0	13	79	332	66	28	18	7	7	0	6	25	9	56	2	0	9	2	.818	0	3- —	—	2.05
1995 Memphis	AA	58	0	0	22	82.2	360	81	38	35	8	3	1	7	27	11	70	5	1	7	3	.700	0	1- —	—	3.81
1996 Memphis	AA	29	0	0	8	42.2	172	38	14	11	4	1	2	1	9	2	47	2	1	3	1	.750	0	1- —	—	2.32
Las Vegas	AAA	19	1	0	9	40.1	165	41	17	13	1	3	1	0	6	2	30	2	0	6	2	.750	0	1- —	—	2.90
1997 Mobile	A	5	2	0	2	5	25	8	5	5	1	0	0	0	3	0	5	0	0	0	0	.000	0	0- —	—	9.00
Rancho Cuca	A+	2	0	0	1	3	13	3	3	2	1	1	0	0	1	0	3	1	0	0	0	.000	0	1- —	—	6.00
Las Vegas	AAA	12	0	0	5	14.1	59	14	8	8	1	0	0	0	6	0	13	3	0	0	2	.000	0	1- —	—	5.02
1996 San Diego	NL	23	0	0	6	29	117	24	10	9	3	1	1	1	10	4	23	1	0	3	1	.750	0	0-0	1	2.79
1997 San Diego	NL	23	0	0	7	24.2	114	28	18	14	5	0	0	2	12	3	21	0	0	2	1	.667	0	0-1	2	5.11
2 ML YEARS		46	0	0	13	53.2	231	52	28	23	8	1	1	3	22	7	44	1	0	5	2	.714	0	0-1	3	3.86

215

Quilvio Veras

Bats: Both   Throws: Right   Pos: 2B-142; PH-7   Ht: 5'9"   Wt: 166   Born: 4/3/71   Age: 27

					BATTING													BASERUNNING				PERCENTAGES		
Year Team	Lg	G	AB	H	2B	3B	HR	(Hm | Rd)	TB	R	RBI	TBB	IBB	SO	HBP	SH	SF	SB	CS	SB%	GDP	Avg	OBP	SLG
1995 Florida	NL	124	440	115	20	7	5	(2 | 3)	164	86	32	80	0	68	9	7	2	56	21	.73	7	.261	.384	.373
1996 Florida	NL	73	253	64	8	1	4	(1 | 3)	86	40	14	51	1	42	2	1	1	8	8	.50	3	.253	.381	.340
1997 San Diego	NL	145	539	143	23	1	3	(3 | 0)	177	74	45	72	0	84	7	9	4	33	12	.73	9	.265	.357	.328
3 ML YEARS		342	1232	322	51	9	12	(6 | 6)	427	200	91	203	1	194	18	17	7	97	41	.70	19	.261	.372	.347

Dave Veres

Pitches: Right   Bats: Right   Pos: RP-53   Ht: 6'2"   Wt: 195   Born: 10/19/66   Age: 31

		HOW MUCH HE PITCHED						WHAT HE GAVE UP											THE RESULTS					
Year Team	Lg	G	GS	CG	GF	IP	BFP	H	R	ER	HR	SH	SF	HB	TBB	IBB	SO	WP	Bk	W	L	Pct.	ShO	Sv-Op	Hld	ERA
1994 Houston	NL	32	0	0	7	41	168	39	13	11	4	0	2	1	7	3	28	2	0	3	3	.500	0	1-1	3	2.41
1995 Houston	NL	72	0	0	15	103.1	418	89	29	26	5	6	8	4	30	6	94	4	0	5	1	.833	0	1-3	19	2.26
1996 Montreal	NL	68	0	0	22	77.2	351	85	39	36	10	3	3	6	32	2	81	3	2	6	3	.667	0	4-6	15	4.17
1997 Montreal	NL	53	0	0	11	62	281	68	28	24	5	6	1	2	27	3	47	7	0	2	3	.400	0	1-4	10	3.48
4 ML YEARS		225	0	0	55	284	1218	281	109	97	24	15	14	13	96	14	250	16	2	16	10	.615	0	7-14	47	3.07

Randy Veres

Pitches: Right   Bats: Right   Pos: RP-24   Ht: 6'3"   Wt: 210   Born: 11/25/65   Age: 32

		HOW MUCH HE PITCHED						WHAT HE GAVE UP											THE RESULTS					
Year Team	Lg	G	GS	CG	GF	IP	BFP	H	R	ER	HR	SH	SF	HB	TBB	IBB	SO	WP	Bk	W	L	Pct.	ShO	Sv-Op	Hld	ERA
1997 Omaha *	AAA	11	1	0	5	15	66	15	11	11	2	0	0	0	5	0	19	0	0	1	1	.500	0	0- -	—	6.60
1989 Milwaukee	AL	3	1	0	1	8.1	36	9	5	4	0	1	0	4	4	0	8	0	0	0	1	.000	0	0-0	0	4.32
1990 Milwaukee	AL	26	0	0	12	41.2	175	38	17	17	5	2	2	1	16	3	16	3	0	0	3	.000	0	1-1	1	3.67
1994 Chicago	NL	10	0	0	1	9.2	43	12	6	6	3	0	1	1	2	0	5	0	0	1	1	.500	0	0-2	2	5.59
1995 Florida	NL	47	0	0	15	48.2	215	46	25	21	6	5	4	1	22	7	31	2	0	4	4	.500	0	1-2	9	3.88
1996 Detroit	AL	25	0	0	11	30.1	153	38	29	28	6	1	3	2	23	4	28	2	0	0	4	.000	0	0-2	3	8.31
1997 Kansas City	AL	24	0	0	7	35.1	152	36	17	13	4	4	5	3	7	1	28	4	0	4	0	1.000	0	1-3	4	3.31
6 ML YEARS		135	1	0	47	174	774	179	99	89	24	13	16	8	74	15	116	11	0	9	13	.409	0	3-10	19	4.60

Jose Vidro

Bats: B   Throws: R   Pos: 3B-36; PH-22; DH-5; 2B-5   Ht: 6'0"   Wt: 185   Born: 8/27/74   Age: 23

					BATTING													BASERUNNING				PERCENTAGES		
Year Team	Lg	G	AB	H	2B	3B	HR	(Hm	Rd)	TB	R	RBI	TBB	IBB	SO	HBP	SH	SF	SB	CS	SB%	GDP	Avg	OBP	SLG
1992 Expos	R	54	200	66	6	2	4	—	—	88	29	31	16	1	31	0	1	2	10	1	.91	5	.330	.376	.440
1993 Burlington	A	76	287	69	19	0	2	—	—	94	39	34	28	3	54	5	4	2	3	2	.60	7	.240	.317	.328
1994 Wst Plm Bch	A+	125	465	124	30	2	4	—	—	170	57	49	51	4	56	5	3	3	8	2	.80	5	.267	.344	.366
1995 Harrisburg	AA	64	246	64	16	2	4	—	—	96	33	38	20	2	37	1	4	3	3	7	.30	5	.260	.315	.390
Wst Plm Bch	A+	44	163	53	15	2	3	—	—	81	20	24	8	0	21	2	2	2	1	0	1.00	1	.325	.360	.497
1996 Harrisburg	AA	126	452	117	25	3	18	—	—	202	57	82	29	2	71	2	9	10	3	1	.75	6	.259	.300	.447
1997 Ottawa	AAA	73	279	90	17	0	13	—	—	146	40	47	22	5	40	1	0	3	2	0	1.00	6	.323	.370	.523
1997 Montreal	NL	67	169	42	12	1	2	(0	2)	62	19	17	11	0	20	2	0	3	1	0	1.00	5	.249	.297	.367

Ron Villone

Pitches: Left   Bats: Left   Pos: RP-50   Ht: 6'3"   Wt: 235   Born: 1/16/70   Age: 28

		HOW MUCH HE PITCHED						WHAT HE GAVE UP											THE RESULTS					
Year Team	Lg	G	GS	CG	GF	IP	BFP	H	R	ER	HR	SH	SF	HB	TBB	IBB	SO	WP	Bk	W	L	Pct.	ShO	Sv-Op	Hld	ERA
1995 Sea-SD		38	0	0	15	45	212	44	31	29	11	3	1	1	34	0	63	3	0	2	3	.400	0	1-5	6	5.80
1996 SD-Mil		44	0	0	19	43	182	31	15	15	6	0	2	5	25	0	38	2	0	1	1	.500	0	2-3	9	3.14
1997 Milwaukee	AL	50	0	0	15	52.2	238	54	23	20	4	2	0	1	36	2	40	3	0	1	0	1.000	0	0-2	8	3.42
1995 Seattle	AL	19	0	0	7	19.1	101	20	19	17	6	3	0	1	23	0	26	1	0	0	2	.000	0	0-3	3	7.91
San Diego	NL	19	0	0	8	25.2	111	24	12	12	5	0	1	0	11	0	37	2	0	2	1	.667	0	1-2	3	4.21
1996 San Diego	NL	21	0	0	9	18.1	78	17	6	6	2	0	1	1	7	0	19	0	0	1	1	.500	0	0-1	4	2.95
Milwaukee	AL	23	0	0	10	24.2	104	14	9	9	4	0	2	4	18	0	19	2	0	0	0	.000	0	2-2	5	3.28
3 ML YEARS		132	0	0	49	140.2	632	129	69	64	21	5	3	7	95	2	141	8	0	4	4	.500	0	3-10	23	4.09

Fernando Vina

Bats: Left   Throws: Right   Pos: 2B-77; PH-3; DH-1   Ht: 5'9"   Wt: 170   Born: 4/16/69   Age: 29

					BATTING													BASERUNNING				PERCENTAGES		
Year Team	Lg	G	AB	H	2B	3B	HR	(Hm	Rd)	TB	R	RBI	TBB	IBB	SO	HBP	SH	SF	SB	CS	SB%	GDP	Avg	OBP	SLG
1997 Stockton *	A+	3	9	4	0	1	0	—	—	6	2	3	0	0	0	0	0	0	0	2	.00	0	.444	.444	.667
Tucson *	AAA	6	19	9	3	0	1	—	—	15	3	5	3	0	1	2	0	0	0	0	—	0	.474	.583	.789
1993 Seattle	AL	24	45	10	2	0	0	(0	0)	12	5	2	4	0	3	3	1	0	6	0	1.00	0	.222	.327	.267
1994 New York	NL	79	124	31	6	0	0	(0	0)	37	20	6	12	0	11	12	2	0	3	1	.75	4	.250	.372	.298
1995 Milwaukee	AL	113	288	74	7	7	3	(1	2)	104	46	29	22	0	28	9	4	2	6	3	.67	6	.257	.327	.361
1996 Milwaukee	AL	140	554	157	19	10	7	(3	4)	217	94	46	38	3	35	13	6	4	16	7	.70	15	.283	.342	.392
1997 Milwaukee	AL	79	324	89	12	2	4	(1	3)	117	37	28	12	1	23	7	2	3	8	7	.53	4	.275	.312	.361
5 ML YEARS		435	1335	361	46	19	14	(5	9)	487	202	111	88	4	100	44	15	9	39	18	.68	29	.270	.334	.365

216

Joe Vitiello

Bats: R Throws: R Pos: RF-16; DH-12; LF-12; PH-12; 1B-1   Ht: 6'3" Wt: 230 Born: 4/11/70 Age: 28

Year Team	Lg	G	AB	H	2B	3B	HR	(Hm	Rd)	TB	R	RBI	TBB	IBB	SO	HBP	SH	SF	SB	CS	SB%	GDP	Avg	OBP	SLG
1997 Omaha *	AAA	13	42	9	1	0	3	—	—	19	5	9	5	0	16	0	0	0	0	0	.00	0	.214	.298	.452
1995 Kansas City	AL	53	130	33	4	0	7	(3	4)	58	13	21	8	0	25	0	0	0	0	0	.00	4	.254	.317	.446
1996 Kansas City	AL	85	257	62	15	1	8	(3	5)	103	29	40	38	2	69	3	0	3	2	0	1.00	12	.241	.342	.401
1997 Kansas City	AL	51	130	31	6	0	5	(4	1)	52	11	18	14	1	37	2	0	0	0	0	.00	2	.238	.322	.400
3 ML YEARS		189	517	126	25	1	20	(10	10)	213	53	79	60	3	131	9	0	3	2	0	1.00	18	.244	.331	.412

Jose Vizcaino

Bats: Both Throws: Right Pos: SS-147; PH-6; 2B-5   Ht: 6'1" Wt: 180 Born: 3/26/68 Age: 30

Year Team	Lg	G	AB	H	2B	3B	HR	(Hm	Rd)	TB	R	RBI	TBB	IBB	SO	HBP	SH	SF	SB	CS	SB%	GDP	Avg	OBP	SLG
1989 Los Angeles	NL	7	10	2	0	0	0	(0	0)	2	2	0	0	0	1	0	1	0	0	0	.00	0	.200	.200	.200
1990 Los Angeles	NL	37	51	14	1	1	0	(0	0)	17	3	2	4	1	8	0	0	0	1	1	.50	1	.275	.327	.333
1991 Chicago	NL	93	145	38	5	0	0	(0	0)	43	7	10	5	0	18	0	2	2	2	1	.67	1	.262	.283	.297
1992 Chicago	NL	86	285	64	10	4	1	(0	1)	85	25	17	14	2	35	0	5	1	3	0	1.00	4	.225	.260	.298
1993 Chicago	NL	151	551	158	19	4	4	(1	3)	197	74	54	46	2	71	3	8	9	12	9	.57	9	.287	.340	.358
1994 New York	NL	103	410	105	13	3	3	(1	2)	133	47	33	33	3	62	2	5	6	1	11	.08	5	.256	.310	.324
1995 New York	NL	135	509	146	21	5	3	(2	1)	186	66	56	35	4	76	1	13	3	8	3	.73	14	.287	.332	.365
1996 NYN-Cle		144	542	161	17	8	1	(1	0)	197	70	45	35	0	82	3	10	3	15	7	.68	8	.297	.341	.363
1997 San Francisco	NL	151	568	151	19	7	5	(1	4)	199	77	50	48	1	87	0	13	1	8	8	.50	13	.266	.323	.350
1996 New York	NL	96	363	110	12	6	1	(1	0)	137	47	32	28	0	58	3	6	2	9	5	.64	6	.303	.356	.377
Cleveland	AL	48	179	51	5	2	0	(0	0)	60	23	13	7	0	24	0	4	1	6	2	.75	2	.285	.310	.335
9 ML YEARS		907	3071	839	105	32	17	(6	11)	1059	371	267	220	13	440	9	57	25	50	40	.56	55	.273	.321	.345

Omar Vizquel

Bats: Both Throws: Right Pos: SS-152; PH-2   Ht: 5'9" Wt: 165 Born: 4/24/67 Age: 31

Year Team	Lg	G	AB	H	2B	3B	HR	(Hm	Rd)	TB	R	RBI	TBB	IBB	SO	HBP	SH	SF	SB	CS	SB%	GDP	Avg	OBP	SLG
1989 Seattle	AL	143	387	85	7	3	1	(1	0)	101	45	20	28	0	40	1	13	2	1	4	.20	6	.220	.273	.261
1990 Seattle	AL	81	255	63	3	2	2	(1	0)	76	19	18	18	0	22	0	10	2	4	1	.80	7	.247	.295	.298
1991 Seattle	AL	142	426	98	16	4	1	(1	0)	125	42	41	45	0	37	0	8	3	7	2	.78	8	.230	.302	.293
1992 Seattle	AL	136	483	142	20	4	0	(0	0)	170	49	21	32	0	38	2	9	1	15	13	.54	14	.294	.340	.352
1993 Seattle	AL	158	560	143	14	2	2	(1	1)	167	68	31	50	2	71	4	13	3	12	14	.46	7	.255	.319	.298
1994 Cleveland	AL	69	286	78	10	1	1	(0	1)	93	39	33	23	0	23	0	11	2	13	4	.76	4	.273	.325	.325
1995 Cleveland	AL	136	542	144	28	0	6	(3	3)	190	87	56	59	0	59	1	10	10	29	11	.73	4	.266	.333	.351
1996 Cleveland	AL	151	542	161	36	1	9	(2	7)	226	98	64	56	0	42	4	12	9	35	9	.80	10	.297	.362	.417
1997 Cleveland	AL	153	565	158	23	6	5	(3	2)	208	89	49	57	1	58	2	16	1	43	12	.78	16	.280	.347	.368
9 ML YEARS		1169	4046	1072	157	23	27	(11	16)	1356	536	333	368	3	390	14	102	34	159	70	.69	76	.265	.326	.335

Jack Voigt

Bats: R Throws: R Pos: LF-35; 1B-19; PH-18; 3B-6; RF-5; CF-2; DH-1   Ht: 6'1" Wt: 175 Born: 5/17/66 Age: 32

Year Team	Lg	G	AB	H	2B	3B	HR	(Hm	Rd)	TB	R	RBI	TBB	IBB	SO	HBP	SH	SF	SB	CS	SB%	GDP	Avg	OBP	SLG
1997 Tucson *	AAA	66	235	64	20	0	5	—	—	99	36	40	43	1	57	1	0	2	4	3	.57	4	.272	.384	.421
1992 Baltimore	AL	1	0	0	0	0	0	(0	0)	0	0	0	0	0	0	0	0	0	0	0	.00	0	.000	.000	.000
1993 Baltimore	AL	64	152	45	11	1	6	(5	1)	76	32	23	25	0	33	0	0	0	1	0	1.00	3	.296	.395	.500
1994 Baltimore	AL	59	141	34	5	0	3	(1	2)	48	15	20	18	1	25	1	1	2	0	0	.00	0	.241	.327	.340
1995 Bal-Tex	AL	36	63	11	3	0	2	(1	1)	20	9	8	10	0	14	0	0	0	0	0	.00	1	.175	.284	.317
1996 Texas	AL	5	9	1	0	0	0	(0	0)	1	1	0	0	0	2	0	0	0	0	0	.00	0	.111	.111	.111
1997 Milwaukee	AL	72	151	37	9	2	8	(5	3)	74	20	22	19	2	36	1	2	1	1	2	.33	5	.245	.331	.490
1995 Baltimore	AL	3	1	1	0	0	0	(0	0)	1	1	0	0	0	0	0	0	0	0	0	.00	0	1.000	1.000	1.000
Texas	AL	33	62	10	3	0	2	(2	0)	19	8	8	10	0	14	0	0	0	0	0	.00	2	.161	.274	.306
6 ML YEARS		237	516	128	28	3	19	(13	6)	219	77	73	72	3	110	2	3	4	2	2	.50	10	.248	.340	.424

Ed Vosberg

Pitches: Left Bats: Left Pos: RP-59   Ht: 6'1" Wt: 190 Born: 9/28/61 Age: 36

Year Team	Lg	G	GS	CG	GF	IP	BFP	H	R	ER	HR	SH	SF	HB	TBB	IBB	SO	WP	Bk	W	L	Pct.	ShO	Sv-Op	Hld	ERA
1986 San Diego	NL	5	3	0	0	13.2	65	17	11	10	1	0	0	0	9	1	8	0	1	0	1	.000	0	0--	0	6.59
1990 San Francisco	NL	18	0	0	5	24.1	104	21	16	15	3	2	0	0	12	2	12	0	0	1	1	.500	0	0-0	0	5.55
1994 Oakland	AL	16	0	0	2	13.2	56	16	7	6	2	1	0	0	5	0	12	1	1	0	2	.000	0	0-1	2	3.95
1995 Texas	AL	44	0	0	20	36	154	32	15	12	3	2	3	0	16	1	36	3	2	5	5	.500	0	4-8	5	3.00
1996 Texas	AL	52	0	0	21	44	195	51	17	16	4	2	1	0	21	4	32	0	0	1	1	.500	0	8-9	11	3.27
1997 Tex-Fla		59	0	0	22	53	239	59	30	26	3	2	4	5	21	6	37	2	1	2	3	.400	0	1-3	8	4.42
1997 Texas	AL	42	0	0	16	41	180	44	23	21	3	1	3	2	15	6	29	1	0	1	2	.333	0	0-1	5	4.61
Florida	NL	17	0	0	6	12	59	15	7	5	0	1	1	3	6	0	8	1	1	1	1	.500	0	1-2	3	3.75
6 ML YEARS		194	3	0	70	184.2	813	196	96	85	16	9	8	5	84	14	137	7	7	9	13	.409	0	13--		4.14

Terrell Wade

Pitches: Left **Bats:** Left **Pos:** SP-9; RP-3   **Ht:** 6'3" **Wt:** 205 **Born:** 1/25/73 **Age:** 25

Year Team	Lg	G	GS	CG	GF	IP	BFP	H	R	ER	HR	SH	SF	HB	TBB	IBB	SO	WP	Bk	W	L	Pct.	ShO	Sv-Op	Hld	ERA
1997 Greenville *	AA	8	6	0	0	12.2	60	15	10	7	3	0	0	0	8	0	14	1	0	0	2	.000	0	0- -	—	4.97
1995 Atlanta	NL	3	0	0	0	4	18	3	2	2	1	0	0	0	4	0	3	1	0	0	1	.000	0	0-0	0	4.50
1996 Atlanta	NL	44	8	0	13	69.2	305	57	28	23	9	5	1	1	47	6	79	2	0	5	0	1.000	0	1-2	4	2.97
1997 Atlanta	NL	12	9	0	1	42	197	60	31	25	6	2	5	2	16	1	35	1	0	2	3	.400	0	0-0	0	5.36
3 ML YEARS		59	17	0	14	115.2	520	120	61	50	16	7	6	3	67	7	117	4	0	7	4	.636	0	1-2	4	3.89

Billy Wagner

Pitches: Left **Bats:** Left **Pos:** RP-62   **Ht:** 5'11" **Wt:** 180 **Born:** 6/25/71 **Age:** 27

Year Team	Lg	G	GS	CG	GF	IP	BFP	H	R	ER	HR	SH	SF	HB	TBB	IBB	SO	WP	Bk	W	L	Pct.	ShO	Sv-Op	Hld	ERA
1995 Houston	NL	1	0	0	0	0.1	1	0	0	0	0	0	0	0	0	0	0	0	0	0	0	.000	0	0-0	0	0.00
1996 Houston	NL	37	0	0	20	51.2	212	28	16	14	6	7	2	3	30	2	67	1	0	2	2	.500	0	9-13	3	2.44
1997 Houston	NL	62	0	0	49	66.1	277	49	23	21	5	3	1	3	30	1	106	3	0	7	8	.467	0	23-29	1	2.85
3 ML YEARS		100	0	0	69	118.1	490	77	39	35	11	10	3	6	60	3	173	4	0	9	10	.474	0	32-42	4	2.66

Paul Wagner

Pitches: Right **Bats:** Right **Pos:** RP-16   **Ht:** 6'1" **Wt:** 209 **Born:** 11/14/67 **Age:** 30

Year Team	Lg	G	GS	CG	GF	IP	BFP	H	R	ER	HR	SH	SF	HB	TBB	IBB	SO	WP	Bk	W	L	Pct.	ShO	Sv-Op	Hld	ERA
1997 Carolina *	AA	12	3	0	1	16	90	25	20	18	3	1	1	1	16	0	20	3	1	0	1	.000	0	0- -	—	10.13
1992 Pittsburgh	NL	6	1	0	1	13	52	9	1	1	0	0	0	0	5	0	5	1	0	2	0	1.000	0	0-0	0	0.69
1993 Pittsburgh	NL	44	17	1	9	141.1	599	143	72	67	15	6	7	1	42	2	114	12	0	8	8	.500	1	2-5	4	4.27
1994 Pittsburgh	NL	29	17	1	4	119.2	534	136	69	61	7	8	4	8	50	4	86	4	0	7	8	.467	0	0-0	2	4.59
1995 Pittsburgh	NL	33	25	3	1	165	725	174	96	88	18	7	2	7	72	7	120	8	0	5	16	.238	1	1-1	1	4.80
1996 Pittsburgh	NL	16	15	1	0	81.2	361	86	49	49	10	5	1	3	39	2	81	7	0	4	8	.333	0	0-0	0	5.40
1997 Pit-Mil		16	0	0	3	18	87	20	9	9	4	3	1	0	13	3	9	3	2	1	0	1.000	0	0-1	0	4.50
1997 Pittsburgh	NL	14	0	0	2	16	79	17	7	7	3	3	1	0	13	3	9	3	2	0	0	.000	0	0-1	0	3.94
Milwaukee	AL	2	0	0	1	2	8	3	2	2	1	0	0	0	0	0	0	0	0	1	0	1.000	0	0-0	0	9.00
6 ML YEARS		144	75	6	18	538.2	2358	568	296	275	54	29	15	19	221	18	415	35	2	27	40	.403	2	3-7	7	4.59

David Wainhouse

Pitches: Right **Bats:** Left **Pos:** RP-25   **Ht:** 6'2" **Wt:** 185 **Born:** 11/7/67 **Age:** 30

Year Team	Lg	G	GS	CG	GF	IP	BFP	H	R	ER	HR	SH	SF	HB	TBB	IBB	SO	WP	Bk	W	L	Pct.	ShO	Sv-Op	Hld	ERA
1997 Calgary *	AAA	25	0	0	9	38	174	46	25	25	5	1	1	3	13	2	24	3	0	2	0	1.000	0	1- -	—	5.92
1991 Montreal	NL	2	0	0	1	2.2	14	2	2	2	0	0	1	0	4	0	1	2	0	0	1	.000	0	0-0	0	6.75
1993 Seattle	AL	3	0	0	0	2.1	20	7	7	7	1	0	0	1	5	0	2	0	0	0	0	.000	0	0-0	0	27.00
1996 Pittsburgh	NL	17	0	0	6	23.2	101	22	16	15	3	1	2	0	10	1	16	2	0	1	0	1.000	0	0-0	1	5.70
1997 Pittsburgh	NL	25	0	0	6	28	137	34	28	25	2	3	1	3	17	0	21	1	1	0	1	.000	0	0-0	1	8.04
4 ML YEARS		47	0	0	13	56.2	272	65	53	49	6	4	4	4	36	1	40	5	1	1	2	.333	0	0-0	2	7.78

Tim Wakefield

Pitches: Right **Bats:** Right **Pos:** SP-29; RP-6   **Ht:** 6'2" **Wt:** 206 **Born:** 8/2/66 **Age:** 31

Year Team	Lg	G	GS	CG	GF	IP	BFP	H	R	ER	HR	SH	SF	HB	TBB	IBB	SO	WP	Bk	W	L	Pct.	ShO	Sv-Op	Hld	ERA
1992 Pittsburgh	NL	13	13	4	0	92	373	76	26	22	3	6	4	1	35	1	51	3	1	8	1	.889	1	0-0	0	2.15
1993 Pittsburgh	NL	24	20	3	1	128.1	595	145	83	80	14	7	5	9	75	2	59	6	0	6	11	.353	0	0-0	0	5.61
1995 Boston	AL	27	27	6	0	195.1	804	163	76	64	22	3	7	9	68	0	119	11	0	16	8	.667	1	0-0	0	2.95
1996 Boston	AL	32	32	6	0	211.2	963	238	151	121	38	1	9	12	90	0	140	4	1	14	13	.519	0	0-0	0	5.14
1997 Boston	AL	35	29	4	2	201.1	866	193	109	95	24	3	7	16	87	5	151	6	0	12	15	.444	2	0-0	1	4.25
5 ML YEARS		131	121	23	3	828.2	3601	815	445	382	101	20	32	47	355	8	520	30	2	56	48	.538	6	0-0	1	4.15

Matt Walbeck

Bats: Both **Throws:** Right **Pos:** C-44; PH-4   **Ht:** 5'11" **Wt:** 188 **Born:** 10/2/69 **Age:** 28

Year Team	Lg	G	AB	H	2B	3B	HR	(Hm	Rd)	TB	R	RBI	TBB	IBB	SO	HBP	SH	SF	SB	CS	SB%	GDP	Avg	OBP	SLG
1997 Lakeland *	A+	4	10	5	1	0	0	—	—	6	4	3	4	1	0	0	0	0	0	1	.00	0	.500	.643	.600
Toledo *	AAA	17	59	18	2	1	1	—	—	25	6	8	4	0	15	0	0	2	0	0	.00	1	.305	.338	.424
1993 Chicago	NL	11	30	6	2	0	1	(1	0)	11	2	6	1	0	6	0	0	0	0	0	.00	0	.200	.226	.367
1994 Minnesota	AL	97	338	69	12	0	5	(0	5)	96	31	35	17	1	37	2	1	1	1	1	.50	7	.204	.246	.284
1995 Minnesota	AL	115	393	101	18	1	1	(1	0)	124	40	44	25	2	71	1	1	2	3	1	.75	11	.257	.302	.316
1996 Minnesota	AL	63	215	48	10	0	2	(1	1)	64	25	24	9	0	34	0	1	2	3	1	.75	6	.223	.252	.298
1997 Detroit	AL	47	137	38	3	0	3	(1	2)	50	18	10	12	0	19	0	0	2	3	3	.50	4	.277	.331	.365
5 ML YEARS		333	1113	262	45	1	12	(4	8)	345	116	119	64	3	167	3	3	7	10	6	.63	28	.235	.277	.310

Jamie Walker

Pitches: Left Bats: Left Pos: RP-50 Ht: 6'2" Wt: 190 Born: 7/1/71 Age: 27

Year Team	Lg	G	GS	CG	GF	IP	BFP	H	R	ER	HR	SH	SF	HB	TBB	IBB	SO	WP	Bk	W	L	Pct.	ShO	Sv-Op	Hld	ERA
1992 Auburn	A-	15	14	0	0	83.1	341	75	35	29	4	4	1	6	21	0	67	4	1	4	6	.400	0	0--	—	3.13
1993 Quad City	A	25	24	1	1	131.2	585	140	92	75	12	10	5	6	48	1	121	12	0	3	11	.214	1	0--	—	5.13
1994 Quad City	A	32	18	0	4	125	569	133	80	58	10	14	3	16	42	2	104	5	1	8	10	.444	0	1--	—	4.18
1995 Jackson	AA	50	0	0	19	58	250	59	29	29	6	3	2	2	24	5	38	4	1	4	2	.667	0	2--	—	4.50
1996 Jackson	AA	45	7	0	13	101	424	94	34	28	7	3	1	8	35	2	79	2	0	5	1	.833	0	2--	—	2.50
1997 Wichita	AA	5	0	0	0	6.2	32	6	8	7	1	1	1	2	5	0	6	0	0	0	1	.000	0	0--	—	9.45
1997 Kansas City	AL	50	0	0	15	43	197	46	28	26	6	2	2	3	20	3	24	2	0	3	3	.500	0	0-1	3	5.44

Larry Walker

Bats: L Throws: R Pos: RF-150; 1B-3; CF-2; PH-2; DH-1 Ht: 6'3" Wt: 225 Born: 12/1/66 Age: 31

Year Team	Lg	G	AB	H	2B	3B	HR	(Hm	Rd)	TB	R	RBI	TBB	IBB	SO	HBP	SH	SF	SB	CS	SB%	GDP	Avg	OBP	SLG
1989 Montreal	NL	20	47	8	0	0	0	(0	0)	8	4	4	5	0	13	1	3	0	1	1	.50	0	.170	.264	.170
1990 Montreal	NL	133	419	101	18	3	19	(9	10)	182	59	51	49	5	112	5	3	2	21	7	.75	8	.241	.326	.434
1991 Montreal	NL	137	487	141	30	2	16	(5	11)	223	59	64	42	2	102	5	1	4	14	9	.61	7	.290	.349	.458
1992 Montreal	NL	143	528	159	31	4	23	(13	10)	267	85	93	41	10	97	6	0	8	18	6	.75	9	.301	.353	.506
1993 Montreal	NL	138	490	130	24	5	22	(13	9)	230	85	86	80	20	76	6	0	6	29	7	.81	8	.265	.371	.469
1994 Montreal	NL	103	395	127	44	2	19	(7	12)	232	76	86	47	5	74	4	0	6	15	5	.75	8	.322	.394	.587
1995 Colorado	NL	131	494	151	31	5	36	(24	12)	300	96	101	49	13	72	14	0	5	16	3	.84	13	.306	.381	.607
1996 Colorado	NL	83	272	75	18	4	18	(12	6)	155	58	58	20	2	58	9	0	3	18	2	.90	7	.276	.342	.570
1997 Colorado	NL	153	568	208	46	4	49	(20	29)	409	143	130	78	14	90	14	0	4	33	8	.80	15	.366	.452	.720
9 ML YEARS		1041	3700	1100	242	29	202	(103	99)	2006	665	673	411	71	694	64	7	38	165	48	.77	75	.297	.374	.542

Todd Walker

Bats: L Throws: R Pos: 3B-40; 2B-8; PH-5; DH-2 Ht: 6'0" Wt: 170 Born: 5/25/73 Age: 25

Year Team	Lg	G	AB	H	2B	3B	HR	(Hm	Rd)	TB	R	RBI	TBB	IBB	SO	HBP	SH	SF	SB	CS	SB%	GDP	Avg	OBP	SLG
1994 Ft. Myers	A+	46	171	52	5	2	10	—	—	91	29	34	32	0	15	0	0	4	6	3	.67	4	.304	.406	.532
1995 Hardware City	AA	137	513	149	27	3	21	—	—	245	83	85	63	1	101	2	1	8	23	9	.72	13	.290	.365	.478
1996 Salt Lake	AAA	135	551	187	41	9	28	—	—	330	94	111	57	11	91	5	2	10	13	8	.62	17	.339	.400	.599
1997 Salt Lake	AAA	83	322	111	20	1	11	—	—	166	69	53	46	3	49	1	2	5	5	5	.50	10	.345	.420	.516
1996 Minnesota	AL	25	82	21	6	0	0	(0	0)	27	8	6	4	0	13	0	0	3	2	0	1.00	4	.256	.281	.329
1997 Minnesota	AL	52	156	37	7	1	3	(1	2)	55	15	16	11	1	30	1	1	2	7	0	1.00	5	.237	.288	.353
2 ML YEARS		77	238	58	13	1	3	(1	2)	82	23	22	15	1	43	1	1	5	9	0	1.00	9	.244	.286	.345

Donne Wall

Pitches: Right Bats: Right Pos: SP-8 Ht: 5'11" Wt: 180 Born: 7/11/67 Age: 30

Year Team	Lg	G	GS	CG	GF	IP	BFP	H	R	ER	HR	SH	SF	HB	TBB	IBB	SO	WP	Bk	W	L	Pct.	ShO	Sv-Op	Hld	ERA
1997 New Orleans *	AAA	17	17	1	0	110	446	109	49	47	13	3	5	1	24	0	84	3	0	8	7	.533	0	0--	—	3.85
1995 Houston	NL	6	5	0	0	24.1	110	33	19	15	5	0	2	0	5	0	16	1	0	1	1	.750	0	0-0	1	5.55
1996 Houston	NL	26	23	2	1	150	643	170	84	76	17	4	5	6	34	3	99	3	2	9	8	.529	1	0-0	0	4.56
1997 Houston	NL	8	8	0	0	41.2	186	53	31	29	8	0	0	2	16	0	25	2	1	2	5	.286	0	0-0	0	6.26
3 ML YEARS		40	36	2	1	216	939	256	134	120	30	4	7	8	55	3	140	6	3	14	14	.500	1	0-0	0	5.00

Jeff Wallace

Pitches: Left Bats: Left Pos: RP-11 Ht: 6'2" Wt: 235 Born: 4/12/76 Age: 22

Year Team	Lg	G	GS	CG	GF	IP	BFP	H	R	ER	HR	SH	SF	HB	TBB	IBB	SO	WP	Bk	W	L	Pct.	ShO	Sv-Op	Hld	ERA
1995 Royals	R	12	7	0	3	44	177	28	20	6	0	1	1	1	15	0	51	3	2	5	3	.625	0	1--	—	1.23
1996 Lansing	A	30	21	0	2	122.1	560	140	79	72	10	8	3	7	66	0	84	12	7	4	9	.308	0	0--	—	5.30
1997 Lynchburg	A+	9	0	0	6	16.1	65	9	3	3	0	1	0	0	10	1	13	1	0	5	0	1.000	0	1--	—	1.65
Carolina	AA	38	0	0	15	43.1	207	43	37	26	3	5	0	1	36	3	39	9	1	4	8	.333	0	3--	—	5.40
1997 Pittsburgh	NL	11	0	0	1	12	50	8	2	1	0	1	1	0	8	1	14	1	0	0	0	.000	0	0-1	3	0.75

Jerome Walton

Bats: R Throws: R Pos: RF-11; LF-9; PH-7; 1B-5; DH-2; CF-2 Ht: 6'1" Wt: 185 Born: 7/8/65 Age: 32

Year Team	Lg	G	AB	H	2B	3B	HR	(Hm	Rd)	TB	R	RBI	TBB	IBB	SO	HBP	SH	SF	SB	CS	SB%	GDP	Avg	OBP	SLG
1997 Frederick *	A+	7	19	4	0	0	1	—	—	7	1	2	5	0	0	0	0	0	1	1	.50	0	.211	.375	.368
1989 Chicago	NL	116	475	139	23	3	5	(3	2)	183	64	46	27	1	77	6	2	5	24	7	.77	6	.293	.335	.385
1990 Chicago	NL	101	392	103	16	2	2	(2	0)	129	63	21	50	1	70	4	1	2	14	7	.67	4	.263	.350	.329
1991 Chicago	NL	123	270	59	13	1	5	(3	2)	89	42	17	19	0	55	3	3	3	7	3	.70	7	.219	.275	.330
1992 Chicago	NL	30	55	7	0	1	0	(0	0)	9	7	1	9	0	13	2	3	0	1	2	.33	1	.127	.273	.164
1993 California	NL	5	2	0	0	0	0	(0	0)	0	2	0	1	0	2	0	0	0	0	1	1.00	0	.000	.333	.000
1994 Cincinnati	NL	46	68	21	4	0	1	(1	0)	28	10	9	4	0	12	0	1	0	1	3	.25	2	.309	.347	.412
1995 Cincinnati	NL	102	162	47	12	1	8	(4	4)	85	32	22	17	0	25	4	3	2	10	7	.59	0	.290	.368	.525
1996 Atlanta	NL	37	47	16	5	0	1	(1	0)	24	9	4	5	0	10	0	1	2	0	0	.00	1	.340	.389	.511
1997 Baltimore	AL	26	68	20	1	0	3	(1	2)	30	8	9	4	0	10	0	0	3	0	0	.00	3	.294	.333	.441

		BATTING																	BASERUNNING				PERCENTAGES		
Year Team	Lg	G	AB	H	2B	3B	HR	(Hm · Rd)	TB	R	RBI	TBB	IBB	SO	HBP	SH	SF		SB	CS	SB%	GDP	Avg	OBP	SLG
9 ML YEARS		586	1539	412	74	8	25	(15 10)	577	237	129	136	2	274	19	16	14		58	29	.67	24	.268	.332	.375

Turner Ward

Bats: B **Throws:** R **Pos:** CF-31; PH-25; RF-23; LF-11   **Ht:** 6'2" **Wt:** 182 **Born:** 4/11/65 **Age:** 33

		BATTING																	BASERUNNING				PERCENTAGES		
Year Team	Lg	G	AB	H	2B	3B	HR	(Hm Rd)	TB	R	RBI	TBB	IBB	SO	HBP	SH	SF		SB	CS	SB%	GDP	Avg	OBP	SLG
1997 Calgary *	AAA	59	209	71	18	3	9	— —	122	44	44	24	0	26	5	0	1		7	1	.88	5	.340	.418	.584
1990 Cleveland	AL	14	46	16	2	1	1	(0 1)	23	10	10	3	0	8	0	0	0		3	0	1.00	1	.348	.388	.500
1991 Cle-Tor	AL	48	113	27	7	0	0	(0 0)	34	12	7	11	0	18	0	4	0		0	0	.00	2	.239	.306	.301
1992 Toronto	AL	18	29	10	3	0	1	(0 1)	16	7	3	4	0	4	0	0	0		0	1	.00	1	.345	.424	.552
1993 Toronto	AL	72	167	32	4	2	4	(2 2)	52	20	28	23	2	26	1	3	4		3	3	.50	7	.192	.287	.311
1994 Milwaukee	AL	102	367	85	15	2	9	(3 6)	131	55	45	52	4	68	3	0	5		6	2	.75	9	.232	.328	.357
1995 Milwaukee	AL	44	129	34	3	1	4	(3 1)	51	19	16	14	1	21	1	1	1		6	1	.86	2	.264	.338	.395
1996 Milwaukee	AL	43	67	12	2	1	2	(2 0)	22	7	10	13	0	17	0	1	1		3	0	1.00	3	.179	.309	.328
1997 Pittsburgh	NL	71	167	59	16	1	7	(5 2)	98	33	33	18	2	17	2	3	1		4	1	.80	1	.353	.420	.587
1991 Cleveland	AL	40	100	23	7	0	0	(0 0)	30	11	5	10	0	16	0	4	0		0	0	.00	1	.230	.300	.300
Toronto	AL	8	13	4	0	0	0	(0 0)	4	1	2	1	0	2	0	0	0		0	0	.00	1	.308	.357	.308
8 ML YEARS		412	1085	275	52	8	28	(15 13)	427	163	152	138	9	179	7	12	12		25	8	.76	26	.253	.338	.394

John Wasdin

Pitches: Right **Bats:** Right **Pos:** RP-46; SP-7   **Ht:** 6'2" **Wt:** 190 **Born:** 8/5/72 **Age:** 25

		HOW MUCH HE PITCHED						WHAT HE GAVE UP											THE RESULTS						
Year Team	Lg	G	GS	CG	GF	IP	BFP	H	R	ER	HR	SH	SF	HB	TBB	IBB	SO	WP	Bk	W	L	Pct.	ShO	Sv-Op	Hld	ERA
1995 Oakland	AL	5	2	0	3	17.1	69	14	9	9	4	0	0	1	3	0	6	0	0	1	1	.500	0	0-1	0	4.67
1996 Oakland	AL	25	21	1	2	131.1	575	145	96	87	24	3	6	4	50	5	75	2	2	8	7	.533	0	0-1	0	5.96
1997 Boston	AL	53	7	0	10	124.2	534	121	68	61	18	4	7	3	38	4	84	4	0	4	6	.400	0	0-2	11	4.40
3 ML YEARS		83	30	1	15	273.1	1178	280	173	157	46	7	13	8	91	9	165	6	2	13	14	.481	0	0-3	11	5.17

Pat Watkins

Bats: Right **Throws:** Right **Pos:** CF-15; PH-3   **Ht:** 6'2" **Wt:** 185 **Born:** 9/2/72 **Age:** 25

		BATTING																	BASERUNNING				PERCENTAGES		
Year Team	Lg	G	AB	H	2B	3B	HR	(Hm Rd)	TB	R	RBI	TBB	IBB	SO	HBP	SH	SF		SB	CS	SB%	GDP	Avg	OBP	SLG
1993 Billings	R+	66	235	63	10	3	6	— —	97	46	30	22	0	44	2	1	1		15	4	.79	4	.268	.335	.413
1994 Winston-Sal	A+	132	524	152	24	5	27	— —	267	107	83	62	3	84	7	1	6		31	13	.70	8	.290	.369	.510
1995 Winston-Sal	A+	27	107	22	3	1	4	— —	39	14	13	10	0	24	0	1	2		1	0	1.00	5	.206	.269	.364
Chattanooga	AA	105	358	104	26	2	12	— —	170	57	57	33	4	53	3	0	4		5	5	.50	7	.291	.352	.475
1996 Chattanooga	AA	127	492	136	31	2	8	— —	195	63	59	30	0	64	7	2	4		15	11	.58	17	.276	.325	.396
1997 Chattanooga	AA	46	177	62	15	1	7	— —	100	35	30	15	1	16	2	0	1		9	3	.75	3	.350	.405	.565
Indianapolis	AAA	84	325	91	14	7	9	— —	146	46	35	24	2	55	1	3	1		13	9	.59	10	.280	.330	.449
1997 Cincinnati	NL	17	29	6	2	0	0	(0 0)	8	2	0	0	0	5	0	1	0		1	0	1.00	1	.207	.207	.276

Allen Watson

Pitches: Left **Bats:** Left **Pos:** SP-34; RP-1   **Ht:** 6'3" **Wt:** 195 **Born:** 11/18/70 **Age:** 27

		HOW MUCH HE PITCHED						WHAT HE GAVE UP											THE RESULTS						
Year Team	Lg	G	GS	CG	GF	IP	BFP	H	R	ER	HR	SH	SF	HB	TBB	IBB	SO	WP	Bk	W	L	Pct.	ShO	Sv-Op	Hld	ERA
1993 St. Louis	NL	16	15	0	1	86	373	90	53	44	11	6	4	3	28	2	49	2	1	6	7	.462	0	0-1	0	4.60
1994 St. Louis	NL	22	22	0	0	115.2	523	130	73	71	15	7	0	8	53	0	74	2	2	6	5	.545	0	0-0	0	5.52
1995 St. Louis	NL	21	19	0	1	114.1	491	126	68	63	17	2	1	5	41	0	49	2	2	7	9	.438	0	0-0	0	4.96
1996 San Francisco	NL	29	29	2	0	185.2	793	189	105	95	28	18	9	5	69	2	128	9	2	8	12	.400	0	0-0	0	4.61
1997 Anaheim	AL	35	34	0	0	199	880	220	121	109	37	5	6	8	73	0	141	8	2	12	12	.500	0	0-0	0	4.93
5 ML YEARS		123	119	2	2	700.2	3060	755	420	382	108	38	20	29	264	4	441	23	9	39	45	.464	0	0-1	0	4.91

Dave Weathers

Pitches: Right **Bats:** Right **Pos:** RP-18; SP-1   **Ht:** 6'3" **Wt:** 220 **Born:** 9/25/69 **Age:** 28

		HOW MUCH HE PITCHED						WHAT HE GAVE UP											THE RESULTS						
Year Team	Lg	G	GS	CG	GF	IP	BFP	H	R	ER	HR	SH	SF	HB	TBB	IBB	SO	WP	Bk	W	L	Pct.	ShO	Sv-Op	Hld	ERA
1997 Columbus *	AAA	5	5	1	0	36.2	148	35	18	13	3	.1	0	0	7	0	35	0	0	2	2	.500	0	0- --		3.19
Buffalo *	AAA	11	11	2	0	68.2	290	71	37	24	7	1	5	0	17	0	51	4	0	4	3	.571	1	0- --		3.15
1991 Toronto	AL	15	0	0	4	14.2	79	15	9	8	1	2	1	2	17	3	13	0	0	1	0	1.000	0	0-0	0	4.91
1992 Toronto	AL	2	0	0	0	3.1	15	5	3	3	1	0	0	0	2	0	3	0	0	0	0	.000	0	0-0	0	8.10
1993 Florida	NL	14	6	0	0	45.2	202	57	26	26	3	2	0	1	13	1	34	6	0	2	3	.400	0	0-0	0	5.12
1994 Florida	NL	24	24	0	0	135	621	166	87	79	13	12	4	4	59	9	72	7	1	8	12	.400	0	0-0	0	5.27
1995 Florida	NL	28	15	0	0	90.1	419	104	68	60	8	7	3	5	52	3	60	3	0	4	5	.444	0	0-0	0	5.98
1996 Fla-NYA	AL	42	12	0	9	88.2	409	108	60	54	8	5	2	6	42	5	53	3	0	2	4	.333	0	0-0	3	5.48
1997 NYA-Cle	AL	19	1	0	5	25.2	126	38	24	24	3	2	1	1	15	0	18	3	0	1	3	.250	0	0-1	0	8.42
1996 Florida	NL	31	8	0	8	71.1	319	85	41	36	7	5	1	4	28	4	40	2	0	2	2	.500	0	0-0	3	4.54
New York	AL	11	4	0	1	17.1	90	23	19	18	1	0	1	2	14	1	13	1	0	0	2	.000	0	0-0	0	9.35
1997 New York	AL	10	0	0	3	9	47	15	10	10	1	0	0	0	7	0	4	2	0	0	1	.000	0	0-1	0	10.00
Cleveland	AL	9	1	0	2	16.2	79	23	14	14	2	2	1	1	8	0	14	1	0	1	2	.333	0	0-0	0	7.56
7 ML YEARS		144	58	0	20	403.1	1871	493	277	254	37	30	11	19	200	21	253	22	1	18	27	.400	0	0-1	5	5.67

Lenny Webster

Bats: Right **Throws:** Right **Pos:** C-97; DH-1; PH-1 **Ht:** 5'9" **Wt:** 195 **Born:** 2/10/65 **Age:** 33

Year Team	Lg	G	AB	H	2B	3B	HR	(Hm	Rd)	TB	R	RBI	TBB	IBB	SO	HBP	SH	SF	SB	CS	SB%	GDP	Avg	OBP	SLG
1989 Minnesota	AL	14	20	6	2	0	0	(0	0)	8	3	1	3	0	2	0	0	0	0	0	.00	0	.300	.391	.400
1990 Minnesota	AL	2	6	2	1	0	0	(0	0)	3	1	0	1	0	1	0	0	0	0	0	.00	0	.333	.429	.500
1991 Minnesota	AL	18	34	10	1	0	3	(1	2)	20	7	8	6	0	10	0	0	1	0	0	.00	2	.294	.390	.588
1992 Minnesota	AL	53	118	33	10	1	1	(1	0)	48	10	13	9	0	11	0	2	0	0	2	.00	3	.280	.331	.407
1993 Minnesota	AL	49	106	21	2	0	1	(1	0)	26	14	8	11	1	8	0	0	0	1	0	1.00	1	.198	.274	.245
1994 Montreal	NL	57	143	39	10	0	5	(2	3)	64	13	23	16	1	24	6	1	0	0	0	.00	7	.273	.370	.448
1995 Philadelphia	NL	49	150	40	9	0	4	(1	3)	61	18	14	16	0	27	0	1	0	0	0	.00	4	.267	.337	.407
1996 Montreal	NL	78	174	40	10	0	2	(1	1)	56	18	17	25	2	21	2	1	0	0	0	.00	10	.230	.323	.322
1997 Baltimore	AL	98	259	66	8	1	7	(3	4)	97	29	37	22	0	46	2	3	1	0	1	.00	10	.255	.317	.375
9 ML YEARS		418	1010	257	53	2	23	(10	13)	383	113	121	109	4	150	10	8	3	1	3	.25	37	.254	.332	.379

John Wehner

Bats: R **Throws:** R **Pos:** PH-20; RF-19; LF-10; 3B-6; CF-1 **Ht:** 6'3" **Wt:** 206 **Born:** 6/29/67 **Age:** 31

Year Team	Lg	G	AB	H	2B	3B	HR	(Hm	Rd)	TB	R	RBI	TBB	IBB	SO	HBP	SH	SF	SB	CS	SB%	GDP	Avg	OBP	SLG
1997 Charlotte *	AAA	31	93	26	5	0	3	(—	—)	40	16	11	6	1	18	0	1	0	3	1	.75	1	.280	.323	.430
1991 Pittsburgh	NL	37	106	36	7	0	0	(0	0)	43	15	7	7	0	17	0	0	0	3	0	1.00	0	.340	.381	.406
1992 Pittsburgh	NL	55	123	22	6	0	0	(0	0)	28	11	4	12	2	22	0	2	0	3	0	1.00	4	.179	.252	.228
1993 Pittsburgh	NL	29	35	5	0	0	0	(0	0)	5	3	0	6	1	10	0	2	0	0	0	.00	1	.143	.268	.143
1994 Pittsburgh	NL	2	4	1	1	0	0	(0	0)	2	1	3	0	0	1	0	0	0	0	0	.00	0	.250	.250	.500
1995 Pittsburgh	NL	52	107	33	0	3	0	(0	0)	39	13	5	10	1	17	0	4	2	3	1	.75	2	.308	.361	.364
1996 Pittsburgh	NL	86	139	36	9	1	2	(1	1)	53	19	13	8	1	22	0	2	0	1	5	.17	3	.259	.299	.381
1997 Florida	NL	44	36	10	2	0	0	(0	0)	12	8	2	2	0	5	1	1	0	1	0	1.00	2	.278	.333	.333
7 ML YEARS		305	550	143	25	4	2	(1	1)	182	70	34	45	5	94	1	11	2	11	6	.65	11	.260	.316	.331

Walt Weiss

Bats: Both **Throws:** Right **Pos:** SS-119; PH-5 **Ht:** 6'0" **Wt:** 175 **Born:** 11/28/63 **Age:** 34

Year Team	Lg	G	AB	H	2B	3B	HR	(Hm	Rd)	TB	R	RBI	TBB	IBB	SO	HBP	SH	SF	SB	CS	SB%	GDP	Avg	OBP	SLG
1987 Oakland	AL	16	26	12	4	0	0	(0	0)	16	3	1	2	0	2	0	1	0	1	2	.33	0	.462	.500	.615
1988 Oakland	AL	147	452	113	17	3	3	(0	3)	145	44	39	35	1	56	9	8	7	4	4	.50	9	.250	.312	.321
1989 Oakland	AL	84	236	55	11	0	3	(2	1)	75	30	21	21	0	39	1	5	0	6	1	.86	5	.233	.298	.318
1990 Oakland	AL	138	445	118	17	1	2	(1	1)	143	50	35	46	5	53	4	6	4	9	3	.75	7	.265	.337	.321
1991 Oakland	AL	40	133	30	6	1	0	(0	0)	38	15	13	12	0	14	0	1	2	6	0	1.00	3	.226	.286	.286
1992 Oakland	AL	103	316	67	5	2	0	(0	0)	76	36	21	43	1	39	1	11	4	6	3	.67	10	.212	.305	.241
1993 Florida	NL	158	500	133	14	2	1	(0	1)	154	50	39	79	13	73	3	5	4	7	3	.70	5	.266	.367	.308
1994 Colorado	NL	110	423	106	11	4	1	(1	0)	128	58	32	56	0	58	0	4	3	12	7	.63	6	.251	.336	.303
1995 Colorado	NL	137	427	111	17	3	1	(0	1)	137	65	25	98	8	57	5	6	1	15	3	.83	7	.260	.403	.321
1996 Colorado	NL	155	517	146	20	2	8	(5	3)	194	89	48	80	5	78	6	14	6	10	2	.83	9	.282	.381	.375
1997 Colorado	NL	121	393	106	23	5	4	(2	2)	151	52	38	66	3	56	2	7	1	5	2	.71	7	.270	.377	.384
11 ML YEARS		1209	3868	997	145	23	23	(11	12)	1257	492	312	538	36	525	31	68	32	81	30	.73	68	.258	.350	.325

Bob Wells

Pitches: Right **Bats:** Right **Pos:** RP-45; SP-1 **Ht:** 6'0" **Wt:** 180 **Born:** 11/1/66 **Age:** 31

Year Team	Lg	G	GS	CG	GF	IP	BFP	H	R	ER	HR	SH	SF	HB	TBB	IBB	SO	WP	Bk	W	L	Pct.	ShO	Sv-Op	Hld	ERA
1994 Phi-Sea		7	0	0	2	9	38	8	2	2	0	0	0	1	4	0	6	0	0	2	0	1.000	0	0-0	0	2.00
1995 Seattle	AL	30	4	0	3	76.2	358	88	51	49	11	1	5	3	39	3	38	6	0	4	3	.571	0	0-1	0	5.75
1996 Seattle	AL	36	16	1	6	130.2	574	141	78	77	25	3	4	6	46	5	94	0	0	12	7	.632	1	0-0	1	5.30
1997 Seattle	AL	46	1	0	19	67.1	304	88	49	43	11	1	2	3	18	1	51	1	0	2	0	1.000	0	2-4	5	5.75
1994 Philadelphia	NL	6	0	0	2	5	21	4	1	1	0	0	0	0	3	0	3	0	0	1	0	1.000	0	0-0	0	1.80
Seattle	AL	1	0	0	0	4	17	4	1	1	0	0	0	1	1	0	3	0	0	1	0	1.000	0	0-0	0	2.25
4 ML YEARS		119	21	1	30	283.2	1274	325	180	171	47	5	11	13	107	9	189	2	0	20	10	.667	1	2-5	6	5.43

David Wells

Pitches: Left **Bats:** Left **Pos:** SP-32 **Ht:** 6'4" **Wt:** 225 **Born:** 5/20/63 **Age:** 35

Year Team	Lg	G	GS	CG	GF	IP	BFP	H	R	ER	HR	SH	SF	HB	TBB	IBB	SO	WP	Bk	W	L	Pct.	ShO	Sv-Op	Hld	ERA
1987 Toronto	AL	18	2	0	6	29.1	132	37	14	13	0	1	0	0	12	0	32	4	0	4	3	.571	0	1-2	3	3.99
1988 Toronto	AL	41	0	0	15	64.1	279	65	36	33	12	2	2	2	31	9	56	6	2	3	5	.375	0	4-6	9	4.62
1989 Toronto	AL	54	0	0	19	86.1	352	66	25	23	5	3	2	0	28	7	78	6	3	7	4	.636	0	2-9	8	2.40
1990 Toronto	AL	43	25	0	8	189	759	165	72	66	14	9	2	2	45	3	115	7	1	11	6	.647	0	3-3	3	3.14
1991 Toronto	AL	40	28	2	3	198.1	811	188	88	82	24	6	6	2	49	1	106	10	3	15	10	.600	0	1-2	3	3.72
1992 Toronto	AL	41	14	0	14	120	529	138	84	72	16	3	4	8	36	6	62	3	1	7	9	.438	0	2-4	5	5.40
1993 Detroit	AL	32	30	0	0	187	776	183	93	87	26	3	3	7	42	6	139	13	0	11	9	.550	0	0-0	1	4.19
1994 Detroit	AL	16	16	5	0	111.1	464	113	54	49	13	3	1	2	24	6	71	5	0	5	7	.417	1	0-0	0	3.96
1995 Det-Cin		29	29	6	0	203	839	194	88	73	23	7	3	2	53	9	133	7	2	16	8	.667	0	0-0	0	3.24
1996 Baltimore	AL	34	34	3	0	224.1	946	247	132	128	32	8	**14**	7	51	7	130	4	2	11	14	.440	0	0-0	0	5.14
1997 New York	AL	32	32	5	0	218	922	239	109	102	24	7	3	6	45	0	156	8	0	16	10	.615	2	0-0	0	4.21
1995 Detroit	AL	18	18	3	0	130.1	539	120	54	44	17	3	2	2	37	5	83	6	1	10	3	.769	0	0-0	0	3.04
Cincinnati	NL	11	11	3	0	72.2	300	74	34	29	6	4	1	0	16	4	50	1	1	6	5	.545	0	0-0	0	3.59

Year Team	Lg	G	GS	CG	GF	IP	BFP	H	R	ER	HR	SH	SF	HB	TBB	IBB	SO	WP	Bk	W	L	Pct.	ShO	Sv-Op	Hld	ERA
11 ML YEARS		380	210	21	65	1631	6809	1635	795	728	189	52	40	38	416	54	1078	73	14	106	85	.555	3	13-26	30	4.02

Turk Wendell

Pitches: Right **Bats:** Left **Pos:** RP-65 **Ht:** 6'2" **Wt:** 195 **Born:** 5/19/67 **Age:** 31

		HOW MUCH HE PITCHED						WHAT HE GAVE UP												THE RESULTS						
Year Team	Lg	G	GS	CG	GF	IP	BFP	H	R	ER	HR	SH	SF	HB	TBB	IBB	SO	WP	Bk	W	L	Pct.	ShO	Sv-Op	Hld	ERA
1993 Chicago	NL	7	4	0	1	22.2	98	24	13	11	0	2	0	0	8	1	15	1	1	1	2	.333	0	0-0	0	4.37
1994 Chicago	NL	6	2	0	1	14.1	76	22	20	19	3	2	1	0	10	1	9	1	0	0	1	.000	0	0-0	0	11.93
1995 Chicago	NL	43	0	0	17	60.1	270	71	35	33	11	3	3	2	24	4	50	1	0	3	1	.750	0	0-0	3	4.92
1996 Chicago	NL	70	0	0	49	79.1	339	58	26	25	8	3	1	3	44	4	75	3	2	4	5	.444	0	18-21	6	2.84
1997 ChN-NYN	NL	65	0	0	21	76.1	345	68	42	37	7	4	3	2	53	6	64	4	0	3	5	.375	0	5-7	2	4.36
1997 Chicago	NL	52	0	0	18	60	269	53	32	28	4	3	3	1	39	5	54	4	0	3	5	.375	0	4-5	2	4.20
New York	NL	13	0	0	3	16.1	76	15	10	9	3	1	0	1	14	1	10	0	0	0	0	.000	0	1-2	0	4.96
5 ML YEARS		191	6	0	89	253	1128	243	136	125	29	14	8	7	139	16	213	10	3	11	14	.440	0	23-28	11	4.45

Don Wengert

Pitches: Right **Bats:** Right **Pos:** RP-37; SP-12 **Ht:** 6'2" **Wt:** 205 **Born:** 11/6/69 **Age:** 28

		HOW MUCH HE PITCHED						WHAT HE GAVE UP												THE RESULTS						
Year Team	Lg	G	GS	CG	GF	IP	BFP	H	R	ER	HR	SH	SF	HB	TBB	IBB	SO	WP	Bk	W	L	Pct.	ShO	Sv-Op	Hld	ERA
1995 Oakland	AL	19	0	0	10	29.2	129	30	14	11	3	1	1	1	12	2	16	1	0	1	1	.500	0	0-0	1	3.34
1996 Oakland	AL	36	25	1	2	161.1	725	200	102	100	29	3	5	6	60	5	75	4	0	7	11	.389	1	0-0	2	5.58
1997 Oakland	AL	49	12	1	16	134	612	177	96	90	21	5	7	8	41	4	68	2	0	5	11	.313	0	2-3	0	6.04
3 ML YEARS		104	37	2	28	325	1466	407	212	201	53	9	13	15	113	11	159	7	0	13	23	.361	1	2-3	3	5.57

John Wetteland

Pitches: Right **Bats:** Right **Pos:** RP-61 **Ht:** 6'2" **Wt:** 215 **Born:** 8/21/66 **Age:** 31

		HOW MUCH HE PITCHED						WHAT HE GAVE UP												THE RESULTS						
Year Team	Lg	G	GS	CG	GF	IP	BFP	H	R	ER	HR	SH	SF	HB	TBB	IBB	SO	WP	Bk	W	L	Pct.	ShO	Sv-Op	Hld	ERA
1989 Los Angeles	NL	31	12	0	7	102.2	411	81	46	43	8	4	2	0	34	4	96	16	1	5	8	.385	0	1-1	1	3.77
1990 Los Angeles	NL	22	5	0	7	43	190	44	28	23	6	1	1	4	17	3	36	8	0	2	4	.333	0	0-1	0	4.81
1991 Los Angeles	NL	6	0	0	3	9	36	5	2	0	0	1	1	1	3	0	9	1	0	1	0	1.000	0	0-0	0	0.00
1992 Montreal	NL	67	0	0	58	83.1	347	64	27	27	6	5	1	4	36	3	99	4	0	4	4	.500	0	37-46	0	2.92
1993 Montreal	NL	70	0	0	58	85.1	344	58	17	13	3	1	2	1	28	3	113	7	0	9	3	.750	0	43-49	0	1.37
1994 Montreal	NL	52	0	0	43	63.2	261	46	22	20	5	5	4	3	21	4	68	0	0	4	6	.400	0	25-35	0	2.83
1995 New York	AL	60	0	0	56	61.1	233	40	22	20	6	1	2	0	14	2	66	1	0	1	5	.167	0	31-37	0	2.93
1996 New York	AL	62	0	0	58	63.2	265	54	23	20	9	1	2	0	21	4	69	1	0	2	3	.400	0	43-47	0	2.83
1997 Texas	AL	61	0	0	58	65	259	43	18	14	5	1	1	0	21	3	63	1	0	7	2	.778	0	31-37	0	1.94
9 ML YEARS		431	17	0	348	577	2346	435	205	180	48	23	15	14	195	26	619	39	1	35	35	.500	0	211-253	1	2.81

Matt Whisenant

Pitches: Left **Bats:** Right **Pos:** RP-28 **Ht:** 6'3" **Wt:** 215 **Born:** 6/8/71 **Age:** 27

		HOW MUCH HE PITCHED						WHAT HE GAVE UP												THE RESULTS						
Year Team	Lg	G	GS	CG	GF	IP	BFP	H	R	ER	HR	SH	SF	HB	TBB	IBB	SO	WP	Bk	W	L	Pct.	ShO	Sv-Op	Hld	ERA
1990 Princeton	R+	9	2	0	2	15	85	16	27	19	3	0	1	3	20	0	25	7	0	0	0	.000	0	0- -	—	11.40
1991 Batavia	A-	11	10	0	1	47.2	208	31	19	13	2	1	1	0	42	0	55	4	2	2	1	.667	0	0- -	—	2.45
1992 Spartanburg	A	27	27	2	0	150.2	652	117	69	54	9	5	6	10	85	0	151	10	6	11	7	.611	0	0- -	—	3.23
1993 Kane County	A	15	15	0	0	71	331	68	45	37	3	8	2	3	56	0	74	8	3	2	6	.250	0	0- -	—	4.69
1994 Brevard Cty	A+	28	26	5	0	160	679	125	71	60	7	6	7	9	82	2	103	18	1	6	9	.400	1	0- -	—	3.38
1995 Portland	AA	23	22	0	0	128.2	544	106	57	50	8	7	4	9	65	3	107	8	0	10	6	.625	0	0- -	—	3.50
1996 Charlotte	AAA	28	22	1	1	121	590	149	107	93	15	8	2	3	101	3	97	30	0	8	10	.444	0	0- -	—	6.92
1997 Brevard Cty	A+	2	1	0	0	3.1	15	3	3	3	0	0	0	0	3	0	4	1	0	0	0	.000	0	0- -	—	8.10
Charlotte	AAA	16	0	0	4	15	73	16	12	12	0	0	0	0	12	0	19	4	0	2	1	.667	0	0- -	—	7.20
1997 Fla-KC		28	0	0	5	21.2	105	19	13	11	0	1	0	3	18	0	20	3	0	1	0	1.000	0	0-0	5	4.57
1997 Florida	NL	4	0	0	2	2.2	19	4	6	5	0	1	0	0	6	0	4	0	0	0	0	.000	0	0-0	0	16.88
Kansas City	AL	24	0	0	3	19	86	15	7	6	0	0	0	3	12	0	16	3	0	1	0	1.000	0	0-0	5	2.84

Devon White

Bats: Both **Throws:** Right **Pos:** CF-72; PH-4 **Ht:** 6'2" **Wt:** 190 **Born:** 12/29/62 **Age:** 35

		BATTING																	BASERUNNING				PERCENTAGES		
Year Team	Lg	G	AB	H	2B	3B	HR	(Hm	Rd)	TB	R	RBI	TBB	IBB	SO	HBP	SH	SF	SB	CS	SB%	GDP	Avg	OBP	SLG
1985 California	AL	21	7	1	0	0	0	(0	0)	1	7	0	1	0	3	1	0	0	3	1	.75	0	.143	.333	.143
1986 California	AL	29	51	12	1	1	1	(0	1)	18	8	3	6	0	8	0	0	0	6	0	1.00	0	.235	.316	.353
1987 California	AL	159	639	168	33	5	24	(11	13)	283	103	87	39	2	135	2	14	2	32	11	.74	8	.263	.306	.443
1988 California	AL	122	455	118	22	2	11	(3	8)	177	76	51	23	1	84	2	5	1	17	8	.68	5	.259	.297	.389
1989 California	AL	156	636	156	18	13	12	(9	3)	236	86	56	31	3	129	2	7	2	44	16	.73	12	.245	.282	.371
1990 California	AL	125	443	96	17	3	11	(5	6)	152	57	44	44	5	116	3	10	3	21	6	.78	6	.217	.290	.343
1991 Toronto	AL	156	642	181	40	10	17	(9	8)	292	110	60	55	1	135	7	5	6	33	10	.77	7	.282	.342	.455
1992 Toronto	AL	153	641	159	26	7	17	(7	10)	250	98	60	47	0	133	5	0	3	37	4	.90	9	.248	.303	.390
1993 Toronto	AL	146	598	163	42	6	15	(10	5)	262	116	52	57	1	127	7	3	4	34	4	.89	3	.273	.341	.438
1994 Toronto	AL	100	403	109	24	6	13	(5	8)	184	67	49	21	3	80	5	4	2	11	3	.79	4	.270	.313	.457
1995 Toronto	AL	101	427	121	23	5	10	(4	6)	184	61	53	29	1	97	5	1	3	11	2	.85	5	.283	.334	.431
1996 Florida	NL	146	552	151	37	6	17	(5	12)	251	77	84	38	6	99	8	4	9	22	6	.79	8	.274	.325	.455

Year Team	Lg	G	AB	H	2B	3B	HR	(Hm	Rd)	TB	R	RBI	TBB	IBB	SO	HBP	SH	SF	SB	CS	SB%	GDP	Avg	OBP	SLG
								BATTING												**BASERUNNING**			**PERCENTAGES**		
1997 Florida	NL	74	265	65	13	1	6	(4	2)	98	37	34	32	2	65	7	0	4	13	5	.72	3	.245	.338	.370
13 ML YEARS		1488	5759	1500	296	65	154	(72	82)	2388	903	633	423	25	1211	54	53	38	284	76	.79	70	.260	.315	.415

Gabe White

Pitches: Left **Bats:** Left **Pos:** SP-6; RP-6   **Ht:** 6'2" **Wt:** 200 **Born:** 11/20/71 **Age:** 26

Year Team	Lg	G	GS	CG	GF	IP	BFP	H	R	ER	HR	SH	SF	HB	TBB	IBB	SO	WP	Bk	W	L	Pct.	ShO	Sv-Op	Hld	ERA
				HOW MUCH HE PITCHED						**WHAT HE GAVE UP**												**THE RESULTS**				
1990 Expos	R	11	11	1	0	57.1	233	50	21	20	3	1	1	3	12	0	42	5	1	4	2	.667	0	0- -	—	3.14
1991 Sumter	A	24	24	5	0	149	626	129	73	54	7	7	6	5	53	0	138	8	0	6	9	.400	0	0- -	—	3.26
1992 Rockford	A	27	27	7	0	187	774	148	73	59	10	9	4	11	61	0	176	9	9	14	8	.636	0	0- -	—	2.84
1993 Harrisburg	AA	16	16	2	0	100	394	80	30	24	4	1	1	2	28	0	80	5	2	7	2	.778	1	0- -	—	2.16
Ottawa	AAA	6	6	1	0	40.1	165	38	15	14	3	0	1	1	6	0	28	2	0	2	1	.667	1	0- -	—	3.12
1994 Wst Plm Bch	A+	1	1	0	0	6	20	2	2	1	0	0	0	0	1	0	4	1	0	1	0	1.000	0	0- -	—	1.50
Ottawa	AAA	14	14	0	0	73	320	77	49	41	11	2	3	2	28	2	63	2	0	8	3	.727	0	0- -	—	5.05
1995 Ottawa	AAA	12	12	0	0	62.1	264	58	31	27	10	1	4	4	17	0	37	2	1	2	3	.400	0	0- -	—	3.90
1996 Indianapolis	AAA	11	11	0	0	68.1	273	69	25	21	6	2	2	1	9	3	51	1	0	6	3	.667	0	0- -	—	2.77
1997 Indianapolis	AAA	20	19	0	0	118	493	119	46	37	10	2	4	6	18	0	62	2	1	7	4	.636	0	0- -	—	2.82
1994 Montreal	NL	7	5	0	2	23.2	106	24	16	16	4	1	1	1	11	0	17	0	0	1	1	.500	0	1-1	0	6.08
1995 Montreal	NL	19	1	0	8	25.2	115	26	21	20	7	3	2	1	9	0	25	0	0	1	2	.333	0	0-0	0	7.01
1997 Cincinnati	NL	12	6	0	2	41	168	39	20	20	6	3	2	1	8	1	25	0	0	2	2	.500	0	1-1	3	4.39
3 ML YEARS		38	12	0	12	90.1	389	89	57	56	17	6	6	3	28	1	67	0	0	4	5	.444	0	2-2	3	5.58

Rondell White

Bats: Right **Throws:** Right **Pos:** CF-151   **Ht:** 6'1" **Wt:** 205 **Born:** 2/23/72 **Age:** 26

Year Team	Lg	G	AB	H	2B	3B	HR	(Hm	Rd)	TB	R	RBI	TBB	IBB	SO	HBP	SH	SF	SB	CS	SB%	GDP	Avg	OBP	SLG
								BATTING												**BASERUNNING**			**PERCENTAGES**		
1993 Montreal	NL	23	73	19	3	1	2	(1	1)	30	9	15	7	0	16	0	2	1	1	2	.33	2	.260	.321	.411
1994 Montreal	NL	40	97	27	10	1	2	(1	1)	45	16	13	9	0	18	3	0	0	1	1	.50	1	.278	.358	.464
1995 Montreal	NL	130	474	140	33	4	13	(6	7)	220	87	57	41	1	87	6	0	4	25	5	.83	11	.295	.356	.464
1996 Montreal	NL	88	334	98	19	4	6	(2	4)	143	35	41	22	0	53	2	0	1	14	6	.70	11	.293	.340	.428
1997 Montreal	NL	151	592	160	29	5	28	(9	19)	283	84	82	31	3	111	10	1	4	16	8	.67	19	.270	.316	.478
5 ML YEARS		432	1570	444	94	15	51	(19	32)	721	231	208	110	4	285	21	3	10	57	22	.72	44	.283	.336	.459

Mark Whiten

Bats: B **Throws:** R **Pos:** LF-44; RF-16; PH-13; DH-7   **Ht:** 6'3" **Wt:** 235 **Born:** 11/25/66 **Age:** 31

Year Team	Lg	G	AB	H	2B	3B	HR	(Hm	Rd)	TB	R	RBI	TBB	IBB	SO	HBP	SH	SF	SB	CS	SB%	GDP	Avg	OBP	SLG
								BATTING												**BASERUNNING**			**PERCENTAGES**		
1990 Toronto	AL	33	88	24	1	1	2	(1	1)	33	12	7	7	0	14	0	0	1	2	0	1.00	2	.273	.323	.375
1991 Tor-Cle.	AL	116	407	99	18	7	9	(4	5)	158	46	45	30	2	85	3	0	5	4	3	.57	13	.243	.297	.388
1992 Cleveland	AL	148	508	129	19	4	9	(6	3)	183	73	43	72	10	102	2	3	3	16	12	.57	12	.254	.347	.360
1993 St. Louis	NL	152	562	142	13	4	25	(12	13)	238	81	99	58	9	110	2	0	4	15	8	.65	11	.253	.323	.423
1994 St. Louis	NL	92	334	98	18	2	14	(6	8)	162	57	53	37	9	75	1	0	2	10	5	.67	8	.293	.364	.485
1995 Bos-Phi		92	320	77	13	1	12	(5	7)	128	51	47	39	1	86	1	0	1	8	0	1.00	9	.241	.324	.400
1996 Phi-Atl-Sea		136	412	108	20	1	22	(9	13)	196	76	71	70	6	127	3	0	1	17	9	.65	12	.262	.372	.476
1997 New York	AL	69	155	57	11	0	5	(4	1)	83	34	24	30	5	47	2	1	0	4	2	.67	6	.265	.360	.386
1991 Toronto	AL	46	149	33	4	3	2	(2	0)	49	12	19	11	1	35	1	0	3	0	1	.00	5	.221	.274	.329
Cleveland	AL	70	258	66	14	4	7	(2	5)	109	34	26	19	1	50	2	0	2	4	2	.67	8	.256	.310	.422
1995 Boston	AL	32	108	20	3	0	1	(0	1)	26	13	10	8	0	23	0	0	1	1	0	1.00	5	.185	.239	.241
Philadelphia	NL	60	212	57	10	1	11	(5	6)	102	38	37	31	1	63	1	0	0	7	0	1.00	4	.269	.365	.481
1996 Philadelphia	NL	60	182	43	8	0	7	(4	3)	72	33	21	33	2	62	1	0	0	13	3	.81	9	.236	.356	.396
Atlanta	NL	36	90	23	5	1	3	(1	2)	39	12	17	16	0	25	0	0	1	2	5	.29	2	.256	.364	.433
Seattle	AL	40	140	42	7	0	12	(4	8)	85	31	33	21	4	40	2	0	0	2	1	.67	1	.300	.399	.607
8 ML YEARS		838	2846	734	113	20	98	(47	51)	1181	430	389	343	42	646	14	4	17	76	39	.66	73	.258	.339	.415

Matt Whiteside

Pitches: Right **Bats:** Right **Pos:** RP-41; SP-1   **Ht:** 6'0" **Wt:** 205 **Born:** 8/8/67 **Age:** 30

Year Team	Lg	G	GS	CG	GF	IP	BFP	H	R	ER	HR	SH	SF	HB	TBB	IBB	SO	WP	Bk	W	L	Pct.	ShO	Sv-Op	Hld	ERA
				HOW MUCH HE PITCHED						**WHAT HE GAVE UP**												**THE RESULTS**				
1997 Okla City *	AAA	10	1	0	3	28	124	30	14	11	1	0	2	0	13	0	11	0	1	1	1	.500	0	1- -	—	3.54
1992 Texas	AL	20	0	0	8	28	118	26	8	6	1	0	1	0	11	2	13	2	0	1	1	.500	0	4-4	0	1.93
1993 Texas	AL	60	0	0	10	73	305	78	37	35	7	2	1	1	23	6	39	0	2	2	1	.667	0	1-5	14	4.32
1994 Texas	AL	47	0	0	16	61	272	68	40	34	6	3	2	1	28	3	37	1	0	2	2	.500	0	1-3	7	5.02
1995 Texas	AL	40	0	0	18	53	223	48	24	24	5	3	3	1	19	2	46	4	0	5	4	.556	0	3-4	7	4.08
1996 Texas	AL	14	0	0	7	32.1	148	43	24	24	8	1	2	0	11	1	15	1	0	0	1	.000	0	0-0	1	6.68
1997 Texas	AL	42	1	0	8	72.2	323	85	45	41	4	2	5	3	26	3	44	3	2	4	1	.800	0	0-4	2	5.08
6 ML YEARS		223	1	0	67	320	1389	348	178	164	31	10	14	6	118	17	194	11	4	14	10	.583	0	9-20	31	4.61

Bob Wickman

Pitches: Right **Bats:** Right **Pos:** RP-74   **Ht:** 6'1" **Wt:** 212 **Born:** 2/6/69 **Age:** 29

Year Team	Lg	G	GS	CG	GF	IP	BFP	H	R	ER	HR	SH	SF	HB	TBB	IBB	SO	WP	Bk	W	L	Pct.	ShO	Sv-Op	Hld	ERA
				HOW MUCH HE PITCHED						**WHAT HE GAVE UP**												**THE RESULTS**				
1992 New York	AL	8	8	0	0	50.1	213	51	25	23	2	1	3	2	20	0	21	3	0	6	1	.857	0	0-0	0	4.11

Year Team	Lg	G	GS	CG	GF	IP	BFP	H	R	ER	HR	SH	SF	HB	TBB	IBB	SO	WP	Bk	W	L	Pct.	ShO	Sv-Op	Hld	ERA
1993 New York	AL	41	19	1	9	140	629	156	82	72	13	4	1	5	69	7	70	2	0	14	4	.778	1	4-8	2	4.63
1994 New York	AL	53	0	0	19	70	286	54	26	24	3	0	5	1	27	3	56	2	0	5	4	.556	0	6-10	11	3.09
1995 New York	AL	63	1	0	14	80	347	77	38	36	6	4	1	5	33	3	51	2	0	4	3	.333	0	1-10	21	4.05
1996 NYA-Mil	AL	70	0	0	18	95.2	429	106	50	47	10	2	4	5	44	3	75	4	0	7	1	.875	0	0-4	10	4.42
1997 Milwaukee	AL	74	0	0	20	95.2	405	89	32	29	8	6	2	3	41	7	78	8	0	7	6	.538	0	1-5	28	2.73
1996 New York	AL	58	0	0	14	79	358	94	41	41	7	1	4	5	34	1	61	3	0	4	1	.800	0	0-3	6	4.67
Milwaukee	AL	12	0	0	4	16.2	71	12	9	6	3	1	0	0	10	2	14	1	0	3	0	1.000	0	0-1	4	3.24
6 ML YEARS		309	28	1	80	531.2	2309	533	253	231	42	17	16	21	234	23	351	21	0	41	20	.672	1	12-37	72	3.91

Chris Widger

Bats: Right **Throws:** Right **Pos:** C-85; PH-6 **Ht:** 6'3" **Wt:** 195 **Born:** 5/21/71 **Age:** 27

Year Team	Lg	G	AB	H	2B	3B	HR	(Hm	Rd)	TB	R	RBI	TBB	IBB	SO	HBP	SH	SF	SB	CS	SB%	GDP	Avg	OBP	SLG
1995 Seattle	AL	23	45	9	0	0	1	(1	0)	12	2	2	3	0	11	0	0	1	0	0	.00	0	.200	.245	.267
1996 Seattle	AL	8	11	2	0	0	0	(0	0)	2	1	0	0	0	5	1	0	0	0	0	.00	0	.182	.250	.182
1997 Montreal	NL	91	278	65	20	3	7	(4	3)	112	30	37	22	1	59	1	2	2	2	0	1.00	7	.234	.290	.403
3 ML YEARS		122	334	76	20	3	8	(5	3)	126	33	39	25	1	75	2	2	3	2	0	1.00	7	.228	.283	.377

Marc Wilkins

Pitches: Right **Bats:** Right **Pos:** RP-70 **Ht:** 5'11" **Wt:** 200 **Born:** 10/21/70 **Age:** 27

Year Team	Lg	G	GS	CG	GF	IP	BFP	H	R	ER	HR	SH	SF	HB	TBB	IBB	SO	WP	Bk	W	L	Pct.	ShO	Sv-Op	Hld	ERA
1992 Welland	A-	28	1	0	8	42	207	49	38	34	2	2	2	4	24	3	42	12	1	4	2	.667	0	1- --		7.29
1993 Augusta	A	48	5	0	14	77	360	83	52	36	4	1	2	13	31	1	73	10	0	5	6	.455	0	1- --		4.21
1994 Salem	A+	28	28	0	0	151	657	155	84	62	15	6	3	2	45	0	90	14	0	8	5	.615	0	0- --		3.70
1995 Carolina	AA	37	12	0	1	99.1	436	91	47	44	8	5	3	11	44	2	80	9	0	5	3	.625	0	0- --		3.99
1996 Carolina	AA	11	3	0	3	24.2	103	19	12	11	1	2	0	2	11	2	19	0	0	2	3	.400	0	0- --		4.01
1996 Pittsburgh	NL	47	2	0	11	75	331	75	36	32	6	3	4	6	36	6	62	5	0	4	3	.571	0	1-5	4	3.84
1997 Pittsburgh	NL	70	0	0	21	75.2	310	65	36	31	7	4	0	4	33	2	47	5	0	9	5	.643	0	2-4	15	3.69
2 ML YEARS		117	2	0	32	150.2	641	140	69	63	13	7	4	10	69	8	109	10	0	13	8	.619	0	3-9	19	3.76

Rick Wilkins

Bats: Left **Throws:** Right **Pos:** C-60; PH-11; DH-2 **Ht:** 6'2" **Wt:** 215 **Born:** 6/4/67 **Age:** 31

Year Team	Lg	G	AB	H	2B	3B	HR	(Hm	Rd)	TB	R	RBI	TBB	IBB	SO	HBP	SH	SF	SB	CS	SB%	GDP	Avg	OBP	SLG
1997 Tacoma *	AAA	17	68	23	8	0	1	(--	--)	34	16	14	8	2	12	0	0	1	0	0	.00	4	.338	.403	.500
1991 Chicago	NL	86	203	45	9	0	6	(2	4)	72	21	22	19	2	56	6	7	0	3	3	.50	3	.222	.307	.355
1992 Chicago	NL	83	244	66	9	1	8	(3	5)	101	20	22	28	7	53	0	1	1	2	2	.00	6	.270	.344	.414
1993 Chicago	NL	136	446	135	23	1	30	(10	20)	250	78	73	50	13	99	3	0	1	2	1	.67	6	.303	.376	.561
1994 Chicago	NL	100	313	71	25	2	7	(4	3)	121	44	39	40	5	86	2	1	2	4	3	.57	3	.227	.317	.387
1995 ChN-Hou	NL	65	202	41	3	0	7	(3	4)	65	30	19	46	2	61	1	0	2	0	0	.00	9	.203	.351	.322
1996 Hou-SF	NL	136	411	100	18	2	14	(6	8)	164	53	59	67	13	121	1	0	10	0	3	.00	5	.243	.344	.399
1997 SF-Sea		71	202	40	6	0	7	(2	5)	67	20	27	18	0	67	0	0	4	0	0	.00	4	.198	.259	.332
1995 Chicago	NL	50	162	31	2	0	6	(3	3)	51	24	14	36	1	51	1	0	1	0	0	.00	8	.191	.340	.315
Houston	NL	15	40	10	1	0	1	(0	1)	14	6	5	10	1	10	0	0	1	0	0	.00	1	.250	.392	.350
1996 Houston	NL	84	254	54	8	2	6	(3	3)	84	34	23	46	10	81	1	0	5	0	1	.00	4	.213	.330	.331
San Francisco	NL	52	157	46	10	0	8	(3	5)	80	19	36	21	3	40	0	0	5	0	2	.00	1	.293	.366	.510
1997 San Francisco	NL	66	190	37	5	0	6	(1	5)	60	18	23	17	0	65	0	0	3	0	0	.00	0	.195	.257	.316
Seattle	AL	5	12	3	1	0	1	(1	0)	7	2	4	1	0	2	0	0	1	0	0	.00	0	.250	.286	.583
7 ML YEARS		677	2021	498	93	6	79	(30	49)	840	266	261	268	42	543	13	9	20	9	12	.43	32	.246	.335	.416

Bernie Williams

Bats: Both **Throws:** Right **Pos:** CF-128; PH-1 **Ht:** 6'2" **Wt:** 205 **Born:** 9/13/68 **Age:** 29

Year Team	Lg	G	AB	H	2B	3B	HR	(Hm	Rd)	TB	R	RBI	TBB	IBB	SO	HBP	SH	SF	SB	CS	SB%	GDP	Avg	OBP	SLG
1991 New York	AL	85	320	76	19	4	3	(1	2)	112	43	34	48	0	57	1	2	3	10	5	.67	4	.238	.336	.350
1992 New York	AL	62	261	73	14	2	5	(3	2)	106	39	26	29	1	36	1	2	0	7	6	.54	5	.280	.354	.406
1993 New York	AL	139	567	152	31	4	12	(5	7)	227	67	68	53	4	106	4	1	3	9	9	.50	17	.268	.333	.400
1994 New York	AL	108	408	118	29	1	12	(8	4)	185	80	57	61	2	54	3	1	2	16	9	.64	11	.289	.384	.453
1995 New York	AL	144	563	173	29	9	18	(7	11)	274	93	82	75	1	98	5	2	3	8	6	.57	12	.307	.392	.487
1996 New York	AL	143	551	168	26	7	29	(12	17)	295	108	102	82	8	72	0	1	7	17	4	.81	15	.305	.391	.535
1997 New York	AL	129	509	167	35	6	21	(13	8)	277	107	100	73	7	80	1	0	8	15	6	.65	10	.328	.408	.544
7 ML YEARS		810	3179	927	183	33	100	(45	55)	1476	537	469	421	23	503	15	9	26	82	47	.64	74	.292	.374	.464

Brian Williams

Pitches: Right **Bats:** Right **Pos:** RP-13 **Ht:** 6'2" **Wt:** 225 **Born:** 2/15/69 **Age:** 29

Year Team	Lg	G	GS	CG	GF	IP	BFP	H	R	ER	HR	SH	SF	HB	TBB	IBB	SO	WP	Bk	W	L	Pct.	ShO	Sv-Op	Hld	ERA
1997 Rochester *	AAA	22	9	0	13	69.1	299	68	33	30	8	3	2	4	23	0	78	1	2	4	3	.571	0	8- --		3.89
1991 Houston	NL	2	2	0	0	12	49	11	5	5	2	0	0	1	4	0	4	0	0	0	1	.000	0	0-0	0	3.75
1992 Houston	NL	16	16	0	0	96.1	413	92	44	42	10	7	3	0	42	1	54	2	1	7	6	.538	0	0-0	0	3.92
1993 Houston	NL	42	5	0	12	82	357	76	48	44	7	5	3	4	38	4	56	9	2	4	4	.500	0	3-6	2	4.83

			HOW MUCH HE PITCHED						WHAT HE GAVE UP												THE RESULTS						
Year Team	Lg	G	GS	CG	GF	IP	BFP	H	R	ER	HR	SH	SF	HB	TBB	IBB	SO	WP	Bk	W	L	Pct.	ShO	Sv-Op	Hld	ERA
1994 Houston	NL	20	13	0	2	78.1	384	112	64	50	9	7	5	4	41	4	49	3	1	6	5	.545	0	0-0	1	5.74
1995 San Diego	NL	44	6	0	7	72	337	79	54	48	3	7	1	8	38	4	75	7	1	3	10	.231	0	0-2	7	6.00
1996 Detroit	AL	40	17	2	17	121	579	145	107	91	21	5	6	6	85	2	72	8	0	3	10	.231	1	2-4	0	6.77
1997 Baltimore	AL	13	0	0	8	24	110	20	8	8	0	0	1	0	18	0	14	1	0	0	0	.000	0	0-1	0	3.00
7 ML YEARS		177	59	2	46	485.2	2229	535	330	288	52	31	19	23	266	15	324	30	5	23	36	.390	1	5-13	10	5.34

Eddie Williams

Bats: Right **Throws:** Right **Pos:** 1B-26; PH-13   **Ht:** 6'0" **Wt:** 210 **Born:** 11/1/64 **Age:** 33

				BATTING														BASERUNNING				PERCENTAGES		
Year Team	Lg	G	AB	H	2B	3B	HR	(Hm	Rd)	TB	R	RBI	TBB	IBB	SO	HBP	SH	SF	SB	CS	SB%	GDP	Avg	OBP	SLG
1997 Albuquerque *	AAA	76	279	102	17	0	29	—	—	206	73	76	37	4	45	8	0	2	0	2	.00	9	.366	.451	.738
1986 Cleveland	AL	5	7	1	0	0	0	(0	0)	1	2	1	0	0	3	0	0	0	0	0	.00	0	.143	.143	.143
1987 Cleveland	AL	22	64	11	4	0	1	(0	1)	18	9	4	9	0	19	1	0	1	0	0	.00	2	.172	.280	.281
1988 Cleveland	AL	10	21	4	0	0	0	(0	0)	4	3	1	0	0	3	1	1	0	0	0	.00	0	.190	.227	.190
1989 Chicago	AL	66	201	55	8	0	3	(2	1)	72	25	10	18	3	31	4	3	3	1	2	.33	4	.274	.341	.358
1990 San Diego	NL	14	42	12	3	0	3	(1	2)	24	5	4	5	2	6	0	0	0	0	1	.00	1	.286	.362	.571
1994 San Diego	NL	49	175	58	11	1	11	(5	6)	104	32	42	15	1	26	3	2	1	0	1	.00	10	.331	.392	.594
1995 San Diego	NL	97	296	77	11	1	12	(4	8)	126	35	47	23	0	47	4	0	2	0	0	.00	21	.260	.320	.426
1996 Detroit	AL	77	215	43	5	0	6	(3	3)	66	22	26	18	0	50	2	0	1	0	2	.00	8	.200	.267	.307
1997 LA-Pit	NL	38	96	23	5	0	3	(1	2)	37	12	12	11	2	25	2	1	1	1	0	1.00	2	.240	.327	.385
1997 Los Angeles	NL	8	7	1	0	0	0	(0	0)	1	0	1	1	1	1	0	0	0	0	0	.00	0	.143	.250	.143
Pittsburgh	NL	30	89	22	5	0	3	(1	2)	36	12	11	10	1	24	2	1	1	1	0	1.00	2	.247	.333	.404
9 ML YEARS		378	1117	284	47	2	39	(16	23)	452	145	147	99	8	210	17	7	9	2	6	.25	49	.254	.322	.405

George Williams

Bats: Both **Throws:** Right **Pos:** C-67; PH-17; DH-1   **Ht:** 5'10" **Wt:** 190 **Born:** 4/22/69 **Age:** 29

				BATTING														BASERUNNING				PERCENTAGES		
Year Team	Lg	G	AB	H	2B	3B	HR	(Hm	Rd)	TB	R	RBI	TBB	IBB	SO	HBP	SH	SF	SB	CS	SB%	GDP	Avg	OBP	SLG
1997 Edmonton *	AAA	3	7	0	0	0	0	—	—	0	0	0	1	0	1	0	0	0	0	0	.00	0	.000	.125	.000
Modesto *	A+	13	44	14	4	0	1	—	—	21	8	6	7	2	14	0	0	1	0	1	.00	0	.318	.404	.477
1995 Oakland	AL	29	79	23	5	1	3	(1	2)	39	13	14	11	2	21	2	0	2	0	0	.00	1	.291	.383	.494
1996 Oakland	AL	56	132	20	5	0	3	(0	3)	34	17	10	28	1	32	3	2	1	0	0	.00	3	.152	.311	.258
1997 Oakland	AL	76	201	58	9	1	3	(2	1)	78	30	22	35	0	46	2	2	1	0	1	.00	2	.289	.397	.388
3 ML YEARS		161	412	101	19	2	9	(3	6)	151	60	46	74	3	99	7	4	4	0	1	.00	6	.245	.366	.367

Gerald Williams

Bats: R **Throws:** R **Pos:** CF-129; LF-39; PH-3; DH-1   **Ht:** 6'2" **Wt:** 190 **Born:** 8/10/66 **Age:** 31

				BATTING														BASERUNNING				PERCENTAGES		
Year Team	Lg	G	AB	H	2B	3B	HR	(Hm	Rd)	TB	R	RBI	TBB	IBB	SO	HBP	SH	SF	SB	CS	SB%	GDP	Avg	OBP	SLG
1992 New York	AL	15	27	8	2	0	3	(2	1)	19	7	6	0	0	3	0	0	0	2	0	1.00	0	.296	.296	.704
1993 New York	AL	42	67	10	2	3	0	(0	0)	18	11	6	1	0	14	2	0	1	2	0	1.00	1	.149	.183	.269
1994 New York	AL	57	86	25	8	0	4	(2	2)	45	19	13	4	0	17	0	0	1	1	3	.25	6	.291	.319	.523
1995 New York	AL	100	182	45	18	2	6	(4	2)	85	33	28	22	1	34	1	0	3	4	2	.67	4	.247	.327	.467
1996 NYA-Mil	AL	125	322	82	19	4	5	(3	2)	124	43	34	19	3	57	5	3	5	10	9	.53	8	.255	.299	.382
1997 Milwaukee	AL	155	566	143	32	2	10	(3	7)	209	73	41	19	1	90	6	5	5	23	9	.72	9	.253	.283	.369
1996 New York	AL	99	233	63	15	4	5	(3	2)	101	37	30	15	2	39	4	1	5	7	8	.47	7	.270	.319	.433
Milwaukee	AL	26	92	19	4	0	0	(0	0)	23	6	4	4	1	18	1	2	0	3	1	.75	1	.207	.247	.250
6 ML YEARS		494	1253	313	81	11	28	(14	14)	500	186	128	65	5	215	14	8	15	42	23	.65	29	.250	.291	.399

Matt Williams

Bats: Right **Throws:** Right **Pos:** 3B-151; PH-1   **Ht:** 6'2" **Wt:** 216 **Born:** 11/28/65 **Age:** 32

				BATTING														BASERUNNING				PERCENTAGES		
Year Team	Lg	G	AB	H	2B	3B	HR	(Hm	Rd)	TB	R	RBI	TBB	IBB	SO	HBP	SH	SF	SB	CS	SB%	GDP	Avg	OBP	SLG
1987 San Francisco	NL	84	245	46	9	2	8	(5	3)	83	28	21	16	4	68	1	3	1	4	3	.57	5	.188	.240	.339
1988 San Francisco	NL	52	156	32	6	1	8	(7	1)	64	17	19	8	0	41	2	3	1	0	1	.00	7	.205	.251	.410
1989 San Francisco	NL	84	292	59	18	1	18	(10	8)	133	31	50	14	1	72	2	1	2	1	2	.33	5	.202	.242	.455
1990 San Francisco	NL	159	617	171	27	2	33	(20	13)	301	87	122	33	9	138	7	2	5	7	4	.64	13	.277	.319	.488
1991 San Francisco	NL	157	589	158	24	5	34	(17	17)	294	72	98	33	6	128	6	0	7	5	5	.50	11	.268	.310	.499
1992 San Francisco	NL	146	529	120	13	5	20	(9	11)	203	58	66	39	11	109	6	0	2	7	7	.50	15	.227	.286	.384
1993 San Francisco	NL	145	579	170	33	4	38	(19	19)	325	105	110	27	4	80	4	0	9	1	3	.25	12	.294	.325	.561
1994 San Francisco	NL	112	445	119	16	3	**43**	(20	23)	270	74	96	33	7	87	2	0	3	1	0	1.00	11	.267	.319	.607
1995 San Francisco	NL	76	283	95	17	1	23	(9	14)	183	53	65	30	8	58	2	0	3	2	0	1.00	8	.336	.399	.647
1996 San Francisco	NL	105	404	122	16	1	22	(13	9)	206	69	85	39	9	91	6	0	6	1	2	.33	10	.302	.367	.510
1997 Cleveland	AL	151	596	157	32	3	32	(7	25)	291	86	105	34	4	108	4	0	2	12	4	.75	14	.263	.307	.488
11 ML YEARS		1271	4735	1249	211	28	279	(136	143)	2353	680	837	306	63	980	42	9	41	41	31	.57	111	.264	.312	.497

Mike Williams

Pitches: Right **Bats:** Right **Pos:** RP-10   **Ht:** 6'3" **Wt:** 195 **Born:** 7/29/68 **Age:** 29

				HOW MUCH HE PITCHED						WHAT HE GAVE UP										THE RESULTS						
Year Team	Lg	G	GS	CG	GF	IP	BFP	H	R	ER	HR	SH	SF	HB	TBB	IBB	SO	WP	Bk	W	L	Pct.	ShO	Sv-Op	Hld	ERA
1997 Omaha *	AAA	20	11	0	6	79	335	71	41	37	10	2	2	1	38	0	68	5	0	3	6	.333	0	5--	—	4.22
1992 Philadelphia	NL	5	5	1	0	28.2	121	29	20	17	3	1	1	0	7	0	5	0	0	1	1	.500	0	0-0	0	5.34

Year Team	Lg	G	GS	CG	GF	IP	BFP	H	R	ER	HR	SH	SF	HB	TBB	IBB	SO	WP	Bk	W	L	Pct.	ShO	Sv-Op	Hld	ERA
		HOW MUCH HE PITCHED						**WHAT HE GAVE UP**												**THE RESULTS**						
1993 Philadelphia	NL	17	4	0	2	51	221	50	32	30	5	1	0	0	22	2	33	2	0	1	3	.250	0	0-0	0	5.29
1994 Philadelphia	NL	12	8	0	2	50.1	222	61	31	28	7	2	3	0	20	3	29	0	0	2	4	.333	0	0-0	0	5.01
1995 Philadelphia	NL	33	8	0	7	87.2	367	78	37	32	10	5	3	3	29	2	57	7	0	3	3	.500	0	0-0	1	3.29
1996 Philadelphia	NL	32	29	0	1	167	732	188	107	101	25	6	5	6	67	6	103	16	1	6	14	.300	0	0-0	0	5.44
1997 Kansas City	AL	10	0	0	4	14	70	20	11	10	1	0	1	1	8	1	10	0	0	0	2	.000	0	1-1	0	6.43
6 ML YEARS		109	54	1	16	398.2	1733	426	238	218	51	15	13	10	153	14	237	25	1	13	27	.325	0	1-1	2	4.92

Mitch Williams

Pitches: Left **Bats:** Left **Pos:** RP-7 **Ht:** 6'4" **Wt:** 205 **Born:** 11/17/64 **Age:** 33

Year Team	Lg	G	GS	CG	GF	IP	BFP	H	R	ER	HR	SH	SF	HB	TBB	IBB	SO	WP	Bk	W	L	Pct.	ShO	Sv-Op	Hld	ERA
		HOW MUCH HE PITCHED						**WHAT HE GAVE UP**												**THE RESULTS**						
1997 Omaha *	AAA	3	0	0	1	8.2	33	6	2	2	1	0	0	0	5	0	8	0	0	0	0	.000	0	0- -	—	2.08
1986 Texas	AL	80	0	0	38	98	435	69	39	39	8	1	3	11	79	8	90	5	5	8	6	.571	0	8- -	—	3.58
1987 Texas	AL	85	1	0	32	108.2	469	63	47	39	9	4	3	7	94	7	129	4	2	8	6	.571	0	6-7	6	3.23
1988 Texas	AL	67	0	0	51	68	296	48	38	35	4	3	4	6	47	3	61	5	6	2	7	.222	0	18-26	1	4.63
1989 Chicago	NL	76	0	0	61	81.2	365	71	27	24	6	2	5	8	52	4	67	6	4	4	4	.500	0	36-47	6	2.64
1990 Chicago	NL	59	2	0	39	66.1	310	60	38	29	4	5	3	1	50	6	55	4	2	1	8	.111	0	16-20	1	3.93
1991 Philadelphia	NL	69	0	0	60	88.1	386	56	24	23	4	4	4	8	62	5	84	4	1	12	5	.706	0	30-39	1	2.34
1992 Philadelphia	NL	66	0	0	56	81	368	69	39	34	4	8	3	6	64	2	74	5	3	5	8	.385	0	29-36	0	3.78
1993 Philadelphia	NL	65	0	0	57	62	281	56	30	23	3	4	2	2	44	1	60	6	0	3	7	.300	0	43-49	1	3.34
1994 Houston	NL	25	0	0	18	20	106	21	17	17	4	2	1	1	24	2	21	1	0	1	4	.200	0	6-8	2	7.65
1995 California	AL	20	0	0	3	10.2	65	13	10	8	1	0	1	2	21	0	9	2	1	1	2	.333	0	0-1	4	6.75
1997 Kansas City	AL	7	0	0	4	6.2	38	11	8	8	2	0	1	0	7	1	10	2	0	0	1	.000	0	0-0	0	10.80
11 ML YEARS		619	3	0	419	691.1	3119	537	317	279	49	33	30	52	544	39	660	44	24	45	58	.437	0	192- -	—	3.63

Shad Williams

Pitches: Right **Bats:** Right **Pos:** RP-1 **Ht:** 6'0" **Wt:** 198 **Born:** 3/10/71 **Age:** 27

Year Team	Lg	G	GS	CG	GF	IP	BFP	H	R	ER	HR	SH	SF	HB	TBB	IBB	SO	WP	Bk	W	L	Pct.	ShO	Sv-Op	Hld	ERA
		HOW MUCH HE PITCHED						**WHAT HE GAVE UP**												**THE RESULTS**						
1992 Quad City	A	27	26	7	0	179.1	748	161	81	65	14	6	6	7	55	0	152	9	1	13	11	.542	0	0- -	—	3.26
1993 Midland	AA	27	27	2	0	175.2	758	192	100	92	16	6	6	3	65	1	91	9	1	7	10	.412	0	0- -	—	4.71
1994 Midland	AA	5	5	1	0	32.1	112	13	4	4	1	0	0	1	4	0	29	2	0	3	0	1.000	1	0- -	—	1.11
Vancouver	AAA	16	16	1	0	86	386	100	61	44	14	3	2	3	30	0	42	6	0	4	6	.400	1	0- -	—	4.60
1995 Vancouver	AAA	25	25	3	0	149.2	627	142	65	56	16	3	3	4	48	2	114	7	1	9	7	.563	1	0- -	—	3.37
1996 Vancouver	AAA	15	13	1	1	75	321	73	36	33	8	4	0	2	28	0	57	2	0	6	2	.750	0	0- -	—	3.96
1997 Vancouver	AAA	40	10	0	7	99	424	98	52	42	13	0	4	5	41	2	52	5	0	6	2	.750	0	0- -	—	3.82
1996 California	AL	13	2	0	3	28.1	150	42	34	28	7	3	1	2	21	4	26	2	0	0	0	.000	0	0-0	0	8.89
1997 Anaheim	AL	1	0	0	1	1	5	1	0	0	0	0	0	0	1	0	0	0	0	0	0	.000	0	0-0	0	0.00
2 ML YEARS		14	2	0	4	29.1	155	43	34	28	7	3	1	2	22	4	26	2	0	0	0	.000	0	0-0	0	8.59

Woody Williams

Pitches: Right **Bats:** Right **Pos:** SP-31 **Ht:** 6'0" **Wt:** 190 **Born:** 8/19/66 **Age:** 31

Year Team	Lg	G	GS	CG	GF	IP	BFP	H	R	ER	HR	SH	SF	HB	TBB	IBB	SO	WP	Bk	W	L	Pct.	ShO	Sv-Op	Hld	ERA
		HOW MUCH HE PITCHED						**WHAT HE GAVE UP**												**THE RESULTS**						
1993 Toronto	AL	30	0	0	9	37	172	40	18	18	2	2	1	1	22	3	24	2	1	3	1	.750	0	0-2	4	4.38
1994 Toronto	AL	38	0	0	14	59.1	253	44	24	24	5	1	2	2	33	1	56	4	0	1	3	.250	0	0-0	5	3.64
1995 Toronto	AL	23	3	0	10	53.2	232	44	23	22	6	2	0	2	28	1	41	0	0	1	2	.333	0	0-1	1	3.69
1996 Toronto	AL	12	10	1	0	59	255	64	33	31	8	2	1	1	21	1	43	2	0	4	5	.444	0	0-0	0	4.73
1997 Toronto	AL	31	31	0	0	194.2	833	201	98	94	31	6	8	5	66	3	124	7	0	9	14	.391	0	0-0	0	4.35
5 ML YEARS		134	44	1	33	403.2	1745	393	196	189	52	13	12	11	170	9	288	15	1	18	25	.419	0	0-3	10	4.21

Antone Williamson

Bats: Left **Throws:** Right **Pos:** 1B-14; PH-9; DH-4 **Ht:** 6'1" **Wt:** 195 **Born:** 7/18/73 **Age:** 24

Year Team	Lg	G	AB	H	2B	3B	HR	(Hm	Rd)	TB	R	RBI	TBB	IBB	SO	HBP	SH	SF	SB	CS	SB%	GDP	Avg	OBP	SLG
		BATTING																	**BASERUNNING**				**PERCENTAGES**		
1994 Helena	R+	6	26	11	2	1	0	—	—	15	5	4	2	0	4	0	0	0	0	0	.00	1	.423	.464	.577
Stockton	A+	23	85	19	4	0	3	—	—	32	6	13	7	0	19	0	1	3	0	1	.00	1	.224	.276	.376
El Paso	AA	14	48	12	3	0	1	—	—	18	8	9	7	0	8	0	0	1	0	0	.00	1	.250	.339	.375
1995 El Paso	AA	104	392	121	30	6	7	—	—	184	62	90	47	3	57	3	0	4	3	1	.75	10	.309	.383	.469
1996 New Orleans	AAA	55	199	52	10	1	5	—	—	79	23	23	19	1	40	1	0	2	1	0	1.00	6	.261	.326	.397
1997 Tucson	AAA	83	304	87	20	5	5	—	—	132	53	41	49	3	41	3	0	1	3	1	.75	12	.286	.389	.434
1997 Milwaukee	AL	24	54	11	3	0	0	(0	0)	14	2	6	4	0	8	0	1	1	0	1	.00	2	.204	.254	.259

Dan Wilson

Bats: Right **Throws:** Right **Pos:** C-144; PH-5 **Ht:** 6'3" **Wt:** 190 **Born:** 3/25/69 **Age:** 29

Year Team	Lg	G	AB	H	2B	3B	HR	(Hm	Rd)	TB	R	RBI	TBB	IBB	SO	HBP	SH	SF	SB	CS	SB%	GDP	Avg	OBP	SLG
		BATTING																	**BASERUNNING**				**PERCENTAGES**		
1992 Cincinnati	NL	12	25	9	1	0	0	(0	0)	10	2	3	3	0	8	0	0	0	0	0	.00	2	.360	.429	.400
1993 Cincinnati	NL	36	76	17	3	0	0	(0	0)	20	6	8	9	4	16	0	2	1	0	0	.00	2	.224	.302	.263
1994 Seattle	AL	91	282	61	14	2	3	(1	2)	88	24	27	10	0	57	1	8	2	1	2	.33	11	.216	.244	.312
1995 Seattle	AL	119	399	111	22	3	9	(5	4)	166	40	51	33	1	63	2	5	1	2	1	.67	12	.278	.336	.416
1996 Seattle	AL	138	491	140	24	0	18	(7	11)	218	51	83	32	2	88	3	9	5	1	2	.33	15	.285	.330	.444

Year Team	Lg	G	AB	H	2B	3B	HR	(Hm Rd)	TB	R	RBI	TBB	IBB	SO	HBP	SH	SF	SB	CS	SB%	GDP	Avg	OBP	SLG
																						BASERUNNING		PERCENTAGES
1997 Seattle	AL	146	508	137	31	1	15	(9 6)	215	66	74	39	1	72	5	8	3	7	2	.78	12	.270	.326	.423
6 ML YEARS		542	1781	475	95	6	45	(22 23)	717	189	246	126	8	304	11	32	12	11	7	.61	54	.267	.317	.403

Enrique Wilson

Bats: Both **Throws:** Right **Pos:** SS-4; 2B-1; PH-1   **Ht:** 5'11" **Wt:** 160 **Born:** 7/27/75 **Age:** 22

Year Team	Lg	G	AB	H	2B	3B	HR	(Hm Rd)	TB	R	RBI	TBB	IBB	SO	HBP	SH	SF	SB	CS	SB%	GDP	Avg	OBP	SLG
1992 Twins	R	13	44	15	1	0	0	— —	16	12	8	4	0	4	4	0	1	3	0	1.00	0	.341	.434	.364
1993 Elizabethtn	R+	58	197	57	8	4	13	— —	112	42	50	14	1	18	6	0	2	5	4	.56	1	.289	.352	.569
1994 Columbus	A	133	512	143	28	12	10	— —	225	82	72	44	5	34	6	0	4	21	13	.62	7	.279	.341	.439
1995 Kinston	A+	117	464	124	24	7	6	— —	180	55	52	25	2	38	2	4	10	18	19	.49	10	.267	.301	.388
1996 Canton-Akrn	AA	117	484	147	17	5	5	— —	189	70	50	31	2	46	4	0	7	23	16	.59	9	.304	.346	.390
Buffalo	AAA	3	8	4	1	0	0	— —	5	1	0	1	0	1	0	0	0	2	2	.00	1	.500	.556	.625
1997 Buffalo	AAA	118	451	138	20	3	11	— —	197	78	39	42	2	41	5	4	4	9	8	.53	7	.306	.369	.437
1997 Cleveland	AL	5	15	5	0	0	0	(0 0)	5	2	1	0	0	2	0	0	0	0	0	.00	0	.333	.333	.333

Scott Winchester

Pitches: Right **Bats:** Right **Pos:** RP-5   **Ht:** 6'2" **Wt:** 210 **Born:** 4/20/73 **Age:** 25

Year Team	Lg	G	GS	CG	GF	IP	BFP	H	R	ER	HR	SH	SF	HB	TBB	IBB	SO	WP	Bk	W	L	Pct.	ShO	Sv-Op	Hld	ERA
1995 Watertown	A-	23	0	0	22	28.2	116	24	10	9	0	1	2	2	6	2	27	2	0	3	1	.750	0	11--	—	2.83
1996 Columbus	A	52	0	0	47	61.1	254	50	27	22	8	5	2	5	16	2	60	4	0	7	3	.700	0	26--	—	3.23
1997 Kinston	A+	34	0	0	34	36.2	146	21	6	6	2	0	1	1	11	0	45	3	0	2	1	.667	0	29--	—	1.47
Akron	AA	6	0	0	6	7	32	8	3	3	1	0	0	1	2	1	8	1	0	0	0	.000	0	1--	—	3.86
Chattanooga	AA	9	0	0	7	10.2	45	9	4	2	0	2	2	0	3	1	3	1	0	2	1	.667	0	3--	—	1.69
Indianapolis	AAA	4	0	0	0	5.2	21	2	0	0	0	0	0	0	2	0	2	0	0	0	0	.000	0	0--	—	0.00
1997 Cincinnati	NL	5	0	0	4	6	30	9	5	4	1	2	0	1	2	0	3	0	0	0	0	.000	0	0-0	0	6.00

Darrin Winston

Pitches: Left **Bats:** Right **Pos:** RP-6; SP-1   **Ht:** 6'0" **Wt:** 195 **Born:** 7/6/66 **Age:** 31

Year Team	Lg	G	GS	CG	GF	IP	BFP	H	R	ER	HR	SH	SF	HB	TBB	IBB	SO	WP	Bk	W	L	Pct.	ShO	Sv-Op	Hld	ERA
1988 Jamestown	A-	14	7	0	5	44	194	47	28	24	3	3	2	0	19	0	29	2	4	2	4	.333	0	2--	—	4.91
1989 Rockford	A	47	0	0	30	65	256	52	16	11	0	3	3	0	11	0	70	7	1	7	1	.875	0	16--	—	1.52
1990 Jacksnville	AA	47	0	0	20	63	246	38	16	15	3	5	2	0	28	2	45	4	0	6	2	.750	0	7--	—	2.14
1991 Indianapols	AAA	27	0	0	4	31	143	26	10	5	3	6	2	1	21	5	23	2	0	1	0	1.000	0	0--	—	1.45
1993 Harrisburg	AA	24	0	0	9	44.2	206	53	30	23	4	4	4	2	19	2	36	3	0	1	0	1.000	0	1--	—	4.63
Wst Plm Bch	A+	8	2	1	3	24.2	88	18	6	4	0	0	0	0	3	0	21	0	0	2	0	1.000	0	0--	—	1.46
1994 Harrisburg	AA	25	0	0	11	35.1	144	32	12	6	3	3	0	2	9	3	27	0	0	4	2	.667	0	0--	—	1.53
Ottawa	AAA	23	0	0	9	28.1	116	27	15	12	6	1	0	0	10	1	17	0	0	2	0	1.000	0	0--	—	3.81
1995 Calgary	AAA	53	0	0	20	50.2	226	59	33	27	8	0	2	0	17	2	40	2	0	4	6	.400	0	2--	—	4.80
1997 Scranton-WB	AAA	39	9	1	9	89.1	371	74	38	34	9	2	3	5	36	4	66	6	1	7	4	.636	0	0--	—	3.43
1997 Philadelphia	NL	7	1	0	1	12	50	8	8	7	4	0	0	2	3	1	8	0	0	2	0	1.000	0	0-0	1	5.25

Jay Witasick

Pitches: Right **Bats:** Right **Pos:** RP-8   **Ht:** 6'4" **Wt:** 205 **Born:** 8/28/72 **Age:** 25

Year Team	Lg	G	GS	CG	GF	IP	BFP	H	R	ER	HR	SH	SF	HB	TBB	IBB	SO	WP	Bk	W	L	Pct.	ShO	Sv-Op	Hld	ERA
1993 Johnson Cty	R+	12	12	1	0	67.2	288	65	42	31	8	4	1	0	19	0	74	5	1	4	3	.571	0	0--	—	4.12
Savannah	A	1	1	0	0	6	27	7	3	3	0	0	0	0	2	0	8	0	0	1	0	1.000	0	0--	—	4.50
1994 Madison	A	18	18	2	0	112.1	443	74	36	29	5	5	3	2	42	0	141	5	0	10	4	.714	0	0--	—	2.32
1995 St. Pete	A+	18	18	1	0	105	425	80	39	32	4	1	4	0	36	1	109	5	1	7	7	.500	1	0--	—	2.74
Arkansas	AA	7	7	0	0	34	161	46	29	26	4	0	0	0	16	1	26	2	0	2	4	.333	0	0--	—	6.88
1996 Huntsville	AA	25	6	0	12	66.2	274	47	21	17	3	3	1	3	26	2	63	2	2	0	3	.000	0	4--	—	2.30
Edmonton	AAA	6	0	0	5	8.2	39	9	4	4	1	1	1	1	6	0	9	2	0	0	0	.000	0	2--	—	4.15
1997 Modesto	A+	9	2	0	1	17.1	75	16	9	8	1	0	0	1	5	0	29	1	0	1	0	1.000	0	1--	—	4.15
Edmonton	AAA	13	1	0	4	27.1	121	25	13	13	3	1	2	0	15	3	17	2	0	3	2	.600	0	0--	—	4.28
1996 Oakland	AL	12	0	0	6	13	55	12	9	9	5	0	1	0	5	0	12	2	1	1	1	.500	0	0-1	0	6.23
1997 Oakland	AL	8	0	0	1	11	53	14	7	7	2	1	0	1	6	0	8	0	0	0	0	.000	0	0-0	1	5.73
2 ML YEARS		20	0	0	7	24	108	26	16	16	7	1	1	1	11	0	20	2	0	1	1	.500	0	0-1	1	6.00

Bobby Witt

Pitches: Right **Bats:** Right **Pos:** SP-32; RP-2   **Ht:** 6'2" **Wt:** 205 **Born:** 5/11/64 **Age:** 34

Year Team	Lg	G	GS	CG	GF	IP	BFP	H	R	ER	HR	SH	SF	HB	TBB	IBB	SO	WP	Bk	W	L	Pct.	ShO	Sv-Op	Hld	ERA
1986 Texas	AL	31	31	0	0	157.2	741	130	104	96	18	3	9	3	143	2	174	22	3	11	9	.550	0	0-0	0	5.48
1987 Texas	AL	26	25	1	0	143	673	114	82	78	10	5	5	3	140	1	160	7	2	8	10	.444	0	0-0	0	4.91
1988 Texas	AL	22	22	13	0	174.1	736	134	83	76	13	7	6	1	101	2	148	16	8	8	10	.444	2	0-0	0	3.92
1989 Texas	AL	31	31	5	0	194.1	869	182	123	111	14	11	8	2	114	3	166	7	4	12	13	.480	1	0-0	0	5.14
1990 Texas	AL	33	32	7	1	222	954	197	98	83	12	5	6	4	110	3	221	11	2	17	10	.630	1	0-0	0	3.36
1991 Texas	AL	17	16	1	0	88.2	413	84	66	60	4	3	4	1	74	1	82	8	0	3	7	.300	1	0-0	0	6.09
1992 Tex-Oak	AL	31	31	0	0	193	848	183	99	92	16	7	10	2	114	2	125	9	1	10	14	.417	0	0-0	0	4.29

Year Team	Lg	G	GS	CG	GF	IP	BFP	H	R	ER	HR	SH	SF	HB	TBB	IBB	SO	WP	Bk	W	L	Pct.	ShO	Sv-Op	Hld	ERA
1993 Oakland	AL	35	33	5	0	220	950	226	112	103	16	9	8	3	91	5	131	8	1	14	13	.519	1	0-0	0	4.21
1994 Oakland	AL	24	24	5	0	135.2	618	151	88	76	22	2	7	5	70	4	111	6	1	8	10	.444	3	0-0	0	5.04
1995 Fla-Tex		29	29	2	0	172	748	185	87	79	12	7	5	3	68	2	141	7	0	5	11	.313	0	0-0	0	4.13
1996 Texas	AL	33	32	2	1	199.2	903	235	120	120	28	2	7	2	96	3	157	4	1	16	12	.571	0	0-0	0	5.41
1997 Texas	AL	34	32	3	1	209	919	245	118	112	33	3	7	2	74	4	121	7	0	12	12	.500	0	0-0	0	4.82
1992 Texas	AL	25	25	0	0	161.1	708	152	87	80	14	5	8	2	95	1	100	6	1	9	13	.409	0	0-0	0	4.46
Oakland	AL	6	6	0	0	31.2	140	31	12	12	2	2	2	0	19	1	25	3	0	1	1	.500	0	0-0	0	3.41
1995 Florida	NL	19	19	1	0	110.2	472	104	52	48	8	5	3	2	47	1	95	2	0	2	7	.222	0	0-0	0	3.90
Texas	AL	10	10	1	0	61.1	276	81	35	31	4	2	2	1	21	1	46	5	0	3	4	.429	0	0-0	0	4.55
12 ML YEARS		346	338	44	3	2109.1	9372	2066	1189	1086	198	64	82	31	1195	32	1737	112	23	124	131	.486	9	0-0	0	4.63

Mark Wohlers

Pitches: Right **Bats:** Right **Pos:** RP-71
Ht: 6'4" **Wt:** 207 **Born:** 1/23/70 **Age:** 28

Year Team	Lg	G	GS	CG	GF	IP	BFP	H	R	ER	HR	SH	SF	HB	TBB	IBB	SO	WP	Bk	W	L	Pct.	ShO	Sv-Op	Hld	ERA
1991 Atlanta	NL	17	0	0	4	19.2	89	17	7	7	1	2	1	2	13	3	13	0	0	3	1	.750	0	2-4	2	3.20
1992 Atlanta	NL	32	0	0	16	35.1	140	28	11	10	0	5	1	1	14	4	17	1	0	1	2	.333	0	4-6	2	2.55
1993 Atlanta	NL	46	0	0	13	48	199	37	25	24	2	5	1	1	22	3	45	0	0	6	2	.750	0	0-0	12	4.50
1994 Atlanta	NL	51	0	0	15	51	236	51	35	26	1	4	6	0	33	9	58	2	0	7	2	.778	0	1-2	7	4.59
1995 Atlanta	NL	65	0	0	49	64.2	269	51	16	15	2	2	0	1	24	3	90	4	0	7	3	.700	0	25-29	2	2.09
1996 Atlanta	NL	77	0	0	64	77.1	323	71	30	26	8	2	2	2	21	3	100	10	0	2	4	.333	0	39-44	0	3.03
1997 Atlanta	NL	71	0	0	55	69.1	300	57	29	27	4	4	4	0	38	0	92	6	0	5	7	.417	0	33-40	1	3.50
7 ML YEARS		359	0	0	216	365.1	1556	312	153	135	18	24	15	7	165	25	415	23	0	31	21	.596	0	104-125	26	3.33

Steve Wojciechowski

Pitches: Left **Bats:** Left **Pos:** SP-2
Ht: 6'2" **Wt:** 195 **Born:** 7/29/70 **Age:** 27

Year Team	Lg	G	GS	CG	GF	IP	BFP	H	R	ER	HR	SH	SF	HB	TBB	IBB	SO	WP	Bk	W	L	Pct.	ShO	Sv-Op	Hld	ERA
1997 Edmonton *	AAA	26	7	0	3	65.2	286	68	33	28	6	1	1	2	23	1	49	2	1	8	2	.800	0	1--	—	3.84
1995 Oakland	AL	14	7	0	3	48.2	219	51	28	28	7	1	2	1	28	1	13	0	0	2	3	.400	0	0-0	0	5.18
1996 Oakland	AL	16	15	0	0	79.2	356	97	57	50	10	1	2	2	28	0	30	3	1	5	5	.500	0	0-0	0	5.65
1997 Oakland	AL	2	2	0	0	10.1	46	17	9	9	2	1	0	1	1	0	5	0	0	0	2	.000	0	0-0	0	7.84
3 ML YEARS		32	24	0	3	138.2	621	165	94	87	19	3	4	3	57	1	48	3	1	7	10	.412	0	0-0	0	5.65

Bob Wolcott

Pitches: Right **Bats:** Right **Pos:** SP-18; RP-1
Ht: 6'0" **Wt:** 190 **Born:** 9/8/73 **Age:** 24

Year Team	Lg	G	GS	CG	GF	IP	BFP	H	R	ER	HR	SH	SF	HB	TBB	IBB	SO	WP	Bk	W	L	Pct.	ShO	Sv-Op	Hld	ERA
1997 Tacoma *	AAA	7	7	0	0	37	157	40	23	21	4	4	2	3	7	0	29	0	2	1	3	.250	0	0--	—	5.11
1995 Seattle	AL	7	6	0	0	36.2	164	43	18	18	6	0	3	2	14	0	19	0	0	3	2	.600	0	0-0	0	4.42
1996 Seattle	AL	30	18	1	0	149.1	672	179	100	95	26	5	3	7	54	5	78	3	1	7	10	.412	0	0-0	0	5.73
1997 Seattle	AL	19	18	0	0	100	451	129	71	67	22	4	2	5	29	2	58	0	0	5	6	.455	0	0-0	0	6.03
3 ML YEARS		56	52	1	0	286	1287	351	190	180	54	9	8	14	97	7	155	3	1	15	18	.455	0	0-0	0	5.66

Tony Womack

Bats: Left **Throws:** Right **Pos:** 2B-152; SS-4; PH-4
Ht: 5'9" **Wt:** 155 **Born:** 9/25/69 **Age:** 28

Year Team	Lg	G	AB	H	2B	3B	HR	(Hm	Rd)	TB	R	RBI	TBB	IBB	SO	HBP	SH	SF	SB	CS	SB%	GDP	Avg	OBP	SLG
1993 Pittsburgh	NL	15	24	2	0	0	0	(0	0)	2	5	0	3	0	3	0	1	0	2	0	1.00	0	.083	.185	.083
1994 Pittsburgh	NL	5	12	4	0	0	0	(0	0)	4	4	1	2	0	3	0	0	0	0	0	.00	0	.333	.429	.333
1996 Pittsburgh	NL	17	30	10	3	1	0	(0	0)	15	11	7	6	0	1	1	3	0	2	0	1.00	0	.333	.459	.500
1997 Pittsburgh	NL	155	641	178	26	9	6	(5	1)	240	85	50	43	2	109	3	2	0	60	7	.90	6	.278	.326	.374
4 ML YEARS		192	707	194	29	10	6	(5	1)	261	105	58	54	2	116	4	6	0	64	7	.90	6	.274	.329	.369

Steve Woodard

Pitches: Right **Bats:** Left **Pos:** SP-7
Ht: 6'4" **Wt:** 225 **Born:** 5/15/75 **Age:** 23

Year Team	Lg	G	GS	CG	GF	IP	BFP	H	R	ER	HR	SH	SF	HB	TBB	IBB	SO	WP	Bk	W	L	Pct.	ShO	Sv-Op	Hld	ERA
1994 Brewers	R	15	12	2	1	82.2	336	68	29	22	3	2	3	4	13	1	85	8	1	8	0	1.000	0	0--	—	2.40
1995 Beloit	A	21	21	1	0	115	490	113	68	58	12	6	2	3	31	0	94	6	5	7	4	.636	0	0--	—	4.54
1996 Stockton	A+	28	28	3	0	181.1	762	201	89	81	14	4	6	3	33	1	142	7	2	12	9	.571	0	0--	—	4.02
1997 El Paso	AA	19	19	6	0	136.1	561	136	56	48	8	8	0	2	25	2	97	9	0	14	3	.824	1	0--	—	3.17
Tucson	AAA	1	1	0	0	7	26	3	0	0	0	0	0	1	1	0	6	1	0	1	0	1.000	0	0--	—	0.00
1997 Milwaukee	AL	7	7	0	0	36.2	153	39	25	21	5	0	0	2	6	0	32	0	0	3	3	.500	0	0-0	0	5.15

Tim Worrell

Pitches: Right **Bats:** Right **Pos:** RP-50; SP-10
Ht: 6'4" **Wt:** 220 **Born:** 7/5/67 **Age:** 30

Year Team	Lg	G	GS	CG	GF	IP	BFP	H	R	ER	HR	SH	SF	HB	TBB	IBB	SO	WP	Bk	W	L	Pct.	ShO	Sv-Op	Hld	ERA
1993 San Diego	NL	21	16	0	1	100.2	443	104	63	55	11	8	5	0	43	5	52	3	0	2	7	.222	0	0-0	1	4.92

Year Team	Lg	G	GS	CG	GF	IP	BFP	H	R	ER	HR	SH	SF	HB	TBB	IBB	SO	WP	Bk	W	L	Pct.	ShO	Sv-Op	Hld	ERA
1994 San Diego	NL	3	3	0	0	14.2	59	9	7	6	0	0	1	0	5	0	14	0	0	0	1	.000	0	0-0	0	3.68
1995 San Diego	NL	9	0	0	4	13.1	63	16	7	7	2	1	0	1	6	0	13	1	0	1	0	1.000	0	0-0	0	4.73
1996 San Diego	NL	50	11	0	8	121	510	109	45	41	9	3	1	6	39	1	99	0	0	9	7	.563	0	1-2	10	3.05
1997 San Diego	NL	60	10	0	14	106.1	483	116	67	61	14	6	6	7	50	2	81	2	1	4	8	.333	0	3-7	16	5.16
5 ML YEARS		143	40	0	27	356	1558	354	189	170	36	18	13	14	143	8	259	6	1	16	23	.410	0	4-9	27	4.30

Todd Worrell

Pitches: Right Bats: Right Pos: RP-65 Ht: 6'5" Wt: 227 Born: 9/28/59 Age: 38

Year Team	Lg	G	GS	CG	GF	IP	BFP	H	R	ER	HR	SH	SF	HB	TBB	IBB	SO	WP	Bk	W	L	Pct.	ShO	Sv-Op	Hld	ERA
1985 St. Louis	NL	17	0	0	11	21.2	88	17	7	7	2	0	2	0	7	2	17	2	0	3	0	1.000	0	5--	--	2.91
1986 St. Louis	NL	74	0	0	60	103.2	430	86	29	24	9	7	6	1	41	16	73	1	0	9	10	.474	0	36--	--	2.08
1987 St. Louis	NL	75	0	0	54	94.2	395	86	29	28	8	4	2	0	34	17	92	1	0	8	6	.571	0	33-43	6	2.66
1988 St. Louis	NL	68	0	0	54	90	366	69	32	30	7	3	5	1	34	14	78	6	2	5	9	.357	0	32-41	1	3.00
1989 St. Louis	NL	47	0	0	39	51.2	219	42	21	17	4	3	1	0	26	13	41	3	3	3	5	.375	0	20-23	3	2.96
1992 St. Louis	NL	67	0	0	14	64	256	45	15	15	4	3	0	1	25	5	64	1	1	5	3	.625	0	3-7	25	2.11
1993 Los Angeles	NL	35	0	0	22	38.2	167	46	28	26	6	3	6	0	11	1	31	1	0	1	1	.500	0	5-8	4	6.05
1994 Los Angeles	NL	38	0	0	27	42	173	37	21	20	4	1	2	1	12	1	44	1	0	6	5	.545	0	11-19	1	4.29
1995 Los Angeles	NL	59	0	0	53	62.1	249	50	15	14	4	1	3	1	19	2	61	2	0	4	1	.800	0	32-36	1	2.02
1996 Los Angeles	NL	72	0	0	67	65.1	285	70	29	22	5	2	2	2	15	1	66	4	1	4	6	.400	0	44-53	0	3.03
1997 Los Angeles	NL	65	0	0	55	59.2	265	60	38	35	12	2	0	0	23	1	61	1	0	2	6	.250	0	35-44	0	5.28
11 ML YEARS		617	0	0	456	693.2	2893	608	264	238	65	29	28	7	247	67	628	23	7	50	52	.490	0	256--	--	3.09

Jamey Wright

Pitches: Right Bats: Right Pos: SP-26 Ht: 6'5" Wt: 203 Born: 12/24/74 Age: 23

Year Team	Lg	G	GS	CG	GF	IP	BFP	H	R	ER	HR	SH	SF	HB	TBB	IBB	SO	WP	Bk	W	L	Pct.	ShO	Sv-Op	Hld	ERA
1993 Rockies	R	8	8	0	0	36	158	35	19	16	1	0	0	5	9	0	26	7	0	1	3	.250	0	0--	--	4.00
1994 Asheville	A	28	27	2	0	143.1	655	188	107	95	6	5	4	16	59	1	103	9	5	7	14	.333	0	0--	--	5.97
1995 Salem	A+	26	26	2	0	171	732	160	74	47	7	3	6	13	72	3	95	16	2	10	8	.556	1	0--	--	2.47
New Haven	AA	1	1	0	0	3	20	6	6	3	0	0	0	1	3	0	0	1	0	1	0	1.000	0	0--	--	9.00
1996 New Haven	AA	7	7	1	0	44.2	167	27	7	4	0	3	0	2	12	0	54	1	1	5	1	.833	1	0--	--	0.81
Colo Sprngs	AAA	9	9	0	0	59.2	246	53	20	18	3	0	1	2	22	0	40	1	0	4	2	.667	0	0--	--	2.72
1997 Salem	A+	1	1	0	0	1	5	1	1	1	0	0	0	0	1	0	1	0	0	1	0	1.000	0	0--	--	9.00
Colo Sprngs	AAA	2	2	0	0	11	44	9	3	2	1	0	0	0	5	0	11	0	0	1	0	1.000	0	0--	--	1.64
1996 Colorado	NL	16	15	0	0	91.1	406	105	60	50	8	4	2	7	41	1	45	1	2	4	5	.500	0	0-0	1	4.93
1997 Colorado	NL	26	26	1	0	149.2	698	198	113	104	19	8	3	11	71	3	59	6	2	8	12	.400	0	0-0	0	6.25
2 ML YEARS		42	41	1	0	241	1104	303	173	154	27	12	5	18	112	4	104	7	4	12	16	.429	0	0-0	1	5.75

Jaret Wright

Pitches: Right Bats: Right Pos: SP-16 Ht: 6'2" Wt: 230 Born: 12/29/75 Age: 22

Year Team	Lg	G	GS	CG	GF	IP	BFP	H	R	ER	HR	SH	SF	HB	TBB	IBB	SO	WP	Bk	W	L	Pct.	ShO	Sv-Op	Hld	ERA
1994 Burlington	R+	4	4	0	0	13.1	62	13	10	8	1	0	1	2	9	0	16	0	0	0	1	.000	0	0--	--	5.40
1995 Columbus	A	24	24	0	0	129	554	93	55	43	9	3	6	13	79	0	113	11	3	5	6	.455	0	0--	--	3.00
1996 Kinston	A+	19	19	0	0	101	413	65	32	28	1	6	3	7	55	0	109	7	1	7	4	.636	0	0--	--	2.50
1997 Akron	AA	8	8	1	0	54	221	43	26	22	4	5	0	0	23	2	59	2	1	3	3	.500	0	0--	--	3.67
Buffalo	AAA	7	7	0	0	45	183	30	16	9	4	0	1	0	19	0	47	2	0	4	1	.800	1	0--	--	1.80
1997 Cleveland	AL	16	16	0	0	90.1	388	81	45	44	9	3	4	5	35	0	63	1	0	8	3	.727	0	0-0	0	4.38

Esteban Yan

Pitches: Right Bats: Right Pos: SP-2; RP-1 Ht: 6'4" Wt: 230 Born: 6/22/74 Age: 24

Year Team	Lg	G	GS	CG	GF	IP	BFP	H	R	ER	HR	SH	SF	HB	TBB	IBB	SO	WP	Bk	W	L	Pct.	ShO	Sv-Op	Hld	ERA
1993 Danville	R+	16	0	0	0	71.1	324	73	46	24	4	3	3	5	24	1	50	3	0	4	7	.364	0	0--	--	3.03
1994 Macon	A	28	28	4	0	170.2	696	155	85	62	15	4	3	13	34	1	121	4	6	11	12	.478	3	0--	--	3.27
1995 Wst Plm Bch	A+	24	21	1	1	137.2	580	139	63	47	3	7	5	10	33	0	89	8	3	6	8	.429	0	1--	--	3.07
1996 Bowie	AA	9	1	0	3	16	75	18	12	10	2	1	1	0	8	0	16	1	1	0	2	.000	0	1--	--	5.63
Rochester	AAA	22	10	0	3	71.2	306	75	37	34	6	3	4	2	18	0	61	4	1	5	4	.556	0	1--	--	4.27
1997 Rochester	AAA	34	12	0	8	119	490	107	54	41	13	1	6	5	37	0	131	5	0	11	5	.688	0	2--	--	3.10
1996 Baltimore	AL	4	0	0	2	9.1	42	13	7	6	3	0	0	3	3	1	7	0	0	0	0	.000	0	0-0	0	5.79
1997 Baltimore	AL	3	2	0	0	9.2	58	20	18	17	3	0	1	2	7	0	4	1	0	0	1	.000	0	0-0	0	15.83
2 ML YEARS		7	2	0	2	19	100	33	25	23	6	0	1	2	10	1	11	1	0	0	1	.000	0	0-0	0	10.89

Dmitri Young

Bats: B Throws: R Pos: 1B-74; PH-19; RF-10; LF-9; DH-1 Ht: 6'2" Wt: 240 Born: 10/11/73 Age: 24

Year Team	Lg	G	AB	H	2B	3B	HR	(Hm	Rd)	TB	R	RBI	TBB	IBB	SO	HBP	SH	SF	SB	CS	SB%	GDP	Avg	OBP	SLG
1991 Johnson Cty	R+	37	129	33	10	0	2	--	--	49	22	22	21	1	28	2	0	2	2	1	.67	1	.256	.364	.380
1992 Springfield	A	135	493	153	36	6	14	--	--	243	74	72	51	3	94	5	0	4	14	13	.52	9	.310	.378	.493
1993 St. Pete	A+	69	270	85	13	3	5	--	--	119	31	43	24	3	28	2	0	5	3	4	.43	7	.315	.369	.441
Arkansas	AA	45	166	41	11	2	3	--	--	65	13	21	9	1	29	2	0		4	4	.50	5	.247	.294	.392

	BATTING																		BASERUNNING				PERCENTAGES		
Year Team	Lg	G	AB	H	2B	3B	HR	(Hm	Rd)	TB	R	RBI	TBB	IBB	SO	HBP	SH	SF	SB	CS	SB%	GDP	Avg	OBP	SLG
1994 Arkansas	AA	125	453	123	33	2	8	—	—	184	53	54	36	14	60	5	1	3	0	3	.00	6	.272	.330	.406
1995 Arkansas	AA	97	367	107	18	6	10	—	—	167	54	62	30	3	46	3	0	3	2	4	.33	11	.292	.347	.455
Louisville	AAA	2	7	2	0	0	0	—	—	2	3	0	1	0	1	0	0	0	0	0	.00	0	.286	.375	.286
1996 Louisville	AAA	122	459	153	31	8	15	—	—	245	90	64	34	8	67	1	0	3	16	5	.76	5	.333	.378	.534
1997 Louisville	AAA	24	84	23	7	0	4	—	—	42	10	14	13	0	15	0	0	0	1	1	.50	1	.274	.371	.500
1996 St. Louis	NL	16	29	7	0	0	0	(0	0)	7	3	2	4	0	5	1	0	0	0	1	.00	1	.241	.353	.241
1997 St. Louis	NL	110	333	86	14	3	5	(2	3)	121	38	34	38	3	63	2	1	3	6	5	.55	8	.258	.335	.363
2 ML YEARS		126	362	93	14	3	5	(2	3)	128	41	36	42	3	68	3	1	3	6	6	.50	9	.257	.337	.354

Eric Young

Bats: Right **Throws:** Right **Pos:** 2B-154; PH-1 **Ht:** 5'9" **Wt:** 170 **Born:** 5/18/67 **Age:** 31

	BATTING																		BASERUNNING				PERCENTAGES		
Year Team	Lg	G	AB	H	2B	3B	HR	(Hm	Rd)	TB	R	RBI	TBB	IBB	SO	HBP	SH	SF	SB	CS	SB%	GDP	Avg	OBP	SLG
1992 Los Angeles	NL	49	132	34	1	0	1	(0	1)	38	9	11	8	0	9	0	4	0	6	1	.86	3	.258	.300	.288
1993 Colorado	NL	144	490	132	16	8	3	(3	0)	173	82	42	63	3	41	4	4	4	42	19	.69	9	.269	.355	.353
1994 Colorado	NL	90	228	62	13	1	7	(6	1)	98	37	30	38	1	17	2	5	2	18	7	.72	5	.272	.378	.430
1995 Colorado	NL	120	366	116	21	9	6	(5	1)	173	68	36	49	3	29	5	3	1	35	12	.74	4	.317	.404	.473
1996 Colorado	NL	141	568	184	23	4	8	(7	1)	239	113	74	47	1	31	21	2	5	53	19	.74	9	.324	.393	.421
1997 Col-LA	NL	155	622	174	33	8	8	(2	6)	247	106	61	71	1	54	9	10	6	45	14	.76	18	.280	.359	.397
1997 Colorado	NL	118	468	132	29	6	6	(2	4)	191	78	45	57	0	37	5	8	5	32	12	.73	16	.282	.363	.408
Los Angeles	NL	37	154	42	4	2	2	(0	2)	56	28	16	14	1	17	4	2	1	13	2	.87	2	.273	.347	.364
6 ML YEARS		699	2406	702	107	30	33	(23	10)	968	415	254	276	9	181	41	28	18	199	72	.73	46	.292	.372	.402

Ernie Young

Bats: R **Throws:** R **Pos:** CF-60; RF-12; PH-9; LF-1 **Ht:** 6'1" **Wt:** 190 **Born:** 7/8/69 **Age:** 28

	BATTING																		BASERUNNING				PERCENTAGES		
Year Team	Lg	G	AB	H	2B	3B	HR	(Hm	Rd)	TB	R	RBI	TBB	IBB	SO	HBP	SH	SF	SB	CS	SB%	GDP	Avg	OBP	SLG
1997 Edmonton *	AAA	54	195	63	10	0	9	—	—	100	39	45	37	1	46	6	1	2	5	2	.71	7	.323	.442	.513
1994 Oakland	AL	11	30	2	1	0	0	(0	0)	3	2	3	1	0	8	0	0	0	0	0	.00	1	.067	.097	.100
1995 Oakland	AL	26	50	10	3	0	2	(0	2)	19	9	5	8	0	12	0	0	0	0	0	.00	1	.200	.310	.380
1996 Oakland	AL	141	462	112	19	4	19	(10	9)	196	72	64	52	1	118	7	3	4	7	5	.58	13	.242	.318	.424
1997 Oakland	AL	71	175	39	7	0	5	(3	2)	61	22	15	19	0	57	2	2	2	1	3	.25	6	.223	.303	.349
4 ML YEARS		249	717	163	30	4	26	(15	11)	279	105	87	80	1	195	9	5	6	8	8	.50	21	.227	.310	.389

Kevin Young

Bats: R **Throws:** R **Pos:** 1B-77; 3B-12; LF-10; PH-8; RF-1 **Ht:** 6'2" **Wt:** 219 **Born:** 6/16/69 **Age:** 29

	BATTING																		BASERUNNING				PERCENTAGES		
Year Team	Lg	G	AB	H	2B	3B	HR	(Hm	Rd)	TB	R	RBI	TBB	IBB	SO	HBP	SH	SF	SB	CS	SB%	GDP	Avg	OBP	SLG
1992 Pittsburgh	NL	10	7	4	0	0	0	(0	0)	4	2	4	2	0	0	0	0	0	1	0	1.00	0	.571	.667	.571
1993 Pittsburgh	NL	141	449	106	24	3	6	(6	0)	154	38	47	36	3	82	9	5	9	2	2	.50	10	.236	.300	.343
1994 Pittsburgh	NL	59	120	25	7	2	1	(1	0)	39	15	11	8	2	34	1	2	1	0	2	.00	3	.205	.258	.320
1995 Pittsburgh	NL	56	181	42	9	0	6	(5	1)	69	13	22	8	0	53	1	4	1	1	3	.25	5	.232	.268	.381
1996 Kansas City	AL	55	132	32	6	0	8	(4	4)	62	20	23	11	0	32	0	0	1	3	3	.50	5	.242	.301	.470
1997 Pittsburgh	NL	97	333	100	18	3	18	(11	7)	178	59	74	16	1	89	4	1	8	11	2	.85	6	.300	.332	.535
6 ML YEARS		418	1224	309	64	8	39	(27	12)	506	147	181	81	6	290	16	9	21	18	12	.60	26	.252	.303	.413

Gregg Zaun

Bats: Both **Throws:** Right **Pos:** C-50; PH-16; 1B-1 **Ht:** 5'10" **Wt:** 170 **Born:** 4/14/71 **Age:** 27

	BATTING																		BASERUNNING				PERCENTAGES		
Year Team	Lg	G	AB	H	2B	3B	HR	(Hm	Rd)	TB	R	RBI	TBB	IBB	SO	HBP	SH	SF	SB	CS	SB%	GDP	Avg	OBP	SLG
1995 Baltimore	AL	40	104	27	5	0	3	(1	2)	41	18	14	16	0	14	0	2	0	1	1	.50	2	.260	.358	.394
1996 Bal-Fla		60	139	34	9	1	2	(1	1)	51	20	15	14	3	20	2	1	2	1	0	1.00	5	.245	.318	.367
1997 Florida	NL	58	143	43	10	2	2	(0	2)	63	21	20	26	4	18	2	1	0	1	0	1.00	1	.301	.415	.441
1996 Baltimore	AL	50	108	25	8	1	1	(1	0)	38	16	13	11	2	15	2	0	0	0	0	.00	3	.231	.309	.352
Florida	NL	10	31	9	1	0	1	(0	1)	13	4	2	3	1	5	0	1	2	1	0	1.00	2	.290	.353	.419
3 ML YEARS		158	386	104	24	3	7	(2	5)	155	59	49	56	7	52	4	4	2	3	1	.75	10	.269	.366	.402

Todd Zeile

Bats: Right **Throws:** Right **Pos:** 3B-160; PH-1 **Ht:** 6'1" **Wt:** 200 **Born:** 9/9/65 **Age:** 32

	BATTING																		BASERUNNING				PERCENTAGES		
Year Team	Lg	G	AB	H	2B	3B	HR	(Hm	Rd)	TB	R	RBI	TBB	IBB	SO	HBP	SH	SF	SB	CS	SB%	GDP	Avg	OBP	SLG
1989 St. Louis	NL	28	82	21	3	1	1	(0	1)	29	7	8	9	1	14	0	1	1	0	0	.00	4	.256	.326	.354
1990 St. Louis	NL	144	495	121	25	3	15	(8	7)	197	62	57	67	3	77	2	0	6	2	4	.33	11	.244	.333	.398
1991 St. Louis	NL	155	565	158	36	3	11	(7	4)	233	76	81	62	3	94	5	0	6	17	11	.61	15	.280	.353	.412
1992 St. Louis	NL	126	439	113	18	4	7	(4	3)	160	51	48	68	4	70	0	0	7	7	10	.41	11	.257	.352	.364
1993 St. Louis	NL	157	571	158	36	1	17	(8	9)	247	82	103	70	5	76	0	0	6	5	4	.56	15	.277	.352	.433
1994 St. Louis	NL	113	415	111	25	1	19	(9	10)	195	62	75	52	3	56	3	0	7	1	3	.25	15	.267	.348	.470
1995 StL-ChN	NL	113	426	105	22	0	14	(8	6)	169	50	52	34	1	76	4	4	5	1	0	1.00	13	.246	.305	.397
1996 Phi-Bal		163	617	162	32	0	25	(10	15)	269	78	99	82	4	104	1	0	4	1	1	.50	18	.263	.348	.436
1997 Los Angeles	NL	160	575	154	17	0	31	(17	14)	264	89	90	85	7	112	6	0	6	8	7	.53	18	.268	.365	.459
1995 St. Louis	NL	34	127	37	6	0	5	(2	3)	58	16	22	18	1	23	1	0	2	1	0	1.00	2	.291	.378	.457

Year Team	Lg	G	AB	H	2B	3B	HR	(Hm	Rd)	TB	R	RBI	TBB	IBB	SO	HBP	SH	SF	SB	CS	SB%	GDP	Avg	OBP	SLG
Chicago	NL	79	299	68	16	0	9	(6	3)	111	34	30	16	0	53	3	4	3	0	0	.00	11	.227	.271	.371
1996 Philadelphia	NL	134	500	134	24	0	20	(9	11)	218	61	80	67	4	88	1	0	4	1	1	.50	16	.268	.353	.436
Baltimore	AL	29	117	28	8	0	5	(1	4)	51	17	19	15	0	16	0	0	0	0	0	.00	2	.239	.326	.436
9 ML YEARS		1159	4185	1103	214	13	140	(71	69)	1763	557	613	529	31	679	21	5	48	42	40	.51	115	.264	.346	.421

1997 Team Statistics

We're always trying to make the Handbook more complete, so you'll be pleased to note we've added information to the Team Statistics section.

We've added three categories to our standings page:

Clinch—the date a team clinched its division

1st—the number of days during the season a team was in first place in its division

Lead—the largest lead a team held during the season

Also included this year in the breakdowns by division are team's records against the other league. American League teams have a split vs. NL teams and National League teams have a split vs. AL teams.

1997 American League Final Standings

Overall

EAST							CENTRAL							WEST					
Team	W-L	Pct	GB	Clinch	1st	Lead	Team	W-L	Pct	GB	Clinch	1st	Lead	Team	W-L	Pct	GB	Clinch	1st	Lead
Baltimore Orioles	98-64	.605	—	9/24	181	9.5	Cleveland Indians	86-75	.534	—	9/23	141	8	Seattle Mariners	90-72	.556	—	9/23	136	6.5
New York Yankees*	96-66	.593	2	—	—	—	Chicago White Sox	80-81	.497	6	—	1	0	Anaheim Angels	84-78	.519	6	—	14	1
Detroit Tigers	79-83	.488	19	—	—	—	Milwaukee Brewers	78-83	.484	8	—	28	2.5	Texas Rangers	77-85	.475	13	—	27	2
Boston Red Sox	78-84	.481	20	—	2	0	Minnesota Twins	68-94	.420	18.5	—	12	1.5	Oakland Athletics	65-97	.401	25	—	11	1.5
Toronto Blue Jays	76-86	.469	22	—	—	—	Kansas City Royals	67-94	.416	19	—	6	0.5							

* represents playoff wild-card berth

East Division

	AT		VERSUS						CONDITIONS					RUNS		MONTHLY						ALL-STAR	
Team	Home	Road	East	Cent	West	NL	LHS	RHS	Grass	Turf	Day	Night	XInn	1-R	5+R	Apr	May	June	July	Aug	Sep	Pre	Post
Baltimore	46-35	52-29	25-23	33-22	32-12	8-7	33-19	65-45	85-60	13-4	33-20	65-44	10-6	28-22	25-20	13-16	20-8	15-12	16-11	18-10	13-16	55-30	43-34
New York	47-33	49-33	29-19	38-17	24-20	5-10	24-26	72-40	85-57	11-9	37-23	59-43	9-9	23-16	39-13	14-13	15-12	17-8	15-11	18-11	17-11	48-37	48-29
Detroit	42-39	37-44	21-27	26-29	24-20	8-7	17-27	62-56	73-69	6-14	32-31	47-52	8-4	17-19	25-26	11-16	14-11	11-15	13-14	16-11	16-11	41-44	38-39
Boston	39-42	39-42	22-26	28-27	22-22	6-9	14-28	64-56	68-74	10-10	22-28	56-56	6-10	24-20	30-27	13-16	9-17	14-15	15-13	16-13	11-14	38-48	40-36
Toronto	42-39	34-47	23-25	29-26	20-24	4-11	24-28	52-58	27-39	49-47	24-35	52-51	5-9	29-30	16-19	11-12	15-13	11-15	13-15	15-15	11-16	40-43	36-43

Central Division

	AT		VERSUS						CONDITIONS					RUNS		MONTHLY						ALL-STAR	
Team	Home	Road	East	Cent	West	NL	LHS	RHS	Grass	Turf	Day	Night	XInn	1-R	5+R	Apr	May	June	July	Aug	Sep	Pre	Post
Cleveland	44-37	42-38	27-28	31-16	19-25	9-6	22-19	64-56	73-65	13-10	29-24	57-51	4-5	19-19	28-26	16-13	15-11	13-11	14-13	16-14	16-13	44-36	42-39
Chicago	45-36	35-45	25-30	26-21	21-23	8-7	19-23	61-58	70-68	10-13	27-23	53-58	9-4	22-18	16-28	8-17	15-11	17-11	13-14	15-15	12-13	43-42	37-39
Milwaukee	47-33	31-50	27-28	22-25	21-23	8-7	23-29	55-54	70-68	8-15	27-33	51-50	4-5	24-32	14-19	12-11	13-14	12-15	16-12	15-15	10-16	39-44	39-39
Minnesota	35-46	33-48	17-38	22-26	22-22	7-8	16-17	52-77	27-41	41-53	19-29	49-65	6-6	16-23	24-32	11-15	12-16	12-13	13-14	8-20	12-16	37-48	31-46
Kansas City	33-47	34-47	25-30	17-30	19-25	6-9	17-34	50-60	55-83	12-11	21-31	46-63	7-8	20-29	21-24	11-12	12-16	13-13	8-19	11-18	12-16	36-46	31-48

West Division

	AT		VERSUS						CONDITIONS					RUNS		MONTHLY						ALL-STAR	
Team	Home	Road	East	Cent	West	NL	LHS	RHS	Grass	Turf	Day	Night	XInn	1-R	5+R	Apr	May	June	July	Aug	Sep	Pre	Post
Seattle	45-36	45-36	30-25	32-23	21-15	7-9	24-18	66-54	38-32	52-40	30-21	60-51	4-7	25-21	31-19	16-11	11-16	20-7	13-13	15-15	15-10	49-38	41-34
Anaheim	46-36	38-42	25-30	30-25	25-11	4-12	18-23	66-55	78-67	6-11	23-23	61-55	5-8	27-25	19-16	12-12	16-12	13-15	19-9	14-15	10-15	44-42	40-36
Texas	39-42	38-43	21-34	31-24	15-21	10-6	23-26	54-59	68-77	9-8	21-16	56-69	5-3	18-29	23-23	14-10	15-13	10-17	11-16	14-17	13-12	43-42	34-43
Oakland	35-46	30-51	22-33	25-30	11-25	7-9	17-26	48-71	58-87	7-10	30-38	35-59	9-6	22-23	14-33	13-13	9-21	12-15	8-19	11-16	12-13	37-52	28-45

Team vs. Team Breakdown

	Ana	Bal	Bos	ChA	Cle	Det	KC	Mil	Min	NYA	Oak	Sea	Tex	Tor
Anaheim Angels	—	4	6	6	7	5	6	7	4	4	11	6	8	6
Baltimore Orioles	7	—	5	5	6	6	7	5	10	8	8	7	10	6
Boston Red Sox	5	7	—	3	6	5	3	8	8	4	7	7	3	6
Chicago White Sox	5	6	8	—	5	4	11	4	6	2	8	5	3	5
Cleveland Indians	4	5	5	7	—	6	8	8	8	5	7	3	5	6
Detroit Tigers	6	6	7	7	5	—	6	4	4	2	7	4	7	6
Kansas City Royals	5	4	8	1	3	5	—	6	7	3	3	5	6	5
Milwaukee Brewers	4	6	3	7	4	7	6	—	5	4	5	5	7	7
Minnesota Twins	7	1	3	6	4	7	5	7	—	3	7	5	3	3
New York Yankees	7	4	8	9	6	10	8	7	8	—	6	4	7	7
Oakland Athletics	1	3	4	3	4	4	4	6	4	5	—	5	5	6
Seattle Mariners	6	4	4	6	8	7	6	6	6	7	7	—	8	8
Texas Rangers	4	1	8	8	6	4	5	4	8	4	7	4	—	4
Toronto Blue Jays	5	6	6	6	5	6	6	4	8	5	5	3	7	—

(read wins across and losses down)

1997 National League Final Standings

Overall

EAST						CENTRAL						WEST					
Team	W-L	Pct	GB	Clinch	1st Lead	Team	W-L	Pct	GB	Clinch	1st Lead	Team	W-L	Pct	GB	Clinch	1st Lead
Atlanta Braves	101-61	.623	—	9/22	169 9	Houston Astros	84-78	.519	—	9/25	153 6.5	San Francisco Giants	90-72	.556	—	9/27	137 6
Florida Marlins*	92-70	.568	9	—	13 2	Pittsburgh Pirates	79-83	.488	5	—	36 1.5	Los Angeles Dodgers	88-74	.543	2	—	34 2.5
New York Mets	88-74	.543	13	—	— —	Cincinnati Reds	76-86	.469	8	—	4 0	Colorado Rockies	83-79	.512	7	—	26 2
Montreal Expos	78-84	.481	23	—	4 0	St. Louis Cardinals	73-89	.451	11	—	4 1	San Diego Padres	76-86	.469	14	—	7 1
Philadelphia Phillies	68-94	.420	33	—	1 0	Chicago Cubs	68-94	.420	16	—	— —						

* represents playoff wild-card berth

East Division

Team	AT Home	AT Road	VERSUS East	Cent	West	AL	LHS	RHS	CONDITIONS Grass	Turf	Day	Night	XInn	RUNS 1-R	5+R	MONTHLY Apr	May	June	July	Aug	Sep	ALL-STAR Pre	Post
Atlanta	50-31	51-30	29-19	38-17	26-18	8-7	27-14	74-47	78-53	23-8	27-21	74-40	10-10	33-20	32-10	19-6	17-11	16-12	17-11	16-11	16-10	57-30	44-31
Florida	52-29	40-41	25-23	34-21	21-23	12-3	18-15	74-55	79-57	17-13	24-28	68-42	9-5	32-22	23-16	15-10	16-11	17-11	13-13	19-10	12-15	48-38	40-36
New York	50-31	38-43	29-19	34-21	18-26	7-8	31-18	57-56	75-60	13-14	38-26	50-48	11-7	21-27	24-19	12-14	18-9	15-12	15-11	13-16	15-12	47-39	31-45
Montreal	45-36	33-48	18-30	26-29	22-22	12-3	24-18	54-66	23-33	55-51	26-26	52-58	4-12	28-25	16-24	12-12	16-12	17-11	10-16	12-17	11-16	43-43	35-41
Philadelphia	38-43	30-51	19-29	26-29	18-26	5-10	12-28	56-66	20-39	48-55	20-31	48-63	5-6	23-20	16-36	8-16	11-18	4-22	10-16	17-10	18-12	24-61	44-33

Central Division

Team	AT Home	AT Road	VERSUS East	Cent	West	AL	LHS	RHS	CONDITIONS Grass	Turf	Day	Night	XInn	RUNS 1-R	5+R	MONTHLY Apr	May	June	July	Aug	Sep	ALL-STAR Pre	Post
Houston	46-35	38-43	27-28	31-17	22-22	4-11	14-27	70-51	26-32	58-46	27-23	57-55	8-11	19-25	27-12	15-11	11-17	14-14	19-7	11-17	14-12	43-43	41-35
Pittsburgh	43-38	36-45	26-29	24-24	22-22	7-8	21-14	58-69	26-28	53-55	26-28	53-55	6-6	22-21	22-26	12-13	14-14	11-16	16-12	15-14	11-14	43-43	36-40
Cincinnati	40-41	36-45	23-32	24-24	20-24	9-6	14-18	62-68	21-34	55-52	21-39	55-47	8-8	18-17	12-28	10-16	13-14	15-13	12-15	12-17	10-16	41-45	35-41
St. Louis	41-40	32-49	21-34	20-28	24-20	8-7	21-17	52-72	62-70	11-19	26-30	47-59	6-11	20-33	21-19	10-16	15-13	14-15	11-17	12-17	10-16	37-50	31-44
Chicago	42-39	26-55	20-35	21-27	18-26	9-6	18-20	50-74	56-76	12-18	44-47	24-47	3-8	24-26	19-20	13-12	15-13	11-17	12-16	13-17	13-12	31-45	37-49

West Division

Team	AT Home	AT Road	VERSUS East	Cent	West	AL	LHS	RHS	CONDITIONS Grass	Turf	Day	Night	XInn	RUNS 1-R	5+R	MONTHLY Apr	May	June	July	Aug	Sep	ALL-STAR Pre	Post
San Francisco	48-33	42-39	31-24	27-28	22-14	10-6	21-20	69-52	74-60	16-12	41-33	49-39	11-3	23-17	18-23	17-7	14-14	16-13	12-15	16-13	15-10	51-36	39-36
Los Angeles	47-34	41-40	32-23	29-26	18-18	9-7	26-25	62-49	72-61	16-13	27-20	61-54	9-8	19-24	24-11	13-11	13-15	13-16	20-7	17-12	15-9	45-42	43-32
Colorado	47-34	36-45	30-25	31-24	13-23	9-7	20-19	63-60	72-60	11-19	42-35	41-44	4-5	19-17	23-25	0-0	12-17	14-15	8-19	17-12	15-9	43-45	40-34
San Diego	39-42	37-44	22-33	27-28	19-17	8-8	17-20	59-66	63-68	13-19	27-29	49-57	11-6	21-16	18-26	9-15	13-15	14-15	16-11	13-17	11-13	38-49	38-37

Team vs. Team Breakdown

	Atl	ChN	Cin	Col	Fla	Hou	LA	Mon	NYN	Phi	Pit	SD	SF	StL
Atlanta Braves	—	9	9	5	4	7	6	10	5	10	5	8	7	8
Chicago Cubs	2	—	7	2	2	3	5	4	6	6	7	6	5	4
Cincinnati Reds	2	5	—	5	5	5	6	6	2	8	8	5	4	6
Colorado Rockies	6	9	6	—	4	7	5	7	4	6	7	5	5	5
Florida Marlins	8	9	6	4	—	7	7	7	4	6	7	5	5	5
Houston Astros	4	9	7	6	4	—	7	8	7	4	6	6	3	9
Los Angeles Dodgers	5	6	5	7	4	4	—	7	6	10	9	5	6	5
Montreal Expos	2	7	5	4	5	3	4	—	5	6	5	8	6	6
New York Mets	7	5	9	5	8	4	5	7	—	7	7	5	3	9
Philadelphia Phillies	2	5	3	7	6	7	1	6	5	—	5	7	3	6
Pittsburgh Pirates	6	5	4	7	4	6	2	6	4	6	—	5	8	9
San Diego Padres	3	5	6	8	6	5	7	3	6	4	6	—	4	5
San Francisco Giants	4	6	7	8	6	8	6	5	8	8	3	8	—	3
St. Louis Cardinals	3	8	6	4	6	3	6	5	2	5	3	6	8	—

(read wins across and losses down)

American League Batting

Tm	G	AB	H	2B	3B	HR	(Hm	Rd)	TB	R	RBI	TBB	IBB	SO	HBP	SH	SF	ShO	SB	CS	SB%	GDP	LOB	Avg	OBP	SLG
Sea	162	5614	1574	312	21	264	(131	133)	2720	925	890	626	53	1110	49	46	49	4	89	40	.69	146	1149	.280	.355	.485
NYA	162	5710	1636	325	23	161	(75	86)	2490	891	846	676	51	954	37	34	70	9	99	58	.63	139	1276	.287	.362,	.436
Cle	161	5556	1589	301	22	220	(96	124)	2594	868	810	617	39	955	37	45	49	8	118	59	.67	152	1181	.286	.358	.467
Bos	162	5781	1684	373	32	185	(90	95)	2676	851	810	514	54	1044	59	21	55	8	68	48	.59	155	1221	.291	.352	.463
Ana	162	5628	1531	279	25	161	(87	74)	2343	829	775	617	37	953	45	40	57	5	126	72	.64	129	1203	.272	.346	.416
Bal	162	5584	1498	264	22	196	(107	89)	2394	812	780	586	44	952	65	46	59	6	63	26	.71	121	1198	.268	.341	.429
Tex	162	5651	1547	311	27	187	(95	92)	2473	807	773	500	39	1116	34	28	52	7	72	37	.66	118	1149	.274	.334	.438
Det	162	5481	1415	268	32	176	(98	78)	2275	784	743	578	37	1164	49	34	47	13	161	72	.69	120	1071	.258	.332	.415
ChA	161	5491	1498	260	28	158	(73	85)	2288	779	740	569	40	901	33	47	60	8	106	52	.67	133	1148	.273	.341	.417
Min	162	5634	1522	305	40	132	(59	73)	2303	772	730	495	32	1121	60	20	56	9	151	52	.74	117	1156	.270	.333	.409
Oak	162	5589	1451	274	23	197	(107	90)	2362	764	714	642	23	1181	49	49	40	9	71	36	.66	133	1221	.260	.339	.423
KC	161	5599	1478	256	35	158	(88	70)	2278	747	711	561	34	1061	42	51	42	5	130	66	.66	108	1176	.264	.333	.407
Mil	162	5444	1415	294	27	135	(56	79)	2168	681	643	494	31	967	58	48	52	7	103	55	.65	123	1118	.260	.325	.398
Tor	162	5473	1333	275	41	147	(68	79)	2131	654	627	487	26	1138	59	38	52	11	134	50	.73	102	1113	.244	.310	.389
AL	1132	78235	21171	4097	398	2477	(1230	1247)	33495	11164	10592	7962	540	14617	676	547	740	109	1491	723	.67	1796	16380	.271	.340	.428

American League Pitching

Tm	G	CG	Rel	IP	BFP	H	R	ER	HR	SH	SF	HB	TBB	IBB	SO	WP	Bk	W	L	Pct.	ShO	Sv-Op	Hld	OAvg	OOBP	OSLG	ERA
Bal	162	8	400	1461	6219	1404	681	635	164	34	51	30	563	31	1139	43	4	98	64	.605	10	59-69	68	.253	.323	.401	3.91
NYA	162	11	368	1467.2	6279	1463	688	626	144	42	34	45	532	41	1165	62	10	96	66	.593	10	51-76	62	.260	.327	.394	3.84
Tor	162	19	336	1442.2	6149	1453	694	628	167	49	37	39	497	29	1150	54	5	76	86	.469	16	34-55	63	.263	.326	.413	3.92
Mil	161	6	367	1427.1	6120	1419	742	669	177	43	36	61	542	25	1016	46	5	78	83	.484	8	44-59	57	.261	.333	.418	4.22
Det	162	13	417	1445.2	6246	1476	790	732	178	37	61	43	552	33	982	51	3	79	83	.488	8	42-64	65	.266	.334	.424	4.56
Ana	162	9	400	1454.2	6365	1506	794	730	202	46	56	54	605	34	1050	57	9	84	78	.519	5	39-66	55	.269	.343	.437	4.52
Cle	161	4	428	1425.2	6260	1528	815	749	181	45	52	51	575	53	1036	59	3	86	75	.534	3	39-54	71	.276	.347	.434	4.73
KC	161	11	393	1443	6277	1530	820	753	186	51	57	54	531	42	961	62	6	67	94	.416	5	29-50	39	.274	.340	.430	4.70
Tex	162	8	382	1429.2	6309	1598	823	745	169	30	58	38	541	40	925	55	6	77	85	.475	9	33-57	42	.283	.347	.439	4.69
ChA	161	6	389	1422.1	6262	1505	833	748	175	43	52	32	575	45	961	71	9	80	81	.497	7	52-70	62	.271	.340	.430	4.73
Sea	162	9	392	1447.2	6368	1500	833	769	192	43	40	66	598	36	1207	57	5	90	72	.556	8	38-65	56	.267	.342	.433	4.78
Bos	162	7	417	1451.2	6440	1569	857	782	149	32	57	70	611	52	987	51	1	78	84	.481	4	40-65	51	.277	.351	.424	4.85
Min	162	10	390	1434	6250	1596	846	796	187	34	47	33	495	31	908	66	6	68	94	.420	3	30-49	52	.283	.342	.454	5.00
Oak	162	2	480	1445.1	6600	1734	946	880	197	44	80	64	642	54	953	51	4	65	97	.401	1	38-61	49	.301	.372	.476	5.48
AL	1132	123	5559	20198.1	88144	21281	11177	10242	2468	573	718	680	7859	546	14440	785	76	1122	1142	.496	98	568-860	792	.272	.341	.429	4.56

American League Fielding

Team	G	PO	Ast	OFAst	E	(Throw	Field)	TC	DP	GDPOpp	GDP	GDP%	PB	OSB	OCS	OSB%	CPkof	PPkof	AVG
Detroit	162	4337	1719	37	92	(35	57)	6148	146	218	122	.560	11	130	48	.73	0	4	.985
Kansas City	161	4329	1630	26	91	(34	57)	6050	168	247	136	.551	14	72	42	.63	0	3	.985
Baltimore	162	4383	1666	23	97	(45	52)	6146	148	208	124	.596	7	149	50	.75	1	12	.984
Toronto	162	4328	1536	28	94	(44	50)	5958	150	185	116	.627	11	77	64	.55	5	8	.984
Minnesota	162	4302	1694	35	101	(35	66)	6097	171	228	142	.623	14	85	46	.65	0	3	.983
New York	162	4403	1705	21	104	(42	62)	6212	156	242	133	.550	19	111	47	.70	0	19	.983
Cleveland	161	4277	1728	30	106	(52	54)	6111	159	235	133	.566	8	126	55	.70	1	3	.983
Oakland	162	4336	1765	37	122	(54	68)	6223	170	252	143	.567	5	131	48	.73	1	4	.980
Texas	162	4289	1666	28	121	(46	75)	6076	155	227	125	.551	9	60	54	.53	9	0	.980
Milwaukee	161	4282	1655	41	121	(56	65)	6058	170	235	142	.604	11	106	52	.67	5	2	.980
Anaheim	162	4364	1592	40	123	(58	65)	6079	140	228	116	.509	19	101	64	.61	1	2	.980
Seattle	162	4343	1572	21	126	(68	58)	6041	143	208	112	.538	3	99	66	.60	0	2	.979
Chicago	161	4267	1439	18	127	(58	69)	5833	131	186	102	.548	16	119	52	.70	3	5	.978
Boston	162	4355	1696	32	135	(69	66)	6186	179	253	145	.573	36	171	53	.76	1	6	.978
American League	1132	60595	23063	417	1560	(696	864)	85218	2186	3152	1791	.568	180	1537	741	.67	27	74	.982

Note: A "GDP Opp" is any situation with less than two out that results in either a double play or a fielder's choice.

236

National League Batting

Tm	G	AB	H	2B	3B	HR	(Hm	Rd)	TB	R	RBI	TBB	IBB	SO	HBP	SH	SF	ShO	SB	CS	SB%	GDP	LOB	Avg	OBP	SLG
Col	162	5603	1611	269	40	239	(124	115)	2677	923	869	562	35	1060	63	73	35	8	137	65	.68	138	1124	.288	.357	.478
SD	162	5609	1519	275	16	152	(75	77)	2282	795	761	604	40	1129	45	63	58	9	140	60	.70	130	1207	.271	.342	.407
Atl	162	5528	1490	268	37	174	(76	98)	2354	791	755	597	45	1160	52	83	52	6	108	58	.65	143	1177	.270	.343	.426
SF	162	5485	1415	266	37	172	(83	89)	2271	784	746	642	72	1120	46	64	59	4	121	49	.71	111	1199	.258	.337	.414
Hou	162	5502	1427	314	40	133	(59	74)	2220	777	720	633	63	1085	100	74	53	4	171	74	.70	104	1221	.259	.344	.403
NYN	162	5524	1448	274	28	153	(74	79)	2237	777	741	550	45	1029	57	58	59	7	97	74	.57	122	1111	.262	.332	.405
LA	162	5544	1488	242	33	174	(85	89)	2318	742	706	498	46	1079	33	105	36	6	131	64	.67	109	1120	.268	.330	.418
Fla	162	5439	1410	272	28	136	(63	73)	2146	740	703	686	55	1074	61	71	42	9	115	58	.66	132	1248	.259	.346	.395
Pit	162	5503	1440	291	52	129	(68	61)	2222	725	686	481	27	1161	92	77	47	7	160	50	.76	105	1168	.262	.329	.404
Mon	162	5526	1423	339	34	172	(81	91)	2346	691	659	420	40	1084	73	72	40	10	75	46	.62	96	1091	.258	.316	.425
StL	162	5524	1409	269	39	144	(68	76)	2188	689	642	543	54	1191	42	58	44	8	164	60	.73	128	1140	.255	.321	.396
ChN	162	5489	1444	269	39	127	(79	48)	2172	687	642	451	41	1003	34	83	38	10	116	60	.66	119	1093	.263	.321	.396
Phi	162	5443	1390	290	35	116	(61	55)	2098	668	622	519	32	1032	40	74	50	8	115	66	.63	105	1152	.255	.322	.385
Cin	162	5484	1386	269	27	142	(73	69)	2135	651	612	518	35	1113	45	75	30	6	190	67	.74	104	1144	.253	.321	.389
NL	1134	77203	20300	3907	485	2163	(1069	1094)	31666	10440	9876	7704	629	15320	773	1030	643	102	1817	841	.68	1646	16195	.263	.333	.410

National League Pitching

Tm	G	CG	Rel	IP	BFP	H	R	ER	HR	SH	SF	HB	TBB	IBB	SO	WP	Bk	W	L	Pct.	ShO	Sv-Op	Hld	OAvg	OOBP	OSLG	ERA
Atl	162	21	374	1465.2	6057	1319	581	518	111	68	46	31	450	56	1196	38	4	101	61	.623	17	37-53	43	.242	.301	.354	3.18
LA	162	6	412	1459.1	6191	1325	645	587	163	74	32	45	546	36	1232	36	14	88	74	.543	6	45-65	75	.241	.313	.389	3.62
Hou	162	16	354	1459	6166	1379	660	594	134	76	42	52	511	25	1138	46	9	84	78	.519	12	37-59	32	.252	.319	.380	3.66
Fla	162	12	404	1446.2	6223	1353	689	615	131	69	45	63	639	41	1188	41	4	92	70	.568	10	39-59	60	.250	.334	.384	3.83
StL	162	5	399	1455.2	6222	1422	708	627	124	81	52	59	536	34	1130	48	8	73	89	.451	3	39-58	48	.259	.329	.380	3.88
NYN	162	7	376	1459.1	6210	1452	709	640	160	63	44	47	504	43	982	47	7	88	74	.543	14	37-55	30	.251	.325	.393	3.95
Mon	162	27	390	1447	6189	1453	740	665	149	72	45	63	557	45	1138	52	4	78	84	.481	14	37-55	30	.266	.339	.435	4.14
ChN	162	6	441	1429	6226	1451	759	705	185	80	57	43	590	51	1072	35	8	68	94	.420	4	37-55	63	.271	.343	.415	4.44
Pit	162	6	451	1436	6291	1503	760	683	143	78	47	64	560	71	1080	61	12	79	83	.488	8	41-59	65	.256	.330	.417	4.28
Cin	162	5	423	1449	6264	1408	764	710	173	75	43	77	558	62	1159	64	7	76	86	.469	8	49-63	74	.256	.330	.417	4.41
SF	162	5	481	1446	6284	1494	793	706	160	76	51	39	578	57	1044	48	10	90	72	.556	9	45-69	85	.270	.340	.412	4.39
Phi	162	13	409	1420.1	6228	1441	840	765	171	81	58	61	616	42	1209	73	12	68	94	.420	7	35-50	38	.280	.352	.437	4.85
SD	162	5	426	1450	6429	1581	891	803	172	71	46	61	596	37	1059	58	7	76	86	.469	2	43-63	43	.280	.352	.435	4.98
Col	162	9	426	1432.2	6417	1697	908	836	196	73	52	67	566	23	870	50	6	83	79	.512	5	38-60	71	.300	.367	.479	5.25
NL	1134	143	5766	20255.2	87397	20190	10427	9454	2172	1004	665	769	7807	623	15497	697	112	1144	1124	.504	113	571-846	770	.262	.333	.409	4.20

National League Fielding

Team	G	PO	Ast	OFAst	E	(Throw	Field)	TC	DP	GDPOpp	GDP	GDP%	PB	OSB	OCS	OSB%	CPkof	PPkof	AVG
Colorado	162	4298	1945	32	111	(46	65)	6354	202	293	176	.601	5	130	54	.71	0	12	.983
Cincinnati	162	4347	1576	27	106	(45	61)	6029	129	171	99	.579	13	139	48	.74	3	1	.982
Philadelphia	162	4261	1547	33	108	(49	59)	5916	134	190	102	.537	16	107	57	.65	2	10	.982
Atlanta	162	4397	1669	30	114	(41	73)	6180	136	189	114	.603	11	124	54	.70	2	1	.982
Chicago	162	4287	1605	39	112	(47	65)	6004	117	205	93	.454	16	146	59	.71	2	13	.981
New York	162	4378	1881	45	120	(48	72)	6379	165	246	134	.545	10	106	44	.71	0	7	.981
Florida	162	4340	1647	32	116	(41	75)	6103	167	236	126	.534	7	95	70	.58	2	3	.981
Los Angeles	162	4378	1561	24	116	(55	61)	6055	104	171	83	.485	11	118	58	.67	0	4	.981
St.Louis	162	4367	1739	28	123	(55	68)	6229	156	215	116	.540	18	134	66	.67	5	3	.980
San Francisco	162	4338	1799	19	125	(53	72)	6262	157	243	133	.547	9	108	73	.60	0	4	.980
Houston	162	4377	1874	31	131	(58	76)	6382	169	255	127	.498	6	92	57	.62	1	6	.979
Pittsburgh	162	4308	1831	34	131	(60	71)	6270	149	246	111	.451	11	109	66	.62	3	4	.979
San Diego	162	4350	1819	36	132	(69	63)	6301	132	214	102	.477	8	171	75	.70	2	1	.979
Montreal	162	4341	1697	30	132	(55	77)	6170	150	218	129	.592	13	192	42	.82	0	8	.979
National League	1134	60767	24190	440	1677	(722	955)	86634	2067	3092	1645	.532	154	1771	823	.68	22	77	.981

Note: A "GDP Opp" is any situation with less than two out that results in either a double play or a fielder's choice.

1997 Fielding Stats

Fielding statistics have evolved considerably over the past decade, and we at STATS always like to stay on the cutting edge. The original range factor was simply total successful chances (putouts + assists) per game played, but the range factor (Rng) you'll find here is a bit more precise: total successful chances *per nine innings*. You'll also find all the old standards, like assists, errors, double plays and games started by position. Another thing you won't find in other sources are our "special" catcher stats, including stolen-base data and one of our personal favorites, Catcher ERA (CERA).

The only important things you need to know before digging in are these: all the fielding stats are unofficial—an assist here or a putout there may change when the official stats arrive in December, but these are very close as they are. The regulars are sorted by range factor, except for the first basemen and the catchers in the first catcher section, which are sorted by fielding percentage. The catchers in the special catcher section are sorted by Catcher ERA. Remember to consider the pitching staff when looking at those CERAs, by the way. Even an All-Star caliber backstop would have had his hands full catching an Athletics staff that finished with a 5.48 ERA. And finally, ties in range or percentage are, in reality, not ties at all, just numbers that don't show enough digits to be unique.

First Basemen - Regulars

Player	Tm	G	GS	Inn	PO	A	E	DP	Pct.	Rng
Joyner,Wally	SD	131	122	1045.2	1027	88	4	85	.996	---
King,Jeff	KC	150	147	1291.0	1217	146	5	136	.996	---
Sorrento,Paul	Sea	139	119	1057.2	929	85	4	91	.996	---
Clark,Will	Tex	100	98	848.1	879	62	4	86	.996	---
Grace,Mark	ChN	148	147	1291.0	1202	120	6	94	.995	---
McGwire,Mark	TOT	152	150	1287.1	1326	94	7	130	.995	---
Snow,J.T.	SF	156	151	1333.1	1308	106	7	135	.995	---
Olerud,John	NYN	146	141	1236.1	1292	119	7	126	.995	---
Segui,David	Mon	125	125	1071.2	1036	87	6	104	.995	---
Martinez,Tino	NYA	150	147	1309.1	1304	104	8	127	.994	---
Brogna,Rico	Phi	145	137	1200.0	1054	117	7	102	.994	---
Clark,Tony	Det	158	157	1383.2	1424	99	10	131	.993	---
Palmeiro,Rafael	Bal	155	151	1356.0	1303	113	10	126	.993	---
Bagwell,Jeff	Hou	159	156	1391.0	1405	136	11	141	.993	---
Thome,Jim	Cle	145	140	1224.2	1234	95	10	124	.993	---
Karros,Eric	LA	162	162	1447.2	1318	120	11	89	.992	---
Conine,Jeff	Fla	145	102	991.2	896	106	8	100	.992	---
Galarraga,Andres	Col	154	150	1325.2	1459	117	15	179	.991	---
Morris,Hal	Cin	89	84	749.0	672	51	7	67	.990	---
McGriff,Fred	Atl	149	148	1263.2	1190	97	13	112	.990	---
Erstad,Darin	Ana	126	120	1083.0	999	65	11	94	.990	---
Stahoviak,Scott	Min	81	71	629.0	606	58	7	68	.990	---
Delgado,Carlos	Tor	119	116	1035.2	963	64	12	98	.988	---
Vaughn,Mo	Bos	131	131	1137.0	1089	73	14	116	.988	---
Thomas,Frank	ChA	97	97	822.2	739	48	11	70	.986	---
Average	---	136	130	1152.1	1114	94	8	109	.993	---

First Basemen - The Rest

Player	Tm	G	GS	Inn	PO	A	E	DP	Pct.	Rng
Amaral,Rich	Sea	14	1	29.0	27	5	0	3	1.000	---
Amaro,Ruben	Phi	1	0	3.0	4	0	0	1	1.000	---
Banks,Brian	Mil	5	2	22.0	9	4	1	0	.929	---
Benjamin,Mike	Bos	4	0	5.0	6	2	0	1	1.000	---
Berryhill,Damon	SF	1	0	4.0	5	0	0	1	1.000	---
Blanco,Henry	LA	1	0	5.2	5	0	0	0	1.000	---
Blowers,Mike	Sea	49	35	296.0	264	25	3	27	.990	---
Bogar,Tim	Hou	1	0	1.0	0	0	0	0	.000	---
Bonilla,Bobby	Fla	2	0	2.2	2	0	0	1	1.000	---
Brede,Brent	Min	15	13	113.2	121	9	1	9	.992	---
Brown,Brant	ChN	12	10	88.2	77	4	2	7	.976	---
Carter,Joe	Tor	42	42	372.0	326	22	1	24	.997	---
Casey,Sean	Cle	1	0	3.0	2	0	0	0	1.000	---
Cianfrocco,Archi	SD	39	22	204.1	217	19	4	17	.983	---
Colbrunn,Greg	Min	64	52	459.0	475	34	6	60	.988	---
Colbrunn,Greg	Atl	14	4	63.1	54	6	1	3	.984	---
Coomer,Ron	Min	9	3	39.0	40	5	0	5	1.000	---
Cooper,Scott	KC	8	2	36.0	27	1	0	4	1.000	---
Cruz,Ivan	NYA	3	0	8.0	7	0	0	0	1.000	---
Daulton,Darren	Phi	3	3	23.0	29	0	0	0	1.000	---
Daulton,Darren	Fla	39	37	248.0	230	17	4	22	.984	---
Diaz,Alex	Tex	1	0	1.0	2	0	0	0	1.000	---
Difelice,Mike	StL	1	0	1.0	1	0	0	0	1.000	---
Edmonds,Jim	Ana	11	10	84.2	85	7	0	5	1.000	---
Eisenreich,Jim	Fla	29	19	159.0	135	11	1	15	.993	---
Fabregas,Jorge	ChA	1	0	2.0	1	0	0	0	1.000	---
Fielder,Cecil	NYA	8	8	67.1	59	6	0	8	1.000	---

First Basemen - The Rest

Player	Tm	G	GS	Inn	PO	A	E	DP	Pct.	Rng
Floyd,Cliff	Fla	9	4	37.1	36	1	1	5	.974	---
Franco,Julio	Cle	1	0	2.0	1	0	0	0	1.000	---
Franco,Julio	Mil	13	13	121.1	109	11	1	20	.992	---
Franco,Matt	NYN	13	3	48.1	50	4	0	5	1.000	---
Frye,Jeff	Bos	1	0	1.0	2	0	0	1	1.000	---
Fullmer,Brad	Mon	8	6	58.2	49	7	1	6	.982	---
Gaetti,Gary	StL	20	4	68.0	61	6	0	8	1.000	---
Garcia,Freddy	Pit	2	1	9.0	14	0	0	2	1.000	---
Gates,Brent	Sea	1	0	1.0	0	0	0	0	.000	---
Giambi,Jason	Oak	51	48	433.1	399	40	5	49	.989	---
Gonzalez,Luis	Hou	1	1	4.0	3	0	0	1	1.000	---
Graffanino,Tony	Atl	1	0	1.0	1	0	0	0	1.000	---
Greene,Willie	Cin	7	6	53.0	47	2	0	2	1.000	---
Gregg,Tommy	Atl	1	0	3.0	3	0	0	0	1.000	---
Hamelin,Bob	Det	7	3	34.0	29	1	0	1	1.000	---
Hansen,Dave	ChN	4	3	29.0	19	2	1	4	.955	---
Harris,Lenny	Cin	11	7	62.0	51	5	1	1	.982	---
Helton,Todd	Col	8	7	57.0	68	10	0	7	1.000	---
Hernandez,Carlos	SD	4	0	7.2	5	3	0	0	1.000	---
Hernandez,Jose	ChN	1	1	8.0	6	0	1	0	.857	---
Hocking,Denny	Min	1	0	1.0	1	0	0	0	1.000	---
Hoiles,Chris	Bal	4	3	26.0	20	3	0	1	1.000	---
Hollins,Dave	Ana	14	14	122.0	107	8	0	10	1.000	---
Houston,Tyler	ChN	2	1	10.0	8	2	0	1	1.000	---
Howell,Jack	Ana	12	4	57.1	44	6	2	4	.962	---
Huskey,Butch	NYN	22	18	156.2	182	10	2	19	.990	---
Huson,Jeff	Mil	21	6	71.0	66	2	0	5	1.000	---
Jaha,John	Mil	27	26	223.0	219	14	2	26	.991	---
Javier,Stan	SF	3	3	21.0	21	0	1	2	.955	---
Jefferson,Reggie	Bos	12	8	80.0	74	5	2	9	.975	---
Johnson,Brian	SF	2	0	6.0	8	0	0	0	1.000	---
Johnson,Mark	Pit	63	58	497.0	541	44	5	48	.992	---
Jordan,Kevin	Phi	25	21	175.1	148	9	2	13	.987	---
Kent,Jeff	SF	13	8	81.2	80	4	0	6	1.000	---
Klesko,Ryan	Atl	22	6	78.0	63	3	0	7	1.000	---
Knorr,Randy	Hou	2	0	12.0	7	2	0	1	1.000	---
Konerko,Paul	LA	1	0	2.0	3	0	0	1	1.000	---
Kreuter,Chad	ChA	2	0	2.0	2	1	1	1	.750	---
Ledesma,Aaron	Bal	5	3	28.0	30	1	0	4	1.000	---
Lee,Derrek	SD	21	12	128.2	131	13	0	12	1.000	---
Lesher,Brian	Oak	3	2	20.0	21	2	0	3	1.000	---
Leyritz,Jim	Ana	15	12	97.2	79	5	2	17	.977	---
Leyritz,Jim	Tex	9	5	53.1	59	2	0	4	1.000	---
Liriano,Nelson	LA	2	0	4.0	5	1	0	0	1.000	---
Livingstone,Scott	SD	2	1	12.2	16	1	0	1	1.000	---
Loretta,Mark	Mil	19	16	147.0	151	7	2	10	.988	---
Mabry,John	StL	49	38	331.2	346	22	1	34	.997	---
Magadan,Dave	Oak	30	10	126.0	123	11	0	15	1.000	---
Manto,Jeff	Cle	6	3	33.0	35	1	0	4	1.000	---
Martinez,Dave	ChA	52	29	284.0	256	24	6	23	.979	---
Martinez,Edgar	Sea	7	7	59.0	68	3	1	5	.986	---
Matheny,Mike	Mil	2	0	3.0	0	0	0	0	.000	---
McGuire,Ryan	Mon	30	17	175.0	158	16	0	20	1.000	---
McGwire,Mark	Oak	102	101	843.2	885	60	6	89	.994	---
McGwire,Mark	StL	50	49	443.2	441	34	1	41	.998	---
McKeel,Walt	Bos	1	0	2.0	2	0	0	0	1.000	---
Merced,Orlando	Tor	1	0	3.0	3	0	0	0	1.000	---
Meulens,Hensley	Mon	3	1	9.2	9	0	0	1	1.000	---

First Basemen - The Rest

Player	Tm	G	GS	Inn	PO	A	E	DP	Pct.	Rng
Miller,Orlando	Det	3	0	8.0	6	0	0	0	1.000	---
Molitor,Paul	Min	12	12	97.1	99	7	1	6	.991	---
Mordecai,Mike	Atl	3	1	11.1	11	2	0	0	1.000	---
Morman,Russ	Fla	1	0	3.0	3	0	0	0	1.000	---
Nevin,Phil	Det	7	2	20.0	22	1	1	0	.958	---
Nilsson,Dave	Mil	74	72	589.2	609	36	6	72	.991	---
O'Neill,Paul	NYA	2	0	1.0	1	0	0	0	1.000	---
Oliver,Joe	Cin	4	2	13.0	14	2	0	0	1.000	---
Orsulak,Joe	Mon	15	11	112.2	111	10	1	4	.992	---
Ortiz,David	Min	11	10	87.0	84	10	1	10	.989	---
Osik,Keith	Pit	1	0	2.0	2	0	0	0	1.000	---
Pagnozzi,Tom	StL	2	1	6.1	6	0	0	1	1.000	---
Perez,Eddie	Atl	6	1	22.1	25	1	0	0	1.000	---
Perez,Eduardo	Cin	67	58	525.0	489	33	2	37	.996	---
Petagine,Roberto	NYN	6	0	18.0	9	3	0	0	1.000	---
Phillips,J.R.	Hou	3	1	11.0	6	0	0	1	1.000	---
Ripken,Billy	Tex	9	3	35.0	34	3	0	4	1.000	---
Robertson,Mike	Phi	5	1	19.0	20	0	0	1	1.000	---
Rodriguez,Henry	Mon	3	2	17.0	22	2	0	2	1.000	---
Rohrmeier,Dan	Sea	3	0	5.0	6	1	0	0	1.000	---
Rose Jr,Pete	Cin	1	0	5.0	6	0	0	0	1.000	---
Sagmoen,Marc	Tex	1	0	1.0	1	0	0	0	1.000	---
Samuel,Juan	Tor	7	4	32.0	21	1	0	4	1.000	---
Seitzer,Kevin	Cle	19	16	146.0	147	13	0	17	1.000	---
Servais,Scott	ChN	1	0	2.0	1	0	0	0	1.000	---
Sexson,Richie	Cle	2	2	17.0	11	1	0	0	1.000	---
Shipley,Craig	SD	4	2	20.2	28	0	2	0	.933	---
Simms,Mike	Tex	2	2	13.0	13	1	1	2	.933	---
Simon,Randall	Atl	6	2	23.0	16	2	0	2	1.000	---
Smith,Mark	Pit	9	6	56.2	58	5	0	1	1.000	---
Sojo,Luis	NYA	2	0	4.0	4	0	0	1	1.000	---
Spiers,Bill	Hou	8	4	40.0	32	1	0	5	1.000	---
Stairs,Matt	Oak	7	1	22.1	20	3	1	2	.958	---
Stanley,Mike	Bos	31	23	226.2	231	19	1	26	.996	---
Stanley,Mike	NYA	12	7	78.0	71	3	0	8	1.000	---
Steinbach,Terry	Min	2	1	8.0	3	0	1	0	.750	---
Stevens,Lee	Tex	62	54	478.0	455	33	3	45	.994	---
Strange,Doug	Mon	1	0	2.1	2	1	0	1	1.000	---
Surhoff,B.J.	Bal	3	3	26.0	21	3	0	4	1.000	---
Sutton,Larry	KC	12	11	110.0	92	7	0	11	1.000	---
Sveum,Dale	Pit	21	10	107.2	105	6	0	10	1.000	---
Sweeney,Mark	StL	4	2	14.1	8	1	0	2	1.000	---
Sweeney,Mark	SD	7	3	30.1	24	3	1	4	.964	---
Taubensee,Eddie	Cin	7	5	42.0	41	2	0	4	1.000	---
Turner,Chris	Ana	2	2	10.0	7	0	0	1	1.000	---
Unroe,Tim	Mil	23	3	61.1	56	6	2	5	.969	---
Valdez,Mario	ChA	47	35	311.2	256	12	0	19	1.000	---
VanderWal,John	Col	5	2	25.0	26	0	0	2	1.000	---
Vitiello,Joe	KC	1	1	6.0	8	0	0	1	1.000	---
Voigt,Jack	Mil	19	11	96.0	82	3	0	15	1.000	---
Walker,Larry	Col	3	3	25.0	22	2	0	3	1.000	---
Walton,Jerome	Bal	5	2	25.0	23	1	0	1	1.000	---
Williams,Eddie	Pit	26	23	187.2	201	8	2	18	.991	---
Williamson,Anton.	Mil	14	12	93.0	82	4	2	6	.977	---
Young,Dmitri	StL	74	68	590.2	603	45	10	50	.985	---
Young,Kevin	Pit	77	64	576.0	618	50	2	48	.997	---
Zaun,Gregg	Fla	1	0	5.0	2	1	0	2	1.000	---

Second Basemen - Regulars

Player	Tm	G	GS	Inn	PO	A	E	DP	Pct.	Rng
Valentin,John	Bos	79	79	707.1	181	259	11	68	.976	5.60
Young,Eric	TOT	154	151	1327.1	319	493	18	111	.978	5.51
Kent,Jeff	SF	148	143	1227.1	323	425	16	104	.979	5.49
Biggio,Craig	Hou	160	155	1384.1	340	503	18	107	.979	5.48
Frye,Jeff	Bos	80	79	703.0	197	228	4	62	.991	5.44
Fernandez,Tony	Cle	109	94	840.1	208	296	10	62	.981	5.40
Womack,Tony	Pit	152	148	1292.2	335	429	20	83	.974	5.32
Baerga,Carlos	NYN	131	122	1048.2	245	371	14	88	.978	5.29
Lemke,Mark	Atl	104	101	849.2	191	308	10	65	.980	5.29
Veras,Quilvio	SD	142	134	1192.1	277	407	11	68	.984	5.16
Vina,Fernando	Mil	78	75	657.1	149	227	7	53	.982	5.15
Alomar,Roberto	Bal	109	103	896.2	203	300	6	66	.988	5.05
Spiezio,Scott	Oak	146	140	1256.0	281	414	7	94	.990	4.98
Lansing,Mike	Mon	144	143	1234.0	280	395	9	97	.987	4.92
Duncan,Mariano	TOT	80	78	638.1	139	210	7	44	.980	4.92
Alicea,Luis	Ana	105	100	890.0	219	267	11	61	.978	4.91
DeShields,Delino	StL	147	137	1226.0	270	397	19	93	.972	4.90
McLemore,Mark	Tex	89	86	742.1	149	254	8	60	.981	4.89
Boone,Bret	Cin	136	127	1115.1	272	333	2	74	.997	4.84
Knoblauch,Chuck	Min	154	154	1316.2	283	425	11	101	.985	4.84
Easley,Damion	Det	137	130	1161.2	233	390	12	83	.981	4.83
Offerman,Jose	KC	101	100	870.0	202	254	9	64	.981	4.72
Cora,Joey	Sea	142	138	1192.2	304	310	17	83	.973	4.63
Garcia,Carlos	Tor	96	93	821.2	167	252	8	50	.981	4.59
Sandberg,Ryne	ChN	126	115	991.1	204	296	8	59	.984	4.54
Morandini,Mickey	Phi	146	143	1220.2	256	350	6	88	.990	4.47
Durham,Ray	ChA	153	153	1339.2	270	395	18	77	.974	4.47
Guerrero,Wilton	LA	91	84	739.2	141	221	4	24	.989	4.40
Average	---	122	118	1031.1	237	336	10	74	.982	5.00

Second Basemen - The Rest

Player	Tm	G	GS	Inn	PO	A	E	DP	Pct.	Rng
Abbott,Kurt	Fla	54	43	374.2	101	116	7	21	.969	5.21
Alexander,Manny	NYN	31	19	170.1	28	64	2	17	.979	4.86
Alexander,Manny	ChN	4	4	34.0	8	8	0	1	1.000	4.24
Alfonzo,Edgardo	NYN	3	1	15.1	4	6	0	0	1.000	5.87
Amaral,Rich	Sea	11	9	81.0	14	23	3	5	.925	4.11
Bates,Jason	Col	22	9	101.1	27	25	0	13	1.000	4.62
Batista,Tony	Oak	1	1	6.0	2	4	0	0	1.000	9.00
Bell,David	StL	23	13	129.0	34	37	2	7	.973	4.95
Bellhorn,Mark	Oak	17	16	135.1	41	56	4	16	.960	6.45
Belliard,Rafael	Atl	7	0	10.2	1	5	0	1	1.000	5.06
Benjamin,Mike	Bos	5	4	37.1	14	11	0	6	1.000	6.03
Berblinger,Jeff	StL	4	1	11.0	4	4	0	2	1.000	6.55
Boone,Aaron	Cin	1	0	2.0	0	0	0	0	.000	.00
Bournigal,Rafael	Oak	7	2	26.0	1	7	0	0	1.000	2.77
Branson,Jeff	Cin	14	6	70.2	17	23	3	7	.930	5.09
Branson,Jeff	Cle	19	15	147.0	21	51	1	10	.986	4.41
Brito,Tilson	Tor	25	22	198.2	28	64	1	14	.989	4.17
Brito,Tilson	Oak	2	2	15.0	3	8	0	5	1.000	6.60
Bush,Homer	NYA	8	1	30.2	8	13	2	2	.913	6.16
Cabrera,Orlando	Mon	4	3	28.0	10	9	0	2	1.000	6.11
Cairo,Miguel	ChN	9	5	54.1	15	15	0	5	1.000	4.97
Candaele,Casey	Cle	9	4	43.1	10	25	0	4	1.000	7.27
Castillo,Luis	Fla	70	64	575.1	129	176	9	44	.971	4.78
Castro,Juan	LA	14	9	81.0	15	28	1	4	.977	4.78

Second Basemen - The Rest

Player	Tm	G	GS	Inn	PO	A	E	DP	Pct.	Rng
Catalanotto,Frank	Det	6	4	34.0	7	9	0	0	1.000	4.24
Cedeno,Domingo	Tex	65	53	484.1	100	162	11	28	.960	4.87
Cianfrocco,Archi	SD	12	8	68.2	16	23	0	8	1.000	5.11
Cordero,Wil	Bos	1	0	4.0	0	3	0	0	1.000	6.75
Counsell,Craig	Fla	51	47	425.2	124	149	3	36	.989	5.77
Crespo,Felipe	Tor	1	1	9.0	1	3	0	1	1.000	4.00
Cromer,Tripp	LA	17	15	126.1	24	36	2	7	.968	4.27
Delgado,Wilson	SF	3	0	10.0	1	3	0	1	1.000	3.60
Diaz,Alex	Tex	1	0	5.0	4	1	0	0	1.000	9.00
Diaz,Eddy	Mil	14	12	107.0	27	35	0	10	1.000	5.21
Duncan,Mariano	NYA	41	39	306.0	65	99	4	20	.976	4.82
Duncan,Mariano	Tor	39	39	332.1	74	111	3	24	.984	5.01
Eenhoorn,Robert	Ana	3	1	11.0	1	1	1	0	.667	1.64
Espinoza,Alvaro	Sea	14	7	60.0	21	23	1	9	.978	6.60
Fonville,Chad	LA	3	3	31.0	0	5	1	0	.833	1.45
Fonville,Chad	ChA	2	0	4.0	0	1	0	0	1.000	2.25
Fox,Andy	NYA	5	4	37.0	8	13	0	4	1.000	5.11
Franco,Julio	Cle	35	34	288.2	69	108	3	23	.983	5.52
Frias,Hanley	Tex	1	0	3.0	0	2	0	0	1.000	6.00
Gallego,Mike	StL	11	6	43.0	9	16	1	3	.962	5.23
Gates,Brent	Sea	21	5	93.0	13	31	1	4	.978	4.26
Gilbert,Shawn	NYN	8	2	14.2	6	1	1	1	.875	4.30
Giovanola,Ed	Atl	1	0	4.0	0	2	0	0	1.000	4.50
Graffanino,Tony	Atl	75	46	475.2	88	178	5	30	.982	5.03
Grebeck,Craig	Ana	26	19	186.0	45	55	0	17	1.000	4.84
Guevara,Giomar	Sea	2	1	10.0	2	5	1	0	.875	6.30
Gutierrez,Ricky	Hou	9	3	33.0	9	3	0	2	1.000	3.27
Halter,Shane	KC	18	7	77.2	16	22	0	5	1.000	4.40
Hansen,Dave	ChN	1	0	2.0	0	0	0	0	.000	.00
Hansen,Jed	KC	31	26	245.2	57	77	1	16	.993	4.91
Hardtke,Jason	NYN	21	9	109.2	25	25	1	7	.980	4.10
Harris,Lenny	Cin	20	13	113.0	25	34	1	6	.983	4.70
Hayes,Charlie	NYA	5	0	7.0	2	1	0	1	1.000	3.86
Hernandez,Jose	ChN	20	10	115.1	31	31	2	3	.969	4.84
Hocking,Denny	Min	15	2	62.1	13	16	0	5	1.000	4.19
Houston,Tyler	ChN	1	0	1.0	1	1	0	0	1.000	18.00
Howard,David	KC	34	28	249.2	66	81	4	25	.974	5.30
Hudler,Rex	Phi	6	3	29.0	11	9	1	2	.952	6.21
Huson,Jeff	Mil	32	18	165.0	37	49	1	9	.989	4.69
Jackson,Damian	Cle	1	0	3.0	0	0	0	0	.000	.00
Jackson,Damian	Cin	3	2	17.0	7	7	1	1	.933	7.41
Johnson,Russ	Hou	3	2	19.0	9	2	0	1	1.000	5.21
Jordan,Kevin	Phi	6	3	34.0	4	11	2	1	.882	3.97
Kelly,Pat	NYA	48	31	302.0	62	92	3	27	.981	4.59
Ledesma,Aaron	Bal	22	15	148.0	32	40	2	8	.973	4.38
Lewis,Mark	SF	29	19	192.2	40	54	6	14	.940	4.39
Liriano,Nelson	LA	17	7	88.2	14	23	2	6	.949	3.76
Livingstone,Scott	SD	1	0	2.0	0	3	0	0	1.000	13.50
Lockhart,Keith	Atl	20	15	116.1	22	36	1	9	.983	4.49
Lopez,Luis	NYN	20	9	100.2	34	40	3	8	.961	6.62
Loretta,Mark	Mil	63	56	497.0	126	170	6	52	.980	5.36
Martin,Norberto	ChA	9	8	78.2	14	25	1	3	.975	4.46
Mejia,Roberto	StL	3	3	18.2	3	6	1	3	.900	4.34
Milliard,Ralph	Fla	8	8	71.0	14	32	0	8	1.000	5.83
Mordecai,Mike	Atl	4	0	9.1	3	2	0	0	1.000	4.82
Nunez,Abraham	Pit	9	2	27.1	5	12	0	1	1.000	5.60
Osik,Keith	Pit	4	0	5.0	1	1	0	0	1.000	3.60
Owens,Eric	Cin	2	2	16.0	0	0	0	0	.000	.00

Second Basemen - The Rest

Player	Tm	G	GS	Inn	PO	A	E	DP	Pct.	Rng
Perez,Neifi	Col	41	39	333.2	105	131	2	40	.992	6.37
Perez,Tomas	Tor	8	7	63.0	15	32	2	3	.959	6.71
Phillips,Tony	Ana	43	42	367.2	78	100	6	21	.967	4.36
Polcovich,Kevin	Pit	2	1	10.0	4	0	0	1	1.000	3.60
Raabe,Brian	Sea	1	1	3.0	0	0	0	0	.000	.00
Raabe,Brian	Col	1	0	6.0	0	3	0	0	1.000	4.50
Randa,Joe	Pit	13	9	84.0	25	41	0	6	1.000	7.07
Reboulet,Jeff	Bal	63	44	416.1	82	132	5	28	.977	4.63
Reed,Jody	Det	41	28	250.0	49	107	2	19	.987	5.62
Reese,Pokey	Cin	8	4	48.2	9	20	0	2	1.000	5.36
Riggs,Adam	LA	8	7	57.0	6	19	0	3	1.000	3.95
Ripken,Billy	Tex	25	23	195.0	41	77	2	18	.983	5.45
Rivera,Luis	Hou	1	0	6.0	3	1	0	0	1.000	6.00
Roberts,Bip	Cle	13	13	93.1	24	31	4	9	.932	5.30
Samuel,Juan	Tor	4	0	18.0	7	6	0	1	1.000	6.50
Sanchez,Rey	ChN	32	28	230.2	51	72	1	16	.992	4.80
Sanchez,Rey	NYA	37	36	306.0	63	101	4	21	.976	4.82
Santangelo,F.P.	Mon	7	1	22.0	5	6	0	2	1.000	4.50
Scarsone,Steve	StL	2	2	18.0	4	2	0	0	1.000	3.00
Sefcik,Kevin	Phi	22	14	136.2	29	45	3	6	.961	4.87
Sheaffer,Danny	StL	3	0	10.0	3	3	0	2	1.000	5.40
Sheets,Andy	Sea	2	1	8.0	2	2	0	0	1.000	4.50
Sheldon,Scott	Oak	1	1	7.0	1	2	0	1	1.000	3.86
Shipley,Craig	SD	16	12	104.0	24	36	1	8	.984	5.19
Shumpert,Terry	SD	7	7	58.0	21	15	1	5	.973	5.59
Sojo,Luis	NYA	72	51	479.0	121	147	5	36	.982	5.04
Spiers,Bill	Hou	4	2	16.2	3	13	0	3	1.000	8.64
Stankiewicz,Andy	Mon	25	11	119.1	20	47	3	9	.957	5.05
Strange,Doug	Mon	3	1	13.2	6	5	0	1	1.000	7.24
Stynes,Chris	Cin	8	8	66.1	10	19	0	2	1.000	3.93
Sveum,Dale	Pit	2	2	17.0	3	5	1	1	.889	4.24
Unroe,Tim	Mil	1	0	1.0	0	0	0	0	.000	.00
Velandia,Jorge	SD	5	2	25.0	7	6	1	1	.929	4.68
Vidro,Jose	Mon	5	3	30.0	5	10	1	1	.938	4.50
Vizcaino,Jose	SF	5	0	16.0	4	4	0	0	1.000	4.50
Walker,Todd	Min	8	6	55.0	11	16	1	5	.964	4.42
Wilson,Enrique	Cle	1	1	10.0	1	3	0	0	1.000	3.60
Young,Eric	Col	117	114	991.2	259	412	15	93	.978	6.09
Young,Eric	LA	37	37	335.2	60	81	3	18	.979	3.78

Third Basemen - Regulars

Player	Tm	G	GS	Inn	PO	A	E	DP	Pct.	Rng
Brosius,Scott	Oak	107	94	825.2	92	205	7	23	.977	3.24
Cirillo,Jeff	Mil	150	148	1294.1	126	318	17	29	.963	3.09
Caminiti,Ken	SD	133	133	1117.0	90	289	24	23	.940	3.05
Orie,Kevin	ChN	112	106	901.0	91	212	9	15	.971	3.03
Fryman,Travis	Det	153	153	1331.2	126	314	10	21	.978	2.97
Mueller,Bill	SF	122	98	916.0	85	217	14	18	.956	2.97
Randa,Joe	Pit	120	111	970.1	66	249	21	24	.938	2.92
Rolen,Scott	Phi	155	155	1337.0	144	290	24	30	.948	2.92
Castilla,Vinny	Col	157	155	1372.0	111	322	21	42	.954	2.84
Alfonzo,Edgardo	NYN	143	127	1117.0	82	268	12	29	.967	2.82
Williams,Matt	Cle	151	148	1284.2	88	299	12	21	.970	2.71
Boggs,Wade	NYA	76	70	611.0	42	141	4	16	.979	2.70
Hollins,Dave	Ana	135	131	1148.1	100	241	29	19	.922	2.67
Berry,Sean	Hou	85	79	629.1	47	138	16	11	.920	2.65

Third Basemen - Regulars

Player	Tm	G	GS	Inn	PO	A	E	DP	Pct.	Rng
Gaetti,Gary	StL	132	127	1075.1	72	244	7	27	.978	2.64
Ripken,Cal	Bal	162	162	1401.0	98	312	22	25	.949	2.63
Strange,Doug	Mon	105	88	803.1	62	171	13	13	.947	2.61
Hayes,Charlie	NYA	98	89	806.0	65	168	13	19	.947	2.60
Palmer,Dean	TOT	141	140	1227.0	99	246	19	18	.948	2.53
Coomer,Ron	Min	119	116	1008.2	66	216	10	20	.966	2.52
Davis,Russ	Sea	117	112	992.0	56	216	18	24	.938	2.47
Sprague,Ed	Tor	129	129	1120.1	106	201	18	19	.945	2.47
Greene,Willie	Cin	103	100	848.0	54	172	16	7	.934	2.40
Bonilla,Bobby	Fla	149	148	1268.2	104	225	22	29	.937	2.33
Snopek,Chris	ChA	82	78	692.0	56	117	16	11	.915	2.25
Naehring,Tim	Bos	68	68	602.1	40	110	3	10	.980	2.24
Zeile,Todd	LA	160	159	1431.1	105	247	26	27	.931	2.21
Jones,Chipper	Atl	152	151	1300.2	77	240	15	18	.955	2.19
Average	---	125	120	1051.0	83	228	15	21	.952	2.67

Third Basemen - The Rest

Player	Tm	G	GS	Inn	PO	A	E	DP	Pct.	Rng
Abbott,Kurt	Fla	4	2	20.2	2	1	1	0	.750	1.31
Alexander,Manny	NYN	1	1	8.0	0	1	0	1	1.000	1.13
Alicea,Luis	Ana	12	8	85.0	5	19	1	1	.960	2.54
Amaral,Rich	Sea	1	0	1.0	0	0	0	0	.000	.00
Andrews,Shane	Mon	18	18	153.2	11	40	6	6	.895	2.99
Arias,Alex	Fla	37	9	130.1	13	19	1	3	.970	2.21
Arias,George	Ana	1	1	8.0	0	3	0	0	1.000	3.38
Arias,George	SD	8	3	48.0	4	13	1	0	.944	3.19
Banks,Brian	Mil	1	1	8.0	2	3	0	0	1.000	5.63
Bates,Jason	Col	6	4	35.1	2	6	0	0	1.000	2.04
Batista,Tony	Oak	4	0	11.0	3	1	0	0	1.000	3.27
Bell,David	StL	35	12	151.2	10	32	4	1	.913	2.49
Bell,Jay	KC	4	3	27.0	2	7	0	3	1.000	3.00
Bellhorn,Mark	Oak	40	37	314.1	31	67	5	8	.951	2.81
Benjamin,Mike	Bos	19	14	136.0	13	39	4	3	.929	3.44
Blanco,Henry	LA	1	0	1.0	0	0	0	0	.000	.00
Blowers,Mike	Sea	10	6	54.0	3	10	1	1	.929	2.17
Bogar,Tim	Hou	14	7	71.0	7	14	1	2	.955	2.66
Boone,Aaron	Cin	13	11	97.1	11	22	3	0	.917	3.05
Booty,Josh	Fla	4	1	13.1	1	5	1	1	.857	4.05
Bragg,Darren	Bos	1	0	1.0	0	0	0	0	.000	.00
Branson,Jeff	Cin	27	8	102.2	12	22	1	4	.971	2.98
Branson,Jeff	Cle	6	4	32.0	2	7	0	2	1.000	2.53
Brito,Tilson	Tor	17	8	91.0	12	14	0	3	1.000	2.57
Brito,Tilson	Oak	10	6	59.0	8	15	2	2	.920	3.51
Candaele,Casey	Cle	1	0	3.0	0	0	0	0	.000	.00
Castro,Juan	LA	3	1	8.0	2	3	0	0	1.000	5.63
Cedeno,Domingo	Tex	3	3	27.0	2	6	0	2	1.000	2.67
Cianfrocco,Archi	SD	38	23	241.0	24	66	2	4	.978	3.36
Coles,Darnell	Col	3	1	12.0	0	3	0	0	1.000	2.25
Cooper,Scott	KC	39	28	260.2	21	54	0	4	1.000	2.59
Crespo,Felipe	Tor	7	7	55.0	8	6	1	0	.933	2.29
Cromer,Tripp	LA	1	1	6.0	0	0	0	0	.000	.00
Diaz,Eddy	Mil	1	0	1.0	0	0	0	0	.000	.00
Eenhoorn,Robert	Ana	5	1	23.0	2	3	1	0	.833	1.96
Espinoza,Alvaro	Sea	1	0	2.0	0	0	0	0	.000	.00
Evans,Tom	Tor	12	11	98.0	9	24	3	1	.917	3.03
Fox,Andy	NYA	11	3	43.1	5	13	0	1	1.000	3.74

Third Basemen - The Rest

Player	Tm	G	GS	Inn	PO	A	E	DP	Pct.	Rng
Franco,Matt	NYN	39	20	191.2	11	48	4	6	.937	2.77
Frye,Jeff	Bos	18	13	124.1	11	31	6	1	.875	3.04
Gallego,Mike	StL	7	3	32.1	1	7	0	0	1.000	2.23
Garcia,Carlos	Tor	4	0	7.0	0	0	0	0	.000	.00
Garcia,Freddy	Pit	10	7	69.0	7	9	3	1	.842	2.09
Gates,Brent	Sea	32	25	224.1	12	49	4	4	.938	2.45
Gilbert,Shawn	NYN	3	1	14.0	1	3	0	0	1.000	2.57
Giovanola,Ed	Atl	8	0	14.1	0	3	0	0	1.000	1.88
Gonzales,Rene	Col	1	0	1.0	0	0	0	0	.000	.00
Graffanino,Tony	Atl	2	0	3.1	1	0	0	0	1.000	2.70
Grebeck,Craig	Ana	15	1	28.1	1	2	0	0	1.000	0.95
Gulan,Mike	StL	3	1	12.0	1	1	0	1	1.000	1.50
Gutierrez,Ricky	Hou	22	17	155.0	10	36	0	3	1.000	2.67
Hale,Chip	LA	2	0	5.0	1	0	0	0	1.000	1.80
Halter,Shane	KC	12	3	41.1	1	4	0	0	1.000	1.09
Hansen,Dave	ChN	51	35	268.1	25	45	6	5	.921	2.35
Hardtke,Jason	NYN	1	0	1.0	0	0	0	0	.000	.00
Harris,Lenny	Cin	13	6	57.2	2	17	0	1	1.000	2.97
Hernandez,Jose	ChN	47	12	183.0	19	28	4	3	.922	2.31
Hocking,Denny	Min	39	8	120.1	14	32	0	2	1.000	3.44
Hoiles,Chris	Bal	1	0	1.0	0	0	0	0	.000	.00
Houston,Tyler	ChN	12	9	75.0	8	19	1	3	.964	3.24
Howard,David	KC	7	4	31.0	3	10	2	1	.867	3.77
Howell,Jack	Ana	24	19	152.0	14	26	1	4	.976	2.37
Hubbard,Mike	ChN	1	0	0.1	0	0	0	0	.000	.00
Huskey,Butch	NYN	15	12	108.0	17	22	7	3	.848	3.25
Huson,Jeff	Mil	2	0	4.0	0	0	0	0	.000	.00
Johnson,Russ	Hou	14	11	106.2	4	22	1	2	.963	2.19
Jordan,Kevin	Phi	12	5	62.0	5	11	2	0	.889	2.32
Konerko,Paul	LA	1	1	7.2	0	0	0	0	.000	.00
Ledesma,Aaron	Bal	10	0	32.0	5	7	1	1	.923	3.38
Lewis,Mark	SF	69	64	530.0	33	103	8	10	.944	2.31
Liriano,Nelson	LA	1	0	0.1	0	0	0	0	.000	.00
Livingstone,Scott	SD	3	1	15.0	1	5	2	0	.750	3.60
Livingstone,Scott	StL	2	1	10.0	0	1	0	0	1.000	0.90
Lockhart,Keith	Atl	11	6	57.2	2	11	2	1	.867	2.03
Lopez,Luis	NYN	4	1	17.2	4	13	1	1	.944	8.66
Loretta,Mark	Mil	15	10	92.0	9	16	1	3	.962	2.45
Mabry,John	StL	1	0	1.0	0	0	0	0	.000	.00
Magadan,Dave	Oak	49	25	233.1	25	54	5	7	.940	3.05
Manto,Jeff	Cle	7	1	27.0	0	4	0	0	1.000	1.33
Martin,Norberto	ChA	17	14	126.0	9	27	1	2	.973	2.57
Martinez,Edgar	Sea	1	0	0.1	0	0	0	0	.000	.00
Miller,Orlando	Det	4	3	28.0	1	7	1	0	.889	2.57
Mordecai,Mike	Atl	19	5	89.2	9	11	0	2	1.000	2.01
Morgan,Kevin	NYN	1	0	2.0	0	1	0	0	1.000	4.50
Nevin,Phil	Det	17	6	86.0	6	13	0	1	1.000	1.99
Norton,Greg	ChA	11	6	67.0	4	15	3	0	.864	2.55
Osik,Keith	Pit	1	0	2.0	0	0	0	0	.000	.00
Pagnozzi,Tom	StL	1	0	1.0	0	0	0	0	.000	.00
Palmer,Dean	Tex	93	92	799.1	72	164	10	10	.959	2.66
Palmer,Dean	KC	48	48	427.2	27	82	9	8	.924	2.29
Paquette,Craig	KC	72	66	585.2	45	128	12	15	.935	2.66
Pena,Tony	ChA	1	0	2.0	0	0	0	0	.000	.00
Pendleton,Terry	Cin	32	25	219.2	14	34	3	1	.941	1.97
Perez,Eduardo	Cin	8	7	57.2	6	14	0	1	1.000	3.12
Perez,Neifi	Col	2	2	12.1	2	4	1	0	.857	4.38
Phillips,Tony	ChA	9	9	73.2	7	12	1	1	.950	2.32

Third Basemen - The Rest

Player	Tm	G	GS	Inn	PO	A	E	DP	Pct.	Rng
Phillips,Tony	Ana	1	1	10.0	0	1	0	0	1.000	0.90
Polcovich,Kevin	Pit	1	0	1.0	0	0	0	0	.000	.00
Pozo,Arquimedez	Bos	4	4	35.1	4	14	1	1	.947	4.58
Raabe,Brian	Sea	2	0	6.0	1	1	0	0	1.000	3.00
Reboulet,Jeff	Bal	12	0	22.0	1	6	1	0	.875	2.86
Reese,Pokey	Cin	8	1	28.1	2	3	0	0	1.000	1.59
Ripken,Billy	Tex	13	7	72.0	4	13	0	2	1.000	2.13
Roberts,Bip	KC	10	9	69.2	3	12	0	1	1.000	1.94
Rose Jr,Pete	Cin	2	1	12.2	0	3	2	0	.600	2.13
Samuel,Juan	Tor	9	7	71.1	3	7	0	2	1.000	1.26
Sanchez,Rey	ChN	1	0	1.0	0	0	0	0	.000	.00
Santangelo,F.P.	Mon	32	25	231.0	17	45	3	0	.954	2.42
Scarsone,Steve	StL	1	1	6.0	0	0	0	0	.000	.00
Sefcik,Kevin	Phi	4	2	21.1	2	3	0	1	1.000	2.11
Seitzer,Kevin	Cle	13	8	79.0	3	20	3	0	.885	2.62
Sheaffer,Danny	StL	30	17	166.1	8	35	2	2	.956	2.33
Sheets,Andy	Sea	21	19	168.0	8	34	6	4	.875	2.25
Sheldon,Scott	Oak	1	0	1.0	0	0	0	0	.000	.00
Shipley,Craig	SD	2	0	3.0	0	0	0	0	.000	.00
Shumpert,Terry	SD	2	1	13.0	1	2	1	0	.750	2.08
Silvestri,Dave	Tex	1	0	2.0	0	0	0	0	.000	.00
Sojo,Luis	NYA	3	0	7.1	1	2	0	0	1.000	3.68
Spiers,Bill	Hou	84	48	497.0	44	129	12	11	.935	3.13
Spiezio,Scott	Oak	1	0	1.0	0	0	0	0	.000	.00
Stankiewicz,Andy	Mon	3	0	3.2	1	2	0	1	1.000	7.36
Stynes,Chris	Cin	3	3	25.0	1	9	0	1	1.000	3.60
Surhoff,B.J.	Bal	3	0	5.0	0	2	0	1	1.000	3.60
Sveum,Dale	Pit	47	39	332.2	17	78	6	4	.941	2.57
Tatis,Fernando	Tex	60	60	529.1	45	90	7	5	.951	2.30
Unroe,Tim	Mil	2	0	4.0	1	3	0	1	1.000	9.00
Valdez,Mario	ChA	1	0	1.0	0	0	0	0	.000	.00
Valentin,John	Bos	64	63	552.2	59	122	11	15	.943	2.95
Velandia,Jorge	SD	3	1	13.0	0	5	1	0	.833	3.46
Ventura,Robin	ChA	54	54	460.2	53	99	7	11	.956	2.97
Vidro,Jose	Mon	36	31	255.1	20	49	3	6	.958	2.43
Voigt,Jack	Mil	6	2	24.0	1	2	0	0	1.000	1.13
Walker,Todd	Min	40	38	305.0	24	70	3	4	.969	2.77
Wehner,John	Fla	7	2	13.2	1	3	0	0	1.000	2.63
Young,Kevin	Pit	12	5	61.0	7	16	3	2	.885	3.39

Shortstops - Regulars

Player	Tm	G	GS	Inn	PO	A	E	DP	Pct.	Rng
Gonzalez,Alex	Tor	125	125	1102.1	209	342	8	77	.986	4.50
Grudzielanek,Ma.	Mon	156	156	1368.1	237	446	32	99	.955	4.49
Renteria,Edgar	Fla	153	149	1328.2	243	415	17	95	.975	4.46
Jeter,Derek	NYA	159	159	1417.0	245	455	18	88	.975	4.45
Rodriguez,Alex	Sea	140	140	1233.2	210	394	24	85	.962	4.41
Bordick,Mike	Bal	153	151	1335.1	224	426	13	95	.980	4.38
DiSarcina,Gary	Ana	153	150	1330.1	226	421	15	87	.977	4.38
Dunston,Shawon	TOT	126	123	979.2	191	281	15	54	.969	4.34
Blauser,Jeff	Atl	149	147	1235.0	204	375	16	80	.973	4.22
Guillen,Ozzie	ChA	139	134	1191.1	207	348	15	77	.974	4.19
Stocker,Kevin	Phi	147	146	1262.1	191	375	11	75	.981	4.04
Gagne,Greg	LA	143	138	1223.0	174	358	16	55	.971	3.91
Average	---	138	133	1171.1	206	387	15	83	.974	4.56

Shortstops - The Rest

Player	Tm	G	GS	Inn	PO	A	E	DP	Pct.	Rng
Abbott,Kurt	Fla	7	6	57.1	10	19	0	6	1.000	4.55
Alexander,Manny	NYN	26	19	167.2	31	65	2	10	.980	5.15
Alexander,Manny	ChN	28	28	226.1	30	83	7	12	.942	4.49
Alfonzo,Edgardo	NYN	12	4	49.0	12	15	0	3	1.000	4.96
Amaral,Rich	Sea	1	0	1.0	0	0	0	0	.000	.00
Arias,Alex	Fla	11	7	60.2	13	18	1	7	.969	4.60
Aurilia,Rich	SF	36	22	223.0	47	91	3	19	.979	5.57
Bates,Jason	Col	16	12	102.0	15	37	3	12	.945	4.59
Batista,Tony	Oak	61	54	468.2	91	169	8	39	.970	4.99
Bell,David	StL	13	9	78.0	10	26	2	4	.947	4.15
Bellhorn,Mark	Oak	1	0	2.0	0	1	0	0	1.000	4.50
Belliard,Rafael	Atl	53	15	219.2	36	64	1	15	.990	4.10
Benjamin,Mike	Bos	16	10	99.1	17	29	2	4	.958	4.17
Bogar,Tim	Hou	80	67	586.1	103	213	5	54	.984	4.85
Bournigal,Rafael	Oak	74	59	524.0	98	192	6	40	.980	4.98
Branson,Jeff	Cin	11	2	42.0	6	11	0	2	1.000	3.64
Branson,Jeff	Cle	2	0	3.0	0	1	0	0	1.000	3.00
Brito,Tilson	Tor	8	5	51.0	13	13	2	6	.929	4.59
Brito,Tilson	Oak	6	4	33.0	5	8	0	1	1.000	3.55
Brosius,Scott	Oak	30	12	120.1	25	39	2	8	.970	4.79
Cabrera,Orlando	Mon	6	0	12.0	1	6	1	1	.875	5.25
Cairo,Miguel	ChN	2	0	5.2	2	3	0	2	1.000	7.94
Castro,Juan	LA	22	12	124.2	19	34	0	6	1.000	3.83
Cedeno,Domingo	Tex	43	30	279.2	44	89	6	28	.957	4.28
Cianfrocco,Archi	SD	5	2	17.0	3	7	1	0	.909	5.29
Collier,Lou	Pit	18	9	92.1	9	36	0	7	1.000	4.39
Cromer,Tripp	LA	10	9	80.0	23	25	1	4	.980	5.40
Delgado,Wilson	SF	1	0	2.0	1	0	0	0	1.000	4.50
Diaz,Eddy	Mil	1	0	1.0	0	0	0	0	.000	.00
Dunston,Shawon	ChN	108	105	829.1	163	226	12	46	.970	4.22
Dunston,Shawon	Pit	18	18	150.1	28	55	3	8	.965	4.97
Easley,Damion	Det	21	7	68.1	9	16	0	0	1.000	3.29
Eenhoorn,Robert	Ana	2	2	18.0	5	4	1	2	.900	4.50
Elster,Kevin	Pit	39	39	336.1	54	123	1	22	.994	4.74
Espinoza,Alvaro	Sea	17	13	118.2	21	34	2	5	.965	4.17
Fernandez,Tony	Cle	10	8	65.2	12	26	1	7	.974	5.21
Fonville,Chad	ChA	2	1	11.0	2	2	1	0	.800	3.27
Fox,Andy	NYA	2	1	10.0	3	3	0	2	1.000	5.40
Frias,Hanley	Tex	12	7	68.0	12	11	0	2	1.000	3.04
Frye,Jeff	Bos	3	0	8.0	2	2	0	0	1.000	4.50

Shortstops - Regulars

Player	Tm	G	GS	Inn	PO	A	E	DP	Pct.	Rng
Weiss,Walt	Col	119	112	971.2	192	372	10	89	.983	5.22
Polcovich,Kevin	Pit	80	75	635.0	121	246	12	38	.968	5.20
Gil,Benji	Tex	106	100	860.2	163	327	19	72	.963	5.12
Meares,Pat	Min	134	129	1131.1	212	415	20	93	.969	4.99
Ordonez,Rey	NYN	118	112	956.1	170	355	9	72	.983	4.94
Vizcaino,Jose	SF	147	140	1221.0	204	444	16	96	.976	4.78
Clayton,Royce	StL	153	145	1287.1	229	450	19	95	.973	4.75
Bell,Jay	KC	149	144	1271.0	226	442	10	103	.979	4.73
Garciaparra,Nom.	Bos	153	152	1344.1	249	450	21	113	.971	4.68
Cruz,Deivi	Det	147	133	1184.0	194	419	13	95	.979	4.66
Vizquel,Omar	Cle	152	149	1307.1	245	428	10	102	.985	4.63
Valentin,Jose	Mil	134	132	1150.1	208	384	20	88	.967	4.63
Gomez,Chris	SD	150	146	1279.2	226	432	15	82	.978	4.63
Reese,Pokey	Cin	110	92	853.1	170	262	15	56	.966	4.56

Shortstops - The Rest

Player	Tm	G	GS	Inn	PO	A	E	DP	Pct.	Rng
Gallego,Mike	StL	10	2	32.0	5	17	0	3	1.000	6.19
Garcia,Carlos	Tor	5	0	18.2	3	3	2	1	.750	2.89
Gates,Brent	Sea	5	1	19.1	2	5	0	2	1.000	3.26
Gilbert,Shawn	NYN	6	1	13.0	4	4	0	1	1.000	5.54
Giovanola,Ed	Atl	1	0	2.0	0	1	0	0	1.000	4.50
Graffanino,Tony	Atl	2	0	2.0	0	2	0	0	1.000	9.00
Grebeck,Craig	Ana	20	10	106.1	16	31	2	8	.959	3.98
Greene,Willie	Cin	0	0	0.0	0	0	0	0	.000	.00
Guerrero,Wilton	LA	5	3	30.2	8	10	0	2	1.000	5.28
Guevara,Giomar	Sea	1	0	2.0	0	1	0	0	1.000	4.50
Gutierrez,Ricky	Hou	64	52	469.1	85	152	8	36	.967	4.54
Halter,Shane	KC	5	4	39.0	9	13	1	3	.957	5.08
Hernandez,Jose	ChN	21	5	83.1	20	32	1	8	.981	5.62
Hocking,Denny	Min	44	32	293.2	61	94	4	28	.975	4.75
Houston,Tyler	ChN	1	0	1.0	0	0	0	0	.000	.00
Howard,David	KC	9	3	42.0	6	15	1	5	.955	4.50
Jackson,Damian	Cle	5	2	23.2	7	7	0	2	1.000	5.32
Jackson,Damian	Cin	6	5	44.0	5	14	0	2	1.000	3.89
Knoblauch,Chuck	Min	1	1	9.0	2	3	1	1	.833	5.00
Larkin,Barry	Cin	63	63	502.2	78	171	5	33	.980	4.46
Ledesma,Aaron	Bal	4	0	7.0	1	2	0	0	1.000	3.86
Liriano,Nelson	LA	1	0	1.0	0	0	0	0	.000	.00
Listach,Pat	Hou	31	28	247.0	26	71	5	12	.951	3.53
Lopez,Luis	NYN	45	26	273.1	41	103	5	21	.966	4.74
Loretta,Mark	Mil	44	29	276.0	51	83	6	23	.957	4.37
Martin,Norberto	ChA	28	23	193.0	27	45	3	11	.960	3.36
Martinez,Felix	KC	12	10	91.0	16	22	1	7	.974	3.76
Miller,Orlando	Det	31	22	193.1	30	64	2	18	.979	4.38
Morandini,Mickey	Phi	1	0	2.0	0	0	0	0	.000	.00
Mordecai,Mike	Atl	4	0	7.0	3	2	0	2	1.000	6.43
Nunez,Abraham	Pit	12	8	71.2	10	23	0	5	1.000	4.14
Ordaz,Luis	StL	11	6	58.1	9	18	1	4	.964	4.17
Orie,Kevin	ChN	2	0	4.0	0	1	0	0	1.000	2.25
Perez,Neifi	Col	45	38	359.0	77	155	6	35	.975	5.82
Perez,Tomas	Tor	32	32	270.2	44	92	1	22	.993	4.52
Reboulet,Jeff	Bal	22	11	113.2	20	28	1	4	.980	3.80
Relaford,Desi	Phi	12	10	93.0	12	31	1	3	.977	4.16
Ripken,Billy	Tex	31	24	213.1	38	64	3	15	.971	4.30
Ripken,Cal	Bal	3	0	5.0	2	0	0	1	1.000	3.60
Rivera,Luis	Hou	6	2	34.0	6	8	2	4	.875	3.71
Sanchez,Rey	ChN	63	24	279.0	49	85	5	12	.964	4.32
Sanchez,Rey	NYA	6	1	23.2	3	9	0	1	1.000	4.56
Santangelo,F.P.	Mon	1	0	1.0	0	1	0	0	1.000	9.00
Sefcik,Kevin	Phi	10	7	63.0	8	14	1	2	.957	3.14
Sheets,Andy	Sea	9	8	73.0	4	26	2	1	.938	3.70
Sheldon,Scott	Oak	12	8	69.2	15	17	2	5	.941	4.13
Shipley,Craig	SD	21	10	114.2	17	37	3	5	.947	4.24
Silvestri,Dave	Tex	1	1	8.0	0	2	0	0	1.000	2.25
Snopek,Chris	ChA	4	3	27.0	5	8	0	2	1.000	4.33
Sojo,Luis	NYA	4	1	17.0	5	4	0	4	1.000	4.76
Spiers,Bill	Hou	28	13	122.1	26	58	6	12	.933	6.18
Stankiewicz,Andy	Mon	14	6	65.2	12	19	0	5	1.000	4.25
Sveum,Dale	Pit	28	13	146.1	29	54	1	14	.988	5.10
Tejada,Miguel	Oak	26	25	227.2	55	67	4	18	.968	4.82
Velandia,Jorge	SD	6	4	38.2	4	11	1	4	.938	3.49
Wilson,Enrique	Cle	4	2	26.0	6	10	1	4	.941	5.54
Womack,Tony	Pit	4	0	4.0	0	1	0	0	1.000	2.25

Left Fielders - Regulars

Player	Tm	G	GS	Inn	PO	A	E	DP	Pct.	Rng
Belle,Albert	ChA	154	154	1333.0	350	1	10	0	.972	2.37
Higginson,Bob	Det	105	90	809.2	195	17	6	6	.972	2.36
Cordova,Marty	Min	101	99	863.2	214	12	2	2	.991	2.36
Anderson,Garret	Ana	130	118	1084.2	260	12	3	1	.989	2.26
Glanville,Doug	ChN	120	80	803.0	184	11	3	2	.985	2.19
Giles,Brian	Cle	82	73	647.1	149	5	3	1	.981	2.14
Greer,Rusty	Tex	148	139	1219.1	280	8	11	0	.963	2.13
Roberts,Bip	TOT	92	79	682.2	155	5	3	1	.982	2.11
Gant,Ron	StL	128	125	1084.1	248	4	6	1	.977	2.09
Surhoff,B.J.	Bal	133	128	1135.0	246	11	2	3	.992	2.04
Gilkey,Bernard	NYN	136	134	1179.2	249	17	3	2	.989	2.03
Bonds,Barry	SF	159	158	1372.1	290	10	5	1	.984	1.97
Gonzalez,Luis	Hou	146	142	1257.2	263	10	5	1	.982	1.95
Cordero,Wil	Bos	137	137	1199.1	248	8	2	3	.992	1.92
Jefferies,Gregg	Phi	124	122	1021.2	211	5	3	3	.986	1.90
Vaughn,Greg	SD	94	88	758.1	153	7	1	0	.994	1.90
Bichette,Dante	Col	128	128	1000.1	208	3	2	0	.991	1.90
Cruz Jr,Jose	TOT	100	98	858.2	176	4	5	1	.973	1.89
Rodriguez,Henry	Mon	126	124	1010.2	197	4	3	2	.985	1.79
Justice,David	Cle	74	73	622.1	115	2	2	0	.983	1.69
Klesko,Ryan	Atl	130	126	992.1	182	3	6	0	.969	1.68
Alou,Moises	Fla	91	85	716.0	123	2	3	0	.977	1.57
Martin,Al	Pit	110	107	929.2	125	8	6	1	.957	1.29
Average	---	119	113	981.2	209	7	4	1	.981	1.99

Left Fielders - The Rest

Player	Tm	G	GS	Inn	PO	A	E	DP	Pct.	Rng
Abbott,Jeff	ChA	5	2	23.0	7	0	0	0	1.000	2.74
Abbott,Kurt	Fla	10	6	45.0	13	0	0	0	1.000	2.60
Abreu,Bob	Hou	10	4	52.0	6	0	1	0	.857	1.04
Amaral,Rich	Sea	39	30	267.2	51	0	0	0	1.000	1.71
Amaro,Ruben	Phi	26	3	79.0	19	0	0	0	1.000	2.16
Anthony,Eric	LA	17	13	111.1	23	2	1	1	.962	2.02
Ashley,Billy	LA	35	31	225.0	39	4	4	0	.911	1.64
Aven,Bruce	Cle	10	2	37.0	8	0	0	0	1.000	1.95
Banks,Brian	Mil	15	13	116.2	19	0	1	0	.950	1.47
Bartee,Kimera	Det	3	0	8.0	2	0	0	0	1.000	2.25
Bautista,Danny	Atl	48	13	189.0	46	1	1	1	.979	2.24
Beamon,Trey	SD	15	6	77.2	15	3	2	0	.900	2.09
Becker,Rich	Min	9	5	52.0	15	0	0	0	1.000	2.60
Benard,Marvin	SF	14	0	38.0	6	1	1	0	.875	1.66
Benitez,Yamil	KC	31	31	264.0	59	0	3	0	.952	2.01
Bieser,Steve	NYN	9	4	41.0	12	1	0	0	1.000	2.85
Blowers,Mike	Sea	5	4	27.0	5	0	0	0	1.000	1.67
Bragg,Darren	Bos	1	0	2.0	0	0	0	0	.000	.00
Brede,Brent	Min	3	1	10.0	3	0	0	0	1.000	2.70
Brosius,Scott	Oak	6	3	28.0	5	0	0	0	1.000	1.61
Brown,Brant	ChN	27	27	195.2	43	3	0	0	1.000	2.12
Brown,Emil	Pit	30	13	149.0	33	1	1	0	.971	2.05
Brumfield,Jacob	Tor	14	11	115.2	29	2	0	1	1.000	2.41
Burks,Ellis	Col	67	17	250.1	53	3	2	0	.966	2.01
Burnitz,Jeromy	Mil	5	2	29.0	5	1	0	0	1.000	1.86
Butler,Brett	LA	47	40	322.1	70	2	0	1	1.000	2.01
Butler,Rich	Tor	3	3	27.0	5	0	0	0	1.000	1.67
Butler,Rob	Phi	4	2	21.2	4	1	0	1	1.000	2.08
Cangelosi,John	Fla	34	12	146.2	34	0	0	0	1.000	2.09

Left Fielders - The Rest

Left Fielders - The Rest

Player	Tm	G	GS	Inn	PO	A	E	DP	Pct.	Rng
Canseco,Jose	Oak	19	17	143.1	25	1	0	0	1.000	1.63
Carr,Chuck	Hou	1	0	1.0	0	0	0	0	.000	.00
Carter,Joe	Tor	41	41	340.2	87	0	3	0	.967	2.30
Cedeno,Roger	LA	13	7	63.0	16	0	0	0	1.000	2.29
Clark,Dave	ChN	24	20	160.0	39	2	2	1	.953	2.31
Clyburn,Danny	Bal	1	0	3.0	0	0	0	0	.000	.00
Coleman,Vince	Det	2	1	13.0	3	0	0	0	1.000	2.08
Coles,Darnell	Col	2	0	5.0	0	0	0	0	.000	.00
Conine,Jeff	Fla	1	0	5.0	0	0	0	0	.000	.00
Cruz Jr,Jose	Sea	49	47	408.0	83	1	3	0	.966	1.85
Cruz Jr,Jose	Tor	51	51	450.2	93	3	2	1	.980	1.92
Cruz,Ivan	NYA	1	0	4.0	1	0	0	0	1.000	2.25
Cruz,Jacob	SF	2	1	6.2	0	0	0	0	.000	.00
Cummings,Midre	Pit	14	11	101.0	19	1	0	0	1.000	1.78
Curtis,Chad	Cle	3	1	7.0	0	0	0	0	.000	.00
Curtis,Chad	NYA	53	48	414.1	77	4	2	1	.976	1.76
Damon,Johnny	KC	48	32	311.1	69	0	1	0	.986	1.99
Daulton,Darren	Fla	1	0	2.0	0	0	0	0	.000	.00
Dellucci,David	Bal	3	0	7.0	4	0	0	0	1.000	5.14
Devereaux,Mike	Tex	5	2	24.0	2	0	0	0	1.000	0.75
Diaz,Alex	Tex	3	2	20.0	6	0	0	0	1.000	2.70
Ducey,Rob	Sea	43	24	229.0	41	2	1	1	.977	1.69
Duncan,Mariano	NYA	6	6	44.0	7	1	1	0	.889	1.64
Dunn,Todd	Mil	19	16	136.1	29	1	3	0	.909	1.98
Dunston,Shawon	ChN	7	5	41.0	16	0	0	0	1.000	3.51
Dunwoody,Todd	Fla	6	5	45.0	6	0	0	0	1.000	1.20
Dye,Jermaine	KC	1	1	5.1	0	0	0	0	.000	.00
Echevarria,Angel	Col	2	0	6.1	0	0	0	0	.000	.00
Eisenreich,Jim	Fla	42	32	288.0	58	1	1	0	.983	1.84
Everett,Carl	NYN	9	5	40.0	10	0	0	0	1.000	2.25
Floyd,Cliff	Fla	24	18	156.2	33	2	1	0	.972	2.01
Fonville,Chad	ChA	1	0	1.0	1	0	0	0	1.000	9.00
Franco,Matt	NYN	1	0	1.0	0	0	0	0	.000	.00
Franklin,Micah	StL	4	1	14.1	2	0	0	0	1.000	1.26
Frye,Jeff	Bos	5	4	36.0	9	2	2	0	.846	2.75
Fullmer,Brad	Mon	2	1	10.0	1	0	1	0	.500	0.90
Garcia,Karim	LA	12	10	81.1	13	0	0	0	1.000	1.44
Gates,Brent	Sea	1	0	2.0	1	0	0	0	1.000	4.50
Giambi,Jason	Oak	68	67	541.1	102	5	2	1	.982	1.78
Gilbert,Shawn	NYN	1	0	2.0	0	0	0	0	.000	.00
Goodwin,Curtis	Cin	32	28	249.1	69	2	0	1	1.000	2.56
Goodwin,Tom	Tex	5	1	12.0	3	0	0	0	1.000	2.25
Grebeck,Craig	Ana	3	3	25.0	6	0	0	0	1.000	2.16
Green,Scarbor.	StL	7	0	27.0	4	0	0	0	1.000	1.33
Green,Shawn	Tor	45	37	337.2	84	0	1	0	.988	2.24
Greene,Willie	Cin	6	4	38.0	3	0	0	0	1.000	0.71
Gregg,Tommy	Atl	5	1	24.1	2	0	0	0	1.000	0.74
Griffey Jr,Ken	Sea	1	0	2.0	1	0	0	0	1.000	4.50
Halter,Shane	KC	10	2	36.0	5	1	0	0	1.000	1.50
Hammonds,Jeffr.	Bal	31	23	207.2	55	2	2	0	.966	2.47
Harris,Lenny	Cin	26	13	132.1	27	0	1	0	.964	1.84
Helton,Todd	Col	13	12	93.2	14	2	0	0	1.000	1.54
Henderson,Rickey	SD	55	50	434.1	109	3	4	0	.966	2.32
Henderson,Rickey	Ana	11	11	92.0	19	0	0	0	1.000	1.86
Hernandez,Jose	ChN	6	1	18.0	4	0	0	0	1.000	2.00
Hidalgo,Richard	Hou	1	1	8.0	1	0	0	0	1.000	1.13
Hocking,Denny	Min	7	5	40.0	12	1	0	0	1.000	2.93
Hollandsworth,To.	LA	80	39	439.1	132	1	2	0	.985	2.72

Player	Tm	G	GS	Inn	PO	A	E	DP	Pct.	Rng
Howard,David	KC	5	1	23.0	4	0	0	0	1.000	1.57
Howard,Thomas	Hou	10	7	68.0	17	0	0	0	1.000	2.25
Hubbard,Trent	Cle	5	3	29.0	3	0	0	0	1.000	0.93
Hudler,Rex	Phi	11	9	76.0	15	0	0	0	1.000	1.78
Hurst,Jimmy	Det	1	0	2.0	0	0	0	0	.000	.00
Huskey,Butch	NYN	30	18	180.0	47	4	3	0	.944	2.55
Huson,Jeff	Mil	8	2	22.1	4	1	0	1	1.000	2.01
Ibanez,Raul	Sea	2	2	12.0	3	0	0	0	1.000	2.25
Incaviglia,Pete	Bal	4	1	12.1	2	0	0	0	1.000	1.46
Ingram,Garey	LA	6	1	17.2	4	0	0	0	1.000	2.04
Jackson,Darrin	Mil	21	9	110.1	25	1	0	0	1.000	2.12
Javier,Stan	SF	5	3	29.0	3	0	0	0	1.000	0.93
Jennings,Robin	ChN	4	1	18.0	4	0	0	0	1.000	2.00
Jones,Andruw	Atl	2	0	3.0	1	0	0	0	1.000	3.00
Jones,Chipper	Atl	3	1	14.2	3	0	0	0	1.000	1.84
Jones,Chris	SD	24	11	114.2	15	3	2	1	.900	1.41
Kelly,Mike	Cin	17	11	110.2	26	0	0	0	1.000	2.11
Kelly,Roberto	Min	1	1	8.0	3	0	0	0	1.000	3.38
Kelly,Roberto	Sea	28	27	238.0	52	1	0	0	1.000	2.00
Kieschnick,Brooks	ChN	26	25	167.0	36	1	2	0	.949	1.99
Kirby,Wayne	LA	9	1	26.0	7	1	0	0	1.000	2.77
Lawton,Matt	Min	58	51	460.1	108	5	2	2	.983	2.21
Lennon,Patrick	Oak	23	16	141.0	38	0	2	0	.950	2.43
Lesher,Brian	Oak	31	26	243.1	61	2	3	0	.955	2.33
Lewis,Darren	LA	23	20	173.1	44	1	1	0	.978	2.34
Listach,Pat	Hou	1	1	4.2	2	0	0	0	1.000	3.86
Long,Ryan	KC	1	0	1.0	1	0	0	0	1.000	9.00
Lowery,Terrell	ChN	5	3	26.0	6	1	0	0	1.000	2.42
Mabry,John	StL	4	3	27.0	6	0	0	0	1.000	2.00
Mack,Shane	Bos	3	0	6.0	0	0	0	0	.000	.00
Malave,Jose	Bos	4	0	10.0	3	0	0	0	1.000	2.70
Manto,Jeff	Cle	1	1	6.0	0	0	0	0	.000	.00
Martinez,Dave	ChA	4	0	7.1	1	0	0	0	1.000	1.23
Mashore,Damon	Oak	28	3	79.0	24	1	0	0	1.000	2.85
May,Derrick	Phi	7	5	39.2	12	1	0	0	1.000	2.95
McDonald,Jason	Oak	18	7	71.1	15	0	1	0	.938	1.89
McGee,Willie	StL	18	9	92.0	15	1	0	1	1.000	1.57
McGuire,Ryan	Mon	21	12	114.2	28	0	1	0	.966	2.20
McLemore,Mark	Tex	1	0	1.0	0	0	0	0	.000	.00
McMillon,Billy	Fla	2	2	16.0	4	0	0	0	1.000	2.25
McMillon,Billy	Phi	19	17	144.1	38	2	2	0	.952	2.49
Mejia,Roberto	StL	1	0	2.0	0	0	0	0	.000	.00
Mendoza,Carlos	NYN	2	1	6.0	2	0	0	0	1.000	3.00
Meulens,Hensley	Mon	8	5	43.0	6	0	0	0	1.000	1.26
Mieske,Matt	Mil	26	21	184.0	33	1	2	0	.944	1.66
Mitchell,Kevin	Cle	1	0	1.0	0	0	0	1	.000	.00
Montgomery,Ray	Hou	2	1	9.2	4	0	0	0	1.000	3.72
Mouton,James	Hou	9	6	56.0	10	0	0	0	1.000	1.61
Mouton,Lyle	ChA	16	5	58.0	16	0	1	0	.941	2.48
Myers,Rod	KC	12	10	93.2	20	0	0	0	1.000	1.92
Nevin,Phil	Det	40	36	308.2	64	4	1	2	.986	1.98
Newfield,Marc	Mil	28	28	204.0	43	0	1	0	.977	1.90
Newson,Warren	Tex	20	15	129.1	31	1	2	0	.941	2.23
Nilsson,Dave	Mil	22	20	141.0	31	1	0	0	1.000	2.04
Nunnally,Jon	KC	1	1	9.0	1	0	0	0	1.000	1.00
Nunnally,Jon	Cin	14	5	46.0	7	1	0	0	1.000	1.57
O'Leary,Troy	Bos	24	20	186.1	37	3	2	0	.952	1.93
Obando,Sherman	Mon	1	0	2.0	0	0	0	0	.000	.00

Left Fielders - The Rest

Player	Tm	G	GS	Inn	PO	A	E	DP	Pct.	Rng
Orsulak,Joe	Mon	37	5	97.1	18	1	0	0	1.000	1.76
Otero,Ricky	Phi	1	0	2.0	0	0	0	0	.000	.00
Owens,Eric	Cin	9	5	50.2	9	0	1	0	.900	1.60
Palmeiro,Orlando	Ana	4	1	13.0	6	0	0	0	1.000	4.15
Paquette,Craig	KC	4	1	10.0	6	1	0	1	1.000	6.30
Perez,Eduardo	Cin	11	9	65.1	12	0	0	0	1.000	1.65
Perez,Robert	Tor	17	12	107.0	19	0	0	0	1.000	1.60
Petagine,Roberto	NYN	1	0	5.0	1	0	0	0	1.000	1.80
Phillips,Tony	Ana	31	29	240.0	48	1	2	0	.961	1.84
Plantier,Phil	SD	3	2	11.1	3	0	0	0	1.000	2.38
Plantier,Phil	StL	10	9	74.0	18	1	0	0	1.000	2.31
Pose,Scott	NYA	28	15	157.2	32	2	0	1	1.000	1.94
Pride,Curtis	Det	34	23	212.2	44	0	1	0	.978	1.86
Pulliam,Harvey	Col	24	3	61.0	14	0	0	0	1.000	2.07
Raines,Tim	NYA	57	51	452.0	78	1	1	0	.988	1.57
Ramos,Ken	Hou	1	0	2.0	0	0	0	0	.000	.00
Rivera,Ruben	SD	2	0	3.0	1	0	0	0	1.000	3.00
Roberts,Bip	KC	82	71	606.2	142	3	3	0	.980	2.15
Roberts,Bip	Cle	10	8	76.0	13	2	0	1	1.000	1.78
Robertson,Mike	Phi	4	4	36.0	8	0	0	0	1.000	2.00
Sagmoen,Marc	Tex	2	0	4.0	0	0	0	0	.000	.00
Sanders,Deion	Cin	37	34	303.1	66	1	1	0	.985	1.99
Santangelo,F.P.	Mon	40	15	168.1	46	1	0	1	1.000	2.51
Scarsone,Steve	StL	1	0	1.0	0	0	0	0	.000	.00
Sheaffer,Danny	StL	13	4	36.0	9	0	0	0	1.000	2.25
Shumpert,Terry	SD	2	0	4.0	1	0	0	0	1.000	2.25
Sierra,Ruben	Cin	12	10	85.0	11	2	0	0	1.000	1.38
Sierra,Ruben	Tor	6	6	54.0	12	0	1	0	.923	2.00
Simms,Mike	Tex	2	1	7.0	1	0	0	0	1.000	1.29
Smith,Mark	Pit	21	20	159.2	26	2	0	0	1.000	1.58
Stairs,Matt	Oak	28	23	197.2	38	2	2	0	.952	1.82
Stevens,Lee	Tex	3	2	13.0	3	0	0	0	1.000	2.08
Stewart,Shannon	Tor	2	1	10.0	4	1	0	0	1.000	4.50
Strange,Doug	Mon	2	0	1.0	0	0	0	0	.000	.00
Strawberry,Darryl	NYA	4	4	30.0	5	0	0	0	1.000	1.50
Stynes,Chris	Cin	38	38	328.2	76	5	2	0	.976	2.22
Sutton,Larry	KC	1	0	1.0	0	0	0	0	.000	.00
Sweeney,Mark	StL	10	4	42.0	6	0	0	0	1.000	1.29
Sweeney,Mark	SD	6	5	46.2	10	0	1	0	.909	1.93
Tarasco,Tony	Bal	7	3	37.0	7	0	0	0	1.000	1.70
Taubensee,Eddie	Cin	6	4	30.2	3	1	0	0	1.000	1.17
Tavarez,Jesus	Bos	4	1	12.0	3	0	0	0	1.000	2.25
Thurman,Gary	NYN	3	0	4.1	1	0	0	0	1.000	2.08
Timmons,Ozzie	Cin	1	1	9.0	0	0	1	0	.000	.00
Tinsley,Lee	Sea	34	28	262.0	57	1	0	1	1.000	1.99
Tomberlin,Andy	NYN	1	0	0.1	0	0	0	0	.000	.00
Trammell,Bubba	Det	13	12	91.2	26	0	0	0	1.000	2.55
Tucker,Michael	Atl	53	21	242.1	56	2	1	2	.983	2.15
Unroe,Tim	Mil	1	0	1.0	0	0	0	0	.000	.00
VanderWal,John	Col	2	2	16.0	2	0	0	0	1.000	1.13
Vitiello,Joe	KC	12	11	82.0	17	0	1	0	.944	1.87
Voigt,Jack	Mil	35	25	237.1	54	5	1	2	.983	2.24
Walton,Jerome	Bal	9	7	59.0	10	0	0	0	1.000	1.53
Ward,Turner	Pit	11	1	17.2	4	0	0	0	1.000	2.04
Wehner,John	Fla	10	2	26.1	3	0	0	0	1.000	1.03
Whiten,Mark	NYA	44	38	365.2	76	0	1	0	.987	1.87
Williams,Gerald	Mil	39	25	245.1	55	3	0	0	1.000	2.13
Young,Dmitri	StL	9	7	56.0	16	0	1	0	.941	2.57

Left Fielders - The Rest

Player	Tm	G	GS	Inn	PO	A	E	DP	Pct.	Rng
Young,Ernie	Oak	1	0	0.1	0	0	0	0	.000	.00
Young,Kevin	Pit	10	10	79.0	17	0	0	0	1.000	1.94

Center Fielders - Regulars

Player	Tm	G	GS	Inn	PO	A	E	DP	Pct.	Rng
Cameron,Mike	ChA	102	99	836.2	297	4	5	1	.984	3.24
Edmonds,Jim	Ana	115	111	967.0	313	9	5	3	.985	3.00
Bragg,Darren	Bos	118	104	945.0	296	9	2	2	.993	2.90
Buford,Damon	Tex	117	102	909.2	282	7	3	5	.990	2.86
Becker,Rich	Min	115	106	932.0	284	5	5	1	.983	2.79
Goodwin,Tom	TOT	145	141	1228.0	367	6	3	0	.992	2.73
Griffey Jr,Ken	Sea	153	153	1330.2	387	9	6	3	.985	2.68
Finley,Steve	SD	140	131	1179.0	338	10	4	3	.989	2.66
Hunter,Brian	Det	162	162	1422.2	408	8	4	0	.990	2.63
Grissom,Marquis	Cle	144	144	1250.2	357	7	3	3	.992	2.62
Williams,Gerald	Mil	129	124	1071.2	301	8	3	4	.990	2.60
White,Rondell	Mon	151	151	1339.0	375	6	3	3	.992	2.56
Johnson,Lance	TOT	105	94	836.1	231	4	7	2	.971	2.53
Lofton,Kenny	Atl	122	121	1047.1	289	5	5	1	.983	2.53
Nixon,Otis	TOT	144	143	1263.2	351	2	2	0	.994	2.51
McCracken,Quin.	Col	133	71	756.0	194	5	4	3	.980	2.37
Sanders,Deion	Cin	77	77	654.2	168	2	3	1	.983	2.34
Lankford,Ray	StL	132	130	1141.1	292	4	9	2	.970	2.33
Hamilton,Darryl	SF	119	112	961.2	245	1	5	0	.980	2.30
McRae,Brian	TOT	148	138	1222.0	308	4	4	2	.987	2.30
Anderson,Brady	Bal	124	123	1096.0	276	1	3	0	.989	2.27
Burks,Ellis	Col	89	89	650.0	154	3	2	2	.987	2.17
Williams,Bernie	NYA	128	127	1122.2	269	2	2	1	.993	2.17
Allensworth,Jerm.	Pit	104	94	837.2	189	5	4	1	.980	2.08
Average	---	125	118	1041.2	290	5	4	1	.987	2.55

Center Fielders - The Rest

Player	Tm	G	GS	Inn	PO	A	E	DP	Pct.	Rng
Abbott,Jeff	ChA	1	0	2.0	1	0	0	0	1.000	4.50
Abreu,Bob	Hou	1	0	1.0	0	0	0	0	.000	.00
Alou,Moises	Fla	54	53	461.2	108	1	0	0	1.000	2.12
Amaral,Rich	Sea	9	2	28.0	9	0	0	0	1.000	2.89
Amaro,Ruben	Phi	37	16	155.1	38	1	1	0	.975	2.26
Anderson,Garret	Ana	27	27	214.1	78	2	0	1	1.000	3.36
Aven,Bruce	Cle	1	0	2.0	2	0	0	0	1.000	9.00
Bartee,Kimera	Det	3	0	6.0	1	0	0	0	1.000	1.50
Bautista,Danny	Atl	1	0	3.0	0	0	0	0	.000	.00
Bell,Derek	Hou	36	34	308.0	65	2	2	1	.971	1.96
Benard,Marvin	SF	6	4	42.0	11	0	0	0	1.000	2.36
Bieser,Steve	NYN	13	7	63.1	18	1	0	0	1.000	2.70
Brosius,Scott	Oak	6	5	43.1	9	0	1	0	.900	1.87
Brown,Adrian	Pit	35	35	306.0	70	3	1	1	.986	2.15
Brown,Emil	Pit	8	3	36.0	16	0	1	0	.941	4.00
Brumfield,Jacob	Tor	24	16	173.0	49	1	0	0	1.000	2.60
Burnitz,Jeromy	Mil	26	19	173.1	50	0	0	0	1.000	2.60
Butler,Brett	LA	49	47	408.1	93	2	0	1	1.000	2.09
Butler,Rob	Phi	14	14	111.0	25	1	0	1	1.000	2.03
Cangelosi,John	Fla	23	15	145.0	38	1	0	0	1.000	2.42
Carr,Chuck	Mil	23	10	113.0	25	1	0	0	1.000	2.07

Center Fielders - The Rest

Player	Tm	G	GS	Inn	PO	A	E	DP	Pct.	Rng
Carr,Chuck	Hou	59	49	434.0	111	3	4	2	.966	2.36
Cedeno,Roger	LA	55	39	376.0	125	1	2	0	.984	3.02
Coleman,Michael	Bos	7	7	60.1	16	0	1	0	.941	2.39
Coleman,Vince	Det	1	0	2.0	0	0	0	0	.000	.00
Cruz Jr,Jose	Tor	4	4	35.0	5	0	0	0	1.000	1.29
Cummings,Midre	Phi	53	50	432.0	113	1	1	1	.991	2.38
Curtis,Chad	Cle	12	4	47.0	17	0	0	0	1.000	3.26
Curtis,Chad	NYA	43	34	330.2	83	2	1	1	.988	2.31
Damon,Johnny	KC	65	51	480.1	155	1	2	0	.987	2.92
Devereaux,Mike	Tex	3	0	4.0	0	0	0	0	.000	.00
Ducey,Rob	Sea	12	4	52.0	14	0	0	0	1.000	2.42
Dunn,Todd	Mil	2	0	3.0	3	0	0	0	1.000	9.00
Dunwoody,Todd	Fla	8	7	65.0	20	0	2	0	.909	2.77
Echevarria,Angel	Col	2	1	11.2	2	1	0	0	1.000	2.31
Eisenreich,Jim	Fla	1	1	8.0	0	0	0	0	.000	.00
Encarnacion,Juan	Det	2	0	3.0	1	0	0	0	1.000	3.00
Erstad,Darin	Ana	1	1	9.0	3	0	0	0	1.000	3.00
Everett,Carl	NYN	71	54	486.0	113	4	4	2	.967	2.17
Floyd,Cliff	Fla	9	7	66.1	20	0	0	0	1.000	2.71
Fonville,Chad	ChA	2	1	9.0	6	0	0	0	1.000	6.00
Frye,Jeff	Bos	5	1	16.0	3	0	0	0	1.000	1.69
Giles,BrianS.	Cle	20	13	125.0	28	0	2	0	.933	2.02
Gilkey,Bernard	NYN	1	0	1.0	2	0	0	0	1.000	18.00
Glanville,Doug	ChN	30	25	218.1	61	1	0	1	1.000	2.56
Goodwin,Curtis	Cin	41	35	330.1	87	1	0	1	1.000	2.40
Goodwin,Tom	KC	96	93	814.0	232	3	1	0	.996	2.60
Goodwin,Tom	Tex	49	48	414.0	135	3	2	0	.986	3.00
Green,Scarbor.	StL	12	5	50.0	15	1	1	0	.941	2.88
Greer,Rusty	Tex	19	12	102.0	38	1	1	0	.975	3.44
Guerrero,Vladimir	Mon	1	0	0.1	0	0	0	0	.000	.00
Guillen,Jose	Pit	4	2	17.2	2	0	0	0	1.000	1.02
Halter,Shane	KC	9	8	60.0	17	0	0	0	1.000	2.55
Hammonds,Jeffr.	Bal	40	36	319.0	94	1	1	0	.990	2.68
Henderson,Rickey	SD	17	16	129.1	40	1	1	1	.976	2.85
Henderson,Rickey	Ana	2	1	10.0	7	0	0	0	1.000	6.30
Hidalgo,Richard	Hou	17	13	133.0	27	0	0	0	1.000	1.83
Higginson,Bob	Det	2	0	4.0	1	0	0	0	1.000	2.25
Hocking,Denny	Min	2	2	16.0	4	0	0	0	1.000	2.25
Hollandsworth,To.	LA	30	25	202.2	51	1	1	0	.981	2.31
Howard,David	KC	2	0	4.2	4	0	0	0	1.000	7.71
Howard,Thomas	Hou	41	35	295.2	73	5	0	1	1.000	2.37
Hubbard,Trent	Cle	1	0	1.0	0	0	0	0	.000	.00
Hudler,Rex	Phi	16	14	113.0	30	1	2	0	.939	2.47
Hurst,Jimmy	Det	1	0	3.0	2	0	0	0	1.000	6.00
Ingram,Garey	LA	1	0	3.0	0	0	0	0	.000	.00
Jackson,Darrin	Min	44	34	308.1	93	4	1	1	.990	2.83
Jackson,Darrin	Mil	9	8	60.0	26	1	0	1	1.000	4.05
Javier,Stan	SF	46	40	353.2	99	1	3	1	.971	2.54
Jennings,Robin	ChN	2	2	12.0	1	0	0	0	1.000	0.75
Johnson,Lance	NYN	66	62	555.0	152	4	4	2	.975	2.53
Johnson,Lance	ChN	39	32	281.1	79	0	3	0	.963	2.53
Jones,Andruw	Atl	57	41	415.1	139	8	2	1	.987	3.19
Jones,Chris	SD	19	13	118.2	30	1	2	0	.939	2.35
Jordan,Brian	StL	14	13	110.0	30	0	0	0	1.000	2.45
Kelly,Mike	Cin	11	3	36.0	10	0	0	0	1.000	2.50
Kelly,Roberto	Min	1	0	2.0	0	0	0	0	.000	.00
Kelly,Roberto	Sea	1	0	2.0	1	0	0	0	1.000	4.50
Kirby,Wayne	LA	16	9	88.1	24	0	0	0	1.000	2.45
Kotsay,Mark	Fla	14	12	113.0	30	2	0	1	1.000	2.55
Latham,Chris	Min	8	4	34.1	10	0	1	0	.909	2.62
Lawton,Matt	Min	23	16	141.1	43	0	3	0	.935	2.74
Lennon,Patrick	Oak	1	0	4.0	4	0	1	0	.800	9.00
Lewis,Darren	ChA	64	19	242.2	91	1	0	1	1.000	3.41
Lewis,Darren	LA	2	1	9.1	5	0	0	0	1.000	4.82
Listach,Pat	Hou	4	4	35.0	7	0	1	0	.875	1.80
Lowery,Terrell	ChN	2	0	4.0	0	1	0	1	1.000	2.25
Mabry,John	StL	6	3	29.1	7	0	0	0	1.000	2.15
Mack,Shane	Bos	43	37	300.0	75	0	0	0	1.000	2.25
Magee,Wendell	Phi	38	35	299.2	95	2	4	1	.960	2.91
Martinez,Dave	ChA	45	42	332.0	104	3	0	0	1.000	2.90
Mashore,Damon	Oak	71	68	557.0	175	9	2	3	.989	2.97
McDonald,Jason	Oak	66	45	435.2	132	2	4	1	.971	2.77
McGee,Willie	StL	18	11	122.1	26	1	1	1	.964	1.99
McGuire,Ryan	Mon	2	0	3.2	1	0	0	0	1.000	2.45
McRae,Brian	ChN	107	103	913.0	243	3	1	2	.996	2.42
McRae,Brian	NYN	41	35	309.0	65	1	3	0	.957	1.92
Mendoza,Carlos	NYN	3	1	18.0	3	0	0	0	1.000	1.50
Montgomery,Ray	Hou	2	0	3.0	2	0	0	0	1.000	6.00
Mouton,James	Hou	39	27	249.1	59	1	0	1	1.000	2.17
Myers,Rod	KC	9	7	67.0	19	0	1	0	.950	2.55
Nieves,Melvin	Det	2	0	5.0	1	0	0	0	1.000	1.80
Nixon,Otis	Tor	102	102	892.0	254	1	1	0	.996	2.57
Nixon,Otis	LA	42	41	371.2	97	1	1	0	.990	2.37
Nunnally,Jon	Cin	46	38	329.0	92	1	2	0	.979	2.54
Ochoa,Alex	NYN	4	3	21.1	5	0	0	0	1.000	2.11
Otero,Ricky	Phi	40	33	309.1	94	4	0	1	1.000	2.85
Owens,Eric	Cin	8	4	37.0	5	0	0	0	1.000	1.22
Palmeiro,Orlando	Ana	45	20	237.1	65	1	1	0	.985	2.50
Phillips,Tony	Ana	2	2	17.0	5	0	0	0	1.000	2.65
Pose,Scott	NYA	3	1	14.1	2	0	0	0	1.000	1.26
Powell,Dante	SF	20	6	88.2	25	0	0	0	1.000	2.54
Pulliam,Harvey	Col	1	0	2.0	1	0	0	0	1.000	4.50
Rivera,Ruben	SD	4	2	21.0	6	0	0	0	1.000	2.57
Roberts,Bip	KC	2	2	17.0	4	2	0	0	1.000	3.18
Santangelo,F.P.	Mon	13	11	104.0	29	0	0	0	1.000	2.51
Scarsone,Steve	StL	1	0	1.0	0	0	0	0	.000	.00
Sheaffer,Danny	StL	2	0	1.2	0	0	0	0	.000	.00
Stewart,Shannon	Tor	40	40	342.2	93	0	2	0	.979	2.44
Sweeney,Mark	SD	1	0	2.0	0	0	0	0	.000	.00
Tarasco,Tony	Bal	8	1	30.0	12	0	0	0	1.000	3.60
Tavarez,Jesus	Bos	29	13	130.1	37	1	1	0	.974	2.62
Thurman,Gary	NYN	4	0	5.2	3	0	0	0	1.000	4.76
Tinsley,Lee	Sea	6	3	35.0	9	1	0	1	1.000	2.57
Voigt,Jack	Mil	2	0	6.1	4	0	0	0	1.000	5.68
Walker,Larry	Col	2	1	13.0	2	0	0	0	1.000	1.38
Walton,Jerome	Bal	2	2	16.0	5	0	0	0	1.000	2.81
Ward,Turner	Pit	31	28	238.2	53	2	0	0	1.000	2.07
Watkins,Pat	Cin	15	5	62.0	11	1	0	0	1.000	1.74
Wehner,John	Fla	1	0	1.0	1	0	0	0	1.000	9.00
White,Devon	Fla	72	67	586.2	150	4	2	1	.987	2.36
Young,Ernie	Oak	60	44	405.1	126	5	3	0	.978	2.91

Right Fielders - Regulars

Player	Tm	G	GS	Inn	PO	A	E	DP	Pct.	Rng
Dye,Jermaine	KC	75	66	600.0	164	7	6	3	.966	2.57
Salmon,Tim	Ana	153	153	1372.2	352	15	11	6	.971	2.41
Nieves,Melvin	Det	101	84	752.1	189	4	4	1	.980	2.31
Mondesi,Raul	LA	159	157	1390.0	338	10	4	1	.989	2.25
Sanders,Reggie	Cin	85	84	753.0	184	4	5	1	.974	2.25
Merced,Orlando	Tor	96	94	827.0	190	10	3	4	.985	2.18
O'Leary,Troy	Bos	119	108	967.2	229	5	4	1	.983	2.18
Sosa,Sammy	ChN	161	161	1416.2	324	16	8	1	.977	2.16
O'Neill,Paul	NYA	146	145	1263.0	293	7	5	1	.984	2.14
Buhner,Jay	Sea	154	153	1326.0	294	5	1	4	.997	2.03
Tucker,Michael	Atl	102	100	828.0	181	4	4	0	.979	2.01
Sheffield,Gary	Fla	132	132	1115.1	230	14	5	1	.980	1.97
Berroa,Geronimo	TOT	83	82	661.1	142	2	4	1	.973	1.96
Guerrero,Vladimir	Mon	84	84	721.0	146	10	12	3	.929	1.95
Burnitz,Jeromy	Mil	124	111	989.1	202	12	7	3	.968	1.95
Hill,Glenallen	SF	97	92	744.2	158	2	9	0	.947	1.93
Ramirez,Manny	Cle	146	145	1253.2	258	10	7	2	.975	1.92
Bell,Derek	Hou	89	87	767.2	160	4	6	1	.965	1.92
Guillen,Jose	Pit	134	130	1108.2	224	9	9	4	.963	1.89
Walker,Larry	Col	150	143	1235.1	230	12	2	5	.992	1.76
Gwynn,Tony	SD	143	143	1203.1	218	8	4	4	.983	1.69
Average	---	120	116	1014.0	224	8	5	2	.976	2.06

Right Fielders - The Rest

Player	Tm	G	GS	Inn	PO	A	E	DP	Pct.	Rng
Abbott,Jeff	ChA	4	2	21.2	7	0	0	0	1.000	2.91
Abreu,Bob	Hou	43	42	375.0	78	4	1	1	.988	1.97
Alou,Moises	Fla	22	7	98.2	18	1	0	1	1.000	1.73
Amaral,Rich	Sea	6	1	14.0	2	0	0	0	1.000	1.29
Amaro,Ruben	Phi	15	6	62.2	18	1	0	0	1.000	2.73
Anderson,Garret	Ana	4	3	27.0	4	0	0	0	1.000	1.33
Anthony,Eric	LA	4	1	14.1	3	0	0	0	1.000	1.88
Aven,Bruce	Cle	2	1	13.0	5	1	0	0	1.000	4.15
Baines,Harold	ChA	1	0	2.0	0	0	0	0	.000	.00
Banks,Brian	Mil	1	0	1.0	0	0	0	0	.000	.00
Barron,Tony	Phi	53	51	454.2	111	3	2	1	.983	2.26
Bautista,Danny	Atl	10	5	63.0	13	0	0	0	1.000	1.86
Beamon,Trey	SD	5	2	25.0	2	0	0	0	1.000	0.72
Becker,Rich	Min	13	5	57.2	18	0	0	0	1.000	2.81
Benard,Marvin	SF	18	7	81.2	10	1	0	0	1.000	1.21
Benitez,Yamil	KC	22	21	174.0	52	0	1	0	.981	2.69
Berroa,Geronimo	Oak	43	42	343.0	71	1	1	1	.986	1.89
Berroa,Geronimo	Bal	40	40	318.1	71	1	3	1	.960	2.04
Bichette,Dante	Col	16	9	90.0	17	1	1	1	.947	1.80
Bieser,Steve	NYN	1	0	1.0	0	0	0	0	.000	.00
Blowers,Mike	Sea	1	0	1.0	0	0	0	0	.000	.00
Bragg,Darren	Bos	41	30	279.1	69	2	3	1	.959	2.29
Brede,Brent	Min	40	34	296.2	64	0	3	0	.955	1.94
Brosius,Scott	Oak	11	9	81.1	11	2	0	0	1.000	1.44
Brown,Adrian	Pit	3	1	12.1	4	0	0	0	1.000	2.92
Brown,Emil	Pit	4	2	20.0	4	1	1	1	.833	2.25
Brumfield,Jacob	Tor	10	8	66.0	9	3	0	0	1.000	1.64
Butler,Rob	Phi	8	0	20.2	4	1	0	0	1.000	2.18
Cameron,Mike	ChA	37	8	105.0	36	1	0	1	1.000	3.17
Cangelosi,John	Fla	6	5	38.1	11	0	0	0	1.000	2.58
Canseco,Jose	Oak	27	27	217.2	49	1	5	0	.909	2.07

Right Fielders - The Rest

Player	Tm	G	GS	Inn	PO	A	E	DP	Pct.	Rng
Carter,Joe	Tor	10	10	90.0	17	1	0	0	1.000	1.80
Cedeno,Roger	LA	4	1	21.0	7	0	0	0	1.000	3.00
Cianfrocco,Archi	SD	2	0	3.0	1	0	0	0	1.000	3.00
Clark,Dave	ChN	1	0	1.0	0	0	0	0	.000	.00
Coomer,Ron	Min	7	7	55.0	17	2	1	2	.950	3.11
Cruz,Jacob	SF	10	3	36.2	12	2	1	1	.933	3.44
Cummings,Midre	Pit	11	8	75.2	18	0	0	0	1.000	2.14
Cummings,Midre	Phi	2	0	2.0	0	0	0	0	.000	.00
Curtis,Chad	Cle	4	1	18.0	3	0	0	0	1.000	1.50
Curtis,Chad	NYA	5	5	40.0	9	0	1	0	.900	2.03
Damon,Johnny	KC	47	35	303.1	99	4	1	3	.990	3.06
Daulton,Darren	Phi	70	70	545.2	132	6	3	3	.979	2.28
Daulton,Darren	Fla	3	1	11.0	0	0	0	0	.000	.00
Davis,Eric	Bal	30	29	244.2	39	0	1	0	.975	1.43
Dellucci,David	Bal	6	4	42.0	15	2	0	0	1.000	3.64
Devereaux,Mike	Tex	24	18	154.0	38	0	0	0	1.000	2.22
Diaz,Alex	Tex	20	19	174.1	42	2	1	0	.978	2.27
Ducey,Rob	Sea	19	4	60.2	12	1	0	0	1.000	1.93
Dunn,Todd	Mil	7	2	20.1	6	0	1	0	.857	2.66
Echevarria,Angel	Col	3	1	10.0	2	0	0	0	1.000	1.80
Eisenreich,Jim	Fla	13	10	89.2	14	1	0	1	1.000	1.51
Encarnacion,Juan	Det	10	9	83.0	21	0	0	0	1.000	2.28
Everett,Carl	NYN	65	42	399.2	103	4	3	1	.973	2.41
Floyd,Cliff	Fla	6	4	35.0	7	2	1	1	.900	2.31
Fox,Andy	NYA	2	0	10.0	2	1	1	0	.750	2.70
Franklin,Micah	StL	9	6	52.0	11	0	0	0	1.000	1.90
Frye,Jeff	Bos	3	2	15.1	4	0	0	0	1.000	2.35
Garcia,Karim	LA	2	0	4.0	0	0	0	0	.000	.00
Giles,BrianS.	Cle	25	11	114.0	23	2	1	0	.962	1.97
Glanville,Doug	ChN	1	0	3.0	2	0	0	0	1.000	6.00
Gonzalez,Juan	Tex	64	64	555.2	127	6	4	1	.971	2.15
Goodwin,Curtis	Cin	1	1	5.0	3	0	0	0	1.000	5.40
Green,Shawn	Tor	46	44	393.2	89	6	2	2	.979	2.17
Greene,Willie	Cin	33	29	239.2	71	1	1	1	.986	2.70
Greer,Rusty	Tex	1	1	6.0	0	0	0	0	.000	.00
Gregg,Tommy	Atl	1	0	2.0	0	0	0	0	.000	.00
Grieve,Ben	Oak	24	22	208.1	39	1	0	1	1.000	1.73
Hall,Joe	Det	1	1	7.0	1	0	0	0	1.000	1.29
Halter,Shane	KC	17	4	55.2	15	0	0	0	1.000	2.43
Hammonds,Jeffr.	Bal	54	40	375.0	91	1	2	0	.979	2.21
Harris,Lenny	Cin	17	9	90.1	14	1	0	0	1.000	1.49
Helton,Todd	Col	2	1	16.0	2	0	0	0	1.000	1.13
Henderson,Rickey	SD	8	8	63.2	11	0	2	0	.846	1.55
Hidalgo,Richard	Hou	1	0	1.0	0	0	0	0	.000	.00
Higginson,Bob	Det	57	51	435.1	91	3	3	0	.969	1.94
Hocking,Denny	Min	12	7	60.0	20	1	0	1	1.000	3.15
Hollandsworth,To.	LA	4	2	18.0	2	0	0	0	1.000	1.00
Howard,David	KC	17	3	63.0	14	3	0	0	1.000	2.43
Howard,Thomas	Hou	18	12	108.2	17	0	0	0	1.000	1.41
Hudler,Rex	Phi	8	3	23.0	5	0	0	0	1.000	1.96
Hurst,Jimmy	Det	10	4	46.0	10	0	0	0	1.000	1.96
Huskey,Butch	NYN	72	68	537.1	131	2	3	1	.978	2.23
Huson,Jeff	Mil	1	0	1.0	1	0	0	0	1.000	9.00
Ibanez,Raul	Sea	6	4	41.0	6	0	0	0	1.000	1.32
Incaviglia,Pete	Bal	14	9	79.0	18	0	1	0	.947	2.05
Jackson,Darrin	Mil	3	3	20.0	4	0	0	0	1.000	1.80
Javier,Stan	SF	95	60	580.0	154	1	3	1	.981	2.41
Jones,Andruw	Atl	95	55	553.2	148	7	5	1	.969	2.52

Right Fielders - The Rest

Player	Tm	G	GS	Inn	PO	A	E	DP	Pct.	Rng
Jones,Chipper	Atl	3	2	18.0	3	0	0	0	1.000	1.50
Jones,Chris	SD	25	4	84.0	28	0	0	0	1.000	3.00
Jordan,Brian	StL	30	24	210.0	52	2	0	0	1.000	2.31
Justice,David	Cle	5	3	27.0	5	1	0	0	1.000	2.00
Kelly,Mike	Cin	31	14	147.0	52	2	2	0	.964	3.31
Kelly,Roberto	Min	57	50	433.1	99	1	0	0	1.000	2.08
Kieschnick,Brooks	ChN	1	1	8.0	3	0	0	0	1.000	3.38
Kirby,Wayne	LA	2	1	9.0	5	0	0	0	1.000	5.00
Latham,Chris	Min	3	0	9.0	1	0	0	0	1.000	1.00
Lawton,Matt	Min	67	59	522.1	129	4	2	1	.985	2.29
Lennon,Patrick	Oak	12	8	66.1	11	0	0	0	1.000	1.49
Lesher,Brian	Oak	3	3	21.0	5	1	0	1	1.000	2.57
Lewis,Darren	LA	1	0	3.0	0	0	0	0	.000	.00
Listach,Pat	Hou	1	0	1.2	0	0	0	0	.000	.00
Livingstone,Scott	StL	1	0	1.0	0	0	0	0	.000	.00
Long,Ryan	KC	4	2	20.0	6	0	0	0	1.000	2.70
Mabry,John	StL	71	61	527.1	96	8	0	1	1.000	1.77
Martinez,Dave	ChA	75	58	507.1	125	3	1	2	.992	2.27
Mashore,Damon	Oak	6	1	19.0	4	0	0	0	1.000	1.89
May,Derrick	Phi	49	26	262.2	57	3	3	1	.952	2.06
McGee,Willie	StL	53	29	297.2	58	4	1	1	.984	1.87
McGuire,Ryan	Mon	22	17	176.2	40	3	2	1	.956	2.19
McMillon,Billy	Phi	2	2	19.0	4	0	0	0	1.000	1.89
Mejia,Roberto	StL	1	1	6.0	0	0	0	0	.000	.00
Mieske,Matt	Mil	52	43	376.2	88	5	3	0	.969	2.22
Montgomery,Ray	Hou	15	13	109.2	19	2	0	1	1.000	1.72
Mordecai,Mike	Atl	1	0	1.0	0	0	0	0	.000	.00
Morman,Russ	Fla	2	1	7.0	0	1	0	0	1.000	1.29
Mouton,James	Hou	14	7	84.0	17	0	0	0	1.000	1.82
Mouton,Lyle	ChA	55	51	413.2	110	1	3	0	.974	2.41
Myers,Rod	KC	10	7	69.0	15	1	0	0	1.000	2.09
Newson,Warren	Tex	44	23	227.2	63	0	3	0	.955	2.49
Nunnally,Jon	KC	8	7	58.0	11	0	0	0	1.000	1.71
Nunnally,Jon	Cin	11	9	79.2	22	1	0	1	1.000	2.60
Obando,Sherman	Mon	14	6	51.0	11	0	0	0	1.000	1.94
Ochoa,Alex	NYN	84	51	513.0	99	7	2	1	.981	1.86
Ordonez,Magglio	ChA	19	17	154.0	43	1	0	0	1.000	2.57
Orsulak,Joe	Mon	26	14	143.0	23	2	0	0	1.000	1.57
Otero,Ricky	Phi	1	0	1.0	0	0	0	0	.000	.00
Owens,Eric	Cin	1	1	8.0	1	0	0	0	1.000	1.13
Palmeiro,Orlando	Ana	4	3	23.0	7	0	1	0	.875	2.74
Pemberton,Rudy	Bos	23	18	155.1	34	2	2	1	.947	2.09
Perez,Eduardo	Cin	1	0	2.0	0	0	0	0	.000	.00
Perez,Robert	Tor	9	4	46.0	16	0	0	0	1.000	3.13
Phillips,J.R.	Hou	3	1	10.1	3	0	0	0	1.000	2.61
Phillips,Tony	ChA	28	25	218.2	67	3	2	1	.972	2.88
Phillips,Tony	Ana	3	3	27.0	6	0	0	0	1.000	2.00
Plantier,Phil	StL	23	23	177.2	34	0	1	0	.971	1.72
Pose,Scott	NYA	17	2	53.1	10	0	0	0	1.000	1.69
Powell,Dante	SF	2	0	3.0	1	0	0	0	1.000	3.00
Pride,Curtis	Det	3	1	9.0	4	0	0	0	1.000	4.00
Pulliam,Harvey	Col	10	4	46.1	8	2	1	0	.909	1.94
Ramos,Ken	Hou	1	0	1.0	0	0	0	0	.000	.00
Reboulet,Jeff	Bal	1	1	9.0	2	0	0	0	1.000	2.00
Rivera,Ruben	SD	4	1	14.0	6	0	0	0	1.000	3.86
Robertson,Mike	Phi	1	1	8.0	0	0	0	0	.000	.00
Rodriguez,Henry	Mon	1	0	1.0	1	0	0	0	1.000	9.00
Sagmoen,Marc	Tex	16	10	97.0	24	0	0	0	1.000	2.23

Right Fielders - The Rest

Player	Tm	G	GS	Inn	PO	A	E	DP	Pct.	Rng
Samuel,Juan	Tor	2	1	9.0	3	0	0	0	1.000	3.00
Santangelo,F.P.	Mon	51	41	354.1	79	3	0	1	1.000	2.08
Sheaffer,Danny	StL	9	3	34.0	4	0	0	0	1.000	1.06
Shumpert,Terry	SD	1	0	1.0	0	0	0	0	.000	.00
Sierra,Ruben	Cin	12	12	100.2	23	1	0	0	1.000	2.15
Sierra,Ruben	Tor	2	1	11.0	1	0	0	0	1.000	0.82
Simms,Mike	Tex	17	9	77.0	22	0	1	0	.957	2.57
Smith,Mark	Pit	22	15	136.2	27	2	0	0	1.000	1.91
Stairs,Matt	Oak	63	44	418.0	85	4	1	0	.989	1.92
Stevens,Lee	Tex	19	18	138.0	27	0	0	0	1.000	1.76
Sweeney,Mark	StL	15	5	66.0	17	0	0	0	1.000	2.32
Sweeney,Mark	SD	13	4	56.0	7	0	0	0	1.000	1.13
Tarasco,Tony	Bal	68	35	356.0	86	4	1	2	.989	2.28
Tartabull,Danny	Phi	3	3	21.0	2	0	0	0	1.000	0.86
Taubensee,Eddie	Cin	5	3	23.2	5	0	0	0	1.000	1.90
Tavarez,Jesus	Bos	4	4	34.0	9	0	0	0	1.000	2.38
Thurman,Gary	NYN	1	0	0.1	0	0	0	0	.000	.00
Tinsley,Lee	Sea	2	0	5.0	2	0	0	0	1.000	3.60
Tomberlin,Andy	NYN	1	1	8.0	2	0	0	0	1.000	2.25
Trammell,Bubba	Det	15	12	113.0	23	1	0	0	1.000	1.91
Turner,Chris	Ana	1	0	5.0	1	0	0	0	1.000	1.80
Unroe,Tim	Mil	1	0	2.0	1	0	0	0	1.000	4.50
VanderWal,John	Col	8	3	35.0	10	0	1	0	.909	2.57
Vitiello,Joe	KC	16	16	100.0	31	0	0	0	1.000	2.79
Voigt,Jack	Mil	5	2	17.0	3	0	0	0	1.000	1.59
Walton,Jerome	Bal	11	4	37.0	14	0	0	0	1.000	3.41
Ward,Turner	Pit	23	6	82.0	14	0	0	0	1.000	1.54
Wehner,John	Fla	19	2	51.2	9	0	0	0	1.000	1.57
Whiten,Mark	NYA	16	10	101.1	26	1	4	0	.871	2.40
Young,Dmitri	StL	10	10	84.0	23	2	2	0	.926	2.68
Young,Ernie	Oak	12	6	70.2	13	0	1	0	.929	1.66
Young,Kevin	Pit	1	0	0.2	0	0	0	0	.000	.00

Catchers - Regulars

Player	Tm	G	GS	Inn	PO	A	E	DP	PB	Pct.
Johnson,Charles	Fla	123	123	1076.2	902	68	0	16	1	1.000
Hoiles,Chris	Bal	87	85	729.2	602	28	0	4	3	1.000
Santiago,Benito	Tor	95	93	819.1	620	39	2	10	7	.997
Mayne,Brent	Oak	83	73	640.2	419	33	2	7	1	.996
Webster,Lenny	Bal	97	73	676.1	532	35	3	5	4	.995
Wilson,Dan	Sea	144	136	1202.0	1050	72	6	14	1	.995
Girardi,Joe	NYA	111	109	979.1	829	54	5	12	11	.994
Manwaring,Kirt	Col	100	95	829.2	488	39	3	8	3	.994
Fletcher,Darrin	Mon	83	79	685.2	607	24	4	5	4	.994
Matheny,Mike	Mil	121	112	929.2	697	57	5	8	7	.993
Lopez,Javy	Atl	117	107	951.0	791	57	6	9	9	.993
Steinbach,Terry	Min	116	112	990.0	654	52	5	4	9	.993
Kreuter,Chad	TOT	80	69	630.1	488	32	4	2	4	.992
Rodriguez,Ivan	Tex	143	139	1201.0	822	74	7	11	3	.992
Ausmus,Brad	Hou	129	113	1032.2	807	74	7	16	6	.992
Johnson,Brian	TOT	98	86	773.2	561	33	5	8	2	.992
Macfarlane,Mike	KC	81	75	664.2	439	19	4	3	9	.991
Difelice,Mike	StL	91	81	690.0	586	65	6	11	12	.991
Oliver,Joe	Cin	106	93	837.0	667	52	7	10	4	.990
Servais,Scott	ChN	118	110	965.2	735	72	8	11	8	.990
Kendall,Jason	Pit	142	139	1218.0	953	101	11	20	7	.990
Lieberthal,Mike	Phi	129	119	1059.0	933	73	12	9	12	.988
Fabregas,Jorge	TOT	113	94	830.2	600	51	8	9	8	.988
Reed,Jeff	Col	78	67	603.0	428	36	6	8	2	.987
Flaherty,John	SD	124	119	1030.1	753	63	11	14	6	.987
Hundley,Todd	NYN	122	116	1006.1	677	55	10	6	7	.987
Piazza,Mike	LA	140	139	1199.1	1044	74	16	11	10	.986
Alomar,Sandy	Cle	119	115	1005.0	742	41	12	11	3	.985
Casanova,Raul	Det	92	83	725.1	543	38	9	7	8	.985
Hatteberg,Scott	Bos	106	93	839.1	574	45	11	13	17	.983
Widger,Chris	Mon	85	78	694.1	516	40	11	2	8	.981
Average	----	108	100	887.1	679	51	6	9	6	.991

Catchers - The Rest

Player	Tm	G	GS	Inn	PO	A	E	DP	PB	Pct.
Berryhill,Damon	SF	51	44	367.2	288	24	3	2	4	.990
Bieser,Steve	NYN	2	0	3.0	2	0	0	0	0	1.000
Borders,Pat	Cle	53	45	399.2	312	19	0	4	5	1.000
Brown,KevinL.	Tex	4	1	13.0	9	0	1	0	0	.900
Castillo,Alberto	NYN	34	18	178.0	142	8	2	0	2	.987
Chavez,Raul	Mon	13	5	67.0	47	7	0	2	1	1.000
Diaz,Einar	Cle	5	1	21.0	18	3	1	0	0	.955
Encarnacion,Ang.	Ana	11	4	45.2	43	4	3	0	0	.940
Estalella,Bobby	Phi	11	8	72.1	49	3	0	0	1	1.000
Eusebio,Tony	Hou	43	42	364.1	297	16	4	4	0	.987
Fabregas,Jorge	Ana	21	11	104.0	81	5	1	1	0	.989
Fabregas,Jorge	ChA	92	83	726.2	519	46	7	8	8	.988
Fasano,Sal	KC	12	10	90.0	53	3	1	2	2	.982
Figga,Mike	NYA	1	1	9.0	6	0	0	0	0	1.000
Fordyce,Brook	Cin	30	23	204.2	162	12	3	1	2	.983
Greene,Charlie	Bal	4	0	5.0	4	0	0	0	0	1.000
Greene,Todd	Ana	26	25	215.1	153	7	0	2	5	1.000
Haselman,Bill	Bos	66	60	529.0	372	40	7	5	17	.983
Hernandez,Carlos	SD	44	32	294.2	234	25	3	3	1	.989
Houston,Tyler	ChN	41	37	321.1	263	16	4	1	6	.986
Hubbard,Mike	ChN	20	15	141.2	120	8	1	0	2	.992

Catchers - The Rest

Player	Tm	G	GS	Inn	PO	A	E	DP	PB	Pct.
Jensen,Marcus	SF	28	19	181.0	106	10	2	1	2	.983
Jensen,Marcus	Det	8	3	34.0	26	1	1	0	0	.964
Johnson,Brian	Det	43	38	340.1	217	9	3	3	0	.987
Johnson,Brian	SF	55	48	433.1	344	24	2	5	2	.995
Karkovice,Ron	ChA	51	45	379.1	261	13	1	1	2	.996
Knorr,Randy	Hou	3	1	10.0	12	1	0	0	0	1.000
Kreuter,Chad	ChA	13	8	79.0	57	3	1	0	0	.984
Kreuter,Chad	Ana	67	61	551.1	431	29	3	2	4	.994
Laker,Tim	Bal	7	4	39.0	28	0	1	0	0	.966
Lampkin,Tom	StL	86	56	549.2	413	35	5	6	6	.989
Levis,Jesse	Mil	78	40	399.2	296	19	2	1	4	.994
Leyritz,Jim	Ana	58	55	489.2	361	39	0	5	9	1.000
Leyritz,Jim	Tex	11	10	87.0	56	5	1	1	1	.984
Machado,Robert	ChA	10	4	46.0	34	3	0	1	1	1.000
Marrero,Eli	StL	17	13	113.1	81	13	3	2	0	.969
Martinez,Sandy	Tor	3	1	12.2	12	2	1	0	0	.933
Marzano,John	Sea	37	24	229.2	191	13	5	4	2	.976
McKeel,Walt	Bos	4	0	5.1	4	0	0	0	0	1.000
Mercedes,Henry	Tex	23	12	128.2	78	4	1	2	2	.988
Miller,Damian	Min	20	15	135.1	85	3	0	1	3	1.000
Mirabelli,Doug	SF	6	1	18.0	16	0	0	0	0	1.000
Molina,Izzy	Oak	48	34	306.2	218	17	2	1	3	.992
Mosquera,Julio	Tor	3	2	18.1	11	1	0	0	0	1.000
Myers,Greg	Min	38	34	293.2	196	11	3	2	2	.986
Myers,Greg	Atl	2	1	9.0	11	2	0	0	0	1.000
Natal,Bob	Fla	4	1	14.0	16	0	0	0	0	1.000
Nevin,Phil	Det	1	0	1.1	1	0	0	0	0	1.000
O'Brien,Charlie	Tor	69	66	592.1	543	39	3	8	4	.995
Osik,Keith	Pit	32	23	218.0	160	13	2	3	4	.989
Pagnozzi,Tom	StL	13	11	83.0	57	2	0	0	0	1.000
Parent,Mark	Phi	38	35	289.0	225	21	1	2	3	.996
Pena,Tony	ChA	30	21	191.1	143	8	0	2	5	1.000
Pena,Tony	Hou	8	6	52.0	48	6	0	1	0	1.000
Perez,Eddie	Atl	64	52	469.2	392	22	5	1	2	.988
Posada,Jorge	NYA	60	52	479.1	367	24	3	3	8	.992
Pratt,Todd	NYN	36	28	272.0	187	21	2	3	1	.990
Prince,Tom	LA	45	23	260.0	221	25	1	5	1	.996
Romero,Mandy	SD	19	9	100.2	96	8	0	0	1	1.000
Rosario,Mel	Bal	4	0	11.0	7	0	1	0	0	.875
Sheaffer,Danny	StL	9	1	19.2	18	1	0	0	0	1.000
Slaught,Don	SD	6	2	24.1	15	3	0	0	0	1.000
Spehr,Tim	KC	17	12	94.0	78	7	0	1	0	1.000
Spehr,Tim	Atl	7	2	36.0	32	4	2	0	0	.947
Stanley,Mike	Bos	15	9	77.0	53	3	1	0	2	.982
Stewart,Andy	KC	4	1	14.2	10	1	0	0	0	1.000
Stinnett,Kelly	Mil	25	9	98.0	81	5	1	1	0	.989
Sweeney,Mike	KC	76	63	579.2	425	30	3	13	3	.993
Taubensee,Eddie	Cin	64	46	407.1	359	24	5	6	7	.987
Turner,Chris	Ana	8	6	48.2	26	2	0	0	1	1.000
Valentin,Javier	Min	4	1	15.0	11	2	0	0	0	1.000
Varitek,Jason	Bos	1	0	1.0	1	0	0	0	0	1.000
Walbeck,Matt	Det	44	38	344.2	240	15	3	2	3	.988
Wilkins,Rick	SF	57	50	446.0	327	36	5	6	1	.986
Wilkins,Rick	Sea	3	2	16.0	9	1	0	0	0	1.000
Williams,George	Oak	67	55	498.0	336	27	6	4	1	.984
Zaun,Gregg	Fla	50	38	356.0	327	21	8	1	6	.978

Catchers - Regulars - Special

Player	Tm	G	GS	Inn	SBA	CS	PCS	CS%	ER	CERA
Lopez,Javy	Atl	117	107	951.0	105	33	4	.31	331	3.13
Girardi,Joe	NYA	111	109	979.1	108	37	17	.34	374	3.44
Piazza,Mike	LA	140	139	1199.1	155	43	9	.28	466	3.50
Webster,Lenny	Bal	97	73	676.1	97	29	6	.30	274	3.65
Difelice,Mike	StL	91	81	690.0	96	34	4	.35	282	3.68
Ausmus,Brad	Hou	129	113	1032.2	93	46	8	.49	434	3.78
Santiago,Benito	Tor	95	93	819.1	79	31	5	.39	350	3.84
Hundley,Todd	NYN	122	116	1006.1	104	25	4	.24	442	3.95
Johnson,Charles	Fla	123	123	1076.2	118	56	6	.47	473	3.95
Oliver,Joe	Cin	106	93	837.0	96	31	6	.32	372	4.00
Fletcher,Darrin	Mon	83	79	685.2	87	16	4	.18	312	4.10
Widger,Chris	Mon	85	78	694.1	139	23	5	.17	320	4.15
Hoiles,Chris	Bal	87	85	729.2	94	20	7	.21	337	4.16
Kreuter,Chad	TOT	80	69	630.1	62	26	11	.42	294	4.20
Casanova,Raul	Det	92	83	725.1	100	28	8	.28	348	4.32
Kendall,Jason	Pit	142	139	1218.0	151	56	5	.37	585	4.32
Servais,Scott	ChN	118	110	965.2	138	46	4	.33	470	4.38
Matheny,Mike	Mil	121	112	929.2	106	37	3	.35	453	4.39
Macfarlane,Mike	KC	81	75	664.2	37	11	1	.30	331	4.48
Johnson,Brian	TOT	98	86	773.2	87	26	6	.30	394	4.58
Alomar,Sandy	Cle	119	115	1005.0	123	39	6	.32	523	4.68
Fabregas,Jorge	TOT	113	94	830.2	98	35	6	.36	436	4.72
Wilson,Dan	Sea	144	136	1202.0	130	56	10	.43	632	4.73
Hatteberg,Scott	Bos	106	93	839.1	123	28	6	.23	445	4.77
Rodriguez,Ivan	Tex	143	139	1201.0	84	47	7	.56	637	4.77
Lieberthal,Mike	Phi	129	119	1059.0	115	40	5	.35	574	4.88
Steinbach,Terry	Min	116	112	990.0	88	29	8	.33	546	4.96
Flaherty,John	SD	124	119	1030.1	175	50	8	.29	575	5.02
Manwaring,Kirt	Col	100	95	829.2	111	28	3	.25	480	5.21
Reed,Jeff	Col	78	67	603.0	73	26	3	.36	356	5.31
Mayne,Brent	Oak	83	73	640.2	80	23	9	.29	396	5.56
Average	—	108	100	887.1	104	34	6	.33	427	4.33

Catchers - The Rest - Special

Player	Tm	G	GS	Inn	SBA	CS	PCS	CS%	ER	CERA
Berryhill,Damon	SF	51	44	367.2	49	17	7	.35	185	4.53
Bieser,Steve	NYN	2	0	3.0	0	0	0	0	0	0.00
Borders,Pat	Cle	53	45	399.2	50	14	1	.28	215	4.84
Brown,KevinL.	Tex	4	1	13.0	1	0	0	0	2	1.38
Castillo,Alberto	NYN	34	18	178.0	13	3	0	.23	85	4.30
Chavez,Raul	Mon	13	5	67.0	8	3	0	.38	33	4.43
Diaz,Einar	Cle	5	1	21.0	8	2	0	.25	11	4.71
Encarnacion,Ang.	Ana	11	4	45.2	8	1	0	.13	29	5.72
Estalella,Bobby	Phi	11	8	72.1	4	1	0	.25	28	3.48
Eusebio,Tony	Hou	43	42	364.1	45	9	0	.20	138	3.41
Fabregas,Jorge	Ana	21	11	104.0	6	2	1	.33	68	5.88
Fabregas,Jorge	ChA	92	83	726.2	92	33	5	.36	368	4.56
Fasano,Sal	KC	12	10	90.0	4	3	0	.75	39	3.90
Figga,Mike	NYA	1	1	9.0	0	0	0	0	3	3.00
Fordyce,Brook	Cin	30	23	204.2	35	6	1	.17	118	5.19
Greene,Charlie	Bal	4	0	5.0	0	0	0	0	3	5.40
Greene,Todd	Ana	26	25	215.1	21	6	2	.29	116	4.85
Haselman,Bill	Bos	66	60	529.0	85	22	2	.26	284	4.83
Hernandez,Carl.	SD	44	32	294.2	54	23	6	.43	159	4.86
Houston,Tyler	ChN	41	37	321.1	49	9	2	.18	172	4.82
Hubbard,Mike	ChN	20	15	141.2	18	4	0	.22	63	4.00

Catchers - The Rest - Special

Player	Tm	G	GS	Inn	SBA	CS	PCS	CS%	ER	CERA
Jensen,Marcus	SF	28	19	181.0	24	10	2	.42	95	4.72
Jensen,Marcus	Det	8	3	34.0	0	0	0	0	12	3.18
Johnson,Brian	Det	43	38	340.1	39	8	3	.21	166	4.39
Johnson,Brian	SF	55	48	433.1	48	18	3	.38	228	4.74
Karkovice,Ron	ChA	51	45	379.1	34	10	4	.29	214	5.08
Knorr,Randy	Hou	3	1	10.0	2	1	0	.50	0	0.00
Kreuter,Chad	ChA	13	8	79.0	7	2	1	.29	37	4.22
Kreuter,Chad	Ana	67	61	551.1	55	24	10	.44	257	4.20
Laker,Tim	Bal	7	4	39.0	7	1	1	.14	19	4.38
Lampkin,Tom	StL	86	56	549.2	77	22	4	.29	220	3.60
Levis,Jesse	Mil	78	40	399.2	46	12	0	.26	176	3.96
Leyritz,Jim	Ana	58	55	489.2	68	31	6	.46	235	4.32
Leyritz,Jim	Tex	11	10	87.0	17	6	1	.35	44	4.55
Machado,Robert	ChA	10	4	46.0	10	4	1	.40	27	5.28
Marrero,Eli	StL	17	13	113.1	16	8	2	.50	63	5.00
Martinez,Sandy	Tor	3	1	12.2	4	1	'	.25	6	4.26
Marzano,John	Sea	37	24	229.2	30	9	2	.30	131	5.13
McKeel,Walt	Bos	4	0	5.1	0	0	0	0	1	1.69
Mercedes,Henry	Tex	23	12	128.2	12	1	0	.08	62	4.34
Miller,Damian	Min	20	15	135.1	7	3	2	.43	61	4.06
Mirabelli,Doug	SF	6	1	18.0	1	0	0	0	9	4.50
Molina,Izzy	Oak	48	34	306.2	43	10	0	.23	166	4.87
Mosquera,Julio	Tor	3	2	18.1	2	1	0	.50	13	6.38
Myers,Greg	Min	38	34	293.2	33	12	4	.36	183	5.61
Myers,Greg	Atl	2	1	9.0	3	1	0	.33	5	5.00
Natal,Bob	Fla	4	1	14.0	0	0	0	0	9	5.79
Nevin,Phil	Det	1	0	1.1	0	0	0	0	11	74.25
O'Brien,Charlie	Tor	69	66	592.1	56	31	4	.55	259	3.94
Osik,Keith	Pit	32	23	218.0	24	10	2	.42	98	4.05
Pagnozzi,Tom	StL	13	11	83.0	7	2	0	.29	52	5.64
Parent,Mark	Phi	38	35	289.0	45	16	2	.36	163	5.08
Pena,Tony	ChA	30	21	191.1	28	3	1	.11	102	4.80
Pena,Tony	Hou	8	6	52.0	9	1	0	.11	22	3.81
Perez,Eddie	Atl	64	52	469.2	64	16	1	.25	169	3.24
Posada,Jorge	NYA	60	52	479.1	50	10	1	.20	249	4.68
Pratt,Todd	NYN	36	28	272.0	33	16	2	.48	113	3.74
Prince,Tom	LA	45	23	260.0	21	15	0	.71	121	4.19
Romero,Mandy	SD	19	9	100.2	15	2	0	.13	51	4.56
Rosario,Mel	Bal	4	0	11.0	1	0	0	0	2	1.64
Sheaffer,Danny	StL	9	1	19.2	4	0	0	0	10	4.58
Slaught,Don	SD	6	2	24.1	2	0	0	0	18	6.66
Spehr,Tim	KC	17	12	94.0	16	4	1	.25	70	6.70
Spehr,Tim	Atl	7	2	36.0	6	4	0	.67	13	3.25
Stanley,Mike	Bos	15	9	77.0	16	3	0	.19	52	6.08
Stewart,Andy	KC	4	1	14.2	2	1	0	.50	5	3.07
Stinnett,Kelly	Mil	25	9	98.0	6	3	1	.50	40	3.67
Sweeney,Mike	KC	76	63	579.2	55	23	3	.42	308	4.78
Taubensee,Edd.	Cin	64	46	407.1	56	11	4	.20	220	4.86
Turner,Chris	Ana	8	6	48.2	7	0	0	0	25	4.62
Valentin,Javier	Min	4	1	15.0	3	2	0	.67	6	3.60
Varitek,Jason	Bos	1	0	1.0	0	0	0	0	0	0.00
Walbeck,Matt	Det	44	38	344.2	39	12	3	.31	195	5.09
Wilkins,Rick	SF	57	50	446.0	59	28	7	.47	189	3.81
Wilkins,Rick	Sea	3	2	16.0	5	1	0	.20	6	3.38
Williams,George	Oak	67	55	498.0	56	15	4	.27	318	5.75
Zaun,Gregg	Fla	50	38	356.0	47	14	2	.30	133	3.36

Pitchers Hitting & Fielding, and Hitters Pitching

What do former hurlers like Wes Ferrell, Jack Stivetts, Erv Brame, Doc Crandall and Don Newcombe have in common? Well, besides knowing a thing or two about tossing a baseball across a little white plate, they were extremely handy with a bat in their hands. All five hit .270 or better for their careers, and Ferrell (38) and Stivetts (35) cracked 73 homers between them. These guys were masters at helping their own cause.

Of course, pitchers at the plate took on a whole new meaning in 1997 with the advent of interleague play. Suddenly, lifelong ALers such as Mike Mussina, Kevin Appier, Pat Hentgen and Chuck Finley found themselves on the other side of a fastball. Which ALers fared best, and which ones won't be clamoring to get rid of the DH anytime soon? You'll find your answer in the following pages.

By the way, if your looking for a few modern-day Ferrells, Crandalls and Stivetts, you won't—their consistant two-way exploits are a thing of the past. That said, let's give Todd Stottlemyre, Jim Bullinger, Tom Glavine, Omar Olivares, etc. their due.

Pitchers Hitting

	1997 Hitting														Career Hitting													
Pitcher,Team	Avg	OBP	SLG	AB	H	2B	3B	HR	R	RBI	BB	SO	SH	SB-CS	Avg	OBP	SLG	AB	H	2B	3B	HR	R	RBI	BB	SO	SH	SB-CS
Acevedo,Juan,NYN	.000	.000	.000	6	0	0	0	0	0	0	0	5	1	0-0	.042	.080	.042	24	1	0	0	0	0	0	1	11	1	0-0
Adams,Terry,ChN	.000	.000	.000	2	0	0	0	0	0	0	0	1	0	0-0	.000	.111	.000	8	0	0	0	0	0	0	1	4	0	0-0
Adamson,Joel,Mil	.000	.000	.000	3	0	0	0	0	0	0	0	0	0	0-0	.000	.000	.000	3	0	0	0	0	0	0	0	0	0	0-0
Aguilera,Rick,Min	.000	.000	.000	0	0	0	0	0	0	0	0	0	0	0-0	.203	.236	.290	138	28	3	0	3	12	11	6	37	16	0-0
Alfonseca,Antonio,Fla	.000	.000	.000	3	0	0	0	0	0	0	0	3	0	0-0	.000	.000	.000	3	0	0	0	0	0	0	0	3	0	0-0
Alvarez,Wil.,ChA-SF	.115	.179	.115	26	3	0	0	0	1	1	2	7	1	0-0	.115	.179	.115	26	3	0	0	0	1	1	2	7	1	0-0
Appier,Kevin,KC	.000	.000	.000	6	0	0	0	0	0	0	0	5	0	0-0	.000	.000	.000	6	0	0	0	0	0	0	0	5	0	0-0
Arocha,Rene,SF	.000	.000	.000	1	0	0	0	0	0	0	0	1	0	0-0	.101	.139	.130	69	7	2	0	0	3	3	3	31	10	0-0
Ashby,Andy,SD	.067	.097	.083	60	4	1	0	0	1	1	2	24	7	0-0	.145	.164	.179	262	38	9	0	0	14	11	6	105	47	1-0
Assenmacher,Pa.,Cle	.000	.000	.000	0	0	0	0	0	0	0	0	0	0	0-0	.083	.195	.111	36	3	1	0	0	3	0	5	12	7	0-0
Astacio,Pedro,LA-Col	.130	.130	.148	54	7	1	0	0	2	1	0	24	11	0-0	.115	.121	.122	279	32	2	0	0	11	7	2	123	37	0-1
Avery,Steve,Bos	.000	.000	.000	1	0	0	0	0	1	0	0	0	0	0-0	.178	.200	.262	409	73	14	4	4	31	31	12	124	39	1-1
Ayala,Bobby,Sea	.000	.000	.000	0	0	0	0	0	0	0	0	0	0	0-0	.067	.067	.100	30	2	1	0	0	2	1	0	13	3	0-1
Aybar,Manny,StL	.143	.143	.143	21	3	0	0	0	0	1	0	9	0	0-0	.143	.143	.143	21	3	0	0	0	0	1	0	9	0	0-0
Bailes,Scott,Tex	.000	.000	.000	0	0	0	0	0	0	0	0	0	0	0-0	.000	.000	.000	0	0	0	0	0	0	0	0	0	0	0-0
Bailey,Cory,SF	1.000	1.000	1.000	1	1	0	0	0	0	0	0	0	0	0-0	.500	.750	.500	2	1	0	0	0	2	0	2	0	1	0-0
Bailey,Roger,Col	.210	.234	.226	62	13	1	0	0	9	2	2	15	5	0-0	.206	.252	.268	97	20	1	1	1	15	8	6	22	11	0-0
Baldwin,James,ChA	.000	.000	.000	3	0	0	0	0	0	0	0	2	1	0-0	.000	.000	.000	3	0	0	0	0	0	0	0	2	1	0-0
Barrios,Manuel,Hou	.000	.000	.000	0	0	0	0	0	0	0	0	0	0	0-0	.000	.000	.000	0	0	0	0	0	0	0	0	0	0	0-0
Batchelor,Ric.,StL-SD	.000	.000	.000	0	0	0	0	0	0	0	0	0	0	0-0	.000	.000	.000	2	0	0	0	0	0	0	0	1	0	0-0
Batista,Miguel,ChN	.000	.000	.000	8	0	0	0	0	0	0	0	5	0	0-0	.000	.000	.000	8	0	0	0	0	0	0	0	5	0	0-0
Bautista,Jose,Det-StL	.000	.000	.000	0	0	0	0	0	0	0	0	0	0	0-0	.100	.118	.100	50	5	0	0	0	2	1	1	17	4	0-0
Beck,Rod,SF	.000	.000	.000	0	0	0	0	0	0	0	0	0	0	0-0	.235	.235	.235	17	4	0	0	0	0	1	0	9	1	0-0
Beckett,Robbie,Col	.000	.000	.000	0	0	0	0	0	0	0	0	0	0	0-0	.000	.000	.000	0	0	0	0	0	0	0	0	0	0	0-0
Beech,Matt,Phi	.167	.167	.200	30	5	1	0	0	1	1	0	14	11	0-0	.136	.136	.159	44	6	1	0	0	2	2	0	18	11	0-0
Belcher,Tim,KC	.000	.000	.000	6	0	0	0	0	0	0	0	1	0	0-0	.122	.135	.159	378	46	8	0	2	18	25	2	143	41	0-1
Belinda,Stan,Cin	.333	.333	.333	3	1	0	0	0	0	0	0	1	0	0-0	.158	.238	.211	19	3	1	0	0	1	3	2	10	3	0-0
Beltran,Rigo,StL	.143	.143	.286	7	1	1	0	0	1	0	0	1	0	0-0	.143	.143	.286	7	1	1	0	0	1	0	0	1	0	0-0
Benes,Alan,StL	.173	.173	.212	52	9	2	0	0	1	3	0	16	2	0-0	.151	.165	.193	119	18	5	0	0	5	8	2	44	9	0-0
Benes,Andy,StL	.218	.246	.255	55	12	2	0	0	4	5	1	14	8	0-0	.139	.174	.191	502	70	14	0	4	29	35	18	219	65	0-0
Benitez,Armando,Bal	.000	.000	.000	0	0	0	0	0	0	0	0	0	0	0-0	.000	.000	.000	0	0	0	0	0	0	0	0	0	0	0-0
Bennett,Shayne,Mon	.000	.500	.000	1	0	0	0	0	0	0	1	0	0	0-0	.000	.500	.000	1	0	0	0	0	0	0	1	0	0	0-0
Bergman,Sean,SD	.231	.231	.308	13	3	1	0	0	2	0	0	7	3	0-0	.140	.140	.233	43	6	1	0	1	3	5	0	16	3	0-0
Bevil,Brian,KC	.000	.000	.000	0	0	0	0	0	0	0	0	0	0	0-0	.000	.000	.000	0	0	0	0	0	0	0	0	0	0	0-0
Bielecki,Mike,Atl	.000	.333	.000	2	0	0	0	0	0	0	1	1	0	0-0	.078	.122	.078	282	22	0	0	0	11	13	14	144	35	1-0
Blair,Willie,Det	.000	.000	.000	4	0	0	0	0	0	0	0	3	0	0-0	.056	.086	.067	90	5	1	0	0	3	5	3	59	8	0-0
Blazier,Ron,Phi	.400	.400	.400	5	2	0	0	0	0	0	0	1	1	0-0	.500	.500	.500	6	3	0	0	0	0	0	0	1	1	0-0
Bochtler,Doug,SD	.000	.000	.000	0	0	0	0	0	0	0	0	0	0	0-0	.000	.000	.000	2	0	0	0	0	0	0	0	0	0	0-0
Boehringer,Brian,NYA	.000	.000	.000	0	0	0	0	0	0	0	0	0	0	0-0	.000	.000	.000	0	0	0	0	0	0	0	0	0	0	0-0
Bohanon,Brian,NYN	.182	.176	.182	33	6	0	0	0	0	4	0	15	1	0-0	.182	.176	.182	33	6	0	0	0	0	4	0	15	1	0-0
Bones,Ricky,Cin-KC	.000	.000	.000	2	0	0	0	0	0	0	0	0	0	0-0	.067	.176	.067	15	1	0	0	0	1	1	2	5	4	0-0
Borland,To.,NYN-Bos	.000	.000	.000	0	0	0	0	0	0	0	0	0	1	0-0	.083	.077	.083	12	1	0	0	0	1	2	0	3	1	0-0
Borowski,Joe,Atl-NYA	.000	.000	.000	0	0	0	0	0	0	0	0	0	0	0-0	.000	.000	.000	2	0	0	0	0	0	0	0	2	1	0-0
Boskie,Shawn,Bal	.000	.000	.000	0	0	0	0	0	0	0	0	0	0	0-0	.184	.228	.270	141	26	5	2	1	9	8	8	42	9	0-0
Bottalico,Ricky,Phi	.000	.000	.000	1	0	0	0	0	0	0	0	1	0	0-0	.111	.111	.222	9	1	1	0	0	0	0	0	7	1	0-0
Bottenfield,Kent,ChN	.000	.000	.000	4	0	0	0	0	0	0	0	3	4	0-0	.231	.254	.231	65	15	0	0	0	3	3	1	22	9	1-0
Brandenburg,Ma.,Bos	.000	.000	.000	0	0	0	0	0	0	0	0	0	0	0-0	.000	.000	.000	0	0	0	0	0	0	0	0	0	0	0-0
Brantley,Jeff,Cin	.000	.000	.000	0	0	0	0	0	0	0	0	0	0	0-0	.118	.143	.132	68	8	1	0	0	5	5	2	23	10	0-0
Brewer,Billy,Oak-Phi	.000	.000	.000	1	0	0	0	0	0	0	0	1	0	0-0	.000	.000	.000	1	0	0	0	0	0	0	0	1	0	0-0
Brocail,Doug,Det	.000	.000	.000	0	0	0	0	0	0	0	0	0	0	0-0	.164	.164	.194	67	11	0	1	0	9	1	0	18	15	2-0
Brock,Chris,Atl	.100	.100	.100	10	1	0	0	0	0	1	0	2	0	0-0	.100	.100	.100	10	1	0	0	0	0	1	0	2	0	0-0
Brown,Kevin,Fla	.125	.182	.139	72	9	1	0	0	4	4	5	25	6	0-0	.122	.182	.135	148	18	2	0	0	5	7	11	53	10	0-0
Bruske,Jim,SD	.167	.167	.333	6	1	1	0	0	0	0	0	1	0	0-0	.167	.167	.333	6	1	1	0	0	0	0	0	1	0	0-0
Bullinger,Jim,Mon	.209	.209	.302	43	9	1	0	1	2	2	0	15	3	0-0	.188	.249	.315	165	31	9	0	4	14	19	13	57	20	1-0
Burba,Dave,Cin	.196	.245	.196	46	9	0	0	0	2	2	1	18	4	0-0	.141	.195	.184	163	23	1	0	2	8	10	9	70	17	0-0
Burke,John,Col	.158	.158	.158	19	3	0	0	0	1	0	0	6	2	0-0	.190	.190	.190	21	4	0	0	0	1	1	0	6	2	0-0
Burkett,John,Tex	.200	.200	.200	5	1	0	0	0	1	0	0	1	0	0-0	.090	.133	.101	424	38	5	0	0	17	14	20	179	47	0-0
Burrows,Terry,SD	.000	.000	.000	0	0	0	0	0	0	0	0	0	0	0-0	.000	.000	.000	0	0	0	0	0	0	0	0	0	0	0-0
Busby,Mike,StL	.500	.500	.500	4	2	0	0	0	0	0	0	2	0	0-0	.500	.500	.500	6	3	0	0	0	0	0	0	3	0	0-0
Byrd,Paul,Atl	.143	.143	.143	7	1	0	0	0	0	1	0	2	2	0-0	.200	.200	.200	10	2	0	0	0	0	1	0	2	2	0-0
Cabrera,Jose,Hou	.000	.000	.000	2	0	0	0	0	0	0	0	0	0	0-0	.000	.000	.000	2	0	0	0	0	0	0	0	0	0	0-0
Cadaret,Greg,Ana	.000	.000	.000	0	0	0	0	0	0	0	0	0	0	0-0	.000	.000	.000	2	0	0	0	0	0	0	0	1	0	0-0
Candiotti,Tom,LA	.094	.121	.094	32	3	0	0	0	0	2	1	10	9	0-0	.114	.137	.128	298	34	4	0	0	11	12	7	71	51	0-0
Carlson,Dan,SF	.000	.000	.000	3	0	0	0	0	0	0	0	0	0	0-0	.000	.000	.000	4	0	0	0	0	0	0	0	0	0	0-0
Carrara,Giovanni,Cin	.000	.000	.000	2	0	0	0	0	0	0	0	2	2	0-0	.000	.000	.000	9	0	0	0	0	1	0	0	3	2	0-0
Carrasco,Hec.,Cin-KC	.000	.000	.000	0	0	0	0	0	0	0	0	0	0	0-0	.056	.056	.056	18	1	0	0	0	0	0	0	12	0	0-0
Casian,Larry,ChN-KC	.000	.000	.000	1	0	0	0	0	0	0	0	1	0	0-0	.000	.000	.000	3	0	0	0	0	0	0	0	2	0	0-0
Castillo,Carlos,ChA	1.000	1.000	1.000	1	1	0	0	0	0	0	0	0	0	0-0	1.000	1.000	1.000	1	1	0	0	0	0	0	0	0	0	0-0
Castillo,Fr.,ChN-Col	.121	.133	.121	58	7	0	0	0	1	5	1	19	10	0-0	.110	.144	.110	326	36	0	0	0	7	13	13	106	40	0-1
Castillo,Tony,ChA	.000	.000	.000	1	0	0	0	0	0	0	0	0	0	0-0	.077	.143	.077	13	1	0	0	0	1	0	1	6	4	0-0
Cather,Mike,Atl	.000	.000	.000	1	0	0	0	0	0	0	0	0	0	0-0	.000	.000	.000	1	0	0	0	0	0	0	0	0	0	0-0
Charlton,Norm,Sea	.000	.000	.000	0	0	0	0	0	0	0	0	0	0	0-0	.093	.152	.116	86	8	2	0	0	6	1	3	50	10	0-0
Christiansen,Jason,Pit	.000	.000	.000	0	0	0	0	0	0	0	0	0	0	0-0	.000	.000	.000	5	0	0	0	0	0	0	0	5	1	0-0
Clark,Mark,NYN-ChN	.030	.086	.076	66	2	0	0	1	3	3	4	31	6	0-0	.056	.082	.079	178	10	1	0	1	6	6	5	77	21	0-0
Clark,Terry,Cle-Tex	1.000	1.000	1.000	1	1	0	0	0	0	0	0	0	0	0-0	.667	.667	.667	3	2	0	0	0	1	0	0	0	0	0-0

	1997 Hitting														Career Hitting													
Pitcher,Team	Avg	OBP	SLG	AB	H	2B	3B	HR	R	RBI	BB	SO	SH	SB-CS	Avg	OBP	SLG	AB	H	2B	3B	HR	R	RBI	BB	SO	SH	SB-CS
Clemens,Roger,Tor	.500	.667	1.000	2	1	1	0	0	1	0	1	0	0	0-0	.667	.750	1.000	3	2	1	0	0	1	0	1	0	0	0-0
Clontz,Brad,Atl	.000	.000	.000	1	0	0	0	0	0	0	0	1	0	0-0	.000	.286	.000	5	0	0	0	0	1	0	2	3	1	0-0
Cloude,Ken,Sea	.000	.000	.000	2	0	0	0	0	0	0	0	0	0	0-0	.000	.000	.000	2	0	0	0	0	0	0	0	0	0	0-0
Colon,Bartolo,Cle	.000	.000	.000	1	0	0	0	0	0	0	0	1	0	0-0	.000	.000	.000	1	0	0	0	0	0	0	0	1	0	0-0
Cone,David,NYA	.000	.000	.000	3	0	0	0	0	0	0	0	2	0	0-0	.153	.191	.173	398	61	8	0	0	26	20	16	88	36	0-1
Cook,Dennis,Fla	.556	.556	.889	9	5	0	0	1	2	2	0	0	0	0-0	.276	.296	.371	105	29	2	1	2	15	9	3	12	8	0-0
Cooke,Steve,Pit	.058	.058	.077	52	3	1	0	0	2	1	0	18	7	0-0	.136	.140	.160	169	23	4	0	0	8	7	0	47	20	0-0
Cordova,Francisco,Pit	.089	.150	.089	56	5	0	0	0	2	0	4	26	8	0-0	.097	.145	.097	72	7	0	0	0	3	2	4	33	10	0-0
Cormier,Rheal,Mon	.000	.000	.000	0	0	0	0	0	0	0	0	0	0	0-0	.185	.202	.217	184	34	4	1	0	14	12	3	43	28	0-0
Corsi,Jim,Bos	.000	.000	.000	0	0	0	0	0	0	0	0	0	0	0-0	.000	.000	.000	1	0	0	0	0	0	0	0	1	0	0-0
Crabtree,Tim,Tor	.000	.000	.000	0	0	0	0	0	0	0	0	0	0	0-0	.000	.000	.000	0	0	0	0	0	0	0	0	0	0	0-0
Crawford,Joe,NYN	.000	.000	.000	11	0	0	0	0	0	0	0	5	0	0-0	.000	.000	.000	11	0	0	0	0	0	0	0	5	0	0-0
Creek,Doug,SF	.333	.333	.333	3	1	0	0	0	1	0	0	1	2	0-0	.250	.250	.250	4	1	0	0	0	1	0	0	2	3	0-0
Crowell,Jim,Cin	.000	.000	.000	2	0	0	0	0	0	0	0	0	0	0-0	.000	.000	.000	2	0	0	0	0	0	0	0	0	0	0-0
Cruz,Nelson,ChA	.000	.000	.000	0	0	0	0	0	0	0	0	0	0	0-0	.000	.000	.000	0	0	0	0	0	0	0	0	0	0	0-0
Cunnane,Will,SD	.357	.438	.500	14	5	0	1	0	4	4	2	4	1	0-0	.357	.438	.500	14	5	0	1	0	4	4	2	4	1	0-0
D'Amico,Jeff,Mil	.000	.000	.000	4	0	0	0	0	0	0	0	3	1	0-0	.000	.000	.000	4	0	0	0	0	0	0	0	3	1	0-0
Daal,Omar,Mon-Tor	.200	.200	.200	5	1	0	0	0	0	1	0	0	0	0-0	.063	.118	.063	16	1	0	0	0	0	1	1	5	0	0-0
Darwin,Dan.,ChA-SF	.111	.111	.167	18	2	1	0	0	0	2	0	11	1	0-0	.135	.150	.212	260	35	10	2	2	13	21	5	141	16	2-0
Darwin,Jeff,ChA	.000	.000	.000	0	0	0	0	0	0	0	0	0	0	0-0	.000	.000	.000	0	0	0	0	0	0	0	0	0	0	0-0
DeHart,Rick,Mon	.000	.000	.000	2	0	0	0	0	0	0	0	2	0	0-0	.000	.000	.000	2	0	0	0	0	0	0	0	2	0	0-0
DeJean,Mike,Col	.333	.333	.667	3	1	1	0	0	0	0	0	1	1	0-0	.333	.333	.667	3	1	1	0	0	0	0	0	1	1	0-0
DeLucia,Rich,SF-Ana	.000	.000	.000	0	0	0	0	0	0	0	0	0	0	0-0	.214	.313	.214	14	3	0	0	0	2	0	2	3	1	0-0
Dessens,Elmer,Pit	.000	.000	.000	0	0	0	0	0	0	0	0	0	0	0-0	.400	.400	.400	5	2	0	0	0	1	2	0	0	0	0-0
Dickson,Jason,Ana	.000	.000	.000	2	0	0	0	0	0	0	0	0	0	0-0	.000	.000	.000	2	0	0	0	0	0	0	0	0	0	0-0
Dipoto,Jerry,Col	.111	.111	.111	9	1	0	0	0	0	0	0	5	0	0-0	.067	.067	.067	15	1	0	0	0	0	0	0	9	1	0-0
Drabek,Doug,ChA	.000	.000	.000	1	0	0	0	0	1	0	0	1	1	0-0	.166	.193	.207	715	119	17	3	2	42	46	17	206	66	0-1
Dreifort,Darren,LA	.143	.143	.143	7	1	0	0	0	0	0	0	5	0	0-0	.182	.182	.182	11	2	0	0	0	0	1	0	7	1	0-0
Duran,Roberto,Det	.000	.000	.000	0	0	0	0	0	0	0	0	0	0	0-0	.000	.000	.000	0	0	0	0	0	0	0	0	0	0	0-0
Eckersley,Dennis,StL	.000	.000	.000	0	0	0	0	0	0	0	0	0	0	0-0	.133	.173	.199	181	24	3	0	3	9	12	9	84	5	0-0
Eischen,Joey,Cin	.000	.000	.000	1	0	0	0	0	0	0	0	0	0	0-0	.000	.000	.000	8	0	0	0	0	0	0	0	3	0	0-0
Eldred,Cal,Mil	.000	.000	.000	3	0	0	0	0	0	0	0	0	1	0-0	.000	.000	.000	3	0	0	0	0	0	0	0	0	1	0-0
Embree,Alan,Atl	.000	.000	.000	0	0	0	0	0	0	0	0	0	0	0-0	.000	.000	.000	0	0	0	0	0	0	0	0	0	0	0-0
Erdos,Todd,SD	.000	.000	.000	1	0	0	0	0	0	0	0	1	0	0-0	.000	.000	.000	1	0	0	0	0	0	0	0	1	0	0-0
Ericks,John,Pit	.000	.000	.000	0	0	0	0	0	0	0	0	0	0	0-0	.083	.083	.111	36	3	1	0	0	2	1	0	13	6	0-0
Erickson,Scott,Bal	.000	.333	.000	2	0	0	0	0	0	0	1	2	2	0-0	.000	.333	.000	2	0	0	0	0	0	0	1	2	2	0-0
Escobar,Kelvim,Tor	.000	.000	.000	0	0	0	0	0	0	0	0	0	0	0-0	.000	.000	.000	0	0	0	0	0	0	0	0	0	0	0-0
Eshelman,Vau.,Bos	.250	.250	.250	4	1	0	0	0	1	0	0	1	0	0-0	.250	.250	.250	4	1	0	0	0	1	0	0	1	0	0-0
Estes,Shawn,SF	.147	.183	.191	68	10	0	0	1	8	3	1	24	7	0-0	.141	.177	.174	92	13	0	0	1	11	4	2	34	13	0-0
Eversgerd,Bryan,Tex	.000	.000	.000	0	0	0	0	0	0	0	0	0	0	0-0	.000	.000	.000	7	0	0	0	0	0	0	0	3	2	0-0
Eyre,Scott,ChA	.500	.500	.500	2	1	0	0	0	0	0	0	0	0	0-0	.500	.500	.500	2	1	0	0	0	0	0	0	0	0	0-0
Falteisek,Steve,Mon	.000	.000	.000	2	0	0	0	0	0	0	0	2	1	0-0	.000	.000	.000	2	0	0	0	0	0	0	0	2	1	0-0
Fassero,Jeff,Sea	.200	.200	.200	5	1	0	0	0	0	0	0	2	0	0-0	.080	.148	.099	212	17	2	1	0	15	5	17	118	39	1-0
Fernandez,Alex,Fla	.152	.219	.242	66	10	6	0	0	3	4	6	20	7	0-0	.152	.219	.242	66	10	6	0	0	3	4	6	20	7	0-0
Fernandez,Osv.,SF	.000	.105	.000	17	0	0	0	0	0	0	1	13	2	0-0	.068	.092	.068	74	5	0	0	0	0	1	1	38	7	0-0
Fernandez,Sid,Hou	.000	.000	.000	1	0	0	0	0	0	0	0	1	0	0-0	.182	.206	.223	539	98	15	2	1	28	34	16	209	67	1-0
Fetters,Mike,Mil	.000	.000	.000	0	0	0	0	0	0	0	0	0	0	0-0	.000	.000	.000	0	0	0	0	0	0	0	0	0	0	0-0
Finley,Chuck,Ana	.000	.000	.000	6	0	0	0	0	1	0	0	2	0	0-0	.000	.000	.000	6	0	0	0	0	1	0	0	2	0	0-0
Florie,Bryce,Mil	.000	.000	.000	0	0	0	0	0	0	0	0	0	0	0-0	.000	.000	.000	5	0	0	0	0	0	0	0	3	0	0-0
Fossas,Tony,StL	.000	.000	.000	0	0	0	0	0	0	0	0	0	0	0-0	.000	.000	.000	1	0	0	0	0	0	0	0	0	0	0-0
Foster,Kevin,ChN	.128	.146	.149	47	6	1	0	0	3	4	1	20	11	0-0	.190	.237	.270	163	31	6	2	1	15	19	9	59	22	2-0
Foulke,Keith,SF-ChA	.154	.154	.154	13	2	0	0	0	0	0	0	4	2	0-0	.154	.154	.154	13	2	0	0	0	0	0	0	4	2	0-0
Fox,Chad,Atl	.000	.000	.000	0	0	0	0	0	0	0	0	0	0	0-0	.000	.000	.000	0	0	0	0	0	0	0	0	0	0	0-0
Franco,John,NYN	.000	.000	.000	0	0	0	0	0	0	0	0	0	0	0-0	.097	.097	.097	31	3	0	0	0	2	1	0	12	3	0-0
Frascatore,John,StL	.000	.000	.000	3	0	0	0	0	0	0	0	2	0	0-0	.000	.083	.000	11	0	0	0	0	0	0	1	9	1	0-0
Gaillard,Eddie,Det	.000	.000	.000	0	0	0	0	0	0	0	0	0	0	0-0	.000	.000	.000	0	0	0	0	0	0	0	0	0	0	0-0
Garcia,Ramon,Hou	.111	.132	.167	36	4	2	0	0	2	5	0	13	7	0-0	.111	.132	.167	36	4	2	0	0	2	5	0	13	7	0-0
Gardner,Mark,SF	.115	.143	.115	61	7	0	0	0	0	2	1	30	3	0-0	.124	.149	.142	330	41	2	2	0	14	14	7	135	40	0-0
Glavine,Tom,Atl	.222	.310	.222	63	14	0	0	0	6	7	7	13	17	0-0	.201	.255	.229	695	140	12	2	1	56	51	49	179	103	1-0
Gomes,Wayne,Phi	.000	.333	.000	2	0	0	0	0	0	0	1	1	0	0-0	.000	.333	.000	2	0	0	0	0	0	0	1	1	0	0-0
Gonzalez,Jeremi,ChN	.100	.163	.100	40	4	0	0	0	1	1	3	12	8	0-0	.100	.163	.100	40	4	0	0	0	1	1	3	12	8	0-0
Gooden,Dwight,NYA	.000	.000	.000	4	0	0	0	0	0	0	0	1	0	0-0	.196	.212	.259	734	144	15	5	7	59	65	13	132	85	1-1
Gordon,Tom,Bos	.000	.000	.000	0	0	0	0	0	0	0	0	0	0	0-0	.000	.000	.000	0	0	0	0	0	0	0	0	0	0	0-0
Gorecki,Rick,LA	.000	.000	.000	0	0	0	0	0	1	0	0	0	1	0-0	.000	.000	.000	0	0	0	0	0	1	0	0	0	1	0-0
Grace,Mike,Phi	.083	.083	.083	12	1	0	0	0	0	0	0	9	0	0-0	.116	.174	.116	43	5	0	0	0	1	0	2	22	3	0-0
Granger,Jeff,Pit	.000	.000	.000	0	0	0	0	0	0	0	0	0	0	0-0	.000	.000	.000	0	0	0	0	0	0	0	0	0	0	0-0
Graves,Danny,Cle-Cin	.000	.000	.000	1	0	0	0	0	0	0	0	1	0	0-0	.000	.000	.000	1	0	0	0	0	0	0	0	1	0	0-0
Green,Tyler,Phi	.308	.308	.423	26	8	3	0	0	2	2	0	5	1	0-0	.222	.222	.375	72	16	8	0	1	4	7	0	23	10	0-1
Greene,Tommy,Hou	.333	.333	.667	3	1	1	0	0	1	1	0	1	1	0-0	.221	.261	.310	213	47	7	0	4	20	19	12	59	15	0-0
Groom,Buddy,Oak	.000	.000	.000	0	0	0	0	0	0	0	0	0	0	0-0	.000	.000	.000	0	0	0	0	0	0	0	0	0	0	0-0
Gross,Kevin,Ana	.000	.000	.000	1	0	0	0	0	0	0	0	1	0	0-0	.161	.201	.220	660	106	19	1	6	41	36	31	277	66	3-0
Guardado,Eddie,Min	.000	.000	.000	0	0	0	0	0	0	0	0	0	0	0-0	.000	.000	.000	0	0	0	0	0	0	0	0	0	0	0-0
Gunderson,Eric,Tex	.000	.000	.000	0	0	0	0	0	0	0	0	0	0	0-0	.000	.143	.000	6	0	0	0	0	1	0	0	4	0	0-0
Guthrie,Mark,LA	.250	.250	.250	4	1	0	0	0	0	0	0	0	1	0-0	.125	.125	.125	8	1	0	0	0	0	0	0	0	1	0-0
Hall,Darren,LA	.000	.000	.000	0	0	0	0	0	0	0	0	0	0	0-0	.000	.000	.000	0	0	0	0	0	0	0	0	0	0	0-0
Hamilton,Joey,SD	.130	.140	.241	54	7	0	0	2	4	6	1	26	9	0-0	.110	.134	.167	227	25	4	0	3	15	14	7	120	30	0-0
Hammond,Chris,Bos	.000	.000	.000	0	0	0	0	0	0	0	0	0	0	0-0	.205	.288	.297	229	47	7	1	4	30	14	27	92	19	0-0

	1997 Hitting														Career Hitting													
Pitcher,Team	Avg	OBP	SLG	AB	H	2B	3B	HR	R	RBI	BB	SO	SH	SB-CS	Avg	OBP	SLG	AB	H	2B	3B	HR	R	RBI	BB	SO	SH	SB-CS
Hampton,Mike,Hou	.137	.190	.178	73	10	1	1	0	6	8	5	21	10	0-1	.165	.233	.189	164	27	2	1	0	22	11	13	47	21	0-1
Haney,Chris,KC	.000	.000	.000	0	0	0	0	0	0	0	0	0	0	0-0	.114	.114	.114	35	4	0	0	0	2	4	0	4	4	0-0
Harkey,Mike,LA	.000	.000	.000	1	0	0	0	0	0	0	0	1	2	0-0	.183	.202	.213	164	30	5	0	0	12	7	3	51	21	0-0
Harnisch,Pe.,NYN-Mil	.000	.000	.000	8	0	0	0	0	0	0	0	3	1	0-0	.116	.144	.153	327	38	12	0	0	25	15	10	89	38	0-2
Harris,Pep,Ana	.000	.000	.000	0	0	0	0	0	0	0	0	0	0	0-0	.000	.000	.000	0	0	0	0	0	0	0	0	0	0	0-0
Harris,Reggie,Phi	.000	.000	.000	0	0	0	0	0	0	0	0	0	0	0-0	.000	.000	.000	0	0	0	0	0	0	0	0	0	0	0-0
Hasegawa,Shige.,Ana	.000	.000	.000	0	0	0	0	0	0	0	0	0	0	0-0	.000	.000	.000	0	0	0	0	0	0	0	0	0	0	0-0
Hawkins,LaTroy,Min	.000	.000	.000	1	0	0	0	0	0	0	0	1	0	0-0	.000	.000	.000	1	0	0	0	0	0	0	0	1	0	0-0
Haynes,Jimmy,Oak	.000	.000	.000	2	0	0	0	0	0	0	0	1	0	0-0	.000	.000	.000	2	0	0	0	0	0	0	0	1	0	0-0
Helling,Rick,Fla-Tex	.071	.071	.071	14	1	0	0	0	0	0	0	5	1	0-0	.087	.087	.087	23	2	0	0	0	1	0	0	8	1	0-0
Henriquez,Oscar,Hou	.000	.000	.000	0	0	0	0	0	0	0	0	0	0	0-0	.000	.000	.000	0	0	0	0	0	0	0	0	0	0	0-0
Henry,Butch,Bos	.000	.000	.000	0	0	0	0	0	0	0	0	0	1	0-0	.139	.166	.166	151	21	1	0	1	10	12	5	30	19	0-0
Henry,Doug,SF	.000	.000	.000	4	0	0	0	0	0	0	0	2	0	0-0	.091	.091	.091	11	1	0	0	0	1	0	0	3	1	0-0
Hentgen,Pat,Tor	.000	.000	.000	7	0	0	0	0	0	0	0	2	0	0-0	.000	.000	.000	7	0	0	0	0	0	0	0	2	0	0-0
Heredia,Felix,Fla	.500	.500	.500	2	1	0	0	0	0	0	0	1	1	0-0	.500	.500	.500	2	1	0	0	0	0	0	0	1	1	0-0
Heredia,Wilson,Tex	.000	.000	.000	0	0	0	0	0	0	0	0	0	0	0-0	.000	.000	.000	0	0	0	0	0	0	0	0	0	0	0-0
Hermanson,Dust.,Mon	.104	.140	.188	48	5	1	0	1	1	1	2	24	5	0-0	.104	.140	.188	48	5	1	0	1	1	1	2	24	5	0-0
Hernandez,Fern.,Det	.000	.000	.000	0	0	0	0	0	0	0	0	0	0	0-0	.000	.000	.000	0	0	0	0	0	0	0	0	0	0	0-0
Hernandez,Livan,Fla	.172	.200	.241	29	5	2	0	0	2	2	1	6	3	0-0	.200	.226	.267	30	6	2	0	0	3	2	1	6	3	0-0
Hernandez,R.,ChA-SF	.500	.500	.500	2	1	0	0	0	0	0	0	1	0	0-0	.500	.500	.500	2	1	0	0	0	0	0	0	1	0	0-0
Hernandez,Xavier,Tex	.000	.000	.000	0	0	0	0	0	0	0	0	0	0	0-0	.027	.077	.027	37	1	0	0	0	2	0	2	20	4	0-0
Hershiser,Orel,Cle	.000	.250	.000	3	0	0	0	0	0	0	0	1	1	0-0	.213	.242	.258	675	144	26	2	0	55	46	23	146	90	6-3
Hill,Ken,Tex-Ana	.500	.500	1.000	2	1	1	0	0	0	2	0	1	1	0-0	.150	.210	.187	326	49	7	1	1	22	21	24	94	66	0-0
Hitchcock,Sterling,SD	.100	.151	.100	50	5	0	0	0	4	1	3	30	8	0-1	.100	.151	.100	50	5	0	0	0	4	1	3	30	8	0-1
Hoffman,Trevor,SD	.333	.333	.333	3	1	0	0	0	0	1	0	1	0	0-0	.130	.130	.174	23	3	1	0	0	1	3	0	7	2	0-0
Holmes,Darren,Col	.158	.150	.316	19	3	0	0	1	2	2	0	9	3	0-0	.130	.160	.261	23	3	0	0	1	2	2	1	11	6	0-0
Holt,Chris,Hou	.090	.103	.090	67	6	0	0	0	6	1	1	33	9	0-0	.088	.101	.088	68	6	0	0	0	6	1	1	33	9	0-0
Holtz,Mike,Ana	.000	.000	.000	1	0	0	0	0	0	0	0	1	0	0-0	.000	.000	.000	1	0	0	0	0	0	0	0	1	0	0-0
Honeycutt,Rick,StL	.000	.000	.000	0	0	0	0	0	0	0	0	0	0	0-0	.132	.210	.148	182	24	3	0	0	13	9	18	44	28	1-0
Hudek,John,Hou	.000	.000	.000	0	0	0	0	0	0	0	0	0	0	0-0	1.000	1.000	1.000	1	1	0	0	0	0	2	0	0	0	0-0
Hudson,Joe,Bos	.000	.000	.000	0	0	0	0	0	0	0	0	0	0	0-0	.000	.000	.000	0	0	0	0	0	0	0	0	0	0	0-0
Hutton,Mark,Fla-Col	.000	.000	.000	3	0	0	0	0	0	0	0	0	0	0-0	.273	.273	.409	22	6	0	0	1	2	1	0	6	1	0-0
Irabu,Hideki,NYA	.000	.000	.000	1	0	0	0	0	0	0	0	0	0	0-0	.000	.000	.000	1	0	0	0	0	0	0	0	0	0	0-0
Isringhausen,Ja.,NYN	.143	.125	.143	7	1	0	0	0	1	1	0	4	1	0-0	.212	.258	.318	85	18	3	0	2	8	10	5	29	7	0-0
Jackson,Dan.,StL-SD	.100	.143	.100	20	2	0	0	0	1	0	1	8	1	0-1	.126	.148	.164	428	54	12	2	0	28	28	10	219	54	0-2
Jackson,Mike,Cle	.000	.000	.000	0	0	0	0	0	0	0	0	0	0	0-0	.185	.214	.259	27	5	2	0	0	3	1	1	4	4	0-0
Jacome,Jason,KC-Cle	.000	.000	.000	0	0	0	0	0	0	0	0	0	0	0-0	.043	.043	.043	23	1	0	0	0	0	1	0	15	2	0-0
James,Mike,Ana	.000	.000	.000	0	0	0	0	0	0	0	0	0	0	0-0	.000	.000	.000	0	0	0	0	0	0	0	0	0	0	0-0
Jarvis,K.,Cin-Min-Det	.000	.000	.000	1	0	0	0	0	0	0	0	0	0	0-0	.161	.175	.194	62	10	2	0	0	4	2	0	21	11	0-0
Johnson,Dane,Oak	.000	.000	.000	0	0	0	0	0	0	0	0	0	0	0-0	.000	.000	.000	0	0	0	0	0	0	0	0	0	0	0-0
Johnson,Jason,Pit	.000	.000	.000	1	0	0	0	0	0	0	0	1	0	0-0	.000	.000	.000	1	0	0	0	0	0	0	0	1	0	0-0
Johnson,Mi.,Bal-Mon	.077	.077	.077	13	1	0	0	0	1	1	0	5	2	0-0	.077	.077	.077	13	1	0	0	0	1	1	0	5	2	0-0
Johnstone,Jo.,SF-Oak	.000	.000	.000	2	0	0	0	0	0	0	0	1	0	0-0	.000	.000	.000	2	0	0	0	0	0	0	0	1	1	0-0
Jones,Bobby,NYN	.129	.169	.161	62	8	2	0	0	4	4	3	18	4	0-0	.123	.147	.143	244	30	5	0	0	16	9	7	89	41	0-0
Jones,BobbyM.,Col	.200	.333	.200	5	1	0	0	0	1	0	1	0	1	0-0	.200	.333	.200	5	1	0	0	0	1	0	1	0	1	0-0
Jones,Doug,Mil	.000	1.000	.000	0	0	0	0	0	0	0	1	0	0	0-0	.200	.333	.200	5	1	0	0	0	0	0	1	2	0	0-0
Jones,Todd,Det	.000	.000	.000	0	0	0	0	0	0	0	0	0	0	0-0	.273	.273	.364	11	3	1	0	0	1	0	0	1	0	0-0
Jordan,Ricardo,NYN	.000	.000	.000	1	0	0	0	0	0	0	0	1	0	0-0	.000	.000	.000	2	0	0	0	0	0	0	0	1	0	0-0
Judd,Mike,LA	.000	.000	.000	1	0	0	0	0	0	0	0	1	0	0-0	.000	.000	.000	1	0	0	0	0	0	0	0	1	0	0-0
Juden,Jeff,Mon-Cle	.140	.178	.186	43	6	2	0	0	1	4	1	24	2	0-0	.103	.125	.167	78	8	2	0	1	2	9	1	48	8	0-0
Kamieniecki,Scott,Bal	.000	.000	.000	2	0	0	0	0	0	0	0	2	0	0-0	.000	.000	.000	2	0	0	0	0	0	0	0	2	0	0-0
Karchner,Matt,ChA	.000	.000	.000	0	0	0	0	0	0	0	0	0	0	0-0	.000	.000	.000	0	0	0	0	0	0	0	0	0	0	0-0
Karl,Scott,Mil	.000	.000	.000	4	0	0	0	0	0	0	0	3	0	0-0	.000	.000	.000	4	0	0	0	0	0	0	0	3	0	0-0
Karp,Ryan,Phi	.000	.000	.000	0	0	0	0	0	0	0	0	0	0	0-0	.000	.000	.000	0	0	0	0	0	0	0	0	0	0	0-0
Karsay,Steve,Oak	.000	.000	.000	0	0	0	0	0	1	0	0	0	0	0-0	.000	.000	.000	0	0	0	0	0	1	0	0	0	0	0-0
Kashiwada,Tak.,NYN	.000	.000	.000	1	0	0	0	0	0	0	0	1	0	0-0	.000	.000	.000	1	0	0	0	0	0	0	0	1	0	0-0
Keagle,Greg,Det	.000	.000	.000	1	0	0	0	0	0	0	0	1	0	0-0	.000	.000	.000	1	0	0	0	0	0	0	0	1	0	0-0
Key,Jimmy,Bal	.000	.000	.000	2	0	0	0	0	0	0	0	2	1	0-0	.000	.000	.000	2	0	0	0	0	0	0	0	2	1	0-0
Kile,Darryl,Hou	.124	.179	.157	89	11	3	0	0	4	7	3	38	10	0-0	.114	.166	.158	368	42	13	0	1	20	24	19	178	48	0-0
King,Curtis,StL	.000	.000	.000	1	0	0	0	0	0	0	0	1	0	0-0	.000	.000	.000	1	0	0	0	0	0	0	0	1	0	0-0
Kline,Steve,Cle-Mon	.000	.000	.000	1	0	0	0	0	0	0	0	1	0	0-0	.000	.000	.000	1	0	0	0	0	0	0	0	1	0	0-0
Kroon,Marc,SD	.000	.000	.000	0	0	0	0	0	0	0	0	0	0	0-0	.000	.000	.000	0	0	0	0	0	0	0	0	0	0	0-0
Kubinski,Tim,Oak	.000	.000	.000	0	0	0	0	0	0	0	0	0	0	0-0	.000	.000	.000	0	0	0	0	0	0	0	0	0	0	0-0
Lacy,Kerry,Bos	.000	.000	.000	0	0	0	0	0	0	0	0	0	0	0-0	.000	.000	.000	0	0	0	0	0	0	0	0	0	0	0-0
Leiter,Al,Fla	.104	.157	.104	48	5	0	0	0	2	1	3	25	2	0-0	.102	.152	.102	118	12	0	0	0	5	2	7	70	9	0-0
Leiter,Mark,Phi	.118	.151	.118	51	6	0	0	0	2	4	2	28	10	0-0	.112	.154	.117	179	20	1	0	0	8	14	9	96	28	0-0
LeRoy,John,Atl	.000	.000	.000	0	0	0	0	0	0	0	0	0	0	0-0	.000	.000	.000	0	0	0	0	0	0	0	0	0	0	0-0
Leskanic,Curt,Col	.000	.000	.000	1	0	0	0	0	0	0	0	1	0	0-0	.167	.194	.267	30	5	3	0	0	2	4	1	12	4	0-0
Levine,Al,ChA	.000	.000	.000	0	0	0	0	0	0	0	0	0	0	0-0	.000	.000	.000	0	0	0	0	0	0	0	0	0	0	0-0
Lewis,Richie,Oak-Cin	1.000	1.000	1.000	1	1	0	0	0	0	0	0	0	0	0-0	.200	.333	.200	10	2	0	0	0	1	1	2	3	1	0-0
Lidle,Cory,NYN	.000	.167	.000	5	0	0	0	0	1	0	1	4	0	0-0	.000	.167	.000	5	0	0	0	0	1	0	1	4	0	0-0
Lieber,Jon,Pit	.121	.177	.155	58	7	2	0	0	1	8	4	23	2	0-0	.123	.167	.162	154	19	6	0	0	8	11	8	62	7	0-0
Ligtenberg,Kerry,Atl	.000	.000	.000	0	0	0	0	0	0	0	0	0	0	0-0	.000	.000	.000	0	0	0	0	0	0	0	0	0	0	0-0
Lima,Jose,Hou	.000	.000	.000	3	0	0	0	0	0	0	0	3	2	0-0	.000	.000	.000	3	0	0	0	0	0	0	0	3	2	0-0
Lloyd,Graeme,NYA	.000	.000	.000	0	0	0	0	0	0	0	0	0	0	0-0	.000	.000	.000	0	0	0	0	0	0	0	0	0	0	0-0
Loaiza,Esteban,Pit	.167	.180	.183	60	10	1	0	0	4	5	1	17	8	0-0	.171	.182	.202	129	22	2	1	0	9	8	2	30	20	0-0
Loiselle,Rich,Pit	.000	.000	.000	1	0	0	0	0	0	0	0	1	0	0-0	.222	.222	.333	9	2	1	0	0	0	2	0	4	0	0-0

	1997 Hitting														Career Hitting													
Pitcher,Team	Avg	OBP	SLG	AB	H	2B	3B	HR	R	RBI	BB	SO	SH	SB-CS	Avg	OBP	SLG	AB	H	2B	3B	HR	R	RBI	BB	SO	SH	SB-CS
Long,Joey,SD	.000	.000	.000	0	0	0	0	0	0	0	0	0	0	0-0	.000	.000	.000	0	0	0	0	0	0	0	0	0	0	0-0
Lopez,Albie,Cle	.000	.000	.000	1	0	0	0	0	0	0	0	1	0	0-0	.000	.000	.000	1	0	0	0	0	0	0	0	1	0	0-0
Lowe,Derek,Sea-Bos	.000	.000	.000	3	0	0	0	0	0	0	0	2	0	0-0	.000	.000	.000	3	0	0	0	0	0	0	0	2	0	0-0
Lowe,Sean,StL	.333	.333	.333	3	1	0	0	0	0	0	0	1	0	0-0	.333	.333	.333	3	1	0	0	0	0	0	0	1	0	0-0
Ludwick,Eric,StL-Oak	.000	.000	.000	2	0	0	0	0	0	0	0	1	0	0-0	.000	.000	.000	4	0	0	0	0	0	0	0	2	0	0-0
Maddux,Greg,Atl	.104	.167	.134	67	7	2	0	0	3	4	5	21	6	1-0	.173	.192	.202	851	147	19	0	2	64	41	19	233	87	4-1
Maduro,Calvin,Phi	.050	.050	.050	20	1	0	0	0	1	0	0	12	1	0-0	.042	.042	.042	24	1	0	0	0	1	0	0	14	1	0-0
Magnante,Mike,Hou	.000	.000	.000	3	0	0	0	0	0	0	0	2	0	0-0	.000	.000	.000	3	0	0	0	0	0	0	0	2	0	0-0
Manuel,Barry,NYN	.000	.000	.000	2	0	0	0	0	0	0	0	1	0	0-0	.000	.100	.000	9	0	0	0	0	0	0	1	4	1	0-0
Manzanillo,Josias,Sea	.000	.000	.000	1	0	0	0	0	0	0	0	0	0	0-0	.000	.000	.000	6	0	0	0	0	0	0	0	3	1	0-0
Martin,Tom,Hou	.000	.000	.000	3	0	0	0	0	0	0	0	1	0	0-0	.000	.000	.000	3	0	0	0	0	0	0	0	1	0	0-0
Martinez,Pedro,Mon	.116	.153	.174	69	8	2	1	0	5	0	3	28	9	0-0	.102	.145	.130	246	25	3	2	0	13	11	10	111	37	0-0
Martinez,PedroA.,Cin	.000	.000	.000	0	0	0	0	0	0	0	0	0	0	0-0	.000	.100	.000	9	0	0	0	0	1	1	1	4	2	0-0
Martinez,Ramon,LA	.190	.190	.214	42	8	1	0	0	5	1	0	11	5	0-0	.152	.164	.178	552	84	11	0	1	29	32	7	181	63	0-2
Mathews,T.J.,StL-Oak	.000	.000	.000	1	0	0	0	0	0	0	0	0	0	0-0	.000	.000	.000	7	0	0	0	0	0	0	0	4	0	0-0
Mathews,Terry,Bal	.000	.000	.000	0	0	0	0	0	0	0	0	0	0	0-0	.391	.391	.522	23	9	3	0	0	3	3	0	8	0	0-0
May,Darrell,Ana	.000	.000	.000	2	0	0	0	0	0	0	0	2	0	0-0	.200	.200	.200	5	1	0	0	0	1	0	0	3	0	0-0
McCarthy,Greg,Sea	.000	.000	.000	0	0	0	0	0	0	0	0	0	0	0-0	.000	.000	.000	0	0	0	0	0	0	0	0	0	0	0-0
McCurry,Jeff,Col	.000	.000	.000	1	0	0	0	0	0	0	0	1	0	0-0	.000	.000	.000	4	0	0	0	0	0	0	0	2	0	0-0
McDonald,Ben,Mil	.000	.000	.000	1	0	0	0	0	0	0	0	1	0	0-0	.000	.000	.000	1	0	0	0	0	0	0	0	1	0	0-0
McElroy,Ch.,Ana-ChA	.000	.000	.000	0	0	0	0	0	1	0	0	0	0	0-0	.242	.242	.394	33	8	3	1	0	4	4	0	9	0	0-1
McGraw,Tom,StL	.000	.000	.000	0	0	0	0	0	0	0	0	0	0	0-0	.000	.000	.000	0	0	0	0	0	0	0	0	0	0	0-0
McMichael,Greg,NYN	.667	.667	.667	3	2	0	0	0	0	0	0	1	0	0-0	.143	.200	.143	14	2	0	0	0	0	0	1	7	0	0-0
Mecir,Jim,NYA	.000	.000	.000	0	0	0	0	0	0	0	0	0	0	0-0	.000	.000	.000	0	0	0	0	0	0	0	0	0	0	0-0
Mendoza,Ramiro,NYA	.000	.000	.000	0	0	0	0	0	0	0	0	0	0	0-0	.000	.000	.000	0	0	0	0	0	0	0	0	0	0	0-0
Menhart,Paul,SD	.000	.000	.000	12	0	0	0	0	0	0	0	4	2	0-0	.000	.000	.000	12	0	0	0	0	0	0	0	4	2	0-0
Mercedes,Jose,Mil	.000	.000	.000	2	0	0	0	0	0	0	0	2	0	0-0	.000	.000	.000	2	0	0	0	0	0	0	0	2	0	0-0
Mercker,Kent,Cin	.156	.224	.222	45	7	1	1	0	3	1	4	23	4	0-0	.093	.129	.130	162	15	4	1	0	4	10	7	79	13	0-0
Mesa,Jose,Cle	.000	.000	.000	0	0	0	0	0	0	0	0	0	0	0-0	.000	.000	.000	0	0	0	0	0	0	0	0	0	0	0-0
Miceli,Dan,Det	.000	.000	.000	0	0	0	0	0	0	0	0	0	0	0-0	.000	.000	.000	17	0	0	0	0	0	0	0	7	0	0-0
Miller,Kurt,Fla	.000	.000	.000	0	0	0	0	0	0	0	0	0	0	0-0	.286	.286	.286	14	4	0	0	0	1	2	0	2	2	0-0
Miller,Travis,Min	.000	.000	.000	0	0	0	0	0	0	0	0	0	0	0-0	.000	.000	.000	0	0	0	0	0	0	0	0	0	0	0-0
Mills,Alan,Bal	.000	.000	.000	0	0	0	0	0	0	0	0	0	0	0-0	.000	.000	.000	0	0	0	0	0	0	0	0	0	0	0-0
Millwood,Kevin,Atl	.000	.077	.000	12	0	0	0	0	0	0	1	8	1	0-0	.000	.077	.000	12	0	0	0	0	0	0	1	8	1	0-0
Mimbs,Michael,Phi	.000	.000	.000	2	0	0	0	0	1	0	0	0	0	0-0	.129	.129	.143	70	9	1	0	0	3	2	0	24	10	0-0
Minchey,Nate,Col	.000	.000	.000	0	0	0	0	0	0	0	0	0	0	0-0	.000	.000	.000	0	0	0	0	0	0	0	0	0	0	0-0
Minor,Blas,Hou	.000	.000	.000	0	0	0	0	0	0	0	0	0	0	0-0	.154	.214	.231	13	2	1	0	0	1	0	0	7	1	0-0
Mlicki,Dave,NYN	.188	.231	.250	48	9	3	0	0	3	3	3	22	3	0-0	.124	.218	.155	97	12	3	0	0	5	5	12	37	15	0-0
Moehler,Brian,Det	.000	.000	.000	3	0	0	0	0	0	0	0	2	0	0-0	.000	.000	.000	3	0	0	0	0	0	0	0	2	0	0-0
Mohler,Mike,Oak	.000	.000	.000	0	0	0	0	0	0	0	0	0	0	0-0	.000	.000	.000	0	0	0	0	0	0	0	0	0	0	0-0
Montgomery,Jeff,KC	.000	.000	.000	0	0	0	0	0	0	0	0	0	0	0-0	.000	.000	.000	2	0	0	0	0	0	0	0	1	0	0-0
Moody,Eric,Tex	.000	.000	.000	0	0	0	0	0	0	0	0	0	0	0-0	.000	.000	.000	0	0	0	0	0	0	0	0	0	0	0-0
Morel,Ramon,Pit-ChN	.000	.000	.000	0	0	0	0	0	0	0	0	0	0	0-0	.000	.000	.000	4	0	0	0	0	0	0	0	2	1	0-0
Morgan,Mike,Cin	.091	.111	.136	44	4	0	1	0	1	2	0	14	9	0-0	.087	.111	.096	469	41	2	1	0	12	14	12	141	57	0-0
Morman,Alvin,Cle	.000	.000	.000	1	0	0	0	0	0	0	0	0	0	0-0	.000	.000	.000	1	0	0	0	0	0	0	0	0	0	0-0
Morris,Matt,StL	.205	.256	.233	73	15	2	0	0	4	6	5	36	2	0-1	.205	.256	.233	73	15	2	0	0	4	6	5	36	2	0-1
Moyer,Jamie,Sea	.333	.333	.333	3	1	0	0	0	0	0	0	0	0	0-0	.143	.213	.156	154	22	2	0	0	10	4	14	51	19	0-0
Mulholland,T.,ChN-SF	.164	.164	.218	55	9	3	0	0	1	2	0	27	4	0-0	.099	.116	.131	505	50	8	1	2	18	13	9	227	38	1-1
Munoz,Bobby,Phi	.300	.300	.400	10	3	1	0	0	2	1	0	1	1	0-0	.196	.211	.286	56	11	2	0	1	6	7	1	17	4	0-0
Munoz,Mike,Col	.000	.500	.000	1	0	0	0	0	0	0	1	1	0	0-0	.200	.500	.400	5	1	1	0	0	1	1	3	4	0	0-0
Murray,Heath,SD	.000	.000	.000	6	0	0	0	0	0	0	0	1	0	0-0	.000	.000	.000	6	0	0	0	0	0	0	0	1	0	0-0
Mussina,Mike,Bal	.250	.250	.250	4	1	0	0	0	0	0	0	1	0	0-0	.250	.250	.250	4	1	0	0	0	0	0	0	1	0	0-0
Myers,Mike,Det	.000	.000	.000	0	0	0	0	0	0	0	0	0	0	0-0	.000	.000	.000	0	0	0	0	0	0	0	0	0	0	0-0
Myers,Randy,Bal	.000	.000	.000	0	0	0	0	0	0	0	0	0	0	0-0	.186	.226	.237	59	11	3	0	0	5	7	3	32	5	0-0
Myers,Rodney,ChN	.000	.000	.000	0	0	0	0	0	0	0	0	0	0	0-0	.000	.000	.000	5	0	0	0	0	0	0	0	4	0	0-0
Nagy,Charles,Cle	.200	.200	.200	5	1	0	0	0	1	0	0	1	0	0-0	.200	.200	.200	5	1	0	0	0	1	0	0	1	0	0-0
Naulty,Dan,Min	.000	.000	.000	0	0	0	0	0	0	0	0	0	0	0-0	.000	.000	.000	0	0	0	0	0	0	0	0	0	0	0-0
Navarro,Jaime,ChA	.000	.000	.000	1	0	0	0	0	0	0	0	0	1	0-0	.154	.166	.196	143	22	6	0	0	1	10	1	51	17	0-0
Neagle,Denny,Atl	.153	.197	.208	72	11	1	0	1	6	7	4	35	9	0-0	.142	.171	.191	282	40	5	0	3	16	26	10	98	39	0-1
Nelson,Jeff,NYA	.000	.000	.000	0	0	0	0	0	0	0	0	0	0	0-0	.000	.000	.000	0	0	0	0	0	0	0	0	0	0	0-0
Nen,Robb,Fla	.000	.000	.000	0	0	0	0	0	0	0	0	0	0	0-0	.000	.000	.000	9	0	0	0	0	0	0	0	1	0	0-0
Nomo,Hideo,LA	.159	.171	.232	69	11	5	0	0	3	2	1	32	5	0-0	.129	.140	.171	210	27	9	0	0	6	9	3	103	20	0-0
Nye,Ryan,Phi	.000	.000	.000	2	0	0	0	0	0	0	0	1	1	0-0	.000	.000	.000	2	0	0	0	0	0	0	0	1	1	0-0
Ogea,Chad,Cle	.000	.000	.000	2	0	0	0	0	0	0	0	1	2	0-0	.000	.000	.000	2	0	0	0	0	0	0	0	1	2	0-0
Ojala,Kirt,Fla	.000	.000	.000	7	0	0	0	0	0	0	0	2	1	0-0	.000	.000	.000	7	0	0	0	0	0	0	0	2	1	0-0
Olivares,Om.,Det-Sea	.600	.600	1.000	5	3	0	1	0	2	2	0	1	0	0-0	.238	.255	.340	206	49	7	1	4	21	23	5	59	13	0-0
Oliver,Darren,Tex	.500	.667	.500	2	1	0	0	0	1	2	0	1	0	0-0	.500	.667	.500	2	1	0	0	0	1	2	0	1	0	0-0
Olson,Gregg,Min-KC	.000	.000	.000	0	0	0	0	0	0	0	0	0	0	0-0	.000	.000	.000	2	0	0	0	0	0	0	0	2	0	0-0
Oquist,Mike,Oak	.250	.250	.250	4	1	0	0	0	0	0	0	0	1	0-0	.250	.250	.250	4	1	0	0	0	0	0	0	0	1	0-0
Orosco,Jesse,Bal	.000	1.000	.000	0	0	0	0	0	0	0	1	0	0	0-0	.169	.250	.169	59	10	0	0	0	2	4	7	25	7	0-0
Osborne,Donovan,StL	.208	.208	.250	24	5	1	0	0	2	2	0	6	1	1-0	.181	.216	.244	221	40	9	1	1	17	19	9	79	23	1-1
Osuna,Antonio,LA	.500	.500	.500	2	1	0	0	0	0	0	0	0	0	0-0	.200	.286	.200	5	1	0	0	0	0	1	1	0	0	0-0
Painter,Lance,StL	.000	.000	.000	1	0	0	0	0	0	0	0	1	0	0-0	.161	.183	.232	56	9	2	1	0	6	5	2	28	7	0-0
Pall,Donn,Fla	.000	.000	.000	1	0	0	0	0	0	0	0	1	0	0-0	.000	.250	.000	3	0	0	0	0	0	0	1	1	0	0-0
Paniagua,Jose,Mon	.000	.000	.000	5	0	0	0	0	0	0	0	3	0	0-0	.000	.111	.000	16	0	0	0	0	1	0	2	10	1	0-0
Park,ChanHo,LA	.176	.236	.255	51	9	4	0	0	5	2	4	21	11	0-0	.141	.197	.197	71	10	4	0	0	5	4	5	31	14	0-0
Patterson,Bob,ChN	.000	.000	.000	1	0	0	0	0	0	0	0	0	0	0-0	.125	.155	.143	56	7	1	0	0	3	4	2	24	6	0-0

	1997 Hitting														Career Hitting													
Pitcher,Team	Avg	OBP	SLG	AB	H	2B	3B	HR	R	RBI	BB	SO	SH	SB-CS	Avg	OBP	SLG	AB	H	2B	3B	HR	R	RBI	BB	SO	SH	SB-CS
Patterson,Danny,Tex	.000	.000	.000	0	0	0	0	0	0	0	0	0	0	0-0	.000	.000	.000	0	0	0	0	0	0	0	0	0	0	0-0
Percival,Troy,Ana	.000	.000	.000	0	0	0	0	0	0	0	0	0	0	0-0	.000	.000	.000	1	0	0	0	0	0	0	0	1	0	0-0
Perez,Carlos,Mon	.172	.197	.250	64	11	2	0	1	3	2	2	31	5	0-0	.156	.200	.257	109	17	3	1	2	4	7	6	52	9	0-0
Perez,Yorkis,NYN	.000	.000	.000	1	0	0	0	0	0	0	0	0	0	0-0	.000	.000	.000	6	0	0	0	0	0	0	0	4	0	0-0
Perisho,Matt,Ana	.000	.000	.000	1	0	0	0	0	0	0	0	1	0	0-0	.000	.000	.000	1	0	0	0	0	0	0	0	1	0	0-0
Person,Robert,Tor	.000	.200	.000	4	0	0	0	0	0	0	1	1	0	0-0	.179	.207	.214	28	5	1	0	0	2	0	1	13	5	0-0
Peters,Chris,Pit	.250	.250	.250	4	1	0	0	0	0	2	0	2	0	0-0	.217	.217	.261	23	5	1	0	0	2	3	0	10	1	0-0
Petkovsek,Mark,StL	.091	.167	.091	11	1	0	0	0	0	0	1	2	1	0-0	.109	.194	.109	64	7	0	0	0	5	2	6	16	4	0-0
Pichardo,Hipolito,KC	.000	.000	.000	0	0	0	0	0	0	0	0	0	0	0-0	.000	.000	.000	2	0	0	0	0	0	0	0	0	0	0-0
Pisciotta,Marc,ChN	.000	.000	.000	1	0	0	0	0	0	0	0	1	0	0-0	.000	.000	.000	1	0	0	0	0	0	0	0	1	0	0-0
Pittsley,Jim,KC	.500	.500	1.000	2	1	1	0	0	0	0	0	1	0	0-0	.500	.500	1.000	2	1	1	0	0	0	0	0	1	0	0-0
Plantenberg,Erik,Phi	.000	.000	.000	0	0	0	0	0	0	0	0	0	0	0-0	.000	.000	.000	0	0	0	0	0	0	0	0	0	0	0-0
Plesac,Dan,Tor	.000	.000	.000	0	0	0	0	0	0	0	0	0	0	0-0	.071	.071	.071	14	1	0	0	0	0	0	0	9	0	0-0
Plunk,Eric,Cle	.000	.000	.000	1	0	0	0	0	0	0	0	1	0	0-0	.000	.000	.000	1	0	0	0	0	0	0	0	1	0	0-0
Poole,Jim,SF	.000	.000	.000	0	0	0	0	0	0	0	0	0	1	0-0	.000	.000	.000	2	0	0	0	0	0	0	0	1	1	0-0
Portugal,Mark,Phi	.000	.000	.000	4	0	0	0	0	0	0	0	2	0	0-0	.191	.222	.249	397	76	15	1	2	27	32	16	77	49	0-0
Powell,Jay,Fla	.500	.500	.500	4	2	0	0	0	0	1	0	1	0	0-0	.222	.222	.222	9	2	0	0	0	0	1	0	5	1	0-0
Quantrill,Paul,Tor	.000	.000	.000	1	0	0	0	0	0	0	0	1	0	0-0	.098	.141	.098	61	6	0	0	0	5	0	3	26	7	0-0
Radinsky,Scott,LA	.000	.000	.000	4	0	0	0	0	0	0	0	4	0	0-0	.000	.000	.000	5	0	0	0	0	0	0	0	4	0	0-0
Radke,Brad,Min	.000	.000	.000	3	0	0	0	0	0	0	0	0	1	0-0	.000	.000	.000	3	0	0	0	0	0	0	0	0	1	0-0
Raggio,Brady,StL	.000	.000	.000	3	0	0	0	0	0	1	0	0	1	0-0	.000	.000	.000	3	0	0	0	0	0	1	0	0	1	0-0
Ramos,Edgar,Phi	.000	.000	.000	3	0	0	0	0	0	0	0	2	1	0-0	.000	.000	.000	3	0	0	0	0	0	0	0	2	1	0-0
Rapp,Pat,Fla-SF	.106	.106	.170	47	5	0	0	1	3	2	0	16	4	0-0	.123	.127	.153	235	29	4	0	1	10	13	1	88	20	0-0
Reed,Rick,NYN	.175	.217	.316	57	10	5	0	1	6	5	3	18	6	0-0	.168	.216	.263	95	16	6	0	1	7	8	6	30	8	0-0
Reed,Steve,Col	.000	.000	.000	1	0	0	0	0	0	0	0	0	0	0-0	.111	.111	.111	18	2	0	0	0	0	0	0	6	2	0-0
Rekar,Bryan,Col	.250	.250	.250	4	1	0	0	0	1	0	0	1	0	0-0	.133	.204	.156	45	6	1	0	0	4	0	4	21	5	0-1
Remlinger,Mike,Cin	.095	.174	.190	21	2	2	0	0	1	6	2	11	3	0-0	.058	.140	.096	52	3	2	0	0	3	7	5	22	10	0-0
Reyes,Al,Mil	.000	.000	.000	0	0	0	0	0	0	0	0	0	0	0-0	.000	.000	.000	0	0	0	0	0	0	0	0	0	0	0-0
Reyes,Carlos,Oak	.000	.000	.000	0	0	0	0	0	0	0	0	0	0	0-0	.000	.000	.000	0	0	0	0	0	0	0	0	0	0	0-0
Reyes,Dennis,LA	.000	.100	.000	9	0	0	0	0	1	0	1	5	1	1-0	.000	.100	.000	9	0	0	0	0	1	0	1	5	1	1-0
Reynolds,Shane,Hou	.113	.145	.170	53	6	3	0	0	3	2	2	31	7	0-0	.147	.172	.203	231	34	7	0	2	14	8	7	104	40	0-0
Reynoso,Arm.,NYN	.241	.281	.345	29	7	0	0	1	3	3	2	15	0	0-0	.155	.206	.205	200	31	1	0	3	12	9	13	81	19	0-0
Rhodes,Arthur,Bal	.000	.000	.000	1	0	0	0	0	0	0	0	1	0	0-0	.000	.000	.000	1	0	0	0	0	0	0	0	1	0	0-0
Rigby,Brad,Oak	.000	.000	.000	3	0	0	0	0	0	0	0	2	0	0-0	.000	.000	.000	3	0	0	0	0	0	0	0	2	0	0-0
Rincon,Ricardo,Pit	.000	.000	.000	1	0	0	0	0	0	0	0	1	1	0-0	.000	.000	.000	1	0	0	0	0	0	0	0	1	1	0-0
Ritchie,Todd,Min	.000	.000	.000	2	0	0	0	0	0	0	0	1	0	0-0	.000	.000	.000	2	0	0	0	0	0	0	0	1	0	0-0
Ritz,Kevin,Col	.057	.154	.057	35	2	0	0	0	4	0	4	15	2	1-0	.155	.224	.190	168	26	3	0	1	14	7	13	76	29	2-1
Rivera,Mariano,NYA	.000	.000	.000	0	0	0	0	0	0	0	0	0	0	0-0	.000	.000	.000	0	0	0	0	0	0	0	0	0	0	0-0
Roa,Joe,SF	.133	.188	.133	15	2	0	0	0	0	0	1	5	0	0-0	.133	.188	.133	15	2	0	0	0	0	0	1	5	0	0-0
Robertson,Rich,Min	.200	.200	.200	5	1	0	0	0	0	0	0	2	0	0-0	.222	.222	.222	9	2	0	0	0	0	0	0	5	0	0-0
Rodriguez,Felix,Cin	.000	.000	.000	3	0	0	0	0	0	0	0	0	1	0-0	.000	.000	.000	3	0	0	0	0	0	0	0	0	1	0-0
Rodriguez,Frank,Min	.000	.000	.000	1	0	0	0	0	0	0	0	0	0	0-0	.000	.000	.000	1	0	0	0	0	0	0	0	0	0	0-0
Rodriguez,Rich,SF	.333	.500	.333	3	1	0	0	0	1	0	1	1	0	0-0	.050	.174	.050	20	1	0	0	0	2	0	3	4	2	0-0
Rogers,Kenny,NYA	.000	.000	.000	3	0	0	0	0	0	0	0	0	0	0-0	.000	.000	.000	3	0	0	0	0	0	0	0	0	0	0-0
Rojas,Mel,ChN-NYN	.000	.000	.000	1	0	0	0	0	0	0	0	0	0	0-0	.119	.119	.136	59	7	1	0	0	1	3	0	32	6	0-0
Rosado,Jose,KC	.000	.000	.000	2	0	0	0	0	0	0	0	1	0	0-0	.000	.000	.000	2	0	0	0	0	0	0	0	1	0	0-0
Ruebel,Matt,Pit	.000	.000	.000	7	0	0	0	0	0	0	0	7	1	0-0	.150	.190	.150	20	3	0	0	0	0	0	1	11	3	0-0
Rueter,Kirk,SF	.138	.176	.138	65	9	0	0	0	5	5	3	14	7	0-0	.110	.158	.110	173	19	0	0	0	8	13	10	43	21	0-0
Ruffcorn,Scott,Phi	.000	.143	.000	6	0	0	0	0	0	0	1	6	1	0-0	.000	.143	.000	6	0	0	0	0	0	0	1	6	1	0-0
Ruffin,Bruce,Col	.000	.000	.000	0	0	0	0	0	0	0	0	0	0	0-0	.081	.148	.095	295	24	4	0	0	13	7	23	143	23	0-0
Rusch,Glendon,KC	.000	.000	.000	3	0	0	0	0	0	0	0	2	0	0-0	.000	.000	.000	3	0	0	0	0	0	0	0	2	0	0-0
Ryan,Ken,Phi	.000	.000	.000	0	0	0	0	0	0	0	0	0	0	0-0	.143	.143	.143	7	1	0	0	0	0	0	0	4	1	0-0
Saberhagen,Bret,Bos	.000	.000	.000	1	0	0	0	0	0	0	0	0	0	0-0	.127	.181	.149	181	23	4	0	0	13	1	12	45	24	0-0
Sager,A.J.,Det	.000	.000	.000	0	0	0	0	0	0	0	0	0	0	0-0	.077	.077	.231	13	1	0	1	0	0	2	0	6	1	0-0
Sanders,Sc.,Sea-Det	.000	.000	.000	0	0	0	0	0	0	0	0	0	0	0-0	.180	.216	.216	111	20	4	0	0	4	7	5	36	17	1-0
Santana,Julio,Tex	.500	.500	.500	2	1	0	0	0	0	0	0	0	0	0-0	.500	.500	.500	2	1	0	0	0	0	0	0	0	0	0-0
Santiago,Jose,KC	.000	.000	.000	0	0	0	0	0	0	0	0	0	0	0-0	.000	.000	.000	0	0	0	0	0	0	0	0	0	0	0-0
Saunders,Tony,Fla	.081	.128	.162	37	3	0	0	1	2	1	2	19	1	0-0	.081	.128	.162	37	3	0	0	1	2	1	2	19	1	0-0
Schilling,Curt,Phi	.173	.181	.185	81	14	1	0	0	4	1	1	32	12	1-0	.161	.175	.178	354	57	6	0	0	14	15	6	122	46	1-0
Schmidt,Jason,Pit	.107	.138	.143	56	6	2	0	0	2	2	2	26	9	0-0	.087	.134	.109	92	8	2	0	0	3	5	5	43	12	0-0
Schourek,Pete,Cin	.167	.167	.292	24	4	0	0	1	1	2	0	8	6	1-0	.172	.196	.213	221	38	3	0	2	12	17	7	61	29	1-0
Scott,Tim,SD-Col	.000	.000	.000	0	0	0	0	0	0	0	0	0	0	0-0	.067	.067	.067	15	1	0	0	0	0	0	0	11	1	0-0
Sele,Aaron,Bos	.000	.000	.000	2	0	0	0	0	0	0	0	1	0	0-0	.000	.000	.000	2	0	0	0	0	0	0	0	1	0	0-0
Serafini,Dan,Min	.000	.000	.000	0	0	0	0	0	0	0	0	0	0	0-0	.000	.000	.000	0	0	0	0	0	0	0	0	0	0	0-0
Service,Scott,Cin-KC	.000	.000	.000	0	0	0	0	0	0	0	0	0	0	0-0	.067	.067	.067	15	1	0	0	0	0	1	0	8	0	0-0
Shaw,Jeff,Cin	.000	.000	.000	3	0	0	0	0	0	0	0	3	1	0-0	.083	.175	.083	36	3	0	0	0	4	0	4	18	2	0-0
Shuey,Paul,Cle	.000	.000	.000	1	0	0	0	0	0	0	0	1	0	0-0	.000	.000	.000	1	0	0	0	0	0	0	0	1	0	0-0
Silva,Jose,Pit	.143	.143	.143	7	1	0	0	0	1	0	0	4	3	0-0	.143	.143	.143	7	1	0	0	0	1	0	0	4	3	0-0
Simas,Bill,ChA	.000	.000	.000	0	0	0	0	0	0	0	0	0	0	0-0	.000	.000	.000	0	0	0	0	0	0	0	0	0	0	0-0
Sirotka,Mike,ChA	.000	.000	.000	1	0	0	0	0	0	0	0	1	0	0-0	.000	.000	.000	1	0	0	0	0	0	0	0	1	0	0-0
Slocumb,He.,Bos-Sea	.000	.000	.000	0	0	0	0	0	0	0	0	0	0	0-0	.091	.091	.091	11	1	0	0	0	0	2	0	6	1	0-0
Small,Aaron,Oak	.000	.000	.000	1	0	0	0	0	0	0	0	0	0	0-0	.000	.000	.000	1	0	0	0	0	0	0	0	0	0	0-0
Smiley,John,Cin-Cle	.100	.100	.125	40	4	1	0	0	0	2	0	10	2	0-0	.145	.185	.185	504	73	14	0	2	21	35	25	183	45	0-0
Smith,Lee,Mon	.000	.000	.000	0	0	0	0	0	0	0	0	0	0	0-0	.047	.090	.094	64	3	0	0	1	2	2	3	42	4	0-0
Smith,Pete,SD	.167	.194	.267	30	5	1	1	0	2	3	1	16	6	0-0	.122	.174	.152	263	32	4	2	0	14	14	17	76	37	0-0
Smoltz,John,Atl	.228	.307	.266	79	18	3	0	0	10	4	9	22	6	1-1	.163	.234	.210	614	100	15	1	4	54	39	56	234	78	3-2
Sodowsky,Clint,Pit	.500	.500	.500	2	1	0	0	0	0	0	0	0	0	0-0	.500	.500	.500	2	1	0	0	0	0	0	0	0	0	0-0

	1997 Hitting														Career Hitting													
Pitcher,Team	Avg	OBP	SLG	AB	H	2B	3B	HR	R	RBI	BB	SO	SH	SB-CS	Avg	OBP	SLG	AB	H	2B	3B	HR	R	RBI	BB	SO	SH	SB-CS
Spoljaric,Paul,Tor-Sea	.000	.000	.000	1	0	0	0	0	0	0	0	0	0	0-0	.000	.000	.000	1	0	0	0	0	0	0	0	0	0	0-0
Spradlin,Jerry,Phi	.000	.000	.000	1	0	0	0	0	0	0	0	1	0	0-0	.000	.000	.000	3	0	0	0	0	0	0	0	2	0	0-0
Springer,Dennis,Ana	.000	.000	.000	3	0	0	0	0	0	0	0	3	0	0-0	.091	.091	.091	11	1	0	0	0	0	0	0	6	0	0-0
Springer,Russ,Hou	.000	.000	.000	1	0	0	0	0	0	0	0	0	0	0-0	.053	.053	.053	19	1	0	0	0	1	0	0	13	3	0-0
Stanifer,Robby,Fla	.667	.750	1.000	3	2	1	0	0	1	1	0	0	0	0-0	.667	.750	1.000	3	2	1	0	0	1	1	0	0	0	0-0
Stanton,Mike,NYA	.000	.000	.000	0	0	0	0	0	0	0	0	0	0	0-0	.545	.583	.636	11	6	1	0	0	1	2	1	1	1	0-0
Stephenson,Gar.,Phi	.094	.121	.125	32	3	1	0	0	0	1	1	16	5	0-0	.094	.121	.125	32	3	1	0	0	0	1	1	16	5	0-0
Stevens,Da.,Min-ChN	.000	.000	.000	1	0	0	0	0	0	0	0	0	0	0-0	.000	.000	.000	1	0	0	0	0	0	0	0	0	0	0-0
Stottlemyre,Todd,StL	.236	.333	.345	55	13	4	1	0	6	4	8	13	5	0-0	.230	.314	.279	122	28	4	1	0	14	6	15	41	14	1-1
Stull,Everett,Mon	.000	.000	.000	0	0	0	0	0	0	0	0	0	1	0-0	.000	.000	.000	0	0	0	0	0	0	0	0	0	1	0-0
Sturtze,Tanyon,Tex	.000	.000	.000	0	0	0	0	0	0	0	0	0	0	0-0	.000	.000	.000	1	0	0	0	0	0	0	0	0	1	0-0
Sullivan,Scott,Cin	.000	.000	.000	7	0	0	0	0	0	0	0	4	2	0-0	.000	.000	.000	9	0	0	0	0	0	1	0	5	2	0-0
Suppan,Jeff,Bos	.000	.000	.000	2	0	0	0	0	0	0	0	1	0	0-0	.000	.000	.000	2	0	0	0	0	0	0	0	1	0	0-0
Swartzbaugh,Da.,ChN	.000	.000	.000	4	0	0	0	0	0	0	0	1	0	0-0	.000	.091	.000	10	0	0	0	0	0	0	1	4	0	0-0
Swift,Bill,Col	.211	.375	.263	19	4	1	0	0	2	2	4	4	4	0-0	.214	.266	.268	224	48	9	0	1	27	15	15	52	29	1-0
Swindell,Greg,Min	.000	.000	.000	0	0	0	0	0	0	0	0	0	0	0-0	.192	.204	.233	240	46	10	0	0	10	13	4	55	33	0-0
Tabaka,Jeff,Cin	.000	.000	.000	0	0	0	0	0	0	0	0	0	0	0-0	.333	.500	.667	3	1	1	0	0	1	0	1	1	1	0-0
Tapani,Kevin,ChN	.136	.208	.136	22	3	0	0	0	2	0	2	12	4	1-0	.146	.186	.171	41	6	1	0	0	2	2	2	20	7	1-0
Tatis,Ramon,ChN	.000	.250	.000	3	0	0	0	0	0	0	1	3	0	0-0	.000	.250	.000	3	0	0	0	0	0	0	1	3	0	0-0
Tavarez,Julian,SF	.000	.000	.000	1	0	0	0	0	0	0	0	1	0	0-0	.000	.000	.000	1	0	0	0	0	0	0	0	1	0	0-0
Taylor,Billy,Oak	.000	.000	.000	0	0	0	0	0	0	0	0	0	0	0-0	.000	.000	.000	0	0	0	0	0	0	0	0	0	0	0-0
Telemaco,Ama.,ChN	.222	.300	.222	9	2	0	0	0	0	0	1	6	0	0-0	.132	.175	.132	38	5	0	0	0	1	1	2	21	4	0-0
Telford,Anthony,Mon	.200	.200	.267	15	3	1	0	0	0	1	0	3	1	0-0	.200	.200	.267	15	3	1	0	0	0	1	0	3	1	0-0
Telgheder,Dave,Oak	.000	.000	.000	2	0	0	0	0	0	0	0	1	0	0-0	.130	.167	.174	23	3	1	0	0	1	1	1	12	5	0-0
Tewksbury,Bob,Min	.200	.200	.200	5	1	0	0	0	0	1	0	1	0	0-0	.132	.178	.150	379	50	7	0	0	20	19	21	147	41	0-0
Thomas,Larry,ChA	.000	.000	.000	0	0	0	0	0	0	0	0	0	0	0-0	.000	.000	.000	0	0	0	0	0	0	0	0	0	0	0-0
Thompson,Justin,Det	.000	.000	.000	2	0	0	0	0	0	0	0	1	0	0-0	.000	.000	.000	2	0	0	0	0	0	0	0	1	0	0-0
Thompson,Mark,Col	.182	.182	.545	11	2	1	0	1	1	1	0	5	2	0-0	.174	.184	.256	86	15	4	0	1	6	3	1	37	9	0-0
Thomson,John,Col	.213	.245	.213	47	10	0	0	0	2	5	2	23	6	0-0	.213	.245	.213	47	10	0	0	0	2	5	2	23	6	0-0
Thurman,Mike,Mon	.500	.500	.500	2	1	0	0	0	1	0	0	1	1	0-0	.500	.500	.500	2	1	0	0	0	1	0	0	1	1	0-0
Timlin,Mike,Tor-Sea	.000	.000	.000	0	0	0	0	0	0	0	0	0	0	0-0	.000	.000	.000	0	0	0	0	0	0	0	0	0	0	0-0
Tomko,Brett,Cin	.139	.162	.167	36	5	1	0	0	2	3	1	14	3	0-0	.139	.162	.167	36	5	1	0	0	2	3	1	14	3	0-0
Torres,Sal.,Sea-Mon	.000	.000	.000	6	0	0	0	0	0	0	0	4	0	0-0	.152	.152	.152	46	7	0	0	0	2	0	0	20	6	0-0
Trachsel,Steve,ChN	.117	.185	.167	60	7	3	0	0	5	4	5	19	11	0-0	.161	.196	.210	224	36	8	0	1	15	15	9	67	31	0-1
Trlicek,Ri.,Bos-NYN	.000	.000	.000	0	0	0	0	0	0	0	0	0	0	0-0	.250	.250	.250	4	1	0	0	0	0	0	0	3	0	0-0
Trombley,Mike,Min	.000	.000	.000	1	0	0	0	0	0	0	0	1	0	0-0	.000	.000	.000	1	0	0	0	0	0	0	0	1	0	0-0
Urbina,Ugueth,Mon	.000	.000	.000	5	0	0	0	0	0	0	0	4	0	0-0	.125	.167	.125	40	5	0	0	0	3	1	2	25	3	0-0
Valdes,Ismael,LA	.088	.133	.105	57	5	1	0	0	0	1	3	17	7	1-0	.110	.133	.120	191	21	2	0	0	8	4	5	69	27	2-0
Valdes,Marc,Mon	.105	.150	.105	19	2	0	0	0	0	1	1	9	0	0-0	.057	.108	.057	35	2	0	0	0	0	1	2	11	0	0-0
Valenzuela,F.,SD-StL	.182	.182	.182	22	4	0	0	0	1	2	0	3	6	0-0	.200	.205	.262	936	187	26	1	10	56	84	8	145	93	0-2
VanLandingham,SF	.115	.148	.154	26	3	1	0	0	1	0	1	13	2	0-0	.122	.137	.165	164	20	4	0	1	6	6	3	85	13	0-0
Veras,Dario,SD	.000	.000	.000	0	0	0	0	0	0	0	0	0	0	0-0	.000	.000	.000	0	0	0	0	0	0	0	0	0	0	0-0
Veres,Dave,Mon	1.000	1.000	1.000	1	1	0	0	0	0	0	0	0	0	0-0	.313	.353	.375	16	5	1	0	0	1	1	1	9	2	0-0
Veres,Randy,KC	.000	.000	.000	0	0	0	0	0	0	0	0	0	0	0-0	.000	.000	.000	4	0	0	0	0	0	0	0	0	0	0-0
Villone,Ron,Mil	.000	.000	.000	1	0	0	0	0	0	0	0	1	0	0-0	.000	.000	.000	2	0	0	0	0	0	0	0	1	0	0-0
Vosberg,Ed,Tex-Fla	.000	.000	.000	0	0	0	0	0	0	0	0	0	0	0-0	.000	.000	.000	2	0	0	0	0	0	0	0	1	0	0-0
Wade,Terrell,Atl	.250	.357	.250	12	3	0	0	0	0	1	2	5	1	0-0	.200	.286	.200	25	5	0	0	0	0	2	3	12	3	0-0
Wagner,Billy,Hou	.000	.000	.000	1	0	0	0	0	0	0	0	0	0	0-0	.000	.000	.000	6	0	0	0	0	0	0	0	2	0	0-0
Wagner,Paul,Pit-Mil	.000	.000	.000	1	0	0	0	0	0	0	0	1	0	0-0	.167	.204	.180	150	25	2	0	0	9	9	7	45	15	0-1
Wainhouse,David,Pit	.000	.000	.000	2	0	0	0	0	0	0	0	0	0	0-0	.000	.000	.000	3	0	0	0	0	0	0	0	0	0	0-0
Wakefield,Tim,Bos	.000	.000	.000	1	0	0	0	0	0	0	0	0	0	0-0	.125	.137	.194	72	9	2	0	1	3	3	1	20	8	0-0
Walker,Jamie,KC	.000	.000	.000	0	0	0	0	0	0	0	0	0	0	0-0	.000	.000	.000	0	0	0	0	0	0	0	0	0	0	0-0
Wall,Donne,Hou	.100	.182	.100	10	1	0	0	0	0	0	1	4	1	0-0	.169	.210	.186	59	10	1	0	0	5	1	3	17	12	0-0
Wallace,Jeff,Pit	.000	.000	.000	0	0	0	0	0	0	0	0	0	0	0-0	.000	.000	.000	0	0	0	0	0	0	0	0	0	0	0-0
Wasdin,John,Bos	.000	.000	.000	0	0	0	0	0	0	0	0	0	0	0-0	.000	.000	.000	0	0	0	0	0	0	0	0	0	0	0-0
Wells,Bob,Sea	.000	1.000	.000	0	0	0	0	0	1	0	1	0	0	0-0	.000	1.000	.000	0	0	0	0	0	1	0	1	0	0	0-0
Wendell,T.,ChN-NYN	.000	.167	.000	5	0	0	0	0	1	0	1	3	0	0-0	.087	.222	.087	23	2	0	0	0	1	0	4	11	1	0-0
Wengert,Don,Oak	.000	.000	.000	0	0	0	0	0	0	0	0	0	0	0-0	.000	.000	.000	0	0	0	0	0	0	0	0	0	0	0-0
Wetteland,John,Tex	1.000	1.000	2.000	1	1	1	0	0	1	1	0	0	0	0-0	.167	.167	.286	42	7	2	0	1	4	8	0	19	9	0-0
Whisenant,Ma.,Fla-KC	.000	.000	.000	0	0	0	0	0	0	0	0	0	0	0-0	.000	.000	.000	0	0	0	0	0	0	0	0	0	0	0-0
White,Gabe,Cin	.111	.111	.111	9	1	0	0	0	0	1	0	7	2	0-0	.063	.118	.063	16	1	0	0	0	0	1	1	11	4	0-0
Whiteside,Matt,Tex	.000	.000	.000	0	0	0	0	0	0	0	0	0	0	0-0	.000	.000	.000	0	0	0	0	0	0	0	0	0	0	0-0
Wickman,Bob,Mil	.000	.000	.000	0	0	0	0	0	0	0	0	0	0	0-0	.000	.000	.000	0	0	0	0	0	0	0	0	0	0	0-0
Wilkins,Marc,Pit	.000	.200	.000	4	0	0	0	0	0	1	1	3	1	0-0	.154	.267	.154	13	2	0	0	0	1	2	2	9	1	0-0
Williams,Brian,Bal	.000	.000	.000	0	0	0	0	0	0	0	0	0	0	0-0	.163	.160	.200	80	13	3	0	0	5	7	0	25	15	0-0
Williams,Mike,KC	.000	.000	.000	0	0	0	0	0	0	0	0	0	0	0-0	.168	.192	.188	101	17	2	0	0	7	7	3	30	22	1-0
Williams,Woody,Tor	.500	.500	.500	2	1	0	0	0	0	0	0	1	0	0-0	.500	.500	.500	2	1	0	0	0	0	0	0	1	0	0-0
Winchester,Scott,Cin	.000	.000	.000	0	0	0	0	0	0	0	0	0	0	0-0	.000	.000	.000	0	0	0	0	0	0	0	0	0	0	0-0
Winston,Darrin,Phi	.500	.667	.500	2	1	0	0	0	0	1	1	0	0	0-0	.500	.667	.500	2	1	0	0	0	0	1	1	0	0	0-0
Witt,Bobby,Tex	.333	.333	1.000	6	2	1	0	1	1	2	0	1	0	0-0	.103	.122	.231	39	4	2	0	1	2	4	1	12	4	0-0
Wohlers,Mark,Atl	.000	.000	.000	2	0	0	0	0	0	0	0	2	0	0-0	.083	.083	.083	12	1	0	0	0	1	0	0	11	1	0-0
Wolcott,Bob,Sea	.000	.000	.000	1	0	0	0	0	0	0	0	0	0	0-0	.000	.000	.000	1	0	0	0	0	0	0	0	0	0	0-0
Worrell,Tim,SD	.200	.294	.200	15	3	0	0	0	3	1	2	8	0	0-0	.116	.164	.130	69	8	1	0	0	6	4	4	34	9	0-0
Worrell,Todd,LA	.000	.000	.000	0	0	0	0	0	0	0	0	0	0	0-0	.074	.107	.148	27	2	0	1	0	1	0	1	20	2	0-0
Wright,Jamey,Col	.125	.176	.146	48	6	1	0	0	4	3	3	22	3	0-0	.108	.165	.149	74	8	3	0	0	7	3	5	35	8	0-0
Wright,Jaret,Cle	.000	.000	.000	3	0	0	0	0	0	0	0	1	2	0-0	.000	.000	.000	3	0	0	0	0	0	0	0	1	2	0-0

Pitchers Fielding and Holding Runners

1997 Fielding and Holding Runners

PitcherTeam	G	Inn	PO	A	E	DP	Pct.	SBA	CS	PCS	PPO	CS%
Acevedo,Juan,NYN	25	47.2	3	9	1	0	.923	9	2	2	1	.44
Acre,Mark,Oak	15	15.2	1	1	0	0	1.000	1	1	0	0	1.00
Adams,Terry,ChN	74	74.0	7	8	0	0	1.000	13	5	0	1	.38
Adams,Willie,Oak	13	58.1	2	10	0	0	1.000	7	1	1	0	.29
Adamson,Joel,Mil	30	76.1	6	9	2	0	.882	6	3	0	1	.50
Aguilera,Rick,Min	61	68.1	6	13	0	1	1.000	9	3	1	0	.44
Alberro,Jose,Tex	10	28.1	3	5	1	1	.889	1	0	0	0	.00
Aldred,Scott,Min	17	77.1	2	7	0	0	1.000	3	0	1	0	.33
Alfonseca,Antonio,Fla	17	25.2	1	3	0	0	1.000	1	1	0	1	1.00
Almanzar,Carlos,Tor	4	3.1	0	0	0	0	.000	0	0	0	0	.00
Alvarez,Wil.,ChA-SF	33	212.0	8	22	2	0	.938	19	4	4	0	.42
Anderson,Brian,Cle	8	48.0	0	11	0	1	1.000	8	3	2	1	.63
Andujar,Luis,Tor	17	50.0	1	7	0	0	1.000	4	1	0	0	.25
Appier,Kevin,KC	34	235.2	24	17	1	3	.976	23	9	0	0	.39
Arocha,Rene,SF	6	10.1	1	4	0	0	1.000	5	0	0	0	.00
Ashby,Andy,SD	30	200.2	16	34	1	1	.980	40	9	1	0	.25
Assenmacher,Paul,Cle	75	49.0	5	6	0	0	1.000	4	1	1	0	.50
Astacio,Pedro,LA-Col	33	202.1	20	38	1	3	.983	20	5	1	0	.30
Avery,Steve,Bos	22	96.2	0	19	0	1	1.000	11	3	1	1	.36
Ayala,Bobby,Sea	71	96.2	11	7	0	1	1.000	8	2	0	1	.25
Aybar,Manny,StL	12	68.0	3	10	2	0	.867	6	2	0	0	.33
Bailes,Scott,Tex	24	22.0	2	6	0	1	1.000	0	0	0	0	.00
Bailey,Cory,SF	7	9.2	0	0	0	0	.000	1	0	0	0	.00
Bailey,Roger,Col	29	191.0	12	53	0	8	1.000	21	2	3	4	.24
Baldwin,James,ChA	32	200.0	15	22	2	0	.949	18	7	0	2	.39
Banks,Willie,NYA	5	14.0	0	4	0	1	1.000	0	0	0	0	.00
Barrios,Manuel,Hou	2	3.0	0	0	0	0	.000	0	0	0	0	.00
Batchelor,Ri.,StL-SD	23	28.2	3	2	1	0	.833	4	1	0	0	.25
Batista,Miguel,ChN	11	36.1	2	6	0	0	1.000	6	2	0	0	.33
Bautista,Jose,Det-StL	32	52.2	5	3	0	1	1.000	6	1	0	0	.17
Beck,Rod,SF	73	70.0	7	4	1	2	.917	3	0	0	0	.00
Beckett,Robbie,Col	2	1.2	0	0	0	0	.000	1	0	0	0	.00
Beech,Matt,Phi	24	136.2	6	18	0	2	1.000	19	2	3	0	.26
Belcher,Tim,KC	32	213.1	23	22	0	1	1.000	11	6	0	0	.55
Belinda,Stan,Cin	84	99.1	3	4	0	0	1.000	22	4	0	0	.18
Beltran,Rigo,StL	35	54.1	4	9	1	0	.929	3	0	0	0	.67
Benes,Alan,StL	23	161.2	13	12	0	3	1.000	20	10	0	1	.50
Benes,Andy,StL	26	177.0	8	14	1	0	.957	31	9	0	1	.29
Benitez,Armando,Bal	71	73.1	1	3	0	0	1.000	22	2	0	0	.09
Bennett,Shayne,Mon	16	22.2	1	1	0	0	1.000	7	2	0	0	.29
Bere,Jason,ChA	6	28.2	1	2	1	1	.750	3	0	0	0	.00
Bergman,Sean,SD	44	99.0	5	20	3	0	.893	23	3	0	0	.13
Bertotti,Mike,ChA	9	3.2	0	0	0	0	.000	2	0	0	0	.00
Bevil,Brian,KC	18	16.1	1	0	0	0	1.000	3	1	0	0	.33
Bielecki,Mike,Atl	50	57.1	4	7	1	1	.917	5	1	0	0	.20
Blair,Willie,Det	29	175.0	9	14	1	2	.958	17	4	1	1	.29
Blazier,Ron,Phi	36	53.2	4	1	0	1	1.000	7	0	0	0	.00
Bochtler,Doug,SD	54	60.1	4	5	2	0	.818	6	1	0	0	.17
Boehringer,Brian,NYA	34	48.0	2	5	0	1	1.000	3	2	0	1	.67
Bohanon,Brian,NYN	14	92.1	2	13	0	0	1.000	14	3	0	0	.21
Bones,Ricky,Cin-KC	31	96.0	8	15	2	1	.920	14	5	0	0	.36
Borland,To.,NYN-Bos	16	16.2	2	1	1	0	.750	2	0	0	0	.00
Borowski,Joe,Atl-NYA	21	26.0	4	3	0	2	1.000	2	0	0	0	.00
Boskie,Shawn,Bal	28	77.0	6	11	0	1	1.000	11	2	0	0	.18
Bottalico,Ricky,Phi	69	74.0	4	5	0	1	1.000	10	3	0	0	.30
Bottenfield,Kent,ChN	64	84.0	5	5	0	0	1.000	16	6	0	0	.38
Bovee,Mike,Ana	3	3.1	0	0	0	0	.000	0	0	0	0	.00
Bowers,Shane,Min	5	19.0	2	2	1	0	.800	2	1	0	0	.50
Brandenburg,Ma.,Bos	31	41.0	5	5	0	0	1.000	3	1	0	0	.33
Brantley,Jeff,Cin	11	11.2	0	0	0	0	.000	0	0	0	0	.00
Brewer,Billy,Oak-Phi	28	24.0	0	4	0	0	1.000	1	0	0	0	.00
Brocail,Doug,Det	61	78.0	6	12	0	0	1.000	10	4	0	1	.40
Brock,Chris,Atl	7	30.2	6	9	0	0	1.000	5	2	0	0	.40
Brown,Kevin,Fla	33	237.1	36	44	1	3	.988	23	4	0	1	.17
Bruske,Jim,SD	28	44.2	2	4	0	1	1.000	6	2	0	0	.33
Bullinger,Brian,Mon	36	155.1	11	30	0	1	1.000	40	5	1	0	.15
Burba,Dave,Cin	30	160.0	13	24	1	0	.974	18	6	0	0	.33
Burke,John,Col	17	59.0	4	6	1	1	.909	17	1	0	0	.06
Burkett,John,Tex	30	189.1	12	27	1	1	.975	17	6	2	0	.47
Burrows,Terry,SD	13	10.1	1	1	0	0	1.000	1	0	0	0	.00
Busby,Mike,StL	3	14.1	0	2	0	0	1.000	5	2	0	1	.40
Byrd,Paul,Atl	31	53.0	6	4	1	0	.909	8	3	0	0	.38
Cabrera,Jose,Hou	12	15.1	1	2	0	0	1.000	0	0	0	1	.00
Cadaret,Greg,Ana	15	13.2	1	0	0	0	1.000	1	0	0	0	.00
Candiotti,Tom,LA	41	135.0	7	24	1	2	.969	24	8	0	0	.33
Carlson,Dan,SF	6	15.1	1	1	0	0	1.000	1	1	0	0	1.00
Carmona,Rafael,Sea	4	5.2	1	0	0	0	1.000	1	0	0	0	.00
Carpenter,Chris,Tor	14	81.1	6	6	1	1	.923	10	6	0	0	.60
Carrara,Giovanni,Cin	2	10.1	0	3	0	0	1.000	1	1	0	0	1.00
Carrasco,He.,Cin-KC	66	86.0	5	10	1	0	.938	7	0	0	1	.00
Casian,Larry,ChN-KC	44	36.1	2	5	0	0	1.000	1	0	0	0	.00
Castillo,Carlos,ChA	37	66.1	1	5	0	0	1.000	12	0	1	0	.08
Castillo,Fr.,ChN-Col	34	184.1	7	21	1	1	.966	28	14	1	1	.54
Castillo,Tony,ChA	64	62.1	3	19	3	0	.880	9	3	1	0	.44
Cather,Mike,Atl	35	37.2	1	7	0	0	1.000	0	0	0	0	.00
Charlton,Norm,Sea	71	69.1	5	13	0	0	.857	10	4	1	0	.50
Chavez,Anthony,Ana	7	9.2	0	4	0	0	1.000	1	0	0	0	.00
Checo,Robinson,Bos	5	13.1	0	0	0	0	.000	1	0	0	1	.00
Christiansen,Jason,Pit	39	33.2	1	4	1	0	.833	5	3	0	0	.60
Clark,Mark,NYN-ChN	32	205.0	11	32	2	1	.956	25	8	0	3	.32
Clark,Terry,Cle-Tex	13	57.0	9	11	1	2	.952	5	3	0	0	.60
Clemens,Roger,Tor	34	264.0	11	39	1	1	.980	19	8	1	2	.47
Clemons,Chris,ChA	5	12.2	1	1	0	0	1.000	2	1	0	0	.50
Clontz,Brad,Atl	51	48.0	0	5	2	0	.714	11	6	0	0	.55
Cloude,Ken,Sea	10	51.0	6	3	1	0	.900	5	2	1	0	.60
Colon,Bartolo,Cle	19	94.0	6	17	5	3	.821	12	2	0	0	.17
Cone,David,NYA	29	195.0	9	13	2	0	.917	30	8	0	1	.27
Converse,Jim,KC	3	5.0	1	0	0	0	1.000	2	0	0	0	.00
Cook,Dennis,Fla	59	62.1	3	10	0	3	1.000	9	2	1	0	.33
Cooke,Steve,Pit	32	167.1	10	29	1	0	.975	26	11	0	0	.42
Coppinger,Rocky,Bal	5	20.0	1	1	0	0	1.000	12	2	0	0	.17
Cordova,Francisco,Pit	29	178.2	16	32	3	3	.941	19	6	1	1	.37
Cormier,Rheal,Mon	1	1.1	0	0	0	0	.000	0	0	0	0	.00
Corsi,Jim,Bos	52	57.2	6	9	1	0	.938	1	0	0	0	.00
Crabtree,Tim,Tor	37	40.2	3	9	0	1	1.000	3	1	0	0	.33
Crawford,Joe,NYN	19	46.1	1	9	0	1	1.000	5	0	2	0	.40
Creek,Doug,SF	3	13.1	1	2	0	0	1.000	2	0	1	0	.50
Crowell,Jim,Cin	2	6.1	2	2	0	0	1.000	0	0	0	0	.00
Cruz,Nelson,ChA	19	26.1	3	1	0	0	1.000	2	0	0	0	.00
Cummings,John,Det	19	24.2	1	5	0	0	1.000	6	0	1	0	.17
Cunnane,Will,SD	54	91.1	12	6	2	2	.900	17	6	0	1	.35
D'Amico,Jeff,Mil	23	135.2	9	12	0	0	1.000	9	3	1	0	.44
Daal,Omar,Mon-Tor	42	57.1	10	11	2	0	.913	4	1	1	0	.50
Darwin,Danny,ChA-SF	31	157.1	8	27	0	2	1.000	14	4	0	1	.29
Darwin,Jeff,ChA	14	13.2	0	1	0	0	.000	0	0	0	0	.00
Davis,Mark,Mil	19	16.1	2	5	0	0	1.000	1	0	0	0	.00
Davis,Tim,Sea	2	6.2	0	1	0	0	1.000	1	0	0	0	.00
delaMaza,Ro.,KC	1	2.0	0	0	0	0	.000	0	0	0	0	.00
DeHart,Rick,Mon	23	29.1	1	5	0	0	1.000	9	1	2	0	.33
DeJean,Mike,Col	56	67.2	5	11	2	0	.889	5	2	0	0	.40
DeLucia,Rich,SF-Ana	36	44.0	2	5	0	2	1.000	7	6	0	0	.86
Dessens,Elmer,Pit	3	3.1	1	1	0	0	1.000	0	0	0	0	.00
Dickson,Jason,Ana	33	203.2	8	20	2	1	.933	12	7	0	0	.58
Dipoto,Jerry,Col	74	95.2	7	11	1	0	.947	9	3	0	0	.33
Dishman,Glenn,Det	7	29.0	3	6	0	1	1.000	1	0	1	0	1.00
Drabek,Doug,ChA	31	169.1	14	20	1	0	.971	22	7	0	1	.32
Dreifort,Darren,LA	48	63.0	4	18	1	0	.957	9	1	0	0	.22
Duran,Roberto,Det	13	10.2	0	1	0	0	1.000	1	1	0	0	1.00
Eckersley,Dennis,StL	57	53.0	3	5	0	1	1.000	7	1	0	0	.14
Eischen,Joey,Cin	1	1.1	0	0	0	0	.000	0	0	0	0	.00
Eldred,Cal,Mil	34	202.0	15	10	0	1	1.000	24	8	0	1	.33
Embree,Alan,Atl	66	46.0	1	7	0	0	1.000	7	1	0	0	.14
Erdos,Todd,SD	11	13.2	2	2	0	0	1.000	2	0	0	0	.00
Ericks,John,Pit	10	9.1	0	2	0	0	1.000	2	0	0	0	.00
Erickson,Scott,Bal	34	221.2	18	42	6	6	.909	27	6	0	1	.22
Escobar,Kelvim,Tor	27	31.0	2	0	1	1	1.000	3	1	0	0	.33
Eshelman,Vaughn,Bos	21	42.2	4	5	1	1	.900	11	1	0	0	.09
Estes,Shawn,SF	32	201.0	10	33	1	3	.977	20	8	4	0	.60

1997 Fielding and Holding Runners

Pitcher,Team	G	Inn	PO	A	E	DP	Pct.	SBA	CS	PCS	PPO	CS%
Eversgerd,Bryan,Tex	3	1.1	0	0	0	0	.000	0	0	0	0	.00
Eyre,Scott,ChA	11	60.2	0	6	0	0	1.000	12	3	2	0	.42
Falteisek,Steve,Mon	5	8.0	1	1	0	0	1.000	2	0	0	0	.00
Fassero,Jeff,Sea	35	234.1	15	35	1	2	.980	26	6	5	0	.42
Fernandez,Alex,Fla	32	220.2	21	40	1	3	.984	18	11	0	1	.61
Fernandez,Os.,SF	11	56.1	3	5	1	0	.889	9	6	0	0	.67
Fernandez,Sid,Hou	1	5.0	0	1	0	0	1.000	2	0	0	0	.00
Fetters,Mike,Mil	51	70.1	2	12	1	1	.933	13	2	1	0	.23
Finley,Chuck,Ana	25	164.0	2	17	0	0	1.000	17	3	3	0	.35
Flener,Huck,Tor	8	17.1	0	0	0	0	.000	1	0	0	0	.00
Florie,Bryce,Mil	32	75.0	5	3	2	1	.800	15	3	0	0	.20
Fordham,Tom,ChA	7	17.1	0	3	0	0	1.000	1	0	0	0	.00
Fossas,Tony,StL	71	51.2	2	16	0	0	1.000	13	1	2	0	.23
Foster,Kevin,ChN	26	146.1	6	14	0	0	1.000	27	6	0	0	.22
Foulke,Keith,SF-ChA	27	73.1	6	11	2	1	.895	12	4	0	0	.33
Fox,Chad,Atl	30	27.1	2	0	0	0	1.000	4	0	0	0	.00
Franco,John,NYN	59	60.0	4	14	0	1	1.000	2	0	0	1	.00
Frascatore,John,StL	59	80.0	5	5	0	0	1.000	16	1	0	0	.06
Gaillard,Eddie,Det	16	20.1	0	0	0	0	.000	3	0	0	0	.00
Garces,Rich,Bos	12	9.0	1	2	0	0	1.000	4	0	0	0	.00
Garcia,Ramon,Hou	42	158.2	9	29	2	3	.950	26	7	0	4	.27
Gardner,Mark,SF	30	180.1	12	28	0	1	1.000	32	15	1	2	.50
Glavine,Tom,Atl	33	240.0	15	35	1	4	.980	12	6	0	0	.50
Gomes,Wayne,Phi	37	42.2	2	2	0	0	1.000	5	3	0	0	.60
Gonzalez,Jeremi,ChN	23	144.0	7	15	2	1	.917	19	2	0	5	.11
Gooden,Dwight,NYA	20	106.1	9	17	0	0	1.000	13	3	2	4	.38
Gordon,Tom,Bos	42	182.2	18	20	2	1	.950	27	6	1	0	.26
Gorecki,Rick,LA	4	6.0	0	0	0	0	.000	1	0	0	0	.00
Grace,Mike,Phi	6	39.0	3	3	0	0	1.000	2	2	0	0	1.00
Granger,Jeff,Pit	9	5.0	0	0	0	0	.000	0	0	0	0	.00
Graves,Danny,Cle-Cin	15	26.0	3	3	1	0	.857	5	1	0	0	.20
Green,Tyler,Phi	14	76.2	6	7	2	2	.867	12	5	1	1	.50
Greene,Tommy,Hou	2	9.0	0	0	0	0	.000	1	1	0	0	1.00
Groom,Buddy,Oak	78	64.2	2	10	0	2	1.000	9	1	3	0	.44
Gross,Kevin,Ana	12	25.1	0	4	0	0	1.000	3	2	0	0	.67
Grundt,Ken,Bos	3	3.2	2	0	0	0	1.000	0	0	0	0	.00
Guardado,Eddie,Min	69	46.0	1	6	0	1	1.000	7	0	1	0	.14
Gubicza,Mark,Ana	2	4.2	1	0	0	0	1.000	1	0	0	0	.00
Gunderson,Eric,Tex	60	49.2	1	3	0	0	1.000	0	0	0	0	.00
Guthrie,Mark,LA	62	69.1	2	13	1	0	.938	12	1	3	1	.33
Guzman,Juan,Tor	13	60.0	1	7	3	0	.727	13	1	0	1	.08
Hall,Darren,LA	63	54.2	3	14	1	2	.944	11	1	1	0	.18
Hamilton,Joey,SD	31	192.2	10	19	1	1	.967	23	9	1	0	.43
Hammond,Chris,Bos	29	65.1	3	10	1	1	.929	5	0	1	0	.20
Hampton,Mike,Hou	34	223.0	16	57	3	6	.961	10	2	4	0	.60
Haney,Chris,KC	8	24.2	1	6	1	0	.875	3	1	0	0	.33
Hansell,Greg,Mil	3	4.2	0	0	0	0	.000	0	0	0	0	.00
Hanson,Erik,Tor	3	15.0	0	0	0	0	.000	3	0	0	0	.00
Harkey,Mike,LA	10	14.2	0	1	0	0	1.000	0	0	0	0	.00
Harnisch,Pe.,NYN-Mil	10	39.2	5	4	0	2	1.000	3	2	0	0	.67
Harris,Pep,Ana	61	79.2	4	14	0	2	1.000	6	5	0	0	.83
Harris,Reggie,Phi	50	54.1	3	3	0	0	1.000	11	2	0	0	.18
Hasegawa,Sh.,Ana	50	116.2	8	21	1	3	.967	7	3	1	0	.57
Haught,Gary,Oak	6	11.1	1	1	0	0	1.000	1	1	0	0	1.00
Hawkins,LaTroy,Min	20	103.1	9	13	1	1	.957	4	2	0	0	.50
Haynes,Jimmy,Oak	13	73.1	6	11	2	2	.895	5	2	0	0	.40
Helling,Rick,Fla-Tex	41	131.0	1	9	1	0	.909	21	11	2	0	.62
Henriquez,Oscar,Hou	4	2.0	0	0	0	0	.000	2	0	0	0	.00
Henry,Butch,Bos	36	84.1	3	17	0	2	1.000	10	1	3	0	.40
Henry,Doug,SF	75	70.2	6	4	1	0	.909	10	3	0	0	.30
Hentgen,Pat,Tor	35	264.0	19	34	1	1	.981	27	11	4	3	.56
Heredia,Felix,Fla	56	56.2	1	0	1	0	.500	4	1	0	0	.25
Heredia,Wilson,Tex	10	19.2	0	3	0	1	1.000	2	1	0	0	.50
Hermanson,Du.,Mon	32	158.1	10	20	2	2	.938	18	7	0	2	.39
Hernandez,Fe.,Det	2	1.1	0	0	0	0	.000	0	0	0	0	.00
Hernandez,Livan,Fla	17	96.1	8	16	1	4	.960	7	3	0	0	.43
Hernandez,R.,ChA-SF	74	80.2	4	10	1	1	.933	13	3	1	0	.23
Hershiser,Orel,Cle	32	195.1	20	29	4	2	.925	12	7	1	0	.67
Hill,Ken,Tex-Ana	31	190.0	17	37	0	2	1.000	27	8	0	0	.30
Hitchcock,Sterling,SD	32	161.0	4	21	2	2	.926	35	4	5	0	.26
Hoffman,Trevor,SD	70	81.1	2	4	1	0	.857	2	2	0	0	.50

1997 Fielding and Holding Runners

Pitcher,Team	G	Inn	PO	A	E	DP	Pct.	SBA	CS	PCS	PPO	CS%
Holmes,Darren,Col	42	89.1	7	15	1	0	.957	8	3	0	0	.38
Holt,Chris,Hou	33	209.2	13	36	1	1	.980	25	11	1	1	.48
Holtz,Mike,Ana	66	43.1	2	9	1	2	.917	8	1	1	0	.25
Holzemer,Mark,Sea	14	9.0	1	4	0	0	1.000	0	0	0	0	.00
Honeycutt,Rick,StL	2	2.0	0	0	0	0	.000	0	0	0	0	.00
Hudek,John,Hou	40	40.2	1	6	0	1	1.000	7	4	1	0	.71
Hudson,Joe,Bos	26	35.2	2	7	0	2	1.000	5	1	0	0	.20
Hurtado,Edwin,Sea	13	19.0	0	6	0	1	1.000	1	1	0	1	1.00
Hutton,Mark,Fla-Col	40	60.1	6	11	0	1	1.000	7	1	0	0	.14
Irabu,Hideki,NYA	13	53.1	1	5	2	1	.750	11	1	1	1	.18
Isringhausen,Ja.,NYN	6	29.2	3	1	0	0	1.000	4	1	0	0	.25
Jackson,Da.,StL-SD	17	67.2	3	10	2	0	.867	11	1	2	0	.27
Jackson,Mike,Cle	71	75.0	5	15	0	4	1.000	4	0	0	0	.00
Jacome,Jason,KC-Cle	28	49.1	4	12	1	1	.941	1	0	1	0	1.00
James,Mike,Ana	58	62.2	2	9	0	0	1.000	7	3	0	0	.43
Janzen,Marty,Tor	12	25.0	3	1	0	0	1.000	2	1	0	0	.50
Jarvis,Ke.,Cin-Det	32	68.0	1	7	0	0	1.000	16	3	0	0	.19
Johnson,Dane,Oak	38	45.2	1	4	2	0	.714	8	0	1	0	.13
Johnson,Jason,Pit	3	6.0	0	0	0	0	.000	2	2	0	0	1.00
Johnson,Mike,Bal-Mon	25	89.2	5	13	1	1	.947	17	2	1	0	.18
Johnson,Randy,Sea	30	213.0	7	20	4	0	.871	29	13	3	0	.55
Johnstone,Jo.,SF-Oak	18	25.0	2	3	0	0	1.000	8	0	1	0	.13
Jones,Bobby,NYN	30	193.1	14	35	1	2	.980	16	5	0	1	.31
Jones,BobbyM.,Col	4	19.1	0	2	0	0	1.000	5	1	0	0	.20
Jones,Doug,Mil	75	80.1	4	8	2	1	.857	5	3	0	0	.60
Jones,Todd,Det	68	70.0	1	4	0	0	1.000	7	1	0	0	.14
Jordan,Ricardo,NYN	22	27.0	0	5	0	1	1.000	4	0	0	0	.00
Judd,Mike,LA	1	2.2	0	0	0	0	.000	2	1	0	0	.50
Juden,Jeff,Mon-Cle	30	161.1	6	15	3	0	.875	56	4	2	1	.11
Kamieniecki,Scott,Bal	30	179.1	15	30	3	5	.938	29	3	1	5	.14
Karchner,Matt,ChA	52	52.2	2	6	0	2	1.000	9	2	0	0	.22
Karl,Scott,Mil	32	193.1	5	28	4	5	.892	13	5	1	0	.46
Karp,Ryan,Phi	15	15.0	1	1	1	0	.667	1	1	0	0	1.00
Karsay,Steve,Oak	24	132.2	7	14	1	1	.840	18	1	0	2	.06
Kashiwada,Ta.,NYN	35	31.1	4	5	1	0	.900	5	1	0	0	.20
Keagle,Greg,Det	11	45.1	4	3	0	1	1.000	6	1	0	0	.17
Key,Jimmy,Bal	34	212.1	12	37	2	3	.961	22	5	6	0	.50
Kile,Darryl,Hou	34	255.2	28	38	1	3	.985	24	4	0	0	.17
King,Curtis,StL	30	29.1	2	5	0	0	1.000	2	0	0	0	.00
Kline,Steve,Cle-Mon	46	52.2	3	5	1	0	.889	11	3	0	0	.27
Krivda,Rick,Bal	10	50.0	6	5	0	1	1.000	9	2	1	0	.33
Kroon,Marc,SD	12	11.1	0	0	0	0	.000	2	0	0	0	.00
Kubinski,Tim,Oak	11	12.2	2	1	0	1	1.000	2	0	0	0	.00
Lacy,Kerry,Bos	33	45.2	4	2	1	0	.857	2	0	0	0	.00
Langston,Mark,Ana	9	47.2	2	12	1	1	.933	3	1	1	1	.67
Leiter,Al,Fla	27	151.1	0	14	0	1	1.000	28	14	2	0	.57
Leiter,Mark,Phi	31	182.2	10	30	3	4	.930	25	5	1	2	.24
LeRoy,John,Atl	1	2.0	0	0	0	0	.000	0	0	0	0	.00
Leskanic,Curt,Col	55	58.1	6	5	0	1	1.000	5	2	1	0	.60
Levine,Al,ChA	25	27.1	5	3	0	1	1.000	3	0	0	0	.00
Lewis,Richie,Oak-Cin	18	24.1	0	4	1	0	.800	4	0	2	0	.50
Lidle,Cory,NYN	54	81.2	5	8	0	0	1.000	5	2	0	0	.40
Lieber,Jon,Pit	33	188.1	16	25	1	1	.976	20	4	0	0	.20
Ligtenberg,Kerry,Atl	15	15.0	1	0	0	1	1.000	4	0	0	0	.00
Lima,Jose,Hou	52	75.0	4	0	0	0	1.000	7	4	0	0	.57
Lira,Felipe,Det-Sea	28	110.2	8	21	2	4	.935	25	3	0	0	.12
Lloyd,Graeme,NYA	46	49.0	3	8	3	1	.786	5	0	0	0	.00
Loaiza,Esteban,Pit	33	196.1	11	26	2	2	.949	30	9	1	0	.33
Loiselle,Rich,Pit	72	72.2	3	7	3	1	.769	5	2	0	0	.40
Long,Joey,SD	10	11.0	2	1	0	0	1.000	5	1	0	0	.20
Lopez,Albie,Cle	37	76.2	4	14	0	1	1.000	17	5	1	0	.35
Lorraine,Andrew,Oak	12	29.2	4	2	0	1	1.000	3	1	0	0	.33
Lowe,Derek,Sea-Bos	20	69.0	3	10	0	0	1.000	6	2	0	0	.33
Lowe,Sean,StL	6	41.1	1	3	2	0	.667	2	0	0	0	.00
Ludwick,Eric,StL-Oak	11	30.2	2	3	0	1	1.000	13	1	0	0	.08
Maddux,Greg,Atl	33	232.2	16	49	3	3	.956	28	8	0	1	.29
Maddux,Mike,Sea	6	10.2	1	1	0	0	1.000	0	0	0	0	.00
Maduro,Calvin,Phi	15	71.0	8	7	1	0	.938	7	3	0	1	.43
Magnante,Mike,Hou	40	47.2	1	7	1	0	.889	7	3	0	0	.43
Mahay,Ron,Bos	28	25.0	1	2	0	0	1.000	3	0	0	0	.00
Mahomes,Pat,Bos	10	10.0	0	0	0	0	.000	0	0	0	0	.00
Maloney,Sean,Mil	3	7.0	0	0	0	0	.000	0	0	0	0	.00

Pitcher,Team	G	Inn	PO	A	E	DP	Pct.	SBA	CS	PCS	PPO	CS%
Manuel,Barry,NYN	19	25.2	2	1	1	0	.750	2	1	0	0	.50
Manzanillo,Josias,Sea	16	18.1	1	1	0	0	1.000	3	2	0	0	.67
Martin,Tom,Hou	55	56.0	1	9	1	0	.909	6	0	1	0	.17
Martinez,Dennis,Sea	9	49.0	5	7	2	0	.857	16	5	0	0	.31
Martinez,Pedro,Mon	31	241.1	7	31	1	1	.974	25	5	0	3	.20
Martinez,PedroA.,Cin	8	6.2	1	0	0	0	1.000	1	0	0	0	.00
Martinez,Ramon,LA	22	133.2	10	20	1	1	.968	20	7	0	0	.35
Mathews,T.J.,StL-Oak	64	74.2	6	8	2	0	.875	13	0	0	0	.00
Mathews,Terry,Bal	57	63.1	5	10	1	0	.938	7	1	0	1	.14
May,Darrell,Ana	29	51.2	0	6	0	1	1.000	2	0	0	1	.00
McAndrew,Jamie,Mil	5	19.1	3	1	1	0	.800	2	2	0	1	1.00
McCarthy,Greg,Sea	37	29.2	2	4	0	0	1.000	4	0	0	0	.00
McCurry,Jeff,Col	33	40.2	3	5	0	0	1.000	6	1	0	1	.17
McDill,Allen,KC	3	4.0	0	1	0	0	1.000	0	0	0	0	.00
McDonald,Ben,Mil	21	133.0	6	16	1	3	.957	24	4	0	0	.17
McDowell,Jack,Cle	8	40.2	3	6	0	0	1.000	5	1	0	0	.20
McElroy,Ch.Ana-ChA	61	75.0	1	12	0	1	1.000	4	0	0	0	.00
McGraw,Tom,StL	2	1.2	0	1	0	0	1.000	0	0	0	0	.00
McMichael,Greg,NYN	73	87.2	9	13	0	2	1.000	11	1	0	0	.09
Mecir,Jim,NYA	25	33.2	4	3	0	0	1.000	6	3	0	0	.50
Mendoza,Ramiro,NYA	39	133.2	11	25	2	2	.947	10	2	0	1	.20
Menhart,Paul,SD	9	44.0	6	4	0	2	1.000	6	3	0	0	.50
Mercedes,Jose,Mil	29	159.0	6	16	3	2	.880	16	7	0	0	.44
Mercker,Kent,Cin	28	144.2	11	22	0	0	1.000	18	4	0	0	.22
Mesa,Jose,Cle	66	82.1	5	6	1	2	.917	5	3	0	0	.60
Miceli,Dan,Det	71	82.2	4	6	0	0	1.000	7	2	0	0	.29
Miller,Kurt,Fla	7	7.1	1	0	0	0	1.000	0	0	0	0	.00
Miller,Travis,Min	13	48.1	8	5	0	0	1.000	7	2	1	0	.43
Mills,Alan,Bal	39	38.2	4	3	2	0	.778	9	1	0	0	.11
Millwood,Kevin,Atl	12	51.1	3	6	0	0	1.000	14	3	0	0	.21
Mimbs,Michael,Phi	17	28.2	0	2	0	0	.500	1	0	0	0	.00
Minchey,Nate,Col	2	2.0	0	2	0	0	1.000	1	0	0	0	.00
Minor,Blas,Hou	11	12.0	1	2	0	0	1.000	0	0	0	0	.00
Miranda,Angel,Mil	10	14.0	1	2	0	0	1.000	2	1	0	0	.50
Misuraca,Mike,Mil	5	10.1	0	0	0	0	.000	0	0	0	0	.00
Mlicki,Dave,NYN	32	193.2	11	17	2	1	.933	31	5	0	0	.16
Moehler,Brian,Det	31	175.1	16	23	1	2	.975	26	5	0	1	.19
Mohler,Mike,Oak	62	101.2	7	18	1	0	.962	14	2	3	1	.36
Montgomery,Jeff,KC	55	59.1	10	5	0	0	1.000	5	2	0	0	.40
Montgomery,St.,Oak	4	6.1	1	0	0	0	1.000	3	1	0	0	.33
Moody,Eric,Tex	10	19.0	1	2	0	0	1.000	4	1	0	0	.25
Morel,RamonPit-ChN	8	11.1	1	2	0	0	1.000	1	0	0	0	.00
Morgan,Mike,Cin	31	162.0	10	23	0	1	1.000	21	5	1	0	.29
Morman,Alvin,Cle	34	18.1	0	2	0	0	1.000	8	0	1	0	.13
Morris,Matt,StL	33	217.0	5	28	5	2	.868	18	6	1	0	.39
Moyer,Jamie,Sea	30	188.2	14	33	0	2	1.000	20	5	1	0	.30
Mulholland,T.,ChN-SF	40	186.2	12	40	4	2	.929	5	3	1	3	.80
Munoz,Bobby,Phi	8	33.1	1	6	1	0	.875	11	2	0	0	.18
Munoz,Mike,Col	64	45.2	3	6	1	2	.900	2	0	0	0	.00
Murray,Heath,SD	17	33.1	1	2	0	1	1.000	3	1	0	0	.33
Mussina,Mike,Bal	33	224.2	18	25	0	0	1.000	15	6	0	0	.40
Myers,Mike,Det	88	53.2	4	8	2	0	.857	6	0	1	0	.17
Myers,Randy,Bal	61	59.2	1	3	0	0	1.000	1	0	1	1	1.00
Myers,Rodney,ChN	5	9.0	2	0	0	0	1.000	2	0	0	0	.00
Nagy,Charles,Cle	34	227.0	16	45	0	1	1.000	34	9	1	2	.29
Naulty,Dan,Min	29	30.2	1	1	0	0	1.000	2	1	0	0	.50
Navarro,Jaime,ChA	33	209.2	15	15	3	0	.909	29	6	0	0	.21
Neagle,Denny,Atl	34	233.1	9	35	1	2	.978	26	2	0	0	.36
Nelson,Jeff,NYA	77	78.2	4	17	0	0	1.000	15	2	0	0	.13
Nen,Robb,Fla	73	74.0	9	7	1	1	.941	9	0	0	0	.00
Nomo,Hideo,LA	33	207.1	16	8	2	2	.923	25	10	0	0	.40
Nye,Ryan,Phi	4	12.0	1	3	0	1	1.000	0	0	0	0	.00
Ogea,Chad,Cle	21	126.1	8	17	5	1	.833	17	8	0	0	.47
Ojala,Kirt,Fla	7	28.2	4	5	0	1	1.000	3	2	0	0	.67
Olivares,Om.,Det-Sea	32	177.1	12	24	2	3	.947	7	4	0	1	.57
Oliver,Darren,Tex	32	201.1	7	23	2	0	.938	24	6	4	0	.42
Olson,Gregg,Min-KC	45	50.0	4	6	1	0	.909	13	4	0	0	.31
Oquist,Mike,Oak	19	107.2	8	10	1	2	.947	7	4	0	0	.57
Orosco,Jesse,Bal	71	50.1	3	6	0	1	1.000	7	1	1	1	.29
Osborne,Donovan,StL	14	80.1	4	10	0	1	1.000	7	3	1	0	.57
Osuna,Antonio,LA	48	61.2	3	13	2	1	.889	4	2	0	0	.50
Painter,Lance,StL	14	17.0	4	3	0	1	1.000	2	1	1	0	1.00

Pitcher,Team	G	Inn	PO	A	E	DP	Pct.	SBA	CS	PCS	PPO	CS%
Pall,Donn,Fla	2	2.1	0	0	0	0	.000	0	0	0	0	.00
Paniagua,Jose,Mon	9	18.0	3	1	0	0	1.000	5	0	0	0	.00
Park,ChanHo,LA	32	192.0	7	27	2	1	.944	15	8	1	0	.60
Patterson,Bob,ChN	76	59.1	4	8	1	1	.923	7	1	0	0	.14
Patterson,Danny,Tex	54	71.0	4	7	0	1	1.000	7	3	1	0	.57
Pavlik,Roger,Tex	11	57.2	3	4	1	1	.875	4	2	0	0	.50
Percival,Troy,Ana	55	52.0	2	2	0	0	1.000	5	1	0	0	.20
Perez,Carlos,Mon	33	206.2	19	37	3	4	.949	15	1	3	1	.27
Perez,Mike,KC	16	20.1	3	3	0	0	1.000	4	3	0	0	.75
Perez,Yorkis,NYN	9	8.2	0	0	0	0	.000	2	0	0	0	.00
Perisho,Matt,Ana	11	45.0	2	7	0	0	1.000	9	1	0	0	.11
Person,Robert,Tor	23	128.1	4	8	1	1	.923	7	4	0	0	.57
Peters,Chris,Pit	31	37.1	2	8	0	0	1.000	5	3	0	0	.60
Petkovsek,Mark,StL	55	96.0	11	19	1	3	.968	11	4	0	0	.36
Pettitte,Andy,NYA	35	240.1	9	43	1	5	.981	21	6	1	8	.30
Pichardo,Hipolito,KC	47	49.0	8	12	0	3	1.000	2	1	1	0	1.00
Pisciotta,Marc,ChN	24	28.1	2	3	0	0	1.000	4	1	1	0	.50
Pittsley,Jim,KC	21	112.0	6	10	1	0	.941	15	3	1	0	.27
Plantenberg,Erik,Phi	35	25.2	2	2	1	0	.800	1	0	0	0	.00
Plesac,Dan,Tor	73	50.1	0	6	0	0	1.000	6	1	0	0	.17
Plunk,Eric,Cle	56	65.2	2	4	2	0	.750	10	2	0	0	.20
Poole,Jim,SF	63	49.1	2	6	2	0	.800	7	2	2	0	.57
Portugal,Mark,Phi	3	13.2	1	2	1	0	.750	2	1	0	0	.50
Powell,Jay,Fla	74	79.2	5	15	4	2	.833	11	3	0	0	.27
Prieto,Ariel,Oak	22	125.0	9	19	5	2	.848	15	3	1	0	.21
Pugh,Tim,Det	2	9.0	0	2	0	0	1.000	0	0	0	0	.00
Quantrill,Paul,Tor	77	88.0	1	17	3	3	.857	11	5	1	0	.55
Radinsky,Scott,LA	75	62.1	3	8	0	2	1.000	3	0	1	0	.33
Radke,Brad,Min	35	239.2	14	31	0	5	1.000	17	7	0	0	.41
Raggio,Brady,StL	15	31.1	1	6	0	0	1.000	7	3	0	0	.43
Ramos,Edgar,Phi	4	14.0	1	2	0	0	1.000	3	1	0	0	.33
Rapp,Pat,Fla-SF	27	141.2	8	20	3	1	.903	15	5	1	1	.40
Reed,Rick,NYN	33	208.1	22	27	2	2	.961	9	6	0	0	.67
Reed,Steve,Col	63	62.1	1	12	1	0	.929	7	2	0	0	.29
Rekar,Bryan,Col	2	9.1	0	4	0	1	1.000	0	0	0	0	.00
Remlinger,Mike,Cin	69	124.0	6	21	1	0	.964	18	1	6	1	.39
Reyes,Al,Mil	19	29.2	1	6	0	0	1.000	1	0	0	0	.00
Reyes,Carlos,Oak	37	77.1	6	11	0	1	1.000	6	0	0	0	.00
Reyes,Dennis,LA	14	47.0	1	16	1	0	.944	7	0	0	1	.00
Reynolds,Shane,Hou	30	181.0	10	31	4	4	.911	11	6	0	0	.55
Reynoso,Ar.,NYN	16	91.1	7	17	1	1	.960	4	1	1	2	.50
Rhodes,Arthur,Bal	53	95.1	4	16	1	1	.952	18	3	1	3	.22
Rigby,Brad,Oak	14	77.2	5	14	1	3	.950	3	1	0	1	.33
Rincon,Ricardo,Pit	62	60.0	3	6	0	0	1.000	7	3	1	0	.57
Rios,Danny,NYA	2	2.1	1	0	0	0	1.000	0	0	0	0	.00
Risley,Bill,Tor	3	4.1	0	0	0	0	.000	1	0	0	0	.00
Ritchie,Todd,Min	42	74.2	3	10	0	2	1.000	7	2	1	2	.43
Ritz,Kevin,Col	18	107.1	13	15	0	3	1.000	27	8	0	0	.30
Rivera,Mariano,NYA	66	71.2	11	9	0	0	1.000	3	0	0	0	.00
Roa,Joe,SF	28	65.2	6	16	1	4	.957	8	3	0	1	.38
Robertson,Rich,Min	31	147.0	7	13	2	2	.909	20	2	4	0	.30
Robinson,Ken,Tor	3	3.1	1	2	0	1	1.000	0	0	0	0	.00
Rodriguez,Felix,Cin	26	46.0	0	2	0	0	1.000	11	4	0	0	.36
Rodriguez,Frank,Min	43	142.1	10	24	2	2	.944	9	4	0	2	.44
Rodriguez,Nerio,Bal	6	22.0	0	5	0	0	1.000	0	0	0	0	.00
Rodriguez,Rich,SF	71	65.1	5	17	1	1	.957	4	2	2	0	1.00
Rogers,Kenny,NYA	31	145.0	13	42	2	4	.965	9	2	4	3	.67
Rojas,Mel,ChN-NYN	77	85.1	2	7	1	0	.900	10	2	0	0	.20
Rosado,Jose,KC	34	203.1	11	24	1	2	.972	13	2	1	2	.23
Rose,Brian,Bos	1	3.0	0	0	0	0	1.000	1	0	0	0	.00
Ruebel,Matt,Pit	44	62.2	3	9	3	0	.800	7	0	0	0	.00
Rueter,Kirk,SF	32	190.2	6	53	0	5	1.000	11	1	6	1	.64
Ruffcorn,Scott,Phi	18	39.2	3	3	1	0	.857	7	1	0	0	.14
Ruffin,Bruce,Col	23	22.0	1	2	0	0	1.000	3	0	0	0	.00
Rusch,Glendon,KC	30	170.1	8	13	0	1	1.000	6	0	0	0	.00
Ryan,Ken,Phi	22	20.2	3	2	0	0	1.000	0	0	0	0	.00
Saberhagen,Bret,Bos	6	26.0	1	2	1	1	.750	4	0	0	1	.00
Sager,A.J.,Det	38	84.0	3	13	0	1	1.000	6	1	1	0	.33
Sanders,Sc.,Sea-Det	48	139.2	6	10	1	0	.941	18	4	1	0	.28
Santana,Julio,Tex	30	104.0	6	15	0	3	1.000	4	1	0	0	.25
Santiago,Jose,KC	4	4.2	0	0	0	0	.000	0	0	0	0	.00
Saunders,Tony,Fla	22	111.1	2	11	2	0	.867	16	7	2	0	.56

1997 Fielding and Holding Runners

Pitcher,Team	G	Inn	PO	A	E	DP	Pct.	SBA	CS	PCS	PPO	CS%
Schilling,Curt,Phi	35	254.1	20	28	1	2	.980	18	8	1	2	.50
Schmidt,Jason,Pit	32	187.2	13	19	0	0	1.000	16	8	0	2	.50
Schourek,Pete,Cin	18	84.2	3	8	0	0	1.000	10	0	0	0	.00
Scott,Tim,SD-Col	17	21.0	4	5	0	0	1.000	3	0	1	0	.33
Sele,Aaron,Bos	33	177.1	10	25	1	2	.972	26	6	1	1	.27
Serafini,Dan,Min	6	26.1	0	1	0	0	1.000	4	2	0	0	.50
Service,Scott,Cin-KC	16	22.1	2	2	0	0	1.000	0	0	0	0	.00
Shaw,Jeff,Cin	78	94.2	12	13	0	1	1.000	5	1	0	0	.20
Shuey,Paul,Cle	40	45.0	3	7	0	0	1.000	6	0	0	0	.00
Silva,Jose,Pit	11	36.1	3	1	0	0	1.000	4	1	0	0	.25
Simas,Bill,ChA	40	41.1	3	3	0	0	1.000	5	1	0	0	.20
Sirotka,Mike,ChA	7	32.0	1	3	1	0	.800	5	2	2	0	.80
Slocumb,He.,Bos-Sea	76	75.0	7	6	1	1	.929	12	1	0	0	.08
Small,Aaron,Oak	71	96.2	5	15	1	2	.952	13	3	0	0	.23
Smiley,John,Cin-Cle	26	154.1	0	16	0	0	1.000	22	5	2	0	.32
Smith,Lee,Mon	25	21.2	1	4	0	0	1.000	9	1	0	0	.11
Smith,Pete,SD	37	118.0	6	24	1	1	.968	17	4	0	0	.24
Smoltz,John,Atl	35	256.0	31	29	2	2	.968	25	10	1	0	.44
Sodowsky,Clint,Pit	45	52.0	3	5	0	0	1.000	6	2	0	0	.33
Spoljaric,Paul,Tor-Sea	57	70.2	6	11	0	1	1.000	8	1	2	0	.38
Spradlin,Jerry,Phi	76	81.2	9	2	0	0	1.000	11	3	1	0	.36
Springer,Dennis,Ana	32	194.2	12	26	2	3	.950	30	8	3	0	.37
Springer,Russ,Hou	54	55.1	5	5	1	1	.909	8	0	0	0	.00
Stanifer,Robby,Fla	36	45.0	2	6	1	1	.889	6	2	0	0	.33
Stanton,Mike,NYA	64	66.2	3	5	0	0	1.000	2	0	1	0	.50
Stephenson,Ga.,Phi	20	117.0	15	14	0	2	1.000	10	8	0	4	.80
Stevens,Da.,Min-ChN	16	32.1	3	1	0	0	1.000	12	2	0	0	.17
Stottlemyre,Todd,StL	28	181.0	12	21	1	0	.971	24	6	1	0	.25
Stull,Everett,Mon	3	3.1	0	0	0	0	.000	1	0	0	0	.00
Sturtze,Tanyon,Tex	9	32.2	0	1	0	0	1.000	1	1	0	0	1.00
Sullivan,Scott,Cin	59	97.1	4	11	2	0	.882	10	0	0	0	.00
Suppan,Jeff,Bos	23	112.1	6	8	3	2	.824	27	2	0	0	.07
Swartzbaugh,Da.,ChN	2	8.0	0	1	0	0	1.000	2	0	0	0	.00
Swift,Bill,Col	14	65.1	4	22	1	2	.963	4	0	0	0	.00
Swindell,Greg,Min	65	115.2	12	11	0	1	1.000	12	1	5	0	.50
Tabaka,Jeff,Cin	3	2.0	0	0	0	0	.000	0	0	0	0	.00
Tapani,Kevin,ChN	13	85.0	4	10	0	0	1.000	6	3	0	0	.50
Tatis,Ramon,ChN	56	55.2	6	10	1	2	.941	2	0	0	0	.00
Tavarez,Julian,SF	89	88.1	5	13	2	2	.900	5	0	0	0	.00
Taylor,Billy,Oak	72	73.0	3	13	0	1	1.000	13	3	0	0	.23
Telemaco,Am.,ChN	10	38.0	3	5	0	0	1.000	5	1	0	0	.20
Telford,Anthony,Mon	65	89.0	7	23	1	1	.968	11	2	1	0	.27
Telgheder,Dave,Oak	20	101.0	9	24	0	4	1.000	13	4	0	0	.31
Tewksbury,Bob,Min	26	168.2	21	30	0	7	1.000	8	2	0	0	.25
Thomas,Larry,ChA	5	3.1	1	0	0	0	1.000	0	0	0	0	.00
Thompson,Justin,Det	32	223.1	11	30	0	3	1.000	31	3	8	0	.35
Thompson,Mark,Col	6	29.2	2	5	0	0	1.000	4	0	0	0	.00
Thomson,John,Col	27	166.1	9	24	2	2	.943	22	7	0	0	.32
Thurman,Mike,Mon	5	11.2	0	4	0	0	1.000	1	0	0	0	.00
Timlin,Mike,Tor-Sea	64	72.2	8	13	1	2	.955	5	2	0	0	.40
Tomko,Brett,Cin	22	126.0	6	9	2	1	.882	11	6	1	0	.64
Torres,Sa.,Sea-Mon	14	25.2	4	5	0	1	1.000	3	0	0	0	.00
Trachsel,Steve,ChN	34	201.1	17	26	2	0	.956	39	10	2	3	.31
Trlicek,Ricky,Bos-NYN	27	32.1	4	5	0	1	1.000	4	1	0	0	.25
Trombley,Mike,Min	67	82.1	6	6	0	2	1.000	7	1	0	0	.14
Urbina,Ugueth,Mon	63	64.1	3	8	1	0	.917	8	0	0	1	.00
Valdes,Ismael,LA	30	196.2	17	28	3	3	.938	22	6	0	2	.27
Valdes,Marc,Mon	48	95.0	9	10	1	1	.950	8	2	0	0	.25
Valenzuela,Fe.,SD-StL	18	89.0	5	24	2	2	.935	13	2	3	0	.38
VanLandingham,SF	18	89.0	6	3	0	2	1.000	21	2	0	0	.10
Veras,Dario,SD	23	24.2	0	0	0	0	.000	5	3	0	0	.60
Veres,Dave,Mon	53	62.0	5	6	1	0	.917	6	2	0	0	.33
Veres,Randy,KC	24	35.1	0	6	1	0	.857	3	0	0	0	.00
Villone,Ron,Mil	50	52.2	3	6	1	0	.900	2	1	1	0	1.00
Vosberg,Ed,Tex-Fla	59	53.0	1	5	1	0	.857	0	0	0	0	.00
Wade,Terrell,Atl	12	42.0	2	5	1	0	.875	17	3	1	0	.24
Wagner,Billy,Hou	62	66.1	2	7	1	0	.900	4	1	1	0	.50
Wagner,Paul,Pit-Mil	16	18.0	1	4	0	0	1.000	4	0	0	0	.00
Wainhouse,David,Pit	25	28.0	2	4	1	0	.857	2	1	0	0	.50
Wakefield,Tim,Bos	35	201.1	9	22	3	1	.912	43	18	0	3	.42
Walker,Jamie,KC	50	43.0	5	6	0	1	1.000	5	0	1	0	.20
Wall,Donne,Hou	8	41.2	2	6	0	1	1.000	8	5	0	0	.63

1997 Fielding and Holding Runners

Pitcher,Team	G	Inn	PO	A	E	DP	Pct.	SBA	CS	PCS	PPO	CS%
Wallace,Jeff,Pit	11	12.0	0	2	0	0	1.000	2	1	0	0	.50
Wasdin,John,Bos	53	124.2	5	11	2	0	.889	20	2	0	0	.10
Watson,Allen,Ana	35	199.0	4	34	3	3	.927	27	1	9	0	.37
Weathers,D.,NYA-Cle	19	25.2	2	2	0	0	1.000	3	1	0	0	.33
Wells,Bob,Sea	46	67.1	7	5	0	0	1.000	9	6	0	0	.67
Wells,David,NYA	32	218.0	7	30	4	3	.902	27	4	4	0	.30
Wendell,Tu.,ChN-NYN	65	76.1	6	12	2	2	.900	8	2	1	0	.38
Wengert,Don,Oak	49	134.0	13	16	1	2	.967	10	5	0	0	.50
Wetteland,John,Tex	61	65.0	1	6	0	0	1.000	2	1	0	0	.50
Whisenant,Ma.,Fla-KC	28	21.2	0	3	2	1	.600	0	0	0	0	.00
White,Gabe,Cin	12	41.0	1	3	0	1	1.000	3	0	0	0	.00
Whiteside,Matt,Tex	42	72.2	9	16	1	1	.962	6	6	0	0	1.00
Wickman,Bob,Mil	74	95.2	6	14	0	4	1.000	19	4	0	0	.21
Wilkins,Marc,Pit	70	75.2	1	4	0	1	1.000	11	5	0	1	.45
Williams,Brian,Bal	13	24.0	1	2	0	0	1.000	0	0	0	0	.00
Williams,Mike,KC	10	14.0	1	1	0	0	1.000	0	0	0	0	.00
Williams,Mitch,KC	7	6.2	0	0	0	0	.000	1	0	0	0	.00
Williams,Shad,Ana	1	1.0	0	0	0	0	.000	0	0	0	0	.00
Williams,Woody,Tor	31	194.2	9	10	1	0	.950	17	9	0	2	.53
Winchester,Scott,Cin	5	6.0	0	1	0	0	1.000	0	0	0	0	.00
Winston,Darrin,Phi	7	12.0	1	0	0	0	1.000	0	0	0	0	.00
Witasick,Jay,Oak	8	11.0	0	0	0	0	.000	0	0	0	0	.00
Witt,Bobby,Tex	34	209.0	10	27	1	2	.974	23	8	1	0	.39
Wohlers,Mark,Atl	71	69.1	7	2	1	0	.900	13	0	0	0	.00
Wojciechowski,St.,Oak	3	10.1	0	4	0	0	1.000	4	0	2	0	.50
Wolcott,Bob,Sea	19	100.0	4	13	1	2	.944	6	2	1	0	.50
Woodard,Steve,Mil	7	36.2	0	2	0	0	1.000	4	1	0	0	.25
Worrell,Tim,SD	60	106.1	8	18	4	2	.867	22	6	0	0	.27
Worrell,Todd,LA	65	59.2	4	10	1	2	.933	7	0	0	0	.00
Wright,Jamey,Col	26	149.2	19	20	3	3	.929	19	9	0	6	.47
Wright,Jaret,Cle	16	90.1	5	10	0	1	1.000	16	1	0	0	.06
Yan,Esteban,Bal	3	9.2	0	0	0	0	.000	2	0	0	0	.00

Hitters Pitching

Player	1997 Pitching											Career Pitching										
	G	W	L	Sv	IP	H	R	ER	BB	SO	ERA	G	W	L	Sv	IP	H	R	ER	BB	SO	ERA
Alexander, Manny	0	0	0	0	0.0	0	0	0	0	0	—	1	0	0	0	0.2	1	5	5	4	0	67.50
Benjamin, Mike	1	0	0	0	1.0	0	0	0	0	0	0.00	1	0	0	0	1.0	0	0	0	0	0	0.00
Boggs, Wade	1	0	0	0	1.0	0	0	0	1	1	0.00	1	0	0	0	1.0	0	0	0	1	1	0.00
Cangelosi, John	1	0	0	0	1.0	0	0	0	1	0	0.00	3	0	0	0	4.0	1	0	0	2	0	0.00
Canseco, Jose	0	0	0	0	0.0	0	0	0	0	0	—	1	0	0	0	1.0	2	3	3	3	0	27.00
Davis, Chili	0	0	0	0	0.0	0	0	0	0	0	—	1	0	0	0	2.0	0	0	0	0	0	0.00
Espinoza, Alvaro	0	0	0	0	0.0	0	0	0	0	0	—	1	0	0	0	0.2	0	0	0	0	0	0.00
Gaetti, Gary	1	0	0	0	0.1	1	0	0	0	0	0.00	1	0	0	0	0.1	1	0	0	0	0	0.00
Gonzales, Rene	0	0	0	0	0.0	0	0	0	0	0	—	1	0	0	0	1.0	0	0	0	0	0	0.00
Howard, David	0	0	0	0	0.0	0	0	0	0	0	—	1	0	0	0	2.0	2	1	1	5	0	4.50
Jackson, Darrin	0	0	0	0	0.0	0	0	0	0	0	—	1	0	0	0	2.0	3	2	2	2	0	9.00
Martinez, Dave	0	0	0	0	0.0	0	0	0	0	0	—	2	0	0	0	1.1	2	2	2	4	0	13.50
O'Neill, Paul	0	0	0	0	0.0	0	0	0	0	0	—	1	0	0	0	2.0	2	3	3	4	2	13.50
Seitzer, Kevin	0	0	0	0	0.0	0	0	0	0	0	—	1	0	0	0	0.1	0	0	0	0	1	0.00
Tomberlin, Andy	0	0	0	0	0.0	0	0	0	0	0	—	1	0	0	0	2.0	1	0	0	1	1	0.00

264

Park Data

In the charts that follow, the first block of columns shows how much the featured team totaled at home, how much opponents totaled against the featured team at its home and the grand totals of both. The second block of columns shows how much the featured team totaled in away games, how much opponents totaled in its away games and the grand totals of both. By combining both the featured team's and opponent totals, most team variance is negated and only the park variance is left.

Now for the Index. In a nutshell, the Index tells you whether the park favors the stat you happen to be looking at. For example, did Chipper Jones have a case when he expressed concern about Turner Field and its adverse effect on home run hitters? In 1997, all National League (we excluded all interleague games when calculating a given Index) batters hit 118 home runs in 5,071 at-bats at Turner Field, a frequency of .0233 HR per AB; in Braves NL road games, the frequency was .0277 HR per AB (135/4,875). Dividing the Home frequency by the Road frequency gives us a figure of 0.84. This number is multiplied by 100 to make it more recognizable: 84. What does an Index of 84 mean? It means it was 16 percent tougher for players to hit home runs at Turner Field than it was in other National-League parks last season. Chipper may have a point!

The greater the Index is over 100, the more favorable the park is for that statistic. The lower the Index is under 100, the less favorable the park is for that statistic. A park that was neutral in a category will have an Index of 100. *E-Infield* refers to infield *fielding* errors.

The indexes for the following categories are determined on a per at-bat basis: 2B, 3B, HR, BB, SO, LHB-HR and RHB-HR. The indexes for AB, R, H, E and E-Infield are determined using per-game ratios. All the other indexes are based on the raw figures shown in the chart.

For most parks you'll notice that we include 1997 data as well as three-year totals (1995-97). However, for parks where there have been changes over the last three years, we never combine data. For Turner Field, 1997 data is shown, and we only give 1995-96 data for comparison's sake. We also include a page which **ranks** the indices for runs, home runs and average from 1995 to 1997. "Alt" is the altitude of the city where the team plays.

Anaheim Angels—Anaheim Stadium

Alt: 160 feet **Surface:** Grass

	1997 Season							1995-1997						
	Home Games			Away Games			Index	Home Games			Away Games			Index
	Angels	Opp	Total	Angels	Opp	Total		Angels	Opp	Total	Angels	Opp	Total	
G	74	74	148	72	72	144	—	227	227	454	225	225	450	—
Avg	.276	.264	.270	.270	.270	.270	100	.277	.260	.268	.274	.279	.276	97
AB	2519	2628	5147	2543	2398	4941	101	7773	8016	15789	7994	7576	15570	101
R	416	369	785	351	331	682	112	1208	1142	2350	1122	1198	2320	100
H	696	693	1389	687	647	1334	101	2153	2084	4237	2191	2112	4303	98
2B	133	132	265	115	121	236	108	386	375	761	370	420	790	95
3B	9	9	18	13	14	27	64	28	18	46	43	42	85	53
HR	80	109	189	67	66	133	136	274	320	594	251	237	488	120
BB	286	263	549	264	287	551	96	840	817	1657	801	881	1682	97
SO	427	506	933	423	443	866	103	1369	1568	2937	1344	1334	2678	108
E	66	60	126	40	51	91	135	197	189	386	165	164	329	116
E-Infield	53	52	105	33	41	74	138	148	135	283	128	118	246	114
LHB-Avg	.280	.263	.273	.270	.252	.263	104	.284	.263	.275	.277	.267	.273	101
LHB-HR	41	40	81	36	21	57	139	147	119	266	130	79	209	123
RHB-Avg	.272	.264	.267	.271	.280	.276	97	.270	.258	.263	.271	.285	.279	94
RHB-HR	39	69	108	31	45	76	134	127	201	328	121	158	279	118

ANAHEIM

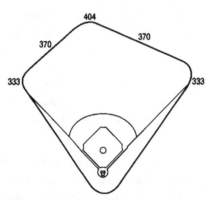

ATLANTA

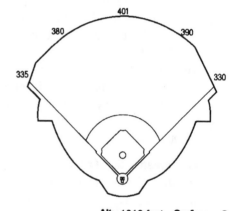

Atlanta Braves—Ted Turner Field

Alt: 1010 feet **Surface:** Grass

	1997 Season							1995-1996						
	Home Games			Away Games			Index	Home Games			Away Games			Index
	Braves	Opp	Total	Braves	Opp	Total		Braves	Opp	Total	Braves	Opp	Total	
G	75	75	150	72	72	144	—	153	153	306	153	153	306	—
Avg	.276	.236	.256	.263	.248	.256	100	.268	.241	.254	.254	.250	.252	101
AB	2491	2580	5071	2501	2374	4875	100	5106	5298	10404	5322	5100	10422	100
R	357	271	628	363	259	622	97	756	595	1351	662	593	1255	108
H	687	610	1297	659	589	1248	100	1366	1279	2645	1350	1277	2627	101
2B	107	116	223	135	104	239	90	241	231	472	233	258	491	96
3B	20	10	30	14	9	23	125	29	21	50	26	25	51	98
HR	68	50	118	87	48	135	84	200	132	332	165	95	260	128
BB	292	223	515	259	194	453	109	514	434	948	536	453	989	96
SO	517	558	1075	530	523	1053	98	885	1205	2090	1080	1127	2207	95
E	64	65	129	42	60	102	121	126	155	281	145	117	262	107
E-Infield	51	53	104	32	52	84	119	98	109	207	91	73	164	126
LHB-Avg	.289	.236	.267	.272	.259	.267	100	.286	.229	.263	.254	.261	.257	102
LHB-HR	35	16	51	46	14	60	79	135	29	164	75	27	102	154
RHB-Avg	.259	.236	.246	.254	.241	.247	100	.248	.248	.248	.253	.245	.249	100
RHB-HR	33	34	67	41	34	75	88	65	103	168	90	68	158	110

Baltimore Orioles—Oriole Park at Camden Yards

Alt: 148 feet **Surface:** Grass

| | 1997 Season | | | | | | | 1995-1997 | | | | | | |
| | Home Games | | | Away Games | | | | Home Games | | | Away Games | | | |
	Orioles	Opp	Total	Orioles	Opp	Total	Index	Orioles	Opp	Total	Orioles	Opp	Total	Index
G	72	72	144	75	75	150	—	226	226	452	228	228	456	—
Avg	.264	.252	.258	.274	.252	.263	98	.267	.259	.263	.271	.262	.266	99
AB	2380	2496	4876	2677	2508	5185	98	7507	7852	15359	8076	7631	15707	99
R	347	312	659	396	300	696	99	1142	1078	2220	1254	1077	2331	96
H	629	630	1259	733	633	1366	96	2001	2033	4034	2185	1999	4184	97
2B	100	105	205	151	135	286	76	340	368	708	439	399	838	86
3B	5	7	12	15	18	33	39	27	31	58	49	49	98	61
HR	93	77	170	83	67	150	121	304	269	573	302	233	535	110
BB	236	244	480	288	263	551	93	870	771	1641	873	856	1729	97
SO	420	522	942	429	511	940	107	1290	1540	2830	1277	1470	2747	105
E	47	38	85	42	57	99	89	157	147	304	131	162	293	105
E-Infield	39	33	72	34	45	79	95	119	116	235	93	122	215	110
LHB-Avg	.280	.254	.267	.293	.251	.274	97	.286	.256	.272	.283	.259	.273	100
LHB-HR	45	34	79	44	33	77	110	167	94	261	173	83	256	104
RHB-Avg	.253	.251	.252	.258	.253	.256	98	.247	.261	.255	.258	.264	.261	98
RHB-HR	48	43	91	39	34	73	132	137	175	312	129	150	279	114

BALTIMORE

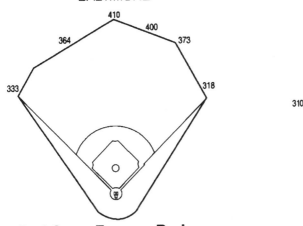

410
400
364
373
333
318

BOSTON

420
379
380
310
302

Boston Red Sox—Fenway Park

Alt: 15 feet **Surface:** Grass

| | 1997 Season | | | | | | | 1995-1997 | | | | | | |
| | Home Games | | | Away Games | | | | Home Games | | | Away Games | | | |
	RedSox	Opp	Total	RedSox	Opp	Total	Index	RedSox	Opp	Total	RedSox	Opp	Total	Index
G	72	72	144	75	75	150	—	225	225	450	228	228	456	—
Avg	.301	.271	.286	.288	.283	.286	100	.299	.275	.287	.273	.274	.274	105
AB	2540	2593	5133	2745	2558	5303	101	7877	8125	16002	8161	7787	15948	102
R	385	365	750	396	415	811	96	1289	1189	2478	1211	1210	2421	104
H	765	703	1468	791	725	1516	101	2358	2236	4594	2228	2136	4364	107
2B	175	165	340	163	134	297	118	530	459	989	402	396	798	124
3B	14	15	29	17	13	30	100	49	41	90	44	40	84	107
HR	82	53	135	88	76	164	85	273	209	482	281	232	513	94
BB	238	259	497	218	301	519	99	856	830	1686	802	928	1730	97
SO	450	470	920	496	429	925	103	1381	1519	2900	1508	1433	2941	98
E	66	40	106	55	57	112	99	237	165	402	186	175	361	113
E-Infield	61	32	93	48	46	94	103	174	123	297	143	130	273	110
LHB-Avg	.315	.290	.302	.282	.283	.282	107	.308	.279	.294	.274	.277	.275	107
LHB-HR	36	26	62	39	25	64	97	123	83	206	134	90	224	90
RHB-Avg	.291	.257	.274	.293	.284	.288	95	.292	.272	.282	.273	.272	.273	103
RHB-HR	46	27	73	49	51	100	77	150	126	276	147	142	289	97

Chicago Cubs—Wrigley Field

Alt: 658 feet **Surface:** Grass

| | 1997 Season | | | | | | | 1995-1997 | | | | | | |
| | HomeGames | | | AwayGames | | | | HomeGames | | | AwayGames | | | |
	Cubs	Opp	Total	Cubs	Opp	Total	Index	Cubs	Opp	Total	Cubs	Opp	Total	Index
G	71	71	142	76	76	152	—	224	224	448	229	229	458	—
Avg	.275	.255	.265	.240	.276	.257	103	.267	.258	.262	.248	.267	.258	102
AB	2388	2457	4845	2588	2496	5084	102	7528	7870	15398	7942	7654	15596	101
R	345	321	666	254	369	623	114	1097	1043	2140	967	1089	2056	106
H	656	626	1282	620	688	1308	105	2008	2028	4036	1971	2046	4017	103
2B	109	111	220	133	164	297	78	358	376	734	418	402	820	91
3B	17	11	28	17	20	37	79	43	40	83	49	48	97	87
HR	70	98	168	45	74	119	148	250	272	522	198	246	444	119
BB	214	266	480	194	272	466	108	705	801	1506	666	801	1467	104
SO	439	514	953	483	462	945	106	1426	1544	2970	1539	1385	2924	103
E	43	64	107	59	50	109	105	187	204	391	181	185	366	109
E-Infield	37	59	96	47	48	95	108	133	161	294	123	151	274	110
LHB-Avg	.301	.258	.275	.247	.268	.259	106	.294	.260	.275	.261	.268	.265	104
LHB-HR	15	28	43	18	30	48	101	67	83	150	72	96	168	93
RHB-Avg	.263	.253	.258	.236	.282	.256	101	.252	.256	.254	.241	.267	.253	100
RHB-HR	55	70	125	27	44	71	176	183	189	372	126	150	276	134

CHICAGO CUBS

CHICAGO WHITE SOX

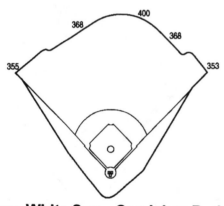

Chicago White Sox—Comiskey Park

Alt: 658 feet **Surface:** Grass

| | 1997 Season | | | | | | | 1995-1997 | | | | | | |
| | HomeGames | | | AwayGames | | | | HomeGames | | | AwayGames | | | |
	WhiteSox	Opp	Total	WhiteSox	Opp	Total	Index	WhiteSox	Opp	Total	WhiteSox	Opp	Total	Index
G	75	75	150	71	71	142	—	228	228	456	225	225	450	—
Avg	.272	.265	.268	.278	.279	.279	96	.277	.264	.270	.281	.280	.280	96
AB	2464	2650	5114	2542	2413	4955	98	7626	8017	15643	8084	7706	15790	98
R	361	375	736	362	405	767	91	1120	1106	2226	1256	1226	2482	89
H	670	701	1371	707	673	1380	94	2110	2118	4228	2270	2159	4429	94
2B	124	145	269	114	132	246	106	352	383	735	422	409	831	89
3B	16	16	32	11	8	19	163	57	48	105	40	40	80	132
HR	65	74	139	78	89	167	81	200	237	437	284	264	548	80
BB	274	254	528	260	283	543	94	905	857	1762	906	913	1819	98
SO	386	487	873	417	397	814	104	1144	1426	2570	1353	1389	2742	95
E	58	42	100	59	51	110	86	167	160	327	203	176	379	85
E-Infield	47	31	78	49	38	87	85	126	113	239	151	121	272	87
LHB-Avg	.277	.269	.273	.280	.288	.284	96	.280	.265	.273	.283	.298	.289	94
LHB-HR	13	33	46	31	45	76	59	71	82	153	123	121	244	64
RHB-Avg	.268	.262	.265	.277	.272	.275	96	.273	.263	.268	.279	.267	.273	98
RHB-HR	52	41	93	47	44	91	99	129	155	284	161	143	304	94

Cincinnati Reds—Cinergy Field

Alt: 869 feet **Surface:** Turf

| | 1997 Season | | | | | | | 1995-1997 | | | | | | |
| | Home Games | | | Away Games | | | | Home Games | | | Away Games | | | |
	Reds	Opp	Total	Reds	Opp	Total	Index	Reds	Opp	Total	Reds	Opp	Total	Index
G	72	72	144	75	75	150	—	225	225	450	228	228	456	—
Avg	.261	.252	.256	.242	.263	.252	102	.266	.254	.260	.253	.267	.260	100
AB	2383	2507	4890	2604	2507	5111	100	7374	7771	15145	7971	7637	15608	98
R	297	352	649	286	353	639	106	1068	1023	2091	1040	1078	2118	100
H	622	631	1253	629	659	1288	101	1961	1970	3931	2014	2037	4051	98
2B	119	151	270	118	127	245	115	412	404	816	361	400	761	111
3B	11	18	29	15	12	27	112	46	54	100	51	46	97	106
HR	65	81	146	64	77	141	108	230	225	455	251	231	482	97
BB	242	255	497	234	257	491	106	859	745	1604	740	782	1522	109
SO	459	548	1007	572	495	1067	99	1425	1548	2973	1686	1487	3173	97
E	43	51	94	59	56	115	85	150	184	334	187	218	405	84
E-Infield	35	38	73	49	45	94	81	118	123	241	131	165	296	83
LHB-Avg	.260	.280	.269	.248	.263	.254	106	.269	.267	.268	.251	.268	.258	104
LHB-HR	29	35	64	26	21	47	137	92	93	185	86	77	163	120
RHB-Avg	.262	.234	.246	.235	.263	.250	98	.264	.246	.254	.254	.266	.260	98
RHB-HR	36	46	82	38	56	94	94	138	132	270	165	154	319	86

CINCINNATI

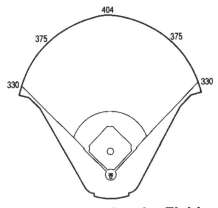

CLEVELAND

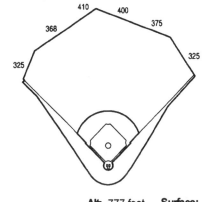

Cleveland Indians—Jacobs Field

Alt: 777 feet **Surface:** Grass

| | 1997 Season | | | | | | | 1995-1997 | | | | | | |
| | Home Games | | | Away Games | | | | Home Games | | | Away Games | | | |
	Indians	Opp	Total	Indians	Opp	Total	Index	Indians	Opp	Total	Indians	Opp	Total	Index
G	75	75	150	71	71	142	—	227	227	454	224	224	448	—
Avg	.288	.272	.280	.285	.279	.282	99	.292	.263	.277	.288	.272	.280	99
AB	2504	2624	5128	2534	2414	4948	98	7695	7997	15692	8052	7622	15674	99
R	397	377	774	390	368	758	97	1285	1038	2323	1294	1083	2377	96
H	721	714	1435	721	673	1394	97	2248	2103	4351	2320	2075	4395	98
2B	135	131	266	137	124	261	98	442	440	882	444	398	842	105
3B	11	7	18	9	15	24	72	40	23	63	26	42	68	93
HR	92	84	176	112	87	199	85	293	219	512	336	260	596	86
BB	296	260	556	271	270	541	99	919	715	1634	861	744	1605	102
SO	438	499	937	415	449	864	105	1209	1504	2713	1254	1403	2657	102
E	47	56	103	46	53	99	98	182	198	380	185	186	371	101
E-Infield	35	43	78	40	47	87	85	118	145	263	133	138	271	96
LHB-Avg	.298	.292	.295	.276	.297	.287	103	.303	.271	.286	.285	.286	.285	100
LHB-HR	48	42	90	49	37	86	97	138	96	234	143	117	260	89
RHB-Avg	.281	.255	.268	.290	.264	.278	97	.283	.255	.269	.291	.259	.276	97
RHB-HR	44	42	86	63	50	113	75	155	123	278	193	143	336	83

Colorado Rockies—Coors Field

Alt: 5282 feet **Surface:** Grass

| | 1997 Season | | | | | | | 1995-1997 | | | | | | |
| | Home Games | | | Away Games | | | | Home Games | | | Away Games | | | |
	Rockies	Opp	Total	Rockies	Opp	Total	Index	Rockies	Opp	Total	Rockies	Opp	Total	Index
G	73	73	146	73	73	146	—	226	226	452	226	226	452	—
Avg	.320	.315	.317	.253	.284	.268	118	.327	.311	.319	.242	.267	.254	125
AB	2542	2675	5217	2489	2419	4908	106	7966	8320	16286	7649	7412	15061	108
R	486	454	940	342	363	705	133	1629	1503	3132	945	1061	2006	156
H	813	843	1656	629	687	1316	126	2604	2589	5193	1851	1981	3832	136
2B	135	163	298	100	142	242	116	464	496	960	327	394	721	123
3B	22	19	41	15	19	34	113	79	72	151	38	50	88	159
HR	110	112	222	105	70	175	119	393	341	734	243	199	442	154
BB	267	237	504	249	272	521	91	822	803	1625	705	842	1547	97
SO	399	397	796	553	379	932	80	1325	1312	2637	1678	1287	2965	82
E	46	71	117	56	51	107	109	201	228	429	193	187	380	113
E-Infield	37	60	97	50	38	88	110	150	169	319	157	128	285	112
LHB-Avg	.347	.330	.337	.266	.304	.287	117	.330	.316	.322	.243	.290	.269	119
LHB-HR	30	50	80	43	34	77	94	96	126	222	80	84	164	124
RHB-Avg	.306	.302	.304	.246	.268	.256	119	.326	.307	.317	.242	.250	.246	129
RHB-HR	80	62	142	62	36	98	140	297	215	512	163	115	278	172

COLORADO

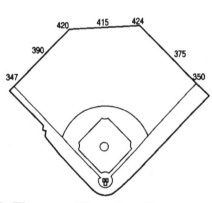

DETROIT

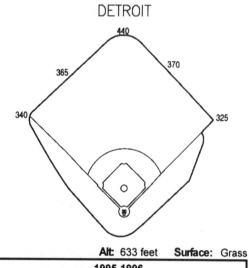

Detroit Tigers—Tiger Stadium

Alt: 633 feet **Surface:** Grass

| | 1997 Season | | | | | | | 1995-1996 | | | | | | |
| | Home Games | | | Away Games | | | | Home Games | | | Away Games | | | |
	Tigers	Opp	Total	Tigers	Opp	Total	Index	Tigers	Opp	Total	Tigers	Opp	Total	Index
G	72	72	144	75	75	150	—	153	153	306	153	153	306	—
Avg	.253	.254	.254	.264	.279	.271	94	.252	.288	.271	.252	.304	.278	97
AB	2353	2525	4878	2636	2531	5167	98	5041	5490	10531	5354	5342	10696	98
R	362	350	712	350	384	734	101	745	965	1710	692	982	1674	102
H	595	642	1237	695	706	1401	92	1269	1583	2852	1348	1625	2973	96
2B	107	111	218	137	129	266	87	226	294	520	259	317	576	92
3B	16	15	31	11	18	29	113	26	32	58	24	40	64	92
HR	83	89	172	75	80	155	118	192	223	415	171	188	359	117
BB	300	247	547	229	270	499	116	569	657	1226	528	663	1191	105
SO	519	449	968	525	445	970	106	1123	895	2018	1132	791	1923	107
E	42	62	104	42	42	84	129	148	116	264	158	121	279	95
E-Infield	35	51	86	32	37	69	130	82	90	172	98	79	177	97
LHB-Avg	.281	.261	.270	.265	.287	.277	97	.256	.294	.281	.259	.318	.297	94
LHB-HR	43	41	84	39	35	74	129	71	101	172	51	90	141	121
RHB-Avg	.236	.250	.243	.263	.272	.267	91	.250	.283	.265	.249	.291	.267	99
RHB-HR	40	48	88	36	45	81	110	121	122	243	120	98	218	115

Florida Marlins—Pro Player Stadium

Alt: 7 feet **Surface:** Grass

	1997 Season							1995-1997						
	Home Games			Away Games			Index	Home Games			Away Games			Index
	Marlins	Opp	Total	Marlins	Opp	Total		Marlins	Opp	Total	Marlins	Opp	Total	
G	75	75	150	72	72	144	—	227	227	454	225	225	450	97
Avg	.264	.239	.251	.256	.266	.261	96	.268	.241	.254	.251	.274	.262	97
AB	2411	2524	4935	2522	2388	4910	96	7457	7686	15143	7860	7568	15428	97
R	325	298	623	337	314	651	92	1025	896	1921	998	1092	2090	91
H	636	602	1238	645	636	1281	93	1997	1850	3847	1975	2073	4048	94
2B	111	102	213	132	108	240	88	314	329	643	383	390	773	85
3B	16	20	36	10	24	34	105	53	56	109	32	57	89	125
HR	57	62	119	69	61	130	91	198	166	364	222	209	431	86
BB	342	300	642	278	258	536	119	853	857	1710	837	861	1698	103
SO	467	560	1027	514	510	1024	100	1449	1617	3066	1570	1497	3067	102
E	53	47	100	58	57	115	83	191	166	357	194	185	379	93
E-Infield	47	38	85	49	46	95	86	137	123	260	137	128	265	97
LHB-Avg	.273	.243	.258	.253	.280	.266	97	.258	.251	.254	.246	.278	.264	96
LHB-HR	12	21	33	19	18	37	87	32	56	88	46	75	121	72
RHB-Avg	.258	.236	.247	.257	.258	.258	96	.273	.234	.254	.253	.271	.262	97
RHB-HR	45	41	86	50	43	93	93	166	110	276	176	134	310	92

FLORIDA

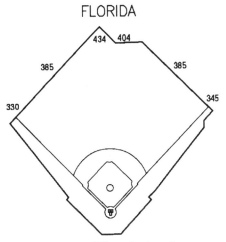

434 404
385 385
330 345

HOUSTON

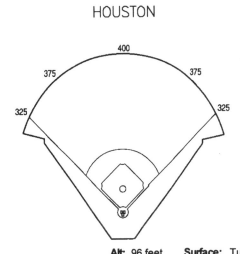

400
375 375
325 325

Houston Astros—The Astrodome

Alt: 96 feet **Surface:** Turf

	1997 Season							1995-1997						
	Home Games			Away Games			Index	Home Games			Away Games			Index
	Astros	Opp	Total	Astros	Opp	Total		Astros	Opp	Total	Astros	Opp	Total	
G	72	72	144	75	75	150	—	225	225	450	228	228	456	—
Avg	.258	.237	.247	.263	.261	.262	94	.263	.248	.255	.269	.280	.274	93
AB	2373	2472	4845	2651	2507	5158	98	7538	7893	15431	8091	7802	15893	98
R	344	258	602	383	333	716	88	1029	901	1930	1198	1156	2354	83
H	613	586	1199	697	655	1352	92	1982	1956	3938	2176	2183	4359	92
2B	141	112	253	153	117	270	100	415	384	799	436	384	820	100
3B	20	15	35	16	4	20	186	40	47	87	47	44	91	98
HR	56	48	104	69	72	141	79	157	159	316	206	233	439	74
BB	263	193	456	323	270	593	82	819	662	1481	887	800	1687	90
SO	469	609	1078	537	448	985	117	1490	1839	3329	1565	1437	3002	114
E	50	58	108	75	62	137	82	191	185	376	252	224	476	80
E-Infield	43	48	91	64	50	114	83	148	147	295	159	164	323	93
LHB-Avg	.265	.247	.254	.270	.269	.269	95	.266	.257	.261	.265	.288	.279	93
LHB-HR	11	20	31	13	30	43	77	24	62	86	43	92	135	66
RHB-Avg	.256	.231	.244	.260	.256	.258	94	.262	.242	.253	.270	.274	.272	93
RHB-HR	45	28	73	56	42	98	79	133	97	230	163	141	304	78

Kansas City Royals—Ewing M. Kauffman Stadium

Alt: 742 feet **Surface:** Grass

| | 1997 Season | | | | | | | 1995-1997 | | | | | | |
| | Home Games | | | Away Games | | | | Home Games | | | Away Games | | | |
	Royals	Opp	Total	Royals	Opp	Total	Index	Royals	Opp	Total	Royals	Opp	Total	Index
G	74	74	148	72	72	144	—	226	226	452	225	225	450	—
Avg	.271	.277	.274	.256	.269	.262	105	.268	.269	.269	.259	.277	.267	101
AB	2563	2663	5226	2528	2423	4951	103	7688	8014	15702	7848	7652	15500	101
R	347	401	748	321	346	667	109	1004	1116	2120	1039	1108	2147	98
H	694	738	1432	646	652	1298	107	2063	2159	4222	2029	2117	4146	101
2B	110	112	222	113	117	230	91	381	362	743	368	391	759	97
3B	20	15	35	14	6	20	166	64	56	120	43	36	79	150
HR	77	91	168	63	81	144	111	176	249	425	206	241	447	94
BB	268	231	499	229	261	490	96	744	706	1450	757	749	1506	95
SO	438	427	865	516	456	972	84	1234	1211	2445	1512	1361	2873	84
E	38	41	79	39	47	86	89	156	180	336	164	186	350	96
E-Infield	28	38	66	32	42	74	87	108	145	253	111	129	240	105
LHB-Avg	.273	.287	.280	.260	.282	.271	104	.273	.278	.276	.270	.283	.276	100
LHB-HR	26	45	71	14	36	50	130	65	112	177	71	101	172	103
RHB-Avg	.269	.270	.270	.253	.261	.257	105	.263	.263	.263	.246	.272	.260	101
RHB-HR	51	46	97	49	45	94	100	111	137	248	135	140	275	88

KANSAS CITY

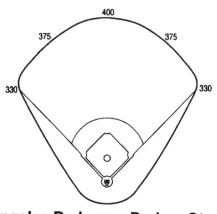

LOS ANGELES

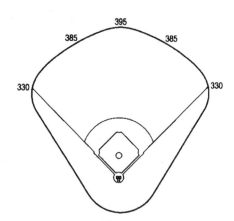

Los Angeles Dodgers—Dodger Stadium

Alt: 270 feet **Surface:** Grass

| | 1997 Season | | | | | | | 1995-1997 | | | | | | |
| | Home Games | | | Away Games | | | | Home Games | | | Away Games | | | |
	Dodgers	Opp	Total	Dodgers	Opp	Total	Index	Dodgers	Opp	Total	Dodgers	Opp	Total	Index
G	73	73	146	73	73	146	—	226	226	452	226	226	452	—
Avg	.265	.224	.245	.268	.255	.262	93	.253	.229	.241	.268	.260	.264	91
AB	2404	2487	4891	2580	2466	5046	97	7432	7712	15144	8032	7655	15687	97
R	303	256	559	349	315	664	84	898	815	1713	1091	1017	2108	81
H	638	558	1196	691	630	1321	91	1879	1766	3645	2149	1988	4137	88
2B	102	94	196	113	136	249	81	259	277	536	362	396	758	73
3B	14	7	21	16	21	37	59	35	18	53	59	49	108	51
HR	70	66	136	82	74	156	90	194	163	357	248	227	475	78
BB	226	225	451	229	256	485	96	697	690	1387	742	787	1529	94
SO	444	551	995	538	559	1097	94	1483	1727	3210	1712	1656	3368	99
E	52	54	106	54	66	120	88	215	203	418	196	187	383	109
E-Infield	48	44	92	43	49	92	100	155	153	308	141	128	269	114
LHB-Avg	.253	.244	.247	.264	.267	.266	93	.241	.241	.241	.265	.260	.262	92
LHB-HR	3	34	37	7	33	40	90	16	80	96	31	99	130	74
RHB-Avg	.270	.206	.243	.269	.246	.260	94	.258	.219	.240	.269	.259	.265	91
RHB-HR	67	32	99	75	41	116	91	178	83	261	217	128	345	80

Milwaukee Brewers—County Stadium

Alt: 672 feet **Surface:** Grass

| | 1997 Season | | | | | | | 1995-1997 | | | | | | |
| | Home Games | | | Away Games | | | Index | Home Games | | | Away Games | | | Index |
	Brewers	Opp	Total	Brewers	Opp	Total		Brewers	Opp	Total	Brewers	Opp	Total	
G	74	74	148	72	72	144	—	227	227	454	225	225	450	—
Avg	.269	.260	.265	.255	.264	.259	102	.277	.278	.277	.262	.269	.266	104
AB	2461	2610	5071	2510	2347	4857	102	7708	8085	15793	7925	7471	15396	102
R	333	338	671	300	348	648	101	1174	1224	2398	1093	1108	2201	108
H	663	679	1342	640	619	1259	104	2133	2247	4380	2077	2012	4089	106
2B	137	144	281	130	110	240	112	404	454	858	416	368	784	107
3B	17	9	26	9	12	21	119	60	45	105	48	45	93	110
HR	53	90	143	73	80	153	90	191	265	456	241	264	505	88
BB	256	256	512	198	243	441	111	855	882	1737	725	855	1580	107
SO	421	494	915	454	433	887	99	1245	1269	2514	1416	1203	2619	94
E	59	50	109	47	45	92	115	200	171	371	178	163	341	108
E-Infield	49	43	92	38	38	76	118	150	130	280	143	128	271	102
LHB-Avg	.276	.249	.262	.259	.287	.273	96	.280	.273	.277	.256	.281	.269	103
LHB-HR	28	34	62	36	39	75	81	73	107	180	94	122	216	79
RHB-Avg	.265	.269	.267	.253	.245	.249	107	.274	.282	.278	.266	.260	.263	106
RHB-HR	25	56	81	37	41	78	98	118	158	276	147	142	289	95

MILWAUKEE

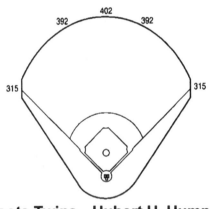

MINNESOTA

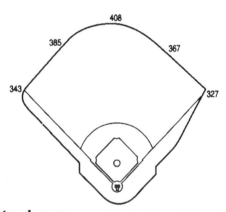

Minnesota Twins—Hubert H. Humphrey Metrodome

Alt: 834 feet **Surface:** Turf

| | 1997 Season | | | | | | | 1995-1997 | | | | | | |
| | Home Games | | | Away Games | | | Index | Home Games | | | Away Games | | | Index |
	Twins	Opp	Total	Twins	Opp	Total		Twins	Opp	Total	Twins	Opp	Total	
G	75	75	150	72	72	144	—	229	229	458	224	224	448	—
Avg	.273	.283	.278	.267	.285	.275	101	.285	.278	.282	.273	.286	.280	101
AB	2571	2707	5278	2542	2428	4970	102	7857	8194	16051	7934	7638	15572	101
R	352	415	767	344	387	731	101	1172	1346	2518	1104	1245	2349	105
H	701	765	1466	678	691	1369	103	2241	2282	4523	2169	2185	4354	102
2B	143	160	303	134	150	284	100	455	494	949	424	458	882	104
3B	15	18	33	20	14	34	91	64	48	112	52	46	98	111
HR	52	87	139	65	88	153	86	172	328	500	183	290	473	103
BB	238	216	454	223	235	458	93	759	788	1547	749	777	1526	98
SO	517	451	968	495	384	879	104	1460	1392	2852	1426	1192	2618	106
E	45	45	90	43	45	88	98	166	180	346	149	180	329	103
E-Infield	36	34	70	34	38	72	93	121	133	254	110	127	237	105
LHB-Avg	.266	.288	.279	.238	.293	.266	105	.271	.277	.274	.247	.296	.274	100
LHB-HR	19	38	57	20	37	57	99	51	145	196	51	124	175	111
RHB-Avg	.276	.279	.277	.283	.279	.281	99	.293	.280	.287	.288	.278	.284	101
RHB-HR	33	49	82	45	51	96	78	121	183	304	132	166	298	98

Montreal Expos—Olympic Stadium

Alt: 187 feet   **Surface:** Turf

	1997 Season							1995-1997						
	Home Games			Away Games				Home Games			Away Games			
	Expos	Opp	Total	Expos	Opp	Total	Index	Expos	Opp	Total	Expos	Opp	Total	Index
G	75	75	150	72	72	144	---	228	228	456	225	225	450	---
Avg	.269	.256	.263	.248	.255	.251	104	.269	.249	.259	.251	.261	.256	101
AB	2523	2602	5125	2500	2354	4854	101	7611	7872	15483	7822	7462	15284	100
R	332	362	694	299	340	639	104	1045	1010	2055	948	998	1946	104
H	679	667	1346	619	601	1220	106	2046	1962	4008	1961	1945	3906	101
2B	174	125	299	135	106	241	118	478	366	844	393	348	741	112
3B	19	21	40	13	16	29	131	50	55	105	33	42	75	138
HR	72	66	138	80	72	152	86	196	197	393	222	221	443	88
BB	206	257	463	172	264	436	101	682	729	1411	588	690	1278	109
SO	492	538	1030	493	484	977	100	1427	1642	3069	1536	1536	3072	99
E	65	44	109	55	39	94	111	213	186	399	189	208	397	99
E-Infield	52	35	87	47	33	80	104	150	117	267	137	146	283	93
LHB-Avg	.275	.251	.263	.243	.264	.253	104	.262	.256	.259	.242	.257	.250	104
LHB-HR	38	23	61	36	25	61	92	92	62	154	87	63	150	101
RHB-Avg	.265	.260	.262	.251	.249	.250	105	.273	.246	.259	.255	.263	.259	100
RHB-HR	34	43	77	44	47	91	82	104	135	239	135	158	293	81

MONTREAL

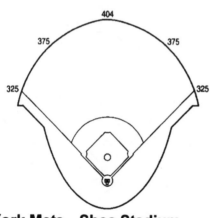

NEW YORK METS

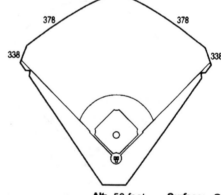

New York Mets—Shea Stadium

Alt: 50 feet   **Surface:** Grass

	1997 Season							1995-1997						
	Home Games			Away Games				Home Games			Away Games			
	Mets	Opp	Total	Mets	Opp	Total	Index	Mets	Opp	Total	Mets	Opp	Total	Index
G	75	75	150	72	72	144	---	228	228	456	225	225	450	---
Avg	.273	.253	.263	.249	.272	.260	101	.268	.258	.263	.264	.274	.269	98
AB	2494	2614	5108	2510	2425	4935	99	7670	8029	15699	7910	7540	15450	100
R	373	312	685	335	319	654	101	1016	956	1972	1095	1072	2167	90
H	681	662	1343	624	660	1284	100	2053	2068	4121	2090	2067	4157	98
2B	134	128	262	104	133	237	107	343	367	710	380	388	768	91
3B	15	16	31	13	17	30	100	53	49	102	56	48	104	97
HR	66	63	129	74	68	142	88	193	203	396	219	220	439	89
BB	266	225	491	239	221	460	103	712	656	1368	684	723	1407	96
SO	431	499	930	508	385	893	101	1421	1511	2932	1581	1273	2854	101
E	59	51	110	49	52	101	105	220	202	422	215	214	429	97
E-Infield	48	41	89	37	43	80	107	157	142	299	149	163	312	95
LHB-Avg	.294	.267	.280	.265	.292	.278	101	.286	.268	.277	.278	.285	.281	98
LHB-HR	40	27	67	35	24	59	112	104	85	189	100	81	181	106
RHB-Avg	.257	.243	.250	.236	.257	.246	102	.254	.250	.252	.254	.265	.260	97
RHB-HR	26	36	62	39	44	83	71	89	118	207	119	139	258	77

New York Yankees—Yankee Stadium

Alt: 60 feet   Surface: Grass

	1997 Season							1995-1997						
	HomeGames			AwayGames			Index	HomeGames			AwayGames			Index
	Yankees	Opp	Total	Yankees	Opp	Total		Yankees	Opp	Total	Yankees	Opp	Total	
G	71	71	142	76	76	152	—	224	224	448	230	230	460	—
Avg	.290	.261	.275	.294	.262	.279	99	.296	.260	.278	.276	.265	.271	103
AB	2412	2492	4904	2807	2619	5426	97	7566	7793	15359	8228	7795	16023	98
R	380	304	684	473	327	800	92	1239	1001	2240	1234	1105	2339	98
H	700	651	1351	826	686	1512	96	2241	2025	4266	2271	2067	4338	101
2B	131	116	247	170	126	296	92	417	381	798	457	404	861	97
3B	13	14	27	9	12	21	142	42	33	75	42	45	87	90
HR	72	65	137	85	69	154	98	217	217	434	224	219	443	102
BB	283	226	509	338	258	596	94	921	756	1677	957	873	1830	96
SO	377	526	903	470	525	995	100	1169	1528	2697	1438	1570	3008	94
E	45	38	83	50	66	116	77	120	160	280	167	220	387	74
E-Infield	39	34	73	38	53	91	86	92	106	198	123	153	276	74
LHB-Avg	.299	.248	.277	.308	.285	.298	93	.302	.259	.284	.280	.272	.277	103
LHB-HR	41	19	60	49	30	79	87	124	80	204	114	86	200	107
RHB-Avg	.283	.268	.275	.283	.249	.266	103	.290	.260	.273	.272	.261	.266	103
RHB-HR	31	46	77	36	39	75	111	93	137	230	110	133	243	98

NEW YORK YANKEES

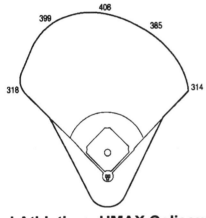

OAKLAND

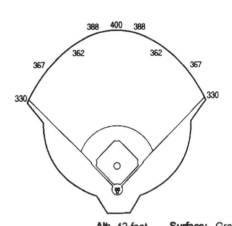

Oakland Athletics—UMAX Coliseum

Alt: 42 feet   Surface: Grass

	1997 Season							1996-1997						
	HomeGames			AwayGames			Index	HomeGames			AwayGames			Index
	Athletics	Opp	Total	Athletics	Opp	Total		Athletics	Opp	Total	Athletics	Opp	Total	
G	73	73	146	73	73	146	—	148	148	296	160	160	320	—
Avg	.269	.303	.287	.249	.298	.274	105	.272	.292	.282	.254	.295	.274	103
AB	2509	2693	5202	2534	2508	5042	103	5040	5377	10417	5633	5524	11157	101
R	347	446	793	329	404	733	108	747	855	1602	790	895	1685	103
H	675	816	1491	631	748	1379	108	1369	1571	2940	1429	1631	3060	104
2B	124	167	291	126	149	275	103	258	315	573	275	315	590	104
3B	9	10	19	9	26	35	53	19	28	47	20	45	65	77
HR	100	87	187	77	92	169	107	203	176	379	217	208	425	96
BB	293	286	579	281	298	579	97	586	546	1132	628	682	1310	93
SO	488	415	903	582	430	1012	86	980	839	1819	1204	890	2094	93
E	52	41	93	50	42	92	101	111	104	215	111	96	207	112
E-Infield	40	33	73	38	32	70	104	79	70	149	85	68	153	105
LHB-Avg	.285	.301	.294	.272	.309	.292	101	.284	.292	.289	.260	.297	.281	103
LHB-HR	44	45	89	21	42	63	131	60	84	144	58	92	150	99
RHB-Avg	.257	.305	.281	.234	.288	.259	108	.265	.292	.278	.250	.294	.270	103
RHB-HR	56	42	98	56	50	106	93	143	92	235	159	116	275	94

Philadelphia Phillies—Veterans Stadium

Alt: 5 feet   **Surface:** Turf

	1997 Season							1995-1997						
	Home Games			Away Games				Home Games			Away Games			
	Phillies	Opp	Total	Phillies	Opp	Total	Index	Phillies	Opp	Total	Phillies	Opp	Total	Index
G	75	75	150	72	72	144	—	228	228	456	225	225	450	—
Avg	.265	.256	.260	.248	.271	.259	100	.264	.256	.260	.252	.268	.260	100
AB	2490	2612	5102	2448	2328	4776	103	7683	7957	15640	7704	7340	15044	103
R	331	372	703	290	394	684	99	980	1110	2090	906	1104	2010	103
H	660	668	1328	607	632	1239	103	2025	2034	4059	1943	1970	3913	102
2B	147	178	325	119	125	244	125	422	469	891	356	364	720	119
3B	17	19	36	14	24	38	89	53	46	99	47	55	102	93
HR	58	77	135	49	82	131	96	164	237	401	169	216	385	100
BB	265	256	521	215	299	514	95	776	800	1576	737	803	1540	98
SO	465	591	1056	472	508	980	101	1420	1690	3110	1493	1433	2926	102
E	45	59	104	57	50	107	93	159	205	364	192	178	370	97
E-Infield	34	44	78	47	43	90	83	120	144	264	138	115	253	103
LHB-Avg	.270	.253	.262	.256	.296	.273	96	.268	.256	.263	.262	.284	.271	97
LHB-HR	21	25	46	21	38	59	78	68	75	143	61	81	142	99
RHB-Avg	.260	.258	.259	.237	.253	.246	105	.258	.255	.257	.241	.259	.251	102
RHB-HR	37	52	89	28	44	72	109	96	162	258	108	135	243	101

PHILADELPHIA

PITTSBURGH

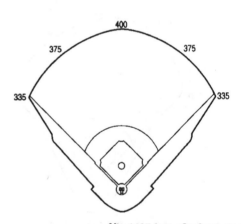

Pittsburgh Pirates—Three Rivers Stadium

Alt: 1137 feet   **Surface:** Turf

	1997 Season							1995-1997						
	Home Games			Away Games				Home Games			Away Games			
	Pirates	Opp	Total	Pirates	Opp	Total	Index	Pirates	Opp	Total	Pirates	Opp	Total	Index
G	72	72	144	75	75	150	—	224	224	448	229	229	458	—
Avg	.264	.271	.268	.262	.271	.266	100	.265	.280	.273	.261	.277	.269	101
AB	2375	2520	4895	2637	2513	5150	99	7514	7958	15472	8100	7742	15842	100
R	333	356	689	343	330	673	107	1046	1181	2227	1035	1074	2109	108
H	626	684	1310	690	682	1372	99	1991	2227	4218	2115	2148	4263	101
2B	130	137	267	138	123	261	108	426	447	873	406	373	779	115
3B	28	18	46	19	14	33	147	55	59	114	52	49	101	116
HR	60	67	127	58	61	119	112	203	215	418	178	226	404	106
BB	225	246	471	230	275	505	98	720	750	1470	701	727	1428	105
SO	511	504	1015	580	471	1051	102	1493	1510	3003	1559	1380	2939	105
E	62	69	131	61	54	115	119	226	217	443	197	196	393	115
E-Infield	53	62	115	50	45	95	126	157	154	311	146	155	301	106
LHB-Avg	.260	.284	.273	.263	.295	.280	98	.271	.291	.281	.264	.292	.277	101
LHB-HR	23	36	59	16	26	42	156	86	78	164	69	86	155	114
RHB-Avg	.265	.263	.264	.261	.252	.257	103	.261	.273	.268	.259	.268	.264	101
RHB-HR	37	31	68	42	35	77	90	117	137	254	109	140	249	101

San Diego Padres—Qualcomm Stadium

Alt: 13 feet   Surface: Grass

	1997 Season							1996-1997						
	HomeGames			AwayGames				HomeGames			AwayGames			
	Padres	Opp	Total	Padres	Opp	Total	Index	Padres	Opp	Total	Padres	Opp	Total	Index
G	70	70	140	76	76	152	—	148	148	296	160	160	320	—
Avg	.261	.270	.266	.273	.288	.281	95	.264	.258	.261	.268	.267	.268	98
AB	2377	2502	4879	2653	2591	5244	101	4987	5252	10239	5698	5470	11168	99
R	309	370	679	382	420	802	92	639	690	1329	823	782	1605	90
H	621	676	1297	725	747	1472	96	1317	1356	2673	1528	1462	2990	97
2B	108	113	221	129	148	277	86	230	228	458	292	283	575	87
3B	4	13	17	10	21	31	59	17	25	42	21	34	55	83
HR	67	82	149	65	66	131	122	134	153	287	145	133	278	113
BB	246	225	471	296	291	587	86	520	459	979	623	563	1186	90
SO	494	488	982	539	479	1018	104	955	1082	2037	1093	1079	2172	102
E	52	51	103	65	49	114	98	131	100	231	123	139	262	95
E-Infield	43	45	88	53	39	92	104	96	78	174	99	99	198	95
LHB-Avg	.290	.269	.280	.301	.294	.298	94	.288	.257	.273	.298	.273	.286	95
LHB-HR	32	36	68	44	22	66	114	65	57	122	84	44	128	104
RHB-Avg	.237	.271	.255	.247	.284	.267	96	.245	.259	.252	.244	.264	.254	99
RHB-HR	35	46	81	21	44	65	131	69	96	165	61	89	150	120

SAN DIEGO

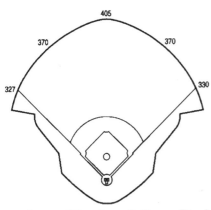

SAN FRANCISCO

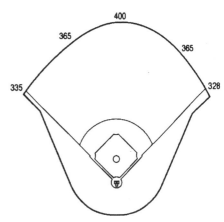

San Francisco Giants—3 Com Park

Alt: 75 feet   Surface: Grass

	1997 Season							1995-1997						
	HomeGames			AwayGames				HomeGames			AwayGames			
	Giants	Opp	Total	Giants	Opp	Total	Index	Giants	Opp	Total	Giants	Opp	Total	Index
G	73	73	146	73	73	146	—	227	227	454	225	225	450	—
Avg	.249	.263	.256	.261	.275	.268	96	.250	.262	.256	.258	.283	.270	95
AB	2387	2567	4954	2541	2405	4946	100	7568	8012	15580	7864	7507	15371	100
R	341	345	686	361	358	719	95	1032	1140	2172	1074	1201	2275	95
H	595	675	1270	664	661	1325	96	1889	2098	3987	2026	2126	4152	95
2B	108	110	218	125	112	237	92	328	380	708	379	379	758	92
3B	17	13	30	19	14	33	91	40	37	77	50	48	98	78
HR	69	67	136	75	71	146	93	227	243	470	222	262	484	96
BB	311	260	571	272	252	524	109	876	798	1674	794	789	1583	104
SO	512	507	1019	506	435	941	108	1624	1495	3119	1643	1245	2888	107
E	62	67	129	53	61	114	113	214	224	438	190	202	392	111
E-Infield	45	58	103	47	48	95	108	149	171	320	142	155	297	107
LHB-Avg	.266	.278	.271	.271	.277	.274	99	.265	.272	.269	.270	.288	.278	97
LHB-HR	42	23	65	41	22	63	104	103	86	189	99	92	191	97
RHB-Avg	.228	.254	.244	.248	.273	.263	93	.239	.256	.248	.249	.281	.265	93
RHB-HR	27	44	71	34	49	83	85	124	157	281	123	170	293	95

Seattle Mariners—The Kingdome

Alt: 400 feet **Surface:** Turf

| | 1997 Season | | | | | | | 1995-1997 | | | | | | |
| | Home Games | | | Away Games | | | Index | Home Games | | | Away Games | | | Index |
	Mariners	Opp	Total	Mariners	Opp	Total		Mariners	Opp	Total	Mariners	Opp	Total	
G	73	73	146	73	73	146	---	227	227	454	225	225	450	---
Avg	.281	.259	.270	.281	.270	.276	98	.283	.264	.273	.280	.278	.279	98
AB	2464	2568	5032	2605	2500	5105	99	7699	7995	15694	8034	7682	15716	99
R	395	376	771	427	358	785	98	1292	1169	2461	1319	1168	2487	98
H	693	666	1359	733	674	1407	97	2180	2109	4289	2248	2136	4384	97
2B	153	137	290	127	142	269	109	489	449	938	410	418	828	113
3B	11	7	18	9	13	22	83	27	33	60	32	51	83	72
HR	113	87	200	118	74	192	106	335	276	611	323	250	573	107
BB	284	280	564	264	262	526	109	907	899	1806	860	839	1699	106
SO	516	603	1119	485	495	980	116	1478	1755	3233	1446	1411	2857	113
E	51	38	89	63	48	111	80	178	139	317	176	163	339	93
E-Infield	48	35	83	55	38	93	89	143	120	263	146	127	273	95
LHB-Avg	.285	.262	.274	.273	.331	.301	91	.284	.281	.282	.277	.303	.290	97
LHB-HR	48	34	82	54	40	94	89	133	111	244	130	102	232	107
RHB-Avg	.279	.258	.268	.286	.237	.262	102	.283	.253	.268	.282	.261	.272	98
RHB-HR	65	53	118	64	34	98	122	202	165	367	193	148	341	106

SEATTLE

405
389
380
331
312

ST. LOUIS

402
372
375
330
330

St. Louis Cardinals—Busch Stadium

Alt: 535 feet **Surface:** Grass

| | 1997 Season | | | | | | | 1996-1997 | | | | | | |
| | Home Games | | | Away Games | | | Index | Home Games | | | Away Games | | | Index |
	Cardinals	Opp	Total	Cardinals	Opp	Total		Cardinals	Opp	Total	Cardinals	Opp	Total	
G	72	72	144	75	75	150	---	153	153	306	156	156	312	---
Avg	.260	.247	.254	.250	.269	.259	98	.269	.243	.256	.253	.266	.259	99
AB	2392	2475	4867	2634	2521	5155	98	5077	5249	10326	5451	5244	10695	98
R	315	296	611	318	343	661	96	706	622	1328	686	723	1409	96
H	622	612	1234	658	679	1337	96	1368	1276	2644	1380	1395	2775	97
2B	126	100	226	116	116	232	103	284	207	491	239	244	483	105
3B	13	9	22	21	21	42	55	31	16	47	34	37	71	69
HR	60	54	114	73	54	127	95	130	135	265	145	146	291	94
BB	255	243	498	237	255	492	107	505	507	1012	482	530	1012	104
SO	487	522	1009	611	498	1109	96	1031	1068	2099	1156	1002	2158	101
E	56	42	98	54	49	103	99	127	91	218	123	136	259	86
E-Infield	43	34	77	47	40	87	92	92	71	163	108	107	215	77
LHB-Avg	.272	.262	.267	.284	.276	.280	95	.280	.262	.271	.276	.278	.277	98
LHB-HR	25	27	52	37	20	57	95	43	62	105	64	54	118	92
RHB-Avg	.250	.236	.243	.223	.264	.243	100	.262	.230	.246	.236	.258	.247	99
RHB-HR	35	27	62	36	34	70	95	87	73	160	81	92	173	96

Texas Rangers—The Ballpark in Arlington

Alt: 551 feet   Surface: Grass

	1997 Season							1995-1997						
	Home Games			Away Games				Home Games			Away Games			
	Rangers	Opp	Total	Rangers	Opp	Total	Index	Rangers	Opp	Total	Rangers	Opp	Total	Index
G	73	73	146	73	73	146	—	226	226	452	227	227	454	—
Avg	.283	.285	.284	.256	.281	.268	106	.285	.280	.282	.263	.280	.271	104
AB	2510	2631	5141	2566	2442	5008	103	7709	8086	15795	7982	7619	15601	102
R	351	387	738	353	354	707	104	1238	1162	2400	1085	1098	2183	110
H	711	750	1461	657	687	1344	109	2194	2261	4455	2100	2130	4230	106
2B	140	132	272	138	138	276	96	413	374	787	435	397	832	93
3B	17	14	31	6	17	23	131	51	52	103	28	46	74	137
HR	85	86	171	86	65	151	110	278	245	523	252	226	478	108
BB	220	270	490	225	230	455	105	875	781	1656	756	815	1571	104
SO	493	414	907	536	426	962	92	1425	1327	2752	1522	1327	2849	95
E	57	55	112	45	50	95	118	162	174	336	149	179	328	103
E-Infield	44	39	83	36	40	76	109	129	124	253	112	141	253	100
LHB-Avg	.297	.292	.295	.261	.283	.272	108	.289	.279	.284	.269	.281	.275	103
LHB-HR	36	42	78	37	29	66	115	117	108	225	90	87	177	126
RHB-Avg	.272	.279	.276	.252	.280	.265	104	.281	.280	.281	.258	.279	.268	105
RHB-HR	49	44	93	49	36	85	107	161	137	298	162	139	301	97

TEXAS

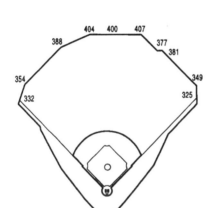

TORONTO

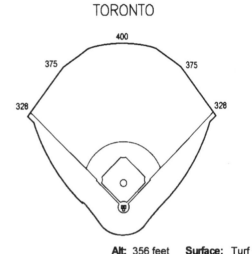

Toronto Blue Jays—SkyDome

Alt: 356 feet   Surface: Turf

	1997 Season							1995-1997						
	Home Games			Away Games				Home Games			Away Games			
	BlueJays	Opp	Total	BlueJays	Opp	Total	Index	BlueJays	Opp	Total	BlueJays	Opp	Total	Index
G	72	72	144	75	75	150	—	225	225	450	228	228	456	—
Avg	.251	.253	.252	.243	.275	.259	97	.254	.263	.259	.257	.269	.263	99
AB	2358	2504	4862	2615	2519	5134	99	7614	7970	15584	7994	7591	15585	101
R	301	281	582	304	347	651	93	987	1102	2089	1026	1112	2138	99
H	593	633	1226	636	692	1328	96	1935	2098	4033	2054	2039	4093	100
2B	125	124	249	126	130	256	103	430	413	843	398	387	785	107
3B	24	11	35	15	11	26	142	55	42	97	46	33	79	123
HR	58	64	122	73	91	164	79	218	245	463	230	242	472	98
BB	237	201	438	205	248	453	102	752	846	1598	711	867	1578	101
SO	476	513	989	533	543	1076	97	1532	1549	3081	1488	1434	2922	105
E	51	46	97	31	70	101	100	168	151	319	158	193	351	92
E-Infield	41	36	77	27	60	87	92	126	109	235	112	135	247	96
LHB-Avg	.287	.240	.259	.255	.273	.265	98	.272	.266	.268	.275	.273	.274	98
LHB-HR	26	26	52	30	45	75	70	74	109	183	92	115	207	92
RHB-Avg	.232	.265	.247	.237	.277	.254	97	.243	.261	.252	.245	.265	.254	99
RHB-HR	32	38	70	43	46	89	85	144	136	280	138	127	265	103

1995-97 Ballpark Index Rankings—Runs per Game

	AMERICAN LEAGUE									NATIONAL LEAGUE								
	HomeGames				AwayGames						HomeGames				AwayGames				
	Gm	Team	Opp	Total	Gm	Team	Opp	Total	Index		Gm	Team	Opp	Total	Gm	Team	Opp	Total	Index
Tex	226	1238	1162	2400	227	1085	1098	2183	110	Col	226	1629	1503	3132	226	945	1061	2006	156
Mil	227	1174	1224	2398	225	1093	1108	2201	108	Pit	224	1046	1181	2227	229	1035	1074	2109	108
Min	229	1172	1346	2518	224	1104	1245	2349	105	ChN	224	1097	1043	2140	229	967	1089	2056	106
Bos	225	1289	1189	2478	228	1211	1210	2421	104	Mon	228	1045	1010	2055	225	948	998	1946	104
Oak*	148	747	855	1602	160	790	895	1685	103	Phi	228	980	1110	2090	225	906	1104	2010	103
Det**	72	362	350	712	75	350	384	734	101	Cin	225	1068	1023	2091	228	1040	1078	2118	100
Ana	227	1208	1142	2350	225	1122	1198	2320	100	Atl**	75	357	271	628	72	363	259	622	97
Tor	225	987	1102	2089	228	1026	1112	2138	99	StL*	153	706	622	1328	156	686	723	1409	96
KC	226	1004	1116	2120	225	1039	1108	2147	98	SF	227	1032	1140	2172	225	1074	1201	2275	95
NYA	224	1239	1001	2240	230	1234	1105	2339	98	Fla	227	1025	896	1921	225	998	1092	2090	91
Sea	227	1292	1169	2461	225	1319	1168	2487	98	NYN	228	1016	956	1972	225	1095	1072	2167	90
Bal	226	1142	1078	2220	228	1254	1077	2331	96	SD*	148	639	690	1329	160	823	782	1605	90
Cle	227	1285	1038	2323	224	1294	1083	2377	96	Hou	225	1029	901	1930	228	1198	1156	2354	83
ChA	228	1120	1106	2226	225	1256	1226	2482	89	LA	226	898	815	1713	226	1091	1017	2108	81

*—Current dimensions began 1996; **—Current dimensions began 1997

1995-97 Ballpark Index Rankings—Home Runs per At Bat

	AMERICAN LEAGUE									NATIONAL LEAGUE								
	HomeGames				AwayGames						HomeGames				AwayGames				
	Gm	Team	Opp	Total	Gm	Team	Opp	Total	Index		Gm	Team	Opp	Total	Gm	Team	Opp	Total	Index
Ana	227	274	320	594	225	251	237	488	120	Col	226	393	341	734	226	243	199	442	154
Det**	72	83	89	172	75	75	80	155	118	ChN	224	250	272	522	229	198	246	444	119
Bal	226	304	269	573	228	302	233	535	110	SD*	148	134	153	287	160	145	133	278	113
Tex	226	278	245	523	227	252	226	478	108	Pit	224	203	215	418	229	178	226	404	106
Sea	227	335	276	611	225	323	250	573	107	Phi	228	164	237	401	225	169	216	385	100
Min	229	172	328	500	224	183	290	473	103	Cin	225	230	225	455	228	251	231	482	97
NYA	224	217	217	434	230	224	219	443	102	SF	227	227	243	470	225	222	262	484	96
Tor	225	218	245	463	228	230	242	472	98	StL*	153	130	135	265	156	145	146	291	94
Oak*	148	203	176	379	160	217	208	425	96	NYN	228	193	203	396	225	219	220	439	89
Bos	225	273	209	482	228	281	232	513	94	Mon	228	196	197	393	225	222	221	443	88
KC	226	176	249	425	225	206	241	447	94	Fla	227	198	166	364	225	222	209	431	86
Mil	227	191	265	456	225	241	264	505	88	Atl**	75	68	50	118	72	87	48	135	84
Cle	227	293	219	512	224	336	260	596	86	LA	226	194	163	357	226	248	227	475	78
ChA	228	200	237	437	225	284	264	548	80	Hou	225	157	159	316	228	206	233	439	74

*—Current dimensions began 1996; **—Current dimensions began 1997

1995-97 Ballpark Index Rankings—Batting Average

	AMERICAN LEAGUE									NATIONAL LEAGUE								
	HomeGames				AwayGames						HomeGames				AwayGames				
	Gm	Team	Opp	Avg	Gm	Team	Opp	Avg	Index		Gm	Team	Opp	Avg	Gm	Team	Opp	Avg	Index
Bos	225	.299	.275	.287	228	.273	.274	.274	105	Col	226	.327	.311	.319	226	.242	.267	.254	125
Mil	227	.277	.278	.277	225	.262	.269	.266	104	ChN	224	.267	.258	.262	229	.248	.267	.258	102
Tex	226	.285	.280	.282	227	.263	.269	.271	104	Mon	228	.269	.249	.259	225	.251	.261	.256	101
NYA	224	.296	.260	.278	230	.276	.265	.271	103	Pit	224	.265	.280	.273	229	.261	.277	.269	101
Oak*	148	.272	.292	.282	160	.254	.295	.274	103	Atl**	75	.276	.236	.256	72	.263	.248	.256	100
KC	226	.268	.269	.269	225	.259	.277	.267	101	Cin	225	.266	.254	.260	228	.253	.267	.260	100
Min	229	.285	.278	.282	224	.273	.286	.280	101	Phi	228	.264	.256	.260	225	.252	.268	.260	100
Bal	226	.267	.259	.263	228	.271	.262	.266	99	StL*	153	.269	.243	.256	156	.253	.266	.259	99
Cle	227	.292	.263	.277	224	.288	.272	.280	99	NYN	228	.268	.258	.263	225	.264	.274	.269	98
Tor	225	.254	.263	.259	228	.257	.269	.263	99	SD*	148	.264	.258	.261	160	.268	.267	.268	98
Sea	227	.283	.264	.273	225	.280	.278	.279	98	Fla	227	.268	.241	.254	225	.251	.274	.262	97
Ana	227	.277	.260	.268	225	.274	.279	.276	97	SF	227	.250	.262	.256	225	.258	.283	.270	95
ChA	228	.277	.264	.270	225	.281	.280	.280	96	Hou	225	.263	.248	.255	228	.269	.280	.274	93
Det**	72	.253	.254	.254	75	.264	.279	.271	94	LA	226	.253	.229	.241	226	.268	.260	.264	91

*—Current dimensions began 1996; **—Current dimensions began 1997

280

1997 Lefty-Righty Stats

Each human being is born almost completely ignorant. The minute one enters the world, he or she begins to acquire knowledge about the universe in which we live. The person receives the wisdom of others, and observes the world firsthand. Through this process, the person may begin to understand *how* and *why* things happen. Ideally, that individual might even contribute to our collective understanding of the universe.

When it comes to platoon data, we remain distressingly ignorant. We know that lefthanded pitchers enjoy an advantage against lefthanded hitters, but we still don't know *why*. Sure, we have *theories*—it's the way the breaking pitch breaks, or the way our brains are wired, or it has something to do with the rotation of the earth—but the truth is that we just don't know for sure.

Looking at it another way, though, you might argue that we don't *need* to know why it happens. "You don't need to understand fluid dynamics, neuroscience or the Coriolis Effect," Ben Franklin might say, "in order to know when to bring in Tony Fossas." The effect *exists; of this there is no doubt. Change pitchers first and ask questions later.*

In the following pages, you'll see which batters need to be pinch-hit for, and which ones ought to be given a chance to play full-time. You'll see which pitchers are likely to get beaten by a lefthanded pinch-hitter with the game on the line. Through careful examination of the empirical data, you might even hit upon the underlying rationale of the platoon principle. If you do, by all means, give us a call here at STATS and release us from our ignorance.

—Mat Olkin

Batters vs. Lefthanded and Righthanded Pitchers

Batter	vs	Avg	AB	H	2B	3B	HR	BI	BB	SO	OBP	SLG
Abbott,Jeff	L	.333	18	6	1	0	0	0	0	1	.333	.389
Bats Right	R	.200	20	4	0	0	1	2	0	5	.200	.350
Abbott,Kurt	L	.315	89	28	7	1	2	11	4	19	.344	.483
Bats Right	R	.252	163	41	11	1	4	19	10	49	.299	.405
Abreu,Bob	L	.182	33	6	3	1	0	6	5	10	.289	.333
Bats Left	R	.265	155	41	7	1	3	20	16	38	.337	.381
Alexander,M	L	.241	83	20	6	2	0	10	5	19	.292	.361
Bats Right	R	.279	165	46	6	2	3	12	12	35	.333	.394
Alfonzo,E	L	.378	135	51	8	1	4	27	18	11	.448	.541
Bats Right	R	.292	383	112	19	1	6	45	45	45	.371	.394
Alicea,Luis	L	.245	110	27	6	0	0	9	11	11	.317	.300
Bats Both	R	.255	278	71	10	7	5	28	58	54	.395	.396
Allensworth,J	L	.278	97	27	5	1	1	6	18	29	.393	.381
Bats Right	R	.246	272	67	13	1	2	37	26	50	.320	.324
Alomar,R	L	.248	113	28	5	0	0	8	9	18	.298	.292
Bats Both	R	.365	299	109	18	2	14	52	31	25	.423	.579
Alomar,Sandy	L	.336	119	40	9	0	5	23	5	11	.363	.538
Bats Right	R	.319	332	106	28	0	16	60	14	37	.351	.548
Alou,Moises	L	.340	97	33	9	2	5	33	21	15	.454	.629
Bats Right	R	.281	441	124	20	3	18	82	49	70	.354	.463
Amaral,Rich	L	.279	129	36	4	0	1	15	6	23	.321	.333
Bats Right	R	.295	61	18	1	0	0	6	4	11	.338	.311
Amaro,Ruben	L	.315	54	17	2	1	0	9	6	8	.383	.389
Bats Both	R	.198	121	24	4	0	2	12	15	16	.293	.281
Anderson,B	L	.281	192	54	11	3	5	23	24	39	.381	.448
Bats Left	R	.291	398	116	28	4	13	50	60	66	.399	.480
Anderson,G	L	.293	184	54	9	1	0	29	2	28	.296	.353
Bats Left	R	.307	440	135	27	2	8	63	28	42	.350	.432
Andrews,Sha.	L	.300	10	3	1	0	2	4	0	1	.300	1.000
Bats Right	R	.185	54	10	2	0	2	5	3	19	.220	.333
Anthony,Eric	L	.500	2	1	0	0	0	1	0	0	.500	.500
Bats Left	R	.236	72	17	3	2	2	4	12	18	.345	.417
Arias,Alex	L	.200	20	4	0	0	0	1	5	3	.360	.200
Bats Right	R	.260	73	19	2	0	1	10	7	9	.349	.329
Arias,George	L	.143	7	1	0	0	0	0	0	1	.143	.143
Bats Right	R	.286	21	6	1	0	0	3	0	1	.286	.333
Ashley,Billy	L	.289	90	26	7	0	5	17	3	26	.312	.533
Bats Right	R	.146	41	6	0	0	1	2	5	20	.255	.220
Aurilia,Rich	L	.280	50	14	6	0	3	9	5	6	.345	.580
Bats Right	R	.269	52	14	2	0	2	10	3	9	.298	.423
Ausmus,Brad	L	.240	96	23	6	0	1	11	7	15	.295	.333
Bats Right	R	.274	329	90	19	1	3	33	31	63	.335	.365
Aven,Bruce	L	.300	10	3	1	0	0	2	0	3	.300	.400
Bats Right	R	.111	9	1	0	0	0	0	1	2	.200	.111
Baerga,Carlos	L	.170	94	16	2	0	1	4	3	16	.196	.223
Bats Both	R	.308	373	115	23	1	8	48	17	38	.339	.440
Bagwell,Jeff	L	.242	120	29	10	0	5	20	39	21	.432	.450
Bats Right	R	.298	446	133	30	2	38	115	88	101	.423	.630
Baines,Harold	L	.272	92	25	6	0	3	19	4	20	.299	.435
Bats Left	R	.308	360	111	17	0	13	48	51	42	.392	.464
Banks,Brian	L	.250	16	4	0	0	0	1	3	5	.350	.250
Bats Both	R	.192	52	10	1	0	1	7	3	12	.236	.269
Barron,Tony	L	.339	59	20	7	1	1	7	7	12	.403	.542
Bats Right	R	.262	130	34	5	0	3	17	5	26	.295	.369
Bartee,Kimera	L	.000	1	0	0	0	0	0	0	1	.500	.000
Bats Both	R	.250	4	1	0	0	0	0	2	1	.500	.250
Bates,Jason	L	.179	28	5	3	0	0	0	5	8	.361	.286
Bats Both	R	.258	93	24	7	0	3	11	10	19	.330	.430
Batista,Tony	L	.150	60	9	3	0	0	2	3	11	.190	.200
Bats Right	R	.227	128	29	7	1	4	16	11	20	.298	.391
Bautista,D	L	.262	61	16	2	0	1	3	3	12	.308	.344
Bats Right	R	.214	42	9	1	2	2	6	2	12	.244	.476
Beamon,Trey	L	.286	7	2	1	0	0	1	0	1	.286	.429
Bats Left	R	.276	58	16	0	0	0	6	2	16	.311	.310
Becker,Rich	L	.156	64	10	2	0	0	3	9	23	.260	.188
Bats Left	R	.282	379	107	20	3	10	42	53	107	.370	.430
Bell,David	L	.280	50	14	4	0	0	2	3	7	.315	.360
Bats Right	R	.174	92	16	3	2	1	10	7	21	.232	.283
Bell,Derek	L	.235	119	28	4	1	1	9	6	23	.270	.311
Bats Right	R	.289	374	108	25	2	14	62	34	71	.366	.479
Bell,Jay	L	.260	173	45	7	0	4	19	18	31	.330	.370
Bats Right	R	.305	400	122	21	3	17	73	53	70	.384	.500
Belle,Albert	L	.295	122	36	7	0	7	21	21	23	.399	.525
Bats Right	R	.270	512	138	38	1	23	95	32	82	.315	.482
Bellhorn,Mark	L	.222	63	14	1	0	2	4	8	26	.310	.333
Bats Both	R	.230	161	37	8	1	4	15	24	44	.330	.366
Belliard,R	L	.357	14	5	1	0	1	2	0	3	.357	.643
Bats Right	R	.175	57	10	2	0	0	1	1	14	.186	.211
Benard,Marvin	L	.214	14	3	0	0	0	0	2	8	.313	.214
Bats Left	R	.230	100	23	4	0	1	13	11	21	.316	.300
Benitez,Yamil	L	.241	58	14	2	0	3	8	4	13	.290	.431
Bats Right	R	.278	133	37	5	1	5	13	6	36	.314	.444
Benjamin,Mike	L	.156	32	5	2	0	0	2	3	6	.229	.219
Bats Right	R	.262	84	22	7	1	0	5	1	21	.276	.369
Berblinger,J	L	.000	1	0	0	0	0	0	0	0	.000	.000
Bats Right	R	.000	4	0	0	0	0	0	0	1	.000	.000
Berroa,G	L	.358	148	53	8	0	7	29	21	28	.444	.554
Bats Right	R	.257	413	106	17	0	19	61	55	92	.342	.436
Berry,Sean	L	.240	75	18	5	0	2	12	4	9	.272	.387
Bats Right	R	.261	226	59	19	1	6	31	21	44	.332	.434
Berryhill,D	L	.342	38	13	2	0	0	5	5	6	.419	.395
Bats Both	R	.233	129	30	6	0	3	18	15	23	.310	.349
Bichette,D	L	.263	133	35	7	0	8	28	9	26	.303	.496
Bats Right	R	.322	428	138	24	2	18	90	21	64	.355	.514
Bieser,Steve	L	.000	2	0	0	0	0	0	0	1	.000	.000
Bats Left	R	.254	67	17	3	0	0	4	7	19	.354	.299
Biggio,Craig	L	.326	138	45	8	2	6	19	26	24	.444	.543
Bats Right	R	.304	481	146	29	6	16	62	58	83	.407	.489
Blanco,Henry	L	.000	1	0	0	0	0	0	0	0	.000	.000
Bats Right	R	.500	4	2	0	0	1	1	0	1	.500	1.250

Batters vs. Lefthanded and Righthanded Pitchers

Batter	vs	Avg	AB	H	2B	3B	HR	BI	BB	SO	OBP	SLG	Batter	vs	Avg	AB	H	2B	3B	HR	BI	BB	SO	OBP	SLG
Blauser,Jeff	L	.312	125	39	9	1	7	20	23	23	.417	.568	Burks,Ellis	L	.280	100	28	2	0	5	17	10	15	.345	.450
Bats Right	R	.307	394	121	22	3	10	50	47	78	.400	.454	Bats Right	R	.293	324	95	17	2	27	65	37	60	.369	.608
Blowers,Mike	L	.321	109	35	4	0	5	17	19	20	.419	.495	Burnitz,J	L	.273	121	33	8	1	3	20	10	26	.343	.430
Bats Right	R	.220	41	9	1	0	0	3	2	13	.250	.244	Bats Left	R	.284	373	106	29	7	24	65	65	85	.393	.592
Bogar,Tim	L	.279	68	19	4	1	1	12	9	9	.363	.412	Bush,Homer	L	.000	0	0	0	0	0	0	0	0	.000	.000
Bats Right	R	.237	173	41	10	3	3	18	15	33	.302	.382	Bats Right	R	.364	11	4	0	0	0	3	0	0	.364	.364
Boggs,Wade	L	.361	72	26	3	0	1	4	7	10	.418	.444	Butler,Brett	L	.333	93	31	5	0	0	4	5	10	.367	.387
Bats Left	R	.274	281	77	20	1	3	24	41	28	.362	.384	Bats Left	R	.264	250	66	3	3	0	14	37	30	.361	.300
Bonds,Barry	L	.295	166	49	11	2	11	26	37	24	.427	.584	Butler,Rich	L	.000	0	0	0	0	0	0	0	0	.000	.000
Bats Left	R	.290	366	106	15	3	29	75	108	63	.455	.585	Bats Left	R	.286	14	4	1	0	0	2	2	3	.375	.357
Bonilla,Bobby	L	.372	113	42	8	0	6	21	9	10	.419	.602	Butler,Rob	L	.167	6	1	0	0	0	2	2	1	.375	.167
Bats Both	R	.278	449	125	31	3	11	75	64	84	.368	.434	Bats Left	R	.301	83	25	9	1	0	11	3	7	.322	.434
Boone,Aaron	L	.364	11	4	0	0	0	0	1	0	.417	.364	Cabrera,O	L	.143	7	1	0	0	0	1	1	1	.250	.143
Bats Right	R	.211	38	8	1	0	0	5	1	5	.231	.237	Bats Right	R	.273	11	3	0	0	0	1	0	2	.273	.273
Boone,Bret	L	.210	100	21	8	0	0	10	18	30	.328	.290	Cairo,Miguel	L	.154	13	2	0	0	0	0	0	2	.154	.154
Bats Right	R	.227	343	78	17	1	7	36	27	71	.288	.344	Bats Right	R	.313	16	5	1	0	0	1	2	1	.421	.375
Booty,Josh	L	1.000	1	1	0	0	0	1	0	0	1.000	1.000	Cameron,Mike	L	.228	114	26	7	1	4	15	18	30	.336	.412
Bats Right	R	.500	4	2	0	0	0	0	1	1	.600	.500	Bats Right	R	.272	265	72	11	2	10	40	37	75	.365	.442
Borders,Pat	L	.259	27	7	2	0	0	0	1	6	.286	.333	Caminiti,Ken	L	.306	144	44	7	0	6	24	24	30	.404	.479
Bats Right	R	.303	132	40	5	1	4	15	8	21	.352	.447	Bats Both	R	.284	342	97	21	0	20	66	56	88	.383	.520
Bordick,Mike	L	.195	154	30	3	0	1	9	8	11	.233	.234	Candaele,C	L	.000	2	0	0	0	0	0	0	0	.000	.000
Bats Right	R	.254	355	90	16	1	6	37	25	55	.304	.355	Bats Both	R	.333	24	8	1	0	0	4	1	1	.360	.375
Bournigal,R	L	.232	69	16	1	0	0	3	6	5	.293	.246	Cangelosi,J	L	.235	51	12	3	0	0	4	5	12	.310	.294
Bats Right	R	.301	153	46	8	0	1	17	10	14	.359	.373	Bats Both	R	.248	141	35	5	0	1	8	14	21	.325	.305
Bragg,Darren	L	.242	120	29	7	0	1	10	13	27	.321	.325	Canseco,Jose	L	.241	79	19	5	0	2	11	9	25	.318	.380
Bats Left	R	.262	393	103	28	2	8	47	48	75	.342	.405	Bats Right	R	.233	309	72	14	0	21	63	42	97	.327	.482
Branson,Jeff	L	.389	18	7	1	0	0	0	1	3	.421	.444	Carr,Chuck	L	.213	47	10	4	0	0	0	3	14	.275	.298
Bats Left	R	.178	152	27	6	1	3	12	13	37	.244	.289	Bats Left	R	.257	191	49	10	2	4	17	14	34	.313	.393
Brede,Brent	L	.286	14	4	0	0	0	2	0	5	.313	.286	Carter,Joe	L	.289	180	52	9	3	6	33	10	27	.328	.472
Bats Left	R	.273	176	48	11	1	3	19	21	33	.350	.398	Bats Right	R	.211	432	91	21	1	15	69	30	78	.266	.368
Brito,Tilson	L	.296	54	16	3	0	0	2	2	10	.333	.352	Casanova,Raul	L	.237	59	14	1	0	1	5	8	11	.338	.305
Bats Right	R	.212	118	25	2	1	2	12	8	28	.264	.297	Bats Both	R	.245	245	60	9	1	4	19	18	37	.301	.339
Brogna,Rico	L	.190	116	22	4	0	1	11	6	30	.228	.250	Casey,Sean	L	.000	2	0	0	0	0	0	1	1	.500	.000
Bats Left	R	.269	427	115	32	1	19	70	27	86	.311	.482	Bats Left	R	.250	8	2	0	0	0	1	0	1	.250	.250
Brosius,Scott	L	.160	125	20	3	0	2	8	8	32	.215	.232	Castilla,V	L	.380	129	49	6	1	11	31	11	18	.434	.698
Bats Right	R	.218	354	77	17	1	9	33	26	70	.275	.347	Bats Right	R	.284	483	137	19	1	29	82	33	90	.335	.507
Brown,Adrian	L	.296	27	8	0	0	1	4	3	4	.367	.407	Castillo,A	L	.192	26	5	0	0	0	1	9	8	.389	.192
Bats Both	R	.167	120	20	6	0	0	6	10	14	.252	.217	Bats Right	R	.212	33	7	1	0	0	6	0	8	.212	.242
Brown,Brant	L	.118	17	2	0	0	0	1	1	0	.211	.118	Castillo,Luis	L	.222	45	10	2	0	0	1	3	9	.271	.267
Bats Left	R	.250	120	30	7	1	5	14	6	28	.297	.450	Bats Both	R	.243	218	53	6	0	0	7	24	44	.318	.271
Brown,Emil	L	.184	38	7	1	0	2	4	5	11	.326	.368	Castro,Juan	L	.100	30	3	2	0	0	0	5	9	.229	.167
Bats Right	R	.175	57	10	1	1	0	2	5	21	.288	.228	Bats Right	R	.178	45	8	1	1	0	4	2	11	.213	.244
Brown,K	L	.250	4	1	0	0	0	0	0	0	.250	.250	Catalanotto,F	L	.000	1	0	0	0	0	0	1	1	.500	.000
Bats Right	R	1.000	1	1	0	0	0	1	0	0	1.000	4.000	Bats Left	R	.320	25	8	2	0	0	3	2	6	.370	.400
Brumfield,J	L	.245	94	23	4	1	1	9	5	11	.283	.340	Cedeno,D	L	.263	76	20	4	0	0	6	6	16	.317	.316
Bats Right	R	.163	80	13	1	0	1	11	9	20	.253	.213	Bats Both	R	.287	289	83	15	6	4	30	21	61	.339	.422
Buford,Damon	L	.252	139	35	5	0	4	14	8	31	.289	.374	Cedeno,Roger	L	.286	84	24	7	0	2	6	8	22	.358	.440
Bats Right	R	.207	227	47	13	0	4	25	22	52	.286	.317	Bats Both	R	.264	110	29	3	2	1	11	17	22	.364	.355
Buhner,Jay	L	.317	126	40	4	1	11	27	29	32	.449	.627	Chavez,Raul	L	.500	10	5	0	0	0	1	0	1	.500	.500
Bats Right	R	.220	414	91	14	1	29	82	90	143	.363	.469	Bats Right	R	.125	16	2	0	0	0	1	0	4	.118	.125

Batters vs. Lefthanded and Righthanded Pitchers

Batter	vs	Avg	AB	H	2B	3B	HR	BI	BB	SO	OBP	SLG	Batter	vs	Avg	AB	H	2B	3B	HR	BI	BB	SO	OBP	SLG
Cianfrocco,A	L	.206	68	14	3	0	3	5	8	26	.299	.382	Cummings,M	L	.289	38	11	2	0	0	2	6	7	.386	.342
Bats Right	R	.263	152	40	9	0	1	21	17	54	.341	.342	Bats Left	R	.261	276	72	20	6	4	29	25	49	.322	.420
Cirillo,Jeff	L	.261	165	43	9	0	3	13	18	22	.354	.370	Curtis,Chad	L	.314	105	33	8	1	4	18	17	17	.403	.524
Bats Right	R	.299	415	124	37	2	7	69	42	52	.372	.448	Bats Right	R	.270	244	66	14	0	11	37	26	42	.344	.463
Clark,Dave	L	.429	14	6	0	0	0	1	1	3	.467	.429	Damon,Johnny	L	.248	117	29	0	1	2	9	8	13	.307	.316
Bats Left	R	.287	129	37	8	0	5	31	18	31	.377	.465	Bats Left	R	.285	355	101	12	7	6	39	34	57	.348	.408
Clark,Tony	L	.265	181	48	6	1	10	35	24	44	.350	.475	Daulton,D	L	.262	84	22	4	1	3	10	11	19	.343	.440
Bats Both	R	.281	399	112	22	2	22	82	69	100	.387	.511	Bats Left	R	.264	311	82	17	7	11	53	65	55	.386	.469
Clark,Will	L	.302	129	39	7	1	3	16	12	20	.366	.442	Davis,Chili	L	.327	147	48	11	0	9	32	18	25	.395	.585
Bats Left	R	.337	264	89	22	0	9	35	37	42	.416	.523	Bats Both	R	.258	330	85	9	0	21	58	67	71	.383	.476
Clayton,Royce	L	.252	139	35	12	1	2	10	8	33	.295	.396	Davis,Eric	L	.382	55	21	5	0	3	7	6	15	.443	.636
Bats Right	R	.270	437	118	27	4	7	51	25	76	.310	.398	Bats Right	R	.262	103	27	6	0	5	18	8	32	.313	.466
Clyburn,Danny	L	.000	1	0	0	0	0	0	0	0	.000	.000	Davis,Russ	L	.248	117	29	7	0	5	19	11	24	.313	.436
Bats Right	R	.000	2	0	0	0	0	0	0	2	.000	.000	Bats Right	R	.281	303	85	22	1	15	44	16	76	.319	.508
Colbrunn,Greg	L	.290	124	36	7	0	4	19	6	25	.321	.444	Delgado,C	L	.254	134	34	14	2	2	16	13	35	.325	.433
Bats Right	R	.272	147	40	10	0	3	16	4	24	.299	.401	Bats Left	R	.265	385	102	28	1	28	75	51	98	.358	.561
Coleman,M	L	.133	15	2	0	0	0	0	0	9	.133	.133	Delgado,W	L	.000	1	0	0	0	0	0	0	0	.000	.000
Bats Right	R	.222	9	2	1	0	0	2	0	2	.222	.333	Bats Both	R	.167	6	1	1	0	0	0	0	2	.167	.333
Coleman,Vince	L	.000	1	0	0	0	0	0	1	0	.500	.000	Dellucci,D	L	.000	2	0	0	0	0	0	0	0	.333	.000
Bats Both	R	.077	13	1	0	0	0	0	0	3	.077	.077	Bats Left	R	.240	25	6	1	0	1	3	4	7	.345	.400
Coles,Darnell	L	.273	11	3	1	0	1	1	0	3	.273	.636	DeShields,D	L	.280	118	33	5	3	1	12	13	13	.358	.398
Bats Right	R	.364	11	4	0	0	0	1	0	3	.417	.364	Bats Left	R	.300	454	136	21	11	10	46	42	59	.357	.460
Collier,Lou	L	.000	4	0	0	0	0	0	0	2	.000	.000	Devereaux,M	L	.227	44	10	2	0	0	1	4	5	.292	.273
Bats Right	R	.152	33	5	0	0	0	3	1	9	.176	.152	Bats Right	R	.179	28	5	1	0	0	6	3	5	.250	.214
Conine,Jeff	L	.248	105	26	1	1	4	15	12	24	.325	.390	Diaz,Alex	L	.292	24	7	0	0	1	5	1	6	.333	.417
Bats Right	R	.240	300	72	12	0	13	46	45	65	.341	.410	Bats Both	R	.197	66	13	4	0	1	7	4	7	.243	.303
Coomer,Ron	L	.415	123	51	11	1	3	24	10	13	.459	.593	Diaz,Eddy	L	.242	33	8	2	1	0	6	1	2	.265	.364
Bats Right	R	.263	400	105	19	1	10	61	12	78	.281	.390	Bats Right	R	.176	17	3	0	0	0	1	0	3	.176	.176
Cooper,Scott	L	.263	19	5	0	1	1	4	0	5	.300	.526	Diaz,Einar	L	.000	3	0	0	0	0	0	0	1	.000	.000
Bats Left	R	.193	140	27	6	0	2	11	17	27	.281	.279	Bats Right	R	.250	4	1	1	0	0	1	0	1	.250	.500
Cora,Joey	L	.364	107	39	10	1	5	26	9	10	.403	.617	Difelice,Mike	L	.234	64	15	2	0	2	10	7	17	.315	.359
Bats Both	R	.285	467	133	30	3	6	28	44	39	.349	.400	Bats Right	R	.240	196	47	8	1	2	20	12	44	.290	.321
Cordero,Wil	L	.287	174	50	11	1	4	19	11	36	.332	.431	DiSarcina,G	L	.209	158	33	3	0	1	9	6	13	.241	.247
Bats Right	R	.278	396	110	15	2	14	53	20	86	.315	.432	Bats Right	R	.261	391	102	25	2	3	38	11	16	.284	.358
Cordova,Marty	L	.212	99	21	5	1	7	20	10	24	.284	.495	Ducey,Rob	L	.111	9	1	0	0	0	0	0	3	.111	.111
Bats Right	R	.258	279	72	13	3	8	31	20	68	.313	.412	Bats Left	R	.299	134	40	15	2	5	10	6	28	.324	.552
Counsell,C	L	.308	13	4	2	0	0	1	2	1	.471	.462	Duncan,M	L	.225	102	23	4	0	0	12	3	25	.255	.265
Bats Left	R	.298	151	45	7	2	1	15	16	16	.367	.391	Bats Right	R	.241	237	57	10	0	1	13	9	53	.274	.295
Crespo,Felipe	L	.222	9	2	0	1	1	2	0	2	.222	.778	Dunn,Todd	L	.241	54	13	3	0	2	6	0	21	.241	.407
Bats Both	R	.316	19	6	0	0	0	3	2	2	.381	.316	Bats Right	R	.219	64	14	2	0	1	3	2	18	.242	.297
Cromer,Tripp	L	.321	28	9	1	0	3	8	2	4	.367	.679	Dunston,S	L	.277	94	26	5	0	3	12	3	13	.293	.426
Bats Right	R	.276	58	16	2	0	1	12	4	12	.317	.362	Bats Right	R	.306	396	121	17	5	11	45	5	62	.317	.457
Cruz,Deivi	L	.214	112	24	5	0	0	8	7	17	.258	.259	Dunwoody,To.	L	.222	9	2	0	0	1	2	0	3	.300	.556
Bats Right	R	.250	324	81	21	0	2	32	7	38	.264	.333	Bats Left	R	.268	41	11	2	2	1	5	7	18	.375	.488
Cruz,Ivan	L	.000	4	0	0	0	0	0	0	2	.000	.000	Durham,Ray	L	.237	177	42	3	0	3	10	12	27	.285	.305
Bats Left	R	.313	16	5	1	0	0	3	2	2	.389	.375	Bats Both	R	.284	457	130	24	5	8	43	49	69	.357	.411
Cruz,Jacob	L	.500	2	1	0	0	0	1	0	1	.500	.500	Dye,Jermaine	L	.286	84	24	5	0	4	8	4	13	.315	.488
Bats Left	R	.130	23	3	1	0	0	2	3	3	.222	.174	Bats Right	R	.212	179	38	9	0	3	14	13	38	.269	.313
Cruz Jr,Jose	L	.258	97	25	4	1	5	18	12	23	.333	.474	Easley,Damion	L	.231	143	33	7	1	7	20	11	29	.299	.441
Bats Both	R	.245	298	73	15	0	21	50	29	94	.309	.507	Bats Right	R	.276	384	106	30	2	15	52	57	73	.383	.482

Batters vs. Lefthanded and Righthanded Pitchers

Batter	vs	Avg	AB	H	2B	3B	HR	BI	BB	SO	OBP	SLG
Echevarria,A	L	.250	8	2	0	0	0	0	0	1	.250	.250
Bats Right	R	.250	12	3	2	0	0	0	2	4	.357	.417
Edmonds,Jim	L	.273	143	39	3	0	6	24	15	20	.342	.420
Bats Left	R	.298	359	107	24	0	20	56	45	60	.378	.532
Eenhoorn,R	L	1.000	1	1	0	0	0	1	0	0	.500	1.000
Bats Right	R	.316	19	6	1	0	1	5	0	2	.316	.526
Eisenreich,J	L	.241	29	7	1	0	0	4	6	5	.361	.276
Bats Left	R	.284	264	75	18	1	2	30	24	23	.342	.383
Elster,Kevin	L	.192	26	5	0	1	0	1	5	11	.313	.269
Bats Right	R	.232	112	26	6	1	7	24	16	28	.331	.491
Encarnacion,A	L	.667	3	2	0	0	1	4	0	0	.667	1.667
Bats Right	R	.357	14	5	1	0	0	0	0	1	.357	.429
Encarnacion,J	L	.167	12	2	1	0	1	2	0	5	.231	.500
Bats Right	R	.238	21	5	0	1	0	3	3	7	.360	.333
Erstad,Darin	L	.302	159	48	7	0	8	31	13	21	.354	.497
Bats Left	R	.297	380	113	27	4	8	46	38	65	.362	.453
Espinoza,A	L	.250	28	7	1	0	0	4	0	5	.250	.286
Bats Right	R	.136	44	6	0	0	0	3	2	7	.191	.136
Estalella,B	L	.125	8	1	0	0	0	0	2	3	.300	.125
Bats Right	R	.429	21	9	1	0	4	9	5	4	.538	1.048
Eusebio,Tony	L	.333	48	16	0	0	1	8	4	6	.385	.396
Bats Right	R	.250	116	29	2	0	0	10	15	21	.356	.267
Evans,Tom	L	.222	9	2	1	0	0	0	2	2	.364	.333
Bats Right	R	.310	29	9	1	0	1	2	0	8	.333	.448
Everett,Carl	L	.208	101	21	6	0	2	9	6	26	.270	.327
Bats Both	R	.260	342	89	22	3	12	48	26	76	.319	.447
Fabregas,J	L	.265	49	13	0	0	1	8	2	9	.288	.327
Bats Left	R	.257	311	80	11	1	6	43	12	37	.284	.357
Fasano,Sal	L	.214	14	3	1	0	0	0	0	3	.214	.286
Bats Right	R	.208	24	5	1	0	1	1	1	9	.240	.375
Fernandez,T	L	.407	123	50	6	1	5	18	7	7	.435	.593
Bats Both	R	.234	286	67	15	0	6	26	15	40	.275	.350
Fielder,Cecil	L	.211	90	19	1	0	1	7	24	29	.379	.256
Bats Right	R	.277	271	75	14	0	12	54	27	58	.350	.461
Figga,Mike	L	.000	1	0	0	0	0	0	0	1	.000	.000
Bats Right	R	.000	3	0	0	0	0	0	0	2	.000	.000
Finley,Steve	L	.263	152	40	5	1	5	20	7	24	.309	.408
Bats Left	R	.260	408	106	21	4	23	72	36	68	.315	.500
Flaherty,John	L	.265	68	18	5	0	1	5	11	8	.367	.382
Bats Right	R	.275	371	102	16	1	8	41	22	54	.314	.388
Fletcher,D	L	.253	75	19	4	0	4	16	3	11	.291	.467
Bats Left	R	.285	235	67	16	1	13	39	14	24	.333	.528
Floyd,Cliff	L	.250	16	4	2	0	0	0	3	6	.368	.375
Bats Left	R	.231	121	28	7	1	6	19	21	27	.352	.455
Fonville,Chad	L	.200	5	1	0	0	0	0	0	0	.200	.200
Bats Both	R	.111	18	2	0	0	0	2	3	4	.238	.111
Fordyce,Brook	L	.152	33	5	1	0	0	2	3	2	.216	.182
Bats Right	R	.238	63	15	4	0	1	6	5	13	.294	.349
Fox,Andy	L	.333	3	1	0	0	0	0	0	2	.333	.333
Bats Left	R	.214	28	6	1	0	0	1	7	7	.371	.250

Batter	vs	Avg	AB	H	2B	3B	HR	BI	BB	SO	OBP	SLG
Franco,Julio	L	.252	111	28	3	0	0	9	26	32	.388	.279
Bats Right	R	.276	319	88	13	1	7	35	43	84	.362	.389
Franco,Matt	L	.227	22	5	0	0	0	1	1	3	.261	.227
Bats Left	R	.284	141	40	5	0	5	20	12	20	.340	.426
Franklin,M	L	.111	9	1	0	0	0	0	0	4	.111	.111
Bats Both	R	.400	25	10	0	0	2	2	3	6	.464	.640
Frias,Hanley	L	.286	7	2	0	0	0	1	0	3	.286	.286
Bats Both	R	.158	19	3	1	0	0	0	1	1	.200	.211
Frye,Jeff	L	.322	115	37	14	0	1	17	10	17	.364	.470
Bats Right	R	.308	289	89	22	2	2	34	17	27	.347	.419
Fryman,Travis	L	.298	151	45	9	0	5	21	15	30	.359	.457
Bats Right	R	.266	444	118	18	3	17	81	31	83	.314	.435
Fullmer,Brad	L	.182	11	2	1	0	0	1	1	2	.250	.273
Bats Left	R	.345	29	10	1	0	3	7	1	5	.387	.690
Gaetti,Gary	L	.277	112	31	6	0	5	18	14	17	.359	.464
Bats Right	R	.244	390	95	18	1	12	51	22	71	.289	.387
Gagne,Greg	L	.256	133	34	9	0	3	14	9	32	.303	.391
Bats Right	R	.249	381	95	11	3	6	43	22	88	.297	.341
Galarraga,A	L	.333	126	42	9	0	10	33	18	24	.426	.643
Bats Right	R	.314	474	149	22	3	31	107	36	117	.378	.570
Gallego,Mike	L	.077	13	1	1	0	0	0	0	3	.077	.154
Bats Right	R	.200	30	6	1	0	0	1	1	3	.219	.233
Gant,Ron	L	.197	122	24	4	2	5	15	17	37	.295	.385
Bats Right	R	.239	380	91	17	2	12	47	41	125	.314	.389
Garcia,Carlos	L	.176	102	18	4	1	1	6	6	17	.227	.265
Bats Right	R	.238	248	59	14	1	2	17	9	43	.264	.327
Garcia,Freddy	L	.273	22	6	1	0	3	5	1	7	.304	.727
Bats Right	R	.000	18	0	0	0	0	0	1	10	.053	.000
Garcia,Karim	L	.000	3	0	0	0	0	0	0	2	.000	.000
Bats Left	R	.139	36	5	0	0	1	8	6	12	.256	.222
Garciaparra,N	L	.266	184	49	12	3	9	30	9	30	.303	.511
Bats Right	R	.320	500	160	32	8	21	68	26	62	.356	.542
Gates,Brent	L	.148	27	4	4	0	0	5	2	4	.207	.296
Bats Both	R	.258	124	32	4	0	3	15	12	17	.317	.363
Giambi,Jason	L	.302	126	38	6	0	6	19	17	28	.397	.492
Bats Left	R	.290	393	114	35	2	14	62	38	61	.350	.496
Gil,Benji	L	.243	74	18	5	2	1	5	9	23	.325	.405
Bats Right	R	.218	243	53	8	0	4	26	8	73	.242	.300
Gilbert,Shawn	L	.143	14	2	0	0	0	0	1	6	.200	.143
Bats Right	R	.125	8	1	0	0	1	1	0	2	.125	.500
Giles,B	L	.295	61	18	2	1	6	15	11		.429	.443
Bats Left	R	.263	316	83	13	1	16	55	48	39	.356	.462
Gilkey,B	L	.288	139	40	11	0	9	27	23	22	.386	.561
Bats Right	R	.235	379	89	20	1	9	51	47	89	.320	.364
Giovanola,Ed	L	1.000	1	1	0	0	0	0	0	0	1.000	1.000
Bats Left	R	.143	7	1	0	0	0	0	2	1	.333	.143
Girardi,Joe	L	.252	103	26	5	0	0	11	10	10	.319	.301
Bats Right	R	.268	295	79	18	1	1	39	16	43	.308	.346
Glanville,D	L	.276	156	43	6	0	3	11	9	8	.317	.372
Bats Right	R	.311	318	99	16	5	1	24	15	38	.341	.403

Batters vs. Lefthanded and Righthanded Pitchers

Batter	vs	Avg	AB	H	2B	3B	HR	BI	BB	SO	OBP	SLG	Batter	vs	Avg	AB	H	2B	3B	HR	BI	BB	SO	OBP	SLG
Gomez,Chris	L	.294	109	32	3	1	2	15	17	19	.386	.394	Guillen,Ozzie	L	.278	108	30	4	2	1	9	7	8	.322	.380
Bats Right	R	.242	413	100	16	1	3	39	36	95	.309	.308	Bats Left	R	.236	382	90	17	4	3	43	15	16	.262	.325
Gonzales,Rene	L	.500	2	1	0	0	0	1	0	0	.500	.500	Gulan,Mike	L	.000	2	0	0	0	0	0	1	2	.333	.000
Bats Right	R	.000	0	0	0	0	0	0	0	0	.000	.000	Bats Right	R	.000	7	0	0	0	0	1	0	3	.000	.000
Gonzalez,Alex	L	.260	123	32	7	1	3	7	11	18	.326	.407	Gutierrez,R	L	.256	78	20	4	0	1	9	5	12	.301	.346
Bats Right	R	.231	303	70	16	1	9	28	23	76	.292	.380	Bats Right	R	.262	225	59	10	4	2	25	16	38	.320	.369
Gonzalez,Juan	L	.297	148	44	7	0	15	40	14	34	.355	.649	Gwynn,Tony	L	.356	163	58	17	1	6	48	11	10	.391	.583
Bats Right	R	.296	385	114	17	3	27	91	19	73	.327	.566	Bats Left	R	.378	429	162	32	1	11	71	32	18	.416	.534
Gonzalez,Luis	L	.250	132	33	3	1	3	15	15	21	.338	.356	Hale,Chip	L	.000	0	0	0	0	0	0	0	0	.000	.000
Bats Left	R	.261	418	109	28	1	7	53	56	46	.348	.383	Bats Left	R	.083	12	1	0	0	0	0	2	4	.214	.083
Goodwin,C	L	.250	56	14	2	0	0	3	9	11	.348	.286	Hall,Joe	L	1.000	2	2	1	0	0	3	0	0	1.000	1.500
Bats Left	R	.254	209	53	9	0	1	9	15	42	.307	.311	Bats Right	R	.000	2	0	0	0	0	0	0	0	.000	.000
Goodwin,Tom	L	.275	160	44	7	1	0	9	9	28	.318	.331	Halter,Shane	L	.286	63	18	1	0	2	4	3	21	.328	.397
Bats Left	R	.254	414	105	19	5	2	30	35	60	.313	.338	Bats Right	R	.267	60	16	4	0	0	6	7	7	.353	.367
Grace,Mark	L	.336	143	48	8	1	3	19	19	9	.412	.469	Hamelin,Bob	L	.209	43	9	1	0	2	4	8	11	.346	.372
Bats Left	R	.313	412	129	24	4	10	59	69	36	.408	.464	Bats Left	R	.280	275	77	14	0	16	48	40	61	.369	.505
Graffanino,T	L	.254	59	15	5	0	3	7	11	12	.361	.492	Hamilton,D	L	.250	104	26	3	1	1	12	11	20	.316	.327
Bats Right	R	.260	127	33	4	1	5	13	15	34	.336	.425	Bats Left	R	.275	356	98	20	2	4	31	50	41	.365	.376
Grebeck,Craig	L	.293	75	22	7	0	0	3	10	8	.372	.387	Hammonds,J	L	.277	148	41	5	3	8	18	13	25	.333	.514
Bats Right	R	.235	51	12	2	0	1	3	8	3	.339	.333	Bats Right	R	.257	249	64	14	0	13	37	19	48	.316	.470
Green,S	L	.143	7	1	0	0	0	0	0	1	.143	.143	Hansen,Dave	L	.286	7	2	0	0	0	0	0	2	.375	.286
Bats Right	R	.083	24	2	0	0	0	1	2	4	.154	.083	Bats Left	R	.313	144	45	8	2	3	21	31	30	.432	.458
Green,Shawn	L	.287	101	29	5	0	0	7	8	27	.339	.337	Hansen,Jed	L	.357	42	15	4	0	0	3	4	11	.413	.452
Bats Left	R	.287	328	94	17	4	16	46	28	72	.341	.509	Bats Right	R	.269	52	14	2	1	1	11	9	18	.381	.404
Greene,C	L	.000	1	0	0	0	0	1	0	0	.000	.000	Hardtke,Jason	L	.286	21	6	0	0	1	5	3	4	.375	.429
Bats Both	R	.000	1	0	0	0	0	0	0	1	.000	.000	Bats Both	R	.257	35	9	2	0	1	3	1	2	.289	.400
Greene,Todd	L	.318	44	14	4	0	3	8	4	8	.375	.614	Harris,Lenny	L	.250	24	6	1	0	0	2	0	2	.250	.292
Bats Right	R	.275	80	22	2	0	6	16	3	17	.301	.525	Bats Left	R	.276	214	59	12	1	3	26	18	16	.335	.383
Greene,Willie	L	.172	99	17	3	0	2	9	18	32	.305	.263	Haselman,Bill	L	.265	102	27	9	0	4	10	8	19	.319	.471
Bats Left	R	.273	396	108	19	1	24	82	60	79	.366	.508	Bats Right	R	.209	110	23	6	0	2	16	7	25	.263	.318
Greer,Rusty	L	.309	178	55	15	0	7	19	28	27	.406	.511	Hatteberg,S	L	.225	80	18	8	1	0	12	11	21	.333	.350
Bats Left	R	.326	423	138	27	3	19	68	55	60	.405	.539	Bats Left	R	.293	270	79	15	0	10	32	29	49	.360	.459
Gregg,Tommy	L	.500	2	1	1	0	0	0	0	0	.500	1.000	Hayes,Charlie	L	.311	135	42	7	0	8	29	18	16	.394	.541
Bats Left	R	.235	17	4	1	0	0	0	1	2	.278	.294	Bats Right	R	.225	218	49	9	0	3	24	22	50	.292	.307
Grieve,Ben	L	.316	38	12	2	0	1	11	5	11	.409	.447	Helton,Todd	L	.200	10	2	0	0	0	0	0	0	.200	.200
Bats Left	R	.309	55	17	4	0	2	13	8	14	.397	.491	Bats Left	R	.289	83	24	2	1	5	11	8	11	.352	.518
Griffey Jr,K	L	.270	196	53	8	1	14	39	14	52	.332	.536	Henderson,R	L	.273	77	21	3	0	4	9	28	17	.481	.468
Bats Left	R	.320	412	132	26	2	42	108	62	69	.405	.699	Bats Right	R	.242	326	79	11	0	4	25	69	68	.378	.313
Grissom,M	L	.261	138	36	8	1	5	18	11	23	.315	.442	Hernandez,C	L	.324	37	12	2	0	1	1	2	6	.359	.459
Bats Right	R	.262	420	110	19	5	7	48	32	66	.317	.381	Bats Right	R	.309	97	30	5	1	2	13	1	21	.316	.443
Grudzielanek,M	L	.224	147	33	10	0	1	12	5	16	.252	.313	Hernandez,J	L	.250	84	21	2	3	3	11	9	19	.319	.452
Bats Right	R	.287	502	144	44	3	3	39	18	60	.323	.404	Bats Right	R	.293	99	29	6	2	4	15	5	23	.327	.515
Guerrero,V	L	.301	93	28	5	1	4	12	6	10	.350	.505	Hidalgo,R	L	.455	22	10	2	0	1	2	1	6	.478	.682
Bats Right	R	.302	232	70	17	1	7	28	13	29	.350	.474	Bats Right	R	.225	40	9	3	0	1	4	3	12	.295	.375
Guerrero,W	L	.220	91	20	1	1	3	8	2	12	.234	.352	Higginson,Bob	L	.301	156	47	8	3	7	35	17	27	.375	.526
Bats Both	R	.316	266	84	9	8	1	24	6	40	.330	.421	Bats Left	R	.297	390	116	22	2	20	66	53	58	.380	.518
Guevara,G	L	.000	1	0	0	0	0	0	0	1	.000	.000	Hill,G	L	.270	111	30	8	0	4	17	7	31	.311	.450
Bats Right	R	.000	3	0	0	0	0	0	0	1	.000	.000	Bats Right	R	.258	287	74	20	4	7	47	12	66	.291	.429
Guillen,Jose	L	.263	99	26	4	0	3	13	6	16	.302	.394	Hocking,Denny	L	.310	84	26	7	1	1	9	6	14	.363	.452
Bats Right	R	.268	399	107	16	5	11	57	11	72	.300	.416	Bats Both	R	.231	169	39	3	1	1	16	12	37	.280	.314

Batters vs. Lefthanded and Righthanded Pitchers

Batter	vs	Avg	AB	H	2B	3B	HR	BI	BB	SO	OBP	SLG
Hoiles,Chris	L	.245	94	23	5	0	5	18	20	24	.385	.457
Bats Right	R	.265	226	60	10	0	7	31	31	62	.371	.403
Hollandsworth	L	.348	46	16	2	0	1	7	1	9	.362	.457
Bats Left	R	.228	250	57	18	2	3	24	16	51	.272	.352
Hollins,Dave	L	.326	175	57	11	0	8	29	17	50	.392	.526
Bats Both	R	.272	397	108	18	2	8	56	45	74	.351	.388
Houston,Tyler	L	.154	13	2	1	0	0	2	0	4	.154	.231
Bats Left	R	.268	183	49	9	0	2	26	9	31	.299	.350
Howard,David	L	.235	51	12	2	1	0	3	3	8	.278	.314
Bats Both	R	.243	111	27	6	0	1	10	7	23	.292	.324
Howard,Thom.	L	.333	18	6	0	1	0	1	1	4	.400	.444
Bats Left	R	.241	237	57	16	0	3	21	25	44	.317	.346
Howell,Jack	L	.261	23	6	2	0	0	4	1	2	.292	.348
Bats Left	R	.258	151	39	5	0	14	30	12	34	.307	.570
Hubbard,Mike	L	.250	36	9	0	0	0	1	0	14	.250	.250
Bats Right	R	.143	28	4	0	0	1	1	2	7	.200	.250
Hubbard,Trent	L	.125	8	1	0	0	0	0	1	3	.222	.125
Bats Right	R	.500	4	2	1	0	0	0	0	0	.500	.750
Hudler,Rex	L	.253	91	23	4	0	5	10	4	20	.284	.462
Bats Right	R	.129	31	4	0	0	0	0	2	8	.206	.129
Hundley,Todd	L	.219	96	21	6	0	3	14	27	33	.391	.375
Bats Both	R	.290	321	93	15	2	27	72	56	83	.395	.601
Hunter,B	L	.264	159	42	8	3	1	9	18	23	.337	.371
Bats Right	R	.271	499	135	21	4	3	36	48	98	.333	.347
Hunter,Torii	L	.000	0	0	0	0	0	0	0	0	.000	.000
Bats Right	R	.000	0	0	0	0	0	0	0	0	.000	.000
Hurst,Jimmy	L	.500	6	3	1	0	1	1	2	1	.625	1.167
Bats Right	R	.000	11	0	0	0	0	0	0	5	.000	.000
Huskey,Butch	L	.338	139	47	8	0	7	26	9	18	.373	.547
Bats Right	R	.265	332	88	18	2	17	55	16	66	.296	.485
Huson,Jeff	L	.286	7	2	0	0	0	2	0	0	.375	.286
Bats Left	R	.199	136	27	3	0	0	9	5	15	.231	.221
Ibanez,Raul	L	.250	4	1	0	0	0	0	0	1	.250	.250
Bats Left	R	.136	22	3	0	1	1	4	0	5	.136	.364
Incaviglia,P	L	.306	72	22	3	0	3	9	8	17	.383	.472
Bats Right	R	.195	82	16	1	0	2	3	3	29	.239	.280
Ingram,Garey	L	.500	6	3	0	0	0	1	1	2	.571	.500
Bats Right	R	.333	3	1	0	0	0	0	0	1	.333	.333
Jackson,D	L	.400	5	2	1	0	1	1	1	0	.500	1.200
Bats Right	R	.161	31	5	1	1	0	1	3	8	.257	.258
Jackson,D	L	.268	97	26	6	0	2	16	3	12	.287	.392
Bats Right	R	.254	114	29	3	1	3	20	3	19	.271	.377
Jaha,John	L	.333	42	14	2	0	6	11	4	7	.391	.810
Bats Right	R	.217	120	26	5	0	5	15	21	33	.342	.383
Javier,Stan	L	.252	135	34	6	0	2	10	16	23	.336	.341
Bats Both	R	.302	305	92	10	4	6	40	40	47	.382	.420
Jefferies,G	L	.333	111	37	5	1	5	21	12	6	.398	.532
Bats Both	R	.233	365	85	20	2	6	27	41	21	.314	.348
Jefferson,R	L	.198	106	21	3	0	0	6	5	28	.267	.226
Bats Left	R	.352	383	135	30	1	13	61	19	65	.383	.538
Jennings,R	L	.000	0	0	0	0	0	0	0	0	.000	.000
Bats Left	R	.167	18	3	1	0	0	2	0	2	.158	.222
Jensen,Marcus	L	.129	31	4	0	0	0	1	3	9	.206	.129
Bats Both	R	.167	54	9	2	0	1	3	5	19	.237	.259
Jeter,Derek	L	.290	169	49	7	0	5	21	19	28	.366	.420
Bats Right	R	.291	485	141	24	7	5	49	55	97	.372	.400
Johnson,Brian	L	.226	93	21	3	1	1	10	6	10	.267	.312
Bats Right	R	.276	225	62	10	2	12	35	13	35	.318	.498
Johnson,C	L	.300	90	27	7	0	5	15	10	21	.376	.544
Bats Both	R	.236	326	77	19	1	14	48	50	88	.339	.429
Johnson,Lance	L	.298	131	39	6	2	1	14	11	8	.350	.397
Bats Left	R	.312	279	87	10	6	4	25	31	23	.379	.434
Johnson,Mark	L	.314	35	11	1	0	0	5	5	11	.390	.343
Bats Left	R	.196	184	36	9	0	4	24	38	67	.336	.310
Johnson,Russ	L	.238	21	5	1	0	0	4	2	3	.304	.286
Bats Right	R	.333	39	13	0	0	2	5	4	11	.395	.487
Jones,Andruw	L	.281	139	39	7	1	7	28	23	31	.383	.496
Bats Right	R	.204	260	53	11	0	11	42	33	76	.300	.373
Jones,Chipper	L	.250	196	49	15	0	1	21	22	37	.324	.342
Bats Both	R	.317	401	127	26	3	20	90	54	51	.393	.546
Jones,Chris	L	.228	57	13	2	0	2	9	6	19	.308	.368
Bats Right	R	.253	95	24	7	0	5	16	10	26	.330	.484
Jordan,Brian	L	.286	35	10	3	0	0	3	4	4	.359	.371
Bats Right	R	.218	110	24	0	0	0	7	6	17	.295	.236
Jordan,Kevin	L	.240	75	18	4	0	4	18	3	10	.259	.453
Bats Right	R	.284	102	29	4	0	2	12	0	16	.284	.382
Joyner,Wally	L	.263	80	21	4	0	3	15	6	13	.307	.425
Bats Left	R	.341	375	128	25	2	10	68	45	38	.407	.499
Justice,David	L	.322	146	47	10	0	11	32	15	22	.380	.616
Bats Left	R	.332	349	116	21	1	22	69	65	57	.432	.587
Karkovice,Ron	L	.214	56	12	1	0	2	4	5	11	.270	.339
Bats Right	R	.159	82	13	2	0	4	14	6	21	.234	.329
Karros,Eric	L	.229	153	35	5	0	6	26	18	22	.306	.379
Bats Right	R	.278	475	132	23	0	25	78	43	94	.336	.484
Kelly,Mike	L	.297	64	19	9	1	3	11	5	16	.343	.609
Bats Right	R	.289	76	22	4	1	3	8	5	14	.333	.487
Kelly,Pat	L	.211	38	8	1	0	0	1	2	12	.250	.237
Bats Right	R	.256	82	21	5	1	2	9	12	25	.354	.415
Kelly,Roberto	L	.298	124	37	10	0	5	24	11	24	.355	.500
Bats Right	R	.287	244	70	16	2	7	35	11	43	.322	.455
Kendall,Jason	L	.297	101	30	8	0	3	10	8	9	.374	.465
Bats Right	R	.294	385	113	28	4	5	39	41	44	.395	.426
Kent,Jeff	L	.230	148	34	7	1	6	21	17	24	.307	.412
Bats Right	R	.257	432	111	31	1	23	100	31	109	.320	.493
Kieschnick,B	L	.286	7	2	0	0	0	1	0	2	.286	.286
Bats Left	R	.193	83	16	2	0	4	11	12	19	.295	.361
King,Jeff	L	.268	149	40	11	0	9	28	32	25	.391	.523
Bats Right	R	.226	394	89	19	1	19	84	57	71	.320	.424
Kirby,Wayne	L	.286	7	2	1	0	0	0	0	0	.286	.429
Bats Left	R	.155	58	9	1	0	0	4	10	12	.279	.172

Batters vs. Lefthanded and Righthanded Pitchers

Batter	vs	Avg	AB	H	2B	3B	HR	BI	BB	SO	OBP	SLG	Batter	vs	Avg	AB	H	2B	3B	HR	BI	BB	SO	OBP	SLG
Klesko,Ryan	L	.198	106	21	2	2	3	14	12	36	.283	.340	Livingstone,S	L	.000	4	0	0	0	0	0	0	0	.000	.000
Bats Left	R	.280	361	101	21	4	21	70	36	94	.349	.535	Bats Left	R	.175	63	11	2	0	0	6	3	11	.206	.206
Knoblauch,C	L	.295	132	39	0	2	3	17	22	12	.404	.394	Lockhart,K	L	.667	9	6	0	2	1	5	1	1	.700	1.444
Bats Right	R	.290	479	139	26	8	6	41	62	72	.386	.415	Bats Left	R	.254	138	35	5	1	5	27	13	16	.314	.413
Knorr,Randy	L	1.000	1	1	0	0	0	0	0	0	1.000	1.000	Lofton,Kenny	L	.336	152	51	6	3	2	22	10	24	.382	.454
Bats Right	R	.286	7	2	0	0	1	1	0	2	.286	.714	Bats Left	R	.331	341	113	14	3	3	26	54	59	.421	.416
Konerko,Paul	L	.250	4	1	0	0	0	0	0	1	.250	.250	Long,Ryan	L	.250	4	1	0	0	0	1	0	2	.250	.250
Bats Right	R	.000	3	0	0	0	0	0	1	1	.250	.000	Bats Right	R	.200	5	1	0	0	0	1	0	1	.333	.200
Kotsay,Mark	L	.000	1	0	0	0	0	0	0	0	.000	.000	Lopez,Javy	L	.330	97	32	4	0	4	14	14	14	.414	.495
Bats Left	R	.196	51	10	1	1	0	4	4	7	.255	.255	Bats Right	R	.284	317	90	24	1	19	54	26	68	.344	.546
Kreuter,Chad	L	.247	77	19	2	0	3	10	9	26	.326	.390	Lopez,Luis	L	.235	51	12	3	0	1	4	5	7	.339	.353
Bats Both	R	.225	178	40	7	2	2	11	20	40	.303	.320	Bats Both	R	.283	127	36	9	1	0	15	7	35	.326	.370
Laker,Tim	L	.000	3	0	0	0	0	1	0	3	.000	.000	Loretta,Mark	L	.255	137	35	4	1	1	14	20	22	.348	.321
Bats Right	R	.000	11	0	0	0	0	0	2	6	.154	.000	Bats Right	R	.302	281	85	13	4	4	33	27	38	.358	.420
Lampkin,Tom	L	.250	36	9	1	0	0	4	4	9	.341	.278	Lowery,T	L	.250	12	3	0	0	0	0	3	3	.400	.250
Bats Left	R	.244	193	47	7	1	7	18	24	21	.333	.399	Bats Right	R	.500	2	1	0	0	0	0	0	0	.500	.500
Lankford,Ray	L	.301	136	41	11	1	12	38	15	39	.368	.662	Mabry,John	L	.266	94	25	6	0	0	10	5	23	.307	.330
Bats Left	R	.292	329	96	25	2	19	60	80	86	.426	.553	Bats Left	R	.289	294	85	13	0	5	26	34	54	.366	.384
Lansing,Mike	L	.299	117	35	10	0	4	16	12	18	.364	.487	Macfarlane,M	L	.200	80	16	4	0	2	12	3	16	.229	.325
Bats Right	R	.277	455	126	35	2	16	54	33	74	.331	.468	Bats Right	R	.254	177	45	10	2	6	23	21	31	.351	.435
Larkin,Barry	L	.447	47	21	4	2	2	11	11	2	.559	.745	Machado,R	L	.000	5	0	0	0	0	0	0	3	.000	.000
Bats Right	R	.282	177	50	13	1	2	9	36	22	.407	.401	Bats Right	R	.300	10	3	0	1	0	2	1	3	.364	.500
Latham,Chris	L	.167	12	2	1	0	0	1	0	5	.167	.250	Mack,Shane	L	.305	59	18	3	0	1	5	5	8	.373	.407
Bats Both	R	.200	10	2	0	0	0	0	0	3	.200	.200	Bats Right	R	.324	71	23	4	0	2	12	4	16	.364	.465
Lawton,Matt	L	.274	84	23	4	0	1	12	13	13	.386	.357	Magadan,Dave	L	.220	41	9	0	0	0	7	6	6	.313	.220
Bats Left	R	.242	376	91	25	3	13	48	63	68	.361	.428	Bats Left	R	.317	230	73	10	1	4	23	44	34	.431	.422
Ledesma,Aar.	L	.375	40	15	2	0	1	5	4	3	.422	.500	Magee,Wendell	L	.100	20	2	1	0	0	3	0	4	.091	.150
Bats Right	R	.333	48	16	3	1	1	6	9	6	.448	.500	Bats Right	R	.221	95	21	3	0	1	6	9	16	.288	.284
Lee,Derrek	L	.250	16	4	2	0	0	0	4	7	.400	.375	Malave,Jose	L	.000	1	0	0	0	0	0	0	1	.000	.000
Bats Right	R	.263	38	10	1	0	1	4	5	17	.349	.368	Bats Right	R	.000	3	0	0	0	0	0	0	1	.000	.000
Lemke,Mark	L	.261	69	18	4	0	1	6	8	10	.329	.362	Manto,Jeff	L	.267	15	4	1	0	1	3	1	5	.313	.533
Bats Both	R	.241	282	68	13	1	1	20	25	41	.300	.305	Bats Right	R	.267	15	4	2	0	1	4	0	5	.267	.600
Lennon,P	L	.337	83	28	6	1	0	13	15	25	.439	.434	Manwaring,K	L	.231	117	27	1	1	0	7	7	25	.270	.256
Bats Right	R	.182	33	6	0	0	1	1	0	10	.182	.273	Bats Right	R	.223	220	49	5	3	1	20	23	53	.302	.286
Lesher,Brian	L	.345	58	20	2	1	3	10	5	6	.391	.569	Marrero,Eli	L	.100	10	1	1	0	0	0	0	4	.100	.200
Bats Right	R	.137	73	10	2	0	1	6	4	24	.179	.205	Bats Right	R	.286	35	10	1	0	2	7	2	9	.316	.486
Levis,Jesse	L	.222	18	4	1	0	0	1	3	3	.333	.278	Martin,Al	L	.326	92	30	4	2	1	16	14	17	.417	.446
Bats Left	R	.291	182	53	6	0	1	18	21	14	.364	.341	Bats Left	R	.281	331	93	20	5	12	43	31	66	.342	.480
Lewis,Darren	L	.266	64	17	1	1	0	4	5	9	.319	.313	Martin,N	L	.346	81	28	1	0	1	13	3	6	.369	.395
Bats Right	R	.267	90	24	3	0	1	11	12	22	.353	.333	Bats Right	R	.273	132	36	6	1	1	14	3	25	.289	.356
Lewis,Mark	L	.290	124	36	7	4	1	15	9	22	.343	.435	Martinez,Dave	L	.259	85	22	1	1	3	8	9	17	.333	.400
Bats Right	R	.253	217	55	7	2	9	27	14	40	.304	.429	Bats Left	R	.291	419	122	15	5	9	47	46	52	.360	.415
Leyritz,Jim	L	.297	118	35	1	0	5	23	23	21	.411	.432	Martinez,E	L	.282	131	37	6	0	4	15	28	21	.413	.420
Bats Right	R	.268	261	70	10	0	6	41	37	57	.364	.375	Bats Right	R	.345	411	142	29	1	24	93	91	65	.469	.596
Lieberthal,M	L	.245	106	26	8	0	5	25	12	13	.319	.462	Martinez,F	L	.091	11	1	0	0	0	0	2	2	.231	.091
Bats Right	R	.246	349	86	19	1	15	52	32	63	.312	.436	Bats Both	R	.300	20	6	1	1	0	3	4	6	.417	.450
Liriano,N	L	.167	12	2	1	0	0	0	1	4	.231	.250	Martinez,S	L	.000	0	0	0	0	0	0	0	0	.000	.000
Bats Both	R	.237	76	18	5	0	1	11	5	8	.280	.342	Bats Left	R	.000	2	0	0	0	0	0	1	1	.333	.000
Listach,Pat	L	.146	41	6	1	0	0	0	1	8	.167	.171	Martinez,Tino	L	.268	231	62	10	2	12	55	22	27	.330	.485
Bats Both	R	.198	91	18	1	2	0	6	10	16	.279	.253	Bats Left	R	.314	363	114	21	0	32	86	53	48	.396	.636

288

Batters vs. Lefthanded and Righthanded Pitchers

Batter	vs	Avg	AB	H	2B	3B	HR	BI	BB	SO	OBP	SLG
Marzano,John	L	.391	23	9	2	0	0	4	3	3	.462	.478
Bats Right	R	.250	64	16	1	0	1	6	4	12	.294	.313
Mashore,Da.	L	.297	74	22	4	1	2	7	14	22	.416	.459
Bats Right	R	.229	205	47	6	1	1	11	36	60	.354	.283
Matheny,Mike	L	.264	110	29	7	1	1	8	5	19	.308	.373
Bats Right	R	.233	210	49	9	0	3	24	12	49	.287	.319
May,Derrick	L	.200	5	1	0	0	0	2	1	0	.333	.200
Bats Left	R	.229	144	33	5	1	1	11	7	26	.263	.299
Mayne,Brent	L	.279	43	12	2	0	0	2	3	9	.326	.326
Bats Left	R	.291	213	62	10	0	6	20	15	24	.346	.423
McCracken,Q	L	.233	86	20	0	0	1	6	9	14	.305	.267
Bats Both	R	.314	239	75	11	1	2	30	33	48	.398	.393
McDonald,J	L	.250	52	13	2	0	0	3	12	15	.391	.288
Bats Both	R	.266	184	49	9	4	4	11	24	34	.352	.424
McGee,Willie	L	.274	95	26	6	1	1	12	7	21	.324	.389
Bats Both	R	.312	205	64	13	3	2	26	15	38	.357	.434
McGriff,Fred	L	.268	183	49	5	1	6	28	25	42	.362	.404
Bats Left	R	.281	381	107	20	0	16	69	43	70	.353	.459
McGuire,Ryan	L	.200	65	13	2	1	1	2	5	11	.257	.308
Bats Left	R	.284	134	38	13	1	2	15	14	23	.349	.440
McGwire,Mark	L	.282	117	33	8	0	12	27	32	40	.436	.658
Bats Right	R	.272	423	115	19	0	46	96	69	119	.380	.643
McKeel,Walt	L	.000	2	0	0	0	0	0	0	1	.000	.000
Bats Right	R	.000	1	0	0	0	0	0	0	0	.000	.000
McLemore,Ma.	L	.267	90	24	6	0	0	3	9	15	.330	.333
Bats Both	R	.259	259	67	11	2	1	22	31	39	.341	.328
McMillon,B	L	.333	15	5	1	0	1	2	3	2	.421	.600
Bats Left	R	.240	75	18	4	1	1	12	3	22	.263	.360
McRae,Brian	L	.278	144	40	8	2	4	9	10	20	.333	.444
Bats Both	R	.230	418	96	24	5	7	34	55	64	.324	.361
Meares,Pat	L	.182	99	18	5	0	1	12	2	19	.243	.263
Bats Right	R	.303	340	103	18	3	9	48	16	67	.347	.453
Mejia,Roberto	L	.167	6	1	1	0	0	1	0	2	.167	.333
Bats Right	R	.000	8	0	0	0	0	1	0	3	.000	.000
Mendoza,C	L	.250	4	1	0	0	0	1	0	1	.500	.250
Bats Left	R	.250	8	2	0	0	0	0	4	1	.500	.250
Merced,O	L	.223	121	27	5	0	4	18	14	26	.312	.364
Bats Left	R	.287	247	71	18	2	5	22	33	36	.372	.437
Mercedes,H	L	.400	15	6	1	0	0	2	2	5	.471	.467
Bats Right	R	.125	32	4	3	0	0	2	4	20	.222	.219
Meulens,H	L	.353	17	6	1	0	2	6	3	5	.429	.765
Bats Right	R	.143	7	1	0	0	0	0	1	5	.250	.143
Mieske,Matt	L	.255	106	27	9	2	3	11	8	14	.304	.462
Bats Right	R	.245	147	36	6	1	2	10	11	36	.297	.340
Miller,Damian	L	.182	22	4	0	0	0	1	0	4	.182	.182
Bats Right	R	.318	44	14	1	0	2	12	2	8	.327	.477
Miller,O	L	.250	32	8	2	1	1	4	2	9	.314	.469
Bats Right	R	.228	79	18	5	0	1	6	3	15	.279	.329
Milliard,R	L	.125	8	1	0	0	0	1	1	0	.222	.125
Bats Right	R	.227	22	5	0	0	0	1	2	3	.346	.227
Mirabelli,D	L	.000	2	0	0	0	0	0	0	1	.000	.000
Bats Right	R	.200	5	1	0	0	0	0	1	2	.333	.200
Mitchell,K	L	.111	18	2	0	0	1	2	2	2	.200	.278
Bats Right	R	.171	41	7	1	0	3	9	7	9	.306	.415
Molina,Izzy	L	.185	54	10	1	1	1	2	1	6	.200	.296
Bats Right	R	.211	57	12	2	0	2	5	2	11	.237	.351
Molitor,Paul	L	.336	113	38	8	0	0	16	13	9	.395	.407
Bats Right	R	.296	425	126	24	4	10	73	32	64	.339	.442
Mondesi,Raul	L	.284	148	42	9	1	7	23	17	19	.355	.500
Bats Right	R	.318	468	149	33	4	23	64	27	86	.362	.553
Montgomery,R	L	.111	27	3	1	0	0	2	1	5	.133	.148
Bats Right	R	.317	41	13	3	1	0	2	4	13	.370	.439
Morandini,M	L	.304	125	38	8	0	0	17	22	14	.417	.368
Bats Right	R	.292	428	125	32	2	1	22	40	77	.356	.383
Mordecai,Mike	L	.176	34	6	1	0	0	1	2	8	.216	.206
Bats Right	R	.170	47	8	1	1	0	2	4	8	.235	.234
Morgan,Kevin	L	.000	1	0	0	0	0	0	0	0	.000	.000
Bats Right	R	.000	0	0	0	0	0	0	0	0	.000	.000
Morman,Russ	L	1.000	1	1	0	0	1	2	0	0	1.000	4.000
Bats Right	R	.167	6	1	1	0	0	0	0	2	.167	.333
Morris,Hal	L	.250	72	18	3	0	0	12	3	13	.286	.292
Bats Left	R	.284	261	74	17	1	1	21	20	30	.339	.368
Mosquera,J	L	.000	0	0	0	0	0	0	0	0	.000	.000
Bats Right	R	.250	8	2	1	0	0	0	0	2	.250	.375
Mouton,James	L	.263	99	26	6	1	3	15	11	16	.336	.434
Bats Right	R	.148	81	12	3	0	0	8	7	14	.225	.185
Mouton,Lyle	L	.280	100	28	4	0	2	11	3	22	.298	.380
Bats Right	R	.261	142	37	5	0	3	12	11	44	.314	.359
Mueller,Bill	L	.282	85	24	7	0	2	10	11	14	.365	.435
Bats Both	R	.295	305	90	19	3	5	34	37	57	.370	.426
Murray,Eddie	L	.281	64	18	2	0	0	7	3	8	.309	.313
Bats Both	R	.184	103	19	5	0	3	11	12	18	.265	.320
Myers,Greg	L	.533	15	8	3	0	1	4	2	1	.556	.933
Bats Left	R	.233	159	37	8	1	4	25	15	31	.297	.371
Myers,Rod	L	.211	19	4	1	0	0	3	3	5	.318	.263
Bats Left	R	.268	82	22	6	0	2	6	14	17	.381	.415
Naehring,Tim	L	.292	72	21	5	1	2	5	16	12	.416	.472
Bats Right	R	.283	187	53	13	0	7	35	22	28	.358	.465
Natal,Bob	L	1.000	2	2	1	0	1	2	0	0	1.000	3.000
Bats Right	R	.000	2	0	0	0	0	1	2	0	.400	.000
Nevin,Phil	L	.307	114	35	10	1	6	21	11	27	.368	.570
Bats Right	R	.175	137	24	6	0	3	14	14	41	.255	.285
Newfield,Marc	L	.241	54	13	2	0	0	7	3	6	.288	.278
Bats Right	R	.223	103	23	6	0	1	11	11	21	.299	.311
Newson,Wa.	L	.077	13	1	0	0	0	0	1	8	.143	.077
Bats Left	R	.224	156	35	10	1	10	23	30	45	.348	.494
Nieves,Melvin	L	.241	112	27	9	0	4	25	15	48	.331	.429
Bats Both	R	.223	247	55	9	1	16	39	24	109	.302	.462
Nilsson,Dave	L	.236	199	47	5	0	4	21	12	47	.282	.322
Bats Left	R	.301	355	107	28	0	16	60	53	41	.388	.515

Batters vs. Lefthanded and Righthanded Pitchers

Batter	vs	Avg	AB	H	2B	3B	HR	BI	BB	SO	OBP	SLG	Batter	vs	Avg	AB	H	2B	3B	HR	BI	BB	SO	OBP	SLG
Nixon,Otis	L	.214	168	36	6	2	1	12	14	18	.273	.292	Paquette,C	L	.228	101	23	5	0	5	21	2	22	.238	.426
Bats Both	R	.287	408	117	12	1	1	32	51	60	.362	.328	Bats Right	R	.232	151	35	10	1	3	12	8	35	.280	.371
Norton,Greg	L	.000	1	0	0	0	0	0	0	0	.000	.000	Parent,Mark	L	.120	25	3	0	0	0	2	3	10	.214	.120
Bats Both	R	.273	33	9	2	2	0	1	2	8	.314	.455	Bats Right	R	.159	88	14	3	0	0	6	4	29	.194	.193
Nunez,Abra.	L	.375	8	3	0	2	0	3	1	3	.444	.875	Pemberton,R	L	.218	55	12	2	0	2	9	3	12	.283	.364
Bats Both	R	.188	32	6	2	0	0	3	2	7	.250	.250	Bats Right	R	.375	8	3	0	0	0	1	1	1	.500	.375
Nunnally,Jon	L	.258	31	8	3	0	1	8	3	9	.343	.452	Pena,Tony	L	.268	41	11	3	0	0	6	5	3	.348	.341
Bats Left	R	.317	199	63	9	4	13	31	28	49	.402	.598	Bats Right	R	.089	45	4	1	0	0	4	5	13	.173	.111
O'Brien,C	L	.267	75	20	10	1	2	10	7	9	.341	.507	Pendleton,T	L	.316	38	12	4	0	0	6	6	3	.409	.421
Bats Right	R	.193	150	29	5	0	2	17	15	36	.296	.267	Bats Both	R	.213	75	16	5	0	1	11	6	11	.272	.320
O'Leary,Troy	L	.277	101	28	9	0	2	18	8	23	.327	.426	Perez,Eddie	L	.170	53	9	2	0	2	6	1	8	.185	.321
Bats Left	R	.317	398	126	23	4	13	62	31	47	.366	.492	Bats Right	R	.232	138	32	3	0	4	12	9	27	.285	.341
O'Neill,Paul	L	.280	189	53	15	0	4	33	20	41	.343	.423	Perez,Eduardo	L	.275	102	28	6	0	8	24	13	19	.362	.569
Bats Left	R	.346	364	126	27	0	17	84	55	51	.427	.560	Bats Right	R	.241	195	47	12	0	8	28	16	57	.299	.426
Obando,S	L	.133	30	4	1	0	1	7	5	8	.278	.267	Perez,Neifi	L	.312	77	24	4	3	2	10	3	9	.333	.519
Bats Right	R	.118	17	2	0	0	1	2	1	6	.167	.294	Bats Both	R	.284	236	67	9	7	3	21	18	34	.333	.419
Ochoa,Alex	L	.224	107	24	4	0	1	10	3	14	.250	.290	Perez,Robert	L	.188	64	12	4	1	0	4	0	13	.188	.281
Bats Right	R	.260	131	34	10	1	2	12	15	18	.338	.397	Bats Right	R	.214	14	3	0	0	2	2	0	3	.214	.643
Offerman,Jose	L	.380	129	49	12	3	0	11	12	22	.433	.519	Perez,Tomas	L	.111	27	3	0	0	0	1	1	5	.143	.111
Bats Both	R	.261	295	77	11	3	2	28	29	42	.327	.339	Bats Both	R	.219	96	21	3	2	0	8	10	23	.299	.292
Olerud,John	L	.276	145	40	9	1	6	38	28	18	.414	.476	Petagine,R	L	.000	2	0	0	0	0	0	0	1	.000	.000
Bats Left	R	.301	379	114	25	0	16	64	57	49	.394	.493	Bats Left	R	.077	13	1	0	0	0	2	3	5	.250	.077
Oliver,Joe	L	.279	86	24	3	0	2	8	9	15	.354	.384	Phillips,J.R.	L	.000	2	0	0	0	0	0	0	2	.000	.000
Bats Right	R	.251	263	66	10	0	12	35	16	43	.299	.426	Bats Left	R	.154	13	2	0	0	1	4	0	5	.143	.385
Ordaz,Luis	L	.000	2	0	0	0	0	0	0	0	.000	.000	Phillips,Tony	L	.245	139	34	8	1	1	12	34	26	.397	.338
Bats Right	R	.300	20	6	1	0	0	1	1	2	.333	.350	Bats Both	R	.286	395	113	26	1	7	45	68	92	.390	.410
Ordonez,M	L	.294	17	5	2	0	1	1	0	0	.294	.588	Piazza,Mike	L	.363	124	45	9	1	7	27	20	20	.450	.621
Bats Right	R	.327	52	17	4	0	3	10	2	8	.352	.577	Bats Right	R	.361	432	156	23	0	33	97	49	57	.426	.644
Ordonez,Rey	L	.270	100	27	3	0	0	11	5	7	.308	.300	Plantier,Phil	L	.154	13	2	0	0	1	1	1	3	.267	.385
Bats Right	R	.195	256	50	2	3	1	22	13	29	.233	.238	Bats Left	R	.259	108	28	8	0	4	17	12	27	.339	.444
Orie,Kevin	L	.207	87	18	4	0	2	10	8	10	.281	.322	Polcovich,K	L	.286	56	16	3	0	2	7	7	9	.379	.446
Bats Right	R	.296	277	82	19	5	6	34	31	47	.370	.466	Bats Right	R	.270	189	51	13	1	2	14	14	36	.341	.381
Orsulak,Joe	L	.000	14	0	0	0	0	1	1	2	.067	.000	Posada,Jorge	L	.310	42	13	4	0	1	5	0	5	.310	.476
Bats Left	R	.250	136	34	12	1	1	6	17	15	.333	.375	Bats Both	R	.233	146	34	8	0	5	20	30	28	.370	.390
Ortiz,David	L	.222	9	2	1	0	0	1	0	3	.222	.333	Pose,Scott	L	.333	15	5	0	0	0	1	0	0	.333	.333
Bats Left	R	.350	40	14	2	0	1	5	2	16	.381	.475	Bats Left	R	.194	72	14	2	1	0	4	9	11	.284	.250
Osik,Keith	L	.375	16	6	1	0	0	0	3	2	.474	.438	Powell,Dante	L	.381	21	8	1	0	1	1	1	6	.409	.571
Bats Right	R	.236	89	21	8	1	0	7	6	19	.292	.348	Bats Right	R	.222	18	4	0	0	0	2	3	5	.333	.222
Otero,Ricky	L	.313	32	10	2	0	0	2	4	3	.405	.375	Pozo,A	L	.000	0	0	0	0	0	0	0	0	.000	.000
Bats Both	R	.235	119	28	4	2	0	1	15	12	.321	.303	Bats Right	R	.267	15	4	1	0	0	3	0	5	.250	.333
Owens,Eric	L	.217	23	5	0	0	0	0	2	3	.280	.217	Pratt,Todd	L	.447	38	17	5	0	2	12	7	8	.553	.737
Bats Right	R	.294	34	10	0	0	0	3	2	8	.333	.294	Bats Right	R	.191	68	13	1	0	0	7	6	24	.257	.206
Pagnozzi,Tom	L	.357	14	5	2	0	0	2	0	1	.357	.500	Pride,Curtis	L	.462	13	6	0	0	0	6	0	3	.500	.462
Bats Right	R	.167	36	6	1	0	1	6	1	6	.189	.278	Bats Left	R	.192	151	29	4	4	3	14	24	43	.301	.331
Palmeiro,O	L	.351	37	13	1	0	0	2	2	1	.385	.378	Prince,Tom	L	.152	33	5	3	0	1	5	3	3	.237	.333
Bats Left	R	.165	97	16	1	2	0	6	15	10	.281	.216	Bats Right	R	.254	67	17	2	0	2	9	2	12	.296	.373
Palmeiro,R	L	.213	225	48	6	0	15	39	17	45	.275	.440	Pulliam,H	L	.306	36	11	2	0	3	5	2	9	.342	.611
Bats Left	R	.278	389	108	18	2	23	71	50	64	.360	.512	Bats Right	R	.258	31	8	1	0	0	4	3	6	.324	.290
Palmer,Dean	L	.240	146	35	5	0	8	17	9	32	.285	.438	Raabe,Brian	L	1.000	1	1	0	0	0	0	0	0	1.000	1.000
Bats Right	R	.263	396	104	26	1	15	69	32	102	.319	.447	Bats Right	R	.000	5	0	0	0	0	0	1	3	.167	.000

Batters vs. Lefthanded and Righthanded Pitchers

Batter	vs	Avg	AB	H	2B	3B	HR	BI	BB	SO	OBP	SLG
Raines,Tim	L	.339	59	20	3	0	1	4	8	5	.412	.441
Bats Both	R	.316	212	67	17	2	3	34	33	29	.400	.458
Ramirez,Manny	L	.350	137	48	13	0	6	26	19	24	.433	.577
Bats Right	R	.321	424	136	27	0	20	62	60	91	.409	.526
Ramos,Ken	L	.000	2	0	0	0	0	0	1	0	.333	.000
Bats Left	R	.000	10	0	0	0	0	1	1	0	.083	.000
Randa,Joe	L	.232	99	23	6	0	2	10	10	11	.303	.354
Bats Right	R	.323	344	111	21	9	5	50	31	53	.383	.480
Reboulet,Jeff	L	.198	101	20	4	0	3	10	9	15	.270	.327
Bats Right	R	.268	127	34	5	0	1	17	14	29	.336	.331
Reed,Jeff	L	.172	29	5	1	0	0	0	0	11	.172	.207
Bats Left	R	.313	227	71	9	0	17	47	35	44	.409	.577
Reed,Jody	L	.233	30	7	0	0	0	2	4	1	.333	.233
Bats Right	R	.183	82	15	2	0	0	6	6	14	.256	.207
Reese,Pokey	L	.172	87	15	3	0	1	6	10	25	.273	.241
Bats Right	R	.232	310	72	12	0	3	20	21	57	.287	.300
Relaford,Desi	L	.267	15	4	0	1	0	3	0	3	.267	.400
Bats Both	R	.130	23	3	1	1	0	3	5	3	.286	.261
Renteria,E	L	.259	108	28	4	0	0	3	13	18	.336	.296
Bats Right	R	.281	509	143	17	3	4	49	32	90	.325	.350
Riggs,Adam	L	.273	11	3	0	0	0	1	3	2	.429	.273
Bats Right	R	.111	9	1	1	0	0	0	1	1	.200	.222
Ripken,Billy	L	.299	87	26	6	1	0	9	1	12	.303	.391
Bats Right	R	.259	116	30	3	0	3	15	8	20	.297	.362
Ripken,Cal	L	.260	181	47	9	0	5	22	19	19	.335	.392
Bats Right	R	.274	434	119	21	0	12	62	37	54	.329	.406
Rivera,Luis	L	.333	6	2	0	0	0	0	0	3	.333	.333
Bats Right	R	.143	7	1	0	1	0	3	1	3	.250	.429
Rivera,Ruben	L	.250	12	3	1	0	0	1	0	6	.250	.333
Bats Right	R	.250	8	2	0	0	0	0	2	3	.400	.250
Roberts,Bip	L	.324	145	47	5	0	2	15	4	18	.340	.400
Bats Both	R	.290	286	83	15	2	2	29	24	49	.347	.378
Robertson,M	L	.000	2	0	0	0	0	0	0	1	.333	.000
Bats Left	R	.222	36	8	2	1	0	4	0	5	.263	.333
Rodriguez,A	L	.299	157	47	11	2	8	25	9	32	.337	.548
Bats Right	R	.300	430	129	29	1	15	59	32	67	.355	.477
Rodriguez,H	L	.218	133	29	6	0	5	14	15	42	.305	.376
Bats Left	R	.254	343	87	22	3	21	69	27	107	.306	.519
Rodriguez,I	L	.321	162	52	10	1	5	25	9	25	.360	.488
Bats Right	R	.310	435	135	24	3	15	52	29	64	.360	.483
Rohrmeier,Dan	L	.500	4	2	0	0	0	1	2	2	.667	.500
Bats Right	R	.200	5	1	0	0	0	1	0	2	.200	.200
Rolen,Scott	L	.282	131	37	11	0	3	24	21	33	.378	.435
Bats Right	R	.284	430	122	24	3	18	68	55	105	.377	.479
Romero,Mandy	L	.200	5	1	0	0	0	0	1	2	.333	.200
Bats Both	R	.209	43	9	0	0	2	4	1	16	.227	.349
Rosario,Mel	L	.000	0	0	0	0	0	0	0	0	.000	.000
Bats Both	R	.000	3	0	0	0	0	0	0	1	.000	.000
Rose Jr,Pete	L	.000	4	0	0	0	0	0	0	3	.000	.000
Bats Left	R	.200	10	2	0	0	0	0	2	6	.333	.200

Batter	vs	Avg	AB	H	2B	3B	HR	BI	BB	SO	OBP	SLG
Sagmoen,Marc	L	.000	3	0	0	0	0	0	0	2	.000	.000
Bats Left	R	.150	40	6	2	0	1	4	2	11	.186	.275
Salmon,Tim	L	.288	139	40	6	0	9	25	32	34	.423	.525
Bats Right	R	.298	443	132	22	1	24	104	63	108	.385	.515
Samuel,Juan	L	.284	67	19	3	2	1	9	6	18	.342	.433
Bats Right	R	.286	28	8	2	2	2	6	4	10	.412	.714
Sanchez,Rey	L	.308	65	20	5	0	1	10	3	9	.333	.431
Bats Right	R	.266	278	74	16	0	1	17	13	38	.301	.335
Sandberg,Ryne	L	.293	116	34	8	0	5	24	12	23	.354	.491
Bats Right	R	.254	331	84	18	0	7	40	16	71	.291	.372
Sanders,Deion	L	.302	126	38	2	1	1	8	6	22	.348	.357
Bats Left	R	.263	339	89	11	6	4	15	28	45	.323	.366
Sanders,R	L	.309	68	21	7	0	4	10	12	15	.420	.588
Bats Right	R	.238	244	58	12	2	15	46	30	78	.326	.488
Santangelo,F	L	.250	80	20	2	0	2	6	8	19	.365	.350
Bats Both	R	.248	270	67	17	5	3	25	42	54	.383	.381
Santiago,B	L	.301	93	28	0	0	6	16	5	21	.333	.495
Bats Right	R	.222	248	55	10	0	7	26	12	59	.259	.347
Scarsone,S	L	.000	2	0	0	0	0	0	0	2	.000	.000
Bats Right	R	.125	8	1	0	0	0	0	2	3	.300	.125
Sefcik,Kevin	L	.245	49	12	1	0	2	5	2	5	.275	.388
Bats Right	R	.286	70	20	2	0	0	1	2	4	.315	.314
Segui,David	L	.295	122	36	6	0	5	9	21	18	.396	.467
Bats Both	R	.312	337	105	16	3	16	59	36	48	.375	.519
Seitzer,Kevin	L	.268	97	26	6	0	2	10	12	10	.345	.392
Bats Right	R	.267	101	27	8	0	0	14	6	15	.306	.347
Servais,Scott	L	.283	92	26	6	0	3	16	6	10	.327	.446
Bats Right	R	.253	293	74	15	0	3	29	18	46	.306	.334
Sexson,Richie	L	.300	10	3	0	0	0	0	0	2	.300	.300
Bats Right	R	.000	1	0	0	0	0	0	0	0	.000	.000
Sheaffer,D	L	.222	63	14	3	0	0	4	4	9	.279	.270
Bats Right	R	.275	69	19	2	0	0	7	4	8	.311	.304
Sheets,Andy	L	.313	16	5	0	0	0	3	4	6	.429	.313
Bats Right	R	.233	73	17	3	0	4	6	3	28	.263	.438
Sheffield,G	L	.343	67	23	4	0	5	13	27	10	.536	.627
Bats Right	R	.233	377	88	18	1	16	58	94	69	.402	.414
Sheldon,Scott	L	.333	6	2	0	0	0	0	0	1	.333	.333
Bats Right	R	.222	18	4	0	0	1	2	1	5	.300	.389
Shipley,Craig	L	.255	47	12	1	0	3	6	2	7	.286	.468
Bats Right	R	.283	92	26	8	0	2	13	5	13	.316	.435
Shumpert,T	L	.600	5	3	1	0	1	3	1	1	.667	1.400
Bats Right	R	.214	28	6	2	0	0	3	0	3	.214	.286
Sierra,Ruben	L	.184	38	7	0	0	1	3	1	11	.205	.263
Bats Both	R	.250	100	25	5	3	2	9	8	23	.303	.420
Silvestri,D	L	.000	1	0	0	0	0	0	0	0	.000	.000
Bats Right	R	.000	3	0	0	0	0	0	0	1	.000	.000
Simms,Mike	L	.235	81	19	5	0	3	13	6	21	.284	.407
Bats Right	R	.300	30	9	3	0	2	9	2	6	.333	.600
Simon,Randall	L	.000	1	0	0	0	0	0	0	0	.000	.000
Bats Left	R	.462	13	6	1	0	0	1	1	2	.500	.538

Batters vs. Lefthanded and Righthanded Pitchers

Batter	vs	Avg	AB	H	2B	3B	HR	BI	BB	SO	OBP	SLG	Batter	vs	Avg	AB	H	2B	3B	HR	BI	BB	SO	OBP	SLG
Slaught,Don	L	.000	5	0	0	0	0	0	2	1	.286	.000	Sutton,Larry	L	.000	4	0	0	0	0	0	1	1	.200	.000
Bats Right	R	.000	15	0	0	0	0	0	3	3	.167	.000	Bats Left	R	.308	65	20	2	0	2	8	4	11	.348	.431
Smith,Mark	L	.212	66	14	1	1	5	10	9	9	.307	.485	Sveum,Dale	L	.196	51	10	1	0	2	9	7	15	.288	.333
Bats Right	R	.323	127	41	12	0	4	25	19	27	.408	.512	Bats Both	R	.275	255	70	19	1	10	38	20	66	.326	.475
Snopek,Chris	L	.217	115	25	7	0	2	17	2	17	.237	.330	Sweeney,Mark	L	.286	7	2	0	0	0	1	0	1	.286	.286
Bats Right	R	.219	183	40	8	0	3	24	16	34	.279	.311	Bats Left	R	.280	157	44	7	0	2	22	20	31	.361	.363
Snow,J.T.	L	.188	133	25	6	0	1	16	23	39	.304	.256	Sweeney,Mike	L	.189	74	14	2	0	1	8	4	12	.228	.257
Bats Both	R	.312	398	124	30	1	27	88	73	85	.415	.595	Bats Right	R	.265	166	44	6	0	6	23	13	21	.339	.410
Sojo,Luis	L	.227	66	15	1	0	1	5	6	4	.288	.288	Tarasco,Tony	L	.160	25	4	0	0	1	1	1	8	.192	.280
Bats Right	R	.342	149	51	5	1	1	20	10	10	.385	.409	Bats Left	R	.213	141	30	8	1	6	25	24	25	.331	.411
Sorrento,Paul	L	.205	39	8	0	0	4	6	4	14	.279	.513	Tartabull,D	L	.000	3	0	0	0	0	0	1	2	.250	.000
Bats Left	R	.275	418	115	19	0	27	74	47	98	.351	.514	Bats Right	R	.000	4	0	0	0	0	0	3	2	.429	.000
Sosa,Sammy	L	.270	141	38	7	0	12	34	15	33	.340	.574	Tatis,F	L	.230	61	14	1	0	1	5	4	11	.277	.295
Bats Right	R	.246	501	123	24	4	24	85	30	141	.288	.453	Bats Right	R	.265	162	43	8	0	7	24	10	31	.305	.444
Spehr,Tim	L	.188	16	3	1	0	1	1	1	5	.235	.438	Taubensee,E	L	.161	31	5	1	0	1	2	0	12	.188	.290
Bats Right	R	.182	33	6	0	0	1	5	1	11	.229	.273	Bats Left	R	.283	223	63	17	0	9	32	22	54	.340	.480
Spiers,Bill	L	.317	41	13	4	1	0	7	9	7	.451	.463	Tavarez,Jesus	L	.211	38	8	2	0	0	3	2	4	.244	.263
Bats Left	R	.320	250	80	23	3	4	41	52	35	.436	.484	Bats Both	R	.129	31	4	1	1	0	6	2	5	.182	.226
Spiezio,Scott	L	.235	149	35	5	1	7	24	17	21	.311	.423	Tejada,Miguel	L	.250	28	7	1	0	1	2	0	2	.276	.393
Bats Both	R	.247	389	96	23	3	7	41	27	54	.295	.375	Bats Right	R	.183	71	13	2	2	1	8	2	20	.227	.310
Sprague,Ed	L	.250	148	37	10	2	7	19	16	31	.327	.486	Tettleton,M	L	.067	15	1	0	0	1	1	0	4	.067	.267
Bats Right	R	.219	356	78	19	2	7	29	35	71	.297	.343	Bats Both	R	.103	29	3	1	0	2	3	3	8	.212	.345
Stahoviak,S	L	.286	14	4	1	0	0	2	2	3	.375	.357	Thomas,Frank	L	.358	106	38	10	0	12	31	16	11	.435	.792
Bats Left	R	.226	261	59	16	0	10	31	22	70	.297	.402	Bats Right	R	.344	424	146	25	0	23	94	93	58	.461	.566
Stairs,Matt	L	.259	85	22	2	0	8	20	12	20	.347	.565	Thome,Jim	L	.275	131	36	6	0	4	22	18	40	.355	.412
Bats Left	R	.311	267	83	17	0	19	53	38	40	.399	.588	Bats Left	R	.290	365	106	19	0	36	80	102	106	.445	.638
Stankiewicz,A	L	.171	35	6	2	0	1	3	2	6	.216	.314	Thurman,Gary	L	.000	3	0	0	0	0	0	0	0	.000	.000
Bats Right	R	.250	72	18	7	0	0	2	2	16	.267	.347	Bats Right	R	.333	3	1	0	0	0	0	0	0	.333	.333
Stanley,Mike	L	.306	144	44	13	0	6	26	28	34	.424	.521	Timmons,Ozzie	L	.500	2	1	0	0	0	0	0	1	.500	.500
Bats Right	R	.291	203	59	12	0	10	39	26	38	.370	.498	Bats Right	R	.286	7	2	1	0	0	0	0	0	.286	.429
Steinbach,T	L	.308	117	36	7	0	4	18	13	25	.374	.470	Tinsley,Lee	L	.308	13	4	2	0	0	1	1	5	.357	.462
Bats Right	R	.227	330	75	20	1	8	36	22	81	.275	.367	Bats Both	R	.183	109	20	4	2	0	5	10	29	.252	.257
Stevens,Lee	L	.284	67	19	4	0	4	12	4	19	.333	.522	Tomberlin,A	L	.000	0	0	0	0	0	0	0	0	.000	.000
Bats Left	R	.304	359	109	20	2	17	62	19	64	.336	.513	Bats Left	R	.286	7	2	0	0	0	0	1	3	.375	.286
Stewart,Andy	L	.333	6	2	1	0	0	0	0	0	.333	.500	Trammell,B	L	.261	46	12	3	0	3	7	5	15	.327	.522
Bats Right	R	.000	2	0	0	0	0	0	0	0	.000	.000	Bats Right	R	.208	77	16	2	0	1	6	10	20	.295	.273
Stewart,S	L	.343	35	12	3	2	0	3	7	8	.452	.543	Tucker,M	L	.283	113	32	5	0	0	12	8	27	.352	.327
Bats Right	R	.271	133	36	10	5	0	19	12	16	.344	.421	Bats Left	R	.282	386	109	20	7	14	44	36	89	.346	.479
Stinnett,K	L	.304	23	7	2	0	0	1	2	4	.360	.391	Turner,Chris	L	.400	10	4	1	1	0	1	2	4	.500	.700
Bats Right	R	.154	13	2	2	0	0	2	1	5	.214	.308	Bats Right	R	.154	13	2	0	0	1	1	3	4	.313	.385
Stocker,Kevin	L	.297	111	33	5	2	1	11	12	13	.376	.405	Unroe,Tim	L	.182	11	2	0	0	1	4	2	7	.308	.455
Bats Both	R	.257	393	101	18	3	3	29	39	78	.323	.341	Bats Right	R	.400	5	2	1	0	1	1	0	2	.400	1.200
Strange,Doug	L	.250	112	28	4	0	0	8	8	21	.300	.286	Valdez,Mario	L	.188	16	3	1	0	0	0	2	6	.316	.250
Bats Both	R	.260	215	56	12	2	12	39	28	55	.348	.502	Bats Left	R	.253	99	25	6	0	1	13	15	33	.356	.343
Strawberry,D	L	.000	7	0	0	0	0	0	1	5	.125	.000	Valentin,J	L	.500	2	1	0	0	0	0	0	0	.500	.500
Bats Left	R	.136	22	3	1	0	0	2	2	4	.208	.182	Bats Both	R	.200	5	1	0	0	0	0	0	2	.200	.200
Stynes,Chris	L	.195	41	8	0	0	1	6	3	4	.250	.268	Valentin,John	L	.221	154	34	12	1	5	12	24	22	.322	.409
Bats Right	R	.389	157	61	7	1	5	22	8	9	.432	.541	Bats Right	R	.337	421	142	35	4	13	65	34	44	.391	.532
Surhoff,B.J.	L	.288	160	46	9	0	3	28	10	21	.335	.400	Valentin,Jose	L	.259	158	41	3	0	2	9	7	35	.299	.316
Bats Left	R	.283	368	104	21	4	15	60	39	39	.348	.484	Bats Both	R	.250	336	84	20	1	15	49	32	74	.315	.449

Batters vs. Lefthanded and Righthanded Pitchers

Batter	vs	Avg	AB	H	2B	3B	HR	BI	BB	SO	OBP	SLG
Vander Wal,J	L	.000	7	0	0	0	0	0	1	2	.125	.000
Bats Left	R	.188	85	16	2	0	1	11	9	31	.266	.247
Varitek,Jason	L	.000	0	0	0	0	0	0	0	0	.000	.000
Bats Both	R	1.000	1	1	0	0	0	0	0	0	1.000	1.000
Vaughn,Greg	L	.237	76	18	1	0	8	20	18	21	.385	.566
Bats Right	R	.211	285	60	9	0	10	37	38	89	.304	.347
Vaughn,Mo	L	.337	196	66	8	0	15	33	30	61	.440	.607
Bats Left	R	.302	331	100	16	0	20	63	56	93	.409	.532
Velandia,J	L	.000	1	0	0	0	0	0	0	0	.000	.000
Bats Right	R	.107	28	3	2	0	0	0	1	7	.138	.179
Velarde,Randy	L	.000	0	0	0	0	0	0	0	0	.000	.000
Bats Right	R	.000	0	0	0	0	0	0	0	0	.000	.000
Ventura,Robin	L	.256	39	10	1	0	0	7	8	4	.375	.282
Bats Left	R	.264	144	38	9	1	6	19	26	17	.372	.465
Veras,Quilvio	L	.194	124	24	5	0	0	5	17	14	.296	.234
Bats Both	R	.287	415	119	18	1	3	40	55	70	.375	.357
Vidro,Jose	L	.213	47	10	3	0	0	3	5	6	.302	.277
Bats Both	R	.262	122	32	9	1	2	14	6	14	.295	.402
Vina,Fernando	L	.253	91	23	2	2	0	8	1	8	.277	.319
Bats Left	R	.283	233	66	10	0	4	20	11	15	.325	.378
Vitiello,Joe	L	.236	72	17	3	0	3	11	7	22	.313	.403
Bats Right	R	.241	58	14	3	0	2	7	7	15	.333	.397
Vizcaino,Jose	L	.240	125	30	6	0	0	12	16	26	.324	.288
Bats Both	R	.273	443	121	13	7	5	38	32	61	.322	.368
Vizquel,Omar	L	.265	151	40	7	0	2	14	9	13	.306	.351
Bats Both	R	.285	414	118	16	6	3	35	48	45	.361	.374
Voigt,Jack	L	.311	90	28	8	2	6	15	11	21	.386	.644
Bats Right	R	.148	61	9	1	0	2	7	8	15	.254	.262
Walbeck,Matt	L	.229	48	11	2	0	0	1	3	5	.275	.271
Bats Both	R	.303	89	27	1	0	3	9	9	14	.360	.416
Walker,Larry	L	.299	144	43	14	0	6	23	17	25	.400	.521
Bats Left	R	.389	424	165	32	4	43	107	61	65	.470	.788
Walker,Todd	L	.357	14	5	1	0	0	3	1	3	.375	.429
Bats Left	R	.225	142	32	6	1	3	13	10	27	.279	.345
Walton,Jerome	L	.250	40	10	1	0	2	6	2	6	.286	.425
Bats Right	R	.357	28	10	0	0	1	3	2	4	.400	.464
Ward,Turner	L	.375	24	9	3	1	1	7	5	2	.483	.708
Bats Both	R	.350	143	50	13	0	6	26	13	15	.409	.566
Watkins,Pat	L	.167	12	2	0	0	0	0	0	2	.167	.167
Bats Right	R	.235	17	4	2	0	0	0	0	3	.235	.353
Webster,Lenny	L	.259	81	21	5	0	3	12	9	15	.330	.432
Bats Right	R	.253	178	45	3	1	4	25	13	31	.311	.348
Wehner,John	L	.000	9	0	0	0	0	1	2	1	.182	.000
Bats Right	R	.370	27	10	2	0	0	1	0	4	.393	.444
Weiss,Walt	L	.192	99	19	3	1	1	6	17	16	.310	.273
Bats Both	R	.296	294	87	20	4	3	32	49	40	.399	.422
White,Devon	L	.188	48	9	1	0	1	8	6	8	.286	.271
Bats Both	R	.258	217	56	12	1	5	26	26	57	.349	.392
White,Rondell	L	.255	137	35	5	2	10	25	8	24	.304	.540
Bats Right	R	.275	455	125	24	3	18	57	23	87	.319	.459
Whiten,Mark	L	.259	81	21	3	0	3	10	11	21	.362	.407
Bats Both	R	.269	134	36	8	0	2	14	19	26	.359	.373
Widger,Chris	L	.277	101	28	8	2	4	19	10	19	.342	.515
Bats Right	R	.209	177	37	12	1	3	18	12	40	.260	.339
Wilkins,Rick	L	.103	39	4	0	0	0	1	4	17	.186	.103
Bats Left	R	.221	163	36	6	0	7	26	14	50	.276	.387
Williams,B	L	.326	141	46	11	0	9	32	31	22	.443	.596
Bats Both	R	.329	368	121	24	6	12	68	42	58	.393	.524
Williams,E	L	.233	30	7	0	0	2	4	3	3	.303	.433
Bats Right	R	.242	66	16	5	0	1	8	8	22	.338	.364
Williams,G	L	.324	68	22	3	0	2	5	7	11	.387	.456
Bats Both	R	.271	133	36	6	1	1	17	28	35	.402	.353
Williams,G	L	.274	157	43	11	0	6	15	7	24	.303	.459
Bats Right	R	.244	409	100	21	2	4	26	12	66	.274	.335
Williams,Matt	L	.281	139	39	10	1	13	31	9	22	.327	.647
Bats Right	R	.258	457	118	22	2	19	74	25	86	.300	.440
Williamson,A	L	.000	2	0	0	0	0	0	1	1	.333	.000
Bats Left	R	.212	52	11	3	0	0	6	3	7	.250	.269
Wilson,Dan	L	.357	129	46	11	0	9	28	11	12	.404	.651
Bats Right	R	.240	379	91	20	1	6	46	28	60	.300	.346
Wilson,E	L	.500	6	3	0	0	0	0	0	1	.500	.500
Bats Both	R	.222	9	2	0	0	0	1	0	1	.222	.222
Womack,Tony	L	.310	129	40	4	1	0	14	9	34	.360	.357
Bats Left	R	.270	512	138	22	8	6	36	34	75	.318	.379
Young,Dmitri	L	.265	83	22	3	0	1	9	7	17	.330	.337
Bats Both	R	.256	250	64	11	3	4	25	31	46	.337	.372
Young,Eric	L	.280	157	44	11	1	3	15	16	11	.358	.420
Bats Right	R	.280	465	130	22	7	5	46	55	43	.359	.389
Young,Ernie	L	.180	61	11	2	0	0	4	8	23	.268	.213
Bats Right	R	.246	114	28	5	0	5	11	11	34	.323	.421
Young,Kevin	L	.360	86	31	6	0	5	19	4	22	.376	.605
Bats Right	R	.279	247	69	12	3	13	55	12	67	.317	.510
Zaun,Gregg	L	.286	14	4	1	0	0	2	5	3	.500	.357
Bats Both	R	.302	129	39	9	2	2	18	21	15	.404	.450
Zeile,Todd	L	.257	140	36	6	0	5	18	23	20	.361	.407
Bats Right	R	.271	435	118	11	0	26	72	62	92	.366	.476
AL	L	.271	--	--	--	--	--	--	--	--	.338	.424
	R	.270	--	--	--	--	--	--	--	--	.341	.430
NL	L	.260	--	--	--	--	--	--	--	--	.334	.403
	R	.264	--	--	--	--	--	--	--	--	.333	.412
MLB	L	.266	--	--	--	--	--	--	--	--	.336	.414
	R	.267	--	--	--	--	--	--	--	--	.337	.421

Pitchers vs. Lefthanded and Righthanded Batters

Pitcher	vs	Avg	AB	H	2B	3B	HR	BI	BB	SO	OBP	SLG	Pitcher	vs	Avg	AB	H	2B	3B	HR	BI	BB	SO	OBP	SLG
Acevedo,Juan	L	.330	88	29	7	0	2	14	14	16	.413	.477	Banks,Willie	L	.214	28	6	2	0	0	2	1	5	.241	.286
Throws Right	R	.245	94	23	6	0	4	12	8	17	.321	.436	Throws Right	R	.150	20	3	0	1	0	1	5	3	.346	.250
Acre,Mark	L	.261	23	6	2	0	0	4	2	2	.320	.348	Barrios,M	L	.500	6	3	1	0	0	0	2	0	.625	.667
Throws Right	R	.349	43	15	4	0	1	5	6	10	.420	.512	Throws Right	R	.333	9	3	1	0	0	4	1	3	.400	.444
Adams,Terry	L	.297	138	41	10	1	1	15	24	27	.405	.406	Batchelor,R	L	.271	48	13	2	0	1	10	9	9	.386	.375
Throws Right	R	.314	159	50	5	0	2	24	16	37	.373	.384	Throws Right	R	.386	70	27	3	0	1	11	5	9	.449	.471
Adams,Willie	L	.333	120	40	14	3	4	26	16	18	.407	.600	Batista,M	L	.258	62	16	4	1	0	5	11	11	.365	.355
Throws Right	R	.280	118	33	8	0	5	23	16	19	.374	.475	Throws Right	R	.274	73	20	3	0	4	15	13	16	.378	.479
Adamson,Joel	L	.238	101	24	5	0	5	11	7	21	.300	.436	Bautista,Jose	L	.234	94	22	1	0	2	10	7	11	.294	.309
Throws Left	R	.280	193	54	9	0	8	28	12	35	.329	.451	Throws Right	R	.381	126	48	9	0	6	24	7	12	.422	.595
Aguilera,Rick	L	.235	115	27	4	2	5	17	10	31	.299	.435	Beck,Rod	L	.234	137	32	1	0	2	14	6	27	.271	.285
Throws Right	R	.275	138	38	6	0	4	20	12	37	.333	.406	Throws Right	R	.265	132	35	6	1	5	19	2	26	.281	.439
Alberro,Jose	L	.349	63	22	5	0	2	14	12	3	.461	.524	Beckett,R	L	.000	2	0	0	0	0	0	0	2	.000	.000
Throws Right	R	.254	59	15	5	0	2	13	5	8	.308	.441	Throws Left	R	.250	4	1	1	0	0	2	1	0	.400	.500
Aldred,Scott	L	.333	72	24	3	0	4	14	2	6	.351	.542	Beech,Matt	L	.221	86	19	3	0	3	10	8	16	.292	.360
Throws Left	R	.320	244	78	21	0	16	49	26	27	.391	.602	Throws Left	R	.290	441	128	23	2	22	62	49	104	.363	.501
Alfonseca,A	L	.323	31	10	1	1	1	6	3	4	.382	.516	Belcher,Tim	L	.278	407	113	24	2	17	50	39	58	.344	.472
Throws Right	R	.325	80	26	8	1	2	11	7	15	.386	.525	Throws Right	R	.297	434	129	28	2	14	65	31	55	.345	.468
Almanzar,C	L	.143	7	1	0	0	1	1	0	2	.143	.571	Belinda,Stan	L	.263	160	42	12	2	6	21	16	43	.343	.475
Throws Right	R	.000	4	0	0	0	0	0	1	2	.200	.000	Throws Right	R	.203	207	42	10	1	5	27	17	71	.275	.333
Alvarez,W	L	.253	154	39	4	0	5	22	16	29	.328	.377	Beltran,Rigo	L	.275	40	11	3	1	1	8	7	11	.367	.475
Throws Left	R	.223	631	141	26	2	13	64	75	150	.306	.333	Throws Left	R	.228	158	36	5	1	2	13	10	39	.272	.310
Anderson,B	L	.314	35	11	1	0	1	5	1	6	.333	.429	Benes,Alan	L	.233	292	68	11	3	8	30	39	73	.325	.373
Throws Left	R	.297	148	44	2	1	6	23	10	16	.331	.446	Throws Right	R	.205	293	60	5	1	5	27	29	87	.279	.280
Andujar,Luis	L	.398	103	41	8	0	6	17	11	13	.452	.650	Benes,Andy	L	.244	336	82	16	4	6	39	31	80	.306	.369
Throws Right	R	.310	113	35	13	1	3	26	10	15	.357	.522	Throws Right	R	.215	312	67	12	1	3	21	30	95	.290	.288
Appier,Kevin	L	.257	467	120	27	1	14	50	50	91	.332	.409	Benitez,A	L	.204	103	21	2	1	3	12	21	38	.339	.330
Throws Right	R	.227	419	95	19	0	10	39	24	105	.268	.344	Throws Right	R	.182	154	28	1	1	4	16	22	68	.282	.279
Arocha,Rene	L	.286	14	4	2	0	0	3	4	1	.421	.429	Bennett,S	L	.143	28	4	1	0	0	1	4	3	.250	.179
Throws Right	R	.406	32	13	1	0	2	9	1	6	.441	.625	Throws Right	R	.298	57	17	4	0	2	7	5	5	.338	.474
Ashby,Andy	L	.286	409	117	18	2	14	55	28	66	.332	.443	Bere,Jason	L	.280	50	14	2	0	2	8	10	8	.403	.440
Throws Right	R	.244	369	90	15	1	3	39	21	78	.289	.314	Throws Right	R	.118	51	6	1	0	2	6	7	13	.250	.255
Assenmacher,P	L	.225	89	20	2	0	3	13	6	26	.278	.348	Bergman,Sean	L	.285	165	47	11	2	4	30	25	30	.374	.448
Throws Left	R	.237	97	23	4	0	2	9	9	27	.299	.340	Throws Right	R	.338	234	79	16	5	7	39	13	44	.378	.538
Astacio,Pedro	L	.270	337	91	18	4	11	44	35	66	.339	.445	Bertotti,Mike	L	.333	9	3	3	0	0	5	1	2	.364	.667
Throws Right	R	.248	439	109	19	3	13	47	26	100	.299	.394	Throws Left	R	.545	11	6	1	0	0	4	1	2	.583	.636
Avery,Steve	L	.403	62	25	4	2	2	9	16	7	.519	.629	Bevil,Brian	L	.375	24	9	1	1	0	6	4	2	.448	.500
Throws Left	R	.304	335	102	20	2	13	60	33	44	.367	.493	Throws Right	R	.194	36	7	2	0	1	5	5	11	.302	.333
Ayala,Bobby	L	.285	165	47	9	1	7	25	25	42	.380	.479	Bielecki,Mike	L	.267	101	27	4	0	3	13	9	25	.327	.396
Throws Right	R	.238	185	44	9	0	7	27	16	50	.298	.400	Throws Right	R	.236	123	29	4	1	6	18	12	35	.307	.431
Aybar,Manny	L	.304	135	41	2	2	7	20	17	18	.381	.504	Blair,Willie	L	.274	347	95	23	1	8	40	25	42	.319	.415
Throws Right	R	.216	116	25	9	0	1	12	12	23	.301	.319	Throws Right	R	.272	334	91	15	3	10	35	21	48	.319	.425
Bailes,Scott	L	.222	36	8	1	0	2	7	5	6	.310	.417	Blazier,Ron	L	.291	79	23	7	1	2	21	8	14	.341	.481
Throws Left	R	.238	42	10	1	0	0	1	5	8	.319	.262	Throws Right	R	.289	135	39	8	0	6	16	13	28	.351	.481
Bailey,Cory	L	.286	14	4	1	0	0	2	2	3	.375	.357	Bochtler,Doug	L	.246	114	28	6	1	3	18	26	27	.383	.395
Throws Right	R	.423	26	11	0	1	1	9	2	2	.448	.615	Throws Right	R	.211	109	23	6	0	0	16	24	19	.353	.266
Bailey,Roger	L	.315	356	112	27	4	11	42	39	44	.383	.506	Boehringer,B	L	.152	66	10	2	0	1	4	12	14	.282	.227
Throws Right	R	.255	385	98	14	3	16	49	31	40	.327	.431	Throws Right	R	.271	107	29	7	0	3	19	20	39	.380	.421
Baldwin,James	L	.277	386	107	28	2	8	55	55	62	.365	.422	Bohanon,Brian	L	.263	76	20	4	0	1	8	5	14	.325	.355
Throws Right	R	.247	396	98	25	5	11	55	28	78	.302	.419	Throws Left	R	.257	292	75	15	3	8	32	29	52	.328	.411

Pitchers vs. Lefthanded and Righthanded Batters

Pitcher	vs	Avg	AB	H	2B	3B	HR	BI	BB	SO	OBP	SLG	Pitcher	vs	Avg	AB	H	2B	3B	HR	BI	BB	SO	OBP	SLG
Bones,Ricky	L	.346	188	65	9	1	8	34	15	18	.391	.532	Carlson,Dan	L	.250	32	8	2	0	3	5	3	7	.314	.594
Throws Right	R	.327	208	68	9	2	4	38	21	26	.396	.447	Throws Right	R	.387	31	12	3	2	2	8	5	7	.459	.806
Borland,Toby	L	.300	30	9	0	0	1	4	8	3	.447	.400	Carmona,R	L	.143	7	1	1	0	0	3	2	2	.333	.286
Throws Right	R	.229	35	8	1	0	1	11	13	5	.471	.343	Throws Right	R	.154	13	2	0	0	1	1	0	4	.154	.385
Borowski,Joe	L	.267	45	12	3	0	0	5	14	5	.441	.333	Carpenter,C	L	.314	172	54	9	0	4	25	16	24	.368	.436
Throws Right	R	.298	57	17	5	0	2	8	6	3	.365	.491	Throws Right	R	.338	160	54	9	0	3	18	21	31	.421	.450
Boskie,Shawn	L	.322	143	46	7	3	8	28	18	18	.396	.580	Carrara,G	L	.261	23	6	0	0	0	1	4	3	.370	.261
Throws Right	R	.290	169	49	17	0	6	25	8	32	.317	.497	Throws Right	R	.421	19	8	0	0	4	8	2	2	.476	1.053
Bottalico,R	L	.257	136	35	8	0	2	17	21	35	.358	.360	Carrasco,H	L	.265	136	36	6	1	4	29	16	27	.358	.412
Throws Right	R	.234	141	33	7	0	5	21	21	54	.335	.390	Throws Right	R	.224	196	44	8	1	3	17	25	49	.320	.321
Bottenfield,K	L	.250	124	31	6	1	1	9	16	26	.340	.339	Casian,Larry	L	.375	64	24	2	0	3	20	1	15	.379	.547
Throws Right	R	.266	192	51	8	0	12	43	19	48	.329	.495	Throws Left	R	.276	87	24	3	0	5	15	7	8	.330	.483
Bovee,Mike	L	.333	6	2	2	0	0	1	0	1	.333	.667	Castillo,C	L	.297	128	38	7	0	8	26	11	24	.345	.539
Throws Right	R	.143	7	1	0	0	1	1	1	4	.250	.571	Throws Right	R	.233	129	30	10	2	1	14	22	19	.346	.364
Bowers,Shane	L	.297	37	11	3	0	1	5	2	4	.341	.459	Castillo,F	L	.263	308	81	20	3	4	36	48	59	.361	.386
Throws Right	R	.356	45	16	3	3	1	10	6	3	.431	.622	Throws Right	R	.326	426	139	26	2	21	68	21	67	.368	.545
Brandenburg,M	L	.386	70	27	11	0	1	12	9	15	.463	.586	Castillo,Tony	L	.184	87	16	1	0	3	13	3	16	.220	.299
Throws Right	R	.234	94	22	2	1	2	16	7	19	.288	.340	Throws Left	R	.356	163	58	16	0	3	34	20	26	.426	.509
Brantley,Jeff	L	.056	18	1	0	0	0	1	6	8	.320	.056	Cather,Mike	L	.205	44	9	1	0	1	3	14	9	.397	.295
Throws Right	R	.308	26	8	1	0	2	5	1	8	.357	.577	Throws Right	R	.159	88	14	6	0	0	9	5	20	.221	.227
Brewer,Billy	L	.257	35	9	1	1	2	7	8	5	.395	.514	Charlton,Norm	L	.312	93	29	5	0	1	21	13	19	.407	.398
Throws Left	R	.185	54	10	1	1	1	9	5	12	.242	.296	Throws Left	R	.313	192	60	10	2	6	39	34	36	.421	.479
Brocail,Doug	L	.275	131	36	5	0	3	15	18	26	.364	.382	Chavez,A	L	.133	15	2	1	0	0	0	2	5	.235	.200
Throws Right	R	.241	158	38	5	1	7	26	18	34	.322	.418	Throws Right	R	.263	19	5	0	0	1	3	3	5	.348	.421
Brock,Chris	L	.268	71	19	6	1	1	10	15	8	.391	.423	Checo,R	L	.273	22	6	2	1	0	1	1	6	.304	.455
Throws Right	R	.319	47	15	2	1	1	11	4	8	.352	.468	Throws Right	R	.207	29	6	3	1	0	3	2	8	.258	.379
Brown,Kevin	L	.244	426	104	16	3	4	34	48	76	.328	.324	Christiansen,J	L	.286	42	12	4	0	1	7	7	13	.388	.452
Throws Right	R	.237	464	110	12	3	6	37	18	129	.278	.315	Throws Left	R	.269	93	25	2	0	1	10	10	24	.352	.323
Bruske,Jim	L	.214	84	18	3	0	2	15	16	13	.343	.321	Clark,Mark	L	.298	359	107	16	6	16	45	38	50	.363	.510
Throws Right	R	.244	78	19	5	0	2	11	9	19	.315	.385	Throws Right	R	.246	431	106	27	5	8	40	21	73	.286	.387
Bullinger,Jim	L	.265	283	75	15	3	7	44	38	30	.360	.413	Clark,Terry	L	.336	125	42	8	1	5	19	15	12	.413	.536
Throws Right	R	.287	314	90	15	1	10	45	36	57	.368	.436	Throws Right	R	.272	103	28	7	0	1	14	8	12	.321	.369
Burba,Dave	L	.296	294	87	19	2	10	34	41	51	.389	.476	Clemens,Roger	L	.205	498	102	21	3	3	32	36	160	.265	.277
Throws Right	R	.218	321	70	16	1	12	45	32	80	.296	.386	Throws Right	R	.222	459	102	20	0	6	27	32	132	.283	.305
Burke,John	L	.364	129	47	10	0	7	23	8	16	.408	.605	Clemons,Chris	L	.344	32	11	1	0	2	6	5	4	.432	.563
Throws Right	R	.293	123	36	7	0	6	23	18	23	.393	.496	Throws Right	R	.348	23	8	1	0	2	7	6	4	.500	.652
Burkett,John	L	.298	396	118	18	2	10	48	20	81	.328	.429	Clontz,Brad	L	.284	74	21	8	0	2	17	8	14	.357	.473
Throws Right	R	.315	387	122	18	2	10	44	10	58	.337	.450	Throws Right	R	.287	108	31	4	1	1	17	10	28	.345	.370
Burrows,Terry	L	.692	13	9	3	0	1	5	4	1	.765	1.154	Cloude,Ken	L	.210	100	21	4	1	3	12	18	22	.333	.360
Throws Left	R	.103	29	3	1	0	0	4	4	7	.235	.138	Throws Right	R	.227	88	20	3	0	5	13	8	24	.306	.432
Busby,Mike	L	.375	24	9	0	0	0	3	3	3	.444	.375	Colon,Bartolo	L	.280	200	56	11	1	5	26	23	35	.353	.420
Throws Right	R	.405	37	15	2	0	2	10	1	3	.410	.622	Throws Right	R	.293	174	51	9	1	7	29	22	31	.382	.477
Byrd,Paul	L	.253	91	23	5	0	1	10	19	14	.382	.341	Cone,David	L	.213	371	79	10	2	11	31	54	109	.315	.340
Throws Right	R	.220	109	24	6	1	5	21	9	23	.298	.431	Throws Right	R	.224	339	76	12	2	6	29	32	113	.294	.324
Cabrera,Jose	L	.095	21	2	0	0	0	3	4	10	.222	.095	Converse,Jim	L	.333	6	2	1	0	1	1	3	1	.556	1.000
Throws Right	R	.148	27	4	1	0	1	4	2	8	.200	.296	Throws Right	R	.167	12	2	0	0	1	2	2	2	.286	.417
Cadaret,Greg	L	.174	23	4	1	0	1	1	2	4	.269	.348	Cook,Dennis	L	.256	90	23	7	1	1	9	10	26	.330	.389
Throws Left	R	.259	27	7	1	1	0	3	6	7	.412	.370	Throws Left	R	.273	150	41	7	2	3	19	18	37	.357	.407
Candiotti,Tom	L	.264	246	65	11	1	11	28	20	30	.326	.451	Cooke,Steve	L	.283	120	34	4	1	3	13	16	23	.389	.408
Throws Right	R	.232	271	63	13	1	10	24	20	59	.303	.399	Throws Left	R	.285	526	150	36	0	12	65	61	86	.361	.422

Pitchers vs. Lefthanded and Righthanded Batters

Pitcher	vs	Avg	AB	H	2B	3B	HR	BI	BB	SO	OBP	SLG
Coppinger,R	L	.219	32	7	0	0	1	3	11	8	.422	.313
Throws Right	R	.311	45	14	4	0	1	4	5	14	.380	.467
Cordova,F	L	.298	346	103	18	2	9	33	28	42	.355	.439
Throws Right	R	.218	330	72	22	0	5	36	21	79	.271	.330
Cormier,Rheal	L	.500	2	1	0	0	0	0	0	0	.500	.500
Throws Left	R	.500	6	3	0	0	1	3	1	0	.571	1.000
Corsi,Jim	L	.221	86	19	5	3	0	15	12	21	.324	.349
Throws Right	R	.276	134	37	5	0	1	16	9	19	.329	.336
Crabtree,Tim	L	.346	78	27	4	1	4	19	6	10	.384	.577
Throws Right	R	.396	96	38	6	0	3	13	11	16	.468	.552
Crawford,Joe	L	.323	31	10	2	0	2	7	3	3	.382	.581
Throws Left	R	.191	136	26	3	0	5	14	10	22	.247	.324
Creek,Doug	L	.300	10	3	1	1	0	3	2	3	.417	.600
Throws Left	R	.225	40	9	3	0	1	5	12	11	.404	.375
Crowell,Jim	L	.143	7	1	1	0	0	1	0	1	.143	.286
Throws Left	R	.500	22	11	1	0	2	5	5	2	.593	.818
Cruz,Nelson	L	.213	47	10	4	0	2	4	2	9	.245	.426
Throws Right	R	.322	59	19	3	0	4	11	7	14	.394	.576
Cummings,John	L	.310	42	13	1	0	0	1	3	4	.356	.333
Throws Left	R	.311	61	19	2	2	3	14	11	4	.417	.557
Cunnane,Will	L	.287	164	47	8	1	4	26	27	35	.385	.421
Throws Right	R	.319	210	67	7	1	7	40	22	44	.397	.462
D'Amico,Jeff	L	.269	264	71	14	2	15	43	24	39	.333	.508
Throws Right	R	.260	262	68	10	1	10	32	19	55	.321	.420
Daal,Omar	L	.370	73	27	7	0	2	23	6	15	.418	.548
Throws Right	R	.331	166	55	10	1	5	20	15	29	.391	.494
Darwin,Danny	L	.309	314	97	21	1	17	45	28	39	.361	.545
Throws Right	R	.264	318	84	11	0	9	32	17	53	.304	.384
Darwin,Jeff	L	.240	25	6	2	0	0	2	4	6	.333	.320
Throws Right	R	.344	32	11	3	1	1	9	3	3	.400	.594
Davis,Mark	L	.286	35	10	0	0	1	5	3	8	.359	.371
Throws Left	R	.367	30	11	1	0	3	8	2	6	.406	.700
Davis,Tim	L	.083	12	1	1	0	0	0	1	6	.214	.167
Throws Left	R	.357	14	5	2	0	1	5	3	4	.471	.714
De La Maza,R	L	.500	2	1	0	0	1	1	1	0	.667	2.000
Throws Right	R	.000	6	0	0	0	0	0	0	1	.000	.000
DeHart,Rick	L	.324	37	12	4	0	1	7	2	10	.350	.514
Throws Left	R	.276	76	21	2	0	6	16	12	19	.371	.539
DeJean,Mike	L	.296	142	42	11	1	3	21	12	19	.348	.451
Throws Right	R	.262	122	32	9	1	1	17	12	19	.343	.377
DeLucia,Rich	L	.160	50	8	2	0	2	6	17	14	.373	.320
Throws Right	R	.260	104	27	6	3	3	17	10	30	.325	.462
Dessens,Elmer	L	.000	4	0	0	0	0	0	0	0	.200	.000
Throws Right	R	.250	8	2	1	0	0	1	0	2	.250	.375
Dickson,Jason	L	.308	438	135	22	0	21	59	34	61	.357	.502
Throws Right	R	.267	378	101	21	1	11	42	22	54	.317	.415
Dipoto,Jerry	L	.295	190	56	15	0	3	35	15	28	.349	.421
Throws Right	R	.281	185	52	6	0	3	25	18	46	.343	.362
Dishman,Glenn	L	.208	24	5	1	1	2	7	2	3	.259	.583
Throws Left	R	.284	88	25	6	2	2	12	6	17	.340	.466
Drabek,Doug	L	.258	310	80	16	2	12	40	46	38	.358	.439
Throws Right	R	.263	342	90	25	2	18	63	23	47	.311	.506
Dreifort,D	L	.184	103	19	2	1	0	5	17	24	.306	.223
Throws Right	R	.217	120	26	8	0	3	19	17	39	.309	.358
Duran,Roberto	L	.200	20	4	1	0	0	1	6	4	.448	.250
Throws Left	R	.176	17	3	1	0	0	7	9	7	.444	.235
Eckersley,D	L	.217	106	23	7	0	2	12	4	22	.252	.340
Throws Right	R	.260	100	26	5	0	7	13	4	23	.295	.520
Eischen,Joey	L	1.000	1	1	1	0	0	1	0	0	1.000	2.000
Throws Left	R	.200	5	1	1	0	0	1	1	2	.333	.400
Eldred,Cal	L	.245	412	101	19	3	14	38	49	69	.332	.408
Throws Right	R	.290	365	106	22	1	17	59	40	53	.363	.496
Embree,Alan	L	.247	73	18	0	0	1	7	9	17	.333	.288
Throws Left	R	.200	90	18	4	0	0	4	11	28	.294	.244
Erdos,Todd	L	.357	28	10	3	0	1	8	2	3	.400	.571
Throws Right	R	.233	30	7	1	1	0	5	2	10	.324	.333
Ericks,John	L	.190	21	4	0	0	0	1	2	3	.261	.190
Throws Right	R	.214	14	3	1	0	1	1	2	3	.313	.500
Erickson,S	L	.248	452	112	21	2	10	47	35	48	.302	.369
Throws Right	R	.267	397	106	14	1	6	37	26	83	.317	.353
Escobar,K	L	.218	55	12	1	0	0	3	12	18	.358	.236
Throws Right	R	.254	63	16	5	0	1	8	7	18	.329	.381
Eshelman,V	L	.225	40	9	3	0	1	4	3	7	.295	.375
Throws Left	R	.360	136	49	15	0	2	25	14	11	.418	.515
Estes,Shawn	L	.241	162	39	8	0	1	20	26	28	.363	.309
Throws Left	R	.218	564	123	14	3	11	46	74	153	.311	.312
Eversgerd,B	L	.500	6	3	2	0	0	1	1	1	.571	.833
Throws Left	R	.667	3	2	0	1	0	1	2	1	.800	1.333
Eyre,Scott	L	.286	42	12	2	1	4	12	6	4	.375	.667
Throws Left	R	.263	190	50	10	0	7	20	25	32	.349	.426
Falteisek,S	L	.200	10	2	0	0	0	1	0	0	.182	.200
Throws Right	R	.333	18	6	1	0	0	4	3	2	.435	.389
Fassero,Jeff	L	.263	175	46	8	1	2	13	14	32	.323	.354
Throws Left	R	.246	731	180	46	2	19	81	70	157	.309	.393
Fernandez,A	L	.289	384	111	22	7	12	42	36	82	.348	.477
Throws Right	R	.192	428	82	18	2	13	42	33	101	.254	.334
Fernandez,O	L	.259	112	29	4	0	5	23	9	18	.311	.429
Throws Right	R	.363	124	45	12	1	4	12	6	13	.392	.573
Fernandez,Sid	L	.250	4	1	0	0	1	1	0	2	.250	1.000
Throws Left	R	.200	15	3	1	0	0	1	2	1	.294	.267
Fetters,Mike	L	.306	111	34	12	0	1	15	11	26	.360	.441
Throws Right	R	.196	143	28	1	2	3	13	22	36	.305	.294
Finley,Chuck	L	.164	61	10	2	0	0	3	14	21	.338	.197
Throws Left	R	.257	552	142	19	2	20	64	51	134	.321	.408
Flener,Huck	L	.591	22	13	1	0	0	3	2	2	.600	.636
Throws Left	R	.397	68	27	6	1	3	13	4	7	.431	.647
Florie,Bryce	L	.211	133	28	7	3	1	18	28	29	.354	.331
Throws Right	R	.309	149	46	7	0	3	24	14	24	.365	.416
Fordham,Tom	L	.200	20	4	2	0	0	5	2	3	.261	.300
Throws Left	R	.295	44	13	1	1	2	10	8	7	.407	.500

Pitchers vs. Lefthanded and Righthanded Batters

Pitcher	vs	Avg	AB	H	2B	3B	HR	BI	BB	SO	OBP	SLG
Fossas,Tony	L	.266	94	25	4	0	0	6	9	28	.337	.309
Throws Left	R	.325	114	37	4	0	7	19	17	13	.409	.544
Foster,Kevin	L	.280	261	73	17	0	13	36	33	43	.357	.494
Throws Right	R	.233	292	68	13	0	14	34	33	75	.311	.421
Foulke,Keith	L	.338	133	45	7	1	5	15	7	25	.369	.519
Throws Right	R	.265	162	43	6	2	8	25	16	29	.346	.475
Fox,Chad	L	.200	35	7	1	0	1	1	9	11	.364	.314
Throws Right	R	.246	69	17	1	1	3	10	7	17	.316	.420
Franco,John	L	.304	46	14	3	0	0	4	5	10	.373	.370
Throws Left	R	.205	171	35	8	0	3	15	15	43	.271	.304
Frascatore,J	L	.214	117	25	4	0	1	11	18	17	.321	.274
Throws Right	R	.269	182	49	5	1	4	22	15	41	.335	.374
Gaillard,E	L	.212	33	7	1	1	1	5	4	3	.289	.394
Throws Right	R	.209	43	9	1	0	1	4	6	9	.300	.302
Garces,Rich	L	.370	27	10	1	0	2	12	4	3	.438	.630
Throws Right	R	.143	28	4	0	0	0	3	5	9	.294	.143
Garcia,Ramon	L	.250	280	70	13	1	10	25	32	51	.329	.411
Throws Right	R	.272	312	85	10	2	10	42	20	69	.330	.413
Gardner,Mark	L	.305	334	102	13	4	13	38	33	66	.367	.485
Throws Right	R	.242	356	86	15	1	15	44	24	70	.288	.416
Glavine,Tom	L	.233	176	41	9	0	4	10	14	28	.292	.352
Throws Left	R	.225	694	156	20	2	16	64	65	124	.292	.329
Gomes,Wayne	L	.250	64	16	4	0	1	12	13	9	.377	.359
Throws Right	R	.290	100	29	5	0	3	12	11	15	.366	.430
Gonzalez,J	L	.232	276	64	8	3	10	30	33	52	.310	.391
Throws Right	R	.241	257	62	17	1	6	29	36	41	.338	.385
Gooden,Dwight	L	.299	211	63	9	1	8	27	31	34	.393	.464
Throws Right	R	.266	199	53	10	0	6	27	22	32	.351	.407
Gordon,Tom	L	.231	363	84	19	2	3	37	46	85	.320	.320
Throws Right	R	.220	323	71	11	0	7	40	32	74	.290	.319
Gorecki,Rick	L	.467	15	7	1	0	2	7	3	1	.556	.933
Throws Right	R	.182	11	2	0	0	1	1	3	5	.357	.455
Grace,Mike	L	.273	77	21	5	0	3	12	7	13	.333	.455
Throws Right	R	.177	62	11	1	0	0	4	3	13	.224	.194
Granger,Jeff	L	.571	7	4	2	0	1	4	3	0	.700	1.286
Throws Left	R	.353	17	6	2	0	2	6	5	4	.500	.824
Graves,Danny	L	.265	49	13	4	0	0	4	8	4	.368	.347
Throws Right	R	.467	60	28	4	1	2	14	12	7	.541	.667
Green,Tyler	L	.286	133	38	8	1	4	16	19	26	.373	.451
Throws Right	R	.215	158	34	7	0	4	25	26	32	.326	.335
Greene,Tommy	L	.267	15	4	1	0	1	4	5	5	.450	.533
Throws Right	R	.300	20	6	1	0	1	1	0	6	.300	.500
Groom,Buddy	L	.231	121	28	5	0	3	14	12	26	.296	.347
Throws Left	R	.346	136	47	8	1	6	21	12	19	.393	.551
Gross,Kevin	L	.268	41	11	1	1	2	7	13	11	.436	.488
Throws Right	R	.345	55	19	2	0	2	10	7	9	.422	.491
Grundt,Ken	L	.500	6	3	1	1	0	1	0	0	.500	1.000
Throws Left	R	.250	8	2	1	0	0	2	0	0	.250	.375
Guardado,E	L	.253	75	19	4	1	4	16	6	26	.309	.493
Throws Left	R	.250	104	26	3	0	3	14	11	28	.331	.365

Pitcher	vs	Avg	AB	H	2B	3B	HR	BI	BB	SO	OBP	SLG
Gubicza,Mark	L	.417	12	5	1	0	1	5	2	3	.500	.750
Throws Right	R	.533	15	8	2	0	1	5	1	2	.563	.867
Gunderson,E	L	.253	91	23	3	0	3	18	8	17	.317	.385
Throws Left	R	.229	96	22	5	0	2	10	7	14	.283	.344
Guthrie,Mark	L	.282	85	24	3	0	3	15	9	18	.351	.424
Throws Left	R	.267	176	47	8	1	9	30	21	24	.340	.477
Guzman,Juan	L	.216	116	25	3	0	4	13	17	25	.319	.345
Throws Right	R	.211	109	23	4	0	10	24	14	27	.304	.523
Hall,Darren	L	.325	83	27	4	0	1	5	10	9	.398	.410
Throws Right	R	.254	122	31	7	1	2	19	16	30	.338	.377
Hamilton,Joey	L	.306	360	110	23	3	14	52	35	43	.372	.503
Throws Right	R	.238	374	89	13	0	8	38	34	81	.310	.337
Hammond,Chris	L	.297	74	22	6	0	1	17	2	19	.312	.419
Throws Left	R	.316	187	59	9	0	4	23	25	29	.398	.428
Hampton,Mike	L	.303	155	47	8	1	3	24	12	21	.353	.426
Throws Left	R	.247	689	170	33	3	13	64	65	118	.311	.360
Haney,Chris	L	.250	28	7	0	0	0	3	0	8	.276	.250
Throws Right	R	.306	72	22	6	0	1	10	5	8	.354	.431
Hansell,Greg	L	.375	8	3	1	0	0	2	1	3	.444	.500
Throws Right	R	.182	11	2	0	0	1	3	0	2	.250	.455
Hanson,Erik	L	.241	29	7	1	0	1	7	4	9	.333	.379
Throws Right	R	.267	30	8	2	0	2	5	2	9	.313	.533
Harkey,Mike	L	.185	27	5	1	0	2	4	2	2	.241	.444
Throws Right	R	.233	30	7	2	1	1	4	3	4	.303	.467
Harnisch,Pete	L	.386	70	27	9	0	2	11	14	5	.488	.600
Throws Right	R	.233	90	21	8	0	4	12	9	17	.300	.456
Harris,Pep	L	.270	111	30	2	1	5	16	19	18	.377	.441
Throws Right	R	.277	188	52	8	2	2	24	19	38	.343	.372
Harris,Reggie	L	.315	89	28	6	2	0	17	24	14	.453	.427
Throws Right	R	.225	120	27	0	0	1	16	19	31	.347	.283
Hasegawa,S	L	.278	176	49	13	0	5	16	19	32	.350	.438
Throws Right	R	.263	262	69	15	2	9	40	27	51	.332	.439
Haught,Gary	L	.200	20	4	0	1	1	3	1	5	.227	.450
Throws Right	R	.348	23	8	3	0	2	5	5	6	.500	.739
Hawkins,L	L	.368	209	77	18	3	12	39	33	27	.453	.656
Throws Right	R	.266	214	57	11	1	7	28	14	31	.320	.425
Haynes,Jimmy	L	.248	141	35	6	0	4	13	21	29	.339	.376
Throws Right	R	.277	141	39	7	0	3	20	19	36	.368	.390
Helling,Rick	L	.220	223	49	11	2	9	30	40	58	.340	.408
Throws Right	R	.246	240	59	10	2	8	33	29	41	.330	.404
Henriquez,O	L	.167	6	1	0	0	0	1	2	1	.375	.167
Throws Right	R	.167	6	1	0	0	0	1	1	2	.375	.167
Henry,Butch	L	.308	65	20	3	0	1	5	4	10	.343	.400
Throws Left	R	.270	256	69	9	2	5	28	15	41	.308	.379
Henry,Doug	L	.240	104	25	5	0	2	15	19	30	.360	.346
Throws Right	R	.274	164	45	8	0	3	21	22	39	.356	.378
Hentgen,Pat	L	.241	511	123	21	4	14	58	44	79	.308	.380
Throws Right	R	.269	484	130	21	3	17	49	27	81	.307	.430
Heredia,Felix	L	.188	69	13	2	1	0	6	11	24	.325	.246
Throws Left	R	.268	149	40	12	0	3	24	19	30	.355	.409

Pitchers vs. Lefthanded and Righthanded Batters

Pitcher	vs	Avg	AB	H	2B	3B	HR	BI	BB	SO	OBP	SLG
Heredia,W	L	.235	34	8	2	0	1	4	9	4	.395	.382
Throws Right	R	.162	37	6	1	0	1	6	7	4	.283	.270
Hermanson,D	L	.232	276	64	12	1	8	33	36	56	.323	.370
Throws Right	R	.236	296	70	14	3	7	30	30	80	.301	.375
Hernandez,F	L	.500	4	2	0	1	0	2	2	2	.667	1.000
Throws Right	R	.600	5	3	2	0	0	5	1	0	.714	1.000
Hernandez,L	L	.248	157	39	8	3	3	11	23	22	.344	.395
Throws Right	R	.214	196	42	9	1	2	21	15	50	.271	.301
Hernandez,R	L	.194	160	31	1	0	2	13	21	50	.287	.238
Throws Right	R	.261	138	36	3	1	5	20	17	32	.344	.406
Hernandez,X	L	.250	72	18	2	0	3	11	11	14	.349	.403
Throws Right	R	.268	123	33	10	0	4	20	11	22	.336	.447
Hershiser,O	L	.282	340	96	21	3	12	49	44	41	.367	.468
Throws Right	R	.263	392	103	12	4	14	48	25	66	.316	.421
Hill,Ken	L	.264	387	102	21	1	12	43	58	47	.359	.416
Throws Right	R	.272	338	92	20	4	7	48	37	59	.343	.417
Hitchcock,S	L	.316	117	37	8	2	4	12	6	18	.370	.521
Throws Left	R	.267	506	135	32	4	20	76	49	88	.329	.464
Hoffman,T	L	.185	157	29	5	2	3	17	9	63	.229	.299
Throws Right	R	.217	138	30	4	1	6	19	15	48	.292	.391
Holmes,Darren	L	.339	180	61	15	2	3	27	20	36	.403	.494
Throws Right	R	.289	180	52	10	0	9	29	16	34	.342	.494
Holt,Chris	L	.302	391	118	27	2	12	55	38	32	.366	.473
Throws Right	R	.226	411	93	13	1	5	27	23	63	.273	.299
Holtz,Mike	L	.198	91	18	5	0	2	10	7	26	.260	.319
Throws Left	R	.263	76	20	5	0	5	16	8	14	.337	.526
Holzemer,Mark	L	.217	23	5	1	0	0	3	4	4	.333	.261
Throws Left	R	.308	13	4	1	0	0	1	4	3	.471	.385
Honeycutt,R	L	.000	1	0	0	0	0	0	0	0	.000	.000
Throws Left	R	.556	9	5	0	0	0	2	1	2	.600	.556
Hudek,John	L	.255	51	13	1	2	2	9	19	11	.465	.471
Throws Right	R	.250	100	25	4	0	6	18	14	25	.353	.470
Hudson,Joe	L	.370	54	20	4	0	0	4	9	6	.477	.444
Throws Right	R	.235	81	19	4	0	1	17	5	8	.295	.321
Hurtado,Edwin	L	.250	28	7	0	0	4	10	6	3	.389	.679
Throws Right	R	.375	48	18	3	1	1	9	9	7	.483	.542
Hutton,Mark	L	.256	90	23	1	3	2	12	13	15	.352	.400
Throws Right	R	.353	139	49	7	1	8	26	13	24	.420	.590
Irabu,Hideki	L	.328	119	39	8	0	9	21	11	25	.379	.622
Throws Right	R	.291	103	30	5	2	6	20	9	31	.354	.553
Isringhausen,J	L	.362	69	25	1	1	2	13	11	13	.451	.493
Throws Right	R	.300	50	15	4	0	1	11	11	12	.419	.440
Jackson,Danny	L	.286	35	10	3	0	1	3	9	8	.457	.457
Throws Left	R	.361	244	88	24	1	10	58	19	24	.406	.590
Jackson,Mike	L	.299	117	35	9	0	0	18	18	18	.391	.376
Throws Right	R	.153	157	24	3	0	3	6	11	56	.221	.229
Jacome,Jason	L	.296	54	16	3	0	7	16	8	9	.381	.741
Throws Left	R	.296	142	42	9	0	3	22	12	18	.355	.423
James,Mike	L	.315	92	29	10	1	0	9	20	22	.434	.446
Throws Right	R	.263	152	40	3	1	3	24	8	35	.321	.355
Janzen,Marty	L	.217	46	10	2	0	1	1	4	4	.280	.326
Throws Right	R	.283	46	13	1	0	3	10	9	13	.400	.500
Jarvis,Kevin	L	.369	130	48	11	0	10	32	10	19	.418	.685
Throws Right	R	.307	166	51	9	1	7	29	19	29	.376	.500
Johnson,Dane	L	.301	83	25	4	1	1	16	15	16	.404	.410
Throws Right	R	.247	97	24	4	0	3	22	16	27	.356	.381
Johnson,Jason	L	.429	7	3	0	1	0	1	1	1	.500	.714
Throws Right	R	.389	18	7	0	0	2	5	0	2	.368	.722
Johnson,Mike	L	.330	194	64	6	1	10	38	21	32	.390	.526
Throws Right	R	.255	165	42	11	0	10	26	16	25	.322	.503
Johnson,Randy	L	.260	77	20	4	0	4	7	5	28	.329	.468
Throws Left	R	.186	681	127	28	1	16	49	72	263	.271	.301
Johnstone,J	L	.270	37	10	3	0	0	3	6	5	.372	.351
Throws Right	R	.235	51	12	4	0	1	14	8	14	.358	.373
Jones,Bobby	L	.237	355	84	18	1	13	49	37	67	.311	.403
Throws Right	R	.248	375	93	17	1	11	34	26	58	.295	.387
Jones,B	L	.250	8	2	0	1	0	3	0	0	.222	.500
Throws Left	R	.394	71	28	8	1	2	13	12	5	.471	.620
Jones,Doug	L	.228	149	34	5	1	3	12	5	42	.258	.336
Throws Right	R	.200	140	28	6	0	1	8	4	40	.224	.264
Jones,Todd	L	.246	134	33	6	0	3	15	16	35	.322	.358
Throws Right	R	.214	126	27	2	0	0	11	19	35	.318	.230
Jordan,R	L	.366	41	15	2	1	0	6	1	7	.400	.463
Throws Left	R	.262	61	16	3	0	1	7	14	12	.395	.361
Judd,Mike	L	.429	7	3	0	0	0	2	0	3	.429	.429
Throws Right	R	.250	4	1	0	0	0	0	0	1	.250	.250
Juden,Jeff	L	.299	281	84	12	1	10	35	49	53	.403	.456
Throws Right	R	.221	330	73	15	1	13	44	23	83	.286	.391
Kamieniecki,S	L	.257	350	90	21	3	8	34	39	51	.330	.403
Throws Right	R	.265	336	89	17	0	12	47	28	58	.325	.423
Karchner,Matt	L	.250	72	18	4	1	1	8	13	11	.360	.375
Throws Right	R	.262	122	32	3	0	3	14	13	19	.333	.361
Karl,Scott	L	.241	116	28	7	0	1	4	10	15	.313	.328
Throws Left	R	.286	644	184	40	3	22	87	57	104	.345	.460
Karp,Ryan	L	.067	15	1	0	0	1	3	4	3	.300	.267
Throws Left	R	.275	40	11	1	0	1	8	5	15	.370	.375
Karsay,Steve	L	.296	287	85	24	4	16	48	32	54	.369	.575
Throws Right	R	.313	259	81	15	2	4	31	15	38	.362	.432
Kashiwada,T	L	.289	45	13	2	0	1	5	9	7	.411	.400
Throws Left	R	.289	76	22	7	0	3	11	9	12	.375	.500
Keagle,Greg	L	.321	109	35	7	1	8	20	11	19	.400	.624
Throws Right	R	.291	79	23	3	0	1	9	7	14	.356	.367
Key,Jimmy	L	.263	137	36	6	0	5	17	18	24	.356	.416
Throws Left	R	.261	667	174	24	4	19	60	64	117	.326	.394
Kile,Darryl	L	.233	486	113	20	1	11	39	53	108	.306	.346
Throws Right	R	.217	438	95	18	3	8	37	41	97	.294	.326
King,Curtis	L	.231	39	9	1	0	0	4	5	5	.311	.256
Throws Right	R	.372	78	29	3	0	0	12	6	8	.414	.410
Kline,Steve	L	.354	82	29	2	2	4	23	3	18	.382	.573
Throws Left	R	.328	134	44	7	0	6	18	20	19	.416	.515

Pitchers vs. Lefthanded and Righthanded Batters

Pitcher	vs	Avg	AB	H	2B	3B	HR	BI	BB	SO	OBP	SLG
Krivda,Rick	L	.385	39	15	4	1	4	10	4	6	.442	.846
Throws Left	R	.315	165	52	13	2	3	23	14	23	.365	.473
Kroon,Marc	L	.130	23	3	1	0	0	2	2	7	.231	.174
Throws Right	R	.407	27	11	3	0	2	8	3	5	.467	.741
Kubinski,Tim	L	.190	21	4	0	0	0	4	5	2	.357	.190
Throws Left	R	.308	26	8	1	0	2	8	1	8	.321	.577
Lacy,Kerry	L	.293	92	27	6	1	4	19	12	8	.375	.511
Throws Right	R	.333	99	33	8	0	3	19	10	10	.387	.505
Langston,Mark	L	.185	27	5	0	0	1	1	3	6	.267	.296
Throws Left	R	.337	166	56	11	0	7	31	26	24	.423	.530
Leiter,Al	L	.204	98	20	2	5	0	5	14	28	.310	.327
Throws Left	R	.249	454	113	20	4	13	67	77	104	.369	.396
Leiter,Mark	L	.316	374	118	29	5	13	66	46	57	.389	.524
Throws Right	R	.268	366	98	29	2	12	55	18	91	.311	.456
LeRoy,John	L	.000	4	0	0	0	0	0	2	2	.333	.000
Throws Right	R	.333	3	1	0	0	0	0	1	1	.500	.333
Leskanic,Curt	L	.312	93	29	7	1	4	20	14	21	.394	.538
Throws Right	R	.240	125	30	4	2	4	22	10	32	.292	.400
Levine,Al	L	.348	46	16	5	0	2	9	8	9	.439	.587
Throws Right	R	.288	66	19	2	0	2	6	8	13	.373	.409
Lewis,Richie	L	.359	39	14	0	1	5	18	4	4	.419	.795
Throws Right	R	.246	57	14	3	0	5	10	14	12	.397	.561
Lidle,Cory	L	.321	137	44	8	2	5	20	10	18	.362	.518
Throws Right	R	.237	177	42	6	0	2	22	10	36	.286	.305
Lieber,Jon	L	.304	378	115	22	6	15	48	34	65	.360	.513
Throws Right	R	.219	356	78	17	1	8	37	17	95	.253	.340
Ligtenberg,K	L	.214	28	6	0	0	2	6	1	9	.241	.429
Throws Right	R	.207	29	6	1	0	2	3	3	10	.281	.448
Lima,Jose	L	.230	122	28	6	1	3	17	8	26	.275	.369
Throws Right	R	.302	169	51	11	1	6	29	8	37	.348	.485
Lira,Felipe	L	.288	226	65	16	1	10	41	25	32	.363	.500
Throws Right	R	.302	222	67	13	2	8	29	30	41	.389	.486
Lloyd,Graeme	L	.279	68	19	5	0	3	9	3	13	.306	.485
Throws Left	R	.300	120	36	7	0	3	21	17	13	.380	.433
Loaiza,E	L	.289	405	117	19	1	7	39	32	54	.348	.393
Throws Right	R	.269	361	97	19	5	10	53	24	68	.322	.432
Loiselle,Rich	L	.309	123	38	7	2	2	18	16	26	.388	.447
Throws Right	R	.238	160	38	3	1	5	21	8	40	.276	.363
Long,Joey	L	.231	13	3	0	0	0	2	1	4	.286	.231
Throws Left	R	.378	37	14	5	0	1	7	7	4	.489	.595
Lopez,Albie	L	.333	153	51	7	1	7	34	17	29	.401	.529
Throws Right	R	.311	161	50	9	1	4	27	23	34	.404	.453
Lorraine,A	L	.371	35	13	4	0	1	5	2	8	.410	.571
Throws Left	R	.348	92	32	8	2	1	15	13	10	.421	.511
Lowe,Derek	L	.348	135	47	12	0	8	24	16	22	.419	.615
Throws Right	R	.208	130	27	4	0	3	16	7	30	.259	.308
Lowe,Sean	L	.419	31	13	3	0	1	9	5	3	.486	.613
Throws Right	R	.326	43	14	2	0	1	8	5	5	.400	.442
Ludwick,Eric	L	.396	53	21	3	0	6	14	5	8	.458	.792
Throws Right	R	.311	74	23	1	0	2	11	17	13	.440	.405

Pitcher	vs	Avg	AB	H	2B	3B	HR	BI	BB	SO	OBP	SLG
Maddux,Greg	L	.213	394	84	16	1	6	31	13	97	.239	.305
Throws Right	R	.255	455	116	15	2	3	25	7	80	.271	.316
Maddux,Mike	L	.294	17	5	1	0	0	2	4	3	.429	.353
Throws Right	R	.455	33	15	5	0	1	7	4	4	.526	.697
Maduro,Calvin	L	.303	109	33	8	1	1	14	24	9	.437	.422
Throws Right	R	.289	173	50	14	2	11	37	17	22	.349	.584
Magnante,Mike	L	.154	39	6	0	0	0	1	4	6	.233	.154
Throws Left	R	.243	136	33	5	0	2	18	7	37	.276	.324
Mahay,Ron	L	.231	39	9	0	0	1	2	7	12	.348	.308
Throws Left	R	.185	54	10	1	0	2	4	4	10	.241	.315
Mahomes,Pat	L	.313	16	5	1	0	1	3	2	2	.421	.563
Throws Right	R	.400	25	10	1	0	1	8	8	3	.543	.560
Maloney,Sean	L	.500	12	6	0	0	1	5	1	2	.500	.750
Throws Right	R	.091	11	1	1	0	0	2	1	3	.267	.182
Manuel,Barry	L	.276	58	16	3	0	3	12	5	14	.333	.483
Throws Right	R	.380	50	19	3	0	3	11	8	7	.475	.620
Manzanillo,J	L	.296	27	8	1	0	1	10	11	6	.500	.444
Throws Right	R	.262	42	11	1	0	2	13	6	12	.340	.429
Martin,Tom	L	.262	61	16	1	0	0	9	10	14	.361	.279
Throws Left	R	.250	144	36	6	0	2	21	13	22	.316	.333
Martinez,D	L	.333	93	31	3	2	5	22	20	9	.447	.570
Throws Right	R	.321	106	34	4	0	3	15	9	8	.403	.443
Martinez,P	L	.183	469	86	14	2	8	29	42	149	.252	.273
Throws Right	R	.184	391	72	10	2	8	33	25	156	.247	.281
Martinez,P	L	.182	11	2	0	0	0	4	0	2	.231	.182
Throws Left	R	.353	17	6	0	1	1	8	7	2	.542	.647
Martinez,R	L	.269	245	66	18	0	7	30	48	47	.384	.429
Throws Right	R	.218	262	57	17	0	7	22	20	73	.288	.363
Mathews,T.J.	L	.323	124	40	8	1	5	21	16	20	.397	.524
Throws Right	R	.213	164	35	3	1	4	12	14	50	.283	.317
Mathews,Terry	L	.256	82	21	8	0	3	14	16	7	.370	.463
Throws Right	R	.273	154	42	5	0	5	18	20	32	.352	.403
May,Darrell	L	.262	84	22	5	0	2	13	9	13	.330	.393
Throws Left	R	.288	118	34	10	2	4	21	16	29	.365	.508
McAndrew,J	L	.244	41	10	1	0	0	8	13	3	.436	.268
Throws Right	R	.368	38	14	4	0	1	8	10	5	.510	.553
McCarthy,Greg	L	.212	52	11	2	0	2	3	6	10	.305	.365
Throws Left	R	.246	61	15	4	0	2	10	10	24	.352	.410
McCurry,Jeff	L	.238	80	19	4	1	3	13	10	6	.319	.425
Throws Right	R	.320	75	24	3	0	4	10	10	13	.400	.520
McDill,Allen	L	.000	4	0	0	0	0	0	2	1	.333	.000
Throws Left	R	.300	10	3	0	0	1	4	6	1	.588	.600
McDonald,Ben	L	.259	255	66	11	2	9	33	27	51	.337	.424
Throws Right	R	.215	251	54	16	2	4	25	9	59	.247	.343
McDowell,Jack	L	.342	79	27	4	0	5	17	10	15	.411	.582
Throws Right	R	.221	77	17	6	0	1	5	8	23	.299	.338
McElroy,Chuck	L	.229	105	24	5	0	2	14	7	18	.272	.333
Throws Left	R	.265	185	49	7	0	3	19	15	44	.325	.351
McGraw,Tom	L	.000	1	0	0	0	0	1	1	0	.500	.000
Throws Left	R	.400	5	2	1	0	0	2	0	0	.333	.600

Pitchers vs. Lefthanded and Righthanded Batters

Pitcher	vs	Avg	AB	H	2B	3B	HR	BI	BB	SO	OBP	SLG
McMichael,G	L	.259	139	36	5	2	3	15	16	39	.338	.388
Throws Right	R	.213	174	37	9	0	5	23	11	42	.259	.351
Mecir,Jim	L	.175	40	7	1	0	2	7	3	11	.233	.350
Throws Right	R	.326	89	29	6	0	3	19	7	14	.384	.494
Mendoza,R	L	.300	250	75	13	1	7	25	17	33	.344	.444
Throws Right	R	.286	287	82	21	1	8	39	11	49	.318	.449
Menhart,Paul	L	.250	72	18	4	1	1	8	8	7	.321	.375
Throws Right	R	.261	92	24	6	0	5	13	5	15	.299	.489
Mercedes,Jose	L	.278	313	87	21	1	12	35	34	36	.348	.466
Throws Right	R	.215	275	59	5	1	12	35	19	44	.275	.371
Mercker,Kent	L	.269	134	36	6	1	3	14	11	13	.327	.396
Throws Left	R	.244	405	99	19	3	13	39	51	62	.328	.402
Mesa,Jose	L	.309	149	46	6	0	1	13	12	25	.364	.369
Throws Right	R	.215	172	37	6	1	6	17	16	44	.286	.366
Miceli,Dan	L	.260	127	33	9	2	5	26	20	26	.365	.480
Throws Right	R	.240	183	44	8	1	8	33	18	53	.304	.426
Miller,Kurt	L	.167	12	2	1	0	0	2	1	4	.286	.250
Throws Right	R	.476	21	10	1	0	2	5	6	3	.593	.810
Miller,Travis	L	.260	50	13	2	0	1	7	5	6	.327	.360
Throws Left	R	.340	150	51	12	0	7	35	18	20	.409	.560
Mills,Alan	L	.333	48	16	5	1	2	10	15	7	.492	.604
Throws Right	R	.240	104	25	5	1	3	13	18	25	.355	.394
Millwood,K	L	.306	108	33	6	0	1	16	14	14	.384	.389
Throws Right	R	.253	87	22	5	0	0	9	7	28	.306	.310
Mimbs,Michael	L	.244	41	10	2	2	1	6	9	12	.380	.463
Throws Left	R	.288	73	21	6	0	5	20	18	17	.447	.575
Minchey,Nate	L	.000	2	0	0	0	0	1	1	0	.333	.000
Throws Right	R	.714	7	5	0	0	0	2	0	1	.714	.714
Minor,Blas	L	.133	15	2	0	0	0	2	2	2	.222	.133
Throws Right	R	.344	32	11	2	0	1	3	3	4	.417	.500
Miranda,Angel	L	.346	26	9	2	0	0	4	3	3	.433	.423
Throws Left	R	.276	29	8	0	0	1	4	6	5	.432	.379
Misuraca,Mike	L	.533	15	8	1	0	3	7	3	1	.611	1.200
Throws Right	R	.233	30	7	4	0	2	6	4	9	.324	.567
Mlicki,Dave	L	.246	362	89	22	5	7	34	40	64	.320	.392
Throws Right	R	.272	386	105	18	1	14	45	36	93	.338	.433
Moehler,Brian	L	.321	374	120	25	4	12	48	32	45	.374	.505
Throws Right	R	.243	321	78	12	0	10	32	29	52	.308	.374
Mohler,Mike	L	.339	115	39	7	0	2	31	11	15	.406	.452
Throws Left	R	.285	270	77	13	1	9	43	43	51	.384	.441
Montgomery,J	L	.267	101	27	3	0	6	16	9	18	.327	.475
Throws Right	R	.217	120	26	4	0	3	16	9	30	.267	.325
Montgomery,S	L	.286	14	4	1	0	1	2	6	0	.500	.571
Throws Right	R	.500	12	6	1	0	1	3	2	1	.533	.833
Moody,Eric	L	.355	31	11	1	0	3	4	1	4	.375	.677
Throws Right	R	.313	48	15	1	0	1	9	1	8	.320	.396
Morel,Ramon	L	.368	19	7	0	0	1	3	1	2	.400	.526
Throws Right	R	.259	27	7	1	1	2	6	6	5	.394	.593
Morgan,Mike	L	.271	291	79	19	4	7	40	25	50	.330	.436
Throws Right	R	.261	329	86	26	4	6	42	24	53	.324	.419

Pitcher	vs	Avg	AB	H	2B	3B	HR	BI	BB	SO	OBP	SLG
Morman,Alvin	L	.268	41	11	1	1	0	7	4	9	.348	.341
Throws Left	R	.267	30	8	1	1	2	6	10	4	.450	.567
Morris,Matt	L	.259	405	105	18	3	8	55	46	80	.333	.378
Throws Right	R	.257	401	103	14	1	4	26	23	69	.306	.327
Moyer,Jamie	L	.322	183	59	8	0	6	20	12	25	.380	.464
Throws Left	R	.234	547	128	21	0	15	50	31	88	.277	.355
Mulholland,T	L	.271	140	38	10	0	2	11	10	13	.327	.386
Throws Left	R	.266	571	152	35	2	22	81	41	86	.324	.450
Munoz,Bobby	L	.313	64	20	4	1	1	10	10	9	.408	.453
Throws Right	R	.360	75	27	9	1	3	24	5	11	.398	.627
Munoz,Mike	L	.337	83	28	3	0	3	13	7	11	.380	.482
Throws Left	R	.255	94	24	4	0	1	11	6	15	.300	.330
Murray,Heath	L	.364	44	16	1	0	1	10	9	7	.472	.455
Throws Left	R	.382	89	34	5	0	2	15	12	9	.472	.506
Mussina,Mike	L	.221	429	95	25	1	14	41	32	110	.276	.382
Throws Right	R	.246	414	102	16	3	13	37	22	108	.288	.394
Myers,Mike	L	.252	107	27	1	1	5	24	13	35	.336	.421
Throws Left	R	.295	105	31	8	0	7	28	12	15	.367	.571
Myers,Randy	L	.188	48	9	1	1	1	5	9	12	.316	.313
Throws Left	R	.225	169	38	6	0	1	13	13	44	.280	.278
Myers,Rodney	L	.333	18	6	0	1	0	5	1	3	.368	.444
Throws Right	R	.333	18	6	0	0	1	2	6	3	.520	.500
Nagy,Charles	L	.279	419	117	23	1	13	49	44	71	.348	.432
Throws Right	R	.286	476	136	25	2	14	59	33	78	.337	.435
Naulty,Dan	L	.268	41	11	3	0	4	10	6	7	.347	.634
Throws Right	R	.247	73	18	4	0	4	13	4	16	.278	.466
Navarro,Jaime	L	.321	396	127	26	4	9	61	49	66	.392	.475
Throws Right	R	.299	469	140	25	1	13	79	24	76	.329	.439
Neagle,Denny	L	.236	174	41	11	1	5	14	8	33	.272	.397
Throws Left	R	.233	700	163	35	5	13	66	41	139	.278	.353
Nelson,Jeff	L	.235	98	23	9	1	3	12	17	23	.364	.439
Throws Right	R	.168	179	30	5	0	4	22	20	58	.252	.263
Nen,Robb	L	.222	144	32	4	0	4	21	20	40	.313	.333
Throws Right	R	.278	144	40	6	2	3	23	20	41	.364	.410
Nomo,Hideo	L	.252	413	104	17	6	9	42	45	107	.330	.387
Throws Right	R	.233	382	89	17	5	14	49	47	126	.325	.414
Nye,Ryan	L	.391	23	9	1	0	1	6	2	5	.429	.565
Throws Right	R	.393	28	11	4	0	1	6	7	2	.528	.643
Ogea,Chad	L	.306	245	75	17	1	8	39	28	39	.378	.482
Throws Right	R	.259	247	64	15	0	5	28	19	41	.317	.381
Ojala,Kirt	L	.556	9	5	0	0	0	1	5	1	.714	.556
Throws Left	R	.225	102	23	2	0	4	8	13	18	.310	.363
Olivares,Omar	L	.305	370	113	24	2	14	60	53	50	.398	.495
Throws Right	R	.243	321	78	18	1	4	38	28	53	.314	.343
Oliver,Darren	L	.246	118	29	6	0	4	15	16	13	.357	.398
Throws Left	R	.275	669	184	37	6	25	83	66	91	.344	.460
Olson,Gregg	L	.253	75	19	5	1	2	19	6	18	.305	.427
Throws Right	R	.328	119	39	3	0	1	17	22	16	.437	.378
Oquist,Mike	L	.260	219	57	11	2	8	29	27	39	.345	.438
Throws Right	R	.271	199	54	10	0	7	25	16	33	.335	.427

Pitchers vs. Lefthanded and Righthanded Batters

Pitcher	vs	Avg	AB	H	2B	3B	HR	BI	BB	SO	OBP	SLG	Pitcher	vs	Avg	AB	H	2B	3B	HR	BI	BB	SO	OBP	SLG
Orosco,Jesse	L	.101	79	8	3	0	1	7	12	26	.215	.177	Poole,Jim	L	.337	83	28	8	0	3	27	10	15	.412	.542
Throws Left	R	.226	93	21	2	0	5	19	18	20	.351	.409	Throws Left	R	.363	124	45	9	0	3	28	15	11	.440	.508
Osborne,D	L	.343	35	12	2	0	0	2	2	9	.378	.400	Portugal,Mark	L	.364	22	8	3	2	0	3	1	2	.391	.682
Throws Left	R	.265	272	72	15	1	10	41	21	42	.316	.438	Throws Right	R	.290	31	9	5	0	0	5	4	0	.361	.452
Osuna,Antonio	L	.192	104	20	6	0	2	6	11	30	.276	.308	Powell,Jay	L	.293	92	27	5	0	0	7	10	24	.371	.348
Throws Right	R	.224	116	26	5	0	4	11	8	38	.272	.371	Throws Right	R	.219	201	44	6	1	3	25	20	41	.292	.303
Painter,Lance	L	.250	24	6	0	1	1	4	2	6	.308	.458	Prieto,Ariel	L	.309	259	80	12	4	8	34	40	47	.405	.479
Throws Left	R	.189	37	7	2	0	0	2	6	5	.302	.243	Throws Right	R	.304	247	75	15	5	8	38	30	43	.381	.502
Pall,Donn	L	.333	3	1	0	0	0	0	0	0	.333	.333	Pugh,Tim	L	.167	18	3	1	0	0	3	3	0	.286	.222
Throws Right	R	.286	7	2	0	0	1	1	1	0	.375	.714	Throws Right	R	.214	14	3	2	0	0	2	2	4	.313	.357
Paniagua,Jose	L	.400	30	12	3	0	1	10	8	2	.537	.600	Quantrill,P	L	.315	130	41	3	0	3	12	11	18	.366	.408
Throws Right	R	.354	48	17	4	1	1	13	8	6	.466	.542	Throws Right	R	.286	217	62	12	1	2	18	6	38	.305	.378
Park,Chan Ho	L	.237	363	86	11	2	13	37	49	73	.330	.386	Radinsky,S	L	.221	86	19	6	1	2	16	7	18	.281	.384
Throws Right	R	.187	337	63	10	1	11	34	21	93	.245	.320	Throws Left	R	.245	143	35	5	0	2	13	14	26	.308	.322
Patterson,Bob	L	.167	96	16	3	1	2	16	4	26	.196	.281	Radke,Brad	L	.291	471	137	28	1	15	52	30	76	.333	.450
Throws Left	R	.267	116	31	7	0	7	16	6	32	.298	.509	Throws Right	R	.221	456	101	24	3	13	52	18	98	.251	.373
Patterson,D	L	.236	110	26	2	2	0	12	14	28	.323	.291	Raggio,Brady	L	.456	57	26	4	0	0	14	7	4	.508	.526
Throws Right	R	.282	156	44	10	0	3	26	9	41	.315	.404	Throws Right	R	.243	74	18	3	0	1	10	9	17	.329	.324
Pavlik,Roger	L	.221	113	25	5	0	1	6	20	20	.336	.292	Ramos,Edgar	L	.391	23	9	1	1	2	5	4	2	.481	.783
Throws Right	R	.315	108	34	10	0	6	19	11	15	.383	.574	Throws Right	R	.207	29	6	3	1	1	2	2	2	.281	.483
Percival,Troy	L	.235	102	24	6	0	2	10	13	42	.331	.353	Rapp,Pat	L	.292	260	76	12	0	7	29	34	40	.372	.419
Throws Right	R	.172	93	16	3	0	4	11	9	30	.257	.333	Throws Right	R	.285	288	82	17	3	9	44	38	52	.373	.458
Perez,Carlos	L	.194	139	27	4	0	2	14	11	20	.257	.266	Reed,Rick	L	.231	385	89	18	2	9	30	24	65	.277	.358
Throws Left	R	.274	654	179	47	9	19	87	37	90	.313	.460	Throws Right	R	.247	393	97	15	3	10	38	7	48	.267	.377
Perez,Mike	L	.200	20	4	0	0	0	3	2	4	.273	.200	Reed,Steve	L	.210	100	21	2	0	5	10	13	15	.319	.380
Throws Right	R	.220	50	11	2	1	2	10	6	13	.316	.420	Throws Right	R	.226	124	28	5	0	5	23	14	28	.312	.387
Perez,Yorkis	L	.400	15	6	0	0	0	2	0	3	.375	.400	Rekar,Bryan	L	.333	21	7	2	0	2	3	4	0	.440	.714
Throws Left	R	.360	25	9	0	2	2	7	4	4	.448	.600	Throws Right	R	.222	18	4	1	0	1	3	2	4	.300	.444
Perisho,Matt	L	.316	19	6	0	0	1	6	6	5	.481	.474	Remlinger,M	L	.241	112	27	4	0	5	16	12	25	.338	.411
Throws Left	R	.325	163	53	6	1	5	23	22	30	.410	.466	Throws Left	R	.217	336	73	27	0	6	34	48	120	.316	.351
Person,Robert	L	.243	251	61	14	1	11	35	35	55	.334	.438	Reyes,Al	L	.333	45	15	1	1	3	11	3	10	.388	.600
Throws Right	R	.267	240	64	19	2	8	38	25	44	.342	.463	Throws Right	R	.236	72	17	5	0	1	9	6	18	.313	.347
Peters,Chris	L	.271	48	13	1	1	3	11	5	5	.352	.521	Reyes,Carlos	L	.327	153	50	7	0	6	20	9	16	.370	.490
Throws Left	R	.281	89	25	6	0	3	14	16	12	.398	.449	Throws Right	R	.305	167	51	9	1	7	26	16	27	.364	.497
Petkovsek,M	L	.262	168	44	7	1	3	18	10	22	.317	.369	Reyes,Dennis	L	.302	43	13	2	0	2	6	8	12	.423	.488
Throws Right	R	.317	205	65	8	5	11	43	21	29	.384	.566	Throws Left	R	.273	139	38	6	1	2	13	10	24	.320	.374
Pettitte,Andy	L	.318	192	61	10	2	1	24	7	32	.343	.406	Reynolds,S	L	.262	370	97	13	2	8	48	35	78	.326	.373
Throws Left	R	.240	718	172	33	2	6	48	58	134	.298	.316	Throws Right	R	.271	339	92	26	1	11	35	12	74	.297	.451
Pichardo,H	L	.301	83	25	2	1	5	10	14	17	.408	.530	Reynoso,A	L	.267	150	40	6	4	2	13	18	22	.347	.400
Throws Right	R	.250	104	26	3	1	2	9	10	17	.316	.356	Throws Right	R	.282	195	55	14	2	5	29	11	25	.330	.451
Pisciotta,M	L	.261	46	12	2	0	1	8	6	10	.346	.370	Rhodes,Arthur	L	.220	118	26	4	0	3	13	6	34	.275	.331
Throws Right	R	.148	54	8	3	0	0	5	10	11	.288	.204	Throws Left	R	.217	226	49	12	1	6	20	20	68	.279	.358
Pittsley,Jim	L	.298	205	61	7	3	8	30	35	25	.403	.478	Rigby,Brad	L	.342	155	53	9	0	7	19	7	13	.365	.535
Throws Right	R	.259	228	59	7	2	7	36	19	27	.319	.399	Throws Right	R	.260	150	39	6	1	7	20	15	21	.323	.453
Plantenberg,E	L	.356	45	16	4	0	1	11	3	5	.408	.511	Rincon,R	L	.235	81	19	6	0	2	10	6	28	.287	.383
Throws Left	R	.170	53	9	6	0	0	7	9	7	.286	.283	Throws Left	R	.227	141	32	3	0	3	12	18	43	.321	.312
Plesac,Dan	L	.189	90	17	2	0	4	14	7	34	.247	.344	Rios,Danny	L	.571	7	4	0	0	2	3	2	0	.667	1.429
Throws Left	R	.291	103	30	3	1	4	14	12	27	.362	.456	Throws Right	R	.556	9	5	0	0	1	4	0	1	.600	.889
Plunk,Eric	L	.277	94	26	3	2	5	12	16	21	.382	.511	Risley,Bill	L	.143	7	1	0	0	1	2	0	0	.143	.571
Throws Right	R	.226	159	36	13	0	7	28	20	45	.313	.440	Throws Right	R	.222	9	2	0	0	1	2	2	2	.364	.556

Pitchers vs. Lefthanded and Righthanded Batters

Pitcher	vs	Avg	AB	H	2B	3B	HR	BI	BB	SO	OBP	SLG	Pitcher	vs	Avg	AB	H	2B	3B	HR	BI	BB	SO	OBP	SLG
Ritchie,Todd	L	.218	110	24	4	0	8	18	12	22	.301	.473	Saunders,Tony	L	.176	85	15	3	0	2	7	9	31	.263	.282
Throws Right	R	.332	190	63	8	2	3	23	16	22	.385	.442	Throws Left	R	.263	320	84	14	2	10	49	55	71	.368	.413
Ritz,Kevin	L	.359	237	85	15	3	11	41	29	31	.425	.586	Schilling,C	L	.232	456	106	21	6	16	51	34	151	.287	.410
Throws Right	R	.295	193	57	14	1	5	23	17	25	.350	.456	Throws Right	R	.215	474	102	28	1	9	41	24	168	.254	.335
Rivera,M	L	.242	153	37	4	0	1	4	9	33	.282	.288	Schmidt,Jason	L	.274	361	99	18	7	11	41	52	79	.364	.454
Throws Right	R	.231	121	28	5	2	4	15	11	35	.289	.405	Throws Right	R	.257	366	94	24	1	5	52	24	57	.318	.369
Roa,Joe	L	.309	123	38	6	1	5	23	11	15	.360	.496	Schourek,Pete	L	.273	66	18	2	1	3	10	5	14	.342	.470
Throws Right	R	.356	135	48	4	0	3	18	9	19	.399	.452	Throws Left	R	.233	258	60	16	1	15	40	33	45	.323	.477
Robertson,R	L	.336	116	39	8	1	2	20	17	21	.426	.474	Scott,Tim	L	.341	44	15	2	1	0	7	5	9	.412	.432
Throws Left	R	.281	463	130	30	1	17	65	53	48	.355	.460	Throws Right	R	.333	45	15	2	2	2	12	2	7	.388	.600
Robinson,Ken	L	.000	4	0	0	0	0	0	1	2	.200	.000	Sele,Aaron	L	.325	378	123	26	4	15	48	49	62	.403	.534
Throws Right	R	.167	6	1	0	0	1	1	0	2	.167	.667	Throws Right	R	.225	325	73	15	2	10	50	31	60	.313	.375
Rodriguez,F	L	.268	82	22	4	0	2	13	12	16	.358	.390	Serafini,Dan	L	.250	20	5	2	0	0	1	4	6	.375	.350
Throws Right	R	.274	95	26	5	1	0	15	16	18	.410	.347	Throws Left	R	.278	79	22	4	1	1	7	7	9	.337	.392
Rodriguez,F	L	.283	233	66	10	2	7	29	38	28	.386	.433	Service,Scott	L	.371	35	13	4	0	1	8	3	10	.421	.571
Throws Right	R	.261	310	81	19	1	5	45	22	37	.315	.377	Throws Right	R	.294	51	15	3	0	1	7	3	12	.327	.412
Rodriguez,N	L	.286	42	12	3	0	2	8	5	6	.347	.500	Shaw,Jeff	L	.242	178	43	11	0	2	18	6	32	.270	.337
Throws Right	R	.214	42	9	4	1	0	7	3	5	.271	.357	Throws Right	R	.212	170	36	4	1	5	11	6	42	.235	.335
Rodriguez,R	L	.314	102	32	4	3	3	14	9	13	.375	.500	Shuey,Paul	L	.235	68	16	1	0	1	7	14	16	.369	.294
Throws Left	R	.229	144	33	5	0	4	21	12	19	.288	.347	Throws Right	R	.330	109	36	6	1	4	21	14	30	.403	.514
Rogers,Kenny	L	.238	101	24	3	0	3	11	13	17	.339	.356	Silva,Jose	L	.390	59	23	7	1	4	13	8	12	.449	.746
Throws Left	R	.288	475	137	23	3	15	75	49	61	.358	.444	Throws Right	R	.319	91	29	5	0	0	12	8	18	.376	.374
Rojas,Mel	L	.258	159	41	8	0	8	28	19	45	.339	.459	Simas,Bill	L	.296	54	16	1	1	3	12	9	15	.397	.519
Throws Right	R	.226	164	37	5	2	7	26	17	48	.319	.409	Throws Right	R	.270	111	30	5	0	3	15	15	23	.364	.396
Rosado,Jose	L	.248	145	36	6	2	7	17	18	33	.325	.462	Sirotka,Mike	L	.269	26	7	1	0	0	2	1	3	.321	.308
Throws Left	R	.268	642	172	28	2	19	75	55	96	.326	.407	Throws Left	R	.296	98	29	5	0	4	7	4	21	.324	.469
Rose,Brian	L	.222	9	2	0	0	0	2	2	3	.364	.222	Slocumb,H	L	.266	143	38	7	1	2	20	25	26	.382	.371
Throws Right	R	.600	5	3	1	0	0	2	0	0	.600	.800	Throws Right	R	.305	151	46	10	0	4	29	24	38	.402	.450
Ruebel,Matt	L	.277	83	23	4	0	2	21	10	11	.351	.398	Small,Aaron	L	.327	168	55	9	3	2	27	18	25	.386	.452
Throws Left	R	.314	172	54	11	3	6	31	17	39	.385	.517	Throws Right	R	.266	203	54	10	0	4	23	22	32	.342	.374
Rueter,Kirk	L	.281	139	39	5	1	4	18	9	19	.322	.417	Smiley,John	L	.383	107	41	7	0	5	14	7	28	.426	.589
Throws Left	R	.261	595	155	34	2	13	49	42	96	.308	.390	Throws Left	R	.280	511	143	26	1	21	77	34	92	.331	.458
Ruffcorn,S	L	.262	65	17	3	2	0	8	18	16	.437	.369	Smith,Lee	L	.255	47	12	2	0	1	4	7	10	.352	.362
Throws Right	R	.284	88	25	11	1	4	25	18	17	.412	.568	Throws Right	R	.364	44	16	2	1	1	10	1	5	.391	.523
Ruffin,Bruce	L	.296	27	8	1	0	1	9	5	11	.406	.444	Smith,Pete	L	.269	223	60	4	1	6	29	30	30	.354	.377
Throws Left	R	.182	55	10	4	0	2	7	13	20	.338	.364	Throws Right	R	.265	226	60	10	0	10	31	22	38	.332	.442
Rusch,Glendon	L	.354	161	57	7	1	9	25	8	26	.386	.578	Smoltz,John	L	.246	524	129	19	3	10	47	41	98	.301	.351
Throws Left	R	.285	523	149	32	2	19	73	44	90	.344	.463	Throws Right	R	.238	442	105	23	1	11	41	22	143	.273	.369
Ryan,Ken	L	.279	43	12	1	1	2	9	5	6	.354	.488	Sodowsky,C	L	.263	80	21	5	0	2	7	13	16	.358	.400
Throws Right	R	.404	47	19	3	1	3	16	8	4	.492	.702	Throws Right	R	.239	117	28	4	0	4	16	21	35	.364	.376
Saberhagen,B	L	.328	61	20	8	0	4	16	9	8	.397	.656	Spoljaric,P	L	.244	123	30	6	1	3	20	13	31	.316	.382
Throws Right	R	.233	43	10	4	0	1	3	1	6	.283	.395	Throws Left	R	.228	136	31	10	1	1	12	23	39	.348	.338
Sager,A.J.	L	.260	150	39	4	2	5	18	12	31	.311	.413	Spradlin,J	L	.270	126	34	6	1	4	15	12	30	.329	.429
Throws Right	R	.256	164	42	7	2	5	29	12	22	.304	.415	Throws Right	R	.277	188	52	10	1	5	31	15	37	.333	.420
Sanders,Scott	L	.286	266	76	22	2	15	44	43	57	.383	.553	Springer,D	L	.262	381	100	29	3	16	60	36	35	.323	.480
Throws Right	R	.270	281	76	16	1	15	56	19	63	.316	.495	Throws Right	R	.271	365	99	21	1	16	52	37	40	.347	.466
Santana,Julio	L	.324	216	70	13	2	5	24	24	31	.400	.472	Springer,Russ	L	.229	96	22	6	0	2	12	13	30	.345	.354
Throws Right	R	.321	221	71	10	2	11	48	25	33	.384	.534	Throws Right	R	.234	111	26	10	0	2	17	14	44	.315	.378
Santiago,Jose	L	.250	8	2	1	0	0	2	0	0	.250	.375	Stanifer,R	L	.327	49	16	3	0	3	11	5	4	.389	.571
Throws Right	R	.385	13	5	0	0	0	0	2	1	.500	.385	Throws Right	R	.233	116	27	3	1	6	17	11	24	.315	.431

Pitchers vs. Lefthanded and Righthanded Batters

Pitcher	vs	Avg	AB	H	2B	3B	HR	BI	BB	SO	OBP	SLG
Stanton,Mike	L	.159	88	14	0	0	0	5	9	20	.253	.159
Throws Left	R	.231	156	36	5	0	3	16	25	50	.341	.321
Stephenson,G	L	.242	178	43	11	3	6	17	18	33	.315	.438
Throws Right	R	.246	248	61	19	0	5	25	20	48	.302	.383
Stevens,Dave	L	.356	73	26	7	1	4	12	11	20	.435	.644
Throws Right	R	.384	73	28	8	1	4	19	15	9	.494	.685
Stottlemyre,T	L	.267	359	96	18	2	11	51	46	67	.354	.421
Throws Right	R	.189	312	59	12	1	5	30	19	93	.253	.282
Stull,Everett	L	.500	8	4	2	0	0	2	2	1	.600	.750
Throws Right	R	.375	8	3	1	0	1	5	2	1	.500	.875
Sturtze,T	L	.328	64	21	3	0	2	15	13	11	.430	.469
Throws Right	R	.348	69	24	5	2	4	12	5	7	.382	.652
Sullivan,S	L	.243	152	37	8	0	7	20	17	27	.324	.434
Throws Right	R	.203	207	42	8	2	5	25	13	69	.265	.333
Suppan,Jeff	L	.280	232	65	15	0	8	40	21	32	.337	.448
Throws Right	R	.330	227	75	13	0	4	22	15	35	.379	.441
Swartzbaugh,D	L	.368	19	7	3	1	1	5	2	2	.435	.789
Throws Right	R	.357	14	5	2	0	0	2	5	2	.526	.500
Swift,Bill	L	.324	136	44	11	2	9	33	18	15	.405	.632
Throws Right	R	.313	131	41	10	2	2	19	8	14	.348	.466
Swindell,Greg	L	.205	151	31	7	2	1	17	3	27	.224	.298
Throws Left	R	.256	277	71	19	2	11	39	22	48	.311	.458
Tabaka,Jeff	L	.000	1	0	0	0	0	0	1	1	.667	.000
Throws Left	R	.167	6	1	0	0	1	1	0	0	.286	.667
Tapani,Kevin	L	.230	174	40	9	1	4	21	9	33	.270	.362
Throws Right	R	.257	144	37	10	0	3	9	14	22	.325	.389
Tatis,Ramon	L	.288	80	23	3	1	2	9	11	10	.380	.425
Throws Left	R	.321	134	43	6	0	11	30	18	23	.401	.612
Tavarez,J	L	.258	124	32	7	1	0	18	17	12	.338	.331
Throws Right	R	.288	205	59	9	1	6	38	17	26	.348	.429
Taylor,Billy	L	.323	130	42	11	2	2	22	18	25	.407	.485
Throws Right	R	.192	146	28	6	0	1	17	18	41	.296	.253
Telemaco,A	L	.303	76	23	9	0	1	9	6	12	.354	.461
Throws Right	R	.304	79	24	7	1	3	17	5	17	.341	.532
Telford,A	L	.232	138	32	4	1	5	15	17	19	.314	.384
Throws Right	R	.239	188	45	2	2	6	24	16	42	.316	.367
Telgheder,D	L	.340	209	71	18	3	9	29	24	26	.403	.584
Throws Right	R	.307	205	63	14	0	6	30	11	29	.341	.463
Tewksbury,Bob	L	.308	351	108	25	2	6	41	22	38	.345	.442
Throws Right	R	.285	323	92	21	2	6	34	9	54	.304	.418
Thomas,Larry	L	.222	9	2	1	0	1	3	1	0	.300	.667
Throws Left	R	.333	3	1	0	0	0	0	1	0	.500	.333
Thompson,J	L	.184	125	23	2	0	4	11	14	37	.266	.296
Throws Left	R	.242	682	165	30	3	16	65	52	114	.294	.365
Thompson,Mark	L	.344	61	21	4	1	4	18	6	5	.397	.590
Throws Right	R	.302	63	19	4	1	4	8	7	4	.400	.587
Thomson,John	L	.316	354	112	15	3	9	49	35	46	.379	.452
Throws Right	R	.273	297	81	21	1	6	36	16	60	.317	.411
Thurman,Mike	L	.267	15	4	2	0	2	4	3	0	.421	.800
Throws Right	R	.143	28	4	1	0	1	5	1	8	.172	.286

Pitcher	vs	Avg	AB	H	2B	3B	HR	BI	BB	SO	OBP	SLG
Timlin,Mike	L	.263	118	31	5	1	3	15	12	19	.331	.398
Throws Right	R	.252	151	38	1	0	5	17	8	26	.292	.358
Tomko,Brett	L	.190	221	42	14	1	9	23	34	43	.300	.385
Throws Right	R	.276	232	64	11	0	5	24	13	52	.312	.388
Torres,S	L	.340	47	16	3	0	1	12	12	5	.467	.468
Throws Right	R	.276	58	16	5	0	1	10	3	6	.344	.414
Trachsel,S	L	.260	377	98	19	3	12	42	32	85	.316	.422
Throws Right	R	.311	408	127	26	1	20	59	37	75	.368	.527
Trlicek,Ricky	L	.327	52	17	3	0	2	14	10	1	.435	.500
Throws Right	R	.268	71	19	3	0	2	7	13	13	.384	.394
Trombley,Mike	L	.211	109	23	4	0	2	13	13	19	.298	.303
Throws Right	R	.267	202	54	7	1	5	26	18	55	.327	.386
Urbina,Ugueth	L	.282	103	29	7	2	4	17	16	23	.378	.505
Throws Right	R	.165	139	23	1	0	5	16	13	61	.242	.281
Valdes,Ismael	L	.262	367	96	19	1	8	36	25	54	.310	.384
Throws Right	R	.206	364	75	16	3	8	29	22	86	.253	.332
Valdes,Marc	L	.250	136	34	8	0	1	13	21	19	.352	.331
Throws Right	R	.234	214	50	9	3	1	24	18	35	.309	.318
Valenzuela,F	L	.313	67	21	4	0	2	9	8	13	.410	.463
Throws Left	R	.291	292	85	14	1	10	41	38	48	.374	.449
VanLandingham	L	.272	162	44	7	2	5	25	31	19	.377	.432
Throws Right	R	.206	175	36	6	2	6	20	28	33	.314	.366
Veras,Dario	L	.237	38	9	5	0	1	10	9	7	.383	.447
Throws Right	R	.306	62	19	2	0	4	10	3	14	.358	.532
Veras,Dave	L	.292	106	31	9	2	2	12	21	21	.409	.472
Throws Right	R	.266	139	37	6	2	3	18	6	26	.304	.403
Veres,Randy	L	.273	55	15	1	0	1	7	4	10	.323	.345
Throws Right	R	.273	77	21	3	0	3	16	3	18	.306	.429
Villone,Ron	L	.353	68	24	0	0	2	13	14	12	.470	.441
Throws Left	R	.229	131	30	3	0	2	13	22	28	.340	.298
Vosberg,Ed	L	.230	74	17	3	0	2	12	8	22	.322	.351
Throws Left	R	.316	133	42	8	2	1	21	13	15	.380	.429
Wade,Terrell	L	.489	45	22	2	0	0	3	1	8	.489	.533
Throws Left	R	.299	127	38	8	0	6	21	15	27	.372	.504
Wagner,Billy	L	.237	38	9	2	0	0	3	5	18	.326	.289
Throws Left	R	.198	202	40	6	0	5	28	25	88	.294	.302
Wagner,Paul	L	.321	28	9	1	0	1	3	4	6	.406	.464
Throws Right	R	.268	41	11	0	0	3	6	9	3	.392	.488
Wainhouse,D	L	.306	36	11	4	0	0	11	8	8	.435	.417
Throws Right	R	.299	77	23		0	2	16	9	13	.386	.429
Wakefield,Tim	L	.269	368	99	23	5	9	38	43	68	.347	.432
Throws Right	R	.244	385	94	20	1	15	50	44	83	.339	.418
Walker,Jamie	L	.275	69	19	3	1	2	16	8	14	.358	.435
Throws Left	R	.267	101	27	3	1	4	17	12	10	.351	.424
Wall,Donne	L	.311	61	19	3	0	4	7	4	6	.354	.557
Throws Right	R	.321	106	34	5	2	4	21	12	19	.400	.519
Wallace,Jeff	L	.118	17	2	1	0	0	0	1	9	.167	.176
Throws Left	R	.261	23	6	1	0	0	3	7	5	.419	.304
Wasdin,John	L	.272	235	64	15	1	10	43	26	33	.341	.472
Throws Right	R	.231	247	57	14	1	8	28	12	51	.271	.393

Pitchers vs. Lefthanded and Righthanded Batters

Pitcher	vs	Avg	AB	H	2B	3B	HR	BI	BB	SO	OBP	SLG
Watson,Allen	L	.254	142	36	6	1	4	19	13	30	.325	.394
Throws Left	R	.285	646	184	33	3	33	96	60	111	.348	.498
Weathers,Dave	L	.354	48	17	2	2	2	11	4	9	.404	.604
Throws Right	R	.356	59	21	2	1	1	13	11	9	.458	.475
Wells,Bob	L	.301	113	34	2	0	3	15	11	21	.370	.398
Throws Right	R	.323	167	54	19	0	8	34	7	30	.352	.581
Wells,David	L	.327	159	52	9	2	3	22	3	23	.344	.465
Throws Left	R	.266	702	187	44	3	21	78	42	133	.311	.427
Wendell,Turk	L	.316	114	36	10	3	4	20	22	16	.431	.561
Throws Right	R	.189	169	32	11	0	3	18	31	48	.314	.308
Wengert,Don	L	.326	270	88	23	0	9	40	23	27	.383	.511
Throws Right	R	.317	281	89	18	1	12	53	18	41	.362	.516
Wetteland,J	L	.167	126	21	4	0	1	10	15	29	.254	.222
Throws Right	R	.200	110	22	7	0	4	12	6	34	.241	.373
Whisenant,M	L	.282	39	11	1	0	0	7	9	9	.451	.308
Throws Left	R	.182	44	8	1	0	0	4	9	11	.321	.205
White,Gabe	L	.500	18	9	4	0	0	5	1	1	.526	.722
Throws Left	R	.221	136	30	8	0	6	15	7	24	.260	.412
Whiteside,M	L	.341	129	44	10	0	3	28	10	14	.389	.488
Throws Right	R	.259	158	41	8	1	1	21	16	30	.328	.342
Wickman,Bob	L	.260	146	38	7	0	1	19	24	29	.364	.329
Throws Right	R	.246	207	51	8	0	7	19	17	49	.310	.386
Wilkins,Marc	L	.246	114	28	6	0	2	11	18	25	.353	.351
Throws Right	R	.239	155	37	5	2	5	16	15	22	.318	.394
Williams,B	L	.273	44	12	2	1	0	7	10	7	.400	.364
Throws Right	R	.170	47	8	4	0	0	6	8	7	.291	.255
Williams,Mike	L	.269	26	7	1	0	1	3	3	6	.345	.423
Throws Right	R	.382	34	13	2	0	0	10	5	4	.463	.441
Williams,M	L	.364	11	4	0	0	1	4	1	2	.385	.636
Throws Left	R	.368	19	7	3	0	1	6	6	8	.520	.684
Williams,Shad	L	.000	2	0	0	0	0	0	1	0	.333	.000
Throws Right	R	.500	2	1	0	0	0	0	0	0	.500	.500
Williams,W	L	.271	395	107	17	3	15	42	46	67	.349	.443
Throws Right	R	.266	353	94	27	2	16	47	20	57	.305	.490
Winchester,S	L	.400	5	2	0	1	0	0	0	0	.500	.800
Throws Right	R	.350	20	7	1	0	1	5	2	3	.409	.550
Winston,D	L	.111	9	1	0	0	1	1	0	1	.200	.444
Throws Left	R	.194	36	7	3	0	3	7	3	7	.275	.528
Witasick,Jay	L	.333	18	6	1	0	1	4	3	3	.429	.556
Throws Right	R	.286	28	8	1	0	1	5	3	5	.355	.429
Witt,Bobby	L	.334	410	137	24	4	20	64	43	50	.398	.559
Throws Right	R	.255	423	108	21	2	13	49	31	71	.303	.407
Wohlers,Mark	L	.225	142	32	4	1	2	15	25	53	.337	.310
Throws Right	R	.223	112	25	4	0	2	12	13	39	.299	.313
Wojciechowski,S	L	.000	3	0	0	0	0	0	0	1	.000	.000
Throws Left	R	.415	41	17	1	0	2	7	1	4	.429	.585
Wolcott,Bob	L	.328	201	66	14	3	14	39	21	21	.390	.637
Throws Right	R	.300	210	63	19	0	8	27	8	37	.339	.505
Woodard,Steve	L	.293	82	24	8	1	3	13	2	19	.310	.524
Throws Right	R	.238	63	15	5	0	2	10	4	13	.304	.413
Worrell,Tim	L	.303	195	59	10	3	5	28	26	26	.388	.462
Throws Right	R	.260	219	57	10	1	9	39	24	55	.340	.438
Worrell,Todd	L	.225	138	31	3	1	7	20	12	33	.287	.413
Throws Right	R	.284	102	29	7	0	5	15	11	28	.354	.500
Wright,Jamey	L	.394	254	100	25	1	8	52	28	21	.453	.594
Throws Right	R	.279	351	98	18	5	11	47	43	38	.372	.453
Wright,Jaret	L	.280	175	49	11	2	4	22	14	26	.335	.434
Throws Right	R	.193	166	32	9	0	5	16	21	37	.293	.337
Yan,Esteban	L	.364	22	8	0	0	2	7	4	2	.462	.636
Throws Right	R	.462	26	12	2	1	1	9	3	2	.531	.731
AL	L	.278	--	--	--	--	--	--	--	--	.353	.445
	R	.267	--	--	--	--	--	--	--	--	.331	.418
NL	L	.270	--	--	--	--	--	--	--	--	.347	.418
	R	.256	--	--	--	--	--	--	--	--	.323	.403
MLB	L	.274	--	--	--	--	--	--	--	--	.350	.431
	R	.261	--	--	--	--	--	--	--	--	.327	.411

Leader Boards

If you want to put your knowledge of the 1997 season to the ultimate test, you've come to the right place. Sure you know that Ken Griffey Jr. led the AL in homers and RBI, sure you know that Tony Gwynn won another NL batting title, sure you know that Roger Clemens won 21 games and that Curt Schilling rang up an astonishing 319 batsmen.

But did you know that Paul O'Neill led the AL with a .428 average with runners in scoring position? Or that Albert Belle grounded into more double plays than anyone in baseball last season? Or that opponents hit a mere .184 off Pedro Martinez—the best figure in the NL? Or how about that Greg Maddux *averaged* an NL-best 3.18 pitches per batter? Or did you know that Cardinals reliever Tony Fossas allowed just 10 percent of his inherited runners to cross the plate?

Of course you didn't!

That's the beauty of the following pages. Our exclusive Leader Boards make you sound like a genius without all the hassle of memorization. Fascinating? Check out our Active Career Leaders. Fun? Check out the Bill James Leaders for '97 in such categories as Cheap Wins and Slow Hooks (and were not talking about a measurement for curveballs). You'll find a little bit of everything in this section, and it all adds up to a whole *lot* of useful information.

1997 American League Batting Leaders

Batting Average

Player, Team	AB	H	AVG
F Thomas, ChA	**530**	**184**	**.347**
E Martinez, Sea	542	179	.330
D Justice, Cle	495	163	.329
B Williams, NYA	509	167	.328
M Ramirez, Cle	561	184	.328
P O'Neill, NYA	553	179	.324
R Greer, Tex	601	193	.321
R Jefferson, Bos	489	156	.319
M Vaughn, Bos	527	166	.315
I Rodriguez, Tex	597	187	.313

On-Base Percentage

Player, Team	PA	OB	OBP
F Thomas, ChA	**649**	**296**	**.456**
E Martinez, Sea	678	309	.456
J Thome, Cle	627	265	.423
M Vaughn, Bos	628	264	.420
D Justice, Cle	582	243	.418
M Ramirez, Cle	651	270	.415
B Williams, NYA	591	241	.408
R Greer, Tex	689	279	.405
P O'Neill, NYA	637	254	.399
T Salmon, Ana	695	274	.394

Slugging Percentage

Player, Team	AB	TB	SLG
K Griffey Jr, Sea	**608**	**393**	**.646**
F Thomas, ChA	530	324	.611
D Justice, Cle	495	295	.596
J Gonzalez, Tex	533	314	.589
J Thome, Cle	496	287	.579
T Martinez, NYA	594	343	.577
M Vaughn, Bos	527	295	.560
E Martinez, Sea	542	300	.554
J Burnitz, Mil	494	273	.553
B Williams, NYA	509	277	.544

Games

C Ripken, Bal	**162**
B Hunter, Det	**162**
A Belle, ChA	161
T Clark, Det	159
D Jeter, NYA	159

Plate Appearances

D Jeter, NYA	**748**
B Hunter, Det	738
N Garciaparra, Bos	734
C Knoblauch, Min	716
R Durham, ChA	711

At Bats

N Garciaparra, Bos	**684**
B Hunter, Det	658
D Jeter, NYA	654
R Durham, ChA	634
A Belle, ChA	634

Hits

N Garciaparra, Bos	**209**
R Greer, Tex	193
D Jeter, NYA	190
G Anderson, Ana	189
I Rodriguez, Tex	187

Singles

G Anderson, Ana	**142**
D Jeter, NYA	**142**
B Hunter, Det	137
C Knoblauch, Min	133
2 players tied with	129

Doubles

J Valentin, Bos	**47**
J Cirillo, Mil	46
A Belle, ChA	45
N Garciaparra, Bos	44
3 players tied with	42

Triples

N Garciaparra, Bos	**11**
C Knoblauch, Min	10
J Damon, KC	8
J Burnitz, Mil	8
5 players tied with	7

Home Runs

K Griffey Jr, Sea	**56**
T Martinez, NYA	44
J Gonzalez, Tex	42
J Buhner, Sea	40
J Thome, Cle	40

Total Bases

K Griffey Jr, Sea	**393**
N Garciaparra, Bos	365
T Martinez, NYA	343
F Thomas, ChA	324
R Greer, Tex	319

Runs Scored

K Griffey Jr, Sea	**125**
N Garciaparra, Bos	122
C Knoblauch, Min	117
D Jeter, NYA	116
2 players tied with	112

Runs Batted In

K Griffey Jr, Sea	**147**
T Martinez, NYA	141
J Gonzalez, Tex	131
T Salmon, Ana	129
F Thomas, ChA	125

Ground Double Play

A Belle, ChA	**26**
J Buhner, Sea	23
M Bordick, Bal	23
E Martinez, Sea	21
J Valentin, Bos	21

Sacrifice Hits

O Vizquel, Cle	**16**
D Cruz, Det	14
M Bordick, Bal	12
4 players tied with	11

Sacrifice Flies

T Martinez, NYA	**13**
K Griffey Jr, Sea	12
J King, KC	12
P Molitor, Min	12
2 players tied with	11

Stolen Bases

B Hunter, Det	**74**
C Knoblauch, Min	62
T Goodwin, KC-Tex	50
O Nixon, Tor	47
O Vizquel, Cle	43

Caught Stealing

B Hunter, Det	**18**
T Goodwin, KC-Tex	16
R Durham, ChA	16
3 players tied with	13

Walks

J Thome, Cle	**120**
E Martinez, Sea	119
J Buhner, Sea	119
F Thomas, ChA	109
T Phillips, ChA-Ana	102

Intentional Walks

K Griffey Jr, Sea	**23**
M Vaughn, Bos	17
C Davis, KC	16
T Martinez, NYA	14
B Surhoff, Bal	14

Hit by Pitch

B Anderson, Bal	**19**
C Knoblauch, Min	17
D Easley, Det	16
P Meares, Min	16
J Cirillo, Mil	14

Strikeouts

J Buhner, Sea	**175**
M Nieves, Det	157
M Vaughn, Bos	154
J Thome, Cle	146
T Clark, Det	144

1997 National League Batting Leaders

Batting Average

Player, Team	AB	H	AVG
T Gwynn, SD	592	220	.372
L Walker, Col	568	208	.366
M Piazza, LA	556	201	.362
K Lofton, Atl	493	164	.333
W Joyner, SD	455	149	.327
M Grace, ChN	555	177	.319
A Galarraga, Col	600	191	.318
E Alfonzo, NYN	518	163	.315
R Mondesi, LA	616	191	.310
C Biggio, Hou	619	191	.309

On-Base Percentage

Player, Team	PA	OB	OBP
L Walker, Col	664	300	.452
B Bonds, SF	690	308	.446
M Piazza, LA	633	273	.431
J Bagwell, Hou	717	305	.425
G Sheffield, Fla	582	247	.424
C Biggio, Hou	744	309	.415
R Lankford, StL	565	232	.411
T Gwynn, SD	650	266	.409
K Lofton, Atl	562	230	.409
M Grace, ChN	653	267	.409

Slugging Percentage

Player, Team	AB	TB	SLG
L Walker, Col	568	409	.720
M Piazza, LA	556	355	.638
J Bagwell, Hou	566	335	.592
A Galarraga, Col	600	351	.585
R Lankford, StL	465	272	.585
B Bonds, SF	532	311	.585
T Hundley, NYN	417	229	.549
V Castilla, Col	612	335	.547
T Gwynn, SD	592	324	.547
R Mondesi, LA	616	333	.541

Games

J Bagwell, Hou	162
C Biggio, Hou	162
S Sosa, ChN	162
E Karros, LA	162
T Zeile, LA	160

Plate Appearances

C Biggio, Hou	744
E Young, LA	718
J Bagwell, Hou	717
E Karros, LA	700
S Sosa, ChN	694

At Bats

M Grudzielanek, Mon	649
S Sosa, ChN	642
T Womack, Pit	641
E Karros, LA	628
E Young, LA	622

Hits

T Gwynn, SD	220
L Walker, Col	208
M Piazza, LA	201
3 players tied with	191

Singles

T Gwynn, SD	152
E Renteria, Fla	143
T Womack, Pit	137
K Lofton, Atl	133
M Piazza, LA	128

Doubles

M Grudzielanek, Mon	54
T Gwynn, SD	49
L Walker, Col	46
M Lansing, Mon	45
R Mondesi, LA	42

Triples

D DeShields, StL	14
N Perez, Col	10
J Randa, Pit	9
W Guerrero, LA	9
T Womack, Pit	9

Home Runs

L Walker, Col	49
J Bagwell, Hou	43
A Galarraga, Col	41
3 players tied with	40

Total Bases

L Walker, Col	409
M Piazza, LA	355
A Galarraga, Col	351
V Castilla, Col	335
J Bagwell, Hou	335

Runs Scored

C Biggio, Hou	146
L Walker, Col	143
B Bonds, SF	123
A Galarraga, Col	120
J Bagwell, Hou	109

Runs Batted In

A Galarraga, Col	140
J Bagwell, Hou	135
L Walker, Col	130
M Piazza, LA	124
J Kent, SF	121

Ground Double Play

F McGriff, Atl	22
B Huskey, NYN	21
G Gaetti, StL	20
5 players tied with	19

Sacrifice Hits

E Renteria, Fla	19
T Glavine, Atl	17
B Butler, LA	15
R Ordonez, NYN	14
2 players tied with	13

Sacrifice Flies

T Gwynn, SD	12
B Gilkey, NYN	12
W Joyner, SD	10
J Kent, SF	10
3 players tied with	9

Stolen Bases

T Womack, Pit	60
D Sanders, Cin	56
D DeShields, StL	55
C Biggio, Hou	47
E Young, Col-LA	45

Caught Stealing

K Lofton, Atl	20
E Renteria, Fla	15
R Mondesi, LA	15
E Young, Col-LA	14
D DeShields, StL	14

Walks

B Bonds, SF	145
J Bagwell, Hou	127
G Sheffield, Fla	121
J Snow, SF	96
R Lankford, StL	95

Intentional Walks

B Bonds, SF	34
J Bagwell, Hou	27
T Hundley, NYN	16
L Walker, Col	14
J Snow, SF	13

Hit by Pitch

C Biggio, Hou	34
J Kendall, Pit	31
F Santangelo, Mon	25
J Blauser, Atl	20
A Galarraga, Col	17

Strikeouts

S Sosa, ChN	174
R Gant, StL	162
H Rodriguez, Mon	149
A Galarraga, Col	141
S Rolen, Phi	138

1997 American League Pitching Leaders

Earned Run Average

Pitcher, Team	IP	ER	ERA
R Clemens, Tor	**264.0**	**60**	**2.05**
R Johnson, Sea	213.0	54	2.28
D Cone, NYA	195.0	61	2.82
A Pettitte, NYA	240.1	77	2.88
J Thompson, Det	223.1	75	3.02
M Mussina, Bal	224.2	80	3.20
K Appier, KC	235.2	89	3.40
J Key, Bal	212.1	81	3.43
J Fassero, Sea	234.1	94	3.61
P Hentgen, Tor	264.0	108	3.68

Won-Lost Percentage

Pitcher, Team	W	L	WL%
R Johnson, Sea	**20**	**4**	**.833**
J Moyer, Sea	17	5	.773
R Clemens, Tor	21	7	.750
A Pettitte, NYA	18	7	.720
O Hershiser, Cle	14	6	.700
S Erickson, Bal	16	7	.696
C Finley, Ana	13	6	.684
B Radke, Min	20	10	.667
W Blair, Det	16	8	.667
D Cone, NYA	12	6	.667

Opposition Average

Pitcher, Team	AB	H	AVG
R Johnson, Sea	**758**	**147**	**.194**
R Clemens, Tor	957	204	.213
D Cone, NYA	710	155	.218
T Gordon, Bos	686	155	.226
J Thompson, Det	807	188	.233
M Mussina, Bal	843	197	.234
K Appier, KC	886	215	.243
C Finley, Ana	613	152	.248
J Fassero, Sea	906	226	.249
P Hentgen, Tor	995	253	.254

Games

M Myers, Det	**88**
B Groom, Oak	78
J Nelson, NYA	77
P Quantrill, Tor	77
H Slocumb, Bos-Sea	76

Games Started

A Pettitte, NYA	**35**
P Hentgen, Tor	**35**
B Radke, Min	**35**
J Fassero, Sea	**35**
6 pitchers tied with	34

Complete Games

P Hentgen, Tor	**9**
R Clemens, Tor	**9**
R Johnson, Sea	5
B Tewksbury, Min	5
D Wells, NYA	5

Games Finished

D Jones, Mil	**73**
H Slocumb, Bos-Sea	61
J Wetteland, Tex	58
R Aguilera, Min	57
R Myers, Bal	57

Wins

R Clemens, Tor	**21**
B Radke, Min	20
R Johnson, Sea	20
A Pettitte, NYA	18
J Moyer, Sea	17

Losses

C Eldred, Mil	**15**
J Baldwin, ChA	**15**
T Wakefield, Bos	**15**
3 pitchers tied with	14

Saves

R Myers, Bal	**45**
M Rivera, NYA	43
D Jones, Mil	36
T Jones, Det	31
J Wetteland, Tex	31

Shutouts

P Hentgen, Tor	**3**
R Clemens, Tor	**3**
6 pitchers tied with	2

Hits Allowed

J Navarro, ChA	**267**
P Hentgen, Tor	253
C Nagy, Cle	253
B Witt, Tex	245
T Belcher, KC	242

Doubles Allowed

J Fassero, Sea	**54**
D Wells, NYA	53
J Baldwin, ChA	53
T Belcher, KC	52
B Radke, Min	52

Triples Allowed

A Prieto, Oak	**9**
J Baldwin, ChA	7
O Hershiser, Cle	7
P Hentgen, Tor	7
5 pitchers tied with	6

Home Runs Allowed

A Watson, Ana	**37**
B Witt, Tex	33
D Springer, Ana	32
J Dickson, Ana	32
4 pitchers tied with	31

Batters Faced

P Hentgen, Tor	**1085**
R Clemens, Tor	1044
J Fassero, Sea	1010
C Nagy, Cle	991
B Radke, Min	989

Innings Pitched

R Clemens, Tor	**264.0**
P Hentgen, Tor	**264.0**
A Pettitte, NYA	240.1
B Radke, Min	239.2
K Appier, KC	235.2

Runs Allowed

J Navarro, ChA	**155**
T Belcher, KC	128
J Baldwin, ChA	128
A Watson, Ana	121
3 pitchers tied with	118

Strikeouts

R Clemens, Tor	**292**
R Johnson, Sea	291
D Cone, NYA	222
M Mussina, Bal	218
K Appier, KC	196

Walks Allowed

K Hill, Tex-Ana	**95**
C Eldred, Mil	89
T Wakefield, Bos	87
D Cone, NYA	86
J Fassero, Sea	84

Hit Batters

T Wakefield, Bos	**16**
A Sele, Bos	15
O Olivares, Det-Sea	13
R Clemens, Tor	12
2 pitchers tied with	11

Wild Pitches

J Baldwin, ChA	**14**
K Appier, KC	**14**
D Cone, NYA	**14**
J Navarro, ChA	**14**
J Fassero, Sea	13

Balks

L Hawkins, Min	**3**
H Irabu, NYA	**3**
P Spoljaric, Tor-Sea	**3**
J Baldwin, ChA	**3**
15 pitchers tied with	2

1997 National League Pitching Leaders

Earned Run Average

Pitcher, Team	IP	ER	ERA
P Martinez, Mon	**241.1**	**51**	**1.90**
G Maddux, Atl	232.2	57	2.20
D Kile, Hou	255.2	73	2.57
I Valdes, LA	196.2	58	2.65
K Brown, Fla	237.1	71	2.69
R Reed, NYN	208.1	67	2.89
T Glavine, Atl	240.0	79	2.96
D Neagle, Atl	233.1	77	2.97
C Schilling, Phi	254.1	84	2.97
J Smoltz, Atl	256.0	86	3.02

Won-Lost Percentage

Pitcher, Team	W	L	WL%
G Maddux, Atl	**19**	**4**	**.826**
D Neagle, Atl	20	5	.800
S Estes, SF	19	5	.792
D Kile, Hou	19	7	.731
P Martinez, Mon	17	8	.680
K Rueter, SF	13	6	.684
J Juden, Mon	11	5	.688
K Brown, Fla	16	8	.667
T Glavine, Atl	14	7	.667
R Martinez, LA	10	5	.667

Opposition Average

Pitcher, Team	AB	H	AVG
P Martinez, Mon	**860**	**158**	**.184**
C Park, LA	700	149	.213
S Estes, SF	726	162	.223
C Schilling, Phi	930	208	.224
D Kile, Hou	924	208	.225
T Glavine, Atl	870	197	.226
An Benes, StL	648	149	.230
T Stottlemyre, StL	671	155	.231
D Neagle, Atl	874	204	.233
I Valdes, LA	731	171	.234

Games

J Tavarez, SF	**89**
S Belinda, Cin	84
J Shaw, Cin	78
M Rojas, ChN-NYN	77
2 pitchers tied with	76

Games Started

J Smoltz, Atl	**35**
C Schilling, Phi	**35**
4 pitchers tied with	34

Complete Games

P Martinez, Mon	**13**
C Perez, Mon	8
M Hampton, Hou	7
J Smoltz, Atl	7
C Schilling, Phi	7

Games Finished

R Beck, SF	**66**
R Nen, Fla	65
J Shaw, Cin	62
R Bottalico, Phi	61
T Hoffman, SD	59

Wins

D Neagle, Atl	**20**
D Kile, Hou	19
S Estes, SF	19
G Maddux, Atl	19
3 pitchers tied with	17

Losses

M Leiter, Phi	**17**
S Cooke, Pit	15
J Lieber, Pit	14
T Mulholland, ChN-SF	13
C Perez, Mon	13

Saves

J Shaw, Cin	**42**
T Hoffman, SD	37
R Beck, SF	37
J Franco, NYN	36
D Eckersley, StL	36

Shutouts

C Perez, Mon	**5**
D Neagle, Atl	4
D Kile, Hou	4
P Martinez, Mon	4
10 pitchers tied with	2

Hits Allowed

J Smoltz, Atl	**234**
S Trachsel, ChN	225
F Castillo, ChN-Col	220
M Hampton, Hou	217
M Leiter, Phi	216

Doubles Allowed

M Leiter, Phi	**58**
C Perez, Mon	51
C Schilling, Phi	49
F Castillo, ChN-Col	46
D Neagle, Atl	46

Triples Allowed

M Clark, NYN-ChN	**11**
H Nomo, LA	**11**
A Leiter, Fla	9
A Fernandez, Fla	9
C Perez, Mon	9

Home Runs Allowed

S Trachsel, ChN	**32**
M Gardner, SF	28
K Foster, ChN	27
R Bailey, Col	27
5 pitchers tied with	25

Batters Faced

D Kile, Hou	**1056**
J Smoltz, Atl	1043
C Schilling, Phi	1009
K Brown, Fla	976
T Glavine, Atl	970

Innings Pitched

J Smoltz, Atl	**256.0**
D Kile, Hou	255.2
C Schilling, Phi	254.1
P Martinez, Mon	241.1
T Glavine, Atl	240.0

Runs Allowed

M Leiter, Phi	**132**
F Castillo, ChN-Col	121
J Wright, Col	113
S Trachsel, ChN	110
C Perez, Mon	109

Strikeouts

C Schilling, Phi	**319**
P Martinez, Mon	305
J Smoltz, Atl	241
H Nomo, LA	233
2 pitchers tied with	205

Walks Allowed

S Estes, SF	**100**
D Kile, Hou	94
H Nomo, LA	92
A Leiter, Fla	91
T Glavine, Atl	79

Hit Batters

K Brown, Fla	**14**
R Bailey, Col	13
5 pitchers tied with	12

Wild Pitches

M Remlinger, Cin	**12**
M Leiter, Phi	11
S Estes, SF	10
H Nomo, LA	10
J Smoltz, Atl	10

Balks

H Nomo, LA	**4**
6 pitchers tied with	3

1997 American League Special Batting Leaders

Scoring Position

Player, Team	AB	H	AVG
P O'Neill, NYA	159	68	.428
F Thomas, ChA	139	58	.417
R Coomer, Min	135	50	.370
J Cirillo, Mil	149	54	.362
D Justice, Cle	127	45	.354
M Stanley, Bos-NYA	100	35	.350
T Salmon, Ana	178	62	.348
D Wilson, Sea	121	42	.347
T O'Leary, Bos	132	45	.341
B Higginson, Det	151	51	.338

Leadoff On-Base%

Player, Team	PA	OB	OBP
T Raines, NYA	252	105	.417
B Anderson, Bal	648	258	.398
D Jeter, NYA	482	190	.394
C Knoblauch, Min	712	278	.390
T Phillips, ChA-Ana	535	208	.389
S Stewart, Tor	189	70	.370
D Mashore, Oak	311	115	.370
O Vizquel, Cle	149	55	.369
J Offerman, KC	382	140	.366
M McLemore, Tex	307	109	.355

Cleanup Slugging%

Player, Team	AB	TB	SLG
M McGwire, Oak	360	217	.603
J Gonzalez, Tex	529	313	.592
J Edmonds, Ana	150	85	.567
M Ramirez, Cle	159	90	.566
J Thome, Cle	152	86	.566
T Martinez, NYA	463	259	.559
E Martinez, Sea	531	296	.557
T Salmon, Ana	317	170	.536
D Nilsson, Mil	229	121	.528
R Jefferson, Bos	344	175	.509

Vs LHP

R Coomer, Min	.415
T Fernandez, Cle	.407
J Offerman, KC	.380
G Berroa, Oak-Bal	.358
D Wilson, Sea	.357

Vs RHP

R Jefferson, Bos	.352
P O'Neill, NYA	.346
E Martinez, Sea	.345
F Thomas, ChA	.344
J Valentin, Bos	.337

Late & Close

S Alomar, Cle	.397
O Vizquel, Cle	.382
D Erstad, Ana	.381
T Martinez, NYA	.378
J Valentin, Bos	.374

Bases Loaded

K Griffey Jr, Sea	.857
J Cirillo, Mil	.625
J Carter, Tor	.600
B Surhoff, Bal	.588
N Garciaparra, Bos	.583

OBP vs LHP

R Coomer, Min	.459
J Buhner, Sea	.449
G Berroa, Oak-Bal	.444
B Williams, NYA	.443
M Vaughn, Bos	.440

OBP vs RHP

E Martinez, Sea	.469
F Thomas, ChA	.461
J Thome, Cle	.445
D Justice, Cle	.432
P O'Neill, NYA	.427

BA at Home

R Greer, Tex	.370
D Justice, Cle	.353
I Rodriguez, Tex	.347
M Vaughn, Bos	.338
R Jefferson, Bos	.337

BA on the Road

F Thomas, ChA	.373
B Williams, NYA	.353
E Martinez, Sea	.339
P O'Neill, NYA	.338
M Ramirez, Cle	.323

SLG vs LHP

D Wilson, Sea	.651
J Gonzalez, Tex	.649
M Williams, Cle	.647
J Buhner, Sea	.627
D Justice, Cle	.616

SLG vs RHP

K Griffey Jr, Sea	.699
J Thome, Cle	.638
T Martinez, NYA	.636
E Martinez, Sea	.596
J Burnitz, Mil	.592

SB Success %

M Cameron, ChA	92.0
C Knoblauch, Min	86.1
B Roberts, KC-Cle	85.7
A Rodriguez, Sea	82.9
O Nixon, Tor	82.5

Times on Base

E Martinez, Sea	309
F Thomas, ChA	296
C Knoblauch, Min	279
R Greer, Tex	279
2 players tied with	274

AB per HR

K Griffey Jr, Sea	10.9
J Thome, Cle	12.4
J Gonzalez, Tex	12.7
T Martinez, NYA	13.5
J Buhner, Sea	13.5

Ground/Fly Ratio

J Franco, Cle-Mil	3.75
D Jeter, NYA	3.05
R Jefferson, Bos	2.19
T Goodwin, KC-Tex	2.14
B Hunter, Det	2.05

GDP/GDP Opp

B Anderson, Bal	0.9
J Damon, KC	3.1
D Martinez, ChA	3.7
M Nieves, Det	3.8
W Boggs, NYA	4.0

% CS by Catchers

I Rodriguez, Tex	56.0
J Leyritz, Ana-Tex	43.5
D Wilson, Sea	43.1
B Santiago, Tor	39.2
J Fabregas, Ana-ChA	35.7

Pitches Seen

D Jeter, NYA	2923
C Knoblauch, Min	2896
B Hunter, Det	2820
R Durham, ChA	2807
2 players tied with	2799

Pitches per PA

J Thome, Cle	4.46
J Franco, Cle-Mil	4.22
J Buhner, Sea	4.20
T Phillips, ChA-Ana	4.15
E Martinez, Sea	4.13

% Pitches Taken

E Martinez, Sea	66.5
J Thome, Cle	65.6
W Boggs, NYA	64.9
S Hatteberg, Bos	63.1
F Thomas, ChA	62.7

Steals of Third

B Hunter, Det	14
C Knoblauch, Min	12
A Rodriguez, Sea	11
O Vizquel, Cle	10
4 players tied with	6

1997 National League Special Batting Leaders

Scoring Position

Player, Team	AB	H	AVG
T Gwynn, SD	146	67	.459
E Alfonzo, NYN	115	48	.417
J Olerud, NYN	130	50	.385
L Walker, Col	140	51	.364
M Piazza, LA	147	53	.361
C Biggio, Hou	123	44	.358
W Joyner, SD	133	47	.353
K Lofton, Atl	111	39	.351
L Johnson, NYN-ChN	89	30	.337
R Sandberg, ChN	112	37	.330

Leadoff On-Base%

Player, Team	PA	OB	OBP
F Santangelo, Mon	185	79	.427
C Biggio, Hou	737	308	.418
R Henderson, SD	350	146	.417
K Lofton, Atl	560	229	.409
J Blauser, Atl	156	61	.391
B Butler, LA	328	125	.381
M Cummings, Pit-Phi	217	81	.373
L Johnson, NYN-ChN	439	162	.369
E Young, Col-LA	645	231	.358
D DeShields, StL	532	188	.353

Cleanup Slugging%

Player, Team	AB	TB	SLG
B Bonds, SF	221	128	.579
R Lankford, StL	199	115	.578
T Hundley, NYN	374	216	.578
A Galarraga, Col	539	299	.555
K Caminiti, SD	470	244	.519
K Young, Pit	298	154	.517
E Perez, Cin	211	108	.512
S Rolen, Phi	288	146	.507
S Sosa, ChN	554	276	.498
D Segui, Mon	438	216	.493

Vs LHP

V Castilla, Col	.380
E Alfonzo, NYN	.378
M Piazza, LA	.363
T Gwynn, SD	.356
B Huskey, NYN	.338

Vs RHP

L Walker, Col	.389
T Gwynn, SD	.378
M Piazza, LA	.361
W Joyner, SD	.341
K Lofton, Atl	.331

Late & Close

T Gwynn, SD	.395
J Blauser, Atl	.382
J Kendall, Pit	.373
M Lewis, SF	.370
J Vizcaino, SF	.368

Bases Loaded

T Gwynn, SD	.615
E Alfonzo, NYN	.600
J Allensworth, Pit	.600
D Bichette, Col	.563
J Kent, SF	.500

OBP vs LHP

M Piazza, LA	.450
E Alfonzo, NYN	.448
C Biggio, Hou	.444
V Castilla, Col	.434
J Bagwell, Hou	.432

OBP vs RHP

L Walker, Col	.470
B Bonds, SF	.455
R Lankford, StL	.426
M Piazza, LA	.426
J Bagwell, Hou	.423

BA at Home

L Walker, Col	.384
T Gwynn, SD	.378
D Bichette, Col	.362
M Grace, ChN	.355
M Piazza, LA	.355

BA on the Road

M Piazza, LA	.368
T Gwynn, SD	.365
L Walker, Col	.346
K Lofton, Atl	.345
W Joyner, SD	.331

SLG vs LHP

V Castilla, Col	.698
R Lankford, StL	.662
A Galarraga, Col	.643
M Piazza, LA	.621
B Bonds, SF	.584

SLG vs RHP

L Walker, Col	.788
M Piazza, LA	.644
J Bagwell, Hou	.630
T Hundley, NYN	.601
J Snow, SF	.595

SB Success %

T Womack, Pit	89.6
S Javier, SF	89.3
R Henderson, SD	87.9
C Biggio, Hou	82.5
B Bonds, SF	82.2

Times on Base

C Biggio, Hou	309
B Bonds, SF	308
J Bagwell, Hou	305
L Walker, Col	300
M Piazza, LA	273

AB per HR

L Walker, Col	11.6
J Bagwell, Hou	13.2
B Bonds, SF	13.3
M Piazza, LA	13.9
T Hundley, NYN	13.9

Ground/Fly Ratio

J Vizcaino, SF	2.29
K Lofton, Atl	2.18
Q Veras, SD	2.14
E Renteria, Fla	2.07
R White, Mon	1.89

GDP/GDP Opp

C Biggio, Hou	0.0
F Santangelo, Mon	1.6
P Reese, Cin	2.0
R Gant, StL	2.3
E Alfonzo, NYN	3.7

% CS by Catchers

B Ausmus, Hou	49.5
C Johnson, Fla	47.5
J Kendall, Pit	37.1
J Reed, Col	35.6
M Difelice, StL	35.4

Pitches Seen

J Bagwell, Hou	2818
T Zeile, LA	2757
C Biggio, Hou	2730
E Karros, LA	2683
S Sosa, ChN	2650

Pitches per PA

T Hundley, NYN	4.30
R Lankford, StL	4.25
R Gant, StL	4.17
T Zeile, LA	4.10
D Hamilton, SF	4.02

% Pitches Taken

R Henderson, SD	68.4
T Zeile, LA	65.7
W Weiss, Col	64.7
J Olerud, NYN	64.0
G Sheffield, Fla	63.5

Steals of Third

D Sanders, Cin	21
T Womack, Pit	16
C Biggio, Hou	14
E Young, Col-LA	10
2 players tied with	9

1997 American League Special Pitching Leaders

Baserunners Per 9 IP

Player, Team	IP	BR	BR/9
R Clemens, Tor	264.0	284	9.68
R Johnson, Sea	213.0	234	9.89
M Mussina, Bal	224.2	254	10.18
J Thompson, Det	223.1	256	10.32
B Radke, Min	239.2	289	10.85
K Appier, KC	235.2	293	11.19
A Pettitte, NYA	240.1	301	11.27
P Hentgen, Tor	264.0	331	11.28
J Moyer, Sea	188.2	237	11.31
D Cone, NYA	195.0	245	11.31

Run Support Per 9 IP

Player, Team	IP	R	R/9
J Moyer, Sea	188.2	162	7.73
T Belcher, KC	213.1	155	6.54
A Pettitte, NYA	240.1	174	6.52
D Drabek, ChA	169.1	121	6.43
A Sele, Bos	177.1	126	6.39
J Fassero, Sea	234.1	164	6.30
W Blair, Det	175.0	122	6.27
C Finley, Ana	164.0	114	6.26
B Radke, Min	239.2	163	6.12
J Burkett, Tex	189.1	128	6.08

Save Percentage

Player, Team	OP	SV	SV%
R Myers, Bal	46	45	.978
D Jones, Mil	38	36	.947
T Percival, Ana	31	27	.871
R Hernandez, ChA	31	27	.871
T Jones, Det	36	31	.861
J Wetteland, Tex	37	31	.838
M Rivera, NYA	52	43	.827
H Slocumb, Bos-Sea	33	27	.818
R Aguilera, Min	33	26	.788
B Taylor, Oak	30	23	.767

Hits per 9 IP

R Johnson, Sea	6.21
R Clemens, Tor	6.95
D Cone, NYA	7.15
J Thompson, Det	7.58
T Gordon, Bos	7.64

Home Runs per 9 IP

A Pettitte, NYA	0.26
R Clemens, Tor	0.31
T Gordon, Bos	0.49
B Tewksbury, Min	0.64
S Erickson, Bal	0.65

Strikeouts per 9 IP

R Johnson, Sea	12.3
D Cone, NYA	10.2
R Clemens, Tor	10.0
M Mussina, Bal	8.7
C Finley, Ana	8.5

GDP per 9 IP

O Hershiser, Cle	1.4
A Pettitte, NYA	1.3
S Erickson, Bal	1.3
O Olivares, Det-Sea	1.1
B Tewksbury, Min	1.1

Vs LHB

R Clemens, Tor	.205
D Cone, NYA	.213
M Mussina, Bal	.221
T Gordon, Bos	.231
P Hentgen, Tor	.241

Vs RHB

R Johnson, Sea	.186
J Mercedes, Mil	.215
T Gordon, Bos	.220
B Radke, Min	.221
R Clemens, Tor	.222

OBP Leadoff Inning

B Radke, Min	.236
R Johnson, Sea	.241
A Pettitte, NYA	.255
R Clemens, Tor	.275
J Key, Bal	.281

BA Allowed ScPos

R Johnson, Sea	.154
J Key, Bal	.179
R Clemens, Tor	.180
M Mussina, Bal	.193
D Cone, NYA	.221

SLG Allowed

R Clemens, Tor	.290
R Johnson, Sea	.318
T Gordon, Bos	.319
D Cone, NYA	.332
A Pettitte, NYA	.335

OBP Allowed

R Clemens, Tor	.273
R Johnson, Sea	.277
M Mussina, Bal	.282
J Thompson, Det	.289
B Radke, Min	.293

PkOf Throw/Runner

S Kamieniecki, Bal	1.63
A Watson, Ana	1.58
A Sele, Bos	1.29
J Key, Bal	1.29
C Finley, Ana	1.27

SB% Allowed

O Hershiser, Cle	33.3
J Dickson, Ana	41.7
O Olivares, Det-Sea	42.9
P Hentgen, Tor	44.4
R Johnson, Sea	44.8

Pitches per Batter

B Tewksbury, Min	3.43
S Erickson, Bal	3.46
D Wells, NYA	3.52
O Hershiser, Cle	3.53
D Springer, Ana	3.55

Grd/Fly Ratio Off

S Erickson, Bal	2.88
C Nagy, Cle	2.32
O Hershiser, Cle	2.23
A Pettitte, NYA	2.11
T Gordon, Bos	1.99

K/BB Ratio

J Burkett, Tex	4.63
R Clemens, Tor	4.29
M Mussina, Bal	4.04
R Johnson, Sea	3.78
B Radke, Min	3.63

Wins in Relief

A Rhodes, Bal	10
D Patterson, Tex	10
B Ayala, Sea	10
A Small, Oak	9
3 pitchers tied with	7

Holds

B Wickman, Mil	28
D Plesac, Tor	27
M Stanton, NYA	26
J Nelson, NYA	22
J Orosco, Bal	21

Blown Saves

N Charlton, Sea	11
M Rivera, NYA	9
M Timlin, Tor-Sea	8
5 pitchers tied with	7

% Inherited Scored

J Nelson, NYA	20.8
B Groom, Oak	20.8
A Benitez, Bal	21.1
M Holtz, Ana	21.4
R Villone, Mil	21.6

1st Batter OBP

J Orosco, Bal	.070
T Percival, Ana	.106
J Wetteland, Tex	.107
M Stanton, NYA	.138
J Nelson, NYA	.143

1997 National League Special Pitching Leaders

Baserunners Per 9 IP

Player, Team	IP	BR	BR/9
P Martinez, Mon	241.1	234	8.73
G Maddux, Atl	232.2	226	8.74
C Schilling, Phi	254.1	271	9.59
R Reed, NYN	208.1	222	9.59
D Neagle, Atl	233.1	259	9.99
I Valdes, LA	196.2	221	10.11
J Smoltz, Atl	256.0	298	10.48
T Glavine, Atl	240.0	280	10.50
C Park, LA	192.0	227	10.64
A Fernandez, Fla	220.2	266	10.85

Run Support Per 9 IP

Player, Team	IP	R	R/9
M Hampton, Hou	223.0	153	6.17
S Estes, SF	201.0	133	5.96
R Bailey, Col	191.0	125	5.89
F Castillo, Col	184.1	119	5.81
H Nomo, LA	207.1	132	5.73
D Neagle, Atl	233.1	147	5.67
K Rueter, SF	190.2	119	5.62
D Kile, Hou	255.2	155	5.46
M Leiter, Phi	182.2	109	5.37
F Cordova, Pit	178.2	106	5.34

Save Percentage

Player, Team	OP	SV	SV%
J Shaw, Cin	49	42	.857
J Franco, NYN	42	36	.857
R Loiselle, Pit	34	29	.853
U Urbina, Mon	32	27	.844
T Hoffman, SD	44	37	.841
D Eckersley, StL	43	36	.837
R Nen, Fla	42	35	.833
R Bottalico, Phi	41	34	.829
M Wohlers, Atl	40	33	.825
R Beck, SF	45	37	.822

Hits per 9 IP

P Martinez, Mon	5.89
C Park, LA	6.98
S Estes, SF	7.25
D Kile, Hou	7.32
C Schilling, Phi	7.36

Home Runs per 9 IP

G Maddux, Atl	0.35
K Brown, Fla	0.38
An Benes, StL	0.46
M Morris, StL	0.50
S Estes, SF	0.54

Strikeouts per 9 IP

P Martinez, Mon	11.4
C Schilling, Phi	11.3
H Nomo, LA	10.1
Al Benes, StL	8.9
J Smoltz, Atl	8.5

GDP per 9 IP

J Thomson, Col	1.4
T Glavine, Atl	1.2
R Bailey, Col	1.2
M Hampton, Hou	1.1
C Perez, Mon	1.0

Vs LHB

P Martinez, Mon	.183
B Tomko, Cin	.190
G Maddux, Atl	.213
R Reed, NYN	.231
D Hermanson, Mon	.232

Vs RHB

P Martinez, Mon	.184
C Park, LA	.187
T Stottlemyre, StL	.189
A Fernandez, Fla	.192
Al Benes, StL	.205

OBP Leadoff Inning

R Reed, NYN	.219
D Neagle, Atl	.236
B Jones, NYN	.241
D Burba, Cin	.260
J Smoltz, Atl	.260

BA Allowed ScPos

D Kile, Hou	.171
T Glavine, Atl	.183
R Martinez, LA	.190
T Candiotti, LA	.192
An Benes, StL	.199

SLG Allowed

P Martinez, Mon	.277
G Maddux, Atl	.311
S Estes, SF	.311
K Brown, Fla	.319
An Benes, StL	.330

OBP Allowed

P Martinez, Mon	.250
G Maddux, Atl	.256
C Schilling, Phi	.271
R Reed, NYN	.272
D Neagle, Atl	.277

PkOf Throw/Runner

I Valdes, LA	1.65
M Gardner, SF	1.57
K Rueter, SF	1.41
M Leiter, Phi	1.34
F Castillo, ChN-Col	1.22

SB% Allowed

T Mulholland, SF	20.0
R Reed, NYN	33.3
M Hampton, Hou	36.4
K Rueter, SF	36.4
C Park, LA	37.5

Pitches per Batter

G Maddux, Atl	3.18
C Perez, Mon	3.35
R Bailey, Col	3.38
R Reed, NYN	3.39
M Morgan, Cin	3.39

Grd/Fly Ratio Off

K Brown, Fla	3.64
S Cooke, Pit	2.87
A Ashby, SD	2.35
G Maddux, Atl	2.31
M Hampton, Hou	2.26

K/BB Ratio

G Maddux, Atl	8.85
C Schilling, Phi	5.50
P Martinez, Mon	4.55
J Smoltz, Atl	3.83
R Reed, NYN	3.65

Wins in Relief

M Wilkins, Pit	9
R Nen, Fla	9
6 pitchers tied with	7

Holds

S Belinda, Cin	28
J Tavarez, SF	26
S Radinsky, LA	26
J Powell, Fla	24
B Patterson, ChN	22

Blown Saves

G McMichael, NYN	11
T Worrell, LA	9
R Beck, SF	8
8 pitchers tied with	7

% Inherited Scored

T Fossas, StL	10.0
A Embree, Atl	14.0
M Remlinger, Cin	16.0
M Wilkins, Pit	16.1
T Adams, ChN	16.3

1st Batter OBP

D Bochtler, SD	.026
D Dreifort, LA	.128
T Hoffman, SD	.147
B Wagner, Hou	.148
M Remlinger, Cin	.160

1997 Active Career Batting Leaders

Batting Average

Player	AB	H	AVG
T Gwynn	8187	2780	.340
M Piazza	2558	854	.334
W Boggs	8453	2800	.331
F Thomas	3821	1261	.330
E Martinez	3818	1210	.317
K Lofton	3314	1047	.316
A Rodriguez	1384	435	.314
R Greer	1837	573	.312
M Grace	5458	1691	.310
P Molitor	10333	3178	.308
H Morris	3255	994	.305
M Ramirez	1938	590	.304
J Bagwell	3657	1112	.304
C Knoblauch	3939	1197	.304
R Alomar	5460	1659	.304
K Griffey Jr	4593	1389	.302
R Jefferson	1721	520	.302
W Clark	5941	1795	.302
G Anderson	1618	487	.301
J Franco	7243	2177	.301
S Mack	2648	795	.300
D Jeter	1284	385	.300
B Larkin	5170	1547	.299
R Mondesi	2306	690	.299
V Castilla	2256	674	.299

On-Base Percentage

Player	PA	OB	OBP
F Thomas	4789	2166	.452
E Martinez	4577	1935	.423
W Boggs	9894	4151	.420
J Bagwell	4407	1803	.409
J Thome	2615	1068	.408
B Bonds	7400	3019	.408
R Henderson	10836	4401	.406
M Piazza	2856	1136	.398
J Olerud	4314	1708	.396
M Ramirez	2258	888	.393
D Magadan	4208	1653	.393
M Vaughn	3771	1481	.393
T Salmon	3151	1236	.392
R Greer	2111	828	.392
C Knoblauch	4564	1784	.391
T Gwynn	8984	3507	.390
T Raines	9552	3686	.386
G Sheffield	4327	1669	.386
K Lofton	3716	1426	.384
M Grace	6214	2384	.384
M McGwire	5630	2148	.382
K Griffey Jr	5256	2002	.381
F McGriff	6648	2530	.381
W Clark	6833	2600	.381
D Justice	3930	1495	.380

Slugging Percentage

Player	AB	TB	SLG
F Thomas	3821	2294	.600
M Piazza	2558	1474	.576
A Belle	4075	2306	.566
K Griffey Jr	4593	2580	.562
J Gonzalez	3663	2041	.557
M McGwire	4622	2570	.556
B Bonds	6069	3343	.551
M Ramirez	1938	1059	.546
L Walker	3700	2006	.542
J Thome	2143	1160	.541
R Klesko	1600	860	.538
J Bagwell	3657	1959	.536
A Rodriguez	1384	739	.534
M Vaughn	3219	1714	.532
T Salmon	2667	1406	.527
K Mitchell	4007	2105	.525
V Castilla	2256	1184	.525
F McGriff	5693	2968	.521
J Canseco	5459	2819	.516
E Martinez	3818	1960	.513
D Justice	3353	1720	.513
R Mondesi	2306	1179	.511
J Edmonds	1841	926	.503
D Strawberry	5074	2548	.502
B Higginson	1396	699	.501

Games

E Murray	3026
P Molitor	2557
C Ripken	2543
H Baines	2463
R Henderson	2460
G Gaetti	2261
C Davis	2255
W Boggs	2226
B Butler	2213
T Raines	2186
R Sandberg	2164
T Gwynn	2095
J Carter	2063
T Phillips	1990
T Pena	1988

Runs Scored

R Henderson	1913
P Molitor	1707
E Murray	1627
T Raines	1475
C Ripken	1445
W Boggs	1422
B Butler	1359
R Sandberg	1318
B Bonds	1244
T Gwynn	1237
T Phillips	1190
C Davis	1170
H Baines	1168
J Carter	1119
J Franco	1104

Runs Batted In

E Murray	1917
C Ripken	1453
H Baines	1423
J Carter	1382
C Davis	1285
P Molitor	1238
G Gaetti	1224
J Canseco	1107
B Bonds	1094
R Sandberg	1061
B Bonilla	1061
A Galarraga	1051
R Sierra	1036
F McGriff	1007
W Clark	1004

Stolen Bases

R Henderson	1231
T Raines	795
V Coleman	752
B Butler	558
O Nixon	557
P Molitor	495
B Bonds	417
J Samuel	383
D DeShields	356
K Lofton	354
M Grissom	345
R Sandberg	344
W McGee	338
E Davis	335
R Alomar	322

Hits

E Murray	3255
P Molitor	3178
W Boggs	2800
T Gwynn	2780
C Ripken	2715
H Baines	2561
R Henderson	2550
T Raines	2439
R Sandberg	2386
B Butler	2375
C Davis	2222
J Franco	2177
W McGee	2118
G Gaetti	2101
J Carter	2083

Home Runs

E Murray	504
M McGwire	387
J Carter	378
B Bonds	374
C Ripken	370
J Canseco	351
H Baines	339
F McGriff	339
G Gaetti	332
C Davis	328
D Strawberry	308
C Fielder	302
K Griffey Jr	294
A Galarraga	288
R Sandberg	282

Strikeouts

C Davis	1580
E Murray	1516
G Gaetti	1486
J Canseco	1471
A Galarraga	1469
J Samuel	1429
D Tartabull	1362
T Phillips	1355
J Carter	1326
M Tettleton	1307
H Baines	1287
R Henderson	1276
P Incaviglia	1267
R Sandberg	1260
F McGriff	1247

AB per HR

M McGwire	11.9
J Gonzalez	14.3
F Thomas	14.9
A Belle	15.0
M Piazza	15.2
J Canseco	15.6
K Griffey Jr	15.6
C Fielder	15.7
R Klesko	16.0
J Thome	16.1
J Buhner	16.2
B Bonds	16.2
D Strawberry	16.5
F McGriff	16.8
M Vaughn	16.9

Doubles

P Molitor	576
E Murray	560
W Boggs	541
C Ripken	517
T Gwynn	460
H Baines	439
R Henderson	426
J Carter	410
R Sandberg	403
T Raines	401
G Gaetti	400
C Davis	392
B Bonilla	372
R Palmeiro	360
B Bonds	359

Walks

R Henderson	1772
E Murray	1333
W Boggs	1328
B Bonds	1227
T Raines	1209
T Phillips	1201
B Butler	1129
C Davis	1107
P Molitor	1049
C Ripken	1016
M Tettleton	949
H Baines	932
M McGwire	890
F McGriff	880
F Thomas	879

K/BB Ratio

W Boggs	0.50
T Gwynn	0.55
M Grace	0.64
E Young	0.66
F Thomas	0.66
G Jefferies	0.71
R Henderson	0.72
T Raines	0.72
D Magadan	0.74
J Reed	0.75
B Bonds	0.78
G Sheffield	0.78
B Butler	0.80
E Martinez	0.82
J Olerud	0.83

GDP/GDP Opp

E Williams	22.8
C Johnson	25.1
L Webster	27.3
T Pena	27.7
M Blowers	28.4
J Franco	28.4
R Gonzales	28.5
A Belle	29.1
B Huskey	29.9
J Lopez	30.3
T Steinbach	30.5
B Gates	30.7
G Myers	30.9
F Thomas	31.1
J Leyritz	31.3

Triples

B Butler	131
T Raines	111
P Molitor	109
L Johnson	107
J Samuel	102
W McGee	93
T Fernandez	90
V Coleman	89
T Gwynn	84
R Sandberg	76
S Finley	69
O Guillen	68
D White	65
R Henderson	59
D Martinez	59

Intentional Walks

B Bonds	260
E Murray	222
T Gwynn	189
C Davis	180
H Baines	173
W Boggs	172
W Clark	145
T Raines	142
K Griffey Jr	142
D Strawberry	127
B Bonilla	118
F Thomas	118
F McGriff	116
M Vaughn	105
C Ripken	103

SB Success %

E Davis	86.1
T Raines	84.8
S Javier	84.7
B Larkin	84.3
R Henderson	81.0
M Grissom	81.0
V Coleman	80.9
K Lofton	79.6
B Hunter	79.4
P Molitor	79.3
R Alomar	79.1
D White	78.9
D Bell	78.4
C Knoblauch	78.2
B Bonds	77.9

AB per RBI

F Thomas	4.5
J Gonzalez	4.6
A Belle	4.7
M McGwire	4.7
M Piazza	4.8
J Canseco	4.9
C Fielder	5.0
J Bagwell	5.1
M Vaughn	5.1
J Buhner	5.1
M Ramirez	5.2
K Griffey Jr	5.3
T Clark	5.3
T Salmon	5.3
R Klesko	5.3

1997 Active Career Pitching Leaders

Wins		Losses		Saves		Shutouts	
D Martinez	241	D Martinez	187	L Smith	478	R Clemens	41
R Clemens	213	D Darwin	172	D Eckersley	389	F Valenzuela	31
D Eckersley	193	D Eckersley	170	J Franco	359	D Martinez	29
G Maddux	184	M Morgan	167	R Myers	319	O Hershiser	25
J Key	180	K Gross	158	D Jones	278	D Gooden	24
O Hershiser	179	F Valenzuela	153	T Worrell	256	G Maddux	23
D Gooden	177	M Langston	150	J Montgomery	256	D Drabek	21
M Langston	174	R Honeycutt	143	R Aguilera	237	D Cone	21
F Valenzuela	173	T Candiotti	142	J Wetteland	211	D Eckersley	20
D Darwin	163	M Gubicza	136	R Beck	199	R Martinez	20
T Glavine	153	D Jackson	131	M Williams	192	M Langston	18
D Drabek	149	B Witt	131	G Olson	173	T Belcher	18
D Cone	148	O Hershiser	123	R Hernandez	165	R Johnson	17
K Gross	142	D Drabek	123	D Plesac	149	M Gubicza	16
C Finley	142	C Finley	120	T Hoffman	135	B Saberhagen	16

Games		Games Started		CG Freq		Innings Pitched	
L Smith	1022	D Martinez	557	D Eckersley	0.28	D Martinez	3908.2
D Eckersley	1021	F Valenzuela	424	F Valenzuela	0.27	D Eckersley	3246.0
J Orosco	956	R Clemens	416	R Clemens	0.26	R Clemens	3040.0
R Honeycutt	797	M Langston	407	B Saberhagen	0.24	F Valenzuela	2930.0
J Franco	771	O Hershiser	394	J McDowell	0.24	D Darwin	2868.0
P Assenmacher	760	J Key	378	G Maddux	0.22	M Langston	2819.2
M Jackson	694	K Gross	368	C Schilling	0.22	O Hershiser	2724.2
D Darwin	683	D Drabek	366	D Martinez	0.22	G Maddux	2598.1
D Plesac	680	G Maddux	365	M Langston	0.20	J Key	2512.1
R Myers	666	T Candiotti	364	K Brown	0.19	K Gross	2487.2
D Jones	653	D Eckersley	361	D Gooden	0.19	T Candiotti	2452.2
D Martinez	639	M Morgan	359	T Wakefield	0.19	D Gooden	2446.2
M Davis	624	D Gooden	351	P Hentgen	0.19	D Drabek	2426.1
M Williams	619	D Darwin	346	R Johnson	0.18	M Morgan	2338.0
T Worrell	617	B Witt	338	T Candiotti	0.18	B Saberhagen	2253.2

Batters Faced		Home Runs Allowed		Walks Allowed		Strikeouts	
D Martinez	16358	D Martinez	364	M Langston	1219	R Clemens	2882
D Eckersley	13363	D Eckersley	341	B Witt	1195	D Eckersley	2379
R Clemens	12428	D Darwin	298	F Valenzuela	1151	M Langston	2365
F Valenzuela	12398	M Langston	291	D Martinez	1146	D Martinez	2087
D Darwin	12056	J Key	249	K Gross	986	F Valenzuela	2074
M Langston	11908	K Gross	230	R Clemens	924	D Gooden	2067
O Hershiser	11351	F Valenzuela	226	C Finley	915	D Cone	2034
K Gross	10791	D Drabek	226	R Johnson	857	R Johnson	2000
G Maddux	10530	G Swindell	213	D Cone	836	D Darwin	1861
J Key	10392	C Finley	211	O Hershiser	831	G Maddux	1820
T Candiotti	10364	T Candiotti	206	D Darwin	825	O Hershiser	1786
D Gooden	10126	M Morgan	205	D Jackson	816	J Smoltz	1769
D Drabek	10034	R Clemens	203	D Gooden	792	S Fernandez	1743
M Morgan	9944	B Witt	198	T Candiotti	790	C Finley	1739
C Finley	9509	O Hershiser	194	M Gubicza	786	B Witt	1737

Earned Run Average

Player	IP	ER	ERA
J Franco	**936.0**	**267**	**2.57**
G Maddux	2598.1	810	2.81
J Montgomery	761.1	246	2.91
J Orosco	1127.1	370	2.95
R Clemens	3040.0	1003	2.97
P Martinez	912.1	304	3.00
L Smith	1289.1	434	3.03
R Myers	828.0	283	3.08
D Jones	865.2	298	3.10
D Cone	2189.0	762	3.13
O Hershiser	2724.2	985	3.25
J Fassero	1084.1	396	3.29
K Appier	1665.1	610	3.30
B Saberhagen	2253.2	826	3.30
D Gooden	2446.2	900	3.31

Winning Percentage

Player	W	L	W%
M Mussina	**105**	**49**	**.682**
D Gooden	177	97	.646
R Johnson	124	68	.646
R Clemens	213	118	.644
D Cone	148	86	.632
G Maddux	184	108	.630
P Martinez	65	39	.625
J Key	180	114	.612
R Martinez	116	74	.611
P Hentgen	82	53	.607
T Glavine	153	99	.607
J McDowell	122	80	.604
D Neagle	65	44	.596
O Hershiser	179	123	.593
J Guzman	70	50	.583

Opposition Batting

Player	AB	H	AVG
S Fernandez	**6793**	**1421**	**.209**
R Johnson	6261	1320	.211
P Martinez	3302	702	.213
M Jackson	3214	698	.217
J Orosco	4096	896	.219
D Cone	8046	1794	.223
R Clemens	11277	2563	.227
R Myers	3032	699	.231
J Montgomery	2824	655	.232
E Plunk	3707	861	.232
J Smoltz	7654	1779	.232
C Schilling	4637	1088	.235
L Smith	4790	1133	.237
N Charlton	2763	654	.237
A Leiter	3274	776	.237

Hits Per 9 Innings

Player	IP	H	H/9
R Johnson	**1734.0**	**1320**	**6.85**
S Fernandez	1866.2	1421	6.85
P Martinez	912.1	702	6.93
M Jackson	885.0	698	7.10
J Orosco	1127.1	896	7.15
D Cone	2189.0	1794	7.38
R Clemens	3040.0	2563	7.59
R Myers	828.0	699	7.60
E Plunk	1003.0	861	7.73
J Montgomery	761.1	655	7.74
J Smoltz	2060.1	1779	7.77
N Charlton	750.0	654	7.85
A Leiter	888.2	776	7.86
C Schilling	1242.2	1088	7.88
L Smith	1289.1	1133	7.91

Homeruns Per 9 Innings

Player	IP	HR	HR/9
G Maddux	**2598.1**	**128**	**0.44**
J Franco	936.0	51	0.49
K Brown	1921.1	113	0.53
D Jones	865.2	53	0.55
D Gooden	2446.2	156	0.57
D Jackson	2072.2	133	0.58
B Swift	1455.0	95	0.59
R Clemens	3040.0	203	0.60
T Glavine	2196.1	147	0.60
K Appier	1665.1	113	0.61
L Smith	1289.1	89	0.62
M Gubicza	2223.1	155	0.63
O Hershiser	2724.2	194	0.64
J Fassero	1084.1	78	0.65
B Ruffin	1268.0	92	0.65

Baserunners Per 9 Innings

Player	IP	BR	BR/9
P Martinez	**912.1**	**1046**	**10.32**
G Maddux	2598.1	2980	10.32
B Saberhagen	2253.2	2611	10.43
S Fernandez	1866.2	2177	10.50
C Schilling	1242.2	1457	10.55
M Mussina	1362.1	1605	10.60
R Clemens	3040.0	3585	10.61
D Eckersley	3246.0	3833	10.63
J Smoltz	2060.1	2499	10.92
J Montgomery	761.1	930	10.99
D Cone	2189.0	2691	11.06
D Gooden	2446.2	3032	11.15
J Key	2512.1	3121	11.18
K Appier	1665.1	2075	11.21
J Smiley	1907.2	2377	11.21

Strikeouts per 9 Innings

Player	IP	K	K/9
R Johnson	**1734.0**	**2000**	**10.38**
P Martinez	912.1	970	9.57
R Myers	828.0	843	9.16
L Smith	1289.1	1251	8.73
R Clemens	3040.0	2882	8.53
P Assenmacher	775.2	735	8.53
E Plunk	1003.0	944	8.47
S Fernandez	1866.2	1743	8.40
D Cone	2189.0	2034	8.36
J Orosco	1127.1	1018	8.13
D Plesac	822.2	742	8.12
C Schilling	1242.2	1119	8.10
M Jackson	885.0	795	8.08
N Charlton	750.0	667	8.00
M Davis	1145.0	1007	7.92

Walks per 9 Innings

Player	IP	BB	BB/9
B Tewksbury	**1658.2**	**272**	**1.48**
B Saberhagen	2253.2	431	1.72
S Reynolds	769.2	161	1.88
G Swindell	1915.2	416	1.95
D Jones	865.2	188	1.95
D Eckersley	3246.0	730	2.02
G Maddux	2598.1	609	2.11
K Tapani	1546.0	372	2.17
M Mussina	1362.1	328	2.17
J Burkett	1597.2	390	2.20
T Mulholland	1707.2	430	2.27
D Wells	1631.0	416	2.30
J Key	2512.1	645	2.31
J Smiley	1907.2	496	2.34
R Aguilera	1101.2	306	2.50

Strikeout to Walk Ratio

Player	K	BB	K/BB
S Reynolds	**661**	**161**	**4.11**
D Jones	721	188	3.84
B Saberhagen	1524	431	3.54
D Eckersley	2379	730	3.26
C Schilling	1119	349	3.21
P Martinez	970	306	3.17
G Swindell	1299	416	3.12
R Clemens	2882	924	3.12
G Maddux	1820	609	2.99
M Mussina	978	328	2.98
R Aguilera	890	306	2.91
B Tewksbury	752	272	2.76
D Neagle	757	278	2.72
P Assenmacher	735	279	2.63
J Fassero	939	358	2.62

1997 American League Bill James Leaders

Top Game Scores of the Year

Pitcher	Date	Opp	IP	H	R	ER	BB	K	SC
R Clemens, Tor	9/7	Tex	9.0	2	0	0	0	14	97
M Mussina, Bal	5/30	Cle	9.0	1	0	0	0	10	95
D Wells, NYA	7/30	Oak	9.0	3	0	0	3	16	94
R Johnson, Sea	8/8	ChA	9.0	5	0	0	3	19	93

Top Game Scores of the Year

Pitcher	Date	Opp	IP	H	R	ER	BB	K	SC
R Johnson, Sea	6/8	Det	8.0	1	0	0	3	15	92
S Sanders, Det	9/9	Tex	9.0	1	0	0	1	8	92
S Woodard, Mil	7/28	Tor	8.0	1	0	0	1	12	91

(BJ) Offensive Win Pct

F Thomas, ChA	.838
E Martinez, Sea	.792
J Thome, Cle	.787
D Justice, Cle	.783
M Vaughn, Bos	.778
K Griffey Jr, Sea	.773
B Williams, NYA	.747
R Greer, Tex	.742
M Ramirez, Cle	.740
T Martinez, NYA	.710

Power/Speed Number

A Rodriguez, Sea	25.6
N Garciaparra, Bos	25.4
D Easley, Det	24.6
K Griffey Jr, Sea	23.7
J Burnitz, Mil	23.0
J King, KC	20.4
D Erstad, Ana	18.9
T Fryman, Det	18.5
B Anderson, Bal	18.0
J Valentin, Mil	17.9

Tough Losses

J Thompson, Det	7
J Baldwin, ChA	6
S Karl, Mil	6
B Tewksbury, Min	5
K Appier, KC	5
B Moehler, Det	5
R Clemens, Tor	4
T Gordon, Bos	4
C Eldred, Mil	4
A Watson, Ana	4
J Mercedes, Mil	4

Runs Created

F Thomas, ChA	153
K Griffey Jr, Sea	152
E Martinez, Sea	140
R Greer, Tex	132
J Thome, Cle	131
M Vaughn, Bos	128
T Martinez, NYA	128
D Justice, Cle	124
M Ramirez, Cle	124
N Garciaparra, Bos	124
T Salmon, Ana	124

Secondary Average

J Thome, Cle	.534
K Griffey Jr, Sea	.485
J Buhner, Sea	.483
F Thomas, ChA	.470
E Martinez, Sea	.439
J Burnitz, Mil	.437
D Justice, Cle	.424
C Davis, KC	.415
T Martinez, NYA	.411
M Vaughn, Bos	.408

Slow Hooks

Blue Jays	22
White Sox	20
Royals	20
Athletics	19
Mariners	17
Angels	16
Red Sox	13
Indians	13
Rangers	13
Orioles	12
Brewers	12
Yankees	12
Twins	11
Tigers	7

Isolated Power (Power Pct)

K Griffey Jr, Sea	.342
J Gonzalez, Tex	.293
J Thome, Cle	.292
T Martinez, NYA	.281
J Burnitz, Mil	.271
D Justice, Cle	.267
C Delgado, Tor	.266
F Thomas, ChA	.264
J Buhner, Sea	.263
P Sorrento, Sea	.245

Cheap Wins

J Moyer, Sea	5
P Hentgen, Tor	4
C Eldred, Mil	4
R Robertson, Min	4
A Sele, Bos	4
J Thompson, Det	4
B Moehler, Det	4
11 pitchers tied with	3

Quick Hooks

Athletics	29
Brewers	26
Tigers	24
Orioles	21
Indians	21
Twins	19
Yankees	18
Red Sox	17
Rangers	17
Royals	16
White Sox	14
Mariners	14
Blue Jays	14
Angels	10

1997 National League Bill James Leaders

Top Game Scores of the Year

Pitcher	Date	Opp	IP	H	R	ER	BB	K	SC
F Cordova, Pit	7/12	Hou	9.0	0	0	0	2	10	95
K Brown, Fla	6/10	SF	9.0	0	0	0	0	7	94
A Fernandez, Fla	4/10	ChN	9.0	1	0	0	0	8	93
Al Benes, StL	5/16	Atl	9.0	1	0	0	3	11	93
P Martinez, Mon	6/14	Det	9.0	3	0	0	2	14	93

Top Game Scores of the Year

Pitcher	Date	Opp	IP	H	R	ER	BB	K	SC
P Martinez, Mon	7/13	Cin	9.0	1	0	0	1	9	93
S Estes, SF	4/26	Hou	9.0	2	0	0	1	9	91
S Estes, SF	7/4	Col	8.2	1	0	0	2	11	91
C Perez, Mon	9/3	Bos	9.0	2	0	0	0	8	91
K Brown, Fla	7/16	LA	9.0	1	1	0	1	8	90

(BJ) Offensive Win Pct

L Walker, Col	.889
M Piazza, LA	.845
B Bonds, SF	.829
J Bagwell, Hou	.812
C Biggio, Hou	.791
T Gwynn, SD	.788
R Lankford, StL	.786
A Galarraga, Col	.764
T Hundley, NYN	.740
K Caminiti, SD	.725

Power/Speed Number

L Walker, Col	39.4
B Bonds, SF	38.4
J Bagwell, Hou	36.0
R Mondesi, LA	31.0
C Biggio, Hou	30.0
S Sosa, ChN	27.3
R Lankford, StL	25.0
A Galarraga, Col	22.0
C Jones, Atl	20.5
R White, Mon	20.4

Tough Losses

P Martinez, Mon	7
Al Benes, StL	7
C Schilling, Phi	6
C Holt, Hou	6
An Benes, StL	5
C Perez, Mon	5
H Nomo, LA	5
13 pitchers tied with	4

Runs Created

L Walker, Col	187
J Bagwell, Hou	153
B Bonds, SF	151
M Piazza, LA	151
C Biggio, Hou	148
A Galarraga, Col	134
T Gwynn, SD	132
R Mondesi, LA	116
R Lankford, StL	115
V Castilla, Col	113

Secondary Average

B Bonds, SF	.620
J Bagwell, Hou	.567
L Walker, Col	.535
R Lankford, StL	.516
G Sheffield, Fla	.477
T Hundley, NYN	.472
J Snow, SF	.414
M Piazza, LA	.408
K Caminiti, SD	.401
C Biggio, Hou	.388

Slow Hooks

Rockies	23
Phillies	15
Expos	13
Padres	13
Mets	12
Marlins	12
Reds	9
Pirates	9
Cardinals	9
Braves	7
Cubs	5
Astros	5
Dodgers	5
Giants	3

Isolated Power (Power Pct)

L Walker, Col	.354
J Bagwell, Hou	.306
B Bonds, SF	.293
R Lankford, StL	.290
M Piazza, LA	.277
T Hundley, NYN	.276
A Galarraga, Col	.267
V Castilla, Col	.243
H Rodriguez, Mon	.235
R Mondesi, LA	.231

Cheap Wins

F Castillo, Col	5
S Hitchcock, SD	5
H Nomo, LA	4
J Wright, Col	4
J Gonzalez, ChN	4
13 pitchers tied with	3

Quick Hooks

Reds	28
Expos	26
Marlins	21
Padres	20
Giants	20
Cardinals	18
Dodgers	17
Mets	16
Pirates	16
Rockies	15
Phillies	14
Braves	13
Cubs	13
Astros	12

Player Profiles

As is our custom each year, we include in the *Major League Handbook* statistical profiles for a few of baseball's brightest stars. Last year, none shone brighter than Mark McGwire. Notice how he stepped up the longball pace in August and September—in a new ballpark, facing unfamiliar pitchers, no less. You'll get to see how impressive Curt Schilling's numbers really were—especially in the second half. And you'll begin to truly appreciate the season-long near-perfection that Randy Myers maintained as he saved 45 games in 46 chances. We'll bet you didn't know that he gave up only 10 extra-base hits all year, though.

If you enjoy these profiles, you might want to check out *STATS Player Profiles 1998,* which has breakdowns like these for *every* major league player.

	Avg	G	AB	R	H	2B	3B	HR	RBI	BB	SO	HBP	GDP	SB	CS	OBP	SLG	IBB	SH	SF	#Pit	#P/PA	GB	FB	G/F
1997 Season	.274	156	540	86	148	27	0	58	123	101	159	9	9	3	0	.393	.646	16	0	7	2419	3.68	105	200	0.53
Last Five Years	.286	464	1499	307	429	70	0	167	375	363	407	29	35	4	2	.431	.667	45	0	15	7306	3.83	282	602	0.47

1997 Season

	Avg	AB	H	2B	3B	HR	RBI	BB	SO	OBP	SLG		Avg	AB	H	2B	3B	HR	RBI	BB	SO	OBP	SLG
vs. Left	.282	117	33	8	0	12	27	32	40	.436	.658	First Pitch	.356	90	32	6	0	8	24	14	0	.443	.689
vs. Right	.272	423	115	19	0	46	96	69	119	.380	.643	Ahead in Count	.439	114	50	9	0	25	50	44	0	.590	1.175
Groundball	.272	103	28	7	0	10	26	22	31	.406	.631	Behind in Count	.165	230	38	6	0	16	27	0	125	.179	.400
Flyball	.216	88	19	3	0	7	13	17	19	.355	.489	Two Strikes	.140	250	35	5	0	14	27	43	159	.269	.328
Home	.315	248	78	18	0	30	60	52	64	.438	.750	Batting #3	.281	128	36	3	0	20	34	36	46	.447	.773
Away	.240	292	70	9	0	28	63	49	95	.354	.558	Batting #4	.265	407	108	24	0	37	87	64	112	.368	.597
Day	.280	193	54	11	0	20	39	41	50	.415	.648	Other	.800	5	4	0	0	1	2	1	1	.833	1.400
Night	.271	347	94	16	0	38	84	60	109	.380	.646	March/April	.322	87	28	8	0	11	25	23	16	.464	.793
Grass	.281	467	131	23	0	51	108	94	136	.405	.657	May	.253	99	25	3	0	8	19	12	20	.325	.525
Turf	.233	73	17	4	0	7	15	7	23	.314	.575	June	.266	94	25	6	0	10	19	11	31	.352	.649
Pre-All Star	.288	299	86	19	0	31	71	50	73	.389	.662	July	.302	86	26	7	0	5	18	12	31	.394	.558
Post-All Star	.257	241	62	8	0	27	52	51	86	.397	.627	August	.211	76	16	2	0	9	18	23	25	.408	.592
Scoring Posn	.232	142	33	12	0	11	63	37	43	.399	.549	Sept/Oct	.286	98	28	1	0	15	24	20	36	.413	.755
Close & Late	.264	87	23	2	0	8	19	26	29	.431	.563	vs. AL	.276	344	95	20	0	33	75	59	95	.383	.622
None on/out	.326	141	46	7	0	21	21	22	38	.417	.823	vs. NL	.270	196	53	7	0	25	48	42	64	.409	.689

1997 By Position

Position	Avg	AB	H	2B	3B	HR	RBI	BB	SO	OBP	SLG	G	GS	Innings	PO	A	E	DP	Fld Pct	Rng Fctr	In Zone	Zone Outs	Zone Rtg	MLB Zone
As 1b	.269	535	144	27	0	57	121	100	159	.389	.639	152	150	1287.1	1326	94	7	130	.995	---	273	223	.817	.874

Last Five Years

	Avg	AB	H	2B	3B	HR	RBI	BB	SO	OBP	SLG		Avg	AB	H	2B	3B	HR	RBI	BB	SO	OBP	SLG
vs. Left	.301	382	115	20	0	45	106	116	100	.467	.707	First Pitch	.370	254	94	18	0	36	88	33	0	.452	.866
vs. Right	.281	1117	314	50	0	122	269	247	307	.418	.654	Ahead in Count	.428	283	121	19	0	57	119	169	0	.642	1.099
Groundball	.325	335	109	17	0	40	85	87	86	.472	.734	Behind in Count	.192	650	125	19	0	41	89	0	309	.204	.411
Flyball	.229	280	64	9	0	29	65	66	77	.388	.571	Two Strikes	.152	710	108	15	0	39	87	161	407	.313	.338
Home	.292	709	207	37	0	80	184	179	187	.442	.683	Batting #3	.277	130	36	3	0	20	34	37	47	.445	.762
Away	.281	790	222	33	0	87	191	184	220	.420	.653	Batting #4	.289	1252	362	65	0	137	319	297	334	.431	.669
Day	.293	584	171	32	0	67	141	147	148	.444	.692	Other	.265	117	31	2	0	10	22	29	26	.412	.538
Night	.282	915	258	38	0	100	234	216	259	.422	.651	March/April	.288	222	64	14	0	21	55	65	58	.451	.635
Grass	.289	1328	384	64	0	146	330	328	361	.435	.667	May	.315	314	99	19	0	33	82	62	63	.431	.691
Turf	.263	171	45	6	0	21	45	35	46	.394	.667	June	.285	281	80	14	0	36	71	72	79	.436	.719
Pre-All Star	.300	911	273	51	0	99	233	222	224	.440	.682	July	.273	253	69	11	0	24	54	50	70	.399	.601
Post-All Star	.265	588	156	19	0	68	142	141	183	.416	.645	August	.270	185	50	4	0	20	46	49	59	.427	.616
Scoring Posn	.282	383	108	25	0	39	201	142	107	.475	.653	Sept/Oct	.275	244	67	8	0	33	67	65	78	.439	.713
Close & Late	.266	218	58	5	0	19	48	76	69	.461	.664	vs. AL	.289	1303	376	63	0	142	327	321	343	.434	.664
None on/out	.284	387	110	16	0	51	51	74	109	.407	.721	vs. NL	.270	196	53	7	0	25	48	42	64	.409	.689

Batter vs. Pitcher (career)

Hits Best Against	Avg	AB	H	2B	3B	HR	RBI	BB	SO	OBP	SLG	Hits Worst Against	Avg	AB	H	2B	3B	HR	RBI	BB	SO	OBP	SLG
Rich Robertson	.600	10	6	1	0	3	7	3	1	.692	1.600	Juan Guzman	.000	11	0	0	0	0	0	2	5	.214	.000
Orel Hershiser	.583	12	7	1	0	3	7	0	3	.583	1.417	Roger Clemens	.085	47	4	1	0	2	2	6	14	.189	.234
John Smiley	.500	10	5	2	0	2	2	3	2	.615	1.300	Rich DeLucia	.105	19	2	1	0	0	0	1	4	.150	.158
Kevin Gross	.455	11	5	0	0	4	7	7	2	.684	1.545	Eric Plunk	.154	13	2	0	0	0	3	2	7	.267	.154
Scott Kamieniecki	.444	18	8	2	0	4	8	2	3	.500	1.222	Matt Whiteside	.154	13	2	0	0	0	0	2	4	.267	.154

321

Randy Myers — Orioles

Age 35 – Pitches Left (flyball pitcher)

	ERA	W	L	Sv	G	GS	IP	BB	SO	Avg	H	2B	3B	HR	RBI	OBP	SLG	GF	IR	IRS	Hld	SvOp	SB	CS	GB	FB	G/F
1997 Season	1.51	2	3	45	61	0	59.2	22	56	.217	47	7	1	2	18	.289	.286	57	20	6	2	46	0	1	55	79	0.70
Last Five Years	3.11	10	18	188	291	0	289.2	121	307	.240	261	46	4	26	134	.315	.362	257	121	38	4	213	5	5	303	320	0.95

1997 Season

	ERA	W	L	Sv	G	GS	IP	H	HR	BB	SO		Avg	AB	H	2B	3B	HR	RBI	BB	SO	OBP	SLG
Home	2.40	1	2	22	30	0	30.0	26	2	10	31	vs. Left	.188	48	9	1	1	1	5	9	12	.316	.313
Away	0.61	1	1	23	31	0	29.2	21	0	12	25	vs. Right	.225	169	38	6	0	1	13	13	44	.280	.278
Day	3.06	0	3	13	18	0	17.2	14	2	8	21	Inning 1-6	.000	0	0	0	0	0	0	0	0	.000	.000
Night	0.86	2	0	32	43	0	42.0	33	0	14	35	Inning 7+	.217	217	47	7	1	2	18	22	56	.289	.286
Grass	1.78	2	3	39	51	0	50.2	38	2	21	48	None on	.223	103	23	3	1	0	0	16	30	.328	.272
Turf	0.00	0	0	6	10	0	9.0	9	0	1	8	Runners on	.211	114	24	4	0	2	18	6	26	.250	.298
March/April	0.00	0	0	10	11	0	10.1	9	0	4	14	Scoring Posn	.220	59	13	2	0	2	17	5	9	.261	.356
May	2.25	0	2	7	12	0	12.0	13	1	3	14	Close & Late	.207	179	37	3	1	2	12	21	51	.290	.268
June	2.00	1	1	8	10	0	9.0	7	0	6	6	None on/out	.186	43	8	2	0	0	0	9	15	.327	.233
July	1.80	1	0	5	9	0	10.0	9	0	4	9	vs. 1st Batr (relief)	.154	52	8	1	0	0	1	9	17	.279	.173
August	1.69	0	0	10	11	0	10.2	6	1	5	6	1st Inning Pitched	.210	210	44	6	1	2	17	20	56	.278	.276
Sept/Oct	1.17	0	0	5	8	0	7.2	3	0	0	7	First 15 Pitches	.209	153	32	6	1	2	12	15	40	.280	.301
Starter	0.00	0	0	0	0	0	0.0	0	0	0	0	Pitch 16-30	.220	59	13	1	0	0	5	7	15	.303	.237
Reliever	1.51	2	3	45	61	0	59.2	47	2	22	56	Pitch 31-45	.400	5	2	0	0	0	1	0	1	.400	.400
0 Days rest (Relief)	0.50	0	0	13	20	0	18.0	16	0	4	14	Pitch 46+	.000	0	0	0	0	0	0	0	0	.000	.000
1 or 2 Days rest	2.49	1	3	18	22	0	21.2	16	1	13	17	First Pitch	.227	22	5	0	0	0	0	2	0	.292	.227
3+ Days rest	1.35	1	0	14	19	0	20.0	15	1	5	25	Ahead in Count	.164	116	19	3	1	1	7	0	48	.164	.233
vs. AL	1.51	2	3	40	55	0	53.2	44	2	17	49	Behind in Count	.303	33	10	1	0	1	7	6	0	.410	.424
vs. NL	1.50	0	0	5	6	0	6.0	3	0	5	7	Two Strikes	.185	119	22	2	1	0	4	14	56	.271	.218
Pre-All Star	1.35	1	3	27	35	0	33.1	29	1	15	39	Pre-All Star	.225	129	29	2	1	1	11	15	39	.306	.279
Post-All Star	1.71	1	0	18	26	0	26.1	18	1	7	17	Post-All Star	.205	88	18	5	0	1	7	7	17	.263	.295

Last Five Years

	ERA	W	L	Sv	G	GS	IP	H	HR	BB	SO		Avg	AB	H	2B	3B	HR	RBI	BB	SO	OBP	SLG
Home	3.14	3	8	91	143	0	143.1	129	13	66	155	vs. Left	.171	216	37	5	2	5	27	35	69	.287	.282
Away	3.08	7	10	97	148	0	146.1	132	13	55	152	vs. Right	.257	871	224	41	2	21	107	86	238	.322	.381
Day	3.63	3	8	85	136	0	136.1	116	16	64	144	Inning 1-6	.000	0	0	0	0	0	0	0	0	.000	.000
Night	2.64	7	10	103	155	0	153.1	145	10	57	163	Inning 7+	.240	1087	261	46	4	26	134	121	307	.315	.362
Grass	3.07	9	13	149	231	0	226.0	203	18	97	246	None on	.237	548	130	24	4	13	13	63	155	.317	.367
Turf	3.25	1	5	39	60	0	63.2	58	8	24	61	Runners on	.243	539	131	22	0	13	121	58	152	.313	.356
March/April	1.11	0	1	28	43	0	40.2	26	1	22	46	Scoring Posn	.254	299	76	14	0	10	111	48	81	.350	.401
May	3.10	0	8	53		0	52.1	55	4	26	61	Close & Late	.245	829	203	36	2	20	109	98	232	.323	.366
June	1.64	3	2	30	47	0	49.1	38	2	13	55	None on/out	.229	236	54	8	2	5	5	24	62	.300	.343
July	5.96	2	4	29	50	0	54.1	65	7	25	51	vs. 1st Batr (relief)	.209	258	54	8	2	3	12	28	72	.287	.291
August	4.18	4	5	29	50	0	47.1	46	8	22	38	1st Inning Pitched	.237	987	234	40	4	23	123	104	279	.309	.356
Sept/Oct	1.97	1	0	34	48	0	45.2	31	4	13	56	First 15 Pitches	.240	739	177	36	3	18	78	79	199	.312	.369
Starter	0.00	0	0	0	0	0	0.0	0	0	0	0	Pitch 16-30	.233	318	74	8	1	7	48	37	102	.311	.330
Reliever	3.11	10	18	188	291	0	289.2	261	26	121	307	Pitch 31-45	.333	30	10	2	0	1	8	5	6	.429	.500
0 Days rest (Relief)	3.66	0	7	57	87	0	78.2	82	8	31	73	Pitch 46+	.000	0	0	0	0	0	0	0	0	.000	.000
1 or 2 Days rest	3.21	7	6	79	116	0	117.2	103	10	53	130	First Pitch	.372	113	42	4	2	2	14	5	0	.398	.496
3+ Days rest	2.51	3	5	52	88	0	93.1	76	8	37	104	Ahead in Count	.167	575	96	15	1	7	39	0	263	.168	.233
vs. AL	2.56	6	7	71	117	0	112.1	104	9	46	123	Behind in Count	.353	184	65	16	1	9	46	57	0	.500	.598
vs. NL	3.45	4	11	117	174	0	177.1	157	17	75	184	Two Strikes	.152	611	93	13	1	7	40	59	307	.226	.211
Pre-All Star	2.55	3	12	110	162	0	162.2	141	9	70	190	Pre-All Star	.230	613	141	25	3	9	70	70	190	.307	.325
Post-All Star	3.83	7	6	78	129	0	127.0	120	17	64	117	Post-All Star	.253	474	120	21	1	17	64	51	117	.325	.409

Pitcher vs. Batter (career)

Pitches Best Vs.	Avg	AB	H	2B	3B	HR	RBI	BB	SO	OBP	SLG	Pitches Worst Vs.	Avg	AB	H	2B	3B	HR	RBI	BB	SO	OBP	SLG
Craig Biggio	.067	15	1	0	0	0	0	3	3	.222	.067	Mark Grace	.429	14	6	0	2	1	6	1	3	.467	.929
Larry Walker	.071	14	1	1	0	0	2	2	4	.176	.071	Bobby Bonilla	.417	24	10	1	0	1	7	6	4	.500	.583
Darrin Jackson	.100	10	1	0	0	0	1	2	0	.250	.100	Jeff Bagwell	.417	12	5	3	0	2	5	1	4	.462	1.167
Ray Lankford	.118	17	2	0	0	0	0	1	2	.167	.118	Luis Gonzalez	.385	13	5	3	0	0	5	1	3	.429	.615
Jose Offerman	.125	16	2	0	0	0	0	1	8	.176	.125	Andres Galarraga	.350	20	7	0	0	3	11	5	7	.480	.800

Curt Schilling — Phillies

Age 31 – Pitches Right

	ERA	W	L	Sv	G	GS	IP	BB	SO	Avg	H	2B	3B	HR	RBI	OBP	SLG	CG	ShO	Sup	QS	#P/S	SB	CS	GB	FB	G/F
1997 Season	2.97	17	11	0	35	35	254.1	58	319	.224	208	49	7	25	92	.271	.372	7	2	4.14	26	118	9	9	267	201	1.33
Last Five Years	3.52	51	41	0	125	125	871.1	219	859	.237	774	157	17	86	336	.287	.375	24	6	4.26	83	110	40	29	1009	831	1.21

1997 Season

	ERA	W	L	Sv	G	GS	IP	H	HR	BB	SO		Avg	AB	H	2B	3B	HR	RBI	BB	SO	OBP	SLG
Home	2.80	7	6	0	20	20	144.2	111	10	32	186	vs. Left	.232	456	106	21	6	16	51	34	151	.287	.410
Away	3.20	10	5	0	15	15	109.2	97	15	26	133	vs. Right	.215	474	102	28	1	9	41	24	168	.254	.335
Day	3.29	7	5	0	13	13	95.2	78	12	17	123	Inning 1-6	.218	734	160	37	4	20	72	45	264	.265	.361
Night	2.78	10	6	0	22	22	158.2	130	13	41	196	Inning 7+	.245	196	48	12	3	5	20	13	55	.294	.413
Grass	3.72	4	4	0	8	8	55.2	50	11	15	73	None on	.212	612	130	29	4	16	16	32	220	.254	.351
Turf	2.76	13	7	0	27	27	198.2	158	14	43	246	Runners on	.245	318	78	20	3	9	76	26	99	.301	.412
March/April	3.80	3	2	0	6	6	42.2	41	6	11	40	Scoring Posn	.209	187	39	11	3	2	59	14	70	.257	.332
May	2.11	4	2	0	6	6	42.2	32	3	10	53	Close & Late	.233	129	30	8	2	2	14	12	35	.296	.372
June	4.54	2	3	0	6	6	39.2	37	6	15	58	None on/out	.229	249	57	12	4	5	5	15	86	.275	.369
July	2.68	2	3	0	6	6	47.0	36	5	8	61	vs. 1st Batr (relief)	.000	0	0	0	0	0	0	0	0	.000	.000
August	1.45	2	0	0	5	5	37.1	25	1	8	52	First 75 Pitches	.218	570	124	24	4	11	46	29	206	.257	.332
Sept/Oct	3.20	4	1	0	6	6	45.0	37	4	6	55	Pitch 76-90	.189	122	23	8	1	4	15	8	39	.235	.369
Starter	2.97	17	11	0	35	35	254.1	208	25	58	319	Pitch 91-105	.274	106	29	8	1	4	11	9	35	.336	.481
Reliever	0.00	0	0	0	0	0	0.0	0	0	0	0	Pitch 106+	.242	132	32	9	1	6	20	12	30	.306	.462
0-3 Days Rest (Start)	0.00	0	0	0	0	0	0.0	0	0	0	0	First Pitch	.333	105	35	12	1	2	12	2	0	.355	.524
4 Days Rest	3.10	14	10	0	30	30	218.0	186	24	43	268	Ahead in Count	.162	543	88	17	5	10	39	0	267	.162	.267
5+ Days Rest	2.23	3	1	0	5	5	36.1	22	1	15	51	Behind in Count	.333	108	36	13	0	6	20	25	0	.463	.620
vs. AL	3.00	1	1	0	3	3	21.0	20	0	4	31	Two Strikes	.159	580	92	18	3	12	42	31	319	.201	.262
vs. NL	2.97	16	10	0	32	32	233.1	188	25	54	288												
Pre-All Star	3.59	9	8	0	19	19	133.0	119	15	37	159	Pre-All Star	.242	492	119	23	4	15	61	37	159	.296	.396
Post-All Star	2.30	8	3	0	16	16	121.1	89	10	21	160	Post-All Star	.203	438	89	26	3	10	31	21	160	.242	.345

Last Five Years

	ERA	W	L	Sv	G	GS	IP	H	HR	BB	SO		Avg	AB	H	2B	3B	HR	RBI	BB	SO	OBP	SLG
Home	3.35	22	23	0	60	60	427.0	369	33	108	457	vs. Left	.239	1580	378	73	13	47	179	122	422	.294	.391
Away	3.69	29	18	0	65	65	444.1	405	53	111	402	vs. Right	.235	1683	396	84	4	39	157	97	437	.280	.359
Day	4.17	16	16	0	44	44	295.1	295	39	66	283	Inning 1-6	.233	2661	621	127	12	68	276	180	721	.284	.367
Night	3.19	35	25	0	81	81	576.0	479	47	153	576	Inning 7+	.254	602	153	30	5	18	60	39	138	.300	.410
Grass	3.51	16	11	0	39	39	271.2	240	41	62	253	None on	.222	2081	461	96	8	56	56	119	558	.267	.356
Turf	3.53	35	30	0	86	86	599.2	534	45	157	606	Runners on	.265	1182	313	61	9	30	280	100	301	.321	.408
March/April	3.60	7	7	0	18	18	125.0	117	13	32	96	Scoring Posn	.250	655	164	35	8	12	230	68	202	.315	.383
May	2.97	11	5	0	25	25	176.0	146	20	45	171	Close & Late	.255	341	87	16	3	11	44	29	74	.332	.416
June	4.38	6	11	0	23	23	150.0	134	21	42	147	None on/out	.232	862	200	45	6	20	20	49	221	.277	.368
July	4.16	8	9	0	23	23	151.1	144	16	52	151	vs. 1st Batr (relief)	.000	0	0	0	0	0	0	0	0	.000	.000
August	2.96	7	5	0	19	19	139.2	121	6	30	157	1st Inning Pitched	.230	460	106	25	3	13	52	45	123	.303	.383
Sept/Oct	3.06	12	4	0	17	17	129.1	112	10	18	137	First 75 Pitches	.233	2141	499	102	11	49	207	135	573	.281	.360
Starter	3.52	51	41	0	125	125	871.1	774	86	219	859	Pitch 76-90	.230	427	98	15	3	12	42	27	106	.276	.363
Reliever	0.00	0	0	0	0	0	0.0	0	0	0	0	Pitch 91-105	.261	371	97	23	1	14	46	23	91	.305	.442
0-3 Days Rest (Start)	0.00	0	0	0	0	0	0.0	0	0	0	0	Pitch 106+	.247	324	80	17	2	11	41	34	89	.318	.414
4 Days Rest	3.64	35	35	0	93	93	648.0	607	64	153	636	First Pitch	.319	433	138	31	3	12	49	14	0	.346	.487
5+ Days Rest	3.18	16	6	0	32	32	223.1	167	22	66	223	Ahead in Count	.175	1718	301	55	9	31	130	0	730	.178	.272
vs. AL	3.00	1	1	0	3	3	21.0	20	0	4	31	Behind in Count	.350	505	177	50	4	27	92	88	0	.446	.626
vs. NL	3.54	50	40	0	122	122	850.1	754	86	215	828	Two Strikes	.171	1781	305	48	7	32	133	117	859	.223	.260
Pre-All Star	3.98	24	29	0	73	73	486.2	457	57	140	448	Pre-All Star	.248	1844	457	90	7	57	216	140	448	.303	.397
Post-All Star	2.95	27	12	0	52	52	384.2	317	29	120	477	Post-All Star	.223	1419	317	67	10	29	120	79	411	.266	.346

Pitcher vs. Batter (career)

Pitches Best Vs.	Avg	AB	H	2B	3B	HR	RBI	BB	SO	OBP	SLG	Pitches Worst Vs.	Avg	AB	H	2B	3B	HR	RBI	BB	SO	OBP	SLG
Ryan Klesko	.000	13	0	0	0	0	0	2	7	.133	.000	Phil Plantier	.545	11	6	3	0	2	5	0	1	.545	1.364
Darrin Fletcher	.031	32	1	0	0	0	4	1	6	.059	.031	Lance Johnson	.500	12	6	0	1	1	3	0	1	.462	.917
Derek Bell	.048	21	1	0	0	0		2	4	.125	.048	Mark Lemke	.484	31	15	1	0	2	5	3	4	.529	.710
Greg Gagne	.056	18	1	1	0	0	2	0	12	.056	.111	Tony Fernandez	.429	14	6	2	1	0	2	2	3	.500	.714
Brad Ausmus	.091	11	1	0	0	0	0	0	3	.091	.091	David Justice	.360	25	9	2	0	3	11	6	5	.484	.800

Manager Tendencies

One of the things about baseball which appeals to many of us is the game's endless opportunity for analysis. . . and few things are analyzed more than managerial decisions. Major League skippers may not have batting averages and slugging percentages to point to at the end of the season, but when it comes time to judge their performance and production, there's no reason we can't take a look at their statistics.

Which manager posted the best stolen-base success rate?

Which skippers were constantly tinkering with their lineups?

Which managers wore out a path to the pitching mound?

It's questions like these that get our second-guessing juices going, and it's questions like these that inspired the following pages, which look at managerial tendencies in a number of situations. Once again, the skippers are compared based on offense, defense, lineups, and pitching use. We don't rank the managers; there is plenty of room for argument on whether certain moves are good or bad. We are simply providing fodder for the discussion.

Offensively, managers have control over bunting, stealing and the timing of hit-and-runs. The *Handbook* looks at the quantity, timing and success of these moves.

Defensively, the *Handbook* looks at the success of pitchouts, the frequency of intentional walks, and the pattern of defensive substitutions.

Most managers spend large amounts of their time devising lineups. The *Handbook* shows the number of lineups used, as well as the platoon percentage. The use of pinch hitters and pinch runners is also explored.

Finally, how does the manager use pitchers? For starters, the *Handbook* shows slow and quick hooks, along with the number of times a starter was allowed to throw more than 120 and 140 pitches. For relievers, we look at the number of relief appearances, mid-inning changes and how often a pitcher gets a save going more than one inning (a rare occurrence these days). The categories include:

Stolen Base Success Percentage: SB/Attempts

Pitchout Runners Moving: The number of times the opposition is running when a manager calls a pitchout.

Double Steals: The number of double steals attempted in 1997.

Out Percentage: The proportion of stolen bases with that number of outs.

Sacrifice Bunt Attempts: A bunt is considered a sac attempt if no runner is on third, there are no outs, or the pitcher attempts a bunt.

Sacrifice Bunt Success%: A bunt that results in a sacrifice or a hit, divided by the number of attempts.

Favorite Inning: The most common inning in which an event occurred.

Hit and Run Success: The hit-and-run results in baserunner advancement with no double play.

Intentional Walk Situation: Runners on base, first base open, and anyone but the pitcher up.

Defensive Substitutions: Straight defensive substitutions, with the team leading by four runs or less.

Number of Lineups: Based on batting order, 1-8 for National Leaguers, 1-9 for American Leaguers.

Percent LHB vs. RHSP and RHB vs. LHSP: A measure of platooning. A batter is considered to always have the platoon advantage if he is a switch-hitter.

Percent PH platoon: Frequency the manager gets his pinch hitter the platoon advantage. Switch-hitters always have the advantage.

Score Diff: The most common score differential on which an intentional walk is called for.

Slow and Quick Hooks: See the glossary for complete information. This measures how often a pitcher is left in longer than is standard practice, or pulled earlier than normal.

Mid-Inning Change: The number of times a manager changed pitchers in the middle of an inning.

1-Batter Appearance: The number of times a pitcher was brought in to face only one batter. Called the "Tony La Russa special" because of his penchant for trying to orchestrate specific match-ups for specific situations.

3 Pitchers (2 runs or less): The club gives up two runs or fewer in a game, but uses at least three pitchers.

Offense

	G	Att	SB%	Pitchout Rn Mvg	2nd SB-CS	3rd SB-CS	Home SB-CS	Double Steals	Out Percentage 0	1	2	Sac Bunts Att	Suc. %	Fav. Inning	Sqz	Hit & Run Att	Suc. %
AL Managers																	
Bell, Buddy, Det	162	233	69.1	4	135-63	25-5	1-4	7	22.7	30.0	47.2	44	86.4	7	3	115	33.0
Bevington, Terry, ChA	161	158	67.1	6	89-48	17-3	0-1	3	16.5	37.3	46.2	62	88.7	8	2	87	31.0
Boone, Bob, KC	82	126	65.1	8	74-34	7-8	1-2	3	19.8	39.7	40.5	43	83.7	1	1	57	42.1
Collins, Terry, Ana	162	198	63.6	5	109-64	16-7	1-1	3	19.7	38.4	41.9	55	83.6	8	0	109	32.1
Garner, Phil, Mil	161	158	65.2	3	95-47	7-6	1-2	2	19.6	33.5	46.8	65	87.7	6	7	98	41.8
Gaston, Cito, Tor	157	177	74.0	7	113-41	18-4	0-1	1	20.3	32.8	46.9	50	82.0	8	1	87	34.5
Hargrove, Mike, Cle	161	177	66.7	5	99-46	17-8	2-5	5	18.6	34.5	46.9	60	88.3	8	3	96	36.5
Howe, Art, Oak	162	107	66.4	1	65-31	5-4	1-1	2	16.8	44.9	38.3	66	81.8	8	0	66	42.4
Johnson, Davey, Bal	162	89	70.8	3	54-24	9-2	0-0	2	16.9	46.1	37.1	59	84.7	7	0	57	38.6
Kelly, Tom, Min	162	203	74.4	4	135-47	15-3	1-2	3	16.7	35.5	47.8	26	84.6	5	2	97	34.0
Muser, Tony, KC	79	70	68.6	2	44-16	4-5	0-1	1	15.7	30.0	54.3	30	90.0	8	3	46	30.4
Oates, Johnny, Tex	162	109	66.1	3	68-32	3-4	1-1	1	22.0	33.0	45.0	38	84.2	7	3	86	32.6
Piniella, Lou, Sea	162	129	69.0	3	72-29	17-10	0-1	8	14.7	46.5	38.8	61	80.3	7	1	64	29.7
Queen, Mel, Tor	5	7	42.9	1	2-4	1-0	0-0	0	14.3	28.6	57.1	1	100.0	3	0	3	33.3
Torre, Joe, NYA	162	157	63.1	3	89-48	10-11	0-0	4	24.2	33.1	42.7	54	75.9	6	3	84	46.4
Williams, Jimy, Bos	162	116	58.6	4	60-42	8-4	0-2	3	25.0	36.2	38.8	30	80.0	6	2	85	44.7
NL Managers																	
Alou, Felipe, Mon	162	121	62.0	5	66-42	9-2	0-2	1	19.0	38.8	42.1	91	85.7	7	8	72	33.3
Baker, Dusty, SF	162	170	71.2	6	105-40	16-4	0-5	2	25.3	34.7	40.0	85	82.4	3	3	143	36.4
Baylor, Don, Col	162	202	67.8	6	112-55	23-6	2-3	10	19.3	44.6	36.1	93	80.6	3	3	147	49.0
Bochy, Bruce, SD	162	200	70.0	5	117-50	22-7	1-3	7	16.0	34.0	50.0	84	77.4	2	6	135	31.9
Cox, Bobby, Atl	162	166	65.1	5	93-43	15-11	0-4	1	20.5	36.7	42.8	112	80.4	5	6	67	31.3
Dierker, Larry, Hou	162	245	69.8	3	142-61	29-12	0-0	10	19.6	40.0	40.4	96	80.2	3	7	131	27.5
Francona, Terry, Phi	162	148	62.2	5	79-48	11-6	2-2	4	18.2	31.1	50.7	91	93.4	5	3	90	27.8
Knight, Ray, Cin	99	178	74.7	10	104-36	28-3	1-6	9	20.8	39.3	39.9	69	73.9	3	6	92	44.6
La Russa, Tony, StL	162	224	73.2	9	140-46	22-10	2-4	10	25.0	32.1	42.9	77	80.5	7	5	137	33.6
Lamont, Gene, Pit	162	210	76.2	12	133-42	27-6	0-3	5	17.6	34.3	48.1	101	81.2	5	1	120	33.3
Leyland, Jim, Fla	162	173	66.5	7	110-53	5-4	0-1	3	23.1	37.6	39.3	91	84.6	1	1	83	25.3
McKeon, Jack, Cin	63	79	72.2	3	47-15	9-5	1-2	4	21.5	35.4	43.0	42	81.0	2	0	27	37.0
Riggleman, Jim, ChN	162	176	65.9	7	100-50	16-6	0-3	6	18.2	35.2	46.6	103	80.6	2	12	143	40.6
Russell, Bill, LA	162	195	67.2	13	113-53	18-6	0-5	8	21.0	36.4	42.6	133	85.0	5	13	145	40.0
Valentine, Bobby, NYN	162	171	56.7	9	79-59	17-9	1-7	4	19.3	39.2	41.5	78	79.5	5	11	120	45.0

Defense

	G	Pitchout Total	Runners Moving	CS%	Non-PO CS%	IBB	Pct. of Situations	Favorite Score Diff.	Defensive Subs Total	Favorite Inning	Pos. 1	Pos. 2	Pos. 3
AL Managers													
Bell, Buddy, Det	162	32	6	50.0	26.2	24	3.6	-2	22	8	ss-12	rf-7	c-1
Bevington, Terry, ChA	161	35	7	14.3	31.1	27	3.9	-2	24	9	cf-15	1b-4	ss-2
Boone, Bob, KC	82	29	6	16.7	31.4	20	6.1	0	7	8	rf-3	c-2	1b-1
Collins, Terry, Ana	162	60	18	50.0	37.4	25	3.6	-2	22	8	cf-5	c-4	3b-4
Garner, Phil, Mil	161	55	12	50.0	31.5	21	3.1	-1	36	8	1b-11	cf-9	c-5
Gaston, Cito, Tor	157	30	10	40.0	45.7	21	3.3	0	6	4	2b-2	ss-2	3b-1
Hargrove, Mike, Cle	161	37	8	37.5	30.1	30	4.5	-1	14	8	2b-6	3b-3	ss-2
Howe, Art, Oak	162	43	11	27.3	26.8	40	5.8	-1	38	8	cf-9	ss-7	lf-7
Johnson, Davey, Bal	162	31	9	44.4	24.2	24	3.6	-2	43	9	c-16	rf-15	lf-3
Kelly, Tom, Min	162	7	0	0.0	35.1	19	3.0	-1	10	8	3b-7	cf-3	None
Muser, Tony, KC	79	20	5	40.0	44.2	12	4.1	-1	14	8	rf-7	3b-4	1b-1
Oates, Johnny, Tex	162	6	2	100.0	44.6	32	5.4	-1	12	8	rf-6	cf-3	c-1
Piniella, Lou, Sea	162	32	7	42.9	39.9	30	4.6	-1	27	9	lf-13	rf-5	2b-4
Queen, Mel, Tor	5	1	0	0.0	50.0	0	0.0	0	0	0	None	None	None
Torre, Joe, NYA	162	14	4	25.0	29.9	29	4.2	0	23	7	2b-12	lf-5	1b-3
Williams, Jimy, Bos	162	108	29	27.6	23.1	40	5.1	-2	16	9	cf-10	c-3	1b-1
NL Managers													
Alou, Felipe, Mon	162	30	12	58.3	15.8	33	4.6	0	40	8	lf-24	3b-8	1b-3
Baker, Dusty, SF	162	93	21	66.7	36.9	37	6.5	0	22	8	3b-7	rf-7	cf-4
Baylor, Don, Col	162	113	25	28.0	29.6	15	2.1	1	36	8	cf-14	lf-10	rf-5
Bochy, Bruce, SD	162	58	15	33.3	30.3	24	3.4	-2	9	8	rf-3	1b-2	2b-5
Cox, Bobby, Atl	162	13	3	66.7	29.7	46	6.7	-2	29	8	lf-10	rf-9	2b-3
Dierker, Larry, Hou	162	35	7	85.7	35.9	25	4.1	-2	26	9	3b-14	ss-4	c-2
Francona, Terry, Phi	162	30	6	66.7	33.5	31	4.8	-2	28	8	rf-12	lf-7	2b-3
Knight, Ray, Cin	99	13	3	33.3	26.3	31	8.1	1	16	8	3b-8	rf-3	2b-2
La Russa, Tony, StL	162	79	22	54.5	30.3	26	3.8	0	18	9	2b-5	3b-4	1b-2
Lamont, Gene, Pit	162	68	10	50.0	37.0	48	7.1	-2	14	8	1b-4	3b-3	lf-3
Leyland, Jim, Fla	162	38	8	62.5	41.4	31	5.0	-1	31	8	1b-14	lf-4	rf-4
McKeon, Jack, Cin	63	18	2	50.0	23.5	12	4.4	-1	7	8	2b-3	cf-2	3b-1
Riggleman, Jim, ChN	162	74	20	65.0	24.9	37	5.6	-1	44	7	ss-14	3b-10	lf-10
Russell, Bill, LA	162	49	11	72.7	30.3	28	4.2	-2	19	8	lf-11	cf-5	c-1
Valentine, Bobby, NYN	162	35	6	66.7	27.8	32	4.7	0	23	7	3b-8	2b-6	rf-5

Lineups

		Starting Lineup			Substitutes					
	G	Lineups Used	% LHB Vs. RHSP	%RHB vs. LHSP	#PH	Percent PH Platoon	PH BA	PH HR	#PR	PR SB-CS
AL Managers										
Bell, Buddy, Det	162	116	49.2	90.9	163	75.5	0.227	4	19	3-1
Bevington, Terry, ChA	161	102	56.7	82.8	127	67.7	0.159	2	39	6-1
Boone, Bob, KC	82	61	54.0	86.3	80	82.5	0.242	2	34	1-3
Collins, Terry, Ana	162	117	68.1	74.3	86	91.9	0.211	0	34	2-1
Garner, Phil, Mil	161	128	48.7	81.8	190	85.3	0.231	2	42	2-0
Gaston, Cito, Tor	157	90	43.5	83.7	71	74.6	0.131	1	19	1-1
Hargrove, Mike, Cle	161	109	49.9	82.9	86	70.9	0.192	2	17	1-0
Howe, Art, Oak	162	133	50.9	87.1	198	79.3	0.345	3	62	2-0
Johnson, Davey, Bal	162	109	48.7	73.5	104	67.3	0.222	1	36	1-0
Kelly, Tom, Min	162	139	41.8	92.6	163	85.3	0.250	2	27	0-2
Muser, Tony, KC	79	71	45.9	91.6	75	82.7	0.180	1	30	2-1
Oates, Johnny, Tex	162	106	51.9	78.7	161	78.9	0.241	6	30	0-0
Piniella, Lou, Sea	162	84	45.5	88.9	147	83.7	0.208	4	35	2-1
Queen, Mel, Tor	5	4	44.4	88.9	3	66.7	0.000	0	1	0-0
Torre, Joe, NYA	162	118	52.9	78.7	75	78.7	0.194	1	70	5-0
Williams, Jimy, Bos	162	97	49.5	75.7	123	75.6	0.291	5	48	3-4
NL Managers										
Alou, Felipe, Mon	162	138	50.0	82.5	205	78.5	0.211	4	22	2-1
Baker, Dusty, SF	162	114	68.0	78.9	212	74.1	0.267	1	17	1-0
Baylor, Don, Col	162	90	39.6	89.7	220	82.7	0.271	4	27	4-1
Bochy, Bruce, SD	162	111	54.2	78.1	291	61.2	0.248	7	26	1-1
Cox, Bobby, Atl	162	87	63.8	66.1	276	65.2	0.188	5	58	2-3
Dierker, Larry, Hou	162	131	30.9	88.3	264	73.5	0.223	2	35	3-1
Francona, Terry, Phi	162	98	61.5	77.8	288	76.7	0.184	3	19	3-0
Knight, Ray, Cin	99	88	61.3	69.6	215	77.7	0.203	2	21	3-0
La Russa, Tony, StL	162	146	48.2	73.1	307	81.1	0.188	3	17	2-0
Lamont, Gene, Pit	162	107	39.0	85.4	225	68.4	0.230	5	28	1-0
Leyland, Jim, Fla	162	105	45.3	93.3	258	75.2	0.253	4	36	1-0
McKeon, Jack, Cin	63	50	37.6	77.8	102	73.5	0.198	0	18	0-2
Riggleman, Jim, ChN	162	127	34.9	86.8	280	77.9	0.249	6	40	4-0
Russell, Bill, LA	162	102	28.1	93.2	267	84.3	0.188	2	38	3-1
Valentine, Bobby, NYN	162	131	51.2	86.6	313	79.6	0.248	11	39	1-1

Pitching

		Starters					Relievers					
	G	Slow Hooks	Quick Hooks	> 120 Pitches	> 140 Pitches	3 Days Rest	Relief App	Mid-Inning Change	Save > 1 IP	1st Batter Platoon Pct	1-Batter App	3 Pitchers (≤ 2 runs)
AL Managers												
Bell, Buddy, Det	162	7	24	12	0	0	417	218	11	65.5	48	28
Bevington, Terry, ChA	161	20	14	18	0	1	389	199	14	67.5	47	24
Boone, Bob, KC	82	9	7	10	2	0	174	92	7	65.5	20	7
Collins, Terry, Ana	162	16	10	15	2	18	400	207	8	66.5	42	12
Garner, Phil, Mil	161	12	26	6	0	1	367	146	6	60.5	23	34
Gaston, Cito, Tor	157	22	13	36	0	1	322	139	6	64.0	42	23
Hargrove, Mike, Cle	161	13	21	14	0	2	429	197	9	65.7	58	24
Howe, Art, Oak	162	19	29	8	0	12	481	264	11	69.6	53	19
Johnson, Davey, Bal	162	12	21	5	0	1	400	191	11	61.4	30	29
Kelly, Tom, Min	162	11	19	8	0	5	390	203	5	61.5	38	16
Muser, Tony, KC	79	11	9	4	0	0	219	94	1	67.1	17	14
Oates, Johnny, Tex	162	13	17	12	0	1	382	207	4	65.2	37	18
Piniella, Lou, Sea	162	17	14	25	4	5	392	201	11	65.6	21	16
Queen, Mel, Tor	5	0	1	1	1	0	14	8	0	71.4	2	2
Torre, Joe, NYA	162	12	18	19	0	4	368	168	14	60.1	33	32
Williams, Jimy, Bos	162	13	17	13	1	2	417	180	11	60.0	27	23
NL Managers												
Alou, Felipe, Mon	162	13	26	15	0	0	390	164	13	56.9	31	19
Baker, Dusty, SF	162	3	20	17	0	2	481	203	4	63.2	36	30
Baylor, Don, Col	162	23	15	2	0	2	427	142	9	52.8	31	15
Bochy, Bruce, SD	162	13	20	3	0	3	426	166	11	51.2	28	15
Cox, Bobby, Atl	162	7	13	23	0	9	374	99	4	52.1	30	32
Dierker, Larry, Hou	162	5	12	13	0	5	354	136	8	48.3	21	19
Francona, Terry, Phi	162	15	14	22	0	1	409	141	9	58.6	23	15
Knight, Ray, Cin	99	7	15	1	0	0	269	99	9	65.4	17	21
La Russa, Tony, StL	162	9	18	16	0	3	399	148	2	62.7	31	29
Lamont, Gene, Pit	162	9	16	9	0	0	451	176	4	61.8	26	28
Leyland, Jim, Fla	162	12	21	18	0	1	404	124	2	64.4	19	29
McKeon, Jack, Cin	63	2	13	5	0	0	154	54	3	60.4	8	9
Riggleman, Jim, ChN	162	5	13	2	0	3	441	213	9	61.0	45	24
Russell, Bill, LA	162	5	17	12	0	3	412	143	5	54.9	35	32
Valentine, Bobby, NYN	162	12	16	4	0	1	376	111	11	55.3	20	22

Player Projections

Establishing the predictable establishes the parameters of our future surprises. This is an annual article, and that was the last line a year ago. Our putative purpose here it to review last year's projections, and learn something from our mistakes. Our real object is to brag about all the good predictions we made, in an ill-fated attempt to bamboozle you into thinking we are some kind of experts.

There are three kinds of players: those who did better than we had predicted they would, those who did worse than we thought they would, and those who did pretty much what we predicted that they would. Sandy Alomar leads off the first group; he's been in the league for ten years, and we had no idea that he was about to deliver a career season:

Sandy Alomar

	G	AB	R	H	2B	3B	HR	RBI	BB	SO	SB	CS	Avg
Predicted	118	384	53	103	20	1	12	49	21	43	4	2	.268
Actual	125	451	63	146	37	0	21	83	19	48	0	2	.324

He out-hit our projection by 56 points, and with more power than expected. Jay Bell played exactly as much as we thought he would, but single-handedly kept Kansas City out of the cellar until the last days of the season:

Jay Bell

	G	AB	R	H	2B	3B	HR	RBI	BB	SO	SB	CS	Avg
Predicted	153	576	79	146	31	4	12	61	61	116	5	5	.253
Actual	153	573	89	167	28	3	21	92	71	101	10	6	.291

Which doesn't even win him the TOPVSWTIJBO97 Award, as the top over performing veteran shortstop with the initials JB of 1997:

Jeff Blauser

	G	AB	R	H	2B	3B	HR	RBI	BB	SO	SB	CS	Avg
Predicted	126	460	68	114	21	2	11	47	58	96	7	4	.248
Actual	151	519	90	160	31	4	17	70	70	101	5	1	.308

Staying with the JB theme, we thought we were presenting a positive, top-end projection for Jeromy Burnitz:

Jeromy Burnitz

	G	AB	R	H	2B	3B	HR	RBI	BB	SO	SB	CS	Avg
Predicted	154	537	93	133	27	4	18	82	83	127	15	6	.248
Actual	153	494	85	139	37	8	27	85	75	111	20	13	.281

Burnitz exceeded the slugging percentage we had projected for him by about 160 points. Damion Easley hit four times as many home runs as we had projected:

Damion Easley

	G	AB	R	H	2B	3B	HR	RBI	BB	SO	SB	CS	Avg
Predicted	97	299	38	73	13	1	5	33	29	44	6	3	.244
Actual	151	527	97	139	37	3	22	72	68	102	28	13	.264

We didn't see Doug Glanville as either a regular or a .300 hitter:

Doug Glanville

	G	AB	R	H	2B	3B	HR	RBI	BB	SO	SB	CS	Avg
Predicted	92	197	22	52	9	1	2	19	7	22	7	4	.264
Actual	146	474	79	142	22	5	4	35	24	46	19	11	.300

And, as a matter of fact, we still don't. Tony Gwynn is usually mentioned here only to point out that he has done again what he always does, but in 1997, he surprised us:

Tony Gwynn

	G	AB	R	H	2B	3B	HR	RBI	BB	SO	SB	CS	Avg
Predicted	135	524	71	176	29	4	7	67	47	23	9	4	.336
Actual	149	592	97	220	49	2	17	119	43	28	12	5	.372

We predicted he would hit .336, and he beat us by 36 points. We missed Mike Lieberthal by only five points, but shorted him on power and playing time:

Mike Lieberthal

	G	AB	R	H	2B	3B	HR	RBI	BB	SO	SB	CS	Avg
Predicted	70	220	20	53	11	0	3	23	17	25	1	1	.241
Actual	134	455	59	112	27	1	20	77	44	76	3	4	.246

Mark McGwire exceeded our projected playing time by 33%, our projected batting average by 13%, and our projected home runs as a percentage of hits by 21%. Put it all together, and he beat the projection by 27 home runs:

Mark McGwire

	G	AB	R	H	2B	3B	HR	RBI	BB	SO	SB	CS	Avg
Predicted	125	405	82	98	16	0	31	80	114	110	1	0	.242
Actual	156	540	86	148	27	0	58	123	101	159	3	0	.274

We have no excuses, either; we should have done better. He'd been healthy for a couple of years, and his power production had been steadily increasing.

Jeff Reed hit twice as many homers on the road as we had projected he would hit altogether:

Jeff Reed

	G	AB	R	H	2B	3B	HR	RBI	BB	SO	SB	CS	Avg
Predicted	108	331	31	86	13	1	4	28	47	62	1	1	.260
Actual	90	256	43	76	10	0	17	47	35	55	2	1	.297

David Segui is almost a match for Sandy Alomar. We had projected that he would do almost the same as we projected for Alomar, and he actually did about the same as Alomar. J. T. Snow actually did what we had projected for Tino Martinez. The following four lines are our projection for Snow, what Snow actually did, our projection for Martinez, and what Martinez actually did:

	G	AB	R	H	2B	3B	HR	RBI	BB	SO	SB	CS	Avg
1.	142	523	68	137	21	1	19	79	54	91	2	3	.262
2.	157	531	81	149	36	1	28	104	96	124	6	4	.281
3.	158	580	83	159	32	1	28	105	69	89	1	1	.274
4.	158	594	96	176	31	2	44	141	75	75	3	1	.296

Martinez and Snow are the same age, essentially the same size. We had presented a "star" projection for Matt Stairs a few years ago:

Matt Stairs

	G	AB	R	H	2B	3B	HR	RBI	BB	SO	SB	CS	Avg
Predicted	82	238	32	66	16	1	7	40	27	35	3	3	.277
Actual	133	352	62	105	19	0	27	73	50	63	3	2	.298

Doug Strange, whom we had projected at .231 with 2 homers, 18 RBI, wound up at .257 with 12 homers, 47 RBI. Finally, of course, there is the presumptive MVP:

Larry Walker

	G	AB	R	H	2B	3B	HR	RBI	BB	SO	SB	CS	Avg
Predicted	135	480	87	138	31	3	26	91	55	88	19	5	.287
Actual	153	568	143	208	46	4	49	130	78	90	33	8	.366

Actually, we had almost the same projection for Larry Walker that we did for Todd:

Todd Walker

	G	AB	R	H	2B	3B	HR	RBI	BB	SO	SB	CS	Avg
Predicted	159	589	90	178	39	4	26	97	56	106	16	9	.302
Actual	52	156	15	37	7	1	3	16	11	30	7	0	.237

This is a segue into the second part of the article, in which we discuss projections which were, in retrospect, outrageously optimistic.

There are more of these than there are of the other type. We make our projections in early October, and in many cases we really have no chance to figure out who is going to be a regular and who isn't. It is my feeling, therefore, that if a player might play, we should project that he <u>will</u> play. Otherwise, we're not telling you what we know.

So we wind up, every year, projecting greatly excessive playing time for any number of players. Sometimes they don't play because they're hurt, sometimes they don't play because they go to Japan, sometimes they don't play because the team signs a free agent, and sometimes they just don't play:

George Arias

	G	AB	R	H	2B	3B	HR	RBI	BB	SO	SB	CS	Avg
Predicted	151	537	76	146	25	3	22	87	43	108	2	1	.272
Actual	14	28	3	7	1	0	0	3	0	1	0	0	.250

Brian Jordan

	G	AB	R	H	2B	3B	HR	RBI	BB	SO	SB	CS	Avg
Predicted	147	520	77	149	27	4	18	83	31	90	22	9	.287
Actual	47	145	17	34	5	0	0	10	10	21	6	1	.234

Brooks Kieschnick

	G	AB	R	H	2B	3B	HR	RBI	BB	SO	SB	CS	Avg
Predicted	146	513	57	142	27	1	18	67	43	99	2	3	.277
Actual	39	90	9	18	2	0	4	12	12	21	1	0	.200

Mark Newfield

	G	AB	R	H	2B	3B	HR	RBI	BB	SO	SB	CS	Avg
Predicted	139	516	74	148	36	1	19	81	39	80	1	1	.287
Actual	50	157	14	36	8	0	1	18	14	27	0	0	.229

Rudy Pemberton

	G	AB	R	H	2B	3B	HR	RBI	BB	SO	SB	CS	Avg
Predicted	140	522	74	165	32	3	19	82	24	80	21	11	.316
Actual	27	63	8	15	2	0	2	10	4	13	0	0	.238

Danny Tartabull

	G	AB	R	H	2B	3B	HR	RBI	BB	SO	SB	CS	Avg
Predicted	125	444	61	111	25	1	19	79	69	127	1	1	.250
Actual	3	7	2	0	0	0	0	0	4	4	0	0	.000

Danny Tartabull may be finished, and I'll miss him as much as you will, but in the case of Arias, Kieschnick, Newfield, Pemberton and Todd Walker, we still believe that these guys can play, if they can stay healthy and get a clean shot at a job.

It is not unusual for our clock to run a couple of years early. We had Matt Stairs projected as a .307 hitter—in 1992. That's extreme, but we often get a year or two ahead of the available opportunities. We projected Ryan Klesko as a .274 hitter with good power in 1992. He got only 14 at bats in 1992 and only 17 in 1993, and only half-time play in 1994.

We had projected (last year) that Todd Greene would hit .278 with 20 homers in 112 games. He played only 34 games in the majors, but hit .290 with 9 homers. Did we miss the boat, or did his manager? You can decide that issue on your own; I'm not here to editorialize. Speaking of Greene, we had been projecting since 1993 that Willie G. would hit 25 to 30 homers if they'd let him. Last year, for the first time, they did:

Willie Greene

	G	AB	R	H	2B	3B	HR	RBI	BB	SO	SB	CS	Avg
Predicted	139	441	69	112	19	2	22	68	51	105	4	3	.254
Actual	151	495	62	125	22	1	26	91	78	111	6	0	.253

Although, in view of what he did after the All-Star break in '96, we should have given him a little more playing time.

Of course, there were a few players last year who played, but just didn't hit what we thought they would hit. These would include:

Carlos Baerga

	G	AB	R	H	2B	3B	HR	RBI	BB	SO	SB	CS	Avg
Predicted	142	584	90	170	30	2	20	93	26	40	8	3	.291
Actual	133	467	53	131	25	1	9	52	20	54	2	6	.281

Bret Boone

	G	AB	R	H	2B	3B	HR	RBI	BB	SO	SB	CS	Avg
Predicted	144	526	66	143	29	2	16	77	37	95	4	3	.272
Actual	139	443	40	99	25	1	7	46	45	101	5	5	.223

Scott Brosius

	G	AB	R	H	2B	3B	HR	RBI	BB	SO	SB	CS	Avg
Predicted	132	450	65	117	22	1	18	57	48	80	5	4	.260
Actual	129	479	59	97	20	1	11	41	34	102	9	4	.203

Quinton McCracken

	G	AB	R	H	2B	3B	HR	RBI	BB	SO	SB	CS	Avg
Predicted	103	356	63	119	20	6	5	38	32	48	22	10	.334
Actual	147	325	69	95	11	1	3	36	42	62	28	11	.292

Scott Stahoviak

	G	AB	R	H	2B	3B	HR	RBI	BB	SO	SB	CS	Avg
Predicted	132	404	66	115	31	2	11	59	56	92	6	4	.285
Actual	91	275	33	63	17	0	10	33	24	73	5	2	.229

Well, I'm several pages into this, and, except for a mention of Willie Greene, I haven't said anything about the things we got right. Believe it or not, there were a few of these.

We grade our projections by measuring the similarity between the actual season and the projection; I've given the details of the system in print several times. If the similarity is 980 or above, we score that as an "A+" projection.

We had seven "A+" projections last year, three of which were for Mike Bordick, John Cangelosi, and Jim Edmonds:

Mike Bordick

	G	AB	R	H	2B	3B	HR	RBI	BB	SO	SB	CS	Avg
Predicted	147	499	47	123	17	2	5	46	45	55	8	4	.246
Actual	153	509	55	120	19	1	7	46	33	66	0	2	.236

John Cangelosi

	G	AB	R	H	2B	3B	HR	RBI	BB	SO	SB	CS	Avg
Predicted	88	188	31	47	7	1	1	11	36	33	13	5	.250
Actual	103	192	28	47	8	0	1	12	19	33	5	1	.245

Jim Edmonds

	G	AB	R	H	2B	3B	HR	RBI	BB	SO	SB	CS	Avg
Predicted	137	497	87	145	28	3	23	80	50	116	3	3	.292
Actual	133	502	82	146	27	0	26	80	60	80	5	7	.291

If the similarity is 960 to 979, we score that a straight "A", and 940 to 959 an "A-". The most common grades for a projection last year were "A-" (there were 69 of those, or 18% of the total projections) and "A" (there were 68 of those). The next most-common grade was "B+" (58), followed by "B" (52). To give you some sense of what that means, I'll give you a few samples of each of those:

Luis Alicea (A)

	G	AB	R	H	2B	3B	HR	RBI	BB	SO	SB	CS	Avg
Predicted	139	396	55	99	20	4	5	42	58	67	12	7	.250
Actual	128	388	59	98	16	7	5	37	69	65	22	8	.253

Moises Alou (A)

	G	AB	R	H	2B	3B	HR	RBI	BB	SO	SB	CS	Avg
Predicted	138	524	87	153	32	3	22	88	52	78	9	7	.292
Actual	150	538	88	157	29	5	23	115	70	85	9	5	.292

Brent Brede (A)

	G	AB	R	H	2B	3B	HR	RBI	BB	SO	SB	CS	Avg
Predicted	61	190	25	52	11	1	3	21	21	38	7	2	.274
Actual	68	189	32	57	12	1	3	23	27	35	5	3	.302

Tony Clark (A)

	G	AB	R	H	2B	3B	HR	RBI	BB	SO	SB	CS	Avg
Predicted	155	568	81	152	24	1	33	103	62	168	1	1	.268
Actual	159	580	105	160	28	3	32	117	93	144	1	3	.276

Chuck Knoblauch (A)

	G	AB	R	H	2B	3B	HR	RBI	BB	SO	SB	CS	Avg
Predicted	155	607	116	183	34	6	10	66	85	87	52	16	.301
Actual	156	611	117	178	26	10	9	58	84	84	62	10	.291

Mike Matheny (A)

	G	AB	R	H	2B	3B	HR	RBI	BB	SO	SB	CS	Avg
Predicted	104	268	26	61	15	1	4	33	17	57	2	1	.228
Actual	123	320	29	78	16	1	4	32	17	68	0	1	.244

Michael Tucker (A)

	G	AB	R	H	2B	3B	HR	RBI	BB	SO	SB	CS	Avg
Predicted	137	462	63	125	20	5	14	60	51	91	10	6	.271
Actual	138	499	80	141	25	7	14	56	44	116	12	7	.283

Russ Davis (A-)

	G	AB	R	H	2B	3B	HR	RBI	BB	SO	SB	CS	Avg
Predicted	139	473	76	124	28	1	20	68	66	116	4	3	.262
Actual	119	420	57	114	29	1	20	63	27	100	6	2	.271

Brian Johnson (A-)

	G	AB	R	H	2B	3B	HR	RBI	BB	SO	SB	CS	Avg
Predicted	101	294	29	77	18	1	7	43	14	47	0	0	.262
Actual	101	318	32	83	13	3	13	45	19	45	1	1	.261

Matt Lawton (A-)

	G	AB	R	H	2B	3B	HR	RBI	BB	SO	SB	CS	Avg
Predicted	129	441	73	120	21	3	13	63	51	66	13	9	.272
Actual	142	460	74	114	29	3	14	60	76	81	7	4	.248

Scott Rolen (A-)

	G	AB	R	H	2B	3B	HR	RBI	BB	SO	SB	CS	Avg
Predicted	143	540	70	154	36	1	17	74	57	89	8	8	.285
Actual	156	561	93	159	35	3	21	92	76	138	16	6	.283

Jermaine Allensworth (B+)

	G	AB	R	H	2B	3B	HR	RBI	BB	SO	SB	CS	Avg
Predicted	136	464	72	124	26	5	5	41	37	80	21	13	.267
Actual	108	369	55	94	18	2	3	43	44	79	14	7	.255

Bill Mueller (B+)

	G	AB	R	H	2B	3B	HR	RBI	BB	SO	SB	CS	Avg
Predicted	139	524	76	151	24	4	3	50	57	61	4	4	.288
Actual	128	390	51	114	26	3	7	44	48	71	4	3	.292

Chris Stynes (B+)

	G	AB	R	H	2B	3B	HR	RBI	BB	SO	SB	CS	Avg
Predicted	83	244	33	70	13	2	4	28	12	15	6	4	.287
Actual	49	198	31	69	7	1	6	28	11	13	11	2	.348

Dmitri Young (B)

	G	AB	R	H	2B	3B	HR	RBI	BB	SO	SB	CS	Avg
Predicted	137	428	57	118	27	3	9	52	27	58	5	4	.276
Actual	110	333	38	86	14	3	5	34	38	63	6	5	.258

Todd Zeile (B)

	G	AB	R	H	2B	3B	HR	RBI	BB	SO	SB	CS	Avg
Predicted	150	563	72	143	29	1	19	81	62	90	1	1	.254
Actual	160	575	89	154	17	0	31	90	85	112	8	7	.268

This is an essentially simple process. If a player has hit .300 over the last several seasons, we project that he will again hit .300. We always predict that Frank Thomas will hit over .300 with 30+ home runs, 100+ RBI and lots of walks. So far, this prediction has turned out alright. We always predict that Rickey Henderson will draw walks, steal bases, and score runs. We never project many stolen bases for Cecil Fielder, or big home run totals for Ozzie Guillen. We think that to do so would probably make our predictions less accurate.

There are some players who are very easy to project, like Travis Fryman and Eric Karros, and there are other players who bounce up and down. Oddly enough, we have had Straight-A projections for Bob Hamelin two years in a row. When a player hits .200 one year and .300 the next, it is amazing how often he will hit about .250 the third year.

We do claim one bit of special knowledge: we know how to read minor league batting statistics. We take pride in our ability to project accurately the production of young players with little major league experience, if they get a chance to play. That's why the chart above contained a number of players with little major league experience before 1997; I wanted to demonstrate (again) that we could project the performance of players based on what they had done in the minor leagues.

But apart from that, it's all pretty obvious. We just basically project that players will continue to do what they have done in the past.

—*Bill James*

Pitcher Projections

Projecting the stats of a major league pitcher is such a daunting task that even Bill James hasn't tackled it. So much can change in a pitcher from year to year—his velocity, the sharpness of his curve, his command, his health, his role—that it's nearly impossible to predict what a pitcher will do with any accuracy.

But it's not *totally* impossible. Thanks to STATS president and CEO John Dewan and systems manager Mike Canter, we have a formula that projects 1998 pitching performances. All pitchers who have 150 games or 500 innnings in their major league careers are covered.

How accurate is our mystical pitching formula? Just ask Rod Beck and Charles Nagy:

Rod Beck

	W	L	ERA	Sv	G	IP	H	BB	SO	BR/9
Predicted	2	4	3.57	36	65	63	57	16	46	10.4
Actual	7	4	3.47	37	73	70	67	8	53	10.1

Charles Nagy

	W	L	ERA	G	IP	H	BB	SO	BR/9
Predicted	15	10	4.02	32	215	233	59	164	11.8
Actual	15	11	4.28	34	227	253	77	149	13.1

Are the projections infallible? Of course not. We didn't really see Darryl Kile or Pedro Martinez coming, though we nearly nailed Martinez' W-L record:

Darryl Kile

	W	L	ERA	G	IP	H	BB	SO	BR/9
Predicted	11	12	4.22	33	194	193	86	185	12.9
Actual	19	7	2.57	34	255.2	208	94	205	10.6

Pedro Martinez

	W	L	ERA	G	IP	H	BB	SO	BR/9
Predicted	16	10	3.07	33	217	179	70	209	10.3
Actual	17	8	1.90	31	241.1	158	67	305	8.4

While the projections may not be perfect, we do think they're the best ones available anywhere. So enjoy.

—Jim Callis

Projections for 1998 Batters

Batter	Age	Avg	G	AB	R	H	2B	3B	HR	RBI	BB	SO	SB	CS	OBP	SLG
Abbott,Jeff, ChA	25	.312	110	260	40	81	16	0	6	33	19	28	5	3	.358	.442
Abbott,Kurt, Fla	29	.259	115	352	48	91	21	4	10	42	27	98	3	2	.311	.426
Abreu,Bob, Hou	24	.256	127	383	49	98	17	7	6	47	44	101	12	9	.333	.384
Alexander,Manny, ChN	27	.232	144	449	65	104	19	4	5	40	34	80	26	10	.286	.325
Alfonzo,Edgardo, NYN	24	.288	153	559	72	161	27	3	9	70	47	66	8	6	.343	.395
Alicea,Luis, Ana	32	.248	125	379	53	94	18	4	5	39	60	65	14	7	.351	.356
Allensworth,Je., Pit	26	.267	148	509	77	136	28	5	5	46	48	91	23	14	.330	.371
Alomar,Roberto, Bal	30	.306	153	582	103	178	31	5	18	77	71	58	27	7	.381	.469
Alomar,Sandy, Cle	32	.280	130	429	56	120	24	1	16	61	18	46	3	2	.309	.452
Alou,Moises, Fla	31	.281	137	502	79	141	30	3	20	88	53	79	8	6	.350	.472
Amaral,Rich, Sea	36	.266	72	158	28	42	9	1	1	14	17	28	9	3	.337	.354
Anderson,Brady, Bal	34	.264	148	573	97	151	27	4	24	68	84	112	25	8	.358	.450
Anderson,Garret, Ana	26	.307	155	606	77	186	37	2	12	91	30	83	8	5	.340	.434
Ashley,Billy, LA	27	.231	93	169	22	39	6	1	8	25	22	67	1	1	.319	.420
Aurilia,Rich, SF	26	.264	69	140	18	37	6	1	3	17	13	18	3	2	.327	.386
Ausmus,Brad, Hou	29	.255	137	428	53	109	20	2	5	40	43	78	12	7	.323	.346
Baerga,Carlos, NYN	29	.276	120	445	66	123	24	1	12	65	23	32	5	3	.312	.416
Bagwell,Jeff, Hou	30	.285	162	586	119	167	39	3	36	122	131	125	23	9	.416	.546
Baines,Harold, Bal	39	.273	132	425	58	116	21	2	17	65	65	59	1	1	.369	.452
Barron,Tony, Phi	31	.268	68	205	24	55	12	0	7	27	12	43	3	2	.309	.429
Bates,Jason, Col	27	.252	71	143	18	36	7	1	3	16	18	32	1	2	.335	.378
Batista,Tony, Oak	24	.262	93	294	39	77	17	1	7	36	21	54	5	4	.311	.398
Bautista,Danny, Atl	26	.242	67	165	20	40	7	1	4	20	11	34	2	2	.290	.370
Becker,Rich, Min	26	.283	144	501	76	142	25	3	11	57	64	121	16	7	.365	.411
Bell,David, StL	25	.242	55	153	15	37	6	1	2	17	9	23	1	1	.284	.333
Bell,Derek, Hou	29	.281	145	565	72	159	26	2	15	84	42	103	27	8	.331	.414
Bell,Jay, KC	32	.258	151	555	78	143	30	4	15	67	62	109	6	5	.332	.407
Belle,Albert, ChA	31	.295	157	606	108	179	41	2	41	125	78	92	8	4	.376	.573
Bellhorn,Mark, Oak	23	.251	110	362	58	91	19	2	9	45	53	95	9	5	.347	.390
Benard,Marvin, SF	28	.267	64	135	21	36	6	1	1	11	16	23	6	4	.344	.348
Benitez,Yamil, KC	26	.254	138	414	49	105	17	2	15	61	25	112	9	7	.296	.413
Berroa,Geronimo, Bal	33	.273	151	568	86	155	24	1	27	93	64	118	6	4	.347	.461
Berry,Sean, Hou	32	.278	122	378	44	105	24	1	13	61	27	60	8	5	.326	.450
Berryhill,Damon, SF	34	.266	71	143	14	38	6	0	2	18	17	24	0	0	.344	.350
Bichette,Dante, Col	34	.295	149	589	88	174	33	2	29	113	33	101	18	9	.333	.506
Biggio,Craig, Hou	32	.281	156	597	116	168	33	3	17	70	82	89	38	9	.368	.432
Blauser,Jeff, Atl	32	.253	127	439	68	111	22	2	12	48	61	95	5	3	.344	.394
Blowers,Mike, Sea	33	.251	100	295	35	74	14	1	10	47	37	81	1	1	.334	.407
Bogar,Tim, Hou	31	.244	107	180	23	44	10	1	2	21	16	30	2	1	.306	.344
Boggs,Wade, NYA	40	.304	120	428	67	130	26	2	5	47	63	43	1	1	.393	.409
Bonds,Barry, SF	33	.276	154	519	117	143	31	3	37	103	141	85	35	10	.430	.561
Bonilla,Bobby, Fla	35	.276	149	561	81	155	31	3	22	90	67	88	3	4	.354	.460
Boone,Aaron, Cin	25	.262	92	252	33	66	16	2	7	33	15	37	6	2	.303	.425
Boone,Bret, Cin	29	.252	136	476	55	120	27	2	11	63	40	92	4	3	.310	.387
Borders,Pat, Cle	35	.241	80	212	18	51	12	1	4	18	10	39	1	1	.275	.363
Bordick,Mike, Bal	32	.244	140	468	46	114	16	1	6	44	39	55	6	3	.302	.321
Bournigal,Rafael, Oak	32	.226	99	265	23	60	10	0	0	20	17	21	2	2	.273	.264
Bragg,Darren, Bos	28	.265	147	479	76	127	31	2	10	55	68	96	18	7	.356	.401
Branson,Jeff, Cle	31	.234	69	145	16	34	7	1	4	16	16	31	1	0	.311	.379
Brede,Brent, Min	26	.300	99	337	55	101	22	3	5	43	43	64	7	4	.379	.427

338

Projections for 1998 Batters

Batter	Age	Avg	G	AB	R	H	2B	3B	HR	RBI	BB	SO	SB	CS	OBP	SLG
Brito,Tilson, Oak	26	.240	70	217	25	52	9	2	3	21	17	41	8	4	.295	.341
Brogna,Rico, Phi	28	.262	121	435	55	114	26	2	17	63	34	98	3	2	.316	.448
Brosius,Scott, Oak	31	.246	101	341	48	84	16	1	12	40	36	66	5	3	.318	.405
Brown,Adrian, Pit	24	.264	53	182	25	48	6	1	1	13	13	22	10	5	.313	.324
Brown,Brant, ChN	27	.256	71	227	28	58	13	2	7	25	14	45	4	5	.299	.423
Brumfield,Jacob, Tor	33	.252	55	155	25	39	9	1	3	15	13	30	6	4	.310	.381
Buford,Damon, Tex	28	.239	111	285	51	68	15	1	7	31	30	59	17	8	.311	.372
Buhner,Jay, Sea	33	.243	147	531	94	129	24	1	40	111	90	159	0	0	.353	.518
Burks,Ellis, Col	33	.273	133	454	86	124	26	3	27	78	52	95	13	4	.348	.522
Burnitz,Jeromy, Mil	29	.262	147	541	90	142	26	5	24	86	77	117	17	10	.354	.462
Cairo,Miguel, ChN	24	.249	95	273	33	68	12	1	1	21	12	25	14	6	.281	.311
Cameron,Mike, ChA	25	.262	148	523	96	137	28	7	21	74	65	139	28	10	.344	.463
Caminiti,Ken, SD	35	.264	142	519	81	137	28	1	26	88	77	107	9	4	.359	.472
Cangelosi,John, Fla	35	.243	99	136	22	33	5	1	1	8	23	24	8	3	.352	.316
Canseco,Jose, Oak	33	.255	107	388	63	99	19	1	24	72	53	106	6	3	.345	.495
Carr,Chuck, Hou	29	.240	80	229	36	55	12	1	2	17	25	41	17	7	.315	.328
Carter,Joe, Tor	38	.240	143	491	60	118	22	2	21	79	34	89	7	2	.290	.422
Casanova,Raul, Det	25	.249	119	366	37	91	15	0	11	42	29	58	1	1	.304	.380
Castilla,Vinny, Col	30	.294	160	618	90	182	30	2	37	103	40	99	5	5	.337	.529
Castillo,Luis, Fla	22	.273	78	271	38	74	7	2	0	16	27	51	21	10	.339	.314
Cedeno,Domingo, Tex	29	.262	119	389	50	102	15	5	4	34	25	76	5	4	.307	.357
Cedeno,Roger, LA	23	.268	127	369	49	99	12	3	3	31	40	71	16	8	.340	.341
Cianfrocco,Archi, SD	31	.246	71	171	19	42	10	1	3	24	11	46	2	1	.291	.368
Cirillo,Jeff, Mil	28	.292	157	568	89	166	39	3	13	77	67	71	6	5	.367	.440
Clark,Dave, ChN	35	.262	106	149	21	39	6	0	5	23	21	34	1	1	.353	.403
Clark,Tony, Det	26	.262	150	568	85	149	24	1	32	111	84	156	1	2	.357	.477
Clark,Will, Tex	34	.294	125	452	72	133	26	2	14	74	65	64	2	1	.383	.454
Clayton,Royce, StL	28	.254	154	574	66	146	26	5	7	53	40	112	31	12	.303	.354
Colbrunn,Greg, Atl	28	.278	98	205	24	57	10	0	7	30	9	30	2	2	.308	.429
Coleman,Michael, Bos	22	.285	88	242	35	69	13	3	8	32	19	63	8	3	.337	.463
Collier,Lou, Pit	24	.271	93	221	29	60	12	1	0	21	16	33	8	4	.321	.335
Conine,Jeff, Fla	32	.282	139	468	61	132	24	2	21	81	60	96	2	1	.364	.476
Coomer,Ron, Min	31	.280	151	532	65	149	29	1	17	87	28	71	4	3	.316	.434
Cora,Joey, Sea	33	.278	142	522	78	145	21	3	7	43	44	40	11	6	.334	.370
Cordero,Wil, Bos	26	.288	125	480	68	138	30	2	13	63	31	88	9	4	.331	.440
Cordova,Marty, Min	28	.280	128	482	71	135	29	3	17	74	47	99	13	6	.344	.459
Counsell,Craig, Fla	27	.299	147	539	78	161	35	6	6	63	56	52	9	4	.365	.419
Crespo,Felipe, Tor	25	.254	93	236	31	60	12	1	6	24	29	32	6	5	.336	.390
Cruz,Deivi, Det	23	.245	141	416	34	102	26	0	2	40	14	48	5	5	.270	.322
Cruz,Jacob, SF	25	.285	136	421	63	120	28	1	8	61	47	68	7	6	.357	.413
Cruz Jr,Jose, Tor	24	.265	157	563	98	149	32	3	28	101	80	136	8	3	.356	.481
Cummings,Midre, Phi	26	.266	127	387	43	103	24	3	5	43	24	69	3	2	.309	.382
Curtis,Chad, NYA	29	.261	125	375	62	98	18	2	12	44	49	63	18	10	.347	.416
Damon,Johnny, KC	24	.289	149	546	80	158	20	9	9	58	46	60	23	9	.345	.408
Daulton,Darren, Fla	36	.237	123	388	55	92	20	2	12	58	72	74	4	2	.357	.392
Davis,Chili, KC	38	.259	132	463	68	120	20	1	23	80	86	97	3	2	.375	.456
Davis,Eric, Bal	36	.236	84	263	42	62	11	1	12	40	39	84	11	4	.334	.422
Davis,Russ, Sea	28	.256	129	429	60	110	26	1	17	59	40	102	4	3	.320	.441
Delgado,Carlos, Tor	26	.268	152	560	78	150	28	2	31	94	67	146	1	1	.346	.491
DeShields,Delino, StL	29	.278	154	561	86	156	22	7	9	55	65	99	52	15	.353	.390

339

Projections for 1998 Batters

Batter	Age	Avg	G	AB	R	H	2B	3B	HR	RBI	BB	SO	SB	CS	OBP	SLG
Difelice,Mike, StL	29	.248	84	230	18	57	11	0	4	24	18	42	1	1	.302	.348
DiSarcina,Gary, Ana	30	.254	146	524	62	133	24	3	5	45	22	33	6	6	.284	.340
Ducey,Rob, Sea	33	.297	86	182	27	54	19	2	4	17	11	40	3	3	.337	.489
Duncan,Mariano, Tor	35	.250	78	260	30	65	14	1	3	28	7	59	3	2	.270	.346
Dunn,Todd, Mil	27	.284	130	395	61	112	27	3	14	58	30	100	7	4	.334	.473
Dunston,Shawon, Pit	35	.263	122	441	48	116	21	3	11	48	11	70	12	5	.281	.399
Dunwoody,Todd, Fla	23	.241	121	361	47	87	15	4	12	45	24	109	13	6	.288	.404
Durham,Ray, ChA	26	.275	157	597	103	164	30	8	11	64	56	96	31	11	.337	.407
Dye,Jermaine, KC	24	.258	145	524	57	135	28	1	18	72	23	107	4	6	.289	.418
Easley,Damion, Det	28	.248	153	557	82	138	26	2	17	67	64	94	19	10	.325	.393
Edmonds,Jim, Ana	28	.290	136	518	90	150	28	2	28	85	57	108	4	4	.360	.514
Eisenreich,Jim, Fla	39	.284	104	278	32	79	15	2	3	33	28	32	4	1	.350	.385
Elster,Kevin, Pit	33	.216	93	329	39	71	16	1	11	48	37	90	2	1	.295	.371
Encarnacion,Juan, Det	22	.291	116	323	50	94	18	3	15	51	21	66	10	2	.334	.505
Erstad,Darin, Ana	24	.296	147	567	100	168	32	4	14	72	57	81	18	10	.361	.441
Estalella,Bobby, Phi	23	.231	89	225	28	52	12	0	10	32	26	60	1	1	.311	.418
Eusebio,Tony, Hou	31	.290	90	252	28	73	13	1	3	37	24	35	1	1	.351	.385
Everett,Carl, NYN	27	.257	112	303	47	78	16	2	9	39	30	70	10	7	.324	.413
Fabregas,Jorge, ChA	28	.263	138	422	38	111	15	0	5	49	27	52	2	2	.307	.334
Fernandez,Tony, Cle	36	.258	78	209	26	54	10	2	4	24	17	25	4	3	.314	.383
Fielder,Cecil, NYA	34	.244	125	454	63	111	16	0	25	80	68	112	0	0	.343	.445
Finley,Steve, SD	33	.268	153	600	100	161	26	6	22	70	55	85	24	9	.330	.442
Flaherty,John, SD	30	.257	135	448	43	115	23	1	11	52	26	63	3	3	.297	.386
Fletcher,Darrin, Mon	31	.260	125	388	41	101	21	1	15	61	29	36	1	1	.312	.436
Floyd,Cliff, Fla	25	.259	100	228	32	59	14	2	7	31	27	56	6	2	.337	.430
Franco,Julio, Mil	36	.250	101	300	41	75	13	1	7	42	46	75	6	3	.350	.370
Franco,Matt, NYN	28	.276	100	185	22	51	12	1	3	23	13	22	1	1	.323	.400
Frye,Jeff, Bos	31	.278	86	273	37	76	18	1	2	27	27	35	9	3	.343	.374
Fryman,Travis, Det	29	.278	157	612	92	170	35	4	21	101	60	114	7	3	.342	.451
Fullmer,Brad, Mon	23	.281	146	558	69	157	34	1	22	80	27	46	4	3	.315	.464
Gaetti,Gary, StL	39	.236	119	423	50	100	19	1	17	60	33	83	2	2	.292	.407
Gagne,Greg, LA	36	.236	127	437	44	103	21	2	8	49	39	94	5	6	.298	.348
Galarraga,Andres, Col	37	.302	146	569	91	172	30	2	34	110	41	155	12	5	.349	.541
Gant,Ron, StL	33	.228	112	382	60	87	18	2	19	61	60	110	14	6	.333	.435
Garcia,Carlos, Tor	30	.263	97	338	41	89	16	2	4	32	20	53	11	6	.304	.358
Garcia,Freddy, Pit	25	.236	86	229	29	54	11	2	11	33	10	52	0	0	.268	.445
Garcia,Karim, LA	22	.245	91	282	36	69	11	3	9	39	16	69	5	4	.285	.401
Garciaparra,No., Bos	24	.293	149	621	104	182	37	9	25	88	39	67	23	9	.335	.502
Gates,Brent, Sea	28	.266	89	305	37	81	18	2	3	35	27	46	2	1	.325	.367
Giambi,Jason, Oak	27	.285	147	526	77	150	40	1	18	82	64	90	1	1	.363	.468
Gil,Benji, Tex	25	.227	89	269	28	61	11	1	5	27	17	86	3	3	.273	.331
Giles,Brian S., Cle	27	.296	149	533	93	158	24	5	24	86	78	59	9	4	.386	.495
Gilkey,Bernard, NYN	31	.269	141	527	81	142	32	2	20	80	63	102	14	10	.347	.452
Girardi,Joe, NYA	33	.263	129	391	46	103	16	2	3	40	26	59	5	3	.309	.338
Glanville,Doug, ChN	27	.264	149	546	65	144	23	3	4	44	22	66	19	12	.292	.339
Gomez,Chris, SD	27	.242	147	541	61	131	22	1	7	58	61	113	6	5	.319	.325
Gonzalez,Alex, Tor	25	.244	140	479	62	117	26	4	13	52	47	119	16	7	.312	.397
Gonzalez,Juan, Tex	28	.295	141	559	89	165	29	3	42	129	39	100	2	1	.341	.583
Gonzalez,Luis, Hou	30	.268	147	511	75	137	31	5	12	73	67	61	12	9	.353	.419
Goodwin,Curtis, Cin	25	.258	79	256	38	66	10	2	1	17	27	48	23	10	.329	.324

Projections for 1998 Batters

Batter	Age	Avg	G	AB	R	H	2B	3B	HR	RBI	BB	SO	SB	CS	OBP	SLG
Goodwin,Tom, Tex	29	.267	147	543	78	145	16	4	2	36	44	82	59	21	.322	.322
Grace,Mark, ChN	34	.300	156	583	87	175	35	2	12	74	77	49	4	3	.382	.429
Graffanino,Tony, Atl	26	.236	121	326	42	77	19	2	7	30	31	74	9	6	.303	.371
Grebeck,Craig, Ana	33	.242	55	99	11	24	7	0	1	8	12	13	0	0	.324	.343
Green,Shawn, Tor	25	.285	148	512	69	146	32	4	17	62	39	98	10	4	.336	.463
Greene,Todd, Ana	27	.285	130	446	65	127	23	0	28	76	24	73	4	3	.321	.525
Greene,Willie, Cin	26	.251	146	501	75	126	22	2	27	83	71	119	4	3	.344	.465
Greer,Rusty, Tex	29	.303	154	588	95	178	38	3	21	90	79	90	5	2	.385	.485
Grieve,Ben, Oak	22	.291	149	556	100	162	35	1	23	105	71	116	3	3	.372	.482
Griffey Jr,Ken, Sea	28	.303	154	588	127	178	34	3	50	128	91	116	14	4	.396	.626
Grissom,Marquis, Cle	31	.271	152	612	92	166	28	4	15	58	46	76	32	12	.322	.404
Grudzielanek,Ma., Mon	28	.278	157	626	81	174	41	3	4	54	27	80	27	9	.308	.372
Guerrero,Vladimir, Mon	22	.318	149	569	87	181	41	6	19	82	43	59	13	10	.366	.511
Guerrero,Wilton, LA	23	.296	120	423	51	125	11	6	2	32	15	59	15	8	.320	.364
Guillen,Jose, Pit	22	.274	144	500	60	137	21	5	14	70	18	80	2	1	.299	.420
Guillen,Ozzie, ChA	34	.254	132	445	52	113	18	3	3	43	15	25	5	5	.278	.328
Gutierrez,Ricky, Hou	28	.261	114	329	39	86	13	2	2	31	27	57	6	4	.317	.331
Gwynn,Tony, SD	38	.348	132	515	68	179	27	3	9	72	39	21	9	4	.394	.464
Halter,Shane, KC	28	.223	78	202	22	45	10	0	2	16	17	43	3	3	.283	.302
Hamelin,Bob, Det	30	.261	118	337	50	88	19	1	19	59	63	85	3	2	.378	.493
Hamilton,Darryl, SF	33	.274	135	514	74	141	20	3	5	45	57	58	14	6	.347	.354
Hammonds,Jeffrey, Bal	27	.262	135	473	79	124	25	3	19	62	44	89	11	4	.325	.448
Hansen,Dave, ChN	29	.280	106	164	16	46	7	0	2	16	28	31	1	0	.385	.360
Hansen,Jed, KC	25	.256	86	234	26	60	12	1	5	24	17	45	5	3	.307	.380
Harris,Lenny, Cin	33	.257	108	218	27	56	10	1	3	22	16	21	9	4	.308	.353
Haselman,Bill, Bos	32	.253	92	249	34	63	14	0	9	36	21	46	2	1	.311	.418
Hatteberg,Scott, Bos	28	.263	125	415	56	109	24	1	11	48	63	76	1	1	.360	.405
Hayes,Charlie, NYA	33	.252	108	274	29	69	13	1	6	36	25	49	2	1	.314	.372
Helton,Todd, Col	24	.327	148	551	91	180	40	4	19	93	72	72	3	3	.404	.517
Henderson,Rickey, Ana	39	.245	118	387	73	95	18	2	8	33	90	79	30	10	.388	.364
Hernandez,Carlos, SD	31	.218	57	124	8	27	4	0	2	11	5	26	1	1	.248	.298
Hernandez,Jose, ChN	28	.239	134	293	44	70	11	3	10	36	21	80	4	2	.290	.399
Hidalgo,Richard, Hou	22	.259	132	413	47	107	26	2	8	49	20	56	6	7	.293	.390
Higginson,Bob, Det	27	.280	149	546	92	153	29	3	26	82	81	101	12	7	.373	.487
Hill,Glenallen, SF	33	.255	120	420	54	107	21	2	16	62	30	95	15	5	.304	.429
Hocking,Denny, Min	28	.240	110	275	30	66	11	2	3	30	17	42	6	5	.284	.327
Hoiles,Chris, Bal	33	.249	124	385	55	96	17	0	19	60	64	97	1	1	.356	.442
Hollandsworth,Todd, LA	25	.259	111	328	43	85	17	2	7	39	26	65	10	6	.314	.387
Hollins,Dave, Ana	32	.254	131	457	80	116	22	2	13	64	73	100	7	4	.357	.396
Houston,Tyler, ChN	27	.248	96	250	24	62	11	1	4	29	12	42	3	2	.282	.348
Howard,David, KC	31	.225	83	200	22	45	8	1	1	19	18	35	4	2	.289	.290
Howard,Thomas, Hou	33	.265	115	294	36	78	14	2	4	29	21	47	8	5	.314	.367
Howell,Jack, Ana	36	.228	80	149	21	34	10	1	9	26	12	36	0	0	.286	.490
Hudler,Rex, Phi	37	.250	86	236	32	59	12	1	9	25	9	50	7	2	.278	.424
Hundley,Todd, NYN	29	.240	73	229	37	55	10	1	14	39	40	60	1	1	.353	.476
Hunter,Brian L., Det	27	.281	155	619	94	174	27	5	4	46	45	105	52	16	.330	.360
Huskey,Butch, NYN	26	.258	144	538	67	139	23	1	23	83	40	104	8	6	.310	.433
Ibanez,Raul, Sea	26	.292	75	243	39	71	15	1	7	36	21	37	4	3	.348	.449
Jackson,Damian, Cin	24	.254	90	291	45	74	13	1	4	23	33	58	16	7	.330	.347
Jaha,John, Mil	32	.275	143	513	88	141	24	1	30	93	74	112	3	2	.366	.501

Projections for 1998 Batters

Batter	Age	Avg	G	AB	R	H	2B	3B	HR	RBI	BB	SO	SB	CS	OBP	SLG
Javier,Stan, SF	34	.256	124	410	62	105	15	2	6	40	47	68	25	5	.333	.346
Jefferies,Gregg, Phi	30	.288	126	490	67	141	26	2	11	59	46	27	17	8	.349	.416
Jefferson,Reggie, Bos	29	.302	139	451	67	136	28	2	15	67	28	93	1	0	.342	.472
Jeter,Derek, NYA	24	.304	159	641	111	195	33	7	9	72	67	105	22	11	.370	.420
Johnson,Brian, SF	30	.263	112	334	33	88	18	2	11	50	15	47	0	0	.295	.428
Johnson,Charles, Fla	26	.241	133	431	48	104	22	1	17	56	59	102	2	2	.333	.415
Johnson,Lance, ChN	34	.289	141	577	82	167	17	8	7	53	37	36	38	11	.332	.383
Johnson,Mark, Cin	30	.234	98	265	40	62	14	1	9	35	44	70	4	3	.343	.396
Johnson,Russ, Hou	25	.258	86	244	33	63	8	1	4	26	23	35	3	3	.322	.348
Jones,Andruw, Atl	21	.263	149	547	85	144	23	1	25	84	60	130	27	16	.336	.446
Jones,Chipper, Atl	26	.294	158	598	107	176	33	5	25	106	86	93	15	5	.383	.492
Jones,Chris, SD	32	.268	78	138	21	37	8	1	5	20	12	36	2	1	.327	.449
Jordan,Brian, StL	31	.283	147	480	67	136	25	3	14	73	26	77	20	8	.320	.435
Jordan,Kevin, Phi	28	.262	72	202	23	53	14	1	4	26	9	23	1	1	.294	.401
Joyner,Wally, SD	36	.293	131	454	56	133	27	1	10	67	65	68	3	3	.382	.423
Justice,David, Cle	32	.283	139	506	82	143	24	2	28	90	86	82	4	4	.387	.504
Karkovice,Ron, ChA	34	.212	45	104	13	22	5	0	4	14	10	28	0	0	.281	.375
Karros,Eric, LA	30	.257	160	622	84	160	30	1	31	102	64	123	8	4	.327	.458
Kelly,Mike, Cin	28	.230	82	183	29	42	11	1	5	21	19	52	6	3	.302	.383
Kelly,Pat, NYA	30	.236	77	195	27	46	12	1	3	21	17	50	5	3	.297	.354
Kelly,Roberto, Sea	33	.280	124	432	57	121	23	2	10	52	25	75	14	7	.319	.412
Kendall,Jason, Pit	24	.300	145	484	73	145	32	3	6	56	47	36	11	6	.362	.415
Kent,Jeff, SF	30	.264	155	546	75	144	31	2	22	83	41	110	6	4	.315	.449
Kieschnick,Br., ChN	26	.253	139	411	46	104	20	0	17	53	38	95	2	2	.316	.426
King,Jeff, KC	33	.242	146	533	72	129	28	2	23	91	73	89	10	4	.333	.432
Klesko,Ryan, Atl	27	.273	150	491	76	134	24	4	27	80	64	122	5	4	.357	.503
Knoblauch,Chuck, Min	29	.296	157	608	120	180	33	7	10	65	96	90	58	16	.392	.423
Konerko,Paul, LA	22	.261	147	528	72	138	23	1	25	83	51	85	2	3	.326	.451
Kotsay,Mark, Fla	22	.253	140	479	79	121	23	2	12	59	50	79	13	4	.323	.384
Kreuter,Chad, Ana	33	.221	75	190	21	42	9	1	3	21	21	52	0	1	.299	.326
Lampkin,Tom, StL	34	.240	97	179	24	43	10	1	4	22	22	23	2	2	.323	.374
Lankford,Ray, StL	31	.278	145	521	95	145	32	4	25	84	84	128	24	10	.379	.499
Lansing,Mike, Mon	30	.267	152	592	77	158	37	2	14	63	43	85	22	8	.317	.407
Larkin,Barry, Cin	34	.286	127	437	82	125	24	3	16	55	73	46	32	6	.388	.465
Lawton,Matt, Min	26	.264	154	519	84	137	27	3	15	71	68	80	13	8	.349	.414
Lemke,Mark, Atl	32	.240	122	413	42	99	14	1	4	32	44	46	2	2	.313	.308
Lennon,Patrick, Oak	30	.308	72	208	33	64	14	1	6	30	24	59	4	3	.379	.471
Lesher,Brian, Oak	27	.261	70	234	33	61	12	1	9	34	22	53	4	3	.324	.436
Levis,Jesse, Mil	30	.266	116	259	30	69	14	0	2	27	39	17	1	1	.362	.344
Lewis,Darren, LA	30	.237	116	152	22	36	4	1	1	13	16	20	11	5	.310	.296
Lewis,Mark, SF	28	.263	136	410	56	108	24	2	9	47	36	79	3	3	.323	.398
Leyritz,Jim, Tex	34	.257	109	335	45	86	14	0	10	53	48	84	1	1	.350	.388
Lieberthal,Mike, Phi	26	.242	138	467	52	113	25	1	15	63	48	67	2	2	.313	.396
Lockhart,Keith, Atl	33	.287	99	251	34	72	15	1	6	32	18	23	4	2	.335	.426
Lofton,Kenny, Atl	31	.310	140	577	107	179	26	6	9	57	59	75	61	20	.374	.423
Lopez,Javy, Atl	27	.287	137	463	56	133	22	2	23	69	32	83	1	2	.333	.492
Lopez,Luis, NYN	27	.252	95	258	29	65	16	1	3	26	14	50	3	3	.290	.357
Loretta,Mark, Mil	26	.281	125	388	49	109	17	3	4	47	36	42	6	5	.342	.371
Mabry,John, StL	27	.281	136	449	52	126	26	1	8	52	35	69	2	2	.333	.396
Macfarlane,Mike, KC	34	.242	95	298	41	72	17	1	12	42	28	57	1	1	.307	.426

Projections for 1998 Batters

Batter	Age	Avg	G	AB	R	H	2B	3B	HR	RBI	BB	SO	SB	CS	OBP	SLG
Mack,Shane, Bos	34	.316	96	272	27	86	15	0	6	36	19	50	4	2	.361	.438
Magadan,Dave, Oak	35	.269	120	279	36	75	17	1	3	32	54	44	1	1	.387	.369
Magee,Wendell, Phi	25	.239	45	142	15	34	8	1	3	15	12	25	2	3	.299	.373
Manwaring,Kirt, Col	32	.223	101	296	20	66	11	1	2	25	24	59	1	1	.281	.287
Marrero,Eli, StL	24	.252	123	381	52	96	18	3	15	55	22	56	7	5	.293	.433
Martin,Al, Pit	30	.286	136	510	80	146	27	4	15	59	51	99	28	11	.351	.443
Martin,Norberto, ChA	31	.276	94	221	30	61	11	2	2	23	7	29	5	3	.298	.371
Martinez,Dave, ChA	33	.276	141	424	62	117	17	4	9	45	48	57	11	6	.350	.399
Martinez,Edgar, Sea	35	.305	145	512	101	156	38	1	25	101	121	88	4	3	.438	.529
Martinez,Tino, NYA	30	.278	158	594	89	165	31	1	33	116	75	88	2	1	.359	.500
Mashore,Damon, Oak	28	.254	99	276	43	70	13	2	4	27	37	69	8	4	.342	.359
Matheny,Mike, Mil	27	.227	128	330	29	75	18	1	5	37	18	74	2	1	.267	.333
Mayne,Brent, Oak	30	.254	101	244	23	62	12	1	3	23	21	35	1	1	.313	.348
McCracken,Qu., Col	28	.316	133	339	62	107	18	4	3	35	36	57	24	10	.381	.419
McDonald,Jason, Oak	26	.242	80	252	44	61	8	3	3	21	39	45	16	8	.344	.333
McGee,Willie, StL	39	.261	108	272	34	71	16	3	3	30	16	59	4	2	.302	.375
McGriff,Fred, Atl	34	.278	151	565	81	157	27	1	24	90	68	112	5	4	.355	.457
McGuire,Ryan, Mon	26	.278	74	227	28	63	14	1	4	24	26	34	4	3	.352	.401
McGwire,Mark, StL	34	.265	154	539	100	143	23	0	52	116	132	152	1	1	.410	.597
McLemore,Mark, Tex	33	.252	124	444	60	112	16	2	3	34	62	67	18	9	.344	.318
McMillon,Billy, Phi	26	.277	112	336	45	93	20	1	8	45	35	73	6	3	.345	.414
McRae,Brian, NYN	30	.262	156	619	98	162	31	7	13	55	67	91	30	11	.334	.397
Meares,Pat, Min	29	.264	146	485	63	128	23	4	10	58	19	88	9	6	.292	.390
Merced,Orlando, Tor	31	.278	130	478	65	133	25	2	14	69	56	76	7	3	.354	.427
Mieske,Matt, Mil	30	.256	105	277	39	71	16	2	9	40	24	53	2	3	.316	.426
Miller,Orlando, Det	29	.252	98	310	33	78	17	3	7	38	15	71	3	3	.286	.394
Milliard,Ralph, Fla	24	.229	94	249	35	57	9	1	3	18	27	43	7	4	.304	.309
Mirabelli,Doug, SF	27	.237	79	156	18	37	8	0	4	19	22	25	0	0	.331	.365
Molina,Izzy, Oak	27	.220	62	186	17	41	7	1	4	19	10	30	1	1	.260	.333
Molitor,Paul, Min	41	.283	133	533	66	151	27	3	10	72	52	68	14	3	.347	.402
Mondesi,Raul, LA	27	.294	159	625	97	184	34	6	27	87	40	113	24	11	.337	.498
Morandini,Mickey, Phi	32	.265	144	547	66	145	26	5	3	40	53	89	17	9	.330	.347
Morris,Hal, Cin	33	.290	96	328	43	95	19	1	7	46	28	50	3	2	.346	.418
Mouton,James, Hou	29	.251	90	219	32	55	14	1	3	22	23	40	17	7	.322	.365
Mouton,Lyle, ChA	29	.272	88	250	30	68	15	1	6	33	22	63	4	3	.331	.412
Mueller,Bill, SF	27	.287	118	415	57	119	21	3	3	40	46	54	3	3	.358	.373
Myers,Greg, Atl	32	.250	77	180	19	45	9	0	4	22	12	31	0	0	.297	.367
Myers,Rod, KC	25	.271	131	332	43	90	18	1	6	35	28	66	17	8	.328	.386
Naehring,Tim, Bos	31	.280	120	421	62	118	23	0	13	57	63	64	2	2	.374	.428
Nevin,Phil, Det	27	.238	81	248	32	59	12	0	9	35	26	65	1	1	.310	.395
Newfield,Marc, Mil	25	.275	139	509	67	140	34	1	13	71	37	88	1	1	.324	.422
Newson,Warren, Tex	33	.234	74	141	22	33	6	0	6	16	28	47	1	1	.361	.404
Nieves,Melvin, Det	26	.244	127	381	56	93	16	2	21	61	39	145	2	3	.314	.462
Nilsson,Dave, Mil	28	.286	150	548	79	157	31	2	19	89	65	84	3	2	.362	.454
Nixon,Otis, LA	39	.257	118	474	63	122	10	1	1	28	56	72	42	13	.336	.289
Norton,Greg, ChA	25	.256	101	313	46	80	16	1	10	43	33	67	5	6	.327	.409
Nunnally,Jon, Cin	26	.270	140	441	78	119	22	5	25	72	64	114	11	8	.362	.512
O'Brien,Charlie, Tor	37	.202	82	233	22	47	13	0	7	26	26	52	0	0	.282	.348
O'Leary,Troy, Bos	28	.286	144	483	67	138	32	5	14	71	42	74	5	3	.343	.460
O'Neill,Paul, NYA	35	.282	142	517	80	146	29	1	19	90	84	84	4	4	.383	.453

Projections for 1998 Batters

Batter	Age	Avg	G	AB	R	H	2B	3B	HR	RBI	BB	SO	SB	CS	OBP	SLG
Ochoa,Alex, NYN	26	.283	96	286	39	81	16	2	5	36	24	36	9	6	.339	.406
Offerman,Jose, KC	29	.276	131	489	68	135	18	5	3	44	68	79	12	9	.364	.352
Olerud,John, NYN	29	.296	153	557	85	165	36	1	21	89	95	62	1	1	.399	.478
Oliver,Joe, Cin	32	.244	118	361	36	88	19	0	13	50	29	66	2	2	.300	.404
Ordonez,Magglio, ChA	24	.286	138	451	55	129	30	1	13	64	25	59	9	9	.324	.443
Ordonez,Rey, NYN	25	.230	119	382	39	88	12	3	1	32	20	38	7	6	.269	.285
Orie,Kevin, ChN	25	.279	137	473	54	132	31	3	11	66	53	75	2	1	.352	.427
Ortiz,David, Min	22	.271	90	221	32	60	16	1	11	41	12	65	1	5	.309	.502
Osik,Keith, Pit	29	.267	61	150	15	40	10	0	2	17	11	22	0	0	.317	.373
Otero,Ricky, Phi	26	.267	46	131	18	35	5	2	0	9	12	12	5	4	.329	.336
Pagnozzi,Tom, StL	35	.236	86	233	21	55	11	1	6	29	12	39	1	0	.273	.369
Palmeiro,Orlando, Ana	29	.274	63	164	22	45	8	1	0	15	17	15	4	2	.343	.335
Palmeiro,Rafael, Bal	33	.271	154	597	94	162	33	2	36	109	76	93	6	2	.354	.514
Palmer,Dean, KC	29	.261	151	559	88	146	27	1	29	92	58	135	3	2	.331	.469
Perez,Eddie, Atl	30	.238	83	223	20	53	10	0	5	24	9	35	0	0	.267	.350
Perez,Eduardo, Cin	28	.265	127	381	56	101	21	2	16	58	42	70	7	3	.338	.457
Perez,Neifi, Col	23	.311	156	602	84	187	40	11	11	66	26	57	10	8	.339	.468
Perez,Tomas, Tor	24	.232	62	177	16	41	8	1	0	13	15	28	2	1	.292	.288
Phillips,Tony, Ana	39	.260	138	519	90	135	20	2	12	49	110	133	12	8	.390	.376
Piazza,Mike, LA	29	.334	154	572	99	191	26	1	38	119	73	94	2	2	.409	.582
Plantier,Phil, StL	29	.256	85	238	34	61	12	0	10	36	28	53	1	1	.335	.433
Polcovich,Kevin, Pit	28	.258	83	248	29	64	11	1	2	22	13	36	4	4	.295	.335
Posada,Jorge, NYA	26	.245	73	159	25	39	9	1	4	21	25	37	2	2	.348	.390
Powell,Dante, SF	24	.242	91	306	50	74	14	1	8	32	32	65	18	9	.314	.373
Pratt,Todd, NYN	31	.281	86	221	35	62	9	1	7	35	25	59	0	2	.354	.425
Pride,Curtis, Bos	29	.256	74	168	27	43	8	3	4	18	20	43	8	4	.335	.411
Raines,Tim, NYA	38	.280	101	354	61	99	16	3	8	44	54	46	10	2	.375	.410
Ramirez,Manny, Cle	26	.318	154	556	100	177	39	1	31	108	87	112	7	5	.411	.559
Randa,Joe, Pit	28	.268	146	497	59	133	28	4	8	58	44	75	7	4	.327	.388
Reboulet,Jeff, Bal	34	.239	101	222	28	53	9	0	3	22	25	38	2	1	.316	.320
Reed,Jeff, Col	35	.258	104	256	29	66	11	1	8	29	36	51	1	1	.349	.402
Reese,Pokey, Cin	25	.220	98	328	39	72	15	1	4	28	29	66	11	4	.283	.308
Relaford,Desi, Phi	24	.240	91	308	38	74	14	1	4	26	26	57	14	5	.299	.331
Renteria,Edgar, Fla	22	.282	153	586	79	165	21	4	5	53	38	92	27	11	.325	.357
Ripken,Billy, Tex	33	.244	72	193	19	47	10	0	2	19	11	23	1	1	.284	.326
Ripken,Cal, Bal	37	.254	162	621	79	158	32	2	19	91	59	78	1	1	.319	.404
Roberts,Bip, Cle	34	.283	108	396	47	112	17	2	2	39	26	55	17	5	.327	.351
Rodriguez,Alex, Sea	22	.328	148	579	106	190	38	3	28	98	49	101	20	7	.381	.549
Rodriguez,Henry, Mon	30	.236	143	504	59	119	26	2	25	78	41	148	2	1	.294	.444
Rodriguez,Ivan, Tex	26	.307	154	612	93	188	34	3	20	85	34	66	5	3	.344	.471
Rolen,Scott, Phi	23	.290	152	555	82	161	40	2	18	83	69	107	12	8	.369	.467
Salmon,Tim, Ana	29	.297	158	589	107	175	31	2	34	112	101	131	6	6	.400	.530
Sanchez,Rey, NYA	30	.251	116	283	30	71	12	1	1	20	14	36	4	3	.286	.311
Sanders,Reggie, Cin	30	.265	137	465	79	123	25	4	24	74	68	129	30	13	.358	.490
Santangelo,F.P., Mon	30	.249	139	369	49	92	22	3	5	37	48	55	6	5	.336	.366
Santiago,Benito, Tor	33	.241	117	395	46	95	17	1	17	54	33	87	1	1	.299	.418
Sefcik,Kevin, Phi	27	.264	61	140	16	37	6	1	1	11	8	14	3	2	.304	.343
Segui,David, Mon	31	.278	149	551	82	153	30	1	18	75	66	69	3	3	.355	.434
Servais,Scott, ChN	31	.248	123	400	41	99	21	0	10	53	33	67	1	1	.305	.375
Sheffield,Gary, Fla	29	.275	148	484	102	133	28	2	30	94	137	79	20	11	.435	.527

Projections for 1998 Batters

Batter	Age	Avg	G	AB	R	H	2B	3B	HR	RBI	BB	SO	SB	CS	OBP	SLG
Shipley,Craig, SD	35	.255	65	137	15	35	7	0	2	13	5	20	3	2	.282	.350
Smith,Mark, Pit	28	.264	83	254	37	67	16	0	11	42	24	49	4	2	.327	.457
Snopek,Chris, ChA	27	.262	71	221	28	58	12	1	5	27	22	36	2	2	.329	.394
Snow,J.T., SF	30	.266	158	572	78	152	25	1	23	92	74	107	3	4	.350	.434
Sojo,Luis, NYA	32	.257	66	183	21	47	7	1	2	17	11	11	2	1	.299	.339
Sorrento,Paul, Sea	32	.257	138	435	61	112	22	0	25	82	57	99	1	1	.343	.480
Sosa,Sammy, ChN	29	.257	153	603	89	155	23	4	37	108	51	156	28	11	.315	.493
Spiers,Bill, Hou	32	.254	136	303	39	77	13	2	4	33	50	48	9	4	.360	.350
Spiezio,Scott, Oak	25	.249	154	555	70	138	30	4	15	75	49	73	7	5	.310	.398
Sprague,Ed, Tor	30	.236	143	521	70	123	27	2	20	68	57	110	0	0	.311	.411
Stahoviak,Scott, Min	28	.259	94	274	40	71	20	1	8	37	34	71	4	3	.341	.427
Stairs,Matt, Oak	30	.282	157	543	78	153	34	1	29	101	64	94	6	5	.357	.508
Stanley,Mike, NYA	35	.261	127	394	64	103	18	1	19	69	63	87	1	1	.363	.457
Steinbach,Terry, Min	36	.242	130	459	52	111	22	1	18	65	37	107	2	2	.298	.412
Stevens,Lee, Tex	30	.271	116	377	54	102	24	1	20	62	35	80	1	1	.333	.499
Stewart,Shannon, Tor	24	.272	148	591	86	161	32	8	5	56	70	78	34	14	.349	.379
Stocker,Kevin, Phi	28	.248	148	544	58	135	23	4	4	49	58	104	8	5	.321	.327
Strange,Doug, Mon	34	.231	107	242	27	56	13	1	6	30	22	50	1	1	.295	.368
Stynes,Chris, Cin	25	.296	156	557	76	165	29	3	10	65	31	37	15	7	.333	.413
Surhoff,B.J., Bal	33	.273	140	506	68	138	25	2	16	72	47	64	3	2	.335	.425
Sutton,Larry, KC	28	.278	110	241	33	67	12	0	8	34	28	35	1	0	.353	.427
Sveum,Dale, Pit	34	.241	101	286	34	69	18	1	10	41	25	68	1	1	.302	.416
Sweeney,Mark, SD	28	.283	123	247	39	70	14	1	5	39	40	42	3	2	.383	.409
Sweeney,Mike, KC	24	.257	138	440	60	113	25	0	15	64	38	53	4	4	.316	.416
Tarasco,Tony, Bal	27	.250	82	220	33	55	9	2	7	26	29	41	9	3	.337	.405
Tartabull,Danny, Phi	35	.247	74	219	30	54	12	1	11	40	42	64	1	1	.345	.461
Tatis,Fernando, Tex	23	.285	142	516	80	147	28	0	25	72	42	93	12	7	.339	.484
Taubensee,Eddie, Cin	29	.263	122	323	42	85	19	1	12	45	30	74	2	2	.326	.440
Tejada,Miguel, Oak	22	.235	129	413	52	97	14	3	12	58	24	90	9	8	.277	.370
Thomas,Frank, ChA	30	.326	149	531	114	173	33	1	38	121	128	73	2	2	.457	.606
Thome,Jim, Cle	27	.294	152	547	119	161	28	2	39	103	134	150	4	3	.433	.567
Tinsley,Lee, Sea	29	.241	55	137	21	33	6	1	2	14	14	38	5	3	.311	.343
Trammell,Bubba, Det	26	.276	131	442	73	122	25	0	31	81	46	106	4	2	.344	.543
Tucker,Michael, Atl	27	.270	147	523	73	141	24	6	14	63	52	112	12	7	.336	.419
Valdez,Mario, ChA	23	.261	68	188	24	49	12	0	6	30	27	48	0	0	.353	.420
Valentin,John, Bos	31	.292	144	568	94	166	39	2	18	80	73	67	11	6	.373	.463
Valentin,Jose, Mil	28	.245	147	502	75	123	29	3	18	72	54	122	18	8	.318	.422
Vaughn,Greg, SD	32	.230	116	387	65	89	19	1	22	69	60	100	8	4	.333	.455
Vaughn,Mo, Bos	30	.291	151	584	99	170	28	1	37	114	89	156	5	3	.385	.533
Velarde,Randy, Ana	35	.260	77	273	43	71	13	1	7	29	39	57	4	2	.353	.392
Ventura,Robin, ChA	30	.269	149	536	81	144	25	1	26	89	82	85	3	3	.366	.465
Veras,Quilvio, SD	27	.259	153	557	92	144	22	4	5	45	93	87	46	21	.365	.339
Vidro,Jose, Mon	23	.256	74	238	26	61	15	1	6	32	14	35	2	1	.298	.403
Vina,Fernando, Mil	29	.262	144	572	84	150	19	7	6	49	38	43	14	9	.308	.351
Vitiello,Joe, KC	28	.248	74	214	23	53	13	1	8	32	21	53	1	0	.315	.430
Vizcaino,Jose, SF	30	.270	152	571	70	154	19	5	3	50	43	87	9	8	.321	.336
Vizquel,Omar, Cle	31	.260	152	569	83	148	21	2	6	54	60	55	33	11	.331	.336
Voigt,Jack, Mil	32	.253	44	99	14	25	6	0	3	16	15	22	1	1	.351	.404
Walbeck,Matt, Det	28	.236	61	148	15	35	6	0	2	15	9	25	1	1	.280	.318
Walker,Larry, Col	31	.302	148	533	102	161	35	3	37	109	59	88	23	6	.372	.587

Projections for 1998 Batters

Batter	Age	Avg	G	AB	R	H	2B	3B	HR	RBI	BB	SO	SB	CS	OBP	SLG
Walker,Todd, Min	25	.294	146	513	73	151	30	3	16	72	47	91	13	7	.354	.458
Ward,Turner, Pit	33	.261	78	184	27	48	11	1	5	23	22	30	4	1	.340	.413
Webster,Lenny, Bal	33	.251	94	231	25	58	12	0	5	27	25	34	0	0	.324	.368
Weiss,Walt, Col	34	.261	141	452	66	118	17	2	4	35	85	67	10	4	.378	.334
White,Devon, Fla	35	.249	111	421	59	105	21	3	10	49	34	92	16	5	.305	.385
White,Rondell, Mon	26	.291	154	597	91	174	33	6	22	82	42	103	23	9	.338	.477
Whiten,Mark, NYA	31	.239	67	159	24	38	6	1	6	22	24	44	5	2	.339	.403
Widger,Chris, Mon	27	.261	88	268	33	70	15	1	9	34	19	50	3	2	.310	.425
Wilkins,Rick, Sea	31	.228	87	193	25	44	9	0	6	25	31	57	1	1	.335	.368
Williams,Bernie, NYA	29	.293	141	547	101	160	32	5	21	86	81	85	14	7	.384	.484
Williams,George, Oak	29	.265	93	260	39	69	15	1	7	35	42	52	1	1	.368	.412
Williams,Gerald, Mil	31	.251	148	442	61	111	27	3	9	46	26	75	15	9	.293	.387
Williams,Matt, Cle	32	.262	146	587	88	154	26	2	34	107	49	118	5	2	.319	.487
Wilson,Dan, Sea	29	.266	143	507	55	135	27	2	14	69	40	81	3	2	.320	.410
Wilson,Enrique, Cle	22	.295	118	369	54	109	14	2	5	35	25	34	10	7	.340	.385
Womack,Tony, Pit	28	.253	151	572	69	145	18	5	2	39	35	88	44	13	.297	.313
Young,Dmitri, StL	24	.270	86	281	36	76	17	2	6	33	23	44	3	3	.326	.409
Young,Eric, LA	31	.288	145	538	89	155	22	4	8	55	59	40	46	17	.358	.388
Young,Ernie, Oak	28	.244	111	340	52	83	16	2	12	48	44	87	4	5	.331	.409
Young,Kevin, Pit	29	.257	128	424	53	109	25	2	18	66	24	103	8	4	.297	.453
Zaun,Gregg, Fla	27	.266	85	214	34	57	11	1	4	25	31	28	2	2	.359	.383
Zeile,Todd, LA	32	.250	148	549	74	137	25	1	25	82	68	100	3	3	.332	.435

Projections for 1998 Pitchers

Pitcher	Age	ERA	W	L	Sv	G	GS	IP	H	HR	BB	SO	BR/9
Adams,Terry, ChN	25	4.01	2	5	26	72	0	83	85	4	42	68	13.8
Aguilera,Rick, Min	36	4.02	2	4	30	60	0	65	65	10	17	56	11.4
Alvarez,Wilson, SF	28	4.08	12	13	0	34	34	214	199	22	92	179	12.2
Appier,Kevin, KC	30	3.28	16	10	0	33	33	228	200	19	71	205	10.7
Ashby,Andy, SD	30	3.57	12	10	0	28	28	184	179	18	45	120	11.0
Assenmacher,Paul, Cle	37	3.19	5	2	5	71	0	48	45	3	15	49	11.3
Astacio,Pedro, Col	28	4.61	14	10	0	34	31	205	209	26	62	147	11.9
Avery,Steve, Bos	28	4.75	7	7	0	23	20	108	107	12	55	65	13.5
Ayala,Bobby, Sea	28	3.83	6	4	6	64	0	87	78	10	36	85	11.8
Bautista,Jose, StL	33	4.81	2	3	0	34	0	58	66	10	14	25	12.4
Beck,Rod, SF	29	3.76	2	4	37	70	0	67	65	9	14	50	10.6
Belcher,Tim, KC	36	4.66	11	14	0	33	33	222	243	27	73	111	12.8
Belinda,Stan, Cin	31	3.43	5	4	0	66	0	76	66	7	31	72	11.5
Benes,Andy, StL	30	3.74	12	11	0	29	29	195	182	19	67	160	11.5
Benitez,Armando, Bal	25	3.65	5	3	8	68	0	69	50	9	44	92	12.3
Blair,Willie, Det	32	4.30	12	12	0	32	32	199	217	22	52	119	12.2
Bochtler,Doug, SD	27	3.63	4	3	0	57	0	62	49	5	39	58	12.8
Bohanon,Brian, NYN	29	5.01	3	5	0	19	9	70	81	8	25	50	13.6
Bones,Ricky, KC	29	5.01	3	5	0	32	17	115	130	15	48	47	13.9
Boskie,Shawn, Bal	31	5.13	4	5	0	31	15	114	132	21	35	70	13.2
Bottalico,Ricky, Phi	28	3.00	2	4	34	66	0	72	54	7	34	78	11.0
Bottenfield,Kent, ChN	29	4.09	4	5	4	59	0	77	79	8	29	57	12.6
Brantley,Jeff, Cin	34	3.19	2	1	10	31	0	31	24	4	11	31	10.2
Brocail,Doug, Det	31	4.37	4	4	3	48	4	70	73	9	27	44	12.9
Brown,Kevin, Fla	33	3.39	15	11	0	33	33	236	231	14	66	183	11.3
Bullinger,Jim, Mon	32	4.59	8	10	0	36	23	147	150	13	70	91	13.5
Burba,Dave, Cin	31	4.03	10	10	0	31	29	172	155	17	78	135	12.2
Burkett,John, Tex	33	4.01	13	11	0	31	31	200	225	21	32	143	11.6
Candiotti,Tom, LA	40	4.24	6	6	0	32	32	191	199	26	55	112	12.0
Carrasco,Hector, KC	28	3.40	5	4	0	63	0	82	71	4	44	66	12.6
Casian,Larry, KC	32	5.63	2	3	0	41	0	32	38	5	13	19	14.3
Castillo,Frank, Col	29	4.79	11	11	0	34	33	184	197	24	69	133	13.0
Castillo,Tony, ChA	35	3.82	5	3	3	61	0	73	74	7	23	43	12.0
Charlton,Norm, Sea	35	5.45	5	3	0	71	0	71	77	6	43	66	15.2
Clark,Mark, ChN	30	4.22	10	14	0	32	31	207	219	22	60	132	12.1
Clemens,Roger, Tor	35	2.91	19	10	0	34	34	257	224	17	66	278	10.2
Clontz,Brad, Atl	27	3.96	4	3	2	61	0	50	51	5	18	37	12.4
Cone,David, NYA	35	3.43	14	8	0	29	29	194	157	18	86	213	11.3
Cook,Dennis, Fla	35	3.88	4	4	0	59	0	65	62	5	30	61	12.7
Cooke,Steve, Pit	28	5.33	7	15	0	32	32	169	192	21	78	112	14.4
Corsi,Jim, Bos	36	3.29	5	2	0	54	0	63	56	3	29	39	12.1
Daal,Omar, Tor	26	4.70	3	4	0	49	4	67	74	7	30	56	14.0
Darwin,Danny, SF	42	4.39	8	10	0	32	24	160	169	21	46	93	12.1
DeLucia,Rich, Ana	33	4.14	3	3	0	43	0	50	44	7	25	47	12.4
Dipoto,Jerry, Col	30	4.30	3	4	25	68	0	90	100	5	38	62	13.8
Drabek,Doug, ChA	35	5.00	10	11	0	31	31	171	189	22	70	110	13.6
Eckersley,Dennis, StL	43	3.76	2	3	33	59	0	55	56	8	7	46	10.3
Eldred,Cal, Mil	30	4.42	10	10	0	28	28	163	156	21	72	98	12.6
Erickson,Scott, Bal	30	4.30	13	12	0	34	33	222	246	20	61	115	12.4
Fassero,Jeff, Sea	35	3.98	16	11	0	35	35	233	233	20	84	206	12.2

Projections for 1998 Pitchers

Pitcher	Age	ERA	W	L	Sv	G	GS	IP	H	HR	BB	SO	BR/9
Fetters,Mike, Mil	33	3.90	4	3	9	54	0	67	67	4	32	60	13.3
Finley,Chuck, Ana	35	4.19	12	10	0	28	28	189	182	21	75	174	12.2
Florie,Bryce, Mil	28	3.82	4	3	0	39	5	73	65	6	41	64	13.1
Fossas,Tony, StL	40	4.86	3	4	0	69	0	50	53	7	24	39	13.9
Foster,Kevin, ChN	29	4.79	8	13	0	29	29	169	162	28	76	124	12.7
Franco,John, NYN	37	3.10	2	3	38	56	0	58	52	3	21	51	11.3
Gardner,Mark, SF	36	4.75	9	13	0	30	30	180	194	27	57	141	12.6
Glavine,Tom, Atl	32	3.37	16	11	0	34	34	238	221	15	78	167	11.3
Gooden,Dwight, NYA	33	5.06	7	9	0	23	22	128	133	17	64	89	13.9
Gordon,Tom, Bos	30	4.15	2	3	35	73	0	89	87	8	38	74	12.6
Groom,Buddy, Oak	32	5.35	4	5	0	76	0	69	81	9	32	48	14.7
Guardado,Eddie, Min	27	4.75	4	4	0	74	0	55	56	9	25	52	13.3
Gubicza,Mark, Ana	35	5.86	2	3	0	8	8	43	47	6	28	21	15.7
Gunderson,Eric, Tex	32	4.15	3	3	0	49	0	39	38	4	15	25	12.2
Guthrie,Mark, LA	32	4.31	4	5	0	63	0	71	74	8	27	58	12.8
Guzman,Juan, Tor	31	4.81	8	10	0	25	25	146	143	18	75	128	13.4
Hamilton,Joey, SD	27	3.93	12	12	0	32	32	199	193	18	71	152	11.9
Hammond,Chris, Bos	32	4.31	3	3	0	32	8	71	78	7	23	52	12.8
Hampton,Mike, Hou	25	3.97	12	12	0	32	32	202	205	16	70	127	12.3
Haney,Chris, KC	29	4.30	3	3	0	17	14	92	104	10	25	45	12.6
Hanson,Erik, Tor	33	4.65	6	8	0	20	20	120	129	12	48	91	13.3
Harnisch,Pete, Mil	31	5.44	4	7	0	17	16	91	93	14	53	53	14.4
Henry,Butch, Bos	29	3.21	5	2	0	36	5	84	81	6	19	44	10.7
Henry,Doug, SF	34	4.13	4	5	0	69	0	72	68	8	34	64	12.8
Hentgen,Pat, Tor	29	3.77	16	13	0	35	35	265	258	29	71	168	11.2
Hernandez,Roberto, SF	33	3.51	3	4	37	73	0	82	71	7	38	92	12.0
Hernandez,Xavier, Tex	32	4.42	3	3	0	50	0	59	62	8	22	55	12.8
Hershiser,Orel, Cle	39	4.66	12	11	0	32	32	199	217	23	70	115	13.0
Hill,Ken, Ana	32	4.59	12	12	0	32	32	210	213	18	105	132	13.6
Hitchcock,Sterling, SD	27	4.63	9	12	0	33	30	173	185	22	59	115	12.7
Hoffman,Trevor, SD	30	2.68	3	3	40	70	0	84	61	9	26	103	9.3
Holmes,Darren, Col	32	4.66	4	4	0	49	4	85	95	9	34	75	13.7
Jackson,Mike, Cle	33	2.80	7	2	5	72	0	74	56	7	27	70	10.1
James,Mike, Ana	30	3.65	5	3	4	62	0	69	62	6	33	55	12.4
Johnson,Randy, Sea	34	2.83	20	7	0	33	33	242	182	20	87	332	10.0
Jones,Bobby, NYN	28	4.13	11	12	0	30	30	194	198	20	63	120	12.1
Jones,Doug, Mil	41	3.00	3	3	36	67	0	75	70	6	15	74	10.2
Jones,Todd, Det	30	3.27	2	3	32	62	0	66	55	4	35	61	12.3
Kamieniecki,Scott, Bal	34	4.18	8	7	0	22	22	127	125	14	47	78	12.2
Karl,Scott, Mil	26	4.68	11	13	0	32	32	198	217	23	69	119	13.0
Key,Jimmy, Bal	37	4.36	12	11	0	33	33	198	198	23	76	133	12.5
Kile,Darryl, Hou	29	3.81	14	13	0	34	34	243	234	19	90	217	12.0
Langston,Mark, Ana	37	5.63	6	9	0	20	20	120	124	18	73	79	14.8
Leiter,Al, Fla	32	4.27	10	11	0	29	29	173	154	12	104	156	13.4
Leiter,Mark, Phi	35	4.69	9	14	0	32	32	190	201	26	67	153	12.7
Leskanic,Curt, Col	30	4.14	4	3	1	60	0	63	62	7	26	65	12.6
Lewis,Richie, Cin	32	5.48	2	3	0	36	0	46	48	8	30	39	15.3
Lieber,Jon, Pit	28	4.36	9	14	0	33	33	190	207	22	51	146	12.2
Lloyd,Graeme, NYA	31	4.33	3	3	0	52	0	52	55	5	19	26	12.8
Maddux,Greg, Atl	32	1.78	22	5	0	34	34	237	193	9	20	173	8.1

348

Projections for 1998 Pitchers

Pitcher	Age	ERA	W	L	Sv	G	GS	IP	H	HR	BB	SO	BR/9
Magnante,Mike, Hou	33	4.32	3	3	0	39	0	50	53	5	17	35	12.6
Martinez,Pedro, Mon	26	2.74	17	9	0	32	32	233	184	20	65	268	9.6
Martinez,Ramon, LA	30	4.17	11	12	0	31	31	190	173	17	97	160	12.8
Mathews,T.J., Oak	28	3.23	5	3	14	65	0	78	65	7	30	74	11.0
Mathews,Terry, Bal	33	4.30	4	4	9	62	0	67	68	8	29	53	13.0
McDonald,Ben, Mil	30	3.78	11	8	0	26	26	162	159	18	44	117	11.3
McDowell,Jack, Cle	32	4.65	5	5	0	15	14	91	95	9	40	70	13.4
McElroy,Chuck, ChA	30	3.55	5	3	3	58	0	66	64	5	24	53	12.0
McMichael,Greg, NYN	31	3.41	6	4	5	73	0	87	82	6	30	79	11.6
Mercker,Kent, Cin	30	4.13	7	8	0	27	21	120	109	15	51	58	12.0
Mesa,Jose, Cle	32	3.30	3	3	32	67	0	79	75	5	26	69	11.5
Miceli,Dan, Det	27	4.84	4	4	0	62	0	67	69	10	33	60	13.7
Mills,Alan, Bal	31	5.32	2	3	0	42	0	44	41	8	32	37	14.9
Mlicki,Dave, NYN	30	4.50	9	12	0	33	27	178	182	21	70	151	12.7
Mohler,Mike, Oak	29	4.55	4	5	0	65	7	95	96	9	52	67	14.0
Montgomery,Jeff, KC	36	3.98	2	3	29	53	0	61	56	10	20	46	11.2
Morgan,Mike, Cin	38	4.23	9	10	0	28	28	151	161	15	46	92	12.3
Moyer,Jamie, Sea	35	4.12	13	9	0	31	31	177	183	24	40	97	11.3
Mulholland,Terry, SF	35	4.77	8	11	0	38	23	164	187	22	45	78	12.7
Munoz,Mike, Col	32	4.60	3	3	0	61	0	45	48	5	19	36	13.4
Mussina,Mike, Bal	29	3.47	16	10	0	34	34	231	214	26	55	208	10.5
Myers,Mike, Det	29	5.37	4	5	3	86	0	57	64	9	30	55	14.8
Myers,Randy, Bal	35	3.66	2	3	48	61	0	59	53	6	27	64	12.2
Nagy,Charles, Cle	31	4.28	14	11	0	33	33	225	234	23	76	159	12.4
Navarro,Jaime, ChA	30	4.56	13	12	0	34	34	219	241	22	76	147	13.0
Neagle,Denny, Atl	29	3.66	15	12	0	34	34	229	229	24	48	162	10.9
Nelson,Jeff, NYA	31	3.04	6	3	0	76	0	77	62	6	33	89	11.1
Nen,Robb, Fla	28	3.27	3	4	34	74	0	77	69	6	29	83	11.5
Nomo,Hideo, LA	29	3.41	14	11	0	33	33	214	169	20	95	230	11.1
Olivares,Omar, Sea	30	5.08	10	10	0	30	29	172	190	19	78	94	14.0
Olson,Gregg, KC	31	4.94	3	4	1	47	0	51	55	5	31	35	15.2
Orosco,Jesse, Bal	41	2.94	5	2	0	69	0	52	35	5	29	48	11.1
Osborne,Donovan, StL	29	4.03	11	11	0	29	29	183	180	23	52	121	11.4
Osuna,Antonio, LA	25	3.00	5	3	9	56	0	69	55	6	26	72	10.6
Patterson,Bob, ChN	39	3.10	5	4	2	77	0	58	47	8	16	56	9.8
Pavlik,Roger, Tex	30	5.23	6	7	0	19	19	105	110	13	57	66	14.3
Percival,Troy, Ana	28	1.98	3	1	35	57	0	59	33	5	23	78	8.5
Petkovsek,Mark, StL	32	3.94	4	4	2	53	0	80	81	8	25	41	11.9
Pettitte,Andy, NYA	26	3.65	16	11	0	35	35	234	237	17	63	166	11.5
Pichardo,Hipolito, KC	28	4.58	3	4	1	50	0	55	61	5	24	36	13.9
Plesac,Dan, Tor	36	3.47	5	3	0	73	0	57	53	5	22	61	11.8
Plunk,Eric, Cle	34	3.34	5	3	0	56	0	70	58	6	32	75	11.6
Poole,Jim, SF	32	5.04	3	4	0	64	0	50	56	6	23	35	14.2
Portugal,Mark, Phi	35	4.17	6	8	0	20	20	121	120	13	44	68	12.2
Powell,Jay, Fla	26	3.51	5	4	0	72	0	77	72	4	35	58	12.5
Quantrill,Paul, Tor	29	4.89	4	6	0	64	7	103	125	13	29	63	13.5
Radinsky,Scott, LA	30	3.81	4	4	3	69	0	59	59	5	21	41	12.2
Radke,Brad, Min	25	4.06	15	13	0	35	35	237	241	36	47	162	10.9
Rapp,Pat, SF	30	4.89	7	11	0	28	26	149	160	12	76	87	14.3
Reed,Rick, NYN	32	3.07	15	9	0	33	31	208	193	22	31	113	9.7

Projections for 1998 Pitchers

Pitcher	Age	ERA	W	L	Sv	G	GS	IP	H	HR	BB	SO	BR/9
Reed,Steve, Col	32	3.49	5	3	0	65	0	67	60	8	20	52	10.7,
Reyes,Carlos, Oak	29	4.79	3	4	0	40	7	92	98	13	39	58	13.4
Reynolds,Shane, Hou	30	3.78	12	12	0	32	32	200	206	17	52	170	11.6
Reynoso,Ar., NYN	32	4.83	3	4	0	11	11	54	62	7	17	28	13.2
Rhodes,Arthur, Bal	28	3.84	5	4	1	52	0	96	86	12	42	103	12.0
Rodriguez,Rich, SF	35	3.74	4	4	0	71	0	65	63	7	20	31	11.5
Rogers,Kenny, NYA	33	4.38	9	9	0	31	25	156	153	18	67	82	12.7
Rojas,Mel, NYN	31	3.54	5	5	5	76	0	84	75	8	34	88	11.7
Rueter,Kirk, SF	27	3.75	10	9	0	28	28	161	160	16	43	89	11.3
Ruffin,Bruce, Col	34	3.79	3	2	4	39	0	38	33	4	20	38	12.6
Sanders,Scott, Det	29	3.90	6	5	0	32	28	173	160	23	65	169	11.7
Schilling,Curt, Phi	31	3.04	15	11	0	32	32	231	199	24	53	264	9.8
Schourek,Pete, Cin	29	4.67	4	6	0	16	15	79	78	10	35	59	12.9
Scott,Tim, Sea	31	3.75	3	2	0	33	0	36	36	3	14	29	12.5
Sele,Aaron, Bos	28	4.89	11	11	0	32	32	171	184	18	77	132	13.7
Shaw,Jeff, Cin	31	3.40	3	5	40	78	0	98	93	9	25	70	10.8
Slocumb,Heathcliff, Sea	32	4.15	3	4	30	76	0	78	78	2	48	75	14.5
Smiley,John, Cle	33	4.13	6	4	0	15	15	85	89	10	23	67	11.9
Smith,Pete, SD	32	5.03	3	5	0	37	15	118	127	21	49	68	13.4
Smoltz,John, Atl	31	2.89	19	10	0	35	35	255	218	21	63	259	9.9
Springer,Russ, Hou	29	4.75	3	4	2	54	0	55	57	8	24	57	13.3
Stanton,Mike, NYA	31	3.80	5	4	2	70	0	71	68	6	29	58	12.3
Stevens,Dave, ChN	28	5.93	1	3	0	27	4	41	48	8	22	28	15.4
Stottlemyre,Todd, StL	33	4.11	11	12	0	30	30	195	188	23	70	171	11.9
Swindell,Greg, Min	33	4.37	5	5	1	64	0	107	118	14	28	69	12.3
Tapani,Kevin, ChN	34	4.55	9	14	0	30	30	194	214	25	52	128	12.3
Tavarez,Julian, SF	25	3.98	5	5	0	76	1	86	92	7	26	52	12.3
Taylor,Billy, Oak	36	3.52	2	3	28	66	0	69	63	4	32	69	12.4
Tewksbury,Bob, Min	37	3.93	12	10	0	29	28	181	205	14	33	105	11.8
Timlin,Mike, Sea	32	3.36	5	3	8	62	0	67	62	6	22	52	11.3
Trachsel,Steve, ChN	27	4.43	10	14	0	33	33	203	202	29	69	146	12.0
Trombley,Mike, Min	31	4.38	4	4	0	59	0	78	79	10	31	62	12.7
Valdes,Ismael, LA	24	3.10	15	9	0	31	31	206	185	17	49	153	10.2
VanLandingham,W., SF	27	5.18	6	9	0	23	22	120	120	12	79	66	14.9
Veres,Dave, Mon	31	3.63	4	4	0	58	0	67	65	5	24	61	12.0
Vosberg,Ed, Fla	36	4.14	3	3	0	57	0	50	53	4	22	40	13.5
Wagner,Paul, Mil	30	4.62	1	2	0	16	5	39	43	4	18	31	14.1
Wakefield,Tim, Bos	31	4.57	12	11	0	34	30	205	199	28	88	144	12.6
Watson,Allen, Ana	27	5.08	11	13	0	33	32	195	212	31	71	136	13.1
Weathers,Dave, Cle	28	5.55	2	2	0	27	5	47	59	4	25	30	16.1
Wells,David, NYA	35	4.01	14	11	0	33	33	220	231	27	45	142	11.3
Wendell,Turk, NYN	31	4.56	4	5	5	67	0	77	75	10	43	67	13.8
Wetteland,John, Tex	31	2.49	3	2	34	61	0	65	47	6	19	67	9.1
Whiteside,Matt, Tex	30	4.58	3	3	0	33	1	59	67	6	21	40	13.4
Wickman,Bob, Mil	29	3.66	6	5	0	73	0	96	90	7	41	71	12.3
Williams,Brian, Bal	29	5.79	2	3	0	22	6	56	68	6	36	42	16.7
Witt,Bobby, Tex	34	5.07	11	13	0	34	32	206	237	26	73	140	13.5
Wohlers,Mark, Atl	28	3.13	3	3	34	73	0	72	64	4	28	96	11.5
Worrell,Todd, LA	38	4.21	2	4	37	67	0	62	64	8	19	63	12.0

These Guys Can Play Too And Might Get A Shot

Which of the following players is going to get a big league opportunity in 1998? That's hard to say, especially because we put the list together in mid-October, a good month before the expansion draft. But if these guys do get a chance, their statistics should resemble the numbers below. They're Major League Equivalencies: not projections but instead a representation of players' 1997 Double-A and Triple-A performance translated into major league terms. Devised by Bill James, MLEs consider a player's level of competition, league, home ballpark and future major league home ballpark. To put it simply, an MLE tells you what the player would have hit last year had he been in the majors, while a projection tells you what he'll hit this year. That said, look for a few of the players below to get a shot in the majors in 1998.

Batter	Age	Avg	G	AB	R	H	2B	3B	HR	RBI	BB	SO	SB	CS	OBP	SLG
Arias,George	26	.255	115	415	62	106	27	1	9	52	34	62	2	4	.312	.390
Aven,Bruce	26	.275	121	425	64	117	26	2	15	72	46	103	8	3	.346	.452
Beamon,Trey	24	.289	90	311	48	90	15	2	3	37	35	60	9	5	.361	.379
Blosser,Greg	27	.279	54	172	28	48	10	0	10	23	23	48	4	2	.364	.512
Brown,Kevin L.	25	.229	116	397	52	91	16	1	16	46	35	115	1	1	.292	.395
Butler,Rich	25	.267	137	513	71	137	26	7	18	66	46	112	14	5	.327	.450
Casey,Sean	23	.347	82	297	39	103	22	0	11	65	22	47	0	1	.392	.532
Clyburn,Danny	24	.279	137	505	79	141	29	3	18	66	46	113	10	4	.339	.455
Cox,Steven	23	.248	131	451	68	112	30	0	11	76	70	93	0	3	.349	.388
Davis,Tommy	25	.282	119	425	64	120	19	1	13	54	37	95	4	1	.340	.424
Dellucci,David	24	.307	107	374	62	115	25	2	18	48	42	74	8	4	.377	.529
Evans,Tom	23	.233	107	361	46	84	15	0	11	49	40	109	0	1	.309	.366
Frias,Hanley	24	.254	132	477	59	121	15	4	4	42	52	74	27	10	.327	.327
Giambi,Jeremy	23	.283	74	254	36	72	12	0	7	38	27	47	2	4	.352	.413
Gibbs,Kevin	24	.285	101	333	66	95	14	2	1	25	43	51	33	12	.367	.348
Gibson,Derrick	23	.366	140	568	108	208	33	2	37	89	35	109	16	8	.403	.627
Hermansen,Chad	20	.249	129	470	67	117	28	3	15	54	45	145	12	5	.315	.417
Hurst,Jimmy	26	.262	115	385	49	101	11	2	18	57	44	126	10	4	.338	.442
Jennings,Robin	26	.255	126	451	55	115	22	3	16	59	46	76	3	3	.324	.424
Lee,Derek	31	.256	75	219	16	56	13	0	3	26	23	36	2	0	.326	.356
Lee,Travis	23	.257	59	214	29	55	13	1	9	32	21	48	1	0	.323	.453
McCarty,Dave	28	.311	121	408	66	127	22	3	16	71	38	79	6	4	.370	.498
Millar,Kevin	26	.297	135	478	65	142	27	1	21	90	39	56	1	2	.350	.490
Monahan,Shane	23	.292	128	480	63	140	28	4	13	84	29	133	15	6	.332	.448
Nixon,Trot	24	.235	130	469	70	110	18	2	17	54	55	90	7	3	.315	.390
Nunez,Abraham	22	.296	47	189	24	56	5	0	0	10	13	29	7	4	.342	.323
Petagine,Roberto	27	.297	129	428	78	127	28	0	27	87	73	96	0	1	.399	.551
Pozo,Arquimedez	24	.272	101	371	54	101	18	0	19	62	32	57	2	3	.330	.474
Raabe,Brian	30	.340	135	533	93	181	35	2	12	74	35	21	0	5	.380	.480
Sexson,Richie	23	.248	115	427	53	106	19	1	28	82	25	91	4	1	.290	.494
Simmons,Brian	24	.237	138	528	87	125	24	9	10	58	59	132	10	12	.313	.373
Simon,Randall	23	.276	133	496	48	137	39	0	10	79	13	79	0	6	.295	.415
Smith,Bubba	28	.242	140	505	55	122	28	0	23	87	49	144	1	1	.309	.434
Towle,Justin	24	.270	119	396	44	107	32	3	7	50	34	79	3	4	.328	.419
Varitek,Jason	26	.234	107	368	55	86	18	0	14	48	39	91	0	0	.307	.397
Velazquez,Andy	22	.286	120	441	55	126	23	9	18	58	27	118	4	3	.327	.501
Ward,Daryle	23	.297	128	445	59	132	22	0	14	76	34	83	2	2	.347	.440
Wilson,Preston	23	.251	70	247	29	62	10	0	14	37	14	76	4	1	.291	.462
Witt,Kevin	22	.251	127	475	54	119	23	3	21	65	26	116	0	0	.289	.444
Wright,Ron	22	.266	91	319	35	85	27	0	11	44	17	85	0	1	.304	.455

Career Projections

Can Ken Griffey Jr. break Hank Aaron's career home run record? Can Harold Baines make it to 4,000 hits, or even top Pete Rose's record total of 4,256? To answer questions like this this, Bill James came up with a formula he called "The Favorite Toy" back in the days when he was still doing the *Baseball Abstract*. For several years, we've run projections based on Bill's formula in the *STATS Baseball Scoreboard*, and last year we began doing so in the *Major League Handbook* as well. We continue the tradition this year; the only difference is that from now on, we'll just call them "Career Projections."

Rather than run the formula, which is fairly complex, we'll just say that the Career Projections use a player's age and recent performance to estimate his chances of reaching the goal. So is it better than 50/50 that Wade Boggs will make it to 3,000 hits? Will Ken Griffey Jr. drive in 2,000 runs before his career is through? Here's what the formula says. (Age here is the player's age as of July 1, 1997.)

— Don Zminda

Player	Age	Current			Home Runs					Hits			RBI	
		H	HR	RBI	500	600	700	756	800	3000	4000	4257	2000	2298
Mark McGwire	33	1201	387	983	94%	63%	27%	15%	8%	—	—	—	1%	—
Barry Bonds	32	1750	374	1094	91%	39%	12%	3%	—	13%	—	—	12%	—
Ken Griffey Jr.	27	1389	294	872	88%	66%	38%	27%	20%	24%	—	—	35%	17%
Juan Gonzalez	27	1045	256	790	78%	41%	20%	13%	7%	10%	—	—	30%	14%
Albert Belle	30	1188	272	867	56%	24%	7%	—	—	10%	—	—	19%	5%
Frank Thomas	29	1261	257	854	53%	23%	6%	—	—	18%	—	—	23%	8%
Sammy Sosa	28	1035	207	642	41%	18%	4%	—	—	5%	—	—	9%	—
Rafael Palmeiro	32	1792	271	958	36%	10%	—	—	—	21%	—	—	8%	—
Jay Buhner	32	1053	253	795	35%	11%	—	—	—	—	—	—	1%	—
Jose Canseco	32	1470	351	1107	35%	15%	—	—	—	—	—	—	—	—
Mo Vaughn	29	960	190	637	33%	13%	—	—	—	8%	—	—	7%	—
Jim Thome	26	617	133	386	31%	14%	3%	—	—	—	—	—	1%	—
Larry Walker	30	1100	202	673	29%	9%	—	—	—	3%	—	—	—	—
Jeff Bagwell	29	1112	187	724	24%	6%	—	—	—	7%	—	—	13%	1%
Fred McGriff	33	1622	339	1007	21%	—	—	—	—	4%	—	—	—	—
Tino Martinez	29	852	157	570	19%	3%	—	—	—	3%	—	—	9%	—
Matt Williams	31	1249	279	837	19%	—	—	—	—	—	—	—	—	—
Vinny Castilla	29	674	124	365	18%	4%	—	—	—	2%	—	—	—	—
Tim Salmon	28	782	153	503	16%	1%	—	—	—	5%	—	—	5%	—
Manny Ramirez	25	590	109	372	15%	2%	—	—	—	12%	—	—	3%	—
Eric Karros	29	891	154	535	12%	—	—	—	—	1%	—	—	—	—
Gary Sheffield	28	1048	180	621	10%	—	—	—	—	—	—	—	—	—
Alex Rodriguez	21	435	64	228	9%	—	—	—	—	18%	—	—	1%	—
Andres Galarraga	36	1752	288	1051	9%	—	—	—	—	—	—	—	—	—
Cecil Fielder	33	1216	302	940	8%	—	—	—	—	—	—	—	—	—
Raul Mondesi	26	690	100	329	6%	—	—	—	—	15%	—	—	—	—
Mike Piazza	28	854	168	533	6%	—	—	—	—	—	—	—	—	—
Ellis Burks	32	1378	209	744	5%	—	—	—	—	—	—	—	—	—
Ryan Klesko	26	447	100	300	5%	—	—	—	—	—	—	—	—	—
Dean Palmer	28	729	163	482	4%	—	—	—	—	—	—	—	—	—
Joe Carter	37	2083	378	1382	2%	—	—	—	—	—	—	—	—	—
Jim Edmonds	27	533	91	294	2%	—	—	—	—	—	—	—	—	—
Tony Gwynn	37	2780	107	973	—	—	—	—	—	97%	—	—	—	—
Cal Ripken	36	2715	370	1453	—	—	—	—	—	95%	—	—	1%	—
Wade Boggs	39	2800	109	933	—	—	—	—	—	49%	—	—	—	—
Roberto Alomar	29	1659	113	653	—	—	—	—	—	28%	—	—	—	—
Chuck Knoblauch	28	1197	43	391	—	—	—	—	—	23%	—	—	—	—
Craig Biggio	31	1470	116	545	—	—	—	—	—	16%	—	—	—	—
Travis Fryman	28	1176	149	679	—	—	—	—	—	14%	—	—	3%	—
Harold Baines	38	2561	339	1423	—	—	—	—	—	14%	—	—	—	—
Mark Grace	33	1691	104	742	—	—	—	—	—	13%	—	—	—	—
Chipper Jones	25	502	74	307	—	—	—	—	—	10%	—	—	4%	—
Bobby Bonilla	34	1810	262	1061	—	—	—	—	—	9%	—	—	—	—
Garret Anderson	25	487	36	234	—	—	—	—	—	9%	—	—	—	—
Marquis Grissom	30	1242	101	458	—	—	—	—	—	8%	—	—	—	—
Bernie Williams	28	927	100	469	—	—	—	—	—	8%	—	—	—	—
Derek Jeter	23	385	20	155	—	—	—	—	—	8%	—	—	—	—
Nomar Garciaparra	23	230	34	114	—	—	—	—	—	7%	—	—	—	—
Carlos Baerga	28	1231	114	623	—	—	—	—	—	6%	—	—	—	—
Kenny Lofton	30	1047	44	309	—	—	—	—	—	5%	—	—	—	—
Delino DeShields	28	1063	49	350	—	—	—	—	—	4%	—	—	—	—
Brian McRae	29	1102	70	405	—	—	—	—	—	4%	—	—	—	—
Ivan Rodriguez	25	948	88	417	—	—	—	—	—	4%	—	—	—	—
Ray Durham	25	446	28	169	—	—	—	—	—	3%	—	—	—	—
Edgar Renteria	21	304	9	83	—	—	—	—	—	3%	—	—	—	—
Jay Bell	31	1369	104	553	—	—	—	—	—	2%	—	—	—	—
John Olerud	28	1064	131	573	—	—	—	—	—	1%	—	—	—	—
Rusty Greer	28	573	67	294	—	—	—	—	—	1%	—	—	—	—

A dash (—) indicates the player has less than a 0.5% chance to reach the specific plateau.

Glossary

% Inherited Scored

A Relief Pitching statistic indicating the percentage of runners on base at the time a relief pitcher enters a game that he allows to score.

% Pitches Taken

The number of pitches a batter does not swing at divided by the total number of pitches he sees.

1st Batter OBP

The On-Base Percentage allowed by a relief pitcher to the first batter he faces in a game.

Active Career Batting Leaders

Minimum of 1,000 At-Bats required for Batting Average, On-Base Percentage, Slugging Percentage, At-Bats Per HR, At-Bats Per GDP, At-Bats Per RBI, and Strikeout-to-Walk Ratio. One hundred (100) Stolen Base Attempts required for Stolen Base Success %. Any player who appeared in 1997 is eligible for inclusion provided he meets the category's minimum requirements.

Active Career Pitching Leaders

Minimum of 750 Innings Pitched required for Earned Run Average, Opponent Batting Average, all of the "Per 9 Innings" categories, and Strikeout-to-Walk Ratio. Two hundred fifty (250) Games Started required for Complete Game Frequency. One hundred (100) decisions required for Win-Loss Percentage. Any player who appeared in 1997 is eligible for inclusion provided he meets the category's minimum requirements.

Bases Loaded

Batting Average with the Bases Loaded

BA ScPos Allowed

Batting Average Allowed with Runners in Scoring Position.

Batting Average

Hits divided by At-Bats.

Blown Save

Entering a game in a Save Situation (see Save Situation in Glossary) and allowing the tying or go-ahead run to score.

Catcher's ERA

The Earned Run Average of a club's pitchers with a particular catcher behind the plate. To figure this for a catcher, multiply the Earned Runs Allowed by the pitchers while he was catching times nine and divide that by his number of Innings Caught.

Cheap Wins/Tough Losses/Top Game Scores

First determine the starting pitcher's Game Score as follows: (1)Start with 50. (2)Add 1 point for each out recorded by the starting pitcher. (3)Add 2 points for each inning the pitcher completes after the fourth inning. (4)Add 1 point for each strikeout. (5)Subtract 2 points for each hit allowed. (6)Subtract 4 points for each earned run allowed. (7)Subtract 2 points for an unearned run. (8)Subtract 1 point for each walk.

If the starting pitcher scores over 50 and loses, it's a Tough Loss. If he wins with a game score under 50, it's a Cheap Win. The top Game Scores of 1997 are listed.

Cleanup Slugging%

The Slugging Percentage of a player when batting fourth in the batting order.

Complete Game Frequency

Complete Games divided by Games Started.

Earned Run Average

(Earned Runs times 9) divided by Innings Pitched.

Fielding Percentage

(Putouts plus Assists) divided by (Putouts plus Assists plus Errors).

Games Finished

The last relief pitcher for either team in any given game is credited with a Game Finished.

GDP

Ground into Double Play

GDP Opportunity

Any situation with a runner on first and less than two out.

Ground/Fly Ratio (Grd/Fly)

For batters, ground balls hit divided by fly balls hit. For pitchers, ground balls allowed divided by fly balls allowed. All batted balls except line drives and bunts are included.

Hold

A Hold is credited any time a relief pitcher enters a game in a Save Situation (see definition below), records at least one out, and leaves the game never having relinquished the lead. Note: a pitcher cannot finish the game and receive credit for a Hold, nor can he earn a hold and a save.

Isolated Power

Slugging Percentage minus Batting Average.

K/BB Ratio

Strikeouts divided by Walks.

Late & Close

A Late & Close situation meets the following requirements: (1)the game is in the seventh inning or later, and (2)the batting team is either leading by one run, tied, or has the potential tying run on base, at bat, or on deck. Note: this situation is very similar to the characteristics of a Save Situation.

Leadoff On Base%

The On-Base Percentage of a player when batting first in the batting order.

LHS

Lefthanded Starter

Offensive Winning Percentage

The Winning Percentage a team of nine Larry Walkers (or anybody) would compile against average pitching and defense. The formula: (Runs Created per 27 outs) divided by the League average of runs scored per game. Square the result and divide it by (1+itself).

On Base Percentage

(Hits plus Walks plus Hit by Pitcher) divided by (At-Bats plus Walks plus Hit by Pitcher plus Sacrifice Flies).

Opponent Batting Average

Hits Allowed divided by (Batters Faced minus Walks minus Hit Batsmen minus Sacrifice Hits minus Sacrifice Flies minus Catcher's Interference).

PA*

The divisor for On-Base Percentage: At-Bats plus Walks plus Hit By Pitcher plus Sacrifice Flies; or Plate Appearances minus Sacrifice Hits and Times Reached Base on Defensive Interference.

PCS (Pitchers' Caught Stealing)

The number of runners officially counted as Caught Stealing where the initiator of the fielding play was the pitcher, not the catcher. Note: such plays are often referred to as "pickoffs," but appear in official records as Caught Stealings. The most common "pitcher caught stealing scenario" is a 1-3-6 fielding play, where the runner is officially charged a Caught Stealing because he broke for second base. "Pickoff" (fielding play 1-3 being the most common) is not an official statistic.

Pitches per PA

For a hitter, the total number of pitches seen divided by total number of At-Bats.

PkOf Throw/Runner

The number of Pickoff Throws made by a pitcher divided by the number of runners on first base.

Plate Appearances

At-Bats plus Total Walks plus Hit By Pitcher plus Sacrifice Hits plus Sacrifice Flies plus Times Reached on Defensive Interference.

Power/Speed Number

A way to look at power and speed in one number. A player must score high in both areas to earn a high Power/Speed Number. The formula: (HR x SB x 2) divided by (HR + SB).

Quick Hooks and Slow Hooks

A Quick Hook is the removal of a pitcher who has pitched less than six innings and given up three runs or less. A Slow Hook occurs when a pitcher pitches more than nine innings, or allows seven or more runs, or whose combined innings pitched and runs allowed totals 13 or more.

Range Factor

The number of Successful Chances (Putouts plus Assists) times nine divided by the number of Defensive Innings Played. The average for a player at each position in 1997:

Second Base: 5.00	Left Field: 1.99
Third Base: 2.66	Center Field: 2.55
Shortstop: 4.56	Right Field: 2.11

RHS

Righthanded Starter

Run Support Per 9 IP

The number of runs scored by a pitcher's team while he was still in the game times nine divided by his Innings Pitched.

Runs Created

A way to combine a batter's total offensive contributions into one number. The formula:
(H + BB + HBP - CS - GIDP) times (Total Bases + .26(TBB - IBB + HBP) + .52(SH + SF + SB)) divided by (AB + TBB + HBP + SH + SF).

Save Percentage

Saves (SV) divided by Save Opportunities (OP).

Save Situation

A Relief Pitcher is in a Save Situation when:

upon entering the game with his club leading, he has the opportunity to be the finishing pitcher (and is not the winning pitcher of record at the time), and meets any one of the three following conditions:

(1) he has a lead of no more than three runs and has the opportunity to pitch for at least one inning, or

(2) he enters the game, regardless of the count, with the potential tying run either on base, at bat, or on deck; or

(3) he pitches three or more innings regardless of the lead and the official scorer credits him with a save.

SB Success%

Stolen Bases divided by (Stolen Bases plus Caught Stealing).

Secondary Average

A way to look at a player's extra bases gained, independent of Batting Average. The formula: (Total Bases - Hits + TBB + SB) divided by At-Bats.

Slugging Percentage

Total Bases divided by At-Bats.

Total Bases

Hits plus Doubles plus (2 times Triples) plus (3 times Home Runs).

Win-Loss Percentage or Winning Percentage

Wins divided by (Wins plus Losses).

About STATS, Inc.

STATS, Inc. is the nation's leading independent sports information and statistical analysis company, providing detailed sports services for a wide array of commercial clients.

As one of the fastest-growing sports companies—in 1994, we ranked 144th on the "Inc. 500" list of fastest-growing privately held firms—STATS provides the most up-to-the-minute sports information to professional teams, print and broadcast media, software developers and interactive service providers around the country. Some of our major clients are ESPN, the Associated Press, Fox Sports, Electronic Arts, MSNBC, SONY and Topps. Much of the information we provide is available to the public via STATS On-Line. With a computer and a modem, you can follow action in the four major professional sports, as well as NCAA football and basketball. . . as it happens!

STATS Publishing, a division of STATS, Inc., produces 12 annual books, including the *Major League Handbook, The Scouting Notebook*, the *Pro Football Handbook*, the *Pro Basketball Handbook* and the *Hockey Handbook* as well as the *STATS Fantasy Insider* magazine. These publications deliver STATS' expertise to fans, scouts, general managers and media around the country.

In addition, STATS offers the most innovative—and fun—fantasy sports games and support products around, from *Bill James Fantasy Baseball* and *Bill James Classic Baseball* to *STATS Fantasy Football* and *STATS Fantasy Hoops*. Check out the latest STATS and Bill James fantasy game, *Stock Market Baseball* and our immensely popular Fantasy Portfolios.

Information technology has grown by leaps and bounds in the last decade, and STATS will continue to be at the forefront as a supplier of the most up-to-date, in-depth sports information available. For those of you on the information superhighway, you can always catch STATS in our area on America Online or at our Internet site.

For more information on our products, or on joining our reporter network, contact us on:

America On-Line — (Keyword: STATS)

Internet — www.stats.com

Toll Free in the USA at 1-800-63-STATS (1-800-637-8287)

Outside the USA at 1-847-676-3383

Or write to:

STATS, Inc.
8131 Monticello Ave.
Skokie, IL 60076-3300

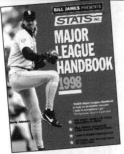

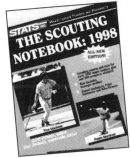
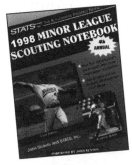

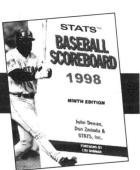

ROUNDING OUT THE STARTING LINEUP...

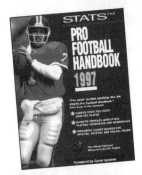

STATS Pro Football Handbook 1997

- A complete season-by-season register for every active NFL player
- Numerous statistical breakdowns for hundreds of NFL players
- Leader boards in a number of innovative and traditional categories
- Exclusive evaluations of offensive linemen
- **Item #FH97, $19.95, Available NOW!** *1998 Edition Available 2/1/98!*

STATS Pro Football Revealed 1997
The 100-Yard War

- Profiles each team, complete with essays, charts and play diagrams
- Detailed statistical breakdowns on players, teams and coaches
- Essays about NFL trends and happenings by leading experts
- Same data as seen on ESPN's *Sunday Night Football* broadcasts
- **Item #PF97, $18.95, Available NOW!** *1998 Edition Available 7/1/98!*

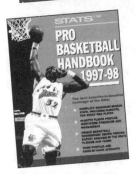

STATS Pro Basketball Handbook 1997-98

- Career stats for every player who logged minutes during 1996-97
- Team game logs with points, rebounds, assists and much more
- Leader boards from points per game to triple doubles
- Essays cover the hottest topics facing the NBA. Foreword by Bill Walton
- **Item #BH98, $19.95, Available Now!**

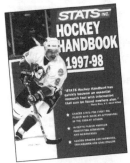

STATS Hockey Handbook 1997-98

- Complete career register for every 1996-97 NHL player and goalie
- Exclusive breakdowns identify player strengths and weaknesses
- Specific coverage for each team, plus league profiles
- Standard and exclusive leader boards
- **Item #HH98, $19.95, Available Now!**

Order from **STATS** INC. Today!

Use Order Form in This Book, or Call 1-800-63-STATS or 847-676-3383 or visit www.stats.com

STATS, Inc. Order Form

Name_____

Address_____

City_____ State_____ Zip_____

Phone_____Fax_____E-mail Address_____

Method of Payment (U.S. Funds Only):
☐ Check ☐ Money Order ☐ Visa ☐ MasterCard

Credit Card Information:
Cardholder Name_____

Credit Card Number_____ Exp. Date_____

Signature_____

Qty.	Product Name	Item #	Price	Total
	STATS All-Time Major League Handbook	ATHA	$54.95	
	STATS All-Time Baseball Sourcebook	ATSA	$54.95	
	STATS All-Time Major League COMBO (BOTH books!)	ATCA	$99.95	
	STATS Major League Handbook 1998	HB98	$19.95	
	STATS Major League Handbook 1998 (Comb-bound)	HC98	$21.95	
	STATS Projections Update 1998 (MAGAZINE)	PJUP	$9.95	
	The Scouting Notebook: 1998	SN98	$19.95	
	The Scouting Notebook: 1998 (Comb-bound)	SC98	$21.95	
	STATS Minor League Scouting Notebook 1998	MN98	$19.95	
	STATS Minor League Handbook 1998	MH98	$19.95	
	STATS Minor League Handbook 1998 (Comb-bound)	MC98	$21.95	
	STATS Player Profiles 1998	PP98	$19.95	
	STATS Player Profiles 1998 (Comb-bound)	PC98	$21.95	
	STATS 1998 BVSP Match-Ups!	BP98	$19.95	
	STATS Baseball Scoreboard 1998	SB98	$19.95	
	STATS Diamond Chronicles 1998	CH98	$19.95	
	Pro Football Revealed: The 100 Yard War (1997 Edition)	PF97	$18.95	
	STATS Pro Football Handbook 1997	FH97	$19.95	
	STATS Basketball Handbook 1997-98	BH98	$19.95	
	STATS Hockey Handbook 1997-98	HH98	$19.95	
	STATS Fantasy Insider: 1998 Major League Baseball Edition (MAGAZINE)	IB98	$5.95	
	STATS Fantasy Insider: 1998 Pro Football Edition (MAGAZINE)	IF98	$5.95	
	Prior Editions (Please circle appropriate year)			
	STATS Major League Handbook '90 '91 '92 '93 '94 '95 '96 '97		$9.95	
	The Scouting Report/Notebook '94 '95 '96 '97		$9.95	
	STATS Player Profiles '93 '94 '95 '96 '97		$9.95	
	STATS Minor League Handbook '92 '93 '94 '95 '96 '97		$9.95	
	STATS BVSP Match-Ups! '94 '95 '96 '97		$5.95	
	STATS Baseball Scoreboard '92 '93 '94 '95 '96 '97		$9.95	
	STATS Basketball Scoreboard/Handbook '93-'94 '94-'95 '95-'96 '96-'97		$9.95	
	Pro Football Revealed: The 100 Yard War '94 '95 '96		$9.95	
	STATS Pro Football Handbook '95 '96		$9.95	
	STATS Minor League Scouting Notebook '95 '96 '97		$9.95	
	STATS Hockey Handbook '96-'97		$9.95	

PUBLICATIONS (STATS books now include FREE first class shipping; magazines — add $2)

FANTASY GAMES

Qty.	Product Name	Item Number	Price	Total
	Bill James Classic Baseball	BJCB	$129.00	
	STATS Fantasy Hoops	SFH	$79.00	
	STATS Fantasy Football	SFF	$69.00	
	Bill James Fantasy Baseball	BJFB	$89.00	

1st Fantasy Team Name (ex. Colt 45's):_____   _____

   What Fantasy Game is this team for?_____

2nd Fantasy Team Name (ex. Colt 45's):_____   _____

   What Fantasy Game is this team for?_____

        NOTE: $1.00/player is charged for all roster moves and transactions.

For Bill James Fantasy Baseball:

Would you like to play in a league drafted by Bill James?　❏ Yes　❏ No

MULTIMEDIA PRODUCTS (Prices include shipping & handling charges)

Qty.	Product Name	Item Number	Price	Total
	Bill James Encyclopedia CD-Rom	BJCD	$49.95	

TOTALS

	Price	Total
Product Total (excl. Fantasy Games)		
Canada—all orders—add:	$2.50/book	
Magazines—shipping—add:	$2.00/each	
Order 2 or more books—subtract:	$1.00/book	
(**NOT** to be combined with other specials)		
Subtotal		
Fantasy Games Total		
IL residents add 8.5% sales tax		
GRAND TOTAL		

For Faster Service, Please Call 800-63-STATS or 847-676-3383
Visit STATS on the World Wide Web at www.stats.com
Fax Your Order to 847-676-0821
STATS, Inc • 8131 Monticello Avenue • Skokie, Illinois 60076-3300

NOTE: Orders for shipments outside of the USA or Canada are Credit Card only.
   Actual shipping charges will be added to the product cost.